GATES TO THE NEW CITY

GATES
TO THE
NEW
CITY

A TREASURY OF
<u>MODERN JEWISH TALES</u>

EDITED AND WITH AN INTRODUCTION BY
HOWARD SCHWARTZ

Jason Aronson Inc.
Northvale, New Jersey
London

10 9 8 7 6 5 4 3 2 1

Library of Congress Cataloging-in-Publication Data

Gates to the new city: a treasury of modern Jewish tales /
    edited by Howard Schwartz.
        p.   cm.
    Bibliography: p.
    Includes index.
    ISBN 0-87668-849-0 (previously ISBN 0-380-81091-3)
        1. Legends, Jewish.   2. Short stories, Jewish.
3. Bible.   O.T.—Legends.   4. Aggada—
Translations into English.   5. Cabala—Fiction.
6. Hasidim—Legends.   I. Schwartz, Howard, 1945-   .
PN6120.95.J5G38   1989
808.83′1′089924—dc20   89-36096

Manufactured in the United States of America.
Jason Aronson Inc. offers books and cassettes. For
information and catalog write to Jason Aronson Inc.,
230 Livingston Street, Northvale, New Jersey 07647.

Howard Schwartz was born in St. Louis in 1945. He attended Washington University and presently teaches at the University of Missouri at St. Louis. He is the author of two books of poetry, *Vessels* and *Gathering the Sparks*, and of several books of fiction, including *Midrashim: Collected Jewish Parables, The Captive Soul of the Messiah: New Tales About Reb Nachman,* and *Rooms of the Soul.* He has also edited three anthologies, *Imperial Messages: One Hundred Modern Parables, Voices Within the Ark: The Modern Jewish Poets,* and *Gates to the New City: A Treasury of Modern Jewish Tales,* and three volumes of Jewish folklore, *Elijah's Violin & Other Jewish Fairy Tales, Miriam's Tambourine: Jewish Folktales from Around the World,* and *Lilith's Cave: Jewish Tales of the Supernatural.* He has also edited *The Dream Assembly: Tales of Rabbi Zalman Schachter-Shalomi. The Diamond Tree: Jewish Nursery Tales From Around the World* will be published in 1991. Schwartz lives in St. Louis with his wife, Tsila, who is a calligrapher, and his three children, Shira, Nathan, and Miriam.

FOR MAURY SCHWARTZ

Two men who live in different places, or even in different generations, may still converse. For one may raise a question, and the other who is far away in time or in space may make a comment or ask a question that answers it. So they converse, but no one knows it save the Lord, who hears and records and brings together all the words of men, as it is written: *They who serve the Lord speak to one another, and the Lord hears them and records their words in His book* (Mal. 3:16).

—Rabbi Nachman of Bratslav

CONTENTS

PREFACE

Exploring Jewish literature is much like undertaking an archeological dig. The first layer one encounters is quite recent—such as the rich body of Hasidic lore, dating from the 18th and 19th centuries. Then one discovers that there is another layer beneath that, the mystical tradition of Kabbalah, which flourished between the 13th and 17th centuries, and which is largely based on the mystical traditions first found in the Talmud and Midrash and other early rabbinic texts. And, of course, these rabbinic commentaries were primarily concerned with interpreting the biblical text. In this way one learns that each generation of Jewish literature looks back to the previous generation, as well as to all the generations before that. This is what we mean by a tradition.

Whereas most writers in this century have been essentially cut off from any kind of tradition, religious or otherwise, many modern Jewish authors have succeeded in drawing on this rich biblical and post-biblical Jewish tradition in their own works. By doing so, they have been able to continue that tradition into the present. This modern tradition is a secular one, and yet, since it draws inspiration from the sacred texts of Judaism, it is an authentic continuation of an ancient tradition more than three thousand years old.

The primary purpose in editing *Gates to the New City* was to collect the best stories by modern Jewish authors who have drawn on this abundant literary tradition in some fashion. No story was included whose source in the Bible, Apocrypha, Aggadah, Kabbalah, folklore, or Hasidic lore could not be documented. Some of these sources were very famous and some were quite obscure, but each and every one can be found in the notes on the stories at the end of the book.

This collection is intended to demonstrate, above all, that for modern Jewish writers the Book is not closed, and the ancient Jewish literary tradition remains a vital source of inspiration even in our own time. Reading these stories with an awareness of this tradition greatly enhances their meaning Finding, for example, that the character of the talmudic heretical sage Elisha ben Abuyah is strongly echoed in Cynthia Ozick's story "The Pagan Rabbi," entirely transforms the way we read that story. Or discovering a midrashic account of a bitter dialogue between Noah and the raven that is remarkably parallel to that between the bird and man in Bernard Malamud's "The Jewbird" gives us new insight into Malamud's famous story.

Indeed, all of these stories are enhanced by an awareness of how they respond to the long and rich tradition of Jewish literature. In order to assist the reader in approaching these stories from this perspective, *Gates to the New City* includes an introduction that provides the necessary historical and literary background. This introduction demonstrates the ways in which the biblical narratives were reimagined in the rabbinic legends and how these legends later took on a life of their own, serving as models for subsequent Jewish texts and providing a sense of inspiration that graces all of Jewish literature.

Those who have been to Israel, and especially to Jerusalem, often marvel at the profound sense of the past that pervades every aspect of daily life. Readers of these stories will come away with a similar sense of past and present bound together into a vision that conveys the rich echoes of the Jewish tradition as they are perceived by some of the finest Jewish authors of this century.

—Howard Schwartz
March 15, 1989
St. Louis

INTRODUCTION

by Howard Schwartz

I

REIMAGINING THE BIBLE

In Genesis there are two versions of the story of how woman was created. One version, which states that God formed Eve from Adam's rib, is the more famous. But there is another version of the creation story: *In the day that God created man, in the likeness of God He made him; male and female He created them* (Gen. 1:27). Most modern readers would not be disturbed by this apparent contradiction, which biblical scholars attribute to the weaving of two separate myths into a single narrative. But to the ancient Jewish sages, who firmly believed that every word in the Torah was divinely inspired, it was a matter of supreme importance that the contradiction be resolved. This they succeeded in doing by proposing that *male and female He created them* referred to the creation of Adam's first wife, whom they called Lilith, while the other version described the creation of Adam's second wife, Eve.[1]

Thus the career of Lilith was launched, and it has been an impressive career by any standard. For once the rabbis had introduced a new element into the biblical narrative, it became necessary to chronicle its history from beginning to end. Because Eve was taken as the model for subsequent women, especially in her submissive behavior toward her husband, Lilith was imagined as her polar opposite.[2] She was especially angered by Adam's insistence that she lie beneath him when they had sex, and when he refused to yield on this issue she pronounced the sacred Name of God[3] and flew out of the Garden of Eden to the Red Sea, where she found new lovers among the demons who lived there. The story goes on to say that Adam complained to God, and God, in turn, sent three angels, Senoy, Sansenoy, and Semangelof, who ordered Lilith to return to her husband. But even when they threatened to kill one hundred of her offspring daily, she refused to return. It was at this point that God created Eve.

Nor does the infamous history of Lilith end there. She was believed to be jealous of Eve's ability to have human children, while her own were merely demons, and thus she was blamed for the high percentage of infant mortality that prevailed. In the Zohar (3:19a) a rite is described whose purpose was to keep Lilith away from the marriage bed. It also became necessary to protect pregnant women and newborn infants from Lilith's vengeance by having them wear amulets to ward off her powers.[4] Lilith's lust was believed to have been so great that whenever a man had nocturnal emissions or sexual fantasies, it was said that he had intercourse with Lilith, and the offspring of these unions were all the demons that populate the world. It was even believed that a man's own demonic children would flock around his deathbed, calling out his name, and that the man's human sons should recite Psalm 91 at their father's funeral in order to protect themselves from these demons, who would otherwise try to steal their inheritance. And all of this involved legend derives from a commentary on the biblical passage *male and female He created them.*[5]

This legend and a great many others like it are known as aggadot (singular: aggadah), a particular form of Jewish legend that appears in the Talmud and later biblical elaborations known as the Midrash.[6] Because the rabbis thought that the answers to all inquiries could be found in the Bible, and especially in the first five books known as the Torah,[7] the whole ethical system of the Jews depended on the interpretation of these particular texts. And, perhaps inevitably, constant meditation on these same laws and legends led the rabbis to invent resolutions to the incomplete narratives and to discover the meaning of obscure passages that are found, in particular, in the early books of the Bible. They sought to reduce, for example, the guilt of Eve which resulted from the sin of the Fall, or to shed light on the childhood of Abraham, the patriarch who was the first to have the perception that there was only one God. For clues, the rabbis searched in the details of the given text, and since there often was little to go on, the conclusions drawn in these cases tended to reflect their creators as much as they resolved the unfinished tale.

Another example of the aggadic-midrashic method concerns Enoch, about whom the Bible says only *And Enoch walked with God, and he was not; for God took him* (Gen. 5:34). This statement, in the midst of a genealogical list, distinguishes Enoch from the others, about whom it is said "and he died." But since even the slightest variation in biblical phrasing was taken to have profound significance, extensive conclusions were drawn from the unusual statement about his death. Enoch came to be described as one of the few righteous men in the evil generation preceding the Flood, who was taken up into Paradise at God's command and taught the secrets of the universe. Then he was returned to earth, to instruct men, and finally he was taken back into heaven, where he was transformed into the fiery angel, Metatron, who became the heavenly scribe, the attendant of the Throne of Glory, the prince of the treasuries of heaven, the ruler and judge of all the hosts of angels, and executor of the Divine decrees on earth—quite a promotion for a figure who appears in only a brief passage in the Bible.[8]

As the examples of Lilith and Enoch make apparent, this imaginative opening out of biblical exegesis was utilized with remarkable freedom, under the circumstances. For in these post-biblical legends we find a literature that flowered under some of the most stringent restrictions ever devised by men. After all, the purpose of many midrashim was not primarily literary; they were an attempt to substantiate a point of the Law, clarify a contradiction in the biblical text, or offer an analogy. Like Adne Sadeh—a midrashic creature who was believed to have been created before man, and who was bound to the earth by his long navel cord and thus could move no farther than it reached—the legends of the Midrash had to remain linked to the biblical passages that served as proof-texts.

In each generation it has been the practice of the Jewish people to return to the Bible for guidance in both ethical and spiritual matters. The radical changes in culture and environment that they experienced over the ages made it necessary to interpret the biblical laws so that they would be applicable to their existence. Thus the Bible, and specifically the Torah, is not only the covenant between the people of Israel and God,[9] but it is also the source of the primary myths of the culture, and the bedrock for all commentary, both in the halakhic, or legal, realm, and in the aggadic, or legendary, realm. Indeed, it is not difficult to understand why all subsequent sacred texts exist in the shadow of the Holy Scriptures.

It is generally acknowledged that some of the narratives in Genesis preserved myths which can be traced back at least four thousand years, and probably more. The actual writing down of these myths was believed to have been begun approximately three thousand years ago. Once the Scriptures were canonized, the Book was regarded as closed. Although the evidence gathered by biblical scholars demonstrates that the texts of the oldest book of the Bible, Genesis, are likely reworkings of the original texts, with subsequent interpolations, we know at least that these scriptural texts have been handed down, virtually unchanged, since the canon of the Hebrew Scriptures was completed around 100 C.E.[10]

Once the canon of the Bible was closed, the creativity of the People of the Book had nowhere to turn but back to the Bible. It was firmly believed that the answers to all questions could be found there, if one only had sufficient breadth and depth of knowledge to understand: "Turn it and turn it over again and again, for everything is in it, and contemplate it, and wax gray and grow old over it, and stir not from it, for you cannot have any better rule than this" (B. Av. 5:25).

However, the need to update the meaning of the Bible extended not only to the laws it contained but also to the stories themselves. These stories retained their immediacy because subsequent generations gave themselves to reimagining the Bible, projecting themselves into the biblical archetypes and reliving the myth in themselves. In this way it was possible for the Aggadah to become a vehicle for the personal and mythic expressions of the people which could then be absorbed into the tradition, as well as a means of permitting the religion to evolve, which it did. The premise here is that a tradition must continually expand its boundaries in order to incorporate all generations at the same time.

Since an entire ethical system also depended on the interpretation of these particular texts, determining the resolution of certain incomplete biblical narratives took on extraordinary importance. Thus, perhaps inevitably, constant meditation on these same myths and legends led the rabbis to invent or discover in some fashion the solution to these incomplete mysteries. These, in turn, often took up motifs that had first appeared in earlier aggadot. In this way the Jewish legendary tradition has reflected a remarkable continuity which underlies the stylistic differences of various stages in the aggadic tradition, "forming," as Martin Buber said, "a second Bible of legends, scattered in innumerable writings, around the nucleus of Scripture."[11]

On first consideration, it is true, the Bible seems to thoroughly overshadow all subsequent Jewish literature. The Bible, and in particular the Torah, is held in such high esteem as the literal Word of God that it has been the focus for post-biblical Jewish literature, both sacred and secular, until this century, much of which presents itself simply as first- or second-level commentary on it. To a remarkable extent this commentary itself is regarded as sacred, since all oral commentary and later written commentary claimed its source in the Oral Law. This companion tradition holds that at the same time Moses received the Torah, the Written Law, at Mount Sinai, he also received the Oral Law, which interpreted the Written Law. So central was this Oral Law considered to be that Rabbi Nehemiah is quoted as saying: "Two Torahs were given, one written and one oral."[12] This spoken commentary was not committed to writing, but was transmitted by word of mouth for many centuries until Judah ha-Nasi, known as Rabbi, compiled and edited the Mishnah, the core of the Talmud, about 200 C.E.[13] Considering the reluctance with which the oral tradition was committed to writing, it is understandable that the rabbis had to seek out a form in which to preserve the laws and legends that constitute it. This structure was from the first an effort to record the discussions of the rabbis, in the form of what appears to be—but in fact is really not—verbatim text. Here, and in the literature that followed, there are constant reminders that the words of the speaker are in a direct line with those handed down from Sinai: "Go and tell them I have a tradition from Rabbi Yohanan ben Zakkai, who heard it from his teacher, and his teacher from his teacher, and his teacher from his teacher, reaching from Moses at Mount Sinai" (B. Hag. 3).

So much importance was placed on the Oral Law that it was soon believed that the primary work, the Torah, could not be understood without it. There is an important midrash in which Moses is sent by God to sit in the classroom of Rabbi Akiba. The fact that Akiba lived over a thousand years after Moses presents no problems in the Aggadah, where time is subordinate to the will of God. Moses finds Akiba's teachings difficult to follow (!) and is astonished when Akiba quotes Moses as the source of his teaching. It seems possible to read in this legend the implicit belief that the later generations had succeeded in contributing to an understanding of the Torah, so that Moses, the predecessor, must turn to his successor, Rabbi Akiba, for a complete understanding of the law that he himself transmitted:

> Rav Yehuda said in the name of Rav: "In the hour when Moses ascended the heights he found the Holy One, blessed be He, sitting and tying crowns for letters. Moses said before Him: 'Master of the Universe! What prevents You from leaving the letters as they are?' The Holy One, blessed be He, said to him: 'There is a man who will live after many generations and Akiba ben Joseph is his name, and he will build on every crown a multitude of halakhot.' Moses said before Him: 'Master of the Universe! Show him to me!' Then the Holy One, blessed be He, said to him: 'Turn around!' Moses then went and sat at the back of the eighth row of Rabbi Akiba's disciples, and he could not understand what they were saying. His strength failed him. When Rabbi Akiba reached a certain point, his disciples said to him: 'Rabbi, from where do you know this?' Rabbi Akiba said to them: 'It is a halakhah of Moses from Mount Sinai.'"
>
> (B. Men. 29b)

In many ways, then, the post-biblical written tradition may be seen as an extension of the oral tradition: instead of regarding what had been set down in writing as fixed, later commentators regarded the tale itself as flexible, as if a single story were being retold and embellished over many generations. There can be no doubt that the acceptance of the practice by which it was possible to embellish the legends of the Aggadah and complete the biblical episodes derived from the nature of the oral tradition. Such a tradition must inevitably come to recognize that no matter how precisely a tale is retold, there is a slow, inevitable, and necessary process of revision that takes place each time it is repeated. Even once the tale has been perfected in some form, minor details of the narrative will continue to evolve. Since a considerable period elapsed before the legends of the oral tradition were recorded in the Talmud and the Midrash, the effects of this inevitable process cannot be underestimated. But being among the world's great storytellers, the Jews recognized that a master storyteller cannot but recast the story in his own vision and style. Just as man was made in God's image, so too do the tales a man tells necessarily bear his imprint.

With the Bible and the Talmud, then, Jewish literature is securely rooted in two thoroughly sacred texts.[11] The Oral Law, as codified in the Talmud, served as the basis of an elaborate structure of commentaries and codes prepared by such masters of the Middle Ages and the Renaissance as Rashi, the Tosafists, Maimonides, and Joseph Caro, forming a continuous chain linked to Sinai. Legal decisions and interpretations were also transmitted by *responsa*, a form of correspondence between rabbis. The resulting body of law, which constitutes the definitive authority and is still in force among Orthodox Jews today, is known as the Halakhah. The Talmud also both contains and later inspired the literature of the Aggadah. But the aura of authority of the Oral Law pales with each subsequent addition to the sacred canon. The rabbis who interpreted halakhic decisions in the post-talmudic *responsa* acknowledged that their additions to the tradition did not have the status of divine revelation. But in the realm of the Aggadah, additions and innovations continued long after the work of the Talmud was brought to a close around 500 C.E., at least until the 12th or 13th century. These later legends, or midrashim, were collected in several major anthologies, the most important of which is the multivolumed *Midrash Rabbah,* whose midrashim came to be widely regarded as a part of the legacy of the Oral Law.

The aggadic tradition is unique in the insight it permits into the process of the evolution and embellishment of the central Jewish myths and legends. In virtually every other mythic tradition the transformation of the central narratives took place early in the culture's development, and this transformation was limited exclusively to the oral phase of the culture which preceded the written phase. Any subsequent embellishment in the written tradition of these cultures was limited to the realm of self-conscious works of art, such as the plays of Sophocles and Euripides. In contrast, the Jewish legendary tradition continued to actively evolve its legends long after the original versions had already been set down in writing. This distinction constitutes one of the primary unresolved paradoxes of the Jewish religion—on the one hand the rabbis did not ignore even the slightest word of the Torah, not even the crown of a letter, as in the story of Moses and Akiba; at the same time, these sacred texts were subject to the often radical revision of the aggadic tradition, which tended to approach them as if they were still oral tales and had never been set down in writing at all. Ultimately, these seemingly polar tendencies were resolved in the creation of a remarkably reverent literature, in which every detail has been carefully weighed with respect to its implications for the primary tenets of Judaism, and especially as to the necessity of upholding the paramount tenet of the religion, the concept of monotheism. It is as if a story had been told and the ones responsible for retelling it had been given the freedom to embellish it as they pleased, within the limitations of very precise and demanding rules. These rules hold that all additions must be demonstrated to be linked to the original text (thus the need for proof-texts); that all additions must clarify and complete missing elements of the original; that they must remain true to the reverent spirit of the original; and that the tone and, to a certain extent, the style must be consistent with the original.

The Aggadah of the Talmud and Midrash and the legends of the Kabbalah and of the Hasidim are unique among the sacred literatures of the world, since virtually every phase in their development can be traced in each subsequent generation. And this evolution continues into secular literature in the form of the folklore of the exiled and oppressed people who also found solace in reimagining the Bible and the subsequent history of their holy men, martyrs, and great rabbis. Although the style of presentation of these folk legends tends to be less didactic and more narrative than that of the Aggadah, the legends themselves are cut from the same cloth.

During the process of this aggadic evolution, elements of the imagination, and ultimately of literary consciousness, worked their way into the midrashic and folk traditions with remarkable freedom. It is possible to detect an increasingly conscious attitude toward the use of literary devices, styles, and techniques. The earliest written midrashim were cast in the style of the Halakhah—precise, terse, and judicial in style and content. Little by little, however, the later midrashim began to break out of this epigrammatic structure and rediscover the narrative expansiveness of the Bible and the oral tradition.

Unlike the fables of Aesop, in which the moral is stated at the end of the fable, the midrashim begin with the biblical passage that is being interpreted, using it as a springboard for the imagination. At the same time, with such intense concentration on a relatively short text, the imaginations of the rabbis were inspired to complete the often unfinished tales of the Torah. As generation followed generation, a larger picture became apparent from the Aggadah, a vision in which image was linked to image, theme to theme, metaphor to metaphor, until finally legend was linked to legend in a way that suggested the possibility of an unbroken bridge of legends built across the gaps in the biblical narratives and chronology. What ultimately was being created was a kind of mono-myth of all creation—even of the time prior to existence—through all of time until the End of Days.

Linking together the disparate legends is the central symbol of the Jewish tradition, the Torah itself. It is a symbol not only of what it contains—the essential sum of all Jewish law and lore—but also a symbol personified in many ways which is received anew by every generation, like an eternal flame handed down from father to son. The Torah is also directly equated with the Tree of Life—*The Torah is a Tree of Life to those who cling to it* (Prov. 3:18). So precious did the sages feel it was that virtually all of the midrashim about the giving of the Torah emphasize the resistance in heaven and on earth. In heaven the angels first objected to God's plan to give this precious gift to the children of Israel. And even though they were overruled, they still resisted Moses during his ascent into Paradise to receive the Torah, almost destroying him in their efforts to stave off one who still wore the earthly raiment. Only the intervention of God saved Moses from the vengeful angels, and ended their near-revolt.[15]

That biblical figures in the Aggadah had become a model for all of Jewish history, into which the Jewish people projected the experiences of their varied history, was recognized by Louis Ginzberg in his seven-volume masterpiece, *The Legends of the Jews*.[16] Ginzberg gathered together a great many of the midrashim and wove them into a continuous narrative of their own, following the order of the Holy Scriptures. In so doing he accomplished for our generation what was the unspoken goal of the aggadic tradition from the first: to write the Book of the Book, a distorted mirror image of the original which reflects its biblical source and yet is also a separate creation in itself.

The primary purpose of the aggadic tradition, then, was to transmit and reinterpret the past for each successive generation. This purpose has at its root a love for the past and a desire to carry it into the future, to keep it alive. The biblical tale, once told, was found to be true for all generations; it was open to reinterpretation as well as retelling in each generation. The Jews have long been a wandering people who have collected tales over the ages and incorporated their own experiences into a common tradition. This is, by definition, what tradition is—receiving and transmitting what has been received. In many ways this legendary literature not only is a peculiar kind of scriptural commentary, but also considers the past from the perspective of the future, searching for oracles that have since been fulfilled, and for clues that will help provide safe passage into the future.

Thus in retelling and rewriting these tales, the rabbis responsible for the midrashim were like jewelers who polished an immense and many-faceted jewel. Each generation turned its gaze to a new facet of the jewel, for the facets of the jewel are infinite. And even so there was never any doubt among them that it was but a single jewel they saw, whose essential structure was eternal and unchanging; the principal jewel, in fact, in the crown of the King whose countless, unqualified blessings are given anew to each generation.

II

THE AGGADIC TRADITION

1.

The continuity of Jewish literature extends across the entire period from the biblical era to the present, unbroken. The legends of the Bible are the foundation on which this tradition has been built, each generation upon the preceding one. The books of the Apocrypha and Pseudepigrapha[17] are modeled directly on the books of the biblical canon, from which the former were excluded, and the latter were written afterward. The legends of rabbinic literature, known as the Aggadah, assume a biblical context within which they elaborate on unfinished aspects of the biblical narratives, such as the evil intentions of the builders of the Tower of Babel, the childhood of Abraham, or how King David evaded the Angel of Death. Since these episodes are not reported in the Bible, the aggadists sought out these solutions themselves, working on the assumption that the missing information is implicit in the biblical narrative. According to tradition, these elaborations belong to the Oral, or Unwritten, Law, which was transmitted on Mount Sinai at the same time as the Torah and is regarded as being part of the legacy Moses received during forty days and nights. But, as will become apparent, they are, in fact, the creations of the longing and imagination of succeeding generations, each of which contributed to these Jewish myths, so that they subsequently continued to evolve. The form and style of the legends of the early rabbinic literature serve as models for the legends of the late rabbinic literature and the Kabbalah, which also emerge out of a context of biblical commentary.[18] As a result a pattern was established in which subsequent genres of post-talmudic literature tend toward a generally exegetical model. This remained the case until the appearance of later midrashim, such as those found in *Pirke de Rabbi Eliezer* (8th-12th century C.E.) and *Sefer Yashar* (13th-15th century C.E.), which utilize a narrative mode more like that of the Bible, while incorporating material derived largely from prior rabbinic collections, such as the Talmud and the midrashim.

The exacting form of the Aggadah does inhibit somewhat the narrative freedom of the legends it relates, while replacing this freedom with a unique structure capable of assimilating a wide range of material, from matters of interpretation to imaginative reports about immense jewels seen at sea.[19] This form permits, as well, the distinctive voices of individual rabbis to be distinguished in their teaching. Yet whatever narrative inhibitions are inherent in the aggadic format are ultimately set free in the folklore that flourished in the Middle Ages, which was the first secular Jewish literature. Here the form of the folktales was blended with the perspective, but not the style, of the legends of the Talmud and Midrash, choosing instead a flowing style like that of a storyteller. This folkloric style is also far freer and less self-conscious, and, of course, less polished than the biblical model, which often reads as if engraved in stone.

The legends and styles of all of these previous periods—the biblical, aggadic, kabbalistic, folkloric, and hasidic—are utilized as models by modern Jewish authors such as S. Y. Agnon, M. J. Berditchevsky, I. L. Peretz, and I. B. Singer. These authors, and virtually all of those represented in this anthology, have discovered new ways to embellish and utilize the old myths, which seem to retain their primal power no matter how many times they are retold. Often these authors draw on a modern stylistic and intellectual perspective while doing this, which in itself brings the legends into a new dimension. The result is a literature that is as much a product of the aggadic tradition as are the legends of the Midrash or the myths of the Kabbalah. For while these modern authors utilize these traditional forms and genres in markedly individual ways, the essential vision of the Aggadah remains unchanged, and in general they retain a tone that is essentially reverent.

The fact is that the process of the evolution of a myth or legend continues each time it is retold. There is even evidence of this evolutionary process taking place at the earliest stages of Jewish literature, involving the myths and legends of Genesis. For it is a firm premise of biblical scholarship in this century that many of the myths found in Genesis existed at least a thousand years before they were written down. Two primary narratives have been observed, that in which God's name is Yahweh (or, in the New Latin version, Jehovah), which is known as the J text, and that in which God's name is Elohim, known as the E text. That these two texts did in fact derive from two separate traditions is underscored by the fact that Yahweh is a singular term, while Elohim is plural.[20]

According to this theory of biblical scholarship, these two texts were woven together by the priestly editors of Genesis. But the possibility also exists that they may have retold the tale of the Exile from Eden in a way quite different from that in which they received it, or at least that the texts they worked with already had transformed the original myth. In *Folklore in the Old Testament*, James G. Frazer, who also wrote *The Golden Bough*, proposes that this legend of the Fall in Genesis may be a retelling of a more ancient myth.[21] He deduces this from the fact that as it stands, the biblical narrative is clearly fragmentary. For while the Tree of Knowledge is given a central role in the episode, no active role is given to the Tree of Life. Yet at the end of the narrative this tree is given as the reason that Adam and Eve were expelled from the Garden:

> So He drove out the man; and he placed at the east of the Garden of Eden the cherubim, and the flaming sword which turned every way, to keep the way to the Tree of Life.
>
> (Gen. 3:24)

On the basis of this evidence, Frazer concludes that an earlier version of the myth involved an active role for the Tree of Life. If so, then it may well have been a myth about the Tree of Life and its natural counterpart, the Tree of Death:

> Accordingly we may suppose that in the original story there were two trees, a Tree of Life and a Tree of Death; that it was open to man to eat of the one and live forever, or to eat of the other and die; that God, out of good will to His creature, advised man to eat of the Tree of Life and warned him not to eat of the Tree of Death; and that man, misled by the serpent, ate of the wrong tree and so forfeited the immortality which his benevolent Creator had designed for him.[22]

That this theory is more than mere speculation is confirmed by the fact that one of the consequences of the eating of the forbidden fruit is human mortality. Why we should regard the expulsion from Eden, rather than the inevitability of mortality, as the primary consequence of the Fall is difficult to comprehend. Thus it appears as if the priorities of the myth have been reversed in the retelling.

If Frazer's thesis is correct—and it does have the ring of truth to it—it demonstrates that even from the earliest period of Jewish literature there was the impulse to retell the old myth from a new perspective—a practice which becomes the *modus operandi* of subsequent Jewish literature, which presumes and incorporates the existence of the old into the new. In this case, it seems likely, the scribes who recorded, interpolated, and reworked the texts of Genesis consciously chose to emphasize the ethical issue of the loss of innocence over the myth of the origin of death, which was the original intent of the tale. However, they retained death as one of the consequences of disobeying the ban on the fruit of the Tree of Knowledge, and thus the tale remains a myth of the origin of death, while becoming, as well, the myth of the Exile from Eden. Now that the Tree of Death had been renamed the Tree of Knowledge, however, they had little use for the Tree of Life. Yet having stripped it of all importance, they were reluctant to eliminate it entirely—perhaps out of some residual reverence to the original myth, or out of the sense that the second tree was still required to provide narrative balance—and chose to retain it, even though its presence made the end of the story obscure and incomplete.

2.

In most cultures the transition from an oral to a written tradition is a dramatic change that tends to regard the written material, after only a few generations, as sacred and eternal in its written form. The inevitability of the evolution of myth, which is presumed in an oral tradition, is replaced with a belief in the permanence of the written form. Such a belief also characterizes the Jewish attitude toward the books of the Bible. Yet, paradoxically, the oral ethic that enabled mythic transformations to take place was also retained. This apparent contradiction was resolved by the recognition of two separate but related traditions: the written and the unwritten. While the text of the Written Law was sacrosanct, the Oral Law was not. It was this conscious retention of the older oral dimension, then, that distinguishes the Jewish religious and literary traditions from others, and was responsible for creating a situation in which it remained possible for the central myths to continue evolving even after they had been written down.

Eventually some of the oral traditions were preserved in writing, usually when they were in danger of otherwise being lost, or to prevent the formation of competing sects, each claiming that the Law as they had received it was the authentic version. As a result it is possible to follow this mythic evolution in texts, although much scholarly debate continues as to their precise dating.[23] A representative example of the kind of evolution that takes place between the biblical source and its aggadic retelling is the legend of the City of Luz. There are four passing references to Luz in the Bible, but it is the first reference that supplies its attributes as a place unique in the world, for it was there that Jacob had the dream of the ladder that reached into heaven, with angels ascending and descending on it (Gen. 28:12):

> And Jacob rose up early in the morning, and took the stone that he had put under his head, and set it up for a pillar, and poured oil upon the top of it. And he called the name of the place Bethel [House of God], but the name of the city was Luz at the same time.
>
> (Gen. 28:18-19)

However, the remaining biblical references to Luz do not shed additional light on the nature of the city. But in the Talmud a legend appears that is linked to this city, which in many ways prefigures the kind of folklore eventually to emerge on a much wider scale in the Middle Ages:

And the man went into the land of the Hittites, and built a city, and called the name thereof Luz, which has remained its name until this day (Judg. 1:26). It has been taught: That is the Luz against which Sennacherib marched without disturbing it, against which Nebuchadnezzar marched without destroying it, and even the Angel of Death has no permission to pass through it. But when the old there become tired of life they go outside the wall and then die.

(B. Sot. 46b)

No further embellishment of this legend of a city in which the inhabitants remain immortal is found in the Talmud.[24] Subsequent development appears in *Genesis Rabbah*. First the biblical passage about Jacob's dream (Gen. 28:12) is quoted in the context of an exegetical discussion, creating the first link between the Luz of Jacob and that referred to in the previously quoted talmudic passage. Then the legend is taken one step further:

Rabbi Abba ben Kahana said: "Why was it called Luz?—Because whoever entered it blossomed forth into meritorious acts and good deeds like a *luz* (nut tree)." The Rabbis said: "As the nut has no mouth (opening), so no man could discover the entrance to the town." Rabbi Simon said: "A nut tree stood at the entrance of the city." Rabbi Leazar ben Merom said in the name of Rabbi Phinehas ben Mama: "A nut tree stood at the entrance of a cave; this tree was hollow, and through it one entered the cave and through the cave the city."

(*Genesis Rabbah* 69:8)

Note how Rabbi Leazar embellishes a detail newly added to the tale by Rabbi Simon—taking the name of the town as a nut tree, the literal meaning of *luz*, he postulates it as the symbol of the city, and places it at the entrance. While it is possible, of course, that this embellishment was part of an earlier tradition that Rabbi Simon was merely recalling, it appears equally possible that the description of the nut tree at the gates of the city is an example of the kind of mythic evolution of which we have been speaking. Certainly the further development presented by Rabbi Leazar, quoting Rabbi Phinehas, takes this motif one step further, embellishing the role of the nut tree: "this tree was hollow, and through it one entered the cave and through the cave the city." Regrettably, this attractive and enticing motif of a city of immortals, almost fairy-tale in nature, was not developed any further until the late medieval period, when it was rediscovered,[25] although the notion of a boundary that the Angel of Death cannot cross appears in the Zohar (4:151a), referring to the Land of Israel as a whole rather than to the City of Luz: "It is the Destroying Angel who brings death to all people, except those who die in the Holy Land, to whom death comes by the Angel of Mercy, who holds sway there." This gradual and meandering kind of development is characteristic of the aggadic tradition, whose evolution is not unlike that of living creatures in this respect. At the same time, this makes reading the Aggadah a treasure hunt in which these kinds of gems lie scattered everywhere in the rich midrashic literatures.

Note also the link between the place in which Jacob had his dream and the city of eternal life. The latter motif of Luz both emphasizes its sacred dimension and confirms the appropriateness of its having been the place where Jacob's vision was revealed: *How full of awe is this place! This is none other than the House of God, and this is the Gate of Heaven* (Gen. 28:17). The ladder of Jacob's dream, after all, is itself an archetype of the link between earth and heaven. Such a link is clearly intended to be regarded in a positive light, but Genesis also contains the inverse of this symbol, the Tower of Babel, whose builders also sought to span the same distance, and were universally condemned for trying to do so in rabbinic literature. These builders, the rabbis felt, were the evil Generation of the Division who failed to recognize the preeminence of God in the world, and foolishly believed they could overthrow heaven; but instead the Lord first confused their language, and then *scattered them abroad from thence upon the face of all the earth* (Gen. 11:8). Jacob's dream, on the other hand, reflects a harmonious exchange between earth and heaven, the world of men and the world of the spirit, *with angels ascending and descending* (Gen. 28:12). In some Hekhaloth and kabbalistic texts, this ladder becomes a metaphor for the mystical ascent, on which the soul of the seeker climbs into heaven. This change from the passive dream of Jacob to the active use of the ladder for ascent accurately reflects one of the primary differences between these early and later periods. By the hasidic era the ladder had come to symbolize the common goal of spiritual purification—the Rungs of the Ladder.[26] In this way the biblical symbol is reinterpreted in every generation, and viewed both from the traditional perspective and from that of the present one.

3.

To illustrate the process by which a midrash evolves and develops, accruing and incorporating new material and variants, the midrashim concerning the death of Cain serve as an excellent example. Since the biblical narrative of Cain is unfinished, the rabbis were left to resolve the story in both a moral and literary sense. Using the tradition of the Oral Law as their justification, and supporting their interpretations with biblical proof-texts, the rabbis embellished the tale of Cain and Abel in many respects. They filled in the sketchy details of the births of the two brothers,[27] the mystery of the origin of their wives,[28] the conflict between the two,[29] the murder of Abel by Cain,[30] the burial of Abel,[31] and the punishment and ultimate fate of Cain. It is this final aspect of the legend that is the particular focus of this discussion.

The end of the biblical narrative about Cain describes his life as an outcast, and concludes by attributing to Cain the founding of the first city.³² After Cain has been cursed to become *a ceaseless wanderer on earth* (Gen. 4:12) he protests the severity of the sentence, and has it modified, as follows:

> Cain said to the Lord, "My punishment is too great to bear! Since Thou hast banished me this day from the soil, and I must avoid Thy presence and become a restless wanderer on earth—anyone who meets me may kill me!" The Lord said to him, "I promise, if anyone kills Cain, sevenfold vengeance shall be taken on him." And the Lord put a mark on Cain, lest anyone who has met him should kill him.
>
> (Gen. 4:13-15)

Of particular interest to the rabbis was the nature of the sign by which God had marked Cain, to signify and protect him in his wanderings. One of the earliest midrashim speculating on this sign appears in *Genesis Rabbah* 22:

> *And the Lord put a mark on Cain* (Gen. 4:15). Rabbi Judah said: "He caused the orb of the sun to shine on his account." Said Rabbi Nehemiah to him: "He caused the orb of the sun to shine! Rather, He afflicted him with leprosy." Rab said: "He gave him a dog." Abba Jose said: "He made a horn grow out of him." Rabbi Levi said in the name of Rabbi Simeon ben Lakish: "He suspended His punishment in abeyance until the Flood came and swept him away."

Of these five alternative accounts³³ of the nature of the mark of Cain, the version that most took in the popular consciousness was that of the horn, which was said to be located on his forehead. The reason for this should be apparent—the horn signified Cain's essentially savage nature, and thus identified him as a wild beast among men. Although it was not apparent at first, the horn was to play an essential role in the most widely accepted account of the death of Cain, which first appears in *Midrash Tanhuma* (Ber. 11) as follows:

> Lamech was Cain's grandson of the seventh generation, and blind. When Lamech went hunting his son would guide him, holding his hand, and tell him when he saw a beast. Thereupon Lamech would draw his bow and kill it. Once he saw a horn between two mountains. "I see an animal's horns!" he exclaimed, and Lamech shot and killed it. But when they went to take it, the child cried out, "It is my grandfather, Cain!" In grief Lamech beat his hands together; accidentally he dealt his child a blow to the head that killed him.

This account soon became the best-known version of the manner of Cain's death, although variants of the legend existed. There was, for example, that proposed originally by Rabbi Simeon ben Lakish, wherein Cain was seen to have found his death along with the other victims of the Flood. But this punishment was unsatisfying in that it did not single out Cain for punishment. The rabbis strongly felt that a decisive punishment for Cain was called for, to set a precedent for future murderers.

Another version of Cain's death appears in the apocryphal *Book of Jubilees* (4:31). Here Cain is said to have been killed when his house fell on him. Just as he had killed Abel with a stone, so was he killed by the stones of the house that collapsed on him.

Midrash Tanhuma (Ber. 11) proposes that Cain's final destiny was in being transformed into the Angel of Death at the time of his punishment, and remaining such until he was killed at the hands of Lamech, at which time "Lamech became transformed into the Angel of Death, thus fulfilling the prophecy, *If Cain shall be avenged sevenfold, truly Lamech shall be avenged seventy and sevenfold* (Gen. 4:24)." It seems likely that this version combines two earlier legends. In one of these, Cain's punishment must have consisted of his being transformed into the Angel of Death, and as such is a powerful origin legend to explain how this terrible angel came into being.[34] The second legend concerns Cain's fatal encounter with his descendant Lamech in the seventh generation.[35]

The first principle of supporting a midrashic interpretation is to link it to a biblical source. Since there is no description of the death of Cain in the Bible, the rabbis turned to the enigmatic passage that is quoted in part in the previous midrash. It reads in full as follows:

> And Lamech said unto his wives:
> Adah and Tsila, hear my voice;
> Ye wives of Lamech, harken unto my speech;
> For I have slain a man for wounding me,
> And a young man for bruising me;
> If Cain shall be avenged sevenfold,
> Truly Lamech seventy and sevenfold.
>
> (Gen. 4:23-24)

In *Midrash Tanhuma* this passage is seen as foretelling Lamech's metamorphosis into the Angel of Death. But most other commentaries on this passage find in it substantiation for the death of Cain at the hands of Lamech, linked to the curse of Cain (Gen. 4:13-15). In this reading, "I have slain a man for wounding me" refers to Cain, who has wounded Lamech by being the ancestor responsible for the curse that hangs over his descendants, and "a young man for bruising me" refers to Lamech's son, Tubal-Cain, who has bruised his father by making him responsible for the death of Cain. Admittedly this reading seems forced, but this kind of literary license is characteristic of the aggadic tradition. In addition, the midrashic rule requiring a proof-text to support a claim makes it the only possible passage to provide the necessary biblical link.

Thus it can be seen how the passage in *Midrash Tanhuma* ingeniously utilizes two existing traditions associated with Cain—the passage concerning Lamech and the midrash that asserts that Cain's sign was a horn. The enigmatic passage about Lamech provides the framework for the narrative of the death of Cain, as well as the conclusion of the tale. The horn is the motif around which the whole tale turns. Together the two fragments provide the necessary link to tradition that gives the midrash its authentic ring. In addition, this version of Cain's death is satisfying in a number of other aspects.

First of all, this midrash brings the tale of Cain to a conclusion, which was of no small importance to the rabbis, who had a strong sense that every tale should have a beginning, a middle, and an ending. In its biblical form the story of Cain was simply incomplete. At the same time, by extending the story seven generations, the principle was established of carrying the biblical story into the future, where the biblical archetype can occur in a new form that still permits recognition of the old. Such a system made possible identification with a biblical patriarch or king, and at the same time permitted incorporating into the Aggadah personal dreams and fantasies.

Next, this midrash provides a unique and appropriate death for Cain, especially fitting in that his slayer is his own descendant. This is a kind of poetic (or, perhaps, midrashic) justice, since Cain slew his own brother. Note, however, that neither Lamech nor his son, Tubal-Cain, can be held responsible for Cain's death, since Lamech was blind, and Tubal-Cain only a child who mistook his ancestor for an animal—which in essence Cain was. It is a case of perfect justice: Cain receives his due from his own offspring, but they are innocent of any crime, though they have in this way repaid Cain for making them accursed, and in this coincidence can be seen, of course, the hand of God. Also, note the presence of Cain's name in that of the descendant who assists in killing him, hinting that Cain, in a sense, killed himself.

Finally, this midrash aptly sets the precedent that a killer shall be slain for his crime, and does not succumb to the alternative interpretation that Cain repented and his repentance was accepted, on the grounds that there had been no previous murder for him to realize the import of his action.[36] This reading also supports the biblical injunction that the punishment for murder be death (Lev. 24:16-17), and avoids setting the precedent that exceptions to this rule be permitted.

It is not surprising, then, that this version of the death of Cain, which became the predominant one, served the needs of the rabbis and accurately reflected their views of the need for and manner of justice and retribution. All subsequent versions of this midrash, such as the following version from the late text *Sefer Yashar* (2:26-31), merely embellish aspects of this midrash, and present the details in an improved narrative form, but do not change it in any essential way:

And Lamech was old and advanced in years, and his eyes were dim so that he could not see, and Tubal-Cain, his son, was leading him one day while they were walking in the field, when Cain, the son of Adam, advanced towards them. Then Lamech was very old and could not see much, and Tubal Cain his son was very young. And Tubal-Cain told his father to draw his bow, and with the arrows he smote Cain, who was yet far off, and he slew him, for he appeared to them to be an animal. And the arrows entered Cain's body although he was distant from them, and he fell to the ground and died. And the Lord requited Cain's evil according to his wickedness, which he had done to his brother Abel, according to the word of the Lord which He had spoken. And it came to pass that when Cain had died, that Lamech and Tubal-Cain went to see the animal they had slain, and they saw, and behold Cain their grandfather was fallen dead upon the earth. And Lamech was very much grieved at having done this, and in clapping his hands together he struck his son and caused his death.

Thus it can be seen that this midrash of Cain's death solves two problems at the same time. First it explicates a difficult passage about Lamech, and at the same time it solves the narrative and moral problem of the ultimate fate of Cain. And despite its intentional usage of existing sources, it still manages to be an original creation of its own. It is in this spirit that the midrashic tradition has been carried into the present in the writings of S. Y. Agnon, I. L. Peretz, and the many other writers whose stories have been included in this collection.

4.

The continuity of style and mode that links the legends of the Talmud and Midrash is preserved in the kabbalistic period.[37] But because of the kabbalistic imperative to perceive the Scriptures from a mystical perspective, changes in the meaning of concepts and legends are common, and are often of a radical nature. A revealing illustration of this kind of transformation can be found by considering the evolution of the concept of the Shekhinah.

In the talmudic and midrashic literatures the term "Shekhinah" designates the personification of God's presence in the world. This use of the term is usually translated as "Divine Presence," and it refers to God's nearness to mankind, as in this homily of Rabbi Akiba: "When a man and wife are worthy the Shekhinah dwells in their midst; if they are unworthy fire consumes them" (Tosefta B. Sot. 17a). In this context the term designates one of the names of God, whose use implies the nearness or presence of God. At this time no attempt was made to suggest that the Shekhinah was in any way independent of God, or to imply that the term referred to a feminine aspect of the Deity. However, the seeds for such an interpretation are contained in legends such as this from the *Mekilta de Rabbi Ishmael* 14:

Whenever Israel went into exile, the Shekhinah, as it were, was with them. When they were exiled to Babylon, the Shekhinah was with them; when they were exiled to Elam, the Shekhinah was with them, as it is said, *And I will set My throne in Elam* (Jer. 49:38).

In this context the presence of the Shekhinah is intended to affirm that God remained true to Israel, and accompanied them wherever they went. But in the kabbalistic period this tradition was expanded to assert that the Shekhinah was the personification of the feminine presence of God. In this expanding myth, the Shekhinah becomes increasingly independent, and at the time of the destruction of the Temple chooses to leave her consort, God, and remain instead with her children, Israel. The exile of the Shekhinah is related in this legend from the Zohar (2;134a):

When the Sanctuary was destroyed and the Temple was burnt and the people driven into exile, the Shekhinah left her home in order to accompany them into captivity. Before leaving, however, she took one last look at her House and the Holy of Holies, and the places where the priests and the Levites used to perform their worship. . . . So in the days to come, when the Holy One, blessed be He, will remember His people, the community of Israel, the Shekhinah will return from exile first and proceed to her House, as the holy Temple will be rebuilt first.

Elsewhere in the Zohar (2;203a) the independent existence of the Shekhinah is further developed:

At the destruction of the Temple the Shekhinah revisited all the spots where she had formerly dwelt, and wept for her habitation and for Israel who had gone into exile and all those righteous ones and saints who perished there. God thereupon said to her: "What aileth thee?" . . . The Shekhinah replied with tears: "Seeing that my children have gone into exile and the Sanctuary is burnt, what is there left for me that I should linger here?" And the answer of the Holy One, blessed be He, was: *Refrain thy voice from weeping, and thine eyes from tears; for thy work shall be rewarded, saith the Lord; and they shall come back from the land of the enemy*

(Jer. 31:16)

The presence of the Shekhinah among the the exiled Israelites is vividly portrayed in the following passage (Zohar 2;176b):

When Israel were journeying in the wilderness, the Shekhinah went in front of them, and they on their side followed her guidance. The Shekhinah was accompanied by all the clouds of glory, and when it journeyed the Israelites took up their march. And when the Shekhinah ascended, the cloud also ascended on high, so that all men looked up and asked *Who is this that cometh out of the wilderness like pillars of smoke?* (S. of S. 3:6). For the cloud of Shekhinah looked like smoke because the fire which Abraham and his son Isaac kindled clung to it and never left it, and by reason of that fire it ascended both as cloud and smoke; but for all that it was perfumed, with the cloud of Abraham on the right and with the cloud of Isaac on the left.

This last passage not only affirms the presence of the Shekhinah among the Israelites during the most archetypal exile of all, the wandering in the wilderness, but it also links the Shekhinah to the patriarchs Abraham and Isaac. The intention clearly is to project the concept of the Shekhinah as a mother-figure to all of Israel back into the biblical text. Certainly the identification of the Shekhinah with the Cloud of Glory described in Exodus that guided the Israelites during the day succeeds in doing just this, and the description of the cloud of smoke creates as well a connection to the sacrifice of the ram on Mount Moriah. The effect is to create a sense of the timelessness of Jewish history, in which the essence of all past events clings to the present like the smoke of the sacrifice to the Cloud of Glory.[38]

The Kabbalists also discerned the presence of the Shekhinah in talmudic legends in which the term was not used, such as the following:

> Reb Lakish said: "An additional soul is given by the Holy One, blessed be He, to a man on every Sabbath eve, and at the end of the Sabbath He takes it away from him."
>
> (B. Ber. 16a)

In the kabbalistic period this extra soul was believed to signify the Sabbath Queen, one of the identities of the Shekhinah, who is said to descend every Sabbath eve, and to remain present for the duration of the Sabbath.

With this kabbalistic initiation, then, the presence of the Shekhinah is fully injected into the tradition. It prepares the way for a series of visions and encounters with the Shekhinah in subsequent literature that are associated, in particular, with the Western Wall of the Temple, also known as the Wailing Wall:

> Once the holy Ari (Rabbi Isaac Luria) said to Rabbi Abraham Halevy, his disciple: "Know that your days are numbered and that you will soon die if you do not do what I tell you; but if you do, you will live yet another twenty-two years. This is what I bid you to do: go to Jerusalem and pour out your prayers before the Wailing Wall and you will prove yourself worthy by seeing the Shekhinah there."
>   Rabbi Abraham went home, shut himself in his house for three days and three nights, clothed himself in sackcloth and ashes, and fasted the whole time. Then he went forth to Jerusalem; he stood before the Wailing Wall in prayer, deep meditation and weeping. The image of a woman, clad in black, appeared to him on the face of the wall. Immediately he fell upon the ground in great fear. Tearing his hair, he cried in a loud voice: "Woe is me, what have I seen?"
>   Finally he fell into a deep slumber and in a dream the Shekhinah appeared to him, clad in fine raiment, and said to him: "Console thyself, My son Abraham;

there is yet hope for thee, and the children of Israel will return to their inheritance, and I will have mercy upon them."

He arose and returned to Safed, and when the Ari saw him, he said to him at once: "Now I know that you have seen the Shekhinah and you can rest assured that you will live another twenty-two years."[39]

In these kabbalistic and post-kabbalistic legends of the Shekhinah it is apparent that at least from a mythological point of view the Shekhinah has become an independent entity. Nevertheless, the Shekhinah was regarded at the same time as being an extension or aspect of the Divinity, which was of course necessary in order to uphold the essential concept of monotheism. True initiates of the Kabbalah were not disturbed by these apparent contradictions, but for others the danger of viewing the Shekhinah as a separate deity was recognized, and explains why the study of the kabbalistic texts was not permitted until a man had reached his fortieth year, was married, and had received rabbinic ordination. Such a person was felt to be grounded enough in the tradition not to be overwhelmed by the kabbalistic metaphors, while younger, more vulnerable men might well be led astray. Such dangers are portrayed in the tale of the Baal Shem retold by Meyer Levin as "The Book Mysteries," in which the son of Rabbi Adam is devoured by the force he sets free in his insistence on studying the Book of Mysteries, which is clearly intended to be a kabbalistic text. S. Ansky's drama *The Dybbuk* also portrays a young yeshivah student who is driven to madness and death after attempting to explore the kabbalistic mysteries on his own. Nor does the evolution of the myth of the Shekhinah end in the kabbalistic period. The implications of the exile of the Shekhinah were expanded in the 16th century by Rabbi Isaac Luria, as explained below. And in the 19th century Rabbi Nachman of Bratslav told the tale "The Lost Princess," included here, which hints at an identification of the Shekhinah with Jung's concept of the *anima*. And this implicit link between Shekhinah and *anima* is made explicit in the story "The Palace of Pearls" by Penina Villenchik, also represented here.

In addition to being potentially dangerous, the texts of the Kabbalah are often obscure. The ten *Sefirot*, which are the emanations of the Divinity, are the foundation on which most kabbalistic thought in the Zohar is based, and are themselves highly metaphorical and esoteric. This fact made it difficult for the essential kabbalistic principles to be transmitted beyond very limited circles. Even after the "discovery" of the Zohar by Moshe de Leon, who attributed his masterly pseudepigraphical work to the 3rd-century talmudic sage Simeon bar Yohai, the spread of its influence was still limited and exclusive. In the 16th century, however, a reformulation of the essential kabbalistic creation myth appeared in the teachings of Rabbi Isaac Luria of Safed, known as the Ari.

The creation of the world in six days and a seventh day for rest, as described in Genesis, had been recast in the Zohar into a far more complex system of ten stages of emanation, the *Sefirot*.[40] In each subsequent phase, the divine substance becomes more manifest, ultimately resulting in the existence of this world. In his reformulation of this myth, the Ari describes these emanations of the Divinity as vessels filled with divine light—the same light that existed after God said *Let there be light. And there was light* (Gen. 1:3) —until the fourth day, when *God made the two great lights: the greater light to rule the day, and the lesser light to rule the night and the stars* (Gen. 1:17). All of these emanations emerged from a single, unseen point, which is the highest and most remote aspect of the Divinity, known as *Ein Sof,* the Endless. These vessels set sail from above to below like a fleet of ships, each carrying its cargo of light. Then somehow—Lurianic doctrine is at a loss to explain why—the frail vessels broke open, split asunder, and all the sparks were scattered, like the dust of the earth and the stars of the sky. This breaking of the vessels is known in Lurianic terms as the Shattering of the Vessels. It is the Lurianic equivalent of the Fall of man. The linkage of the Creation with the Fall is intended to reveal them as part of a single process, for the Fall brought about a change in existence that was as profound as the changes that took place during the six days of Creation. As a result of the Shattering of the Vessels, the sparks of light that were contained in the vessels were scattered everywhere in the world. The whole had split apart. The Fall had taken place.

But the mythic cosmology of the Ari does not conclude with the Shattering of the Vessels—it is far too concerned with the issue of restoration. Rather, it proposes that this was but the first in a two-stage process. And the second stage of this process is that of restoration and redemption, or *Tikkun.* The Ari called this phase Gathering the Sparks, and in his view it was the destiny of the Jews to seek out and gather these scattered sparks, no matter how far they had flown and how well they were hidden. This process was described by one of the disciples of the Ari, Israel Sarug, in 1631:

> Traces of the divine light adhered to the fragments of the broken vessels like sparks. And when the fragments descended to the bottom of the fourth and last world, they produced the four elements, and when all these became materialized, some of the sparks still remained within. Therefore it should be the aim of everyone to raise these sparks from where they are imprisoned in this world and to elevate them to holiness by the power of their soul.[41]

However, the Shattering of the Vessels not only provided a purpose for the Children of Israel, but also explained the exile of the Shekhinah, as formulated by the primary disciple of the Ari, Hayim Vital:

And behold, when the Temple was destroyed the Shekhinah went into exile among the *kelippot* (shattered vessels which have been reduced to mere shells), because the souls that had been exiled there no longer had sufficient strength—as a result of their sins—to free themselves. Therefore the Shekhinah . . . descended among them in order to gather in the soul-sparks . . . to sift them from the *kelippot*, to raise them to the sphere of holiness, and to renew them and bring them down again into this world in human bodies. Thus you may understand the mystery of the exile of the Shekhinah.[42]

Note how well this myth not only expresses the essential aspects of the process of Gathering the Sparks, but also incorporates the concept of the exile of the Shekhinah, as if these essentially separate myths had always been integrally related. This is one more example of how each subsequent phase of the aggadic tradition recreates the past phases within itself, and thus reinterprets the past for the present generation.

This mythic explanation for the fallen state of the world, combined with a vision of redemption involving the combined efforts of Israel and the Shekhinah, rapidly took root in the Jewish world and more than any other myth or legend was responsible for imbuing a kabbalistic fervor among the masses, which led directly to the rise of the false messiah Shabbatai Sevi in the 17th century, and led, as well, to the emergence of Hasidism in the 18th century, founded by Israel ben Eliezer, known as the Baal Shem Tov.

A close examination of the traditional elements the Ari used in his mythic retelling includes the biblical version of Creation, the Fall, and the entire kabbalistic system of emanation. Yet it emerges as a new myth, one of the last to be added to the Jewish tradition and one which quickly became an integral part of it. For like all new myths it recombines elements of the old in a new fashion, which nevertheless transforms it into something new. That this myth of the Fall and restoration should find such wide acceptance came about because of its apparent links to past traditions, which made it possible for it to be recognized as having been implicit in the earlier texts. It had grown from within, and although it presented a new transformation, the seeds were still recognizable. From this perspective the myth of the Ari existed all along, but awaited the Ari to be revealed.

Also present in the Ari's Creation myth, but not as apparent at first, are centuries of longing for the coming of the Messiah, to which the Gathering of the Sparks must undoubtedly be linked. Both the Ari and his primary disciple, Hayim Vital, were regarded in their time as precursors of the Messiah, if not as Messiah ben Joseph, who precedes the coming of Messiah ben David, and prepares the way. This messianic tradition has its roots in the Bible, as well as in all the subsequent sacred literature. But in the kabbalistic period the myth of the Messiah grew to epic proportions not unlike that of the growth of the myth of the Shekhinah. Detailed legends describe the Mes-

siah's abode in Paradise, known as the Bird's Nest, and the legends of his
coming are filled with vivid details of tremendous conflict and upheaval before the Messiah initiates the End of Days. And this kabbalistic impetus is
also incorporated into the Ari's myth with the belief that when the sparks
have finally been gathered, they will be restored to the vessels, which will
themselves have been restored, and the world will be returned to its primordial condition. This, of course, is the very result of the coming of the Messiah, and it is in this way that the Ari's myth reflects this messianic longing.

   Thus it should be apparent that certain myths of the Jewish people were
transmitted to succeeding generations with their power undiminished. Each
generation had to seek out its own means of expressing this myth, in a manner appropriate to its own time. The successive generations of Jewish literature can be seen as ongoing attempts to report the transformations of their
primal myths in their own age. It is this mythic dimension of the religion
which has played an immense role in its perpetuation in our own age.

5.

In addition to the emergence of the Zohar and other kabbalistic literature in
the Middle Ages, there was also the blossoming of folklore. Stressing narrative, and open to the influences of the folklores of surrounding cultures,
these folktales and fairy tales, lacking the sacred seal of the previous literatures, were forced to fend for themselves, as a new kind of oral tradition, and
to await the first serious collectors of Jewish folklore, such as Micha Joseph
Berditchevsky and S. Ansky. To a considerable extent the subjects of this
folklore are identical to those of the earlier sacred literatures. There are a
multitude of legends about the ten lost tribes, the miracles of the Prophet
Elijah, and the births, deaths, and wonders of the greatest rabbis, heroes,
holy men, and scholars. There are also many tales about the supernatural, in
which demons and dybbuks play important roles.

   This medieval folklore differs from the preceding sacred literatures, however, in that it is not restricted by the ethical prerogative of the talmudic and
midrashic literatures, nor is it tied to proof-texts. Instead it is attracted to the
miraculous and imaginative, as well as to tales of quests and other great un-
dertakings. A moral element is still present, but it is the kind of clear-cut
moral found, for example, in *Aesop's Fables*. Above all, it is not a self-conscious literature, as is that of the Aggadah of the Talmud and Midrash, nor is
it concerned with the mystical (in contrast to the supernatural) dimension as
is the Kabbalah. In this respect it is not unlike the kinds of folklore that
emerge naturally out of every culture, much of it borrowed from other cultures, and recast in a Jewish context.

   Here are to be found complete cycles of legends about King David and
King Solomon, and a substantial body of tales in which Elijah appears in dis-

guise to provide some form of salvation. It is apparent that these folktales reflect a simpler, more fundamental grasp of religious elements, while at the same time they are more grounded in a realistic perspective, except in the kinds of enchanted tales in which it is recognized that a flight of fancy is desired. Here too can be found those aggadic motifs which appealed to the popular imagination; for the inclination to embellish and extend existing myths and legends is just as intense as it is in the sacred literatures. At the same time, it is apparent that the powerful influence of the Oral Law, which lends its sacred aura to the legends of the Talmud and Midrash, is considerably diminished in medieval folklore. And while one consequence of this absence of the sacred aura is a distance that enters into the narration of the tale, which does not presume that the tale is necessarily true, at the same time there is an even greater liberation of the imagination than in the earlier literatures, now that its foremost commitment is no longer primarily to the affirmation of the sacred tradition.

Unfortunately, while we can be certain that the primary sacred texts have been carefully preserved, it is apparent that a great deal of folklore, which was never written down, has been lost. In fact, considering its exclusion from the sacred tradition, it is remarkable that so much of this oral tradition has survived. Among the best collections of this literature are M. J. Berditchevsky's *Mimekor Yisrael,* which is available in English, and the still untranslated collection *Sefer Maaysiot* ("The Book of Tales") by Mordecai ben Yehezkel.

In the late Middle Ages there also appeared a religious folklore, religious in that its origins came from within rabbinic circles. Its themes, of course, are primarily concerned with spiritual and moral issues, although moral themes are also prevalent in the secular folklore. A good example of such religious folklore is *Shivhei ha-Ari,* the tales about the Ari, Rabbi Isaac Luria, which has been translated into English as *In Praise of the Ari.* This collection includes tales about the miraculous birth of the Ari, his miracles, including that of transporting a king who was asleep in his palace to a pit in a field, where he was forced to sign his seal to a proclamation protecting the Jews, and his teachings. There are in addition tales about dybbuks, demons, and legends current in his time. The Ari's primary disciple, Hayim Vital, is also the subject of a volume of tales, modeled on those of the Ari, known as *Shivhei Rabbi Hayim Vital.* It is in this period that the sacred and the secular Jewish literatures flow closest together. And the subsequent hasidic literature, which turned to the tales of the masters of Safed for their model, maintains, to a considerable extent, the practice of incorporating secular legends, especially when it is possible to interpret in them some kind of religious dimension.

Many of the primary themes of medieval Jewish folklore have demonstrated an attraction for modern Jewish authors as well. Both Sholom

Aleichem and I. L. Peretz are represented with very different tales about Elijah, "Elijah the Prophet" and "The Magician," respectively. In Sholom Aleichem's story, Elijah carts off a child in a sack, as a punishment for falling asleep at the Seder, while Peretz's Elijah is an accomplished magician who uses his powers to assist the poor. Still another vision of Elijah appears in S. Y. Agnon's "The Revelation of Elijah," where much of the mystery of the tale revolves around the true identity of the Elijah in the title, who is first identified as an unlearned Jew. An example of a folktale about Elijah which is still current is Kamelia Shahar's "The Poor Man and Eliyahu the Prophet" (Eliyahu is Hebrew for Elijah).[43]

Other popular themes of folklore include that of the Golem, the man created out of clay in the legends of Rabbi Judah Loew of Prague, known as the Maharal, which appears in the stories of Yudl Rosenberg ("How the Golem Was Created" and "The End of the Golem") and Lajos Szabolcsi ("The Moon, the Mercenary and the Ring"). There is also a variety of tales about supernatural animals and places—the imaginary animal that haunts a synagogue in Franz Kafka's "The Animal in the Synagogue"; the talking bird that appears to be an incarnation of a Jew in Bernard Malamud's "The Jewbird"; and the girl transformed into a duck in Jeremy Garber's "The Tale of the Duck."

Another common motif in both ancient and modern folklore concerns the demonic element. I. B. Singer is perhaps best known for his tales about spirits, imps, dybbuks, and demons, which populate his short stories much as they populated the folk beliefs of the Jews of Eastern Europe and Russia from the Middle Ages until the upheavals of this century. "The Dybbuk," by Romain Gary, has as its premise the assumption that the soul of a murdered Jew has settled in the body of a Nazi soldier. With this metaphor does Gary observe how tainted were the Nazi murderers, and how the blood of their victims came to haunt them. At the same time, Gary's dybbuk observes all of the qualities of the traditional dybbuk, and it is this blend of the traditional and the new that gives the story so much of its power. In "The Wandering Spirit of Léon Mitrani," by Isaac Goldemberg, one man, Jacobo Lerner, is possessed by the spirit of another, Léon Mitrani:

> Toward the middle of 1934, Jacobo Lerner began to feel that he had been possessed by the spirit of Léon Mitrani, that Mitrani had taken refuge within him and was nourishing himself with his blood. From that moment on, his life, until then discreet, defined by a walk in the evening through the Parque de la Reserva or by an afternoon of love with doña Juana, began to be disturbed by strange events, until the compact order of his days tumbled like a castle made of sand.

In this tale Goldemberg is completely faithful to the traditional notion of the dybbuk, while still managing to relate this occurrence from a modern perspective that implies, by its very nature, the psychological dimension of the event—that is, in experiencing this possession Don Jacobo Lerner is experiencing some kind of psychological aberration. The fascination Goldemberg's story is able to engender derives from the author's dual perspective, for he never openly refutes the concept of the dybbuk as superstition, yet, at the same time, he casts the kind of doubt on it that is characteristic of a psychological perspective.

One of the most popular themes among modern Jewish writers, both of fiction and poetry, is the legend of Lilith, which has greatly revived in popularity in recent years. Moyshe Kulbak's "Lilith" is the creation of Benye's imagination and the incarnation of his lust. This follows the tradition of Lilith as the demon of sexual fantasy, with whom the dreamer has intercourse in his imagination, conceiving in this way all the demons that populate the world. A similar incarnation is found in Jiri Langer's "The Woman in the Forest," from *Nine Gates to the Chassidic Mysteries*. Note that the enticing feminine figure in this tale (who is not named as Lilith, but who exhibits every one of Lilith's characteristics) has long blond hair, revealing a secret longing for non-Jewish women who are, of course, unattainable. A very similar episode is found in David Pinski's story "The Temptations of Rabbi Akiba," except that the temptress here is even more blatant and daring, and Rabbi Akiba starts to succumb to her power. This story is saying that sexual attraction is such a powerful force that even Rabbi Akiba—who entered Paradise in peace and departed in peace, while his three companions, themselves great sages, were destroyed—even Rabbi Akiba cannot resist. Primo Levi's "Lilith in the Lager" transplants the Lilith legend to a concentration camp, and the juxtaposition is highly effective. Identifying one of the girls in the concentration camp as Lilith, Tischer proceeds to relate the full cycle of Lilith legends, from her role as Adam's first wife to a succubus and child-destroying witch to the Bride of God. This latter evolution appears in a bizarre kabbalistic legend where Lilith, noting that the Shekhinah has departed from God and gone into exile with her people Israel, brazenly offers to take her place, and, strange to say, God accepts her as His mistress until the time the Shekhinah shall come out of exile. In the context of the concentration camp, the massive disruptions of life on earth are revealed to be a result of this terrible union.

All of these stories have emphasized the seductive aspect of Lilith's nature and ignored, for the most part, her alter ego, the child-destroying witch. That being the case, the accomplishment of David Meltzer's "From the Rabbi's Dreambook" is all the more apparent, for in this brief tale Meltzer takes these two essentially unrelated aspects of Lilith's nature and unites them into one in much the same way that Jakov Lind links the legends of Lilith and Eve in "The Story of Lilith and Eve." Lilith enters Meltzer's story intent on suffocating a child, fully manifesting her witchlike role. When confronted with the rabbi her intentions change in a flash to that of the temptress, against whom the rabbi, although aware of her original intentions, is helpless. Lind's story is intended to demonstrate another polarity, that between Lilith, the incarnation of passion and independence, and Eve, who comes to represent the rabbinic vision of the model of womanhood: loyal, passive, and acquiescent, although in the episode of the Fall she was easily led astray. Lind's story suggests that every woman demonstrates both of these personality poles, to some extent, and attempts to restore the original unity that was divided, mythologically, into projections of separate figures.

The obvious power of the Lilith legends emerges in every one of these modern tales, demonstrating beyond a doubt the eternal nature of the mythic archetype, which is as true for the present generation as it was for those that preceded it. But in the stories of Primo Levi, David Meltzer, and Jakov Lind, in particular, there is a conscious awareness on the part of the authors that by changing the context of a legend (as in the case of Levi) or by combining disparate myths (as in the cases of Meltzer and Lind) a primary transformation can take place that mirrors the authors' own understanding, for example, of Gestalt psychology, which teaches how psychological projections can be traced back to their source in the human psyche.

6.

The last major phase of Jewish literature produced before the 20th century is that of Hasidism. This sect was founded in the 18th century by Israel ben Eliezer, known as the Baal Shem Tov (Master of the Good Name), or by the acrostic BeShT. The Baal Shem gathered around him disciples, known as Hasidim, with whom he shared his teachings, which emphasize the need for *kavanah*, or spiritual concentration, in prayer in particular and in every other kind of activity. As a result, the Hasidim actively sought out spiritual enlightenment, attempting to perceive the presence of the Creator or the Shekhinah in every situation. In this active approach to religious experience the Hasidim are not unlike the Sufis or, especially, the Zen Buddhists.[44] Hasidism also emphasizes the mystical dimension, as do these other sects, and in this the Hasidim should be seen as the spiritual heirs of the Kabbalists, and especially of the teachings of the Ari. Above all, Hasidism was a product of messianic longings and the sense that in the Baal Shem and some of the later hasidic masters, figures of the stature of the sages of the past had come again into the world. This belief provided a renewed sense of meaning, and enabled the Hasidim to bring about an extraordinary reanimation of the process of spiritual growth in Judaism. Although this dimension of Hasidism began to decline in the 19th century, the abundance of teachings and tales that was produced in a relatively short period is equal to that of any earlier period. And the possibilities of spiritual expression they demonstrate set in motion a process that has revived and inspired Judaism in the present century.

After the death of the Baal Shem, his scribe of eight years, Rabbi Dov Baer, published *Shivhei ha-Besht*, a volume of legends and myths that had become associated with the Baal Shem. (It has been translated into English as *In Praise of the Baal Shem Tov*, translated and edited by Dan Ben-Amos and Jerome R. Mintz.) Many of the tales in this volume, which concern the birth, childhood, and later life of the Baal Shem, have parallels to earlier rabbinic literature, notably to the legends of the Ari reported in *Shivhei ha-Ari*. The master-disciple relationship of the Baal Shem and his Hasidim, about whom volumes of tales were produced after their deaths, was duplicated in subsequent generations. The result is a rich literature of over three thousand texts, some of which are available in English in Martin Buber's *Tales of the Hasidim* and in Meyer Levin's *Classic Hasidic Tales* as well as in other collections. These texts are a product of the sacred literatures of the Bible, Talmud, Midrash, and Kabbalah, but what is less apparent is the influential role of medieval folklore. For hasidic tales incorporate elements of the narrative similar to those found in folktales, as well as the miracles, enchantments, witches, and demons that are so familiar in folklore and fairy tales. Imposed on this archetypal substructure are figures of angels and spirits, a supernatural aspect of hasidic literature that is found in a great many tales.

In combining the sacred intentions of the Aggadah with the narrative freedom of the folktale, Hasidism produced a body of literature that is the direct result of the previous genres, sacred and secular. If there is any one key to understanding the Hasidim, it is this profound sense of dialogue with the past, as is suggested in the words of Rabbi Nachman of Bratslav, one of the key rebbes, as the hasidic masters were called, which serves as the epigram to this book. And from the present perspective it does appear that some of the hasidic rebbes, including the Baal Shem, Rabbi Levi Yitzhak of Berditchev, and Rabbi Nachman, were among the most inspired figures of Jewish history.

To a considerable extent, most modern stories based on hasidic models retell existing legends about major figures in Hasidism, especially the Baal Shem Tov. Often these stories combine related legends and create transitions between them. The most popular source for these recreations has been *Shivhei ha-Besht*. S. Ansky retells a famous tale in "A Good Laugh," and Israel Zangwill utilized the entire legend cycle to create his novella *Master of the Good Name*, from which "Watch Night" has been excerpted. M. J. Berditchevsky approached this legend cycle in two ways, much as did Martin Buber. Berditchevsky offered closely literal versions in *Mimekor Yisrael* and also retold the tales in longer and freer recastings, such as "Two Worlds." This dual approach characterizes the career of Berditchevsky, where the line between the scholar and the creative artist is often blurred. Rabbi Zalman

Schachter retells the stories with the kind of oral flourish that is often missing from the majority of modern reworkings, where a polished literary style often sacrifices the oral aspect of the presentation.

From a literary perspective, one of the finest and most valuable retellings of the tales of the Baal Shem (as well as those of Rabbi Nachman of Bratslav) is Meyer Levin's *Classic Hasidic Tales*, whose original title was *The Golden Mountain*. Working from penny pamphlets of hasidic tales that he purchased in Paris, Levin approached these sources with both reverence and literary insight, and the results are extraordinarily moving tales that go a long way toward recreating the mystique that surrounds the legend of the Baal Shem.

Most fascinating and central to the retelling of the legends of the Baal Shem and the later Hasidim is the work of Martin Buber. Buber's two earliest publications were *Tales of Rabbi Nachman* and *The Legend of the Baal Shem*. In these books he took extensive liberties with the tales for the purpose of arriving at a highly polished and original literary style. Even from the first, Buber had a distinct vision of Hasidism, which primarily emphasized its spiritual dimensions and downplayed all other aspects. In the case of the tales of Rabbi Nachman, Buber deleted major portions and recast others to reflect his personal vision. Where, for example, in the original version of one of the tales of the Baal Shem, a rabbi is delayed by the breaking of a wheel of his wagon, and unable to continue his journey, in Buber's version, "The Revelation," he experiences a vision so intense he is unable to continue:

> A great whirl enveloped him, and he moved along in it, in the midst of confused and confusedly revolving things. . . . Now the whirl forced him to look up, and he saw the things of the world, but dislodged from their places and lost in confusion. It seemed to him as if an abyss had opened up beneath him, greedy to swallow up heaven and earth. The rabbi felt the whirl swell in his own heart, and he knew the darkness from within.[45]

Buber often uproots the narrative from the realm of the literal and down-to-earth and transplants it into a mystical realm. From the point of view of scholarship this kind of transformation may be dubious, and Buber was, in fact, frequently attacked on these grounds. But from the point of view of the aggadic tradition, Buber's recreations are supreme examples of the tradition's serving to inspire subsequent revisions of the original.

Later Buber came back to these tales of the Baal Shem and those of later rebbes in his seminal collection *Tales of the Hasidim*. Here Buber stayed much closer to the sources and limited his involvement in the text to matters of editing and style. Even so, the tales in this collection have also been criticized as being unrepresentative, in that Buber excised material that he did not deem appropriate to his vision of Hasidism. On the other hand, Buber's editing permits the reader to focus on what might well be called the aggadic element in these tales, which emerges with clarity and illumination.[46]

While less well known than the tales of the Baal Shem, the subsequent hasidic literature is one of the richest of the aggadic tradition. It consists of the tales of what Buber calls the Early Masters and the Later Masters, as well as a voluminous exegetical literature. Although it is obvious that the tales of the Baal Shem served as the primary model for the tales of subsequent masters, the format is flexible enough that the individual qualities of the various rebbes easily emerge. The effect of groups of tales about individual rebbes is to create a kind of legendary history based on anecdote that is both attractive in itself and a valuable resource for the modern Jewish writer. Much of the compelling quality of both these sources and the modern retellings derives from the fact that the rebbe is an ideal subject for an anecdote. As a result it is not uncommon for a modern writer to invent a hasidic rebbe rather than turn to a historical figure, as do Yehuda Yaari in "Reb Yeshaiah Argues with God," Leslie A. Fiedler in "The Dancing of Reb Hershl with the Withered Hand," and David Slabotsky in "The Death of Rabbi Yoseph." What is apparent, above all, is that the love of legend demonstrated by the Hasidim has easily transmitted itself into the creative imagination of our own time, where hasidic lore has been recognized as one of the most accessible and moving of all Jewish traditions.

In the stories of the modern Jewish authors who have utilized these aggadic legends, the source lies like a seed in the center of the fruit of the modern creation, while the modern element has, in a sense, fused with the ancient. Much of the power of this modern literature derives from the reader's experience of this fusion. Whether the starting point derives from a myth, legend, or ritual, or even from a halakhic ruling, there is inevitably a process of both preservation and transformation that takes place.

For the authors of such works there is also the opportunity to participate in the evolution of the archetypal myths that serve as the foundation of Western culture, and as well, of course, at the center of Judaism. For it is important to recognize, above all, that the process that is taking place is essentially mythic, and that it is the fundamental, compelling quality of myth which explains the momentum of this mythic evolution over so many centuries, even into the present. This also helps explain the lasting attraction of the tradition, even to those who do not necessarily identify with its religious goals.

The aggadic tradition, then, is more than the preservation of the past, as symbolized by the coffin of Joseph that the Israelites carried beside the Tabernacle in the wilderness. It is a continuing process of the reintegration of the past into the present. Each time this recurs, the tradition is transformed, and must be reimagined. And despite the inevitability of this metamorphosis, the essential aspect of the tradition remains eternal and unchanging. This is how the Jewish people view life in this world. On one level it is a blessing that has been given, and on another it is transitory and illusory. This dual awareness exists at all times, for neither this world nor the world to come can be ignored. In contrast to the Hindu world view, for example, which dismisses this world, and seeks to escape from the cycle of rebirths, or that of the skeptics, who insist that nothing exists beyond this world, this contrast of the worldly and the eternal is the essence of the Jewish vision. In aggadic terms this correspondence is the natural harmony of the earthly Jerusalem and the heavenly Jerusalem, for the one cannot exist without the other.

III

RABBI NACHMAN OF BRATSLAV: FORERUNNER OF MODERN JEWISH LITERATURE

The emergence, in the present century, of a flourishing modern Jewish literature was made possible by the evolution from a sacred written tradition to a consciously literary, secular one. A key figure in this transition was the hasidic master Rabbi Nachman of Bratslav (1770-1810). From his mother's side, Rabbi Nachman was the great-grandson of the Baal Shem Tov, founder of Hasidism. From his father's side, Nachman was a descendant of the famous Rabbi Judah Loew of Prague, known as the Maharal, to whom legend attributes the creation of the Golem, a man made out of clay. Thus from his birth the greatest expectations were held for Rabbi Nachman, and in light of these it is not surprising that he believed from a young age that his destiny was a great one, perhaps even messianic in nature.

In the 17th century there had been a great messianic uproar centered around Shabbatai Zevi, who ultimately proved to be a false messiah by converting, under duress, to Islam. But before that happened, hundreds of thousands of euphoric Jews made preparations to sell their possessions and follow him to the Land of Israel. Unlike Shabbatai Zevi, Rabbi Nachman never openly declared a messianic role for himself,[47] nor did he succeed in acquiring more than a small circle of Hasidim who accepted him as a *tzaddik*, much less a messianic figure. Yet since his death Rabbi Nachman's importance has continued to grow so that he now stands as one of the most highly regarded figures of Hasidism after the Baal Shem.

Perhaps the primary reason for Rabbi Nachman's importance lies in the tales that he told. For in the last years of his life Rabbi Nachman chose to clothe his teachings in the garb of fairy tales about unhappy kings, lost princesses, and loyal ministers. Despite their apparent simplicity, however, these tales are actually complex and mysterious allegories. Thus Nachman was the first rebbe to make the telling of tales the primary method of conveying his teachings. While previous hasidic masters, including the Baal Shem, had been the subject of a rich body of miracle tales, and some masters, such as the Baal Shem and Rabbi Levi Yitzhak of Berditchev, told occasional brief *maasehs*, none had made a practice of telling tales as a primary method of instruction. But this is precisely what Rabbi Nachman did in the last four years of his life, and these tales have achieved international renown and now exist in English in five translations.[48]

The reasons that led Rabbi Nachman to begin telling tales are veiled in mystery, but some surmises can be made. During most of his life Nachman alternated between periods in which he felt a mythic sense of destiny and all-pervasive meaning, and periods of deep despair and the sense that he knew nothing. Eventually, he came to regard these periods of despair as inevitable, and even incorporated them into his vision, teaching that a descent must precede every ascent. With such teachings Nachman came to function almost as a therapist to his disciples, leading them through the depths as well as to the heights. Even after the death of his young son, Shlomo Ephraim, and the abandonment of any messianic aspirations he may have held either for himself or his son, Nachman did not retreat into silence, but discovered a new form of expression for his messianic impulses—the tales he began to tell in his final years. It is in these tales that Rabbi Nachman finally embraced his true destiny.

Since Jewish folklore had flourished as an oral tradition among the common folk (if not among the rabbis) since at least the early Middle Ages, it was not an illogical mode of expression for Nachman. However, it must be remembered that this folklore had never achieved anything like the status of the various sacred literatures, and not until the late Middle Ages was any effort made to record these tales. Eventually some of them were preserved in collections that became widely known, such as *The Masseh Book* (translated into English by Moses Gaster) and *Tzene Rene* (as yet untranslated).

It is apparent, however, that despite the low status of folklore, and its universal as opposed to specifically Jewish character, Nachman felt drawn to this mode of expression in a powerful way. One clue for this attraction can be found in the dreams of Nachman that have been preserved. The most striking quality is their similarity to Nachman's tales, as in the following excerpt:

As I ascended the mountain, I saw a golden tree with branches of gold. From the branches hung all sorts of vessels that were like those depicted in the book. Inside those vessels were other vessels that were made out of these vessels and the letters in them. I wanted to take the vessels from there, but I couldn't because the thicket did not permit me to go through.[49]

Often these dreams also seem like condensed versions of one of Nachman's epic tales, such as "The Master of Prayer" or "The Seven Beggars," as the following dream, recorded in its entirety, demonstrates:

> Once I saw in my dream that I woke up in a forest which was endless and I wanted to return. One came to me and said: "In this forest one can never come to its end for it is so long it is infinite and all the instruments and the vessels of this world are made from this forest." He showed me a way to get out of the forest. This way brought me to a river. I wanted to come to the end of the river. A man came and said: "It is impossible to reach the end of the river, for the river is boundless. All the people of this world drink from the source of this river." But then he showed me a way to go out through the river. Then I came to a mill which stood at the side of the river, and someone came and said to me: "Here is ground the food for all the people in the world." And I again entered the forest where I saw a smith working, and entered into the smithy and they told me: "This smith makes the vessels for the whole world."[50]

Such dreams raise the possibility that Nachman based his tales on his dreams, elaborating on them in the retelling. However, it is not possible to confirm this hypothesis, since none of the surviving dreams contains material that was directly incorporated into the tales.

Most of all, the essential qualities of the enchanted world of fairy tales, with its solutions that inevitably draw on the magical, and the ability of the good to prevail despite the odds, were all enormously appealing to Nachman, and reflect his own world vision, in which the power of faith can surmount any obstacle.

The tale "The Lost Princess," for example, has as its primary motif a theme that commonly reappears in world folklore as a quest in which a prince sets out to rescue a princess who has fallen under an evil spell.[51] For the uninitiated, this tale is simply one more variant on a common theme. But among Nachman's Hasidim it was understood that this and all of Nachman's tales contained meanings hidden from all but those who knew how to seek them out. Thus among the Bratslav Hasidim, Nachman's tales are regarded as sacred texts, and are studied from every angle and subjected to the same thorough exegesis as are the sacred Scriptures.[52]

In *Sichos ha-Ran* (*The Wisdom of Rabbi Nachman*, 180), Rabbi Nachman is quoted by Rabbi Nathan, his scribe, as saying: "Even a *tzaddik* who searches after lost things is himself sometimes lost, as it is written: *They shall search and be lost* (Ps. 83:18)." This statement reveals the personal dimension of "The Lost Princess"—that Nachman identified with the loyal minister who devotes his life to the quest of finding the lost princess. Nachman's statement about the lost *tzaddik* is also a comment on the necessity of accepting the futility and extended effort that is required for a successful ascent. From an early period the princess in "The Lost Princess" was identified with the

Shekhinah, the Sabbath Queen and Bride of God, and in some readings the messenger who seeks her is identified as the Messiah. Thus the tale can be understood to mean that once the Messiah has found the Shekhinah and brought her out of exile, then he will be free to usher in the End of Days. Or, conversely, it could mean that when the Messiah does come, the Shekhinah will voluntarily end the exile she chose at the time of the destruction of the Temple in Jerusalem.

That the lost princess was intended to represent the Shekhinah was confirmed by Rabbi Nathan in his introduction to Rabbi Nachman's tales:

> Behold, the first story about the king's daughter who is lost is the mystery of the Shekhinah in exile. . . . And this story is about every man in every time, for this entire story occurs to every man individually, for everyone of Israel must occupy himself with this *Tikkun,* namely to raise up the Shekhinah from her exile, to raise her up from the dust, and to liberate the Holy Kingdom from among the idolators and the Other Side among whom she has been caught. . . . Thus one finds that everyone in Israel is occupied with the search for the king's daughter, to take her back to her father, for Israel as a whole has the character of the minister who searches for her.

> (*Sippure Maasiot,* pp. 7-8)

"The Lost Princess" also contains other hints of this kabbalistic allegory. The king's six sons and one daughter can be seen to represent the seven days of creation. It would be natural to identify the first six days in which the world was created as masculine, and the day of rest as feminine. In the Jewish view, of course, the seventh day is the Sabbath, and one of the identities of the Shekhinah is that of the Sabbath Queen.

An even more disguised allegory is that of the three giants who rule over the animals, the winged creatures, and the winds, that the minister encounters in his search for the lost princess. Each one carries a giant tree. In terms of the fairy tale, this detail merely serves to confirm their great size and strength. But to those familiar with kabbalistic allegory, the giants may be seen to represent Adam Kadmon, the primordial man whose creation serves as the transition from the unmanifested aspect of God known as *Ein Sof* to the world as we know it. In that case the tree the giant holds would certainly refer to the kabbalistic Tree of Life, which designates the stages in the process of emanation from nonexistence to existence known as the ten *Sefirot.* The diagram of this Tree of Life is often found combined with a drawing of Adam Kadmon, and the two have been traditionally linked, since their meanings intersect. Both of these examples, that of the six sons and one daughter and that of the giants carrying a tree, demonstrate how well Rabbi Nachman was able to suggest esoteric Jewish concepts in the universal language of fairy tales. So well integrated are they that only one searching for the hidden meanings that Rabbi Nachman made abundantly clear did exist would consider them allegorically.

It is also apparent that Rabbi Nachman made use of common folk motifs in his tales in part because he recognized the biblical archetypes glimmering beneath the surface of the traditional fairy tale, and had found a way to relate these folk motifs to his Hasidim by forcing them to consider them from the traditional Jewish perspective. He perceived that in this way his teaching would be revealed to them, but would remain concealed from others, who would be misled by the simple surface of the tales.

Even more obviously intended to serve as a commentary on *Maaseh Bereshith*, the Work of Creation—that is, the process by which the world came into being—is Rabbi Nachman's famous last tale, "The Seven Beggars." First, the overall structure of the story, with the tale of the seven beggars serving as a frame for other tales within tales, implies the seven days of creation. As in the biblical myth of creation, the seventh day and the seventh beggar are singled out for particular emphasis. The seventh day, of course, represents the Sabbath, while the seventh beggar may be seen as the representative of the messianic era, if not of the Messiah himself. Note that the tales of the first six beggars are told, but that of the seventh beggar remains mysteriously untold, with the final observation by Rabbi Nathan: "Nor will we be worthy to hear it until the Messiah comes in his mercy, may he come speedily in our days, Amen."

It also seems likely that Nachman intended each of the beggars to represent one of the biblical patriarchs. Thus the blind beggar represents Isaac, who was blind; the deaf beggar represents Abraham, who was deaf to the noise of the world, so intently was he concentrated on the Covenant between God and himself; the beggar with the crooked neck represents Aaron, brother of Moses and the first high priest of Israel—as the high priest his duty is to unite Israel and God, and his affliction focuses on the neck, which links the head (God) to the rest of the body (Israel); the hunchbacked beggar represents Jacob, whose hunchback symbolizes the power of "the small which contains the great," just as Jacob is identified in the Aggadah as the pillar that supports the entire world; the beggar with no hands represents Joseph, a master of the spiritual powers sometimes associated with the hands (keeping in mind that each beggar explains that he does not in fact suffer from his deformity, quite the opposite); and the seventh beggar, who has no feet, can be seen as the representative of the Messiah, who has not yet come—when he is about to arrive we will enter the era of the "footsteps of the Messiah."

The clearest indication of the concern of this tale with *Maaseh Bereshith* comes in the tale of the blind beggar. He recounts a meeting of those whose memories reached back to the early phases of creation. One remembers "the moment when they plucked the apple from the branch"; the second recalls "the moment that the candle burned"; the third the precise "moment when the fruit was formed"; the fourth "the moment that they extracted the seed to plant the fruit"; the fifth "the wise men who discovered the seed"; the sixth "the taste of the fruit before it entered the fruit"; the seventh "the fragrance of the fruit before it entered the fruit"; and the eighth "the appearance of the fruit before it attached itself to the fruit." The beggar who is telling the story has a memory that reaches back even further, to "the time before there was anything—that is the Void." In this sequence Nachman suggests the nine stages of emanation of the kabbalistic *Sefirot* that brought the world into being. The tenth stage, which precedes all of the others, goes unremarked because it is that of *Ein Sof,* that aspect of God which remains hidden and unknown from every man. These stages of emanation are the kabbalistic equivalent of the seven days of creation, although they are far more abstract and obscure. The fact that this tale within a tale is the first to be told emphasizes its role as an allegory about creation, and of the importance of an understanding of the mysteries of creation, which are particularly difficult to comprehend.

Further kabbalistic allegories are to be found in the tales "The Portrait," "The Royal Messenger," "The Letter," and "The Tale of the Menorah." The central symbol of "The Portrait" is clearly intended to designate the *Pargod,* the curtain referred to in kabbalistic literature behind which the Holy One sits on His Throne of Glory. This symbol thus personifies the hidden aspect of God, known as *Ein Sof.* In the early Hekhaloth texts, describing journeys to Paradise, and in the later kabbalistic texts, the *Pargod* is described in great detail. The side facing God is, of course, hidden, but all souls are said to be woven into the other side, facing the angels, which has been described as a kind of archetypal screen on which flickers all of past and future destiny.

The primary purpose of the *Pargod* is to serve as a reminder that complete knowledge of the Divinity is beyond the capacity of humans; they may travel so far, all the way into Paradise, but they can never probe the mystery of God Himself. Not even the angels are permitted to know that aspect of God; only the Shekhinah, the Divine Presence and Bride of God, and the supreme angel, Metatron, are permitted behind the *Pargod.*

The kabbalistic concept of the Shekhinah, including its use in "The Lost Princess," converges with the archetypal symbolism of the collective unconscious, as proposed in the theories of C. G. Jung.[53] These, then, are the same symbols that are largely repeated in world mythology, and commonly appear as dream symbols as well. These symbols have, from the first, an eternal aspect, and by virtue of their role in the evolution of the Jewish religion also have assumed particular characteristics of the religion.

In this way the ground was prepared for a full-scale allegorical reading of the Torah such as is found in the Zohar. There every symbol is refined to reach its underlying archetype. The concept of the Shekhinah, for example, which dates from the talmudic era, was permitted to evolve until a myth had been formed about the Bride of God, whose particular concern is the destiny of Israel. This myth includes the separation of the Shekhinah from her spouse at the time of the destruction of the Temple in Jerusalem, and thus links the destiny of Israel with that of the Shekhinah, since they will come out of exile at the same time.

This myth of the Shekhinah can easily be recognized, in Jungian terms, as an *anima* figure, as Jung called the symbolic feminine aspect of every man. (For women this symbolic figure is known as the *animus*.) This is that part of the psyche that must be integrated in order to achieve wholeness, or what Jung calls Individuation. This also is the symbolic inner figure identified as the elusive muse sought after by generations of poets, whom Robert Graves calls "the White Goddess." In Jungian terms the exile of the Shekhinah might therefore be seen as a psychic dislocation of the Jewish nation brought about by their exile from the Promised Land. And there are many Jews, Zionists in particular, who firmly believe that Jews can find peace of mind only by making their home in the Land of Israel.

Rabbi Nachman's ability to integrate kabbalistic concepts into the straightforward and essentially simple fairy-tale narrative was possible because Nachman seemed to comprehend instinctively the personal psychic dimensions of both modes. He seems to have recognized how each mode has its source in the inner world and its own laws, which are quite independent of those of the "real" world. Furthermore he seems to have understood, as have psychologists since Jung, the nature of the psychological process of projection. Certainly for this kind of literature to succeed it is necessary for the author to somehow descend into his unconscious, and to report back the mythic and archetypal drama as it is reflected there. Nachman perceived, for example, that the exile of the Shekhinah concerned him in the most personal way possible. The Shekhinah was not only lost to Israel as a whole, but also to him individually, and it was possible and necessary to set off on the quest to restore her to her former position of glory. The quest described in "The Lost Princess," then, is not just a fairy-tale quest, or an allegory of the exile of the Shekhinah (although it is both), but must be understood as a mirror of a crucial drama of the psyche. The ability of Nachman to personalize these mythic elements of Judaism by transmuting them into the universal language of fairy tales was a bold act with profound implications.

This suggests the process by which the myth of the Shekhinah evolved in the first place, and one possible approach of the modern reader to a literature making use of such symbolic figures. Starting with a psychic truth, such as the existence of the *anima*, the Jewish myth projects the presence of such a figure who is concerned with her people as a whole just as a man's own *anima* is concerned with his spiritual and emotional life. The modern reader might then be well advised to attempt to relate to his or her own psychic reality the mythological projections that were the starting points of this mythology in the first place. This is not an intellectual process, but a spiritual and emotional one. What it requires, above all, is that the reader be open to the psychic truths that serve as the foundation for the entire aggadic tradition. Then the mythology that finds its first expression in the Bible and is cultivated throughout all subsequent Jewish literature will once again exercise its compelling power, making possible a personal contact not only to the tradition itself, but also to all the generations that have received and transmitted it until this time.

This link between kabbalistic thinking and the theory of archetypal symbolism as proposed by Jung is strongly prefigured in Rabbi Nachman's tale "The Portrait." The concept of the archetype is itself clearly defined in this tale:

> Now there is a country that contains within it all countries. And in that country there is a city that contains all the cities of that country that contains all countries. And in that city there is a house that contains all houses of that city that contains all the cities of that country that contains all countries. And in that house is a man who bears within him all of this.

In "The Portrait" the king represents, of course, the Holy One who "is hidden from men. He sits behind a curtain and is far from the people of his land." This king's distance, which has the effect of causing distortions of the truth among his people, is a source of mystery and confusion. No one possesses the portrait of this king because it is impossible to obtain. Yet, paradoxically, at the end of the tale "the face of the king was revealed, and the wise men saw him." This does not mean to imply that the most hidden and recondite secrets of the Divinity will be revealed to those who steep themselves in the mysteries of the Kabbalah, but rather that immersion in these mysteries makes possible a knowledge about the Divinity previously impossible among men.

The key revelation is that the king "cannot bear the lies of the kingdom." God is pained by falsehood and imperfection in the world, although, ironically, it exists because of His distance from His creation. This paradox, which cannot be resolved simply, is at the core of Nachman's complex vision of existence, and of the central kabbalistic vision itself, in which the further the distance from *Ein Sof,* the hidden aspect of God, the further the distance from the source of truth itself, and the greater the distortions that come into being.

At the end of Rabbi Nachman's tale "The Spider and the Fly" is another passage which defines, for all practical purposes, the inexhaustible aspect of the archetype (symbolized by the image worn by the maiden), and the fact that it is essentially independent of the vessel through which it expresses itself:

> He saw that among the myriads of prisoners he had taken there was a beautiful maiden. The maiden possessed every loveliness that was to be found on earth, the beauty of form that was felt as sweet water under the fingers, the beauty of the eyes that was as a caress of the hands, and the beauty that is heard like the sound of bells touched by the wind. But when the king looked upon her, he saw that her beauty was not her own, but that it came forth like a perfume out of the tiny image that she wore upon herself. And it was this image that contained all forms of beauty, and because it was upon her, it seemed that all those forms of beauty were her own.

The tale "The Royal Messenger" is focused on the question of the existence of God: "The king had sent a letter to a wise but skeptical man, who, in his faraway province, refused to accept it." The quest to the end of the world to discover if the king actually exists represents the extensive kabbalistic quest for knowledge of the Divinity. Despite evidence of the greatness of the king, the skeptical man remains unsatisfied that proof of the king's existence has been given.

This tale is enhanced by comparison with Nachman's tale "The Letter," an allegory about a prince who receives a letter and recognizes the handwriting of his father, the king. Also related is "The Portrait," previously discussed, about the king who lives behind a curtain and thus cannot be seen. In these two tales the nonappearance of the king is not a source for skepticism about his existence, but in "The Royal Messenger" the difficulty of accepting the paradox of a God who must remain hidden, and thus ultimately unknown, is presented in its most powerful form, with the skeptic receiving the final word.

Both "The Royal Messenger" and "The Letter" have a remarkable parallel to Franz Kafka's famous parable "An Imperial Message," which they preceded by more than a hundred years. In Kafka's parable an emperor gives his deathbed message to his faithful messenger to deliver "to you, the humble subject, the insignificant shadow cowering in the remotest distance before the Imperial sun; the Emperor from his deathbed has sent a message to you alone." Due to insurmountable obstacles, it becomes impossible for this message to be delivered, so that the reader remains uncertain of whether the message actually has been sent; whether, indeed, the Emperor, the messenger, and the message even exist, or whether the "humble subject" has merely daydreamed the whole incident.

In Kafka's parable, as well as those of Rabbi Nachman, one likely meaning is that which proposes that the emperor or king is intended to represent God. The letter sent may be identified as the Torah, containing all truth, or as the very existence of the world around us. In Kafka's parable the "humble subject" deeply believes in the existence of the letter, and that but for the obstacles, "If [the messenger] could reach the open fields how fast he would fly, and soon doubtless you would hear the welcome hammering of his fists on your door." In Nachman's "The Royal Messenger," on the other hand, the letter arrives, but the recipient pays no attention to its contents, instead concerning himself solely with the question of the existence of the author of the letter. We suspect that Kafka's peasant would not have been assailed by these doubts! But the most fortunate of all is the prince in "The Letter" who recognizes the handwriting of his father, i.e., the *tzaddik* who recognizes the Creator through His creation. Thus in these three parables the essence of the world views ranges from total belief in the existence of God the Creator ("The Letter"), to belief in God's existence but inability to receive the message sent by God to man ("An Imperial Message"), to doubt in the existence of the Creator, despite evidence to the contrary ("The Royal Messenger"). These parables can be seen to represent, respectively, the views of the believers ("The Letter"), the religious existentialists ("An Imperial Message"), and the atheists ("The Royal Messenger").

In general, Rabbi Nachman's view is closest to that held by the prince in "The Letter"—he has recognized the Creator and His creation. It is natural, then, that the key figure reappearing in Nachman's tales is the *tzaddik*, the spiritual guide that every rebbe sought to be to his Hasidim. Certainly the central figure of the Master of Prayer in the story of the same title is clearly intended to be such a *tzaddik*. It is the clarity of vision of the Master of Prayer that enables the initial confusion of the world in this tale to be eventually overcome. Likewise, the tale "Harvest of Madness" emphasizes the necessity that the *tzaddik* retain his clarity of vision even if he seems to be mad in the eyes of the world. Here the king and his counselor are the only ones spared the general madness brought on by the harvest, which because it is so extensive is virtually unavoidable. This tale of Nachman's is identical in theme to a Sufi folktale collected by Idries Shah in *Tales of the Dervishes*.[54] The only difference is that in the Sufi tale the madness is carried by water, rather than wheat. The Sufi tale, which Shah calls "When the Waters Were Changed," concerns a warning given that on a certain date all the waters in the world which had not been specially preserved would disappear, to be renewed with different water, which would drive men mad. Only one man listens to this warning and stores water for himself. And when the waters stop flowing and then begin to flow again, he finds that men have begun to think in an entirely different way, and have lost their memories of what has happened. They regard this last sane man as mad, and resulting isolation leads him, eventually, to drink from the new water, despite the consequences, because he cannot bear the loneliness of being different from everyone else. After he does drink of their water he becomes like everyone else, and they regard him as a madman who has been restored to his sanity.

Another tale dealing with madness and sanity is "The Prince Who Thought He Was a Rooster." Here a prince who has been given up as mad is finally restored to sanity by the action of the wise man who pretends to share his madness, and, gaining his confidence in this way, eventually influences him to function again as a human being. In his own comment on this tale Rabbi Nachman makes it clear that the story is intended as an allegory of the role of the *tzaddik*, who must be prepared to descend to the level of those he hopes to influence: "In this way must the genuine teacher go down to the level of his people if he wishes to raise them up to their proper place."

A further kabbalistic allegory is found in Nachman's "The Tale of the Menorah," which illustrates the central kabbalistic concept of *Tikkun*, of redemption and restoration. This concept is an integral part of Isaac Luria's cosmological theory about the Shattering of the Vessels and the Gathering of the Sparks. *Tikkun* is identical to the process of Gathering the Sparks—of bringing together that which has been scattered, and restoring that which has been broken.

In Rabbi Nachman's tale the son constructs his menorah out of the defects of those who observe it. We may assume that the craftsman was familiar with those before whom he demonstrated his skills. The primary purpose of the menorah in this tale is to make these others aware of their own defects, since this awareness is the first and most essential step before the act of *Tikkun* can take place. In this way the menorah serves symbolically as the *tzaddik* should serve his Hasidim—making them aware of their defects so that they can begin the process of *Tikkun*. This reading of the tale can be summarized in the talmudic phrase "Anyone who finds a flaw finds his own flaw" (B. Kid. 70a).

Rabbi Zalman Schachter, however, suggests another way of approaching this tale. His view can be summed up in what might be called "The Tale of the Opal": An opal's most distinguishing feature is the fire in its center, but this fire is also its flaw. When seen from one angle, the fire resembles nothing more than a crack, but from another perspective it is the most beautiful part of the opal. Thus what appears to be the defect in the menorah is what makes it unique and more beautiful. Rabbi Schachter feels that this interpretation, which emphasizes Rabbi Nachman's belief in the essential polarity of existence, preserves the complexity of his vision.

The craftsman who creates the menorah may also be seen to represent God, while the menorah is God's creation, the world. In such a reading the seven branches of the menorah may be seen as the seven days of creation described in Gen. 1:1-24. In this case the light of the flames of the menorah can be identified with the primordial light that came into existence on the first day, when God said *Let there be light, and there was light* (Gen. 1:3), and was present until the creation of the sun and moon on the fourth day (Gen. 1:14-19).[55] If this tale is read as an allegory of the creation of the world, Nachman may be seen to be saying that the defects are the defects of this world and that God created the world out of the defects in it. Nor does this conflict with the traditional view of creation, since *God formed man out of the dust of the earth* (Gen. 2:6).

It is interesting to note that Rabbi Nachman, as well as being a forerunner of the modern Jewish literary tradition, was also one of the very last great figures in the oral tradition. For him the *maaseh* could only be told orally, but fortunately these tales have been preserved because he was blessed with a highly responsible *sopher*, or scribe, Rabbi Nathan (Nussan) of Nemerov. It is as if Rabbi Nachman's soul had its source in the oral tradition, while Rabbi Nathan's derived from the written, for their mutual effort was required in order to bring Rabbi Nachman's tales back from the highest heavens, where his Hasidim believed he received them.

That Rabbi Nachman was willing to permit his tales to undergo the folk process in which the tale is never told twice in exactly the same fashion is apparent by his decision, on occasion, to tell the tales on a Friday night, the start of the Sabbath. During the Sabbath, of course, the ban against writing was in effect, and it was therefore necessary for Nachman's Hasidim to retell the tale among themselves many times in order not to lose any of it, until the Sabbath came to an end. Only then could Nathan write down the tale, already likely to have undergone the process of recasting that naturally occurs with every retelling of a tale.

That the Bratslav Hasidim believed that Rabbi Nachman had the stature of the ancient patriarchs and prophets and that his storytelling was a continuation of an unbroken tradition is demonstrated in this remarkable prayer, which they invoked before the telling of tales:

> Master of the Universe, Thou workest wonders in every generation through the true *tzaddikim* of every generation, as our fathers have related to us, all the great deeds and wonders and great miracles that Thou hast performed in each generation through Thy true *tzaddikim* from the beginning of time unto this day. In this generation too there are of certainty *tzaddikim* and true wonder-workers. Therefore may Thou in Thine abundant mercy grant and help me and strengthen and animate me so that I may be worthy to tell the tales of the true *tzaddikim*, of all that happened to them in their days, both to them and their children, and all the great and awe-inspiring wonders and signs which they performed both in secret and in public, and all the holiness and revelation of God which they effected in the world; all this may I merit to hear well with my ears and heart, and meditate and always retell them.[56]

All in all, Rabbi Nachman told thirteen primary tales[57] which are those most frequently included in the various editions of his stories. In addition there are a number of brief, lesser-known tales, including "Harvest of Madness," "The Royal Messenger," "A Letter," and "The Prince Who Thought He Was a Rooster," previously discussed, all of which are included in this collection.

Before his death Rabbi Nachman directed his Hasidim to burn all his writings. (His tales, told orally and recorded by his scribe, Rabbi Nathan, were exempted from this order.) Nachman's first disciple, Simeon (Shimon), carried out this order directly after Nachman's death, as Rabbi Nathan describes with obvious distress:

> Before Rabbi Nachman departed from this world, he left instructions to burn all his writings which, secreted in a special box, no one had been permitted to read. Immediately after his soul left him and his clothes were being removed, Rabbi Simeon hastened to open the box, took out all the hidden manuscripts, carried them to the stove, built a fire, and consigned them to the flames. I followed after him, in order to sniff the sacred fumes of the awesome Torah whose enjoyment was denied to our generation.[58]
>
> (*Yeme Maharnat*)

After Rabbi Nachman's death the impact of his tales rapidly emerged from the limited circle of Bratslaver Hasidim to the world at large. This was in part because of the universal appeal of the tales and in part because Nachman himself came to be recognized as the most charismatic hasidic figure since the Baal Shem; the fact that he was the Baal Shem's great-grandson only emphasized this link.[59] Because Nachman had chosen to tell his tales in Yiddish (although Nathan, his scribe, later translated them into Hebrew, and the traditional text includes both languages), he had significant influence on the modern Yiddish literary tradition. For with the model of Nachman's broad acceptance in Yiddish to support them, the formative figures of modern Yiddish literature, especially Sholom Aleichem and I. L. Peretz, had the confidence to write in their native tongue. And because their stories were published in the widely circulated Yiddish newspapers of Eastern Europe and Russia, they soon possessed an enviable following among Yiddish-speaking Jews.

The wide currency of Nachman's tales also proved influential in other direct and indirect ways. Nachman's style was the direct model for Yiddish writers such as Der Nister and Dovid Ignatow.[60] But more important, the break Nachman had made with the past by the mere telling of his allegorical fairy tales created an atmosphere in which it was possible to approach the sacred literatures from a consciously literary perspective. It is hard to imagine the career of I. L. Peretz, for example, without the existence of Nachman as his predecessor. Peretz was aware, of course, that Nachman had been the first to utilize folklore in a literary creation. Peretz himself made good use of the folktales that his friend S. Ansky, author of *The Dybbuk*, gathered in his capacity as one of the first collectors of Jewish folklore.

Above all, it was Rabbi Nachman's ability to sustain a mythological vision of existence "at the meeting place between the truth of the soul and the truth of the cosmos," as Arthur Green states in his exemplary biography of Nachman, *Tormented Master* (p.347), that has served to inspire subsequent Jewish authors. For Nachman had an intuitive ability to enter into the world of the sacred and to discover the secret by which a mythic kingdom could be made to flourish. That secret he has succeeded in transmitting to his successors, who have acknowledged his role as progenitor, and have sought, in turn, to keep alive the Jewish literary tradition.

IV

S. Y. AGNON, I. L. PERETZ, AND I. B. SINGER: MODERN MASTERS OF THE AGGADAH

All of the categories of sacred and secular literatures have been drawn upon by modern Jewish authors. The two primary literary traditions which have utilized these traditional sources are associated with the primary Jewish languages, Hebrew and Yiddish.[61] Each of these literatures is characterized by two distinct literary approaches: the realistic and the parabolic. The realistic approach, exemplified by writers such as Mendele Mokher-Seforim and Abraham Reisen among Yiddish writers, was largely divorced from the models of traditional Jewish literature, [62] although the style of the realistic folktale was an important influence. But this realistic literature looked primarily to the trends of the current European literatures, and let these serve as its primary models.

The allegorical writers, on the other hand, saw themselves as being directly in the aggadic tradition. Turning to the various categories of sacred literature, including that of the Hasidim, and to medieval folklore, these writers, S. Y. Agnon, I. L. Peretz, and I. B. Singer, in particular, sought their models from the past. Of course, they were also familiar with various 20th-century literatures, and drew on these sources as well. This conjunction of the ancient and modern proved a fertile meeting ground in which these two rich literatures, the Hebrew and the Yiddish, could each take root. Once again, the tradition demonstrated its flexibility by incorporating the past into the present and the present into the past.

While Hebrew and Yiddish literatures each represent a separate literary tradition with its own history and primary figures, there were, in fact, considerable links between the two. Of primary importance was the fact that many of the Yiddish writers first wrote in Hebrew, and several of the Hebrew writers began in Yiddish. This is true of major figures in both fiction and poetry, such as I. L. Peretz, whose Hebrew contribution is highly

49

valued, although he is primarily recognized as one of the preeminent Yiddish writers. S. Y. Agnon, on the other hand, wrote some of his first stories in Yiddish, and Zalman Shneur made equally valuable contributions in both languages.

It happened that both the Hebrew and Yiddish literary traditions were dominated at an early stage by a great master—Agnon[63] in Hebrew literature, and Peretz in Yiddish. More so, perhaps, than any other modern Jewish writer, Agnon sought to create a literature that was theologically compatible in all ways with the ancient tradition. The persona that Agnon projected was that of a devout, observant Jew who steeped himself solely in the sacred writings, and whose technique it was to borrow and build upon the biblical and aggadic traditions in much the same way that Israel has built new cities over ancient ones. Because of his exquisite use of Hebrew, and the traditional lore in which he was steeped, Agnon was able to create a body of texts closer to the spirit of the original, in terms of style and language, than those created by anyone else in this century, for they are, in fact, cut from the very same cloth.

At the same time, Agnon was also able to write in an abstract, surreal style, not unlike that of Franz Kafka. Agnon insisted, however, that even these surreal writings were a logical extension of the traditional sources, and he strongly resisted the notion that more recent writers had influenced his style. In particular, he stoutly denied that Kafka's writings had had a seminal influence on his own, and went so far as to claim that he had not even read the works of Kafka.[64]

It has been argued that Agnon's stories and novels do not lend themselves to translation, since they are so closely based on traditional sources, and that translation is, to use Bialik's image, like kissing the bride through the veil. But despite the inherent difficulties, enough seems to have survived in translation for Agnon, who received the Nobel Prize in 1966, to have developed an international reputation that places him in a class with such key 20th-century writers as Kafka, Jorge Luis Borges, Pär Lagerkvist, and Isak Dinesen.

Agnon's use of sources is well illustrated in his "Fable of the Goat," which is based on a folktale about a goat that discovers an enchanted cave offering passage directly to and from the Holy Land. The delicious taste of the goat's milk in this tale derives from the fact that it has been grazing in the Holy Land. And when the father, in his mistaken grief, kills the goat when it returns without his son, who has sent it to guide his father to the Holy Land, he also kills his link to that place, and causes the secret location of the enchanted cave to be lost.

The aggadic prototype for this fable is likely to be found in the legends concerning the Cave of Machpelah (such as B. Bab. Bat. 57b-58a and *Pirke de Rabbi Eliezer* 36), in which the bodies of Adam and Eve were said to be buried—perfectly preserved—along with those of the Patriarchs, and which was filled with the aroma of the Garden of Eden, suggesting the cave was located in the vicinity of the Garden. This belief is directly stated in the Zohar (1:57b). A parallel motif is also found in the hasidic legend about the journey of the Baal Shem Tov to the Holy Land (*Shivhei ha-Besht* 11). Here robbers offer to show the Baal Shem "a short way to the Land of Israel through caves and underground passages." But when the Baal Shem entered the cave "he saw there *the flaming sword which turned every way* (Gen. 3:24)," meaning that the way was closed to him. Also standing behind this fable of Agnon's is the messianic tradition that when the End of Days arrives "the righteous who were buried abroad . . . will roll through underground caves until they reach the Land of Israel. And when they reach the Land of Israel He will put the spirit of life into them and they will stand up" (*Midrash Tanhuma*, ed. Buber, 1:214).

The Israel Folktales Archives in Haifa has collected five variants of this folktale, some about a goat, some a cow. One of these is remarkably close to Agnon's version of the tale, suggesting that he himself may have heard the tale, and retold it in a way that is quite close to the original, except for elements of style and interpretation, which, of course, are central in Agnon's writing. A translation of this orally collected folktale is as follows:

In Yemen, in a village near Tzena, lived a very poor Jew who scarcely earned enough for himself and his family. Every day he went out to the fields with the few poor goats he had. In the evening he milked them and sold their milk cheaply. Only very poor people would buy the milk from him for all the Jews had their own goats and cows who were taken to graze by Arab shepherds, but our poor Jew would himself go to the fields for his goats to graze and he went to a great deal of trouble to find them grazing land. When he returned in the evening, before nightfall, to his home, he was tired, worn out, and broken.

One day the poor man got sick. He did not go out to the grazing land and asked his two sons, aged fourteen and ten, to go in his stead.

The two rose in the morning and went to look for grazing land. But they did not find any for they took the wrong road.

Suddenly one of the goats left the herd and the elder son followed it to bring it back. The goat started to run, the son ran also. The goat fled and the son followed. He called to his younger brother: "Return home meanwhile with the other goats and I'll follow with the stubborn one."

So the younger brother returned with the goats and the elder continued to chase the fleeing goat. Time passed, and the elder brother failed to return home. His family began to worry, and as more time passed, their worry increased. The next day they began to pray for his well-being and even fasted. But he did not return home.

The goatherd's son continued to pursue the goat until towards evening he followed it to a wonderful site where he saw oranges radiating like the sun, apple trees illuminating like the moon, pears full of juice, olive groves and vineyards.

Among the various trees ran streams of pure clear water to refresh the soul and delight the eye.

The goat splashed about in the clear water and drank of it, then rubbed itself against the tree trunks. The son, intoxicated by the sight before his eyes, which seemed to him to resemble the Garden of Eden, could not leave the place. He ate of the fruit trees and his desire was great to stay there and continue to enjoy the goodness and beauty of the place.

The goatherd's son took a piece of paper and wrote: "Dear father, I am in an enchanted place containing all the delights and beauties of the world, a veritable Garden of Eden. Please, father! Leave your impoverished home and come here to enjoy all the goodness of the site. And you will never again suffer poverty and deprivation for God showed me the way and the goat led me here."

When he finished writing, he took the note and put it in the goat's ear and the goat returned to the poor goatherd's home.

The goat returned to the goatherd's home alive and well. When it arrived, the entire household hastened to greet it, but their pain was great when they saw that the goat had returned without the son and without any sign of what had come to pass with them.

The household believed that the son had been killed and would not return home. They immediately began to weep and eulogize the loss of their poor boy. When they got up from the days of mourning the bereaved father took the goat and out of deep sorrow and pain at the death of the son, slaughtered it, for he could not bear to look at the cause of his son's death. Morning and evening the goat reminded him of his beloved son and the cause of his death.

After the father slaughtered and sold the miserable goat flesh for a pittance, he suddenly found the note in its ear. He quickly read it and immediately regretted his rash behavior. What a pity that the goat could not show him the way to where his son was, the site of happiness and plenty, of rest and tranquillity.

The poor father remained wretched until the end of his days and never again heard anything about his elder son. And the son continued to enjoy the delights of the place which was like the Garden of Eden, and waited anxiously for his father and family to come. He never understood what prevented his father and family from coming to him.[65]

Assuming that this version of the folktale was familiar to Agnon, there are some valuable conclusions that can be drawn about the kinds of changes Agnon makes in the tale. First of all, the place the young man is led to by the goat in the folktale is obviously intended to be the Garden of Eden, and this identification does not go unremarked. Agnon, while retaining reference to the Garden of Eden, identifies the place the young man comes to as the Land of Israel, specifically, the holy city of Safed. In doing so he transforms the meaning of the tale, which becomes instead an allegory of the process of separation between the older and younger generations that Agnon, who emigrated to Palestine from Poland, was intimately familiar with. The cave, which does not appear in the folktale, becomes, in Agnon's rendering, a magical link between the old country and the Land of Israel, which both parents and their children longed for. The fact that such a cave is unknown, and thus such a link between countries does not exist, is explained by the fact that the goat was killed, and therefore could not lead the father to his son. In this way Agnon has made the story much more poignant to his Hebrew readers, themselves immigrants. Note Agnon's insertion of biblical phrases into the tale when the father discovers his error and cries out, "My son, my son, where are you? My son, would that I might die in your stead, my son, my son!" These moving lines are taken from the words of King David, on hearing of the death of his son, Absalom (2 Sam. 19:1). For the Hebrew reader familiar with the biblical text, there can be no doubt about the origin of this speech, and the emotional context of the original is easily transferred to the modern tale, enriching it in many respects.

In conclusion, it is apparent that while Agnon has undoubtedly been true to the source, he has also subtly introduced new elements which have enhanced and enlarged the scope of the meaning of the original, while preserving its original intent. This approach is characteristic of a substantial part of Agnon's work, because it was his intent both to enhance and transmit the sources he was drawn to. In many other cases, however, Agnon's use of source material is far more restricted, and his reworkings of the original much more extensive. Yet even in these cases it is possible to recognize in his narratives the imprint of the tradition that stands behind them, and on which his stories and novels have been built.

While some literary critics have argued that Agnon is a self-contained phenomenon, something akin to James Joyce, whose work does not serve as a model to younger writers of the present generation, the opposite is true of Peretz, whose work became the primary model for much subsequent Yiddish literature. Drawn to both the midrashic and hasidic models, in particular, Peretz was almost always true to his sources, but not in the literal way of M. J. Berditchevsky. He would reinterpret and embellish, but at the same time always keep the essence of the original in focus. Peretz saw this as his primary role as a writer—to receive and transmit the essential Jewish spirit contained in these tales.

One of the most remarkable aspects of Peretz's career was his use of the folklore brought to him at the end of folktale expeditions by his friend S. Ansky, the author of The Dybbuk. Peretz made direct use of the tales Ansky brought him, and in so doing performed a great service. Another primary source for Peretz is the hasidic tale. Steeped in hasidic lore, Peretz in many cases combined and linked various tales and wove them into a seamless fabric.

An example of Peretz's use of sources can be seen by comparing his story "The He-Goat Who Couldn't Say No" with the hasidic tale of Reb Menahem Mendel of Kotzk on which it is based, which appears in Martin Buber's Tales of the Hasidim: The Later Masters (pp. 288-89) as "The Sacred Goat":

Rabbi Yitzhak of Vorki was one of the very few who were admitted to Rabbi Mendel during the period when he kept away from the world. Once he visited Kotzk after a long absence, knocked, entered Rabbi Mendel's room and said in greeting: "Peace be with you, Rabbi."

"Why do you say rabbi to me?" grumbled the rabbi of Kotzk. "I am no rabbi! Don't you recognize me! I'm the goat! I'm the sacred goat. Don't you remember the story?

"An old Jew once lost his snuffbox made of horn, on his way to the House of Study. He wailed: 'Just as if the dreadful exile weren't enough, this must happen to me! Oh me, oh my, I've lost my snuffbox made of horn!' And then he came upon the sacred goat. The sacred goat was pacing the earth, and the tips of his black horns touched the stars. When he heard the old Jew lamenting, he leaned down to him, and said: 'Cut a piece from my horns, whatever you need to make a new snuffbox.' The old Jew did this, made a new snuffbox, and filled it with tobacco. Then he went to the House of Study and offered everyone a pinch. They snuffed and snuffed, and everyone who snuffed it cried: 'Oh, what a wonderful box! Wherever did you get it?' So the old man told them about the good sacred goat. And then one after the other they went out on the street and looked for the sacred goat. The sacred goat was pacing the earth and the tips of his black horns touched the stars. One after another they went up to him and begged permission to cut off a bit of his horns. Time after time the sacred goat leaned down to grant the request. Box after box was made and filled with tobacco. The fame of the boxes spread far and wide. At every step he took the sacred goat met someone who asked for a piece of his horns.

"Now the sacred goat still paces the earth—but he has no horns."

As can be seen by comparing this tale with that of Peretz, he has been essentially faithful to the narrative. What he has added to the tale, above all, is a sense of identification with the ram, which broadens our understanding of the extent of its sacrifice. The enchanted goat described here is a figure directly out of mythology, whose essence is Jewish because of the link his horns create between earth and heaven, which in this parallels the function of Jacob's ladder. Peretz invents the story of the origin of the ram's horns (it grazed in the ruin of a synagogue)—a practice that is an essential aspect of aggadic tradition. This source of nourishment for the goat (who grazes, in particular, at two spots—that of the Tabernacle and where Jewish blood had been shed) explains the enormous growth of its horns. In this way Peretz makes the goat a symbol of the Jewish tradition, which makes possible contact with God.

On the other hand, Peretz omits from his version the connection between Reb Mendel and the goat. Reb Mendel asserts that he is the goat. But by the end of the tale it is apparent that he means this metaphorically, in that he, like the goat after its horns have been cut off, has been bound to this world.

Peretz also turns the tale into a call for the Messiah, having the goat hook "the points of his horn around the moon, to hold her" and ask: "Isn't it time yet for the Messiah to come?" This sets off a cosmic echo, in which the ram's question reaches all the way to God's Throne of Glory. This ability of the ram to have its question—which is also mankind's question—reach into the highest heavens would eventually, Peretz implies, have succeeded in bringing the Messiah. But when the ram's horns are cut off, due to the goat's compassion and men's selfishness, the coming of the Messiah is delayed—who knows for how long?

Peretz played a pivotal role in bringing modern Jewish readers and writers to regard the old tradition as a treasure house of riches which could be drawn upon. Peretz pointed the way this could be done, and because he himself was a pure vessel, he succeeded in transmitting, as well, the essential reverence with which the aggadic tradition is best understood.[66]

Through most of the history of Yiddish literature the dominant figures were Mendele Mokher-Seforim, Sholom Aleichem, I. L. Peretz, and, before his accusations of apostasy, Sholem Asch. However, all of these figures have been eclipsed in the past twenty years by the major role Isaac Bashevis Singer has come to play. Singer's receipt of the Nobel Prize in 1979 was confirmation not only of his world stature but also of the validity of the modern Yiddish tradition. Singer is one of the last of the dying tradition of Yiddish literature and possibly its greatest exemplar. Like Peretz and Sholom Aleichem, Singer has published his stories and novels in the *Jewish Daily Forward*. And like the earlier Yiddish masters, Singer has mined the aggadic tradition for much of his subject matter. But unlike most of them he is a writer who is as fascinated with the eccentricities of the flesh as he is with the mysteries of existence.

Singer's emigration to the United States in 1935 and the subsequent destruction of the Polish Jewish communities by the Nazis in World War II created a situation in which he had to turn, of necessity, to his memory and imagination for subject matter. So great has his success been that for many readers Singer's descriptions of life in prewar Poland form the basis for their conception of this period. To his detractors, Singer's character portraits, with their emphasis on the grotesque and the tension between the sacred and the sexual, are overworked and exaggerated. But Singer has always emphasized the primary role of the imagination in his stories and novels. It is a tribute to the power of his imagined worlds that this dispute has long continued to smolder.

Spurred by the acclaim received by his first story to be translated into English (by Saul Bellow), "Gimpel the Fool," and by his natural attraction to the short-story form, Singer has continued to work in this genre, and the regular appearance of many of his stories in *The New Yorker* and other magazines has broadened his audience immeasurably, as, of course, did the receipt of the Nobel Prize. Although Singer is a highly accomplished writer in every style and format he has tried, his greatest successes have come in the realm of the short story, where he must be numbered among the masters in world literature.

Singer is, above all, a storyteller. Even the demons and imps who frequently narrate his stories demonstrate the same keen if somewhat ironic intelligence as their creator, and like him they carefully observe every situation and attempt to penetrate every mystery. Singer is a master of irony and satire, modes that are rarely encountered in the traditional literature. While some Yiddish readers have regarded Singer's use of irony and satire in conjunction with sacred sources as a betrayal, others accept it as an evolution in style, where the essence of sources still remains essentially intact.

Such a use of irony characterizes Singer's story "Sabbath in Gehenna," which appears here in book form for the first time. The legend of Gehenna,[67] which is introduced in the Talmud as the inverse of everything Paradise represents, is based on the biblical Valley of Gehinnom and biblical passages about the punishment of sinners, such as that found in Psalm 11:6: *Upon the wicked He will cause to rain coals; fire and brimstone and burning wind shall be the portion of their cup.* There the souls of sinners are subjected to a painful process of purification for eleven months before they are permitted to ascend to the heavenly abode. This parallel between Paradise and Gehenna is made explicit in the following passage:

> Each person has two portions, one in the Garden of Eden and the other in Gehenna. If a person is worthy and righteous, he takes his share and that of his fellow in the Garden; while if he has incurred guilt and is wicked, he takes his share and that of his fellow in Gehenna.
>
> (B. Hag. 15a)

The nature of Gehenna and the punishments of the wicked are portrayed in detail in a variety of talmudic passages, such as this one:

> The Holy One, blessed be He, punishes the wicked in Gehenna for twelve months. First he forces them to enter the cold, then to enter a fire, and then to enter the snow, where they say "Woe, woe."
>
> (Y. Sanh. 29b)

These punishments and others are embellished in subsequent texts, such as the *Midrash Rabbah* and the Zohar. It is in the Zohar (2:251a) that we find the issue of Sabbath in Gehenna dealt with directly:

> Every Sabbath eve, when the day becomes sanctified, heralds go out to all those compartments of Gehenna announcing: "Cease punishing the sinners, for the Holy King approaches and the Day is about to be sanctified. He protects all!" Instantly all punishment ceases, and the guilty have a respite. But the fire of Gehenna does not let off from those who never observed the Sabbath. Since they did not observe the Sabbath before, they will have no respite forever. An angel whose

name is Santriel, which means God is my Guardsman, goes and fetches the body of the sinner. He brings it to Gehenna before the eyes of the guilty, and they see how it has bred worms. They know the soul of such a sinner has no respite from the fire of Gehenna. And all those guilty who are there surround that body and proclaim over it: "This person is guilty, for he would not regard the honor of his Master, he denied the Holy One, blessed be He, and denied the Torah. Woe to him! It had been better for him never to be created and not to be subjected to this punishment and this disgrace!"

Rabbi Yehuda said: "After the Sabbath goes out the angel comes and takes that body back to its grave, and both the body and the soul are punished, each in its own way."

And all this takes place while the body is still well preserved. But once the body is decayed, it no longer suffers all these punishments. The guilty ones are punished in their bodies and their souls, each with a suitable punishment, so long as the body in the grave is intact. But when the body breaks down the punishment of the soul ceases. He who must leave Gehenna leaves, and he who must find rest has rest. He who must become ashes and dust under the feet of the pious turns to ashes and dust—to each one is done what is suitable for him.

As a former yeshivah student in Warsaw, I. B. Singer became acquainted with the full range of traditional sources, including the Torah, the Talmud, and the Midrash, and he also explored on his own the esoteric world of the Kabbalah and its primary text, the Zohar. Blending details about Gehenna accumulated in these sources, Singer presents a critical view of hell that is a distorted extension of the hellish present. Despite his use of authentic sources, the primary difference between these and Singer's story is substantial because Singer chooses to regard the whole in a satirical light, and identifies the sufferers as Yiddish writers who have all been condemned to Gehenna for their sins. Taking a slanted look at both traditional sources and the present by bringing his ironic vision to them is quite characteristic of Singer, and probably accounts for much of his literary success as well as for the animosity felt for him by the traditionalists.[68] The object of the story, then, is to satirize the Yiddish writing community as much as it is to use the traditional sources for Gehenna. The irony is particularly pointed when the Yiddish writers decide, even in Gehenna, that the thing to do is to start a newspaper, and Singer creates a great deal of comedy out of this situation.

To readers unfamiliar with the rich body of Jewish legends and folklore, the stories and novels of I. B. Singer have a fantastic, startling quality that is almost surreal. But to the reader familiar with these sources, Singer's writings are immediately recognizable as a fusion of the ancient tradition with Singer's individual vision. Thus Singer's best writings must be acknowledged not only as literary masterpieces but also as a valuable storehouse of the folklore and superstitions of the hasidic community that was current during his childhood, which they accurately reflect.

V

MODERN JEWISH LITERATURE AND THE ANCIENT MODELS

The vision first formulated in the Bible and sustained and developed throughout the subsequent phases of Jewish literature has continued uninterrupted into this century in the writings of Jewish authors of many nationalities. These include Nobel Prize winners such as the Hebrew author S. Y. Agnon and the Yiddish author Isaac Bashevis Singer, as well as major figures such as the Yiddish writers Mendele Mokher-Seforim, I. L. Peretz, Sholom Aleichem, S. Ansky, David Pinski, Der Nister, Sholem Asch, and Itzik Manger; the Hebrew writers Hayim Nachman Bialik, M. J. Berditchevsky, Haim Hazaz, Yehuda Yaari, M. J. Feierberg, Pinhas Sadeh, and David Shahar; the German writers Martin Buber, Franz Kafka, Else Lasker-Schüler, Franz Werfel, Stefan Zweig, and Jakov Lind;[69] the French writers André Schwarz-Bart, Edmond Jabès, Albert Memmi, Romain Gary, and Elie Wiesel; the Spanish writers Isaac Goldemberg, Mario Satz, and Jorge Plescoff; the Hungarian writers Lajos Szabolsci, Arnold Kiss, and Péter Ujvári; the Czech writers Jiri Langer and Ladislav Grosman; the Judezmo writers Kamelia Shahar and Alfredo Sarrana; and the English-language writers Israel Zangwill, Bernard Malamud, Cynthia Ozick, Hugh Nissenson, Meyer Levin, Don Jacobson, Milton Steinberg, Leslie A. Fiedler, and Francine Prose.

Before proceeding further, it would be useful to consider why these authors have sought inspiration in the ancient Jewish literary tradition, and how in the process they have contributed to that same tradition and kept it alive.

Among the literary schools of Modernism, two dominant models have arisen. One is primarily concerned with the external landscape, and the other is concerned with exploration of the inner, or spiritual, world. Realism is the dominant style to emerge from those authors for whom the outer world has remained the central subject, while those whose primary impulse is to map out the inner life have utilized the symbolism associated with dreams, my-

thology, legends, and various kinds of religious texts, and their primary literary mode has been an allegorical one. To a large extent the Jewish writers
who have sought inspiration in the ancient sources manifest an impulse toward self-exploration, and therefore largely utilize the allegorical or parabolic
mode.[70]

Of course, this movement toward the use of parable has not been limited
to Jewish authors by any means; it crosses the entire spectrum of modern
masters such as Jorge Luis Borges, Gabriel García Marquez, and Italo Calvino. But while Borges draws his inspiration from a multitude of traditions
and does not owe allegiance to any one, S. Y. Agnon was able to focus all of
his energies into sustaining and rejuvenating a literary tradition that reaches
back almost three thousand years. Very few modern authors have had the
opportunity to work within such a tradition, and virtually all of the authors
represented here feel enhanced by their heritage, and the opportunity to receive and transmit it. In contrast, many modern authors feel outside of all
tradition, and as a result have evolved bleak and narrow world visions, such
as that of Samuel Beckett. Naturally, there is a wide variety of styles and
techniques that are used by the one hundred authors whose work is included
here. Each conceives of his relationship to the ancient tradition in his own
terms, and in fact may vary his approach from story to story. But the essential fact is that these writers do not regard their long religious and cultural
traditions as a burden, but rather as an invaluable blessing.

The advantages of working within a tradition have been amply demonstrated in the past, notably by Dante and Milton. While it is true that the
modern environment does not offer the broadly based support that medieval
Christian culture provided Dante, the Jewish literary tradition, which has remained unbroken, has left a remarkably deep imprint on a substantial number of modern Jewish authors. At the same time these authors have opened
themselves to the various types of modern literature that have emerged in
this century, and have utilized these various approaches in exploring and
mining the ancient tradition. The result, as this collection is intended to
demonstrate, is that this ancient, essentially mythological literature, the Aggadah, emerging out of a legalistic element, the Halakhah, has lent itself perfectly to an infinite variety of manifestations.

The arrangement of the stories in this anthology according to the categories of Jewish literature, beginning with the Bible, is intended to indicate the
primary and/or earliest source and model on which the modern author has
based his material. A comparison of this source and the later work is the first
logical step to take in order to begin to explicate the modern tale.[71] To fully
appreciate the creative process of the modern author in retelling the ancient
tale, it is necessary to observe the elements of each version that coincide, and
those that diverge. The parts that are traditional serve as the frame on which
the modern author weaves his retelling, and the parts that are original consti-

tute the new directions the tale takes. At their best, these tales are able to bring the ancient myths through a new evolution. Jakov Lind, for example, in his tale "The Story of Lilith and Eve" manages to bring together two separate but closely related legends, that of Lilith, Adam's first wife, and that of Eve. In this retelling, Lilith and Eve must ultimately be recognized as poles of the same personality, rather than as separate individuals. What Lind has done, in fact, is to repair the original split, wherein Eve symbolized all positive qualities (from a rabbinic perspective) and Lilith all the negative ones. Out of this process of projection emerged two opposite figures—Eve, loving, receptive and sexually passive, and Lilith, independent, dominating, and sexually active. Lind's story is an assertion that the time has come to reunite these polar aspects which are present in all women, and shows us how this can be done in a metaphorical manner, integrating these opposing aspects into one complete personality.

In some cases this modern material is so similar to the ancient sources as to be almost indistinguishable, while there are also stories in which the influence of the sources is far more remote and sometimes disguised. The tales about the Baal Shem Tov, founder of Hasidism, written by Israel Zangwill, S. Ansky, M. J. Berditchevsky, and Meyer Levin, for example, are based directly on the tales published by the Baal Shem's Hasidim in volumes such as *Shivhei ha-Besht*. These authors do not really alter the tales, but simply bring a literary eye to them, combining those tales that can readily be linked, and polishing the narrative. Martin Buber's versions of these same legends, however, in the volume *The Legend of the Baal Shem*, take a great many liberties. In this case, and that of Buber's *The Tales of Rabbi Nachman*, Buber's primary impulse was clearly a literary rather than scholarly one, and even when he veers away from the original, he remains a master of style and expression. Buber's later versions of these same *maasehs* in *Tales of the Hasidim*, on the other hand, are much closer to the original sources. In both cases, however, the early and the later, Buber sought out tales that confirmed his pure vision and avoided those that did not. Those he chose he then revised to conform to his own literary views, and all of these bear Buber's distinct imprint.[72]

While the sources for all of these tales of the Baal Shem are usually not difficult to locate, there are also stories such as Cynthia Ozick's "The Pagan Rabbi," which is based in a subtle, allusive way on the prototype of the talmudic heretic Elisha ben Abuyah, known as Aher.[73] Likewise, Primo Levi's "Lilith in the Lager" transports the legend of Lilith out of its familiar context, and transfers it to a concentration camp, which soon comes to seem like an appropriate place, after all, for demons to be loose. So too does Mario Satz link the number tattooed on a concentration camp inmate and the esoteric four-letter Name of God, known as the Tetragrammaton, subjects which on the surface seem impossibly disparate. These stories of Ozick,

Levi, and Satz utilize the ancient sources in unexpected but effective ways. In the case of the majority of the stories collected here, however, there is more of a balance between the traditional source and the process of reimagining that takes place.

The central paradox of this type of modern Jewish literature is that it is essentially a secular literature which makes extensive use of symbols drawn from a sacred tradition. This raises a key question about the intentions of the authors who choose to draw upon this rich tradition—are their objectives directed primarily toward the sacred or toward the secular? This question is complicated by the awareness that had some authors working in this genre, S. Y. Agnon in particular, lived a thousand years ago, much of what they wrote would undoubtedly have been accepted into the sacred tradition. The fact, then, that Agnon's writings are not regarded as sacred does not necessarily reflect his most secret desires about how they should be perceived. On the other hand, it is likely that had Dante lived today he would have found it virtually impossible to create a masterpiece such as the *Divine Comedy*. Missing today is the wide acceptance of Christian principles that served as the foundation on which Dante built his literary cathedral.

The fact remains that circumstances have made it necessary for Jewish authors drawn to the ancient tradition to recognize that their writings are by necessity a blend of the sacred and secular. If we are able to perceive the sacred element as representative of an authentic religious impulse, which utilizes a powerful, numinous symbolism, we should be able to accept that the primary motivation for both ancient and modern authors to write has not changed very much over the centuries. What has changed is our perspective toward the literature that is a product of such experience. Essentially, the claim that this literature derives from a sacred source, or was handed down as part of the oral tradition, has been rejected. Nevertheless, the primary impulse behind these writings has remained the same, and for this reason the most reasonable way to regard them is as a continuation of the Jewish literary tradition, making that tradition broad enough to incorporate both sacred and secular elements.

The methods by which modern Jewish authors are inspired by and make use of these traditional sources are diverse. In terms of the amount of ancient material incorporated into the modern work, this ranges from mere allusions and echoes of the source material to the actual incorporation of the source into an expanded retelling. This retelling itself may range from the reverent to the ironic, and may in some cases be literal and in others a radical reworking. The following examples should clarify these possibilities, and indicate the degree to which the source material serves as a starting point for the modern author.

A good example of a modern tale which is built almost entirely on its sources is David Shahar's "On the Life and Death of Abbaye." Abbaye was a prominent talmudic sage, and in the manner of the Talmud, scattered references to his life are to be found throughout the text, among his hundreds of legal comments and decisions. Shahar first located all of these passages, and then wove them together to form a consistent vision of Abbaye which at the same time incorporates virtually all of the sources. His virtuosity in smoothly juggling the various texts results in a highly coherent tale. This is far more of an accomplishment, however, than may at first appear to be the case. Abbaye was an eccentric among the sages; he believed so fully in the world of spirits and demons that he was afraid to be left alone in the privy, and had a lamb accompany him there as a child. Shahar is taken with his personality, and because of his skill in weaving transitions between legends, he is able to accomplish what are the novelist's finest skills—bringing a character to life and at the same time imprinting on the narrative his own vision of Abbaye.

To assist this process of fleshing out Abbaye's character, Shahar does not hesitate to incorporate his own experiences—such as that of observing a great juggler—as well as to utilize other traditional sources—such as the traditional belief, found, for example, in *Midrash Tanhuma*, ed. Buber, Ber. 27, that demons are born from every issue of semen that goes to waste. To protect himself in that house of demons, the privy, Abbaye composed a prayer. And Shahar makes use of this information to suggest, according to the way he has linked together the legends, that in this act we gain insight into the role of religion in Abbaye's life, where the Lord took the place of those who had offered him protection in this world, protection being something he valued above all else.[74]

"On the Life and Death of Abbaye" is an extreme example in that it is based on so many fragmentary talmudic legends, two dozen in all. More often there are one or two primary sources, and rarely more than a few, that the modern Jewish author has utilized. "The Flying Letters" by David Einhorn, for example, is based entirely on two sources. The first is the aggadah that before Moses broke the first tablets, he saw that "the writing had disappeared from them" (Y. Taan. 4:68c); that is, the letters had flown to heaven. The second source is a Yiddish folktale that makes use of the motif of the flying letters, but reworks it in a significant way. In this case the letters of the Torah of one community abandon the scroll of the Torah because the people abandoned the way of the Torah. They then arrive, like a swarm of bees, in another community, and rearrange themselves on a blank scroll that had not yet been written.

Einhorn retells the legend in the brisk style of the folktale. It is not likely that he has embellished it at all, except in a stylistic sense. It is not necessary for the reader to be aware of the original talmudic legend that stands behind this tale, but certainly that knowledge enhances the meaning of the tale, and creates a certain tension in its meaning which results from comparing the two versions of the motif of the flying letters. In the first the moral seems to be that the text of the Torah is immortal, and the ascent of the letters to heaven demonstrates this in a metaphorical manner. In the Yiddish folktale, the letters decide on their own that the community in which they are to be found no longer observes their teachings. This too is a metaphor for the fact that since the people have abandoned the Torah, the Torah, which is frequently personified, can be seen as spurned, and therefore leaving on its own volition to seek out a more hospitable community. The tale is of course an explicit warning that God's grace, as personified in the presence of the Torah, can be lost if the divine commandments are not observed.

Sometimes these modern fictions are based almost directly on a single source. Such is the case of "Yaish and the Angels" by Hayim Hazaz. It is the story of the ascent of Yaish into the heavens, and although there is a specific tradition of heavenly journeys, that of Merkavah Mysticism,[75] Hazaz seems to have turned for his source to one famous talmudic legend about the ascent of Moses into heaven to obtain the Torah, during which he encounters the scorn of the angels, as follows:

Rabbi Joshua b. Levi said: "When Moses ascended to Heaven, the ministering angels said to the Holy One, blessed be He, 'Master of the Universe, what has one born of a woman to do among us?' 'He has come to receive the Torah,' was the Divine answer. 'What!' they said to Him, 'Art Thou about to bestow upon frail man that cherished treasure which has been with Thee for nine hundred and seventy-four generations before the world was created?' The Holy One, blessed be He, then called upon Moses to refute their objections. Whereupon Moses thus pleaded, 'Master of the Universe, I fear lest they consume me with the fiery breath of their mouths.' Thereupon God told Moses to take hold of the throne of His Divine Majesty. Moses then said unto Him: 'Master of the Universe, what is written in the Torah which you are about to give me?' '*I am the Lord, thy God, who brought you out of the land of Egypt*' (Ex. 20:2). Moses then said to the angels: 'Did you go to Egypt and serve Pharoah? Of what use can the Torah be to you?' The angels at once confessed that the Holy One, praised be He, was right in his intention to give the Torah to man. Soon after this, every one of them became so friendly with Moses that each of them disclosed to him some useful secrets, and even the Angel of Death revealed something to him."

Rabbi Joshua b. Levi said further: "When Moses ascended before the Holy One, blessed be He, Satan appeared before Him and said, 'Master of the Universe, where is Thy Torah?' 'I have given it to the earth,' He answered. So Satan went to the earth, saying to it, 'Where is the Torah?' '*God alone,*' answered the earth, '*understandeth her way*' (Job 28:8). Satan then went to the sea and was told, 'She is not with me.' He then went to the deep, and was told, 'She is not with me.' Satan then returned and said to the Holy One, blessed be He, 'Master of the Universe, I have searched throughout the earth for the Torah but could not find it. Then the Lord said to him, 'Go to the son of Amram [Moses].' Satan went to Moses and said to him, 'Where is the Torah that the Holy One, blessed be He, gave thee?'

'Who am I that the Holy One should give me the Torah?' replied Moses in a surprised tone. The Lord then said to Moses, 'Moses, art thou a liar?' 'Master of the Universe!' Moses pleaded before Him, 'such a treasure which Thou hast and art delighted with every single day, shall I claim the credit of obtaining for myself?' Whereupon the Holy One, blessed be He, said unto Moses, 'Because thou hast belittled thyself, I will cause the Torah to be called in conjunction with your name,' as it is said, *Remember ye, the Torah of Moses my servant"* (Mal. 3:22).

(B. Shab. 88b-89a)

The framework of "Yaish Meets the Angels" by Hayim Hazaz is parallel to that of this talmudic legend, while the primary difference lies in the nature of the characters of Moses and Yaish. Moses is far more confident of his mission, while Yaish is something of a buffoon who does not really appreciate the miracle of his ascent. This type of character is developed through the novel *Yaish,* from which this episode has been excerpted. In this episode Yaish is cast in the unlikely role of Moses, and responds, of course, as himself rather than as the patriarch. The primary differences between the talmudic version, then, and that of Hazaz are found in the character of the protagonists, while all other factors remain constant. Nevertheless, the Hazaz tale manages to attain a quality unique from its source by utilizing to the maximum the lighter tone made possible by the nature of Yaish's personality.

Another kind of satire is found in a novel by one of the most attractive Yiddish figures, Itzik Manger. Manger was first and foremost a poet; he wove aggadic themes into balladlike poems which later became the words to a great many popular Yiddish songs. But Manger also wrote a novel, *The Book of Paradise,* that is a comic masterpiece. Originally intended to be the first of three novels, it had the misfortune to be published just as the Germans invaded Warsaw, and the storehouse in which the copies were kept was burned. Only a few copies survived. After the war Manger found he was no longer able to evoke a comic mood, and abandoned the other two planned volumes. But the existing volume is a satire of the midrash about the infant in the womb:

> During pregnancy a light shines upon the head of the child, by which it sees from one end of the world to the other. In the morning the angel takes it, carries it into the Garden of Eden and shows it the righteous who sit there in glory with crowns on their heads. . . . In the evening he carries it into Gehinnom, and shows it the sinners, whom the wicked angels beat with fiery staves. . . . At the end of nine months the angel fillips the baby on the nose, extinguishes the light at his head, and brings him forth into the world against his will. It then forgets whatever it has seen, and as soon as it comes forth unto the world, it cries.[76]

This legend has been taken as an explanation for both the presence of the indentation above the lip and that of a large nose. Manger chooses the second of these possibilities, which has far more humorous potential, and proposes that Shmuel-abba, an angel, has been ordered to descend to this world and be reborn as an infant. But rather than lose his memory, the independent Shmuel-abba puts a piece of clay on his nose and gets the angel bringing him to the world drunk on Messiah wine (which, according to a midrash, has been saved from before the Creation for the coming of the Messiah). The drunken angel only twists the clay, and Shmuel-abba is born remembering everything, which he begins at once to tell. This serves as the framework for a satire about the patriarchs, told in a mock midrashic fashion. In this tale Isaac, who was known to have a weakness for venison, now lives in Paradise, where every day he takes a piece of chalk and, although he is blind, still marks off the finest part of the Messiah Ox—the ox that will not be slaughtered and eaten until the Messiah comes, according to another midrash. Two of these satirical midrashim have been excerpted here: "Adam and Eve Return to the Garden" and "The Star and the Angel of Death." It was possible to excerpt this material because of the tale-within-tale structure of *The Book of Paradise*, which is itself very much in the aggadic tradition, despite its satirical intentions.

Far more allusive in his use of sources is Hugh Nissenson in his story "Forcing the End." Setting his story in modern Israel, Nissenson retells the talmudic episode of the escape of Rabbi Yohanan ben Zakkai from Jerusalem during the Roman siege. Although there was a famine, the Zealots, who controlled the city, refused to let any living person leave. Therefore Yohanan ben Zakkai pretended that he had died, and was carried outside of the city in a coffin by his disciples, with whom he later established a major yeshivah at Yavne. The story is told in the Talmud as follows:

Abba Sikra, the head of the Zealots of Jerusalem, was the son of Rabban Yohanan ben Zakkai's sister. Yohanan sent for him, saying: "Come to me in secret." When he came, Yohanan said to him: "How long will you act in this way and kill the world with hunger?" Abba Sikra said to him: "What shall I do? If I say anything to the other Zealots they will kill me." Then Yohanan said to him: "Find a way for me to escape from the city; perhaps there will be some succor." Abba Sikra said to him: "Pretend to be ill, and let all the world come to ask about you. And take something putrid and put it next to you, and they will say that you died, and let only your disciples come in to you, and let no one else come in, lest they notice that you are light of weight, for they know a living person is lighter than a dead one."

So he did. Rabbi Eliezer walked on one side of the "body" of Yohanan, and Rabbi Yehoshua on the other side. When they came to the gate, the guards wanted to stick their lances into Yohanan. But Abba Sikra said to them: "The Romans will say, 'They pierced their master!'" They wanted to push him. But Abba

Sikra said to them: "They will say, 'They pushed their master!' " Then they opened the gate for him and he was taken out.

When Yohanan reached Vespasian, he said: "Peace be unto you, O king!" But Vespasian said to him: "You have incurred two death sentences. One, because I am not king and you have called me king; and the other, because if I am king, why did you not come to me before this?" Yohanan said to him: "As for your saying that you are not king, you are about to become king, for were you not king, Jerusalem would not be delivered into your hands. And as for your saying that if you are king why did I not come to you before this, the Zealots who are among us did not let me come."

In the meantime a messenger came from Rome and said to Vespasian: "Rise, for Caesar has died and the notables of Rome have decided to elect you as king."

Vespasian had put on one shoe, and wanted to put on the other, but it did not go on. He wanted, then, to take off the first shoe, but it did not come off. He said: "What is this?" Rabban Yohanan said to him: "Be not concerned. Good news has come to you, and it is written, *Good news maketh the bones fat*" (Prov. 15:30). "But what is its remedy?" asked Vespasian. Rabban Yohanan answered: "Let a person, whom you hate, come and pass in front of you, for it is written, *A broken spirit drieth the bones*" (ibid. 17:22). He did so, and the second shoe could be put on.

Then Vespasian said to him: "I am going away, and shall send another man to take my place. However, ask something of me and I shall give it to you." He said to him: "Give me Yavne and its sages, the dynasty of Rabban Gamliel, and a physician to heal Rabbi Tzaddok."

(B. Git. 56a-b)

By retelling this talmudic tale in a different period, with another rabbi— Rabbi Jacobi—Nissenson is able to create a remarkable effect of continuity between the generations, as well as increase our empathy for the talmudic episode, to which the reader can return with a new perspective, drawn from the present. Nissenson emphasizes this continuity in this exchange:

And twisting the tuft of hair below his mouth, Jacobi says, "You're looking at the Holy City through my eyes."
 "The past?"
 He shrugs. "The future, too. What's the difference? They're one and the same."

This time it is Rabbi Jacobi who feels he must escape from Jerusalem in order to establish a yeshivah at Yavne. And like his predecessor, Yohanan ben Zakkai, he has himself smuggled out of the city in a coffin. The reader, noting these parallels, cannot help being caught up, as well, in the realistic details of present-day Israel. And it is these that have the final word in this retelling, in which having escaped in a coffin, Rabbi Jacobi is soon discovered to have been murdered in Yavne. Thus are the parallels and differences between the two times clearly drawn. In this case, it is safe to say, the reader unfamiliar with the talmudic episode will miss much of the point of Nissenson's story, although the tale itself is a riveting one.

Another tale that exists in two time periods simultaneously is Aharon Appelfeld's "In the Wilderness." Appelfeld describes in simple, almost abstract terms the journey of the Israelites wandering in the wilderness as described in Exodus and the subsequent midrashim, while at the same time telling the story of victims of the Holocaust traveling from one city to another. Clearly Appelfeld intends to demonstrate that the experience of the Jews during the Second World War, while unique, was at the same time prefigured by the biblical episode that is of such central importance.

The survivors in Appelfeld's story encounter a landscape parallel in many ways to that of the Israelites in the Egyptian wilderness. In a central episode the survivors reach a wide lake, which clearly represents the Red Sea in the biblical tale. Here there is no parting of the waters, as happened in Exodus, but instead there is a miracle of sorts, as the water sinks into the earth, making passage possible: "Marvelous blossoms suddenly speckled the landscape. . . .The lake came into its own. Birds hovered overhead. . . . Itzik climbed down and said 'The water is sinking.' "

The accessibility of food in the midrashim about the crossing at the sea—"The sea yielded to the Israelites what each desired. If a child cried out as it lay in the arms of its mother, she needed but stretch out her hand and pluck an apple or pomegranate and quiet it" (*Exodus Rabbah* 21:10)—is transferred in Appelfeld's story into an abundance of fish that suddenly become available as the waters sink: "Startled fish were seen in their last attempt to dart away from the shallow water. Itzik would grab a handful and say, 'There are lots of little fish.' "

So too is there a parallel in Appelfeld's tale about the central episode of the Song of the Sea. In the midrashic version the singing is an incredible act of unity among the people, an assertion of determination to continue, in which "even the embryos in their mother's wombs opened their mouths and uttered song before God" (*Mekilta de Rabbi Ishmael* on Ex. 15:1). This assertion of tribal unity appears as well in "In the Wilderness": "Bodies were throbbing, mouths let out cries, questions which merged into a chorus of incantations rejoicing at every discovery."

So too does Appelfeld emphasize this mythological link to the biblical episode by including a story about the angel of death, told by one of the survivors:

The fire was blazing on, the *shochet* made offerings and told us a story about his father who had struggled with the angel of death for many years, until his struggle had become well known. At times he had played sly tricks on the angel, and at times the angel of death had played tricks on him. They had waged war on one another for forty years and at the age of ninety-five the angel had got the better of him.

There are also nightmarish tortures the refugees experience in a wasteland like that described in Exodus. At one point, the horse sinks into the mud as if it were quicksand.

As for the pillar of flame that guided the Israelites in the wilderness, Appelfeld's survivors identify it with the horse that is finally lost to them for good: "Only now did we know that a living pillar had walked before us, protecting us all the way." And, as in the Egyptian wilderness, it is a place transformed into a mythical landscape: "Every object was luminous as though seen for the first time."

Here the role of Moses is played by a *shochet*,[77] a ritual slaughterer, who, like Moses, "feared we would turn to idolatry, since there was one who said: a stone." So too do the people in Appelfeld's story lose patience with the *shochet*, as did the Israelites with Moses: ". . . the *shochet* had misled us. He promised us miracles from God in the wilderness and what did he show us?" And in the end of his tale Appelfeld echoes the death of Moses, who climbed Mount Nebo at the end of his life and whose body was never found, since, according to the Aggadah, he received "the Kiss of the Shekhinah" (B. Sot. 13b) and was taken wholly into the Divine Presence:

> Towards morning the *shochet* kissed our foreheads and said he was requested to leave early. We ran behind but couldn't catch up with him.

Quite often a modern author chooses to continue a story that somehow appears unfinished. A good example of a tale of this kind is Stefan Zweig's "Legend of the Third Dove." This is the last dove that Noah released, which signaled that the waters had significantly subsided so that the land had reappeared. Zweig tells the tale of "the journey and the fate of the third dove." In the process he makes use of another tradition, that of the wanderer who has no home, which first appears in the biblical tale of Cain, and is further embellished in the Christian legend of the Wandering Jew whose presence was reported in every generation. Here it is this third dove, the symbol of peace, who can find no rest:

> It whirred up and flew over our world, in order to find peace, but no matter where it flew, everywhere there were these streaks of lightning, this thundering of men; everywhere there was war. . . . As yet the dove has not found rest, nor mankind peace, and sooner than that it may not return home, it may not rest for all time.

The reader will marvel at how well this allegory builds on its three primary sources: the biblical narrative, the motif of the eternal wanderer, and the tradition that the dove is a symbol of peace. Zweig's narrative also forges links between the biblical motif of the Flood as a symbol of destruction, stating that "a Flood had again come." Thus it indicates that the Flood can serve as a metaphor for the kind of chaos that still threatens the world. Stories of this quality can only be regarded as the logical culmination of the literary tradition begun in the Bible, and evidence that this tradition is still alive and flourishing.

It is also possible for a story to be based on a traditional concept rather than a legend. This is the case with many of the stories included here that are based on kabbalistic themes. Here primary kabbalistic concepts such as that of the *Pargod*, the curtain that hangs before the Throne of Glory,[78] or of *zimzum*, the contraction of God that made possible the creation of the world, serve as the starting points for tales such as Rabbi Nachman's "The Portrait," M. J. Berditchevsky's "Illusion," David Shahar's "The Death of the Little God," and "The Disappearance" by Edmond Jabès.

In the case of Nachman's tale, as well as others of his such as "A Letter" and "The Royal Messenger," God is represented by a king, and the *Pargod* by the curtain that conceals him. This tale serves to make the same point as does the kabbalistic concept of the *Pargod*—that is, that God's true nature is irrevocably hidden from the knowledge of men. There is a long tradition, of course, of allegories in which God is represented as a king. Other examples in this collection are "Illusion" by M. J. Berditchevsky, "The Tale of the Palace" by Tsvi Blanchard, and "The Castle in the Kingdom" by Francis Landy.

"Illusion" by M. J. Berditchevsky and "Three Vows" by S. Y. Agnon illustrate the concept of *Alma d'Shikra*, meaning World of Illusion or World of Lies. The title of Berditchevsky's story in the original Hebrew is *Ahizat Enayim* (literally, "seizing the eyes"), which translates with some difficulty as "illusion," "delusion," "mirage," "chimera," or perhaps "sleight of hand." However, the closest meaning is a term used in Hindu teachings, *maya*. The classic legend defining *maya* is, it is of interest to note, identical in many respects to the Agnon story.

The Hindu tale tells of a Hindu prophet who approaches one of the gods, Arjuna, and asks to be taught the secrets of *maya*. The god agrees, but asks that the prophet first bring him a glass of water from a house at some distance from them in the desert. The prophet agrees, and hurries off to the house. When he arrives there it is almost evening, and the people take him in, share their dinner, and convince him that he must not try to return at night. He remains that night, nor does he leave the next day. He becomes enamored of the daughter of his hosts, and in the end he stays and marries her. They are married for twelve years and have three children. One day a tidal wave passes through the desert and uproots their house, carrying off the man's wife and in-laws. He fights the waves with two children in one arm, and one in the other. A wave tears away the single child, and as he reaches for it with both arms he loses hold of the other two children, and is carried downstream a great distance before the world grows dark. At last he wakes up to find himself covered by a shadow. It is the god Arjuna, leaning over him. The god is saying: "I have been waiting at least five minutes—have you brought my water yet?"

This story serves to define the term *maya* as the illusion of life in this world, which seems so real to us, yet which is in fact only an illusion created by the gods. The concept of *ahizat enayim* differs slightly from *maya* in that the moral is not the meaninglessness of existence, but a reminder that all existence emanates from God, and ultimately has no existence apart from the Divinity.

Berditchevsky's tale is clearly an allegory in which the king represents God, and the cities the king builds and destroys, "in order to build better and more beautiful ones," are actually illusions. The effort to get past the gate in order to discover the truth, only to find another gate behind it, reminiscent of Kafka's "Before the Law," is a metaphor intended to show that ultimate truth is beyond the understanding of men. Finally those seeking entrance to the palace are reminded of this fact by a man who tells them: "There is no palace here, no grand ballrooms, no walls or gates, no building, no doors; all of it is one enormous illusion." Then the man is identified as the Baal Shem Tov, and in fact the allegory of the king and his kingdom is a teaching of the Baal Shem, found in the book *Kether Shem Tov (The Crown of the Good Name)*. The Baal Shem's parable about God is as follows:

A mighty king built a great palace with many chambers, one within the other. Many walls were round about it, each surrounded by the other. Only one gate was open, and opposite it were many doors. He who entered saw many beautiful pictures and costly vessels. The king dwelt in the innermost chamber, far removed from him who entered. When they had finished building the palace, the princes of the realm and the great men of the land were invited to come to the king. But when they came to the palace gate, they found it barred and the doors locked. They now asked one another in surprise, "How shall we enter, seeing that such a multitude of walls separate us?" They looked at the gate and pondered. They saw nothing but wall upon wall. Thus they stood a long time, until finally the king's son came and spoke to them: "Know ye not that my father is exceedingly wise and practised and skilled in the art of conjuring up false images? Behold, the entire palace is unreal. There is no wall here, no gate, and no door—it is all an illusion. It bears the semblance of reality to him who looks upon it. But in very truth, the space here is empty—it stretches unconfined in all directions."

David Shahar's use of the kabbalistic notion of *zimzum* in "The Death of the Little God" is truly astonishing. In the first place, *zimzum* is one of the most esoteric concepts of Kabbalah, which was formulated to explain how

God could be ever-present and still leave a place for the existence of the universe. According to this concept, God first contracted in order to make room for the world, a notion not very far off from the astronomical theory that the universe was once contracted all at one point and then proceeded to expand, and will someday revert to the process of contraction. Shahar makes an inspired connection between the kabbalistic concept and the present-day theological position that God is dead. For God to die, in Shahar's tale, is for Him to contract and shrink away, as He does for the man who is obsessed with the notion that God is growing smaller, and whose death comes after a dream in which he discusses with his father, who is no longer living, the imminent death of God:

> . . . his father sat on the table, crossed his arms over his chest, which was covered only by the thin vest, and said, "Now tell me what's going on in the world."
>
> "The world is growing bigger, Father, and God is growing smaller. . . . God is growing smaller, Father, and now, already, compared to an ant, God looks like a flea compared to an elephant. He is still alive, wriggling and writhing under the weight of the world He created, but it is only a matter of time before His death agonies cease."
>
> "And how long will it take before He disappears?" asked his father, his face becoming serious.
>
> "Two or three weeks, perhaps less."
>
> "Then this is the end."
>
> "Yes, this is the end."

The impact of this story comes largely because the reader cannot help but be fascinated at the man's belief that God is growing literally smaller, which becomes ludicrous when presented in this concrete fashion, while it is far more acceptable in the abstract concept of *zimzum*. At the same time, the modern reader cannot help but recognize the echo of the death-of-God debate in this story, and marvel at how well it is able to create a new perspective on that issue as well. Above all, the story is the moving narrative of an isolated man whose fear took the form of a kabbalistic concept made concrete, and whose accidental death shortly after the dream of the imminent death of God seems to be a confirmation of his obsession, ironic as that may seem.

Edmond Jabès, on the other hand, echoes the original kabbalistic usage of the term *zimzum* in his brief narrative "The Disappearance." In addition, Jabès hints at a parallel between *zimzum* and human introspection when he describes the process as "God, within himself," who "comes to terms with the Face." The writing of Jabès is in many ways in a direct line with the Talmud, and at the same time his work is obviously a new departure in which his fragmented style creates the impression that his words are an echo and response to a dialogue which has already lasted four thousand years.[79]

It is also possible for the modern author to utilize the traditional source by creating a narrative that is its precise opposite. Naturally such a narrative depends on the reader's recognition and awareness of the source. Two examples in this mold are "In the End" by Rabbi Jack Riemer and "Midrash of the Alphabet" by Rabbi Yehiel Poupko. "In the End" describes the End of Days in the same style as the Creation is described at the start of the Bible. The parallel underscores the irony that one is the beginning and the other the end. The images are also intended to echo the threat of atomic chaos hanging over the world. "Midrash of the Alphabet" is an even more bitter retelling of the famous legend from the Zohar about God's decision to create the world through the letter Bet, first letter of *Bereshith* ("in the beginning"). For in the kabbalistic vision the letters of the Hebrew alphabet are sacred vessels through which any kind of creation can be accomplished. This is a logical corollary to the belief that words have the power of the Word. Thus, for example, the four-letter Name of God known as the Tetragrammaton had such great power because it was God's Name, and those who knew the well-kept secret of how to pronounce the Name possessed the unlimited powers of the Divinity. The original legend in the Zohar is, in part, as follows:

When the Holy One, blessed be He, was about to make the world, all the letters of the Alphabet were still embryonic, and for two thousand years before the Holy One, blessed be He, came to create the world, all the letters presented themselves before Him in reversed order. The letter Tau advanced in front and pleaded: "May it please Thee, O Lord of the world, to place me first in the creation of the world, seeing that I am the concluding letter of *Emet* (Truth) which is engraved upon Thy seal." The Holy One, blessed be He, said to her: "Thou art worthy and deserving, but it is not proper that I begin with thee the creation of the world, since thou art destined to serve as a mark on the foreheads of the faithful ones who have kept the Law, and through the absence of this mark the rest will be killed; and further, thou formest the conclusion of *Met* (death)." The Shin then came to the fore and pleaded: "Oh Lord of the world, may it please Thee to begin with me the world, seeing that I am the initial letter of Thy name *Shaddai* (Almighty) and it is most fitting to create the world through that holy name." Said He in reply: "Thou art worthy, thou art good, thou art true, but I will not begin through thee the creation of the world, since thou formest part of the group of letters expressing forgery." Having heard this, the Shin departed. . . . In this manner all of the remaining letters of the alphabet, except for the Bet and the Aleph, presented themselves and were sent back to their places by the Holy One, blessed be He. Then the Bet entered and said: "O Lord of the world, may it please Thee to put me first in the creation of the world, since I represent the benedictions offered to Thee on high and below." The Holy One, blessed be He, said to her: "Assuredly, with thee I will create the world, and thou shalt form the beginning in the creation of the world." The letter Aleph remained in her place without presenting herself. Said the Holy One, blessed be His Name: "Aleph, Aleph, wherefore comes thou not before Me like the rest of the letters?" She answered: "Because I saw all the other letters leaving Thy presence without any success. What, then, could I achieve there? And further, since Thou hast already bestowed on the letter Bet this great gift, it is not meet for the Supreme King to take away the gift which He has made to His servant and give it to another." The Lord said to her: "Aleph, Aleph, although I will begin the creation of the world with the letter Bet, thou will remain the first of the letters. My unity shall not be expressed except through thee, on thee shall be based all calculations and operations of the world, and unity shall not be expressed save by the letter Aleph."

(Zohar, 2b-3b)

This legend from the Zohar[80] serves as a reminder of the polar nature of the world—for every positive word that a letter begins with, there is also a negative one. The personification of the letters also serves to present the kabbalistic belief in the power of letters and words, and emphasizes the honor held by the letter Bet in its role as the first letter of the Torah. (In fact, the Zohar contains an epic treatise on the subject of just the word *Bereshith* and the letter Bet.) Finally, the legend points out that even the letters are not free of the longing for individual honor that so haunts all of mankind.

Rabbi Poupko's "Midrash of the Alphabet" utilizes the essential structure of the kabbalistic legend, but retells it in a chilling, bleak manner in which the letters all shrink away from the ill fate of having to begin the word that stands for the Kingdom of Night, the Holocaust, that in Rabbi Poupko's view must be seen as having cosmic implications. In this way does Rabbi Poupko manage to invert the polarities of the original legend, and emphasize the evil qualities rather than the good. In psychological terms, the figure of the original legend was positive, while the ground concealed the negative qualities. In Poupko's version this figure/ground configuration has been reversed, and the evil aspects are dominant.

There are also cases in which a writer may only hint at the use of the traditional motif and of the sacred or secular tradition. This link may not even be consciously recognized by the reader, but may still play a role in his or her response. One such case is Cynthia Ozick's story "The Shawl." On first reading this story we are almost certain to be struck by the pervasive images of suffering it contains. Drawing from authentic memoirs of the Holocaust, Cynthia Ozick has condensed into this brief tale a moving fragment that manages to sound the true depths of the suffering of the victims of the Holocaust. Less apparent at first is the kernel of hope that sustains the desperate mother—the notion, which barely reaches her consciousness, that all other hope having been lost, the shawl itself will somehow sustain her infant.

Of course the shawl is not magical, and the fate of the child is tragic. Yet the mother's irrational faith in the powers of the shawl reveals a great deal about the human impulse to sustain ourselves on hope alone when all ra-

tional justification for it has been lost. And it is just this seeking after a supernatural salvation when all other hopes have been denied that is one authentic
source of the spontaneous literature we call folklore. It is out of frustrated
hope that folklore, which is hope against hope, arises, and "The Shawl"
gives us great insight into this process.

Imagine, for a moment, a story called "The Magic Shawl." In this tale a
mother escaping a great devastation with her child is able to protect and sustain the child through the powers of the magical shawl she has received from
some traditional source, such as a wise old man, or a fairy godmother.
Themes such as this are the very stuff of which folklore is made. When we
read such tales we share the sense of danger of the protagonist, and the relief
that comes with the magical deliverance. Rarely does it cross our minds that
such a tale has emerged out of tragedy, and that the tragedy has been transformed by the tale so that a victory may be achieved at least in the world of
the imagination, if not in reality.

This, then, is the valuable lesson we learn from Cynthia Ozick's tale,
where the shawl is the projected image of the hope against hope of the
mother, a hope that is ultimately in vain. For it is out of this vain hope that
the kernel of the folktale arises, to console us in later generations. But for the
generation of the Holocaust there was only a brief, imagined hope, and
when even that was gone the taste was bitter indeed. Like the driven mother
we hope in vain that the child will somehow be saved, and like the mother
we briefly put a vain hope in the efficacy of the shawl. But this is no folktale,
and, like the mother, we are ultimately doomed to disappointment. In this,
and all other of these cases, it is the new perspective brought to ancient
sources that permits the modern author to assert his or her own vision, and
to explore in his or her own way the literary possibilities of the subject.

A consideration of the wide range of potential approaches to the same
subject is also a useful method of examining these stories. Several stories included here, for example, consider the Fall from grace. One of these, "Paradise" by Franz Kafka, makes the remarkable assertion that the expulsion
from Eden was a blessing in disguise, since it would otherwise have been necessary to destroy the Garden. Thus Kafka postulates the continued existence
of the Garden, even into our own age, as an ideal of perfection that can only
serve to inspire. Nachman Rapp, in "The Eden Angel," retells the story of
the Fall and expulsion from Eden very much in the biblical mold. However,
he adds to the narrative an angel sympathetic to Adam and Eve who shares
in their temptation and expulsion, losing, in the process, his angelic nature to
become human instead. "Generation" by Nessa Rapoport suggests that the
Fall was a sexual one, and that we succumb to it all over again each time we
indulge our sexual natures. Rabbi Harold S. Kushner's "The Tree of Id"
proposes that the narrative of the Fall be viewed primarily in psychological

terms, and identifies the Tree of Knowledge with that part of the psyche which is the source of instinctive behavior.[81]

Each of these narratives uses the myth of the Fall as its starting point, but each finds it leading to a different conclusion, draws a different lesson, and thus views the original narrative from a different perspective. Part of the power in these tales comes from the fact that they compel readers to reconsider the old narrative at the same time they are presented with the new. The tension of the divergences between the old and new and the delight the new vision brings to the old provide a considerable satisfaction in themselves. Of further edification is the recognition that each of these tales is also a modern form of midrashic interpretation of the original narrative of the Fall. Together these stories expand the boundaries of meaning of the original myth, and make that meaning far more personal and pertinent. Finally, they serve as proof of the profundity of the original and of the attention it continues to attract.

There is also found in this collection a cluster of stories concerning the *Akedah*, the binding of Isaac by Abraham. In "Abraham" Franz Kafka imagines an Abraham "who was prepared to satisfy the demand for a sacrifice immediately, with the promptness of a waiter, but was unable to bring it off because he could not get away, being indispensable." Jakov Lind's "The Near Murder" retells the story of the *Akedah* from a modern, almost psychiatric perspective in which a father hears a voice command him to kill his only son, and he attempts to obey. This dimension of the tale, always present in the biblical narrative, but in a more latent fashion, is truly horrifying when made overt, and refashions the reader's view of the *Akedah* for all time. My own story "The Dream of Isaac" takes the radical step of substituting for the ram in the biblical narrative a goose. This substitution ultimately provides the link between the legendary action of Abraham and the necessary act of cutting the umbilical cord. It is an illustration of what might be called "midrashic license." Michael Strassfeld's "Isaac" is powerfully identified with its subject, and implies an unsuspected link between Abraham and the ram, which, after it is considered, provides a valuable new perspective on the ancient tale. "Isaac" by Barry Holtz links the binding of Isaac with the blessing of the firstborn, in which Jacob deceives Isaac by pretending to be Esau. Such linking of two biblical episodes, causing them to shed light on each other, is one of the most common aggadic devices. "The Tale of the Ram" by Tsvi Blanchard also suggests a new perspective from which to regard the *Akedah*—as an act less significant in itself than for the fact that it took place at the very moment that the ram, which had been created before the root of the world, chose to goie the Messiah, delaying the time of his arrival. "Rivka on Mount Moriah" by Laya Firestone bas Rivka (Toblerru), Isaac's wife, return to the place of the *Akedah* before giving birth to Jacob and Esau, implying that the struggle of the twins in the womb, which is amply described in the midrashic literature, was the turning point in her life, as the binding was in the life of Isaac.

The *Akedah* has long remained one of the most central and perplexing episodes in the Bible, and the range of these interpretations strongly suggests that it has lost none of its power, nor is its essential meaning any more certain at this time than when it was first written down. And each of these stories, in its own way, refutes the simplistic interpretation that the *Akedah* should merely be regarded as a test by God of Abraham, or as an event intended to demark the elimination of human sacrifice by the Jews. For these authors, certainly, the original tale has retained its mystery, which grows with each subsequent interpretation, rather than being diminished.[82]

The choice of the authors who have utilized traditional sources in the ways outlined here must be recognized, above all, as an act of affirmation. At every stage in the evolution of Jewish literature there have been those prepared and even anxious to declare that the Book was closed, and that all that came afterward lacked significance. These authors, on the contrary, insist that the tradition is still alive, and that the ancient tale may still be retold in new ways. Their desire is clearly, as Edmond Jabès puts it, "To be in the book . . . to be part of it. To be responsible for a word or a sentence, a stanza or chapter."[83]

As these examples have demonstrated, these authors have sought out their own roles and relationships with the tradition, while retaining the right to embellish as they see fit. These embellishments are the lifeblood of this particular type of literature, for it is understood that once a tale is frozen in one form, it becomes an object for analysis, not a living force; much of the power of the retelling comes from the new perspectives on the old tale that are made possible.

VI

TOOLS OF
INTERPRETATION

Surely this instruction which I enjoin upon you this day is not too baffling for you, nor is it beyond reach. It is not in the heavens, that you should say: "Who among us can go up to the heavens and get it for us and impart it to us, that we may observe it?" Neither is it beyond the sea, that you should say, "Who among us can cross to the other side of the sea and get it for us and impart it to us, that we may observe it?" No, the thing is very close to you, in your mouth and in your heart, to observe it.

(Deut. 30:11-14)

The words of the Torah have many meanings. Sparks fly in different directions. Each word may catch a different spark.

(B. Kid. 30b)

The Bible serves not only as the primary sacred scripture for the West, but as the source of our central myths. These myths have become so entwined with all aspects of our lives that they have taken on the quality of archetypal symbols. It is into these symbols that the culture as a whole projects its hopes and dreams, permitting the mythic archetypes to assert their power.

As in any system of symbols, then, it is necessary to explicate the symbolic intent. This requires a mastery of the meaning of the primary symbolism. Fortunately, the need for interpretation has long been recognized in the Jewish tradition, and the act of explication held in high esteem. Many editions of the Hebrew Bible are printed with the commentaries of Rashi and others, and these commentaries have taken on the aura, over time, of the sacred texts they explicate, even though they often disagree as to the correct interpretation of the biblical text. However, the acceptance of opposing views has been recognized since the talmudic period, because of the cordial relation between the schools of Hillel and Shammai, which is apparent from the following talmudic statement:

77

About Hillel and Shammai: Notwithstanding the fact that one school prohibits what the other allows, that one declares unfit what the other declares fit, the disciples of the two schools have never refrained from intermarriage. Likewise, as regards Levitical cleanliness and uncleanliness, where one school declared clean what the other declared unclean, nevertheless they never hesitated to help one another in the work which according to the other faction might not be considered clean.

(B. Yeb. 13)

In fact, it was the act of exegesis that was held in highest esteem as the best means of understanding the sacred text at hand. And not only for the sacred Scriptures, but also for dreams: "A dream left uninterpreted is like a letter unread" (B. Ber. 55a). Before the accepted ruling on the Halakhah, the Law, was reached by majority opinion, polar and contradictory interpretations were offered. The following midrash, from *Genesis Rabbah* (1:15), amply demonstrates how conditioned the rabbis were to opposing viewpoints:

The school of Shammai maintains that heaven was created first, while the school of Hillel holds that earth was created first. In the view of the school of Shammai this is like the case of the king who first made his throne and then made his footstool. According to the school of Hillel, this is to be compared to a king who builds a palace—after laying the foundation he builds the upper portion. Discussing this matter, Rabbi Yonathan said: "As regards creation, heaven was first; as regards completion, earth was first." Rabbi Simeon observed: "I am amazed that the fathers of the world engage in controversy over this matter, for surely both were created at the same time, like a pot and its lid."

One further legend, from the Talmud, relates the remarkable circumstances in which the majority opinion of the rabbis overruled both Rabbi Eliezer ben Hycranos and God Himself:

Rabbi Eliezer used every possible argument to support his opinion, but it was not accepted by the other sages. Then he said: "Let this carob tree prove that the Halakhah is as I state it is." The carob tree then uprooted itself and moved a distance of one hundred (and according to others four hundred) ells. But the sages said: "The carob tree proves nothing."

Then Rabbi Eliezer said: "Let the waters of the spring prove that I am right." Then the waters began to flow backward. But again the sages said that this proved nothing.

Then Rabbi Eliezer spoke again and said: "Let the walls of the house of study prove that I am right." And the walls were about to collapse when Rabbi Yehoshua said to them: "If scholars are discussing a halakhah, why should you interfere?" Thus they did not fall, in deference to Rabbi Yehoshua, but neither did they straighten out, out of respect for Rabbi Eliezer, and they are inclined to this day.

Rabbi Eliezer then said: "If the law is as I say, let heaven prove it." Thereupon a *bat kol,* a heavenly voice, came forth and said: "Why do you quarrel with Rabbi Eliezer, whose opinion should prevail everywhere?"

Rabbi Yehoshua then stood up and said: *"The Law is not in heaven"* (Deut. 30:12). "What does this mean?" asked Rabbi Yermiyahu. "It means that since the Torah was given to us on Mount Sinai, we no longer require a heavenly voice to reach a decision, since it is written in the Torah: *Follow after the majority"* (Ex. 23:2).

Later Rabbi Nathan encountered Elijah, and asked him: "What did the Holy One, blessed be He, do at that time?" And Elijah replied: "He smiled and said: 'My children have overruled Me, My children have overruled Me!' "

(B. Bab. Met. 59b)

From this example it is apparent that the rabbis regarded the very act of explication of the Torah as a divine injunction, and their decisions so inviolate that not even God could overrule them. The necessity for this interpretation goes back to the original existence of both a written and an oral law, the latter intended to explicate the former. Thus the need for commentary was regarded as a necessity from the very giving of the Torah on Mount Sinai, and we find it said in the Talmud concerning commentary: "Prior to the time of Solomon, the Torah was like a basket without handles, but when Solomon came he affixed the necessary handles" (B. Eruv. 21b).

It is also of interest to note that while the ruling on a law was always observed and quoted in all decisions related to it, the opposing viewpoints were not deleted from the Talmud, and thus are not disregarded. The existence of these rabbinic debates assisted immeasurably in the creation of an atmosphere in which a variety of interpretations became possible.[84]

The oldest and most elementary method of scriptural exegesis consisted of locating one passage in the Bible to explicate another. From this method evolved more intricate techniques for a close reading of the text, including the seven rules, or *middoth*, of Hillel, which were later expanded to thirteen *middoth* by Rabbi Ishmael. These rules were primarily formulated to reach an understanding of the Halakhah, and were intended to assist in the establishment of general principles that could be deduced from the text. Their primary focus is on the *peshat*, or literal meaning, but some of them are couched in general enough terms that they are able to serve as justification for less literal readings as well. Later Rabbi Eliezer ben Jose, a disciple of Rabbi Akiba, formulated thirty-two rules for aggadic exegesis.[85]

In addition to rules of exegesis there were also other techniques for extracting meaning from a text. Four particularly common techniques which gained their widest acceptance during the kabbalistic period (13th–17th centuries C.E.), are *gematria, notarikon, temurah,* and *tziruf.* In *gematria* the numerical value of the letters is added up, and words with identical totals are assumed to be related. By this technique, for example, the ladder Jacob saw reaching into heaven could be related to Mt. Sinai, since the numerical total of *sullam* ("ladder") is 130, the same as that of *Sinai.* After all, both the ladder and the Torah, received on Mt. Sinai, connect earth and heaven, each in its own way. *Notarikon* takes the letters of a word as the initial letters of an acrostic. By this method the first word of the Torah, *Bereshith* ("in the beginning"), for example, can be said to represent in Hebrew the phrase "In the beginning God saw that Israel would accept the Torah." By the same technique the same word can allude to the phrase "He created the sky, the earth, the heavens, the sea, and the abyss." *Temurah* substitutes one letter for another, and *tziruf* rearranges a word to make it into another—i.e., an anagram. These methods tend to encourage a kind of free association, but also lend themselves to manipulation by those intent on confirming a particular reading of the text.

One valuable medium for the preservation of early biblical exegesis both of the halakhic and the aggadic nature was the translations of the Bible into Aramaic known as the Targumim. In these translations interpretations were incorporated into the texts, expanding and clarifying the narrative. In this way the Targumim, particularly those edited in Palestine, prefigure the later midrashic collections, such as *Pirke de Rabbi Eliezer, Sefer Yashar,* and *The Chronicles of Jerahmeel,* that gather aggadic interpretations from various sources and weave them into a continuous narrative. Needless to say, many of these interpretations altered the meaning of the original text. The Targum on the story of the Tower of Babel, for example, makes overt the challenge to the Divinity that is only implicit in the biblical text; the nonitalicized words are the addition of the Targum:

And they said, "Come, let us build us a city, and a tower whose top comes up to *heaven, and let us make us* an idol on the top of it and let us put a sword in its hand, and it will make formations for battle before Him, before we are scattered over the face of the earth."*

(Targum Pseudo-Jonathan on Gen. 11:4)

From a very early period interpretations of an allegorical nature also emerged as an accepted, albeit controversial, method of explication. One of the earliest allegorical interpretations appears in Hosea 12:5, with the suggestion that Jacob's struggle with the angel may have been a struggle in prayer rather than a physical contest. A further illustration is the interpretation of Jeremiah's prophecy (29:10) that the exile would end after seventy years, which appears in the Book of Daniel (9:2 and 9:24). Here the prophecy is interpreted to mean seventy weeks of years, to give hope for redemption from the Greek rule of that period.

Additional allegorical readings appear in the apocryphal book *The Wisdom of Solomon* (10:10), where Jacob's ladder is viewed as a symbol of Divine Providence, and in the writings of Josephus, who interprets the Tabernacle allegorically, equating, for example, the Holy of Holies with the heavens.

But among early allegorists, the master was Philo of Alexandria. Philo constructed an entire system of biblical interpretation based on allegory, in which every finite detail is seen as an allegory of some higher truth. Ironically, Philo's writings had very little direct impact on later Jewish tradition, but furnished a foundation stone to Christianity; his approach to interpreting the Old Testament was used as a prophecy for the New Testament. Philo's failure to influence the Jewish tradition is due to the implications of his approach, which appears to sacrifice the literal meaning for an allegorical one, reducing the patriarchs to mere abstractions. Philo interprets, for example, God's command to Abraham to *Depart from thy land, and from thy kindred, and from thy Father's house* (Gen. 12:1) to mean "by Abraham's country the body, and by his kindred the outward senses, and by his father's house uttered speech."[86]

It might appear that the rejection of Philo's extreme approach would have brought about a general rejection of the allegorical method, but this was not the case. Rather, it was a rejection, for a time, of Philo's highly abstract, all-encompassing metaphysical interpretation, and its apparent denial of the literal meaning of the text (although Philo himself defended the literal meaning, while remaining vague on the subject of how it related to the allegorical one). It was not until the kabbalistic period that such thoroughly abstract allegories came to flourish and found acceptance in the tradition.

On what grounds, then, was allegory retained as a tool of interpretation by the talmudic sages? Primarily as a means to explain some passages of the Scriptures that were difficult to interpret in any other way. Allegorical interpretations were necessary, for example, to explain anthropomorphic expressions about God, so as to protect the principle of monotheism and sustain the conception of God as an incorporeal Being. At the same time, their belief in the Torah as the repository of all truth led the rabbis to assume that a literal interpretation of a passage from the Torah could not fully exhaust its meaning. Allegorical interpretations made it possible for some passages, in particular, to express more profound meanings than those conveyed by the literal reading.

Since the sages, and Rabbi Akiba in particular, saw it as their duty to explicate each and every word of the Torah, even what might seem to be insignificant, they were forced to come to grips with passages that did not lend themselves to any apparent interpretation. We read in Genesis, for example, that *Abram and Nahor took to themselves wives, the name of Abram's wife being Sarah and that of Nahor's wife Milcah, the daughter of Haran the father of Milcah and Iscah* (Gen. 11:27-29). There is no further mention of Iscah, and the rabbis were at a loss as to how to identify her. This dilemma was solved in the talmudic period by Rabbi Isaac, who observed, "Iscah was Sarah, and why was she called Iscah? Because she foresaw the future by divine inspiration" (B. Sanh. 69b). With no other evidence to go on, Rabbi Isaac turns to

the root of "Iscah," *sachah*, which means "to see, gaze or prognosticate."
(This interpretation was later quoted by Rashi, commenting on Gen. 11:29.)
From this he draws his clearly allegorical explanation, in which Iscah represents that pole of Sarah's personality which functioned as a seer. For tradition has it that Abraham was a great soothsayer, but that Sarah was even
greater. Normally Sarah was the devoted wife of Abraham, but when she
served as a vessel of the divine word she touched on another aspect of her
personality, and thus could be identified by another name. In this way does
Rabbi Isaac solve the mystery of Iscah's identity while incorporating the tradition of Sarah's prophetic abilities. Iscah, then, is an extension of Sarah's
personality beyond its normal bounds, which in a mythological system is inevitably identified as a separate individual.

That the role of allegory was recognized as an accepted method in which
to garb teachings is apparent from the following parable, which defines the
ties between body and soul:

> Antoninus said to Rabbi: "The body and the soul can both free themselves from
> judgment. Thus, the body can plead: 'The soul has sinned, the proof being that
> from the day it left me I have lay like a dumb stone in the grave.' While the soul
> can say: 'The body has sinned, the proof being that from the day I departed from
> it I fly about in the air like a bird and commit no sin.' " Rabbi replied: "I will tell
> you a parable. To what may this be compared? To a human king who owned a
> beautiful orchard which contained splendid figs. Now, he appointed two watch-
> men therein, one lame and the other blind. One day the lame one said to the blind:
> 'I see beautiful figs in the orchard. Come and take me upon thy shoulder, that we
> may procure and eat them.' So the blind one carried the lame one, and they pro-
> cured the figs and ate them. Some time later the owner of the orchard came and
> inquired of them: 'Where are those beautiful figs?' The lame one replied: 'Have I
> feet to walk with?' And the blind one replied: 'Have I eyes to see with?' What did
> the king do then? He placed the lame upon the blind and judged them together. So
> will the Holy One, blessed be He, bring the soul and the body together, and judge
> them as one, as it is written, *He shall call to the heavens from above, and to the earth,*
> *that He may judge His people* (Ps. 50:4). *He shall call to the heavens from above*—this
> refers to the soul; *and to the earth, that He may judge his people*—to the body."
>
> (B. Sanh. 91a-b)

The principle of allegorizing an entire book of the Bible was established by
Rabbi Akiba's defense of the inclusion of the Song of Songs in the sacred
canon. There was resistance to this poem on the grounds that its imagery is
highly erotic, and that it does not concern itself at all with the Divinity. It
was only after Akiba's suggestion that the Song of Songs could be read as the
love between God and Israel (rather than as that between a man and a
woman) that opposition to its inclusion was finally quelled.[87] At this point
the technique of allegorical interpretation of Scripture was fully established,
and statements in support of it began to appear: "Let not the allegoric

method appear to you as slight, for by means of the allegorical method one may sometimes get at the true meaning of the scriptural words" (*Song of Songs Rabbah* 1:8). Nevertheless, the rabbis continued to resist a great many of the interpretations of the allegorists, fearing that the method might be used against Judaism by the followers of a religion such as Christianity. This reservation remained a point of contention between the rabbis throughout the talmudic and midrashic periods, and allegory did not receive full sanction as a primary approach to the interpretation of the Torah until the kabbalistic era. At that time allegory was codified as one level of interpretation in the system identified by the acronym *PaRDeS*.[88] This exegetical approach was of the greatest value in perpetuating the expectation that any passage of the Torah is subject to multiple levels of meaning.

The method of interpretation known as *Pardes* was most likely invented, or at least codified, by Moshe de Leon, author of the Zohar, according to the widely accepted findings of Gershom Scholem. Moshe de Leon was also the author of a volume, since lost, entitled *Sefer Pardes*. Scholem speculates that this volume was a theoretical treatise of *Pardes* as a method of explication, a concept which in any case dates from the same period, the 13th century.

PaRDeS is an acronym for four levels of understanding: *peshat, remez, drash* and *sod*. *Peshat* is the literal level. *Remez* is the first hint of another level of meaning; in literary terms it is the use of metaphor. *Drash* stands for midrash, when the interpretation takes the form of a legend, or, in literary terms, of allegory, which itself is simply an extended metaphor.[89] *Sod* is the level of mystery, of Kabbalah. Its literary meaning must remain inseparable from its religious meaning: entry into the realm of the transcendent. The existence of the level of *sod* is also a reminder that metaphor is a kind of veil, and that ultimate truth transcends it and must remain imageless and unknown, like the remotest aspect of God, known in Kabbalah as *Ein Sof*.

Applying the terms of *Pardes* retrospectively to the Song of Songs, it is apparent that when the poem is viewed as depicting the love between a man and a woman, it is being viewed from the literal level of *peshat;* while when it is seen as an expression of love between God and Israel, as in Rabbi Akiba's interpretation, it is being viewed from the third level of *drash*, of allegory. In this and many other cases the second level of *Pardes, remez,* is actually more of a transitional phase, wherein the reader first recognizes the use of simile, metaphor, or allusion. It is not unlike recognizing the connotation of a word, rather than the denotation. When the entire metaphor has been revealed, as in Akiba's interpretation, it achieves the level of *drash*. The fourth level, *sod,* was added during the kabbalistic period. In fact, it was certainly the reason for Moshe de Leon to formulate the system of *Pardes,* since it codified the kabbalistic vision of the Zohar as an integral part of the Jewish system of explication. It should be apparent that such a system of interpretation offered assurance for the continued existence of contrary interpretations of the same text, which could simply be seen as signifying differing levels of meaning. Furthermore, a system that posits four simultaneous levels of understanding, from the most concrete to the most abstract, is well suited to develop a rich literary tradition whose works can be approached no matter how obscure they may appear.

The choice of the word *Pardes* as the acronym for this system derives from its use in the talmudic legend about the four sages who entered *Pardes*. This is without a doubt one of the key legends in all of Jewish literature, and probing its meaning offers a vivid opportunity to demonstrate how the meaning of the term *Pardes* can itself be understood in terms of these four levels of understanding. Its use in the Talmudic literature also demonstrates that the system Moshe de Leon later expanded and codified had been in use in a less formal sense for many previous generations.

On the literal level *Pardes* refers to an orchard. The word is still in common usage for that meaning in modern Hebrew. On the level of *peshat* it is just that, an orchard, an enclosed place where fruit is grown. On the next level, of *remez*, we recall that *Gan Eden*, the Garden of Eden, was also an orchard. That is enough to imply a deeper meaning of the word. On the third level of meaning, *drash*, the term *Pardes* is interpreted by the famous legend in B. Hag. 14b, about the four sages who entered *Pardes*, as follows:

> The rabbis taught: Four sages entered *Pardes*, and they are: Ben Azzai, Ben Zoma, Aher,[90] and Rabbi Akiba. Rabbi Akiba said to them: "When you arrive at the stones of pure marble, do not say 'Water, water.' "[91] Ben Azzai looked and died.[92] Ben Zoma looked and lost his mind.[93] Aher cut the shoots.[94] Only Rabbi Akiba entered in peace and departed in peace.[95]

Observe how well this legend manages to work on two levels at the same time—the essential factor in forming an allegory. On the literal level the sages have entered an orchard. This is confirmed when Aher cuts the shoots. On the other hand, there is no doubt that this aggadah is using *Pardes* to refer to Paradise. But "Paradise" itself is only an allegory whose meaning becomes apparent when the legend is viewed from the perspective of the level of *sod*, of mystery. Here Paradise is a metaphor for mystical contemplation, and *Pardes* refers to the enticing but dangerous realms of mystical speculation and contemplation, symbolized by a heavenly ascent. The subject of their contemplation was either what is known as *Maaseh Bereshith*, the Work of Creation, or *Maaseh Merkavah*, the Work of the Chariot. These terms refer to the two biblical episodes in which the Kabbalah was best able to root itself, and thus all kabbalistic literature is linked, in some respect, to one of these two central concerns.

Maaseh Bereshith is the mystery of Creation, and *Maaseh Merkavah* is the mystery of the heavenly chariot in the vision of Ezekiel. On the basis of the

אין דורשין פרק שני חגיגה

report in B. Hag. 14b, the rabbis concluded that such mystical contemplation was too dangerous a path to be left to any but the fully initiated. The
following dictum from the Mishnah (B. Hag. 13) demonstrates this rabbinic
concern about such activity:

> One should not discuss the laws concerning illegal union before three, nor the cre-
> ation before two, nor the divine chariot with even one individual, unless he is a
> wise man with much knowledge of his own. Anyone who tries to ascertain these
> things, it were better for him had he never come into the world. . . . Search not
> into that which is concealed from thee; that which is hidden from thee do not try
> to penetrate; consider only that which thou hast permission. Thou must have
> nothing to do with mysteries.

But the tale of the four who entered Paradise (for this is how it was commonly understood) impressed others in an entirely different way. For this
legend also became an entry into the mysteries of *Pardes* by an esoteric Jewish sect, who actively sought to engage in the mystical contemplation of
Maaseh Merkavah. This form of contemplation, at first limited to a small circle of initiates, later was injected into the common tradition by the acceptance of the Zohar as a text written by the talmudic sage Simeon bar Yohai,
who lived in the 3rd century. For this is the claim Moshe de Leon made in
the 13th century for his masterful work of pseudepigraphy, and the claim
was accepted; the work was demonstrated to be a forgery only in this century as a result of the research, in particular, of Gershom Scholem.[96]

This sect sought, by engaging in mystical contemplation, to discover the
means to enter *Pardes*, which in their metaphorical system was represented
by the heavenly Paradise. The texts produced by this sect are called Hekhaloth texts, since they describe travels through the palaces (*hekhaloth*) of
heaven. As is the case with the alchemists, it is impossible to ascertain
whether they believed in and sought after actual heavenly journeys, or
whether it was implicit that the heavenly journey itself was a metaphor for
the mystical ascent, in which the palaces signify degrees of spiritual elevation.
In any case, Scholem speculates that this sect actively engaged in techniques
to bring about mystical experiences, including the use of yogalike positions,
and the singing of rhythmical hymns in unison for long periods of time.[97]
Standard Jewish practices of purification were also used, including the *mikvah* (ritual bath), fasting, and extensive prayer. Emphasis was also placed on
the power of the word—on amulets containing invocations and, above all,
the secret of the pronunciation of the ineffable Name of God, the Tetragrammaton.

Either to record their experiences or to prepare a guidebook for mystical
ascent, this sect authored a number of texts that describe in great detail the
process of the heavenly ascent, as well as the palaces of heaven.[98] Using

B. Hag. 14b, the passage about the four who entered *Pardes,* and the apocryphal *Book of Enoch* as their models, the Hekhaloth texts explore the upper Paradise in extensive detail. The primary figures to make the ascent are Enoch, who, it will be recalled, *walked with God and was not* (Gen. 5:24); Rabbi Akiba, who "ascended in peace and descended in peace" in an alternate phrase used in the talmudic discussion of the episode;[99] and Rabbi Ishmael ben Elisha, a talmudic sage, who, like Rabbi Simeon bar Yohai, became identified as a bearer of the mystical tradition.

These *Hekhaloth* texts prefigure the later kabbalistic treatises, and can be regarded as expanded commentaries on the subject of *Maaseh Merkavah,* the Work of the Chariot. They introduce the metaphor of the heavenly ascent as the ultimate allegory for mystical contemplation, and it remains such throughout subsequent Jewish literature, where it is a motif used extensively by the Kabbalists and Hasidim.[100]

Returning to the concept of *Pardes* as a system of interpretation, it can now be recognized as a method directing the reader through subsequent plateaus of meaning. While primarily designed to explicate the Torah, it is also applicable to all literature, sacred as well as secular, and can serve as a highly sophisticated tool of interpretation. It is a technique especially useful, both in its religious and literary dimensions, for coming to terms with the tales collected here, which like the legends that are their source, exist on several levels simultaneously. Some, of course, are intended to be understood primarily on the simplest level, quite literally. But most touch on all four levels at the same time, and as such are far richer than may be apparent on first reading.[101]

Consider, for example, the tale "The Lost Princess" by Rabbi Nachman of Bratslav. Cast as a fairy tale, the *peshat,* or literal meaning, of the story is simply an extension of the enchanted world of kings and princesses that all fairy tales engender, as well as a model mirroring the relationship between father and daughter. Its link to the Jewish tradition seems nonexistent, except as part of an expression of folklore that had flourished since the early Middle Ages. Clearly, if the tale has some tie to the sacred tradition, an interpretation must be sought at the allegorical level. The key is to recognize the king as a symbol for God, while the lost princess is a metaphor for the Shekhinah, the kabbalistic "Bride of God." Making this identification is to read the tale at the level of *remez.* Recasting the entire tale in terms of the myth of the Shekhinah, who has gone into exile along with her people, Israel, and who is sought after by the king's minister, who may be seen as a *tzaddik* or perhaps even the Messiah, the tale forms itself into a fully developed allegory, and thus reaches the level of *drash.* But to come to an understanding of this mysterious tale at the highest level of *sod,* of mystery, it is necessary to glimpse the secret of how the minister will finally free the princess, thus how the Shekhinah will finally be brought out of exile.

Rabbi Nachman intentionally clothed his kabbalistic allegories in the garb of the common fairy tale in order to permit his tales to reveal their mysteries to his Hasidim according to the ability of each to understand. Nachman made it clear to his Hasidim that his tales did contain great secrets, for those who could comprehend them.

As a further illustration, consider S. Y. Agnon's "Fable of the Goat." This tale, which exists as a folktale in at least five variants, concerns a goat that leads its owner through a cave to the Promised Land. On the level of *peshat* the story can be seen simply as an embellishment of the folktale on which it is based. The magical occurrence of the cave will be seen from this perspective as an expression of the enchantment that is such a common motif in folktales and fairy tales. But if the reader notes in the separation of father and son a hint of the predicament of those who emigrated to Israel and those who stayed behind, then the direction of the allegory can be discerned. At this point the reading has passed the level of *remez* and reached that of *drash*. It should not be difficult for readers to achieve this understanding of the story, but few will succeed in reaching into the realm of *sod*, where the tale must be internalized. From this perspective the cave comes to symbolize the path within the self that leads one to emerge from the exile of self-alienation to discover the Promised Land within. Such self-realization is the true goal of kabbalistic literature, as it was the true goal of the alchemists, whom the world regarded as being concerned with the transmutation of lead into gold, and whose true calling, that of transmuting the leaden soul into the golden one, was concealed.

A third illustration is provided by the tale of I. L. Peretz entitled "The Hermit and the Bear." This is a story that refuses to be read only on the literal level. It suggests that the methods of the hermit in moving the river, in seeking to wake the world-soul, and in taming the bear are the esoteric techniques of the Kabbalist, who can concentrate great powers to achieve an end. These are the powers called upon by Rabbi Judah Lowe in the legend-cycle of the Golem, the man of clay who comes to life in the folk legend that prefigures the Frankenstein myth of our own time.

These implications in Peretz's tale are intended to direct the reader beyond the first level of *Pardes* to the second, of *remez*, where the struggle can be viewed in its abstract form as the classic confrontation of good and evil. This reading, in turn, leads to the logical allegorical meaning, in which the struggle of the hermit and the bear can be seen as the eternal conflict between the flesh and the spirit in everyone. This reading reaches the level of *drash*. But to achieve an understanding at the level of *sod* would require insight into the quest of the hermit to awaken the soul of the world, which is sleeping. Such insight would require not necessarily the ability to wake this soul, but at least the ability to recognize the existence of the soul that sleeps, and of the possibility of every person, working independently or together, to wake that sleeping soul within himself. Peretz also makes it quite clear that devoting one's energy solely to taming the bear, i.e., our unbridled desires, will not serve the quest of trying to awaken the world-soul, for, as he writes, "the hermit who now sleeps together with the bear will not wake the soul of the world." And asleep, how can the hermit continue his quest?

This story, then, despite its folktale exterior and its jaunty manner, has at its core a truth that Peretz has clothed in allegory for the same purpose that the Kabbalists invented similar allegories. Whether or not the reader lifts the veils hiding that truth depends on his or her ability to reach these higher levels of comprehension. But for those capable of reaching that far, this truth glows like a fiery jewel at the center of Peretz's tale.

At this point it should be apparent that this exegetical method is concerned not only with demarking particular levels of interpretation, but also with the natural process of arriving at a full understanding of these profound tales, which begins, naturally, with their link to the literal and familiar, and leads us, step by step, to the transcendental. Like the ascent into Paradise that was the goal of the Merkavah mystics, the goal of the reader should be a spiritual ascent. These tales, then, are not mere entertainment or embellishment of familiar themes, but attempts to construct around a kernel of truth a labyrinth in which some readers will wander without ever penetrating to the core, and in which others will quickly find their way.

VII

A NOTE
ON THE CATEGORIES

It is the premise of this anthology that the stories in each of the subsections, or books, were inspired by some aspect of the Jewish literary tradition. The seven books, based on biblical, apocryphal, aggadic, Merkavah, kabbalistic, folkloric, and hasidic themes, represent the seven primary categories of Jewish literature, apart from liturgical or secular poetry. These mythic developments are ordered chronologically, as they evolved, although folklore flourished independently during several periods, especially during the kabbalistic and hasidic periods.

The inclusion of a story in one of these books is intended to propose that the earliest legend on which it is based derives from the category into which it has been placed. The legend of the *Lamed-vov Tzaddikim* derives from the Talmud, although tales of the *Lamed-vov* are most widespread in the hasidic period. The cluster of stories concerning the *Lamed-vov* have been placed in the earlier, aggadic section, but the notes on these stories consider later legends as well. Other legends, such as those about the Messiah, have distinctive developments associated with particular periods. Therefore there are stories about the Messiah in the biblical, aggadic, kabbalistic, and hasidic books.

The nature and development of the seven categories are discussed in the preceding essays in this introduction. The first essay, "Reimagining the Bible," focuses on biblical and aggadic themes. "The Aggadic Tradition" traces the development of legends in the talmudic, midrashic, kabbalistic, folkloric, and hasidic periods. "Rabbi Nachman of Bratslav: Forerunner of Modern Jewish Literature" considers the role of this key hasidic rebbe in the transition from a sacred to a secular literature. "S. Y. Agnon, I. L. Peretz, and I. B. Singer: Modern Masters of the Aggadah" considers the three major figures of the modern period working in the aggadic tradition. "Modern Jewish Literature and the Ancient Models" compares and contrasts a number of modern tales and their sources. "Tools of Interpretation" presents methods by which this kind of literature, with an established tradition be-

90

hind it, can best be approached. Included are discussions of legends and concepts deriving from the aggadic, Merkavah, and kabbalistic periods.

The reader is advised to consult the appropriate note for each story. The Notes on the Stories section has been prepared to demonstrate the links of each story to specific Jewish legends or traditions. Sources are listed and often quoted from at length. Parallel motifs and subjects for further reference are also included. The notes begin on p. 645; they follow the order of the stories and list the page on which each story begins along with its title and author.

The focus of the individual books is as follows:

Book I: Biblical Themes

The stories in this section are all based on themes deriving from the first five books of the Bible, known as the Torah, or the Five Books of Moses. Postpentateuchal themes are not represented for reasons of space, and because the primary Jewish archetypal figures—Adam and Eve, Cain and Abel, Noah, Abraham, Isaac and Jacob and their wives, Joseph and Moses—all emerge in the first five books of the Bible. Many of the legends used in these stories are aggadic in origin, and are included in this section because of their biblical focus. The order of the stories follows the chronology of the Bible.

Book II: Apocryphal Themes

The books of the Apocrypha were omitted from the Jewish Bible, although they are preserved in the Catholic Bible. The books of the Pseudepigrapha were generally written after the biblical period, but were based directly on the biblical models, in the hope of being accepted as part of the sacred Scriptures, which they were not. The brevity of this section testifies to its lack of influence, although The Book of Enoch served as a primary model for the Hekhaloth texts of Merkavah Mysticism (see Book IV, "Themes of Merkavah Mysticism"). Most of the apocryphal themes drawn on (using the term in a broader sense, to include the Pseudepigrapha as well), such as that of Gehenna, do not achieve their full development until later in the aggadic or kabbalistic periods. All of the apocryphal texts referred to in the notes to these stories can be found in The Apocrypha and Pseudepigrapha of the Old Testament, edited by R. H. Charles. (See the Bibliography for details about this and all other books referred to in the Introduction and Notes on the Stories.)

Book III: Aggadic Themes

The stories in this book take as their starting point the legends of the Talmud and Midrash. The first part of the Talmud, the Mishnah, was completed in the 2nd century C.E., and the second part, the Gemara, was completed in the 5th century. The midrashic period, which begins upon the completion of the Talmud, is generally designated as between the 5th and 13th centuries. Together the legends of the Talmud and Midrash are referred to as the Aggadah. (See note 6 to the Introduction for a discussion of this term.) The legends of the Aggadah are primarily concerned with completing the biblical narratives or recording tales associated with the great talmudic sages, such as Rabbi Akiba. The aggadic sources focused on biblical figures can be found in Book I, "Biblical Themes." The remaining aggadic themes are included in Book III.

Book IV: Themes of Merkavah Mysticism

The title and placement of this book were recommended by Professor Gershom Scholem as appropriate. A discussion of Merkavah Mysticism can be found on pp. 86-87. The primary motif of the heavenly journey also serves as the central metaphor for the mystical contemplation associated with the Merkavah mystics. All of the stories in this section consider this theme of ascent, except for "The Portrait" by Rabbi Nachman of Bratslav, which focuses on the concept of the *Pargod*, the curtain said to hang before the Throne of Glory. The only Hekhaloth text to have been translated in full into English to date is *3 Enoch or The Hebrew Book of Enoch*, edited and translated by Hugo Odeberg. See also *Jewish Gnosticism, Merkabah Mysticism, and Talmudic Tradition* by Gershom Scholem.

Book V: Kabbalistic Themes

The kabbalistic period can be designated as running between the 13th century, in which the Zohar was "discovered" by Moshe de Leon, and the 17th-century debacle of the false Messiah Shabbatai Zevi. Most stories based on kabbalistic themes focus either on kabbalistic concepts, such as *zimzum* and *gilgul*, or on kabbalistic myths associated with figures such as the Shekhinah or the Messiah. These concepts and myths are considered both earlier in this introduction and in the Notes on the Stories. To locate all material on a particular theme, consult the General Index.

Book VI: Themes of Folklore

The dominant themes of Jewish folklore—those concerned with demons, such as Lilith, with the exploits of the Golem, and with the tales of Elijah—are grouped in clusters in this section. There is also a cluster of stories mirroring tragic events, which represent another important category of Jewish folklore. Folklore stands apart from the other categories included, which are all types of sacred literatures, although the apocryphal texts were not accepted as such. A discussion of the characteristics of Jewish folklore can be found on pp. 26-30. The Notes on the Stories amplifies on the sources drawn from, and provides background information about these sources.

Book VII: Hasidic Themes

The dominant figure of Hasidism, the Baal Shem Tov, is the focus of five of the stories in this book, and other hasidic masters, including Abraham the Angel and Rabbi Nachman of Bratslav, are also represented. Hasidic concerns, such as messianic longings, are also the subject of several stories. Other stories of hasidic derivation can also be found in earlier sections of the anthology, where they have been placed because the specific theme they are concerned with derives from an earlier period. The major hasidic developments took place in the 18th and 19th centuries, although there is a flourishing hasidic movement today in both Israel and the United States. Some of the stories included concern present-day rebbes as well as the ones of the past.

VIII
THE BOOK
OF THE BOOK

In Memory of Louis Ginzberg

In that country was only to be found one book. No one knew how or when the Book had first appeared, but it was believed by all to be the first book ever written, and that the stories it recorded had been handed down for centuries before finally being written down. At the same time the Book was a history of everything that had ever happened. It started with the story of how the sun had entered the world, and concluded with the stories of the kings and prophets whose words still ruled the kingdom. It was the custom of these people to read from the Book three times each day, when the sun rose in the morning, and just before and after it had set. But there were also a few among them whose sole duty it was to spend their days reading the Book, and this was considered to be the highest calling in the land.

Still fewer were a small group of writers who had devoted themselves to the strange practice of trying to rewrite the Book. Some of them would simply work from memory and write for years without referring to the original, while others would make up stories that would shed light on particular legends in the Book. In both cases these new legends were considered to have great importance, and were studied by the full-time readers as a commentary on the Book. Such a tradition will probably seem foreign, for we find it disturbing if one work too closely resembles any other. However, the people in this country had no doubt about this tradition, because it had been derived from one of the parables which appeared in the Book. This parable was about a mirror that reflected back whatever it was that the one on the other side of it was missing. If it was night when they looked into the mirror, the mirror reflected day, and if day, night; while if they were young the mirror would reflect how they would look when they were old, and if old, then how they had looked when they were young. In addition, if one was worried about a loved one who had been out to sea too long, or could not recall

94

the face of a parent who had passed away, the mirror would reply to these and all other questions. In some ways it was like a window that always looked out on the same landscape, but what it reflected changed from season to season. Little by little the replies to their questions would take form in front of them. And this is what the authors who rewrote the Book were trying to preserve—the forms that took shape when they phrased their questions as they stood in front of the mirror.

Thus it happened, after the Book had been read and rewritten for many centuries, that one of these writers realized that all of the others had rewritten so many of the legends that they had created a new version of the same Book, the Book of the Book. And he gathered these new legends from every source he could find, and wove them together to form a single story, a history that reflected the history in the Book like the changing landscape in the parable of the mirror. And in this way it was finally recognized that for centuries the Book had been trying to give birth. And now that the new Book had appeared, the people believed that they were as blessed as those who had lived when the Book had first been written down, who had been relieved of the burden of preserving it by word of mouth. And before long the legend arose that one day the Book would again give birth, and it was a common belief that when this third Book appeared men would discover another dimension, one it is impossible to reflect in any mirror. A third eye with which to see—this is what they awaited.

NOTES TO THE
INTRODUCTION

1. In the Talmud (B. Eruv. 18a) an alternate legend is given in which *male and female He created them* is understood to mean that a single being was created with a male face looking forward and a female face looking back. Later God separated them into two beings.

2. Lilith's independent and assertive nature has not been lost on modern Jewish feminists, who have proposed her rather than Eve as a role model, despite the demonic nature of her later history as a succubus and child-destroying witch. She has also been made the namesake of *Lilith Magazine*, a Jewish-feminist journal.

3. This is the Name YHVH or Yahweh (later translated as Jehovah). Those who held the secret of how to pronounce the Ineffable Name possessed the power of the Name, the power to create and destroy. This most sacred Name of God is known as the Tetragrammaton, and the secret of its pronunciation was closely guarded by the high priest. But since the destruction of the Temple this pronunciation has been lost. However, to avoid accidental correct pronunciations of the Ineffable Name during prayer—which would have profound consequences—another divine name, Adonai or the Lord, has traditionally been substituted.

4. A typical text for such an amulet reads as follows: "OUT LILITH! I adjure you, Lilith, in the Name of the Holy One, blessed be He, and in the names of the three angels sent after you, Senoy, Sansenoy and Semangelof, to remember the vow you made that wherever you find their names you will cause no harm, neither you nor your cohorts; and in their names and in the names of the seals set down here, I adjure you, Queen of Demons, and all your multitudes, to cause no harm to a woman while she carries a child nor when she gives birth, nor to the children born to her, neither during the day nor during the night, neither through their food nor through their drink, neither in their heads nor in their hearts. By the strength of these names and seals I so adjure you, Lilith, and all your offspring, to obey this command" (*Sefer Raziel* 43b).

5. The primary source for the Lilith legend is the *Alphabet of Ben Sira* 47. Other sources include B. Shab. 151b; B. Eruv. 18b, 100b; B. Nid. 24b; Zohar 1:34b, 3:19a; Zohar Sitre Torah 1:14a-b; and *Yalkut Reubeni* on Gen. 2:21 and 4:8. According to the traditional doctrine, God is incapable of error. Why, then, did the match of Lilith and Adam fail? Rabbi Zvi Magence suggests that it was

necessary to create a negative as well as a positive example—Adam and Eve constituting the latter.

6. The term "Aggadah" has both a specific and a more general meaning. In the narrow sense the term refers to the body of legends that appear within the Talmud itself. (These legends constitute about a quarter of the Talmud, and most were collected in the 16th-century volume *Ein Yakov*.) In a broader sense, "aggadah" can refer to any post-biblical Jewish legend, and is frequently used in contrast to the term "Halahkah," meaning the law. This implies that there are two kinds of major realms of traditional study, that of defining and expounding on the law (Halahkah) and all of the remaining material, which may be grouped under the category of Aggadah, and consists primarily of legends. The term "Midrash" (from the root *darash*, meaning both "to search out" and "to expound") likewise has a double usage. In the narrow sense it refers to all post-talmudic legends up to the kabbalistic period, which begins in the 13th century. But in the broader sense it is interchangeable with the term "aggadah" to denote a Jewish legend (a midrash) or the body of Jewish legends (the Midrash). For more on the Talmud, see note 13.

7. The term "Torah" refers to both the Five Books of Moses and also, in a broader sense, to the whole of Jewish law and lore.

8. The primary sources for the Enoch legend are the three Books of Enoch. *The Book of Enoch (1 Enoch)* and *The Slavonic Book of Enoch (2 Enoch)* are included in *The Apocrypha and Pseudepigrapha of the Old Testament*, volume 2, edited by R. H. Charles. *The Hebrew Book of Enoch (3 Enoch)* has been translated into English by Hugo Odeberg. Enoch's transformation into Metatron is described in this last book, chs. 10-25.

9. On Shavuoth, many Sephardic communities read a *ketubah* (wedding contract) for the marriage of God and Israel, which was written by Israel Najara in the 16th century in Safed. See note 88 below for a partial translation of the text.

10. C.E. stands for Common Era, and is equivalent to A.D. B.C.E. stands for Before the Common Era, and is equivalent to B.C.

11. From "Myth in Judaism," in *On Judaism*, p. 106.

12. *Song of Songs Rabbah* on Song of Songs 1:2.

13. The Talmud consists of two interrelated texts. The older is the Mishnah, which was committed to writing around 200 C.E., and the second is known as the Gemara, which passed from oral to written form approximately 500 C.E., and which is a commentary on the Mishnah. Traditionally, the pages of the Talmud reflect this relationship: the text of the Mishnah appears in bold type in the middle of the page, surrounded by the Gemara in smaller type, while both are surrounded by, in even smaller type, traditional commentaries by Rashi, the Tosafists, Hananel ben Hashiel (d. 1055), and others. The Mishnah is actually far more complex than a commentary or interpretation of the Bible, in the way that we understand the term "interpretation." When we attempt to interpret a text, our goal is to understand what the author was trying to say at the time he said it. The Mishnah, on the other hand, finds an appropriate passage on which to base its innovations, and then elaborates extensive rules and regulations which often come to seem remote from their source. An entire legal world can spring up from a brief, seemingly simple biblical law. The complex

system of *eruvim*, for example, which permits establishing fictitious boundaries, involves the symbolic *mingling* (*eruv*—a mixture) of time and space, and allows a Jew to engage in otherwise forbidden practices such as cooking on a holiday for the upcoming Sabbath or carrying things within a city on the Sabbath. While its origin is the biblical injunction to sanctify the Sabbath, its application goes far beyond this basic commandment and takes on a life of its own.

14. Even during the talmudic era, this constituted a great amount of learning to master, as this passage demonstrates: "Our rabbis were taught: 'Eighty disciples did Hillel have; thirty of them were worthy that the Shekhinah should rest upon them, as it did upon Moses, our teacher; thirty of them were worthy that the sun should be stopped for their sake, as it did before Joshua; and twenty were ordinary. The superior among them was Yonathan ben Uziel, the inferior among them was Rabbi Yohanan ben Zakkai. It was related of Rabbi Yohanan ben Zakkai that he did not leave unstudied the Bible, the Mishnah, the Gemara, the Halakhot, the Aggadot, subtle points in the interpretation of the biblical laws, the special points in rabbinic enactment, the restrictive and nonrestrictive rules, rules of analogy, astronomy, geometry, the whisper of the angels, the whisper of the evil spirits, and the whisper of palm trees, foxes, fables, major affairs and minor affairs. And since the most inferior of all was so great, how much the more was the most superior of all? It was said of Yonathan ben Uziel that when he studied the Law every bird that flew overhead was instantly consumed in flames' " (B. Suk. 28).

15. B. Shab. 88b-89a. This myth of the giving of the Torah over the angel's objections is both parallel to and at the same time exactly the opposite of the myth of Prometheus. Prometheus stole the fire of the gods and gave it to men; in the Jewish myth God Himself has to overrule the protests of the angels in order to transmit the eternal flame that is the Torah to the people of Israel.

16. The first four volumes contain Ginzberg's compilation and retelling of the aggadic sources, the fifth and sixth volumes contain valuable notes, and the seventh volume is an extensive Index. A single-volume condensation of the first four volumes, *The Legends of the Bible,* is available.

17. See R. H. Charles, *The Apocrypha and Pseudepigrapha of the Old Testament.* Although the Apocrypha and Pseudepigrapha were excluded from the canon of sacred Jewish texts, their intentions were fully religious in nature. They were never far away from the sacred city, camped outside the gates.

18. Ezekiel's vision of a *merkavah*, a chariot, and a central talmudic passage (B. Hag. 14b) about four sages who entered Paradise—only one, Rabbi Akiba, emerged in peace—serve as the models for the Hekhaloth texts of Merkavah Mysticism, a particular category of texts which Gershom Scholem identifies as post-talmudic and pre-kabbalistic. See the stories in Book IV, "Themes of Merkavah Mysticism," and the appropriate notes.

19. "Rabbi Yohanan was sitting and lecturing: 'In the future the Holy One, blessed be He, will bring jewels and pearls the size of thirty cubit square, twenty ells in height and ten in width, and will place them at the gates of Jerusalem.' And one disciple sneered at him: 'We do not even find a jewel as large as the egg of a turtle dove and you say we shall find jewels of such sizes?' Thereafter it happened that the same disciple was on a boat on the high sea, and he saw angels

who sawed jewels and pearls the size of thirty ells square, boring holes in them twenty ells in height and ten in width. He asked them, 'For whom is this?' And they answered: 'The Holy One, blessed be He, will place them at the gates of Jerusalem.' When he returned he said to Rabbi Yohanan: 'Lecture, Rabbi, for all you said is true, as I have seen it for myself!' " (B. Bab. Bat. 74). Further tales about the gates of Jerusalem are "The Six Days and the Seven Gates" by Yitzhak Navon and "The Golden Gates of Jerusalem" by Matti Megged.

20. It was a practice of the early Jewish people to identify the names of the gods of their neighbors as one of the many names of the Jewish Divinity. The primary Canaanite god was El, and Elohim was the term used to refer to the multiple Canaanite gods, which was taken over by the Jews as a Name for their one God. There are said to be seventy-two Names of God in all, including common ones such as Adonai (used to substitute for Yahweh, the most secret and powerful Name of God, known as the Tetragrammaton); Shaddai (meaning "mountains"—obviously once having referred to a pagan mountain god); and HaShem (meaning "The Name").

21. Frazer's *Folklore in the Old Testament* has been edited by Theodore H. Gaster, with additional commentaries, as *Myth, Legend and Custom in the Old Testament;* see pp. 32-34.

22. *Myth, Legend and Custom in the Old Testament,* p. 33.

23. In the case of *Pirke de Rabbi Eliezer,* for example, it has been variously dated as originating between the 8th and 12th centuries C.E. In addition, it is generally recognized that much of its material is based on earlier sources.

24. The likely reason that Luz was identified as a city of immortals is that Luz also refers to the one bone in the body which never decomposes.

25. A medieval Jewish fairytale about a quest to the city of Luz can be found in *Dos Buch fun Nissyonoth,* edited by Israel Osman. The modern Hebrew author Yakov HaCohen has also written a play based on this legend, *The City of Luz.*

26. See Martin Buber's *The Rungs of the Ladder.*

27. The midrashim trace Cain's seemingly innate evil character to his conception, which they attributed to the serpent, who is said to have fathered Cain with Eve, while Adam was the father of Abel. Thus all generations have descended from the seed of Cain or of Abel and his brothers, such as Shem. (See 1 Chron. 1:1.) The seed of Cain was believed to have manifested itself in the persons of Ishmael and Esau, while Isaac and Jacob were descended from the seed of Shem (*Pirke de Rabbi Eliezer,* ch. 21).

28. In the midrash it is stated that Cain and Abel each were born with twin sisters, who served as their wives, plus one other sister, born with Abel and his twin. "Rabbi Joshua ben Karchan said: 'Only two (Adam and Eve) entered the bed, and seven left it, including Cain and his twin sister, and Abel and his two twin sisters' " (*Genesis Rabbah* 22:2).

29. The nature of the conflict is thus portrayed in *Genesis Rabbah* (22:7): "About what did they quarrel? 'Come,' they said, 'let us divide the world. One took the land and the other the movables. The former said, 'The land you stand on is mine,' while the latter retorted: 'What you are wearing is mine.' One said 'Strip'; the other retorted: 'Fly.' Out of this quarrel *Cain rose up against his brother Abel and slew him* (Gen. 4:8). . . . Judah Berebbi said: 'Their quarrel was

about the first Eve (Lilith).' Said Rabbi Aibu: 'The first Eve had returned to
dust. Then about what was their quarrel?' Said Rabbi Huna: 'An additional
twin was born with Abel, and each claimed her. The one claimed: "I will have
her, because I am the firstborn" while the other maintained. "I must have her,
because she was born with me." ' "

30. There was general agreement that Cain killed Abel with a stone, although
Rabbi Simeon said that he killed him with a staff (*Genesis Rabbah* 22:8).

31. Since no one had previously died, there was no precedent for burial. Furthermore, the ground was reluctant to accept Abel's body. In some versions it is
said that a sparrow burying its mate demonstrated the principle of burial, and
in others it is said that Abel's body remained unburied until after the death of
Adam. It was possible to bury Adam because, according to another midrash,
the dust from which he had been formed had been gathered from the four corners of the earth (*Pirke de Rabbi Eliezer*, ch. 21).

32. A late midrashic collection, *The Chronicles of Jerahmeel*, states: "Cain was the
first to surround a city with a wall, for he was afraid of his enemies" (24:2).

33. A sixth account appears in *Pirke de Rabbi Eliezer* (ch. 21): " 'Master of the Universe!' Cain pleaded, '*My sin is too great to be borne* (Gen. 4:13), for it has no
atonement.' This confession was accounted to him as repentance. 'Moreover,'
he continued, 'one will arise and slay me by pronouncing Thy Great Name
against me.' What did the Holy One, blessed be He, do? He took one letter
from the twenty-two letters in which the Torah is written, and set it upon
Cain's arm like a tattoo, that he should not be killed." Another version has it
that the letter was affixed to his forehead. Note that this version amplifies on
the nature of the death Cain fears—brought about by the power of the Ineffable Name rather than by the brutal revenge of those aware of his crime. The
unexpected notion that Cain's reply to God was reckoned as repentance can be
found in *Pesikta Rabbati* (50:5), as follows: "Adam met Cain and asked: 'My
son, how is it that your case turned out this way?' Cain replied: 'I resolved repentance and was delivered.' When Adam heard this, he began to strike his
own face, saying: 'Is such the great power of *Teshuvah* (repentance)? I did not
know.' "

34. Note how the continuity of the existence of the Angel of Death is provided for
by Lamech's taking over that role after Cain, although this legend does not suggest how long he was condemned to this incarnation, and who succeeded him
in the role.

35. It is interesting to note one interpretation that the rabbis did not propose is that
Cain's curse to be "a fugitive and a wanderer" was intended to last for all time.
While the seeds of Cain were seen as a plague to future generations, the Midrash does not carry Cain beyond the generation of the Flood. But this motif of
the eternal wanderer suggested by the biblical curse of Cain is fully developed
in the Christian legend of the Wandering Jew, and it seems possible that the
legend of Cain served as a prototype to that of the Wandering Jew. According
to this legend, as Jesus (Yehoshua ben Yosef) was carrying the cross on the way
to Golgatha he stumbled and came to rest against the house of a Jew, Ahasuerus, who emerged from his house and ordered Jesus to leave, perhaps out of
fear of being implicated as a sympathizer. Jesus replied by saying that he would

leave, but that the man would wander until he came back, i.e., until the Second Coming. This initiated the legend of the Wandering Jew, who subsequently appeared in tales told in every generation and in many places. Like Cain, he was a man marked for his sin—in this case the sign that marked him was his inability to die. His role came to be that of one who witnessed all that came to pass, and also that of a man obsessed with the search for his death. The story "The Wandering Jew" by David Slabotsky, included in this volume, relates how he finally succeeded in this quest.

36. In *The Chronicles of Jerahmeel* (24:3) reference is made to "Lamech, who slew Cain in the seventh generation, after Cain had confessed his sin, repented, and his punishment had been suspended until the seventh generation." This late version combines Cain's repentance with the legend of the death of Cain at the hands of Lamech.

37. The kabbalistic period can be defined as the period from the writing of the Zohar in the 13th century C.E. until the debacle of Shabbatai Zevi in the 1660s.

38. See Marc Bregman, "Past and Present in Midrashic Literature," in *Hebrew Annual Review* 2 (1978), pp. 45-59.

39. *Shivhei ha-Ari*, as quoted in Zev Vilnay, *Legends of Jerusalem*, pp. 165-66.

40. For more information about the ten *Sefirot*, see Gershom Scholem, "Emanation and the Concept of the *Sefirot*" and "Details of the Doctrine of the Sefirot and Their Symbolism," in *Kabbalah*, pp. 96-116.

41. Quoted in Gershom Scholem, *Shabbatai Sevi*, pp. 40-41.

42. Hayim Vital, *Sha'ar haGilgulim* 166:15, quoted in Gershom Scholem, *Shabbatai Sevi*, p. 43.

43. This tale was collected orally by the author as part of the ongoing effort to collect the folklore of Jews of various ethnic nationalities in Israel, which are preserved in the Israel Folktale Archives in Haifa, directed by Dov Noy of Hebrew University and Aliza Shenhar of Haifa University. The original language of this tale is Judezmo, the name given to the modern form of Judeo-Españole, which is also known as Ladino.

44. See Harold Heifetz, ed., *Zen and Hasidism*.

45. Martin Buber, *The Legend of the Baal Shem*, p. 65.

46. It is interesting to note that I. B. Singer recently turned to the subject of the Baal Shem for the first time, in the short novel *Reaches of Heaven*. Faced with the fact that the legends of the Baal Shem are well known, Singer chose to ignore these legends and produced instead a version of his own which concentrates on the character of the Baal Shem and downplays the miracles associated with him. Perhaps it was Singer's goal to humanize the Baal Shem in order to communicate his pure and almost innocent world vision to those who fail to respond to the mystical realm. But the Baal Shem who emerges in Singer's novel is strangely demythologized and largely indistinguishable from any one of a multitude of spiritual seekers. As a result, Singer's detached narrative falls far short of the fascination engendered by the original myth.

47. Although Rabbi Nachman did not publicly declare such a messianic role for himself, it appears that he may have viewed himself as the possible *tzaddik hador* or potential Messiah ben Joseph of his generation, who would prepare the way for the coming of Messiah ben David. See Arthur Green's biography of

Nachman, *Tormented Master,* for a full discussion of Nachman's messianic aspirations. For more on Shabbatai Zevi, see Gershom Scholem's *Shabbatai Sevi.*

48. These are *Classic Hasidic Tales* by Meyer Levin (which also includes versions of the tales of the Baal Shem Tov); *The Tales of Rabbi Nachman* by Martin Buber; *Beggars and Prayers* by Adin Steinsaltz; *Nachman of Bratslav: The Tales* by Arnold J. Band; and *The Thirteen Stories of Rebbe Nachman of Breslev,* translated by Ester Koenig, edited by Mordechai Kramer. See the Bibliography for additional details of publication. Other Nachman tales will be found in *Yenne Velt: The Great Works of Jewish Fantasy and the Occult.*

49. From *Fragments of a Future Scroll* by Zalman Schachter, p. 99. This book contains the most extensive translation of Nachman's dreams available in English, pp. 95-100. Additional dreams are reported in Arthur Green's *Tormented Master,* pp. 165-66.

50. *Fragments of a Future Scroll,* Schachter, pp. 99-100.

51. Compare the following passage from an Italian folktale, "The Enchanted Palace," whose theme and setting are in many ways identical to that of "The Lost Princess," with a similar passage from that tale:

"The queen arrived. With cries, embraces, slaps in the face, kisses and shakes, she did her best to awaken Fiordinando. But realizing she would not succeed, she began weeping so violently that instead of tears a few drops of blood trickled down her cheeks. She wiped the blood off with her handkerchief, which she placed over Fiordinando's face. Then she got back into her carriage and sped straight to Peterborough" (*Italian Folktales,* selected and retold by Italo Calvino, p. 235).

"And after the troops had passed, a carriage came by, and in the carriage sat the daughter of the king. She stopped near him, and left the carriage, and sat down next to him, and recognized him. And although she shook him very strongly, he did not wake up, and she began to lament. . . . Not long afterwards he woke up and asked his servant: 'Where am I?' And the servant told him all that had happened. . . . Then the minister saw the kerchief and asked: 'From where did this come?' And the servant told him that the lost princess had written on it with her tears. So the minister took it and lifted it up towards the sun, and then he saw the letters written with her tears, and he read all that she had written" ("The Lost Princess," retold by Meyer Levin).

52. On his deathbed Rabbi Nachman told his Hasidim that he would continue to be their rebbe even after his death, and therefore a successor need not be appointed. His Hasidim have observed this bequest, although all other Hasidim traditionally appoint a new rebbe upon the death of the old one. For this reason the Bratslaver Hasidim are sometimes called "the Dead Hasidim." Two groups of Bratslaver Hasidim can be found in present-day Jerusalem, and a third group in B'nai Brak, outside Tel Aviv. Every year, on the *yartzeit* of Rabbi Nachman's death, his Hasidim read his tales out loud in an extended ceremony.

53. See Jung, *The Archetypes and the Collective Unconscious,* vol. 9 of *The Collected Works of C. G. Jung.*

54. New York: Dutton, 1967, p.21.

55. Reference to the origin of this primordial light is found in *Genesis Rabbah* (3:4):

"Rabbi Simeon ben Jehozadak asked Rabbi Samuel ben Nachman: 'As I have heard that you are a master of aggadah, tell me from what the primordial light was created?' He replied: 'The Holy One, blessed be He, wrapped Himself therein as in a robe and radiated with the luster of His majesty from one end of the world to the other.' " This metaphor is developed further in *Pirke de Rabbi Eliezer* 3: "Whence were the heavens created? From the light of the garment with which He was robed. He took this light and stretched it as it is written, *Who coverest thyself with light as with a garment, who stretched out the heavens like a curtain* (Ps. 104:2)."

56. "The Poetry of Hassidism" by Koppel S. Pinson, *The Menorah Journal*, autumn 1941, p. 304.

57. The thirteen "canonical" tales are: "The Lost Princess," "The Master of Prayer," "The Seven Beggars," "The Broken Betrothal," "The Cripple," "The Bull and the Ram," "The Prince Who Was Made Entirely of Precious Stones," "The Spider and the Fly," "The Rabbi's Son," "The Sage and the Simpleton," "The King's Son and the Servant's Son," "The Portrait," and "The Burger and the Beggar." All thirteen are found only in *Nachman of Bratslav: The Tales* and *The Thirteen Stories of Rebbe Nachman of Breslev* among the English-language editions.

58. The parallel of this episode with one involving Franz Kafka is remarkable and noteworthy. On his deathbed Kafka directed his friend and mentor Max Brod to burn all his unpublished writings—novels, stories, journals, diaries, and letters. Brod gave his word, then promptly published all of this material, which resulted in Kafka's being acclaimed as one of the seminal figures of 20th-century literature. Had Brod followed Kafka's expressed wish, as did Rabbi Simeon, Kafka would probably be known, if at all, as an obscure Czech writer who published only a handful of stories in his lifetime and left no other legacy. One of the first articles to bring attention to the parallels between Kafka and Rabbi Nachman was "Franz Kafka and Rabbi Nachman" by Rabbi Jack Riemer, *Jewish Frontier*, Fall 1961.

59. All his life Rabbi Nachman was obsessed with the Baal Shem, and as a child he spent many hours praying on the grave of the Baal Shem in Medzhibozh. See Green, *Tormented Master*, p. 28.

60. A long, Nachman-like tale by Der Nister called "A Tale of Kings" can be found in *Yenne Velt: The Great Works of Jewish Fantasy and the Occult*, edited and translated by Joachim Neugroschel. Ignatow published a novel, *The Hidden Light*, which has not yet been translated from Yiddish, that is based entirely on Nachman's tale "The Seven Beggars."

61. Outside of the modern Hebrew and Yiddish literary traditions, there is no other fully developed modern tradition, although there are to be found individuals writing in at least a dozen languages who have utilized traditional sources and found inspiration in them. For a further discussion of the sources of some of these authors, see the next section of this introduction, "The Links of Modern Jewish Literature to the Ancient Models," and the notes to the individual stories.

62. While this is true regarding their literary form, it should be noted that Men-

dele's style was filled with folk sayings, proverbs, talmudic phrases, etc. In this respect Agnon has always been viewed as an heir of Mendele.

63. Agnon's preeminence was, however, not apparent from the first. For a time M. J. Berditchevsky was regarded as the leading figure, and Agnon was considered an interesting, if somewhat esoteric, writer of hasidic tales.

64. The Israeli writer Yehuda Yaari, who was a friend of Agnon's for forty years, recounts the anecdote that he was once in Agnon's house and noticed Kafka's collected works in a bookcase. He asked Agnon how he could insist that he hadn't read Kafka, since he owned all of his books. Agnon replied that the books weren't his, but belonged to his wife!

65. "A Story With a Goat" from *The Holy Amulet: Twelve Jewish-Yemenite Folktales,* collected by Rachel Seri, edited and annotated by Aliza Shenhar, No. 11, pp. 44-47. Translated from the Hebrew by Evelyn Abel.

66. On the other hand, Peretz found less to utilize of the halakhic tradition, and was a leader of the Haskalah. This splitting of the halakhic and aggadic is a development of this century, but it may not necessarily be a negative one, for it permits the Aggadah to retain its power even among those who do not accept the rule of the Halakhah.

67. For more on Gehenna see the note to "Sabbath in Gehenna," p. 661, and *Hell in Jewish Literature* by Samuel J. Fox.

68. The source of Singer's isolation from the Yiddish writing community derives from the hostile reception he received at the time of his arrival in the United States when, as the younger brother of Israel Joshua Singer, who had already established himself as a major Yiddish novelist, Singer found that he had immediate access to the crucial Yiddish newspaper the *Jewish Daily Forward* and its editor, Abraham Cahan. Virtually simultaneous with his arrival, the *Forward* began to serialize a novel of his, a fact which quickly brought him into opposition with a large number of jealous Yiddish writers who had already been in this country many years without having so much as their pictures appear in that newspaper. As he relates in the third volume of his autobiography, *Lost in America,* Singer was then broke and desperate for the fifty dollars he received for each installment, although he regarded then and still regards this novel as a complete failure (and leaves it unnamed, and, of course, untranslated). This fact, coupled with his unearned early prominence, led to his immediate isolation within the community of Yiddish writers, a situation that has continued up to the present. It is worth observing that the effects of Singer's initial isolation and rejection by the Yiddish writers have been profound. After Singer's emergence as an international success, he was in a position to direct attention to the rich Yiddish literary tradition, but invariably he has chosen not to. Instead, he has always singled out non-Yiddish authors such as Tolstoy and Balzac as his primary influences, while perpetuating the illusion that his writings are unique in Yiddish, when in fact they are deeply influenced by the tradition of Mendele Mokher-Seforim, I. L. Peretz, Zalman Shneur, Sholem Asch, and, of course, his brother, I. J. Singer. Unfortunately, Singer's claim to uniqueness has gone essentially unquestioned by Western critics, and the result has been little impetus to explore and translate many other important Yiddish figures, such as Der Nister, Dovid Ignatow, and Y. Y. Trunk, who subsequently have

fallen into obscurity because of the inaccessibility of the Yiddish language to most readers. In this way an entire literary tradition has suffered grave damage because of a jealousy-engendered literary quarrel.

69. Although Jakov Lind is known primarily as the author of *Soul of Wood* and several other novels written in German, in recent years he has switched to writing in English. His two stories in this collection, "The Story of Lilith and Eve" and "The Near Murder," are from an as yet unpublished manuscript of stories titled *The Stove*, which were written in English.

70. For a further discussion of the use and interpretation of allegory, see the next section of the Introduction, "Tools of Interpretation."

71. To assist this comparison, the Notes on the Stories section indicates the apparent sources on which the stories are based. The availability of English translations of these texts is indicated in the Bibliography.

72. Hayim Nachman Bialik took these same kinds of liberties in editing, with N. Ravnitsky, *Sefer ha-Aggadah*, an important aggadic collection which has not yet been translated into English.

73. See the note to "The Pagan Rabbi," p. 676-677.

74. For a list of many of the sources used in "On the Life and Death of Abbaye," see p. 671-672.

75. For a discussion of Merkavah Mysticism, see pp. 83-87. See also the stories and notes in Book IV, "Themes of Merkavah Mysticism."

76. *Tanhuma Pekude* 3 and *The Chronicles of Jerahmeel* 9:1-8.

77. The unlikely association of Moses with a *shochet* is explained by the tradition that it was Moses who was taught the correct procedure of slaughtering animals by God, and in turn transmitted it orally to the people. Also, while the Jews were journeying in the desert, they were permitted to eat only of the meat of the sacrifices that were brought into the Tabernacle (B. Men. 29a).

78. For a further discussion of the *Pargod*, see p. 40.

79. The theme of *zimzum* also plays a prominent part in Jay Neugeboren's novel *The Stolen Jew*.

80. Ben Shahn's book *The Alphabet of Creation* retells the same legend.

81. Other stories concerned with the Fall are "Before the Law" by Franz Kafka, "The Tree of Life and the Tree of Death" by Howard Schwartz, "Adam and Eve Return to the Garden" by Itzik Manger, and "True Joy" by Kamelia Shahar; see these stories and the appropriate notes.

82. Other tales gathered around a single theme include those based on the legend of the *Lamed-vov Tzaddikim*, such as "The Prince Who Was Made Entirely of Precious Stones" by Rabbi Nachman of Bratslav, "The Hidden Tzaddik" by S. Y. Agnon, "The Legend of the Just Men" by André Schwarz-Bart, "One of the Just Men" by Elie Wiesel, and "The Unrecognized Just Men" by Albert Memmi. There are also several tales on the theme of Lilith, including "The Temptations of Rabbi Akiba" by David Pinski, "Watch Night" by Israel Zangwill, "Lilith" by Moyshe Kulbak, "Lilith in the Lager" by Primo Levi, "From the Rabbi's Dreambook" by David Meltzer, and "The Woman in the Forest" by Isi Langer.

83. Edmond Jabès, *The Book of Questions*.

84. Perhaps because of the early splits with the Samaritans, who insisted that only

the Pentateuch was sacred of the books of the Bible, and with the Karaites, who denied the validity of the Talmud, the rabbis took care to create a system of interpretation that avoided the kinds of conflict associated with various fundamental sects, which permit only the narrowest, most literal reading of the Scriptures.

85. The seven rules of Hillel can be found in *The Fathers According to Rabbi Nathan*, ch. 37, as well as in Sifra 3a and B. Sanh. 7b. The thirteen principles of Rabbi Ishmael are printed in the Jewish Daily Prayer Book. A translation can be found in *The Authorized Daily Prayer Book*, pp. 14-15. In B. Git. 67a there are references to rules formulated by Rabbi Ishmael's rival, Rabbi Akiba. A discussion of these principles of Hillel and Rabbi Ishmael and those of Rabbi Eliezer ben Jose, including translations of the rules, can be found in *Introduction to the Talmud and Midrash* by Hermann L. Strack, pp. 93-98.

86. Philo, *On the Migration of Abraham*, ch. II.

87. The marriage between God and Israel that Rabbi Akiba discerned in the Song of Songs is a theme later found in the Zohar (Prologue 8a). Describing the forthcoming wedding, on Shavuoth, the day of the Giving of the Torah, Rabbi Simeon bar Yohai is quoted as saying: "O my sons, happy is your portion, for on the morrow the bride will not enter the bridal canopy except in your company; for all those who help to prepare her adornments tonight will be recorded in the book of remembrance, and the Holy One, blessed be He, will bless them with seventy blessings and crown them with crowns of the celestial word." Also, in many Sephardic congregations, prior to the Torah reading on the first day of Shavuoth, a *ketubah* (marriage contract) is read, betrothing God and Israel. The most widely used text of such a *ketubah* is that of the Safed mystic and poet Israel Najara (c. 1550-1625 C.E.), a partial translation of which follows: "Friday, the sixth of Sivan, the day appointed by the Lord for the revelation of the Torah for His beloved people, the Invisible One came forth from Sinai. The Bridegroom, Ruler of rulers, Prince of princes, said unto the pious and virtuous maiden, Israel, who had won His favor above all others: 'Many days wilt thou be Mine and I will be thy Redeemer. Be thou My mate according to the law of Moses and Israel, and I will honor, support and maintain thee, and be thy shelter and refuge in everlasting mercy. And I will set aside for thee the life-giving Torah, by which thou and thy children will live in health and tranquility. This Covenant shall be valid and established forever and ever.' Thus an eternal Covenant, binding them forever, has been established between them, and the Bridegroom and the bride have given their oaths to carry it out. May the Bridegroom rejoice with the bride whom He has taken as His lot, and may the bride rejoice with the Husband of her youth."

88. *Pardes* was originally a Persian word meaning an enclosed area. In the Bible it is used to mean "orchard" (see S. of S. 4:13). In rabbinic Hebrew it takes on the additional meaning of "Paradise," after the Greek *paradeisos*, which is used in the Septuagint to translate *Gan Eden* (the Garden of Eden).

89. The concept of *drash* is multifaceted. It refers, above all, to a method of exegesis practiced by the talmudic sages and their disciples and successors. This method involves deriving the essential meaning from a scriptural source by examining both its explicit and implicit meaning. In many cases a passage is explicated by a

legend, or a midrash. These legends are frequently intended to be understood as allegories. It is in this way that allegory can be identified as one of the dimensions of *drash*.

90. Aher ("the Other") is the name given to Elisha ben Abuyah, toward whom the rabbis demonstrated great ambivalence, refusing to refer to him by his own name, but retaining many of his statements in the Talmud. See note 95.

91. The advice is not to be taken in by any mirage that might turn them from their quest.

92. The Kabbalists later interpreted Ben Azzai's death as a mystical experience in which he gave up his soul. It is sometimes associated with what is known as "the kiss of the Shekhinah," in which a man gives up his soul in a moment of mystical ecstasy. Such was the nature of the death of Moses, according to the Talmud (B. Bab. Bat. 17a). See the note to "The Death of Moses" by Franz Werfel, p. 659-660.

93. Becoming obsessed with the experiences of this heavenly ascent (i.e., mystical contemplation) caused Ben Zoma to lose first his reason and then his life. See the note to "The Fate of Ben Zoma" by Milton Steinberg, p. 675.

94. This enigmatic phrase is generally understood to mean that Aher (Elisha ben Abuyah) became an apostate. The same metaphor is used in connection with Adam's Fall (*Genesis Rabbah* 19). Today most scholars believe his apostasy was some form of Gnostic dualism. This theory is supported by the following talmudic legend (B. Hag. 15a): "Aher saw [in Paradise] that permission was granted to Metatron to sit and write down the merits of Israel. Said Aher: 'It is taught that there is no sitting on high and no emulation of the Holy One, blessed be He. Perhaps—God forbid!—there are two powers in heaven!' Thereupon the angels led Metatron forth, and punished him with sixty fiery lashes, saying to him: 'Why didst thou not rise before Him when thou didst see Him?' Permission was then given to Metatron to strike out the merits of Aher. A *bat kol* [a heavenly voice] went forth and said: *'Return, ye backsliding children* (Jer. 3:22)—all except Aher.'"

95. Thus Rabbi Akiba was the only one of the four sages to survive intact the mystical initiation.

96. See Scholem, *Major Trends in Jewish Mysticism*, 5th lecture, "The Zohar: The Book and Its Author," pp. 156-204.

97. For a detailed discussion of the Merkavah mystics, see Scholem, *Jewish Gnosticism, Merkabah Mysticism and Jewish Tradition*, chs. 2-3, pp. 9-30.

98. Only one of the Hekhaloth texts has been published in full in English. This is *3 Enoch or the Hebrew Book of Enoch*, edited and translated by Hugo Odeberg. However, an English translation of another important text, *Hekhaloth Rabbatai*, has been prepared by Morton Smith based on the as yet unpublished critical Hebrew edition of Gershom Scholem. Translations of other Hekhaloth texts are in process by Alan Segal, David Halprin, and Itamar Gruenfeld, In *Jewish Gnosticism, Merkabah Mysticism and Jewish Tradition*, pp. 5-7, Scholem lists eight known Hekhaloth manuscripts.

99. B. Hag. 15b. This passage elaborates on Akiba's experience in Paradise: "Rabbi Akiba was also in danger of being pushed away by the angels, but the Holy One, blessed be He, said to them: 'Leave this old scholar, for he is worthy to

avail himself of My glory.' " This passage is clearly intended to echo the legend of the ascent of Moses into the heavens (Shab. 88b-89a) to obtain the Torah. Once again, the rabbis were drawing a parallel between Moses and Akiba, who were the guiding lights of their generations. See p. 7.

100. In one tale of the Baal Shem he describes his ascent into Paradise until he reached the palace of the Messiah (*Shivhei ha-Besht* 41). In another, the Baal Shem describes how he climbed on the living ladder formed by the prayers of his Hasidim into Paradise, and was about to fetch a glorious bird when those nearest the ground lost patience, and the ladder collapsed (Buber, *Tales of the Hasidim: Early Masters*, pp. 54-55). In another tale the Baal Shem describes Paradise in terms of levels of spiritual ascent which echoes the concept of *Pardes*: "I once entered Paradise. A great multitude of men from among Israel were there with me beneath the Tree of Knowledge of Good and Evil. But when I was led underneath the Tree of Life, there were but few of them. And when I was led into the innermost Paradise, there were still fewer, until their number was exceedingly small" (*Shivhei ha-Besht* 18).

101. Moshe ben Yitzhak HaPardesan has suggested the theoretical possibility of a fifth level of *Pardes—nitzraf*, suggesting purification through unification—in which all four other levels of interpretation might be forged into one, permitting the text to be perceived simultaneously in all its levels of meaning as a total unity and wholeness, not unlike that which is the goal of Gestalt psychology.

BOOK I
BIBLICAL
THEMES

The Tale of the Menorah
by Rabbi Nachman of Bratslav

Once there was a young man who left his home and traveled for several years. Afterward, when he returned home, he proudly told his father that he had become a master in the craft of making menorahs. He asked his father to call together all those who practiced this craft, that he might demonstrate his unrivaled skill for them.

That is what his father did, inviting to their home all those who practiced this craft in that town. But when his son presented the menorah he had made to them, not everyone found it pleasing in their sight. Then his father went to each and every one and begged them to tell him the truth about what they thought of it. And at last each one admitted that they found a defect in his son's menorah.

Then the father reported to his son that the menorah was not pleasing in the eyes of everyone, and that many of the craftsmen had noted a defect. To this the son asked to know what was the defect the craftsmen had found, and it emerged that each of them had noted a different defect. And it was true that what one craftsman had praised, another had found defective; nor did they agree on what was the defect in the menorah, and what was the most beautiful aspect of it.

And the son said to his father: "By this have I shown my great skill. For I have revealed to each one his own defect, since each of these defects was actually in he who perceived it. It was these defects that I incorporated into my creation, for I made this menorah only from defects. Now I will begin its restoration."

Translated from the Hebrew sources
by Tsila and Howard Schwartz

The Seven Lights of the Lamp
by Moshe ben Yitzhak HaPardesan

In the beginning God created the Heavens and the Earth. And God said: "Let there be Light, and there was Light." But it was not until the fourth

111

day that God created the lights we know, the Greater Light to rule during the day, and the Lesser Light to rule at night. What, then, was the first light that shone in the beginning, when the Spirit still hovered over the face of the waters? Now, it is forbidden to ask what was above, below or before the three strokes of the letter Bet of *Bereshith* that stands at the beginning of the Torah. But we may ponder the Aleph of *Or*, the Light that shone within the Bet, shining out through its open side and illuminating all that comes after. This primordial Light was, as it were, but a momentary flicker that radiated from one tiny jewel of the many myriad of jewels in the crown of the Holy One, blessed be He, when He wrapped Himself in His *tallit* of Light at the time of the creation of the World. It was by this Light that Adam was permitted to see from one end of the universe to the other. And the first man saw all of his descendants in every generation, each generation and its wicked ones, each generation and its righteous ones, until the coming of the Messiah. Now, some say that this Light shone for only thirty-six hours—one hour for each of the thirty-six righteous ones who support the world in each generation. But according to others, so long as the first man and woman were of one mind and of one body, there was no evil in the world and the Light shone for them in the garden. But it was by the brilliance of that very Light that they saw the Tree of Knowledge, ate from it and fell from grace, becoming two, and thus the Light was dimmed. Now some say that Adam shaped what remained of the Light into a luminescent pearl and gave it to Eve. And she took it unto herself and it is this very Light that still shines at the head of every innocent child in the womb of its mother, to calm its fears and to light its way into the Light of this world. But others tell that Eve, afraid it would be taken away because of the Fall, hid the pearl of Light in the bed of the River Pishon that flowed from Eden.

Now it was Noah who, at God's behest, fetched the glistening jewel from that river. And he called it *Tzohar*, set it inside a lamp, and hung it high upon the Ark—first to serve as a beacon to guide the creatures who were permitted to enter, and then to shed its supernal Light for twelve months, to calm the fears of those within the Ark. And some say that when the Ark came to rest upon the Mount, that jewel of Light was fetched again unto the heavens, unto the wheel of the sun. And later it was given again into the hands of our father Abraham as an astrolabe, which he wore as a jewel around his neck, and all the potentates of the East and West attended at his gate to hear him read the stars.

But others say that Noah's glowing jewel fell from the Ark upon the Mount, and came to rest far below, where it was covered by darkness for many generations. And it was into that pit of darkness that Joseph was cast by his brothers. And when night fell on that accursed day, in that base pit, Joseph's fears were calmed to see a glow shining not from above but from below. And so his hands dug out the glowing object, a jewel buried so many centuries, with no source but itself to sustain its golden glow. And Joseph took the glowing jewel down into Egypt when he was sold into slavery. And its Light sustained him in the darkness of the dungeon. So he set the jewel into the base of his cup, and peering into its Light he was able to interpret dreams and foretell distant times. And it was this divining cup which by stealth held the brothers of Joseph in Egypt, and by its Light all the tribes of Jacob followed in their path.

Now some say that Joseph's cup was placed by those who mourned him in his coffin and that the primeval Light was hidden yet again while Israel suffered in Egyptian bondage. And it was found again only when Moses raised the coffin from the depths of the Nile where it lay hidden, to accompany Israel on their Exodus from Egypt. But others tell that the Light continued to shine far out in the desert. And Moses was led unto it, unto the bush that burned but was not consumed. And that it was from the jewel, buried at the base of the bush, that the flames curled up, green and gold and black and red. And that when Moses, commanded by God, cast down his staff the snake which it became took the jewel unto itself and becoming Moses' staff again returned with him to Egypt to answer the call of God.

And so it was that when it came time to depart, the primal Light as a pillar of fire led Israel from the dungeon of Egypt out into the Wilderness of Sinai.

And then, despite the Giving of the Law, there came that deed which dimmed the Light. Yet after the Calf had been burnt and ground to powder, and strewn upon the water, and the children of Israel had drunk of it, the Holy One spoke again and commanded Moses that a Lamp be made as an everlasting beacon of repentance. And Moses commanded Bezalel to make the Lamp to stand between the people and their Lord. And Bezalel, who knew how to arrange the letters with which heaven and earth were created, set the jewel within the base of the Lamp. And so, when the Lamp was kindled, its seven lights stood with three on each side bowing in, submissive to their Lord, the face of Light, that burned between. And so did God instruct Moses: "When you kindle the Lights, the seven Lights shall give Light toward the face of the Lamp." And that Lamp burned before the altar down on earth to light the sacrifices that Israel offered in penance for their sins, until that accursed day when the sacrifices ceased and the Temple ascended from on earth to heaven.

And yet, behold, the Lamp has not been dimmed. For it shall shed its Light before the Heavenly Altar until the End of Days. And how do we know that? Come and see what it says in Scripture: "The seven Lights *shall* give Light." AMEN, AND SO MAY IT BE HIS WILL.

In the Beginning

by Zalman Shneur

And at once God stretched, stirring all His members, as though He would cast all Chaos off Him.

"He is awake, by now He is awake—He is awake by now—" thus, with curiosity and the bewilderment of veneration, the surrounding Chaos kept whispering and at the same time, deep within it was a ferment, swelling and rising like dark dough into which some yeast had been thrown.

And God in confusion, as if but half awake, was rubbing His eyes, lazily brushing off the last imperceptible cobwebs of the withered eternities, after which He looked about Him and saw nothing. Then He fell into Thought: He fell into Thought and began rummaging in His drowsy consciousness.

Ponderously, wearily did His conceptions work, but at last: "So," said He, "this is *I* . . . *I* signifies *I* . . . and all about Me is this . . . this—"

Muttering as if in delirium Chaos itself repeated His words after Him and breathed as if it were suffocating. Which, in the language of the Void, signified: "I am ready; let them take me, let them knead me, let them . . . let them do with me what they will. . . ."

And thereupon God became gentle and content, since He, the Incomparable One, was He, and because all that which was around Him was something else. And suddenly He broke into a smile of divine gentleness and happiness, smiling upon illimitability.

From the faint smile of God was born the first nimbus, the first-created light, and rays surged forth from His lips in a white, soft billow. They spread out all around like enormous radiant tentacles, striving to grope for something amid Chaos, to illumine something, but found nothing and, like an echo, returned to whence they had come, spreading over the majestic misty image of God and illuminating Him.

"Oh, how great, how vast all this is!" God voiced His wonder naively as He, the Incomparable One, beheld the wild, mighty forms by the faint reflection of His smile. He drew one foot out of the depths of Chaos, then drew out the other, and knew not where to put them down. And Chaos echoed His wonder.

And, not knowing where to put His immeasurably mighty hands in the half-light, God placed them together and by chance, without intent, almost idly, rubbed one against the other.

And suddenly—

Suddenly, because of this unintentional gesture, something great took place.

Enormous masses of Chaos, like colorless matter, rolled up between the hands of God and burst into spirals of flame. The twin suns of Sirius broke forth, Neptune began to sway, Saturn hung in the air; comets scattered fanwise and plunged into Chaos to a majestic, thunderous refrain. They rushed on, whirling, and poured forth virginal sultry rays in their flight.

The Lord Himself, in all the majesty of His nebulous image, was magnificently illumined by their awesomely enchanting reflection, as a sable nightcloud is illumined by lightning flashes.

Translated from the Yiddish
by Moshe Spiegel

In the Beginning

by Lilly Rivlin

When God set out to create Heaven and Earth, He found nothing but *Tohu Va' Vohu*, namely Chaos and Emptiness. Faced by the Deep, God's spirit wavered. In that atomic second, He became aware of Another. It was the pulse of the Universe: a Throbbing Spirit whirling in the Chaos. In that space I and Thou encountered. During that Absence, Energy was born. And He wanted to replicate that second, that memory of creation which He called Order. The Throbbing Spirit called it Love. And the Throbbing Spirit directed Love toward the Chaos, and the Heavens and the Seas divided. And God gave Order to the Energy, and there was Light. And the Throbbing Spirit danced in a golden light until there was Fire. God watched the Fire glow within the Seas and dreamed Jewels. And God and the Throbbing Spirit embraced in Dream and Reality, and there was Spirit and Matter. And God pulled the Light from the bowels of the Fire, and there was Day and Night. Throbbing Spirit loved with such force that the Skies trembled and the Seas boiled, and there was Lightning. The Heavens wept with joy, and there was rapture in the universe.

Throbbing Spirit and God combined Love and Order. She created the Grass, Herbs, and Trees to reciprocate to the Sun, Moon, and Stars. And on growing globules of Energy, He placed land-beasts and creeping things, while the Throbbing Spirit pulsed and kept time. The Throbbing Spirit changed Her rhythm as She encountered the growing globules of Energy, gaining momentum and movement. And the Wind moved among the Heavens and the Seas, along globular islands of Energies sowing grass, herbs, and trees, stroking land-beasts and creeping things with life. And Earth revolved in the Deep.

God sought the Throbbing Spirit in the Wind to ask Her: "What final Order?" "An image of you," She replied. And so God took some of every

Element He had created and made Adam. But He took nothing from the Wind. And Adam who was but an image of God existed. And the Throbbing Spirit of Chaos and Emptiness had also faced the Deep and created. She took the Elements and made an image. And She breathed life into Lilith. But the Wind had not passed through Adam, and He could not remember the birth of Love which gave forth Energy. You know the rest of the myth. Adam now knows the myth. He has felt the Throbbing Spirit in the Wind.

The Creation of Man

by Morris Rosenfeld

When the Lord created our wonderful world, He asked nobody's advice, and did as He pleased—all after His own will, in accordance with His own plans: He worked at it long, and He did it well.

When He was about to create man, things did not go so well, and He summoned the seventy angels who encompass His throne: "Listen to Me, My mighty ones, I have called you here that you may offer your advice on how man is to be made. Help Me, children, to create him, but take good counsel. He must resemble us, and he must be without faults and blemish, for I shall crown him as a ruler, and I shall give him of My flame: he shall freely rule over air, and earth, and ocean. Before him shall fall the bird in the air, the fish in the water and the wild lion in the chase."

The angels became frightened: "If man, who is nothing but foam and smoke, were to rule the air, he would soon enter heaven." And they replied to God: "Make him in our image; give him reason, give him power, but give him no wings. No, he shall have no wings, for he will fly with his sword. Let him not enter heaven who rules the earth."

"You are right," the Lord answered, "your decision is good; but one exception I shall make, but one exception; listen to Me: Let the poet be winged. He shall receive My highest rank. I will open the heavens to the master of song. And I shall choose an angel among you who shall be ready day and night to attach the wings to him whenever his holy song will rise."

Translated from the Yiddish
by Leo Wiener

Before

by Penina Villenchik

A long time ago, before anything had a name, we didn't know that we were man or woman, human or animal, male or female. When the wild reeds bowed their heads in the wind, we bowed our heads too, for it was the same spirit-breath that breathed through us every second, every hour, every day of our lives. At dawn when the brilliant orange squash blossoms opened gently, gently at the first warm kiss of sun, we too opened our eyes and un-curled from sleep, stretching wide, stretching far, rejoicing as every part of our bodies came to life again. And when the rains came forth, loving Earth so much that she grew fruits and berries and nuts to feed us with, we were full of her joy and we loved each other and we grew our own children to eat Earth's joys, her fruits, so that the rains would come again and visit her.

It was before we were called man or woman, even before we could speak one word. In those days we prayed with our entire beings, in the wind, in the sun, in the rain; every second, every day, every hour of our lives; at the rising of the sun and the dark of the moon, at the birth of the son and the death of the grandmother, at the wedding of two lovers, at the buzzing of the Spring. We breathed, we bowed, we laughed, we wept. This was before we called it prayer.

In the End

by Rabbi Jack Riemer

In the end, man destroyed the heaven and the earth. The earth had been tossing and turning, and the destructive spirit of man had been hovering over the face of the waters. And man said: Let me have power over the earth. And it was so. And man saw that the power tasted good, and so he called those that possessed power wise, and those that tried to curb power he called weak. And there was evening, and there was morning, the seventh day.

And man said: Let there be a division among all the peoples of the earth. Let there be a dividing line, or a wall, between those that are for me and those that are against me, and it was so. And there was evening, and there was morning, the sixth day.

And man said: Let us gather all of our resources into one place, and let us create instruments of power to defend ourselves: let us make a radio to mold men's minds, and a draft to control their bodies, and flags and symbols of power to capture their souls. And it was so. And there was evening, and there was morning, the fifth day.

And man said. Let there be censorship to divide the light from the darkness. And it was so. And man made two great censorship bureaus, to control the thoughts of men, one to tell only the truth that he wanted to be heard abroad, and one to tell only the truth that he wanted to be heard at home. And it was so. And there was evening, and there was morning, the fourth day.

And man said: Let us create weapons that can kill millions and hundreds of millions from a distance, and let us make clean bombs, and let us learn sanitary germ warfare, and let us make guided missiles. And it was so. And there was evening, and there was morning, the third day.

And man said: Let us make God in our image. Let us say that God thinks what we think, that God wants what we want, that God commands what we want Him to command. And man found ways to kill, with atomic power and with radiation fallout, those that were living, and those that were not yet born, and he said: This is God's will. And it was so. And there was evening, and there was morning, the second day.

And then, on the last day, a great cloud went up over all the face of the earth, and there was a great thunder over all of the face of the earth, and there was a great cry that reached up from over all of the earth, and then man, and all of his doings, was no more. And the earth rested on the last day from all of man's labors, and the universe was quiet on the last day from all of man's doings, which man in his folly had wrought. And there was nothing. There was no more evening, and there was no more morning—there was no more day.

The Arrival of Eve

by Francine Prose

"Eve was not fashioned from Adam's rib," the patriarch had said. "She was created in another place, a distant country. But one day, after Adam had been alone in the Garden for several months, she knocked on the gates of Paradise.

" 'Who are you, and what do you want?' asked Adam. For, though he could not help noticing Eve's beauty, he had experienced nothing, in those first months, which might have prepared him to deal with strangers.

" 'I am Eve,' the woman replied. 'I want to come inside the gates.'

" 'What will you do here?' asked Adam.

" 'I will bring you suffering,' she answered, 'I will listen to the snake, and eat the apple. I will introduce evil into the world.'

"And Adam, who had at first been undecided about this newcomer, immediately opened the gate and admitted her to Paradise."

Before the Law

by Franz Kafka

Before the Law stands a doorkeeper. To this doorkeeper there comes a man from the country and prays for admittance to the Law. But the doorkeeper says that he cannot grant admittance at the moment. The man thinks it over and then asks if he will be allowed in later. "It is possible," says the doorkeeper, "but not at the moment." Since the gate stands open, as usual, and the doorkeeper steps to one side, the man stoops to peer through the gateway into the interior. Observing that, the doorkeeper laughs and says: "If you are so drawn to it, just try to go in despite my veto. But take note: I am powerful. And I am only the least of the doorkeepers. From hall to hall there is one doorkeeper after another, each more powerful than the last. The third doorkeeper is already so terrible that even I cannot bear to look at him." These are difficulties the man from the country has not expected; the Law, he thinks, should surely be accessible at all times and to everyone, but as he now takes a closer look at the doorkeeper in his fur coat, with his big sharp nose and long, thin, black Tartar beard, he decides that it is better to wait until he gets permission to enter. The doorkeeper gives him a stool and lets him sit down at one side of the door. There he sits for days and years. He makes many attempts to be admitted, and wearies the doorkeeper by his importunity. The doorkeeper frequently has little interviews with him, asking him questions about his home and many other things, but the questions are put indifferently, as great lords put them, and always finish with the statement that he cannot be let in yet. The man, who has furnished himself with many things for his journey, sacrifices all he has, however valuable, to bribe the doorkeeper. The doorkeeper accepts everything, but always with the remark: "I am only taking it to keep you from thinking you have omitted anything." During these many years the man fixes his attention almost continuously on the doorkeeper. He forgets the other doorkeepers, and this first one seems to him the sole obstacle preventing access to the Law. He curses his bad luck, in his early years boldly and loudly; later, as he grows old, he only grumbles to himself. He becomes childish, and since in his yearlong contemplation of the doorkeeper he has come to know even the fleas in his fur collar, he begs the fleas as well to help him and to change the doorkeeper's mind. At length his eyesight begins to fail, and he does not know whether the world is really darker or whether his eyes are only deceiving him. Yet in his darkness he is now aware of a radiance that streams inextinguishably from the gateway of the Law. Now he has not very long to live. Before he dies, all his experiences in these long years gather themselves in his head to one point, a question he has not yet asked the doorkeeper. He waves him nearer, since he can no longer raise his stiffening body. The doorkeeper has to bend low toward him, for the difference in height between them has altered much to the man's disadvantage. "What do you want to know now?" asks the doorkeeper; "you are insatiable." "Everyone strives to reach the Law," says the man, "so how does it happen that for all these many years no one but myself has ever begged for admittance?" The doorkeeper recognizes that the man has reached his end, and, to let his failing senses catch the words, roars in his ear: "No one else could ever be admitted here, since this gate was made only for you. I am now going to shut it."

Translated from the German
by Willa and Edwin Muir

Paradise

by Franz Kafka

The expulsion from Paradise is in its main significance eternal: Consequently the expulsion from Paradise is final, and life in this world irrevocable, but the eternal nature of the occurrence (or, temporally expressed, the eternal recapitulation of the occurrence) makes it nevertheless possible that not only could we live continuously in Paradise, but that we are continuously there in actual fact, no matter whether we know it here or not.

Why do we lament over the fall of man? We were not driven out of Paradise because of it, but because of the Tree of Life, that we might not eat of it.

We are sinful not merely because we have eaten of the Tree of Knowledge, but also because we have not yet eaten of the Tree of Life. The state in which we find ourselves is sinful, quite independent of guilt.

We were fashioned to live in Paradise, and Paradise was destined to serve us. Our destiny has been altered; that this has also happened with the destiny of Paradise is not stated.

We were expelled from Paradise, but Paradise was not destroyed. In a sense our expulsion from Paradise was a stroke of luck, for had we not been expelled, Paradise would have had to be destroyed.

God said that Adam would have to die on the day he ate of the Tree of Knowledge. According to God, the instantaneous result of eating of the

Tree of Knowledge would be death; according to the serpent (at least it can be understood so), it would be equality with God. Both were wrong in similar ways. Men did not die, but became mortal; they did not become like God, but received the indispensable capacity to become so. Both were right in similar ways. Man did not die, but the paradisiacal man did; men did not become God, but divine knowledge.

He is a free and secure citizen of the world, for he is fettered to a chain which is long enough to give him the freedom of all earthly space, and yet only so long that nothing can drag him past the frontiers of the world. But simultaneously he is a free and secure citizen of Heaven as well, for he is also fettered by a similarly designed heavenly chain. So that if he heads, say, for the earth, his heavenly collar throttles him, and if he heads for Heaven, his earthly one does the same. And yet all the possibilities are his, and he feels it; more, he actually refuses to account for the deadlock by an error in the original fettering.

Since the Fall we have been essentially equal in our capacity to recognize good and evil; nonetheless it is just here that we seek to show our individual superiority. But the real differences begin beyond that knowledge. The opposite illusion may be explained thus: nobody can remain content with the mere knowledge of good and evil in itself, but must endeavor as well to act in accordance with it. The strength to do so, however, is not likewise given him, consequently he must destroy himself trying to do so, at the risk of not achieving the necessary strength even then; yet there remains nothing for him but this final attempt. (That is moreover the meaning of the threat of death attached to eating of the Tree of Knowledge; perhaps too it was the original meaning of natural death.) Now, faced with this attempt, man is filled with fear; he prefers to annul his knowledge of good and evil (the term "the fall of man" may be traced back to that fear); yet the accomplished cannot be annulled, but only confused. It was for this purpose that our rationalizations were created. The whole world is full of them, indeed the whole visible world is perhaps nothing more than the rationalization of a man who wants to find peace for a moment. An attempt to falsify the actuality of knowledge, to regard knowledge as a goal still to be reached.

Translated from the German
by Will and Edwin Muir

The Eden Angel

by Nachmann Rapp

Knowing that the Blessed Lord created man on the eve of Sabbath, at twilight, it has been found that man was the last creation. The sages have it that the Lord did this intentionally, so that should man become haughty, the very smallest mosquito would rise up and say: I preceded you in the deeds of creation! Whether it is so, or not so, it was God's will, blessed be His name, and who shall presume to say to the Creator: What is this that You are doing?

But no one saw the bright wise smile on the face, as it were, of God when He said to the angels: Let us make man in our image. Not one of the angels grasped what was about to happen. They saw God smile, and smiled with Him. For is it not known that the heavenly angels are beams of light irradiated by the luminance of God Himself? They shine with His light and never fade, for the light of the Lord shall never die.

The Creator set about molding a creature different from every living, shining being in the heavens. Creation of man was still swathed in mystery, and no one knew what it was to be. But when the clay fermented between the Creator's fingers, the clay of which man was made, the Lord God knew that this time a creature would emerge exceeding in importance every other creation in the universe. A being that needs much kindness and mercy to survive; a great deal of beauty and glory so that he may not despair, and a great deal of bitterness and sorrow that he may value his beauty, and not envy the light of the angels. It was as though the Lord had created a second world, not a heavenly one, another one—in which this newly born creature, man, could live out his utterly strange existence.

It did not take long and man was made. With his first breath, instilled by God, he opened his eyes and looked straight into the countenance of the Creator. Man was beautiful in his earliest form. His innocent gaze appealed to the Creator and He decided to keep him close by and to establish his world not far from the Godly heavens. And so He gave man the Garden of Eden, the wondrous Garden, which blossomed a little out of the way and was not inhabited by angels. The woman, too, whom God created for man, was given him in the Garden of Eden. For both man and his wife were fashioned of one clay; the same innocence in their gaze, and the resplendent glow of heaven, lit by the angels, dazzled their eyes. The Garden of Eden cooled them with its shade and refreshed them with its living fragrances.

All that existed in the Garden was blessed with the vivid character of nature in blossoming fruition. The fruit was goodly to eat, and the waters flowed calmly, between stone hillocks and undulating vines. The beasts and birds called out their song as though they had never been there. At night the earth was covered with fresh dew, which glittered at dawn in a harmony of color, beneath the face of the sun. Man and his wife walked the garden sensing the mysterious miracle around them, but not knowing what it was. So passed days and nights. No anxieties or yearning touched their human hearts. Angels did not enter the Garden, they were captives of the light of heaven, and the rays of glory which they spread bound them to the endless light of the Creator. They were His will and His existence. They shone with His light and were ready to shine thus for all eternity even as the eternal light of their Creator. Together with the Lord God, the angels smiled at man's creation, but when the deed was done, they no longer gave it thought. They did not care what he was doing there in the out-of-the-way Garden, the strange parkland, that peculiar creature named man.

And man walked Eden without worry or desire. Like the birds and the insects, the snakes and the animals, he walked there, lapping with his tongue from the spring waters when thirst dried his palate, and plucking with his teeth from the cherry tree when his stomach rumbled with hunger. Sometimes, during his slow, purposeless strolls, he would meet the woman created for him. She would come towards him, her mouth reddened by the juice of pomegranates, or her hair wet from a dip in the waters. He would look at her as he did at the other garden residents, pass her by, and continue on his way. She would do the same. Days and weeks passed by, and they led their peaceful lives, their inane lives. The angel appointed over the Garden of Eden did not distinguish them from the other creatures of Eden, from those who walked on four roaring a hollow roar, or from those who crawled the dust in constant silence. And the miracle of man's creation which had roused the angels' wonder slowly receded and faded away.

On the day that, by chance, woman tasted of the Tree of Knowledge and gave her man a taste of the forbidden fruit, there was great upheaval in the skies. The Eden angel was thrown into confusion by what he saw, and he, too, blundered. This is what happened: When the woman bit into the forbidden apple, she felt a certain warmth spreading through her body, a warmth she had not known before. The warm feeling ebbed swiftly, and her bare limbs then began to shiver. She pressed her hands to her breast and then to her belly and felt a strong need to cover her body. Fear came upon her and she started to run. With his first bite, man was struck by the same fear. In great shock he threw the remains of the apple to the ground, and they both darted wildly through the greenery like frightened birds. The angel watched them with astonishment and could not understand what had happened to these strange creatures. He went to the spot where they had both been standing, and no longer found them there. On the ground he saw the piece of apple. —Was this the cause of fear? pondered the angel. He picked up the bitten apple and studied it. The fruit of one of the Garden trees, could this change God's will and judgment? They had put it to their lips and had bitten into it with their teeth. And so? Was that so frightening? He put the apple to his lips and calmly started to chew.

And then, utter confusion. Pain surged up in the angel's heart and sorrow enveloped him. Where were they, the two creatures, man and his wife? He wanted to walk with them in the Garden, to look at their faces, and to pace, step by step, along with them. Strong yearning for them swept over him. The Garden stretched large and empty; flourishing trees, blossoming flowers, crawling insects and animals on four. But they, the two of them, whom sudden fear had uprooted, had kindled with a will and tremendous craving of their own—they were gone!

Bewildered he stood there, overcome by a desire to run and find the two who had fled in fear. Without them the Garden of Eden was bare, the heavens cold and hollow, the light—frozen illumination without radiance, the angels and their singing—mere instruments of music with no trend or emotion of their own. How beautiful were the two when fear struck their hearts, flashed in their eyes, and thus set them apart from the other creatures of the Garden! He would go to them, find them and be with them, and this new revelation would ease him in its glow.

In vain did the angels call on him to join them in song. He stood in the Garden, trapped in his great longing for the two people. His friends, the angel choir, seemed foolish and empty to him. The angels had already sung "Holy" three times, yet he stood there basking in the new revelation, torn by painful yearning. Until news of the tasting of forbidden fruit reached the supreme throne and He Himself, Creator of the Universe, ordered the expulsion of the two from the Garden of Eden, condemned to death and eternal wandering over the face of the earth.

Now the angel saw them. They stood there guilty and terrified. God's voice thundered at them and they cowered in fear. Then the curse of God descended upon them, the curse of death. The fear in their eyes turned to bewilderment. They looked at each other. The angel thought he saw hatred in their eyes, a readiness to attack and to trample one another at the flick of an eyelid. But immediately a smile lit their faces and happiness shone there. Man stroked his woman's head with his broad hands and pressed her to his chest; joyfully they turned together to the gates of Eden, and together they burst into happy laughter. Death did not terrify them; they had found a source of intoxicating joy, a power more valid than death.

The angel stood watching them; two great teardrops gathered in his eyes and dropped to his chest. How would he find a way to accompany the two, to drink of their joy and eat the bitter fruit of their sorrow? His ears heard the echo of their gay laughter, his eyes saw their pain and fear. What wonderful creatures these were! Outweighing, in their fear and their joy, all the frozen glory of all the heavens.

Suddenly the angel trembled. Such thoughts, how do they come to me, an angel? My place is with the heavenly entourage, to live forever and to relate the deeds of the Lord. I must leave this place and return to heaven! But he felt his body grow heavy; his feet rooted to the soil and his wings would not spread for flight. He sank to the ground and wept in agony. He did not remember eating of the forbidden fruit. All he felt was utter longing for the two exiles of the Garden of Eden, the two frightened people who had raised their voice in laughter, and who bore springs of new hope in their hearts.

The realm of eternity in the heavens carefully observes its laws, time and moments. The singing of angels never ceases and no one is absent from the heavenly host. Long since, a very long time ago, there had been the case of two, whom God Himself had banished from the Garden of Eden. The angels no longer remembered them. Praise of the Universe and the Creator filled their days and their nights. Only one angel could not forget those two, and his longing renewed itself day by day. He walked among the angels like an alien. His sapphire eyes did not glow, nor did his white wings glisten like the others. At times, sadness would descend upon him during the singing; he would stop, sigh deeply, and thus disrupt the heavenly chorus. No one knew the source of disharmony, and a great shudder would tremble through the choir, and reach the heavenly throne. In the cold beam of the heavens, the angel was drawn to the light and shadow of the Garden of Eden, where the two had lived, had become aware of themselves, and from which they had been banished. But the gates of Eden were heavily guarded. A stern fiery angel, with sharp-edged sword in his hand, guarded the gate, that no one might enter or leave. There, beyond the gate, were the traces of his first longings, and he could not reach them. He walked, therefore, in the cold light of heaven and scorched his heart with burning tears.

One day, the miracle occurred. There, in the garden of miracles, his eyes traced the four principal rivers which stream forth from the Garden of Eden, out and onward in a silvery flow, to slake the thirsty soil. He gazed into the waters and a great desire awoke in his heart. To dip his burning body in this cool stream; his flaming flesh would fall into the cold current and disappear into its depths. He would no longer walk about in the cold light, torn with unfulfilled yearnings. He would extinguish this flaming angel body of his in the waters which streamed towards the two banished ones, to whom his heart reached out in longing.

Gripped by the forceful urge, he leaped into the River Gihon. The heat of his body churned the river waters into a swirl of seething waves. The oncoming current cooled the turbulent whirlpool and extinguished the angelic fires; his body lost its heavenly translucent glow. With closed eyes, he whirled and rolled along with the current, and felt the penetrating chill of the waters. At times the waters still stormed around his rolling body, throwing sheets of boiling spray into the air. Until, at last, the river calmed, and flowed serenely on its path. The angel became aware of a sharp pain in his ribs and a suffocating thickness in his throat. He opened his eyes and was immediately engulfed by an enveloping darkness. There he lay, washed up on a rock at the side of the river in the darkness of night. The river rippled in the wind with incessant sound. The angel lay, shivering with cold, on the river bank.

Translated from the Yiddish
by Miriam Silver

Generation

by Nessa Rapoport

When Adam saw the world through the eyes of God he knew that it was good. The rivers flowed according to their way, the earth was flowering, and the sky was suspended over it all, like a breath.

It was a time of great wonder, when Adam looked at the created things. He saw the birds of the air flying, and the beasts of the field asleep. He saw vines, roots, stems, petals, trunks, and leaves. And seas, lakes, rivers, falls, oceans, pools, and streams. He saw each perfect in its state, and so would always be.

Adam, sprung from the earth of the world, locked his feet to the land. And when Eve was taken from him to be given, he thought she had always been. But she, born in separateness, saw how becomings were hidden in their present skins, as she, in him. She knew that the fruit contained the seed, and that only the falling away of flesh brings its release. This was the way of things to Eve, and the grass that stood in stillness for Adam flickered for her like a snake.

Adam, the world is good, she said. Tide and wind, moon swollen, then thin, the seas rise to rain to ripen the fruit, and look, we are part of the changing.

Don't change, Adam cried, but Eve wove her arm as she'd seen the grass move, undulating, beautiful, and Adam watched the leaves part and the fruit plucked in her hand.

Good, she said, her cheeks flushed with sweetness, the syrup staining her mouth. And Adam saw the white fruit flesh broken around the red skin. He saw Eve's belly swelled by the fruit, and everything opened for him. And he looked at Eve and felt in her the girl she had been, and watched her stomach rise and fall with the children she would bear for him. Her face distended by fruit became the old woman she would be, and the span of the world burst into space. All he could do was choose to be part of it or be chosen to be. And so he stretched out a trembling hand, and said: I am a man. Let me eat.

The Tree of Id

by Rabbi Harold S. Kushner

But of the tree of the knowledge of good and evil thou shalt not eat.
(Gen. 2:17)

Now the serpent was more cunning than any beast of the field. And he said unto the woman, "Has God indeed said, 'You shall not eat of any tree of the garden'?" And the woman answered, "Of the fruit of the trees in the garden we may eat, but of the fruit of the tree in the middle of the garden, the tree of the Knowledge of Good and Evil, God has told us we may not eat, nor may we touch it." And the serpent said to the woman, "That is because God knows that in the day you eat of it, your eyes will be opened and you will be like God, knowing good and evil." And the woman saw that the fruit of the tree was a temptation to the palate and a delight to the eyes, but she said, "No, we shall obey the Lord our God." And her husband too said, "Indeed, how shall we make ourselves different from the way the Lord created us?" And they did not eat.

And they heard the sound of the Lord God walking in the garden toward the cool of the day. And the Lord God called unto the man and his wife and said, "Because I have seen that you are God-fearing people and have done My will, I shall reward you greatly. You shall live in peace in the midst of the other animals; their ways shall be your ways, and their patterns and purposes yours. You shall not work for your food, but shall find it on the ground and pluck it from the trees, even as the beasts do. You shall bear children without pain and without apprehension, without love and without passion, and when they are old enough to find their own food, you shall send them out into the world and forget them. You will never need to cry and never laugh, for I shall give you warm days, full bellies, and a placid existence."

And the man and his wife continued to live in the Garden of Eden, eating each day from the Tree of Id, which some call the Tree of Life. And they were naked, but they were not ashamed, and made themselves no clothes. They found shelter, as the animals did, in caves and under trees, and built themselves no homes. They never saw a wheel or lit a fire. They heard the songs of birds, but they themselves wrote no music, no poetry, and of course, they never cut down trees for paper. And they never cried and never laughed, as God had promised them.

And the grass grew high around the Tree of Knowledge of Good and Evil till it covered it completely and hid it from view, for there was no human being on earth to tend it.

The Tree of Life and the Tree of Death
by Howard Schwartz

In the beginning there were two trees, the Tree of Life and the Tree of Death. The Tree of Life rose up like a ladder into the heights, with angels ascending and descending on it, and the Tree of Death grew through the depths of the earth like a great root, in a vast abyss that extended from one end of the world to the other, and continued on from there, reaching to the ends of the universe. And never, ever, could that tree be uprooted, for, strange to say, it served as the cornerstone for all existence, as well as the foundation that supported the Tree of Life.

Now there were those who believed that the Tree of Life and the Tree of Death were counterparts which completed each other, and some of these people went as far as to assert that they might even be the same tree, the same endless trunk encircling the worlds. But the majority were certain that the two trees were opposites, and that everything about the one excluded the other. These people assumed that the two trees had been placed in this world to provide a test for mankind. For if the first father chose to taste the fruit of the Tree of Life, eternal life would be given to him and his descendants. But if he did not, mortality would become the rule. According to this myth, God sat back for centuries while this test was taking place, drawing His breath back and forth through countless stars, waiting for the man to make his choice.

Now how is it possible that in all those centuries the man did not approach either tree, the Tree of Life or the Tree of Death? Perhaps because the garden was so abundant that the man had no need to seek out either one. He merely had to reach out wherever he stood to taste a new fruit, for there was such an abundance of fruit trees in that garden that he never returned to the same tree twice. Or perhaps he avoided both trees, and thus the test, because he had been made in the image of God, after all, and thus had received some of the knowledge that had previously been known to God alone. Thus he may have sensed that even to approach the two trees that grew in the center of the garden was forbidden. Or perhaps he may have worshiped them, and accepted from the first that such fruit was sacred, and not to be tasted.

In this way a great many centuries passed, in which all of existence flourished, for God had permitted the world to remain abundant until the man had made his choice. At last He grew impatient, and one night while the man was sleeping God extracted one of his ribs, and with it created the first woman. And when the man awoke in the morning and saw her lying next to him, he could not take his eyes away from her face, yet all the while he felt the pain of a wound that would never heal. That night the man knew her ripeness for the first time, and the next day the woman brought him as a gift of love the fruit of the Tree of Life, which she had picked, unaware that he held it sacred. But when the man saw what she had done, he grew frightened and refused to taste the fruit (which would have given him eternal life), and told the woman to take it back and to leave it as an offering beneath the tree from which it had been taken. But when the woman did this, and bent down to place the fruit at the foot of the Tree of Life, she glimpsed the abyss in which the Tree of Death was growing. And that was enough. For while the Tree of Life bears fruit, the Tree of Death does not. But merely to look into its dark abyss is sufficient to cause all who do so to become mortal. And because the woman did not understand what she saw there, she brought the man to that place, and he looked down, and when he lifted up his eyes the Tree of Life had disappeared, and the garden along with it, and the wilderness stretched before them in every direction.

Lilith Recollects Genesis
by Wendy Laura Frisch

They crept through the haze of the last dark hour. Swans like sentinels along the riverbank straightened to survey them as they passed. Clouds rolled slowly off the water, which looked gray and oily in the mist. The girl discerned a spiny creature gliding silently in midstream. She felt her heartbeat quicken and convulse, knew herself a trespasser and could not speak to tell the man her fear. She sensed malevolent pressure of eyes behind her, force of spectral forest halflives closing in for a kill. She felt creatures stirring all around her. The slightest movement of leaves set her teeth on edge, her flesh rippling. She knew the signs.

Rejecting God and gravity a fish crashed upward, shattering the water's surface and thrashing in a momentary agony of light. Startled, the girl grasped the hands of her companion, clamped them fast to her own, but felt no pulse and let them fall. The man pulled her close to his body. It was not what she wanted. Always it would come to this; she craving only the lightness of fingertips, a grazing, glancing embrace and then to walk on fearless, needing no master nor teacher nor guide. She was content with nearness. He wanted many sons. She craved fingertips. He gave her elbows and armpits and sweaty palms. No kiss on the mouth; she could not hear it, could not swallow it at all. Here death was, but for his greedy hunting of her sex he could not see it, could not hear the screech owl's singing, would never understand that song.

Adam and Eve Return to the Garden

by Itzik Manger

Before a densely branched, wide-spreading apple tree, the angel Laibl
stopped. We, that is, my friend Pisherl and I, also stopped. Laibl whispered,
"You see it, fellows. This is the Tree of Knowledge. This is the tree from
which Eve plucked the apple; and that fool Adam was persuaded to taste it.
You know the story; it's written in the Bible."

We stood and stared. It seemed to me that the Tree of Knowledge was a
tree like any other in Eden; nevertheless, there was something different
about it. Because of this tree, Adam and Eve had been driven from Eden. A
wind sounded in the branches, but though the apples trembled, not one of
them fell.

The moon that had been following us all this while cast its silver glow over
the tree. It was something wonderful to behold. The angel Laibl whispered,
"Let's hide nearby. You'll see something nice."

"What, for instance?" we asked, but he did not reply. He pointed at a
bush, and we hid ourselves behind it. We lay still and waited. I don't recall
how long we lay there. It might have been an hour, perhaps less. The angel
Laibl suddenly pricked up his ears. We heard footsteps.

"Psst . . ." Laibl put a finger to his lips. "Psst . . . they're coming."

"Who? Who, Laibl?"

"Adam and Eve."

We saw two figures approaching the Tree of Knowledge. One of them
was dressed in a frock coat and a top hat. The other wore hoopskirts and a
hat with a long ostrich feather.

"That's it—that one," said the man with the top hat, pointing. "That's
the one, Eve. Right here, on this spot, you gave me the cursed apple to
taste."

The woman in the hoopskirts sighed. She folded her hands over her heart.
I could see tears in her eyes. *"Ah oui.* This is it, Adam. It was the cursed serpent that persuaded me to it."

"And *à cause de toi*, we've lost our happiness, Eve. That incomparable Paradise."

"It was a good life in Paradise, Adam, but that . . . that cursed . . ."

"Right . . . right, Eve," Adam replied, his finger pointing at his wife.
"She, that cursed . . ."

"I meant the serpent, Adam. But you're pointing your finger at me."

"I too mean the serpent, Eve. And . . . I point my finger at you."

They began to quarrel. Each called the other every name under the sun.
Eve grabbed a handful of Adam's hair. She herself might not have escaped

unscathed, except that a miracle took place. An apple fell from the Tree of Knowledge, bounced off Adam's top hat, and fell to the grass.

"Don't touch it, Eve," Adam cried in a strange voice. "Don't touch it, I implore you, in God's name."

"God forbid," Eve said, clasping her hands together. "I can still taste that other apple."

They seated themselves under the tree. Adam reminded her of the fine times in Eden before their great sin. Eve's eyes glistened. "Ah, Adam. How good it was. We'll never see such times again."

"We were naked, unashamed, and happy," sighed Adam.

"Let's take off our clothes, Adam, and be naked, unashamed, and happy again."

They got up and started to tear off their clothes. The stars twinkled wickedly in the sky. "Adam, I can't. The clothes have grown fast to my body," Eve sighed.

"Mine too." Adam bowed his head. They stood awhile with their heads bent, two lost figures in the light of the Eden moon. "Let's beg pardon for our sins. Let's beat our breasts," said Adam haltingly. "Maybe He will forgive us."

They stood, facing the stars. The man in the top hat and the woman in the hoopskirts began to beat their breasts with their fists, whispering piously, imploring their Maker to forgive them, and to be shown the way back into Eden.

The wind, that all this while had been tickling the leaves on the Tree of Knowledge, suddenly leaped down. Adam and Eve were frightened; they took to their heels as fast as they could go.

Translated from the Yiddish
by Leonard Wolf

True Joy
by Kamelia Shahar

Eliyahu the Prophet and his disciple Elisha, with whom he was wandering hrough the roads of the Land of Israel, one day saw someone who was tilling the soil and in a very black mood, muttering and cursing at the cows. It was noon. His wife came with a meal all ready, his mother came with a jug of wine. The man stopped work, sat down, ate and drank, but neither the tasty food nor the good wine nor the kindness of his wife and mother succeeded in changing his mood.

Eliyahu the Prophet, who had been watching the man, approached him and said, "Tell me, why are you in such bad spirits? I see you're neither hungry nor thirsty. You have a wife and mother who love you and look after you. What is it you're lacking? Why are you sad?"

"And why should I be satisfied with my luck? Because I've got to walk behind my cows from morning till night to earn bread from the sweat of my brow? There are people who live in palaces, enjoying the good things of this world, while I've got to suffer and work hard for each little piece of bread! Damn the day when Adam and Eve ate the forbidden fruit! If they hadn't eaten it, we'd still be living in the Garden of Eden, without having to work in order to survive. If I'd been in Adam's place, Eve could've said whatever she wanted, I wouldn't have listened to her!"

"Me too," the wife said. "If I'd been in Eve's place, I wouldn't have listened to the snake."

"You're speaking like ignorant people," the mother said. "You shouldn't criticize the actions of others without first putting yourselves in their place."

Eliyahu the Prophet, who had been listening to the conversation in silence, said to the old woman, "One can see that you've had a lot of experience in life. And as for what concerns you," he said to the husband and wife, "in a short while you'll have the opportunity to prove if you're capable of resisting temptation." And he left.

The tiller returned to work, but he had hardly begun when he saw, buried in the earth, a little metal box! He bent down to seize it—and right there saw a second and third box. Immediately he called his wife and mother and showed them the boxes. On the first one was written: "Whoever opens me will be wealthy."

"You see?" the mother said. "Didn't I tell you that this stranger who passed through here was a messenger of God? Open it, you're going to find a treasure for sure."

He opened it and marveled at it: the little box was full of jewels. "We're rich!" he said. "Now let's see what's in the second box." Taking it in his hand, he saw that on the box was written: "If gold makes you happy, open me."

"What a question!" the man said. "The richer a person is, of course the happier he is!"

"My son," the mother said, "that's not true. Health is a treasure more precious than all the gold in the world."

The tiller didn't respond. He opened the second little box, which was filled with ducats, and out of happiness began to sing and dance with his wife. A little afterwards, remembering the third little box, he took it in his hand to open it, but saw written on it: "Whoever opens me loses all that he has."

"I'm not so stupid as to risk all the gold and jewels we've found because of curiosity. The best thing," he said, "would be to bury the box and forget about it."

"You're stupid for not wanting to open it!" his wife exclaimed. "No doubt there's some other treasure inside of it; open it and look. If it's empty, we'll throw it away. How can we lose what we already have? It's ours! Who can take it away from us?"

At first the husband didn't want to listen to her, but she insisted so much, she begged, cried and threatened so much, that finally he was convinced and opened the little box. As soon as he did this, a fierce wind began blowing and a torrent of rain came down which carried away all the treasures they had found.

Then Adam and Eve appeared in front of them, and at the same time a voice said, "Don't judge others till you put yourselves in their place. What happened to you happened to Adam and Eve. You couldn't resist temptation either."

The tiller's mother, seeing her son and daughter-in-law sad and humbled, told them, "My children, enough with believing only in riches. The truly happy person is the one who's content with what God gave him."

Time passed. Eliyahu the Prophet, accompanied by Elisha, came back to the same place. And this is what their eyes saw: the tiller was tilling; his mother and his wife were bringing him food, and with them was a child, who the man took in his arms, kissed and hugged.

Eliyahu said to him, "I see that you're working hard, but it seems to me that you're happy. Am I right?"

"Yes, holy man," the tiller answered. "I recognize you. God be blessed, you opened my eyes. We're happy now, we lack for nothing; most of all, God made us content by giving us a child who is more precious than all the treasures in the world."

Satisfied to have put this covetous husband and wife on the right road, Eliyahu the Prophet spread his hand, blessed them, and went away.

Translated from the Judezmo
by Stephen Levy

The Story of Lilith and Eve
by Jakov Lind

Before God created Eve, the legend tells us, he created Lilith, but Lilith left Adam, as she could never agree with him, in smaller and larger matters, while Eve became Adam's true wife, that is, a woman who is always in agreement with her man. Lilith left, but not for good. The legend tells us she returns to haunt Adam as lust.

Once upon a time there was a man who was haunted by Lilith. The demon had disguised herself in the clothes of an ordinary, simple, agreeable woman and came to visit Adam when he was alone.

Why are you on your own? Lilith asked. Where is your woman, the one who came to replace me?

She is out in the country, she went to visit relatives, and she will return soon. She will not be pleased to find you here, for she fears you.

Why should my sister be afraid of me? asked Lilith. I am as simple in my heart as she is. I am as good and kind as she is. I love my parents and I love my children, the same as she. But I don't think as she does, our difference is hidden in the mind, not in our bodies.

I believe you, said Adam, and I love you, but I need a peaceful life.

Have it your way, said Lilith, have your peaceful life. I am just your other woman, and I will not leave you, but will love you as I always did.

Adam looked into her eyes and said no more. Her eyes were like doors wide open into a world he had almost forgotten, and he stepped inside.

They were in each other's arms and mouth when Eve returned. Lilith and Adam are united, she thought. Stay with me, sister. I will bring food to your bed. She brought food and drink to the bed for them and retired to a far corner of the house, where she crouched at the stove to keep herself warm, and went into a trance. She left her own body and entered the body of her sister Lilith and thus she embraced and kissed Adam and felt his love for her as she had never known it before.

But I am your Eve, said Lilith. Why do you love me so passionately? You never loved me with such passion before.

Adam laughed and said: You will leave with dawn and I will not see you for a long time. If I am passionate it's because our happiness is but short.

How can you say that? said Lilith. I will be here tomorrow and the day after and so for the rest of your life. Why do you love me so passionately? Do you think I am the one I look? I am Eve speaking through my sister's mouth.

You are joking, laughed Adam. I know you will leave at the dawn and will not be back for quite some time.

Lilith, who was Eve now, kissed him and said: I wish this were so, but alas I cannot leave you. I will stay with you, because you are full of fire for this other woman whose body I have now taken over. Look at me carefully and tell me whether you don't see that I am your wife Eve?

Eve sits in the far corner of the house, said Adam. But when he looked he could not see her there. What he saw were the flames from the stove.

The Poet of Irsahab

by Else Lasker-Schüler

Nine hundred sixty-nine was Methuselah's age when he died. That very noon he was standing in the huge marketplace of Irsahab, with his fingers hanging down, the twigs of his long arm-branches, and his hoary head mournfully drooping to the ground.

The boys and girls kissing in his cozy hiding place and the children playing their games under his shadow were frightened by his gloominess. Then along came his son Grammaton and comforted him. This was his youngest child, the only one by his last, his hundredth, wife, whom curiosity had led to marry a man as old as heaven. And thus it was that Grammaton looked with blue eyes, for Methuselah was closer to the faraway blue than to the earth. And Methuselah said to his son Grammaton: "I shall die today, for I cannot live without Mellkabe, my nurse." Mellkabe had been buried that morning, and her lullabies were still lulling up to Methuselah from her grave. He heard all kinds of pet names, and thus Methuselah sank into the grave next to her. And an old raven alighted on the edge of his resting place; the raven's name was Enoch and he was Methuselah's father. After a dark transmigration he finally came back to the world as a raven for having insulted Vishnu, the God of the neighboring nation. And besides him, the aged man, who was as old as heaven, left three sons and a measureless flock of children's children. The two eldest sons were twins and five hundred years old, and Grammaton, his late offspring, who bore so much celestial goodness in his face, had been born at the same time as the new constellation Pegasus. Now Grammaton was a poet and that was his misfortune, for he couldn't tell the difference between two and three, nor had he ever been involved in the buying and selling of his father's lands and cattle. And he realized, as his five-hundred-year-old pair of brothers explained, that his father's bequests could be divided in two but not in three parts, so Grammaton waived his claim with noble tears in his blue eyes. But ever since, his grandfather in the guise of a raven gave him no peace. He perched upon his shoulder, his dreamy head of curls, and once Grammaton, fully unaware of the close blood kinship of the bird, heard him speaking in an ominous tone. But the ebony creature's suspicions made his heart fierce until his soul arose under the morning's radiance and filled up with gold. And he thought to himself, I can stamp my golden thoughts only in stars and signs in the column that holds up the roof of my father's house. But the cunning twins called him a sneak who was trying to make off with their property, and he was driven from father Methuselah's rich garden. And since the column holding up the roof of his father's house was the temple of his art, he began hating his brothers and could hardly wait for the day when one would slay the other, as Cain had slain Abel.

And his hate extended to the children and children's children and he scattered an ill harvest among them, and one wrested another from the face of the earth. But then they grew up again just as quickly, from child's child's child to child's child's child's child, and if a father died, his son would replace him that night. And Grammaton realized that the whole city was his kith and kin, and his hatred grew from cousin to cousin and he trampled the sassy child that ran into his legs—before it could some day return on a future star as the son's son's son of some coming great-nephew. And he succeeded in exterminating the Methuselah dynasty, which was all the inhabitants of the city; and even the temple, the column holding up his father's house, was not spared by him. And only the raven could not die, it perched in the hollows of his shoulders, and he, Grammaton, sat on the tail of a stone monkey and sang:

i! ü! hiii e!!
i! ü! hiii e!!

Translated from the German by
Joachim Neugroschel

The City Coat of Arms
by Franz Kafka

At first all the arrangements for building the Tower of Babel were characterized by fairly good order; indeed, the order was perhaps too perfect, too much thought was taken for guides, interpreters, accommodation for the workmen, and roads of communication, as if there were centuries before one to do the work in. In fact the general opinion at that time was that one simply could not build too slowly; a very little insistence on this would have sufficed to make one hesitate to lay the foundations at all. People argued in this way: The essential thing in the whole business is the idea of building a tower that will reach to heaven. In comparison with that idea everything else is secondary. The idea, once seized in its magnitude, can never vanish again; so long as there are men on the earth there will be also the irresistible desire to complete the building. That being so, however, one need have no anxiety about the future; on the contrary, human knowledge is increasing, the art of building has made progress and will make further progress, a piece of work which takes us a year may perhaps be done in half the time in another hundred years, and better done, too, more enduringly. So why exert oneself to the extreme limit of one's present powers? There would be some sense in doing that only if it were likely that the tower could be completed in one generation. But that is beyond all hope. It is far more likely that the next generation with their perfected knowledge will find the work of their predecessors bad, and tear down what has been built so as to begin anew. Such thoughts paralyzed people's powers, and so they troubled less about the tower than the construction of a city for the workmen. Every nationality wanted the finest quarters for itself, and this gave rise to disputes, which developed into bloody conflicts. These conflicts never came to an end; to the leaders they were a new proof that, in the absence of the necessary unity, the building of the tower must be done very slowly, or indeed preferably postponed until universal peace was declared. But the time was spent not only in conflict; the town was embellished in the intervals, and this unfortunately enough evoked fresh envy and fresh conflict. In this fashion the age of the first generation went past, but none of the succeeding ones showed any difference; except that technical skill increased and with it occasion for conflict. To this must be added that the second or third generation had already recognized the senselessness of building a heaven-reaching tower; but by that time everybody was too deeply involved to leave the city.

All the legends and songs that came to birth in that city are filled with longing for a prophesied day when the city would be destroyed by five successive blows from a gigantic fist. It is for that reason too that the city has a closed fist on its coat of arms.

Translated from the German
by Willa and Edwin Muir

Legend of the Third Dove
by Stefan Zweig

In the Book of the Beginning of Time is told the story of the first dove, and of the second, which Forefather Noah sent from the Ark for a message, as the gates of heaven closed and the waters of the deep dried up. Yet the journey and the fate of the third dove: who has ever told it? On the peak of Mount Ararat stood stranded the rescuing ship, which in its bosom cradled all life spared from the Flood, and as the Forefather's glance from the mast saw only billow and wave, waters without end, he sent out a dove, the first, that it might bring him some message of whether land was yet to be seen anywhere, under the overcast skies.

The first dove, so it is told there, arose and spread its wings. It flew toward east and then toward west, but water still lay over all. Nowhere did it find respite from its flight, and gradually its wings began to grow lame. Thus it returned to the only secure place in the world, the Ark, and it fluttered around the resting ship on the mountaintop, until Noah stretched out his hand and took it home into the Ark with him.

Seven days he now waited, seven days in which no rain fell and the waters subsided; then he took a dove once again, the second, and sent it out for news. In the morning the dove flew out, and as it came back at eventide, behold, it carried, as a first sign of a liberated earth, an olive leaf in its beak. Thus Noah learned that the treetops had already reached out over the waters, and that the test had been endured.

After another seven days he once again sent out a dove, for news, the third, and it flew out into the world. In the morning it flew out, but in the evening it did not return; day after day Noah waited, yet it did not come back. Then our Forefather knew that earth was free, and that the waters had gone down. Of the dove, however, of the third, he never learned again, nor did mankind ever do so; never was her legend made known until our very own day.

Now this was the third dove's journey and destiny. In the morning it flew out of the stuffy chamber of the ship, in which, in the dark, the crowded animals growled with impatience, and there was a crowding of hooves and claws and a dreary sound of howling and whistling and hissing and barking; out of these crowded quarters it had flown out into the endless expanse, out of the darkness into the light. But as it now lifted its wings into the clarity of light, into the light-clear air sweetly seasoned by rain, at once freedom hovered about it, and the grace of the Unbounded One. The waters gleamed of their depth, green shone the forests like damp moss, early morning's vapor rose white from the meadows, and the fragrant fermentation of the plants sweetened the meadows through and through. Brilliance fell mirroring from the metallic heavens; on the mountain battlements the rising sun shone in endless reddening dawn; like red blood the sea glistened from it; like hot blood the blossoming earth steamed of it. Godlike it was to behold this waking, and with a happy glance the dove rocked itself in smooth gliding over the purple world; over lands and seas it flew and gradually became, in its dreaming, a flying dream itself. Like God Himself, it was the first now to see the freed earth, and of its looking there was no end. Long since now it had forgotten Noah, that Whitebeard of the Ark, and its mission; long since, the idea of its returning. For the world had now become its home, and the heavens its very own house.

So the third dove flew, faithless messenger of the Forefather, over the empty world, ever farther and farther, borne on by the storm of its happiness, by the wind of its blissful restiveness; on it flew, ever on, until its wings grew tired and its feathers heavy. Earth drew it down to itself with weighty force; deeper and deeper sank the exhausted wings, so that they were already grazing the tops of the moist trees—and on the evening of the second day it finally let itself sink into the depths of a forest, which was as yet nameless, like all else in that Beginning of Time. In the thicket of branches it hid and rested from its air-filled journey. Underbrush covered it, wind rocked it to sleep; it was cool in the branches during day and warm in the sylvan dwelling of the night. Soon it forgot the windy heavens and the lure of distance; the green vaulting enclosed it, and time grew abundant over it without numbers.

It was a woods of our nearby world that the lost dove had chosen for its home; but as yet no humans dwelt therein, and in this solitude it gradually became a dream itself. In darkness, in the green of night, it nested, and the years passed it by and death forgot it—for all those animals, that one of each kind which had still seen the first world before the Flood, they cannot die, and no hunter has the power to do anything against them. Invisibly they nest in the inexplorable folds of earth's dress, and so did this dove in the forest's depth. From time to time there came, of course, some presentiment over it of the presence of humans; a shot rang out and ricocheted a hundred-fold in the green walls; woodcutters struck against the trunks, so that the darkness resounded roundabout; the soft laughter of those in love who, entangled in each other's embraces, went off to the side, cooed mysteriously among the boughs; and the singing of children looking for berries sounded thin and far-off. The sunken bird, wrapped like a cocoon in foliage and dream, heard these sounds of the world off and on, but it listened to them without fear and remained in its darkness.

At one time during these days, however, the entire forest began to roar, and it thundered as if earth were breaking in two. Through the air flew whistling, black, metallic masses, and wherever they fell, earth sprang up in shock, and the trees broke like stems of straw. Men in colored clothing threw death at one another, and the terrible machines hurled fire and conflagration. Bolts of lightning flew from earth into the clouds, and thunder after them; it seemed as if the land were about to spring into the skies or as if the sky wanted to fall down on earth. The dove started up from its dream. Death and annihilation were above it; as did the waters once, so now fire swelled over the world. Suddenly it spread its wings and soared up on high, in order to look for another home for itself other than the collapsing forest—a place of peace.

It whirred up and flew over our world, in order to find peace, but no matter where it flew, everywhere there were these streaks of lightning, this thundering of men; everywhere there was war. A sea of fire and blood flooded earth as once upon a time; a Flood had again come; and hastily the dove soared through our lands, to spy a place of rest, and then to soar up on high to the Forefather, to bring him the olive leaf of promise. But nowhere was it to be found these days; ever higher swelled the flood of destruction over mankind, ever farther on the fire ate its way through our world. As yet the dove has not found rest, nor mankind peace, and sooner than that it may not return home, it may not rest for all time.

None has seen it in our days, the mythical dove gone astray, the one seeking peace, and yet it flutters over our heads, fear-ridden and already weary of wing. Off and on, but only by night, when we start from our sleep, we hear a rustling sound high in the air, a harried chase in the dark, disturbed flight and forlorn fleeing. On its wings hover all our black thoughts, in its fear hang all our desires; and the one who, behold, hovers trembling between earth and sky, the dove gone astray—it is only our own fate it proclaims, the faithless messenger of long ago, to the Forefather of mankind. And again, as did thousands of years past, there lies a world, waiting that someone reach out to it a hand and recognize that there has now been testing enough.

Translated from the German
by Emery George

The Fleeting Rainbow

by Ladislav Grosman

Left eye half-shut, brow pensively wrinkled, Yidele Froehlich stood in the door of the wooden shed here in the marketplace, where he sold fruits and vegetables, and looked out into the street. His expression serious, he seemed to be pondering the question of the world's doom or salvation—a mysterious question—which occupied his mind.

A few steps away, three little ragamuffins frolicked and acted up in a naughty manner, as though the square belonged to them. Screaming and shouting, they threw mudpies at each other, without regard to passersby, without regard to Yidele Froehlich, who could have interfered, but so far merely watched and kept quiet.

Three boys, two of them identical twins, in patched-up shirts and torn short pants, had long before come to his attention. Every day for the past year, they gathered around the melon counter like three hungry bees, drawn by the red pulp of the sweet watermelon. Yidele did not drive them away. On the contrary. He did his best to gain their confidence. And that he did.

"As God Himself is my witness, I would slice up my soul, just like a melon, to be able to offer these three a sprinkling of knowledge from the Holy Scriptures," he muttered to himself. "Knowledge which their own father could not and did not bestow upon his neglected children. Blessed be the memory of their father, Emanuel. Such a nice sweet-sounding name. Emanu-el, God be with us. But that atheist did not acknowledge God. He carried Him in his name, but not in his heart. May he rest in peace. He lived like an atheist and died like one; and in ignorance and desolation grew his three sons, children of the street. And where in heaven did this Jewish father find such names—Augustin, Sylvester, and Frankie?"

Yidele Froehlich took charge of them. And he knew how! He was not reckless, so as not to overwhelm them with learning right at the outset. He began slowly and carefully, for there would be nothing worse than seeing them scatter like sparrows on a rooftop, when hit by a rock.

"Do you know, boys," he once asked in his melodious, persuasive voice, "do you know why God appeared to Moses in the bushes rather than in a garden, a meadow or an orchard? Why, I ask you," continued Yidele Froehlich, over an open book, lightly swaying his gaunt body, "why, I ask you, did God need to appear to Moses in a hot, sun-parched desert, in thorny bushes, that ignited and burned and burned, but miraculously did not burn up, when He could have appeared to him, say, on a lawn, in an orchard, or in a flowerbed among roses?"

The three barefoot urchins, their heads shaven, sat without stirring, but tense, ready to fly away, like three soap bubbles. They sat on a short cot, fashioned out of flat boards, looking up at flytraps, those long, sticky strips of paper hanging from the ceiling. Flies blackened the yellow paper bait, stuck to the strip. They were dead. Others, caught by their transparent wings only moments earlier, were still swinging their legs in the air. And in the silence that followed the question, the steady sound of obstinate buzzing could be heard.

"Well, who among you would like to answer that? Perhaps you, Frankie, or you, Sylvester?" Yidele Froehlich called on the lads one by one. He happily performed the holy work of a voluntary teacher, since he had no customer at the moment. It had been in the spring that he first took charge of them.

Now, with the summer and its ripe watermelons at an end, it was different. The boys knew many a thing already and, at times, questioned endlessly. In such moments of bliss, Yidele Froehlich fed the mouths of the three small brothers with prunes and watermelon, and their souls with fragments from the Scriptures—acts which he deemed indispensable.

"Which one of you knows when the greatest silence prevailed? A silence that quivered with joy and excitement, as only the impatient human heart can, and at the same time, shook fearfully as only human knees can?" asked Yidele Froehlich in a tuneful and heightened voice. "Well, which one of you knows?" He wanted to hear how the children of Israel received the Ten Commandments on Mount Sinai and his soul swelled with pride as the three boys recited the Decalogue in unison and by heart. This material they had absorbed at the beginning of the summer.

Now, as the rain fell and winds shook the wooden structure, it occurred to Yidele that he could repeat the story of the Flood, about Noah and the Ark, the symbol of God's promise never to punish the human race again. And so, casually, he asked the boys, who couldn't wait for the storm to end, whether they knew what was in the world before it came to be.

They laughed out loud. How could there be anything before there was a world?

"That, exactly, is the big mistake." Yidele raised a bony finger, intending to tell them that even before the Creation there arose out of God's will seven things of matter, in outline—for example, the Old Testament in outline, the Holy City of Jerusalem in outline—but he never completed the thought, for the sky outside the window suddenly cleared.

The rain had ended, and the boys, as though shot from a cannon, bolted out of the hut. Nothing could stop them. They leaped over brooks and waded through puddles, yelled and shouted and threw mudpies at each other, without regard to Yidele Froehlich, who watched their play and waited for them to return, but they did not.

Like a huge red melon, the sun broke through the clouds, wildly carried by the wind, illuminating the square. Chimneys turned red, store signs paled and the black, still-wet pavement shone like a mirror. Somewhere on the east horizon, there appeared an irresistible something. . . .

"Where are you running?" called Yidele.

"To catch the rainbow," shouted Frankie, running, without a backward glance. There were certain matters Yidele knew nothing about, though the three of them did. They knew how and where it is possible to catch a rainbow. Basically, it is quite simple. One must get to the river while the rainbow drinks from it. Every rainbow should drink immediately following its birth, but not all of them succeed. It all depends on how big and how well curved it is. If it is not big enough and curved enough, it will die, like an infant unable to get its mother's milk. It is not true that rainbows are painted by angels using the tips of their wings; seven angels, that is, one for each color. Nor is it true that children are brought by storks. Rainbows are born of storms and all regular storms carry one in their belly each summer, and sometimes two, in which case they are twins, just like Augustin and Sylvester. If, on the other hand, the rainbow is too small and weak and its mouth can't reach the river's surface to drink right after birth, it dies from thirst, for it is born thirsty, just like a baby. It is best, of course, to catch a rainbow just after a storm, after the thunder has died down and the lightning stopped, and especially in places uninhabited by people. Rainbows are shy, even timid, and prefer silence. They cannot bear loud noises. Those successful in catching a rainbow can stop worrying; happiness and riches will be theirs. Indeed, were the three of them to gain much wealth, their mother would not need to go on washing and housecleaning, would not have to leave at dawn and return late at night, and sometimes she could even buy them shirts and sandals. . . .

Through a shortcut, jogging, they reached Sandrick. Sandrick is a bare hill just outside of town. It is isolated and round like the miller's belly. At its foot flows the Cirka River. It is here the rainbows come to drink. Now they could see it with their own eyes! The river was within reach, and over it arched a huge rainbow in beautiful, clear, rich colors. Only the narrow, dark, unplowed field separated them, and the greenish swamp with the tall rush around which they had to go to get through the narrow strip of willows bordering the river. That swamp . . .

They arrived, out of breath, but the sun hid behind the clouds and the sky grew dark once again. The rainbow was gone! It started drizzling.

"Let's go in the water!" shouted Frankie to his twin brothers, and dropped his shorts.

Sylvester and Augustin shed their shirts by the old oak with the crusty bark, and all three of them jumped into the water. They allowed the swift current to carry them, screaming with delight, and did not notice that the air had cooled. It began hailing. They laughed joyfully. "Hailstones, hailstones, hailstones!" Soon, however, their enthusiasm waned. The water felt cooler too, and the hailstones grew bigger and bigger, pelting their backs and heads. At last the water became unbearable. They found some shelter under the spreading oak tree. Pale and shivering, they dressed quickly and in silence, and when the hailing stopped, set out to return, reaching the marketplace just as the sun had set.

Yidele Froehlich stood facing the wall, as though whispering to it. He did not even turn when they entered. He stood erect, eyes shut, and prayed. He knew the evening prayer by heart. They wanted to leave.

"Now, what did you bring?" asked Yidele suddenly.

Smirking, damp, they remained guiltily silent.

"Did you catch the rainbow?" asked Yidele, and divided some carrots and prunes among them.

"We were too late, it was gone! The rainbow was gone!" said Frankie, the oldest, swallowing the prunes with the pits. "Too bad," he added. "We could have gotten rich, could have had money, could have helped Mother."

"Money? Money isn't everything. Rich?" Yidele looked at them and around his shed in amazement. He leaned out the window to hang the carbide lamp on the hook of the outer wall, and caught sight of the pile of melons, which could not be carried into the shed night after night. Now he turned to the boys, the light from the lamp outside illuminating his smile.

"How about a fiery castle, my pigeons, wouldn't you like that?"

"Oh, yes," they cried enthusiastically.

"Clever people, long before you tried to catch the rainbow and, in so doing, forgot all about its divine beauty," said Yidele Froehlich, and continued: "I don't know; perhaps when you are older, you will have a teacher who will lead you out of ignorance into light. He will tell you that the rainbow is nature's phenomenon and that it is a breakdown of the colors of light in raindrops. But let him, the clever one, explain to you, what is light, if not a gift from God? What are colors? What are raindrops?"

The boys remained silent, shivering from the cold. The shed was in almost total darkness.

Yidele Froehlich frowned. Who knows what is light, what are colors, what are raindrops?

Translated from the Czech
by Bianca Baar

The Ark

by Cecil Helman

Abandoned by God, the ark floats aimlessly and empty on a plain of sea. Only Noah and the lions remain. There are many lions, multiplying as fast as the forty years since the Flood began. All the other animals aboard, all the flesh and fowl, have either eaten or been eaten by one another. Even the men have died; drowned, one by one, beneath the years.

Noah, alone now among the roars, stands on the splintered wood of the upper deck. The lions circle below, thoughtfully, searching for the stairs of the gangway up. Over him creak the riggings, to which tired generations of doves have returned, every evening—their beaks empty.

The sky reddens. At the foot of the gangway the lions crowd for the final rush, jostling among themselves. Suddenly, small shadows fall over their faces; from every horizon white clouds of doves flow towards the ark. Even through old eyes, Noah can see how each dove holds in its beak an olive branch, a crumb, or a piece of cloth. They swoop down joyfully towards him—

The lions and doves hold Noah, for a long instant, like a plucked flower between two soft fingers. . . .

The Rainbow

by Aaron Sussaman

Vodka, not milk, was his drink, and plenty of it, but in that whole sprawling neighborhood of Brooklyn where I grew up there never was a finer milkman than Moshe Halpern. Every morning, however hung over he might be from the night's excesses, he would arrive on time to make his deliveries. And unlike other milkmen he never rushed through his route, sitting in a modern milk truck and gripping a chilly wheel linked to hundreds of horsepower. In what can only be called Old World style, Moshe rumbled through his route, sitting on an old uncovered wooden wagon and gripping chilly reins linked to one donkey.

And what a donkey! Yellow-eyed, burry-hided, with a tail sparser than the tail feathers of an aged eagle, this devoted beast may have looked little enough to squeeze through the Pearly Gates, but he could pull over ten times his weight in milk.

For many years people sadly predicted that this donkey would outlive his beloved master, who was rumored not only to be older than the Milky Way but to have drunk in his lifetime a whole Milky Way of vodka. And to their sorrow their prediction came true. One morning in my eighth year of milk-drinking and Moshe's unreckonable year of milk-delivering, he suddenly tumbled from his wagon in pain, was rushed to the hospital, and died there of advanced cirrhosis of the liver.

He was greatly mourned and even more greatly missed. In the refrigerated milk brought by the modern service that took over his territory, people tasted only progress. In Moshe's at best lukewarm milk, gotten from who knows what ancient cows, they had tasted a lost world.

Thanks to the goodness of the people, as well as to the fact that there was no such thing as a donkey pound where old, unemployed donkeys were put to sleep, the poor donkey was tethered to a pole behind the synagogue to wait out his days. There even he, a dumb beast, mourned. He wouldn't drink, not even buttermilk, which he loved. He wouldn't eat, not even candy. All he would do was stand there, swinging his great lanternlike head at people who looked at him, as if he were trying to see some speck of Moshe in them.

It wasn't long before the effects of not drinking or eating began to tell on him. He grew restless, as if with fever. His yellow eyes burned with unnatural brightness. And several times he escaped his tether and did almost humanly delirious things, like eating the laundry hung out on people's clotheslines. And when he'd been retethered, he'd lie down, roll on the ground, and bray and bray. To this day I can still hear that braying, so wild, so desperate, like the sound of someone trying to work the rusty pump of a dried-up well.

One cold rainy morning I woke up from a terrible dream in which Moshe the milkman had appeared to me, shrugged and said: "A man has to work. Down below I was in the milk business. Up above I'm in the rainbow business. But if somebody doesn't stop the sky from falling, then the rainbow I've delivered this morning will be lost." Springing out of bed, I ran to seek the rabbi for an explanation, but before I found him I spotted the dead donkey. He was lying on his back, propping up with his four stiff legs a sky in which a fragile rainbow was shimmering.

Abraham

by Franz Kafka

Abraham's spiritual poverty and the inertia of this poverty are an asset, they make concentration easier for him, or, even more, they are concentration already—by this, however, he loses the advantage that lies in applying the powers of concentration.

Abraham falls victim to the following illusion: he cannot stand the uniformity of this world. Now the world is known, however, to be uncommonly various, which can be verified at any time by taking a handful of world and looking at it closely. Thus this complaint at the uniformity of the world is really a complaint at not having been mixed profoundly enough with the diversity of the world.

I could conceive of another Abraham for myself—he certainly would have never gotten to be a patriarch or even an old-clothes dealer—who was prepared to satisfy the demand for a sacrifice immediately, with the promptness of a waiter, but was unable to bring it off because he could not get away, being indispensable; the household needed him, there was perpetually something or other to put in order, the house was never ready; for without having his house ready, without having something to fall back on, he could not leave—this the Bible also realized, for it says: "He set his house in order." And, in fact, Abraham possessed everything in plenty to start with; if he had not had a house, where would he have raised his son, and in which rafter would he have stuck the sacrificial knife?

This Abraham—but it's all an old story not worth discussing any longer. Especially not the real Abraham; he had everything to start with, was brought up to it from childhood—I can't see the leap. If he already had everything, and yet was to be raised still higher, then something had to be taken away from him, at least in appearance: this would be logical and no leap. It was different for the other Abrahams, who stood in the houses they were building and suddenly had to go up on Mount Moriah; it is possible that they did not even have a son, yet already had to sacrifice him. These are impossibilities, and Sarah was right to laugh. Thus only the suspicion remains that it was by intention that these men did not ready their houses, and—to select a very great example—hid their faces in magic trilogies in order not to have to lift them and see the mountain standing in the distance.

But take another Abraham. One who wanted to perform the sacrifice altogether in the right way and had a correct sense in general of the whole affair, but could not believe that he was the one meant, he, an ugly old man, and the dirty youngster that was his child. True faith is not lacking to him, he has this faith; he would make the sacrifice in the right spirit if only he could believe he was the one meant. He is afraid that after starting out as Abraham with his son he would change on the way into Don Quixote. The world would have been enraged at Abraham could it have beheld him at the time, but this one is afraid that the world would laugh itself to death at the sight of him. However, it is not the ridiculousness as such that he is afraid of—though he is, of course, afraid of that too and, above all, of his joining in the laughter—but in the main he is afraid that this ridiculousness will make him even older and uglier, his son even dirtier, even more unworthy of being really called. An Abraham who should come unsummoned! It is as if, at the end of the year, when the best student was solemnly about to receive a prize, the worst student rose in the expectant stillness and came forward from his dirty desk in the last row because he had made a mistake of hearing, and the whole class burst out laughing. And perhaps he had made no mistake at all, his name really was called, it having been the teacher's intention to make the rewarding of the best student at the same time a punishment for the worst one.

Translated from the German
by Clement Greenberg

The Near Murder
by Jakov Lind

Once upon a time there was a man who was very old, who had a wife who was very old, but they had no children. They had everything they needed: houses, gardens, food, wine and money. They owned horses, cattle and dogs, plantations, fishing grounds and large woods. They were healthy, strong, wise, and beloved by everyone in the country. They had everything but children and for this they were sad.

The woman said to the man: "I met a stranger yesterday who told me I will have a child before I die." "What did you say?" asked the husband. "I laughed," said the woman. "Why did you laugh?" asked her husband. "Because I am old," she said, "and an old woman cannot have a child. That's why I laughed." "Pity, you laughed," said the man. "Why?" "Because the stranger might have been someone who knows more than you and I do," said the man. And so it was. The woman became pregnant and bore a son. Their happiness was now complete. One day the man returned from his work and as he walked home, he heard a voice behind him: "Take your son and kill him." When the man turned around, there was no one who could have spoken to him.

How can I kill my son, he asked himself, it is insane. But again the voice spoke at his neck and said: "Kill your son" before he entered his house.

"Why are you sad?" asked his wife. And he told her what the voice had said to him. The woman cried; what more could she do? Her husband was the lord over everyone in that land and he would not listen to her anyway.

One morning he asked his son to go with him. "Take your gun," he said, "we are going for a hunt." "What game?" asked the son. The old man said nothing, but walked silently, his eyes cast down, his gun slung across his shoulder.

When they reached the wood, the man said to his son: "I must listen to an inner voice and this voice has told me to kill you."

As the son saw no way out from the forest, which also belonged to his father, and saw men with guns ready all over the place, he knew that this was his end. "All right," he said to his father. "Shoot."

The father tied his son to a tree, lifted his gun and was about to pull the trigger when a voice at his back said: "Don't be insane. I just wanted to know whether you were ready to kill him. As I see you are, let him go, and kill a goat instead." And not far from him, the man suddenly saw a goat, which hadn't been there before. The goat had caught its horns in the thicket and was struggling to get away. The father aimed his gun at the goat and killed it. He untied his son, said not a word, and they both walked silently back to their home. The woman was happy to see her son alive. She had given up hope.

Later at night, she asked her husband: "Why did you behave so strangely? Why did you want to kill him?"

"It's not him I wanted to kill. It's your doubt, your laughter, I wanted to destroy."

"But you didn't," said the woman.

"No, I didn't," said the man. "A voice told me I should let him live." The name of the son was Isaac—which means Laughter—who later inherited all of his father's estates and lived to a ripe old age.

The Dream of Isaac
by Howard Schwartz

for Laya and Tom Seghi

It is said that as he grew older Isaac put the journey to Mount Moriah out of his mind. Even to Rebecca, his wife, he would not speak of what had happened. So circumspect did he become that by the time of his marriage at the age of forty no one could remember the last time he had been heard to speak on the subject. So it seems likely that during the period in which his wife was expecting a child the old memory came to his mind even less often, for Rebecca had grown ripe with her waiting, which was already much longer than the old wives had estimated.

On one such night, while he and Rebecca were sleeping side by side, Isaac dreamed for the first time of the sacrifice that had taken place almost thirty years before. But this dream was even more real than the actual incident, for then his confusion had saved him from his fear, and now all the terror he had not noticed was with him as a faceless man chained him to a great rock and held a knife against his neck. He felt the blade poised to press down when the sun emerging from behind a cloud blinded them both, and at the same time they heard the frantic honking of a goose whose gray and white feathers had become entangled in the thorns of a nearby bush. It was then that the fierce and silent man, whom Isaac now knew was his father, put down the blade and pulled the bird free from the thorns and berries, and as he brought it back Isaac saw how it struggled in his hands. Then, when the goose was pressed firmly to the rock, Isaac watched as his father pulled back the white throat and drew the blade. He saw especially how white was the neck and how cleanly the blade cut through. At last Abraham put down the blade and unbound his son and they embraced. It was then that Isaac opened his eyes, felt the arms of his wife as she tried to wake him, and heard her whispering that the child was about to be born.

When Isaac understood he sat up in bed and hurried from the room to wake the midwife who had been living with them for almost three weeks. Two hours later Rebecca gave birth, first to one son and then to another, the first who was hairy, his skin red, and the second who came forth with his hand on his brother's heel. Isaac found himself fascinated as he watched the midwife wash the infants in warm water. The first son, whom they came to call Esau, was born with an umbilical cord that was dark purple, the color of blood. But his second son, whose name became Jacob, had a cord that was soft and white as pure wax. It was this perfectly woven rope that Isaac found most intriguing, for reasons he could not comprehend. And he sensed a strange terror as he unsheathed a knife and drew the blade to sever this last link between what was and what will be. For it was then the dream of that night came back to him, and he saw in the same instant how the hands of his father had held down the goose, and how the sharp blade had cut across its neck, soft and white, like the severed cord he held in his own hands.

Isaac

by Michael Strassfeld

The dream—I am lying looking up, and at first I see the knife, long and cold, reflecting the light of the dawn, its brightness hurting my eyes. Then I see the arm, long, hairy, gripping the knife tightly, powerfully; the arm is taut but steady, strong but true. There is something admirable about the arm.

For a long time, I cannot see the face, it is hidden in the brightness of the knife, though at times a shadow flickers through the light.

Then the face becomes clearer, it is familiar, very familiar, but just as I am about to shout aloud my recognition, the face changes and becomes that of an ugly animal—a ram.

The knife descends, I wake up screaming.

This dream is an evil omen. But of what? Of my death? It is true that I feel my age, that I have had a long, hard, and yet uneventful life. I want to enjoy my remaining days surrounded by my wife and my sons. I thought to escape the dream but instead it occurs more frequently now than ever before. What does it mean?

If it foretells my death, then I should bless my children, now, while I still live. Esau, my firstborn, shall by right of birth be doubly blessed. Though I have tried to hide this, I have always felt inexplicably drawn to him, my hairy hunter, more than to Jacob. Esau is a good son who tries to please. I wish he would spend less time at the hunt, each morning going out with bow and arrow, each evening bringing home the day's kill; though I must confess of late a growing fondness for venison stew—a treat for an old man.

Jacob is more like me; he is quiet, studious, and a little overshadowed by his older brother. He should be more aggressive, but the rigors of life will teach him that he must wrestle with the woes of reality in order to prevail in this world.

Well, listen to the ramblings of an old man; let me call Rebecca, who has been my eyes since I've become blind, and tell her to send Esau to fetch venison over which I will bless him.

Isaac

by Barry Holtz

Now in old age, quiet in his tent, eyes dim, lost in reverie, he turns and hears the untroubled steps of his elder son trudging toward the open air, red body (color of stones the father can barely see) made redder still by sun and wind, pursuit of game and calm unworried sleep on stone and desert sand—common pleasures of a common man—pure desire, pure response, the uncomplicated rest of the simple.

Isaac, the sightless one, smiles—his keen ear discerns the heavy step of this hunter loaded down with the tools of his animal trade. The taste of game in the old man's mouth, the satisfaction with this, the chosen son (the inheritor by birth who walks with heavy, but unworried step); his mind slips back to darkness, to peace, the calm repose of his later days.

Clatter from the next tent startles him, sounds of cooking—at work, his wife Rebecca, perhaps, or even the boy, the other son, the white-skinned one, learning at his mother's side the deceptive acts of womanhood, of stirring, ladling, boiling the brew, fiery potions that inflame the brain, fulfill desire with a wave of the hand, potions that could calm an old man's pain, lift an enormous rock from a well, deceive appointed order of heaven and hell.

Unnerved, excited now, the terrible future before his eyes, his mind returns to an unescaped past, decades back to his father's home, the unforgotten journey, the climb alone; he, the quiet son atop the silent hill, knife upraised in his father's hand, the cloud, the whirling madness of divine command—"Again? In this generation too?" he shouts, eyes open, the unchanging darkness before him.

Anxiously seeking a shape, a form, his mind grasps for Esau, Esau alone in the open air—unafraid, a part of it—his young, hairy body red, blending into stone and animal worlds—part of the wild, safe from all but natural terrors, his life defined by taste and smell, the hunt, the thrill of simple mastery. Isaac falls back assured. Recalling the power of his blessing and this the rightful inheritor, the son who smells of land and dew, he smiles—it is certain, on the elder the blessing will fall. The crooked son, deceiving with his cookery, has stolen but a birthright, and not the generations. The future lies in Esau's image, destiny on his red shoulders. A vow escapes those ancient lips: "He may deceive the birthright, that sullen, quiet one, but never the blessing, my blessing never." And calmed, he sinks deep into innocent sleep.

The Tale of the Ram

by Rabbi Tsvi Blanchard

Reb Zvi said: "All the hidden things in the universe are hidden together in one small back section of Heaven. There the Messiah waits for the time when he is to come. There also live all of the other great hidden things. There lived the ram which was sacrificed in place of Isaac. And when you are together in eternity, what you are at your deepest begins to show. And the ram, in a fit of rage at being locked up in a room for so long, gored the Messiah.

"When he came before the Heavenly Court, the Holy One, blessed be He, said: 'Ordinarily, the first time an animal gores it is considered as if it were an accident. But you are a ram with knowledge and wisdom. You are a ram who is like a person, and a person is always considered responsible for the damage that he does. You have gored the Messiah. This shall be your punishment: you shall be put to death, and it shall occur as soon as possible.' With that the ram was transported to the next sacrifice to be made on the face of the earth. He found himself on Mount Moriah, replacing the boy whose father was no longer going to sacrifice him."

Reb Hayim Elya asked: "How badly wounded was the Messiah?" Reb Zvi replied: "So badly that he will come only when his wound is healed."

Rivka on Mount Moriah

by Laya Firestone

When Eliezer journeyed in search of a wife for Isaac, he came to Aram Naharaim at dusk, stopped with his camels, and had them kneel at the well from which the women drew water. There he prayed for God to reveal the chosen woman: she would be the one willing to draw water, tirelessly, for those who thirsted.

And Rivka drew water for Eliezer and his camels, until all had drunk long draughts and finished drinking. In gratitude, Eliezer knelt before Abraham's God, thanking him for continuing to reveal his kindness. Then he followed Rivka to her father's home, where food and lodging were provided, gifts given, and Abraham's mission told. Upon questioning, Rivka did not hesitate or delay. She simply said, "I will go."

So Rivka traveled to Isaac, entered his mother's empty tent, and rekindled its warm glow. And Isaac loved his wife Rivka and was comforted. For almost twenty years, Rivka spread her branches over him, until he no longer thirsted. He wanted fruit. And he prayed to God for his barren wife who, like a tree standing amidst the fragrance of blossoms, withheld her bloom yet another year.

Spring returned. At last, Rivka's roots spread deep underground, seeking out darker waters. The sap from many seasons spiraled within her, gathering in her womb like countercurrents coupled, the fullness of one part filling the slimness of the other, forming a perfectly intertwined circle. Thus she conceived.

But the swirl within terrified her, as if it were the center of a great abyss. She watched as her outer shape expanded, signifying the mystery mingled within her growing beyond reason. She lost sight of her feet and strained to keep them grounded. The new life struggled within her. She could no longer sleep, nor could she rest. As her body became fuller, she felt herself becoming weightless as an empty shell, combustible as tinder. Dark and light fought furiously within her until she thought the friction would ignite her. "How," she asked the other women, "can I bear this?" The women answered with home remedies, tales of pregnancies, miscarriages, and deliveries. But Rivka was not set at ease. She became volatile. She wished first that she had not conceived, then that she herself had not been conceived.

In desperation, she set out to Mount Moriah. She ascended on the path that Abraham had trod with Isaac, cutting her feet on the jagged stones. As she strained to climb higher, she began to labor, holding on tight to the gnarled and twisted mountain brush. Thus she arrived at the very rock where, years before, Isaac had been bound and a ram sacrificed in his place. The rock was enormous in size and it radiated a timeless quality. She reached to touch it and lost her balance entirely, falling until she lay stretched out, breathless, upon it. She felt herself tied and bound, one knot upon another, and suddenly she could see Abraham's glinting knife. She heaved in pain. And then she heard the voice of the angel calling, "Abraham, Abraham," and she became calm.

She lay on the rock, at length, as time reeled around her. She watched the stars appear, and then the chilling moon. She waited. When the sun finally burst forth, she rose from the rock and sang to God:

> The years have grown in me;
> Like wood rings in the tree
> They've rounded.
> Patterns of winter winds
> Swirled tightly,
> Circles of summer sun
> Spread wide.
> The whorls remain coiled within:

Here—coiled like a spring,
There—extended like an open hand.

I'm getting thicker now.
It takes more than a breeze
To rustle me.
I stand impervious to the rain
And rarely do I chill.
The sun itself must wage battle
To dry or drain me.

Surely I could make a brilliant fire—
I would crackle in a blaze,
Snapping as I burned.
My years consumed would render
A final pile of ashes—
Soft as chalky dust
And caustic.

But don't reduce me to ashes.
Let me rise among the green,
Tall and rooted,
Abundant with seed.
Let me bear fruit,
Let it ripen,
One, and then another,
Until
There will return to earth
What has been turned in me—
The years,
Patterns,
And circles—
To unwind
Endlessly.

And God said to Rivka: "Two will come from you, one stronger than the other. The elder will serve the younger."

Then Rivka descended from the mountain and returned to her tent. She lay down to rest and, for the first time in months, she slept deeply. She dreamed of a storm, thundering in her being, and a violent thrust shook her from within. A torrent streamed down her and she awoke. Her body convulsed with its bittersweet fruit and she watched as her blood-red son emerged, followed by another holding fast on his heel: Esau and Jacob, unwinding from their double coil.

Jacob at the River

by *Joel Rosenberg*

Jacob alone at the river Yabbok. The moon's reflection dances on the blackness of the waters. All is quiet. Work, wealth and procreation of the past three Sabbaths of years sent on ahead. Do they exist, now that they've disappeared beyond the waters? Jacob, self-stripped, stands to his knees in water, searching its crests in vain for his reflection. And the river gleams, obsidian, unyielding—giving back only a twinlike name: Yabbok. Yaakob. Yabbok. Yaakob.

"Surely, I am just like water," Jacob says to no one. "Smooth and devious. I can flow where paths are cut for me. I'm flexible. I bend to serve. I nourish. I create life. I can fertilize, and make things grow. But I can also steal away whatever sits within my grasp. I stay alive only by keeping on the move. I stop and I shall dry up, vanish. I am always on the run. To live is but to run. I live in borders between lands, but I am not a land, only the contours of a land, and even then, not my own land. I have no house. I am no house. The moon is dancing at my knees. She mocks me. I am no one. I am chaos. I am going mad. I am the Empty Space of God. I am the Kings of Edom. Tohu, Bohu, Tihamat, Leviathan, Behemoth and Rahab. *Where have all my labors gone?* They've turned to water, lapping at my knees with the dancing moon, unsaying my name. Yabbok. Yabbok."

Jacob, stripped of kin and wives, of soldiers and of bodyguard, of concubines and servants, animals and wealth, of amulets and godlets, standing empty in the lapping Yabbok, slowly goes berserk. He kicks and thrashes at the water, screaming: "Bless me! Bless me!" He throws his body at the swells and ripples, tumbling and frothing, pounding up explosions of thin water sheets that mingle with the moonlit river-mist, a luminous and radiant halo of pulverized droplets enveloping the raging madman. Yaakob wrestling the churning Yabbok ceaselessly throughout the night, piercing the countryside and forests with the echoing cry "Bless me! Bless me! Give me a name! Give me a name! Bless me! Bless me! . . ."

Some villagers upon a hill beyond the Yabbok's southern shore, hearing these sounds, grow frightened. "A *melammu!* Look at this, a cloud of God! There will be earthquakes, famine, rains held back—or worse: invaders from the North!" But drawing near, they see this play of northern lights give way to human form. It is a madman, thrashing at the river "He is not from here," they tell each other. "He's a stranger. A berserk soothsayer, possibly a prophet or a dervish. Or a beggar, following those caravans of Syrian migrants that passed through a while ago; he's hoping for their table scraps, a coin or two, a quaff of ale. We'd better calm him down, though, he'll wake up the animals and children, the whole place will be a bedlam. Why, the cats are howling up a storm already. Let's go call that huntsman from Seir. You know, that hardy, hairy fellow, he's a match for *this* one, he'll know what to do."

And Jacob goes on pouring all his frenzy at the Yabbok, trying to shape its crests and swells into the letters of the alphabet and into words, to carve out names with fingernails, and shape the flowing stream into a text and into commentaries, but in vain. Into the night he raves, the pieces of the shattered and reshattered moon falling around his legs. He stumbles on a hidden rock, gouging his inner thigh. The cloud of slammed-up sheets of water streaks with red. An edge of pain creeps in the taunts and challenges. "A name! A naaaaame!"

And then, as if by gradual stages, the incessant churning seems to undergo a change. It is slowly interlaced with silences. These grow into a cloak, a mantle of a stillness, almost a straitjacket. The sounds of crickets, chirping birds and barking dogs intrude. The madman feels a long yearned counterweight answering his heaves and thrashes. Hands reach out to grab his wrists and pin them down. The water beads into a thousand moons against the surface of a hairy shoulder, droplets like the eyes of Argus staring back at him. He sees his beard and face—his own—look back at him a thousandfold. He smells the smell of hides, the blood of venison, the taste of leeks and garlic. The waters of the river Yabbok have become a man.

They stand anchored against each other like the two legs of a wishbone, pushing isometrically, moving not north, not south, affixed dead center, lodged against each other in what seems an everlasting impasse. And he sees that he cannot win over him. He touches him upon his inner thigh. He claps the inner thigh of Jacob while he wrestles him. He says: "Let me get out of here; the sun is coming up!" He says: "But I won't let you go until you bless me." So he asks him: "What's your name?" He says: "Jacob." He says: "Your name is not to be called Jacob anymore, but Israel, one-who-fights-the-god. For you have fought with gods and people, and you've won."

Their discourse trades this way amid their unremitting standoff. (In the telling of it, an exchange of pronouns makes it hard to tell who speaks, until the one gives to the other his new name.) Then Israel summons one last question: "Tell me, and what's *your* name?" He says: "Why should you ask my name?" And there he blesses him.

Jacob came to call the place "the Face of God" (Penuel), because, he'd later say, "I've seen God face-to-face, and yet my life was spared."

The sun gleams red upon him as he finishes fording the Face of God. He walks on into Ammon favoring one side—his wounded thigh. No longer prisoner of a double. No more running from his shadow. No more living in the interstices. At last, landed, asymmetrical and aged. Somewhere, not far from here, is home.

The Plague of Darkness
by Dan Jacobson

It had been a day like any other in South Africa. Now that it was over even the indefatigable cabinet ministers, who worked so hard making laws to segregate white from black, put down their papers and rested; devout theologians, who night after night conned their scriptures for texts to justify these laws, closed first their heavy tomes and then their weary eyes; incorruptible judges, who punished the breakers of the law, were able to relax at last. All over South Africa people went to sleep in the usual way. Safe, protected, segregated, the whites stretched themselves out on their beds, and their servants did the same in the backyards of houses or in dormitories on the top of blocks of flats. Other Africans slept in their new, mass-produced huts in the townships around the cities, or in their old hovels of flattened iron, sacking and mud on farms and in shanty-towns.

Watchmen dozed over their braziers on city corners, telephone operators nodded in front of their quiet exchanges, policemen slumped over the counters of their charge offices, maintenance men on mines yawned in brightly lit offices and took their eyes off the dials they were supposed to be watching. The night was cloudless, moonless, starlit, silent on the veld, silent even in the cities, where only an occasional police patrol car moved about with its headlights brushing the empty streets before it, or some lover drove back reluctantly to his bachelor room. Machines clattered and roared in the printing works of the morning newspapers, but long before dawn most of the people who had been working in these offices were asleep too.

The sky lightened slowly. The stars lost their glitter; what had been black before was now gray; long silver streaks appeared in the east, wavered, fell back, sprang forward again; faintly, tenuously, other colors appeared, blue and rose in the sky, brown on the earth. But hardly anyone saw this; not even those whose work usually had them up by that time. Some of them heard their alarm clocks ringing, opened their eyes, saw how dark it still seemed to be and went back to sleep. People working on night shift wondered irritably when their reliefs would be coming, drank coffee from their vacuum flasks, and fell into a doze, and remained asleep, for no one came to wake them. No one could come.

The sun rose clear above the horizon; it shone on the mountains of the Drakensberg and the bald earth of the Karroo; on the mine dumps of Johannesburg and the white coasts of the Peninsula; on the sugar plantations of Natal and the tangled bush of the lowveld; on railway lines, airports, oil refineries, building sites, fuming refuse heaps in the middle of the shanty-towns. The country was revealed, as on every other day, in a strong, clear, unmodulated light.

But the streets, the roads between *dorps* in the country, the dusty double tracks that ran through the veld from farm to farm, all remained deserted. Until, groping, staggering, crawling on hands and knees, shrieking, cursing, praying, men and women emerged from their houses and huts. They tripped down flights of stairs; they clutched at one another in passageways; they stumbled over curbstones and fell into the streets; they bruised themselves against walls, blundered into parked cars; they tumbled out of moving trains onto embankments and into tunnels. Mothers screamed for their children, and children lay in their beds and yelled in terror at the darkness around them; men tore at their eyelids and found that they were open—yet they could not see.

Many people lost their lives within minutes of waking. Switches in factories were accidentally thrown by the fumbling hands of watchmen who had slept, and the machines began to devour the boots and blankets and car bodies they had been making the previous evening, and then began devouring themselves and the unfortunate people who stumbled into them. Men and women plunged to their deaths from balconies; they drowned themselves in their private swimming pools; they gassed themselves in their kitchens, electrocuted themselves in their bathrooms; they were burned in the fires they started; they fell down lift shafts and died in hospital beds because there was no one to attend to them.

As dangerous as those who had lost their sight were the few who had not slept and whom the plague of blindness was slower in striking. Demented by terror, some drove home in their cars and did not stop for the people they crushed in the streets; some clubbed at the people around them, at their clumsy crawlings and clawings; most of them shrieked with a strange kind of relief when they found that they too had suddenly been stricken by blindness. Announcers on the radio, who had earlier uttered appeals for calm that no one had asked them to deliver, were now shrieking obscenities over the air; the telephone exchanges were deluged with calls that went unanswered; over Jan Smuts Airport great jet planes from Europe circled and turned north, unable to land, their pilots unable to make sense of what they heard on their radios.

Yet, considering that within a couple of hours everyone in the country was totally blind, there were relatively few fires, few floods; no gasworks exploded; no trains ran into one another at high speeds; no mines collapsed. A strange calm fell upon particular houses, farms, streets, even on whole towns and villages, as the first terror the day had brought began to give way to exhaustion. Those who were safe groped about cautiously—touching, feeling, calling to one another, resting where they lay or sat. Fewer screams were heard; people clung to one another for company; they sank into the darkness, unable to help themselves, forced to put their trust in it and in each other.

Food was passed from hand to hand, and people drank together at running taps; they echoed each other's prayers; they waited for help from the outside world to come; they repeated to each other the rumors and stories they heard. They comforted each other, sang hymns, huddled together closely, and more closely still, as close as they could get. They sat in great rings in the streets, hands interlinked, or apart in couples that clung to one another; they strained to hear known voices and were grateful for the sympathy expressed in unknown ones.

How long the calm lasted in each place none could say; and no one knew why it would suddenly leave him and his neighbors. Then people shrieked and flailed around them as they had done in the first terrible minutes after waking to their blindness. But, though the calm might leave one group, one street, one *dorp* or town, it passed on to another, which no longer resisted the darkness, but submitted to it patiently. Under thornbushes, on the verandas of houses, in parks and roadsides and beds, men and women welcomed everything soft, gentle, nourishing, delicate that came to them out of the darkness. Much of what they touched, heard and smelled was new to them and yet deeply familiar; so familiar that to all of them it was as if they had experienced this darkness before and dreamed in it of the touch of fingers in their hair, or of the sound of the voices that whispered hoarsely in their ears, or of the smell of sweat and perfume in their nostrils.

Hands caressed faces lingeringly, following contours seen but never felt; people uttered endearments they had not known they could use; outbursts of laughter were followed by sighs, the touch again of hands, lips, legs, bodies. The fulfillment of their longings revealed to them what their longings had always been; sightless, shameless, beyond loss, they gained what they had not known they had missed until it was given to them.

Then, with that sharp crackling sound that a bolt of lightning makes when it is directly overhead and is heard as well as seen, sight returned to them all, in an instant. They were blinded at first by it, as they had been previously by darkness. A great cry of relief rose to the sky, to the sun itself, which stood over the country at high noon. The visitation was over. Men and women got to their feet slowly, their hands across their brows. It was impossible for them to see at once what was around them: each single thing their eyes fell upon seemed to jump separately into its place, as if the world were reassembling itself before their startled eyes. Trees, houses, factories, trains, ironstone *kopples*, pillars, walls, flickered and then were still, in place, standing there as if they had never been lost, never become so many unknown, unidentifiable surfaces and weights.

The dead and injured lay still; the living rose and breathed, hardly daring to blink, lest they should again be plunged into darkness. The cry of thanksgiving rose again and again; and then it died away suddenly, as people saw whose hands they were holding, who it was that had comforted them and whom they had comforted, with whom they had exchanged their entreaties and endearments; as they recognized what the longings were that they had fulfilled in the secrecy given them by darkness. And the cry of relief became momentarily one of regret for what they were losing; then changed into one of fury.

In disgust, remorse and fear, more murders were committed, and more people took their own lives after sight had been restored to them than when they had been in darkness. This last fact was striking proof, the government declared in one of its numerous official statements after the catastrophe, of how necessary it is for the protection of both white and black that the two groups should be segregated from one another even more carefully than in the past. And millions nodded their shamed agreement.

And the Almighty, wearily foreseeing this unwelcome conclusion to the lesson He had intended to give His people in South Africa—a conclusion utterly familiar to Him, in its essentials, from many other times and places—changed His mind, and let the South Africans of all races wake up in the morning with their vision unimpaired, after all. The crowds rose from their segregated trains to work, as on every other day, in the jobs allotted to them by the Reservation of Occupations Act.

In the Wilderness

by Aharon Appelfeld

It grew slowly, like a tree sprouting leaves, snow melting, a body arising and going forth. This spring came after a harsh winter. Fountains gushed forth flooding the soil. It was a cosmos of water, at dawn and dusk clad in most exquisite shades, clean twofold rosiness, a fusing of heaven and earth. The circling mountains in the distance were but auspicious harbingers of approaching days when, if the sun stayed out, one would feel the ground under one's feet again.

It was an early spring sun that shone; its rays were still chilly. At times the wheels would hit gravel, a stump of wood, or hardening soil. It was still too soon to set one's feet down. Black rocks emerged from the water, angry remnants of another eon. Showing above the surface, their contortions took on a familiar human expression: a female head, a body coiled before leaping.

Forms implicit in inanimate objects were here delineated explicitly and turned toward you with a look of primeval wrath.

A vast lake; we were forced to avoid the hills since, like saturated walls, they quaked under alternating heat and cold, and spewed forth huge stones which sank without echo. The topsoil was soft but beneath it were solid layers on which the horse could tread and the wheels turn. The horse would lift his head, survey the surroundings in search of a bit of land which would support his weight, but, since there was no such thing in sight, he dragged on in whichever direction his legs carried him. From time to time a cloud would drift up from the mountains, descend, and hurl its waters down on the plain in an attempt to turn the universe back to winter and the domain of water and lightning. The wagon would stop, and the horse anchor his hooves. Then things changed. The rain stopped, bubbles burst on the surface and you felt that the water was being absorbed. Someone thrust his head out of the wagon and said, "The water is going down." Needless to say, it was an illusion. The wheels showed no real change.

The horse was heading northwards, as the sun indicated; there was no reason for changing direction. The plain revealed no variety; on all sides lay the very same scene.

One day, at nightfall, the horse stopped dead in his tracks. At first they tried beating him, but he held out like an obstinate slave refusing to betray his master. What was the meaning of this halt which seemed to imply that he recognized something? The water was shallow by now and one could see the soil and the rotting roots. There were no clouds on the horizon.

Only later did things become clear. A hidden current was swirling underneath, unperceived by the human eye. These were no stagnant waters, as we had assumed. The thawing mountains replenished them through underground channels, with a rushing flow.

How long did we remain standing by the water's edge? For many days the horse showed no desire to go on. He stood still as though waiting for a sign, and his sunken legs were our measuring stick. Then he started moving. Plants emerged from the water; in the distance they looked as if they were floating, though one knew they had roots attaching them to the soil. The horse would linger, nipping a flower or a leaf. Marvelous blossoms suddenly speckled the landscape. The lake came into its own. Birds hovered overhead. Stems were still below eye level and the horizon was in full view. Itzik climbed down and said, "The water is sinking."

Beautiful days followed. The horse didn't move on and we felt the water trickling through while bits of soil emerged. Startled fish were seen in their last attempt to dart away from the shallow water. Itzik would grab a handful and say, "There are lots of little fish."

The horse was chewing. His calm munching meant that the danger had passed, and now there was nothing for us to do but watch the water's slow trickling. We stood near a rock, a black lump all holes inside. It looked as if only the skeleton was left. But here it was a landmark from which you could see the universe. The *shochet* left the cart; his face was pallid from the long journey. He too sat upon the rock.

God was with us again. Blue and blue ran together, water lilies were blossoming, birds glided in the air, creating in flight a kind of expanding flow. The *shochet* drawing the blade across the fowl's neck looked like a priest offering his sacrifice. We lit a bonfire; smoke rose up spreading in all directions, settled like a cloud and was scattered in the misty night. These were the sights before us; they created expectancy, the joy of solitude, the desire to kneel down and embrace the rock and drink of the water and watch the stalks. The horse stood still and left us standing. For a moment it seemed as though the war had never existed. Bodies were throbbing, mouths let out cries, questions which merged into a chorus of incantations rejoicing at every discovery. The fire was blazing on, the *shochet* made offerings and told us a story about his father who had struggled with the angel of death for many years, until his struggle had become well known. At times he had played sly tricks on the angel, and at times the angel of death had played tricks on him. They had waged war on one another for forty years and at the age of ninety-five the angel had got the better of him.

Now the *shochet* began to speak; all throughout the war they had silenced him but now he began to speak. The water went on sinking; the horse's legs could be seen. He carried his agony silently all the way, as though waiting for a stretch of land on which to lay his body. His legs shed their hair, revealing deep sores. Itzik tore his shirt and bandaged the sores. The horse's face bore no signs of pain. A kind of smile wove itself on his young features. Who will carry us across the sparse green plain? He had a human expression, a self-control that astonished us. He neither moaned nor asked for our help. Occasionally he would turn his head back.

He didn't want to stretch himself out on the wet soil; we didn't make him sit, assuming that he knew what he was doing. He had led us across floods, thrashing his way in the current, and who were we to give advice?

The plants had grown taller, and were bare at their roots. Only now could we examine the damage done by the winter rains. Not a single stretch of land was left unchurned. The soil was completely wrinkled, and looked like a bit of uneven stitching, waves of hardened lava which keep their shape only in a moderate temperature. We felt somehow uneasy, looking at the drying soil that began to block our view. We could no longer see the wide open spaces; swaying stems became an unchanging sight.

Suddenly the horse sank to the ground, his neck sprawled out. Itzik fell to his knees and tried to whisper something to arouse him. What came over Rivka? At the sight of the horse she started crying. All these years she hadn't cried and now tears came to her eyes.

Our horse, that was all we could say; something had been taken away from us. Our legs sinking in the mud could bear no more.

The *shochet* tried to break the silence since something had to be said. There was the cart huddled like a corpse. "That was a horse," said the *shochet*. "That was a horse," said Itzik. Each meant something else. Only the words were the same. "Who will lead us?"—they didn't ask that. It was too frightening a question to be asked.

Plants blocked our way. A stone on which to lay our heads. How did we stay alive?—or perhaps we only imagined that we were alive. From time to time Rivka would raise her head out of the pit as if to testify that we were indeed alive. "After the war . . ." said Itzik, reminding us of the fact. The *shochet* looked about from the top of the rock, his beard fluttering in the breeze. How long did we sit there? Who whispered, prompting us to go on? You couldn't measure our course; it was infinity itself. Distances indicated no changes. Only the gurgling of water was heard from afar. We harnessed ourselves to the cart, the *shochet* carrying the traces on his shoulders, Itzik on the right, Shmil on the left. We assumed it to be a cart, since it had carried us all the way, but we didn't realize that the horse had lent it its life. The horse died and the wagon fell to bits along with it. Its rotten beams started to crumble.

We had to flee the place. Had the horizon been open we would have set out toward it. It was concealed by the bush, which had grown over our heads; only the *shochet* could see beyond it.

"Our horse"—this no longer referred to anything in particular; we had been robbed of something, and the body sensed its nakedness. Only now did we know that a living pillar had walked before us, protecting us all the way. Itzik took off his coat, and we saw that the wound was still festering on his back.

We reached a stream, stripped off our clothes and sat down to rest. "Children," the butcher said suddenly, as though awaiting that moment all along. We were ready to hear a voice, to welcome a breeze that would cleanse our bodies. We sensed that he had something to tell us but he held it back, perhaps fearing discord.

The days were huge. The stream crept on slowly, willows sheltered us, the sun softened the ground. It seemed that the howl would be wrenched from us at any moment, and a rock would roll down the hill.

The *shochet* froze in silence. He probably saw that our readiness was incomplete or perhaps he feared we would turn to idolatry, since there was one who said: a stone. Every object was luminous as though seen for the first time.

Now the days that came were different. The sky grew clearer and higher. There were the sounds of animals and peasants nearby. Itzik took out an axe and sharpened it on the stone. Facing him sat Shmil running his knife over a strap. It was the same as during the days we spent disguised in Count Paritzki's farmyard working with the peasants in the field. And why did we run away from him? The horse pulled us away, and when we wanted to go back we couldn't; it was raining. And what happened to the horse? The horse died. And why did he die? Because he saw that the only choice was to return to Count Paritzki. And why didn't we go back now? Because the horse had misled us. It wasn't the horse; the *shochet* had misled us. He promised us miracles from God in the wilderness, and what did he show us? Rivka misled us; she was scared of the young Count. Itzik and Shmil sharpened their knives, sparks flying. And the *shochet*? He must have seen the clouds gathering, his heart growing numb again.

Come, children, let us pour oil over the stone. As soon as we pour oil, flames will rise. Drop the hatchets and take a wooden dish, because the place is holy. Rivka got up and took the bowl.

Paritzki never existed. You just imagine him to be a landowner. Who ever heard of a landowner taking risks for the sake of a Jew? So who was he? He was a pillar of strength that watched over us. The horse you say; our wise men already dealt with that and said, "A horse goes only where it is told to go."

That was an unforgettable night. Dusk lingered in the sky and stars were about to come out. "Paritzki never existed; he was a phantom. If we annihilate his defiled body we shall see the pure flame." Other things were said which cannot be repeated.

Itzik and Shmil dropped the hatchets and knives and were silent. Their faces were fixed upon the fire. Only Rivka remained standing in the dark. Towards morning the *shochet* kissed our foreheads and said he was requested to leave early. We ran behind but couldn't catch up with him.

Translated from the Hebrew
by Tirza Sandbank

The Third Tablet of the Covenant
by Moshe ben Yitzhak HaPardesan

We learn that Moses remained on the summit of Mount Sinai neither eating nor drinking for forty days and for forty nights. During the day he was instructed in the Written Torah, and during the night he learned the Oral Torah from the mouth of the Holy One Himself. Each day from sunrise to sunset Moses, like one who is called to read from the sacred scroll, stood in awe and read as the Written Torah was revealed, word by word written by the Finger of God upon the two tablets of sapphire glowing with a supernal light even in the midday sun. And the writing rose up before Moses like fire, black as a raven upon white fire pure as snow, curling up as the locks of hair upon the head of the Ancient of Days. And each lock was made of innumerable hairs and each hair was as radiant as the golden glow of the sun. But as the sun set each day, Moses sat as well, and swaying gently to and fro began to learn the Oral Torah from the Mouth of the Holy One Himself.

Now, it is said that the Oral Torah contained not only all the seventy interpretations of each and every letter and word of the Written Torah, but also every question and its answer that every student of the wise would raise in all the coming generations. And even Moses, the greatest of the prophets and the wisest of the sages, could not retain the limitlessness of this teaching. So on the last day, Moses rose before the Holy One and said: "Master of the Universe, I know that it is Thy will that not all of Thy words be written. But the mystery of Thy unwritten word is too great for me to bear. May it be Thy will that these words be written as well." And the Holy One answered: "The words of My Mouth are not to be written as the writing of My Hand, but you are permitted to record the heads of the sections of the words of My Mouth, as a disciple may record the words of his master, so that none of My words shall be forgotten, but may be handed down from you to your disciples and from them to their disciples in every generation." So Moses fashioned a tablet of stone and took up a flint to scratch with his own hands what he learned at night from the Mouth of the Holy One, blessed be He. But as he touched flint to stone, he saw within the tablet the words forming themselves, and each new facet revealed and contained boundless depths, glittering with the distant light of Torah.

Now at the end of the forty days and nights, Moses arose and took up the two sapphire tablets, one in each arm. But the stone tablet of the Oral Law he placed within his *tallit*, next to his heart, and girded his outer garment to begin the descent. But when he approached the camp and saw the Calf and the people rising up to laugh, he was seized with a towering rage, and cast the tablets from his hands. Immediately they crashed to the earth; the burning letters of the Written Torah flew up to heaven and the glowing sapphire was dimmed. Then all was silent, as Moses stood glaring down at the people. But then was heard a distant rumble, and from the heavens a great angel with the head of a bird appeared. And plummeting down with outstretched talons, it plucked the Oral Torah from Moses' heart and slowly ascended back into the heavens.

The Flying Letters

by David Einhorn

Once, long ago, in legendary times, there were two Jewish communities. The first community was ruled by a devilish tyrant who hated all men, especially the Jews. He issued a decree confiscating all the books in the Jewish community and ordered them burnt. He forbade the Jews, under penalty of death, to write or copy any religious works.

The Jews of this community, however, were very devout and very learned. They knew the Torah by heart and continued to teach it to their children by word of mouth. In order that the ritual of taking the scrolls from the Ark should not be forgotten, they fashioned a blank piece of parchment the exact length and width of a scroll, and a blind man who was very learned recited the portion for the week, as if he could see the written words.

The second community lived under the rule of a king that was kind and just. They enjoyed equal rights and privileges with the rest of the population. But the Jews in this community quickly forgot their Torah. Their synagogue remained closed even on the Sabbath. Only once a year, on the Day of Atonement, they assembled in the synagogue to listen to the cantor pray for them and hear him read from the Torah.

On the night before Yom Kippur, the sexton came to the synagogue in order to make it ready for the Holy Day. He suddenly saw the little doors of the Holy Ark open. He watched in silent wonder as scores of alphabet letters flew out from the inner darkness of the Ark, like swarms of angry bees tossed out by a concealed hand. The letters arranged themselves in lines and rows. Like an unfurled fiery scroll, they flew out through the open window and disappeared in the dark blue sky of the night.

"The Torah has abandoned us!" the sexton cried with terror in his voice.

"No, it is you who have abandoned the Torah," a voice from the Ark answered.

On that Yom Kippur day when the scrolls were taken from the Ark and unrolled before the assembled congregation, the worshipers were horrified to see the white parchment blank, as though nothing had ever been written upon it.

On that same day a miracle happened in the synagogue of the oppressed Jewish community. When the Jews took out their blank scroll and unrolled it, they were amazed to see that the white sheets were covered with letters and lines. Every letter was in its place. Not one was missing. The blind reader suddenly regained his sight and joyfully read the Torah to the whole congregation.

Sometime after that Jews from the first community visited the second community. They told their more fortunate brothers how hard life was under the rule of the tyrant. They also told them about the miracle that had happened in their congregation. It was then that the Jews who lived in the second community realized where the letters of their Torah had disappeared.

They brought their persecuted brothers to their community and established a great and famous college that produced many noted and distinguished scholars. And the city became known to all Jews throughout the world as "The Second Jerusalem."

Translated from the Yiddish
by Gertrude Pashin

The Chest of Herbs and the Golden Calf
by Martin Buber

Since ancient times there stood in the city of Rome a mighty tower. This tower was protected by seven iron portals ranged one before the other, and each was secured with many strong and ingenious locks. It had always been the custom, as far back as anyone remembered, for each king on the day of his coronation to have a new lock placed beside all the others on the seventh and outermost portal. This usage was so old and had been maintained by so many generations that its meaning had gradually slipped out of memory.

It happened then that the Emperor died, and all the great leaders repaired to council to choose a new ruler. There was one deemed worthy by all, and the leaders addressed him: "Sire, it is the wish of the people that you rule over us."

He made answer: "As you see, I stand prepared to do whatever you desire. I must, however, make one condition upon which I will consent to assume the burden of the crown. You must give me written assurance that your will and the will of the people shall submit without resistance to my first imperial command."

They were much afraid and asked, "What is it you intend to impose on us?"

"I will say nothing further until I have your written assurance."

Then the leaders held counsel, and it was decided to do what their newly chosen Emperor required. Thereupon they raised him to the throne and placed the crown on his head. The next day he summoned the leaders and addressed them in this manner: "What I require of you is not a very great thing. I desire to see what is within the old locked tower with the iron portals. Therefore, let the gates be opened."

When the leaders heard this, they cried out in fear, "Oh Sire, what you command seems a most grave undertaking. Many were the kings that ruled this city, yet none ever thought to open the tower. It has ever been the first act of each new king to place a new lock on the outer gate, that new dignity might be lent to this ancient mystery. Your curiosity seeks to overturn a shrine honored for a hundred generations. We are afraid. Some pestilence may issue from the open gates and spread through the city."

"Save your words," said the Emperor. "It only remains for you to open the tower, that I may enter and see what is within."

The smiths of the city were summoned, and after much effort the gates came open. While people and council stood fearfully aside, the Emperor summoned his courage and was the first to enter. Soon leaving behind him the few who had dared to follow, he wandered alone from chamber to chamber, searching every room and passage and finding all empty until he came at last to a small cell in the depths of the tower. There, glittering in the dim light, stood a chest wrought of solid gold and inscribed with an indecipherable seal. When the Emperor raised the lid, waves of subtle odor suffused the air. The chest was laden with all manner of herbs that cover the earth, both highland and lowland, and all as green and ripe with mounting sap as when the hand reaching into the soil had plucked them from the earth's womb. Astonished, the Emperor fell to marveling: "How is this possible! These herbs have had neither light nor sustenance these last thousand years, and yet they are as fresh as on the day when the sun lured them from the earth's domains." But all around him, there was only silence.

He returned to his men and commanded them to take the chest upon their shoulders and bear it to the palace. Presently he sent a messenger into the city to summon all the servants of the gods, the mages and the augurers. When they were gathered before him, the Emperor spoke:

"It is my urgent desire to know by what secret these herbs live, that have endured in freshness this last millennium in the old locked tower. If you fail to satisfy me in this, you will have sealed your deaths."

They replied, "Long live our lord, the Emperor! May he grant us of his mercy some short respite, that we may examine what is set down in the old writings and, if that does not suffice, scan the heavens to see what they reveal."

The Emperor said, "You shall have the course of a single moon."

Each day they buried themselves in the old scripts, and at night raised their eyes to consult the stars. On clouded nights they listened to the voices of the water. But they were unable to find an answer anywhere, and their days were spent in vain. On the last day of the period of grace, all the people abandoned their customary labor and occupations and gathered beside the seers. All gave themselves over to fasting, and their prayers rose toward the gods.

At this time there lived in the city of Rome a man who had seen a century pass within his lifetime. He had seven sons who were greatly respected for their wisdom and held in honor by the multitude; they belonged to the highest order of the priesthood. But every morning, before concerning themselves with their daily affairs, they took their way to the house of their aged father, where they greeted him and received his blessing. On this last day of the month of grace, however, for the first time in his old age, he found himself completely alone. It was not till evening, when the sons had returned from the council, that they gathered around him. "My sons," he said, "what made this day different from all the others? Why did you not follow your good custom and come to me as usual?"

"Father," they said, "we cannot answer. We are overcome with sorrow. This night we must leave you alone to your old age."

When their father heard this, he stared at them intently, and his gaze seemed to pierce their souls. "Tell me the whole story," he commanded. Then they told him of the chest found in the locked tower, of the Emperor's demands, and of the fate that awaited them. The old man spoke: "If this is what troubles you, there is nothing to fear. The secret is known to me, and tomorrow at sunrise, if you will take me to the Emperor, I will reveal it to him." Then the sons fell at his feet; they kissed his hands and exclaimed, "Bless you, father. You have saved our lives."

The next morning they bore the old man on their shoulders to the palace and led him into the throne room. "Sire," they said, "it was your desire to understand the secret of the herbs. We have come that your desire may be satisfied."

Then the old man addressed the Emperor. "My lord," he said, "if you will incline toward me—I know this matter thoroughly and how it has been handed down from antiquity. Once there was a king over Rome of the race of Eliphas, the son of Esau. It was he that built the tower and girdled it with seven iron gates. He ordered the golden chest to be placed within and had the chest filled with sixty myriads of different herbs, one for each of Israel's six hundred thousand souls. Over the chest he intoned this curse: 'The while these herbs are fresh and green, let Israel flourish; but when these herbs go dry, let the bough of Israel wither and be razed from the earth.' Then he locked the chest in the deepest and innermost recess of the tower and caused the outer gates to be shut, that no one might gain entrance to the herbs to water them, that no grain of earth might give them sustenance and no breath of air penetrate the dark depths of the tower to warm them. He then ordained that each of his successors who ruled in Rome after him place a new lock on the seventh and outermost gate. In this manner he thought to wither the herbs and raze Israel from the earth. But, as you see, his magic was powerless. After a thousand years without food or light, the herbs continue to flourish. Now, Sire, if you will incline but a little more closely, I will reveal the last secret.

"One of my ancestors, who was a wise man and a mage and had traveled the length and breadth of the world, had occasion to pass through the land of the Jews and traverse the ruins of their cities. He wandered day and night through that country's desolate stretches, when one night his journey was stayed by a profound darkness. It was one of those nights when the unearthly hold dominion over the elements and tolerate no mortals. He sought refuge in a deep, deserted cave and lay down on the bare floor to rest.

"But no rest came to him. The earth trembled, and he heard far beneath him in the depths of the cliff and high above him in the air sounds as of a dialogue of spirit voices. He heard a laugh that caused his heart to quake, and then he heard the voice of the mountain spirit say, 'Behold that train of crowned shades fleeing restlessly as if driven from cliff to cliff. Those are the dead kings who, while living, sought to guard the tower in which Israel's fate is locked. Let us laugh at the fools. Their efforts were in vain and must ever remain so, for there is but one way that the people of Israel can be razed from the earth: if the Jews do ever celebrate the night of their deliverance over the chest containing the six hundred thousand herbs, then the golden calf demon that they worshiped on the way out of Egypt will be reborn from the vital essence of the herbs and, having long awaited his return to life in the invisible realms, will acquire mastery of the world and destroy Israel. But this cannot happen while the chest is protected by seven locked gates.'

"Thus spoke the voice of the mountain spirit. The other made answer, and the voices discoursed tenderly of the banished children of the desolate land. In this manner the wanderer spent the night. When he left the place at daybreak, he encountered two shepherds driving their herds up the mountain. When they saw him they recoiled in fear, and one said to the other, 'Behold the stranger who has slept in the cave of the prophets.'

"When my ancestor grew old and sensed the departure of his soul, he entrusted the secret to his eldest son, and he in turn to his. In this way I heard it from my father. Now, Sire, you and I are the only ones who know it, since I have not yet confided it to any of my sons."

When the Emperor had heard the old man's words, he rewarded him suitably and sent him home. Then he commanded his servants to summon the most skillful goldsmiths and metal workers in the city. He showed them the chest he had discovered in the tower and ordered them to construct another that would be identical in size, shape and beauty of workmanship. After enjoining them to silence on penalty of their lives, he supplied them with all the gold they would need and gave them a secluded part of the palace in which to work. It was not long before they were finished and brought the chest to the Emperor. He filled it with precious stones and riches of all sorts, and dispatched a servant to summon the Chief Rabbi of the city. When he arrived, the Rabbi was received with great honor by the Emperor, who dismissed all of his retainers so that he and the Rabbi were left completely alone.

Then the Emperor addressed the Rabbi: "As you know, it is not long since I assumed power. I know full well that there is no loyalty to be found among my subjects and allies, who only await the hour to rise against me that they may destroy my power and seize my possessions. Therefore I will reveal to you a thing that must remain a secret between us. This chest is filled with all the gems and valuables I could gather. You will take them into your house and keep them in your possession until I require them. I cannot tell what the next day may bring." Then he opened the chest and showed the Rabbi that it was filled with riches and said, "Keep this chest with you always, and be ever watchful of it. Whatever your momentary occupation, you must keep it beside you. Let it serve as your desk, your bed, your board. As you have seen, it contains all my wealth; I will one day require it of your safekeeping."

The Rabbi answered, "I accept the Emperor's trust and will do what he commands." And that night the Emperor sent a golden chest to the Rabbi's house which was really the chest with the herbs.

The Rabbi placed it in his study, and from that time on it was his desk, his bed and his board. At the Passover feast he would use no other board for the Seder. When the Rabbi stood and raised his glass to begin the blessing, "This is the feast of the Lord . . ." he heard, of a sudden, a voice cry out with great urgency, "Praised be the true Judge! There is something impure in the house." The Rabbi was shocked and fell silent, but then he thought, "What if this is only some trick of my senses?" He took up the goblet once more and began the blessing. Again a great voice cried out, "Praised be the true Judge! There is something impure in the house." But the Rabbi did not heed the voice and continued with the blessing. He emptied the goblet and leaned back among the cushions, but before he could raise the unleavened bread, the voice echoed fearfully, "Praised be the true Judge! There is something impure in the house." At this they all rose trembling, and the Rabbi's sons cried, "Father, how long will you continue to ignore this?" The Rabbi and his family searched the house thoroughly, but they were unable to find anything that was impure and did not know what to do. The Rabbi dispatched a servant to summon all the important men of the congregation and invite them to his house.

The Rabbi received his guests with these words, "This night I would have you do me the honor of celebrating the Seder with me."

"We are greatly pleased to do what you wish," they answered and sat down around the chest to begin the Seder with the Rabbi. Once more the voice called out its warning in tones whose resonance shook the house to its foundations. "You have all heard it," said the Rabbi. Each one took a candle and they searched every room but it was all in vain. They could find nothing impure or leavened. At length the Rabbi overcame his fear and told his guests, "We have searched throughout the house and found nothing. There is but one place left—the chest upon which we are eating."

Then, because he believed the voice, the Rabbi told his guests how the chest had come into his possession. He raised the lid, and clouds of incandescent and breathtaking vapors surged from the chest so that they were nearly overcome. Wave after wave of new vapors poured into the room, twisting and turning and engulfing each other until they finally began to congeal into a single mass. Before the eyes of the assembled rabbis, there arose a creature of horrible aspect, somewhat like the image of a calf but with the wings and fangs of a monstrous bird of prey. The creature hovered trembling in the air, transparent and seemingly incapable of reality. Its eyes were formless liquid fires and its breath a mist of ice and cloud.

The company was amazed and asked themselves, "What punishment has God in store for us? Why has He visited this image of terror upon us on this holy night?" But the Rabbi began to address God with forceful and eloquent words, and his soul was lifted up in prayer and tears. Then a voice descended from heaven and said, "Let the Rabbi write the Holy Name upon the brow of this creature. Let him write the Name on its heart and on its feet, and the creature will perish." The Rabbi drew the Holy Name upon the creature's brow, and its head sagged weakly to one side. He wrote the Name on its heart, and it ceased to breathe. He wrote the name on its feet, and it crumpled before him. Then, rising like a cloud, it disappeared into space. The company was overcome with great joy. But the Rabbi said, "This is a day of tidings. Go in peace, each to his own home." Then each one went to his own home and joyfully made the Seder. Their happiness was so great that no sleep came to them, and they spent the whole night waking like the wise men at Bene-Berak.

In the early morning the Emperor's men came for the chest. When the Rabbi appeared in the palace with the Emperor's servants, the ruler rushed forward and raised the lid. The herbs had put out buds and shoots and were fresher than before. The Emperor was amazed and demanded, "Was this chest opened?" Then the Rabbi told the events of the night.

When the Emperor heard, his soul was humbled.

Translated from the German
by David Antin

A Tent of Dolphin Skins
by Rabbi Marc A. Gellman

> *And make for the tent a covering of*
> *tanned ram skins, and a covering of*
> *dolphin skins above.*
>
> (Ex. 26:14)

When the children of Israel escaped from Egypt, the dolphins of the Red Sea were waiting for them, chirping with happy dolphin sounds, and splashing the blue waters of the Red Sea with their flat tails.

Suddenly the people heard the terrible sound of Pharaoh's great army chasing them from Egypt. Long spears clanking, and horses' hoofs pounding the dry earth as they pulled the war chariots with the metal wheels and the pointed hubs. "We are trapped!" they screamed, "If we go back to Egypt, Pharaoh and his great army will kill all of us." About this the people were absolutely right. "If we go forward we will all drown in the Red Sea." But about this the people were quite wrong. Moses raised his arm and God split the Red Sea right down the middle, so that two huge walls of water stood straight up with a narrow path of dry Red Sea bottom in between.

The sight of the Red Sea split in half was amazing and confusing to the children of Israel, but can you imagine just how amazing and confusing it was for the fish? The fish would be swimming along, minding their own business, when suddenly they were in midair—which is nowhere—if you're a fish! Fish, fish, and more fish just kept plopping through the wall of water and flopping around on the dry hallway of the bottom of the Red Sea. The dolphins tried to save their friends the fish. They swam quickly along the edge of the walls of water chirping a warning, in Fish, "Don't go there!" But very few fish were as smart as the dolphins and many just kept swimming, right into the air. Some asked, "Where?" But by the time they asked, they were already there—in midair—which is nowhere—if you're a fish. Many fish flopped to death, but some of the smarter fish listened and were saved.

Meanwhile, the children of Israel and their herds and their flocks and their wagons had started to walk down the hallway of dry Red Sea bottom between the two huge walls of water. This presented another problem for the kindly dolphins. Occasionally one of the sheep or goats would wander through the walls of water and find themselves at the bottom of the Red Sea—which is nowhere—if you're a sheep or a goat. So the dolphins would gently nudge them back through the wall of water onto dry land.

When the great army of Pharaoh arrived at the Red Sea, they too were amazed and confused. The Pharaoh did not remember the Red Sea as having a hallway of dry land right down the middle, but when he saw the children of Israel and their flocks and their herds and their wagons almost across to the other side, he ordered his army to chase them and kill them. This presented the kindly dolphins of the Red Sea with still another problem. In addition to warning the fish about swimming into the air, and keeping the flocks from wandering into the water, the dolphins also tried to slow down the great army of Pharaoh. They would flick their tails through the walls of water over the army and cause such a shower that the dry Red Sea bottom turned to mud, and the mud clogged up the heavy wheels of the war chariots, and the great army of Pharaoh got stuck.

God warned the dolphins when the walls of water were about to collapse, but they did not listen. They just kept warning the fish, nudging the sheep and goats, and flicking water on the army of Pharaoh. Suddenly the walls of water came crashing together and the Red Sea was whole again. But many dolphins were pulled down, down, down, to the bottom of the Red Sea. Down onto the sharp spears of Pharaoh's spear carriers, down onto the sharp pointed hubs of Pharaoh's war chariots.

The next day, among the junk of Pharaoh's army which washed ashore, many dead dolphins were found. The children of Israel complained to Moses, saying, "This place stinks! Let's get out of here now!" But God commanded Moses to gather the dolphin skins so that they might be sewed together to make a large cover for the golden box which would hold the holy words which would be given in the middle of the desert of Sinai. God hoped that when people saw the tent of dolphin skins, they would remember that they did not leave Egypt and become a free people without a lot of help from the dolphins.

When the children of Israel left the Red Sea and walked into the Sinai desert, the dolphins of the Red Sea were waiting for them, chirping their happy dolphin sounds, and splashing the blue waters of the Red Sea with their flat tails.

The Death of Moses
by Franz Werfel

When Moses on his mountain saw that the verdict of the court had been reached about him, he donned sackcloth and ashes, drew a small circle around himself, stood inside it, and said: "I shall not move from this place until the verdict has been annulled."

And he fasted and began a great praying and imploring, so that the foundations of heaven and the orders of creation quivered and quaked. And from this prayer, a tempest came over heaven and earth, so that both thought that the Lord's will had come upon the world to smash it and renew it. Then the heavenly voice thundered: "God's will has not yet come to smash and renew his world."

What did God do? He summoned Achzesiel before his countenance, the angel ruling proclamations, the herald of the heights, and he said to him: "Hurry down, herald, and have them close the gates of the heavenly fortress, for a man's prayer is sounding up to me mightily."

And he sent after the herald three serving angels: Michael, Gabriel, and Sagsagel, who had gone out before the man's prayer. For Moses' prayer was a cutting, dreadful sword, and nothing could hold before it.

And in that hour, Moses spoke to God:

"Lord and king of the world, You have chosen me that I may teach Your people, and my work and effort are not concealed from You. You know the bitterness and patience that I sacrificed to You until I erected Your Law and established Your commandment in their souls. I did all this, and, full of solace, I thought: As I have seen them in the desert, in wandering and torment, so shall I see them in their ownership and happiness! Just look: Under Your festive sky, they move in scores and build bridges to the blessed valley. And You speak the word to me: 'Thou shalt not cross this Jordan.' My Lord, do not smash Your Scriptures in me, in which You say: 'On his day shalt thou reward the worker for he is poor, and his soul yearns for it, and let not the sun go down upon it, so that he may not cry to the Lord and so that you may not become sinful!' And should this be the compensation for the worker Moses after forty years of effort before they became a loyal and holy people?"

And while Moses thus spoke to God, the grimmest and most wicked of the angels, Samael, the head of the Satanhood, was waiting for Moses' death. He said: "When will the hour come when Moses is gone and I descend and call for the soul of the man of whom it is said: 'Never in Israel shall there be a prophet like Moses, who knows the Eternal One face to face'? When will Michael, my radiant brother, and I laugh in my triumph?"

This was heard by Michael, the clear angel, next to the Lord, and he said: "What, you blasphemer laugh and I weep! Do not delight! I fell, but I stand up again, and now I sit in darkness, but the Eternal One is my light."

Now the final hour was broached for Moses. And he threw himself down and prayed to God: "Lord, my king: If I am not permitted to cross into my land Israel, which I see before my eyes, then remove the shining of dignity from my head, remove from me the Moses who was a leader and a general of Your will, and leave me here, so that I may live in this world and not die!"

God's voice then went to Moses and replied:

"If I do not kill you in this world, how shall I bring you alive in the next world?"

The holy man now beat his breast more wildly and began to plead: "Lord, my king, if You will not allow me to go across to the Land of Israel and I may not even live in these mountains as a poor charcoal burner, then let me be like a forest animal, trotting through the preserves, so that I may eat herbs and drink of the waters! I only want to live and breathe and enjoy the world!"

God then spoke a word, and it meant:

"Enough!"

And Moses bit into the earth and raged against the ground and roared: "I want to be a bird, reeling through the four areas of heaven, and through the sunset I return home, weary, to my nest! And if You do not grant me this, then let me be the stupid grass on the shore or the motionless stone in the gap. Only let me live!"

God then repeated the same word:

"Enough!"

And Moses held his peace and bowed, seeing that nothing could save him from the road of death. . . . And he said: "A rock untottering He stands there. His works have no flaw. A God without falsehood, just and straight is He."

After saying this, he took a scroll and wrote the Name of God upon it, and while he was writing, the deadline came and the beginning of his dying.

And God sent out His serving angels Gabriel and Michael to get the soul of Moses. But they beat their wings about their faces and turned away.

The Lord then sent dreadful Samael to get the soul of Moses.

Samael rejoiced and armed himself fiercely and girded himself with the sword of terror and wrapped himself in the cruel cloud. Thus did he descend.

But when he saw Moses sitting there and writing the Name of God and resting in a measureless brilliance, which spread out from him like an angel, the devil trembled and grew weak.

But Moses had felt him coming and leaped gloriously out of his flame and said:

"What do you want, blasphemer?"

"Your soul," replied the shivering Satan.

"You shall not get my soul, you have no power over me, I am the strongest of all dwellers of the world."

"What does your strength consist in?" cried Samael.

And Moses replied:

"On the day I was born, I spoke to my father and mother and I could walk instantly, and I was never suckled with any milk. And at three months,

I prophesied from the Law, which was lent to me from the fiery flame, and I went out and entered the palace.

"At eighty, I performed signs and wonders in Egypt and split the sea and led my people through it.

"The bitter water I turned into sweet, and I slew the kings of the giants, Sichon and Og.

"From God's right hand, I received the Law in fire, and at the peak of the world I ordered the sun to stand still and the moon, and I struck them with this staff and brought them down. Go away, Satan, what can you do against me?"

And Moses struck the blasphemer with his staff, so that he howled and fled.

Now, only one moment was left for Moses, and the heavenly voice announced the end of his dying.

"Lord of the world," Moses said to God, "remember the bramble bush and the forty days and forty nights of Sinai, and do not deliver me into the hand of the angel of death."

And the heavenly voice said: "Do not be afraid, I myself will take care of you and your funeral." Then God and His seraphim descended from the highest heavens. The angels bedded Moses on Bussus and lifted him a bit, so that he rested across from the Land of Israel. In this hour, God called the soul with a sweet voice: "My daughter, one hundred twenty years were ordained for you to abide in this body. Come and do not tarry."

And the soul replied, sweet and soft: "A hundred and twenty years I was permitted to dwell in this pure body, and there is no bad smell on it, no worm and no decay. I love it; let me remain."

"Leave, soul," said God. "You will live by my throne and among my hosts."

"Lord of the world," said the soul even more softly, "I have never touched a woman since you appeared to me. I beg you, let me stay in this body."

God kissed him and took the soul from his mouth with that kiss. And God wept and said:

"Who shall rise for me against the wicked?

"Who shall stand for me against the evildoers?"

Translated from the German
by Joachim Neugroschel

BOOK II
APOCRYPHAL
THEMES

The Royal Messenger

by Rabbi Nachman of Bratslav

The king had sent a letter to a wise but skeptical man, who, in his faraway province, refused to accept it. He was one of those men who think too much, who complicate their lives by complicating small things. He couldn't understand, not in the slightest, what the king might want of him: "Why would the sovereign, so powerful and so rich, address himself to me, who am less than nothing? Because he takes me for a philosopher? There are more important ones. Could there be another reason? If so, what reason?"

Unable to answer these questions, he preferred to believe the letter a misunderstanding. Worse: a fraud. Worse yet: a practical joke. "Your king," he said to the messenger, "does not exist." But the messenger insisted: "I am here, and here is the letter; isn't that proof enough?" —"The letter proves nothing at all; besides, I haven't read it. And by the way, who gave it to you? The king in person?" —"No," confessed the messenger. "It was given to me by a royal page. In his name." —"Are you sure of that? And how can you be sure that it comes from the reigning sovereign? Have you ever seen him?" —"Never. My rank does not permit or warrant it." —"Then how do you know that the king is king? You see? You don't know any more than I."

And without unsealing the letter, the sage and the messenger decided to learn the truth once and for all. They would go to the end of the world, they would question the very last of mortals, but they would know.

At the marketplace, they accosted a soldier: "Who are you and what do you do?" —"I am a soldier by trade and I am in the king's service." —"What king?" —"The one to whom we swore allegiance; this land is his. We are all here to serve him." —"Do you know what he looks like?" —"No." —"Then you have never seen him?" —"Never."

The two companions burst into laughter: "Look at him! This man in uniform insists upon serving someone he has never seen and will never see!"

Further on, they met an officer: yes, he would willingly die for the king; no, he had never had the honor of seeing him, neither from close by nor from afar.

A general; same questions, same answers, clear and precise. He, too, thinks of nothing but to serve the king, he lives only for him and by him; and yet, even though he is a general, he cannot boast of ever having set his eyes upon the king.

"You see?" says the skeptical sage to the messenger. "People are naïve and credulous, and rather foolish; they live a lie and are afraid of the truth."

Retold from the Yiddish and Hebrew sources
by Elie Wiesel

The Menorah

by Theodor Herzl

Once there was a man who deep in his soul felt the need to be a Jew. His material circumstances were satisfactory enough. He was making an adequate living and was fortunate enough to have a vocation in which he could create according to the impulses of his heart. You see, he was an artist. He had long ceased to trouble his head about his Jewish origin or about the faith of his fathers, when the age-old hatred reasserted itself under a fashionable slogan. Like many others, our man, too, believed that this movement would soon subside. But instead of getting better, it got worse. Although he was not personally affected by them, the attacks pained him anew each time. Gradually his soul became one bleeding wound.

This secret psychic torment had the effect of steering him to its source, namely, his Jewishness, with the result that he experienced a change that he might never have in better days because he had become so alienated: he began to love Judaism with great fervor. At first he did not fully acknowledge this mysterious affection, but finally it grew so powerful that his vague feelings crystallized into a clear idea to which he gave voice: the thought that there was only one way out of this Jewish suffering—namely, to return to Judaism.

When his best friends, whose situation was similar to his, found out about this, they shook their heads and thought that he had gone out of his mind. How could something that only meant an intensification and deepening of the malady be a remedy? He, on the other hand, thought that the moral distress of modern Jews was so acute because they had lost the spiritual counterpoise which our strong forefathers had possessed. People ridiculed him behind his back, some even laughed right in his face, but he did not let the silly remarks of people whose judgment he had never before had occasion to value throw him off his course, and he bore their malicious or good-natured jests with equanimity. And since his behavior otherwise was not irrational, people in time left him to his whim, although some used a stronger term, *idée fixe*, to describe it.

In his patient way our man over and over again displayed the courage of his convictions. There were a number of changes which he himself found hard to accept, although he was stubborn enough not to let on. As a man and an artist of modern sensibilities he was deeply rooted in many non-Jewish customs, and he had absorbed ineradicable elements from the cultures of the nations among which his intellectual pursuits had taken him. How was this to be reconciled with his return to Judaism? This gave rise to many doubts in his own mind about the soundness of his guiding idea, his *idée maitresse*, as a French thinker has called it. Perhaps the generation that had grown up under the influence of other cultures was no longer capable of that return which he had discovered as the solution. But the next generation, provided it were given the right guidance early enough, would be able to do so. He therefore tried to make sure that his own children, at least, would be shown the right way; he was going to give them a Jewish education from the very beginning.

In previous years he had let the festival which for centuries had illuminated the marvel of the Maccabees with the glow of candles pass by unobserved. Now, however, he used it as an occasion to provide his children with a beautiful memory for the future. An attachment to the ancient nation was to be instilled early in these young souls. A menorah was acquired, and when he held this nine-branched candelabrum in his hands for the first time, a strange mood came over him. In his remote youth, in his father's house, such little lights had burned and there was something intimate and homelike about the holiday. This tradition did not seem chill or dead. The custom of kindling one light with another had been passed on through the ages.

The ancient form of the menorah also gave him food for thought. When had the primitive structure of this candelabrum first been devised? Obviously, its form had originally been derived from that of a tree: the sturdy stem in the center; four branches to the right and four to the left, each below the other, each pair on the same level, yet all reaching the same height. A later symbolism added a ninth, shorter branch which jutted out in front and was called the *shammash* or servant. With what mystery had this simple artistic form, taken from nature, been endowed by successive generations? And our friend, who was, after all, an artist, wondered whether it would not be possible to infuse new life into the rigid form of the menorah, to water its roots like those of a tree. The very sound of the name, which he now pronounced in front of his children every evening, gave him pleasure. Its sound was especially lovely when it came from the mouth of a child.

The first candle was lit and the origin of the holiday was retold: the miracle of the little lamp which had burned so much longer than expected, as well as the story of the return from the Babylonian exile, of the Second Temple, of the Maccabees. Our friend told his children all he knew. It was not much but for them it was enough. When the second candle was lit, they repeated what he had told them, and although they had learned it all from him, it seemed to him quite new and beautiful. In the days that followed he could hardly wait for the evenings, which became ever brighter. Candle after candle was lit in the menorah, and together with his children the father mused upon the little lights. At length his reveries became more than he could or would tell them, for his dreams would have been beyond their understanding.

When he had resolved to return to the ancient fold and openly acknowledge his return, he had only intended to do what he considered honorable and sensible. But he had never dreamed that on his way back home he would also find gratification for his longing for beauty. Yet what befell him was nothing less. The menorah with its growing brilliance was indeed a thing of beauty, and inspired lofty thoughts. So he set to work and with an expert hand sketched a design for a menorah which he wanted to present to his children the following year. He made a free adaptation of the motif of the eight arms of equal height which projected from the central stem to the right and to the left, each pair on the same level. He did not consider himself bound by the rigid traditional form, but created again directly from nature, unconcerned with other interpretations which, of course, continued to be no less valid on that account. What he was aiming for was vibrant beauty. But even as he brought new motion into the rigid forms, he still observed their tradition, the refined old style of their arrangement. It was a tree with slender branches; its ends opened up like calyxes, and it was these calyxes that were to hold the candles.

With such thoughtful occupation the week passed. There came the eighth day, on which the entire row of lights is kindled, including the faithful ninth candle, the *shammash,* which otherwise serves only to light the others. A great radiance shone forth from the menorah. The eyes of the children sparkled. For our friend, the occasion became a parable for the enkindling of a whole nation. First one candle; it is still dark and the solitary light looks gloomy. Then it finds a companion, then another, and yet another. The darkness must retreat. The young and the poor are the first to see the light; then the others join in, all those who love justice, truth, liberty, progress, humanity and beauty. When all the candles are ablaze everyone must stop in amazement and rejoice at what has been wrought. And no office is more blessed than that of a servant of light.

Translated from the German
by Henry Zohn

The Seventh Millennium
Der Nister

The women spoke in their familiar Yiddish mixed with words of prayer, and told always of the same things, in story form, and mostly about the city of Jerusalem. How for instance a cave had recently been discovered there, and when one entered the cave one walked and walked until one saw some sort of light from far away. And when one came nearer to the site from which the light shone, one came upon a white-gray elder seated at a table over a book. One saw immediately that this was Elijah the Prophet. The proof: near him lay a *shofar* with which to trumpet when the Messiah comes in order to inform the world of the redemption and recall the Jews to Eretz Israel. And when one turned to him and asked: when will the end come? his reply was brief: when the Sabbath will come to the world, the seventh millennium according to the world's reckoning by which we reckon. Well, the story-tellers said, we're almost there: it is now the eve of Sabbath, the sixth millennium, and if we will be worthy, the God-fearing storytellers added, our share will be added on from the unholy to the holy, and the Sabbath will come sooner by virtue of the charity we give with a full hand and joyful heart, and we will have the good fortune to hear the *shofar* sounded by that elder who daily awaits the redeemer who is to come soon, soon, in our time, Amen.

Translated from the Yiddish
by Evelyn Abel

Sabbath in Gehenna
by Isaac Bashevis Singer

On the Sabbath, as is known, the fires do not burn in Gehenna. The beds of nails are covered with sheets. The hooks on which the wicked males and females hang—by their tongues for gossip, by their hands for theft, by their breasts for lechery, by their feet for running after sin—are concealed behind screens. The piles of coals and snow on which the transgressors are flung are hidden by curtains. The angels of destruction put away their fiery rods. The sinners who remain pious even in Hell (there are such) go to a little synagogue where an iniquitous cantor intones the Sabbath prayers. The free-thinkers (there are many of them in Gehenna) sit on logs and converse. As is usually the case with enlightened ones, their topic is how to improve their

lot, how to make a better Gehenna. That wintry late Sabbath afternoon a
sinner named Yankel Farseer was saying:

"The trouble with us in Hell is that we are selfish. Every sinner thinks
only about his own business. If he believes that he can save his behind from a
few lashes by the angel Dumah, he is in seventh heaven. If we could create a
united front, we would not be in need of private intercession. We would
come out with demands—"

When he uttered the word "demands," his mouth began to water. He
choked and puffed. Yankel was and remained a fat man with broad shoulders, a round belly, short legs. He had long hair around his bald spot and
grew a beard—not a kosher beard as the pious in paradise have, but a rebellious one, every hair of which points at revolution. A little delinquent who
braided his long hair in a pony tail tied with a wire he tore out of a bed of
nails asked:

"What kind of demands, Comrade Yankel?"

"First, that the week in Gehenna should not last six days, but that we
should have a four-day week. Secondly, that each villain should get a six-
week vacation during which he should be permitted to return to earth and
break the ten commandments without being punished. Thirdly, that we
should not be kept away from our beloved sisters, the female sinners. We
will ask for sex and free love. Fourthly—"

"Dreams of a chopped-off head!" said Chaim Bontz, a former gangster.
"The angel Dumah is not afraid of your demands and petitions. He does not
even bother to read them. The saints in Paradise use them for toilet paper."

"What do you propose?"

"The angels, like the humans, understand one thing—blows. We must
arm ourselves. Rub out the angel Dumah, storm the court of heaven, break a
few ribs among the righteous. Then we must take over Paradise, Leviathan,
the Wild Ox, the sanctified wine, all the other good things. Then—"

"Arm ourselves?" a petit bourgeois who had fallen into Hell for swindling
cried out. "Where will you get arms in Hell? They don't give us a single
knife or fork. The fiery coals we eat we have to pick up with our naked fingers. Besides, Gehenna does not last longer than a year except for Sabbath
and holidays. I am supposed to end my term on the day after Purim. If we
begin a conspiracy now, the term may be prolonged. Do you know the punishment for conspiring against the angel Dumah?"

"This is the misfortune of us sinners," Yankel Farseer yelled out. "Everyone is only for himself. How about the wicked who will come after us?
Every day new transports arrive. What will happen to them? This year is not
so bad yet, it has twelve months. The next year will be a leap year, all of
thirteen months."

"It is not my duty to worry about all the wicked in the world," replied
the swindler. "I happen to be an innocent victim. All I did was to forge a

signature. I shed ink, not blood. Those who murder, set fire to houses, and cause children to perish in the flames, those who stab and rape are not my brothers. If I were in charge here, I would keep them until the end of the 6,000th year!"

"Didn't I say that every sinner is out for himself?" Yankel Farseer spoke. "If we cannot unite, the angels can do to us as they please. In that case, why the idle talk? Let's play cards and finish out the rest of the Sabbath."

"Comrade Yankel," a sinner with eyeglasses spoke up, "may I say something?"

"Say. Talk doesn't change anything."

"My opinion is that we should concentrate mainly on culture. Before we come with maximal demands like six-week vacations, with sex, and with free love, we must show the angels that we are sinners with spiritual goals. I propose that we publish a magazine."

"A magazine in Gehenna?"

"Yes, a magazine, and its name should be *The Gehennanik*. When you sign a petition, the angels take one look at it and they throw it away, or they blow their noses into it. But a magazine they would read. The righteous in paradise expire from boredom. They are overfed with the secrets of the Torah. They want to know what's going on in Hell. They are curious about our view of the world, our way of thinking, our sex fantasies, and most of all are they intrigued by the fact that we are still atheists. A series of articles, *The Atheists in Gehenna*, would become a smash hit in Paradise. Of course, we would also publish a gossip column and a lot of special Hell pornography. The saints would have something to enjoy and to complain about."

"Silly babble! I'm going to sleep." Chaim Bontz yawned.

"Who is going to do all this scribbling and how will this help us?" asked a sinner with a hoarse voice.

"You don't have to worry about who will do the writing," said the sinner with the eyeglasses. "We have a lot of writers here. I was a writer on earth myself. I was condemned to Hell because I was supposed to be a rabble rouser. Every Monday and Thursday, I changed my opinion. When it was profitable to preach communism I became an ardent Communist and likewise, I preached capitalism when that paid. They heaped accusations against me. But the fact is that I had many readers and they wrote me enthusiastic fan letters. It is true that I changed my opinions like gloves, but were my readers any more consistent? Here in Hell—"

A sinner who looked young and had long hair reaching down to his shoulders asked, "Why publish a magazine? Why not open a theater? We have here a shortage of paper. Besides, it's so hot here that the magazine will catch fire. The righteous are all half blind and don't understand our modern language and are not accustomed to our spelling. My advice is that we should organize a theatrical group."

"A theater in Hell? Who's going to play? And who's going to attend? They punish us day and night."

"We will play on Sabbaths and all holidays."

"Are there any scripts in Gehenna?"

"I have an idea for a play—a love affair between a sinner and a saint."

"What kind of love affair? The wicked and the saints never meet."

"I have thought it through thoroughly. My hero is lying on his bed of nails and screaming. He is an opera singer by profession and so wracked with pain that he breaks out into an aria. She, the saint, hears his song and falls madly in love with his voice. Then—"

"The saints in paradise are all deaf."

"This one happens not to be deaf."

"Well, then, what follows?"

"To be able to meet him, she asks for permission from the angel Eshiel to dress up like a demon and to become one who dispenses lashes in Gehenna. Permission is granted and so the two lovers meet. She is supposed to whip him, but when the angel Dumah looks away, she covers him with kisses and they soon reach a point where they cannot be one without the other."

"Melodrama of the worst kind!"

"What do you want to play in Gehenna—*Migdal Oz* by Mosheh Chayim Luzzato? Our sinners love action. A play like this would give the actors an opportunity to sing a song, to dance, and to make a couple of spicy jokes."

"Assuming that it will work, what would be the result?"

"Theater is the best form of propaganda. It may very well be that the saints and the angels will visit our theater to see our plays. And between one act and the other, we would explain to them our point of view, our situation, and our philosophy."

"Your play is not realistic, and your plan is not realistic. Where will we play—among the piles of coals? The saints will not come here. All day long they are busy with the secrets of the Torah and with munching Leviathan. In the evening they are afraid to leave paradise."

"What are they afraid of?"

"A couple of murderers and rapers managed to escape from Gehenna. They prowl around at night. They have already killed several saints and have tried to ravish Sarah bas Tovim."

"I hear this for the first time."

"Of course, as long as we don't have any magazines, no one is informed about anything. The magazine would give us news and explain—"

"Fantasies, fantasies," called out a sinner who had been a politician on earth. "Culture will not solve our problem and neither will the theater. What we really need is a progressive political party built on democratic principles. We don't need to come out with impossible demands, Comrade Yankel. We should be satisfied with a minimum. I have heard from a very reliable source that there is a liberal group among the angels who are asking for reforms in Gehenna."

"What kind of reforms?"

"They want us to have a five-day Gehenna week. Besides Saturday and holiday, we should be given a week vacation in the World of Illusions. Some of them would request that the nails on the beds of nails should be two millimeters shorter. I was told that there is some change in their attitude towards homosexuality, lesbianism and certainly masturbation. We could do a lot, but we need money."

"Money?" all the sinners called out with one voice.

"Yes, money. What do you know? 'And money answereth all things,' Ecclesiastes has said. If we had money we could achieve everything without revolutions, without petitions, without culture. In Gehenna—as everywhere else—everybody has his price. You are all greenhorns. I know Gehenna from top to bottom and inside out. With money we could even—"

The politician wanted to tell his listeners what else could be accomplished with money in Gehenna, but at that instant the Sabbath ended. The fires leaped up again. The nails on the beds of nails began to glow with heat again. The punishing demons grabbed up their rods and a lashing, and a whipping, and a hanging, and wailing erupted once more. The politician who just spoke about money winked an eye toward one of the older demons and both of them left—where, no one knew. Most probably to play cards and to engage in conversation about some non-kosher Gehenna business.

Translated from the Yiddish
by the author

The Book of Mysteries
by Meyer Levin

When the children of Horodenka ceased to sing, Israel was no longer content to remain in that place. He wandered again, and returned to the town of Okup, where he had been born. There he became the watcher of the synagogue.

The desire for knowledge came into him; and the joy that was given him by flowers and beasts in the forest was no longer sufficient. His mind was afire and thirsty, but his thirst could be quenched only by those waters that had cooled for ages deep in the deepest wells of mystery, and the fire within him was of the sort that burns forever, and does not consume.

The innermost secrets of the Cabbala were for him, and they were only as stars of night against the sun. For to him would be revealed the Secret of Secrets.

The boy lived in the synagogue. But since the time for the revelation of his power was yet far away, he did not show his passion for the Torah to the men of the synagogue. By day, he slept on the benches, pretending to be a clod. But as soon as the last of the scholars blew out his candle and crept on his way toward home, Israel rose, and took the candle into a corner, and lighted it, and all night long he stood and read the Torah.

In another city the Tsadik, Rabbi Adam, master of all mysteries, waited the coming of his last day. For in each generation one is chosen to carry throughout his lifetime the candle that is lighted from heaven. And the candle may never be set down. And the soul of the Tsadik may not return to eternal peace in the regions above until another such soul illuminates the earth.

Rabbi Adam was even greater than the Tsadikim who had been before him. For in the possession of Rabbi Adam was the Book that contains the Word of eternal might.

Though Rabbi Adam was not one of the Innocent souls, he had led a life so pure that this Book had been given into his hands. Before him, only five human beings had possessed the knowledge that was in the Book of Adam. The Book was given to the first man, Adam, and it was given to Abraham, to Joseph, to Joshua ben Nun, and to Solomon. And the seventh to whom it was given was the Tsadik, Rabbi Adam.

This is how he came to receive the Book.

When he had learned all Torah, and all Cabbala, he had not been content, but had searched day and night for the innermost secret of power. When he knew all the learning that there was among men, he said, "Man does not know." And he had begged of the angels.

One night Rabbi Adam arose from his sleep. He walked into a wilderness. Before him stood a mountain, and in the side of the mountain was a cave. And that was one mouth of the cave, whose other mouth was in the Holy Land. It was the cave of the Machpelah, where Abraham lies buried.

Rabbi Adam went deep into the cave, and there he found the Book.

All of his life Rabbi Adam had guarded the secret of knowledge. Gazing into it, he had grown old, and he had come to see with the grave eyes of one who sees to the end of things.

And when he saw himself growing old, he began to ask, "What will become of my wisdom?"

Then he rose, and looked to the Lord and said, "To whom, Almighty God, shall I leave the Book of Wisdom? Give me a son, that I may teach him."

He was given a son. His son grew, and became learned in the Torah. The Rabbi taught his son all that there was in the Torah. And he said, "My son learns well." He began to teach his son the Cabbala. His son was sharp in understanding. But when the boy had learned the secrets of the Cabbala, he asked no more. Then the old heart of Rabbi Adam was weary and yearned for death. "My son is not the one," he said.

Night after night Rabbi Adam prayed to the Almighty that he might be relieved of the burden of knowledge. And one night the word came to him, saying, "Give the Book into the hands of Rabbi Israel, son of Eleazer, who lives in Okup."

Rabbi Adam was thankful, for now he might give over his burden, and die. He said to his son, "Here is one book in which I have not read with you."

His son asked, "Was I not worthy?"

"You are not the predestined vessel," said Rabbi Adam. "You would break with the heat of the fluid."

Then he said to his son, "Seek out Rabbi Israel, in the city of Okup, for these leaves belong to him. And if he will be favorable toward you and receive you as his servant and instruct you in his Torah, then count yourself happy. For, my son, you must know that it is your fate to be the squire who gives into the hands of his knight the sword that has been tempered and sharpened by hundreds of divine spirits that now lie silent under the earth."

Soon Rabbi Adam died. His son did not think of himself, but thought only of fulfilling the mission his father had given into his charge. He deserted the city of his birth and, taking with him the leaves of the Book, went in search of that Rabbi Israel of whom his father had spoken.

The son of Rabbi Adam came to the town of Okup. He wished to keep secret the true reason of his coming, so he said, "I am seeking a bride. I would marry, and live my life here." The people of the town were delighted, and felt greatly honored because the son of the Tsadik, Rabbi Adam, had chosen to live among them.

Every day he went to the synagogue. There he encountered scholars, and holy men, and rabbis. He asked them their names. But he did not meet with anyone called Rabbi Israel, son of Rabbi Eleazer.

Often, when all the others had gone from the synagogue, Rabbi Adam's son remained studying the Torah. Then he noticed that the boy who served in the synagogue also remained there, he saw that the eyes of the boy were bright with inner knowledge, and that his face was strained with unworldly happiness.

Rabbi Adam's son went to the elders of the house of prayer and said to them, "Let me have a separate room in which to study. Perhaps I shall want to sleep there sometimes when I study late into the night. Then give me the boy Israel as a servant."

"Why has he chosen the boy Israel, who is a clod?" the elders asked.

Then they remembered that Israel was the son of Rabbi Eleazer. "He has chosen him to honor the memory of his father, Eleazer, who was a very holy man," they said.

When the boy came to serve him, the son of Rabbi Adam asked, "What is your name?"

"Israel, son of Eleazer."

The master watched the boy, and soon came to feel certain that this was indeed the Rabbi Israel whom he sought.

One night he remained late in the synagogue. He lay down on a bench, and pretended to be asleep. He opened his eyes a little, and he saw how the boy Israel arose and took a candle and lighted it, and covered the light, standing in a corner and studying the Torah. For many hours the boy remained motionless in an intensity of study that the rabbi had known only in his father, the Tsadik, Rabbi Adam.

All night long the boy studied. And when the sunrise embraced his candle flame, he slipped down upon the bench, and slept.

Then the rabbi arose and took a leaf from the holy book his father had given him, and placed the leaf on the breast of Israel.

Soon the boy stirred, and sleeping reached his hand toward the page of writing. He held the page before his eyes, and opened his eyes and read. As he read, he rose. He bent over the page of mysteries, and studied it, and his whole face was aflame, his eyes glowed as if they had pierced into the heart of the earth, and his hands burned as if they lay against the heart of the earth.

When full day came, the boy fell powerless upon the bench, and slept.

The rabbi sat by him and watched over him until he awoke again. Then the rabbi placed his hand upon the boy's hand that held the leaf out of the book. The rabbi took the other pages of the book, and gave them to him, saying: "Know, that I place in your hands the infinite wisdom that God gave forth on Mount Sinai. The words that are in this book have been entrusted only in the hearts of the chosen of the chosen. When no soul on earth was worthy to contain its wisdom, this book lay hidden from man. For centuries it was buried in unreachable depths. But always there came the time for its uncovering, again it was brought to light, again lost. My father was the last of the great souls to whom it was entrusted. I was not found worthy of retaining it, and through my hands my father transmits this book to your hands. I beg of you, Rabbi Israel, allow me to be your servant, let me be as the air about you, absorbing your holy words, that otherwise would be lost in nothingness."

Israel answered, "Let it be so. We will go out of the city, and give ourselves over to the study of this book."

* * *

The son of Rabbi Adam went with Israel to live in a house that stood outside of the town. There, day and night, they were absorbed in the study of the pages that contained the words of all the mysteries.

Israel was as one who feeds on honey and walks on golden clouds. His soul swelled with tranquil joy, and his heart was filled with the peace of understanding. Often, he went with the leaves of the book into the forest, and there, the words of the book were as the words spoken to him by the flowers and by the beasts.

But the son of Rabbi Adam was eaten by that upon which he fed, and yet his hunger grew ever more insatiable. The grander the visions that opened before him, the greater was the cavern within himself. And he was afraid, as one who stands on a great height and looks downward.

Each day, his eyes sank deeper, and became more red.

Rabbi Israel, seeing the illness that was come into his companion, said to him, "What is it that consumes you? What is it that you desire?"

Then the son of Rabbi Adam said, "Only one thing can give me rest. All that has been revealed to me has set me flaming with a single curiosity, and each new mystery that is solved before me only causes a greater chaos in my mind, and a greater hunger in my heart."

"What is the one thing that you desire?"

"Reveal the Word to me!"

"The Word is inviolate!" cried Rabbi Israel.

But the son of Rabbi Adam fell on his knees and cried, "Until I see the end of all wisdom, I cannot come to rest! Call down the highest of powers, the Giver of the Torah Himself, force Him to come down to us, otherwise I am lost!"

Then the Master shrank from him. He said, "The hour has not yet come for His descent to earth."

His companion was silent. He never pleaded with Israel again.

But each day Rabbi Israel saw his face become darker, and his body become more feeble. The hands were weak, and could hardly turn a leaf.

Rabbi Israel was torn with pity for his companion.

At last he said, "Is it still your wish that we name the Giver of the Torah, and call Him to earth once more?"

The son of Rabbi Adam remained silent. But he lifted his eyes to the eyes of Rabbi Israel. They were as the eyes of the dead come to life.

"Then we must purify our souls, that they may reach the uttermost power of will."

On Friday, the two rabbis went to the mikweh, where they bathed in the spring of holy water. From Sabbath to Sabbath they fasted, and when they reached the height of their fast they went again to the mikweh, and purified themselves in the bath.

On the second Friday night they stood in their house of prayer. They called upon their own souls and said, "Are you pure?" Their souls answered, "We have been purified."

Then Rabbi Israel raised his hands into the darkness, and cried out the terrible Name.

The son of Rabbi Adam raised his arms aloft, and his feeble lips moved as he repeated the unknowable Word.

But in the instant that the word left those lips, Israel touched him and said, "My brother, you have made an error! Your command was wrongly uttered, it has been caught by the wind, it has been carried to the Lord of Fire! We are in the hands of death."

"I am lost," said the son of Rabbi Adam, "for I am not pure."

"Only one way is left to us," cried Rabbi Israel. "We must watch until day comes. If one of us closes an eyelid, the evil one will seize him, he is lost."

Then they began to watch. They stood guard over their souls. With their eyes open they watched. And the hours passed. They stood in prayer, and the hours passed.

But as dawn came, the son of Rabbi Adam, enfeebled by his week of purification, and by the long struggle against the darkness of night, wavered, his head nodded, and sank upon the table.

Rabbi Israel reached out his arm to raise him. But in that moment an unseen thing sped from the mouth of Rabbi Adams's son, and a flame devoured his heart, and his body sank to the ground.

All of the knowledge of Power that the Baal Shem Tov ever possessed was contained in the secret book that he had received from Rabbi Adam.

After the Baal Shem had returned from his journey to the Ancient Land, he prepared for his journey to eternity.

Then Rabbi Adam came down to the Baal Shem Tov and said, "You have no more need of this Book. The Book is in your heart."

Rabbi Israel asked, "Who shall have it after me?"

That was the Book of Mysteries that had been given only to seven. It was given to Adam, and to Abraham, to Joseph, and to Joshua ben Nun, to Solomon, and to Rabbi Adam, and to Rabbi Israel, son of Eleazer.

And the eighth one to possess the Book of Wisdom shall be Messiah, Son of David.

The Baal Shem Tov and Rabbi Adam went up into the mountains. They found a great stone. Rabbi Adam touched the stone, and the stone split open. Within the stone, Rabbi Israel placed the Book of Wisdom. Then he touched the stone, and the stone closed.

Angel Rolling the Heavens Together
by Jerred Metz

At the end of time this will happen: when the souls of air, dust, stone, plants, creatures and men stream toward the gate and all the words and sounds and letters signing sounds crown the sky, when everything seeks gate and passage through the sky, in a place of the world, a point in air where no one looked, an angel appears. Other angels surround him—some no bigger than fleas, but white and whose wings beat loud as thunder, some the size of men and women, robust and smelling of work and long flight, some big as stars, showering the sky with threads of light. One angel tears the tongue from a liar's mouth, another buries living sinners in dust, a third drops a ship on a courtyard filled with thieves. But this angel does not move with the other angels toward a distant point singing as they fly. This angel will roll the heavens together and so stands still, his eyes burning, his jaws shut against the strong and growing stink.

Skilled in knots and cloth, a sailmaker or one who coils baskets from plaited straw, he bends to his knees and winds and furls the air. As he furls, he names God from the least name to the most secret and when he speaks the last the world becomes a snail shell, the moon and sun at the rim, the planets and stars clustered in tight swirls at the center. Coiling backward, the angel enters the shell and comes out an eon later, horns on his head, himself a snail now, who drags the heavens slowly toward the Ever Present.

BOOK III
AGGADIC THEMES

The Spider and the Fly

by Rabbi Nachman of Bratslav

Perhaps you think I will tell you everything, so that you may be able to understand my story. I will begin to tell the story.

There was a king who fought a great battle against many nations, and won the battle, and took thousands of prisoners from among all the nations. Every year, on the day of his victory, he caused a great feast to be made; and to the conqueror's festival there came princes and emperors from all the kingdoms of the world. He would have clowns at his festival, to entertain him and his guests with imitations of the different peoples of the world. The comedians would dress themselves in long cloaks, with scarves over their heads, as Arabs of the desert; and then they would appear as Turks, and as Spaniards, and they would make themselves fat as Germans, and they would make fun of whomever they pleased; and naturally they did not forget to put on long beards and to scratch themselves like Jews.

The king sat and watched the clowns, and tried to guess when they were Arabs, or Germans, or Spaniards, or Jews. Then he ordered that the Book of Nations be brought to him and he looked in the Book of Nations to see how well the clowns had portrayed the different peoples. For the comedians, too, had looked in that book.

But while the king sat over the open volume, he noticed a spider that crept along the edge of the page; then he saw that a fly stood upon the open page. With its thin hairlike legs the spider pulled itself up the side of the book, then it reached its legs slowly over the side of the book, trying to crawl onto the page where the fly stood.

Just then a wind came and blew on the page so that it stood erect, and the spider could not reach the fly. Then the spider turned away, and for a while it crept along the table, as if it had forgotten the fly. Slowly and carefully it put out its feet, and then it stood still for a moment, as if it were waiting to hear a sound.

When the wind was gone, the page fell back to its place; then the spider turned and crept in a circle, coming nearer and nearer again to the edge of the book, until it clambered up the sides of the pages, and its little specks of eyes peered over the clifflike top of the book onto the wide plain where the fly remained standing. And the spider lifted its claw onto the page.

Once more the wind came, and blew the page upward, and the spider fell

away from the edge, and could not reach the fly. This happened several
times, but at last the wind was quiet for a long while, and the spider returned
to the book, and crept up the side, and placed its feet upon the open page,
and drew its body up onto the page. In that instant, the wind blew hard, and
turned the page over entirely upon the spider, so that he lay on his back between the pages of the book.

He tried to crawl out, but he could only crawl a little way, and he could
not turn himself aright, and though he moved with all his strength he could
only go a little further into the darkness that pressed upon him between the
pages of the book; and there he remained, until nothing remained of him.

As for the fly, I will not tell you what he did.

But the king saw all that had happened, and he knew that what he saw
was not a simple thing, but that there was a meaning intended for him in
what he had seen; and it was as though he heard a message vaguely through
thick walls. Then he fell into deep thought, trying to understand what had
happened before his eyes; the guests at the festival saw the king was lost in
thought, and did not disturb him.

For a long while the king leaned over the book, wondering, but he could
not find a meaning to what he had seen; at last he became very tired, and his
head leaned further over the page until it lay upon his spread arms, and he
slept. Then he dreamed.

He dreamed that he sat upon his throne in his palace, and over him hung
his portrait, and according to the custom in the palaces of kings, his crown
hung over his portrait. He sat there, holding a precious image in his hands.
Suddenly, hosts of people began to pour out of the image. He threw the
thing away from him.

Then the sleeping king saw how the people that rushed out of the image
turned, and climbed above him, and cut his head from his portrait. They
seized his crown and hurled it into the mud. Then they ran toward him with
their knives drawn, to kill him.

In that instant, a page out of the book upon which he slept stood erect
and shielded him, so that the oncoming horde could do him no harm; when
they had turned away, the page fell back into its place in the book.

Once more the angry people rushed to kill him, and the page stood before
him and shielded him so that they had to turn back. Seven times they rushed
upon him, and seven times they were prevented from harming him.

Then the king in his sleep was eager to see what was written on the leaf
that had so well protected him, and what nation out of the Book of Nations
might be represented there. But as he was about to look at the page, he was
overcome by a terrible fear; the edges of his hair felt like ice. He began to
scream.

The princes and the emperors who were his guests heard the king screaming in his sleep, and wanted to shake him that he might awake out of his

frightful dream, but it was forbidden to touch the king while he slept. Then they began to shout, and to beat upon drums, and to make wild noises that might awaken the king, but he did not hear them, and only trembled, and cried out, and shouted with fear as he slept over the Book of Nations.

Then a high mountain came to him and said, "Why are you screaming so? I was asleep for many ages, and nothing could awaken me, but your screams have broken my sleep!"

"How can I keep from screaming?" cried the king. "See how all the people are assembled, how they come against me with their drawn knives! They will kill me! And I have nothing to protect me but this little sheet of paper!"

"As long as it stands before you, you have nothing to fear," said the mountain. "I too have many enemies, but that same leaf has protected me, and I am not afraid. Come, and I'll show you my enemies."

They went, and the king saw myriad upon myriad of warriors assembled at the foot of the mountain; they were shouting and dancing and loudly blowing their trumpets.

"Why do they sing so gaily, and why do they dance so triumphantly?" the king asked of the mountain.

"Each time one of them thinks of a plan by which they may come up on me, they become wild with joy, and hold a feast, and they dance and sing in triumph," said the mountain. "But the same page protects me by what is written upon it, just as you are protected."

Then the king saw that a tablet stood on the top of the mountain, but because the mountain was very high, he could not read what was written on the tablet.

Behind them, however, was another stone on which this was written: "He that has all his teeth may come up to the top of the mountain."

The king thought, "Surely there are many people who can easily go up this way." But he looked on the ground and saw that they were not pebbles, but teeth of men and beasts upon which he trod, and all over the side of the mountain there were little mounds of teeth.

For the Power of the Name had caused a grass to grow on the sides of that mountain, and this grass was such that it drew out the teeth of all those who passed over it. The enemies from below tried to ride over it on the backs of swift horses, or in wagons, thinking that thus they would not touch the grass; nevertheless their teeth fell from them, and they could go no further up against the mountain.

When the king had seen this, he returned to the place of his own dream, and saw that now his own enemies, who were the people that had rushed out of the image, took up the head of his portrait and placed it back upon the shoulders; then they took the crown out of the mud, and washed it, and hung it in its accustomed place.

And then the king awoke.

At once he looked into the book, to see what was written on the page that had protected him. And he found that that page in the Book of Nations was the page of the Jews. He read carefully what was written there, and he began to understand the truth, and he said, "I will become a Jew."

But when he had become a Jew he was not yet satisfied, and cried, "The whole world must know the truth, and I will make all the peoples in the world into Jews."

But he could not think of a way by which he could show the truth to the whole world, and cause all men to become Jews, so he decided, "I will go and seek a sage who can tell me the meaning of everything in my dream, and then I shall know how to do what I want to do."

The king disguised himself as a simple traveler, and took two companions, and went out to seek a wise man.

Wherever he went he asked, "Is there anyone here who can explain a dream?" Though he traveled all over the earth, he could find no one who understood the meaning of his dream. But at last he was told of a sage who lived in a place that had no name.

When the king had been to every place that had a name, he continued to seek, and at last he reached a place where there were no hills or trees or rivers, no houses, and no beasts; and there was a man.

"What is the name of this place?" the king asked.

And the man answered him, "This place has no name." Then the king knew that he had come to the end of his journey, and that this man was the sage who could tell him the meaning of his dream. So he told the wise man the truth about himself. "I am no simple traveler," he said, "but a king who has won many battles and conquered many nations; and now I would like to know the true meaning of my dream."

The sage answered that he could not give him the meaning of his dream, but that if the king would wait until a day that was not in a month, he might himself learn what he wanted to know. "For on that day," the wise man said, "I gather the seeds of all things and make them into a perfume. And when the perfume is spread all about you, you will have the power to see for yourself all that you desire to know."

The king said, "I will wait."

He waited. And there came a time when he no longer knew the day and the month. Then the wizard brought him a perfume, and burned the perfume until it rose all about the king. And in the cloud the king began to see.

He saw himself as he had been even before he had become himself; he saw his soul as it waited in readiness before coming down to this world, and he saw his soul being led through all the worlds above and below, while a voice cried, "If there is anyone who has evil to say of this soul, let him speak!" But the soul passed through all the regions, and not one voice was raised against

it. Then the king saw his soul in readiness to go down and live upon earth.
But at that instant someone came hurrying, running, crying, "Hear me,
God! If this soul goes down on earth, what will there remain for me to do?
Why was I created!"

The king looked, to see who it was that cried out so against his soul's
going down to earth, and he saw that it was the Evil One himself!

And the Evil One was answered: "This soul must go down on earth. As
for you, you must think of something to do." Upon this, the Evil One went
away.

Then the king saw his soul being led through the high regions, from one
heaven to another, until at last it stood before the Court of highest heaven,
ready to take its oath to go down and live on earth. And still the Evil One
had not returned. Before the soul was given oath, a messenger was sent to
bring the Evil One before the Throne. The Evil One came, and brought with
him a wizened old man whom he had known for a very long time. And as he
came up with the bent old man, he was laughing, and chuckling, and smiling
to himself, and he said, "I've thought of a way out of it all! You can let this
soul go down on earth!"

Then the king saw his soul go down on earth, and he saw himself born,
and he saw everything that had happened to him on earth; he saw how he
had become king, and how he had gone out in battles, and slaughtered peoples, and won victories, and taken prisoners.

He saw that among the myriads of prisoners he had taken there was a
beautiful maiden. The maiden possessed every loveliness that was to be
found on earth, the beauty of form that was felt as sweet water under the
fingers, the beauty of the eyes that was as a caress of the hands, and the
beauty that is heard like the sound of bells touched by the wind. But when
the king looked upon her, he saw that her beauty was not her own, but that
it came forth like a perfume out of the tiny image that she wore upon herself.
And it was this image that contained all forms of beauty, and because it was
upon her, it seemed that all those forms of beauty were her own.

And only the very good and the very wise can go higher upon this mountain, for no more may be told.

Retold from the Yiddish and Hebrew sources
by Meyer Levin

The Prince Who Was Made
Entirely of Precious Stones

by Rabbi Nachman of Bratslav

There was a king who had no children, and he was greatly troubled with the thought that after his death his kingdom would pass into the hands of strangers. So he called to him all the physicians and all the magicians of his realm, and commanded them to make use of their learning and of their magic, that a prince might be born to the royal family. But they were of no help to him.

At last in despair he turned to the Jews who lived in his kingdom, for, he said, "I have heard that among the Jews there are secret saints whose prayers can bring whatever is in the heavens down on earth." So he commanded the Jews to bring one of these saints to the palace.

In each generation there are thirty-six men whose virtue bears up the world: they live unknown among other men, and they are called hidden Tsadikim. When the king commanded that one of them be brought to the palace, the Jews did not know where to turn, but one man went up to another, asking, "Might you be one of the secret Tsadikim?"

There was a shoemaker in a village; he lived quietly, earning bread for himself and his family, working each day, but resting on the Sabbath. Then all the people in the village bethought themselves that they had never known him to do any wrong, and they said to one another, "He must be a secret Tsadik!" But when they came to him and asked him, he only said, "I don't know anything about it. I am a shoemaker." Still, the word went from one village to another, and at last it came to the king that in a certain village there lived a shoemaker who was really a hidden Tsadik, but who said he knew nothing about it.

The king commanded that the man be brought before him, and when the Tsadik stood in the palace, the king spoke to him in a friendly way, saying, "You know that all your people are in my power, and I can do good or ill to them as I please. Therefore I ask you in a friendly way to pray that my queen may have a child."

The Tsadik went into a little room and spoke to God. Then he returned to the king. "Within a year," the Tsadik said, "a child will be born to the queen." And he went home to his village and made shoes.

Before the year had passed, the queen gave birth to a daughter. The little girl was so beautiful that whoever looked once upon her never ceased wondering at her loveliness; and she was so clever that when she was four years old she could play music upon many instruments, and speak all the languages of mankind. Emperors and sages came from distant lands to look upon and speak with the child.

At first the king was happy with his daughter, but then he grew discontented, for he wanted a son to rule after him, in order that his kingdom might not fall into strange hands. So he commanded that the secret Tsadik should again be brought before him.

But when the king's messenger went to seek out the Tsadik, he was told that the man had died.

The king said, "Let the Jews find another Tsadik!" So the Jews asked of one another, and sought amongst themselves, until they found another of the thirty-six secret Tsadikim, and they told the king where he was, and the king sent for him and said to him in a friendly way, "If you do not help me, remember that your people are in my power."

Then the Tsadik answered, "I will help you, if you will give me what I ask."

"I will give half of my possessions for a son!" the king cried.

"Then," said the Tsadik, "you must bring me precious stones, for in every jewel there is a quality of good, and the secret virtues of the jewels are written in the angel's book. Bring me every kind of precious stone, for I have need of them all."

The king commanded that jewels be brought. And from all parts of the world there were brought to him the largest and purest of precious stones: a diamond as radiant as a falling star, a pearl as white as an infant's smile, a ruby deep as a friendly eye, and sapphire, agate, carbuncle, and opal stones. These the king gave to the Tsadik who took them and crushed them into a powder; the powder he poured into a goblet of wine. Then he gave half of the wine to the king to drink, and the queen drank the other half.

"You will have a son," said the Tsadik, "who will be made entirely of precious stones, and who will have all the virtues of all the jewels in the world." Then he went home.

A son was born to the queen.

Now the king was completely happy, for he had a son to reign after him. And though the child appeared to be made like all other children, and not made of precious stones as the Tsadik had predicted, the king was satisfied, for the boy was even more beautiful than his sister, and he too was able to speak all the languages of mankind when he was four years old, and he knew besides all the wisdom of the world, so that rulers came from far places to ask advice of him.

But when the little girl saw the emperors and sages coming to court to seek her younger brother, and no longer for her sake, and when she heard the beauty and the wisdom of her brother constantly praised, while she was forgotten, she became jealous of her brother. Only one thing pleased her. "They said he would be made entirely of precious stones," she remembered, "but he is made like all of us."

One day as he was carving wood with a sharp knife, the prince cut his finger. His sister ran to bind up his finger, but as she looked into the wound she saw a gleaming sapphire there.

Then her jealousy turned to hatred, and she thought only of how she could be revenged upon her brother.

There was consternation in the palace because of the prince's injury, and when the princess saw how the king was troubled, and the people anxious, and the servants ran everywhere, she thought, "I too will be ill, and then they will remember me!" So she pretended to be sick.

Physicians were sent to her, but they could not find out the cause of her illness; at last the magicians were called, but none of the magicians could help her. She lay in her bed, and thought with hatred of her brother, and how he was indeed made of precious stones, and her jealousy gave her no rest. Then the sorcerer who was the most cunning of all the king's magicians came to the little girl, and as soon as he saw her he said, "You are not ill, but are only pretending illness!" She looked into his wicked eyes, and they were like two hard stones pressing upon her. Then she told the sorcerer the truth.

"I am not ill," she said, "but I cannot bear my brother's beauty; he is so beautiful that no one any longer remembers me." Then the princess begged the wizard: "Tell me," she cried, "is there no way to bewitch a person, so that all his body will become covered with itching sores?"

"There is a way," the wizard said. "I can make a charm against him."

But the clever little princess thought, "What if another magician should come, and break your charm? Then my brother will be beautiful again."

"If the charm is buried in water," the sorcerer replied, "it can never again be broken."

So they made an evil charm against the prince, and they bound their sorcery in a silken cloth and threw it into a deep pool where it could never again be found.

Then the prince's tender skin became red, and broke; sores appeared on his face and hands, and there were itching and leprous sores all over his body.

The king was terrified, the entire kingdom was in mourning because of the loathsome disease that had come upon the beautiful prince. Every physician and every sage hurried to the palace to try to heal the suffering boy. They covered him with balm and with ointments, but the sores remained upon him, and he tore at his loathsome skin.

The physicians said, "He cannot be cured."

Then the king cried, "It is the Jews who have brought this thing upon me!" and he commanded that the Jews cause the boy to be healed of his sores.

Once more the Jews sought amongst themselves for a secret Tsadik. And they found that Tsadik who had brought about the birth of the prince, and he was brought again to the palace.

"See what you have done!" the king cried. "You promised me a son who would be made entirely of precious stones, and instead he is covered with sores."

"Let me go into a little room where I may be alone," said the Tsadik. Then he went into a tiny chamber, and closed the door, and stood alone and spoke to God.

"It was not to bring glory upon myself that I did this thing," said the Tsadik, "but it was for the glory of your Name that I said that a child would be born, all made of precious stones. And now, see how my words have been fulfilled; the boy is covered with sores."

Then the truth was revealed to the Tsadik, for he knew that nothing happened without reason, and that the depths of loathsome sin must be felt before the heights of purest beauty may be known. And he came out and said to the king, "A sorcerer has made a charm against the prince, to cover him with evil. The charm has been buried in water, so that it may not be destroyed."

The king was terrified, for he thought that the prince would never be well again. "Is there nothing that can be done?" he begged. "Is there no magician more powerful than the evil one who has done this thing?"

"Since the charm has been buried in water," the Tsadik said, "there is only one way in which it can be broken. The magician who made the charm must be found, and he also must be thrown into the water."

"Take all the magicians of my kingdom," cried the king, "and throw them into the sea! If only my son will be well!"

Then he issued a decree that on the very next day every wizard, sorcerer, and magician in his realm should be thrown into the water.

When the princess heard this decree, her guilt made her afraid, for she thought, "Now the charm will be found out, and they will know that I have done this thing to my brother." So she ran to the pond, to take the charm out of the water before anyone else would find it there. But as the princess leaned far over the pond seeking for the evil charm, she fell into the water herself, and she sank to the bottom of the deep pool.

Then the servants hurried through the palace crying, "The princess has fallen into the pool!" and there was crying and wailing everywhere.

But when the Tsadik heard them he only smiled and said, "Now the prince will be well."

And so it was as he said. The sores upon the body of the prince began to close, and to dry up, and to fall away. And as the wounds fell away, the sickly skin became dry and hard, and it slipped from him as a cloud from the face of the sun; then the prince stood healed and shining before them, and their eyes were scarcely strong enough to look upon the dazzling brilliance of the boy, for now anyone might see that the prince was indeed made entirely of precious stones.

And he had all the virtues of all the jewels in the world.

Retold from the Hebrew and Yiddish sources
by Meyer Levin

The Hidden Tzaddik

by S. Y. Agnon

The hidden *tzaddik*—who was he? Before I tell of his deeds I will tell how he was discovered and by whom.

There was a gaon who suffered from headaches and couldn't study To-rah. He searched through his deeds and found nothing apart from the sin of closing his eye to a regulation of the Council of the Four Lands, which said that no man would be appointed to any holy post for money, even if he was wise and worthy of the post, reading the text "gods of silver . . ." to say a judge made such for money, and here, one member of his *beit din* had been appointed for money, his father-in-law having given the congregation money so they should make him a *dayan*. And the gaon knew that his troubles of Torah-neglect were all only because of this. He started rebuffing the man and treating him according to the law on gods of silver, it being a *mitzvah* to disregard him. The man's father-in-law was a wealthy tax collector and had a powerful arm, and most of the town's inhabitants were subject to him; he demanded redress for the insult to his son-in-law, and sorely troubled the gaon. The gaon found himself between two sources of trouble, neither of which was dispelled by the other.

The gaon had a relative in our town, one of the town's councilors, Reb Nahman David, one of the grandsons of Rabbi Nahman the Keeper-of-the-Seal and Rabbi David Prager the Head-of-the-State: these two distinguished families had intermarried and one of the outcomes was Reb Nahman David, whose heart was as great as his distinction, and as great as both together was his love of Torah and love of people, planted in him by his fathers. One day Reb Nahman David happened to come to the place where his relative the gaon lived. He went to visit him.

He found him lying on a rickety bed in a low house, where sewage water flowed in an open gutter outside his window. The tax collector owned a water mill, and had made a kind of engine to turn the wheels, closing the place where the water came out so that it filled up and overflowed its banks until the water rose to a level where it picked up all the dirt, then opening the plug so the water flowed out with the dirt, bringing the clean water to the mill where it turned the wheels, then pouring out the bad water. And where did he pour it? In front of the gaon's window. And another thing—he had prevented him receiving his allowance from the congregation fund, and the people of his household weren't even able to cook a meal.

Reb Nahman David said to his relative the gaon: "Rabbi, my fathers left me a house and I have added a room to it, so that if a guest comes to my house I won't have to say that my place is too cramped to lodge him for the night, and my wife is the daughter of a *talmid hakkam* and learned in hospitality. Come with me to my town, and stay with us. We won't trouble you with unnecessary things nor lay any burden upon you, light or heavy."

The gaon considered his relative's words and didn't say yes or no. But he continued thinking it over. The conflict was difficult: Whether I win, or whether my adversaries win, either way I won't be able to study Torah with a clear mind. Yet, if I'm here I at least shame some of the people so they don't bow to gods of silver. Another thought came, and said: All this time I've lived here not one of my relatives has come here, and now that this one's come perhaps it's for my good that he's come. But am I entitled to leave my congregation for my own good?

Reb Nahman David was a merchant and a man of Torah, and his discourse was pleasant. Each time he came to the gaon's, the gaon would greet him gladly and listen attentively to whatever he told him about, be it about their illustrious fathers, the pride of the province, or about Bichach and its sages. And when he left he would spend a little time with his relatives, the people of the gaon's house, and tell them of the qualities of the town of Bichach, which was surrounded by forests and mountains with living water coming from the mountains and fresh soothing breezes blowing among the trees and the governor of the town gracious to the Jews, and the people of the town quiet, conducting their affairs with trust and avoiding disputes. And as for the people of his house, his wife knew the ways of her fathers, loved her relatives and respected all people, and the sons and daughters followed in their mother's steps.

After several days Reb Nahman David said to his relative: "Today or tomorrow all my business here will be finished, and, God willing, with the full moon I'll be returning home. If you agree to come with me, Rabbi, I will prepare a place for you in the carriage."

· That day the gaon saw that all those who loved him were worried. He asked them: "What are you worried about?" They told him that slanders had been told about him to the governor of the town, and the governor was a hard gentile, and could trap him in plots that he wouldn't get out of, God forbid. The gaon was alarmed, fearing that this surfeit of troubles might make him start cursing his enemies. He said: "I'd better get away from here than curse one of Israel." And he added: "If I stay here it's clear I'll become

idle in Torah, and if I go to my relative's possibly I won't be so idle. At all
events, I have to leave here to save myself from the persecutor."

He came to Bichach and Reb Nahman David gave him a room with a bed
and a table and a lamp, and he didn't even lack a full set of the Six Orders
and Rav Alfass and a part of Rambam and Four Columns—things of which
not every town could proudly say it didn't lack all these. And the people of
Reb Nahman David's house served the gaon and didn't keep him away from
his studies.

Here I leave the gaon and return to the hidden *tzaddik*. Later I will speak
of them together. As it is written, *mercy and truth met righteousness and peace
kissed*. Mercy is the hidden *tzaddikim* who enhance God's mercies in the
world, truth is those true sages whose Torah is the Torah of truth; righteousness is those secret *tzaddikim* whose righteousness allows the world to exist,
peace is the sages of whom we have learned that they spread much peace in
the world.

So much for the sermon. From here on, the story.

There was a craftsman in our town, a maker of stoves. He made new ones
and mended old ones. He dressed like the masters of the lesser crafts, in German trousers and a garment of fringes with a kind of short coat over it, and
his wide-brimmed hat rose from his coat to cover his head. His shoes were of
fiber, and he carried a sack in which were the tools of his trade and halves of
bricks and mortar and clay. He lived at the edge of the town on the way to
the village behind the forest close to the Strypa, in a clay house which looked
like the earth and was as low as the earth. He spoke little, never saying a
word except in dire need. When he came in to do a job he would say Lord
save, and when he left he smiled in blessing. These were but the outskirts of
his ways.

During the time when the gaon came to his relative's house they were
putting in a new stove, even though this was summertime, when no stove
was necessary, for it is the custom of the wealthy to put in summer requirements in winter and winter requirements in summer.

The gaon heard the sound of a hammer. He came in and saw a stove
being made. The gaon said: "Many precepts have been taught around
stoves. I'll observe the injunction: Better is the seeing of the eyes." He stood
there watching how the craftsman worked and was astonished. And it was
not only the craftsman's work that astonished him, but also the craftsman
himself, for the motions of his hands and all his movements were immaculate.

All my life I've grown up among sages, the gaon thought to himself, and I
never saw one of them who took such meticulous care not to waste even the
slightest gesture. And this craftsman, this simple man, each of his movements
is guided by thought, and I'd heard he was of the ignorant folk, and not pious ignorant.

The heavens took pity on him and said to him: It's because you long to learn every good measure that you see the thoughts of your heart in the craftsman's work, but there is neither wisdom here nor even the shadow of wisdom.

The gaon started searching inside himself: For what sin was he being deluded? The heavens took pity on him and said to him: The craftsman has a craftsman's ways. What does it mean that he has a craftsman's ways? The works of masters of the craft are in his hands. When he learned from his master he learned from his deeds, as had his master before him, and his master's master before him, back to the first masters of craft among whom were *tannaim* and *amoraim*, except that the *tannaim* and the *amoraim* did all their deeds for the sake of heaven while the craftsmen of our days do according to the commandment of men, learned by rote.

The gaon rejoiced at having come across a man in whom one could see a reflection of the *tannaim* and the *amoraim*. He began following the craftsman, who, in turn, avoided him. He's a journeyman, thought the gaon, he's afraid of wasting time and idling at the expense of his employer. He waited for him until evening, since it is the way of craftsmen to lay down their work in the evening and leave for home. When evening came and the craftsman laid down his work the gaon accosted him and started speaking to him. The craftsman replied in a low tone, and before he replied he whispered several words in Aramaic between his lips. The gaon noticed that even in this low answer there was perfect wisdom, and saw how careful the craftsman was, not even letting a word out of his mouth without preparing his tongue in advance. And how did he prepare it? In the language of the Targum, which was a mean between the holy language and the profane one. The gaon grew increasingly sorry that he had discovered this *tzaddik* only to have the other avoid him.

Because of his headaches the gaon wore a light hat. One day his headaches were overpowering. He raised his hat above his forehead. A great light streamed from his forehead, beaming out, like the foreheads of those whose thoughts have never wandered when the *tefillin* were on their head.

The craftsman saw this and smiled.

The gaon asked him: "Why did you smile?" He replied: "I smiled from joy." He said: "Wherefore joy?" He said: "I saw on your forehead that you carry out the precept of *tefillin* as prescribed, and I rejoiced." He said: "What did you see?" He told him. He said to him: "I don't see it and you see it, that means that it is given to you to see what not every eye sees, which means that you are shown what is not shown except to the select of a generation. I know who you are. You can't conceal yourself from me any more."

The craftsman made no reply.

The gaon spoke again: "I know that you are a great *tzaddik*. You may be one of the thirty-six upon whom the world stands, and now that I've seen you I won't let you go until you reveal to me by what good deeds you have attained to this."

The craftsman answered: "What have I done to you to make you say things like that? If people hear I'll be a laughingstock."

The gaon said: "I could command you by the force of the Torah to obey me and to answer my question. But what is the Torah of a man like me against such humility as yours? If your excellency permits, I shall accompany you to your home."

The craftsman lowered his eyes and said: "*And the earth hath He given unto men.* In the entire earth all are equal. If you want to walk with me we can go together."

The two walked as one man and did not speak. The one did not speak because of the end of the verse which begins *The heavens are the heavens of the Lord,* and the other didn't speak because of the beginning of the verse which ends *and the earth hath He given unto men,* for He, the Blessed, is gracious to His creatures and allows all living things to walk upon the earth under the Lord's sky.

The two walked together in silence. Their silence alone spoke the righteousness of the Lord.

They came to the end of the town, near the Strypa, to a place where today you find the long bridge. On one side rose two or three clay houses, and on the other side a herdsman grazed his herd. And a still small voice rose upwards from below and dropped downwards from above, joining in the conversation of the field and the sound of the waters of the Strypa.

They reached a mound of earth. The craftsman stretched out his hand and said: "This is where I live." As there was no house there the gaon understood that the *tzaddik* dwelt inside the mound. He turned his eyes to him and said: "If you permit me to come in, I'll come in with you." The craftsman answered: "If you want to come, come. But there isn't a chair to sit on in my house." He said: "And what do you sit on?" He pointed to the ground with his hand.

The craftsman bent down and moved a stone and said to the gaon: "Don't be offended that I'm going first, it's to show you the way that I'm going first."

The gaon heard and was astonished at how well the *tzaddik* knew how to conceal his actions: It's to show you the way that I'm going first, he says, and that's Gemara, the master of the house goes in first.

As he entered, the master of the house put his mouth to the *mezzuzah* and kissed it, and said: "A man can love his home, for it gives him shelter from storm and from rains, and the sign of a home is a *mezzuzah*."

At this the gaon was illuminated in several aspects of the *mezzuzah* precepts. He raised his hands in thanksgiving and said: "Blessed is He Who has brought me here." And to the craftsman he said: "Tell me whence you attained to this light."

The craftsman sighed from his heart and said: "How is this man searched out, his hidden places sought out? How has this man been exposed and his secret discovered?"

The gaon repeated: "I won't leave you until you tell me by what you have attained to such light."

The craftsman lowered his eyes and said: "If I have any favor, it is because I make stoves."

The gaon called out in wonder: "Because you make stoves?"

"Because I mend old stoves."

The gaon asked again: "And only because of that?"

"And because I build new stoves."

The gaon said: "But there are many makers of stoves and they have not attained to what you have."

He said: "Because with every stove I make I take great care to make it right, and people come and warm themselves by it and do not get to feel anger against the Creation."

He said: "And only because of this?"

He said: "When people don't feel anger they are easy with each other, and when people are easy with each other then the judgment upon them is easy and turns anger to mercy."

The gaon asked: "If so, why did you sigh before?" He said: "Winter is coming on and a great frost is coming to the world and there are many broken stoves and many stoves are worn out and many stoves are blocked, and there are many houses still without stoves."

The gaon said: "If so, you can fix what needs fixing and make what needs making."

He said: "My time has come, and I can't prolong my life any more."

He said: "You can pray for yourself." He said: "I can't." He said: "Why?" He said: "Because my strength is gone, because I've become publicly known." He said: "Apart from me no one knows what you are." He said: "Known to many or known to one is still known." He said: "Pray for yourself and attain long life." He said: "It isn't worth it." He said: "Why not?" He said: "After becoming known my life is no longer worthwhile in my eyes." The gaon sighed. He said: "Why do you sigh?" He said: "For a great *tzaddik* who is about to leave this world." He said: "The world doesn't need me, the lack has already been filled by another."

The gaon wept and said: "Woe is me that because of my sin a *tzaddik* is leaving the world." He said. "Not for the sin of others but for my own sin, because I took pleasure in the light of the precept that I saw on your forehead, and delighted in it." He said: "As much as that." He said: "The precepts were not given for any other reason than to give delight to our Creator." The gaon said: "And what will a man like me do, who when he fulfills a precept properly is happy, and what will others do, who sense the burden of the precepts without their joy?" The craftsman slapped him on the arm joyfully and said melodiously: "The children of Israel—I am their atonement—the weary of exile, persecuted by gentiles, broken by troubles, rushing about to seek food for their houses, and stretching their necks to the yoke of the Lord's precepts because so the Torah has commanded, who is like unto them and who can be compared with them."

The gaon sat for a long while as if stunned. Then he said to the craftsman: "Please allow me to stay with you." The craftsman nodded and said: "It's a *mitzvah* to hear the words of the wise. Until they come to take my soul you can sit with me, and afterwards you can go back to where you live and I shall prepare my way."

The gaon sat with the craftsman for three days and three nights and they studied as one man and did not stop except for reading of *Shema* and for prayer. Some say they stopped of themselves and others say that an announcement came from heaven to tell them the time for prayer, since the Holy One blessed is He desires the prayer of *tzaddikim* even if it involves Torah-neglect. The tiniest part of the terrible things the hidden one revealed during their studies I know. Because it is the glory of God to conceal a thing, I keep silence on them.

By now the people of Reb Nahman David's house were anxious about the fate of their relative, the gaon, who had vanished. They remembered that they'd last seen him with the maker of stoves. They went to him to seek him. All the people of Reb Nahman David's house went, and with them half the town. By the time they'd reached the town's outskirts they'd been joined by the rest of the townspeople.

They came to the house of the craftsman. They had never been there and didn't know it was a dwelling place, because the house was as low as the ground. When they arrived there everyone said: "Here is the home of the maker of stoves." And this is one of the wonders that they tell of, that one could not see the shape of a house and yet they knew it was the craftsman's home. To me this is no wonder. Everything that has to be revealed is revealed.

They heard a voice coming out of the house, sometimes a voice asking and sometimes a voice answering. A child of about four, of Reb Nahman David's household, who had tagged along behind his mother, said that he heard the voice of a bird from the heavens. Since no one saw any bird or heard a bird's voice they ignored what the child said, and listened to hear the voices coming out of the house. Those who stood near the house peeped inside.

They saw the gaon sitting in front of the craftsman, on the floor, the former asking and the other answering, and the questions and answers were of high and terrible things that not every mind could endure. And they knew that the craftsman was full of wisdom and knowledge of God, since it was not the gaon's way to step four paces without Torah, and now that they saw him sitting in front of the craftsman like a pupil in front of his rabbi they understood that he had found one of twice his stature. They stood in awe and listened. Some there were who attained to hearing a word or even two, and some attained more and heard whole phrases. But only the select of the select heard that the craftsman was interpreting to the gaon the two strokes between the Yod and the Ayin of *abiy'a*. From the terror of the Lord and the glory of His majesty they stood as mute. These were the fathers and forefathers of the precious men of Bichach who are filled with Torah and awe and make themselves mute.

Someone came to himself and said: "Well, if so it means that the rabbi is here at the stove maker's."

Reb Nahman David heard this and said: "We have to go in." He went first of all to bathe in the Strypa and washed his hands in the water and washed them again. He did this five or six times and came back and repeated: "Well then, we have to go in."

He looked around to all sides and saw the child of his household hanging on to his mother's apron, the child I mentioned before, who said he heard the voice of a bird.

Reb Nahman David said to the child: "Son, come with me." And no one in Bichach knew, not that day and not all the years of his life, that this child had been chosen in the covenants of God to be one of the hidden *tzaddikim*, in place of the maker of stoves, for the Shekhinah had already come from Her heights of sanctity to receive his spirit. That was what the child had heard like the sound of a bird in the heavens from between the wings of the Shekhinah. If the Lord helps me I will yet tell the story of the child. They went inside, the two of them—Reb Nahman David and the boy of his household—and one other.

The craftsman got up from the ground and whispered: "My end is close and my time has come." He laid his hand on the child's head and said: "God be gracious unto thee, my son." The gaon stood up and went out.

All the people of the town encircled him and cried out in awe: "Rabbi, Rabbi, who is this craftsman that you have spent three days and three nights in succession with him?"

The gaon sighed and said: "Would that I had spent all my days with him. And you, my brothers and friends, take care not to raise your voices nor belittle him when the Shekhinah comes to him." And the gaon said no more, for his words ceased and the springs of his eyes opened and he broke into weeping.

The gaon's relatives left to escort the gaon to Reb Nahman David's house, and some of the people of the town didn't move and remained standing in front of the craftsman's house.

The craftsman opened a door and said: "Hear me, please, people of Bichach, go to your homes in peace, and afterwards whoever wants to may come and accompany me to my last resting place."

After they had all gone he came out and went down to the river and washed and returned to his house. He took his pallet and a clean sheaf of straw and went up to the cemetery and into the booth where the dead are purified, so that the bearers would not have to work too hard over him when they came to carry him to the grave. From there he went to the burial society.

All the men of the society came, the washers and the purifiers and those who bring out the dead and those who carry the bed and the ministrants and the gravediggers and at their head the community leaders and the beadles who keep the watch over death and life. They all lowered their heads because of the great light burning in his face. And he too lowered his head, out of respect for the holy men of Israel who treat the dead of Israel in order to bring them to a grave of Israel. They stood facing him in a row and waited for him to begin.

He said to them: "Blessed are you and known as doers of true charity, do not be angry at me for troubling you. In all my life I have never troubled a man, nor asked a favor of flesh-and-blood, but there is no power over the day of death. Now that I am dying I ask of you—be gracious to me and bury me in the plot where the stillborn are buried and do not place a tombstone on my grave."

They said to him: "Rabbi, why will you do a thing like that to us and why should we not place a tombstone on your grave? How many afflicted men there are, how many needful of mercy, who if they see the holy tombstone of your burial place will come to your grave and pray for themselves?" He said to them: "The master of mercy will have mercy on his merciful ones, and let them not regard a heap of dust. And you, doers of charity, be gracious to me and do not place a tombstone on my grave, so that people do not come and trample on the graves of the stillborn." They said to him: "We will observe your command and do nothing against your will."

He raised himself from the ground and lifted his hands and blessed them and the town. Then he said: "It is good to dwell among the people of the Lord, the holy people of Israel, but my time has come to leave you."

After they'd gone he put on his shrouds, spoke the *Shema Yisrael*, greeted the four corners of the sky, then closed his eyes and delivered his soul to the master of souls.

This approximately is the story of the hidden one who attained to what he attained because he mended old stoves and made new ones so that Israel could warm themselves by their light and because all that he did he did with perfection and so attained to what he attained.

Translated from the Hebrew
by Richard Flantz

The Stars of Heaven
by S. Y. Agnon

There once was a man Moshe, Reb Moshe Shoham, the upright storyteller of the holy congregation of Dolina. He was a great saint and mastered the teachings both revealed and hidden. He never left the tent of Torah nor did he walk for one moment without it. The great men of the generation were his teachers, and the holiest, above all others, was Reb Israel Baal Shem Tov. Moshe was like a child in the palace of the Baal Shem Tov. All the treasures of his teachings were in his heart and on his lips. He related his master's words with the wisdom God had placed in his mind. He also recorded a small portion of them.

The man Moshe was very humble. He did not write down the Besht's words out of conceit, but for himself alone, so as to arouse his pure soul to love and serve the Blessed One. His son came later and brought out the words in a book, *The Words of Moses*.

Once Reb Moshe had difficulty understanding a saying of the Baal Shem Tov, may his memory be for a blessing, that the rabbi of Polonnoye had written in his book *The Generations of Ya'akov-Yosef*, and which began, "I heard this from my teacher." He took his prayer shawl and phylacteries and went to Polonnoye.

At that time, the author of *The Generations of Ya'akov-Yosef* had neared the end of his days and was quite old, for the Besht had blessed him to attain the years of Joseph the Patriarch, of whom it is written, *And Joseph lived one hundred and ten years*. He had already squeezed out almost all the time allotted him and was about to take leave of the earth. The wrath of age had shriveled his body and reduced his limbs to those of a one-year-old baby. He was placed in a cradle which hung from the ceiling because of bugs.

Reb Moshe came to Reb Ya'akov-Yosef and asked him to explain the saying. As soon as Reb Ya'akov-Yosef heard the name of his master, the Baal Shem Tov, his face began to burn like torches and like lightning. He raised his head from the cradle and began to rock himself until the walls shook and the vessels of the house moved more and more fervently. And thus he explained and interpreted the saying with awe and fear, sweating and trembling, until the day passed and it was night. The heavens had become filled with stars, yet he continued his explanation.

After he finished speaking he stretched his right hand toward the window and asked, "Moshe, do you see the stars of heaven? They seem small, but truly each and every star is as great as the breadth of the entire world. Thus is each and every saying of my teacher the Baal Shem Tov. From a distance they appear to be small but truly each is as great as the breadth of the entire world."

Translated from the Hebrew
by Jeremy Garber

The Legend of the Just Men
by André Schwarz-Bart

Our eyes register the light of dead stars. A biography of my friend Ernie could easily be set in the second quarter of the twentieth century, but the true history of Ernie Levy begins much earlier, toward the year 1000 of our era, in the old Anglican city of York. More precisely, on March 11, 1185.

On that day Bishop William of Nordhouse pronounced a great sermon, and to cries of "God's will be done!" the mob moiled through the church square; within minutes, Jewish souls were accounting for their crimes to that God who had called them to him through the voice of his bishop.

Meanwhile, under cover of the pillage, several families had taken refuge in an old disused tower at the edge of town. The siege lasted six days. Every morning at first light a monk approached the moat, crucifix in hand, and promised life to those Jews who would acknowledge the Passion of our very gentle Lord Jesus Christ. But the tower remained "mute and closed," in the words of an eyewitness, the Benedictine Dom Bracton.

On the morning of the seventh day Rabbi Yom Tov Levy gathered the besieged on the watchtower. "Brothers," he said to them, "God gave us life. Let us return it to him ourselves by our own hands, as did our brothers in Germany."

Men, women, children, dotards, each yielded a forehead to his blessing and then a throat to the blade he offered with the other hand. The old rabbi was left to face his own death alone.

Dom Bracton reports, "And then rose a great sound of lamentation, which was heard from here to the St. James quarter. . . ."

There follows a pious commentary, and the monk finishes his chronicle so: "Twenty-six Jews were counted on the watchtower, not to mention the females or the herd of children. Two years later thirteen of the latter who had been buried during the siege were discovered in the cellar, but almost all of these were still of suckling age. The rabbi's hand was still on the hilt of the dagger in his throat. No weapon but his was found in the tower. His body was thrown upon a great pyre, and unfortunately his ashes were cast to the wind, so that we breathe it and so that, by the agency of mean spirits, some poisonous humors will fall upon us, which will confound us entirely!''

This anecdote in itself offers nothing remarkable. In the eyes of Jews, the holocaust of the watchtower is only a minor episode in a history overstocked with martyrs. In those ages of faith, as we know, whole communities flung themselves into the flames to escape the seductions of the Vulgate. It was so at Speyer, at Mainz, at Worms, at Cologne, at Prague during the fateful summer of 1096. And later, during the Black Plague, in all Christendom.

But the deed of Rabbi Yom Tov Levy had a singular destiny; rising above common tragedy, it became legend. To understand this metamorphosis, one must be aware of the ancient Jewish tradition of the Lamed-Vov, a tradition that certain Talmudists trace back to the source of the centuries, to the mysterious time of the prophet Isaiah. Rivers of blood have flowed, columns of smoke have obscured the sky, but surviving all these dooms, the tradition has remained inviolate down to our own time. According to it, the world reposes upon thirty-six Just Men, the Lamed-Vov, indistinguishable from simple mortals; often they are unaware of their station. But if just one of them were lacking, the sufferings of mankind would poison even the souls of the newborn, and humanity would suffocate with a single cry. For the Lamed-Vov are the hearts of the world multiplied, and into them, as into one receptacle, pour all our griefs. Thousands of popular stories take note of them. Their presence is attested to everywhere. A very old text of the Haggadah tells us that the most pitiable are the Lamed-Vov who remain unknown to themselves. For those the spectacle of the world is an unspeakable hell. In the seventh century, Andalusian Jews venerated a rock shaped like a teardrop, which they believed to be the soul, petrified by suffering, of an "unknown" Lamed-Vovnik. Other Lamed-Vov, like Hecuba shrieking at the death of her sons, are said to have been transformed into dogs. "When an unknown Just rises to Heaven," a hasidic story goes, "he is so frozen that God must warm him for a thousand years between His fingers before his soul can open itself to Paradise. And it is known that some remain forever inconsolable at human woe, so that God Himself cannot warm them. So from time to time the Creator, blessed be His Name, sets forward the clock of the Last Judgment by one minute."

The legend of Rabbi Yom Tov Levy proceeds directly from this tradition of the Lamed Vov. It owes its birth also to a singular occurrence, which is the extraordinary survival of the infant Solomon Levy, youngest son of Rabbi Yom Tov. Here we reach the point at which history penetrates legend and is absorbed by it, for exact details are lacking and the opinions of the chroniclers are divergent. According to some, Solomon Levy was one of thirty children who received Christian baptism during the massacre. According to others he (ineptly butchered by his father) was saved by a peasant woman who sent him along to the Jews of a neighboring county.

Among the many versions current in thirteenth-century Jewish stories we note the Italian fantasy of Simeon Reubeni of Mantua; he describes the "miracle" in these terms:

"At the origin of the people of Israel there is the sacrifice accepted by one man, our father Abraham, who offered his son to God. At the origin of the dynasty of the Levys we find again the sacrifice accepted by one man, the very gentle and luminous Rabbi Yom Tov, who by his own hand slit the throats of two hundred and fifty of the faithful—some say a thousand.

"And therefore this: the solitary agony of Rabbi Yom Tov was unbearable to God.

"And this too: in the charnel house swarming with flies was reborn his youngest son, Solomon Levy, and the angels Uriel and Gabriel watched over him.

"And finally this: when Solomon had reached the age of manhood, the Eternal came to him in a dream and said, 'Hear me, Solomon; listen to my words. On the seventeenth day of the month of Sivan, in the year 4945, your father, Rabbi Yom Tov Levy, was pitied in my heart. And therefore to all his line, and for all the centuries, is given the grace of one Lamed-Vovnik to each generation. You are the first, you are of them, you are holy.' "

And the excellent author concludes in this manner: "O companions of our ancient exile, as the rivers go to the sea all our tears flow in the heart of God."

Authentic or mistaken, the vision of Solomon Levy excites general interest. His life is carefully reported by Jewish chroniclers of the time. Several describe his face—narrow, pensive, somewhat childlike, with long black curls like a floral decoration.

But the truth had to be faced: His hands did not heal wounds, no balm flowed from his eyes, and if he remained in the synagogue at Troyes for five years, praying there, eating there, sleeping there always on the same hard bench, his example was commonplace in the minuscule hell of the ghettos. So they waited for the day of Solomon Levy's death, which might put an end to debate.

It occurred in the year of grace 1240 during a disputation ordered by the sainted King Louis of precious memory. As was customary, the Talmudists of the Kingdom of France stood in one rank facing the ecclesiastic tribunal, where was noticed the presence of Eudes de Chateauroux, Chancellor of the Sorbonne, and the celebrated apostate Jew Nicholas Donin. In these singular disputations, death hovered over every response of the Talmudists. Each spoke in turn in order to distribute equitably the threat of torture.

At a question of Bishop Grotius relative to the divinity of Jesus, there was a rather understandable hesitation.

But suddenly they saw Rabbi Solomon Levy, who had until then effaced himself like an adolescent intimidated by a gathering of grownups. Slender and slight in his black gown, he steps irresolutely before the tribunal. "If it is true," he whispers in a forced tone, "if it is true that the Messiah of which our ancient prophets spoke has already come, how then do you explain the present state of the world?" Then, hemming and hawing in anguish, his voice a thread, "Noble lords, the prophets stated that when the Messiah came sobs and groans would disappear from the world—ah—did they not? That the lion and the lamb would lie down together, that the blind would be healed and that the lame would leap like—stags! And also that all the peoples would break their swords, oh, yes, and beat them into plowshares—ah— would they not?"

And finally, smiling sadly at King Louis, "Ah, what would they say, sire, if you were to forget how to wage war?"

And these were the consequences of that little oration as they are revealed in the excruciating Book of the Vale of Tears: "Then did King Louis decide that our brothers of Paris would be condemned to a Mass, to a sermon, to the wearing of a yellow cloth disc and a sugar-loaf hat and, as well, to a considerable fine. That our divine books of the Talmud would be burned at the stake against an isolated tree in Paris as pettifogging and lying and dictated by the Devil. And that finally, for public edification, into the heart of the Talmudic flames would be cast the living body of that Just Man, that Lamed-Vovnik, that man of sorrows—oh, how expert in sorrows—Rabbi Solomon Levy, since then known as the Sad Rabbi. A tear for him."

After the auto-da-fé of the Just Man, his only son, the handsome Manasseh, returned to that England whence his ancestors had once fled.

Peace had reigned over the English shores for ten years; to the Jews it seemed permanently enthroned. Manasseh settled in London, where the renown of the Just Men set him at the head of the resurgent community. As he was very graceful of form and speech, he was constantly asked to plead the cause of the Jews, who were daily accused of sorcery, ritual murder, the poisoning of wells, and other affabilities. In twenty years he obtained seven acquittals, which was indeed remarkable.

The circumstances of the seventh trial are little known. It concerned a certain Eliezer Jetryo, whom rumor accused of having stabbed a communion wafer, thereby putting the Christ to another death and spilling the blood of the Sacred Heart, which is the dry bread of the Host. This last acquittal disturbed two powerful bishops. Shortly, arraigned before the tribunal of the

Holy Inquisition, Manasseh heard himself accused of the crime from which he had so recently exculpated Eliezer Jefryo.

He was obliged to undergo the Question Extraordinary, which was not repeated—that being forbidden by the legislation in force—but simply "continued." The court records show him infected by the evil spirit of taciturnity. And therefore on May 7, 1279, before a gallery of some of the most beautiful women in London, he had to suffer the passion of the wafer by means of a Venetian dagger, thrice blessed and thrice plunged into his throat.

"It is thus," a chronicler writes naïvely, "that after having defended us in vain before the tribunals of men, the Just Manasseh Levy rose to plead our cause in Heaven."

His son Israel did not seem bound to follow that dangerous path. A suave, peaceful man, he had a small cobbler's shop and wrote elegiac poems with the tip of his hammer. So great was his discretion that his rare visitors never arrived without a shoe in hand. Some assure us that he was well versed in the Zohar, others that he had barely the intelligence of a dove, whose gentle eyes and moist voice he also had. A few of his poems have become part of the Ashkenazic ritual. He is the author of the celebrated selihah "O God, cover not our blood with thy silence."

So Israel was quietly fashioning his own little world when the edict of expulsion burst upon the Jews of England. Always levelheaded, he was among the last to quit the island; they made first for Hamburg but settled later for slow progress toward the Portuguese coast. At Christmas, after four months of wandering, the caravel entered the harbor of Bordeaux.

The little shoemaker made his way furtively to Toulouse, where he passed several years in a blessed incognito. He loved the southern province; the Christian manner there was gentle, almost human. He had the right to cultivate a plot of ground, he could practice trades other than usury, and he could even swear an oath before a court as if, a Jew, he spoke with the tongue of man. It was a foretaste of Paradise.

There was only one shadow on the picture. A custom called the Cophyz required that every year on the eve of Easter the president of the Jewish community present himself in a plain gown at the cathedral, where the Count of Toulouse, to the strains of the Mass, administered a blow in the face with great ceremony. But over the centuries the custom had been singularly refined; in consideration of fifty thousand écus, the Count satisfied himself with a symbolic slap at six paces. So it went until Israel was recognized by an English emigrant and duly "denounced" to the faithful of Toulouse. They plucked him from his shop, blessed him, his father, his mother, all his ancestors and all his descendants, and willy-nilly he accepted the presidency, which had become a position of no danger.

The years flowed by with their train of griefs and small joys, which he persisted in translating into poetry, and on the sly he turned out a few pairs of shoes now and then. In the year of grace 1348 the old Count of Toulouse died; his son had been raised by excellent tutors, and decided to administer the Easter slap.

Israel presented himself in a long shirt, barefoot, on his head the obligatory pointed hat, two vast yellow discs sewn to the whiteness of his chest and back; on that day he had seventy-two years behind him. A huge crowd had gathered to see the slap. The hat rolled violently to the ground. According to the ancient custom Israel stooped to pick it up and thanked the young count three times; then, supported by his coreligionists, he made his way through the screaming press of the mob. When he arrived at home his right eye smiled with a reassuring sweetness. "It is only a matter of habit," he told his wife, "and I am already entirely accustomed to it." But over the cheek marked by four fingers his left eye wept, and during the night that followed, his aged blood turned slowly to water. Three weeks later he displayed signal weakness by dying of shame.

Rabbi Mattathias Levy, his son, was a man so well versed in the mathematical sciences, astronomy and medicine that even certain Jews suspected him of trafficking with the Devil. His agility in all things was notorious. Johanan ben Hasdai, in one of his anecdotes, compared him to a ferret; other authors sharpen the description, indicating that he seemed always in the process of fleeing.

He practiced medicine in Toulouse, Auch, Gimont, Castelsarrasin, Albi, Gaillac, Rabastens, Verdun-sur-Garonne. His condition was that of the Jewish doctors of the time. In Auch and Gaillac they accused him of poisoning sick Christians; in Castelsarrasin they accused him of leprosy; in Gimont he was a poisoner of wells. In Rabastens they said he used an elixir whose base was human blood, and in Toulouse he cured with the invisible hand of Satan. In Verdun-sur-Garonne, finally, he was hounded as a propagator of the fearsome Black Death.

He owed his life to the patients who kept him posted, hid him and spirited him away. He was often reprimanded but he always found, ben Hasdai says, "strange reasons for opening his door to a sick Christian." In several places his death was reported. But whether he was thrown into the Jew pit at Moissac, burned alive at the cemetery in Auch, or assassinated in Verdun-sur-Garonne, one fine day the ferret would make his sad appearance in a synagogue. When King Charles VI, on the good advice of his confessor, published the edict of expulsion of the Jews of France, Rabbi Mattathias Levy was hidden away in the neighborhood of Bayonne; a step or two and he was in Spain.

There he died very old, in the middle of the following century, on the immense white slab of the *quemadero* in Seville. Around him, scattered among the fagots, were the three hundred Jews of the daily quota. It is not even known whether he sang in his agonies. After an ordinary life, this lackluster death casts doubt on his quality as a Just Man. . . . "Nevertheless," writes ben Hasdai, "he must be counted as of the illustrious line, for if evil is always manifest, striking, good often dons the clothing of the humble, and they say that many Just Men died unknown."

On the other hand his son Joachim bore eloquent witness to his vocation. Before he was forty he had composed a collection of spiritual decisions as well as a dizzying description of the three cabalistic *sephiroth*—Love, Intelligence, Compassion. He possessed, legend says, one of those faces of sculptured lava and basalt of which the people believe that God models them veritably in his own image.

On that level the persecutions did not trouble him. Always noble and grave, he reigned over his disciples, who had come from all corners of Spain, and spoke to each of them the language of his death. In a polemic that has remained famous, he established definitively that the reward of the persecuted is the Supreme Delight—in which case it is obvious that the good Jew does not feel the horrors of torture. "Whether they stone him or burn him, whether they bury him alive or hang him, he remains oblivious; no complaint escapes his lips."

But while the illustrious Lamed-Vovnik discoursed, God, through the intervention of the monk Torquemada, concocted divinely the edict of permanent expulsion from Spain. Through the black night of the Inquisition the decree fell like a bolt of lightning, marking for many Jews immediate expulsion from earthly existence.

To his great shame Rabbi Joachim managed to reach Portugal without bearing personal witness to his own teachings. There John III charitably offered the exiles a sojourn of eight months in return for a mutually agreeable entrance fee. But seven months later, by a singular aberration, that same sovereign decreed that he would now spare the lives of those Jews leaving his realms without delay, and this in return for a mutually agreeable exit fee. For lack of savings Rabbi Joachim saw himself sold as a slave with thousands of other unfortunates; his wife was promised to the leisures of the Turk and his son Chaim promised to Christ and baptized abundantly in several convents.

A doubt hovers over the rabbi's death. A sentimental ballad locates it in China, by impalement, but the most cautious writers admit their lack of sure knowledge. They suppose that his death was worthy of his teachings.

The infant Chaim knew a prodigious fate. Raised in a convent and ordained a priest, he remained a faithful Jew under the soutane, but his superiors, satisfied of his apparent good conduct, delegated him to the Holy See in 1522 with a sizable group of "Jewish priests" assigned to the edification of the papal entourage. Leaving for Rome in soutane and biretta, he ended at Mainz in black caftan and sugar-loaf hat; there the survivors of the recent holocaust welcomed him with pomp.

Treated and regarded as animals, the Jews were naturally avid for the supernatural. Already the posterity of Rabbi Yom Tov had broken all the bounds of the ghetto. From the Atlantic coast to the interior of Arabia, every year on the twentieth day of the month of Sivan a solemn fast took place, and the cantors chanted the selihoth of Rabbi Solomon ben Simon of Mainz:

> *With tears of blood I bewail the holy community of York.*
> *A cry of pain springs from my heart for the victims of Mainz,*
> *The heroes of the spirit who died for the holy name.*

The arrival of Chaim Levy, come surging from the depths of monasteries, seemed as miraculous as the deliverance of Jonah; the abyss of Christianity had rendered up the Just Man.

Blessed, cherished, circumcised, he leads a life of ease. They present him generally as a tall, thin, cold man. A witness alludes to the unctuously monotonous flow of his voice, and to other ecclesiastical traits as well. After eight years as a recluse in the synagogue, he marries a certain Rachel Gershon, who shortly offers him an heir. A few months later, betrayed by a coreligionist, he is escorted back to Portugal. There his limbs are broken on the rack; lead is poured into his eyes, his ears, his mouth and his anus at the rate of one molten drop each day; finally they burn him.

His son Ephraim Levy was brought up piously in Mannheim, Karlsruhe, Tübingen, Reutlingen, Augsburg, Regensburg—all cities from which the Jews were no less piously chased. In Leipzig his mother died, out of breath. But there he knew the love of a woman and married her.

The margrave was not at all devout, no more was he greedy or wicked; he was simply short of money. So he fell back on the favorite game of German princes, which consisted of chasing the "infamous" and retaining their worldly goods. Young Ephraim fled with his new family to Magdeburg, whence he started for Brunswick, where he set out on the road to the death of Just Men, and was laid low by a stone that hit him in Kassel.

He is hardly mentioned in the chronicles; the scribes seem to avoid him. Judah ben Aredeth devotes barely eight lines to him. But Simeon Reubeni of Mantua, the gentle Italian chronicler, evokes "the undulating curls of Ephraim Levy, his laughing eyes, his graceful limbs moving as if in dance. They say that from the day he knew his wife, whatever befell him he never ceased to laugh, so the people named him the Nightingale of the Talmud, which perhaps indicates excessive familiarity toward a Just Man."

These are the only lines that describe the charming person of the young Ephraim Levy, whose happiness in love seems unworthy of a Lamed-Vovnik. Even his last agony failed to soften the rigor of the Jewish historians, who do not mention its date.

His son Jonathan had a more commendable life. For many years he criss-crossed Bohemia and Moravia—a peddler of the secondhand, and a prophet. When he entered the gates of a ghetto he began by unwrapping his glass trinketry; then, the day's small business over and the bundle done up and knotted at his feet, he lectured passersby on the Torah, on the angels, on the imminent arrival of the Messiah.

A reddish beard covered his face even to the periphery of his eyes and, a more cruel disgrace still, his voice had a falsetto resonance, but he possessed, the chronicle says, "a story for each of our sufferings."

In those days all the Jews of Europe wore the uniform of infamy ordered by Pope Innocent III. After five centuries of this catechism, its victims were curiously transmuted. Under the pointed hat, the *pileum cornutum,* solid citizens thenceforth imagined two small horns; at the base of the spine, where the cloth disc began, the legendary tail could be guessed at; no one was any longer unaware that Jewish feet were cloven. Those who stripped their corpses were amazed, and saw an ultimate witchcraft in these bodies now so human. But as a general rule no one touched a Jew, dead or alive, except with the end of a stick.

During the long voyage that was his life, Rabbi Jonathan struggled often against cold, hunger, and the ordinance of Pope Innocent III. All the parts of his body testified forcefully to that. Judah ben Aredeth writes, "In the end, the Just Man no longer had a face. In Polotsk, where he turned up in the winter of 1552, he had to give up his bundle. A happy indiscretion having betrayed his quality as a Lamed-Vovnik, his sicknesses were healed, he was married, he was admitted to the seminary of the great Yehel Mehiel, where eleven years passed for him like one day."

Then Ivan IV, the Terrible, annexed Polotsk in a thunderclap!

As we know, all the Jews were drowned in the Dvina except those who would kiss the Holy Cross, prelude to the saving aspersion of holy water. The Czar indicating a desire to exhibit in Moscow, duly sprinkled, "a couple of wriggling little rabbis," his minions proceeded to the methodical conversion of Rabbi Yehel and Rabbi Jonathan. When all else had failed, they were tied to the tail of a small Mongol pony, and then their remains were hoisted to the thick branch of an oak, where two canine cadavers awaited them. Finally, to this oscillating mass of flesh was affixed the famous Cossack inscription, "Two Jews, Two Dogs, All Four of the Same Religion."

The chroniclers prefer to end this story on a lyric note. Thus Judah ben Aredeth, ordinarily so dry: "Ah, how the mighty have fallen!"

* * *

On Tuesday the fifth of November, 1611, an aged servant asked entrance to the Grand Synagogue of Vilna. Her name was Maria Kozemenieczka, daughter of Jesus, but she had raised a Jewish child and perhaps, she finished timidly, the Jews would act jointly to save him from conscription?

Assailed with questions, she first swore by all the saints that the child had been "engendered" in her by a peddler at the side of the road "in passing." Then she admitted having picked him up the day after the Russian annexation at the gates of the former ghetto of Polotsk, and finally she offered what was accepted as the truth: once cook in the household of the late Rabbi Jonathan, she had received the boy from the hands of the young wife as the Russians broke down the door. In the night she had fled to her native village. She would be old some day; she felt tender; she kept the innocent for her own; that was all. "And may you all forgive me," she concluded in a sudden shower of tears.

"Return to your village," the rabbi said to her, "and have the young man come here. If he is properly circumcised, we will pay for his release."

Two years went by.

The prudent rabbi of Vilna had breathed not a word to any man, and congratulated himself on it. But one night, leaving the temple, he bumped into a young peasant planted under the porch, haggard, his features drawn with fatigue, his eyes gleaming with an emotion in which arrogance battled fear. "Hey, you, old rabbi, I seem to be one of your people, so tell me what you have to do to be a dog of a Jew."

The next day, bitterly: "Pig in a sty, Jew in a ghetto, we are what we are, huh?"

A month later: "I'd like to respect you but I can't do it; it's as if I was disgusted, a feeling in the belly."

Started on the way of frankness, he told them of his anger and his shame, of burying himself in the Army. He had deserted in the middle of the night on an irrevocable impulse. "I woke up, just like that, and I heard them all snoring, good Christian snores. 'Jezry, Jezry,' I said to myself, 'you didn't come out of the belly you thought, but a man is what he is and if he denies it he's a pig!' " On that violent thought he had knocked out the sentry and then a passerby, whom he stripped of his clothing, and like an animal off into the night he had headed for Vilna, a hundred and twenty-five miles from his garrison.

Men who had known his father, the Just Jonathan Levy, came rushing from all the provinces. First struck by his coarseness, they made overtures, analyzed his expression. They say it took him five years to resemble Rabbi Jonathan; he burst into laughter finding that he had Jewish hair, Jewish eyes, a long nose with a Jewish curve. But they were always worried about the crazy peasant who slumbered in him; now and then rages shook him, he spoke of "getting out of this hole," uttered blasphemies at which they stopped their ears. After which he enclosed himself in an attentive, studious, suffering silence for weeks on end. In his famous *Story of a Miracle* the prudent rabbi of Vilna reports, "When he did not understand the meaning of a Hebrew word, the son of the Just Men squeezed his head between his heavy peasant hands, as if to tear out the dense Polish gangue."

His wife revealed that he cried out in his sleep every night, calling now upon Biblical figures and now upon a certain St. John, the patron saint of his Christian childhood. One day when the service was at its height he fell full length, beating at his temples with his huge fists. His madness was immediately recognized as holy.

According to the rabbi of Vilna, "When the Eternal at last took pity upon him, Nehemiah Levy had replaced, one by one, all the pieces of his former brain."

The life of his son, the curious Jacob Levy, is nothing more than a desperate flight from the implacable "benediction" of God. He was a creature of thin, elongated limbs, a languid head, the long, fearful ears of a rabbit. In his passion for anonymity he hunched his back to the extreme, as if to mask his height from men's eyes, and as a hunted man buries himself in a crowd, he became a simple leatherworker, a man of nothing.

When the talk turned to his ancestors, he claimed that there had been an error in his case, arguing from the fact that he felt nothing within himself except perhaps terror. "I am nothing more than an insect," he said to his indiscreet courtiers, "a miserable insect. What do you want of me?" The next day he had disappeared.

Happily, heaven had joined him to a talkative woman. A hundred times she had sworn to keep silence, but always one fine morning, leaning toward a neighborly ear: "He doesn't seem like much, does he, my husband?" she would begin slyly. And under the absolute seal of confidence the secret made its way like a fired train of powder. The rabbi sent for the modest tooler of leather, and if he did not offer him his own ministry, he assured him that he was blessed of all men, dangerously radiating glory. So it happened in all the towns the couple passed through. "So that he could never savor the quietude of obscure men," writes Meir of Nossack, "God placed a female tongue at his side as a sentinel."

In the end Jacob, his patience exhausted, put away his wife to burrow into an alley in the ghetto at Kiev, where he quietly carried on his trade. They found him soon enough, but out of fear that he would disappear again, they only verified his presence now and then with a discretion equal to his own. Observers record that he straightened up to his full height, that his eyes cleared, and that three times in less than seven years he gave in to unfeigned gaiety. Those were happy years, they say.

His death fulfilled everyone's expectations: "The Cossacks locked a group in the synagogue and demanded that all Jews present strip naked, men and women. Some had begun to take off their clothes when a simple man of the people came forward whom a subtle rumor had identified with the celebrated dynasty of the Levys of York. Turning toward the tearful group, he hunched his shoulders suddenly and in a quavering voice broke into the selihoth of Rabbi Solomon ben Simon of Mainz: 'With tears of blood, I bewail . . .'

"They cut short the chant with one blow of a cleaver, but other voices had already taken up the plaint, and then still others; then there was no one to sing, for all was blood. . . . So did things come to pass among us in Kiev on 16 November, 1723, during that terrible *hadaimakschina.*" (Moses Dobiecki, *History of the Jews of Kiev.*)

His son Chaim, called the Messenger, was bequeathed his father's modesty. He gleaned instruction from everything, from rest as from study, from things as much as from men. "The Messenger heard all voices and would have accepted the reproach of a blade of grass."

And yet in those days he was himself quite a blade of a man, built like a Pole and so hale that the ghetto dwellers feared for their daughters.

The evil-minded insinuate that his unmarried state was not unconnected with his sudden departure from Kiev. Actually it was on the express injunction of the elders that he was obliged to take his place near the Baal Shem Tov—Rabbi Israel ben Eliezer, the divine Master of the Name—in order, they said, to add to his knowledge and to refine his heart.

After ten years of retreat on the most savage slopes of the Carpathians, the Baal Shem Tov had established himself in his natal village of Miedzyborz, in Silesia, whence his light streamed forth on all Jewish Poland. They came to Miedzyborz to heal ulcers, resolve doubts, or cure themselves of demons. Wise men and fools, the simple and the depraved, noble reputations and the run-of-the-mine faithful milled together around the hermit. Not daring to reveal his identity, Chaim Levy did his chores as a handyman, slept in the barn reserved for the sick, and awaited, trembling, the luminous glance of the Baal Shem Tov. Five years passed thus. He had merged so thoroughly with his identity as a servant that pilgrims from Kiev did not recognize him.

His only apparent talent was for the dance; when the reels formed to lighten the heart of God, he leaped so high in the air and cried out so enthusiastically that many Hasidim were offended. He was relegated permanently to the ranks of the sick; he danced among them for their pleasure.

Later, when everything was known, he was also nicknamed the Dancer of God.

One day the Baal Shem received a message from the old Gaon of Kiev. Immediately he ordered it proclaimed that a Just Man was concealed at

Miedzyborz. All the pilgrims were interrogated—the sick, the wise, the possessed, rabbis, preachers. The next day it was noticed that the handyman had fled. Testimony streamed in immediately, each contributed his own anecdotes: the vagabond of the barn danced at night, took care of the sick, and so on. But the Baal Shem Tov, wiping away a tear, said simply, "That one was healthy among the sick, and I did not see him."

News filtered in as if drop by drop.

They learned that poor Chaim was wandering through the countryside preaching in public squares or practicing odd and humble crafts—for example that of the bonesetter, who used only his two hands (and who treated both humans and animals). Many chronicles point out that he preached only reluctantly, as if under the domination of an officiating angel. After fifteen years of that mad solitude, he became so popular a figure that a number of stories identify him with the Baal Shem Tov himself, of whom he was said to have become the wandering incarnation. In the abundance of ancient parchments we cannot separate entirely the commonplace from the miraculous. It is certain nevertheless that the Messenger often stayed in a village without delivering himself of any message but his medicine, so that he passed doubly unnoticed.

But his legend traveled faster than he did, and soon they recognized him by certain signs: first his tall lumberjack's build and his face ridged with scars, and then the famous missing right ear, ripped off by Polish peasants. From then on it was noticed that he avoided the larger cities, where his description was common knowledge.

One night during the winter of 1792 he arrived in the neighborhood of the small town of Zemyock, in the canton of Moydin, in the province of Bialystok. He fainted away at the door of a Jewish home. His face and his boots were so worn, so hardened by the cold, that at first he was mistaken for one of the innumerable peddlers who crisscrossed Poland and the "zone of Jewish residence" in Russia. It was necessary to amputate his legs at the knee. When he was better they came to appreciate his manual talents and his skill as a copyist of the Torah. Every day his host trundled him to the synagogue in a wheelbarrow. He was a human husk, a poor unfortunate, but he performed small services and was consequently not a great burden. "He spoke," writes Rabbi Moshe Leib of Sasov, "only of material things like bread and wine."

The Just Man was in his wheelbarrow, like a living candle planted in a dim corner of the synagogue, when it happened that the village rabbi erred in the interpretation of a holy text. Chaim raised an eyebrow, rubbed his one ear, cleared his throat carefully, rubbed his ear again—to hold back the truth of God is grave, grave. . . . Finally, rubbing his ear one last time, he brought himself upright with one hand on the edge of the wheelbarrow and requested the right to speak on the text. He was then assailed with questions.

Suffering a thousand deaths, he answered brilliantly to all of them. To make
the disaster perfect, the old rabbi of Zemyock was transported into a sobbing
ecstasy:

"Lord of the worlds," he cried between two sobs, "Lord of souls, Lord of
Peace, admire with us the pearls that drop suddenly from that mouth! Ah,
no, my children, I cannot now remain your rabbi, for this poor wanderer is a
far wiser man than I. What have I said? Far wiser? Only far wiser?"

And advancing, he embraced his horrified successor.

Translated from the French
by Stephen Becker

One of the Just Men

by Elie Wiesel

One of the Just Men came to Sodom, determined to save its inhabitants
from sin and punishment. Night and day he walked the streets and markets
preaching against greed and theft, falsehood and indifference. In the beginning, people listened and smiled ironically. Then they stopped listening: he
no longer even amused them. The killers went on killing, the wise kept silent, as if there were no Just Man in their midst.

One day a child, moved by compassion for the unfortunate preacher, approached him with these words: "Poor stranger. You shout, you expend
yourself body and soul; don't you see that it is hopeless?"

"Yes, I see," answered the Just Man.

"Then why do you go on?"

"I'll tell you why. In the beginning, I thought I could change man. Today, I know I cannot. If I still shout today, if I still scream, it is to prevent
man from ultimately changing me."

Translated from the French
by Lily Edelman and the author

The Unrecognized Just Men

by Albert Memmi

Naturally, I am exempted from work, am I not, for all that, one of the
busiest people in the realm?

An old tradition has it that the continuity of the world rests on Thirty-six

Just Men. Yet no one knows this, and no one is supposed to know it, not even those who have this mission. For were they to lose this anonymity, they would not be anything anymore, and from this there would arise some great calamities for the world—they are, and it is necessary that they should be, the unrecognized Just Men.

Am I not a prince myself? A cousin of the king, in any event, and perhaps more? Unrecognized, to be sure, that is how it was probably always supposed to be, but not by all, not by myself, at any rate—that makes the sole difference.

But, for precisely this reason, should I not be on the watch over all things? Over my royal cousin, over the public weal, and over my own person?

Translated from the French
by Emery George

The Holy of Holies

by Albert Memmi

It was the first and the only time, thank God, that a conqueror was able to penetrate into our city—and its amazement, the moment it arrived at the tabernacle! It was getting ready to lay bare our God, so mysterious, of Whom we hardly speak, and in Whom, all nations agree, resides our invincibility to this very day. While, hearts pounding, they expected to see a fabulous being, a rare animal, at the very least an unusual object, what was there to be found there at the moment they entered the Holy of Holies? Nothing, nothing; a perfectly empty space.

This, at least, is the version of the historians, one that we have never contradicted, for reasons that one can surmise. The precise account of the event is one I know better than anyone else, since the high priest is also a member of our family. Some minutes beforehand, alerted to the possibility that the fall of the city might be imminent, the high priest transported the Ark to a safe place.

That now is the way all the speculations of philosophers the world over were born concerning the nature of our God. They say it may be only an absence, a communal nostalgia, a negative cement for our collective spirit, a phantom of the virtues we do not possess, etc., etc. So then, I will put the question: If they have been this loquacious about this nothing, what could they have said, had there been something there?

Translated from the French
by Emery George

The Building of the Temple

by Franz Kafka

Everything came to his aid during the construction work. Foreign workers brought the marble blocks, trimmed and fitted to one another. The stones rose and placed themselves according to the gauging motions of his fingers. No building ever came into being as easily as did this temple—or rather, this temple came into being the way a temple should. Except that, to wreak a spite or to desecrate or destroy it completely, instruments obviously of a magnificent sharpness had been used to scratch on every stone—from what quarry had they come?—for an eternity outlasting the temple, the clumsy scribblings of senseless children's hands, or rather the entries of barbaric mountain dwellers.

> Translated from the German
> by Clement Greenberg

Temple-Builders

by Dennis Silk

One-winged angels with hods gather moodily before the temple-builders. *Just a cubit more,* says Hiram. *Windows of light,* says Solomon.
   Who can control this work-gang of unruly djinns? Hovering between moon and set-square, they're so flighty you must play them like kites.
   Twilight twists its queer fingers, halfway between this and that.
   Hiram and Solomon have enough on their hands. They dare to channel the long thought from there, to shape it under their mild hats. All the foreign wives have gone to sleep. Measure bruises the forehead.

Scroll of Fire

by Hayim Nachman Bialik

All night long the flaming seas had boiled and tongues of fire had spread themselves above the Temple Mount. Stars sprang off the heat-seared vault of heaven and earthward poured bright flames on flames. Had God then spurned His throne and shattered His own crown to bits?

And shreds of reddened clouds laden with blood and fire strayed in the vast, vast spaces of the night, recounted there among the far-off mountains the raging of the God of Vengeance and told His wrath among the desert rocks. Had God then rent His royal robe and scattered to the wind its fragments?

And there came the terror of God upon the distant mountains and a trembling seized the sullen desert rocks: the God of Vengeance, the Eternal One, the God of Vengeance shone forth!

Behold the God of Vengeance, Himself in all His glory calm and awesome, sitting on a throne of fire in the heart of a sea of flame! His robe is purple flame and His footstool burning coals. Leaping flames have encompassed Him. A cruel dance burns around Him. Upon His head flame rages, gulping greedily the void of the world. And He, calm and awesome, sits with His hands against His heart. He causes the flames to spread with the glance of His eyes and deepens the fire pits with the movement of His lids. Give glory to the Eternal, O dancing flames, give glory to the Eternal, O dance of flame and fire!

And when dawn blossomed on the mountains and pale mists stretched in the valleys, then did the seas of flame grow silent and the tongues of fire sink down from the burnt Temple of the Eternal, upon the Temple Mount. And the ministering angels had gathered as was their custom in choruses of Holiness to sing the song of dawn. And they opened the windows of the firmament and inclined their heads full toward the Temple Mount to see if the Temple doors were opened and if the cloud of incense smoke ascended. And they saw, and behold the Eternal, the God of Hosts, Ancient of Days, sitting in the morning twilight over the desolation! His garment was a pillar of smoke and His footstool dust and ashes; His head bowed low between His arms and mountains of sorrow on His head. Silent and desolate, sitting and gazing at the ruins, His eyelids darkened with the rage of all the worlds and in His eyes congealed was the Great Silence. And all the Temple Mount still smoked hills of ashes, hills of embers and smoking brands were massed together, and whispering coals in heaps and heaps, sparkling like mounds of carbuncles and rubies in the stillness of the dawn.

And the Lion of Fire that had couched upon the altar always, day and night, even he—extinguished, one orphaned lock from his mane's edge flickering, trembling and expiring on the heap of burnt stones in the stillness of the dawn. And the ministering angels knew what God had done to them, and they trembled exceedingly, and all the stars of morning shuddered with them, and the angels veiled their faces with their wings, for they feared to look upon the sorrowing of God.

And their song was turned that morning into silent lamentation and a thin still wailing. Silently they separated and wept, each angel by himself, and all the world in silence wept with them. And one soft sigh, soft and deep, arose from the end of the earth and spread itself and was shattered into a muted weeping. The heart of the world was broken, and God no longer could restrain Himself. And the Eternal awoke and roared like a lion and smote His hands together, and the Shekhinah arose from over the ruins and went into the hidden places.

Translated from the Hebrew
by Ben Aronin

The Angel and the World's Dominion
by Martin Buber

There was a time when the Will of the Lord, Whose hand has the power to create and destroy all things, unleashed an endless torrent of pain and sickness over the Earth. The air grew heavy with the moisture of tears, and a dim exhalation of sighs clouded it over. Even the legions that surround His throne were not immune to the hovering sadness. One angel, in fact, was so deeply moved by the sufferings he saw below, that his soul grew quite restless. When he lifted his voice in song with the others, a note of perplexity sounded among the strains of pure faith; his thoughts rebelled and contended with the Lord. He could no longer understand why death and deprivation need serve as connecting links in the great Chain of Events. Then one day, he felt to his horror that the eye of All-Being was piercing his own eye and uncovering the confusion in his heart. Pulling himself together, he came before the Lord, but when he tried to talk, his throat dried up. Nevertheless, the Lord called him by name and gently touched his lips. Then the angel began to speak. He begged God to place the administration of the Earth in his hands for a year's time, that he might lead it to an era of well-being. The angelic bands trembled at this audacity. But at that same moment, Heaven grew radiant with the brightness of God's smile. He looked at the suppliant with great love, as He announced His agreement. When the angel stood up again, he too was shining.

And so a year of joy and sweetness visited the Earth. The shining angel poured the great profusion of his merciful heart over the most anguished of her children, on those who were benumbed and terrified by want. The groans of the sick and dying no longer disturbed the world's deep, surging harmony. The angel's companion in the steely armor, who only a short time before had been rushing and roaring through the air, stepped aside now, waiting peevishly with lowered sword, relieved of his official duties. The Earth floated through a fecund sky that left her with the burden of new vegetation. When summer was at its height, people moved singing through the full, yellow fields; never had such abundance existed in the memory of living man. At harvest time, it seemed likely that the walls would burst or the roofs fly off, if they were going to find room to store their crops.

Proud and contented, the shining angel basked in his own glory. For by the time the first snow of winter covered the valleys, and dominion over the Earth reverted into God's hands, he had parcelled out such an enormous bounty, that the sons of the Earth would surely be enjoying his gifts for many years to come.

But one cold day, late in the year, a multitude of voices rose heavenwards in a great cry of anguish. Frightened by the sound, the angel journeyed down to the Earth and, dressed as a pilgrim, entered the first house along the way. The people there, having threshed the grain and ground it into flour, had then started baking bread—but, alas, when they took the bread out of the oven, it fell to pieces, and the pieces were unpalatable; they filled the mouth with a disgusting taste, like clay. And this was precisely what the angel found in the second house and in the third and everywhere that he set foot. People were lying on the floor, tearing their hair and cursing the King of the World, who had deceived their miserable hearts with His false blessing.

The angel flew away and collapsed at his Master's feet. "Lord," he cried, "help me to understand where my power and judgment were lacking."

Then God raised his voice and spoke: "Behold a truth which is known to me, and only to me from the beginning of time, a truth too deep and dreadful for your delicate, generous hands, my sweet apprentice—it is this, that the Earth must be nourished with putrefaction and covered with shadows that its seeds may bring forth—and it is this, that souls must be made fertile with flood and sorrow, that through them the Great Work may be born."

Translated from the German
by Jerome Rothenberg

Yaish Meets the Angels

by Hayim Hazaz

Now Yaish knew that God had granted him the power to look into the shining mirror and see visions while awake.

A great, overwhelming joy, like a flame of fire in a field of thorns, seized him. All morning long he trembled and recited hymns. His heart melted within him out of abundance of delight.

When he returned home from the bathhouse—it was Friday—after he had lunched and slept, he rushed to the synagogue. Ah, thank God, it was empty, not a soul was there. He went in, opened the ark and chanted a psalm aloud.

"My soul thirsts for the Lord, the living God.

"When shall I come to see the face of God?"

Immediately afterward, he sat down and recited the story of Isaac's sacrifice, then the penitential prayers and then mystical petitions. These he recited until the people assembled for the Sabbath Eve service.

On that particular Sabbath he rejoiced even more than he did during his own seven-day wedding feast. He sang many Sabbath hymns, toasted "good health" and drank beyond measure. He drank in honor of the ministering angels, the moon, Mari Salem Shabazi, Rabbi Simeon Bar Yochai and all the other saints who dwell in Paradise. In the end he fell, like Sisera in his day, at the feet of his wife and slept.

In the course of days he repeated that which he had done, concentrating upon his mystical intentions. He imagined that he would rise again to where the sun and moon both graze. Having risen, he found himself standing in a place which he did not recognize. He had never been there before in his life.

This was an eerie place where trees and herbs grew from the sky. The likes of which have no match in our own fields nor was their name known in our parts. They looked as if they were drawn the way the moon and the sun are: all done in heaven's colors. The void was filled with lustrous light: twilight hues, the glow of the heaven's expanse which turned to gold at midday, the brilliance of distant places which opened out toward the sky, the infinite light, the green hue which encompasses the world and the vague, hidden light—bright on the inside but dark on the outside, and similar lights, concealed from the sight of men, which the eye is powerless to sustain and the mouth to describe. Here and there, the grass was strewn with the leaf-fall of the sun, the tatters of sky and rays of light. Green and white lightning fragments and meteor tails appeared like fallen palm branches. The air was warm, as the heart is warm when it is full of yearning and longing. A deep, total and all-encompassing silence, deeper than the stars in their courses and the ball of the sun, flooded him, and he was washed by it and became oblivious of his self, of his body.

Because the silence was so very heavy, Yaish did not sense it at first. He stood bewildered and amazed, his eyes fixed upon those hues and lights. Later, when he came to himself, he grew frightened. The silence terrified him. It seemed that it lay in ambush for him, lay siege to him and hounded his very steps. Everything was stopped. There was no sound, no motion. Time stood still and all the universe had grown taut like a bow, waiting behind him in a state of surcease.

Trembling and frightened he froze in his place. His heart pounded, he found it difficult to breathe, and his lips contorted in a pitiful smile as if to assuage the terror within him. Slowly, carefully, secretly, he rolled his eyes sideways but saw nothing. He lowered his head to the earth and closed his eyes as if shutting himself out from the world. He sank into himself. Only he and his soul.

For a long time he stood. Then the white light smote his eyes and he bestirred himself. He opened his eyes and saw band after band of angels walking one after the other. There were young angels of uniform size and gait. They were little, and pretty like white geese, and were wrapped in white wings. They all looked alike.

He wanted to run away from them.

"I have nothing to do with them," he thought.

But before he could do so, the first band of angels had already caught up with him.

He took hold of himself, smiled at them and said:

"I don't know your custom but nevertheless I greet you as the custom is in our parts."

They glanced at him as they walked and asked: "Where are your wings?"

He answered: "In the wash tub."

They immediately passed his words from one to another. "He says in the wash tub. He says in the wash tub."

The first band made its way out and the second came into view. They turned to him and wondered: "Why are you clipped? Why don't you have any wings?"

He took on an excess of courage and answered: "His mind is greater than the fowl's."

Immediately they passed on his words one to another: "He says: 'His mind is greater than the fowl's.' He says: 'His mind is greater than the fowl's.' "

The second band made its way out and the third came into view.

They said: "Who are you?"

He answered: "A creature."

They asked again: "What kind of creature?"

He answered: "The righteous man *lives* by his faith!"

For what is called *Yaish* in Arabic means *lives* in Hebrew.

The third band made its way out and the fourth came into view.

They said to him as did their predecessors: "Who are you, clipped-winged one?"

He said: "A Jew."

"A Jew?" They stood wondering. But an angel who had been standing in mid-heaven and reciting "Bless the Lord Who is the blessed" said: "I'm his relative, flesh of his flesh."

"And why are you without wings?"

"Because were I to grow wings and feathers, I would cover you, the heaven, the skies and all the world."

And so the fifth band and the sixth and the seventh. When the last band arrived, they began pushing, shoving and tormenting him.

He stood frightened and drove them away.

"Home, home, home—flats full of feathers." He waved his hands and shouted as one shouts at geese and chickens.

"Keep away from me—or you'll endanger your lives."

They all jumped back.

Only one of them, a white, rotund angel whose wings hung limp because of his obesity, held his ground and chattered at him:

"How do we endanger our lives?"

"Say Amen, and get away safely," Yaish made bold. "If any angel, even a double or triple angel, even a Seraph, or a Cherub or a heavenly being, flies over me, he will burn to a cinder."

"How now does he burn, if he flies over you?" the angel queried.

"Because I'm made of fire," Yaish said in an exaggerated and threatening tone.

"And what if you are made of fire?" he said, as if this were the most natural thing.

"It is written: 'The fire of Law is opposite his right hand.' The words of the Torah are like fire and whoever approaches them is burnt."

"Where's it written, why's it written?"

"Do you know any Torah?"

"It is not in the heavens."

Yaish saw that they knew nothing of the Torah and he was pleased.

"And I know the entire Torah," he said proudly.

"And in what way are you so different now that you know the Torah?"

He soon realized the bent of the conversation and did not know what he might answer.

He began speaking in order to change the subject.

"What do you do?" he asked. "Where are you going?"

The angel, who was the most loquacious of the group, answered: "Under our Creator's orders."

Yaish sweetened his tone, smiled and asked: "How old are you, wingy?"

The other responded somewhat vaguely: "I was born yesterday."

"My chick, I'm the dust under your feet," Yaish joked with him. "Let me ask you a question."

"Ask, wingless one, ask."

"What are you, male or female?"

"As you wish."

"I wish you male."

"Good."

"Males are more important, more complete, superior. As our Sages said:

'There are three things that man does not desire: weeds in his crops, vinegar in his wine and a female among his children.' "

The angel let his head rest between his wings. He stood like a dull school-boy, pondering the matter over and over again. He said nothing.

"By your leave, may I ask you a question?" Yaish once again said gently.

"Ask, wingless one, ask."

"Tell me! What sort of birth did you have?"

The angel looked up at him in astonishment as if Yaish had asked him a very difficult question.

"How were you born?" Yaish explained.

"I don't know, since I haven't been born as yet, even once."

"You haven't been born? From where do you come?"

"From there." He lifted his wing toward heaven.

"Have you a mother?"

"I don't know."

"Perhaps a bird hatched you?"

"Perhaps."

"What do you eat?"

"What do I eat?" He cast his eyes backward toward his companions and stood confounded like one who had never heard of such a thing.

"Manna?"

"Manna," the angel repeated like a pupil repeats after his teacher.

"Manna. 'And it is like white grain and tastes like a honey wafer.' It is the bread which the angels eat, and is absorbed in all their limbs, as Scripture says. 'Man eats the bread of the mighty.' "

"I don't know."

"Perhaps *matzot?*"

"I don't know anything."

"*Matzot*—the unleavened bread which the Children of Israel ate when they left Egypt."

"I don't understand what you're saying."

"You are an ignoramus, with all due respect. You haven't learned Torah. Our Sages were quite right when they said: 'The Torah was not given to the ministering angels.' "

"If you don't eat, then you don't know Torah?"

"Certainly. Our Sages have said: 'No flour—no Torah.' "

"And have you eaten?"

"Certainly. I'll pull out your feathers and roast you and eat you from head to foot."

After a while they took their leave of him gaily and affectionately. One lifted his wing and the other his thigh and they took off.

Yaish remained behind and followed them with his eyes. After a few minutes one of them turned round and glided. In a moment, he dropped and came running to him with spread wings, and beat against his feet.

He was a little angel, soft and white as a gosling, all feathers. A fluffy, pretty ball of feathers. He had the face of an infant, eyes like the moon, and his mouth looked like a rosebud.

Yaish bent toward him and passed his hand along his feather-back, squeezing him between his wings. His heart was pounding as if he had turned his hand to sin.

"What's wrong, angel mine?" he whispered in an agitated and excited voice. "What's wrong, my Cherub?"

He seized him, lifted him high and glanced at his body and his glowing brightness. He hugged and fondled him and kissed his face. Then he began to play with him; he would let him fly and catch him, let him fly and catch him.

"O, Light of my Eye!" He threw him upwards, crying joyfully.

"Caught!" He grasped him with both hands with delight and affection.

"God bless you!" Again he threw him upwards.

"Caught!" He grasped him.

"Be blessed!" He swung him from side to side and cast him ten cubits high.

"Delicious!" He caught him under his wings and his hands were filled with feathers, pleasure and softness.

"Bravo, bravo!" He lifted him above his head and cast him into empty space.

"O my Joseph!" He caught him and pressed him to his heart.

And so the angel would fly several rounds, rise and descend, rise and descend, his face shining and glowing with much joy and frolicking. Until like a bird he lighted upon him and hung on to his chest.

Yaish stretched his hand, removed him and cast him below.

"Enough, enough," he said, "Wait a minute. Let me ask you a question."

The angel folded his wings, looked at him and stood still.

"What's your name?" Yaish said to him.

He was silent and gave no answer.

"Can't you talk?"

He answered: "I do not know my name."

Yaish said to him: "All right. Tell me how you were created. . . . What are you like, what do you do and what is God's power within you?"

He answered: "You created me."

Yaish stood dumbfounded.

"I . . . I . . . When did I create you, how—and with what? Why do you make such false accusations against me?"

He responded, "Don't you fast."

"Yes, I fast. What then?"

"I was created out of this pious act of yours."

"So—o," Yaish concluded and his face beamed.

"So, so, so."

The angel lifted his wings above his head and waved several times.

"They've given you my food and that's why you've become so fat?"

"I was created out of your pious acts, and I am nurtured from them every time you fast."

"That's ve—ry good." Yaish nodded his head, smiling with great pleasure. "Then you're m—ine. You're my son. O my soul, my liver. Let me hug you and kiss you—my angel, my angel son!"

He embraced him and kissed him.

"From now on, my child, you must listen to me and do whatever I command you. You must honor me as you've been bidden to do in the Torah. You do know what the Torah says about honoring your father?"

"What Torah? What honor?"

The angel glanced at him sideways as he stood with his wings dropped to his side and his head turned about.

"Haven't you gone to school? Don't you have a *mari* to teach you?"

"No school and no *mari*."

"Next time I'll bring a *Humash* and teach you the *Shema*, the prayers and the responses."

"The Torah was not given to the angels."

"Aren't you my son?"

"Correct, but I'm an angel."

"But you are my son. It is quite improper that I should have a son who is an ignoramus, God forbid! You are obliged to fulfill my will and God's will. You must learn Torah."

"It is not in the heavens."

"All right, my child," Yaish agreed unwillingly. "As you wish and in accordance with the local custom. But you must fulfill the commandment to honor your father. You must obey me and help me in everything necessary."

"Good."

"Not that way. Say, with God's help."

"With God's help."

After some time the angel returned, jumped upon him, clung to his chest and held on to him.

"Please let me go."

"Why do you want to leave me?" Yaish fondled his hand.

"By your leave, let me go, my time is up." He wriggled and flapped his wings against his chest.

"All right," agreed Yaish, "I'll let you go but you must promise to visit me again."

"With God's help."

The angel then spread his wings, circled two or three times and disappeared from sight.

Translated from the Hebrew
by Ezra Spicehandler

The Angel

by Jiri Langer

Everybody has a special light burning for him in the higher world, totally different from the light of every other person. When two friends meet in this world, their lights up above unite for a moment, and out of the union of the two lights an angel is born. However, the angel is only given sufficient strength to live one year. If the two friends meet again within the year they give the angel a further lease of life. But if they do not see each other for a whole year the angel wastes away and dies for lack of light. The Talmud bids us, when we see a friend whom we have not seen for a whole year, to bless God for "raising the dead." This is a strange commandment indeed, since neither of us has died. Whom then has God raised from the dead? Surely none other than the languishing angel whose lease of life is renewed each time we meet.

Translated from the Czech
by Stephen Jolly

The Sacrifice

by I. L. Peretz

Once upon a time there was a great lord who had a palace among gardens by the edge of the sea.

The lord was a widower; he had decided not to remarry, because of his two daughters, Sarah and Rebecca.

One day the lord stood at a window in his palace, watching how his daughters spent their time.

The older, Sarah, sat on a bench in the park, embroidering. He knew when she was embroidering—she was making a curtain for the Ark of the Law in the synagogue, a beautiful velvet curtain, with gold and silver em-

broidery, and set with precious stones. She was a pious soul, and a fine nee-
dlewoman.

The other, Rebecca, was busy among the flowers, picking the loveliest of
them to make a bouquet. He knew whom the bouquet was for—for him, for
her father. She was devoted to him.

His eyes turned to the sea, and his heart wondered why there were no
ships coming towards his palace with suitors for his daughters. He wanted
the joy of seeing them married.

Suddenly he saw a boat approaching the shore. The oars lay still. There
was someone in the boat, but he lay senseless, unmoving, one arm hanging
motionless over the side. Was the man ill, had the sun struck him, and he
had fainted?

The lord ran down and called his servants together, and ran off with them
to the shore. His daughters followed him.

The boat drifted ashore; they pulled it in. A young man lay in the boat,
unconscious.

"He is so handsome!" cried Rebecca.

But Sarah was already busy attending to him. She got a litter prepared,
and took him to the palace, and put him to bed. She tried to revive him, but
without success.

The lord said: "I'm going to ride to the town for a doctor." The servants
saddled a horse.

Rebecca said: "I'm going into the garden to pick some flowers for him.
He is so handsome! It will be nice for him to see the flowers when he opens
his eyes."

But Sarah stayed at the bedside, trying to make him comfortable. And she
prayed quietly for him.

The sun was setting. Shadows were creeping about in the sickroom. Suddenly the door opened, and a figure in black, with black wings, came in.

"Who are you?" Sarah cried out, frightened.

"The Angel of Death! I have come for this young man's soul."

"Don't take him!" Sarah pleaded. "He is so young and handsome! He is
asleep. Look, how he smiles in his sleep. He is dreaming, a happy dream, a
dream of life!"

"You love him?" said the Angel of Death. "Would you purchase a few
minutes of life for him?"

"A few minutes? And with what?"

"You have lovely black hair. Give me your hair."

"Take it!"

The Angel of Death took a knife from under the folds of his long black
mantle, and cut off all Sarah's hair.

Then he vanished.

He came back a few minutes later. From the garden came the sound of Rebecca singing as she gathered the flowers.

"Let me buy another few minutes of life for him!" Sarah cried. "Let me see him open his eyes!"

"You want to see his eyes? What will you give me for that?"

"What do you want?"

"I want colors—the white of your body, the red of your lips, the blue of your eyes."

"Take them!"

"Only for a few minutes."

"Yes, for a few minutes!"

Sarah's form was now shriveled, her lips were faded, her eyes dead.

Again the Angel of Death vanished. From the garden came the sound of Rebecca singing, coming nearer.

"She will be here soon!" Sarah said to herself. She wasn't sure whether the thought pleased her or frightened her.

The Angel of Death appeared the third time.

"You're back so soon!" Sarah stammered.

"Do you want to buy another two minutes for him?"

"Yes!"

"Those fine teeth of yours!"

"Take them!"

The young man has not yet opened his eyes. And Rebecca's step is already heard on the stairs.

"What more can I give you?" Sarah asks in desperation.

"Your life! Your life, your soul for his!"

"Take it!"

"Not here!" said the Angel of Death. "Go into your room, and lie down on your bed. That is how you will die."

"And he?"

"He will live! He will live a full life!"

Sarah went to her room, and the Angel of Death followed.

At that moment Rebecca entered the sickroom, singing, her arms full of flowers.

The young man opened his eyes, and stretched his arms out to Rebecca.

"My love!" he cried.

"My love!" she answered.

Translated from the Yiddish
by Joseph Leftwich

From the Beyond

by Sholem Asch

The queer story of Boruch Mordecai happened quite a number of years ago, exactly how many I could not say. He fell sick—nobody seems to remember with what—and declined so rapidly that they had to send for Solomon, the head of the burial brotherhood. Solomon entered the room, looked once at Boruch Mordecai, and ordered the company to light candles and say Psalms. Boruch Mordecai's wife let out a scream and began to tear her hair; the children sent up a heartrending wail; half the village heard and came crowding into the street—none of which did any good. For when Solomon the burial man held a goose feather to Boruch Mordecai's nose there was no sign of breath. It was all over—at any rate, that is what everyone believed.

Solomon and an assistant lifted poor Boruch Mordecai from the bed and placed him on the pile of straw on the floor. But no sooner was Boruch Mordecai stretched out with the candles at his feet, than he suddenly sneezed. In less time than you can count ten, that house was empty, except for Boruch Mordecai; for everyone fled in terror, even Boruch Mordecai's wife; even Solomon the burial man, who was used to dead people, more used to them, in fact, than to the living. But he was not used to people who were both dead and alive, and no such case had ever been heard of in the village. When they crept back into the house, they found Boruch Mordecai sitting up on the straw and looking round him vaguely. He was repeating, in a weak voice: "Sarah! Make me a bowl of grits."

Boruch Mordecai did not realize what had happened. It was only later, when he had become well, that they told him of the candles and the Psalms and the preparations for the burial. And then he actually remembered, not what had taken place about him, but his visit to the other world. He had been in heaven and had seen the Dark Angel, who consigns people to the other place. Yes, the Dark Angel had come up to him, up to Boruch Mordecai, and had asked him, "Well, what's your name?" as though he—the Dark Angel, that is—was already sure of his man. Indeed, he got hold of Boruch Mordecai by the lapel of his coat, as much as to say, "You come along with me." But at this point another angel, with white wings and a kind face, interfered. Boruch Mordecai was of the opinion that this was the archangel Gabriel but could not be sure. At any rate, Gabriel, or whoever else it was, called out: "Take it easy, there! No grabbing, if you don't mind. Because first of all we have to find out where this man belongs; which means that we have to hold a trial." And at a distance Boruch Mordecai saw people standing in cerements, with prayer shawls over them; and all the people nodded approvingly at the archangel Gabriel.

"I guess," added Boruch Mordecai, reflectively, "those must have been my forefathers, pleading for me with their good deeds. I also saw my father, God's peace be with him, and my grandfather, Reb Chanan, who, as you know, was a great saint. My father, peace be upon him, even stretched out his hand to me in welcome. At least, I think he did. I can't remember it too clearly," went on Boruch Mordecai. "Because at this point someone, maybe the angel Gabriel, flicked me with his finger on my nose, and said: 'Boruch Mordecai, you're not wanted here yet.' And that's when I opened my eyes."

And having finished this recital Boruch Mordecai suddenly realized something, for he murmured, in another tone of voice:

"Bless us all! Doesn't that mean that I've already been in the beyond? I've been in the world after this!"

From that day on the Jews of the village began to treat Boruch Mordecai with a certain respect and even to fear him a little. A man who had been in the beyond! To some extent they even avoided him. If they saw him coming toward them on the same side of the street they crossed over; that is, if he had not seen them first, because it would not have done to offend him. And if they had to stop and speak to him, they said "Good morning" hurriedly and timidly, as if he was liable to fly into a rage, and they cut the conversation short and slipped away as quickly as they could.

Boruch Mordecai soon became aware of the respect, mingled with fear, which he inspired; and this filled him with a pride and self-confidence which he had never known before. He began to display a certain touchiness. If he wasn't called up to the reading of the Law in the synagogue at the point which he thought his due, if someone got in his way accidentally at the ritual baths, if someone fell foul of him in the marketplace, and offered a peasant a better price for a sack of grain or a bushel of potatoes, Boruch Mordecai would pull his belt tighter, and say, significantly:

"I don't stand for that sort of thing. I'm a man who's already been in the beyond, in the world after this."

Hearing the words "the beyond," and "the world after this," the offenders shrank back, muttering apologetically: "Why, Boruch Mordecai, I meant no harm; there's nothing to get angry about."

As time went on, Boruch Mordecai developed a possessive attitude toward "the beyond," as though his visit had given him prescriptive rights. He remembered the incident with increasing clarity; and when he heard that someone had died, had "gone to the other world," he would say with a shrug: "Oh, I've been there," and make a rather contemptuous gesture, as though he could not understand why people made such a fuss about it or even talked about it at all.

So, whether people wanted to listen or not, whether they tried to avoid him or not, Boruch Mordecai would insist on recounting the details of his

visit. He would come upon a group sitting on the bench before the ritual
baths in the cool of the evening or before the stove in the synagogue some
winter afternoon, and he would begin to talk. The topography of "the other
world" became clearer and clearer, his relations with the Dark Angel and
with Gabriel more and more intimate. Also his own role increased and took
on character.

"I wasn't a bit afraid of them," he said. "Take my word for it, a man who
knows how to use his tongue doesn't have to be afraid of anybody. The
main thing in life is to be able to stand up for your rights, and to speak up."

Thereupon he shifted his hat to the back of his head, poked his fingers
into his dusty beard, scratched himself vigorously, and went into details.

"Lying there on the straw, after Solomon the burial man put me down, I
kept saying to myself, 'Well, now, let's see what's going to happen.' And all
of a sudden who do you think turns up, if not *he*—you know, the Dark One,
the Dark Angel, the soul-snatcher—grabs me by the lapel, and asks me:
'Name, please.' Just like that, as if he already had me! I didn't answer him
right away. So he tugs me, and says, 'Come along.' I suppose you think I
was frightened. Not a bit of it. 'Listen, you,' I say to him, 'I don't doubt for
a minute you're a very important sort of person, the Dark Angel himself and
all that, and I guess it's your business to try to grab everybody who turns up
in these parts and cart them off to the other place. Oh, yes,' I say, 'I know all
about that, don't you worry. I know your profession. All the same, take it
easy. Do you think we're still in that miserable, sinful world which I've just
left? With its police, and officials, and magistrates, and what not, where anybody can come into your store and drag you off to the police station, without a reason, without a by-your-leave? Oh, no, this is the world beyond, the
world of truth and judgment. They don't do things that way here. They
have a system here, they have justice, they have law and order. I know that,
because I've read the good books. So take it easy, because you can't frighten
Boruch Mordecai. And if you start anything crooked or irregular, I know
exactly what to do and where to lodge a complaint. I'll report you right
away to the Throne. I may have been a nobody down there, in the world
I've left, but I'm a somebody here. I'm one of the grandsons of Abraham, I
am a child of the Covenant. And Moses himself taught me the Torah and
the word of God at the foot of Sinai. I have a friend at court, if you know
what I mean. If you've got anything against me, a complaint, or accusation,
you know where to lodge it. You're not judge and executioner all rolled in
one,' I say to him. Because what did I have to be afraid of? My record's
clean. I've never eaten meat and butter together, I haven't spent my money
in the beer saloons, or gone dancing with strange women. I tell you, if you
know your life's been kosher, and there's nothing on your conscience, you
take a very different tone. And all around me stood my saintly forefathers, in
cerements and prayer shawls, and they nodded and said: 'Good for you,

Boruch Mordecai! Speak up for your rights! Don't let him try any of his games on you.'

"Well, I didn't. It's not in my nature. And you should have seen him; yes, I mean the Dark Angel himself. The moment I spoke up he softened, used a different tone of voice. 'Why, Boruch Mordecai,' he said, 'I'm not dragging you. I'm taking it easy. I'm only telling you that you've got to be put on trial like anybody else. You've got to appear before the heavenly court.'

" 'Sure,' I say. 'Everybody has to do that, and I'm ready for it, too. I'm kosher through and through, not a mark against me. I'll stand up before the Judge of the Universe, and I'll speak up. What do you think I did, in that world I've just come from? You can be sure I didn't sleep in a feather bed and drink wine in the morning—or at any other time. No,' I say, 'it was a life of labor, morning until night and through half the night. Summer and winter, heat and cold, and never a bellyful of potatoes. I brought up my children decently, made them go to school and learn the holy books. I'll stand up before the Judge of the Universe, and I'll show him the bruises on my shoulders, from the sacks I carried to the villages and farmhouses. I'll show him the welts on my sides, where the police lashed me because I couldn't afford to pay for my peddler's licence. So what are they going to do here, in this world of justice? Lash me again? I had enough of that in the other world, down there; I had enough of it to make up for all the sins I committed and didn't commit. I'll speak right out to the Judge of the Universe. What have I got to be afraid of? I've brought with me a wagonful of prayers and Psalms— all the prayers and Psalms I said in the world below.'

"Well," continued Boruch Mordecai, "you should have seen all of them open their eyes. I mean the members of the heavenly court, the angels and archangels, the whole divine council. Not a word was uttered against me. I tell you that's the main thing, to be able to open your mouth, and speak up for yourself. Even in the life beyond, in the world after death.

"They listened without interrupting me once. And when I was finished the archangel Gabriel came up to me, flicked me under the nose, and said, in a laughing way, 'Reb Boruch Mordecai, you can go back to your wife and children. You're not wanted up here yet.' So I took off my hat to him— because there's no sense in being a boor, is there?—and took myself off."

Years later, when Boruch Mordecai really died, he lay three days and three nights on his bed. They were afraid to go near him. Who could tell? Perhaps Boruch Mordecai was having it out a second time with the divine council, and perhaps it would end up the same way as before. After all, he was a man who knew how to stand up for his rights.

Translated from the Yiddish
by Maurice Samuel

The Star and the Angel of Death

by Itzik Manger

I heard the sound of beating wings. Looking up, I saw the glittering of fires at a great distance; many, many little fires. They kept coming closer; the beating of wings became stronger, swifter.

I was astonished. I had never, until then, heard such a beating of wings. "Who can it be?" I thought, straining my eyes. I saw an angel with huge black wings. He had a thousand eyes that flickered, threatening and red, through the white moonlit night. In his hand, the angel with the black wings carried a sword. "It's the Angel of Death," I realized. "No doubt, he's flying down to earth. Here in Eden, no one is afraid of him, but there, on earth, they tremble before him. No sooner do they hear the flapping of his wings than they are overcome with fear. Jews run to the synagogue to recite psalms; their wives hurry to wail at the graveyards, to ward him off. But it's said that nothing helps. Whom the Angel of Death must take, he takes. No amount of weeping or praying can help."

The angel with the black wings came closer and closer. He waved his huge sword about, making it clear that he was flying on serious business . . . a very, very serious mission.

A star detached itself from the Eden sky. It flew to greet the angel with the black wings and detained him. "Angel of Death, where are you flying?" asked the star, shuddering. I could not tell whether it shuddered for fear or for pity.

The black-winged Angel of Death answered, "I'm flying down to earth, where I'm supposed to gather the soul of a bride and bring it to the throne of God." My heart began to throb. "The soul of a bride," I thought. "Pisherl's sister is a bride." Then I remembered that the Eden brides had nothing to fear from the Angel of Death, and I felt reassured.

The star trembled and shook and pleaded. "Turn back, angel with the black wings. What do you want with the poor earthly bride? Have pity on her. Let her delight in her flowers, her love, and her dreams."

"Ah—a new pleader for justice," said the Angel of Death angrily. "Who asked you for your pity? Your duty is to shine; then shine away in good health, and don't mind other people's business."

But the star would not let up. He began to argue with the black angel, trying to persuade him: "That earthly bride is not my sister; she isn't even a relative. It's only that I saw her eyes once when she turned them up. It's only that I heard a sigh of hers once . . . a murmur. She was wishing on me, asking me to send her love to her betrothed."

"Why are you telling me this?" the black-winged angel asked sternly.

"Do you mind not standing in my way? I'd cut a fine figure, indeed, if I were to be as sentimental as you are."

The star all but sobbed. It pleaded with tears in its eyes and trembled all over. "Have you no pity for a life so young? Only nineteen years old altogether. Think a bit. Nineteen years old."

"You're something of a poet, I see," said the angel scornfully. "But it would be a lot better for you if you forbore to disturb my work."

"You're a brute and a murderer," said the star sadly. "You have a heart of stone. You aren't moved by any plea. But just remember what I tell you. . . ."

"What is there for me to remember?"

"Remember," said the star piously, "remember what is written in the Passover song about the kid . . ."

"And what does it say there?" asked the Angel of Death, ironically.

"In the song about the kid, it is written that in the end, the Lord of the Universe will come and he will slay the Angel of Death."

I saw the Angel of Death tremble. The star had reminded him of his own end. It was a remarkable shudder: the fear of death, for himself.

I was curious to know how all of this would end. Would the angel with the black wings turn back? Would the earthly bride open her eyes tomorrow morning, as always? Would she rejoice in the sun, in her flowers, in her loved one?

Evidently not. The Angel of Death whirled his sword about. Sparks all but flew from it. He spread his huge black wings and flew on.

"You're going . . ." called the star in a broken voice.

"I must," the angel answered harshly. Without further ado, he disappeared.

I could still see his gleaming eyes in the distance; I could still hear the sound of his beating wings. The star fell somewhere into the Eden grass and sought consolation among the crickets.

Strange thoughts entered my head. In the same moonlit night, I had heard the cries of children who did not want to be born; and the harsh, firm "I must" of the angel with the thousand eyes who was flying down to earth to extinguish a life.

Translated from the Yiddish
by Leonard Wolf

The Six Days and the Seven Gates

by Yitzhak Navon

On the day the king of Ammon went to Egypt the verdict was sealed. And the men of Jerusalem clapped their hands in woe and said:

"What will become of us now, for all the Arabs have encompassed us, from the River Euphrates even unto Egypt?"

There was a certain old man there; while they sat and grieved, he sat and laughed.

"Why are you laughing?" they asked him.

"Why do you grieve?" he asked in reply.

"Because war approaches," they replied, "and our enemies are cruel, and we do not know which of our sons will be killed, and what will happen to our little ones, and who will be the victor and who the vanquished."

He laughed and said: "Of you the sages said: 'No man recognizes his own miracle.' Do you not see that it has all been brought about by the Holy One, blessed be He, to produce a miracle the like of which the world has never seen before?"

"And what will become of Jerusalem?" they asked.

He said to them: "He that does not love Jerusalem, what does he see in her? Stones and dust! And he that loves her, what does he see in her? Radiance and light! She is won only by suffering; she responds only to him who woos her with yearning and supplication, and gives his soul for her sake."

Before a few days had passed, the Land was on fire in every corner—North and South and East. And the children of Israel went forth to war and put their lives in jeopardy, and they were victorious everywhere until they reached Jerusalem.

Seven gates there were in the walls of Jerusalem, and they did not know by which gate they should enter, for every gate leapt forward, dancing before them, and said:

"Enter through me, for I deserve you more than any of them."

The Holy One, blessed be He, sat in the Heavenly Assembly, with the ministering angels on His right hand and His left.

"Which gate deserves to have the redemption come through it?" He asked them. "For two angels do not perform the same mission, nor two gates bring the same salvation."

And they did not know what to answer. Michael rose and said:

"Master of the World! All are beautiful, all are deserving. Summon the gates and let them present their pleas before Thee, and Thou shalt choose one of them."

Said the Holy One, blessed be He:

"As thou livest, so will I do!"

Then He beckoned with His finger and a kind of fiery tongue descended and struck the Jaffa Gate.

"Speak thou first," He said.

The Jaffa Gate leapt forward and said:

"Master of the World! I am the gate! Two roads go forth from me: one to Hebron, to the Tombs of the Patriarchs who founded Thy people, and one to Jaffa, where the Prophet Jonah suffered for Thy sake. May their virtues speak for me before Thee, that the redemption may be brought about through me. Let the young men of Israel enter through me, and I shall protect them; if all the winds in the world were to come and blow at me, they would not shift me from my place. And I shall make a covenant with the Tower of David, which is on my right hand, and we shall be of one counsel together."

As the Jaffa Gate spoke, Gabriel wrote down his plea, and the angels congregated together and said:

"True, it is deserving, it is deserving."

Then the Shechem Gate reared up on its pillars, higher than any part of the wall, and cried with a loud voice:

"I am the gate from which the road goes to Shechem, where stands Mount Gerizim, the Mount of the Benedictions, and Mount Eval, the Mount of the Maledictions. The maledictions have all been fulfilled. Now fulfill Thou the blessings. And if the sons of the tribes enter through me, Judah and Ephraim will become one band and one kingdom."

When leave was given, the Zion Gate leapt forward and said:

"Master of the World! I am the gate after which Thy Holy City was named Zion. Look down from Heaven and see, behold from Thy sacred habitation: I am all over wounds and bruises, fissures and fractures. All Thy calamities and tribulations have passed over me: Israel struck at me trying to enter, and the Arabs struck at me to stop them. And was it not I alone who opened myself in the War of Independence and let the young men of Israel enter Thy Holy City?"

As it spoke, the ministering angels wept and said:

"It is deserving, it is deserving!"

And they could not look upon its sorrow.

Then the Dung Gate trembled and said:

"Master of the World! See how I stand before Thee, poor and humble, shamed and degraded, half of me buried in the ground. Over me generation after generation has cast its refuse and I bowed myself, saying: 'Better the refuse of Jerusalem than the jewels of the whole world!' And when, if not now, wilt Thou fulfill in me Thy promise: 'He that lifteth the needy out of the dunghill'? Nor is that all, for every day I gaze at the Western Wall, see it in its wretchedness, and soothe it with words of consolation."

And the Wall shook itself and said:

"It has spoken the truth!"

Then the Holy One, blessed be He, said to Michael:

"Fine counsel thou gavest Us to summon the gates and listen to their pleas! Now that We hear, Our Heart is touched and Our Eyes burn with pain. See what counsel thou gavest!"

Then Michael replied:

"Sufferings cleanse the gates. Now that we have heard four gates, we cannot refrain from hearing the other three, for it might be said, Heaven forbid, that there is partiality in the Heavenly Assembly!"

Then the Flower Gate leapt forward and said:

"Heaven forbid that the young men of Israel should enter through the Dung Gate. On the contrary, let them go in through the Gate of Flowers, for if they enter through me, I shall pluck my flowers and crown the heads of our dear ones with them."

Hardly had it finished speaking, when a great cry was heard, and the angels saw the prophet Jeremiah tearing his garments and crying:

"Master of the World! How long will the Heavenly Assembly pile up words? Our sons are being killed there below, and you are debating by which gate they shall enter!"

Gabriel wished to rebuke him, but the Holy One, blessed be He, said to him:

"Let Jeremiah be, for he prophesied the Destruction, and the embers of his prophecy still glow and burn his tongue!"

Then the Holy One, blessed be He, gave leave, and the New Gate, in the West, shook and said:

"Master of the World! I am the least of the gates and I have no right of seniority, but I am lowly and humble, so that a tiny hillock seems to me a mighty mountain. And all the time my heart has been sore, for the legions of the sons of Ammon have been standing on my back and showering the Children of Israel with fire. How often have I tried to shake them off, but could not cast them down! Let me be credited with the virtue of my sorrow."

The angels said:

"It is humble, and small, and fitting for Israel!"

But the Court decreed:

"The gate is new, and is not numbered among the Seven Gates."

And the gate went aside into its corner and wept.

Before they could say anything more, a great wind came, and the voice of Moses, the son of Amram, thundered out from the banks of the Jordan and cried:

"How long will the Heavenly Assembly remain in session? You are a cruel court, for all night the Children of Israel are held down on Ammunition Hill and their blood flows to the Jordan, while you sit and debate!"

The ministering angels tried to silence him, but Moses protested and said: "I will not obey you!"

"Moses, Moses," they said to him. "This is the Court and thou canst not disturb it."

Then Michael came forward to the Almighty and said:

"The night is over and done, but the sun does not wish to shine."

"For what reason?"

He said to Him:

"Because if it rises in the East it will blind the eyes of the Children of Israel, who come from the West," he replied.

Then the Holy One, blessed be He, said to him:

"Go and tell the sun that since the days of Gideon there is no changing the order of creation!"

Michael went out and came back, and said:

"It refuses to emerge from its sheath!"

"Scourge it until it emerges!" said the Holy One, blessed be He.

Then Michael scourged it with sixty rods of fire until the sun emerged from its sheath. And it wept as it shone, seeking a cloud to hide its face, but not finding one, for those were the days of Iyar.

Then the Holy One, blessed be He, gave a sign, and a spark of fire descended and struck the Mercy Gate. The Mercy Gate leapt from its place and began to cry. Its voice was indistinct, for it is blocked on both sides, one side for mercy and one side for repentance.

"Master of the World!" it said. "For many generations my mouth has been sealed with stones. All the other gates may be opened or may be closed, but my entrance is blocked and large stones are embedded in my throat. From here the Shekhinah, the Divine Presence, went into exile, and from here She is destined to return. I look out upon the Mount of Olives, and to me men have come all through the years and wept upon my neck and pressed me, saying: 'Open thyself, open, that the Shekhinah may enter in.' And I weep and say: 'Since the day the Temple was destroyed, an iron wall has risen between Israel and their Father in Heaven. Leave me alone, and go entreat your Father in Heaven.' "

Before it had finished speaking, a cry of agony was heard, rending the seven firmaments. The angels looked down and saw Rachel tearing her hair.

"Master of the World!" she cried. "How long wilt Thou lead my sons to the slaughter? Didst Thou not say to me, 'Refrain thy voice from weeping, and thine eyes from tears, and thy children shall come again to their own border'? Was it of living children Thou didst speak, or of the dead?"

And the ministering angels hid their faces in shame. Then the Holy One, blessed be He, said to her:

"Rachel, my daughter! What I have promised I shall fulfill, and thine eyes shall see it. We shall hear one more gate, and decide."

He stretched forth His hand and a flame descended upon the Lions' Gate. His voice thundered forth and He said to it:

"Speak!"

The Lions' Gate shrank, and did not say a word.

"Speak!" said the Holy One, blessed be He, but it still refused.

Then He scourged it with a rod of flame until it spoke:

"Master of the World! Every moment I can see from here, on the eastern side, soldiers of Israel on the hills and on Mount Scopus, and at the feet of the gates I see them falling, scorched by fire. Let them enter by any gate, so long as not another single one of them falls!"

When the Holy One, blessed be He, heard this, said He to it:

"Since thou hast belittled thyself, and held the lives of the young men dearer than thine own glory, I hereby decree that they shall enter through thee, and from thee shall salvation come to my Holy Mount. Let the young lions enter through the Lions' Gate!"

And before an hour passed, a flood of Israel's youth broke through the Lions' Gate in iron cars, and thence on to the Temple Mount and the sanctities of Israel.

Translated from the Hebrew
by Misha Louvish

The Golden Gates of Jerusalem

by Matti Megged

Jerusalem has seven gates, which correspond to the seven days of the week as well as to the seven ages between the war of Gog and Magog and the coming of the Messiah. And the seven days came together upon Mount Moriah and prostrated themselves before the Throne of Mercy, and each one of them spoke in turn, saying: "I shall place the royal crown on the head of the Messiah."

The First Day, the day of semen, spoke first and said that except for him, no one born of woman would come into the world, and therefore no one would expect the Messiah to come.

Then the Second Day, the day of dust and ashes, to which we all return, spoke up and said in his own praise that but for him the creatures of the world would be fruitful and multiply and fill the whole world, until there would be no room left for the Messiah to come.

Then the Third Day, the day of righteousness and light, said that if not for his deeds, the Messiah could not come.

Against him argued the Fourth Day, the day of darkness and sin, that did not the sons of Adam see evil and sin, they could never attain righteousness.

The Fifth Day, the day of the voice and the word, also had many reasons and arguments of his own.

And the Sixth Day, the day of the works of creation, rose up and tried to outshout all of the others.

And the Seventh Day shone above them all and remained silent. And why was he silent? Because he was certain that it was he who was destined to place the royal crown on the head of the Messiah, for he is the day that came after the completion.

And the Holy One, in whose hands lay the choice, came and placed the crown into the hands of the Seventh Day, and said to him: "You shall bring the Messiah."

Translated from the Hebrew
by the author and Howard Schwartz

The Messiah at the Gates of Rome

by Der Nister

According to legend, the Messiah sits at the gates of Rome, sore-ridden and leprous, and bandages, unbandages, rebandages his sores. . . .

Dawn. At first the singer sees fog where his glance is directed. Then it begins to lift, and from afar a city begins to show itself to him: houses, walls, one higher than the other, one above the other, also whole city quarters, some evident on hillsides, others at their feet—in valleys.

It is still early. The city still sleeps. But one feels a great disquiet in her sleep. As if she will soon awake and after her sinful night open her eyes outward to the day—again onto day, night, and sin.

Now it's already light. From the city people start to leave, and to the city, from various far-off corners and roads, drawn, arriving, alighting, begin to arrive peasants from faraway villages to provide the town with food. Tradesmen, peddlers, soldiers, cripples, tax collectors, serfs, magicians, beggars, and whores, come from all corners of the land to provide for the town's nightly pleasures. And all those who leave the city and those who enter it, all who pass through the gates, feel obliged in passing, to spit on the sores of the man seated there. Some spit on his head, some on his face, some on his clothes and rags. Sometimes he wipes away the spittle, but for the most part he sits frozen and mute, as though it is not at him that they spit.

Now the singer starts to wail and his limbs to quiver. He sees that shining face spat upon by wild, gross soldiers, tradesmen, peddlers, cripples, and whores. Phrases and half-phrases of old liturgists, of old sorrowful folk singers come to his mind, and together with them he moves, and together with one of them he calls out, as if wounded:

"My wounds have not softened
And my bruises are terrible
And my eyes have grown dim
Searching for my glorious redeemer."

He seeks solace and finds none. His only relief is in imagining himself in the other's place, as if it were the other who was sore-ridden and spat-at, and as if it were he who took upon himself the other's disgrace, the other's silence, and the other's knowledge that his fate has been predetermined by a lofty destiny, and that his fate is a privileged, a great gift bestowed by gracious hands.

Translated from the Yiddish
by Evelyn Abel

Forcing the End

by Hugh Nissenson

Having refused a chair, Rabbi Jacobi stands in front of my desk, pulling the tuft of white beard that sprouts beneath his underlip.

"All I want," he says, "is your permission to leave the city, go to Yavneh, open up a school there, and teach."

"Yes, I understand, Rabbi, but unfortunately, under the circumstances, I must refuse you permission."

"What circumstances?"

"For one thing, you'll be safer here."

"Really?" he asks. "Look out the window and tell me what you see."

"Jaffa Road."

"Look again."

I rise to my feet. The street, the entire city has vanished. We are in a wilderness, where a white haze has effaced the boundary between the earth and the azure sky. Mount Scopus is a barren rock, illuminated on its eastern slope by the morning sun. Huge, yellowish limestone boulders, tinged with red, reflect the glaring light. The ruins of buildings? It's impossible to tell. They seem to have been strewn indiscriminately on the parched ground shimmering from the rising heat. Only an ancient, twisted oak, with shriveled leaves, grows there, just below my window, and as I watch, a jackal which has been sleeping in the shade rises unsteadily, its pink tongue lolling from its jaws, and pisses against the tree trunk: a short spurt of urine, in which, suddenly dropping from the cloudless sky, a starling immerses itself for an instant, fluttering its wings and catching a few drops in its gaping beak.

And twisting the tuft of hair below his mouth, Jacobi says, "You're looking at the Holy City through my eyes."

"The past?"

He shrugs. "The future, too. What's the difference? They're one and the same."

"That's impossible."

"Nevertheless, God help us, it's true," he says, covering his face with his hands. As he has been speaking, a Sammael, one of our new, self-propelled rocket launchers, roars up Jaffa Road in the direction of the Russian compound. Its two rockets, capable of carrying nuclear warheads, are covered by canvas.

Jacobi twists that tuft of beard between the thumb and forefinger of his right hand. Is he a hypnotist, or what? I read over his dossier, open on my desk, once again. He was born in Jerusalem in 1917 and was ordained at the age of nineteen. After that, for twelve years, he was the rabbi of the small town of Arav in the southern Galilee, where he also worked as a clerk in the local post office because he refused any remuneration for teaching Torah. His wife died last year, and he lost his only son at the age of sixteen to nephritis. The boy was also a precociously brilliant scholar, of whom his father said at his death, "I am consoled by the fact that my son, may his memory be blessed, fulfilled the purpose for which man was created—the study of the Holy Law."

For the last eight years, Jacobi has lived in Jerusalem, teaching a select group of students in a small Talmud Torah on Adani Street. He has been in constant conflict with the rabbinate over its acquisition of extensive property, and with the government over its policy of retaliatory raids for terrorist attacks.

My secretary, Dora, whose husband was killed two years ago by an Arab grenade while serving on reserve duty in Gaza, comes into my office and whispers excitedly in my ear, "Sunday, at dawn."

"How do you know?"

"Yoram's sister heard it from her husband."

"Who's her husband?"

"The pilot."

"What's the matter with you? You know how tight security is. It's just another rumor."

She adds without conviction, "Yoram's sister swears it's the truth," and sighs. She has aged extraordinarily in the last two years; her lips are as wrinkled as an old woman's.

"No, there's still time," Jacobi says. "Not much, but enough. At least enough for me to go to Yavneh, open my school, and plant a few lemon trees. They're very delicate, you know, but I love the odor of the blossoms, don't you? Sweet but spicy. An unusual combination." He goes to the door and says, "Tell me the truth. Do you honestly believe that this time we'll achieve a lasting peace?"

"Absolutely."

"By force of arms?"

"Of course."

"Really? How I admire your faith. Let me tell you something, my friend. A secret. When I'm in Yavneh, and if one day I'm planting a sapling and I hear that the Messiah himself has arrived, do you know what I'll do? Finish planting the sapling, and then go to welcome him." He opens the door. "Did you know that lemons turn yellow only after they've been picked? It's a fact. They remain green and bitter on the tree. You have to store them for months before they turn yellow and ripen."

"Not any more," Dora says. "A specially heated storage plant forces them to ripen in four or five days."

"Is that so? How hot?"

"I'm not sure."

"As hot as this?" he asks, and in the sweaty palm on his right hand he holds up a yellow lemon. "From the new storage plant in Yavneh, by the way, and fully ripe, as you can see; juicy too, with a wonderful smell. . . ."

He passes it under Dora's nose.

"Right?" And closing his eyes and inhaling deeply, he recites the traditional benediction, " 'Blessed art Thou—the Eternal, our God, King of the Universe—who hath given fragrance unto fruit.' " Then he smiles, and says, "This one, for your information, was picked from a tree four and a half days ago and then stored at exactly 22°C." He twirls it in the air. "Why, one could almost imagine it's the world: cut off from its source, mercifully ignorant of its state; and just think: some minute malfunction of some machine in that storage plant, for example, or more likely some human error, and the temperature rises only three or four degrees, and look at it now! That marvelous color splotched brown. See? This whole side has changed its color; faintly, but changed, nevertheless, and it's gotten soft—feel it—rotten . . ."

"Where is it?" Dora cries out. "I know. Up your sleeve." But, shaking his head, Jacobi replies, "No, it was only a trick. Well, not exactly that, but . . ."

"What?" she asks, in a peculiar, strident voice that makes Jacobi stare at her. She looks him straight in the eye.

"It's true about you and your brother, isn't it?" he asks, but she says nothing. She and her brother Menachem are reputed to be important members of the Knives, a new, illegal organization allegedly responsible for the murders of a prominent writer who advocated trying to make peace with the Arabs by restoring to them all their territory which we now occupy, and an eighteen-year-old pacifist who, last fall, refused to register for the draft.

Leaving the door open, she goes into the outer office and, with an unlit cigarette dangling from her wrinkled lips, sits down at her desk and pecks away with one finger at some official form, in triplicate, stuffed into her old Remington typewriter. Jacobi follows her. Six of his students from the Talmud Torah on Adani Street crowd around him, speaking Yiddish in hushed, agitated voices. One boy, not more than fifteen, fixes his dark eyes on me and grimaces. He's deformed in a way I've never seen. His right arm is normal, but the left, hanging loose, reaches his knee.

Two days later, at about four, while I'm having my afternoon glass of tea and a butter cookie, I idly glance out of the window again. Four soldiers, in battle dress and armed with submachine guns, are patrolling the street. Each one has inserted a thirty-round magazine into his weapon, behind the trigger guard, and has taped another magazine at right angles to the first, to facilitate rapid reloading. Their footfalls, I notice, are muffled by the sandbags which last night were heaped up, waist high, against the walls of the buildings.

Then, at a command from their sergeant, they break rank, to allow a funeral procession to pass down the center of the street. Four bearded men, dressed in black kaftans, are carrying an unpainted pine coffin on their shoulders. Behind them, three women, with fringed black shawls over their heads, are howling at the top of their lungs. In spite of the sandbags, the din is terrific. About to shut the window, I notice that the boy with the long arm is also following the coffin. With his good hand, he rhythmically pounds his chest, and his narrow face is twisted by the same grimace he gave me—a grimace that bares his yellow upper teeth to the gums.

"Who is it?" I shout down. "Who's died?" But the howling women, who are now scratching their cheeks with their fingernails, drown me out.

"Answer me," I yell louder, and the boy with the long arm raises his face.

"Our master," he yells back. "The Light of the World."

"Rabbi Jacobi?"

He nods, and Dora, who has been standing behind me, rushes down to the street, where I can see her arguing with one of the pallbearers, who has trouble balancing the coffin and rummaging in his pocket for some papers at the same time. When she returns, she says, "They've gotten permission to bury him in Arav."

"Arav?"

"Next to his kid."

"What about transportation?"

"Two horse-drawn carts, if you can believe it."

"Who authorized them to leave the city?"

"What's-his-name. Oh, you know who I mean. That Litvak from the Ministry of Interment who dyes his hair. Kovner."

"Are you sure?"

"Yes," she says. "I'm sure." And she glances at her briefcase, on the filing cabinet, in which she keeps the yellowing document, signed by Kovner, which authorized the burial of her husband, with full military honors, on Mount Herzl.

The next morning, Shmelke Kalb, who works in an office across the street, throws open my door, waving a newspaper in my face. As usual, he's wearing a steel helmet; not because he's the air-raid warden in charge of the block, but because he suffers from skin cancer, a discolored blotch on his forehead, and puts on the helmet whenever he has to go outside, to protect himself from the sun.

"Have you read about Jacobi?" he asks.

"No, but I'm sorry, in a way."

"What're you talking about? Are you crazy? He's deserted the city. And five or six more of his students have already joined him in Yavneh."

"But that's impossible. The man's dead. I saw his funeral procession."

"A sealed coffin?"

"Yes."

"It was a trick to smuggle him out of the city."

"What're you saying?"

"Some of his students nailed him into a coffin and smuggled him out of the city two days ago. It's all here, in this morning's paper, along with some kind of manifesto for some new kind of school he wants to start."

"Let me see that," I tell him, and then read aloud:

" 'We shall be as the disciples of Aaron, loving peace, pursuing peace, and teaching Torah which alone sustains the Jews who, if they faithfully follow its Holy Principles, will be redeemed by them, and then redeem all mankind, in God's good time . . .' "

Dora has come to the door; Kalb lowers his voice: "They say Kovner has disappeared without a trace."

At one—during critical times like these, we grab a sandwich for lunch at the office—I turn on the radio for the latest news.

". . . which will demand from each of us the greatest sacrifice . . . credence, which, although . . . New York . . ."

I can catch only a word now and then because of the noise: columns of Sammaels, rattling the windowpanes, have been roaring up the stre et for the last two hours. I twist the knob, and unexpectedly, in a perfectly audib le voice, the announcer says that Rabbi Jacobi's body, spattered with dried blood, was discovered in Yavneh early this morning in front of a vegetar ian restaurant on the Rishon-Lezion road. A preliminary coroner's report has established that the distinguished religious leader was stabbed once throu gh the heart with a penknife, and died instantly, between 2 and 3 a.m. The district superintendent of police reports that no fingerprints were found on the weapon, but he has been quoted that he is confident that the criminal or criminals will soon be apprehended because of a peculiar aspect of the case. The distinguished rabbi's jaws were pried open after his death, and a yellow lemon inserted in his mouth. . . .

Another Sammael, which makes it impossible for me to hear Dora shouting from the outer office, where she's been pecking away at the Remington.

"What?" I ask.

"Green," she says. "The idiot. Not yellow, green."

On the Life and Death of Abbaye

by David Shahar

Abbaye never saw his father in his life, so he loved his mother deeply. Only when he had grown a bit and was a boy of about six or seven did she disclose to him that she was not his mother but just his nursemaid. Nevertheless, he continued to love her and call her mother. She told him that his father had died after his mother conceived, and that his mother had died giving birth to him. As he matured he did not alter his relations toward the old, good nursemaid. When he mentioned her in his speeches—and this occurred frequently, even in the house of study—he would say "the matriarch said to me." Abbaye the man could no longer say "mother" as he had in his childhood, for in truth she was not his mother. Yet remarkably, the very absence of this private connection led Abbaye to elevate his nursemaid, by means of the appellation "the matriarch," to the higher level of a woman who is a mother in her soul.

If not for the love with which the nursemaid loved the orphan and if not for her knowledge of how to impart this to him, she would surely have damaged the joyousness imbedded in him. Furthermore, he would have counterfeited the natural rhythm that quivered within him from womb and from birth. He would laugh so much simply from love of life that his teacher and master Rabbah feared for him lest he be seized by frivolousness and cast off the life of the spirit which prepares the soul for the world to come. But as we well know, all his fears proved groundless.

As for the rhythm deep in his blood, he would entertain his aged teacher with the egg game. Abbaye would play before Rabbah with eight eggs, throwing one and catching another without any of them touching. I once saw, in a movie featuring some of the greatest performers of the circus world, a master artist who juggled eight colored wooden bottles. He received circusdom's grand prize for his wondrous integration with the rhythm of the laws of gravity and acceleration, so wondrous that while the wooden bottles were in flight he himself would fly, executing acrobatic leaps. Later, I was privileged to see him perform in person when the Coliseum Circus came to Jerusalem. It was fascinating to observe the tension of joy not only in his face but in every movement and flutter of his arm and leg muscles and his entire body that set the wooden bottles in motion and entered into their acceleration with that total linkage of heart and soul which alone made it possible to overcome the rhythm, to dominate it, and which caused the first effervescence of joy to quiver in every tissue and orifice of his body, to quiver from all the danger hovering over the mouth of the abyss.

The danger of falling is the constant hidden danger of any deviation from the cadence. Most men, and especially those who are called in our day "men of the spirit" or "experts in the humanities," of every stripe, do not even feel their own falling because they are usually crawling on the bottom of the deepest possible chasm. But even these men, who are completely insensate toward rhythms and who, therefore, cannot feel deviations from them, nevertheless sense, at least, the absence of one of the manifestations of harmony—the absence of happiness. They comfort themselves with the proverb that he who increases knowledge increases sorrow, without relating to the accuracy and the truth of the saying. All knowledge that is cut off from wisdom is sad in itself as well as saddening to all who look upon it, and contains nothing to cause rejoicing until such time as it links itself to wisdom, as it is said, *For to the man, that is good in His sight, He gives wisdom, and knowledge, and joy,* and therefore, *Happy is the man who finds wisdom*—wisdom is the path, and the path is the harmony of the rhythms, and every high-wire artist who walks along a rope stretched over the mouth of the abyss, and every black who dances to jazz, is closer in his way to wisdom than the crippled-spirited scientist who knows with strict accuracy the chemical formula of the blood coursing in the veins of the acrobats and the dancers.

Abbaye was a greater man than that charming young circus acrobat because of his inner rhythm. He did not juggle wooden bottles, which remain unbroken when they fall, but fragile eggs, which require a higher degree of rhythmic precision. And all this he did not with the rigorous practice regimen of the professional but as a pleasant diversion during free moments, when he would rest from the other cadence in which he immersed his life. Because of his delicate feelings for rhythms he did not tend to mingle them together, as it says of him in the Talmud: "Abbaye said, 'When the matriarch said to me, "Bring some *kutach*," I could not study.' " In our days we call this food *kutach* by the names yogurt, *lebeniah*, or *leben* mixed with bread crumbs.

When Abbaye sailed on the surface of the rhythm of study, anything at all, even the most trivial, belonging to another wave or a different frequency than his own would destroy his equilibrium, for with him study was not just an external affair of the conscious mind. Even the beloved nursemaid, who was the one creature in the entire world who was close to him, would, with her meager request to bring her a bowl of *kutach*, make him fall from the waves of study, just as she would, with the same tiny supplication, knock him from the rope he walked on in his free playful moments. This refined sensitivity to different kinds of waves was linked to the basic purity within him, the purity based on the distinction and differentiation of different fundamentals, the recoiling from before everything that served as a barrier cutting him off from the essence of things

This purity, like his inner rhythm and the love of life fermenting within him, had already been uncovered in his childhood. In the days when they were still schoolchildren Abbaye and Rava would sit in front of Rabbah and learn. Once Rabbah said to them, "Whom do we bless?" They answered him, "God." Asked Rabbah, "And where does God dwell?" Rava pointed to the roof-sky, in other words, to the ceiling above their heads, while Abbaye went outside and motioned toward the heavens. Rabbah told them, "Both of you will be wise." The difference between the two future wise men was revealed in their childhood. Rava with his abstract, theoretical approach indicated the general direction in its logical, mathematical, schematic form, whereas Abbaye, who felt the essence of things and the resonance of their waves with all his two hundred and forty-eight organs and three hundred and sixty-five sinews, could not bear the ceiling, which separated him from God who dwells in heaven, and distorted the waves passing through it. He therefore went outside in order to point directly, without any barriers, to the source of emanation.

I noted that the nursemaid was the one and only living creature in the whole world who was close to him. Her heart ached for him during the immense loneliness of his childhood, so she raised a lamb who would go into the outhouse with him.

Truly, every man is alone, particularly in the outhouse. He is much more alone there than he can possibly imagine in these our shortsighted days. The orphan boy Abbaye both knew of and felt abysmal loneliness in the outhouse, but the lamb, raised by his nursemaid in her great compassion, preserved him not only from loneliness but more important from the gaping hole itself which is none other than the devils' chasm.

The angels who accompany man on the paths of his life walk with him everywhere he goes except to the privy. Consequently, he who enters an outhouse turns to his angels and says: "Be thou honored, oh holy honored ones, servants of the Most High, and give thou honor to the God of Israel! Depart from me while I enter and do my will, and then I will return to thee." For as long as he remained a child and the lamb, who entered the outhouse with him, served as a living link to the tangible, vital world, Abbaye felt relieved after he said the accepted prayer. But when he grew up and became a leader of the Jews, and the little lamb raised by the matriarch was no longer at his side, his awareness of and terror of the devils' abyss increased within him to such an extent that the prayer changed in his mouth to a cry for help. As it is written: "Abbaye said: 'A man must not pray thusly, lest they leave him and go. Instead he should say, "Guard me, guard me! Help me, help me! Draw near unto me, draw near unto me! Wait for me, wait for me from when I enter until I leave, for this is the way of men." ' "

His greatest fear was the fear "lest they leave him and go." Father and mother had left him from the moment he breathed the air of the world. When he opened his physical eyes to the concrete world the dim memory of the two figures remained, growing ever more distant until swallowed by the night of the day of earthly life. Since then, the fear "lest they leave him and go" would return and hover every time he entered the demon-filled privy.

The world is full. Emptiness prevails only in the superficial type of consciousness that both creates flowery platitudes and finds them where they do not exist, as in the exact and exhaustive expression "the world and all its fullness." The expanse of the universe is filled with angels and devils, for behold, our cosmos is the world of confusion, a mixture of angels and devils. In a place where angels do not tread, there reign devils. Since, to this day, no one has carried out deep comprehensive research on the subject, we still do not know what the reason is—or what the reasons are—that several outhouses were the demons' particular favorites and were therefore quite dangerous, like the famous privy in Tiberius into which no one would enter, even by day, except in pairs.

In order to send a regular devil fleeing one says: "Thou wast closed up; closed up wast thou. Cursed, broken, and destroyed be the Son of Clay, Son of Defilement, Son of Filth as Shamgaz, Merigaz, and Istamai." However, to the demon of the privy known as Bar Shirikai Pandai, one should speak thusly: "On the head of a lion and on the snout of a lioness did we find the demon Bar Shirikai Pandai; with a bed of vetch I hurled him down and with the jawbone of an ass I smote him."

One can assume that the Kabbalah refers mainly to these children of Shirikai Pandai in its saying concerning the devils who are born from every issue of semen that goes to waste. The demon, like every monster, is a creature lacking proportion. In visible monsters, one sees the hideousness of a limb or limbs that deviate from the proper sizes or that are attached to each other in abnormal numbers or ways, or a conspicuous lack of equilibrium of its spiritual characteristics. As to devils, absence of proportion is ensconced in the kernel of their essence with regard to the two primary foundations from which all creatures are composed, in other words, the physical and the spiritual foundations. Surprisingly, it is the physical foundation which is deficient in demons because their bodily gestation was halted and did not reach completion, leaving them neither here nor there. They are not totally spiritual, for they are invested with the first portion of physicality, but neither are they dressed in a tangible body, for their gestation never lasts to the point of birth. Their existence in and of itself is one of pain and suffering from belonging to both here and there, that is, total lack of belonging. Worse than these sufferings is the torment of the naked striving of a force that will never be capable of actually doing anything because of the absence of bodily tools.

I possess no additional information on the situation of Abbaye in the privy during his adulthood other than the prayer he composed. It is very likely that after the death of the lamb which his nursemaid raised for him in his childhood he was left without any helper in this world of ours, even though he was married. His wife was no help to him in contrast to the wife of his childhood friend and adult rival. In truth, it is told of Rava's wife that she would place a nut in a copper mug and rattle it to and fro every time her husband eased himself. Furthermore, after he was made head of the yeshivah and the menace of demons increased—for clearly the danger lies mainly in their envy of human beings—she made a window in the outhouse door and rested her hand on his head whenever he sought relief.

Abbaye's wife did not rattle nuts in copper cups, nor did she cut windows in privy doors in order to put her hand on her husband's head to ward off flying devils and naked demons that are not perceived by the senses. Perhaps Abbaye never asked that of her. It is even possible that he hid from her his great fear stemming from the disappearance of the two figures, becoming ever more distant until swallowed by the night of the sea of earthly life. And perhaps the cry of his prayer, "Guard me, guard me! Help me, help me! Draw near unto me, draw near unto me! Wait for me from when I enter until I leave, for this is the way of men," he carried within his heart, his lips alone moving so that his voice would not be heard by her ears.

Huma was her name in Israel, and she was, as they say, a real woman with healthy urges. She loved to eat the finest food and to drink much wine. Abbaye was careful to keep from her, in his heart, everything that was beyond her perception and perceptions, yet with equal care he would dote on her, granting all her desires. In his physical love for her he would even slake her thirst with gigantic pitchers of wine called *shoprazin*, although he himself abstained. Before she was married to the joyful and quickbodied "Great One of the Generation" she managed to wed twice and bury both her husbands, who were flushed from her heart and forgotten from the moment she heard Abbaye's laugh and saw his muscles dance as he made eight eggs fly heavenward at once and caught them without even one touching another. When she married him he fulfilled all the hopes she had rested on him, if not more. His urges were even stronger than her own. Once, when it became clear to him that he was unable to subjugate his passion for other women, he went off and, sunk in sorrow, leaned against the bolt of a door. An old man came by and recited to him: "He who is greater than his fellows, his urges too are greater than theirs." But in the end Abbaye did not have a long life with Huma. Even he walked the path of the two husbands who preceded him.

When Abbaye died, the facing cliffs of the river Hedekal came together in a kiss. The banks of the mighty torrent seemed to draw nigh from the great number of people accompanying his casket who filled the bridge. As with every man, however, Abbaye too, died alone. Among the vast multitude who escorted "the vessel that was emptied of its contents" walked Rava, his surviving friend.

One day, after Abbaye's death, Rava returned home from a session of the rabbinical court and his wife noticed that his face did not bear its normal expression. She approached him, looked him over and asked, "Who was at the court today?" Rava replied, "Abbaye's wife." His wife became silent and continued to stare at him. He then related that Huma, Abbaye's wife, had appeared in court for him to determine her legal food allowance from her late husband's estate. Rava gave his decision, at which point the widow said to him: "Grant me wine!" Rava hesitated, then told her: "I know that Nahmani, My Comforter—thus everyone affectionately called Abbaye during his life—did not drink wine and therefore it is not just that I apportion you also wine from his possessions." Huma replied, "On your life, my master, he would give me drink from a *shoprazin* like this." And as she showed him her arm it became uncovered and a light shone in the court.

Rava's wife did not ask him additional questions nor did she utter a sound. She went over to a trunk, took from it the *kolpi*, the bar with which a chest is enclosed, went outside to Huma, and began beating her with the rod in her hand. She screamed and struck her until she chased her out of the entire city of Mahoza. "You killed three," she shouted at her, "and you came to kill another!"

If one of the professional eulogists of our day would have sought to portray Abbaye's death, he would certainly have said of him that he was slain on the altar of love. In any case, it is certain that in that grand rhythm of life and death, Abbaye was interwoven wholly with the rhythms of life.

Translated from the Hebrew
by Jeremy Garber

The Temptations of Rabbi Akiba
by David Pinski

Heavens, how stern and pious a Jew this Rabbi Akiba was! Scarcely his peer to be found in all Judea.

He devoted all his days and all his nights to the Holy Law, studying it himself and expounding it to others. The number of his disciples was a veritable army, and whoever heard the Torah from his lips felt that he drank from the very source of life.

Not only did he teach the Torah's word, but also how to live its very spirit, how to purge oneself of gaiety; for laughter, play and mirth all led to sin.

He, too, dwelt in all simplicity, renouncing every earthly pleasure. He was deeply in love with his wife, the beautiful Rachel, the wise and learned daughter of Kalba-Sabua. But in order to belong entirely to the Torah he even parted from his sweet beloved and became an ascetic.

This was a sore burden to him. He longed deeply for his wife, and he was still a man in the very prime of life. In order not to weaken, and to make sure of maintaining this separation and his pious seclusion, he made a vow to himself that he should not return to his wife until he acquired twelve thousand disciples. This he did because he held that an oath was as a wall around holy retirement. He would have to keep his word and his absence from his wife would thus be ensured.

This fortitude, however, caused him to be unrelenting toward every one else. What he could do, all must be able to do. And he demanded of all the strictest abstention from the sins of the flesh, excoriating with barbed words the desire for women in the hearts of men.

Whereupon the weaklings—those who could not withstand the woman-lust in their hearts and were wracked by the sins of the flesh—spoke thus of Akiba:

"Merely because he was able to part from his wife is no proof that he is above temptation. Let Satan but approach him in the form of a naked woman and lust will suddenly befall him like an enemy from ambush, and rob him of all his senses, even as a thief robs his victim in the night."

And they added to their prayers an entreaty that God should lead the Rabbi into such temptation. And, to their own punishment, God heard their prayers.

When Rabbi Akiba left his wife he also left the city in which she dwelt. This he did not so much from personal choice, lest the proximity of his wife allure him, but rather for her sake, lest his nearness too much affect her. And in order that his wife, in her feminine weakness, should not follow him to the new place in which he intended to settle, he did not for a long time establish himself anywhere, journeying from city to city and from land to land.

And once, in his peregrinations, he came to a land in which remarkable customs and manners prevailed. One of these customs was to sweeten the nights of the honored guests with the company of women.

And it happened that when the ruler of this land learned of Rabbi Akiba's arrival and the importance of his guest, he sent to him for the night two beautiful damsels, the most beautiful in his realms. In the manner of women both beauties did their best to heighten their charms and increase the power of their attraction. They freshened themselves in the bath; the enchanting odor of their youthful bodies they rendered more intoxicating than ever with rare perfumes; they arrayed themselves seductively like brides on the wedding night. And they came to Rabbi Akiba in radiant half-nakedness, with an inviting smile upon their cherry lips, with the fire of passion and voluptuousness in their sparkling eyes.

They knew that they were going to a highly honored guest, but they did *not* know that they would encounter a very handsome man of gigantic stature. When they beheld him their passion flamed still higher, and each tried to display before him the most enticing allurements of her person.

"Come to me," said one.

"Come to me," invited the other.

And they passed close to him with their naked bodies, and each praised her person and its charms, and the pleasures it afforded.

"My body is as white as the full moon."

"And my body is as rosy as the rising sun."

"In my embrace you will lie as softly as in warm down."

"And in my arms you will feel the tender warmth of newly shorn lambs' wool."

"The kiss of my lips is like the wine of Damascus."

"And my lips are like the round grapes in which the sunbeams have chosen their home."

And thus they continued—the firmness of their breasts, the velvety softness of their skin, the ravishing delight of their legs, and the intoxication of their tenderness. One wrapped him about with her dark hair; the blond tresses of the other likewise enmeshed him. And with the passing of the hours their lust increased; their naked bodies turned and writhed, wracked and tortured by rising desire.

"Come, take me!" implored the one.

"Come, take me!" panted the other.

But Rabbi Akiba sat between them and—spat. For a whole night he sat between them and spat, looking neither upon one nor the other. He did not try to distract his mind with Torah thoughts, for he did not wish to bring the

Torah into the company of two naked women. He simply tried to work himself into a feeling of repulsion, to rouse within him a powerful resistance.

And thus he sat and spat—more vehemently, more impatiently than ever, with rising disgust, with increasing aversion. At last, however, he became calm, indifferent, ice-cold.

At first the two beautiful damsels looked at him in astonishment. Why was he spitting so? Why did he not touch them? Was he a fool? Was he crazy? Were they not beautiful enough? Not young enough? Not passionate enough?

They questioned him; he vouchsafed no reply. Then they were on the point of leaving him, when they looked at him again and saw how handsome he was, and gazed once more into his eyes and saw wisdom itself beaming out of them. Then they forgot his remarkable behavior, disregarded his incessant spitting, threw their nakedness and the fire of their bodies upon him, and pleaded and begged and groaned, calling to him in their intoxication.

"Take *me!*"

"Take *me!*"

The whole night passed in this way. In the morning, weary and exhausted, they went to the ruler and complained to him against Rabbi Akiba. In despair, they cried out, "Sooner death than another time with that man!"

The ruler sent for Rabbi Akiba and questioned him.

"Why did you not act toward the women I sent in to you as the sons of man act with women? Are they not beautiful? Are they not human, like you? Has not He, who created you, likewise created them?"

If Rabbi Akiba had replied that, in spending the night with them in the manner of the sons of man with woman, he would have committed a sin, then the ruler would surely become angry. Did his hospitality then lead to sin? Was his hospitality an incentive to wrongdoing?

Rabbi Akiba's wisdom saw this at once, and with an altogether innocent expression he replied, "What could I do? Before they came to me they must surely have eaten impure things, and the odor from them was that of carrion meat, impurities, reptiles."

And Rabbi Akiba quickly left this land with its remarkable hospitality, happy in the consciousness that he had overcome the greatest of temptations—filled with thanks to God for having so wonderfully given strength to his heart.

As the number of his disciples at this time had reached to twelve thousand, and as the wall that separated him from his wife thereby crumbled, he went back to her. As he came to the door of his house he heard a strange woman say to his wife, "Are you happy that your husband is returning after having acquired twelve thousand disciples?"

"I should be still happier," answered his wife, "if he returned with twenty-four thousand."

And Rabbi Akiba did not open the door of his house, nor did he go in to his wife. Once again he imposed upon himself separation from his mate, and erected a new wall about himself, with a vow that he should not approach his wife until he acquired four and twenty thousand disciples. And again he left, to wander through cities and lands, to spread the word of God and assemble disciples.

From now on he became more severe than ever in his religious demands, and his condemnations grew harsher. One who, like him, had triumphed over such great temptations, had full right to demand similar continence and willpower on the part of others. And he was wont to mock, jeer and jest at all who committed a sin.

He had forgotten the saying: "Believe not thyself until the day of thy death." And in Heaven it was decreed that he should be reminded of it.

One day his travels led him to a beautiful spot, through woods and fields. It was a wonderful day. The sun, midway in the sky, did not burn, but laughed and sang of the splendor of existence, pouring out joy upon the entire land, upon wood and field, upon tree and grass. All the birds and beasts and insects laughed and sang together with it. Rabbi Akiba, filled with the great gladness, forgot the passage of the Torah that was running through his mind and across his lips but a moment before, and could not remove his glance from the sunny splendors that surrounded him.

Suddenly it seemed as if some one had thrust him backward. But it was nobody. It was his own blood, and the blow that he had felt was the throb of his own heart.

Were not his eyes deceiving him? He opened them wide and looked again, intently.

No. His eyes saw clearly. A wondrously beautiful naked girl at the top of a palm tree.

He could not believe his eyes, but there was the girl looking down at him, smiling at him so enticingly, intoxicating him with the pearly whiteness of her teeth.

She was so beautiful and entrancing that the sun had forgot its wedding procession. It had stopped in its path—this shining star—and had enfolded the maiden's naked body in its rays, coloring it a rosy red and filling its veins with red wine.

Rabbi Akiba, too, stopped in his path, unable to move from the spot, unable to tear himself away from the dazzling vision. His heart palpitated, his body burned, his tongue became dry. He stood dumbfounded, and could not himself hear how he barely managed to utter, "Who are you?"

And the vision upon the tree laughed seductively down to him.

"Come up and I will tell you."

"What are you doing there?"

"Come up, and you shall see."

"Are you gathering dates?"

"What need have I of them? I feed myself and feed others with my own sweetness. Do you not wish to taste it?"

"Why are you naked?"

"So that the sunbeams may enjoy me, and the wind, and the hills, and the valleys, and the heavens, and God."

"How can you lie there so?"

"I have a couch here made of leaves and branches—a soft couch for me and for those whom I invite to enjoy me. Soft is my bed and fragrant—but even softer and more fragrant am I. Will you not feel us?"

And in utter forgetfulness, filled with a single intense desire, Rabbi Akiba approached very close to the tree and scarcely had breath to ask, "How can I get to you?"

The glorious vision uttered a magic laugh.

"Were you, then, never a little boy? What did you do when a tempting apple nodded to you from among the branches of an apple tree? You removed your clothes, made yourself as light as possible, and climbed up the tree after the beautiful, ripening fruit. Am I less than the fruit? Is it not worthwhile to climb up after me? Or are you old, and have your bones become hard, and is climbing now beyond your years and your strength? Take off your clothes; you will have no need of them in any case, up here. Make yourself light, and with all the youth that has now been born anew in you, climb up to me. . . ."

Enchanted and intoxicated, as hastily as possible, whipped on by driving impatience, Rabbi Akiba cast off his clothes and seized the trunk of the palm tree, beginning to climb aloft. With his naked hands and feet around the shaggy bark, with his burning eyes riveted upon her above, drinking in her beauty, sucking in the warm ruddiness of her veins, he did not notice that his skin was being scratched and torn by the bark of the tree, and that blood was beginning to flow over his body. He climbed higher, ever higher.

And her magic eyes drew him on as if with ropes and her fascinating voice was as a guide to him. From between her pearly teeth it poured forth like wine that robbed the senses.

"Come! Co-o-ome! Co-o-ome!"

But when he had climbed half the height of the palm he suddenly came to himself. It was as if a cold wind had icily bedewed him and had blown something away from before his eyes, making him see the complete ludicrousness and unworthiness of his position. He, the renowned master, teacher and judge among the Jews, climbing, half-naked, up a tall tree, driven and goaded on by lust! He threw himself down, rather than descended, from the tree, rolled himself into a ball at its foot, and burst into bitter tears.

A malicious, mocking voice spoke above him:

"Had it not been decreed in Heaven that you and your Torah should be protected, your life at this moment would not be worth a straw."

Rabbi Akiba wept more bitterly than ever, striking his breast and beating his head.

He dressed and continued on his way. The sun no longer shone; heaven and earth were veiled in grayish fog, and the laughter and song of the surrounding scene now ceased. Or perhaps it merely seemed so to him because his heart was bitter and his soul grieved; he looked neither to right nor to left and his ears were deaf to the outer world.

He felt ashamed and debased. And he knew that henceforth he would not mock those who had committed sin.

Now he understood the weakness of man, and how plentifully life was strewn with dangers, and his lips muttered acridly, "All of us here below are even as criminals who are released on bail, and a net of transgression is spread over all existence."

Translated from the Yiddish
by Isaac Goldberg

The Garden of *Shir Hashirim*
by Arthur Waskow

When the rabbis were still arguing over what ought and what ought not to be regarded as part of the Biblical canon, some of them felt *Shir Hashirim*—in its sexuality, its earthiness, its not-one-mention of the Name of God—was troubling. But Rabbi Akiba said, "All the Writings are holy, but the Song of Songs is the Holy of Holies."

Akiba may have felt the same auras that we felt from *Shir Hashirim*. He said it was the love story of God and the People Israel, and he may have felt that to know God as lover was to be in Eden grown up. But I have a fantasy about Akiba, as well.

There is a story that Akiba and three other great rabbis had a powerful mystical experience of "going into *Pardes*"—the garden, the orchard. Paradise. We do not know what they saw there; but one went mad, one died, and one plucked up the Root of Being and denied there was a Judge or Justice in the world. Only Akiba, says the Talmud, came out unharmed.

What was this *Pardes*? I imagine that they walked into the garden of *Shir Hashirim*. They found there goats and flowers, sexuality and love. They did not see the God of Sinai or of Eden; they did not hear the Name of God at all. They knew this was the ultimate experience. And so one died in shock; one went mad because he could not fit this moment with his Torah; one gave up the Torah because this seemed more real; and only Akiba knew that this *was* Torah. Only Akiba, and he came out unharmed—but singed a little, enough to say the Song was holiest of all. And singed enough to be the only one of the rabbis to proclaim the coming of Messiah. For once you have lived in the Garden of the Song, how can you not believe Messiah has come?

The Four Who Entered *Pardes*

by Howard Schwartz

Four sages, Ben Azzai, Ben Zoma, Elisha ben Abuyah, and Rabbi Akiba, made their way to the cave of Machpelah, and by following the scent of cedars that bore a hint of Paradise, they discovered the route the souls of the righteous follow in order to reach the Garden of Eden. They knew that once every hundred years the gates of Eden were opened for as long as the blink of an eyelash, and by many signs they had become convinced that the time was soon approaching for the gates to open in that generation.

In this they proved to be correct, and due to the vigilance of Rabbi Akiba, who alone among them had his eyes open at the instant the gates flew apart, and pulled in the others behind him, they managed to make their way into the earthly Paradise. There they hurried to seek out the tree in the center of the Garden. Which tree was this?—the Tree of Knowledge, for this tree forms a hedge around the Tree of Life. And the only pathway from the one tree to the other is hidden somewhere in the massive trunk of the Tree of Knowledge, which takes five hundred years to encircle.

Therefore it was necessary to choose the correct passage around this tree. Those who started in the wrong direction were unlikely ever to return. But on this matter the sages could not agree. Ben Azzai argued that they must cleave to the right, since the letters of the Hebrew alphabet are written that way. But Ben Zoma argued that they must cleave to the left, since the Tree of Life had been created first of all things in the Garden, and therefore their direction was backward, into the past, and not forward, into the future. Elisha, too, preferred to cleave to the left, for he had always sought to comprehend the secrets of creation. Yet Akiba insisted that they must cleave to the right, for that is where the Throne of Mercy can be found, while the Throne of Justice belongs to the left.

So it was that the four sages parted ways for the first time, and Ben Zoma and Elisha ben Abuyah followed the way that led to the left. Little did they know that in that direction lay an intricate labyrinth, impossible to penetrate. It was there that Ben Zoma lost his mind and Elisha abandoned his faith. And what of Ben Azzai and Rabbi Akiba, who cleaved to the right? They soon found the sole path that leads to the Tree of Life.

But what they did not know was that the Tree of Life is only visible from one side. On all other sides nothing of it can be seen. From where the two sages found themselves there was nothing but two paths branching from the one that had brought them to that place. It was here that Ben Azzai and Rabbi Akiba finally parted ways. Ben Azzai observed that if they each took the path in one direction, one of them might eventually arrive at the Tree of Life. Rabbi Akiba concurred. Then Ben Azzai chose the way that led to the left, for he said that it was necessary in order to seek out the balance. But Akiba continued to cleave to the right, for he believed that one must remain unwaveringly on the same path in order to reach the goal.

Ben Azzai soon discovered that he had made his way into a mirage that stretched like an endless desert on every side. And when he looked into that abyss, he lost his life. But Rabbi Akiba made his way to the threshold of the Tree of Life, and found himself standing before the *Pargod,* the curtain that hangs before the Throne of Glory. Inscribed there in black fire on white were the letters that spelled out the first word, *Bereshith,* in the beginning.

Slowly, with all of time still to unfold, Akiba began to read the letters of that word from right to left, starting with the first letter, Bet. And he saw from the first that the path led from the circumference of the letter to the dot in the center, and because he never wavered from that path, he inevitably found himself standing before the gate of the Garden of Eden, which can always be opened from the inside, and departed in peace.

The Cave of Machpelah
by Howard Schwartz

So it was that in order to reach Paradise, where they hoped to recover the sacred Book of Raziel, the four sages, Ben Zoma, Ben Azzai, Ben Abuyah and Rabbi Akiba, first journeyed from Jerusalem to Hebron, to the sacred cave of Machpelah. For they knew that the soul of every man and woman who dies must first pass through that cave, on its way to Paradise. The cave was located at the end of a field, its entrance guarded by an iron door which dated from the time of our forefathers. The doorkeeper was an old Jew who assumed they had come to visit the burial place of the Patriarchs Abraham, Isaac and Jacob and their wives. He directed them to cross two empty caves and then to descend twenty-four steps in a narrow passage, in order to come to the six tombs on which the names of the Patriarchs and their wives are engraved on stone.

Each of the sages purchased a candle from the old man and they passed through the outer caves as he had directed them. Inside they saw by the light of the candles that these caves were filled with barrels containing bones of people, which had been taken there because the cave was a holy resting place. When they reached the tombs of the Patriarchs they stopped to pray, and afterwards Rabbi Akiba took out a map of the letter Bet, which he had inscribed on parchment, and held it up to the candle. To progress any further in the cave without guidance was impossible; there in the third cave all passages seemed to come to an end. Yet Akiba also knew that the bodies of Adam and Eve were believed to have been laid to rest in this same cave. In fact, Abraham was said to have discovered the cave while chasing after a calf he planned to slaughter for the three angels who had come in disguise to visit him, and he was said to have discovered the bodies of our first parents there. Then, knowing that at the time of the resurrection of the dead those buried in the cave would be the first to rise up, he wished to be buried there himself, and eventually purchased the cave from Ephron, who did not suspect its true value.

Akiba still held the map up to the light, but he could find no clue that would guide them in continuing their journey. Finally he put down the candle and sat down, placing the parchment in front of the tomb of Abraham. It was then that the miracle they had been waiting for so long came to pass. Although the map was no longer illumined by the light, it continued to glow by itself in the dark. Ben Zoma was the first to notice it, then all the others saw that a light, growing steadily brighter, was emerging as if from inside the map. Soon the letter Bet itself began to glow apart from the parchment, and all of the sages, knowing that they were witnessing a miracle, sat still for a long time and did not speak. As Akiba bent over the map, what he saw in its mirror was a beautiful garden surrounded by an aura, with a river winding through it. There were three women, who resembled each other like sisters, and sometimes seemed to blend into one figure, one woman, seated outside the entrance of a cave. Akiba beckoned the others to look into the map. They too saw the mirror and the garden reflected inside it, and when the vision faded it was replaced by another, of the four sages traveling downstream in a small wooden boat. Akiba pointed out the sign on the side of the boat—it was the letter Bet!

And no sooner did the sages raise their eyes from the map than they saw the light it cast illuminating the tomb of Abraham, and while they watched the tomb was transformed. It grew young and old, large as the planet they stood on and small as the star that rose above it in the sky. And at the same time they realized that the Patriarch sleeping inside it was both dead and alive, and ruled that sacred place and all those who entered within its boundaries. Then they understood that all of them must pass beyond that tomb, that there was no other choice, that this was precisely the route they had been seeking and the knowledge they needed in order to retrieve the sacred Book of Raziel; more than that, that this route was their destiny.

Now the map no longer revealed any visions, yet it continued to glow. It was Elisha ben Abuyah who understood that it could serve to guide them through the cave. And as he lifted the map, the light it cast lit up a small passage at the back of the inner cave, and one by one the four sages crawled through to the other side. No sooner had they crossed into this secret cave than they saw two beautiful bodies stretched out on their couches, candles burning at the head of their resting places, while a sweet scent pervaded the cave. Adam and Eve! The four sages stood back in awe. The sight of the perfectly preserved bodies of our first parents and at the same time the first, unforgettable fragrance of Paradise was more than they could comprehend. Even stranger was that Akiba believed he saw in the face of Adam something that reminded him of the face of his own father; it was Adam, yet at the same time it was the face of his father. And each of the other sages, too, saw his own father's face in the face of the first father. Whispering to the others, Akiba recalled the legend that when Adam had brought Eve into the cave he had wanted to go further because he had scented the fragrance of Paradise, but a heavenly Voice called out to him, "Enough!" Now none of the sages would have been surprised had the same Voice called out to them, but the parchment in Akiba's hand continued to glow, and they knew they were destined to journey further into the cave.

Now the letter began to glow with a light so bright it was no longer possible to look at it directly, as if its mirror were reflecting a hidden sun. The sages saw that the light it cast led directly to a passage near the ceiling of the cave, that they could reach by climbing along the sides. Ben Azzai, the youngest of the four, assisted each of the others in reaching this passage, then followed after them. When he climbed down into the other side he found them standing in awe by a stream that flowed slowly through the center of the new passageway, and like them he could barely believe what he saw at the side of the stream—a small wooden boat, the same one they had seen in the mirror of the map, and inscribed on its side was the letter Bet. This letter must have been engraved with a pen of flaming fire, for the fire in the letter still burned, although it did not cause the boat to be consumed.

A new scent arose from the wood of the boat, also an unforgettable fragrance, for it had been formed from one of the cedars inside of Eden. The sages could find no sign of the presence of anyone else—and then they observed the absence of any oars. "How are we to guide ourselves without any oars?" asked Ben Azzai. But even as he asked he knew the answer: they must let the current carry them. So without any further questions the sages carried the boat into the water and climbed inside it. Almost at once the slow current caught it up and the boat began to move downstream, with no sound filling the air except for the sweet singing of the waters.

The Four Who Sought to Re-enter the Garden

by Moshe ben Yitzhak HaPardesan

Once, long ago, there were four ancient sages who longed to return to a famous garden, to again ponder and partake, each in his own way, of the wondrous fruits they knew grew there. After wandering for many years, they arrived at the awesome wall that surrounded the garden and followed it for many months until they found the gate, massive and impenetrable. In joy and expectation they gave thanks that they had been permitted to return to the entrance of the garden. After praying that they be found worthy to enter the garden and partake of its fruits, they arose together and, as one man, with great reverence, solemnly knocked upon the gate three times. The sound of their wordless plea could be heard echoing cavernously through the vast reaches of the great garden. However, the gatekeeper did not appear to let the sages enter. For he was tending and nurturing, with great love, the Tree which bore the wondrous fruits that grew in the garden. Now the gatekeeper did hear the knocking of the sages on the gate. Indeed, it is said that it was he who, disguised sometimes as a poet, sometimes as a storyteller, had faithfully directed their steps to the gate. However, when they finally arrived, the gatekeeper was far within the garden, and the journey back to open the gate would be long and arduous. Moreover, a younger master of Torah, whom the gatekeeper had already admitted into the garden, had partaken of the fruits and become intoxicated with their sweetness. Tormented by their supernal succulence, it was he who distracted the attention of the gatekeeper by telling him stories pregnant with deep but hidden meaning. So when the gatekeeper finally heard the three knocks of the four ancient sages, although he wanted to hurry to let them in as well, he was detained, torn between tending the fruits of the Tree and unraveling the mysteries they had inspired. So the four ancient sages continued to wait, reverently standing at the entrance to the garden, fervently praying that the gatekeeper might appear. And, some say, they are still waiting there until this very day.

Ben Azzai

by M. J. Berditchevsky

Ben Azzai was one of the four great sages of the Talmud who entered paradise seeking God. His soul desired Torah more than any other man. Day and night he did not depart from its tent, and would sit and interpret and the fire flared around him and the words became like unto the day when they were given on Sinai.

The daughter of Rabbi Akiba, born to him by the daughter of Kalbah Savua, saw this student and loved him with a love as strong as death. She waited for him twelve straight years, as her mother had for her husband. Finally his brothers and his father's house pestered him to wed her, for he refused to build his house, saying: "The world will be sustained through others."

Once he was sitting in the evening and occupying himself with his Torah when he saw his teacher's daughter standing by him. He said to her: "My daughter, bring me a jug of water that I may wash my hands." And she hurried and ran and brought him a pitcher of water. When he saw the water in her hand he began to expound on the biblical verse *Who has measured the waters in the hollow of his hand?* and he delved into the matter of the divine chariot until the morning broke, while she stood and saw the vision. . . . And it came to pass that when the dawn rose and he lifted up his eyes and saw her standing by him, he asked her: "Did you stand here all night?" She answered yes. Said he to her: "Please go to your father's house." And she said: "Will I not merit to serve you and wash your feet?" And she wept.

In the highest heaven this thing was counted against him as a sin.

It was also said concerning him: *If you find honey, eat only till you are satiated.* For he gazed and died. And there are those who say that he died a martyr's death, that they seized him in the study house when he was immersed in his recitation and killed him.

Translated from the Hebrew
by Jeremy Garber

The Death of Ben Azzai

by Rabbi Milton Steinberg

In the hall of Ben Azzai's home in Tiberias, Akiba, Ben Zoma and Elisha waited for their host. He had not been at the door to greet them when they entered. He was, the porter informed them, meditating in his study. Indeed, he had locked himself in two days before and had not come out since. Servants had entered his room to bring their master food and once to inform him of the disaster at Jerusalem. Except for those brief moments no one had seen him.

Seated on divans the three discussed the depressing news of the day before. They considered it from every conceivable angle, debated as to what should be done, and speculated anxiously over whether it would be possible to restrain the outraged populace. On one fact only they agreed immediately—their impotence against the Romans.

Elisha had to drive himself to attend the conversation with even half-hearted interest. He could not talk or care about an issue so remote as the rebuilding of the Temple. A more intimate sorrow, the parting from Beruriah, possessed him. The subject of discontinuing the meetings of the four would also have to wait for a time when, ceasing to feel, he could think again.

The rasp of curtain rings called their eyes to the door. There Ben Azzai stood, framed in the lintel and posts, his hands groping feebly before him.

There was in his eyes a glittering vacancy, an intent absence of sight such as they had never seen before. Without a word of greeting he walked to the center of the room and stood trembling as with the ague. Akiba half-rose to help him. But Ben Azzai began to speak, so softly that they could scarcely hear. Yet had he shrieked he could not have captured their attention more completely. Akiba sat down on the edge of his chair.

"For years," he intoned, "I have sought Him in vain. His footsteps, the imprint of His hand, the signature of His wisdom are all about me. On every leaf, in each mote, in the industry of the ant, the rage of the lion, the cunning of the spider, I detected traces of His presence. In Scripture I held His letter of love. Most of all, I felt closest to Him within my own mind and heart. But when I looked inward, lo, He was gone as though He had just passed from sight. And I stood like one who knows that his beloved is in the chamber with him, who senses her presence, recognizes the fragrance of her perfumes, who yearns to touch her but cannot. And I said to myself with Job:

'Behold, I go forward, but He is not there;
And backward, but I cannot perceive Him:
On the left hand, where He worketh, but I cannot behold Him;
He hideth Himself on the right, that I cannot see Him.'

"Long ago, I concluded that my body was a wall between us. Wherefore I fasted and denied myself the desire for woman in order to break it through. And when they asked me why I would not fulfill the first commandment of

Scripture, 'Be fruitful and multiply,' I told them that mankind and its future generations could be maintained by others.

"It was a long, dark, weary way I traveled. But never did I doubt that I would arrive at my destination to drink there from the fountains of salvation. Then Elisha almost persuaded me that there was nothing beyond the veil—that my painful quest was a pilgrimage to nowhere.

"I hated him for murdering my dreams. Hush, Elisha, hear me out. Now I thank you because through your denial I was driven to the truth. For I had mistaken the demiurgic world-soul for God. Was it to be marveled at, if, having aimed at an illusory target I could not hear my arrow strike? Now since my discovery, my progress has been rapid. I am almost at the end of the road. Stay here, my friends, and watch while I walk through the last curtains and enter into His Presence. With you I would share the glory of the moment that is coming."

The three men sat transfixed, their skin crawling with terror. Even Ben Zoma was frozen into quiet, as Ben Azzai circled waveringly to face the wall. Standing before the blank expanse of plaster, he raised his hands and beat weakly, rhythmically against it, chanting a strange perversion of the Song of Songs:

"The winter is going, the rains are passing, the blossoms appear in the fields, the voice of the dove is heard at last. Open unto me, my beloved, my perfect one!"

Then his hands were still and there came as though across long leagues of distance a voice hushed with awe and wonder:

"The veil is lifting. The wall is breaking through. Light flows over me and an intoxication as of wine. There is sweetness, too, sweetness within and everywhere. 'And God saw all which He had made and behold, it was good.' It is good, all good, aglow with light. The whole world is aglow with light . . . brighter and brighter . . . too bright to see, too dazzling, for no man may see Thee and live. I have asked after Thee, sought Thee in the night watches, and called out of the depths. Now do I, Simeon the son of Azzai—see—I see . . ."

He stiffened in a spasm, then his shoulders drooped forward onto the wall. Slowly he slid to the floor until he sat cross-legged; his great shaggy head scraped down along the plaster and came to rest between his knees.

Akiba, the first to reach him, groped for his wrist.

"He is dead," he cried out incredulously. "Blessed be the Righteous Judge."

Elisha and Ben Zoma repeated the ancient formula after him. For a full moment the three stood so. Then they carried Ben Azzai to a couch. His large form was surprisingly light, like a shell from which all inner substance has been burned.

The Fate of Ben Zoma

by Rabbi Milton Steinberg

One morning Simeon ben Zoma failed to appear at a lecture at which he was expected. At first no one took the fact seriously, not even after casual inquiry disclosed that he had arrived in Usha the preceding day. Always erratic, he had become increasingly undependable. Joshua and Akiba took over his classes.

But when Simeon was not present at vesper worship in the synagogue that night, his colleagues grew concerned. A disciple, dispatched to the inn where he lodged, brought back the report that the luggage of the missing sage was in his room but that no one at the tavern had seen him since the evening before. A quiet search was instituted. By midnight every house in Usha had been visited without yielding a trace of him.

Thoroughly alarmed, the sages, disciples and townspeople procured fagots and lanterns, divided themselves into groups, allocated districts about the village to one another, and set out to hunt for him in the countryside.

Joshua, Akiba and Meir joined a party assigned to one of the main highways. Spread out on both sides of the road, where Joshua walked so that he might be spared the difficulty of traversing broken fields, they moved forward slowly, torches glaring in an irregular line, calls passing back and forth. By the time they came to a crossroad the lights had burned out. Only the blue glow of stars shone on a marble pillar of Hermes, God of Wayfarers, which marked the intersection of routes. There they gathered about Joshua for consultation.

Into the whispers of the group a faint weird chanting penetrated. Instantly they were quiet. Peering through the darkness in the direction of the sound, Meir was the first to see something white shimmering eerily at a distance. The superstitious among them, already unnerved, trembled with fear. Shrinking, they made their way forward in a body. Leaves rustled, dead branches snapped underfoot; the wind hummed an accompaniment to the incessant intoning.

At the foot of a plane tree his friends found Simeon. He gave them no heed when they encircled him. Crouched, he crooned without pause:

"From the earth to the firmament is a distance of five hundred years' journey. And from the topmost firmament to God's throne is an equal distance. And the upper firmament is so close to the lower that a bird flying between them would brush both with each stroke of his fluttering wings. Even as it is written, 'The spirit of God hovered.' So short is the interval between things celestial and earthly. And yet so far that man cannot span it. It is written in Scripture, *V'noshantem ba-aretz.* 'Ye shall grow old in the land.' Now the numerical value of the phrase 'Ye shall grow old' is 852. So long was the duration of the first Commonwealth to have been before the Exile. And yet it endured only 850 years. What secret shall this discrepancy conceal?"

Joshua spoke to him. He continued to babble scriptural quotations.

Meir clutched Joshua's arm.

"Master," he asked, "what does it mean? Has Simeon . . . ?"

"God pity him," the old sage replied, "he is mad."

Sick at heart, two disciples lifted Simeon by his arms, raised him to his feet and half-carried him back to Usha. With each step he quoted biblical verses, interpreting them with an insane, fantastic ingenuity.

In the quiet streets of Usha, the townsfolk stood about in assemblies of stirring shadows. A murmur of horror swept through them when they heard Simeon's speech and the explanation of it whispered hastily to them by his companions. Then they fell silent, retiring uneasily to their homes or gathering before the doors of the tavern into which the stricken sage was borne.

The Fire at Elisha's Grave

by Rabbi Milton Steinberg

On a night of angry winds and dripping rain, two peasants brought the news to Meir.

"Rabbi, Elisha's grave has been struck by lightning."

Shadows danced along the wall as the west wind blew in through the open door and shook the lamplight. The little room, chill with winter, was suddenly colder.

Meir turned to Beruriah, asking a silent question.

Fleetingly, her eyes came alive with pain. She nodded her head and looked away.

Meir picked up his cloak, threw it about his shoulders and left the house. Their bodies hunched against the gale, the three men made their way through the streets of the sleeping village, passing the darkened synagogue and the sprawling buildings of the Academy, where in one window a lone light burned, throwing a splash of yellow luminosity across the wet cobblestones. Like shadows they moved. Like wraiths, memories haunted Meir: the message from Elisha saying that he was mortally ill in Caesarea; the room where he lay dead, his body attended by a palsied old Greek called Nicholaus; the long slow journey back to Galilee; and the hours of coaxing before the authorities would allow him to be interred even outside the sacred confines of the town's cemetery.

Meantime, they left the city behind them and, reaching the crest of a bleak hill, stopped to peer through the gloom.

One of the men clutched Meir's arm.

"See, Rabbi," he whispered, pointing ahead, "there it is."

From a mound a column of smoke rose uncertainly into the darkness.

Overawed, the peasants would go no farther. Alone, Meir came to the side of the grave and looked down. A bolt of lightning had struck the place. A piece of wood, either the marker or a fragment of the coffin, hissed as it smoldered.

"Come back, Rabbi," one of the peasants called. "It is an omen from God, a judgment on the heretic."

Unhearing, unresponding, Meir contemplated his master's resting place. Long since the season's rains had gullied it. Now the lightning had broken it open altogether. He must return and tend it, he thought. But he could not bear to leave him, even until dawn, so exposed to the elements.

Slowly, as in a trance, he slipped his cloak from his shoulders and draped it like a blanket over the spot.

" 'Sleep through the night,' " he prayed, quoting the words of Boaz to another tired traveler.

Then he bethought himself of the poor shattered body before him, and of the weary search that had worn it into death. He recalled its beauty in youth, and set against it its likeness in old age, black hair turned white, eyes burned out like ashes, a face drawn with despair and lips too tired and too discouraged to speak. He wept silently, the tears streaming down his cheeks to mingle with the rain that beat upon them.

Thunder rolled in the misty vault of the heavens. From the cemetery down the hill, from the grave at his feet and from out dead yesterdays ghosts came stealing. And he wept not alone for his master, but for himself as well, for a woman who rarely smiled, for sweet children who slept near by, for a people crushed and persecuted, for all the sons of men, their aches of the body and soul, and their dreams that die.

The Pagan Rabbi

by Cynthia Ozick

> *Rabbi Jacob said: "He who is walking along*
> *and studying, but then breaks off to remark,*
> *'How lovely is that tree!' or 'How beautiful is that*
> *fallow field!'—Scripture regards such a one*
> *as having hurt his own being."*
> *—from The Ethics of the Fathers*

When I heard that Isaac Kornfeld, a man of piety and brains, had hanged himself in the public park, I put a token in the subway stile and journeyed out to see the tree.

We had been classmates in the rabbinical seminary. Our fathers were both rabbis. They were also friends, but only in a loose way of speaking: in actuality our fathers were enemies. They vied with one another in demonstrations of charitableness, in the captious glitter of their scholia, in the number of their adherents. Of the two, Isaac's father was the milder. I was afraid of my father; he had a certain disease of the larynx, and if he even uttered something so trivial as "Bring the tea" to my mother, it came out splintered, clamorous, and vindictive.

Neither man was philosophical in the slightest. It was the one thing they agreed on. "Philosophy is an abomination," Isaac's father used to say. "The Greeks were philosophers, but they remained children playing with their dolls. Even Socrates, a monotheist, nevertheless sent money down to the temple to pay for incense to their doll."

"Idolatry is the abomination," Isaac argued, "not philosophy."

"The latter is the corridor to the former," his father said.

My own father claimed that if not for philosophy I would never have been brought to the atheism which finally led me to withdraw, in my second year, from the seminary. The trouble was not philosophy—I had none of Isaac's talent: his teachers later said of him that his imagination was so remarkable he could concoct holiness out of the fine line of a serif. On the day of his funeral the president of his college was criticized for having commented that although a suicide could not be buried in consecrated earth, whatever earth enclosed Isaac Kornfeld was ipso facto consecrated. It should be noted that Isaac hanged himself several weeks short of his thirty-sixth birthday; he was then at the peak of his renown; and the president, of course, did not know the whole story. He judged by Isaac's reputation, which was at no time more impressive than just before his death.

I judged by the same, and marveled that all that holy genius and intellectual surprise should in the end be raised no higher than the next-to-lowest limb of a delicate young oak, with burly roots like the toes of a gryphon exposed in the wet ground.

The tree was almost alone in a long rough meadow, which sloped down to a bay filled with sickly clams and a bad smell. The place was called Trilham's Inlet, and I knew what the smell meant: that cold brown water covered half the city's turds.

On the day I came to see the tree the air was bleary with fog. The weather was well into autumn and, though it was Sunday, the walks were empty. There was something historical about the park just then, with its rusting grasses and deserted monuments. In front of a soldiers' cenotaph a plastic wreath left behind months before by some civic parade stood propped against a stone frieze of identical marchers in the costume of an old war. A banner across the wreath's belly explained that the purpose of war is peace. At the margins of the park they were building a gigantic highway. I felt I was making my way across a battlefield silenced by the victory of the peace machines. The bulldozers had bitten far into the park, and the rolled carcasses of the sacrificed trees were already cut up into logs. There were dozens of felled maples, elms, and oaks. Their moist inner wheels breathed out a fragrance of barns, countryside, decay.

In the bottommost meadow fringing the water I recognized the tree which had caused Isaac to sin against his own life. It looked curiously like a photograph—not only like that newspaper photograph I carried warmly in my pocket, which showed the field and its markers—the drinking-fountain a few yards off, the ruined brick wall of an old estate behind. The caption-writer had particularly remarked on the "rope." But the rope was no longer there; the widow had claimed it. It was his own prayer shawl that Isaac, a short man, had thrown over the comely neck of the next-to-lowest limb. A Jew is buried in his prayer shawl; the police had handed it over to Sheindel. I observed that the bark was rubbed at that spot. The tree lay back against the sky like a licked postage stamp. Rain began to beat it flatter yet. A stench of sewage came up like a veil in the nostril. It seemed to me I was a man in a photograph standing next to a gray blur of tree. I would stand through eternity beside Isaac's guilt if I did not run, so I ran that night to Sheindel herself.

I loved her at once. I am speaking now of the first time I saw her, though I don't exclude the last. The last—the last together with Isaac—was soon after my divorce; at one stroke I left my wife and my cousin's fur business to the small upstate city in which both had repined. Suddenly Isaac and Sheindel and two babies appeared in the lobby of my hotel—they were passing through: Isaac had a lecture engagement in Canada. We sat under scarlet neon and Isaac told how my father could now not speak at all.

"He keeps his vow," I said.

"No, no, he's a sick man," Isaac said. "An obstruction in the throat."

"I'm the obstruction. You know what he said when I left the seminary. He meant it, never mind how many years it is. He's never addressed a word to me since."

"We were reading together. He blamed the reading, who can blame *him?* Fathers like ours don't know how to love. They live too much indoors."

It was an odd remark, though I was too much preoccupied with my own resentments to notice. "It wasn't what we read," I objected. "Torah tells that an illustrious man doesn't have an illustrious son. Otherwise he wouldn't be humble like other people. This much scholarly stuffing I retain. Well, so my father always believed he was more illustrious than anybody, especially more than your father. *Therefore,*" I delivered in Talmudic cadence, "what chance did I have? A nincompoop and no *sitzfleish.* Now you, you could answer questions that weren't even invented yet. Then you invented them."

"Torah isn't a spade," Isaac said. "A man should have a livelihood. You had yours."

"The pelt of a dead animal isn't a living either, it's an indecency."

All the while Sheindel was sitting perfectly still; the babies, female infants in long stockings, were asleep in her arms. She wore a dark thick woolen hat—it was July—that covered every part of her hair. But I had once seen it in all its streaming black shine.

"And Jane?" Isaac asked finally.

"Speaking of dead animals. Tell my father—he won't answer a letter, he won't come to the telephone—that in the matter of the marriage he was right, but for the wrong reason. If you share a bed with a Puritan you'll come into it cold and you'll go out of it cold. Listen, Isaac, my father calls me an atheist, but between the conjugal sheets every Jew is a believer in miracles, even the lapsed."

He said nothing then. He knew I envied him his Sheindel and his luck. Unlike our fathers, Isaac had never condemned me for my marriage, which his father regarded as his private triumph over my father, and which my father, in his public defeat, took as an occasion for declaring me as one dead. He rent his clothing and sat on a stool for eight days, while Isaac's father came to watch him mourn, secretly satisfied, though aloud he grieved for all apostates. Isaac did not like my wife. He called her a tall yellow straw. After we were married he never said a word against her, but he kept away.

I went with my wife to his wedding. We took the early train down especially, but when we arrived the feast was well under way, and the guests far into the dancing.

"Look, look, they don't dance together," Jane said.

"Who?"

"The men and the women. The bride and the groom."

"Count the babies," I advised. "The Jews are also Puritans, but only in public."

The bride was enclosed all by herself on a straight chair in the center of a spinning ring of young men. The floor heaved under their whirl. They stamped, the chandeliers shuddered, the guests cried out, the young men with linked arms spiraled and their skullcaps came flying off like centrifugal balloons. Isaac, a mist of black suit, a stamping foot, was lost in the planet's wake of black suits and emphatic feet. The dancing young men shouted bridal songs, the floor leaned like a plate, the whole room teetered.

Isaac had told me something of Sheindel. Before now I had never seen her. Her birth was in a concentration camp, and they were about to throw her against the electrified fence when an army mobbed the gate; the current vanished from the terrible wires, and she had nothing to show for it afterward but a mark on her cheek like an asterisk, cut by a barb. The asterisk pointed to certain dry footnotes: she had no mother to show, she had no father to show, but she had, extraordinarily, God to show—she was known to be, for her age and sex, astonishingly learned. She was only seventeen.

"What pretty hair she has," Jane said.

Now Sheindel was dancing with Isaac's mother. All the ladies made a fence, and the bride, twirling with her mother-in-law, lost a shoe and fell against the long laughing row. The ladies lifted their glistering breasts in their lacy dresses and laughed; the young men, stamping two by two, went on shouting their wedding songs. Sheindel danced without her shoe, and the black river of her hair followed her.

"After today she'll have to hide it all," I explained.

Jane asked why.

"So as not to be a temptation to men," I told her, and covertly looked for my father. There he was, in a shadow, apart. My eyes discovered his eyes. He turned his back and gripped his throat.

"It's a very anthropological experience," Jane said.

"A wedding is a wedding," I answered her, "among us even more so."

"Is that your father over there, that little scowly man?"

To Jane all Jews were little. "My father, the man of the cloth. Yes."

"A wedding is not a wedding," said Jane: we had had only a license and a judge with bad breath.

"Everybody marries for the same reason."

"No," said my wife. "Some for love and some for spite."

"And everybody for bed."

"Some for spite," she insisted.

"I was never cut out for a man of the cloth," I said. "My poor father doesn't see that."

"He doesn't speak to you."

"A technicality. He's losing his voice."

"Well, he's not like you. He doesn't do it for spite," Jane said.

"You don't know him," I said.

He lost it altogether the very week Isaac published his first remarkable collection of responsa. Isaac's father crowed like a passionate rooster, and packed his wife and himself off to the Holy Land to boast on the holy soil. Isaac was a little relieved; he had just been made Professor of Mishnaic History, and his father's whims and pretenses and foolish rivalries were an embarrassment. It is easy to honor a father from afar, but bitter to honor one who is dead. A surgeon cut out my father's voice, and he died without a word.

Isaac and I no longer met. Our ways were too disparate. Isaac was famous, if not in the world, certainly in the kingdom of jurists and scholars. By this time I had acquired a partnership in a small book store in a basement. My partner sold me his share, and I put up a new sign: "The Book Cellar"; for reasons more obscure than filial (all the same I wished my father could have seen it) I established a department devoted especially to not-quite-rare theological works, chiefly in Hebrew and Aramaic, though I carried some Latin and Greek. When Isaac's second volume reached my shelves (I had now expanded to street level), I wrote him to congratulate him, and after that we corresponded, not with any regularity. He took to ordering all his books from me, and we exchanged awkward little jokes. "I'm still in the jacket business," I told him, "but now I feel I'm where I belong. Last time I went too fur." "Sheindel is well, and Naomi and Esther have a sister," he wrote. And later: "Naomi, Esther, and Miriam have a sister." And still later: "Naomi, Esther, Miriam, and Ophra have a sister." It went on until there were seven girls. "There's nothing in Torah that prevents an illustrious man from having illustrious daughters," I wrote him when he said he had given up hope of another rabbi in the family. "But where do you find seven illustrious husbands?" he asked. Every order brought another quip, and we bantered back and forth in this way for some years.

I noticed that he read everything. Long ago he had inflamed my taste, but I could never keep up. No sooner did I catch his joy in Saadia Gaon than he had already sprung ahead to Yehudah Halevi. One day he was weeping with Dostoyevski and the next leaping in the air over Thomas Mann. He introduced me to Hegel and Nietzsche while our fathers wailed. His mature reading was no more peaceable than those frenzies of his youth, when I would come upon him in an abandoned classroom at dusk, his stocking feet on the windowsill, the light already washed from the lowest city clouds, wearing the look of a man half-sotted with print.

But when the widow asked me—covering a certain excess of alertness or irritation—whether to my knowledge Isaac had lately been ordering any books on horticulture, I was astonished.

"He bought so much," I demurred.

"Yes, yes, yes," she said. "How could you remember?"

She poured the tea and then, with a discreetness of gesture, lifted my dripping raincoat from the chair where I had thrown it and took it out of the room. It was a crowded apartment, not very neat, far from slovenly, cluttered with dolls and tiny dishes and an array of tricycles. The dining table was as large as a desert. An old-fashioned crocheted lace runner divided it into two nations, and on the end of this, in the neutral zone, so to speak, Sheindel had placed my cup. There was no physical relic of Isaac: not even a book.

She returned. "My girls are all asleep, we can talk. What an ordeal for you, weather like this and going out so far to that place."

It was impossible to tell whether she was angry or not. I had rushed in on her like the rainfall itself, scattering drops, my shoes stuck all over with leaves.

"I comprehend exactly why you went out there. The impulse of a detective," she said. Her voice contained an irony that surprised me. It was brilliantly and unmistakably accented, and because of this jaggedly precise. It was as if every word emitted a quick white thread of great purity, like hard silk, which she was then obliged to bite cleanly off. "You went to find something? An atmosphere? The sadness itself?"

"There was nothing to see," I said, and thought I was lunatic to have put myself in her way.

"Did you dig in the ground? He might have buried a note for goodbye."

"Was there a note?" I asked, startled.

"He left nothing behind for ordinary humanity like yourself."

I saw she was playing with me. "Rebbetzin Kornfeld," I said, standing up, "forgive me. My coat, please, and I'll go."

"Sit," she commanded. "Isaac read less lately, did you notice that?"

I gave her a civil smile. "All the same he was buying more and more."

"Think," she said. "I depend on you. You're just the one who might know. I had forgotten this. God sent you perhaps."

"Rebbetzin Kornfeld, I'm only a bookseller."

"God in his judgment sent me a bookseller. For such a long time Isaac never read at home. Think! Agronomy?"

"I don't remember anything like that. What would a Professor of Mishnaic History want with agronomy?"

"If he had a new book under his arm he would take it straight to the seminary and hide it in his office."

"I mailed to his office. If you like I can look up some of the titles—"

"You were in the park and you saw nothing?"

"Nothing." Then I was ashamed. "I saw the tree."

"And what is that? A tree is nothing."

"Rebbetzin Kornfeld," I pleaded, "it's a stupidity that I came here. I don't know myself why I came, I beg your pardon, I had no idea—"

"You came to learn why Isaac took his life. Botany? Or even, please listen, even mycology? He never asked you to send something on mushrooms? Or having to do with herbs? Manure? Flowers? A certain kind of agricultural poetry? A book about gardening? Forestry? Vegetables? Cereal growing?"

"Nothing, nothing like that," I said excitedly. "Rebbetzin Kornfeld, your husband was a rabbi!"

"I know what my husband was. Something to do with vines? Arbors? Rice? Think, think, think! Anything to do with land—meadows—goats—a farm, hay—anything at all, anything rustic or lunar—"

"Lunar! My God! Was he a teacher or a nurseryman? Goats! Was he a furrier? Sheindel, are you crazy? *I* was the furrier! What do you want from the dead?"

Without a word she replenished my cup, though it was more than half full, and sat down opposite me, on the other side of the lace boundary line. She leaned her face into her palms, but I saw her eyes. She kept them wide.

"Rebbetzin Kornfeld," I said, collecting myself, "with a tragedy like this—"

"You imagine I blame the books. I don't blame the books, whatever they were. If he had been faithful to his books he would have lived."

"He lived," I cried, "in books, what else?"

"No," said the widow.

"A scholar. A rabbi. A remarkable Jew!"

At this she spilled a furious laugh. "Tell me, I have always been very interested and shy to inquire. Tell me about your wife."

I intervened: "I haven't had a wife in years."

"What are they like, those people?"

"They're exactly like us, if you can think what we would be if we were like them."

"We are not like them. Their bodies are more to them than ours are to us. Our books are holy, to them their bodies are holy."

"Jane's was so holy she hardly ever let me get near it," I muttered to myself.

"Isaac used to run in the park, but he lost his breath too quickly. Instead he read in a book about runners with hats made of leaves."

"Sheindel, Sheindel, what did you expect of him? He was a student, he sat and he thought, he was a Jew."

She thrust her hands flat. "He was not."

I could not reply. I looked at her merely. She was thinner now than in her early young-womanhood, and her face had an in-between cast, poignant still at the mouth and jaw, beginning to grow coarse on either side of the nose.

"I think he was never a Jew," she said.

I wondered whether Isaac's suicide had unbalanced her.

"I'll tell you a story," she resumed. "A story about stories. These were the bedtime stories Isaac told Naomi and Esther: about mice that danced and children who laughed. When Miriam came he invented a speaking cloud. With Ophra it was a turtle that married a blade of withered grass. By Leah's time the stones had tears for their leglessness. Rebecca cried because of a tree that turned into a girl and could never grow colors again in autumn. Shiphrah, the littlest, believes that a pig has a soul."

"My own father used to drill me every night in sacred recitation. It was a terrible childhood."

"He insisted on picnics. Each time we went farther and farther into the country. It was a madness. Isaac never troubled to learn to drive a car, and there was always a clumsiness of baskets to carry and a clutter of buses and trains and seven exhausted wild girls. And he would look for special places—we couldn't settle just here or there, there had to be a brook or such-and-such a slope or else a little grove. And then, though he said it was all for the children's pleasure, he would leave them and go off alone and never come back until sunset, when everything was spilled and the air freezing and the babies crying."

"I was a grown man before I had the chance to go on a picnic," I admitted.

"I'm speaking of the beginning," said the widow. "Like you, wasn't I fooled? I was fooled, I was charmed. Going home with our baskets of berries and flowers we were a romantic huddle. Isaac's stories on those nights were full of dark invention. May God preserve me, I even begged him to write them down. Then suddenly he joined a club, and Sunday mornings he was up and away before dawn."

"A club? So early? What library opens at that hour?" I said, stunned that a man like Isaac should ally himself with anything so doubtful.

"Ah, you don't follow, you don't follow. It was a hiking club, they met under the moon. I thought it was a pity, the whole week Isaac was so inward, he needed air for the mind. He used to come home too fatigued to stand. He said he went for the landscape. I was like you, I took what I heard, I heard it all and never followed. He resigned from the hikers finally, and I believed all that strangeness was finished. He told me it was absurd to walk at such a pace, he was a teacher and not an athlete. Then he began to write."

"But he always wrote," I objected.

"Not this way. What he wrote was only fairy tales. He kept at it and for a while he neglected everything else. It was the strangeness in another form. The stories surprised me, they were so poor and dull. They were a little like the ideas he used to scare the girls with, but choked all over with notes, appendices, prefaces. It struck me then he didn't seem to understand he was only doing fairy tales. Yet they were really very ordinary—full of sprites, nymphs, gods, everything ordinary and old."

"Will you let me see them?"

"Burned, all burned."

"Isaac burned them?"

"You don't think I did! I see what you think."

It was true that I was marveling at her hatred. I supposed she was one of those born to dread imagination. I was overtaken by a coldness for her, though the sight of her small hands with their tremulous staves of fingers turning and turning in front of her face like a gate on a hinge reminded me of where she was born and who she was. She was an orphan and had been saved by magic and had a terror of it. The coldness fled. "Why should you be bothered by little stories?" I inquired. "It wasn't the stories that killed him."

"No, no, not the stories," she said. "Stupid corrupt things. I was glad when he gave them up. He piled them in the bathtub and lit them with a match. Then he put a notebook in his coat pocket and said he would walk in the park. Week after week he tried all the parks in the city. I didn't dream what he could be after. One day he took the subway and rode to the end of the line, and this was the right park at last. He went every day after class. An hour going, an hour back. Two, three in the morning he came home. 'Is it exercise?' I said. I thought he might be running again. He used to shiver with the chill of night and the dew. 'No, I sit quite still,' he said. 'Is it more stories you do out there?' 'No, I only jot down what I think.' 'A man should meditate in his own house, not by night near bad water,' I said. Six, seven in the morning he came home. I asked him if he meant to find his grave in that place."

She broke off with a cough, half artifice and half resignation, so loud that it made her crane toward the bedrooms to see if she had awakened a child. "I don't sleep any more," she told me. "Look around you. Look, look everywhere, look on the windowsills. Do you see any plants, any common house plants? I went down one evening and gave them to the garbage collector. I couldn't sleep in the same space with plants. They are like little trees. Am I deranged? Take Isaac's notebook and bring it back when you can."

I obeyed. In my own room, a sparse place, with no ornaments but a few pretty stalks in pots, I did not delay and seized the notebook. It was a tiny affair, three inches by five, with ruled pages that opened on a coiled wire. I read searchingly, hoping for something not easily evident. Sheindel by her melancholy innuendo had made me believe that in these few sheets Isaac had revealed the reason for his suicide. But it was all a disappointment. There was not a word of any importance. After a while I concluded that, whatever her motives, Sheindel was playing with me again. She meant to punish me for asking the unaskable. My inquisitiveness offended her; she had given me

Isaac's notebook not to enlighten but to rebuke. The handwriting was recognizable yet oddly formed, shaky and even senile, like that of a man outdoors and deskless who scribbles in his palm or on his lifted knee or leaning on a bit of bark; and there was no doubt that the wrinkled leaves, with their ragged corners, had been in and out of someone's pocket. So I did not mistrust Sheindel's mad anecdote; this much was true: a park, Isaac, a notebook, all at once, but signifying no more than that a professor with a literary turn of mind had gone for a walk. There was even a green stain straight across one of the quotations, as if the pad had slipped grassward and been trod on.

I have forgotten to mention that the notebook, though scantily filled, was in three languages. The Greek I could not read at all, but it had the shape of verse. The Hebrew was simply a miscellany, drawn mostly from Leviticus and Deuteronomy. Among these I found the following extracts, transcribed not quite verbatim:

Ye shall utterly destroy all the places of the gods, upon the high mountains, and upon the hills, and under every green tree.

And the soul that turneth after familiar spirits to go a-whoring after them, I will cut him off from among his people.

These, of course, were ordinary unadorned notes, such as any classroom lecturer might commonly make to remind himself of the text, with a phrase cut out here and there for the sake of speeding his hand. Or I thought it possible that Isaac might at that time have been preparing a paper on the talmudic commentaries for these passages. Whatever the case, the remaining quotations, chiefly from English poetry, interested me only slightly more. They were the elegiac favorites of a closeted Romantic. I was repelled by Isaac's Nature; it wore a capital letter, and smelled like my own Book Cellar. It was plain to me that he had lately grown painfully academic: he could not see a weed's tassel without finding a classical reference for it. He had put down a snatch of Byron, a smudge of Keats (like his scriptural copyings, these too were quick and fragmented), a pair of truncated lines from Tennyson, and this unmarked and clumsy quatrain:

> And yet all is not taken. Still one Dryad
>   Flits through the wood, one Oread skims the hill;
> White in the whispering stream still gleams a Naiad;
>   The beauty of the earth is haunted still.

All of this was so cloying and mooning and ridiculous, and so pedantic besides, that I felt ashamed for him. And yet there was almost nothing else, nothing to redeem him and nothing personal, only a sentence or two in his rigid self-controlled scholar's style, not unlike the starched little jokes of our correspondence. "I am writing at dusk sitting on a stone in Trilham's Inlet Park, within sight of Trilham's Inlet, a bay to the north of the city, and within two yards of a slender tree, *Quercus velutina*, the age of which, should one desire to measure it, can be ascertained by (God forbid) cutting the bole and counting the rings. The man writing is thirty-five years old and aging too rapidly, which may be ascertained by counting the rings under his poor myopic eyes." Below this, deliberate and readily more legible than the rest, appeared three curious words:

Great Pan lives.

That was all. In a day or so I returned the notebook to Sheindel. I told myself that she had seven orphans to worry over, and repressed my anger at having been cheated.

She was waiting for me. "I am so sorry, there was a letter in the notebook, it had fallen out. I found it on the carpet after you left."

"Thank you, no," I said. "I've read enough out of Isaac's pockets."

"Then why did you come to see me to begin with?"

"I came," I said, "just to see you."

"You came for Isaac." But she was more mocking than distraught. "I gave you everything you needed to see what happened and still you don't follow. Here." She held out a large law-sized paper. "Read the letter."

"I've read his notebook. If everything I need to fathom Isaac is in the notebook I don't need the letter."

"It's a letter he wrote to explain himself," she persisted.

"You told me Isaac left you no notes."

"It was not written to me."

I sat down on one of the dining-room chairs and Sheindel put the page before me on the table. It lay face up on the lace divider. I did not look at it.

"It's a love letter," Sheindel whispered. "When they cut him down they found the notebook in one pocket and the letter in the other."

I did not know what to say.

"The police gave me everything," Sheindel said. "Everything to keep."

"A love letter?" I repeated.

"That is what such letters are commonly called."

"And the police—they gave it to you, and that was the first you realized what"—I floundered after the inconceivable—"what could be occupying him?"

"What could be occupying him," she mimicked. "Yes. Not until they took the letter and the notebook out of his pocket."

"My God. His habit of life, his mind . . . I can't imagine it. You never guessed?"

"No."

"These trips to the park—"

"He had become aberrant in many ways. I have described them to you."

"But the park! Going off like that, alone—you didn't think he might be meeting a woman?"

"It was not a woman."

Disgust like a powder clotted my nose. "Sheindel, you're crazy."

"I'm crazy, is that it? Read his confession! Read it! How long can I be the only one to know this thing? Do you want my brain to melt? Be my confidant," she entreated so unexpectedly that I held my breath.

"You've said nothing to anyone?"

"Would they have recited such eulogies if I had? Read the letter!"

"I have no interest in the abnormal," I said coldly.

She raised her eyes and watched me for the smallest space. Without any change in the posture of her suppliant head her laughter began; I have never since heard sounds like those—almost mouselike in density for fear of waking her sleeping daughters, but so rational in intent that it was like listening to astonished sanity rendered into a cackling fugue. She kept it up for a minute and then calmed herself. "Please sit where you are. Please pay attention. I will read the letter to you myself."

She plucked the page from the table with an orderly gesture. I saw that this letter had been scrupulously prepared; it was closely written. Her tone was cleansed by scorn.

" 'My ancestors were led out of Egypt by the hand of God,' " she read. "Is this how a love letter starts out?"

She moved on resolutely. " 'We were guilty of so-called abominations well-described elsewhere. Other peoples have been nourished on their mythologies. For aeons we have been weaned from all traces of the same.' "

I felt myself becoming impatient. The fact was I had returned with a single idea: I meant to marry Isaac's widow when enough time had passed to make it seemly. It was my intention to court her with great subtlety at first, so that I would not appear to be presuming on her sorrow. But she was possessed. "Sheindel, why do you want to inflict this treatise on me? Give it to the seminary, contribute it to a symposium of professors."

"I would sooner die."

At this I began to attend in earnest.

" 'I will leave aside the wholly plausible position of so-called animism within the concept of the One God. I will omit a historical illumination of its continuous but covert expression even within the Fence of the Law. Creature, I leave these aside—' "

"What?" I yelped.

" 'Creature,' " she repeated, spreading her nostrils. " 'What is human history? What is our philosophy? What is our religion? None of these teaches us poor human ones that we are alone in the universe, and even

without them we would know that we are not. At a very young age I understood that a foolish man would not believe in a fish had he not had one enter
his experience. Innumerable forms exist and have come to our eyes, and to
the still deeper eye of the lens of our instruments; from this minute perception of what already is, it is easy to conclude that further forms are possible,
that all forms are probable. God created the world not for Himself alone, or
I would not now possess this consciousness with which I am enabled to address thee, Loveliness.' "

"Thee," I echoed, and swallowed a sad bewilderment.

"You must let me go on," Sheindel said, and grimly went on. " 'It is false
history, false philosophy, and false religion which declare to us human ones
that we live among Things. The arts of physics and chemistry begin to teach
us differently, but their way of compassion is new, and finds few to carry
fidelity to its logical and beautiful end. The molecules dance inside all forms,
and within the molecules dance the atoms, and within the atoms dance still
profounder sources of divine vitality. There is nothing that is Dead. There is
no Non-life. Holy life subsists even in the stone, even in the bones of dead
dogs and dead men. Hence in God's fecundating Creation there is no possibility of Idolatry, and therefore no possibility of committing this so-called
abomination.' "

"My God, my God," I wailed. "Enough, Sheindel, it's more than
enough, no more—"

"There is more," she said.

"I don't want to hear it."

"He stains his character for you? A spot, do you think? You will hear."
She took up in a voice which all at once reminded me of my father's: it was
unforgiving. " 'Creature, I rehearse these matters though all our language is
as breath to thee; as baubles for the juggler. Where we struggle to understand from day to day, and contemplate the grave for its riddle, the other
breeds are born fulfilled in wisdom. Animal races conduct themselves without self-investigations; instinct is a higher and not a lower thing. Alas that we
human ones—but for certain pitifully primitive approximations in those few
reflexes and involuntary actions left to our bodies—are born bare of instinct!
All that we unfortunates must resort to through science, art, philosophy, religion, all our imaginings and tormented strivings, all our meditations and
vain questionings, all!—are expressed naturally and rightly in the beasts, the
plants, the rivers, the stones. The reason is simple, it is our tragedy: our soul
is included in us, it inhabits us, we contain it, when we seek our soul we
must seek in ourselves. To see the soul, to confront it—that is divine wisdom.
Yet how can we see into our dark selves? With the other races of being it is
differently ordered. The soul of the plant does not reside in the chlorophyll,
it may roam if it wishes, it may choose whatever form or shape it pleases.
Hence the other breeds, being largely free of their soul and able to witness it,

can live in peace. To see one's soul is to know all, to know all is to own the peace our philosophies futilely envisage. Earth displays two categories of soul: the free and the indwelling. We human ones are cursed with the indwelling—' "

"Stop!" I cried.

"I will not," said the widow.

"Please, you told me he burned his fairy tales."

"Did I lie to you? Will you say I lied?"

"Then for Isaac's sake why didn't you? If this isn't a fairy tale what do you want me to think it could be?"

"Think what you like."

"Sheindel," I said, "I beg you, don't destroy a dead man's honor. Don't look at this thing again, tear it to pieces, don't continue with it."

"I don't destroy his honor. He had none."

"Please! Listen to yourself! My God, who was the man? Rabbi Isaac Kornfeld! Talk of honor! Wasn't he a teacher? Wasn't he a scholar?"

"He was a pagan."

Her eyes returned without hesitation to their task. She commenced: " 'All these truths I learned only gradually, against my will and desire. Our teacher Moses did not speak of them; much may be said under this head. It was not out of ignorance that Moses failed to teach about those souls that are free. If I have learned what Moses knew, is this not because we are both men? He was a man, but God addressed him; it was God's will that our ancestors should no longer be slaves. Yet our ancestors, being stiff-necked, would not have abandoned their slavery in Egypt had they been taught of the free souls. They would have said: "Let us stay, our bodies will remain enslaved in Egypt, but our souls will wander at their pleasure in Zion. If the cactus-plant stays rooted while its soul roams, why not also a man?" And if Moses had replied that only the world of Nature has the gift of the free soul, while man is chained to his, and that a man, to free his soul, must also free the body that is its vessel, they would have scoffed. "How is it that men, and men alone, are different from the world of Nature? If this is so, then the condition of men is evil and unjust, and if this condition of ours is evil and unjust in general, what does it matter whether we are slaves in Egypt or citizens in Zion?" And they would not have done God's will and abandoned their slavery. Therefore Moses never spoke to them of the free souls, lest the people not do God's will and go out from Egypt.' "

In an instant a sensation broke in me—it was entirely obscure, there was nothing I could compare it with, and yet I was certain I recognized it. And then I did. It hurtled me into childhood—it was the crisis of insight one experiences when one has just read out, for the first time, that conglomeration of figures which makes a word. In that moment I penetrated beyond Isaac's alphabet into his language. I saw that he was on the side of possibility: he

was both sane and inspired. His intention was not to accumulate mystery
but to dispel it.

"All that part is brilliant," I burst out.

Sheindel meanwhile had gone to the sideboard to take a sip of cold tea
that was standing there. "In a minute," she said, and pursued her thirst. "I
have heard of drawings surpassing Rembrandt daubed by madmen who
when released from the fit couldn't hold the chalk. What follows is beautiful, I warn you."

"The man was a genius."

"Yes."

"Go on," I urged.

She produced for me her clownish jeering smile. She read: " 'Sometimes
in the desert journey on the way they would come to a watering place, and
some quick spry boy would happen to glimpse the soul of the spring (which
the wild Greeks afterward called naiad), but not knowing of the existence of
the free souls he would suppose only that the moon had cast a momentary
beam across the water. Loveliness, with the same innocence of accident I discovered thee. Loveliness, Loveliness.' "

She stopped.

"Is that all?"

"There is more."

"Read it."

"The rest is the love letter."

"Is it hard for you?" But I asked with more eagerness than pity.

"I was that man's wife, he scaled the Fence of the Law. For this God preserved me from the electric fence. Read it for yourself."

Incontinently I snatched the crowded page.

" 'Loveliness, in thee the joy, substantiation, and supernal succor of my
theorem. How many hours through how many years I walked over the cilia-
forests of our enormous aspiring vegetable-star, this light rootless seed that
crawls in its single furrow, this shaggy mazy unimplanted cabbage-head of
our earth!—never, all that time, all those days of unfulfillment, a white space
like a desert thirst, never, never to grasp. I thought myself abandoned to the
intrigue of my folly. At dawn, on a hillock, what seemed the very shape and
seizing of the mound's nature—what was it? Only the haze of the sun-ball
growing great through hoarfrost. The oread slipped from me, leaving her illusion; or was never there at all; or was there but for an instant, and ran
away. What sly ones the free souls are! They have a comedy we human ones
cannot dream: the laughing drunkard feels in himself the shadow of the
shadow of the shadow of their wit, and only because he has made himself a
vessel, as the two banks and the bed of a rivulet are the naiad's vessel. A
naiad I may indeed have viewed whole: all seven of my daughters were once
wading in a stream in a compact but beautiful park, of which I had much

hope. The youngest being not yet two, and fretful, the older ones were told to keep her always by the hand, but they did not obey. I, having passed some way into the woods behind, all at once heard a scream and noise of splashes, and caught sight of a tiny body flying down into the water. Running back through the trees I could see the others bunched together, afraid, as the baby dived helplessly, all these little girls frozen in a garland—when suddenly one of them (it was too quick a movement for me to recognize which) darted to the struggler, who was now underwater, and pulled her up, and put an arm around her to soothe her. The arm was blue—blue. As blue as a lake. And fiercely, from my spot on the bank, panting, I began to count the little girls. I counted eight, thought myself not mad but delivered, again counted, counted seven, knew I had counted well before, knew I counted well even now. A blue-armed girl had come to wade among them. Which is to say the shape of a girl. I questioned my daughters: each in her fright believed one of the others had gone to pluck up the tiresome baby. None wore a dress with blue sleeves.' "

"Proofs," said the widow. "Isaac was meticulous, he used to account for all his proofs always."

"How?" My hand in tremor rustled Isaac's letter; the paper bleated as though whipped.

"By eventually finding a principle to cover them," she finished maliciously. "Well, don't rest even for me, you don't oblige me. You have a long story to go, long enough to make a fever."

"Tea," I said hoarsely.

She brought me her own cup from the sideboard, and I believed as I drank that I swallowed some of her mockery and gall.

"Sheindel, for a woman so pious you're a great skeptic." And now the tremor had command of my throat.

"An atheist's statement," she rejoined. "The more piety, the more skepticism. A religious man comprehends this. Superfluity, excess of custom, and superstition would climb like a choking vine on the Fence of the Law if skepticism did not continually hack them away to make freedom for purity."

I then thought her fully worthy of Isaac. Whether I was worthy of her I evaded putting to myself; instead I gargled some tea and returned to the letter.

" 'It pains me to confess,' " I read, " 'how after that I moved from clarity to doubt and back again. I had no trust in my conclusions because all my experiences were evanescent. Everything certain I attributed to some other cause less certain. Every voice out of the moss I blamed on rabbits and squirrels. Every motion among leaves I called a bird, though there positively was no bird. My first sight of the Little People struck me as no more than a shudder of literary delusion, and I determined they could only be an instantaneous crop of mushrooms. But one night, a little after ten o'clock at the crux of summer—the sky still showed strings of light—I was wandering in this place, this place where they will find my corpse—' "

"Not for my sake," said Sheindel when I hesitated.

"It's terrible," I croaked, "terrible."

"Withered like a shell," she said, as though speaking of the cosmos; and I understood from her manner that she had a fanatic's acquaintance with this letter, and knew it nearly by heart. She appeared to be thinking the words faster than I could bring them out, and for some reason I was constrained to hurry the pace of my reading.

" '—where they will find my corpse withered like the shell of an insect,' " I rushed on. " 'The smell of putrefaction lifted clearly from the bay. I began to speculate about my own body after I was dead—whether the soul would be set free immediately after the departure of life; or whether only gradually, as decomposition proceeded and more and more of the indwelling soul was released to freedom. But when I considered how a man's body is no better than a clay pot, a fact which none of our sages has ever contradicted, it seemed to me then that an indwelling soul by its own nature would be obliged to cling to its bit of pottery until the last crumb and grain had vanished into earth. I walked through the ditches of that black meadow grieving and swollen with self-pity. It came to me that while my poor bones went on decaying at their ease, my soul would have to linger inside them, waiting, despairing, longing to join the free ones. I cursed it for its gravity-despoiled, slow, interminably languishing purse of flesh; better to be encased in vapor, in wind, in a hair of a coconut! Who knows how long it takes the body of a man to shrink into gravel, and the gravel into sand, and the sand into vitamin? A hundred years? Two hundred, three hundred? A thousand perhaps! Is it not true that bones nearly intact are constantly being dug up by the paleontologists two million years after burial?'—Sheindel," I interrupted, "this is death, not love. Where's the love letter to be afraid of here? I don't find it."

"Continue," she ordered. And then: "You see I'm not afraid."

"Not of love?"

"No. But you recite much too slowly. Your mouth is shaking. Are you afraid of death?"

I did not reply.

"Continue," she said again. "Go rapidly. The next sentence begins with an extraordinary thought."

" 'An extraordinary thought emerged in me. It was luminous, profound, and practical. More than that, it had innumerable precedents; the mythologies had documented it a dozen dozen times over. I recalled all those mortals reputed to have coupled with gods (a collective word, showing much common sense, signifying what our philosophies more abstrusely call Shekhinah), and all that poignant miscegenation represented by centaurs, satyrs, mermaids, fauns, and so forth, not to speak of that even more famous mingling in Genesis, whereby the sons of God took the daughters of men for brides, producing giants and possibly also those abortions, leviathan and behemoth, of which we read in Job, along with unicorns and other chimeras and monsters abundant in Scripture, hence far from fanciful. There existed also the example of the succubus Lilith, who was often known to couple in the medieval ghetto even with prepubescent boys. By all these evidences I was emboldened in my confidence that I was surely not the first man to conceive such a desire in the history of our earth. Creature, the thought that took hold of me was this: if only I could couple with one of the free souls, the strength of the connection would likely wrest my own soul from my body—seize it, as if by a tongs, draw it out, so to say, to its own freedom. The intensity and force of my desire to capture one of these beings now became prodigious. I avoided my wife—' "

Here the widow heard me falter.

"Please," she commanded, and I saw creeping in her face the completed turn of a sneer.

" '—lest I be depleted of potency at that moment (which might occur in any interval, even, I assumed, in my own bedroom) when I should encounter one of the free souls. I was borne back again and again to the fetid viscosities of the Inlet, borne there as if on the rising stink of my own enduring and tedious putrefaction, the idea of which I could no longer shake off—I envisaged my soul as trapped in my last granule, and that last granule itself perhaps petrified, never to dissolve, and my soul condemned to minister to it throughout eternity! It seemed to me my soul must be released at once or be lost to sweet air forever. In a gleamless dark, struggling with this singular panic, I stumbled from ditch to ditch, strained like a blind dog for the support of solid verticality; and smacked my palm against bark. I looked up and in the black could not fathom the size of the tree—my head lolled forward, my brow met the trunk with all its gravings. I busied my fingers in the interstices of the bark's cuneiform. Then with forehead flat on the tree, I embraced it with both arms to measure it. My hands united on the other side. It was a young narrow weed, I did not know of what family. I reached to the lowest branch and plucked a leaf and made my tongue travel meditatively along its periphery to assess its shape: oak. The taste was sticky and exaltingly bitter. A jubilation lightly carpeted my groin. I then placed one hand (the other I kept around the tree's waist, as it were) in the bifurcation (disgustingly termed crotch) of that lowest limb and the elegant and devoutly firm torso, and caressed that miraculous juncture with a certain languor, which gradually changed to vigor. I was all at once savagely alert and deeply daring: I chose that single tree together with the ground near it for an enemy which in two senses would not yield: it would neither give nor give in. "Come, come," I called aloud in Nature. A wind blew out a braid of excremental malodor into the heated air. "Come," I called, "couple with me, as thou didst with Cadmus, Rhoecus, Tithonus, Endymion, and that king Numa Pompilius to whom thou didst give secrets. As Lilith comes without a sign, so come thou. As the sons of God came to copulate with women, so now let a daughter of Shekhinah the Emanation reveal herself to me. Nymph, come now, come now."

" 'Without warning I was flung to the ground. My face smashed into earth, and a flaky clump of dirt lodged in my open mouth. For the rest, I was on my knees, pressing down on my hands, with the fingernails clutching dirt. A superb ache lined my haunch. I began to weep because I was certain I had been ravished by some sinewy animal. I vomited the earth I had swallowed and believed I was defiled, as it is written: "Neither shalt thou lie with any beast." I lay sunk in the grass, afraid to lift my head to see if the animal still lurked. Through some curious means I had been fully positioned and aroused and exquisitely sated, all in half a second, in a fashion impossible to explain, in which, though I performed as with my own wife, I felt as if a preternatural rapine had been committed upon me. I continued prone, listening for the animal's breathing. Meanwhile, though every tissue of my flesh was gratified in its inmost awareness, a marvelous voluptuousness did not leave my body; sensual exultations of a wholly supreme and paradisal order, unlike anything our poets have ever defined, both flared and were intensely satisfied in the same moment. This salubrious and delightful perceptiveness excited my being for some time: a conjoining not dissimilar (in metaphor only; in actuality it cannot be described) from the magical contradiction of the tree and its issuance-of-branch at the point of bifurcation. In me were linked, *in the same instant*, appetite and fulfillment, delicacy and power, mastery and submissiveness, and other paradoxes of entirely remarkable emotional import.

" 'Then I heard what I took to be the animal treading through the grass quite near my head, all cunningly; it withheld its breathing, then snored it out in a cautious and wisplike whirr that resembled a light wind through rushes. With a huge energy (my muscular force seemed to have increased) I leaped up in fear of my life; I had nothing to use for a weapon but—oh, laughable!—the pen I had been writing with in a little notebook I always carried about with me in those days (and still keep on my person as a self-shaming souvenir of my insipidness, my bookishness, my pitiable conjecture and wishfulness in a time when, not yet knowing thee, I knew nothing). What I saw was not an animal but a girl no older than my oldest daughter, who was then fourteen. Her skin was as perfect as an eggplant's and nearly of that color. In height she was half as tall as I was. The second and third fingers of her hands—this I noticed at once—were peculiarly fused, one slotted into the other, like the ligula of a leaf. She was entirely bald and had no ears but rather a type of gill or envelope, one only, on the left side. Her toes displayed the same oddity I had observed in her fingers. She was neither naked nor clothed—that is to say, even though a part of her body, from hip to just below the breasts (each of which appeared to be a kind of velvety color-less pear, suspended from a very short, almost invisible stem), was luxuri-antly covered with a flossy or sporelike material, this was a natural efflores-cence in the manner of, with us, hair. All her sexual portion was wholly visi-ble, as in any field flower. Aside from these express deviations, she was com-mandingly human in aspect, if unmistakably flowerlike. She was, in fact, the reverse of our hackneyed euphuism, as when we say a young girl blooms like a flower—she, on the contrary, seemed a flower transfigured into the shape of the most stupendously lovely child I had ever seen. Under the smallest push of wind she bent at her superlative waist; this, I recognized, and not the exhalations of some lecherous beast, was the breathlike sound that had alarmed me at her approach: these motions of hers made the blades of grass collide. (She herself, having no lungs, did not "breathe.") She stood bobbing joyfully before me, with a face as tender as a morning-glory, strangely phos-phorescent: she shed her own light, in effect, and I had no difficulty in con-fronting her beauty.

" 'Moreover, by experiment I soon learned that she was not only capable of language, but that she delighted in playing with it. This she literally could do—if I had distinguished her hands before anything else, it was because she had held them out to catch my first cry of awe. She either caught my words like balls or let them roll, or caught them and then darted off to throw them into the Inlet. I discovered that whenever I spoke I more or less pelted her; but she liked this, and told me ordinary human speech only tickled and amused, whereas laughter, being highly plosive, was something of an assault. I then took care to pretend much solemnity, though I was lightheaded with rapture. Her own "voice" I apprehended rather than heard—which she, un-able to imagine how we human ones are prisoned in sensory perception, found hard to conceive. Her sentences came to me not as a series of differen-tiated frequencies but (impossible to develop this idea in language) as a dif-fused cloud of field fragrances; yet to say that I assimilated her thought through the olfactory nerve would be a pedestrian distortion. All the same it was clear that whatever she said reached me in a shimmer of pellucid per-fumes, and I understood her meaning with an immediacy of glee and with none of the ambiguities and suspiciousness of motive that surround our hu-man communication.

" 'Through this medium she explained that she was a dryad and that her name was Iripomoňoéià (as nearly as I can render it in our narrowly limited orthography, and in this dunce's alphabet of ours which is notoriously im-pervious to odoriferous categories). She told me what I had already seized: that she had given me her love in response to my call.

" ' "Wilt thou come to any man who calls?" I asked.

" ' "All men call, whether realizing it or not. I and my sisters sometimes come to those who do not realize. Almost never, unless for sport, do we come to that man who calls knowingly—he wishes only to inhabit us out of perversity or boastfulness or to indulge a dreamed-of disgust."

" ' "Scripture does not forbid sodomy with the plants," I exclaimed, but she did not comprehend any of this and lowered her hands so that my words would fly past her uncaught. "I too called thee knowingly, not for perversity but for love of Nature."

" ' "I have caught men's words before as they talked of Nature, you are not the first. It is not Nature they love so much as Death they fear. So Corylylyb my cousin received it in a season not long ago coupling in a harbor with one of your kind, one called Spinoza, one that had catarrh of the lung. I am of Nature and immortal and so I cannot pity your deaths. But return tomorrow and say Iripomoňoéià." Then she chased my last word to where she had kicked it, behind the tree. She did not come back. I ran to the tree and circled it diligently but she was lost for that night.

" 'Loveliness, all the foregoing, telling of my life and meditations until now, I have never before recounted to thee or any other. The rest is beyond mean telling: those rejoicings from midnight to dawn, when the greater phosphorescence of the whole shouting sky frightened thee home! How in a trance of happiness we coupled in the ditches, in the long grasses, behind a fountain, under a broken wall, once recklessly on the very pavement, with a bench for roof and trellis! How I was taught by natural arts to influence certain chemistries engendering explicit marvels, blisses, and transports no man has slaked himself with since Father Adam pressed out the forbidden chlorophyll of Eden! Loveliness, Loveliness, none like thee. No brow so sleek, no elbow-crook so fine, no eye so green, no waist so pliant, no limbs so pleasant and acute. None like immortal Iripomoňoéià.

" 'Creature, the moon filled and starved twice, and there was still no end to the glorious archaic newness of Iripomoňoéià.

" 'Then last night. Last night! I will record all with simplicity.

" 'We entered a shallow ditch. In a sweet-smelling voice of extraordinary redolence—so intense in its sweetness that even the barbaric stinks and wind-lifted farts of the Inlet were overpowered by it—Iripomoňoéià inquired of me how I felt without my soul. I replied that I did not know this was my condition. "Oh yes, your body is now an empty packet, that is why it is so light. Spring." I sprang in air and rose effortlessly. "You have spoiled yourself, spoiled yourself with confusions," she complained, "now by morning your body will be crumpled and withered and ugly, like a leaf in its sere hour, and never again after tonight will this place see you." "Nymph!" I roared, amazed by levitation. "Oh, oh, that damaged," she cried, "you hit my eye with that noise," and she wafted a deeper aroma, a leeklike mist, one that stung the mucous membranes. A white bruise disfigured her petally lid. I was repentant and sighed terribly for her injury. "Beauty marred is for our kind what physical hurt is for yours," she reproved me. "Where you have pain, we have ugliness. Where you profane yourselves by immorality, we are profaned by ugliness. Your soul has taken leave of you and spoils our pretty game." "Nymph!" I whispered, "heart, treasure, if my soul is separated how is it I am unaware?"

" ' "Poor man," she answered, "you have only to look and you will see the thing." Her speech had now turned as acrid as an herb, and all that place reeked bitterly. "You know I am a spirit. You know I must flash and dart. All my sisters flash and dart. Of all races we are the quickest. Our very religion is all-of-a-sudden. No one can hinder us, no one may delay us. But yesterday you undertook to detain me in your embrace, you stretched your kisses into years, you called me your treasure and your heart endlessly, your soul in its slow greed kept me close and captive, all the while knowing well how a spirit cannot stay and will not be fixed. I made to leap from you, but your obstinate soul held on until it was snatched straight from your frame and escaped with me. I saw it hurled out onto the pavement, the blue beginning of day was already seeping down, so I ran away and could say nothing until this moment."

" ' "My soul is free? Free entirely? And can be seen?"

" ' "Free. If I could pity any living thing under the sky I would pity you for the sight of your soul. I do not like it, it conjures against me."

" ' "My soul loves thee," I urged in all my triumph, "it is freed from the thousand-year grave!" I jumped out of the ditch like a frog, my legs had no weight; but the dryad sulked in the ground, stroking her ugly violated eye. "Iripomoňoéià, my soul will follow thee with thankfulness into eternity."

" ' "I would sooner be followed by the dirty fog. I do not like that soul of yours. It conjures against me. It denies me, it denies every spirit and all my sisters and every nereid of the harbor, it denies all our multiplicity, and all gods diversiform, it spites even Lord Pan, it is an enemy, and you, poor man, do not know your own soul. Go, look at it, there it is on the road."

" 'I scudded back and forth under the moon.

" ' "Nothing, only a dusty old man trudging up there."

" ' "A quite ugly old man?"

" ' "Yes, that is all. My soul is not there."

" ' "With a matted beard and great fierce eyebrows?"

" ' "Yes, yes, one like that is walking on the road. He is half bent over under the burden of a dusty old bag. The bag is stuffed with books—I can see their raveled bindings sticking out."

" ' "And he reads as he goes?"

" ' "Yes, he reads as he goes."

" ' "What is it he reads?"

" ' "Some huge and terrifying volume, heavy as a stone." I peered forward in the moonlight. "A tractate. A tractate of the Mishnah. Its leaves are so worn they break as he turns them, but he does not turn them often because there is much matter on a single page. He is so sad! Such antique weariness broods in his face! His throat is striped from the whip. His cheeks are folded like ancient flags, he reads the Law and breathes the dust."

" ' "And are there flowers on either side of the road?"

" ' "Incredible flowers! Of every color! And noble shrubs like mounds of green moss! And the cricket crackling in the field. He passes indifferent through the beauty of the field. His nostrils sniff his book as if flowers lay on the clotted page, but the flowers lick his feet. His feet are bandaged, his notched toenails gore the path. His prayer shawl droops on his studious back. He reads the Law and breathes the dust and doesn't see the flowers and won't heed the cricket spitting in the field."

" ' "That," said the dryad, "is your soul." And was gone with all her odors.

" ' My body sailed up to the road in a single hop. I alighted near the shape of the old man and demanded whether he were indeed the soul of Rabbi Isaac Kornfeld. He trembled but confessed. I asked if he intended to go with his books through the whole future without change, always with his tractate in his hand, and he answered that he could do nothing else.

" ' "Nothing else! You, who I thought yearned for the earth! You, an immortal, free, and caring only to be bound to the Law!"

" ' He held a dry arm fearfully before his face, and with the other arm hitched up his merciless bag on his shoulder. "Sir," he said, still quavering, "didn't you wish to see me with your own eyes?"

" ' "I know your figure!" I shrieked. "Haven't I seen that figure a hundred times before? On a hundred roads? It is not mine! I will not have it be mine!"

" ' "If you had not contrived to be rid of me, I would have stayed with you till the end. The dryad, who does not exist, lies. It was not I who clung to her but you, my body. Sir, all that has no real existence lies. In your grave beside you I would have sung you David's songs, I would have moaned Solomon's voice to your last grain of bone. But you expelled me, your ribs exile me from their fate, and I will walk here alone always, in my garden"—he scratched on his page—"with my precious birds"—he scratched at the letters—"and my darling trees"—he scratched at the tall side-column of commentary.

" ' He was so impudent in his bravery—for I was all fleshliness and he all floppy wraith—that I seized him by the collar and shook him up and down, while the books on his back made a vast rubbing one on the other, and bits of shredding leather flew out like a rain.

" ' "The sound of the Law," he said, "is more beautiful than the crickets. The smell of the Law is more radiant than the moss. The taste of the Law exceeds clear water."

" 'At this nervy provocation—he more than any other knew my despair—I grabbed his prayer shawl by its tassels and whirled around him once or twice until I had unwrapped it from him altogether, and wound it on my own neck and in one bound came to the tree.

" ' "Nymph!" I called to it. "Spirit and saint! Iripomoňoéià, come! None like thee, no brow so sleek, no elbow-crook so fine, no eye so green, no waist so pliant, no limbs so pleasant and acute. For pity of me, come, come."

" 'But she does not come.

" ' "Loveliness, come."

" 'She does not come.

" 'Creature, see how I am coiled in the snail of this shawl as if in a leaf. I crouch to write my words. Let soul call thee lie, but body . . .

" ' . . . body . . .

" ' . . . fingers twist, knuckles dark as wood, tongue dries like grass, deeper now into silk . . .

" ' . . . silk of pod of shawl, knees wilt, knuckles wither, neck . . .' "

Here the letter suddenly ended.

"You see? A pagan!" said Sheindel, and kept her spiteful smile. It was thick with audacity.

"You don't pity him," I said, watching the contempt that glittered in her teeth.

"Even now you don't see? You can't follow?"

"Pity him," I said.

"He who takes his own life does an abomination."

For a long moment I considered her. "You don't pity him? You don't pity him at all?"

"Let the world pity me."

"Goodbye," I said to the widow.

"You won't come back?"

I gave what amounted to a little bow of regret.

"I told you you came just for Isaac! But Isaac"—I was in terror of her cough, which was unmistakably laughter—"Isaac disappoints. 'A scholar. A rabbi. A remarkable Jew!' Ha! He disappoints you?"

"He was always an astonishing man."

"But not what you thought," she insisted. "An illusion."

"Only the pitiless are illusory. Go back to that park, Rebbetzin," I advised her.

"And what would you like me to do there? Dance around a tree and call Greek names to the weeds?"

"Your husband's soul is in that park. Consult it." But her low derisive cough accompanied me home: whereupon I remembered her earlier words and dropped three green house plants down the toilet; after a journey of some miles through conduits they straightway entered Trilham's Inlet, where they decayed amid the civic excrement.

Outfoxing the Fox

by Cynthia Ozick

"There ran the little fox," the storyteller said, "on the Temple Mount, in the place where the Holy of Holies used to be, barren and desolate, returned to the wild, in the generation of the Destruction. And Rabbi Akiva was walking by with three colleagues, Rabbi Gamliel, Rabbi Elazar, and Rabbi Joshua, and all four saw the little fox dash out. Three of the four wept, but Akiva laughed. Akiva asked, 'Why do you weep?' The three said, 'Because the fox goes in and out, and the place of the Temple is now the fox's place.' Then the three asked Akiva, 'Why do you laugh?' Akiva said, 'Because of the prophecy of Uriah and because of the prophecy of Zechariah. Uriah said, "Zion shall be plowed as a field, and Jerusalem shall become heaps." Zechariah said, "Yet again shall the streets of Jerusalem be filled with boys and girls playing." So you see,' said Rabbi Akiva, 'now that Uriah's prophecy has been fulfilled, it is certain that Zechariah's prophecy will also be fulfilled.' And *that*," said the storyteller, "is pedagogy. To predict not from the first text, but from the second. Not from the earliest evidence, but from the latest. To laugh out loud in that very interval which to every reasonable judgment looks to be the most inappropriate—when the first is accomplished and future repair is most chimerical. To expect, to welcome, exactly that which appears most unpredictable. To await the surprise which, when it comes, turns out to be not a surprise after all, but a natural path." Again she lifted her head. "The hoax is when the pedagogue stops too soon. To stop at Uriah without the expectation of Zechariah is to stop too soon. And when the pedagogue stops too soon, he misreads every sign, and thinks the place of the priest is by rights the place of the fox, and takes the fox and all its qualities to be right, proper, and permanent; and takes aggressiveness for intelligence, and thoughtfulness for stupidity, and diffidence for dimness, and arrogance for popularity, and dreamers for blockheads, and brazenness for the mark of a lively personality. And all the while the aggressive and the brazen one is only a fox!—a false and crafty creature running in and out of a desolation and a delusion. The laughter of Akiva outfoxes the fox."

The Homily of the Roses
by Arthur A. Cohen

It is said, if I recall the passage correctly, that one of our ancient rabbis was a gardener. I cannot remember his name. (I quote sources poorly. Since all of us, you no less than myself, are sources, it isn't relevant to remember the original. In any case, I cannot remember the rabbi's name and it does not matter. We have so many ancient teachers.)

The ancient rabbi raised roses.

He would go out into the desert each morning, and there, among the rocks, he would grow roses, sheltered from the heat, but nourished by the reflected light of the sun. He never raised very tall roses, nor were his roses very beautiful. They were stunted roses and all his roses were red, but their thorns were tough and fibrous, sufficient protection against the small lizards who made their home in the clefts of the rocks.

The rabbi raised roses with stubborn defiance and they responded. They were nourished by his quiet affection and they were hearty. Of course they would die. When they died, one by one, over each dead rose the rabbi would say one word of the *Kaddish*, scratching a mark in the sand until all seventy-five words had been spoken, and then, the *Kaddish* completed, he would gather the broken stems, the rotting petals, the dead buds and bury them in places on the mountainside along with seedlings so that other rose-bushes would grow forth. In time the entire mountainside before his cave was covered with rosebushes.

You may well ask, Did that holy man ever pick a rose for himself? He did not. Picking was not the purpose. Planting and watching the struggle, saying the *Kaddish* and planting again was enough. That is the homily. Now, let each of us think about its meaning. (Throats cleared, feet shuffled but no one spoke. After some minutes Simon began once more.) We have waited long enough. What do you think, sir from Chicago? You decline the honor. Or you from Detroit, no idea? You, Pittsburgh? You, Newark? None. Not any. Don't fidget. Give them some wine. All right. I will proceed.

Interpretation I

There are two possible meanings to the homily. The first is appropriate and correct, but not completely relevant. Like all interpretations the ground-work comes first

In the case of the homilies of the rabbis (the lives of the saints, as the others call them) the first interpretation is founded upon actual history. Our rabbi—let his name, for the moment, be Yohanan ben Zakkai, a saint of a rabbi, a rabbi of a saint—lived in the time of the Roman conquerors, those that are later called Edom (to signify Christians) and at that time called, simply, simplistically, Romans.

The Romans threatened to destroy us and, in fact, very nearly accomplished their objective. What were we then? We were roses planted in the craggy soil of the Holy Land, soil that could not bring forth without nurture, without water, without sustenance and care.

And we were roses of but one color. That signifies that we were united, but having only the strength of single-mindedness we were both strong and weak, strong in that we were determined, breathing with a single breath, an integrated people, but weak in that single colors define unanimity without the presence of antibodies, foreign agents, diversities from which resilience and tensility derive.

So. We were strong and weak. And red. Blood. Clear and simple. The Adamic color, the color of our soil, the color of our blood. Red. And strong though we were, we had the strength of knobbly men, bowlegged giants, powerful but without mobility and speed. And so we died. Picked off one by one. Our petals fell until by the time of Masada we were vanquished.

But then, let us say, the Holy One, blessed be He, had a kind of mercy upon us and loving our stupid loyalty, our single-mindedness, our sacrifice, our obduracy, having spoken over us prayers of mourning, he replenished us until from a single bush we covered the mountainside, as in fact we are everywhere on the face of the earth.

Interpretation II

Let us update the interpretation. Let us make it real. It is our time, our palpable time, the time we can hear rumbling and taste bitter.

The same roses. But of weaker strain. The thorns less testy, less provocative. Few in number, no longer mighty, huddling together in the countryside, in sections of the cities, isolated, cut off from the side of the mountain. Granted the soil is indulgent, full of acid and fertilizer, and we have grown. We were once sixteen million. Now we are cut back to ten. We will grow up again.

But the thorns are no longer fibrous. Little brownish pockets on the surface of the green. Grasp them between your thumb and index finger and break them off clean, not a prick, no blood at all. Not their blood surely. None of their blood. But ours, red no less than before, pouring forth from myriad apertures, pouring, pouring. Yours as well as mine. And do you think your planting of green, your real green, your fake green, your backed green, your strong-armed green, will stop the flow of red?

Your money is no power unless your power be in blood. To fight red you must spill red and you must, knowing that you are separated and alone, combat their red with your own. Elsewise their viscous fluids, their sap, their watery corpuscles will dilute your red until it is no more, no more yours, no longer blood, no longer red.

And the earth will be replenished and no less than before a prayer will be spoken, but when the petals are gathered, and the stems, and the thorns, and the roots and all these are planted with a new seedling, the rosebushes that will grow up will be smaller with each generation, more stunted, more stubbly, until finally nothing but midgetry and dwarfdom will be seen in the land.

A Song of Children

by David Meltzer

It is said that the newborn sing holy songs upon arriving into new light.

They are blind for several days because they watch creation's light fade from within. They watch the sky upon their eyelids washed clean of stars and moons and comets whose tails spark letters, numbers, and notes of music.

For many days they are deaf as the voice within gives way to the voices without. It takes some time for the child to speak words that link him to our language. By that time he is fully born on earth and no longer a child.

For many days the child remains immune to disease as alphabets of formation and resistance cohere within.

It is said a child accepts the presence of God without question.

It is said a child lives like an acrobat, a tumbler, in constant motion, with no sense of time's gravity, its shape or course. Leaping and dancing from day to night, he engages constantly with what the moment brings.

It is said that when a child sings it is the song we spend the rest of our lives trying to learn. We see the ancient one sit quietly with wrinkled flesh, used-up, slowly sliding off old polished bones, slowly turning into powder. We see the ancient one sit quietly and notice how much he looks like wrinkled newborn ones. It is as if we are all born with the same face and die with the same face and in between this living and dying hold to a face we think sets us apart from others.

We who have heard the ancient one sing are stirred by the sameness of his song to the song the child sings. The old man has his history, his memory, to share with the child who has no memory or history. The child has his song and often they are heard singing together.

BOOK IV
THEMES OF MERKAVAH MYSTICISM

The Portrait

by Rabbi Nachman of Bratslav

There was once a king who had a wise counselor. One day the king approached him and said: "There is a certain king who seals his documents with the words: 'A great and awesome man, a man of truth and humility.' I know that this king is in fact a great man. For his kingdom is surrounded by a sea and a fleet of ships with cannons roams this sea, keeping people from drawing near. And at the edge of this sea there is a swampy bog and men stand in danger of drowning there. This swamp encircles the kingdom and the only way to walk through the mire is on a narrow path, wide enough for only one person. Here, too, cannons are stationed. When one comes to do battle, cannons are poised to shoot. And so, one cannot draw near the king. All this I do know, yet, I don't know why this king signs his documents 'A man of truth and humility.' This remains a mystery to me. I want you, counselor, to bring me a portrait of this king."

Now the counselor's king had the portraits of all other kings, but no king had a portrait of this great and humble king, for he is hidden from men. He sits behind a curtain and is far from the people of his land.

The wise man went to that land. He thought: "I really must discover the nature of this land. What better way to find out than through the pranks and humor of the land?" To really know the heart of something, one must be able to mock that thing, to make fun of it. Of course, there are several types of mockery and jest for humor may be used in many ways. One sort is when one wholly intends to hurt his friend through his words. When the friend lifts his eyes and looks back, the prankster says: "Oh, I was only joking." As it says, "Like a madman who casts firebrands, arrows and death, so is the person who deceives his friend and says: 'Am I not in sport?' " Then there is another sort of jest: We all know that one may joke good-naturedly, with the best of intentions, and still one's friend may be wounded by these joking words. And there are still other sorts of humor and jest. . . .

Now there is a country that contains within it all countries. And in that country there is a city that contains all the cities of that country that contains all countries. And in that city there is a house that contains all houses of that city that contains all the cities of that country that contains all countries. And in that house is a man who bears within him all of this. There is one there who is laughing; he clowns and pulls all the pranks of that land.

317

The wise man gathered together a great sum of money and went to that house. And there he saw that they were acting out all sorts of pranks and jokes. From the pranks he understood that the country was shot through with lies. Through coming to know the humor of the land, he saw how they cheated and shortchanged men in business; he saw the "justice" of the magistrate court, whose judges were full of lies and took bribes. He went to a higher court. And there too, all was lies. Through the joking and jesting, they showed all these things. So the wise man understood from this that the entire land was fraught with lies and deception, stripped of all truth.

The wise man left the house and did business in the land. He let himself be cheated, and he sought justice before the judges. And they were filled with lies. If on one day someone gave them a bribe, by the next day they wouldn't even recognize him. So the wise man proceeded to a higher court. And there too, all was lies. He went to the Senate and the men there were full of lies and bribes.

Finally, the wise man came to the king himself. He asked the king: "Over whom are you king? For this land is shot through with lies; not a shred of truth can be found." And he began to tell of the lies of the kingdom. When the king heard his words he pressed his ear to the curtain that concealed him and listened intently. For he was astonished that there was a man in his kingdom who could recognize the lies. Now the royal officers who heard the man's words were enraged. But the wise man went on, enumerating the lies of the land. He added: "One might think that the king, too, would be like his people; that he too would love falsehood. But now I see that you are a man of truth. And precisely because of this you are far from them. For you cannot bear the lies of the kingdom."

The wise man began to praise the king exceedingly. And the king was very humble. For his greatness and his humility were one. Such is the way of a humble man. The more he is praised and magnified, the smaller and more humble he becomes. And as the wise man offered more praise, exalting and magnifying the king, the king grew smaller and more humble till he became nothing at all. And at that moment the king could not withhold himself any longer, and he tore open the curtain to see this wise man, as though to say: who is this person who knows and understands all this?

The face of the king was revealed, and the wise man saw him. He made a portrait and brought it to the king.

Translated from the Yiddish and Hebrew sources
by Elliot Ginsburg

The Wandering of a Soul
by Mendele Mokher-Seforim

It was the time (and I don't mean our time, God forbid!) when boy-husbands were boarding with their in-laws, fathering, and sitting with folded arms in the synagogue. I say (he says) that I don't mean our time because the words "it came to pass," as our sages say, always herald a lot of trouble. Our trouble is that young husbands in those days were not as smart, except in their own matters, as young husbands in our time. Nowadays, young husbands do not know their own goals as they did in the past, and they are useless; quite simply because they need the kind of things that impractical idlers, much to our distress, and whether earlier or later, are lacking; and no one is prepared to speak out and berate them for it. It would be like making fun of a pauper for not closing some great business deal, or making fun of a mute for not talking, or a lame man for not dancing, or a cripple for not standing straight. But useless to themselves (maintain the moderns), those of the past couldn't even pin a tail on a donkey, that is to say, lie down for the nation of Israel. They couldn't pursue their own goals, and, woe to them and to their lives, they never gave a second thought to, never moved heaven and earth for, the goals of the Jewish people! . . . They were lazy and moldy, they never formed groups or unions, they never tried to hold assemblies, not at their own expense, coming or going. They had feet, but not for walking; mouths, so to speak, but not for talking or sermonizing. May such sluggishness befall our worst enemies! What did they understand, what did they know? . . . Stocks and bonds?—No! Funds?—No.—"Culture"?—Forget it!—Well, then what? Nothing!

They yawned, went to synagogue, rose for midnight prayers, lamented the destruction of Jerusalem, peered into holy books, studied the Scriptures, and learned how to be broken Diaspora-Jews with their fine, highfalutin Friday-night prayers: "How beautiful . . . ! "

"Because of our sins we were driven out."

It was for all these things that the wrath was poured out on those poor creatures. The beginning of all wisdom is: Get wisdom. But today, the beginning and end of all wisdom is to hell with the fathers, the past. "Ugh!" they say. "Ugh!" for old, bygone days! That is the entire wisdom, really quite Jewish, in the manner of a wise and intelligent people, the "People of the Book,"—and that, I'm afraid, is the trouble! . . .

But that says the author, is neither here nor there.

And we can believe him, for, as it turns out in the end, his intentions really do lie elsewhere.

What I'm after, he says, is to tell what happened to me once in those days, when, as is the custom of sons-in-law, I was rooming and boarding with my mother- and father-in-law. My father-in-law, a simple man, fine and well-to-do, took me in, like a rare and precious thing, an earnest student, took me from the yeshivah for his one and only beloved daughter, the apple of his eye. It's hard to say how old I was because there was so much confusion about my age, and there was no way of untangling it. My mother counted my years after a great conflagration at the time of my birth. My grandmother, however, calculated after some great panic, and my aunts had different reckonings altogether. But whatever it was, and be that as it may, all I know is that when I got married, my face was pale, smooth, and beardless, like a boy's.

During the first few years of our marriage, nothing much happened. . . . All I knew how to do was pray, eat my mother-in-law's meals, and study. It never even occurred to me to do the tomfooleries that people sometimes do—and my wife didn't get any children. . . . In the beginning, I would simply come home to eat and drink—and that was all. Not to hear a nasty word, not to notice a nasty grimace. But then a slight change took place. I noticed peculiarities about my mother-in-law, a wry face, a pouting, and I was supposed to know what it was all about. But what I didn't know didn't hurt me—I merely went about my business and ate heartily. Little by little, the reason for her pouting was explained to me. First by way of hints, *allusions*, insinuations, that is to say, she meant—*children!* How could a Jew not have children! . . . And next, my mother-in-law told me in so many words, with a simple straightforward *explanation:* "Listen!" she argued, highly excited, as though I had stomped on her toes. "Listen! You've been married for two whole years already and—nothing! . . . Husbands who got married at the same time as you have been fathers for ages already, some with one child, some with two. They're mature and responsible, they know what their goals are. . . . How happy they are, and how happy their parents are! And you? A fine husband you are!"

And next, they worked around this matter *in secret.* I would often find my mother-in-law sitting with other women—neighbors, wives of rabbinical managers, women who administered the ablutions to women at the bathhouse, and my own wife in the middle, with downcast eyes red from weeping, and all the women whispering, winking at one another. An old Gentile woman (if you'll excuse my mentioning her in the same breath) also joined them a couple of times. It turned out that they were sitting there, wondering why my mother-in-law hadn't gotten any grandchildren from her daughter, that is to say, my wife. And they were using household remedies on her. Naturally, the old Gentile woman and the local healer had their fingers in the pie, along with the women who had been mothers many times over.

But I never thought about any tomfooleries. I ate heartily and studied heartily.

Now since *allusions* didn't help, and *explanations* didn't help, and *secrets* didn't help, my mother-in-law finally resorted to *homiletical discourse*, i.e., sermons. She was a marvel at sermonizing. The minute she opened her mouth, out came pouring, as from a sack full of holes, a preacher, a torrent of speech, helter-skelter, higgledy-piggledy, hugger-mugger, Gentile sayings all mixed up with (please excuse my mentioning them in the same breath) Talmudic quotations (it sounded moronic) spiced with the bittersweet language of Yiddish prayers for women, so that it would have the proper Jewish flavor.

Her sermons about me were based on the verse: "My son-in-law is indecent." And she demonstrated at length that it was indecent of me to do this, and do that. . . . Indecent, like the peasant's proverb "Neither fish nor fowl," which in Yiddish goes: "No bah, no moo, no cock-a-doodle-doo!" So what was I then? A dummy! That's what! And a further indecency: Any other father-in-law would take his son-in-law to the rebbe of Khandrikev—long may he live!—and if not personally, then through one of his followers, to turn the son-in-law into a decent human being. . . . And he would prosper, with "children and money,"—as it says in the Sabbath prayer. But as for me, she would exclaim—glaring at her poor husband, who had to put up with everything from her: As for me, oh God in heaven! It should happen to her worst enemies! I simply wasn't decent, amen, amen! . . .

When I hear the sermons of preachers nowadays, they fit me like a six-fingered glove. I merely look at them in pity, these poor people affecting wisdom, no doubt knowing very well, as well as I do, that their wise sayings are bogus, a swindle, a put-on. But my mother-in-law's sermons hooked into my heart like leeches, they sucked out my blood. I still ate her food as heartily, I still studied heartily, but it just didn't taste quite right anymore. Something was itching, nibbling in my head, and I would sometimes daydream for minutes at a stretch, with bulging eyes, at random. But still, I was all right, there was no danger. I couldn't botch up my youth, until the time came for me to decide on one of the Jewish professions: teaching Hebrew school, running a store, keeping a tavern, for instance, and thereby become my own boss. But then a dybbuk got hold of me, the Evil Spirit himself, in the guise of a Hasid, and tried to talk me into the devil knows what, lead me off to the devil knows where. . . .

My Evil Spirit, the Hasid, was an ugly little mannikin with all the gestures, all the charm befitting such a person. His way of speaking was exquisite, he could talk holes into your head. For telling stories, there was never a creature like him, there isn't now, and there never will be, in all the world. The skies were open to him, he could do what he wanted to there, the gates of hell and of paradise stood open for him. Angels and demons were his servants, fire and water his playthings. . . . His stories could capture a person's soul. If he wanted, his stories could cast a sweet sleep on a person, a warmth flowed through all parts of your body, and you felt a delicious scratching. If he licked his fingers and smacked his lips—you would get an urge to drink, simply to have a sip of spirits. . . .

That was my Evil Spirit, the one that caught hold of me (may all Jews be spared the like).

"Listen, shlemiel!" the Evil Spirit would start reproving me. "Just how long are you going to stay a shlemiel anyway? What can come of all this studying, day and night? Talmud—Shmalmud! You can brood over the Talmud all you wish, like a mother hen, but you won't hatch any children—and what's the sense of it anyway? You're a grown man, you shlemiel! . . . What a pity, I swear, such a young man. . . . I wouldn't care if you were a rationalist, an old recluse separated from your wife, a bookworm with a beard—to hell with him, the heretic! Keep sitting, keep swaying, get hemorrhoids, go through the Forty-nine Steps of Uncleanliness, and so much for you, you'll never get out! But you shlemiel, you're still a boy, you've still got time to exorcise the rationalist in you and become a decent man, a gifted person. Get on the right path while you still have time, and follow me, don't lag behind other young husbands, children of good families, don't lag behind, I tell you, and come . . . come. . . . Others may say to you: Come to Kandrivek, or come to Yehupets, to the rebbe of Yehupets, but I say to you: Boiberik! There are lots of rebbes around, you know, all of them alike, none of them, thank God, in any way sluggish about Jewishness—may they be healthy and strong! But all of them together are nothing but a garlic peel compared with the rebbe of Boiberik, long may he live. —Come, I tell you, come to Boiberik, he'll be able to help you. He's really an expert in barren women, the rebbe of Boiberik. Besides, your eyes will open when you look at his radiant face. 'You will warm youself in his light,' you frozen yeshivah student, you cold rationalist you. Like the noble children of Israel, you will see the Shekhinah, the Divine Radiance, upon his face, and you'll be so enthusiastic that, like them, you will eat at his court and drink. . . . You've got the possibility now, you're boarding with your in-laws, you haven't touched your wife's dowry yet. Later on, I hope, you'll pawn something, you'll steal your wife's last bit of jewelry—and you'll take a wagon, or you'll walk, to Boiberik! . . ."

That was how the Evil Spirit talked, and how he talked me into things. And when he saw he hadn't gotten very far, that moralizing didn't help, he tried getting to me with alcohol. He would smack his lips wordlessly, and so tantalizingly that I got a yen for a shot of brandy. It began with drinks on anniversaries of people's deaths, and then one drink led to another, brandy to conclude a section of the Talmud in synagogue, a celebration here, an anniversary there, to sanctify the new moon, to usher in the new month, a holiday here, a Sabbath there, a social drink, and then finally, a brandy-for-its-own-sake drink. As a result, I went so far once that I was literally out of my skin, that is to say, my mind left my body, it leaped out of my flesh, I was intoxicated, in seventh heaven!

The things that I, or, more precisely, my soul, heard and saw if it were humanly possible, in heaven, can scarcely be described in human speech. I'll try anyway, as far as I can, only for the sake of my readers really, because my readers are very curious, they're dying to know about what goes on in heaven, in the world to come.

First of all, I was welcomed by an extremely long nose, as thick and swollen as a mountain, fiery red, slightly dazed, like a flame of burning alcohol, and studded over with warts, and moistened by wellsprings of sweat. After the nose came its owner, reeling, barely keeping himself on his feet, just barely. . . . Lot—the chief cup-bearer of the wine reserved for the righteous at the coming of the Messiah—Lot, in all his glory, more in the spirit than in the flesh, and then an oracular voice boomed out as from a huge, empty barrel: "Make way, make room, for our guest, Ployne the son of Sosye! . . ." Upon hearing this voice, I was overcome with trembling, like a woman in childbirth. The chief cup-bearer smeared my lips, and poured a hundred-proof bitter drop into my mouth, and I felt like a new man!

"I know," he said to me, "what you want, and why you've come. The voice of your mother-in-law, praying for her daughter, your barren wife, is rending the heavens. The healer's incantations are moving heaven and earth. I was ordered to welcome you, fortify you with a bit of liquor, and lead you to the first division of our judicial apparatus, or as you call it down there, the first tavern, and since you're a bookworm and thereby under the supervision of the Angel of Study, we'll have to appeal to him, and he'll make sure your request goes to where it has to go. . . . Well, have another drink, and come along!"

And then he actually took me and carried me, the way a demon carries a scholar, so fast that my head swam. All at once, he threw me, *pow!* I landed on my feet all alone and suddenly there was light throughout my body. And I looked up and saw a palace before me five hundred leagues high, all of marble and fine gold. And the palace had five hundred enormous gates, and each enormous gate five hundred tiny gates. Between them stood the Angels of Wisdom, the Angels of Intelligence, the Angels of the Talmud, the Guardian Angels of Hasidism, the Guardian Angels of Enthusiasm, the Guardian Angels of Religious Ecstasy. And I saw something like two fearfully long flashes of lightning crackle out of the palace, and a shape of a hand clutched a heap of black fire and made crowns for the letters in the Torah. My ankles buckled in terror and I collapsed on my face. I felt a hand touching me, and I heard a voice calling me: "Please stand up, you mortal. The Guardian Angel of Study has heard your mother-in-law's prayer!" And I could feel a frost run over my whole body, my teeth were chattering with cold, and, getting to my feet, I saw a cold angel before me, a hunk of ice!

"It is I," he said, "your angel, the Angel of Rationalist Scholars and Yeshivah Students, the Overseer of the Guardian Angels of the Talmud. Come, I shall take you, as I have been ordered, to the Guardian Angel of Conception, that is to say, of Pregnancy."

And the cold angel took me and carried me so fast, the way a demon carries a scholar, the cold devoured me, and I fainted dead away. Suddenly— *pow!* I was standing on my feet, and a delicious warmth was pouring through all my parts. I raised my eyes and saw a palace of five hundred stories, constructed of all kinds of gems and jewels, in a beautiful garden with all sorts of plants: roses, flowers, and trees—a delight for the eyes. And above them, a dark blue curtain was spread with a golden moon on the center and diamond stars, all looking like a lovely summer night. The garden was full of thousands of paths running every which way, both open and concealed, and there were angels strolling about in couples, kissing one another, pouring out a sweet, tender song. Amuriel, the Guardian Angel of Love, armed with a bow and arrow, was shooting, and playing with cherubs, like children, lying hidden among dense branches. And his arrows hit their marks. At each shot, a cherub would spring from his hiding-place. . . . It was delightful to stand there watching. Something lured me on, as when you recite the Song of Songs. And then I heard Amuriel's voice calling my name:

"Ployne the son of Sosye!"

"Here I am," I said, "I'm ready!"

"If you're ready, then fine! I've been expecting you and I'm about to fulfill your request."

Having spoken these words, he turned to another angel and said: "Go and open the treasury of souls and bring me a lively little soul for this man." The angel hurried off on his errand, but soon he came back empty-handed.

What was wrong? They couldn't open the treasury, the key was gone!

There was an uproar, the angels scurried about in alarm, seeking high and low, until they found out, alas, that the rebbe of Boiberik had the key! Opening the hole in heaven through which the prayers from Boiberik came, they pleaded with the rebbe: "Damn it, give us the key for a barren woman!" But they were wasting their breath, he stuck to his guns: "No—let the woman come to me! . . ."

Amuriel became furious at the rabbi of Boiberik and poured out his anger on me and on all Jews: "You Jews are simply impossible! You grab the keys to all treasures, and you want to make us guardian angels your servants. You push in everywhere, and no rage in heaven is complete without you. . . .

"Where are you crawling?" he yelled at me. "Your place is down there in the Jewish district with the other Jews! What's a Jew doing up here? Kick him out!"

I got punched and kicked so much that I lost my senses. And when I opened my eyes, I found myself lying in bed in my own little cubicle, with the family standing around me, all talking at once: "He's come back from the dead! He's alive again!"

What was wrong? Can you imagine, I had been lying in a coma for three days!

A person lying in a coma looks dead, as everyone knows. His body is here in this world, but his soul is gone, it's hovering in heaven, as they say. There, they decide his fate: Should he come, should he go? Is he a goner, a new-comer. Should he come back to earth, where he came from, should he go on to the world to come? While they cast lots for his coming and going, the man's soul wanders freely around heaven, seeing wondrous sights. Very marvelous tales from olden days are told or else can be found in ancient tomes. These tales were told by people who had gone to heaven in a coma and then come back. Rabbi Joseph, the son of Joshua ben Levi (says the Talmud), was very ill and fell into a deathlike coma. When he regained con-sciousness, his father asked him: What did you see there? And the son told him that he saw something topsy-turvy—the lowered were raised, and the raised were lowered. . . . His father asked him: What about sages and schol-ars, how do things look for us up there? And the son replied, short and sharp: The same (so to speak) as here! . . . And he told him other, similar things.

Thus, if the whole matter of a coma is so important, no one will be sur-prised that people, big and little, young and old, fell upon me like locusts when I regained my strength, they were dying to have me tell about what was happening in heaven, and what was new up there. They were so eager that they drooled as they gazed at me in deep respect. If I had been smart, I would have known which side my bread was buttered on, in fact, I could have earned my bread and butter like many other heavenly people among us, who made an income from their comas. Like them, I could have told tales, vast exaggerations, and if the fools had heard them they would have loved them, and I would be swimming in gold. But I was a raw youth, boarding with my in-laws, I knew only the Talmud and little of the bitter taste of earning one's living at hard work. So, fool that I was, I stuck to the truth, and only told people what I knew. I told the same thing to our rabbi, Lord preserve him. He asked me, as a scholar: "How are things for us Jews up there?" I replied: "They don't want us."

It was dreadful to see his face, the poor man, as he heaved a deep, heartfelt sigh.

And now, after all these things, my Evil Spirit, the Hasid, urged me all the more strongly with his dishonest gestures:

"So you see, simpleton, how revered and venerated he is up there, may God preserve him! C'mon, say something. . . ."

"It should only happen to our worst enemies," I muttered under my breath, remembering the abuse I had heard.

"So what!" he said, "what's the difference if they talk among themselves? But he *is* powerful, he *does* hold the world in his hands, and he does have the key to the treasures, and he can make decisions. . . . Just go to Boiberik! I simply don't understand what's eating you."

And something was really eating me! Boiberik was eating me! To me and to everyone around me, it seemed absolutely weird! And Jewish stubbornness was eating me, and having to put aside the Talmud, to which I had been accustomed ever since childhood. But on the other hand, I have to admit that, except for the reason that forced me to go there, I got to like Boiberik, it grew on me. Weird as the people of Boiberik may appear, if you look hard, you'll find a few virtues in them. They're very devout. Gloom and worry are sins, ugh! The rabbi of Boiberik said people should be merry. All of them, young or old, rich or poor, maintain a comradely tone with one another. They're not so dry, not so cold, with somber troubles, like the Jews in my town. They can sometimes have a drink and dance a jig, not necessarily at Purim or the Feast of the Torah, but on an ordinary weekday. I was all prepared to follow my Evil Spirit, when suddenly something happened. . . .

My wife—can you imagine!—got pregnant without the Boiberik rebbe and she up and gave birth to twin boys!

This weakened my Evil Spirit a bit. Boiberik became less important to me, and I stood there like a Jew on the Sabbath, with one foot inside the prescribed Sabbath area and one foot outside it—I didn't know whether I was coming or going! I was neither here nor there!

Translated from the Yiddish
by Joachim Neugroschel

Mysteries of the Chariot

by Rabbi Milton Steinberg

The foot of Ben Zoma pressed nervously on the treadle of the loom, sending the shuttle back and forth in jerking flight. Like a harp player's, his fingers flowed over the threads. The weaver's frame stood against the doorway of his workshop, the web of warp and woof cutting the light with thin lines and drawing fine black tracings over the houses and men beyond. But his eyes saw no further than the intertwining strands and their pattern, so tightly did his thoughts hold him.

It was sinful to hate Elisha. But how could one cherish love for a blasphemer to whom Scripture itself was no sanctity? And his denials, unspoken as they were, were insidious. There were times when even he, Simeon the son of Zoma, was seduced into wondering. . . .

A spasm shook his body, his hands faltered in their automatic movement. For a moment he contemplated the vista which opened before him. Its bleakness chilled him. Deliberately he submerged himself in the comforting warmth of old researches.

"And the spirit of God hovered"—what mystery lay hidden here in that word suggestive of the circling motion of a bird, as though the Presence were in some way akin to a winged thing?

"Over the face of the waters"—but the world, its rivers and its seas had not yet been called into being. Might it be, as some Greek believed, that water was a primeval substance as old as God, that the creative word had given to material things not existence, but only form?

"Let us make man in our image. . . ."

Wild surmises gleamed in his eyes as he dwelt on the baffling plural pronoun. The shuttle darted more quickly, Ben Zoma's body twisted, his lips writhed suddenly. Who, he asked himself, was with Him in that awesome moment when man was conceived in the womb of Eternity?

Snapped by his uneven touch, a filament sagged across the web in lifeless spirals. Disturbed in its rhythm, his thinking leaped from one cryptic passage of Scripture to another . . . from the mystery of creation to that of revelation, to the vision of the chariot which Ezekiel saw when he was among the exiles by the River Chebar.

"The four creatures . . . and each had four faces . . . wheels within wheels . . . and their rims were full of eyes." . . . He tried to visualize it, but it was too complex to be conceived, too intricate to be interpreted.

". . . a firmament like the color of a terrible ice . . . the likeness of a throne, as the appearance of a sapphire stone . . . the likeness as the appearance of a man . . . colored like the bow that is in the cloud in the day of rain . . ."

His foot pressed with increasing ferocity on the treadle. The strip of woven cloth mounted apace, until it blotted out the world, leaving him only the dizzy intertwining of myriad threads that lost themselves in convolutions about one another. . . .

My Grandfather
by Arnold Kiss

His picture is in front of me—a handsome man with a serious face, his thick black hair heavily streaked with gray, his glance stern at first but upon closer investigation sadly meditative. An unusual sadness radiates from those deep eyes.

The old doctor from Miskolc is dressed in a Hungarian festive suit that was popular around 1848. He loved his country passionately. He hid Hungarian *honvéds* in his house after the collapse of the Revolution, and received a stiff jail sentence for it. His great-grandfather too had lived in Miskolc, and because of family tradition, the old gentleman used to say with respectful pride that his family was one of the oldest Hungarian-Jewish families.

He must have been sixty-five when one of his arms became paralyzed. He was a widower. His eyes were afflicted with cataracts and he moved in with his only daughter and son-in-law, my father, the rabbi of Ungvár. There he lived, at the twilight of his life, the old doctor from Miskolc, the respected former *rashekol* of the Jewish community of Miskolc. I remember him from my childhood. He especially liked me, his oldest grandchild. He often took me on his lap and told me unusual, beautiful stories in his somewhat husky, quietly sad voice. Before the High Holy Days, in the small hours of the cool September mornings when the autumn night left behind fine veils of fog above the Carpathian peaks, my grandfather took me by the hand and led me to the *Selichos* service in the synagogue, which stood on a slope with its small candlelights flickering in the dark of the night. Although he was supposed to lead me, I walked briskly almost ahead of him, swinging a lamp in my hand on the dark streets, while with bleary eyes he walked leaning heavily on my arm.

My grandfather had a meticulously elaborate family tree drawn with primitive artistry. He would often lay the old, faded piece of paper with its pale writing on the table in front of him and explain to me, in a voice half serious half joking, the mysteries of that large many-branched tree, the ancestry of his forefathers. The Hungarian branch reached into the distant times, to the Jews who lived in the period of the conquest. His father was a licensed interpreter, his grandfather a famous, pious talmudic scholar. Maria Theresa, Louis the Great, Matthias, contemporary churchmen, dignitaries, merchants, teachers; poor, struggling, suffering, and persecuted men followed one another on the branch of his Hungarian ancestors.

There was another branch; it led to German lands. One ancestor had been a relative of the great rabbi of the thirteenth century, Rabbi Meir of Rothenburg. Another branch showed the medieval poet Susskind von Trimberg, and a stern, black-bearded rabbi from Worms, an ascetic, wild-haired chorister, and a fanatical Jewish martyr from Regensburg. There were also pious, wigged women, dreamy-eyed mothers who died young.

Then there were the Italians. There was an exegete named Lonzo among them who, according to family legend, had once polemicized with a scholarly bishop about God's religion.

The Russian and Lithuanian branches were made up mainly of ancestors who held communal posts.

The refugee Spanish Jews also played an important role. One of them wandered across the seas on board a ship for long years before he settled in Holland.

With adventurous, mythical turns, the fabulous family tree reached as far as biblical times and then suddenly, jumping from heroes to bards, it came to rest at Mordecai, the son of Kish, the Persian minister. The beautiful eyes of Queen Esther lit up when the tree reached her. Then it climbed to Boaz, the sheaf-binding landowner. It embraced the flowing, scented hair of Naomi and Ruth, and finally came to a halt at the most distant of ancestors, the harp-playing King David.

Outside, the windstorm howled and shook the old runways of the window, and in the kitchen the Slovak servant girl sang a melancholic song. Sitting in his huge armchair, in the long autumn evenings, my grandfather mused over the worn pieces of paper. The dim light of the green-shaded lamp painted shadows on the walls of the small room; the ancestors came to visit. I squatted in front of him and watched the trembling forefinger of his left hand as it slid along the family tree and listened with fascination to his quiet words about the ancestors, the forefathers, as if an old, forgotten song had come to life in the eerie calm.

One day my grandfather became seriously ill. It happened in the autumn, around the Feast of Tabernacles. My grandfather and I had wandered about in the thicket of the Ung, gathering branches for *Hoshano Rabbo*. He caught a cold then. He hovered between life and death for weeks. My mother's eyes were red from crying and she devotedly kept vigil at the sickbed of her father, whom she idolized. My father prayed in the synagogue with sad lamentations and with name-changing chants for the gravely ill man, his father-in-law, so that the Angel of Death would not find Akiba, the son of Rachel, whose name he had changed. The *Moloch Hamoves* would never again find the son of Akiba.

I did not hear my grandfather's beautiful tales for a long time. I was concerned and afraid that I would never hear them again. He was running a high fever; his hands and forehead were hot as he lay unconscious on the bed.

Nonetheless, God helped him. He counted my mother's tears—only God could keep count of them—and in His great mercy He found that they had filled the chalice of sorrow; and He listened to my father's sad psalms. My grandfather slowly recovered.

On a late autumn afternoon, basking in the fading sunshine, my convalescing grandfather sat in a large armchair in the arbor. The white flowers of the apple tree kept falling on his silvery hair. He unfolded the family tree again and looked at the map of the ancestors with dreamy eyes. He drew me near him with his healthy arm and for the first time since his illness he began to tell a story.

His voice was soft and melodic like the sound of a harp. He stroked my hair and began his story.

* * *

My little boy, I have come home from very far. I almost thought that I would never find the way home, to you whom I love so dearly. I had a dream, a beautiful dream, perhaps it wasn't even a dream. . . .

I was in Heaven, my son. I can't even tell you how beautiful everything is there. The huge antechamber is studded with heavenly garnets and fiery rubies. The multitude of stars that glitter like so many diamonds, the sweet, enchanting song of the angels, and the wondrous, blue celestial roads that are in Heaven are hidden from the people who live on earth. The thousands of enchanted trees are covered with fabulously beautiful flowers that, when the wind rushes through them, play heavenly music. And God's throne! How can I describe to you that enormous brightness or the singing of the *serafim;* the zithers that play by themselves; the stars that glitter like so many diamonds, the sweet enchanting sound of the praising angels' trumpets; the enchanted melodies of hidden violins? No, my son! I cannot describe to you all that beauty.

Just imagine, my little boy, how I cried with happiness when an angel took me by the hand and led me to my mother and father, who had left me an orphan in this world such a long time ago. My dear mother embraced me again and her warm tears fell on my cheeks: "Thank Heaven I can see you again, my dear son! I have waited for you for such a long time!" My father embraced me a hundred times and blessed me as he did when I was a child.

Then they took me by the hand. My mother grasped one, my father took the other.

"Let's go, my son," my father said solemnly. "We are going to visit your ancestors, your grandfathers and great-grandfathers. It is proper that we should introduce you, their distant grandchild, to them."

My heart was beating fast. I would see them at last, the ancestors whose memory is preserved in the family tree.

We walked and walked in Heaven. Miraculously, no one gets tired in Heaven. It is easy to walk there, there are no thorns and prickles like down here on earth.

Then I saw them. I came up to my grandfather, the former licensed interpreter of Miskolc. He was a kind-faced, smiling man. He softly embraced me and kissed me many times. My grandfather and grandmother on my mother's side were also very happy to see me. My grandmother, a pretty, blue-eyed young woman, said, "I remember you. I used to rock your cradle, but I had to depart from earth too soon."

And I saw the long line of great-grandfathers and great-grandmothers—my ancestors who lived in the time of Maria Theresa, Louis the Great, and Matthias, the men who played prominent roles in the community and the synagogue, the poor teachers, the persecuted and long-suffering great-great-grandfathers and great-great-grandmothers. Every one of them embraced me. Naturally, the farther we went visiting, the less familiar my ancestors were to me.

I saw the great Rabbi Meir of Rothenburg, my famous ancestor. There was an unusual turbanlike hat on his head, his gray beard glittered, and his deep eyes sparkled with such brilliance that they looked like precious stones. There were handcuffs on his wrists because he was jailed in his earthly life for his love of the sacred Torah. But in Heaven, the handcuffs on his wrists changed to shining gold. They were no longer tight but soothingly smooth as if they had been made of velvet. When I reached him, the great Rabbi Meir of Rothenburg was bent over the Torah, absorbed in the sacred writing. He put his arm on my shoulder but his eyes rested on me only fleetingly. Small wonder, he must have been visited by numerous grandchildren in the course of time.

I also saw my other famous great-great-grandfather: Susskind, the poet of Trimberg. He was playing a golden harp; in Heaven everyone is allowed to devote himself to his favorite profession. He had just finished a poem when I reached him and kindly told me of the many good things he had heard of the Hungarian branch of his family.

I also saw my martyred ancestor from Worms. He was the stern rabbi with the black beard. I also heard the chanting of my ascetically thin ancestor, the cantor. I stood in front of my stern ancestor from Worms in respectful awe. He merely glanced at me and quickly blessed me. My ancestor from Regensburg was singing a fanatical psalm and praying; he had little time for me. However, my pious, God-fearing great-great-grandmothers welcomed me lovingly. They discovered resemblances between me and some of my ancestors and touched my face with their soft, velvety fingers. They told me that I had a grandson down on earth and that he—so they heard—especially resembled me. You are that grandson, my little boy.

There was a beautiful but very sad young woman among my ancestors. The other great-great-grandmothers talked about her in whispers. She had had a sad life. She left the parental home against the will of her parents for a poor boy whom she loved very much. Her parents disowned her, but God forgave her and took her into Heaven because of her great capacity for love.

Passing along the long, winding roads, through my Spanish, Russian, and Lithuanian ancestors, I reached Mordecai the son of Jair the son of Shimei the son of Kish. His shoulders were covered with purple and on his chest was a diamond decoration that the king of Persia had given him. There were masked, merry people around him dancing to sweet music. God himself had decorated him with a beautiful star in his hair, the sparkle of which cast brightness around him.

Mordecai loved his people and was prepared to sacrifice his life for them.

There was also the beautiful Queen Esther, his sister, amid respectful admiration. They were celebrating the eternal feast of Purim.

I also saw my ancestor Boaz, the harvester of Bethlehem. His face was cheerful and handsome. Even the usually sad Naomi stood by him smiling. With her flowing hair, the sheaf-binding girl was singing the sweet songs of springtime. All of them kissed me and let me go on.

Finally, I reached the great ancestor who is shining at the top of the highest branch of my family tree: the harp-playing King David. His crown glittered and he played a beautiful, sweet song on the harp. I have never seen a handsomer man in my life. He had a large, respectful court. I fell to the ground in front of my most illustrious ancestor and he smiled at me kindly without interrupting his song. And I, too, mingled with the other admirers, grandchildren, and descendants.

My father and mother were the happiest of all. They kissed and hugged me endlessly. I, too, was very, very happy to see them again.

Two weeks passed this way. Yet I became quieter and quieter. I have no idea what kind of sadness got hold of me amid all that happiness.

My father and mother noticed my sadness. They caressed and pampered me and questioned me about my behavior.

Suddenly, tears began rolling down my cheeks and my heart and forehead became hot. In that moment I realized why I was so sad. Then I told my father, crying, "I am longing for my daughter and grandson. I'd like to go home to my family, to Ungvár, where they are waiting and crying for me. Don't be angry with me, my dear parents, because I want to leave you."

My parents loved me very much. They had never denied me anything. They prayed and implored God to let me come home to you. And God permitted me to come home to you for a little longer.

That is how I came home to you, my little son. That is how I recovered and that is what I dreamed about my family tree and that is how I awoke from my miraculous dream.

That was the end of the story of my grandfather, who has been lying in the cemetery for so long; who had, at one time, rocked me on his knees while explaining his family tree, and to whom, according to my great-grandmother, I bear such an amazing resemblance.

Translated from the Hungarian
by Andrew Hendler

Heaven's Wagon Driver

by Péter Ujvári

Golden drips and opal teardrops trickled down on the the seven-armed candelabrum. Rabbi Meir of Promishlan was praying for the arrival of the Sabbath. As his soul yearned for the Sabbath, the sky opened up above him glittering. He had never seen anything like that.

In the brightly shining hall of the *metivta,* a man wearing a sheepskin coat drove his small horses about joyfully. Bright-faced pious men gathered together and nodded kindly after him.

The soul of Rabbi Meir of Promishlan was filled with horror. How could such a dirty wagon driver be allowed to trot his horses in Heaven as if he were on the road? As he remained wrapped up in his amazement, he did not even notice that the door of his room opened and the keyhole, like the gates of a synagogue, widened, and through it the angels of the weekdays left and the angels of the Sabbath arrived. He did not even notice that his soul, which had been resting on his lips, slid downward and would have fallen on the ground if an angel had not embraced it. The soul attached itself to the angel, who carried it to Heaven.

Suddenly, he stood in the dazzling brightness of Paradise. Indeed, the wagon driver was still trotting his horses on the diamond-paved road.

"Begging your pardon," said the rabbi to the angel guarding the entrance, "but how come you tolerate such a creature among the heavenly beings?"

"Well," responded the angel and smiled, "he's been here for a long time."

The rabbi of Promishlan fell into deep thought. Then he turned to the angel again. "Although I've never seen anyone driving a wagon up here or trotting his horses on the Sabbath, he must be a heavenly being and must have done a great deal of good in his earthly life."

"That one?" the angel laughed. "Just look at his load. Even the rack of his wagon is full of evil deeds and that heavy load is all his. True, the one good deed, the only good deed among the many evil ones, is also his. But that was the result of a truly good deed. And that one opened the doors of Heaven for him."

The rabbi was amazed. He began to realize that the laws of Heaven were different from man-made ones. On earth, it was thought, one sin was enough to condemn a person to damnation; in Heaven, even one good deed brought salvation.

"Please," the rabbi said humbly, "tell me about the meritorious deed of that driver, which must indeed be great and weighty to outbalance so many misdeeds."

The angel laughed even more uproariously. "Not in the least! Why should it be so meritorious? As I think of it, I cannot even say that it was a meritorious deed. It was just humane. That's all. They still love that sort of thing around here. You cannot even imagine what great confidence mankind enjoys up here. You could be a drunkard, a gambler, or a woman chaser, but be humane only once and you'll be seated on such a golden chair that you wouldn't change places even with a king. Take that driver. He was a crude, wicked man. He never prayed and swore endlessly. He despised the Hasidim and gave them a chase whenever he could. Yet, what do you think he did once? He was driving on the highway of Belz toward Shokal. The snow reached the knees of the horses and he walked alongside them so that they could pull the wagon more easily. The horses suddenly reared and the driver tripped and nearly fell. It was a man lying under the snow. The driver swore and whipped the horses. But then he pulled them back. After all, he was not going to leave that fool there, even though he had gone to sleep under the snow. First, he gave the man a kick, but then he started pulling him out of the snow. He leaned over him, rubbed his chest with snow, and poured brandy into his mouth through the tightly squeezed teeth. As the man slowly revived, Reb Srulche lifted him on the wagon like a sack of flour and took off his own sheepskin coat and spread it over him. And do you know who that man was whom the driver pulled out of the snow and saved from death? A Hasid, whose kind he despised and who was on his way to the *tzaddik* of Belz. The driver cursed the Hasid when he learned his identity, yet he put the horse blanket on him. He ridiculed him and laughed at him, yet he drove him as far as the house of the *tzaddik* of Belz and helped him off the wagon. "Hey, you," he yelled after the Hasid, "don't tell your saint that I drove a fool to his house."

"I understand, I understand," said the rabbi of Promishlan, and his eyes were filled with emotion.

"Wait," the angel said. "There is more. The Hasid of the *tzaddik* of Belz lived for two more years, then died. Since he could not return to Belz, he came here. He did not stop until he reached the Merkavah. Then he looked around and pulled on his beard cheerfully. 'I swear,' he exulted, 'I feel as if I were in Belz. Perhaps Belz is more beautiful.' He grabbed a golden stool and was about to sit down in front of the Lord. 'Hey, listen,' a chief angel called out, 'nobody lives here without a companion. Choose someone to be your companion in salvation.' The Hasid responded happily, 'I'll choose Reb Srulche, the wagon driver.'

"A hundred angels spread out in Heaven searching. But no driver. The Hasid was told to choose another companion, but he remained obstinate. He did not want anyone else. He wanted the driver who had dug him out of the snow. And if the driver was not up there yet, he would wait. With that he withdrew and waited for some twenty years. Then, one day, the driver died.

"In the *metivta,* the *Knesset Haggedoloh* convened to judge the newcomer. A large golden scale was placed on a golden table. The driver stood in front of the table, and next to it his sins swarmed like worms. The angels swept his sins with their wings into one of the plates of the scale. It sank with a squeak. A teardrop from the compassionate eyes of the Lord fell into the empty plate, but even that could not move the scale. The judges lowered their heads sadly as they were about to pronounce judgment. But then someone pulled open the ivory gate of the *metivta.* It was the Hasid, who stood on the threshold panting. 'Wait! In the name of the Lord, wait! I want my companion!' He ran to the judges and placed a snowball in the empty plate of the scale. The snowball glittered. That glitter was warm and lively like a smile. 'That's how he smiled when he rescued me,' the Hasid said. 'That's his smile.'

"The scale shook and the plate with its horrible load began to rise. On the foreheads of the seventy-one judges as many expressions of mercy gleamed. They pronounced the decision. The driver was to remain in Heaven.

"Reb Srulche scratched his head. 'My hat! And just what am I going to do among you? I don't give a hoot about praying and singing. And then, without a horse a driver is only half a man. I can see it already; I'll be bored to death.'

"The Lord showed compassion toward the driver and said, 'Give him a wagon and a horse so that he may have a good time to his heart's delight.'

"You see," concluded the angel, "that's how the driver got to Heaven."

There were still a few Sabbath angels in Heaven opening their wings in preparation for descending to earth. The guardian angel softly lifted the soul of the rabbi of Promishlan and placed it on an angel's wing. The rabbi reached his home in a few moments, praised the Lord, and exulted that mankind, if it remained humane, would be saved from damnation.

Translated from the Hungarian
by Andrew Hendler

The Celestial Orchestra

by Howard Schwartz

Once it happened that Reb Nachman woke up in the middle of the night, and instead of the deep silence that usually pervaded, he heard something like a faint music. At first the sound was no more than that of an approaching wind, but soon he could make out that it was actually a kind of music.

What could it be? He had no idea. But he continued to hear that music, ever so faintly, sometimes present, sometimes about to disappear. Nor did it grow any louder, so he had to strain to listen. One thing was certain, though: Reb Nachman felt drawn to this music, as if it were a message he was trying to receive, that was coming to him from a great distance.

Then Reb Nachman got up and went into his study and sat down by the window. And yes, from there the music seemed slightly louder, as if he were a little closer to its source. And now it did not disappear, but it remained very faint. Nor was he able to identify it with any instrument with which he was familiar—it did not sound like a violin or a flute; not like a bass fiddle and not like a drum. Nor did it have the sound of a voice or voices. If only he were able to hear it better, he thought, he might be able to identify its source.

Then Reb Nachman left the house and walked outside. He walked out into the field beyond the gate, under a sky crowded with stars. There he had no memory, except for questions that concerned the origin of the mysterious music. And while his eyes were fixed on the heavens, the ground remained unknown beneath his feet. And for that time he did not impose patterns on distant stars or imagine the life they might sustain. Nor did he count the gift of the stars as riches. Instead he listened for a long, long time.

At first Reb Nachman thought that what he heard was seamless, and was coming from a single instrument. But after a while he was almost able to separate the instruments that wove their music together so well. Yet this new knowledge did not satisfy his longing and curiosity; in fact, it only served to whet it. Where was this distant music coming from? Surely it was not drifting there from any orchestra in Bratslav, or from anywhere else in this world, of that Reb Nachman was certain. No, this was some kind of celestial music, music of the spheres.

It was then that Reb Nachman realized how much he wanted to follow that music and discover its source. And this longing grew so great that Reb Nachman became afraid that his heart might break. Then, while he was staring up into the stars, he saw a very large star fall from its place in the heavens and blaze across the sky like a comet. And he followed that first star to fall, and shared its last journey. And somehow it seemed to Reb Nachman that he was falling with that star, and was caught up in that same motion, as if he had been swept away by an invisible current, and he closed his eyes and let himself be carried.

That is how it happened that when Reb Nachman opened his eyes again he found himself seated inside a chariot of fire that blazed its way across the heavens. And he did not have time to wonder how this had happened, or what it meant, but only to marvel in awe as the wonders of the heavens passed before his eyes. Before him he saw two kinds of luminaries: those which ascended above were luminaries of light; and those which descended below were luminaries of fire. And it was then, when his eyes had become adjusted to the sudden illuminations that crossed his path, that Reb Nachman became aware of a presence beside him, and he began to perceive a dim body of light.

That is when the angel who drove the chariot first spoke to him, and said: "Welcome, Reb Nachman. I am the angel Raziel. You should know that your calling and your prayers have not gone unheard in Heaven. This chariot has been sent to bring you to the place you long for, the source you are seeking."

And with each word that the angel Raziel spoke, the light that surrounded his ethereal body grew brighter, until he appeared to Reb Nachman as a fully revealed being. This was the first time that Reb Nachman had ever been face to face with an angel. And yet, strange to say, he did not feel the fear he would have expected, but rather felt as if he had been reunited with a long-lost companion.

It was then that Reb Nachman saw the chariot approach some kind of parting of the heavens, which resembled a line drawn across the cosmos. As they drew closer, he saw that it was actually an opening through which an ethereal light emerged. Raziel recognized the question taking form in Reb Nachman's mind, and he said: "We are approaching the place where the Upper Waters and the Lower Waters meet. This is where the Upper Worlds are separated from the Lower Worlds, and what belongs to the spheres above is divided from what belongs to the spheres below."

No sooner did the angel finish speaking than the chariot approached close enough to that place for Reb Nachman to catch a glimpse of what lay on the other side. And what he saw was a magnificent structure suspended in space. And from that glimpse he knew that whatever it was, no human structure could begin to compare with it. But then, before he had time to question the angel, the chariot passed through that very aperture, to the complete astonishment of Reb Nachman, for it was no higher than a hand's breadth. It was at that moment that Reb Nachman grew afraid for the first time, for he realized that he was flying through space at a great height, and he did not dare to look down. Then he said to the angel: "How is it possible that we have passed through that place which is no more than three finger-breadths?"

Raziel said: "In your world of men, Reb Nachman, it is possible to contain a garden in the world. But in this kingdom it is possible to contain the world in a garden. How can this be? Because here, whoever opens his heart to the Holy One, blessed be He, as much as the thickness of a needle, can pass through any portal."

Even as Raziel spoke these words Reb Nachman had already been captured by the radiant vision that loomed ahead. And again, without his having to ask, Raziel replied: "The place you are about to be taken to, Reb Nachman, is the very one you have been seeking. But since even this chariot is not permitted to approach much closer to that sacred place, you must soon depart from it and remain suspended in space, like the Sanctuary you see before you."

And without any other explanation, Reb Nachman realized that the wonderful structure he saw must be the Celestial Temple, after which the Temple in Jerusalem had been modeled, and with which it was identical in every aspect, except for the fire that surrounded the heavenly Sanctuary. For the marble pillars of this heavenly miracle were surrounded by red fire, the stones by green fire, the threshold by white fire, and the gates by blue fire. And angels entered and departed in a steady stream, intoning an unforgettable hymn to a melody Reb Nachman heard that day for the first time, but which he recognized as if it had been familiar to him all the days of his life.

It was then Reb Nachman realized that he was no longer within the chariot, but was suspended in space without hands or feet for support. And it was then, with his eyes fixed on that shimmering vision, that Reb Nachman was able to distinguish for the first time the Divine Presence of the Shekhinah hovering above the walls and pillars of the Temple, illuminating them, and wrapping them in a glowing light that shone across all of Heaven. It was this light that he had seen from the other side of the aperture, before the chariot of fire had crossed into the Kingdom of Heaven. And so awestruck was Reb Nachman to witness the splendor of the Shekhinah that he suddenly experienced an overwhelming impulse to hide his face, and he began to sway in that place and almost lost his balance. And had it not been for the angel Raziel speaking to him at that instant he might have fallen from the great height. And the angel said: "Take care, Reb Nachman, and know that the Temple remains suspended by decree of the Holy One, blessed be He. And you must remember, above all, to keep your eyes fixed on its glory, if you are not to become lost in this place. For should you turn away from the Temple for as long as a single instant, you would risk the danger of falling from this height. Even a mere distraction would take you to places unintended, from which you might never return. So too you should know that no living man may enter into that holy dwelling place and still descend to the world of men. For no man could survive the pure fire that burns there, through which only angels and purified souls can pass."

And it was then, when he had regained his balance, that Reb Nachman finally discovered the source of the celestial music that had lured him from his house in a world so far removed, and yet so close. And when he followed that music to its source in the Celestial Temple his eyes came to rest on concentric circles of angels in the Temple courtyard. Then he realized that the music he had been hearing was being played by an orchestra of angels. And when he looked still closer he saw that each of the angels played a golden vessel cast in the shape of a letter of the Hebrew alphabet. And each one had a voice of its own, and one angel in the center of the circle played an instrument in the shape of the letter Bet.

And as he listened to the music, Reb Nachman realized it was that long note which served as its foundation, and sustained all of the other instruments. And Reb Nachman marveled at how long the angel was able to hold this note, drawing his breath back and forth like the Holy One Himself, who in this way had brought the heavens and the earth into being. And at that moment Reb Nachman was willing to believe that the world only existed so that those secret harmonies could be heard. And he turned to the angel Raziel, who had never left his side, and once more the angel knew what he wished to know, and said: "The score of this symphony is the scroll of the Torah, which commences with the long note of the letter Bet, endless and eternal, and continues with each instrument playing in turn as it appears on the page, holding its note until the next letter has been sounded, and then breathing in and out a full breath."

And when Reb Nachman listened to that music he arrived at a new understanding of the Torah, and realized that among its many mysteries there was one level on which it existed only as pure music. And he was also aware that of all the instruments in that orchestra, it was that of the letter Bet which spoke to him and pronounced his name. Then the angel Raziel turned to Reb Nachman and said: "The souls of all men draw their strength from one of the instruments in this orchestra, and thus from one of the letters of the alphabet. And that letter serves as the vessel through which the soul of a man may reveal itself. And your soul, Reb Nachman, is one of the thirty-six souls that draw their strength from the vessel of the letter Bet, which serves as its Foundation Stone, and holds back the waters of the Abyss."

And then it happened that when the angel Raziel said the word "Abyss," Reb Nachman forgot all of his warnings for one instant, and glanced down at the world so far below. And the next thing he knew was that he felt like a falling star. And that is when he realized that he was still standing in the field beyond the gate, following the first star that had fallen, which had now disappeared. And the celestial music, though faint once more, still echoed in his ears.

The Tale of the Amulet
by Howard Schwartz

In Memory of Rose Rubin

After the passing of his grandmother, Rayzel, Reb Hayim Elya inherited the library of sacred books that had belonged to his grandfather, Reb Zev ben

Simha Leib, who had died ten years before. Among those books there was one very old leather-bound volume of the *Sefer Raziel*, written by hand, and Hayim Elya recognized at once that this was the jewel of his grandfather's library.

Then it happened that as Hayim Elya leafed through the pages of that book, a small parchment fell from it onto the table. And that parchment was worn and faded, and it was difficult to make out the text, which was inscribed inside the shape of a flame. And Hayim Elya was filled with curiosity when he saw it, and when he picked it up and studied it he had a very strange sensation, for it seemed to stir his spirit and waken his soul.

It took Hayim Elya several hours, but at last he succeeded in deciphering the words of the text written there. And this is the text he transcribed:

> May the Holy One, blessed be He, let me behold the worlds on high. Open to me the gates of *peshat*, the gates of *remez*, the gates of *drash*, the gates of *sod*, all the gates of *Pardes*. Let the heavens open to receive me, let me gaze upon the radiance of the angels, let me enter each and every palace. Open my mouth and let me utter a song before the Throne of Glory. Let me gaze into the flames of the *Pargod*, into the black flames of the past, into the white flames of the future. Let me read the history written in the Book of Life, let me taste of its sweetness as did Ezekiel.

When Reb Hayim Elya had finally deciphered this text, he realized that the parchment must have belonged to an amulet, and that the amulet must have had a magical purpose, although he was not certain what it was. Then Hayim Elya showed the parchment to Tselya, his wife, and even though she was a *sopher*, she had never seen a similar design, and also wondered at its purpose. Then they decided that all of them would take the text to Reb Zvi, to see if he could identify it.

Now Reb Zvi was not surprised to see Hayim Elya and Tselya and their child that day. For the night before he had dreamed that Hayim Elya had pointed out a passage to him in the Bible, and when he had awakened, he had recalled it, and marked that place. But Reb Zvi had not expected anything like the parchment, which he recognized at once, although he had never before seen one like it. And what purpose did that amulet serve? For every amulet has a specific function, either to ward off demons like Lilith and the effects of the Evil Eye, or to be used for magical purposes. And Reb Zvi recognized at once that the parchment had been the text of an amulet that had been used in order to enter *Pardes*, the upper realms, as did Enoch in his generation, and Rabbi Akiba in his. For with the protection of the amulet it was possible to ascend and descend in peace, as Akiba had.

Then Reb Zvi said: "This parchment, Hayim Elya, belonged to an amulet that was once used for purposes of the mystical ascent. For he who wore the amulet in which this parchment was contained would shortly be taken up into Paradise."

And Hayim Elya asked: "But how did this ascent take place?"

And Reb Zvi replied: "There are many possible paths, as I explained to you in the tale of the King's treasure. One can be taken up in the Merkavah, the Divine Chariot, as was Enoch; or ascend the ladder that reaches from earth to Heaven, on which Jacob saw angels ascending and descending; or be transported to that place by means of the power of the Name. But in each and every case it is only the potency of the incantation inscribed on this parchment, contained within the amulet, that can protect those still among the living from destruction."

When Hayim Elya heard this, he was filled with longing to make that ascent, for he was one of those who are drawn like a moth to the flame that burns eternally in Paradise. And Reb Zvi read all this in his face, and he said: "Do not be deceived, Hayim Elya. This parchment cannot provide ascent by any of those paths."

"But why not, Rebbe?" Hayim Elya pleaded. "I am certain it is authentic."

"That is true," said Reb Zvi, "but the parchment by itself is powerless. It cannot release its power unless it is accompanied by the same amulet for which it was written, for no other could ever work. No, Hayim Elya, that way is blocked for you, and an angel guards it with a flaming sword that turns in every direction. But do not despair—for there is still another path."

"What is it, Rebbe?" begged Hayim Elya, who had almost abandoned hope.

Then Reb Zvi said: "This path is hinted at in the parchment, in the words 'let me taste of its sweetness as did Ezekiel.' And what does this refer to? You answered this question for me last night, Hayim Elya, in a dream. In the dream you brought me the *Tanach* and asked me to explain a passage in the *Sefer Ezekiel*."

"Tell me, Rebbe, what was that passage?" asked Hayim Elya. "For I do recall speaking to you in a dream last night, but I have forgotten what we said."

"Listen, Hayim Elya," said Reb Zvi, opening the Bible to the place he had marked. "This is the passage you pointed out:"

> And when I looked, behold, a hand
>   was put forth unto me;
> and, lo, a scroll of a Book was therein;
> and He spread it before me,
> and it was written without and within
> And he said unto me: "Son of Man, eat
>   this which thou findest;

eat this scroll, and go, speak unto
the House of Israel."

Then did I eat it; and it was in my
mouth as honey for sweetness.

Then it happened that just as Reb Zvi finished reading this passage, Sharya, the infant daughter of Reb Hayim Elya and Tselya, crawled up to that table and took the parchment in her hand and brought it to her mouth. And when Reb Zvi and Hayim Elya saw this, both of them understood it was a sign, and at that moment Hayim Elya realized what must be done, which had already been apparent to Reb Zvi. And Hayim Elya said: "Now I know that I must eat this parchment, as Ezekiel ate that scroll."

And when Reb Zvi saw that Hayim Elya understood, he handed the parchment to him and said: "Yes, take this parchment, Hayim Elya, and pronounce the blessings over both wine and bread, and eat."

But Hayim Elya did not fully understand this command. And he hesitated and said: "But why both blessings, Rebbe? Why not only the blessing over bread?"

And Reb Zvi replied: "The blessing over bread serves only to bless the parchment; the second blessing serves to bless the ink as well. For the blessing over wine will transform the letters of the words into rivers that will flow from within, and the blessing over bread will make the words nourishing in your sight. Furthermore, if you only pronounced one blessing, and not both, there could be the danger that you would succeed in the ascent, but might not be able to return to this world."

Then Reb Hayim Elya pronounced the blessings over wine and bread, and he ate the parchment, and it was like the honey of manna to his taste, and he felt the rivers of words begin to flow. And in the vision that took form before his eyes, he saw the scroll of the Book that had been revealed to Ezekiel, and the scroll was unrolled, and the letters of that scroll burned in his sight like flames, black fire on white. And Hayim Elya read out loud the words that were written there without and within, and Reb Zvi, who shared in this vision, witnessing the scroll and hearing the words that Hayim Elya spoke, took down those words so that a record would exist in this world.

And in the black fire of the letters Hayim Elya read the history of his family, from the days of Abraham until that time. And in the white fire he read the future, until the End of Days. And when he looked up at last, he was amazed and terrified to discover that somehow he had ascended to a very high place, and was hovering there, like a dove above its nest. And before him shimmered a vision more vivid than anything he had ever seen in his life. For there he saw the Celestial Temple that exists in Paradise, which is torn down and rebuilt every day as a reminder of the destruction of the earthly Temple in Jerusalem. And Hayim Elya saw the Celestial Temple reconstructed in his sight, from the first cornerstone until the final stone was in place. And when he gazed upon the splendor of the Temple in all its glory, he knew that his soul had been numbered among the blessed. But at the same time he began to fear that the splendor was more than a man may gaze upon and live, and then he shut his eyes.

When he opened his eyes again, Reb Hayim Elya found himself standing beside Reb Zvi and Tselya, and realized that he had never stopped speaking during the whole of the vision, for he had never stopped reading the words written in that Book. And Reb Zvi had taken down all that he had said, and Tselya had observed all that had transpired. And Hayim Elya saw that a glowing aura surrounded Reb Zvi's face. Then Reb Zvi smiled and said:

"Normally, Hayim Elya, you serve as my scribe. But this time it was my honor to serve as yours. Because of you, I too had a glimpse into that Book whose sweetness Ezekiel was permitted to taste. And because of you I have shared in his blessing, for once a blessing has been brought to our People, it can be renewed by those who reach that rung of the ladder. And today, Hayim Elya, you stood on that rung, nor did you fall off. But tell me, please, did you close your eyes because you could not bear to gaze upon such majesty, or because you could not bear to see the Temple torn down?"

And Hayim Elya considered Reb Zvi's question, and he said: "I sensed that had I continued to observe that unveiled splendor, I might have been blinded, and I also felt in danger of cutting the silver cord by which every man's soul is attached. But now I also realize that I am grateful I was spared witnessing the Temple being torn down, for this way it will remain in my memory as it is in all its glory."

Then Reb Zvi said: "Just after you shut your eyes, Hayim Elya, and before the scroll was rolled up, I glanced at it and read there that you had inherited the volume of the *Sefer Raziel* from the side of your grandmother, Rayzel, and not from that of your grandfather. And it was also revealed that your grandmother had been named for that very angel, Raziel, for that is the guardian angel of your family, and that book and parchment have been in your family since the days of the first Temple. Who knows how many times that parchment, folded inside the amulet, protected whoever used it against the dangers of the ascent? But once the amulet had been lost, the parchment was unable to serve its purpose, until you deciphered the meaning of the reference to Ezekiel. This, Hayim Elya, you did by yourself, as must be the case, though Sharya and I took you as close as we could. Now the parchment has fulfilled its purpose, and the Book has been transcribed for another generation."

The Apocalyptic Chariot Race
by Aaron Sussaman

This morning I was sitting on a park bench with a friend, Sasha Edelstein, talking and feeding pigeons. Many years ago Sasha suffered terribly in a Nazi concentration camp, losing everything but the will to live. Now he's a wisp of an old man retired on all the money he made in this country he calls "the land of hope."

"Is all right," he asked me suddenly, tossing his last peanut to those over-fed birds, "if I take a little snooze? You won't be offended? I'm getting to be really a sleepyhead." And then, leaning back and closing his eyes, he fell asleep almost immediately. When he started tipping toward his end of the bench, I caught him and braced him against me, letting his head rest on my shoulder.

I've never urged Sasha to talk to me about the Holocaust, but whenever the mood has come upon him and he has, I've listened.

Sometimes he's said that he wished he could have experienced, after all the horror of it was over, the emotional release that some other survivors experienced. Some, he's told me, had been able to cry, cry even in public places and in front of strangers. And others, they had been able to laugh. Yes laugh, laugh bitterly and too loudly, like madmen, as if they'd discovered that life was nothing but a joke whose terrible point they'd finally gotten.

And also he's sometimes talked about a dream he's long been haunted by.

"It's apocalyptic, but in Technicolor," he's said, as if to try to mitigate its somberness.

In the dream, somewhere up in the sky God and Hitler are having a fierce chariot race. Hitler is driving a chariot of fiery darkness drawn by black horses. He is cracking a whip over their heads, making blood-red smoke pour from their nostrils. And God is driving a chariot of heavenly light drawn by white horses, and promising in a voice ten times more booming than the one which boomed over Mount Sinai, "Don't worry, Edelstein, I will win!" Hitler's chariot has two wheels, God's has only one. And whereas God races fairly, Hitler is constantly trying to ram God's remaining wheel to eternal smithereens. Nevertheless, the race is fearsomely close. One time Sasha will dream that Hitler is ahead. Another time he'll dream that God is ahead. If Hitler wins, Sasha is convinced, then death will be an everlasting concentration camp. Only if by some miracle God wins will death be green pastures and Sasha, like countless others, be saved.

When Sasha suddenly awoke from his snooze, sitting stiffly upright and blinking with grateful dismay to find himself still among the living, I couldn't help wondering if he'd just had the dream again, and who was ahead this time.

Somehow he must have guessed what I was wondering, because he smiled and said, "No, for weeks I haven't had that dream. But I'll tell you something. The last time I had it, I could have sworn that Hitler was down to one wheel too. Now how do you suppose that happened?"

BOOK V
KABBALISTIC THEMES

The Lost Princess

by Rabbi Nachman of Bratslav

There was a king who had six sons and but one daughter; he loved his
daughter more than any of his other children, and passed many hours in her
company; but one day while they were together the princess displeased the
king, and he cried out, "May the devil take you!"

There seemed nothing amiss that night when the princess went to bed.
But in the morning she could not be found.

Then the king tore his hair for grief and guilt. "It is because of what I
cried out," he said, "that she is gone."

Then the second to the throne, seeing the king in despair, arose and cried,
"Give me a servant, and a steed, and gold, and I will go out and seek the
princess."

For a long time he rode through wasteland and desert in search of the
missing maiden. Once as he passed in a desert he saw a road at the edge of
the sand, and he thought, "I have ridden so long in the desert without meeting anyone. Perhaps the road will lead me to the city."

The road led him to a great castle guarded by hosts of warriors. The
prince was afraid they would not allow him to enter the castle, but nevertheless he dismounted from his steed, and went up to them; and they allowed
him to pass through the gate. Then he came in upon a magnificent courtyard, and saw a marble palace before him. He went into the palace, and
walked through halls that were studded with alabaster pillars. Guards stood
in all the passageways, but no one questioned him, and he went from room
to room until he came to the chamber of the throne, and there a king was
seated. Tables laden with delicate foods were along the walls of the room;
the prince ate of the delicacies; then he lay down in a corner of the chamber
where he might not easily be seen, and he watched to see what would happen.

Musicians played upon their instruments, and sang before the king; soon
the king held out his hand and commanded that the queen be brought. Then
the music became more joyous, and people danced in the court, and made
merry, and drank, for the queen would soon appear.

When the queen came into the chamber she was given a smaller seat next
to the throne; the wanderer looked upon her and saw that she was indeed
the princess he sought. And as she looked out over the room she saw the

man withdrawn into an obscure corner, and she recognized him. She got down from her throne and went to him and said, "Do you not know me?"

"You are the princess!" he said. "But how have you come to this place?"

"The king let fall an angry word," she said. "He cried, 'May the evil one take you!' and this is the palace of evil."

"The king is grief-stricken because of what he has done, and I have sought for you these many years," the wanderer told her. "How may I take you away?"

"You cannot take me from this place," she said, "except that you first go and select a place for yourself, and there you must remain for an entire year, thinking only of my deliverance, longing and hoping to rescue me, and on the last day of the year you must not eat a particle of food, but must fast, and on the last night of the year you must not sleep; then you may come to me."

He did as she told him to do. He went into the desert and remained there an entire year, and at the end of the year he did not sleep, and did not eat, but returned toward the palace of the evil one. On the way, he passed a beautiful tree heavily laden with ripe fruit, and a terrible desire came over him to taste of the apples, so he went and ate. At once he fell into a deep sleep, and he slept for a very long time. When he awoke he saw his servant standing beside him, and he cried out, "Where am I?"

"You have slept many years," the servant said; "I have waited by you, while I lived on the fruit."

Then the wanderer went to the palace and came to the princess; and she cried, "See what you have done! Because of a single day, you have lost eternity! For if you had come on that day, you might have rescued me. I know that it is difficult to refrain from eating, and it is especially difficult on the last day, for the evil spirit was strong in you on that last day. But you must go again and choose a place and remain there another year, praying, and longing, and hoping to deliver me; on the last day of that year you may eat, but you must drink no wine, for wine will cause you to sleep, and the most important thing of all is not to sleep."

He went back to the wilderness, and did as she had told him to do, but on the last day, as he was returning toward the palace, he saw a flowing spring. He said to his servant, "Look, the fountain of water is red, and it has an odor as of wine!" Then he knelt and tasted of the spring, and at once fell to the ground and slept. He slept for many years.

And in that time a great army of warriors passed on the road; among them were mounted riders, and carriages, and at last there came a great carriage drawn by fourteen steeds. The princess was in that carriage; but when she saw the wanderer's servant on the road, she ordered the carriage to be halted, and she went down and saw the wanderer sleeping, and she sat by him and wept. "Poor man," she said; "so many years you have sought me, and yet because of a single day you have lost me, and see how you must suffer, and how I suffer because of that day!'' Then she took her veil from her face; she wrote upon the veil with her tears, and left it beside him; and she got into her carriage and rode away.

After he had slept seventy years, the man awoke and asked his servant, "Where am I?" The servant told him what had happened, of the army that had passed, and how the princess had wept over him. Just then the wanderer saw the veil lying beside him, and he cried, "Where does this come from?"

"The princess left it for you," the servant said. "She wrote upon it with her tears."

He who was second to the throne held the veil up to the sun, and saw the marks of her weeping, and read of her grief at finding him so, and read that she was gone from the first palace of the evil one, but that he must now seek her in a palace of pearls that stood on a golden mountain. "Only there, you may find me," the princess had written.

Then the wanderer left his servant and went alone in search of the princess.

For many years he wandered among mankind, asking and seeking for the palace of pearls upon the mountain of gold, until he knew that it was to be found upon no chart, and in no land inhabited by men, and in no desert, for he had been everywhere. But still he searched in the wilderness, and in the wilderness he came upon a giant who carried a tree that was greater than any tree that grew in the world of men. The giant looked upon the wanderer and said, "Who are you?"

He answered, "I am a man."

"I have been so long in the wilderness," said the giant, "that it is many years since I have seen a man." And he looked at the man.

The man said, "I seek a palace built of pearls upon a golden mountain."

The giant laughed, and said, "There is no such place on earth!"

But the man cried, "There is! There must be!" and he would not give up his seeking.

Then the giant said, "Since you are so obstinate, I'll prove to you that there is no such place on earth. I am the lord over all the animal kingdom, and every beast that runs over the earth, from the greatest to the tiniest, answers to my call. Surely if there were such a place as you seek, one of my creatures would have seen it." So he bent and blew on the ground, making a sound that was narrow as the call of wind in the grass, and wide as the rustling of leaves; his call spread like spreading water, and at once the beasts of the earth came running, leaping toward him: the timid gazelle and the wild tiger and every creature from the beetle to the great elephant, all came, and he asked of them: "Have you seen a palace of pearls built on a golden mountain?"

The creatures all answered him, "No."

Then the giant said to the man, "You see, my friend, there is no such place at all. Spare yourself, and return home."

But the man cried, "There is, there must be such a place! And I must find it!"

The giant pitied him, and told him, "I have a brother who is lord over all the creatures of the air; perhaps one of them has seen this place, for birds fly high."

Then the man went further into the wilderness, until he found another giant who carried a great tree in his hand. "Your brother has sent me to you," he said. And he told the giant of his quest. The giant whistled into the air, and his cry was like the sound of all the winds that murmur and shriek high over the earth; at once every winged creature, insect and eagle, answered his call. But none had seen a palace of pearls upon a golden mountain.

"You see," said the giant, "there is no such place at all. You had better return home, and rest yourself."

But the man cried, "There is, there must be such a place, and I will not rest until I find it!"

At last the second giant said, "I have a brother who is lord over all the winds. Go to him, perhaps he can help you."

After many years the wanderer came to the third giant, who carried a still greater tree in his hand; and the wanderer told the giant what he sought.

Then the giant opened wide his mouth, and the call he hurled over the world was like the tumult of colliding heavens. In that instant, all the winds over the earth came rushing to him, and he asked them, "Have you seen a palace of pearls upon a mountain of gold?" But none of them had seen such a thing.

"Someone is jesting with you, and has sent you on a fool's quest," the giant said to the man. "Better go home, and rest yourself."

But the man cried, "There is, there must be such a place!" Just then another wind came hastening to the giant, and lay breathless and weary at his feet.

"You have come late!" the giant cried angrily, and he lifted the great tree to lash the wind. "Why did you come tardily to my call?"

"Master," the wind said, "I came as soon as I could, but I could not come sooner, for I had to carry a princess to a mountain of gold on which there stands a palace built of pearls."

The man heard, and was overjoyed. "Can you take me there?" he begged. The wind answered, "I can."

Then the master of the winds said to the man, "You will have need of gold, where you are going, for in that city all things are of high worth." And he took a wonderful purse, and gave it to the wanderer. "Whenever you put your hand into this bag," the giant said, "you will find it filled with gold, no matter how much gold you draw out of it."

Then the wind took up the wanderer and set him down upon the golden mountain.

The wanderer saw the palace of pearls that stood within a wonderful city, and the city was surrounded by many walls guarded by warriors. But he put his hand into his marvelous purse, and gave them gold, and they let him pass, and when he came into the city he found that it was a pleasant and beautiful place. Then he lived there for a long while, and there the princess lived, but in the end, with wisdom and righteousness, he took her home to the king.

Retold from the Yiddish and Hebrew sources
by Meyer Levin

A Letter

by Rabbi Nachman of Bratslav

When I look upon the heavens,
the work of Your fingers.
(Ps. 8:4)

Once there was a prince who became separated from his father, the king. The boy yearned for reunion with his father, but he was too far away to reach him. Then one day he received a letter from his father. The letter filled him with joy and desire. "Oh, if only I could see my father again!" he cried. "If only I could just touch him. If only he would stretch out his hand to me. I would gladly take his hand and kiss each finger. Oh, my father! My teacher! My light! If only I could touch your hand!"

While he was yearning and wishing for his father's hand, a thought came to him. "Do I not have my father's letter? And is this letter not written by his hand? And is not the *handwriting* of the king something akin to his *hand*?" He treasured and fondled the letter and said happily to himself over and over again: "The handwriting of the king—the hand of the king."

Translated from the Yiddish
by Rabbi Jack Riemer

The King Who Loved Music
by Rabbi Levi Yitzhak of Berditchev

There once was a king who so loved music that he directed his musicians to play before him at a certain hour each morning. Those who came at the appointed time and performed received a reward, and those who arrived early, even before sunrise, received a double reward. But whether they arrived at the appointed time or earlier, they came not for the sake of the reward but only out of love for the king. For many years all went well. The musicians delighted in playing each morning before the king, and the king delighted in hearing their music.

When, at last, the musicians died, their sons sought to take their places. But, alas, they had neither mastered the art of their fathers nor had they kept their instruments in proper condition. Worse still, the sons no longer loved the king as did their fathers but set their eyes only upon the reward, blindly following their fathers' custom of arriving early each morning at the palace to perform. But the harsh sounds that emerged were so offensive to the ear, that after a time the king no longer listened to their music. Intent upon the reward, however, greed closed the sons' eyes to this reality, and they continued to come each day to play as usual.

Still, there were among the sons of the old musicians some who recognized that they were not worthy to play before the king. And they were determined to correct the situation. They set about the difficult task of relearning the forgotten art. Before coming to the king, they would now first try to tune their instruments, and in so doing would often arrive late. Upon entering the king's court and hearing the racket of the other musicians who were already present, they sought out an obscure corner for themselves where they could play undisturbed in accordance with their ability. It was there that they gathered each morning to perform, remaining long after the other musicians had departed so that they might improve their skill. And long before leaving their homes for the palace each morning they continued to struggle with their poor instruments. The king was aware of their efforts and it was good in his eyes. For even though they did not play with the same talent as their fathers, still they strove, within their limits, to once more bring joy to the king. Thus was their music received by the king with favor.

Translated from the Hebrew
by Samuel Dresner

An Imperial Message
by Franz Kafka

The Emperor, so it runs, has sent a message to you, the humble subject, the insignificant shadow cowering in the remotest distance before the imperial sun; the Emperor from his deathbed has sent a message to you alone. He has commanded the messenger to kneel down by the bed, and has whispered the message to him; so much store did he lay on it that he ordered the messenger to whisper it back into his ear again. Then by a nod of the head he has confirmed that it is right. Yes, before the assembled spectators of his death—all the obstructing walls have been broken down, and on the spacious and loftily mounting open staircases stand in a ring the great princes of the Empire—before all these he has delivered his message. The messenger immediately sets out on his journey; a powerful, an indefatigable man; now pushing with his right arm, now with his left, he cleaves a way for himself through the throng; if he encounters resistance he points to his breast, where the symbol of the sun glitters; the way, too, is made easier for him than it would be for any other man. But the multitudes are so vast; their numbers have no end. If he could reach the open fields how fast he would fly, and soon doubtless you would hear the welcome hammering of his fists on your door. But instead how vainly does he wear out his strength; still he is only making his way through the chambers of the innermost palace; never will he get to the end of them; and if he succeeded in that nothing would be gained; he must fight his way next down the stair; and if he succeeded in that nothing would be gained; the courts would still have to be crossed; and after the courts the second outer palace; and once more stairs and courts; and once more another palace; and so on for thousands of years; and if at last he should burst through the outermost gate—but never, never can that happen—the imperial capital would lie before him, the center of the world, crammed to bursting with its own refuse. Nobody could fight his way through here, least of all one with a message from a dead man.—But you sit at your window when evening falls and dream it to yourself.

Translated from the German
by Willa and Edwin Muir

Illusion

by M. J. Berditchevsky

In a far-off land, a land far across the sea, a great king sits upon his lofty throne. He alone is the ruler in that land. He builds cities and then destroys them, builds them in beauteous splendor and afterward tears them down, in order to build better and more beautiful ones. And when he builds he does wondrous things.

Now the day has come when he begins to build a palace, a great palace whose width and breadth exceed anything ever built before or after. There are towers and fortresses on it, grand halls and rooms without number, each one different from the next, and each one is built in front of the other in progression. Each room has an entrance and a gate, ascending and descending stairs, anterooms and chambers.

In front of the palace is a large courtyard built of black marble superimposed on white marble, and behind the courtyard is a grand and spacious garden in which are lovely trees, beautiful shady spots where the trees whisper together; and there are ponds and brooks that pass through the garden from one end to the other, and on them are suspended bridges made of net as strong as a bowstring. In front of the garden is uncultivated land which stretches without end and this in turn is surrounded by a great wall, and in front of the wall is a partition, and in front of that mountains.

Only one gate opens onto the main road, and across from this gate all the doors are built, and through this one gate all of the beauty within can be seen, every hue and color of the rainbow, every image and form.

And there in the last room the king sits upon his throne in all his glory. And he calls all of his servants, and he invites all of his people from every corner of the land, to come and see what he has built, all of its power and splendor. And so they come in long lines, old and young, large and small, to see the magnificence and the beauty.

And all of a sudden the gate is locked, and the doors are all shut. . . .

So they try to open the gate, but it is as if they have all been blindfolded, and they cannot find it. Some look here and others there, these climb up and those try to dig a tunnel.

But in front of them are partitions that stand before more partitions.

And as soon as they tear one down, behold a second one bigger and more difficult to penetrate appears, and they toil and struggle for many days.

When will it end? When will they find the entrance?

And so they kept toiling and striving until a man who had eyes in his head came to that place and said to them: "You are the greatest fools in the world! Why do you drive yourselves so? Why do you struggle in vain? When will you know that He Who Builds for Eternity is wise in a wisdom unknown to you and not perceived by your senses, and He is the Master of the wondrous illusion. . . . There is no palace here, no grand ballrooms, no walls, no gates, no buildings, no doors; all of it is one enormous illusion! You think you are seeing, while in fact there is nothing to be seen."

Like this story, so too are all the worlds, all that does or does not fill their spaces, everything felt, perceived or understood because they are seen or imagined by us as things outside and separate from us; in truth they are nothing of and by themselves; they depend only on the Word from His Mouth, praised be He, and He and they are all one. It is just that the Holy One, praised be He, has hidden Himself in that which is apparently revealed. He can be seen by His garments and He is hidden from the eyes of His creatures, for in this is His Greatness, that He hides Himself in what can be seen, and reveals Himself in what is hidden.

So it was told in the name of the man Israel ben Eliezer, the Baal Shem Tov.

Because he can see what is revealed in the hidden, and he can see what is beyond the illusion . . . with this ability to see, he wants to redeem Israel, to redeem the people not by Torah or *mitzvot*, laws or customs, but by seeing, for by vision he can penetrate the light that is hidden and that is surrounded by the net of optical illusions.

And the moment that he uncloaks the world, at that precise moment that he stands directly in front of the Essence itself and face to face with the One Absolute, then his soul is exalted. His soul leaves its confines and penetrates the depths of the world, the depths of the heavens.

He enters into and behind the illusion.

And a sound from on high is heard. . . .

The sound is the voice of the world at that moment that he enters that which is hidden in the world, the sound of existence at that moment that he receives his light from the spark of the Divine Presence.

There under the glorious throne—it is like the whiteness of the diamond.

But woe to them, to the people who see but do not know what they are seeing, who stand and know not before what they are standing, who hear and know not what they are hearing. Woe to him, to the man who does not know the secret that is in the obvious, and the revealed that is in the secret; woe to those who take everything as it seems and appears without looking at what is above and what is below.

And there above and below is where the essence of things begins—

These things are understood by every ear that knows how to hear, and every eye that knows how to see, it is understood by all those to whom the Divine Presence talks from within their hearts . . . these are the ones that experience the splendor of the world, who see the wondrous perfection, who know and hear the voice from on high. . . .

And as soon as the voice of the Lord knocks upon the doorposts of their hearts, immediately they leave the lower world and ascend God's ladder, they ascend with awesome reverence.

What is all this awe?

That is what those who are blind ask because they do not see, and those who are deaf, because they do not hear, and the ones who are not like the others. They mock those who sit in the heavens and say to them: "If your words are true and your spirits are lifted, why don't we see what you see? Why don't we hear what you hear?"

To what can this be likened? So spoke once the man Israel. There were musicians with instruments of music and song in their hands, and they succeeded in making music, playing upon their harps, and people heard the sound of music and the spirit of life raised them up and they got up and danced, and the dances went with the singing voices, and the steps with the beats of the song.

A deaf man was there and he had never heard the beauty of music in his life, and he was amazed and he thought to himself, Is it just because these ones move their fingers on these things and pluck them this way and that, that these people dance and make different movements?

Now who will incline his ear to the melody of the song?

So too are these people who hear not the voice from on high.

And he, the man Israel, hears, he hears everything, he hears all that the heavens say and the earth tells, he hears the words of all living creatures, all the birds in the sky, all the trees on the ground and also what the silence speaks.

He hears what is not to be heard. . . .

Translated from the Hebrew
by Pamela Altfeld Malone

Three Vows

by S. Y. Agnon

There once was a tale of an emperor who ruled over many states that were filled with the children of Israel. One day the emperor passed a study house and heard the voice of a scribe reading from the Song of Songs: "I have made you swear, daughters of Jerusalem, with harts or gazelles, lest you raise up or stir up love, until it please."

The emperor stood and listened. He listened as the scribe continued to interpret: "What are the three vows in the song? One, that the Holy One, blessed be He, has made the people Israel swear that they will not go up to the Land of Israel with a strong hand. The second is that He has made Israel swear that they will not stir up rebellion against the nations of the world. Even though the nations rule tyrannically over Israel, they will not rebel, but instead will lovingly accept their sorrows until the time of salvation arrives when God will redeem them from among the peoples and raise them up to the Land of Israel. The third is that the Holy One caused the nations to swear that they will not oppress Israel overly much."

The emperor pondered on these words with astonishment for an entire day: "Is it possible that the Jews, a people who are mournful, downcast, delivered into the hands of others and oppressed by every regime, is it possible that the Holy One found it necessary to make them vow not to rebel against the nations of the world? What if they did rise up? If I sent one legion against them I would sweep them off the face of the earth."

The emperor puzzled over the scribe's words and found no explanation for them. He sent for the princes of Israel and asked them his questions, but they did not know what to answer him. He sent for the wise men of Israel, but they, too, gave no reply.

Then the emperor became enraged and said: "Behold, I give you one year's time. If you answer me all will be well, but if not I will expel all the Jews from every province in my kingdom."

One month passed, then two months, then three until the whole year was over, but no one came to explain to the emperor why it was necessary for God to make Israel vow not to rebel against the nations of the world. He ordered that the Jews be driven out from every state in his kingdom. Because there were so many Jews, the exodus lasted one year.

During the expulsion the Jews were so upset, overworked, and exhausted that no one thought to seek advice. When they reached a field outside the empire, however, they began to look at themselves and said, "When our forefathers were in Egypt and numbered 600,000 the Holy One raised up a leader for them, Moses our Teacher, peace be upon him. Now, therefore, when we are more than 600,000, God will certainly not leave us leaderless. We surely have a leader even now, but he is hidden and does not reveal himself to his generation."

They stood up and proclaimed, to the accompaniment of thirteen shofars, "Whoever knows himself to be the leader of the generation and says nothing will be placed under a ban."

One old man arose and said, "I am he, this generation's leader. Remove from me all traces of a ban and I will go to the emperor and explain the three vows."

They arose and revoked the ban. As the old man stood and spoke to them he was already standing near the emperor.

When the emperor saw a man he did not recognize standing by him in his bedroom he was seized by trembling and shaking. The old man said to him, "I am the one who has come forward to explain the questions you are puzzling over. Come with me to the garden and I will make it known to you." Why the garden? Because the emperor's bedroom was filled with statues of their gods, so the old man did not want to stand there. The old man continued, saying, "Perhaps you fear to leave, but do not fear. For had I sought to do you evil I would have already done so. Behold, several companies of soldiers stand on guard before your palace door, but none were able to prevent me from entering your chamber." They went out. As they were leaving the old man said to him, "Look at this watch." As the emperor looked at the watch the old man pushed him into the world of fantasy.

It seemed to the emperor that one state was rising up in arms against him. He became angered and sent a legion there to restore order. The legion fell into the rebels' hands. Not one soldier survived. The emperor then sent another legion and another until he had thrown against them all his forces. All fell into the hands of the rebels and were killed.

The emperor had a legion of valiant men that had conquered many provinces for him. He loved the legion both because it had conquered many provinces and because it gave him a reputation across the land. He called this legion and told them, "Go forth and battle my enemies until you wipe them from the earth." They all grabbed their swords and went off to fight against the rebellious state. The rebels engaged them in battle with sword and spear, lance and bow. With a mighty arm they poured out their weapons upon the emperor's men. They struck with furious anger, each man beside his comrade. They killed and did not spare. Whoever escaped their hands fell into the hands of the nearby menfolk, who came at them with iron axes. Whoever escaped the menfolk fell into the hands of the women, who broke open their heads with large rods used for poking coals and with small rods used for knitting wool. They felled them all as one, and left the emperor neither horse nor rider, neither swordsman nor swordbearer.

The emperor saw himself alone in the field without his forces, without horse, rider, or palace guard, without food, without anything. He removed his fine coat and began to tear at his flesh. Then hunger seized him and he desired to return to his land.

With his whole spirit he longed to go to his land and kingdom. He began to go along on foot but he could not find the way. He thought he found the right path but when he reached its end he saw that it was not the way. Meanwhile, his feet became uncovered and his clothing torn. He did not appear to be a king.

After several days he reached a small village in another province. He saw a farmer standing and plowing his soil. He turned toward the farmer and said to him, "I am hungry. Give me something to eat." The farmer cursed him angrily and said, "You are not sick. If you want to eat, go work." Disappointed, the emperor left him and went on his way.

He entered the village and approached a Jew. The Jew saw a poor man with downcast eyes standing in his doorway. He brought him into his home and gave him food and drink. When he finished his meal, the Jew prepared a bed for him. The emperor stretched out on the Jew's bed, became drowsy, and slept. When he awoke the Jew set before him a table and gave him food and drink. Thus it was for one day, two days, three days, seven days, and for thirty days. The emperor dwelled with the Jew, ate from his loaf and slept on his bed, but the Jew did not ask him for any payment. Nor did he ask him how long he would remain. And he would comfort him in his sorrow and say to him, "Trust in the Lord is a mighty thing, for God has salvation."

The emperor's soul cleaved to the God of Israel, and to Israel His people, for among all the nations there are none compassionate, helping, or partaking in the suffering of others like Israel. The emperor already forgot all the evil that he had done to the Jews and yearned, desired, and sought to become a part of this people. After two or three years he passed the knife over his flesh, circumcised himself and became a convert.

He went to a city, entered a study house, and began to learn Torah. The men of the city saw this man busying himself with Torah and were good to him and gave him enough to live on.

He sat in the study house and read the Torah, the Prophets, and the Writings. He studied the Mishnah, Midrash, the ordinances, the Gemara, and the legends. He prayed, put on phylacteries, and observed all the commandments of the Torah.

In the same city was a homely, slovenly old maid who could not find a man to come and cover her head, she was so repulsively ugly and poor. The emperor heard of her, and sent her a message that he would marry her, for since he wanted to cling to the arm of Abraham our father, peace be upon him, he paid no attention to her ugliness or poverty. He married her and she bore him two sons. He would sit in the study house and study Torah, and she would launder the clothing of the townspeople and support him, herself, and her two sons from the labor of her hands.

One day the emperor stood at the window of the study house and looked outside. His study house faced the river. If a man stood at the window and looked at the river he could see the river and all that was close to it.

At the same time his wife went out to the river to wash laundry with her two small sons. One was in her arms, while the other dragged along behind her, grabbing onto the hem of her dress or to the laundry that dangled down her back. The older son leaned over and fell in the river. His mother saw and jumped into the river with his little brother in her arms. Her husband saw and began to shout. As he shouted he awoke.

The old man asked the emperor, "Why are you shouting?" He replied,

"My wife and children are drowning in the river." He asked, "Where is there a river here and where are a wife and children? Are you not standing in the garden of the emperor's house and are you not the emperor?"

He looked around him and found himself standing in the garden as in the beginning with an old man standing by him. Said the emperor to himself, "I have seen this old man before, but I do not know when."

The old man said to him, "Look at the watch in your hand." The emperor looked and saw that not even an hour had passed from the moment the old man first appeared, and behold how many things had happened to him in this short span! A state rebelled against him, all his armies were slain, he found himself alone in a field and he lost his way and came to a certain village and asked a farmer for something to eat, and the farmer railed at him, and he went to a Jew who gave him food and drink and a bed to sleep on and he lived with the Jew and his soul cleaved to the God of Israel and he passed a knife over his flesh and circumcised himself and walked to a city and entered a study house and studied Torah, and married a daughter of Israel and gave birth through her to two sons, and finally his wife and her children drowned in a river and he saw them drowning but was not able to save them. Now, after all this, he finds himself standing in the garden of his house and the same old man stands over him.

The emperor stood speechless for a long time. Then he gazed at the old man and asked him, "What is this?" Said the old man, "You see, emperor, if we wish, behold we are able, but what shall we do? For the Holy One, blessed be He, has caused us to swear that we will not rebel against the nations of the world. And if you doubt this story, look at your flesh and see that you are circumcised."

Even this is from the stories of our rabbi, Israel Baal Shem Tov, which I heard from the mouth of the Hasid Reb Efraim, lover of God, may he live, who heard it from the mouth of the saint Reb Nachum from Rachmistrivka, may this saint's memory be for a blessing, who heard it in the name of the Baal Shem Tov, whose soul is in the treasure house of heaven, who said, "Even we could do thus. But we do not want this, that this gentile will be like us by circumcising himself."

Translated from the Hebrew
by Jeremy Garber

The Tale of
Rabbi Gadiel the Infant

by S. Y. Agnon

Rabbi Gadiel was born by virtue of the Torah, which his father taught the
babes of Israel. And when Rabbi Gadiel came out into the world air he was
so small that one could hardly tell that he was human. When he came of age
for education his father began to instruct him in the commandments and in
piety. And he made him a *tallit katan* with fringes fringed of early fleece and
shaved the hair of his head on the gravesite of Rabbi Shimon ben Yohai on
Lag Ba'Omer and left him side curls, and carried him about in the pocket of
his clothes morning and evening to the great synagogue to say "Blessed is He
and blessed is His Name" and to answer "Amen, may His Great Name be
blessed." And when the cantor said the blessing, Rabbi Gadiel would repeat
after him "Blessed is He and blessed is His Name" and answer "Amen"
with all his might. And Rabbi Gadiel would lift up his voice until the doorposts trembled and none would know from where came the voice because
he was hidden inside his father's pocket.

And when he came of age for Mikra his father took him and set him
down on the tobacco box and opened before him the five books of Torah
and studied Torah with him and interpreted for him the words of living
God, until he learned the whole Torah and could read Mikra and Targum
and knew discourse and he learned Mikra, Mishnah, customs and legends,
the Babylonia Talmud and the Jerusalem Talmud, Sifra and Sifré, Tosefta
and *Mekilta*, *Sefer Yetsirah*, the letters of Rabbi Akiva and *Sefer Hatmunah*.
And if his father dozed off in the middle of his teachings, Rabbi Gadiel
would get off the tobacco box and sit at the edge of the pages of the book
and examine the flourish of the letters and the roundness of the letters, the
big letters and the small letters. When his father awoke and did not see him,
he was persuaded that the child was with his mother, and not knowing that
he stood between the pages he closed the book and turned to his affairs, leaving Rabbi Gadiel to stand among the letters, studying and poring over and
studying all that he had learned, and he was diligent in his studies and exceedingly successful in Torah and wisdom.

And so that these words might not be construed as mere exaggeration,
God forbid, we see fit here to describe how small Rabbi Gadiel actually was.
It happened that a phial of olive oil was set down for the Hanukah candle
and Rabbi Gadiel fell into the phial and sat there until his father came to light
the candle and only when he poured the oil into the candelabrum could
Rabbi Gadiel jump out, his face shining and his fragrance as the fragrance of
good oil. And because Rabbi Gadiel was so small his father feared to put him

down in public lest he be trampled on by passersby and he carried him in the
fold of his clothes, and when he went to market to do trade with the nations
of the world, Rabbi Gadiel would lie in the corner of his *tallit* and listen to
the conversation of his father and the conversation of the people, what his
father said to them and what they said to him, and in this way he learned the
tongue of Greece and the tongue of Edom and the tongue of Ishmael and all
the other tongues of the nations and he could converse in their tongues in an
exemplary fashion.

One day several of the wickedest men of the nations of the world who
were envious of Rabbi Gadiel's father came together and said: "How long
will this Jew usurp us and rob us of our livelihood? The time has come to
remove him from this world." One said to the other: "But for fear of the
authorities we would swallow him alive." And one stood and said: "These
Jews' Pesach is approaching; come let us take a corpse and put it in the Jew's
house and say, 'One of ours he killed, for his *matzot* he killed, to bake them
in blood he killed,' and we will go and call the judges of the town and the
elders of the community and they will arrest him with iron chains and lead
him out to be executed and we will have our revenge on him, and moreover
we will have his wealth and divide it amongst us." But they did not know
how to go about it. So one among them, resolved in his mind, advised the
others: "It is their custom on the eve of their Pesach to drink four cups of
wine and leave one large goblet on the table, the prophet Elijah's cup it is
called; come, let us fill a skin-bottle with blood and stir up the household on
the eve of Pesach, and while the Jew and his family are confounded we will
pour out the wine from Elijah's goblet and fill it with blood, and we will alert
the king's guards and community elders and they will put him in shackles
and arrest him in jail and sit in judgment over him and kill him and we will
take our revenge on him." They all heard and said, "It is well," and they
spread a rumor that "a lad of ours has been lost" and they agitated over the
imaginary loss and they incited the wicked of the nations to seek vengeance
from Israel.

On the eve of Pesach various knaves and scoundrels from the nations
came together with axes and hatchets to kill and destroy and wipe out the
seed of Israel. And because Rabbi Gadiel's father was a community elder
that year they came to him first, according to the adage "Begin with the
greatest," in order to upset his home and its inhabitants. Rabbi Gadiel's father and his family were reclining around the table and telling of the exodus
from Egypt that night when the door opened with a great clamor and a
horde of soldiers entered and set the house in turmoil. The family looked on
and were afraid because fear of the nations befell them. They stood cowering, this one wailed and that one wailed, and Rabbi Gadiel, who was so
small, jumped into Elijah's cup and his proximity remained unknown, and

he stayed inside Elijah's cup until their priest came and raised the cup and drank all the wine so that the blood could be poured into the cup.

Rabbi Gadiel remained inside this wicked man and the knave was unaware of his presence because his intestines were exceedingly coarse from eating a thousand pigs and drinking a thousand measures and he could feel nothing. Rabbi Gadiel remained inside this wicked man but he did not sit and wait for his body to become a part of the knave's body and their flesh to become one; instead he reflected on the seven wisdoms and the seventy tongues so as not to reflect on matters of Torah in such a place as this.

After the Gentiles had filled the cup with blood, they placed guards around it and ran in great confusion and called the elders of the community and the judges of the town and showed them the blood and said: "See how these Jews take our lives and suck our blood to drink on their holidays?" A great anger immediately filled the community elders and they took Rabbi Gadiel's father and his mother and his brothers and his sisters and they put them in iron chains and they lowered them into a ditch and they tortured them with various tortures while they waited for the execution order to arrive from the king.

The matter was brought before the king and his ministers and Rabbi Gadiel lay inside the belly of the knave and fed off Elijah's cup and reflected on matters of wisdom and rhetoric and the fables of the nations and conversation of men. And the kingdom was a benevolent kingdom that year and they did not judge crime without investigation and examination. They investigated and examined very closely and brought all those who had been present to bear witness and chief among them was the priest. And they swore in the priest with an age-long oath and said to him: "Open your mouth and give your evidence." The priest pronounced "his fear" from the heart and swore that all his words were true and just and prepared to begin his evidence. And what did Rabbi Gadiel do? He rose into the wicked man's throat and began to poke around with his finger inside the knave's throat. The knave felt the poking in his gullet and was unable to emit a single word. His claims remained blocked up and the wicked gentleman was disgraced. The king shouted and said: "Open your mouth." And what did Rabbi Gadiel do? He began to speak from inside the knave's throat and in the knave's tongue and told all that had come to pass. The scoundrels all bowed their heads in shame and the king and his ministers stood shaking and aghast for they had almost spilt innocent blood and, God forbid, destroyed a large community of Israel which had done no wrong. They immediately punished the wicked and set free the imprisoned in great honor and hung the priest on a tree. Thus was he repaid by God for what he had conspired to do to the Jews.

And thus hung the priest all day until came the prophet Elijah, of blessed memory, and kicked the knave and took Rabbi Gadiel out of his belly and wrapped him in the corner of his cloak and brought him to the hot springs of

Tiberias and bathed him there and anointed him in pure olive oil and immersed him into the flowing waters of the persimmon and dressed him in a gown of light and led him into one of the caves of the just and there he sat with him and studied the prosecution of the wicked who so oppress the children of the Lord.

And Rabbi Gadiel still sits in the yeshivah of the just and faithfully records every crime with which the nations of the world defame the children of the Lord. And when God's day shall come, that great and awful day, Rabbi Gadiel shall go forth from his place and he shall put on his garments of vengeance and shall be clad with zeal as a cloak and he shall speak to the Gentiles and show the nations and roar against them so saying: "Such and such you did, such and such you said." And they shall have no excuse, the ministers of the nations, to refute him and they shall go into the holes of the rocks and into the caves of the earth, as it is written, and they shall go into the holes of the rocks and the caves of the earth for fear of the Lord and for the glory of His majesty when He ariseth to shake terribly the earth.

(So ends the tale of Rabbi Gadiel the infant but unended are all his tales.)

Translated from the Hebrew
by Evelyn Abel

The Castle in the Kingdom

by Francis Landy

Once there was a castle in a kingdom on a high mountain. There the king sat and reigned. He had a council that met in secret in a chamber hollowed out under the cup of the mountain; all the sages of the world met there. But strangely none was seen to have left his home, nor was absent for any length of time. The chamber was a hemisphere, the color of the night sky, engraved with stars and constellations. Each man sat under the sign of his own kingdom, and interpreted the movement of the stars. In this way the king was the master of destiny, and thus he ruled his kingdom.

Now there were many Jews in that kingdom, who were fearful that the king would impose harsh laws or taxes on them, or exile them or forcibly convert them, and so they conspired against the king. But all their conspiracies came to naught. For the king would go privately to each Jew, from the humblest to the richest, and tell him of his secret council, and swear him to silence. Then the Jew would say to himself, "Who am I, and what is my life, that the king has so favored me? Whatever happens, at least I will be safe." And so no one knew that others knew of the existence of the council, and, for the sake of appearances, each entered the conspiracy, and each plot failed, because none willed it to succeed. And thus the king still sits on his throne.

In a different version of the parable, it was the entire people that decided to rebel against the king, and the king visited each of his subjects and told him of his council, and all happened exactly as in the first version.

No one knows whether there really is a council, or whether it is a fabrication, whereby the king preserves his throne.

Those who recorded the parable also handed down interpretations of it, some of which have survived. One refers to the Jews who, if they all united in the service of God, would overthrow the king of this world, and the dominion of evil would pass away for ever; and also to the tyrants and oppressors, who say to the Jews, "We are stronger than you, look at us," who treat the individual Jew favorably, to separate him from his people; they are the subtle tyrants, whose weapons of extermination are rational and unspoken, till we are all half or quarter Jews, till our very language hardly betrays us.

A second interpretation, arising out of this, is political. The king and his wise men rule the world, watching the stars, predicting events, the rise and fall of exchange and commodity, listening, consulting, till all believe that they know what they do, and are at their service. Every so often the rulers come to their subjects, saying, "Choose me: I have a secret council, a wisdom unknown to others," and they choose them, to forget what they lack, their desire for justice, for keeping faith.

The third interpretation may be termed psychological. The king rules the castle as a man rules himself, with a mixture of guile and compassion. The *yetzer* wishes to escape from fetters, and the king loves and cherishes him, for he too has a part in his story, and is tamed and nourished. Ultimately he will be free, so the king tells him—"I read it in the stars." He tells him that he has a secret council, which weighs and chooses his destiny, that the world is full of signs, for his eyes alone. And so he constructs his story, rounds it optimistically, with pattern and purpose. Without this assurance, the king's rule would fail. And perhaps he has no assurance.

The last interpretation that is remembered is that the king is God, who dwells in and beyond the world. The starred chamber is the night sky, the entire universe. We believe that there is a destiny, a pattern in experience, or rather God comes to each worshiper in turn, and tells him that He knows the movement of the stars, and all has its place and purpose, and he too, its image, inspired by His breath, has his own unique consummation and revelation. And so they wait for the coming of the Messiah, and God waits too, and no one knows if there is a Messiah, or what is his destiny. Then each worshiper is distanced from the other by his knowledge and terrible conviction: for my sake alone the universe was created.

The Tale of the Palace

by Rabbi Tsvi Blanchard

There was once a king with a large treasure of gold and jewels which he wished to reserve for those of his subjects who loved him. He built a large treasure house near his palace, and spent his days there surrounded by his treasure. The king instructed his servants to bring his guests to see him in his treasure house: It was a long and difficult journey to his palace, and only those who had a great desire to see the king would even begin the trip. When they had arrived they would come into the treasure house, and there delight in conversing with the king, and in enjoying his treasure with him. When they returned to the settled areas of the land they told their fellow subjects of the king and of his great treasure.

Soon many who loved the king's treasure far more than the king were journeying to the palace. They pretended to desire audience with the king, they repeated the ancient formulas of reverence, and they were full of praise for the king. But they gloried in viewing the great store of gold and jewels which surrounded the king. The king, saddened to see this, resolved to make the way to his treasure so difficult that only those who truly loved him would ever reach the storehouse of his wealth.

The king took some of his treasure and built a magnificent garden in widening circles around his treasure house. He planted shrubs, trees and flowers of many varieties so that there were always blossoms or fruit in the garden. He kept the climate mild. The enticing odors, the enchanting smells, the pleasant greenery were truly as fine as the gold and jewels the king had spent to create the garden. Those who sought the king and his treasure had first to pass through the winding pathways of his garden. Many were those who paused forever in the garden, bewitched by the delight. Here they tasted of the goodness they sought, and they remained for the rest of their lives rapt in the sensuous joy the king had made.

As a stronger barrier, the king made another garden of his jewels and gold. He took only a small portion of his fortune, and crafted it into a cache to be hidden at the exit from the garden of plants and trees. Any who passed would find this cache hidden amidst the second garden. Surely, they would say, we have found the home of the king and the king's treasure. There they remained, studying these wondrous gems, and lost in the fine shafts of light which reflected off the gold of the second garden. They shuddered with joy at finding the hidden cache. Most lost all interest in finding the king.

Such is the way of people, thought the king, their greed is limited only by their imagination. They do not think that there is greater wealth than that which they see before them in my plants, and in the jewels I have set for them to find. Now, only those who sought the king alone would find him. They would marvel at the beauty of his creations, but their search would not cease for it was the king whom they sought to see and not his wealth. The king, when they had found him, would lead them back through his gardens. They would travel over hidden paths among the jewels of the garden and among the plants, flowers and trees. They would see the beauty of these gardens as a part of the immensity of the fortune of the king. There, in the fullness of the king's presence, they would sit, crowns upon their heads, delighting in the brilliance of the king and his wealth.

Kabbalists

by I. L. Peretz

In bad times the finest merchandise loses its value, even the Torah—the best of all wares. And thus of the big yeshivah of Lashtshivo, there remained only the principal, Reb Yekel, and one of his students.

The principal was an old, lean Jew, with a long unkempt beard and extinguished eyes. Lemech, his favorite pupil, was a tall, slight, pale-faced youth, with black curly locks, sparkling, dark-rimmed eyes, dry lips, and an emaciated throat, showing a pointed Adam's apple. Both the principal and his pupil were wearing tattered garments showing their naked breasts, for they were too poor to buy shirts. With great difficulty the principal dragged a pair of peasant's boots on his feet, while the student, with stockingless feet, shuffled along in a pair of shoes far too big for him. The two alone remained of all the once famous yeshivah.

Since the impoverished townspeople had begun to send less and less food to the yeshivah and to offer fewer invitations for free meals to the students, the latter had left for other towns. Reb Yekel, however, resolved to die and be buried at Lashtshivo, while his favorite pupil was anxious to be present to close his beloved master's eyes.

Both frequently suffered the pangs of hunger, and lack of food resulted in many sleepless nights. After a good many hungry days and sleepless nights, there arises an inclination to study the Kabbalah. Since they were already forced to lie awake at night and go hungry during the day, why not at least derive some benefit from such a life? At least that way they could avail themselves of their long fasts and mortifications of the body to force open the gates of the invisible world and get a glimpse of all the mysteries it contains, of angels and spirits.

And thus the two of them had been studying the Kabbalah for some time. They were seated at a long table in the empty lecture room. Other Jews had already finished their midday meal, but for these two it was still before breakfast. But this was not unusual for them. His eyes half-shut, the principal spoke, while his pupil, his head leaning on both hands, listened.

"There are," the principal said, "four degrees of perfection. One man knows only a small portion, another a half, while a third knows an entire melody. The Rebbe, of blessed memory, knew, for instance, an entire melody. And I," he added sadly, "I have only been vouchsafed but a single scrap, this tiny." And he measured a tiny portion of his lean, emaciated finger, and continued: "There are melodies which require words. That is the lowest degree. There is also a higher degree; it is a melody that requires no words, it is sung without words—as a pure melody. But even this melody requires a voice and lips to express itself. And the lips, you understand, pertain to matter. The voice itself, though it belongs to the higher aspects of the physical world, is still material in essence. We may say that the voice stands on the borderline between matter and spirit. In any case, the melody that is dependent upon voice and lips is not yet pure, not yet entirely pure, not completely spirit.

"The truest, highest melody, however, is that which is sung without any voice. It resounds in the interior of a man, vibrating in his heart and in all his limbs.

"And that is how we are to understand the words of King David, when he says in the Psalms: *'All my bones utter thy praise!'* The melody should vibrate in the marrow of our bones, and such is the most beautiful song of praise addressed to the Lord, blessed be His Name. For such a melody has not been invented by a being of flesh and blood; it is a portion of that melody with which the Lord once created the universe; it is a part of the soul which He has breathed into His creation. It is this melody that the heavenly hosts sing."

The sudden arrival of a ragged fellow, a carrier, a rope around his hips, interrupted the discourse. Entering the room, he placed a dish of soup and a piece of bread upon the table before the head of the yeshivah, and said in a rude voice: "Reb Tevel sends this food for the teacher." And on the way out he added: "I'll come for the dish later!"

Torn from the celestial harmonies by the sound of the messenger's voice, the principal slowly and painfully rose from his seat and dragged his feet in their heavy boots to the water basin near the door, where he performed the ritual ablution of his hands. He continued to speak the whole time, but with less enthusiasm, while the pupil followed him with shining, dreamy eyes, straining his ears.

"I have not even been found worthy," said the teacher sadly, "to know the degree at which this can be attained, nor do I know through which of the celestial gates it enters. You see," he added with a smile, "I know well the necessary mortifications and prayers, and I will communicate them to you, even today."

The eyes of the student were wide, and his mouth fell open; he was literally swallowing every word his master uttered. But the master interrupted himself. He performed the ritual ablution of the hands, dried them, and recited the prescribed benediction. Then he returned to the table and broke off a piece of bread, reciting with trembling lips the prescribed blessing. His shaking hands then seized the dish, and a moist vapor covered his emaciated face. He put down the dish on the table, took the spoon into his right hand, while warming his left at the edge of the dish. All the time he munched with his toothless gums the morsel of bread over which he had said the blessing.

When his face and hands were warm enough, he wrinkled his brow and extended his thin, blue lips and began to blow on the soup.

All this time the pupil was staring at him. But when the trembling lips of the old man stretched to meet the first spoonful of soup, a pang seized the pupil's heart. Covering his face with his hands, he drew back into himself.

A few minutes later another man came in, also carrying a bowl of soup and a piece of bread.

"Reb Yosef sends the student his breakfast," he said.

The student did not remove his hands from his face. Putting down his own spoon, the teacher rose and went to him. For a moment he looked down at the boy with eyes full of pride and love. Then he touched his shoulder and said in a friendly and affectionate voice: "They have brought you food."

Slowly and unwillingly the student removed his hands from his face. He seemed to have grown paler still, and his dark-rimmed eyes were burning with an even more mysterious fire.

"I know, Rabbi," he said, "but I am not going to eat today."

"Are you going to fast the fourth day?" asked the teacher, greatly surprised. "And without me?" he added in a somewhat hurt tone.

"It is a particular fast day," replied the student. "I am fasting today for penance."

"What are you talking about? Why must you do penance?"

"Yes, Rabbi, I must do penance, because a while ago, when you had just started to eat, I transgressed the commandment which says, 'Thou shalt not covet.' "

Late in the night the student woke up his master. The two were sleeping side by side on benches in the old lecture hall.

"Rebbe, Rebbe!" called the student in a feeble voice.

"What's the matter?" the teacher said, jumping up frightened.

"Just now, I have been upon the highest summit."

"How is that?"

"I don't know how myself, Rebbe," replied the pupil in an almost inaudible voice. "Since I could not find sleep, I plunged myself into your lecture. I was anxious at any costs to learn that melody. Unable, however, to succeed, I was greatly grieved and began to weep. Everything in me was weeping, all my limbs were weeping before the Creator of the Universe! I recited the prayers and formulas you taught me; strange to say, not with my lips, but deep down in my heart. And suddenly, I was dazzled by a great light. I closed my eyes, yet I could not shut out the light around me, a powerful dazzling light."

"Yes!" said the old man, leaning over him.

"And in the midst of the strange light I felt so strong, so light-hearted. It seemed to me as if I had no weight, as if my body had lost its heaviness and that I could fly."

"Yes! Yes!"

"And then I felt so happy, lively, full of laughter. My face remained motionless, my lips never stirred, and yet I laughed. I laughed so joyously, so heartily, so frankly and happily."

"Yes, yes, in supreme exultation!"

"Then something began to hum in me, as if it were the beginning of a melody."

The teacher jumped up from his bench and stood by his pupil's side. "And then? And then?"

"Then I heard how it was singing in me."

"And what did you feel? What? What? Tell me!"

"I felt as if all my senses were closed and shut tight; and there was something singing in me, just as it should, without words, just so . . ."

"How? How?"

"No, I can't say. At first I knew, then the song became . . ."

"What did the song become? What?"

"A sort of music, as if there had been a violin in me; as though Yone the musician were sitting in my heart and playing one of the tunes he plays at the Rebbe's table. But it sounded much more beautiful, nobler and sadder, more spiritual; and all this was voiceless and tuneless, mere spirit."

"You have been blessed!"

"And now it is all gone," said the pupil, growing very sad. "My senses have again woken up, and I am so tired, so terribly tired that I . . . Rebbe!" the student suddenly cried, "Rebbe, recite with me the confession of the dying. They have come to fetch me; they require a new singer in the celestial choir. There is a white-winged angel—Rebbe—Rebbe—*Shema Yisroel, Shema*. . ."

Everyone in the town wished to die such a death, but the teacher found that it was not enough.

"Another few fast days," he said, "and he would have died quite a different death. He would have died by a kiss from the Shekhinah!"

Translated from the Yiddish
by A. S. Rappoport

The Hermit and the Bear

by I. L. Peretz

Once upon a time there was a man who couldn't stand injustices. So he handed over his shop to his wife, and he sat at home, shut up in his room, studying Torah, both the written and the mystic secret doctrine.

But he seems to have found injustices at home too, among his own household, so he decided to become a hermit—he left his home and he sat in the *beth hamedrash*, studying.

But the injustices of the world followed him into the *beth hamedrash*. Even at night a nightwatchman would come in to warm himself at the stove, or a poor traveler came to snatch a few hours of sleep, or someone in the town couldn't sleep, and came and talked. No matter what they talked about he heard only injustices, only injustices.

So he left the town and went out into the wide world to find a town without injustices. He didn't find one. The same world everywhere.

Then he left civilization behind, and went through one forest and another, over valley and hill, till he came to a river. He didn't know the name of the river. There was an old ruined palace on its shore, far away from every town or village. There he decided to live, there he sat all the time studying Kabbalah.

But you can't run away from injustices. Sometimes the river rose, and capsized boats, broke off big chunks of meadowland with the grass on it, or even sown fields. The fish in the river fought among themselves all the time. He couldn't rest, he couldn't sleep, there was nowhere to escape from it.

He lay awake and thought and thought—he wanted to discover where all these injustices originated, where they came from. He reached the conclusion that the injustices came because the soul of the world had gone to sleep. The idea isn't as fantastic as it sounds.

For instance—that lesser world, a man, as long as his soul is awake he does what is useful and of benefit to himself, systematically, rationally all his limbs obey the soul. But when a man is asleep the soul, the master over the body, is asleep, then the body tosses and turns, throws itself about without any plan or order, each limb separately, on its own, without any rational, coherent idea behind it—a man may even do himself an injury while he is asleep.

Injustices are committed without any reason; the world tosses and turns, with no plan, with no order. The soul of the world has fallen asleep, and each separate part does something different, not for the good of the whole.

Do you follow? Yes or no—that was his idea.

He decided that he must awaken the soul of the world. When the soul was awake there would be a system in the world, there would be an end to this tossing and turning without aim or purpose, and the separate limbs of the world would stop hitting out at each other.

But how does one waken the soul of the world?

There are several answers to this question in the sacred writings. You only have to do what is necessary, say what is necessary. To do that you must have complete belief and devotion and ecstasy. You must give yourself up to it heart and soul, with absolute self-surrender, or else the words fly away into empty space, into the void, and nothing is accomplished.

You must create something that has wings to fly, and a soul that knows where to fly, and what to demand there!

Now that is not possible during the day. You are deep in meditation, when suddenly a crow caws, or a thrush sings, or you hear a peasant at the plow swearing because the ground is hard, and blunting his share.

It is better at night, best at midnight. So that is when he tried it.

It worked! He felt it worked! Another night, another night, another night. . . .

But the wrathful spirit of the river discovered what he was doing, and said—"No!" And as soon as the hermit was filled with devotion and ecstasy the spirit of the river gave it a push, and the waves rose and seethed and boiled, and huge waves dashed out on to the shore. There was such a noise and commotion that the hermit's thoughts capsized like the boats on the river.

Then the hermit realized that he had no option but to shift the river with its wrathful spirit further back. Because he had no wish to leave his ruined palace and go to look for another abode away from the river. Who knows how long he would have to search, and perhaps he would never find anything suitable, and meanwhile there were all these injustices destroying the world!

Now shifting back the river was an easy matter for him. He had a spell that would do it. He kept another additional fast day, and after the fast was over he pronounced the spell, and the river shifted.

That made the spirit of the river furious. But there was nothing he could do about it. The spell had been pronounced! He stirred up the waters, however, so that they rose higher and higher, and huge waves stood up and crashed down upon the shore. Then he took one huge wave and hurled it straight at the ruined palace where the hermit lived, and the wave turned into a black shaggy bear, and the bear ran with blazing eyes round and round the ruined palace, and every time the hermit tried to concentrate, with devotion and ecstasy, the bear roared and growled, and upset the hermit's thoughts.

What could the hermit do? He wouldn't dream of killing the bear! That would be an injustice! For how was the bear guilty? Why shouldn't the bear live?

Then the hermit thought he would pacify the bear. Make him behave himself! Even if he was a bear he could be made to understand what was at stake! He would lift up the bear, elevate his soul, raise it higher.

So one morning the hermit stood at a corner of his ruined palace, and looked down at the bear. The bear saw him, and started roaring and growling, and tried to rush at him, with his eyes blazing wildly.

The bear glared up at the hermit, and the hermit looked down at the bear with compassion and love. There was a war between both pairs of eyes, the eyes with compassion and love, and the eyes with hate and fury.

But the hermit's eyes were stronger, and prevailed over the bear's eyes.

The war lasted a very long time, the war between those two pairs of eyes, between two hearts and two souls.

But when the sun began to rise in the east, all was quiet. By the time the sun reached its zenith in the sky the bear lay docilely in front of the ruin like a submissive dog. And when the sun set the bear stood up and sent a beseeching glance towards the hermit; then he went up to the gate, and asked to be admitted, whining like a dog that the gate should be opened.

The hermit had prevailed. The savage bear had submitted to him—he was whining: "Let me in! I shall serve you like a dog! I shall lie at your feet, look into your eyes faithfully and loyally, read your wish in them, and when you are thinking I shall be quiet, motionless."

Then the hermit opened the gate and let the bear in. And the bear lay down at the hermit's feet, and his eyes said:

"You are my lord! You are my god! I believe in you! You are my hope! Your thoughts are holy—what you mean to do will restore the world!"

The hermit stroked the bear affectionately, his own bear, the bear that believes in him—then he fell into deep thought, how to accomplish what he wants to do, to waken the soul of the world.

But now he can no longer think as he had thought before. He no longer has his whole soul. With every step that brought the bear up higher towards him, he had descended down to the bear.

He feels weary, his lids fall over his eyes, and he stumbles towards his couch.

The bear follows him, and lies down beside the bed.

Injustices will not cease. The bear has become a bit of man, and the man a bit of bear. And the hermit who now sleeps with the bear can not awaken the soul of the world.

Translated from the Yiddish
by Joseph Leftwich

The Amulet

by M. Z. Feierberg

I woke up crying in the middle of the night.

"What is it, Hofni?" asked my mother, awakened too by the sound of my tears. "What are you crying for?"

"I'm scared, mama, I'm so scared. Please light the candle for me, please do."

"But why should you be scared, Hofni?" my mother asked in an unsteady voice. "Of what?" She quickly lit the kerosene lamp, trimming back the wick to keep it from burning too brightly.

"I'm so scared, mama. I had a dream, and when I woke I couldn't remember it. And now I've been lying in bed for a whole hour and I can't sleep. It's so scary to be up all alone in the middle of the night."

"Don't be a silly thing," my mother said in a thin, hoarse voice, and fell asleep again.

I turned to stare directly at the dim lamp. The silence that prevailed in the house was broken only by the snoring of the sleepers, which sounded slowly and in sequence like an orchestrated theme. The lamp stood at one end of a table over most of which it cast its light, throwing into relief the half-empty water jug that had been set out for hands to be washed before prayer in the morning. Farther on a thick pall of darkness covered everything. The two chairs by the table seemed awfully ominous and black; the light made its way up through the house from the lamp to the ceiling, where it played back and forth harmonically, dancing and jigging before yielding to the pitch-black darkness beyond it, which had a shape and form of its own and seemed terribly thick, black, and crude. The black half-jug was like a monstrous apparition. I turned to stare again at my mother's bed, but all I could make out was the sideboard and the corner of her pillow. My mind was a perfect blank. I lay without stirring, unconscious of whether I was awake or asleep. . . . Gradually, I began to think again—yet not to think either, but to precariously feel, as though a sound like a bell had rung in my ear and restored me to my senses, so that I remembered that I was awake, and began dimly and disconnectedly to associate the lamp, the wick, the light, and on and on . . . and all kinds of other just as vague things and sensations, or so it seemed:

demons, ghosts, my father, the rabbi, the fair . . . and still other things too
that I couldn't name. Something was terribly wrong—but what? I couldn't
sleep—but why not? And where was my mother? I wasn't in a magic circle in
the forest or in the Great Synagogue . . . I could feel the pillow beneath me
. . . yes, I was lying on it. I wanted to cry, but it would make my mother
angry. I decided to say the *Shema*. My mother had once told me that whenever she was frightened at night she said the *Shema*. But my hands were unclean for prayer. I could have leaned over to the water jug and washed them,
I even wanted to, but I couldn't. My will was too weak to make me obey it.
I couldn't even take my hands out from under the covers. I wanted to wake
my mother, but I was afraid to make a sound. . . .

It was an awful, an intolerable situation. Without realizing it, I had begun
to cry again, at first at intervals and in an almost inaudible whisper, alternately releasing a sob and stopping to listen to it and contemplate the way it
calmed and revived me: I was not, after all, alone by myself; there was this
other thing beside me. My own voice was a sign of life, and where there was
life, fear vanished. My sobs proceeded as though by themselves in short, low
bursts that periodically grew longer and louder in progression. . . .

"Hofni, what is it?" my mother called out in distress, waking again from
her sleep. "Why are you crying, Hofni?"

The sound of her voice immediately broke the bad spell and brought me
back to myself.

"What *is* the matter, Hofni?" she asked again anxiously, when I awoke a
second night crying once more. "What is it, son? What are you crying for
this time?"

"Oh, mama, I'm so afraid! I saw the old holy man in my dream, the one
grandmother told me about. Oh, mama, let me into bed with you and I'll tell
you all about it. . . . Don't you remember the old holy man that grandmother told us about? She said that he was my grandfather, I mean my great-
grandfather, and he lived in Polonnoye in Chmielnicki's time—didn't you
also tell me all about Chmielnicki and the holy man?—and now I saw him in
my dream, and he went dressed in white shrouds to Chmielnicki's army, and
he said: 'Go ahead and kill me, I surrender my soul to be a martyr of God!
Hear, O Israel, the Lord is one!' And then they killed him. . . . Ah, mama,
are there still holy men now too? Does the blood still come up to your knees
in Polonnoye? And why aren't there holy men in our village too? My friend
Shlumiel told me that in Chmielnicki's time the boys didn't study in the
heder. But once Chmielnicki came to a heder, and he found it full of boys,
and the rabbi and his assistants were teaching them to read, and the rabbi
said to them: 'Don't be afraid, children, we're leaving this filthy, contami
nated world to these cossacks, and we, in the name of our God, are going to
paradise to the holy fathers Abraham, Isaac, and Jacob.' And while Chmiel-

nicki was slaughtering the children, the rabbi said the *Shema* with them, and he said it very loud so that all the mothers came too, and the cossacks killed them too, and they poured their blood on the babies. And then the fathers came too, and they killed them too, and they poured the blood on the mothers. And then—Shlumiel told me all this—all the blood was mixed together, the children's and the rabbi's and the assistants' and the rabbi's wife's and her children's and the mothers' and the fathers', and it flowed like a stream through the city streets until it came to the river, and it turned that red too. Oh, mama, mama, it's so awful!"

My mother bent over me and said, hugging me in her arms: "Don't be afraid, Hofni, don't. Tomorrow I'll have the old midwife come, and she'll rub you down with an egg so that you won't be afraid anymore."

"Zalman," said my mother to my father when he came home from the fair, "it's too much for me. For the past five nights Hofni has awakened with the most awful crying fits. The midwife rubbed him with an egg, and I even had the gypsy woman come, but he just cries and cries. During the day he wastes away in the heder, and when evening comes—the rabbi's assistant told me—he begins to tremble at his own shadow and sobs and screams. It's too much for me. What am I to do?"

"He's just being a foolish little boy!"

And turning to me, my father asked:

"What are you crying for, fool?"

"I'm afraid, papa. I'm afraid of the dark, and of the shadows too. . . ."

"If you were to listen to me, Zalman," my mother said, "I'd advise you to take him to the holy rabbi, may he live. I don't like it, and I have a feeling that it's nothing to make light of. Please, forget about your business and go with him to the rabbi. Do you hear me?"

"Forget about my business?" asked my father with bitter irony. "That's easy enough, there's little to forget in the first place. But where am I to get the money to pay for the journey and for the warm clothes to travel with in weather like this? I won't do it. You're just a woman; you don't know a thing and you can't. I have my reasons, but you won't and can't understand them . . . even if I had the money and the clothing, I wouldn't go. I have reasons that you can't understand! There's no one, no one for me to go to—do you understand me now? But of course you don't! How could you? I'm a man with an open wound in his heart—but what do you know about Hasidism? Even in the *klayzl* hardly anyone understands; even those who go to the rabbi don't understand . . . woe to evil days such as these! The heart is covered with ashes! Heresy, free thought, superficiality, hard times, and exile—and all the while the flame is growing dimmer, the flame is going out. . . . The old rabbi Shneur Zalman is dead. What our hasidic leaders used to understand in the old days, what I learned from my fathers, next to whom I'm not even like a dog lapping at the sea, our rabbi himself doesn't understand today. Don't look so astonished. You're a woman and you can't understand, but we're a shepherdless flock nowadays. We have no father, none. Do you hear me? We have no one to lean on but our Father in heaven. I'm not going. I won't . . ."

"I beg you," my mother pleaded, "don't sin before God with your talk. It's not for the likes of us to stick our heads between mountains."

"Let me be. You're a woman and you don't know a thing. I may be a poor, downtrodden, itinerant Jew, but a Jew I still am . . . and I know what a 'degree' is. I know what the degree of the Baal Shem Tov was, the degree of the Maggid of Mezritsh, the degree of the Grandfather of Shpola, the degree of the Old Man of Chernobyl. But you don't know what a degree is at all. You think of it in the ordinary sense of the word, but you've never understood the holy books—there are secrets that you can't begin to understand. I shouldn't even be talking about them to a woman. Even in the *klayzl* almost no one understands anymore—because you might as well know that a degree isn't simple. It's something very, very deep. I have my reasons that you can't understand . . . if only I could be sure that at least the rabbi knew what a degree was . . . but I doubt even that . . . wherever I look things are falling apart! All that our fathers built is falling apart! And my heart tells me that the worst is yet to come. Everything will be laid waste. All Judaism will be laid waste because of the sins of this generation. I don't know what will become of this son Hofni of ours. A man needs a point of connection— that's also something you can't understand—and the less holiness there is, the more he connects with the *klipa*. And there's no strong tree in sight, no *tzaddik* to protect us. . . . No, I won't go. I'd do better to take him to Shemaiah the Kabbalist. True, he's not one of us; he's a misnagid who thinks that the great chain stopped with Rabbi Isaac Luria and Hayyim Vital, so that he denies that divine inspiration still exists and won't hear of the sacred line of descent from the Baal Shem Tov to the old rabbi Shneur Zalman—that's another secret you can't understand—but a little is still better than nothing. At least he knows the meaning of a degree. . . . Yes, I'll go to him and to no one else."

My mother washed my face, scrubbing my mouth, teeth, and eyes, neatly curled my long earlocks, and helped me into my Sabbath suit, over which she put my winter coat after cleaning it of the layer of mud and dirt that clung to it from the autumn rains. Then she set my cap straight on my head and said, after studying me for a moment and nodding with satisfaction:

"Now listen, Hofni, be a good boy. You're going with your father to Rabbi Shemaiah the Kabbalist, and Rabbi Shemaiah is a great man, your father says, a fine Jew, and a person of high degree. Master of the Universe, one could wish that you grew up to be the same! And really, Hofni, you could some day be like him if you wanted. It would certainly be no disgrace to your holy forefathers, of whom you wouldn't need to feel ashamed even if you were greater than him. Now run along and be a good boy, so that he needn't be cross with you."

"Do you know where you're going?" my father asked me as we stepped from the house.

"To Rabbi Shemaiah the Kabbalist, papa."

"And who is Rabbi Shemaiah the Kabbalist; do you know?"

"Rabbi Shemaiah is a fine Jew, a great Jew. That's what mama told me."

"And that's all? He's a Kabbalist and a man of degree besides! And why are you going to him, Hofni?"

"Why? It must be because of what you told mama."

"Ah, Hofni, if only you understood! Yes, I told your mama, but all she cares about is worldly things, earning a living and getting along in this life. That's why she's upset about your crying. She makes a big fuss over it, but I know it doesn't mean a thing. You're just being a silly, foolish boy, that's why you cry. Really now, why should you cry? What do you see that's worth crying about? You don't have to worry about a living, and as for spiritual things, you're still too young for them. You certainly aren't crying because the Shekhinah is in exile! But because the opportunity presented itself, I'm taking you to Rabbi Shemaiah anyway. It's a good introduction to the study of Torah and the fear of heaven to see the face of an honest man, and men like Rabbi Shemaiah"—my father heaved a sigh—"are becoming scarcer all the time. Who knows whether in your generation they'll still be found at all? The times mock us to our faces. We can feel how this world is no longer our own, how our lives are no longer our lives, how everything has changed on account of our sins . . ."

My father didn't finish his thoughts because he had suddenly noticed that we were standing knee-deep in mud. Taking me in his arms, he rescued me from the quagmire and put me down on a wooden plank that lay by the side of the road. We worked our way along step by step, picking out a path among boards and bits of stone. More than once my father had to help me by picking me up and carrying me from one clear stretch to the next until we reached the Kabbalist. The mud in his front yard was so deep that my father had to pick me up once more and carry me across it. He opened the door and we found ourselves standing in the Kabbalist's prayer room.

"Does the Kabbalist live here in the *klayzl*, papa? I think this must be a *klayzl*, don't you?"

"It's his own private *klayzl*. But he has a house too."

And addressing one of the occupants of the room, my father asked:

"Is the Kabbalist at home?"

"He is."

My father opened a second door that led to the house and we entered a long, dark hallway. He opened another door and we entered a small room.

A rectangular table, painted red, stood several feet from the window. A long bookshelf, across from which were two wooden chairs, ran parallel to it. Along one of the table's short sides stood a stool, and opposite it, at the head of the table, a large chair, in which sat a white-haired old man who was staring intently at a large, thick book that lay on the wood top before him.

My father made a noise, in order, I guessed, to attract the old man's attention.

The Kabbalist looked up and let his glance roam over each corner of the room before it came to rest on my father and me. It frightened me terribly. Sunk deep in their sockets, his large, dark eyes made me think of burning coals; above their slit, guarded pupils loomed a high, white forehead, furrowed up and down with many wrinkles; his earlocks hung down in dishevelment, his beard was long, his gaunt, sallow cheeks had a bluish tincture like that of a corpse. I was too petrified to look back. It was awesome, his gaze; his head seemed holy and majestic to me, though I couldn't have said why. My mind worked its way through a furious profusion of fantasies and thoughts, but all were left off in the middle, and the one thing I knew in the end, the only thing I felt, was that here was a different, a magical and holy world. The room was small and sparse; the Jew sitting in it was no less thin and haggard-looking than all Jews; but what a difference nonetheless! I could feel deep within me how utterly exalted he was, how much holiness and purity were in the air of his small room.

"Well, well, Zalman," the Kabbalist declared. "What brings you here, and who is the young man?"

"The young man is my son, rabbi. Boys will be boys. For the past several nights he's awakened from his sleep crying and screaming terribly. And during the day he wastes away in the heder like a melancholic."

The old man turned to stare at me, and I clutched in fear at the tails of my father's coat.

"Does he study in the heder?"

"Yes, rabbi, with Gad the melamed."

"Does he say the *Shema* every night?"

"He does."

"His *tsitsis* are in order?"

"They are."

"And the *mezzuzahs* in your house too?"

"The *mezzuzahs* too."

"It's nothing, nothing at all; he's a silly boy and he cries. But Zalman, if these little ones cry over nothing, how much is there for us grown men to cry over! Ah, Zalman, tell me, what will become of this son of yours? I'm not saying, God forbid, that you'll expose him to the *klipa*, but I'm afraid may the devil stop his ears—that it may lure him in spite of himself. Who knows what the future holds in store? The Messiah hasn't come, there's nowhere left to turn. Our generation has lost the power of expectancy; we no longer have men of faith; the inner mind has shrunk to nothing; the Shekhinah refuses to descend from her ten spheres. . . . Let me tell you a deep truth, though it isn't easy to fathom: the fathers who send their children to secular schools, the free-thinkers who read forbidden books—none of them have any choice, because holiness has departed this world on account of our many sins. And because holiness has departed and left a vacuum behind, Samael has spread his nets and goes forth to stalk souls. It's as clear as day for whoever has eyes to see . . . holiness is gone from the world . . . woe, woe, woe is us!" The old man raised his voice in a wail. "We no longer have a foothold in this world! There's no room for us anymore! We're in exile together with the Shekhinah. . . ."

I didn't understand a word but the conversation moved me deeply. I understood one thing: that the situation was desperate, the battle fierce. The Evil Urge was a hard opponent. He was an angel—a bad one of course, but an angel nevertheless. Ah, I thought to myself, what can this dreary, muddy, dirty world be worth that we should have to fight for it and suffer for it so much? Hadn't my mother once told me that little babies had to be watched in their cribs so that the demons didn't choke them at night? Even little babies in their cribs had to fight for their lives! And the struggle would go on forever, forever!

"Here's an amulet for you," said my father, interrupting my thoughts. "The rabbi has given it to you. Go to the rabbi and he'll tie it around your neck. Go!"

He took my hand and led me to the Kabbalist.

The Kabbalist tied the amulet around my neck and said in a trembling voice:

"Your name is Hofni? Be a good Jew, Hofni!"

"Amen!" answered my father. He took me by the hand and we left.

I felt like a hero when we left. I was a soldier, I'd been issued my arms—now the fight was up to me.

Translated from the Hebrew
by Hillel Halkin

The Rebbe's Whip

by S. Ansky

Once there came before Reb Shmelke two litigants: a poor man and a well-connected burgher before whom all trembled. Reb Shmelke heard out both sides and gave his verdict in favor of the poor man. The rich man became angry and said he would not submit to the decision. Reb Shmelke replied calmly, "You *will* submit. One must obey a judgment rendered by a rabbi." By then the wealthy man was furious and began screaming, "I laugh at you and all your rabbis." Now Reb Shmelke rose to his full height and cried out, "You must carry out my verdict this very moment! If not, I'll take my whip!"

The burgher was completely beside himself with rage and began heaping insults and curses on the rabbi. Reb Shmelke then shoved his table drawer open a bit. Suddenly, out there sprang the *Nahash Hakadmoni*, the primeval serpent, and wrapped itself around the rich man's neck. Well, well. There was quite a to-do. The rich man shouted and wept, "*Gevald*, Rebbe, forgive me! I will do anything you command, only take away the snake!" Said Reb Shmelke to him, "You must warn your children and your children's children to follow the rebbe and fear his whip." And he removed the snake.

Translated from the Yiddish
by Jeremy Garber

The Death of the Little God
by David Shahar

At ten to seven the *shamash* of the hospital, a bearded Jew with side-curls, knocked on my window. I don't know why he knocked on the window and not at the door. Perhaps he wanted to see whether I was in, or perhaps it was a habit that he had carried over from his days as a beadle at the Central Synagogue when he had had to summon the "good Jews" (as he called them) to midnight prayers. At all events his knocking shattered my dream. The moment I opened my eyes and saw his big head pressed close to the window-pane I knew that the meaning of his visit was that the Little God was dead, but looking at his abundant, untidy beard and at his blinking eyes I refused to believe it.

Startled, I jumped out of my bed and hurriedly opened the door. He came in without uttering a word and, nonchalantly sitting down on a chair, he smoothed his beard with both his hands and placed its tip in his mouth, chewing it with his false teeth. At the same time his eyes roamed over the room till they rested on a picture of a naked woman reclining on her elbow and staring indifferently at the world. The expression on his face hardened and he quickly looked away from the picture to the bookcase. Next to the gaudy pocket books there stood six heavy, old, calf-bound volumes worn at the edges with years and use. For a minute he hesitated, but then he got up and looked at the volumes. I glanced at him sideways, ready to see on his face an expression of wonder mixed with disappointment, for the six calf-bound volumes were neither Talmudic commentaries nor prayer books but the first edition of Hugo's *Les Misérables*, which appeared about one hundred years ago in Brussels.

He pulled out the middle volume, wiped the dust off the cover with his sleeve, sniffed at the smell of old books which it gave off, and glanced at me to see whether I was ready to go or whether he had time to look at the book. I prepared two cups of coffee, one for him and one for myself. He opened the book in the middle, frowned at the sight of the Latin characters, shut it, and returned it to its place with a dry and bored face, like one accustomed to all sorts of oddities. He recited *shebakol* over the coffee and drank it slowly and deliberately. After I too had finished my cup it suddenly occurred to me to sweep the floor, but I did not do so because I did not want to delay him too long.

We went out and only after we had started walking was I seized by a hot and cold fever and by the need to hurry. I had to make haste lest I should be too late. I walked quickly, taking big strides, till we reached the bus stop. We both jumped onto the bus without paying attention to the people who were standing in the queue. Perhaps they did not protest or shout at us because they could see that we were agitated and pressed for time. If there had been any young people in the queue, people who stand up for their rights and who are quick to get angry, they would doubtless have tried to prevent us from boarding the bus, but in fact there were only some old and weak Jews, experts in suffering and accustomed to being deprived of their due, and they did not say a word. They looked at us with their sad eyes and murmured, "Ay, ay." Perhaps they even understood that we were hurrying to the chamber of the dead, on the floor of which the Little God was lying cold and silent, covered with a white sheet and with candles burning all around him.

In the bus the *shamash* took out a tin box which had once been ornamented with colored pictures but which now showed a white, worn-away, tinny nakedness. He opened it and took out half a cigarette—all the cigarettes in the box had been cut in half. He put the cigarette in an amber holder and lit it. Looking at him, I wondered what was going on in the head of the old Jew. He was wearing a black hat, his face was wrinkled and brown like old parchment, and his red, flattened nose dipped into the sea of his mustache and beard. The holes in his socks peeped above his heavy boots and even from afar he gave off a smell of stale sweat mixed with Turkish tobacco. All in all he looked old and calm amid sorrow and disasters and many funerals—the funerals of my generation and of the generation which preceded mine. It was he who had seen my grandfather to his grave, and now he would accompany the Little God, who had died in his very prime if not in the bloom of his youth.

On the way to the hospital we passed many people and they all looked strange and distant and absorbed in their own business. Only a few of them walked calmly; mostly they had tense and worried faces and the children alone seemed happy.

I ran into the hospital and the *shamash* hurried after me. I wanted to go up into the ward where the Little God had been lying and to ask the chief nurse, "How's the Little God? Is he any better? I am here, ready to do everything that's necessary." But he drew me to the chamber of the dead. Before I entered it he held me and rent the lapel of my jacket and then took out of his pocket a small black skullcap, which he put on my head. I knew that he would do everything that was necessary—that he would conclude the business with the Chevra Kedisha, decide on the site of the grave, and handle all the other funeral arrangements. He was the only solid basis in the void and formlessness, around which the darkness was in flux on the face of the deep.

When I went into the chamber of the dead I saw the long body of the Little God, enshrouded in white sheets, stretched out full length on the floor. My tremulousness vanished completely and one great wish took hold of me—to run out and to escape from the place as quickly as possible. Most of the candles around the corpse had already burned out and only a few were still flickering in the stench of the room. In a corner an old blind man was sitting and reciting psalms—a task which had occupied him for the last forty years, ever since he had been hired for the job. The *shamash* put an end to the silence in which he had been immersed since he knocked on my window at ten to seven, leaned toward me, whispered in Yiddish, "A finever," and then went out to collect the ten men needed for the *minyan*.

"That means that this *minyan* is going to cost me a fiver," I said to myself. "Half a pound each." I went to the corpse, lifted the white sheet a bit, and saw a thin cold arm on which death had spread a greenish yellowness. "That's forbidden, that's forbidden," somebody suddenly called out. The man who had stuck his red face into the chamber nodded at me as if I were a naughty child. I hurriedly covered the arm and went outside.

"You," he said to me, "are you a relative of the deceased?"

I did not know how to answer him satisfactorily so I started to fumble in my pockets, looking for my cigarettes. The man stuck the red swollen fingers of his left hand into the packet and nimbly extracted a cigarette. He jingled the collection box which he was holding in his right hand. I remembered him from my early childhood. He always followed funerals with a sad face, rattling his collection box and calling out, "Charity wards off death, charity wards off death." It was said that he owned two buildings in the Mahne-Yehudah quarter and one in Nachlat Shivah. His daughter was a nice buxom girl and all the boys used to talk about her reverently till she married an English policeman and went with him to England when the British left the country.

"I was a lodger in his apartment," I answered him.

"Ah?" He threw out the syllable like a question mark while he lit the cigarette.

"I lived in his apartment," I repeated.

"He was a good man," he declared, after blowing out a cloud of smoke through the nostrils of his big red nose, which was pitted like a sieve. He looked around and, seeing no one nearby, put his face close to mine and whispered confidentially, as if we were two old friends, "A good man, but a bit touched . . . too much thinking."

Only after the second cigarette did it occur to me to put a coin in his box. Since the coin was safely in the box, and since none of the deceased's family—or anyone else, for that matter—had come, as people say, to pay their last respects, and since the *minyan* of beggars whom the *shamash* had gathered were the only people in sight, he fluttered his eyes, made a curtsy in the French fashion of all things, and went on his way. After he had gone one of the *minyan* of beggars approached me, inspected me from head to foot, and finally murmured sympathetically and compassionately. "A small family, eh?" Then as a consolatory afterthought of a more philosophical order he added, "It is not good that a man should be alone."

"I am not one of his family," I answered him. "I live in his apartment. He had a two-room apartment and I live in one of the rooms."

"So . . . so . . . And what did he die of?"

"A brick fell on his head," I told him.

He rolled his eyes in wonder, as if I had told a joke in bad taste, turned his back, and rejoined his companions.

"It really is like an odd joke," I reflected. "He was walking along harmlessly enough past the scaffolding of a seven-story apartment house under construction when a brick fell on his head; he instantly lost consciousness and died two days later. And that's that. All over. And indeed he once told me in a moment of confidence that his whole life was nothing but a joke. 'All in all,' he said, 'I am nothing but a practical joke of somebody else's making.' "

And who was that somebody? He certainly meant his Little God. He had a sort of theory that God was small. Once he had gathered a couple of students around him and for two hours he had expounded his views about the divinity; ever since, he had been nicknamed "The Little God." In his big, lucid, somewhat childish handwriting he had even left a paper entitled "Reflections on Man's Concept of the Dimensions of God in Time and Space." Several days before the brick fell on his head he had started to translate the paper into English. "It seems," he told me, "that not until the gentiles accept my views will Jewish scholars listen to my system." He was a physicist by profession, and until he dedicated himself to his idea about the dimensions of God, which are, according to him, much smaller than we can imagine—indeed so small that our minds cannot grasp their smallness—up to the time he sank into big thoughts about the smallness of God, he was, one might say, like everybody else, or at any rate like any other man of science. He was tall and thin and stooped, his eyes were gray and slanting, deep wrinkles ran down from his longish nose to the sides of his mouth, flaxen tufts flapped from the sides of his bald head, and all in all he looked as if he were constantly apologizing for his long figure and big arms and awkward hands and, in general, for occupying space in the world. One could not tell how old he was. Sometimes, when he smiled, he looked like a giant baby. But usually he did not smile and sadness flowed down his face, an ancient sadness.

It's strange that he was happy—when he wasn't sad. He would sing and even dance and drink heavily—but it's perhaps as well not to go into the details of his behavior when he was happy, for at the end of each attack of happiness he would fall into the hands of a Greek prostitute and talk lovingly to her, in Yiddish of all languages, till he fell asleep on her lap. On such occasions he would also wave his fists and shout at the top of his voice that he hated humanity. "I love men, and better still, women, but humanity, dear God, I hate humanity. I can love Yankil or Shmeril or Beril"—he would hit the table with his fists—"but *giwald, geschrien*, I hate Jewry." Even when he sobered up and was in control of all his faculties he would avoid any human contacts, and things came to such a pass that he was often attacked by a fear of crowds. Then he would shut himself up in his room, close the shutters, draw the curtains, plug his ears with cotton wool, and cringe on the edge of his couch, praying silently to his Little God to save him from humanity.

When I came to rent the room in his apartment about a year before he died, his condition was already pretty serious—or so his colleagues and other people who knew him thought. He himself was sure he had climbed as high, in spirit, as a man could. By then he had already abandoned his work in the Physics Department "in order to dedicate myself to philosophical contemplation," as he said. His colleagues nodded sagely and talked of the "attacks" which more and more often laid him low. For a long time he had gone out of his way to avoid people and disdained to enter buses or restaurants or cinemas. Apart from going out in the early morning or late in the evening to do his daily shopping, with which even he could not dispense, apart from these excursions which he undertook as if compelled by the devil, he would sit shut up in his room sailing on his thoughts about the concepts of God. He would sit for two or three weeks, or sometimes even for a month, until happiness started to ferment in his limbs. The hummings and whisperings that emanated from his room at an ever increasing tempo gave me advance notice of such happiness. Like a volcano on the verge of bursting out, he would walk up and down in his room, turn on the radio, open the curtains, and lift the shutters to let in the sunshine and noise of the street like an overflowing river. Finally he would wash, shave his month-old beard, put on a white shirt, don his Sabbath suit—the only one in his cupboard—and run out like a prisoner escaping from jail.

During the last year of his life his whole income consisted only of the rent he received from me and of a small allowance made to him by one of the Zionist institutions. Throughout the time I lived in his apartment he only once told me about his life in the past and about his family—and that was when he was brought home by the fat, aging Greek prostitute. I learned from him that his father had been a Zionist of some standing, important enough to have a settlement named after him. He had two sisters, one a communist who had married a gentile, and the other, who had remained single, a doctor who had specialized in tropical diseases and had gone to care for the Negroes in Central Africa. Had he told more, perhaps I could have found some clue to the way of life of the daughters of the Zionist who had not had the good fortune to immigrate to Israel and who had been murdered by the Nazis, but the Little God was not communicative and I had to content myself with what he divulged.

And so during the last months of his life he was driven from seclusion to the most dubious and strange friendships, and from elation and belief in his original thinking, a belief bordering on a strange boastfulness, to the depths of despair. Then one night, some two weeks before that brick fell on his head, he gave me a terrible fright.

From eleven o'clock that night a wintry cold had prevailed over the sleeping world and a silent wind had brought layers of low cloud which completely covered the sky and the sickle of moon. I had closed the window and made my bed. I had fallen asleep a few minutes after I had gone to bed and would have gone on sleeping happily till morning had I not been woken by a muffled cry of fright which set my nerves on edge.

The Little God was groaning in his room like a wounded jackal. Then suddenly he came and knocked faintly at my door. I braced myself, overcame my fear, and even remembered to arm myself with a ruler before I slowly opened the door, ready to strike him over the head if he jumped at me in his madness. His long body was clad in pajamas which were too short for him and his feet were bare. As soon as he appeared in all his shame and awkwardness I let the ruler drop and pushed it under the bed with my foot. He stood in the middle of my room like a man fleeing a catastrophe and urgently in need of shelter who suddenly finds that the anticipated shelter is illusory.

"Excuse me," he muttered, "please excuse me. I shouted in my sleep. I must have given you a real fright. I myself was frightened to death— otherwise I would not have shouted. But now it's all over and I must go back to bed. Yes, I must go back to sleep, but really I'd prefer to remain here with you a little while, a little longer, for I'm afraid to go back to sleep. These nightmares are worse than hell. Perhaps you'd like to come to my room and I'll make you tea? Till I calm down?"

"No," I said to him, "I'll make some tea. You just sit down here."

He obeyed me and sat down on a chair. He knew he could not have made tea, for his hands were still trembling. He held his cup with both hands but it shook and tea dripped onto his hands and knees.

In his dream his father had come to him. He was wearing only a sleeveless vest and short underpants, and the Little God burst out laughing and his heart wept and his teeth chattered and his eyes shed tears. "How is it, Father," he said, and he pointed at him, but his laughter and the chattering of his teeth choked his voice, "how is it that all of a sudden you decided to put on short underpants like a modern dandy? All your life you have worn long woolen underpants because of the chronic cold you have had since your youth."

"Here in Eretz Israel," said his father, "one does not need woolen underpants."

"What are you saying, Father? This is not Eretz Israel! Look, the fields around us are covered with snow and the trees are standing naked and a frosty wind penetrates to the marrow."

"Stuff and nonsense, my boy, you're talking nonsense."

While the Little God was talking to his father the scene changed to the father's study. A blue Keren Kayemet collection box was standing on the table with the carved legs. A map of Palestine, with all the Keren Kayemet land colored green, was hanging on the eastern wall. Opposite the map, on the western wall, the faces of Herzl and Nordau stared down from within their golden frames. When the Little God approached the pictures in order to examine them more closely he was confronted by the faces of his two sisters. The sisters, he saw, looked as they had when they were in their first year at the gymnasia. His father went to the table and spread out on it an issue of the *Welt,* the Zionist organ, which grew and grew till it covered the whole table. Then his father sat on the table, crossed his arms over his chest, which was covered only by the thin vest, and said, "Now tell me what's going on in the world."

"The world is growing bigger, Father, and God is growing smaller." His father jerked his head back and laughed heartily in the way he used to laugh when he was in a good humor. Protruding veins twined on his forehead and his belly heaved as he laughed and laughed until tears came to his eyes and his voice choked and one could not tell whether he was laughing or crying.

"God is growing smaller, Father, and now, already, compared to an ant, God looks like a flea compared to an elephant. He is still alive, wriggling and writhing under the weight of the world He created, but it is only a matter of time before His death agonies cease."

"And how long will it take before He disappears?" asked his father, his face becoming serious.

"Two or three weeks, perhaps less."

"Then this is the end."

"Yes, this is the end."

On hearing this his father jumped off the table and started to knock his head against the map of Israel. He knocked his head and cried out with pain, knocked and cried, and with each knock his body became smaller, and his son knew that only he could save him but his whole body became stiff and numb and he could not move a limb. He froze with cold and fright and saw how his father was becoming smaller and smaller, knocking his head against the wall and vanishing, till nothing remained of him but the reverberations of the knocking.

Translated from the Hebrew
by H. M. Daleski

The Disappearance
by Edmond Jabès

The day's freedom consists in the light's secret climb back to the beginnings of the shores deserted by men.

The heart beats in the emptiness of the astonished body. Its form will come from the *other*.

Thus the world will form the world in freeing it.

Thus God, within Himself, will come to terms with the Face.

The sage dipped his reed pen into the inkwell, pulled it out, and held it for a few moments, as if in doubt, above the page where he had not noted anything yet that day. Then, to his pupil's surprise, he drew a small circle in a corner of the blotter he always kept within reach.

"This circle," he said, "which the blotter has made into a point invaded by night, is God."

"Why did you want the circle to turn into a black point? And why should this stain among so many others on your blotter be God?" the disciple asked.

"Your question is that of the Lord," replied the sage.

"If my question is that of the Lord," said the disciple, "I know now that God has created me in His image."

* * *

At this time before time, when life was only a bare death with weak lungs, one insignificant point in space contained, like a bubble, all the wanderings of the worlds.

When it burst it freed the universe, but gave form to exile.

God had disappeared, existing only in Creation.

Being the Principle of Unity—a circle tightening in infallible memory of the circle—He was going to become the dazzling center of clear absence.

Never again will we escape exile.

The book is among its true stages.

Translated from the French
by Rosmarie Waldrop

Mirror and Scarf

by *Edmond Jabès*

> *"We will gather images and images of images until the last—which is blank. This one we will agree on."*
>
> —Reb Carasso

Mordohai Simhon claimed the silk scarf he wore around his neck was a mirror.

"Look," he said, "my head is separated from my body by a scarf. Who dares give me the lie if I say I walk with a knotted mirror under my chin?

"The scarf reflects a face, and you think it is made of flesh.

"Night is the mirror. Day the scarf. Moon and sun reflected features. But my true face, brothers, where was it lost?"

At his death, a large scar was discovered on his neck.

The meaning of this anecdote was discussed by the rabbis.

Reb Alphandery, in his authority as the oldest, spoke first.

"A double mirror," he said, "separates us from the Lord, so that God sees Himself when trying to see us, and we, when trying to see Him, see only our own face."

"Is appearance no more than the reflections thrown back and forth by a set of mirrors?" asked Reb Ephraim. "You are no doubt alluding to the soul, Reb Alphandery, in which we see ourselves mirrored. But the body is the place of the soul, just as the mountain is the bed of the brook. The body has broken the mirror."

"The brook," continued Reb Alphandery, "sleeps on the summit. The brook's dream is of water, as is the brook. It flows for us. Our dreams extend us.

"Do you not remember this phrase of Reb Alsem's: 'We live out the dream of creation, which is God's dream. Evenings, our own dreams snuggle down into it like sparrows in their nests'?

"And did not Reb Hames write: 'Birds of night, my dreams explore the immense dream of the sleeping universe?

"Are dreams the limpid discourse between the facets of a crystal block?" continued Reb Ephraim. "The world is of glass. You know it by its brilliance, night or day."

"The earth turns in a mirror. The earth turns in a scarf," replied Reb Alphandery.

"The scarf of a dandy with a nasty scar," said Reb Ephraim.

> (*"Words are inside breath, as the earth is inside time."*
> —Reb Mares.)

And Yukel said:

"The bundle of the Wandering Jew contains the earth and more than one star."

"Whatever contains is itself contained," said Reb Mawas.

The story I told you, as well as the commentaries it inspired, will be recorded in the book of the eye. The ladder urges us beyond ourselves. Hence its importance. But in a void, where do we place it?

> (*"God is sculpted."*
> —Reb Moyal.)

Translated from the French
by Rosmarie Waldrop

The Angel of the Alphabet

by David Meltzer

At the end of a sentence. The dot. A stop. A black circle. Its edges rainbow like petroleum like linoleum like bubbles blown out of plastic hoops. The period. The end. A stop.

Black round sphere on the page. Black dot holding all the alphabets and words inside itself.

Did you ever see the angel who wears a curved and no doubt jewel-powered device of glass and metals looped about into mad-scientist spires and gyres and all of it hooked to transistor batteries worn around his arms like snakes? He puts his mouth on a tuba mouthpiece and blows four notes which you can see moving up the tubing and turning into one black dot rushing up through loops and hoops of metals and glass. The black dot goes up to the top shaped like an upside-down icecream brass cone and out it goes. Into the air. Straight to the open book's blank page and it lands right in the white center.

Black dot in the center of a page surrounded by white. The period. The end. A stop.

Another angel who wasn't in the room before appears through the roof in a flurry of splashing light like overflowing fireworks. And lands before the large open book and shuts his eyes and slowly lets his wings fold together. Light remaining from his flight falls onto the floor where it dissolves like snowflakes.

—I am the Angel of the Alphabet, he says to the open book.

The book says nothing.

But the black dot widens in the page's center and opens like a yawn like an apple sliced into many sudden wedges. And the Angel of the Alphabet seems pleased and flutters his wings like a helicopter and arises to the ceiling and soaks through it like sunlight.

Period. The end. A stop. The room is empty again. Its walls as white as blank pages in the book. There is nothing in the room. Period. Except the book which is on a round table made from sturdy wood and engraved and carved with stars, moons, alphabets, hieroglyphs, petroglyphs, runes going around the edges of the table.

Letter into letter into letter. The black dot splinters into black shapes of lovely designs. Flowers quickly blossoming. People walking. Each letter as it forms itself looks like something remembered from life. An ox, a coathook, a dancer, a room, a staff, a pitchfork, a stem, a seed, a weed.

Letters appear on the page and meet each other to form words. They stand in groups and sing. They discuss each other's meanings. They remember and they forget.

A black angel spreads its black wings through a wall of the room and enters. He is happy to see the page of the book alive with his blackness. His shadow is like a letter on the white wall.

A white angel, entirely white, spreads its wings and enters through the wall as if breaking through water after diving deep into a lake and then pushing up and up to where sunlight wobbles and shatters on the water.

The two angels stand side by side before the book. Their black and white shadows.

And we know that the black angel shuts his eyes as if asleep and all the letters and words float to him and he inhales them as if smelling a stew. And we know how he then turns an eye-blinking white from head to toe, dazzling.

And we know how the white angel smiles to see the book page suddenly empty of marks. And we are ready when he shuts his eyes and the pages of the book turn faster than a cartoon and become a small snowstorm which the white angel inhales and, to our amazement, turns a magnificent black.

And later, when the sun and moon and stars have turned inside out into letters and pages and words and books, and a century of amazing seconds has gone, and it's hard to know what's happening, but nobody's worried, a comforting voice says to you or me or to nobody in particular that the black dot is the planet of the alphabet. The alphabet atom. All alphabets live in harmony in the period. The stop. The end.

And the blank page, white and empty, is the alphabet's sky.

And sometimes what has been said seems to be true. The letters and words are stars in the white sky of the page. Or the white page is part of a huge letter with dots and spots of black sky poking through it.

And now what do you say if we start all over again?

At the end of a sentence. Dot. Stop. Black circle. Beginning again.

Midrash of the Alphabet

by Rabbi Yehiel Poupko

Twenty-six generations before the creation of the world, the twenty-two letters of the alphabet descended from God's crown. They gathered around God, each one vying to be the instrument of creation.

The first to step forward was Tav. "Master of the Universe, it is through me that You will give the Torah to Israel by the hand of Moshe. Let it be Your will to create the world through me."

But God answered, saying, "No, it will not be you because in the days to come I will place you as a sign of death on the foreheads of men."

And Shin came forward. "Master of the Universe, create Your world through me since Your own name, Shaddai, begins with me."

But God answered, saying, "You are the first letter of the word *sheker*— lie—and I will not create My world through you."

And Resh stepped forward begging to be chosen. "I who am the first letter of the word *rahamim*—mercy—should certainly be chosen to create Your world."

But God answered, saying, "No, for you, Resh, stand at the head of the word *ra*—wicked—and you cannot be chosen."

And so it went. Each letter successively came before God begging to be chosen—only to be told of its evil essence and its unsuitability to serve as God's tool.

Until it came to the turn of the letter Bet. When Bet came before God, he pleaded, "Master of the Universe, may it be Your will to create the world through me since every person daily will praise You through me, saying 'Barukh—Blessed be the Lord forever and ever.' And God granted the petition of Bet, saying "Blessed be he that comes in the name of the Lord." And God created the world through Bet as it is written "Bereshith—in the beginning—God created the heaven and earth."

And when, in the beginning, God pondered the creation of the Kingdom of Night, lo, the letters that had eagerly rushed to His aid earlier in cosmic time, each one vying to be the instrument of creation, could not be found. Their deafening clamor, once heard at the creation of the Kingdom of Light, was no more. All that could be heard was the chaotic, primordial spirit of God, fluttering over the vast emptiness. And God summoned all the letters to appear before Him, but lo, they had all abandoned their stations in the four crowns that uphold the universe. And so the spirit of God hovered over the world, searching and searching for His lost letters, calling out, wailing like a lost dove, "Where are you, where are you? What has become of My beloved ones?"

But the holy letters did not answer Him. As He cried in despair, the angel Katriel came before Him and said, "Master of the Universe, do You not know where Your letters can be found? They have all fled to the one sanctuary left on earth."

And God did not know whereof Katriel spoke. And so Katriel took Him to Jerusalem, to the Wall, and there, in its cracks and holes hewn out of rock by centuries of prayer, there had the letters taken refuge.

And God said to the letter Tav, "It is My will to create the Kingdom of Night through you because I have set you as a sign of death upon the foreheads of men."

Tav replied, "Oh, Master of the Universe, true, in Your eyes I may be a sign of death. But since the receiving of the Torah at Sinai, the people of Israel have made of me a sign of the Torah. I am the first letter of the word Torah. I shall not be the tool to create the Kingdom of Night."

God then said to the letter Shin, "You are the first letter of the word sheker and so you are the symbol of lying and deceit. Therefore it is My will to create the Kingdom of Night through you."

And the Shin replied, "True, as You see it I stand for lying and deceit; but the people of Israel, through their actions have understood that I am the first letter of the word shalom. I am the sign of peace. And so the Kingdom of Night cannot be created through me."

God then said to the letter Resh, "You are the first letter in the word *ra*—evil. You are the symbol of evil and wickedness. Therefore it is My will to create the Kingdom of Night through you."

And the Resh replied, "True, as You see it I stand for evil and wickedness, but the people of Israel, through their actions, have understood that I am the first letter of the word *rahamim*—mercy. I stand for love and kindness and mercy. Through me the Kingdom of Night cannot be created."

And so it went for each and every letter. Each letter was told of its evil essence and its suitability to be God's tool in creating the Kingdom of Night; and each letter rebelled, telling God that they no longer belonged to the evil qualities, for the actions of the people of Israel had transformed them into holiness.

All this, all this and it seemed as if God would have no means by which to create the Kingdom of Night—until it came time for the letter Aleph. All the letters had rebelled except for Aleph, for God had a power over Aleph that He did not have over the other letters. All the other letters are of this world and the world above, of God and of person, spiritual and physical. But the letter Aleph is only of God and of the world above—completely spiritual. It has no sound: it cannot be pronounced. It is *all* God, *all* spiritual. The only letter that the people of Israel heard at Sinai was the silent Aleph, the first letter in God's name, the first letter in the word *emet*—truth. So God took the holiest letter of all, the humblest letter of all, the letter of Sinai, the letter of His name, the first letter of *emet*—truth. He took away Aleph from *emet* and left *met*—death. And with Aleph, God created the Kingdom of Night.

The Mind of Genesis

by David Slabotsky

Rabbi Mikhal used to say: "For the study of Torah one must have the Mind of Genesis, otherwise one becomes lost in the doctrine." Illustrating the Mind of Genesis Rabbi Mikhal related the following tale:

"Rabbi Yehuda lived in the ghetto of Zlochtov where he studied Talmudic Law at the hand of Rabbi Lev. A dedicated man, Rabbi Yehuda would stay in his room for days on end with a single phrase which Rabbi Lev had assigned to him. Yet it was clear to Rabbi Yehuda, in spite of his devotion, that his soul would ultimately perish in the elegant disputes of Talmudic Law, for while his fellow disciples grew strong in their faith, scholarship merely succeeded in leading him farther and farther away from the source of the Torah, and rather than bringing a deepening joy to his daily life it was turning him into a bitter sage and souring his faith.

"Rather than come to grief through the wisdom of others, Rabbi Yehuda devised the following plan: Since the Torah was equally holy in all Its parts, every word and every letter possessed the gateway into eternal life and profound understanding. Choosing a single letter, he could reach in its union with the Sacred Name to the Sacred Name Itself. Not knowing which of the letters to choose, he settled upon the Aleph, the first in the alphabet.

"Rabbi Yehuda drew the Aleph on his wall with a piece of chalk and sat before it with great devotion, representing as it did the entire Torah. He no longer visited Rabbi Lev and was never seen in the study hall or synagogue of Zlochtov. The Aleph had become his only resource, his only form of worship. The Aleph sustained him even on the Sabbath and the Day of Atonement.

"Time passed and Rabbi Yehuda discovered that he was no longer able to distinguish between the Aleph and the wall on which it had been drawn, and rather than discontinue meditation he simply included the wall along with the Aleph in his mental devotions.

"Time passed and Rabbi Yehuda discovered that he was no longer able to distinguish the wall on which the Aleph had been drawn from the adjoining walls of his room, and rather than discontinue meditation he simply included those walls along with the Aleph in his mental devotions.

"Time passed and Rabbi Yehuda was forced to include the entire ghetto of Zlochtov along with Rabbi Lev and the disciples, all of Galicia, Poland and Russia, Europe, America and the Orient. In fact he carried in his mind at one time the entire creation including the planets and the kingdom of heaven.

"Time passed and the universe proceeded without interruption from its source through the mind of Rabbi Yehuda, who, sustained by the Sacred Name, no longer sought out the doctrines or laws of his faith."

Concerning this tale a student asked Rabbi Mikhal: "Regardless of his perfection can one be called a rabbi and not participate in the doctrine or law?" Rabbi Mikhal replied: "What participation could you expect from such a man? His mind is the Mind of Genesis. The sun may rise and set, the days are days and the nights are nights, but still in Rabbi Yehuda's mind the Lord has not as yet divided between them."

Aleph/Bet

by Jorge Plescoff

Still feeling the midday heat in my half-closed eyes, I couldn't help but notice the white piece of paper that was lying in the place where my good friend had been.

Opening it, I saw to my surprise that it contained a single letter of the Hebrew alphabet, Aleph.

I could have thrown it away, but I kept it in my hand. Aleph. I walked slowly, absorbed both by the possible meaning of the letter and the blue of the sky. The sky is blue in my city. It's a good blue, a real blue, not a painted one. It's so blue that it hurts. It encircles the sun with its mystical cloak. But I was traveling by foot and in this way, I arrived at a little synagogue that was almost on my way. "Hear O Israel," the voices intoned; with Aleph in hand, I was looking for its meaning.

All the bodies leaned over the books, so no one noticed my arrival. I sat in a corner waiting for the services to end. When the prayer leader descended from the platform I went up to him, handing him the paper. His eyes looking at the letter questioned me while his mouth repeated "Aleph." "Yes," I answered, "but what does it mean?" He put his finger over his mouth in a gesture of silence, returned the paper to my hand, and walked away. The scene repeated itself several times with various members of the congregation until one of them, observing perhaps my growing irritation, took the paper and wrote "Bet" on the other side.

An Aleph and Bet were written on their respective sides of my piece of paper without my understanding their meaning.

But it couldn't go on like this. Boiling inside, I threw the paper away. I stood in the synagogue alone, without the sky, without water, and with the fire that was tormenting me.

It was cold and dark and I regretted having read it.

Besides, I'm not a Jew. I mean, I am a Jew, well, I entered the covenant, but it never really affected me. It's not that I deny God's existence, on the contrary, but has anyone ever seen him?

Witches don't affect me, nor do spiders, although I wouldn't want to be poisoned to death. But this little matter of the paper was beginning to annoy me. However, this is one of my faults, if I want to know something, I won't back off.

I left the synagogue and made my way to Mount Zion, for "Out of Zion shall go forth the Law." It's strange that I should remember those words. An Aleph and a Bet in my hands and a promise in my thoughts.

God promised many things to my people: a benediction for each suffering. The latter have been accumulated over the last millennia; the former is yet to be seen. Of course we believe that the calf is cast and we don't see under our feet. But, after all, *Out of Zion shall go forth the Law*, the Aleph and the Bet.

And the calf was made of gold, today it is iron. What would Moses have done? Would he hurl a computer at us? A small one, a compact, pocket-size, one, made in Hong Kong. And forty more years until a generation is burned.

But I have to know what Aleph and Bet are.

I looked at the paper again, and there it was, clear, black on white, a Bet. When I turned it over I didn't believe my eyes. The paper was blank, white, without any mark of what had been there. Had anything been there? I looked and looked but found nothing. There was no Aleph to be found. The Bet was all I had left. Disillusioned, I lost all interest and I angrily walked away from there, without the paper, without the law, but with a great desire to forget. I walked along with a firm stride until an old man leaning on a doorpost called me over to him. He whispered the first line of Genesis in my ear: *The Beginning created Elohim the heavens and the earth.*

He smiled and I, without comprehending, took the book and looked at that sentence which began with the letter Bet. But the Aleph was not included. His smile remained, indicating the Bet.

"And the Aleph?" I asked.

"The Beginning created Elohim."

"The God of Israel?" I shouted.

"Neither Aleph nor Bet," I heard with all my ears. And I fainted right there on the spot.

When I regained consciousness, I no longer asked myself, I only smiled.

Translated from the Spanish
by Yishai Tobin

The Alphabet Came to Me
by Jerome Rothenberg

the Alphabet came to me in a dream he said I am Alphabet take your light from me & I thought you are numbers first before you are sound you are the fingers' progression & you end in the fist a solid mass against the world but the alphabet was dark like my hand writing these words he rose not as light at first though issuing from light but fear a double headed body with the pen a blacker line at center *A* began it but in Hebrew not a vowel a choked sound it was the throat the larynx stopped the midrash said contained all sound sound of alphabet initial to all speech as one or zero called it WORK OF CREATION in my dream a creature more than solid more than space or mass or distance & he said all numbers & all sounds converge here but I knew it I said that I would count my way into the vision grooved thus with numbers & with sound the distances to every side of us as in a poem

Staraya Ushitza's Rabbi

by Isaac Goldemberg

Someone asked him for the meaning of time one day. He wanted forty days to think it over. He took to the woods and camped out in a cave. Ideas swirled in his head. He undressed from head to toe. He purified himself in the water running over the rocks. He made the darkness his bed. He crawled down endless tunnels till his hands bled. He recited passages from the Bible under his breath. And he sometimes wondered if he had died. Meanwhile circles got deeper around his eyes. His memory started slipping. Bats had swarmed into the cave. He could hear them copulating in the silence. Gradually he was losing his patience. He went deeper into the cave. He figured his children might be out looking for him. He answered in a voice like thunder: Time is in the Kabbalah. Time is an ostrich's egg. Time is a devil with a thousand horns. He tried to think but mirages ravaged his mind.

Translated from the Spanish
by David Unger

The Number of the Name

by Mario Satz

Did Lionel ever think that his hands could be used for something better than writing and caressing the worn back of a book? His hands, which weren't ugly, nevertheless possessed the rigidity of the Arabic *hamsah* and the Hebrew *yad* with which one reads the Pentateuch. Even while playing with his magnifying glass, with the crystal sphere that would rub against his dark trousers now and again as if it wanted to communicate its translucent virtues to his body, his fingers would remain together, almost motionless, serious. His wife, who never spoke to me of Lionel as a lover out of modesty or a lack of experience, was silent about his nonexistent caresses. When he moved his hands to explain some number or letter to me, the Kabbalist would pay less attention to his gestures than to his words, and less to his words than to his meaning, which always evaporated after being understood, and so quickly that I could hardly understand what my friend was pointing at, when, after scratching his beard, in his particular way, another maxim or phrase shook my heart in the work of his sanguine conversation.

"The greatness of an invisible God," Lionel used to say, "rests on our being able to love his absence as well."

And thus, as remote as the gestures of Sedar, from the imaginary dancer who was irrationally moved by love, Lionel would repeatedly speak to us about the desert. A place, perhaps, that he may have never known, but that corresponded with his most brilliant meditations. As if, through the secret passageway of the metaphors in the choice of his words and the turn of a phrase, one could see from afar a small cave in Pekiin, in the Upper Galilee, where Rabbi Shimon bar Yohai and his son Rabbi Eliezer meditated, buried to the waist, patiently caressing the sand, while the Roman soldiers tortured the Jews for not succumbing and not accepting the laws of the invader. A double concealment and revelation, the cavern, a minimum amount of nourishment, the continuous meditation and finally the sanctity of which the Zohar tells. The life of that great master and his son was the perfect model of sanctity for Lionel. That is why he didn't mind living in the misery of Sixth Street, poor and apart, surrounded by a few friends—Tim, until his death, Asparagus, Max Ferdinand, and so many other madmen and vagabonds who would come to his house to eat every Saturday, sharing the eucharistic monologue more than the bread of a man for whom the Holocaust, the most irrefutable proof of the absurdity of the world, made him understand even after denying it that he was a Jew and would continue to be one forever. That meant more than the precepts and phylacteries, living and radiating light, *or lagoyim*, "a light unto the nations," mentioned by the prophets. Below Lionel's hand, the place where the wrist is lost in the forearm, underneath the skin, the Name was tattooed, more than a numeral, a destiny, more than a number, an accusation.

Remembering his tale of the apparition of the Name and the epileptic attack that followed the discovery set my feelings on end. It happened, naturally, after Lionel already knew how to read Hebrew and was familiar with the *gematria* value of the letters. It was the kind of summer afternoon when New York smells like a burned ashcan, sweat, and chewing gum. He was thinking of the Tetragrammaton. Of the mystery of its timelessness and, at the same time, its immanence . . . How can one not enter, by the guttural, aspirate sound of that extraordinary language, the lost and buried roads, dark and despite all, throbbing of a modality of being that, understood even in its final tremblings, reveals the greatness of Jewish genius, the jealous guardian of the Alphabet of the World? The modality of being which, understood as Lionel understood it, could offer in our infamous and raucous times an oasis of meditation and living waters to those who, with the reverence of a prayer on their lips, approach the Tetragrammaton. The fact that they stopped pronouncing it after a certain historical period does not mean that its significance has disappeared; it shows that in certain periods, Ferdinand would say, "the great kings bury their treasures." If there are three tenses—past, present, and future—there is something that unfolds them in space, that spreads them in the magnetic field of the memory, until from out of their respective capsules they unite in order to synthesize the most incredible fruit of the human imagination: God. Then, for Lionel, every mental, linguistic, or visual formation was the echo felt by man upon hearing the divine cry of his innards. Nothing more than the echo of an inaudible sound that, no matter how we searched for it, climbing from the precipice to the mountain, we would never detect in the very source of its waves. In this way the Tetragrammaton was no more than a package, a perfect system of communicative vessels through which the waters of eternity flowed. Lionel was seated on a bench in Tompkins Square, observing the movements of a squirrel on a branch: jumping, winking, hiding, and animal fear. He counted two, three, four acorns taken by the squirrel to its nest. He thought of the numbers and then afterward of the roundness of the acorns. He thought of the Kabbalists who gave names of fruits to their works: *The Garden of the Pomegranates* of Cordovero; *The Walnut Orchard* of Chilatilla. He thought of the Hebrew word *Pardes*, "Paradise," which enclosed in itself the squaring of the circle of the exegesis, the verbal key that opened the door of the Book of Books. All of this in the jumping steps of the squirrel, a little infantile creature, sensitive and timid. And suddenly, there he was, in the immense kitchen of the concentration camp, carrying food, hardly having arrived from the other place, from the icy room where two laughing soldiers had marked his hand forever with the number 56.510. Mother and Father dead. Dead or disappeared? Only in a kitchen that smells of sauerkraut and horrible sausages. Little Lionel, shipwrecked and forced to drink the seawater, the juice of the seaweed, so as not to die from pain and absurdity. Then, again in the square, the hand that passes over, as if it were filling the space between the numbers with a complete succession of fears, the tattoo that is about to turn into a revelation. But one irony still remains, a whiplash from the past, which, when entering his memory, awakens an old German teacher, a fragile and proud Hebraist, to whom an uncouth Nazi captain says: "The most absurd thing about you Jews is that you write backward, from right to left, thus revealing the perversity that the Fuehrer justifiably accuses you of. When we begin, you are finishing, and when you finish, we are beginning. There is only room for one of us in this world, professor."

And after seeing how they brought him to his death, at the precise moment when the squirrel lets an acorn fall to the ground and Lionel becomes startled, his notebook opens to the page that contains the Tetragrammaton. The reading almost comes out automatically: Yod, He, Vav, He, four letters and their respective numbers from right to left, 10 (something strange happens at the top of his heart), 5 (no, no it cannot be), 6 (all the blood evaporates from his body), 5 (he shouts in silence like someone who has had his tongue removed in his first infancy) . . . Yes! Yes! . . . Lionel jumps up from the bench and runs away holding his notebook, while his arm with the numerical tattoo of the Name bursts into flames and turns into burning coals. . . . Into burning coals or crystal?. . . It is attached and not attached to his body. It is the serpent that Moses hurls before the Pharaoh; it is the leprous arm of one of Bar Kochba's soldiers; it is the stump of an arm from a golden statue; it is the transparent sail of a mad windmill; it is the thin oar of a Phoenician boat; it is Samson's arm destroying the Philistine temple; it is his mother and his father; it is Berlin and the sirens; it is Chopka and the raspberry bushes in the forest; it is the center branch of the menorah; the arm of the reflection and the self; it is the arm of his pregnant wife; it is a palm tree in the Sinai; the coral pierced by the repeated flow of the Red Sea; it is the arm of Adam choosing the fruits of Paradise; it is the arm of Maimonides binding the phylacteries; it is the arm of Solomon writing the Song of Songs; it is the arm gleaming in the light, that conceals a thousand flashes of lightning and their diagrams in the sky; it is his usual arm that is and is not, that reveals itself to him and rises up to his face flooded with tears on the Brooklyn Bridge, pressing his eyes of man with his hand, lavishing himself with the rest of his body in a network of trembling that doesn't stop. The earth splits open, the immense bridge crumbles, the ground smells of urine and abandoned newspapers. The hour dissolves into minutes, then into seconds, then into microns, then into atoms and protons that seethe in his brain. He is in the middle of a whirlpool of blue fire, in the beginning of the world where the suns split open like hot quartz, and the birth of stars is repeated like an image viewed from a thousand different angles. He falls and at the same time is elevated toward his inner sky. At night he wakes up in a hospital: a black nurse smiles at him, tender, from a far-off blues. . . .

Translated from the Spanish
by Yishai Tobin

The Generation of the Flood
by Mark Mirsky

Fifteen cubits upward did the waters prevail; and the mountains were covered. And all flesh perished that moved upon the earth, both fowl, and cattle, and beast, and every swarming thing that swarmeth upon the earth, and every man, all in whose nostrils was the breath of the spirit of life, whatsoever was in the dry land, died. And He blotted out every living substance which was upon the face of the ground, both man, and cattle, and creeping thing, and fowl of the heaven: and they were blotted out from the earth; and Noah only was left, and they that were with him in the ark.

Genesis 7: 20-23

. . . after the primordial light was withdrawn there was created a "membrane for the marrow," a k'lifah, and this k'lifah expanded and produced another. As soon as this sec-

ond one came forth she went up and down till she reached the "little faces." She desired to cleave to them and to be shaped as one of them, and was loth to depart from them. But the Holy One, blessed be He, removed her from them and made her go below. When He created Adam and gave him a partner, as soon as she saw Eve clinging to his side and was reminded by his form of the supernal beauty she flew up from thence and tried as before to attach herself to the "little faces." The supernal guardians of the gates, however, did not permit her. The Holy One, blessed be He, chid her and cast her into the depths of the sea where she abode until the time that Adam and his wife sinned. Then the Holy One, blessed be He, brought her out from the depth of the sea and gave her power over all those children, the "little faces" of the sons of men, who are liable to punishment for the sins of their fathers. She then wandered up and down the world. She approached the gates of the terrestrial paradise, where she saw the Cherubim, the guardians of the gates of Paradise, and sat down near the flashing sword, to which she was akin in origin. When she saw the flashing sword revolving, she fled and wandered around the world and, finding children liable to punishment, she maltreated and killed them. All this is on account of the action of the moon in diminishing her (original) light. When Cain was born this k'lifah tried for a time without success to attach herself to him, but at length she had intercourse with him and bore spirits and demons. Adam for a hundred and thirty years had intercourse with female spirits until Naamah was born. She by her beauty led astray the "sons of God," Uzza and Azael, and she bore them children and so from her went forth evil spirits and demons into the world. She wanders about at night time, vexing the sons of men and causing them to defile themselves.

. . . Said R. Simeon, "Alas for the blindness of the sons of men, all unaware as they are how full the earth is of strange and invisible beings and hidden dangers, which could they but see, they would marvel how they themselves can exist on the earth."

The Zohar: Genesis

It was the waters that overwhelmed them. All the fountains of the great deep broken open, the windows of the Heavens rattled with the blast of rain. Upper world and lower world which they had put themselves between with spells, curses, anagrams, rushed together, a clap, a mighty wave, blotted all.

It was the earth which was corrupt. Not just man, uplifted speck of clay, or his brothers, animals that ran four-footed, or birds that flew above him, even clusters of insects that swarmed, or finally seed sprouting in humus, rot, up into the blighted barley and wheat, but corruption had seeped into the very salt crystal, sand, splinter of rock so that the whole of it, curved and shuddering obscenely, stank in the eye.

So we can hardly imagine that generation. It started with Adam's disgust, Eve. After Abel's death he couldn't look at her. He had heard all this talk of sin, evil, crime, but it meant nothing, too confusing, hard to grasp, he took a bite in a bad apple, wasn't even a taste to that fruit. They'd been punished. He was afraid. Something done that wasn't supposed to be, but too thin for him to smell, touch, taste.

Then the blood, losing—the word death the angel had uttered palpable. And he looked between Eve's legs where Abel and Cain had come from and it was ugly. He got down on his knees and sniffed it. The smell was awful, not as he had thought it before. He saw stretch marks on her tummy, her breasts drooped, that black bush where he thought sometimes he might slip back down into the garden, now stank of blood, sweat, piss, seemed like the gate to that place, death. And he was afraid. He stayed away from her. Slept by himself.

She came. Mist, fine air, perfume of clover blossom, iris, lily, split herself in two, a sister. They lay down beside him with gauzy limbs rubbed along his body, fluttering, drawing the sweetness out of her pistil, sucking until his temples hammered with joy and he swooned, "Enough! Enough!" at their ticklings leaving his body rosy, a host of tiny creatures like herself taking wing from each spore of the lump, seed, he threw up, progeny of Lilith, first wife of the first Adam, that clay man under them both, flying off to copulate like flies, seeking out not only Cain but bears, lions, calves, trees, flowers, even the cleft of the rock.

Cain! Cain! The cursed one, and the smell of murder, scorpions, toads, snakes, scurrying out of the way, turning on the sand as he hears the soft giggling call of girls behind him and sees them hanging back a few yards, suddenly bashful, trying to stuff breasts back in the thin stuff of their dresses, drawing the veil, mischievous, across faces.

His sister, a twin, among them and he feels the mark on his forehead fiery, the sweat of his brow scalding drop by drop as she too skips showing her long girlish legs, the length of them up to her waist as the desert wind whips their skirts lifting them . . . they dart about him, just out of touch. He cries, a bitter voice, is this his punishment, faint as the spike of hunger goes through him, comes out between his legs as he speaks her name, Naamah, Naamah, the seed in his hands only it is not his sister who is standing in front of him now, her blue eyes watching him steadily over the edge of the half veil which outlines the chisel of her nose and chin. The smell of flowers, soft yellow puffs, a carpet of them. He strikes at her but the fingers touch his just as he swings down and the cool stroke stops him, he can't help it as the hand reaches out, he does feel it and is dazzled, so icy, the seed pumps from him again and again as she strips off the bandages from her glowing olive face, the soft red berries of her lips helping him to find the apple breasts, pear buttocks, purple flesh of the dark plum its veined flesh between his teeth, he can not hold her, eat her, die within her enough. Her wrappings are off, throttled between her legs, squeezing, trying to possess the quick, laughing creature, he aches, Cain, he is sick, as the shape draws off him filled with his creation, his shining grandmother, first Eve, the *k'lifah*.

The sand is wet and scummy under his feet as he stands shaky. His forehead is cold. He has lost something. Now he is alone and for the first time since his hands struck out at Abel, he shivers.

Momma," he cries. "Momma."

* * *

Was it Enoch who caused it? Enoch who seeking Cain sought to understand the invisible as well as the visible world, collecting the secrets of generation, calling upon his ancestor, the ancient Adam, six hundred and fifty years old, to speak of the mysteries in the Garden, taking down the words of Uzza and Azael as they shriveled into dust, learning the secret names of the presences, tapping the streams of light that bubbled in the earth, setting down the language of the leaves, birds, summoning the demons to his aid, befriending the angels.

While his nephews, nieces, cousins, children, children's children, all but one of the issue of his loins were swarmed in murder, adultery, sodomy, bestiality. Leaning over his shoulder, reading the leaves, they became skilled in the divination of the spirits. Some lay with cattle in the field, garlanding the bull's horns, perfuming the cow's hindquarters. Others fell in love with trees, entreating sap from the oak, maple, cherry; grafting their human flesh into the branches. Others shaped partners from the earth itself, molding the clay into breasts, mouth, arms, manipulating the likeness of their sleeping fantasies, breathing quickness into the limbs. Aye, the earth itself—corrupt. Fetid with human blood, see, it steamed of heat, and man lay down upon his ancient mother and made love to her. Death: when Enoch's fingers fell from the pages of the book, Methuselah turned them, seeking within the leaves that Adam brought out of the Garden, the pathway to his father and his father's father. And after him, Lamech, and Noah after him, the bright essences who danced about his chair and brought him stories of the upper, lower world could not enlighten man on that: one terrible key that had been turned to lock him out.

They raged, at last, the generation of the Flood. Stamped their feet upon the earth, abusing it, defiling it, deliberately, hoping the upper world would take notice. Cut their bodies, crippled themselves, refused to spawn with humankind, ate their babies. Stopped up fountains of goodness, mercy, drove off the angel that came down to plead with them. Death! Death! They were sick of it. They would pervert the whole world, upper, lower, real and dreamed, until they were set free. Noah! Free! Free!

What good was this turning of pages? Adam had died. Cain had died. Enoch was dead. Kenan. Mahalalel, Lamech, Mehuhael, Irad, Adah, Seth. And a whole numberless host.

What was the sin of the generation of the Flood?
They corrupted the earth.
Man sinned, why call the earth corrupt?
Man is the "essence of the earth," he can infect the earth with his own corruption.
Why were the animals extinguished too?

He had perverted them, even to the birds of the air, even the insects are of his foulness.

How?

He did not allow the upper and lower waters to "meet in conjunction," he intervened in all natural process, prevented its intercourse, his violence, abstract, overreaching, was impossible. The measure of sin was not filled up, however, until he destroyed his own seed.

If men, even their children, were skilled in magic and divination, how is it they had no foreknowledge of the Flood?

They did, but they thought they could avert the catastrophe as they were on good terms with the angel in charge of fire, and the angel in charge of water.

How did the Flood come about?

"Measure for Measure." Man had wasted his "warm fluid" upon the ground. So, bubbling up from below, "all the fountains of the Great Deep were broken open," hot, burning waters scalded him. From above, "and the windows of Heaven were opened," it fell in cold sheets. The giants stood upon the springs.

The manner of their death was as follows: scalding water spurted up from the abyss, and as it reached them it first burnt the skin from the flesh, and then the flesh from the bones, the bones then came asunder, no two remaining together, and thus they were completely blotted out.

Said God to them: "You wish to undo the work of my hands; your wish shall be fully granted, for every living thing that I have made will I blot out from the face of the earth. I will reduce the world to water, to its primitive state, and then I will form other creatures more worthy to endure."

Woe to those sinners, since they will not rise from the dead on the day of the last judgment . . . they were blotted out.

The Zohar

The Coming of the Messiah
by Franz Kafka

The Messiah will come as soon as the most unbridled individualism of faith becomes possible—when there is no one to destroy this possibility and no one to suffer its destruction; hence the graves will open themselves. This, perhaps, is Christian doctrine too, applying as much to the actual presentation of the example to be emulated, which is an individualistic example, as to the symbolic presentation of the resurrection of the Mediator in the single individual.

The Messiah will come only when he is no longer necessary; he will come only on the day after his arrival; he will come, not on the last day, but on the very last.

Translated from the German
by Clement Greenberg

Rabbi Joseph Della Reina

by Asher Barash

In the city of Safed there lived a great Kabbalistic scholar called Rabbi Joseph Della Reina, who had five students so devoted to him that they would not leave him for a moment and were always ready to fulfill his wishes.

One day, Rabbi Joseph said to them: "My children, the time has come for me to take action. We can no longer suffer Samael, or Satan, to rule the earth, and we must bring the Messiah to replace him."

"Master," they cried, "we are at your service and are ready to go through fire and water for your sake."

"If that is so," he replied, "go and purify yourselves and change your clothing. Make yourselves ready for the third day, for on the third day we will set out on a journey and not return until we have brought the final redemption for Israel and the whole world."

The students leapt to their feet and eagerly went to bathe and change their clothes. They prepared provisions for the journey and came back to their rabbi on the third day. They found him praying in the *beit midrash*, dressed in spotless garments, and concentrating deeply with his head buried in his hands.

Realizing that they had entered, he lifted his head and said: "May it be God's will to help us in our holy task."

The students answered: "Amen, may it be His will," and then they all left for Meiron to pray at the tomb of Rabbi Simeon ben Yohai, spending the night there.

During the night, Rabbi Simeon ben Yohai appeared to Rabbi Joseph in a dream and said: "Why do you attempt a task which you can never succeed in, however fervently you wish it?"

"I am doing it neither for my own honor, nor for that of my family," Rabbi Joseph replied, "but for the glory of heaven and for the sake of Israel. I am convinced that God will help me."

Rabbi Simeon ben Yohai blessed him, and disappeared.

Then they went to Tiberias and entered a thick forest nearby, where they sat and studied Kabbalah for three days without a pause. Next they went and bathed in Lake Kinneret, immersing themselves twenty-six times in accordance with the mystic number of God's holy name.

Towards evening on the third day, they prayed together with extraordinary fervor, concentrating on every word in their prayers, and pronouncing them with purity of thought. Then Rabbi Joseph called on the prophet Elijah to appear to him and tell him how he should proceed. As they fell upon their knees, Elijah appeared before them, saying: "What is your request, and what can I do for you?"

Rabbi Joseph stood up, bowed before the prophet, and said: "Welcome to you, savior of Israel! I have not troubled you to come hither for my sake, but in order to fight in God's holy cause as you did once in the days of King Ahab. Now, I beseech you, show me the way whereby I may conquer Samael and bring about the redemption of the world."

"The task you have undertaken," answered Elijah, "is too difficult for you, and you will not succeed; for the sins of the world have strengthened the hand of Samael. You would only be able to conquer him with a purity of body and soul beyond the power of normal man. If you do succeed, blessed will you be, but my advice is to leave the task, lest you be hurt by Samael and his supporters."

"Grant me strength and courage, prophet, for I have sworn not to return home until I have raised Israel from the dust. I am prepared to lay down my life for the honor of God, so, I beseech you, show me and my pupils what we should do."

"Stay together with your disciples," Elijah answered, "in an open field far from the habitation of men so that you see no living soul. Remain there for twenty-one days eating only what is necessary to keep yourselves alive. Eat a little less every night until you have trained yourselves to eat nothing at all. Just inhale the scent of spices and herbs in order to keep your bodies fresh and to give yourselves strength to talk with the angels who will come to visit you. At the end of twenty-one days, pronounce the holy names and call upon the angel Sandalphon to come to you. When he comes with all his host, inhale the smell of spices, for a dreadful fear will descend upon you and a great weakness before the thunder and lightning."

Rabbi Joseph and his disciples did exactly as they had been instructed. They spent every moment of the twenty-one days discussing kabbalistic lore until they left all the material part of themselves behind them and became elevated in spirit. On the twenty-first day they prayed with especial devotion, asked pardon for all their sins and for the sins of all Israel. Then they cried in a loud voice: "Answer us, O Lord, answer us!" and they called on the name of Sandalphon. At once the heavens opened and Sandalphon descended with all his host, with chariots of fire and flaming horses—an army roaring like the ocean in tumult.

Rabbi Joseph and his disciples fell on their faces in great terror, but they remembered in time to smell the spices which strengthened and revived them. However, they were still unable to stand on their feet, but lay instead prostrate on the ground.

Sandalphon turned to Rabbi Joseph and said: "Son of man, you creature of flesh and blood, why did you dare to disturb the heavenly angels?"

In a trembling voice Rabbi Joseph replied: "Give me strength and courage and I will speak before you."

The angel touched him, saying: "Stand and speak!"

Rabbi Joseph, fortified by the angelic touch, stood up, slipping off his shoes in deference to the holy angel, while his disciples lay on the ground, unable to rise. Then he said:

"Welcome, angel of the heavenly host, and welcome to all your holy army. Almighty God knows full well that I call you not for my own glory nor for the glory of my family but solely for the glory of God Himself, the Ruler of all. Hear my prayer and instruct me how to fight against Samael and all his party so that I may remove evil from the world and bring perfect redemption to the descendants of Abraham, Isaac and Jacob."

"Your words are noble and fair. All the heavenly host, the seraphim and the cherubim, are waiting for God to take vengeance and for the redemption of Israel to come by the hand of the Messiah. But this you should know—as yet, you have done nothing. If you only knew the might and the power of Samael, you would never undertake this impossible task. How can I help you, for I myself do not know the extent of Samael's power nor how to overthrow him? Only the archangels Katriel and Metatron know the extent of Samael's power—but could you stand before the terror of those archangels whom no mortal has yet looked upon and lived? If you were terrified at my coming and almost swooned away, how will you stand before them? Nevertheless, the truth of the matter is, that if you could manage to achieve your desire, then your reward would be great and none could be compared to you among men."

"I know that I am only a small and insignificant mortal," replied Rabbi Joseph, "but I have sworn to lay down my life if necessary for the sake of God—yea, I will even sacrifice my spirit and my blood for the Almighty. So instruct me, heavenly angel, what I must do to bring down the archangels Katriel and Metatron from heaven to visit the earth!"

"Do the same as you have done until now," the angel answered him. "Omit none of the fasting and bathing and prayers. Continue for forty days and then, after the forty days are completed, call upon the two archangels in the name of God. Pray to God yourselves that He should give you strength to bear the holy and terrifying sight lest your souls faint before it. Ask the archangels for strength and power and they will tell you of the ways of Samael and how you may overthrow him."

Sandalphon disappeared heavenward in a whirlwind while the disciples still lay terrified on the ground.

When he had departed, they rose trembling to their feet, and Rabbi Joseph said to them: "Be strong and of good courage. Let us carry out the instructions of the angel."

"We are ready," they replied at once, "and we heard everything that the angel told you, even though we were lying on the ground."

They then walked away from that spot until they reached a certain mountain where they found a cave in which to dwell. There they stayed for forty days purifying themselves as they had been instructed until they felt that they had left their bodies completely behind them and were almost living in the next world.

On the fortieth day they went to the Arabah through which flows the brook of Kishon and bathed in its waters. Then they prayed amid much weeping, plucked off a myrtle branch which they bent into a circle, and within its circle formed a ring by holding hands. Next they fell on their faces in prayer and, using one of the Holy Names, called upon the two archangels to descend.

The moment they called, the whole earth shook, the sky clouded over darkly, there was thunder and lightning, and the heavens themselves opened. Then the two archangels descended with all their hosts, and were about to strike Rabbi Joseph and all his disciples dead with thunderbolts. However, the rabbi and his pupils prevented them by repeating the Holy Name, not with their lips, but in their minds, and they fell prostrate with arms outspread.

In great anger the two archangels thundered: "What mortal has dared to use the sceptre of the Holy One to call us?"

Rabbi Joseph could not reply, for his soul had almost swooned away, and his disciples lay like corpses beside him.

Then the archangel Metatron touched him and said: "Why have you angered us? Why did you not respect the honor of your Creator?"

The angel's touch revived him a little and Rabbi Joseph murmured weakly: "Strengthen me and I will speak."

Katriel stretched out his wing and touched him with it, saying: "See, I have given you strength. Now speak and tell me your answer."

The rabbi stood up and cried: "Almighty God knows that I have not called upon you in rebellion nor in sin but for the sake of His honor, in order to redeem Israel, His chosen people, from the dust. It is you, reverend archangels, who should perform the task of fighting God's battles, the battles of the Lord of Hosts. Therefore, I call upon you in His holy name to tell me of the powers of Samael and how I may overthrow his rule."

"That is a hard question," answered the angels. "It is through the sins of Israel that Samael has become strong, and there is no one who can dislodge him from his place among the stars, for he is surrounded by three sets of defenses through which no creature may pass—only God Himself in all His Holiness and Might, if He should so decree."

Rabbi Joseph wept aloud: "After all the suffering we have undergone in the name of the Almighty in order to reach you, will you look upon our sorrow and refuse to help us?"

The archangels were stirred by compassion and replied: "Listen, Joseph! We know in heaven of your earnest desire and we approve of it. But the time has not yet come, nor has the heavenly decree been issued. Nevertheless, by virtue of your knowledge of the dreadful secrets of kabbalah and your use of the Holy Names, we are duty bound to show you the way. If you should succeed, your reward would indeed be great."

"Reverend angels," he pleaded, "strengthen me to the best of your power and I shall turn neither to the right nor the left until I have completed my purpose, for I know that the Almighty will assist me and I shall not fail."

"Well," began the angels, "you should know that Samael has two mighty lines of defense on one side—a wall of iron stretching from earth to heaven, and the ocean. On the other side, he has a very strong defense—a mountain covered with snow whose peak reaches to heaven. You must pass through these three defenses in order to climb Mount Seir and bring judgment upon the tribe of Esau. Now, turn toward Mount Seir and omit nothing of what we tell you.

"On your way, you will meet an enormous pack of black dogs. They are the hounds of Samael, sent to confound your purpose, but do not be afraid. Pronounce the Holy Name and they will turn away and flee. From there you will make your way to the snow-capped mountain, and as soon as you mention the secret Name derived from the phrase '. . . white as snow in Salmon,' the mountain will be uprooted and will disappear as though it had never existed.

"As you continue on your way (if you do not weaken in your purpose) you will eventually reach the ocean whose waves will tower above you like mountains. There you must use the secret Name derived from the phrase 'The voice of the Lord is over the mighty waters' and the waters will at once recede, the land appear, and you will walk across the dry earth.

"After that, you must proceed on your way till you reach the iron wall which stretches from the earth to heaven. Now take a knife in your hand and write on it the secret Name derived from the phrase 'a sword for God and for Gideon.' You will be able to cut through the wall with this knife and make an opening through which you can pass. But be sure to hold the doorway open until you have all passed through, lest one should be left behind, when it closes.

"Next, you reach Mount Seir and climb up the mountain. At that moment, we shall dislodge Samael from his throne and he will fall next to you. Now you must have two metal tabs ready, each engraved with the Holy Name, and when you see Samael and his mate, Lilith, fleeing from you and hiding in a cave, pursue them into the cave and you will find them in the likeness of two black dogs, male and female. Do not be afraid, but tie one of the metal tabs to each of their necks and they will stand still, unable to move. Then you can fix chains around their necks and they will follow you together with all their cronies, and you will know that God has blessed your work.

"You must bring them to justice on Mount Seir where a trumpet will blow loud and long, the Messiah will appear, and the full redemption will take place. But beware of one thing—if Samael or his mate beg and plead for food or drink to save themselves from death, do not listen to them and do not give them anything at all. If you do, you will pay for it with your life."

With these words, the two archangels disappeared in a whirlwind, and the disciples leaped to their feet with great rejoicing, for they had heard all that the angels had said.

Rabbi Joseph and his disciples followed all the instructions with the greatest care, preparing the two metal tabs and the knife, and then they all set out for Mount Seir. On their way, they met huge packs of black dogs which surrounded them, snarling viciously and baring their fangs. They pronounced the Holy Name and the dogs scattered, disappearing into thin air.

After another day's journey, towards evening they reached the snow-capped mountain whose peak reached to heaven. Rabbi Joseph pronounced the appropriate secret Name and the mountain disappeared as though it had never existed. They traveled on for another few days, and on the third day, at the first light of dawn, they came to an enormous sea whose waves were like mountains about to swallow them up. Again, they pronounced the appropriate secret Name and were able to pass through on dry land.

Within a few hours they reached the iron wall. Rabbi Joseph took out the special knife engraved with God's name, and he cut an opening in the wall shaped like a door, holding it open until all of his disciples had passed through. The last of the five was, however, a little slow and did not manage to bring his foot through the opening before it closed. His foot was at once trapped in it and he began to cry: "My teacher and master, save me—my foot is caught in the iron!" Rabbi Joseph took out the knife again and cut the metal around his foot, freeing it from the wall. However a sort of iron ring was left fixed permanently around his ankle.

They ascended Mount Seir, climbing until the evening when they found a small rise with one or two caves in it. Then they perceived two shapes falling towards the earth. They ran after them, pursuing them into one of the caves, and as they entered, they found two black dogs there, a male and a female.

With his right hand, Rabbi Joseph fixed a tab on the male dog and with his left on the female, his disciples hurrying to chain them up as soon as he had finished his task. When they saw that there was no way of escape, the two dogs assumed human form, with the addition of black wings filled with shining eyes. They began to beseech Rabbi Joseph to give them a few crumbs of bread or a drop of water to save them from dying before reaching the top of the mountain, but he refused to listen and gave them nothing.

As they proceeded up the mountain, with the two captives weeping and pleading for a little food, and the others rejoicing over their victory, Rabbi Joseph said joyfully: "Who would believe that this is the day we have all been waiting for, when it will be proclaimed among all the nations of the world that the Lord is King of the Universe!"

But Samael answered: "I knew that you would succeed and that our fate was sealed. So now, kind sir, what have you to fear in granting our request? We are all under your command and you can do with us as you please. Take pity, therefore, and give us something to revive us so that we can survive for the trial."

But Rabbi Joseph merely rebuked him: "You are wasting your breath—I will give you nothing."

As they approached the top of the mountain, Rabbi Joseph took out a piece of scented myrrh to smell, and gave it to his disciples to smell too, for they were weary after their long journey. "If you will not give me anything to eat," said Samael, "at least let me smell the myrrh to refresh myself—otherwise you will have only a dead prisoner to rejoice over."

Rabbi Joseph held it out from the distance for Samael to smell, and at that very moment a flame leaped from Samael's mouth, consuming the myrrh in Rabbi Joseph's hand. At once the chains snapped, the metal tabs dropped off, and he and his supporters took command. They attacked the disciples, three of whom fell dead on the spot before the terrible roaring of Samael, Lilith, and their followers. The remaining two went out of their minds and began barking like dogs, and Rabbi Joseph was left alone.

The mountain started to smoke and a voice was heard saying: "Woe to you, Joseph, for failing to obey your orders. You gave Samael spices to smell and now he will pursue you and trouble you both in this world and in the world to come."

Rabbi Joseph stumbled away, weeping and mourning, and he continued to lament until the day of his death.

Translated from the Hebrew
by Murry Roston

The Fettered Messiah

by Yehoshua Bar-Yoseph

Towards evening, after Hayim had finished his day at the *heder*, he would run to Aunt Sarah's.

He liked to be in her somber-looking room, when it was filled with shadows in the twilight.

And Sarah, in her slow old voice, would begin telling the story:

. . . The face of the scholar quivered as he sat over his folios, alone amid the large shadows in the prayer-house—because he heard the Messiah quiver in pain. The Messiah strained at his shackles . . .

And so, the man rose from his studies. He covered his shoulders with a white mantle, placed the Holy Book under his armpit and walked out through the open window. . . .

Filled with wrath and indignation, the man strode across the darkness of the clouds. He was now ready to reach the verge of heaven with his white mantle and from there to swoop down to the dark dungeon of the Messiah and undo his shackles. . . .

But suddenly the skies darkened and terrifying lightning flashed, illuminating everything with a dazzling white glare, and the loud thunder reverberated. . . . The black-bearded man who wore the white mantle began to tremble, and his face became very pale . . . for he saw a huge black dog rise from the couch where the Messiah lay in chains. As the black dog advanced from the fettered Messiah towards the scholar in the white mantle, he loomed as large as the Jermak Mountain. The eyes of the dog were like two green suns. His teeth were like sharp rocks of red and violet fire, and when he gritted them there was lightning and thunder and a loud creaking noise, and white smoke came out of his nostrils. The monster shook his head violently, and a great golden candlestick leaped up to rest on his head. That was the sacred candlestick of the Temple in Jerusalem which Satan had stolen when the Temple was destroyed. The candlestick had turned pale with fury and humiliation and it now shone with a golden fire. . . . The candlestick on the dog's brow danced a mourner's dance. Eight black flames leaped from it and swallowed the surrounding sparks of fire. Making long strides, the hound drew near, stride by stride; the heavens were set quaking by each step and at each motion of his heavy yet sinuous body, a tremulous roar was heard from afar.

The scholar in the white mantle shrank back in fear and raised his face to Heaven.

He who sits in Glory surrounded by a bright blue light and golden angels heard the supplication. The azure sky smiled gently and little by little grew brighter. Terror was now gone from the eyes of Rabbi Joseph de la Reina and they became tranquil in the reflected radiance. From on high came the singing of Psalms and gold-white angels hovered around the scholar's head, whispering into his ears.

Thereupon Rabbi Joseph took courage and firmly strode towards the huge dog. And as he strode, this great scholar murmured the names of holy angels and the Exalted and Awesome Name of the One Who is Omnipresent and Everlasting.

And lo and behold—a miracle! The dreadful monster which had been advancing with the sureness of a devouring beast towards its prey, now began to retreat in fear before the lean man murmuring prayers. Nor was that all. With every step he took in withdrawing, the dog shrank in size while the horrendous colors of his mouth and eyes became fainter and fainter. The fiery candlestick detached itself from the head of the beast and flew away. Now in place of a terrifying monster was a miserable little cur, wagging its tail and rolling its eyes and fawning at the feet of the man.

Now, the white-mantled scholar thought to himself as he smiled into his black beard, the time has come to cast this monster out of this world and out of the other world too! And so he caught the cur by the scruff of his neck and began carrying him towards the Dark Mountain. For only the Dark Mountain would swallow up the monster and not throw him back to the sinister forces who would restore his carcass to life. For seven days and seven nights the scholar was to travel, just as the angels had whispered to him, across seas and land and hills and dales, over high mountains and through deep precipices. He was to give the dog no bread to eat nor water to drink, until he perished of hunger and thirst. When the man saw that the dog had no more life in him, he was to fling the carcass into the black abyss, return to Safed, immerse himself in the pool of the Saintly Scholar Rabbi Isaac Luria and purify his soul of every stain or blemish. Only then was he to return to this place and proceed without interruption or interference to the dungeon where the Messiah was imprisoned in chains. Then with his pure hands would he rid the Redeemer of his shackles and bring Redemption to the Jews and to mankind. . . .

For forty-nine days and forty-nine nights, seven times seven days and nights, as the angels enjoined him, the white-mantled scholar dragged the cur toward the Dark Mountain. The beast grew weaker and weaker.

At first, the wretch tried to win the man's heart by wagging his tail. It had a pitiable-looking tail like a worn-out old broom, every shake of which evoked much compassion in the Rabbi's heart; it was as if he were witnessing infants in death agony, or women expiring in childbirth, or old men pleading for another day of life. But Rabbi Joseph de la Reina was firm.

Then the dog made his green eyes look sad and sick. Though the hues of the Satan still skulked in them, he filled them with the tears of innocent suffering; he dropped his eyes and raised them a trifle, in plea and supplication. But Rabbi Joseph de la Reina remained firm and gave the dog neither food nor drink.

Finally the dog tried with his voice. He whimpered and he wailed like an injured dove, like a sick child, like a hungry orphan, like a bridegroom pleading against the murder of his bride under the wedding canopy, like a sinner in his penitence, like an old beggar woman thrown out into the street. The wretch wept and howled and his echoes resounded far and wide. But Rabbi Joseph knew these were the wiles of Satan, so he stopped his ears and, gritting his teeth, he dragged the dog along to his appointed grave in the Dark Mountain.

Three days before they reached the black abyss the dog feigned death and made his own carcass feel as heavy as a mountain. The man in the white mantle did not flinch. Sweating and panting, he dragged the carcass to the brink.

Then Rabbi Joseph stood still for a moment to take a pinch of snuff. He had had neither food nor drink for forty-nine days and nights and he wished to refresh himself just a trifle with the scent of the snuff before the final effort. To make sure that the monster did not escape, he placed his foot on the neck of the dog when he opened the snuff-box and raised the fragrant powder to his nostrils.

He sniffed one pinch and then another and thanked God in his heart for the success of his undertaking thus far. He felt a sense of satisfaction that it was he, Rabbi Joseph de la Reina, who had been elected by Him Who dwells on High—he, of all men, to bring about the Redemption of Israel and the world.

But here the wily beast caught the familiar scent of man's self-satisfaction. Greatly encouraged by it, he summoned his remaining strength for a new effort. With a smile of dissembled meekness in his green eyes, he sighed a deep sigh of resignation and spoke like a human being. Humbly, he said:

"You are much to be envied, you, who are but mortal flesh and blood, that you have achieved what has been denied to greater men in bringing me to these nethermost depths. My end has come and I have but one request. Do, I beseech you, after you have flung me down, pray to All-Highest for my lost soul. May He of the Blessed Glory take compassion on me and join the holy sparks that are in my soul to those of the Righteous of the Universe. . . ."

With these words the wretch succeeded in stirring up pride in the man's heart. Rabbi Joseph de la Reina smiled to himself and thrust another pinch of snuff into his nostrils, saying: "Perhaps I will pray to His Blessed Name, not for your sake, but for the sake of the holy sparks in your unclean soul. . ."

The dog closed his eyes in abject humility and then opened them with a smile of despair, as if begging for pity. In a voice which sounded like a prayer he entreated: "Before you fling me down, will you please let me sniff some of your snuff so that I may overcome somewhat the pangs of my inescapable death?"

The man in the white mantle, who had withstood the dog's tears and whimperings, could not withstand this plea. The angels had warned him against giving the beast anything to eat or drink—but this was snuff and was permissible, he thought to himself. He bent toward the black dog and opened the snuffbox. . . . Fire burst forth from the monster's nostrils and consumed the snuff. The smoke incense curled up from the box and rose to the arch-father of all abomination. Unwittingly Rabbi Joseph de la Reina had offered incense to the Prince of Pollution.

The powers of the monster returned. He leaped to his feet, rising as tall as a mountain. His eyes again filled with life and shone like two green suns. His teeth grew hard as flinty rock; lightning flashed and thunder roared as he gnashed them in fury. The fiery candlestick leaped once more upon his head. His claws grew sharper. . . .

The man clad in the white mantle, in his bewilderment, forgot the combination of holy names and holy letters which would protect him from the power of Satan.

The black dog sprang upon him and, thrusting his sharp teeth into the Rabbi's heart, began to eat his flesh and to drink his blood.

Nothing was left but the white mantle of Rabbi Joseph de la Reina. Then it fell into the black abyss. . . .

And so the Messiah remains shackled to this day. . . .

Translated from the Hebrew
by M. Z. Frank

The Pangs of the Messiah
by Moshe Smilanski

1

At the foot of Mt. Atzmon, tallest of the mountains in the Manesseh Region, which overlooks all of Galilee, at the gate of the tomb of Rabbi Simeon ben Yohai, sat the *shamash* Rabbi Yose, a shoot out of the stock of the Baal Shem Tov. Rabbi Yose watched over the Eternal Lamp that was on the holy tomb, lest it go out and lest, God forbid, the world should return to emptiness and void.

Rabbi Yose was wretchedly poor and downtrodden all the forty years of his life. He received his post as *shamash* as a legacy from his father, may he rest in peace. Rabbi Yose, his wife, and his only daughter and her husband, who was a fisherman along with the gentile fishermen in Tiberias, sustained themselves from Saturday night to Friday on very scanty food. The rabbi's face was withererd and wrinkled like that of an old man. However, it was not from worrying over a livelihood nor from pursuing mammon that he had become old, rather . . . this secret should only be revealed to a few and only whispered in the ear: he was one who reckoned the End of Days. From the day he came of age, his soul was stirred by the calculations of the coming of the Messiah and he studied and meditated on them. And from the time he returned from the yeshivah that is in Safed to his father's house in Meron, and became, after his father's passing, the *shamash* at the holy tomb, Rabbi Yose immersed himself in computing the End of Days. No man knew this secret of his. He bared his heart to no one. Only to his humble wife did he sometimes reveal the last digit of his calculations. She would listen to him and nod her head in agreement. She would agree and sigh with a broken heart. However it was not because of "The End" that she sighed. She herself never ceased from her own calculations, *prutah* after *prutah*, in order to honor the Sabbath. Her husband's salary was one *megidieh* a week, and his part of the charity received from abroad from the Rabbi Meir Baal ha-Nes box came to one *megidieh* per month. Her son-in-law the fisherman only brought fish home for the Sabbath. It was the worry of providing enough, especially for the Sabbath, that was on her mind.

Rabbi Yose did not compute the "End of Days" for pleasure. Year after year he kept at it, he even worked at night as well as by day, one number combination after another, one numerical pair after another, until he swam in a sea of numerology. And he found many "Ends of Days." "Ends of Days" that proved false, heaven preserve us! But to the one correct "End" he had not yet come. The Devil would intervene. Sometimes Rabbi Yose would be standing on the right path, and the holy spark would light the way before him and behind him. And sometimes he would feel in his whole being that the thing was near, very near, he could almost feel it within his grasp. One more day with a clear mind, just two more days and the "End" would be in the palm of his hand . . . and behold, a troubling thought: there were riots in the land, days of destruction were decreed; evil deeds were done that had in them the desecration of Israel and the Torah. Then Rabbi Yose would rend his garments, put on sackcloth and ashes, and he would fast at the gate of the tomb, mourn as if for one who had died. Every calamity that befell the Jewish people was his calamity. Every degradation was his. For what did he have in this world if not the glory of Israel and the Torah?—And then from much sorrow and an aching heart, his mind would become confused, and he would forget the order of his calculations and his deductions, that had been as clear to him as the sun in the afternoon. All the threads that connected and joined together would unravel. The light vanished and a heavy darkness pressed on him. And after he had rested from his sad emotional state, he would again begin from the beginning. Begin and work and struggle and discover. And then again disaster and misfortune. Again and again, the Devil would intervene.

Truly, the twenty-two years that he had served at the holy tomb were not spent in vain. For they were full of work. Only on the Sabbath and Holy Days were his heart and mind not on his calculations. Then all of him was given to the greater spirit—to honor and take pleasure and be made glad by its light. And also he did not pursue his work on the regular fast days and during the forty days of fasting that he imposed on himself as a yearly obligation: then he would mourn for the disappearance of the Divine Presence. Except for these days, all of his days and nights were dedicated to the holy work. Every morning, after immersion and prayer, he would entrust the watching of the Eternal Lamp to his young granddaughter, who would watch the lamp intently. Then he would go out to wander in the surrounding area. And he didn't return home until time for the afternoon prayer. He had his meal in his knapsack, a small piece of bread made with coarse flour; he would wash his hands in the streams and he would sing the blessing over the food to the rocks and it would echo back to him. In all the surroundings there was no rock he didn't know, no blade of grass he had not investigated, no cave which he had not entered to its very end. He even knew the Dervishes and the Haji. He knew them and their language and their customs. He spoke a clear Arabic, and from all of them—the rocks and the grass, the caves and the mountains, the Dervishes and the common folk—he extracted very fine threads and wove them together into his computation of the "End of Days." And who knows? Had not the time for the afternoon prayer come and interrupted his thinking and pondering as well as breaking the magical thread that connected him with his surroundings and the distant holy traces that had passed through here thousands of years ago—who knows—it is possible that he would have come one fine day to the "End" . . . but his obligation halted him, and he returned to the cave and the tomb and to his house at the foot of the mountains. The magic thread had been broken, and tomorrow he would begin to weave it again. In the evenings he would return alone to the cave, a grease candle in one hand and the Zohar in the other. He had also at his side a crumpled piece of paper and a tiny pencil that had become ancient from so much use. He would read, compute, and write. There was no end to the numbers. Great were the searchings of the heart . . . and then the hour of midnight would arrive. Again duty would call. Rabbi Yose would devote himself to the midnight prayer and he would weep in a bitter voice over the disappearance of the Divine Presence and over the woe of the Jewish people. He would forget his everyday world, and so too he would forget his numbers. After the midnight prayer he would have a necessary but snatched sleep, and then quickly he would awaken to serve the Creator.

When the morning became light, he could be found in the cave, pale as a corpse. His heart was empty, his mind was empty, all of him was shattered like a broken vessel and he was near fainting. If his good wife had not brought him a glass of tea at this time, he might have actually passed out.

However, as already stated, Rabbi Yose did not toil in vain for twenty-two years of his life. Many things became clear to him. Even if all the kings of the east and west and all the holy men in Israel had come, they couldn't have moved him an inch from his point of view. He had found three numbers of the Year of Redemption. He knew the thousand, the hundred, and the digit number. All of these had been tried and tested. He only hadn't found the decade number. That was where the problem was. What was it? That was the secret! And he felt with all his heart that the moment was near, that there was no possibility that it would be held off much longer . . . What are the years of our lives?—seventy, and if in strong health, eighty. The sign must come in his time. This knowledge was as clear to him as the sun.

And then something happened and he almost had the fourth number: the decade. A great light was revealed to him and he almost had the number within his grasp. And then again the work of the Devil . . . the light was revealed to him by a young girl, and by her was it hidden away. And this is what happened:

2

On a Friday, before morning, Rabbi Yose immersed himself three times, prayed and prepared the Eternal Lamp, filling it with pure olive oil. He ordered his granddaughter to watch the lamp with seven eyes, then he took his stick and knapsack and went off in the field to wander among the rocks. In a little while he came upon a wildflower that charmed him. The flower's unusual fragrance, its look of enchantment, and its wondrous form told him that a secret was contained in this wildflower. It was clear to him that this wildflower was not like any of the other flowers of the field. Rabbi Yose turned his steps toward it. Even before he got to the rock from under which the wondrous flower sprouted, Rabbi Yose lifted his head and saw something—and he almost lost his breath: next to the wondrous flower a female bent on her knees and she was touching the flower with her fingers and examining it with her eyes. In another minute the Divine Name would have been uttered by him, he was so astounded. There was no doubt in his mind that Satan, in the form of a woman, stood before Rabbi Yose, and the Devil's intention was clear: to confuse Rabbi Yose's mind so that he wouldn't discover the flower's meaning. But before Rabbi Yose could utter a word, the female stood up and turned her eyes to him. And the eyes were black and innocent like the eyes of a child, and they were full of an endless sadness; and a holy spark of fire flickered from within her eyes.

"Peace to you, old man! Are you not Rabbi Yose, the *shamash* who watches over the holy tomb of Rabbi Simeon ben Yohai?"

And her voice—a gentle sound of heartfelt prayer, pure like the dew of morning and full of the warmth and spirit of the midnight prayer.

"Peace unto you, daughter. Yes, I am the *shamash*. What is your wish, what your request? Tell me!"

And only after his mouth had said these words did Rabbi Yose really look at the one who stood before him—and his soul froze within him. From her knees on down, her legs were bare, her arms were bare, the hair on her head was uncovered, and it was in ringlets that fell on her neck.

Again suspicion grew in his heart and his face turned white.

"Who are you?" He asked in a hard voice, angry and trembling at once.

"I am a worker. I come from the nearby *moshav* that is behind the mountain."

"And what is your name?"

"Ruhamah."

"And what are you doing with this?"

"I am seeking God, the God of Redemption who is zealous for His people and will visit the rightful punishment on those who blaspheme Him."

Rabbi Yose was confused and astonished by what his eyes saw and what his ears heard. He had heard something about the *moshavs* which had been built in the land: that the men worked the land, and the women worked there like men in the fields. But he had never seen them, and his heart was not inclined to favor them, he kept himself away from them as if from evil: their purpose was to rebel against both the earthly and the heavenly kingdoms—and one must not tempt the Devil . . . and behold, now one of these stood before him. But what was the holy sadness in her eyes? What was the eternal lamp that appeared in the pupils of her eyes? And what was the grace that pervaded her face which was browned by the sun? And she spoke in the name of the Lord, and she was consumed with religious fervor . . . a strange riddle.

"Why do you look at me that way, old man? Because I am dark? The sun has turned me brown. Because my heart is blacker than my face? The sorrow of my people has blackened it. Old man, why are the cities built on their mounds, while jackals run through Jerusalem?"

"My daughter, the holy people have not yet filled the measure of their punishment. The End has not yet come."

" 'The measure of their punishment' ?—their blood is forsaken, their glory, their Torah. They have no yesterday and no tomorrow. There is no meaning to their lives and their death is a disgraceful death. With what else must their measure be filled?"

The *shamash*'s heart melted like wax and his warm tears choked his throat. Suddenly he lifted his head and said in a strong voice:

"Do not despair, my daughter, and do not be amazed! The End is not far off. I have seen it, and it is near; I have beheld it, and it is now. The time is near. Tried and proven. Clear as the sun."

And the old man was shaken by his own words; he jumped back and shook like a leaf. This was the first time his secret had escaped his lips, and before whom? Before a young, barefoot, bareheaded girl. For shame!

Now things had changed: the young girl stood as if enchanted and paid rapt attention to the words of the old man.

"Is it correct and true what they say about you, old man, that you are one who reckons the End of Days?" And suddenly the girl sank to the ground and a laugh broke from her mouth. And the laugh fragmented and scattered all around, falling on the rocks and among the thickets in the valley, and its echoes returned and fell over the heads of the *shamash* and the girl, who stopped laughing and stood there. Even she was pale as chalk.

"No, old man, this is not the way! You, who are pure and upright, reckon the End of Days in this cave while they, the sinners, defile the land. They have sold God and Redemption for a profit, and there is no one who cares, no one who will seek revenge for those who blaspheme against the Lord. From without hatred consumes, and from within slavery destroys. No, old man, you will not build up the land with prayers. It will be ransomed by sweat and blood. Do you see this wildflower? If its seed falls in a place that has soaked up sweat and blood, it will sprout and grow a certain decade of years."

The *shamash* was shaken. It was as if someone had whipped him in the face. He awakened from his sleep, the spell of enchantment, for the forthright words of the girl fell upon him, and he straightened himself up and cried out:

"Daughter! How many? How many? Oh, tell me, please, how many?"

But the girl didn't hear him and she did not face him. Her gaze wandered away into the distance, as if it sought help from the rocks and the valleys. And from her lips hard and bitter words escaped as if by themselves:

"Not by our sweat and not by our blood did this wildflower bloom. The people were sold for a Golden Calf . . ." and her other words were lost among the rocks. And the *shamash* fell on his face to the ground and prayed and entreated: "My God, God of Mercy! Please reveal to me only this one thing: how many years does this wildflower live?"

But his prayer fell and died among the rocks. There was total silence. His spirit sank. . . .

Before sunset, Rabbi Yose returned to the cave with a definite decision in his mind: after Sabbath, he would gird up his loins and go down to the *moshav* that was behind the mountain, to find the girl and find out from her about the flower.

But in the afternoon he heard his son-in-law telling his wife that the fishermen had brought up from the Kinneret in their nets the body of a young girl.

"A young girl? A Hebrew? What did she look like?" cried the *shamash* with fear. But at that very moment the voice of his granddaughter caused him alarm: "Grandfather, Grandfather! The Eternal Lamp is about to go out! Hurry, hurry!" The *shamash* almost collapsed. He ran to the cave, to the Eternal Lamp, that was almost extinguished, God forbid. . . .

3

After the Holy Sabbath, after *havdalah*, Rabbi Yose went down to Tiberias and from there to the small *moshav* that was behind the mountain, and he spoke with the fishermen who had brought the body of the girl up from the Kinneret, and with the members of the *moshav* and with the local rabbi. On Sunday with darkness he returned to Meron, more shattered and broken than before.

The things he had heard gave birth to difficult thoughts in his mind.

Her friends, who rent their clothes, all of them, and sat *shivah* for their friend, had told him that about two months before she had separated herself off from them and she would walk in the mountains, and until Friday when she was brought up from the waters of the Kinneret, they did not know what she was doing.

The fishermen told him that on Friday around two hours before noon they saw a young girl from the distance, coming down from the mountains. Her head looked upward and she continued to walk forward farther, farther . . . the water came up to her neck, it passed over her head—she was no more . . . they quickly rushed to her aid, they spread out their nets in that place . . . and they brought her up without any sign of life. . . .

And the local rabbi told him, trembling and whispering into his ear, that on the eve of Sabbath the sun had detained itself from setting until after the gravediggers had returned from the cemetery . . . and the gravediggers had sworn to the local rabbi that the clods of earth that were thrown on the grave stood up like an arc over the boards and would not fall down upon them . . . and it was with a great deal of effort that they filled the dirt in a mound. . . .

Hard days came to Rabbi Yose, the likes of which he had rarely seen.

The *shamash* suddenly knew something that he had never known since he had become a man. This young girl, who had drowned in the waters of the Kinneret, had become more dear to him than a daughter, than a wife or anyone else. In his whole life he had never been drawn or closely bound to anything. He was dedicated to the work that he had to do. He gave all of himself to holiness . . . and this one—it was as if she herself was a part of the holiness. . . .

, Nevertheless he mourned hard for her.

Had she killed herself? Why? What were they, the signs of glory that had been shown to her from Heaven? And was there reparation for her soul? Or was her fate like the fate of all disembodied souls—difficult and perpetual reincarnations without rest?

And in his distress he turned for help to the holy Baal Shem Tov. More than once or twice the guidance of the BeShT stood him through his trials.

He placed the Eternal Lamp in the safekeeping of his granddaughter, and he also put his wife in charge of it. Then he put on sackcloth, and ashes on his head, and he went off to wander in the mountains. He mourned and fasted for three days and three nights. He ate no bread, drank no water, and gave his eyes no rest. He sent out his plea to the holy Baal Shem Tov to illuminate his soul and to stand it before the Glorious Throne of Judgment, to seek compassion, mercy, and purification for her soul, so that she would not suffer the hard punishment that awaited her. Nor did he refrain from asking that the secret of the flower, the wondrous wildflower, be revealed.

For all of those three days a storm was in the mountains. Northern winds broke out of their hiding places, howling and raging, tearing up plants and vegetation, moving stones from their places, dislodging the foundations of the mountains. The face of Mt. Atzmon was dark with anger. Its sharp rocks protruded and grew sharper, the mountaintop reached skyward as if to give one last warning to the whole world. What was the warning about? The face of Yodefat, visible between the mountains of Zebulun, was more innocent than it had ever been. This would not have been so, except that the storm had ripped the outer crust that had formed on it over a long period of time, leaving it standing there naked before all. The great caves opened their mouths wider and wider, as if the storm had enlarged them, and a sound of weeping and lamentation went up painfully from the smiting wind and circled the mountains and the valleys and rolled into every crevice and ravine, and filled the spaces of the whole world. Were these not the voices of the afflicted and martyred now stealing forth with the wind from the caves in which they'd been sealed? The sun's light grew dark. Mourning lay heavy on the top of Gush Halav, as if the sorrow were increased seventy times over, blacker than black it was—hollowed out with bloody tracks. Only the top of Mt. Tabor, which looked out from the rocks in the area, was round and green as it always was, and it had its own light, hope and faith and a spirit of courage hovered over it, soothing, encouraging, bringing the good news of Redemption.

And on the fourth night a heavy sleep fell on Rabbi Yose. And in his dream, a night vision, he was standing in a long room that was full of light and holiness, and before him, on a golden throne, sat the holy BeShT in all his glory and alone and he spoke to Rabbi Yose

"My son, what is the fear that has brought you to me?"

"My rabbi and my teacher, please gaze upon the face of your servant. My heart is in my question and a Jewish soul is in my request: the soul of one who sins by taking his own life, is there any mercy for such a soul in the Seat of Judgment?"

"There is not."

"Only this one time look kindly upon your servant. Is it only impurity that can cause a person to take his own life or can an excess of holiness?"

"Only impurity, my son."

A heavy sigh burst forth from the old *shamash*'s heart and it caused the palace to shake.

"What is it, my son, that makes you sigh?"

"Oh holy one, I mourn for the disgrace of the Jewish people. Their glory has been brought down to the lowest of the low and the disgrace causes our sons and daughters to kill themselves."

"My son, do your words not refer to the one who was brought up from the Kinneret on Sabbath Eve?"

A spark of hope lit the darkness in the old man's heart. He was stirred up and he said, "Yes, oh holy one. My soul is in my question and the reparation of the soul of this one is my request. I know her and she is pure and good."

The BeShT sighed. The foundations of the world trembled.

"My son, it was told to me from behind the curtain. It is an edict."

"And what is the fate of this disembodied soul?"

A deadly silence reigned in the palace. The *shamash* bent his knee and bowed his head from the burden of his grief.

And the BeShT was enveloped with sadness.

Then a still voice was heard:

"My son, the time has come to reveal to you the beginning of the End."

The *shamash* trembled like a falling leaf and he lifted up his eyes in supplication to the BeShT.

"My son, lift the curtain from the window and see what is behind the curtain."

With quaking knees the *shamash* went to the window of the palace and lifted one corner of the curtain. Next to a marble pillar he stood, bound with iron chains, the Messiah . . . and a hidden hand, the hand of a young girl, removed the shackles from his arms and legs.

A loud cry came from Rabbi Yose and he fell prostrate on the floor. The young girl who stood there removing the chains of the Messiah, she was the one he had seen with the wildflower.

And then he awoke and behold, it had been a dream, and his spirit was troubled and he prayed: "Master of the Universe! Was it Your will to reveal to me only a little and conceal from me more? When will the sign be?"

But the heavens were cold and silent.

Worn out, depressed and dejected, the *shamash* returned home. And he
guarded the thing in his heart.

4

Years passed. Rabbi Yose, the *shamash*, grew very old. His daughter became
a widow. Her husband's boat was torn apart by the waters of the Kinneret
and he was drowned. The granddaughter, who watched the Eternal Lamp,
got married. At this time she was expecting; it was the beginning of her pregnancy. The poverty in the house increased. While the mouths to feed were
many, the income didn't change. The granddaughter's husband was also a
fisherman. And he made no more money than his father-in-law, may he rest
in peace. But it was not worrying over a livelihood or raising children that
had aged Rabbi Yose. The cloud that had covered his thoughts since he had
met the young girl had not lifted to the present day. And he experienced
many difficult times, days of doubt and troublesome thoughts. And there
was that which the heart did not dare divulge to the mouth. The iron wall
was about to crumble, and he began to have doubts, and he was almost on
the point of insanity. The blood of Israel spilled like water. The glory of Israel became an object for ridicule. Enough shame and anger. Still the foot-
prints of the Messiah were not yet seen. Every day brought with it only the
pangs of the Messiah—but the Messiah was not. Rabbi Yose would sometimes become strong as a lion and he would be comforted from the heavy
sorrow that pressed on his heart: "If not now . . . it cannot be far off . . . if I
am not worthy, my son will be worthy." And from these comforting
thoughts he would jump as if a scorpion had stung him. He would return to
his thoughts: "Can it truly not be in my time?"

There was one thought he couldn't get out of his head; it chilled his blood
and stopped his heart from beating. And there was a worry he hid in his
heart, not even revealing it to himself. It was like a rot penetrating his bones.
The Lord had not given him a male offspring. This and something more: he
had learned from his father, who had learned from his father, who had received it from his grandfather, that on the nineteenth of Kislev, on that day
the *tzaddik* Rabbi Shneur Zalman was released from prison, the one who was
to proceed the coming of the Messiah was to be born. Rabbi Yose had never
aspired to great things. But the Devil had his ways, and every time Rabbi
Yose's wife conceived, and after that his daughter, his mind would work by
itself without the permission of its owner, computing the period of pregnancy and the count reckoned—the nineteenth of Kislev. And when Rabbi
Yose would catch himself doing this, he would become frightened and he
would spit at whoever it was and he would rebuke whoever it was and he
would turn his steps to the tomb. Rabbi Yose was not a man of good fortune. His wife's first pregnancy ended in miscarriage. The second brought

him his daughter. And after that his wife was not able to conceive. He had not been worthy of a male child. His daughter's first pregnancy brought him his granddaughter. And after that his daughter's womb closed also. And behold, now it was his granddaughter who was expecting, and when his wife whispered to him about the first signs of the granddaughter's pregnancy, he made a vow to himself that he would not think or ponder this in any form or fashion. And when he would find himself entertaining light thoughts of that kind he would beat his breast and run with all his strength to the tomb, as if he wanted to seize it by the horns and be saved from the persecution of someone.

However, in a corner hidden in the deepest recesses of his heart, under a mound of ash, there lived a spark of hope. . . .

5

The nineteenth of Kislev began on Sabbath day. Therefore the eve of the nineteenth was the evening in which the Sabbath was consecrated. Rabbi Yose had always been accustomed to adding his own candle to the tomb of the *tzaddik* on that evening. Then after evening prayer, he would drink to life and taste the salted fish that his good wife would prepare for that evening. Since the days of his youth he had loved this tasty dish. This time, Rabbi Yose performed his regular duty at the Sabbath meal which his wife had prepared on the grand scale as she always had all of her days: fine bread, meat, and fish. Since the morning, Rabbi Yose was wrapped in the spirit of a song, sad and heart-stopping, one of the Bratzlav melodies which he particularly loved. He hummed it under his breath when he went to the *mikveh* and when he wore the *tefillin* and when he prepared the Eternal Lamp and also when he prepared the wood chips for his wife in honor of the Sabbath, as well as when he looked with pleasure at his wife's work, how she prepared and salted the great fish that the granddaughter's husband had brought that very day from Tiberias. It was a wondrous fish. Since the day he was born, Rabbi Yose had never seen one like it. It was big and fat and fresh, wriggling under the knife as if it were fighting for its life. Who knew if it held within it a reincarnation of a disembodied soul. . . .

In the afternoon, as Rabbi Yose stood washing his hands before the meal, his granddaughter passed by him; she was very pregnant, and she was busy getting the house in order for the Sabbath. She smiled at him with great affection, for she loved him very much. And a shadow flickered over the face of Rabbi Yose; was it of pleasure or sadness? At that moment it would be hard to determine. And as his wife chanced to enter the room at that moment, she bent her head and whispered quietly into his ear:

"There's still another month before the birth. May the Lord guard her from all evil and sickness."

"Mmmmmmm!" the old man mumbled as if he wanted to say something but couldn't get ordinary language out of his mouth before he had said the blessing over the meal and before he broke the bread and tasted it.

What the old man had wanted to say, if he had wanted to say something, was hidden from those who sat at the table. And only one thing was clear to all of them, that his good spirits, which he had had since morning, had suddenly vanished. A cloud of worry hovered over him and covered his face.

"What is bothering him? And how did I upset him?" the old woman wondered and she chewed her food with remorse; she did not know what she was feeling remorse about. A piece of the *challah* bread and the radish dipped in oil in honor of the Sabbath stuck in her throat.

Still the *shamash* was busy with holy work at the cave and the Eternal Lamp, and the sun was ready to set. Its rays turned the waters of the Kinneret to gold; they could be seen between the mountains. The horizon was peaceful, the sky was as clear as crystal, and only in the most northern extremity over Mt. Hermon a tiny cloud the size of the palm of a man's hand appeared. The gatekeeper, the dark Haji, had been watching over the Eternal Lamp from Sabbath's eve to Sabbath's end since the days Rabbi Yose's father, may he rest in peace, served as *shamash* at the tomb. The gatekeeper looked with his left eye, for his right had been blind since he was a child, toward the peaceful Kinneret, which was dead calm, and toward the little cloud that was right over the old man's head. The gatekeeper nodded, indicating suspicion. But Rabbi Yose paid no attention to the gatekeeper, the Kinneret, or the small cloud over his head, because he was ready to receive the Sabbath Queen. He immersed himself again in the *mikveh* that was in the cave, he put on the white underwrap and over that the velvet capote that he had received as an inheritance from his father, may he rest in peace, and he tied a silk sash around his waist. His hose were white as snow and his sandals had been pressed that day by his granddaughter. On his head he wore the three-cornered fur-trimmed hat. His face radiated with divine light. As usual, he prepared the Eternal Lamp that was before the tomb. He poured in the oil, enough to last somewhat beyond the end of Sabbath, and he turned over the watch to the Haji, who fulfilled his watch faithfully and honestly. Never had there been any mishap or accident when he was in charge.

Rabbi Yose was still doing this and that when his wife appeared at the threshold. Her face was full of worry, confusion, and distress and she signaled to him that he should come over to her. Her lips were moving but her voice could not be heard. Rabbi Yose paid no attention until the gatekeeper called her to his attention. Then Rabbi Yose looked at his wife and didn't understand what she was trying to tell him or what the mute whisper on her lips was all about. And he mumbled against her to himself, because she disturbed him at this time, and he came up to her and said:

"What has you so agitated that you have come to me?"

"Yose, Yose, listen, Yose . . . hear me . . . our granddaughter . . . Yose, our granddaughter . . ."

"What about her? What about the granddaughter, tell me?"

"Oh, Yose, she's about to give birth. Pains, birth pangs, have seized her. Oy, run pray to the Holy One . . ."

Suddenly, there appeared a spark of light on Rabbi Yose's face. He grabbed his wife and looked at her with happiness.

"My dear wife, why are you frightened? Let us lift up our hands and give thanks to the Master of the Universe for this great gift of love."

"Old man, your mind is playing tricks on you. She is having trouble . . . danger . . . do not tempt the Devil. There is still a month to go."

"Quiet, fool, do not cry out to high heaven. What's a month, what's a year, what's a generation? It's like a drop in the bucket, dust on the scales to the Will of the Almighty. Old woman, old woman, little fool, it is light for the nineteenth of Kislev. Behold, this one that comes today is the hope. Woman! Bring candles! I order you with a husband's command. Bring out all the candles! Pour all the oil, woman! Let us kindle candles and oil, let us make a great kindling, old woman! Open your mouth in song, sing a song! Let us sing! Let us be joyful, come, come! Bend an ear, hear it! Behold the sound of the trumpet of the Messiah, hear it break forth from the mountains, ascending. The Day of Retribution has come, Day of Restitution, Day of Salvation. Old woman. Light has broken through the darkness . . . a great light will illuminate us."

"Have you both gone crazy or have you left the straight and narrow? The *shofar* can be heard from Safed, the time to light the candles has arrived . . . and you old people are lovemaking."

The voice of the old Haji gatekeeper roused Rabbi Yose from his visionary dream and caused him to tremble. The old woman also trembled and looked at him with prayer and supplication as if she wanted mercy for herself, her husband, and for the one who was about to give birth and for the whole world.

"Old woman, the blessing over the candles, the sanctification of the Sabbath before all else. Woman, the candles!"

The old woman hurried to go and Rabbi Yose lit an extra candle at the tomb to honor the Sabbath, then he returned home to hear the blessing over the Sabbath candles. But the candles had just been lit, the words of the blessing had just died on the old woman's lips, when behold . . . the old man stood rooted to the spot.

A strange shrieking voice could be heard passing from one end of the earth to the other. A wild laugh, a venomous hoot, full of nerve and force. The mighty cracking of a whip was in the air. Scorn, mocking, perpetual noise . . . opposite this voice there answered from every side and corner, every rock and cave, behind every stone and bush, different voices that a man's ear had never heard since the earth was footstool to the sky. A wild, screaming voice. A voice of protest. A voice of anger, accusing, speaking evil. A voice saturated with blood and lust . . . and the face of the heavens was covered with black and heavy clouds that were like an iron partition between Heaven and earth. And a storm broke out of the north toward Hermon with the force of tens of thousands of chariots of fire. And the storm howled and bellowed and ate up Heaven and earth. It overturned, swept up, and destroyed everything it found in its way. It uprooted trees, toppled houses, moved mountains. A great storm came to the Kinneret. Gale after gale went up and swallowed everything on the face of the water. And the water leaped out of its boundaries and was ready to destroy the world and everything on it. A stench of pestilence, destruction and death pervaded everything. The End of the World had come. As if all creation was giving its last breath and was dying at once. There was no one to stand in the breach, no one to stop the destruction. The way to Heaven had been sealed off. The Gates of Mercy were locked. And the Deep opened her mouth wide without restraint.

There were only three people whose minds didn't abandon them, and who remained standing at their posts.

The gatekeeper, blind in one eye, sheltered the Eternal Lamp with his body and his cloak, so the wind would not do it any harm.

The old woman lit her five candles, a candle for every living soul in the house, and one more tiny candle, a sixth, for the one who was yet to come into the world. And behold, the wind came to the four corners of the house to turn it over on the old woman and the granddaughter who was about to give birth and the candles . . . but the old woman kept her place. She spread out her silk apron, her mother's Sabbath apron, peace be with her, and she shielded the candles with it. And the storm could not get to them.

And Rabbi Yose—the wings of his coat, his side locks, and beard all blew about in the wind. His black eyes shone like two fiery torches. And he did not cease to sing songs and praises raised on high. One minute he would run to the tomb and goad the old Haji on and encourage him, the next he would run home and watch his wife and lift her spirits. And the very next moment he would lift his ear and listen raptly to the quiet sigh that penetrated the door of the house and made a path for itself in the storm. And he encouraged his granddaughter and he prayed for her well-being.

"Old man, old man!" The whispering voice of the Haji reached his ear and he saw the gatekeeper motioning to him with his hand and calling him. And Rabbi Yose went up to him.

"Old man! There is no remedy or solution except to placate her wrath."

"Whose wrath?"

The gatekeeper bent his head close to Rabbi Yose's ear and whispered, "The Kinneret's."

"Why? What?"

"She is angry. Because of the fish that you take from her every Friday to honor the Sabbath Queen. The Kinneret is jealous."

"Your mouth speaks lies!"

"Don't get angry. You are a wise *shumush*. I am an experienced gate-keeper. I have heard it from the mouths of the elders. In the first six days of Creation the Kinneret was the wife of Allah. And on the seventh day, your Queen took her place. And from that day she has carried her sorrow and jealousy with secret intent. The Devil tried to soothe her, and she, the fool, kicked him away. Only once in a great while she rebels and protests against Heaven. As if she were not shamed enough it is compounded because her glory and her fish are taken from her, making her distress all the greater! And then, when her anger erupts she cannot be restored except by the flesh of one of the daughters of Israel who prepares the fish. With this only will her anger be placated."

"Idol worship!" cried out Rabbi Yose, and he spat at the Haji.

"Not idol worship, old man. Your worship. Your Sabbath. The Kinneret was yours and will be yours again, but she will not be avenged except by your blood. Do you not remember the one the fishermen brought up out of the Kinneret with their nets? She wanted to give herself to the Kinneret, so that she would be redeemed, but the girl wasn't worthy. Another will be worthy."

"Silence!"

"I will not be silent. You have no solution, old man, except to promise her the flesh of the one who is about to give birth. And if not—we are lost. The lamp that is on the tomb will go out in a little while. The candles in front of your wife will turn over. Already the apron is rent to shreds. And the whole world will return to nothingness and void. The forces below have overcome the forces above. Promise her, old man, and we will all be saved for her sake."

"Old Asmodeus, put a stopper on your mouth! I know you! I recognize you! You have just been covering yourself with the skin of a gatekeeper all your days. Your day has come, behold, it has come! This one who is about to be born is a light for the nineteenth of Kislev—the news of Redemption is in his mouth. Behold, I will say it in his name, that the one who is about to be born will broadcast his arrival, and all of your arguments will be stopped, you will be turned into a mound of ash, and all of the forces that you have gathered to turn the world upside down will amount to nothing, zero. Behold me, I call out his name: Messiah!"

And before the name had died on Rabbi Yose's lips, from within the house there came a thin whistling sound. The candles before the old lady remained upright. The wind and the storm and the strange voices were as if they never had been. The gatekeeper, the old Haji, was carried and tumbled away in the air, and he disappeared like a speck of dust in the wind. And Sabbath peace came to every corner of the world.

Rabbi Yose lifted his hands on high, and his mouth was full with song, thanksgiving, and praise.

"Yose, Yose, a good Sabbath and a good sign! Our granddaughter gave birth to a girl for good luck!"

Rabbi Yose fell prostrate to the ground and fainted.

6

And at night, when a heavy sleep fell upon Rabbi Yose, the BeShT in all his glory came alone to Yose and said these words:

"Yose, my son, do not be grieved. This great-granddaughter that was born to you with the sanctification of the Sabbath—in her time will the beginning of the vision be, which I will show you."

And the old man trembled greatly and he asked:

"Oh holy one, what is the name that I shall call her?"

"Lift your eyes and look in the corner of the room."

"Behold me . . ."

Rabbi Yose lifted his eyes to the corner of the room—and his heart froze within him. She stood across from him. The legs were bare from the knees on down, the arms were bare, and the hair, uncovered, was in ringlets and fell on her shoulders; and tangled and entwined in her hair were the tendrils of the seaweed from the belly of the Kinneret, and her eyes were big and black and they were full of a spark of holiness, and they were full of a pure and silent prayerfulness.

"This one? Her name?" asked Rabbi Yose, trembling.

"Yes, Yose, my son, her name. Your great-granddaughter is nothing else but a reincarnation of the soul of this one."

"Oh wise one . . . is she not the one . . . then her soul was redeemed?"

"Do not pursue what is too wondrous for you. Great are the searchings of the heart. Do what I have told you. It was told to me from the other side of the curtain."

On the Sabbath, with the gathering of a *minyan* of worshipers from Safed and Tiberias at the tomb of Rabbi Simeon ben Yohai at the time of the Torah reading, Rabbi Yose named his great-granddaughter with a name in Israel "Ruhamah." And after the Sabbath, before the *havdalah* candle had gone out, Rabbi Yose died peacefully. And he lay with his forefathers.

Within the period of a year, the old lady, Rabbi Yose's wife, also died. And the widowed daughter, the granddaughter, her husband, and the little girl all went from Meron and settled in the *moshav* that was on the other side of the mountain. And the granddaughter's husband became a worker of the land. He soaked the earth with the sweat of his brow and he ate the produce of his land. Because thus was it written and explained word for word in the will of Rabbi Yose which he left to his household after him.

Translated from the Hebrew
by Pamela Altfeld Malone

A Message from the Messiah
by Howard Schwartz

One day Reb Nachman spoke to his Hasidim of the Shattering of the Vessels and of the Gathering of the Sparks. Of how the vessels had emanated from the *Ein Sof,* the Beginning before which there was no beginning, filled with primordial light. And how these vessels had somehow shattered, scattering sparks of light everywhere in the world. And how it was the purpose of every Jew to search for those sparks no matter where they were hidden, so that the vessels might someday be restored. For since waking that day Reb Nachman had felt as if he had come close to an understanding of this divine mystery that was still concealed from him, although he felt its presence as if it were palpable. Therefore he spoke to his Hasidim in the hope that one of them might be the vessel through which this secret would be revealed.

So it was that Reb Nachman encouraged each of his Hasidim to question him that day. And because Reb Shimon had been Reb Nachman's first disciple, it was his honor to ask the first question. And Reb Shimon said: "Tell me, Rebbe, where shall I search for the sparks that must be gathered?"

And Reb Nachman said: "Look first, Shimon, in your own soul. For a man's soul consists of many sparks. And from where do these sparks come? From the light given off by great men after their death. For you must know that no longer does a man inherit a single *neshamah.* Remember: there were only six hundred thousand *neshamahs* created at the beginning of time, and the same number were present at Mount Sinai to receive the Torah. But today there are more Jewish bodies than there are Jewish souls. Therefore the souls of men have become fragmented, and it is a rare soul indeed that is inherited from a single source. Even in my own soul I have recognized the sparks of many souls—of the souls of Moses, of Shimon bar Yohai, of the Ari, and, of course, of the Baal Shem Tov. In addition I have recognized sparks of the souls of both Messiah ben Joseph and Messiah ben David. And the seventh soul is one that had not been reborn since the days of the Wandering in the Wilderness. So long had it searched for a resting place."

After Reb Nachman had spoken his Hasidim were silent, for they too sensed the mystery hovering above them. Finally Reb Nussan, Reb Nachman's scribe, spoke up and said: "But tell me, Rebbe, why did the vessels split apart in the first place?"

And Reb Nachman replied without any hesitation: "It is little understood, Nussan, that it was the destiny of the vessels to shatter, just as seed pods break open when they are ripe and cast their seeds into the wind."

With these words the current quickened and carried all of them a little closer to the edge of a waterfall, and all of them became afraid, and none of the others dared to speak. But at last one other spoke up, Reb Naftali, the musician, who played many instruments, but when he played the violin, the music evoked in all who heard it long lost memories of the Garden of Eden, and left a taste as sweet as manna. And Reb Naftali said: "All of us, Rebbe, seek to gather the sparks. But who will restore the vessels so that they can contain the divine light?" And to this question not even Reb Nachman dared to reply, for the restoration of the vessels could not be accomplished by any man.

But that night Reb Nachman had a dream that was a crystal vision, in which the veil was at last torn away from the mystery that had hovered among them like a dove above its nest. In that dream Reb Nachman found himself in the Holy Land, in the holy city of Safed, where the Ari, Rabbi Isaac Luria, had made his home. And the path Reb Nachman followed led him directly to a *beit knesset* in that city. And the walls of that House of Prayer were made of stone, and the shape of the building was round, so that it resembled a dome. And when Reb Nachman entered there he found that the Ark of the Covenant had been placed in the center of that House of Prayer. And the curtains of the Ark had been pulled back so that the scrolls of the Torah were revealed, and there were seven scrolls inside that Ark.

It was at that moment that the door of the *beit knesset* opened and a man entered there whose face was glowing. And when this man saw that Reb Nachman was already there, he said: "I hope I have not kept you waiting." And Reb Nachman said: "There is only one for whom I am waiting, and that is for the Redeemer who shall restore the shattered vessels." And the man replied: "It is he who has sent me here with a message to deliver to you." And he took out a sealed letter from beneath his white robe and gave it to Reb Nachman. And when Reb Nachman had broken open the seven seals he saw that the words were written in large Hebrew letters, and that the script of the letters was similar to that of the Torah.

And Reb Nachman was staggered to receive such a message. And he said to the man: "Where have you come from?" And he replied: "I have come from a kingdom quite distant from here, from a place more than two years' journey from where the ten lost tribes live, on the other side of the River Sambatyon." And Reb Nachman said: "Then how have you come to this place?" And the messenger replied: "I traveled in the underground caverns that cross the earth, through which all souls will travel to reach Jerusalem at the End of Days, when the Messiah takes his place among men."

And when he heard this Reb Nachman grew afraid. And he said: "What is your name?" And the man said: "I am the spirit of Hayim Vital. In the afterlife I have been made the messenger of the Messiah, just as I was the messenger of the Ari."

And in the presence of Hayim Vital Reb Nachman was in awe, for it was through the pure vessels of Hayim Vital's writings that the sacred teachings of the Ari had been preserved and transmitted. And then Reb Nachman remembered that he had just received a letter from the Messiah. And he opened the letter and this time the letters of the words burned in his vision, black flames illuminated by white. And at that very moment Reb Nachman stepped outside his body and his soul broke into blossom. And when he looked up he saw the twenty-two letters of the alphabet flying everywhere around him like dark birds. And then he saw that every letter was actually a vessel filled with light, and that every one of them understood what it meant to receive. And he saw that when the vessels became so full that they overflowed, they spilled sparks of light into the world, and each spark was a primal seed taking root wherever it touched down.

Then Reb Nachman woke up, and as he lay back on his bed and remembered this dream he felt as if he had swallowed one of those sparks, for inside him a sun seemed to be growing ripe. And every word Reb Nachman spoke to his Hasidim that day was inscribed in their memories and took root in their souls. And those were the very same words that the Messiah had written in the message that he had sent.

The Two Souls of Professor Scholem
by Howard Schwartz

To fully grasp the paradox of Professor Scholem you must know that two souls have been incarnated into the same body. One of these is the soul of a Kabbalist, one of the most daring and wise, who, like Rabbi Akiba, could ascend into Paradise and descend in peace. This soul was once the soul of a disciple of Moses de Leon, who sat with his master during the years that he was writing the *Zohar*, and reluctantly obeyed his master's command that he tell no one that Moses de Leon and not Simeon bar Yohai was the true author of the *Zohar*. But because he obeyed his master's wish, and remained silent, the soul of this disciple left his body restless and unsatisfied, and wandered like the Wandering Jew for six centuries until it was reborn as one of the two souls of Professor Scholem. This soul found it necessary to immerse itself in the deep waters of the *Zohar* and other Kabbalistic texts in order to thrive. And the soul had no doubt that it would convince the human it inhabited to devote his life to the study of precisely those texts.

On the other hand, Professor Scholem's second soul: a German scholar, one of the best of that breed. Meticulous, persistent, with one eye for detail and one for overview. And this soul, which had been promised to a pliable lad, was diverted on this lad's death to the same Professor Scholem, where it found itself caught up, virtually caged, with the soul of the mad Kabbalist— mad from the point of view of the scholar's soul, in that the other soul refused to follow the scholar's soul into the realm it preferred, Mathematics. And because of the contrary soul's resistance, the young professor soon realized that he would never become the best in the field. Then the scholar's soul was struck with its moment of supreme illumination. It understood that it could free itself of the struggle with the contrary Kabbalistic soul by giving that soul its complete freedom: the scholar's soul would simply follow after him, taking notes. That solved everything.

The Messiah's Overcoat
by Aaron Sussaman

My grandfather picked me up and cradled me in his arms, letting my head rest on the bushy gray pillow of his beard. I had stayed up late to listen to him and the other men in the study house of the synagogue tell stories about the Messiah, and now I was so sleepy I could hardly keep my eyes open.

He carried me outside into the night, wrapping part of his overcoat around me for a blanket, and headed down the long, moonlit hill toward his house. It was like being curled up in a bed that was slowly bobbing along high above the world.

I closed my eyes and thought of the stories, full of sweetness and ache, that I'd heard. I loved the one about how the soul of all the Jewish people sat with the Messiah in his palace, waiting with him, her grave eyes, like his, seeing to the end of things. I loved best of all my grandfather's own story about how God took the moon away from the world for one day, and the world wept because until then it didn't know what need it had of the moon—that was how the Jews would weep, and be lost, if the hope of the Messiah were taken away for even one day.

I could hear my grandfather, as though from far off, singing me a lullaby in Yiddish. It was a song about what the world would be when the Messiah came. What good things to eat and drink, what wisdom from King Solomon, what music from King David, what stars in the sky, like eyes that shine with tears when the joy of the heart overflows.

The button on my grandfather's coat that had been rubbing gently against my forehead, like a little secret wanting inside, got quieter and quieter and finally grew still. I fell asleep.

There, in his arms, I dreamed of the Messiah. He looked like my grandfather, but he glowed. He was sitting on a cloud, smiling, because God had just told him that it was time to put on his overcoat and come down to earth. So he stood up and he put on his overcoat and he started buttoning the buttons. I became very sad. I looked at all the buttons he had to button, and it seemed to me there were more of them than stars in the sky. I was sure it would take him forever to finish.

When I awoke, my grandfather was tucking me in bed. "Grandfather," I asked, muddled with sleep and innocence but wanting so to understand, "why does the Messiah have to wear an overcoat when he comes? Can't he just come in his pajamas?"

My grandfather smiled softly, giving the ancient, wistful shrug of the wise, and kissed me good night.

The True Waiting
by Elie Wiesel

Having concluded that human suffering was beyond endurance, a certain Rebbe went up to heaven and knocked at the Messiah's gate.

"Why are you taking so long?" he asked him. "Don't you know mankind is expecting you?"

"It's not me they are expecting," answered the Messiah. "Some are waiting for good health and riches. Others for serenity and knowledge. Or peace in the home and happiness. No, it's not me they are awaiting."

At this point, they say, the Rebbe lost patience and cried: "So be it! If you have but one face, may it remain in shadow! If you cannot help men, all men, resolve their problems, all their problems, even the most insignificant, then stay where you are, as you are. If you still have not guessed that you are bread for the hungry, a voice for the old man without heirs, sleep for those who dread night, if you have not understood all this and more: that every wait is a wait for you, then you are telling the truth: indeed, it is not you that mankind is waiting for."

The Rebbe came back to earth, gathered his disciples and forbade them to despair:

"And now the true waiting begins."

Translated from the French
by Lily Edelman and the author

The Palace of Pearls

by Penina Villenchik

It begins with Aleph, the first letter of the Hebrew alphabet. Aleph, the infinite seed; Beth, the first shelter, the womb; Gimel, the initial step, the weaning away; Daleth, the door to the world.

It begins with a few letters and a few names: Penina, Perla, Pearl, the name of her great-grandmother; Shekhinah, how God's mate is called; Samuel, name of her grandfather.

The names lead to a kingdom of words: Adam—Man, Adamah—Earth, Shamayim—Heavens, Nahar—River, Midbar—Wilderness, Ruah—Wind, Mayim—Waters, Etz—Tree, Hayim—Life. With each word Penina reclaimed a fragment of a vessel that had been shattered when her ancestors were scattered all over the earth. She regained a vocabulary which her soul leaped to speak as a hungry fish leaps to the surface of the water to consume a few choice crumbs. She had not realized how hungry she was until she began to eat.

Then the Land of Israel, Herself, began to call to Penina through the Hebrew. In a dream her grandfather Samuel holds out a scroll of the Torah for her to read. As she comes closer to look, he clasps the Torah to his chest with the love of a husband for his wife. He holds Her so close to him. Penina beholds their bond with awe.

"Union such as ours is possible only in the Land of Israel," explains her grandfather. "It occurs when the Shekhinah lives with God.

"Shekhinah is a new rose, slowly unfolding Her secrets. She will urge you up the path little by little, round and round until you reach Her sacred center, the Holy of Holies. Many tears it will take to open its gates, many tears hardening into milk-white pearls. In this way you will have built Her palace yourself, from your own innermost longing: each pearl a death and a rebirth, a divine sphere which you exude from your tough shell. Most difficult of all, you will give birth to yourself.

"But first you have to leave behind the limbo in which you were born, in which your father and mother were born. Return to the Land of the Torah. Her soil is rich and potent, full to bursting as a ripe pomegranate, at Rosh Hashanah, the head of the year."

Penina awoke. On the shelf above her head, her grandfather's Bible lay open at Lekh Lekha: "Go from your land and your kindred and your father's house to the land which I shall show you."

It begins with Aleph, the first letter of the Hebrew alphabet. Hebrew: the language her father could barely read, let alone understand; the language whose Torah her grandfather could barely understand, though for some reason which he could not even name, he believed in it; the language her great-grandfather had held so sacred he would speak it only on the Sabbath. Hebrew bore in the soul of each letter the history of hundreds of generations who lived before her and now lay buried under the muted earth. At last Penina was ready to go to Israel, as her grandfather had instructed her, to find the palace of pearls.

She reached the hills of Jerusalem in midsummer.

The dry heat was a warm hand caressing the world. Scents of hummus and falafel and fresh-baked bread, Turkish coffee ground with cardamon seed, tea minted with nana leaves; fragrance of honeysuckle and lemony acacia and sweet roses; rich red baking earth always underfoot.

Women in rainbow dresses: Mediterranean turquoise and queenly vermilion, pale amethyst and flaming orange, golden ocher and pine-dark emerald; in the swarming marketplace luscious honeydews and casaba melons, shimmering peaches, squashes, peppers inviting her to squeeze, to rattle, to taste.

Sounds drifted on the air like birds: the mournful song of the minaret awakened her each morning even before the cock's crow, grayish babble of old men and young men chanting in the synagogues on Friday evening; the sheep's bell and the goat's bell clanging softly in four-footed time in the distant wadis; the everchanging wind named Ruach was a veil wrapping itself around and around the pine trees and the hills, helplessly moaning through the cracks of windows and doors like a lonely, old widow.

Now Penina was bound to find where She lived, to enter the palace of pearls which her grandfather had described.

She went to the marketplace, to the synagogue, to the university, asking everyone she met where the palace of pearls could be found. Nobody could tell her.

The man who sold cheeses and olives in the marketplace joked bitterly, "Palace of pearls? You'd be more likely to find a palace of pigs in this country! We don't even let ourselves dream of such riches here. Who ever heard of such a thing since Solomon's Temple?"

The men finished praying in the synagogue, then they listened to her question and considered it well before answering: "Palace of pearls? There may have been one in Solomon's time, but we do not hold with such ostentatious displays of adoration nowadays. Our temple is the plainest sort, as you can see."

Then Penina asked a professor of Bible in the university, "Where can I find the palace of pearls, the abode of the Shekhinah?"

The learned man frowned and then spoke to her as if addressing a very small child, "My dear, we don't take that subject seriously here. You had best ask somewhere else."

She was at a loss where to turn next. But then a student who had over-heard her brief conversation with the professor approached her and said, "You are looking for the palace of pearls? I'll take you there. Let's go." His smile beckoned and Penina followed him, fascinated by his beautiful black curly hair and his lean, long limbs. He was a wild, young horse.

They walked in the hot sun of late afternoon to the outskirts of the city, far from the marketplace, far from the synagogue, far from the university. After several hours of walking in silence, the young stallion turned to her and suggested, "Let's sit and talk first before I bring you to the palace. Tell me about your quest, where you have come from and how you came to search for the palace of pearls."

With great relief Penina poured out her story of longing, how she had come from a soulless country, how her grandfather had shown her the bliss-ful union with his beloved Torah which was possible only in Israel.

Then the student began to recite to her the progress of his own quest, but it was not with words so much as with his eyes that he told her. She was transfixed by those coruscations of black onyx. His voice wound like weeds around her ears. "Now I am ready to show you my palace. Come." It was dusk as he led Penina by the hand up to a windy hilltop. And then she saw, indeed, there it stood at last in glistening splendor, the palace of pearls.

Penina had never beheld such beauty. Walls constructed entirely of pearl—every size, shape, and hue. The great entry doors were framed in tiny seed pearls, transparent as teardrops, and the roof was shingled in pure mother-of-pearl, reflecting the setting sun. She could not speak but went over to touch the magnificent structure.

"Don't touch," he commanded from behind her. "First promise you'll stay here forever."

Then Penina remembered her grandfather's words: "Only if you show me where the Torah is," she returned.

His face shriveled. "I am not Jewish," he confessed bitterly. A wind shiv-ered through his entire body, a roaring emerged from his depths and opened his mouth wider and wider, until his whole body was swallowed inside. Then the entire palace came tumbling down, turning into a thick brown cloud of choking dust.

The student with the curly mane was gone. The palace was gone. Over-come by loss, Penina wept and wept until the cloud of dust became a mud puddle at her feet. Hope was gone.

But in the dark puddle, she began to discern the reflection of a beautiful young woman. She knelt at the edge of the pool and saw that the woman was speaking, soundlessly at first, then faintly until the words were barely audible.

"Do not despair, wandering one," soothed the woman. "This palace was only a mirage, built by the uncircumcised. I have been imprisoned inside it for as long as I can remember. As soon as you asked for me, the student was required to give me up. Believe me, he wanted his illusions to crumble but he had built them with such care that he could not raze them himself."

The vision vanished and Penina arose from her knees to survey the darkening hills and wadis around Jerusalem. Night was settling in the crevices of the earth, night was caressing the scorched slopes and hilltops with cool fingertips.

She let her feet guide her and so she wandered across the silent hills, unafraid. With each footstep, each crunch of dry ground, the earth spoke. "I shall protect you from the night terrors in these hills. Only trust in me and I shall lead you where you must go."

Then Penina saw in the distance a small stone hut built right into the face of the mountain. In the thickening moonlight she could barely distinguish a human form squatting before the hut. The sounds of a flute trickled into her ears and she longed to follow them, but she was wary of strangers by now and would not fall into the pit of kindness so easily.

She approached the hut cautiously, ready for a barking voice or a rough hand, but it was only a blue-robed boy with soft red-feathered hair. She could not resist that softness, reaching out to touch his head. He arose, answering her with joy on his reed flute. He was graceful as the Great Blue Heron.

She understood that he would guide her to the place. They wandered over the hillsides together in the moonlight, the strange bird speech of his flute encouraging her onward. The blue-robed boy was teaching her with his music to walk lovingly, patiently all over the earth's body.

Then her foot stumbled on something lying on the ground. It was not a rock or a bush. She picked it up. It was a festival drum shaped like an hourglass and blue as the flowing robes of the boy whom she followed.

Gently Penina began to tap the drum on its calfskin face with the heel of her hand. Tap, tap, tap, tap, the ground vibrated in her feet, deeper and deeper, resounded in the most untouched crevices and cracks, faint, faintly, faintly, the almost imperceptible tremor of a heart beneath the earth beating louder and deeper, louder and deeper, until all hearts were one heart breathing together, beating together, and all beings buried beneath Her crust filtered up through the furrows and folds of earth, beating, beating.

Flute notes on the wind bade her follow. The mouth of a cave gaped open before them. A final beat of the blue drum and she heard the lonely hoot of an owl from deep within, begging her to enter.

"But I can't come in yet," Penina cried. "I must go back home and play on this drum for my family so they will understand that She is here, the heart beating in the Land of Israel. Exiled from Her land since Her people were expelled, She has now returned. She fills the Land of Israel with Her Presence."

"You can never go back," the boy warned on his flute, "once you know what you know."

She refused to believe him. Still holding the drum, she walked away from the cave. She started tapping again, but this time the beating became fainter and fainter the further she went from the cave until it died entirely. She knew she would never be able to play the drum for her family. Like the Emperor's nightingale this drum could sound only in its native land. This knowledge was a sword that pierced her heart. A horrid gaping emptiness where her family had been. And Penina wept as if her heart would pour out of her body.

She walked back blindly, crunching earth, her steps slow and deliberate as the approach to a holy temple. Tapping, tapping all the while with the heel of her hand on the soft brown calfskin face until the beating began again. She reached the mouth of the cave where he stood waiting for her. Three pairs of sandals lay just outside the entrance. She hesitated, then took off her own and the barefoot boy took her hand.

They went down, down, down in darkness. The drum gave off a blue light by which they saw their way. They came to a narrow slit in the cave wall. He bade her peer inside.

She saw a torch-lit room lined with scrolls—Torahs of every size and color, and great tomes of Talmud, Midrash, and holy books. In the middle of this treasure was an old bent man, clad in rags nearly the color of the stone on which he sat. He turned around instantly, sensing her. Penina could not help herself. She came to where he sat. His finger stroked her damp cheek.

"Yes, weep, my daughter, weep, for the gate of tears is the only entrance into this palace. What is your name?"

"Penina," she said.

"Yes, Penina, little Pearl. Welcome to the true palace of pearls where your tears have joined to my son's fire."

She looked and surely, the boy's hair was flaming, his eyes were sparkling.

"Ah, Penina," said the sage and then, "Thank you, my son, for bringing her here safely. You see," he went on, "my son and I have been living here in this cave since before you were born. Here we have been practicing the wisdom of the Torah. By all the knowledge therein we sought to make the Shekhinah appear in Israel, for though always present, She is often hidden. Only a woman able to hear Her voice could find this cave. Countless people have walked by it and never noticed the drum. Countless others have picked it up and never attempted to play it. Hundreds have tried to make it sound, but only one could coax it alive. Now that you have returned to Israel, you can forge new links in the golden chain which my son and I have striven to keep from breaking.

"For there is more wisdom here than we can ever penetrate, more understanding than we can bear alone." He motioned towards the books, which were glowing. "These books contain your life and breath."

Penina beheld the beautiful young woman of the puddle, now perched like an owl among the volumes, and marveled at how she had at last discovered the palace. "I came to know Her first in ways that were never in books. I didn't know what I was looking for, only that I was looking. My grandfather showed me in a dream that She dwells in Israel and inhabits the Torah. So I came and found this drum."

"Penina, your search has been rewarded," announced the old rabbi. "I give you my only son in marriage, the last link in our family chain. He has grown and thrived on the soil of Israel. Be fruitful and multiply, my children. Play the drum and the flute together. In coming generations your music will reverberate throughout the universe."

Once more Penina heard the plaintive hoot of an owl as the rabbi, his flesh the color of ancient parchment, became one with his books. The rabbi's son stood by her side. Together they listened to the sublime music the books emitted. It was the voice of the Torah singing Herself.

The son of the rabbi took Penina's hand and she floated up. His touch was so gentle that the dead and the not-yet-born arose in her. He clasped her to his chest as if she were his Torah. Pestle pressed into mortar. Night poured onto the sweltering hills. There was rain and a stream flowed in the desert. God embraced His Shekhinah once again.

The Tale of the Garden
by Rabbi Tsvi Blanchard

Reb Zvi had a fault. He arrived on time. Hasidim say that the greatest of the masters were beyond time, some even beyond space. But Reb Zvi was not. He remained rooted to the earth, and imprisoned by space. Worse, it was by his own will that he lived in time and accepted its demands. Yet it happened that Reb Zvi was tricked into transcending time.

Reb Zvi had a special room off his house where he held prayers with his Hasidim. He also gave *divrei Torahs* to his followers in a hall near his home. On days when he was to speak he rose early and walked alone before arriving at the hall. On one of these walks he passed a walled garden. The secluded garden intrigued him, and he quickly located an entrance. His first glimpse showed a garden so beautiful that he knew he would need to remain for many hours to enjoy it. He was very tempted to stay, but he remembered his *d'var Torah* of that day, and he decided to return the following day. As he was about to leave, a young woman, who seemed to be the keeper of the garden, appeared at the wall and beckoned him to enter. Nonetheless he turned and went his way.

The next day he rose earlier than before and went directly to the garden. He hoped he would have enough time to explore it, but again, the garden disclosed itself as wondrous beyond the limits of his time. Just as before, the young woman beckoned him to enter. He knew that to enter would mean being very late for his *d'var Torah*. The woman was somehow harder to resist than before, and Reb Zvi had to use all his power to turn away. This same scene was repeated many times. Reb Zvi would arise earlier, go to the garden, and find that it revealed an even deeper aspect than before, that it promised delights which demanded more time than he had to give. Each time the maiden increased her entreaties that he enter, offering him free access to the garden and all its delights. But each time Reb Zvi refused, knowing that he must go his way. Life made its demands, people were waiting.

At last Reb Zvi reached the moment when all hung in the balance. He had gone the whole night without sleep but still lacked sufficient time. Now he stood at the entrance to the garden, facing the maiden, her face more radiant than ever before. True, others needed him; true, he was a rebbe. But he was also human, and he knew that if he were ever to enter the garden it must be now. He entered.

As he had expected, he became lost in the garden. For eons the woman guided him from flower to flower and from tree to tree. She revealed to him colors beyond his imagination, and depth beyond his own soul. For longer than the Holy One took to create the world, Reb Zvi lived the night of his deepest dreams, holding near what before he had sensed only at a distance. Reb Zvi had often cautioned his followers about the dangers of the spiritual search. To become yourself might mean to be caught in the swirling windstorm of one's infinite possibilities, some of which, God forbid, might cause a man to be lost. Now he himself was lost in the swirl. He realized at last that he had slipped beyond time and was living out all his incarnations, his *gilgulim*, at once.

The maiden also pained him. He understood that she was his self facing him as a woman. He had dreamed of fulfilling the holy Zohar by finding the woman who was himself. Now, having found her, he felt entrapped in a self that was not he. The maiden offered a simple solution: "Unite with me and remain in the garden." "But what of my Hasidim," said the rebbe, "what of my wife and children?" "Here," she answered, "here, there are all the Hasidim that have ever been or will be, all the wives of all your incarnations, and all their children."

Reb Zvi remained puzzled. Then in a flash his reply came to him like a Kabbalist's magic formula, breaking the seals which barred his way. He said: "I claim my wife, the daughter of Rivchin, and my two sons Duvid Moshe and Yisroel, and *my* daughter who made me Yaakov Zvi."

With this he found himself standing before his Hasidim. He had arrived in time.

The Tale of the Spark

by Rabbi Tsvi Blanchard

Reb Zvi said: "There is a man I know, let us call him Hayim. Hayim's life and mine crossed in a very strange way. Hayim is a writer. He was a writer who had very tenuous connections with Judaism. Nor did his writings reflect any particularly Jewish concerns. And then his path crossed mine. And afterwards things turned around in a whole different direction for Hayim. He started becoming involved in Jewish matters. He caught on immediately, and people recognized at once that he had talent in the area. It was apparent to everyone that this was what he was supposed to be doing.

"As time passed Hayim got better and better at this, until he was almost an expert at the Aggadah. He could tell stories like the old rebbes. If you gave him a drop of water, he made a whole ocean out of it. The problem was that Hayim kept saying to himself, 'Why is it that I'm so good at this, but at *mitzvahs* I'm not so good?' It was like living in two different countries. But how could it be? How could a person have this close a connection to Torah on one side, and on the other side it was like a different world? It was as if he were an ordinary person as far as *mitzvahs* are concerned, but something very special whenever he would start communicating spiritually.

"Every time I would see Hayim he would ask me this question, but not openly. This was the question of his life. It was as if the sun were shining on one side of the ocean, and on the other side some days were cloudy, and some days the sun shined. Finally his *neshamah* came to me and said, 'I have to know the answer to this question.' So I told the *neshamah* this story:

" 'In the beginning, as everyone knows, the world was created and the vessels could not hold the sparks. The vessels were smashed and the light went everywhere. But they don't think about what it really means to be a spark. A spark is not a whole fire. A flame is a whole fire. A spark is a part of a fire. It can kindle an amazing blaze. If you have an arid, dry house, one little spark can turn the whole thing into a huge fire.

" 'In our generation, *Bazaman Hazeh*, the world is very dry. So you'll sometimes find not a whole fire, but a spark. And once that spark is released it will burn a whole house. It will create a light that people can see for fifty miles. But it's only one little spark when it starts. So in our time you don't look for the whole fire, you look for the spark. Things today are fragmented. There are very rare occasions when a person is a whole fire. People who are sparks have to find out what it is that illuminates them. And they'll know, because it will start a blazing fire. That's the story.'

"When the *neshamah* of the writer Hayim had heard this story, it asked me: 'But is a spark enough?' And I replied: 'I'll tell you another tale. There once were two people who were traveling in a forest in the winter. And they had meant to get to a town by day. But they didn't succeed, and they had to spend the night in the cold, dangerous forest. They needed a fire desperately, because without a fire not only might they freeze to death, but they might be attacked by wolves. So they decided that they had to try to build a fire. And it would be easy to build a fire, since the forest is filled with dry wood. But there are no sparks. So they looked around, and they found a very small rock. They thought that perhaps if they broke the rock, and hit the parts together, they might get one small spark. Of course, they would have preferred a big, glowing coal. A glowing coal is always better than a rock to start a fire with. But in a forest you don't find big, glowing coals. And after many hours of labor they succeeded in starting the fire. And one of them said, "You know, I would have preferred a glowing coal, but a spark is enough." ' "

The Magic Spark

by *Miriam Goldman*

Who has not been waked by a dream we were just this second dreaming but can't recall though it holds us in its net? Or huddling in our warmth, wake so panicked we begin to count our wasted days because we remember everything—the place, the gestures, the ominous familiar words.

I am sitting on a cliff above a river deep and broad enough for ships. The river is empty, the air which has weight and density is hard to breathe. A small black barge creeps by, smoke rising from the coals like mist. At once I know the coals aren't coals. They are my mother and my father burning. Running along the edge, I try to shout and call them back but my throat is locked. Still straining I wake up, words I hoped were buried and forgotten cold and bitter in my mouth. Eyes closed against the light, I see the smoking barge float down the river with the tide. What shall I do with such a dream? The dream is mine forever. I know then that I am exiled, banished as we all are from our childhood. And though I'm not yearning to go back, though I have no deep nostalgia for those boggy green May meadows, I long for those I loved, even for a few I didn't know I loved . . . for their loved lost voices.

My grandmother, Rifka, sang her stories. It pleased me when I was little that her maiden name meant *fire*. She sang like a gypsy, her voice thrown out harsh and clear with sweetness lurking in it. Sometimes after singing, she would stand, clap her hands, and dance. *Hopf! Hopf!* A stately woman, she turned in place with the lightest beating of her heels but slowly, carefully, because she had a sick heart and easily grew dizzy, not falling, but toppling full length like a tree that has been axed. Her apron pocket held everything in daily use that was most important: her glasses, her pills, the last letters from Austria and Israel, and a white lawn handkerchief folded into a square, with her initials and blue flowers embroidered in a garland. Now she carried a letter informing her of the extinction of her uncle's and her cousin's entire family. The uncle's name is also Feuer, and this frightens me. Several times a day she takes the letter from her pocket, spreads it on the kitchen table, and yet once again reads it to herself, mouthing the words in a whisper loud enough for me to hear. Then holding my hands between her palms both to comfort me and to make certain I won't escape through however many verses, she begins to sing—about Elijah, the prophet; about Jonah trying to escape the eye of God by hiding in the belly of the whale; and she sings a long tale about a king and queen who have a vineyard in which there blooms an almond tree on which there grows a branch that holds a nest in which there lives a little bird. One night the old king dies and calamity overwhelms everyone and everything, even the little bird. *Lulinke, mein vögele. Lulinke, mein kind.* The song is a lullaby. Hush, my child—Sleep, my little bird—the refrain soothes between the verses. *Seufzer, Thränen, Trage, Not* . . . begins a Bach aria with oboe obbligato. I listen to the letters, I listen to the songs, I listen to my mother and my father worry and reminisce until the peach pit I am sucking turns as smooth as glass. What fascinates children about such stories? I hear the refrain and the oboe obbligato. My grandmother taught me that to sing is happy though the songs are sad. I like sad songs the best. Why else do we sing if not to celebrate some ancient living woe?

The young man who came to our house to teach me Yiddish read happy poems and stories. His last name meant "teacher." He was Mr. Malamud. No first name. When he was born, his mother and his father weighed him, looked him over, turned him this way and that, and named him Mr. Malamud. He dressed in brown to match his thick fine hair, richer than his delicate features and his deep-blue eyes. I considered he was old not just because my parents said he was *ein alter Bucher* (which doesn't mean old boy, only bachelor) but because as we sat reading side by side, I could see his rosy cheeks were a map of tiny broken veins, and also because frequently during our lesson, he would wipe his palms with a pristine handkerchief, a gesture that reminded me of how my grandmother used her folded handkerchief to wipe her tearing eyes. We read in tandem: I, haltingly; he, liltingly in a gentle girlish voice. At Hanukah, we read Sholem Aleichem's memoir about Hanukah. In that story there are feasting, pranks, and laughter. Also mysterious dark edges. The living room was brilliant but by some magic you knew the house had corridors and closets. In the middle of the gaiety, Sholem Aleichem brings on a speechless servant he calls *die Sheina Yedeya Lisha*. Her black strands of hair hang over her glistening fat cheeks while she herself is wrapped in a greasy apron redolent of potato pancakes, the delicious golden *latkes* everyone has been devouring. Reading about her, Mr. Malamud laughs until he chokes and sputters. I don't recall my teacher trying to explain the author's wit in transforming the simple son of the Passover Haggadah into the simple *latke*-maker. But though the fat shy servant left me uncomfortable and sad, when Mr. Malamud fell into his spasm, I too laughed so wildly I fell off my chair and had to be picked up. I laughed not only because laughter is infectious but because Sholem Aleichem's cook reminds me of Mr. Malamud's landlady. We have never met her but he says she is in love with him. That's hilarious. But more, when he excuses himself from eating the bacon and eggs she prepares for him every morning, she offers to make the bacon kosher. Or cook ham if that is better. Show me how! Just show me how! That is really funny. So though our laughter joined, as sometimes is the case, Mr. Malamud and I laughed for different reasons.

I liked Sholem Aleichem but in order to read him I must come in from playing. So in those years, the great writer was outdistanced for me as a teller of tales by a friend of the family whose name was Chaim Cohen. Chaim Cohen and Mr. Malamud were both pure souls — *edele menschen*. There comparison stopped. Where Mr. Malamud was merely a bachelor, Chaim Cohen was a wild man — a *wilder mensch* — which is certainly more interesting. If Mr. Malamud rented a single room and walked miles to save a dime, Chaim Cohen occupied space in the land of poverty. His only house was his house of prayer where he spent hours studying the Talmud and the Torah. More hours in winter than in summer, when he roamed the streets. His pants, a color between ashes and green rust, were wider than a woman's skirt. His shirt was not the cleanest—a euphemism—the buttonless cuffs intimate with soups and tea. Against the winter cold and the heat of summer he wore an old coat of my father's whose coat was also old but new compared to Chaim's. How did he make his living? He didn't. He just lived. Find Chaim, my mother would say, and he arrived in time for Sabbath. Two or three nights a week she would send to find him because she was cooking or baking something that he liked. Once in a while he brought a present. A *katchkale!* he announced, laying the duckling in its bloody paper bag on the counter by the sink. Or he would have a whole fish wrapped in newspaper, or from his pocket hold out a single lemon. Now he was the donor, and he opened his reddened eyes, rubbed his stubble beard, and talked. He was a learned man, respected for his knowledge. Come, Mirale, he invited, and I would sit on his lap, my face half turned away because he smelled of feathers. To this day I don't know what feathers smell like except they must smell like Chaim Cohen. I think I was inhaling overlays of soap like varnish that had been dampened down with too little water and I may have been smelling out the misery of his fate—he ended his days in the state mental hospital. I didn't mind his smell too much. His stories captivated me; he, himself, was enmeshed and captivated in the telling. To this day I'm possessed by the legend of the "shattered vessels."

Listen! Are you comfortable, Mirale? I rest my hand in his spongy one and he is answered. Once upon a time in the very beginning when God was busy creating the world, He worked with joy giving full scope to His imagination. He was so prodigious, His ideas so full to bursting, though He knew the time had come to stop He kept creating on and on. In His joy He made too much. Birds, moons, fishes, flies, and so on until the world was crammed too full to breathe.

How can that be? my mother asks. I can't believe that He could blunder so. After all—

Excuse me, Clara, but you don't know everything. Excuse me, I don't mean to insult you. Did you know, for example, that the Unnamable One, blessed be His Name, detests perfection? Did you know that? He does. He detests perfection and so allows Himself a few mistakes, like fashioning some humankind, not exactly minor mistakes we must admit. So . . . having created too much, having crammed the world too full, what should He do? Gently he moves his knees to rock me and playing my assigned role, I ask, What did He do? And Chaim echoes, What did He do? I'll tell you. Again He went to work, this time turning out hundreds of shining vessels and into these holy vessels He cast all the light. Now in one stroke He had room.

Does light really take up room?

Of course. Let's look around together and you will see that light floods every inch of space. If this second the candles should burn down and leave us here sitting in the dark, what would we see? Nothing. Does nothing take up space? But light flows into every corner and fills up every crack just like the sea. Whence we say seas of light. A tree, as a great poet said, what is a tree but a column of green light? And if a poet didn't say so, he should have and I will say it for him. So then, when the light was poured into the vessels and contained, immediately there was room. The universe is in half-darkness, from the vessels emanates a marvelous glow only—but—there is room. The problem has been solved. But then, a terrible occurrence. By some accident that has never been explained, the vessels were broken and shattered. The light escaped. The sparks flew everywhere. Some were lost eternally. But others fell in a shower of sparks to earth. A lucky accident. Now we have not just a glow that is half-darkness, now we have light. Not as much as in the beginning—but light—and here and there, a little room.

Then magic sparks are all around us?

Yes, they are all around us. Why can't we see them? They are buried, hidden. Ages have passed over them. Could you, yourself, find a spark? Mirale, you might. Anything is possible.

You are right, Chaim, my father comments. That was a lucky accident. The Divine One may not like perfection but His accidents are perfect. If not for that accident, we might be sitting this Shabat in darkness, a total power failure.

The next days I walk with my eyes searching every inch of ground. Not only must I be careful never to step on the cracks in the sidewalk which open up and swallow you, I'm looking for a magic spark, certain beyond a doubt I'll find one. I have made a tremendous pact with the Almighty, a promise He would be foolish to resist. At picnics I circle the base of trees; in winter, plunge headlong like a drunkard into drifts of snow; at Revere Beach, instead of building fortresses I sift mounds of sand. I find a penny. Not a spark. So I dream about it. In a forest of stone columns carved with hieroglyphics, I pick up a little stone and when I rub the surface clean and hold it to the sun, I see a clear unbroken well of light. Joy fills me to the brim. The Magic Spark glows in my hand like the reflection from a distant fire. I feel that I can fly.

Now it is years later. My husband and I and our two young daughters live at the edge of a small oak wood. One of our neighbors is a geologist and he delights in dropping chunks of semiprecious stones for the neighborhood children to find. One day it is our children's turn and they come running from the woods with a large crude amethyst, insisting the event is so important they must stay home from school. After showing me the stone, they run into the road and smash the amethyst in two. Did you do that so you could each have one? I ask. No, says the elder. I smashed it to see if I could find the light. See how the outside is just white? the younger asks. But where we broke it open, you can see lavender and purple lights.

Will you break it again so I can have a piece?

No, they answer. You can look at ours.

I look at them instead. And since they are very young and for a little while the future is far away, like all mothers, I tell myself with pride: I only dreamed about it but the children found it. That night at bedtime, I tell them the story of the shattered vessels and the sparks. Listen! Once upon a time in the very beginning . . .

How the Rabbi of Kalev Freed a Song
by Manasseh Unger

Every soul comes to the earth to accomplish a purpose, the Rabbi from Kalev taught his Hasidim. It is the duty of every man to strive to release the holy spark from the lower creations and bring that spark back to the God-head. My soul—continued the Rabbi—is of the *olam ha-nigun*, the world of song. I came into the world to bring back into our domain all the songs that have fallen to the Evil Power.

And then the Rabbi and his Hasidim would go to the mountain where they could hear diverse sounds. The monotonous murmuring of a little brook, the sighing of a hot afternoon breeze, and sometimes the melancholy lament of a mournful shepherd. For the Rabbi said that the true *nigun* is not the already assembled tones, but those that, coming from the world of song, are still wandering about the spaces of the world.

"Every day at a certain hour, different tones and voices come down. Sometimes an endless sorrowing cry. Then all who listen sorrow without knowing why, and feel their heart yearn to something. At another time, happy joyful tones fall. Then people feel lighthearted and gay. And from all these scattered tones, men make song, but they do not understand how to find the original song.

"I was created in this world to gather melodies and bring them to their true home. . . ."

The Hasidim listened attentively but understood little. They would see the Rabbi lie down on the earth and strain his ears—listen, now the earth sings a song of praise—and sometimes bending his ear to a tree—now the tree is singing. The Hasidim listened after him, wanted to understand, but they heard nothing except the brushing of a breeze in the twigs of the tree. . . .

The Rabbi used also to teach the Hasidim how to pray. "The important thing in prayer is to become one with the Infinite," said the Rabbi, "and that is possible through the power of song. Why? Because songs lead to yearning, and yearning to oneness. And if you want to understand what it means to yearn then you must get up very early before the sun has gilded the peaks of the mountains, and go alone to a wood in the hills. There you will understand what it means to yearn. There you will know how to pray. . . ."

And so one used to see lonely Hasidim scattered on all the paths, or-phaned, going about with their hands hidden in their girdles, their eyes lifted to the skies, experiencing their solitude. They would listen to the songs of the birds, to the running of a brooklet and sometimes stand by a shepherd to carefully note his singing. The Rabbi was always among them to teach them to understand the true sense of the song.

The shepherd would begin to feel at home among the Hasidim. He would leave his sheep to God's care, lay himself down on the grass in the fresh dew with his face to the rising sun, and begin to sing his peasant songs. He sang a verse, then played on his pipes. The Rabbi, hidden in a corner, would listen to the shepherd's song. For the Rabbi said that the shepherd sings with feeling, but he knows not what he sings. He is grown one with nature, he listens to the tones that come from the world of song, but he does not understand them.

The Rabbi gathered his Hasidim to listen to the shepherd. The Hasidim came from all sides. They heard soft plaintive words that the shepherd sang now and then:

> kalah kalah how far you are
> mountain mountain how great you are
> mountain mountain go away from here
> then to my kalah I'll be near.

And the Rabbi said to the Hasidim: "Do you know where this melody comes from? It is the yearning song that the *Knesset-Israel* sings to the *Shekhinah*, and the right way to sing it is this:

> Shekhinah Shekhinah how far you are
> Exile Exile how great you are
> Exile Exile go away from here
> So to Shekhinah I may come near."

The Rabbi had freed the melody and brought it back to its true sense and since then this song is chanted by the Hasidim as the *bishtokikut nigun*.

Translated from the Hebrew
by Edward Robbin

BOOK VI
THEMES OF FOLKLORE

Harvest of Madness
by Rabbi Nachman of Bratslav

One day the king summoned his counselor and told him of his anguish: "I have read in the stars that all those who will eat of the next harvest will be struck with madness. What shall we do, my friend?"

"Nothing could be more simple, Sire," replied the counselor, "we shall not touch it. Last year's harvest is not yet exhausted. You have but to requisition it; it will be ample for you. And me."

"And the others?" scolded the king. "All the subjects of my kingdom? The faithful servants of the crown? The men, the women, the madmen and the beggars, are you forgetting them? Are you forgetting the children, the children too?"

"I am forgetting nobody, Sire. But as your adviser, I must be realistic and take all possibilities into account. We don't have enough reserves, not enough to protect and satisfy everyone. There will be just enough for you. And me."

Thereupon the king's brow darkened, and he said: "Your solution does not please me. Is there no other? Never mind. But I refuse to separate myself from my people and I don't care to remain lucid in the midst of a people gone mad. Therefore we shall all enter madness together. You and I like the others, with the others. When the world is gripped by delirium, it is senseless to watch from the outside: the mad will think that we are mad too. And yet, I should like to safeguard some reflection of our present glory and of our anguish too; I should like to keep alive the memory of this determination, this decision. I should like that when the time comes, you and I shall remain aware of our predicament."

"Whatever for, Sire?"

"It will help us, you'll see. And thus we shall be able to help our friends. Who knows, perhaps thanks to us, men will find the strength to resist later, even if it is too late."

And putting his arm around his friend's shoulders, the king went on: "You and I shall therefore mark each other's foreheads with the seal of madness. And every time we shall look at one another, we shall know, you and I, that we are mad."

Retold from the Hebrew and Yiddish sources
by Elie Wiesel

The Prince Who
Thought He Was a Rooster

by Rabbi Nachman of Bratslav

Once there was a prince who fell into the delusion of thinking he was a rooster. He took off all his clothes, sat under the table, and refused to eat any food but corn seeds. The king sent for many doctors and many specialists, but none of them could cure him.

Finally a wise man appeared before the king, and said: "I think that I can cure the prince." The king gave him permission to try.

The wise man took off his clothes, crawled under the table and began to munch on corn seeds. The prince looked at him suspiciously, and said: "Who are you, and what are you doing here?"

The wise man answered: "Who are you, and what are you doing here?"

"I am a rooster," answered the prince belligerently.

"Oh really? So am I," answered the wise man quietly.

The two of them sat together under the table until they became accustomed to each other. When the wise man felt that the prince was used to his presence, he signaled for some clothing. He put on the clothing, and then he said to the prince: "Don't think that roosters can't wear clothing if they want to. A rooster can wear clothes and be a perfectly good rooster just the same."

The prince thought about this for a while, and then he too agreed to put on clothes.

After a time, the wise man signaled to have food put under the table. The prince became alarmed and he said: "What are you doing?" The wise man reassured him. "Don't be upset. A rooster can eat the food that human beings eat if he wants to, and still be a good rooster." The prince considered this statement for a time, and then he too signaled for food.

Then the wise man said to the prince: "Do you think that a rooster has to sit under the table all the time? A rooster can get up and walk around if he wants to and still be a good rooster." The prince considered these words for a time, and then he followed the wise man up from the table, and began to walk.

After he began dressing like a person, eating like a person, and walking like a person, he gradually recovered his senses and began to live like a person.

Retold from the Yiddish and Hebrew sources
by Jack Reimer

Fable of the Goat

by S. Y. Agnon

The tale is told of an old man who groaned from his heart. The doctors were sent for, and they advised him to drink goat's milk. He went out and bought a she-goat and brought her into his home. Not many days passed before the goat disappeared. They went out to search for her but did not find her. She was not in the yard and not in the garden, not on the roof of the house of study and not by the spring, not in the hills and not in the fields. She tarried several days and then returned by herself; and when she returned, her udder was full of a great deal of milk, the taste of which was as the taste of Eden. Not just once, but many times she disappeared from the house. They would go out in search for her and would not find her until she returned by herself with her udder full of milk that was sweeter than honey and whose taste was the taste of Eden.

One time the old man said to his son, "My son, I desire to know where she goes and whence she brings this milk which is sweet to my palate and a balm to all my bones."

His son said to him, "Father, I have a plan."

He said to him, "What is it?"

The son got up and brought a length of cord. He tied it to the goat's tail.

His father said to him, "What are you doing, my son?"

He said to him, "I am tying a cord to the goat's tail, so that when I feel a pull on it I will know that she has decided to leave, and I can catch the end of the cord and follow her on her way."

The old man nodded his head and said to him, "My son, if your heart is wise, my heart too will rejoice."

The youth tied the cord to the goat's tail and minded it carefully. When the goat set off, he held the cord in his hand and did not let it slacken until the goat was well on her way and he was following her. He was dragged along behind her until he came to a cave. The goat went into the cave, and the youth followed her, holding the cord. They walked thus for an hour or two, or maybe even a day or two. The goat wagged her tail and bleated, and the cave came to an end.

When they emerged from the cave, the youth saw lofty mountains, and hills full of the choicest fruit, and a fountain of living waters that flowed down from the mountains; and the wind wafted all manner of perfumes. The goat climbed up a tree by clutching at the ribbed leaves. Carob fruits full of honey dropped from the tree, and she ate of the carobs and drank of the garden's fountain.

The youth stood and called to the wayfarers: "I adjure you, good people, tell me where I am, and what is the name of this place?"

They answered him, "You are in the Land of Israel, and you are close by Safed."

The youth lifted up his eyes to the heavens and said, "Blessed be the Omnipresent, blessed be He who has brought me to the Land of Israel." He kissed the soil and sat down under the tree.

He said, "Until the day breathe and the shadows flee away, I shall sit on the hill under this tree. Then I shall go home and bring my father and mother to the Land of Israel." As he was sitting thus and feasting his eyes on the holiness of the Land of Israel, he heard a voice proclaiming:

"Come, let us go out to greet the Sabbath Queen."

And he saw men like angels, wrapped in white shawls, with boughs of myrtle in their hands, and all the houses were lit with a great many candles. He perceived that the eve of Sabbath would arrive with the darkening, and that he would not be able to return. He uprooted a reed and dipped it in gallnuts, from which the ink for the writing of Torah scrolls is made. He took a piece of paper and wrote a letter to his father:

"From the ends of the earth I lift up my voice in song to tell you that I have come in peace to the Land of Israel. Here I sit, close by Safed, the holy city, and I imbibe its sanctity. Do not inquire how I arrived here but hold onto this cord which is tied to the goat's tail and follow the footsteps of the goat; then your journey will be secure, and you will enter the Land of Israel."

The youth rolled up the note and placed it in the goat's ear. He said to himself: When she arrives at Father's house, Father will pat her on the head, and she will flick her ears. The note will fall out, Father will pick it up and read what is written on it. Then he will take up the cord and follow the goat to the Land of Israel.

The goat returned to the old man, but she did not flick her ears, and the note did not fall. When the old man saw that the goat had returned without his son, he clapped his hands to his head and began to cry and weep and wail, "My son, my son, where are you? My son, would that I might die in your stead, my son, my son!"

So he went, weeping and mourning over his son, for he said, "An evil beast has devoured him, my son is assuredly rent in pieces!"

And he refused to be comforted, saying, "I will go down to my grave in mourning for my son."

And whenever he saw the goat, he would say, "Woe to the father who banished his son, and woe to her who drove him from the world!"

The old man's mind would not be at peace until he sent for the butcher to slaughter the goat. The butcher came and slaughtered the goat. As they were skinning her, the note fell out of her ear. The old man picked up the note and said, "My son's handwriting!"

When he had read all that his son had written, he clapped his hands to his head and cried, "*Vay! Vay!* Woe to the man who robs himself of his own good fortune, and woe to the man who requites good with evil!"

He mourned over the goat many days and refused to be comforted, saying, "Woe to me, for I could have gone up to the Land of Israel in one bound, and now I must suffer out my days in this exile!"

Since that time the mouth of the cave has been hidden from the eye, and there is no longer a short way. And that youth, if he has not died, shall bear fruit in his old age, full of sap and richness, calm and peaceful in the Land of the Living.

Translated from the Hebrew
by Barney Rubin

The Animal in the Synagogue
by Franz Kafka

In our synagogue there lives an animal about the size of a marten. One can often get a very good view of it, for it allows people to approach to a distance of about six feet from it. It is pale blue-green in color. Nobody has ever yet touched its fur, and so nothing can be said about that, and one might almost go so far as to assert that the real color of its coat is unknown, perhaps the color one sees is only caused by the dust and mortar with which its fur is matted, and indeed the color does resemble that of the paint inside the synagogue, only it is a little brighter. Apart from its timidity, it is an uncommonly quiet animal of settled habits; if it were not so often disturbed, it would doubtless scarcely be in this place at all, its favorite haunt being the latticework in front of the women's compartment; with visible delight it sinks its claws into the lattice, stretching itself and gazing down into the main chamber; this audacious attitude seems to please it, but the beadle has instructions never to tolerate the animal's being on the lattice, for it would get used to the place, and that cannot be permitted on account of the women, who are afraid of the animal. Why they are afraid is not clear. True, at a first glance it looks frightening, particularly the long neck, the triangular face, the upper teeth, which jut out almost horizontally, and on the upper lip a row of long, obviously hard, pale bristles, which extend even farther than the teeth—all that may be frightening, but it does not take one long to realize how harmless this whole apparent horror is. Above all, it keeps away from human beings, it is more shy than a denizen of the forest, and seems to be attached only to the building, and it is doubtless its personal misfortune that this building is a synagogue, that is, a place that is at times full of people. If only one could communicate with the animal, one could, of course, comfort it by telling it that the congregation in this little town of ours in the mountains is becoming smaller every year and that it is already having trouble in raising the money for the upkeep of the synagogue. It is not impossible that before long the synagogue will have become a granary or something of the sort and the animal will then have the peace it now so sorely lacks.

To be sure, it is only the women who are afraid of the animal, the men have long ceased to bother about it, one generation has pointed it out to the next, it has been seen over and over again, and by this time nobody any longer wastes a glance on it, until now even the children, seeing it for the first time, do not show any amazement. It has become that animal which belongs to the synagogue—why should not the synagogue have a special domestic animal not found anywhere else? If it were not for the women, one would hardly be aware of the animal's existence any more now at all. But even the women are not really afraid of the animal, indeed it would be more than odd to go on being afraid of such an animal, day in, day out, for years, for decades. Their excuse is that the animal is usually much nearer to them than to the men, and this is true. The animal does not dare to go down below where the men are, it has never yet been seen on the floor. If it is stopped from getting on the lattice of the women's compartment, then at least it wants to be at the same height on the opposite wall. There, on a very narrow ledge scarcely two inches wide, which extends round three sides of the synagogue, the animal will sometimes flit to and fro, but mostly it sits quietly curled up on a certain spot opposite the women. It is almost incomprehensible how it so easily contrives to use this narrow path, and it is remarkable to see the way it turns round up there when it gets to the end, for after all, it is by now a very old animal, but it does not shrink from taking a most daring leap into the air, nor does it ever miss its foothold, and having turned in midair it runs straight back again the way it came. Of course, when one has seen this several times one has had enough of it, and there is no reason why one should go on staring. Nor is it either fear or curiosity that keeps the women fidgeting about; if they were to pay more attention to their prayers, they might be able to forget all about the animal; the devout women would certainly do so if the others, who are in the great majority, would let them, but these others always like attracting attention to themselves, and the animal provides them with a welcome pretext. If they could and if they dared, they would long ago have enticed the animal to come yet closer to them, so that they might be more frightened than ever. But in reality the animal is not at all eager to approach them, so long as it is left alone it takes just as little notice of them as of the men, and probably what it would like best would be to remain in the hiding place where it lives in the periods between the services, evidently some hole in the wall that we have not yet discovered. It is only when prayers begin that it appears, startled by the noise. Does it want to see what has happened? Does it want to remain on the alert? Does it want to be in the open, ready to take flight? It is in terror that it comes running out, it is in terror that it performs its capers, and it does not dare to withdraw until the divine service is at an end. It naturally prefers being high up because that is where it is safest, and the places where it can run best are the lattice and the ledge, but it does not always stay there, sometimes too it climbs down farther towards the men; the curtain of the Ark of the Covenant hangs from a shining brass rod, and this seems to attract the animal, it quite often creeps towards it, but when it is there it is always quiet, not even when it is right up close to the Ark can it be said to be causing a disturbance, it seems to be gazing at the congregation with its bright, unwinking, and perhaps lidless eyes, but it is certainly not looking at anybody, it is only facing the dangers by which it feels itself threatened.

In this respect it seemed, at least until recently, to be not much more intelligent than our women. What dangers has it to fear, anyway? Who intends it any harm? Has it not been left entirely to itself for many years? The men take no notice of its presence, and the majority of the women would probably be miserable if it were to disappear. And since it is the only animal in the building, it has no enemy of any kind. This is something it really ought to have come to realize in the course of the years. And though the divine service, with all its noise, may be very frightening for the animal, still, it does recur, on a modest scale daily and on a grander scale during the festivals, always regularly and without ever a break; and so even the most timid of animals could by now have got used to it, particularly when it sees that this is not the noise of pursuers, but some noise that it cannot understand at all. And yet there is this terror. Is it the memory of times long past or the premonition of times to come? Does this old animal perhaps know more than the three generations of those who are gathered together in the synagogue?

Many years ago, so it is recounted, attempts were really made to drive the animal away. It is possible, of course, that this is true, but it is more likely that such stories are mere inventions. There is evidence, however, that at that time the question whether the presence of such an animal might be tolerated in the house of God was investigated from the point of view of the Law and the Commandments. Opinions were sought from various celebrated rabbis, views were divided, the majority were for the expulsion of the animal and a reconsecration of the house of God. But it was easy to issue decrees from afar, in reality it was simply impossible to catch the animal, and hence it was also impossible to drive it out for good. For only if one could have caught it and taken it a long distance away could one have had anything approximating to a certainty of being rid of it.

Many years ago, so it is recounted, attempts were really still made to drive the animal away. The beadle of the synagogue says he remembers how his grandfather, who was also beadle, liked to tell the story. As a small boy his grandfather had frequently heard talk about the impossibility of getting rid of the animal, and so, fired by ambition and being an excellent climber, one bright morning when the whole synagogue, with all its nooks and crannies, lay open in the sunlight, he had sneaked in, armed with a rope, a catapult, and a crookhandled stick. . . .

Translated from the German
by Ernst Kaiser and Eithne Wilkins

The Jewbird
by Bernard Malamud

The window was open so the skinny bird flew in. Flappity-flap with its frazzled black wings. That's how it goes. It's open, you're in. Closed, you're out and that's your fate. The bird wearily flapped through the open kitchen window of Harry Cohen's top-floor apartment on First Avenue near the lower East River. On a rod on the wall hung an escaped canary cage, its door wide open, but this black-type longbeaked bird—its ruffled head and small dull eyes, crossed a little, making it look like a dissipated crow—landed if not smack on Cohen's thick lamb chop, at least on the table, close by. The frozen foods salesman was sitting at supper with his wife and young son on a hot August evening a year ago. Cohen, a heavy man with hairy chest and beefy shorts; Edie, in skinny yellow shorts and red halter; and their ten-year-old Morris (after her father)—Maurie, they called him, a nice kid though not overly bright—were all in the city after two weeks out, because Cohen's mother was dying. They had been enjoying Kingston, New York, but drove back when Mama got sick in her flat in the Bronx.

"Right on the table," said Cohen, putting down his beer glass and swatting at the bird. "Son of a bitch."

"Harry, take care with your language," Edie said, looking at Maurie, who watched every move.

The bird cawed hoarsely and with a flap of its bedraggled wings—feathers tufted this way and that—rose heavily to the top of the open kitchen door, where it perched staring down.

"Gevalt, a pogrom!"

"It's a talking bird," said Edie in astonishment.

"In Jewish," said Maurie.

"Wise guy," muttered Cohen. He gnawed on his chop, then put down the bone. "So if you can talk, say what's your business. What do you want here?"

"If you can't spare a lamb chop," said the bird, "I'll settle for a piece of herring with a crust of bread. You can't live on your nerve forever."

"This ain't a restaurant," Cohen replied. "All I'm asking is what brings you to this address?"

"The window was open," the bird sighed; adding after a moment, "I'm running. I'm flying but I'm also running."

"From whom?" asked Edie with interest.

"Anti-Semeets."

"Anti-Semites?" they all said.

"That's from who."

"What kind of anti-Semites bother a bird?" Edie asked.

"Any kind," said the bird, "also including eagles, vultures, and hawks. And once in a while some crows will take your eyes out."

"But aren't you a crow?"

"Me? I'm a Jewbird."

Cohen laughed heartily. "What do you mean by that?"

The bird began dovening. He prayed without Book or tallith, but with passion. Edie bowed her head though not Cohen. And Maurie rocked back and forth with the prayer, looking up with one wide-open eye.

When the prayer was done Cohen remarked, "No hat, no phylacteries?"

"I'm an old radical."

"You're sure you're not some kind of a ghost or dybbuk?"

"Not a dybbuk," answered the bird, "though one of my relatives had such an experience once. It's all over now, thanks God. They freed her from a former lover, a crazy jealous man. She's now the mother of two wonderful children."

"Birds?" Cohen asked slyly.

"Why not?"

"What kind of birds?"

"Like me. Jewbirds."

Cohen tipped back in his chair and guffawed. "That's a big laugh. I've heard of a Jewfish but not a Jewbird."

"We're once removed." The bird rested on one skinny leg, then on the other. "Please, could you spare maybe a piece of herring with a small crust of bread?"

Edie got up from the table.

"What are you doing?" Cohen asked her.

"I'll clear the dishes."

Cohen turned to the bird. "So what's your name, if you don't mind saying?"

"Call me Schwartz."

"He might be an old Jew changed into a bird by somebody," said Edie, removing a plate.

"Are you?" asked Harry, lighting a cigar.

"Who knows?" answered Schwartz. "Does God tell us everything?"

Maurie got up on his chair. "What kind of herring?" he asked the bird in excitement.

"Get down, Maurie, or you'll fall," ordered Cohen.

"If you haven't got matjes, I'll take schmaltz," said Schwartz.

"All we have is marinated, with slices of onion—in a jar," said Edie.

"If you'll open for me the jar I'll eat marinated. Do you have also, if you don't mind, a piece of rye bread—the spitz?"

Edie thought she had.

"Feed him out on the balcony," Cohen said. He spoke to the bird. "After that take off."

Schwartz closed both bird eyes. "I'm tired and it's a long way."

"Which direction are you headed, north or south?"

Schwartz, barely lifting his wings, shrugged.

"You don't know where you're going?"

"Where there's charity I'll go."

"Let him stay, papa," said Maurie. "He's only a bird."

"So stay the night," Cohen said, "but no longer."

In the morning Cohen ordered the bird out of the house but Maurie cried, so Schwartz stayed for a while. Maurie was still on vacation from school and his friends were away. He was lonely and Edie enjoyed the fun he had, playing with the bird.

"He's no trouble at all," she told Cohen, "and besides his appetite is very small."

"What'll you do when he makes dirty?"

"He flies across the street in a tree when he makes dirty, and if nobody passes below, who notices?"

"So all right," said Cohen, "but I'm dead set against it. I warn you he ain't gonna stay here long."

"What have you got against the poor bird?"

"Poor bird, my ass. He's a foxy bastard. He thinks he's a Jew."

"What difference does it make what he thinks?"

"A Jewbird, what a chuzpah. One false move and he's out on his drumsticks."

At Cohen's insistence Schwartz lived out on the balcony in a new wooden birdhouse Edie had bought him.

"With many thanks," said Schwartz, "though I would rather have a human roof over my head. You know how it is at my age. I like the warm, the windows, the smell of cooking. I would also be glad to see once in a while the *Jewish Morning Journal* and have now and then a schnapps because it helps my breathing, thanks God. But whatever you give me, you won't hear complaints."

However, when Cohen brought home a bird feeder full of dried corn, Schwartz said, "Impossible."

Cohen was annoyed. "What's the matter, crosseyes, is your life getting too good for you? Are you forgetting what it means to be migratory? I'll bet a helluva lot of crows you happen to be acquainted with, Jews or otherwise, would give their eyeteeth to eat this corn."

Schwartz did not answer. What can you say to a grubber yung?

"Not for my digestion," he later explained to Edie. "Cramps. Herring is better even if it makes you thirsty. At least rainwater don't cost anything." He laughed sadly in breathy caws.

And herring, thanks to Edie, who knew where to shop, was what Schwartz got, with an occasional piece of potato pancake, and even a bit of soupmeat when Cohen wasn't looking.

When school began in September, before Cohen would once again suggest giving the bird the boot, Edie prevailed on him to wait a little while until Maurie adjusted.

"To deprive him right now might hurt his school work, and you know what trouble we had last year."

"So okay, but sooner or later the bird goes. That I promise you."

Schwartz, though nobody had asked him, took on full responsibility for Maurie's performance in school. In return for favors granted, when he was let in for an hour or two at night, he spent most of his time overseeing the boy's lessons. He sat on top of the dresser near Maurie's desk as he laboriously wrote out his homework. Maurie was a restless type and Schwartz gently kept him to his studies. He also listened to him practice his screechy violin, taking a few minutes off now and then to rest his ears in the bathroom. And they afterwards played dominoes. The boy was an indifferent checker player and it was impossible to teach him chess. When he was sick, Schwartz read him comic books though he personally disliked them. But Maurie's work improved in school and even his violin teacher admitted his playing was better. Edie gave Schwartz credit for these improvements though the bird pooh-poohed them.

Yet he was proud there was nothing lower than C minuses on Maurie's report card, and on Edie's insistence celebrated with a little schnapps.

"If he keeps up like this," Cohen said, "I'll get him in an Ivy League college for sure."

"Oh I hope so," sighed Edie.

But Schwartz shook his head. "He's a good boy—you don't have to worry. He won't be a shicker or a wifebeater, God forbid, but a scholar he'll never be, if you know what I mean, although maybe a good mechanic. It's no disgrace in these times."

"If I were you," Cohen said, angered, "I'd keep my big snoot out of other people's private business."

"Harry, please," said Edie.

"My goddamn patience is wearing out. That crosseyes butts into everything."

Though he wasn't exactly a welcome guest in the house, Schwartz gained a few ounces although he did not improve in appearance. He looked bedraggled as ever, his feathers unkempt, as though he had just flown out of a snowstorm. He spent, he admitted, little time taking care of himself. Too much to think about. "Also outside plumbing," he told Edie. Still there was more glow to his eyes so that though Cohen went on calling him crosseyes he said it less emphatically.

Liking his situation, Schwartz tried tactfully to stay out of Cohen's way, but one night when Edie was at the movies and Maurie was taking a hot shower, the frozen foods salesman began a quarrel with the bird.

"For Christ sake, why don't you wash yourself sometimes? Why must you always stink like a dead fish?"

"Mr. Cohen, if you'll pardon me, if somebody eats garlic he will smell from garlic. I eat herring three times a day. Feed me flowers and I will smell like flowers."

"Who's obligated to feed you anything at all? You're lucky to get herring."

"Excuse me, I'm not complaining," said the bird. "You're complaining."

"What's more," said Cohen, "even from out on the balcony I can hear you snoring away like a pig. It keeps me awake at night."

"Snoring," said Schwartz, "isn't a crime, thanks God."

"All in all you are a goddamn pest and freeloader. Next thing you'll want to sleep in bed next to my wife."

"Mr. Cohen," said Schwartz, "on this rest assured. A bird is a bird."

"So you say, but how do I know you're a bird and not some kind of a goddamn devil?"

"If I was a devil you would know already. And I don't mean because of your son's good marks."

"Shut up, you bastard bird," shouted Cohen.

"Grubber yung," cawed Schwartz, rising to the tips of his talons, his long wings outstretched.

Cohen was about to lunge for the bird's scrawny neck but Maurie came out of the bathroom, and for the rest of the evening until Schwartz's bedtime on the balcony, there was pretended peace.

But the quarrel had deeply disturbed Schwartz and he slept badly. His snoring woke him, and awake, he was fearful of what would become of him. Wanting to stay out of Cohen's way, he kept to the birdhouse as much as possible. Cramped by it, he paced back and forth on the balcony ledge, or sat on the birdhouse roof, staring into space. In the evenings, while overseeing Maurie's lessons, he often fell asleep. Awakening, he nervously hopped around exploring the four corners of the room. He spent much time in Maurie's closet, and carefully examined his bureau drawers when they were left open. And once when he found a large paper bag on the floor, Schwartz poked his way into it to investigate what possibilities were. The boy was amused to see the bird in the paper bag.

"He wants to build a nest," he said to his mother.

Edie, sensing Schwartz's unhappiness, spoke to him quietly.

"Maybe if you did some of the things my husband wants you, you would get along better with him."

"Give me a for instance," Schwartz said.

"Like take a bath, for instance."

"I'm too old for baths," said the bird. "My feathers fall out without baths."

"He says you have a bad smell."

"Everybody smells. Some people smell because of their thoughts or because who they are. My bad smell comes from the food I eat. What does his come from?"

"I better not ask him or it might make him mad," said Edie.

In late November Schwartz froze on the balcony in the fog and cold, and especially on rainy days he woke with stiff joints and could barely move his wings. Already he felt twinges of rheumatism. He would have liked to spend more time in the warm house, particularly when Maurie was in school and Cohen at work. But though Edie was good-hearted and might have sneaked him in in the morning, just to thaw out, he was afraid to ask her. In the meantime Cohen, who had been reading articles about the migration of birds, came out on the balcony one night after work when Edie was in the kitchen preparing pot roast, and peeking into the birdhouse, warned Schwartz to be on his way soon if he knew what was good for him. "Time to hit the flyways."

"Mr. Cohen, why do you hate me so much?" asked the bird. "What did I do to you?"

"Because you're an A-number-one trouble maker, that's why. What's more, whoever heard of a Jewbird? Now scat or it's open war."

But Schwartz stubbornly refused to depart as Cohen embarked on a campaign of harassing him, meanwhile hiding it from Edie and Maurie. Maurie hated violence and Cohen didn't want to leave a bad impression. He thought maybe if he played dirty tricks on the bird he would fly off without being physically kicked out. The vacation was over, let him make his easy living off the fat of somebody else's land. Cohen worried about the effect of the bird's departure on Maurie's schooling but decided to take the chance, first, because the boy now seemed to have the knack of studying—give the black bird-bastard credit—and second, because Schwartz was driving him bats by being there always, even in his dreams.

The frozen foods salesman began his campaign against the bird by mixing watery cat food with the herring slices in Schwartz's dish. He also blew up and popped numerous paper bags outside the birdhouse as the bird slept, and when he had got Schwartz good and nervous, though not enough to leave, he brought a full-grown cat into the house, supposedly a gift for little Maurie, who had always wanted a pussy. The cat never stopped springing up at Schwartz whenever he saw him, one day managing to claw out several of his tailfeathers. And even at lesson time, when the cat was usually excluded from Maurie's room, though somehow or other he quickly found his way in at the end of the lesson, Schwartz was desperately fearful of his life and flew from pinnacle to pinnacle—light fixture to clothestree to doortop—in order to elude the beast's wet jaws.

Once when the bird complained to Edie how hazardous his existence was, she said, "Be patient, Mr. Schwartz. When the cat gets to know you better he won't try to catch you any more."

"When he stops trying we will both be in Paradise," Schwartz answered. "Do me a favor and get rid of him. He makes my whole life worry. I'm losing feathers like a tree loses leaves."

"I'm awfully sorry but Maurie likes the pussy and sleeps with it."

What could Schwartz do? He worried but came to no decision, being afraid to leave. So he ate the herring garnished with cat food, tried hard not to hear the paper bags bursting like firecrackers outside the birdhouse at night, and lived terror-stricken closer to the ceiling than the floor, as the cat, his tail flicking, endlessly watched him.

Weeks went by. Then on the day after Cohen's mother had died in her flat in the Bronx, when Maurie came home with a zero on an arithmetic test, Cohen, enraged, waited until Edie had taken the boy to his violin lesson, then openly attacked the bird. He chased him with a broom on the balcony and Schwartz frantically flew back and forth, finally escaping into his birdhouse. Cohen triumphantly reached in, and grabbing both skinny legs, dragged the bird out, cawing loudly, his wings wildly beating. He whirled the bird around and around his head. But Schwartz, as he moved in circles, managed to swoop down and catch Cohen's nose in his beak, and hung on for dear life. Cohen cried out in great pain, punched the bird with his fist, and tugging at its legs with all his might, pulled his nose free. Again he swung the yawking Schwartz around until the bird grew dizzy, then with a furious heave, flung him into the night. Schwartz sank like stone into the street. Cohen then tossed the birdhouse and feeder after him, listening at the ledge until they crashed on the sidewalk below. For a full hour, broom in hand, his heart palpitating and nose throbbing with pain, Cohen waited for Schwartz to return but the broken-hearted bird didn't.

That's the end of that dirty bastard, the salesman thought and went in. Edie and Maurie had come home.

"Look," said Cohen, pointing to his bloody nose swollen three times its normal size, "what that sonofabitchy bird did. It's a permanent scar."

"Where is he now?" Edie asked, frightened.

"I threw him out and he flew away. Good riddance."

Nobody said no, though Edie touched a handkerchief to her eyes and Maurie rapidly tried the nine times table and found he knew approximately half.

In the spring when the winter's snow had melted, the boy, moved by a memory, wandered in the neighborhood, looking for Schwartz. He found a dead black bird in a small lot near the river, his two wings broken, neck twisted, and both bird-eyes plucked clean.

"Who did it to you, Mr. Schwartz?" Maurie wept.

"Anti-Semeets," Edie said later.

Eliyahu the Prophet

by Sholom Aleichem

It isn't good to be an only child, to be doted on anxiously by your father and mother, "of seven the only one remaining." Here—don't stand, there—don't go. This—don't eat, that—don't drink. Your head—cover it, your throat—wrap it. Your hands—hide them. Your nose—blow it. Ah, it isn't good, it just isn't good to be an only child. And a rich man's son at that. My father is rich. He's a money-changer. He goes around from shop to shop with a sack of coins exchanging silver for small change and small change for silver. That's why his fingers are always black and his nails chipped. He works very hard. When he comes home at night he is exhausted and worn out. "My legs are finished," he moans to my mother. "My legs are finished. There's nothing left of my legs."

Nothing left? It's possible. But then again, his business is thriving. That's what everyone says, and everyone is envious of us because the business is good and very good at that. My mother is pleased. So am I. "The kind of Pesach I will have this year, I wish for all Jewish children, God be praised."

That's what my mother says and she thanks God because we are having such a wonderful Pesach. And I do too. But how am I going to make it through the days until that wonderful seder?

I barely make it to Pesach, that beloved Pesach. They have outfitted me like a king, as befits a rich man's son. But what good is it. I am not allowed to play outdoors—I might catch a cold. I am not allowed to run around with the poor children—I am a rich man's son. Such beautiful clothes and no one to show them off to. A pocketful of nuts and no one to play with.

It's no good to be an only child, overprotected, of seven the only one remaining and a rich man's son at that.

My father puts on his best long coat and goes off to *shul* to pray. My mother says to me, "Do you know what? Lie down a little. Take a little nap. Then you'll be able to stay up with us for the whole seder. You will ask your father the Four Questions." Am I crazy? Do you think I could sleep before a seder? "Remember now, at the Pesach seder you are not allowed to fall asleep, because if, God forbid, you do fall asleep, then right away Eliyahu the Prophet will appear with a big sack on his back. Pesach night Eliyahu the Prophet goes around looking for anyone who falls asleep at the seder and takes him away in his sack." Ha-ha! *I* fall asleep at the seder? *I?* Even if it lasts all night, until the crack of dawn. What happened last year, Momma? "Last year you fell asleep right after the *Kiddush*." So how come Eliyahu the Prophet didn't come to me with his sack then? "Then you were only a little boy but this year you are a big boy, this year you are old enough to ask your father the Four Questions. This year you have to recite along with your father the *Avadim hayinu*—'Slaves were we.' This year you have to eat fish and soup and knaidlach with us. Quiet—here comes your father from *shul*."

"*Goot yontiff!*"

"*Goot yontiff!*"

Thank God. My father finishes reciting the *Kiddush*. So do I. My father drinks down the first glass of wine. So do I. And a full one at that, down to the last drop. "Look at that, down to the last drop!" my mother exclaims to my father, and then she says to me, "A full glass of wine? You'll fall asleep!" Ha-ha! *I* fall asleep? *I?* Even if it lasts all night, until the crack of dawn. Just ask Poppa how well I polished off the Four Questions, how well I read the Haggadah, how I swayed back and forth over the *siddur* and sang the *Avadim hayinu*. My mother keeps her eyes glued to me and smiles as she says to me, "You will fall asleep, fall asleep . . ." Ah, Momma, Momma! It seems to me that if a person had eighteen heads, just hearing those words would make him fall asleep! Just try to stay awake when you have the words, "Fall asleep, fall asleep . . ." sung into *your* ear.

Obviously, I fall asleep.

I fall asleep and dream that my father is already at the portion of the Haggadah *Sh'foach chamt'chah*. My mother is getting up from the table to open the door in order to welcome Eliyahu the Prophet. That would be a fine how-do-you-do if Eliyahu the Prophet were to come in, as my mother described, with a sack on his back and say to me, "Come, young man." And whose fault would it be? Momma's—because of her "Don't fall asleep! Don't fall asleep." And just as I am thinking these thoughts—Aha!—I hear the scraping of the door and my father stands up and calls out loud, "Welcome!" I look toward the door and sure enough—yes, it's him. He's walking toward me, walking toward me—so slowly, you can barely hear him. He's a fine-looking Jew, Eliyahu the Prophet. An old man. An old man with a curly gray beard down to his knees. The face is aged, yellowed, wrinkled but handsome and filled with goodness. And his eyes—ah, his eyes! Gentle, kind, friendly, loving, trusting eyes. Bent over, leaning on a huge staff, with a sack on his back, he silently, oh so silently, without a word, comes straight toward me.

"Well, young man, climb into my sack and come with me!" So says this old man to me and yet with such kindness, with such gentleness, such sweetness.

I ask him, "Where to?" He responds, "You'll know soon enough." I don't want to, but he bids me to come again. I plead with him, "How can I go with you when I am a rich man's son?" He replies, "So if you are a rich man's son, what's so special about that?" I go on, "I am my parents' only child." This does not impress him. "To me you're not an only child." I try again. "But I am watched over, of seven the only one remaining. If they see that I'm gone," I continue, "they will not endure it. They will die—especially my mother." He gazes at me, the old man, with benevolence in his eyes, and says to me as gently and sweetly as before, "If you don't come with me, then sleep soundly but sleep forever, forever." I begin to cry. "Does that mean I will die? They won't endure it, especially Momma." "If you don't want to die, then come with me. Say goodbye to your parents and come." "But after all, how can I go when I am an only child, of seven the only one remaining?" Now he becomes a little more stern. "For the last time, young man, decide one way or the other: either you say goodbye to your mother and father forever and come with me or stay here, but fall asleep forever. Forever."

Having said these words, he takes a step away from me and is about to go out the door. What should I do now? Go with the old man, God knows where, to be eternally lost? My parents would die. An only child, of seven the only one remaining. Stay here and sleep forever? That means I myself would die. I stretch both hands out pleadingly to him with tears in my eyes. "Eliyahu the Prophet! Good, beloved, generous Eliyahu! Give me one minute to think about it!" He turns his fine, old, yellowed, wrinkled face, with the curly gray beard down to his knees toward me, looks at me with his fine, good, loving, trusting eyes, and says to me with a smile, "I will give you one minute to think about it, my child, but no more than one minute."

And the old man leans on his huge staff and waits . . . .

* * *

Now I ask you—in that one minute, what could I possibly think that would permit me not to go with the old man and yet not sleep forever? Just go ahead. Try to guess!

Translated from the Yiddish
by Aliza Shevrin

The Revelation of Elijah

by S. Y. Agnon

There was an old poor man who frequented the study house of the Baal Shem Tov. He had a full beard and girded himself with a leather belt, and, since his name was Elijah, he was called Elijah the Prophet. Even the eminent Hasidim whose names were all David, Rabbi David of Mikulov, Rabbi David Pirkes, Rabbi David of Ostrog, Rabbi David Leikes, and Rabbi David the Elder, the Maggid of Kolomyya, all five Rabbis David, the Baal Shem's treasured men, called him Elijah the Prophet. They did not want to preface his name with "Rabbi" because he appeared to be ignorant. On the other hand, they did not want to omit the title, for the Torah says, "Thou shalt glorify the aged," and though he had no learning he was certainly old. Therefore they called him Elijah the Prophet, as if referring to the prophet himself, may he be remembered for a blessing.

It happened that a prominent man in the city was to circumcise his newborn son. He went to ask the Baal Shem to be the godfather and received his assent. He then entered the disciples' study house.

He saw the old poor man warming himself by the light of the oven and said to him, "I am making a circumcision feast. If you come to my home you surely won't leave hungry."

One of the disciples stirred and said, "Even if you do not invite him he will come, for the Holy One, blessed be He, said to Elijah, 'I swear that Israel will not perform a circumcision unless you see it with your own eyes.' "

The old man nodded his head and said, "I will come." The former had referred to the prophet Elijah, the angel of circumcisions, while the latter had referred to himself.

The disciples noted [disapprovingly] that the old man should have said, "God willing": "Man does nothing but what the Holy One wills. Without God's help, man would be nothing. Yet here this fellow says, 'I will come,' and fails to mention the name of God, as if the promise were his to fulfill!"

The day of the son's circumcision arrived. The whole city came. The Baal Shem Tov sat on a high-backed chair with the prophet Elijah, may he be remembered for a blessing, and brought the baby into the covenant of Abraham our Father, peace be upon him.

Then the baby's father held a circumcision feast. The Baal Shem sat at the head of the table and his students sat around him. The Baal Shem's face blazed. He put down his glass, leaned his head back and sat in silence. His teeth, however, rattled against each other and his body shook. His students were silent.

The Baal Shem brought his head forward and opened his discourse with the verse *Behold, I will send you Elijah the Prophet* (Mal. 3:23). He elaborated on the verse, speaking with awe and terror, with joy and trembling until he concluded with, "Happy is he who has seen him. And happy is he who has greeted him and was in turn greeted."

After he had finished speaking he got up from his seat and went away, his students behind him.

As they walked they meditated on their master's teachings, each one according to his ability. But the pleasure each took in these meditations was equal. This one's pleasure was as great as that one's.

Their master gazed at them with a kind expression on his face.

One spoke up, saying, "We know that Elijah is often with our teacher. May our teacher uncover our eyes that we may see Elijah." Another added, "And greet him."

The Baal Shem nodded his head to them and said, "God willing."

When they arrived at his house, he locked the door and they went into their study house.

A bit before the afternoon prayers the father of the newly circumcised baby came to the study house. He saw the old man standing before the oven and said to him, "Didn't I say that you should come?"

He replied, "I did what I said I would do."

The students heard and said to him, "How can you speak thusly? Behold, we did not see you."

He said to them, "He who saw, saw."

"What is the meaning of these words?" they asked him.

He replied, "He who must see, sees."

They turned their faces from him, because "a man who speaks lies shall not stand before my eyes."

The Baal Shem entered the study house and listened to the whole matter. He smiled at the old man and said, "I saw you." And the old man smiled at the Baal Shem and said, "You saw me."

The disciples listened and said, "Our Master said this only to shield the old man from disgrace, but the old man should have kept silent. Yet not only did he not keep silent but he smeared lie upon lie!"

The old man left and went on his way.

They began to discuss whether when God said to Elijah, "I swear that Israel will not perform a circumcision unless you see it with your own eyes," it was to reward or to punish him. Some said it was a reward for his zealotry for the sake of the Lord of Hosts, as it is written, *I have been very jealous for the Lord, the God of hosts.* Others said that it was nothing but a punishment for speaking evil of Israel as it also says *for the children of Israel have forsaken Thy Covenant.* Said the Holy One to Elijah, "You are eternally zealous. You were zealous at Shittim concerning incest and here you are zealous about the Covenant. You have been spreading slander against My children, claiming they do not fulfill the Covenant. With your own eyes you will see that they do fulfill it."

One of the group spoke up, saying, "When our master agreed to uncover our eyes to see Elijah we should have asked him when." Said another, "We could still ask him when." They agreed that whoever saw their master first would ask. It turned out that the one who gave the advice saw him first but did not remember "he who is remembered for a blessing." Thus it was on that day, on the morrow, and the day after, that they did not ask the Baal Shem their question.

What happened to this man happened to all his fellows also. When their master spoke to them they forgot and did not ask. When they departed from him they remembered. Forgetfulness is a serious thing, for one is liable to forget what he desires. Therefore, a man who holds a request in his heart should be careful to request his heart not to forget the request at the propitious moment.

"Blessed is He who brings to mind forgotten things," said one of the disciples. "Our Elijah has pulled up his roots from our study house. He has not shown himself here for several days."

Another spoke up, saying, "He is ashamed to appear before us because we made him lie."

Someone else said, "One cannot say that he is a liar, for did not our master say that he saw him?"

The door opened and the old man entered.

One of the disciples said to him, "We called you to mind and you came. If we had only recalled 'he who is remembered for a blessing' he would have come."

The old man nodded his head in agreement.

Said one of the four Rabbis David to Rabbi David the Elder, "I doubt whether he knows who 'he who is remembered for a blessing' is."

The Baal Shem entered, sat down, and began to teach Torah. The disciples sat and listened while the old man stood half awake, half asleep.

The Baal Shem lifted himself up and said, "I received this teaching from the mouth of Elijah."

The old man stirred and nodded his head.

After the Baal Shem finished speaking he returned to his room and locked the door. The disciples sat and went over the words of their master.

One of the group stood and said, "Did you see the old man? When our master said, 'I received this teaching from the mouth of Elijah,' the old man nodded to him."

The door opened and the Baal Shem came into the study house. He gazed at the disciples and asked them, "Why were you laughing?" They told him why. He said to them, "May he be remembered for a blessing for nodding his head to me. Thus he showed me that I did not alter anything I received from his mouth."

Then they knew that this old man must be Elijah the Prophet. They sought to greet him, but now they could not find him.

They said, "He will come for the afternoon prayers." The time came for the afternoon prayers, then the evening prayers, then the morning prayers, but he did not come. They said, "He will come tomorrow or the day after." One morning arrived and a second morning, a third and a fourth, but he did not come.

Their teacher told them, "Be not sorrowful. Just as you saw him, so shall you merit seeing him."

They forgot to ask him when this would be. Even during the evening following the Sabbath, a time of readiness for the coming of Elijah, with singing of table songs written about the prophet, they forgot and did not ask.

The Baal Shem sat on his chair while his students stood before him and sang songs for the departed Sabbath. The door opened and a villager entered with a staff and a knapsack. They wanted to push him out. The Baal Shem, however, told them, "Let him be. His sorrows brought him here."

The Baal Shem arose from his chair and greeted him. The disciples saw this and were dumbfounded. Here was a man who not only clearly walked farther than the distance permitted to walk on the Sabbath, but he brought with him a staff and a knapsack as well. Even if one set aside the matter of distance, one knew he had transgressed the prohibition against carrying goods from one area to another. Yet in spite of all this, their master stood up and greeted him.

The Baal Shem took him, seated him to his right, and said, "I see that your soul presses upon you with sadness. Have sorrows befallen you?"

The villager sighed and said, "It's not good, Rabbi Israel, not good. We are in great trouble."

The Baal Shem's face began to change color, each shade darker than the one before. He leaned his head backward. Then he turned his head to the villager and asked him, "What happened?"

The villager began to speak. "You know, Rabbi Israel, that we have a great craftsman in our village. He made us a workshop and filled it with fine, lovely vessels, and prepared for us everything we needed. We lacked nothing from him. It was our responsibility to maintain the vessels. But we neither watched over them nor maintained them. They began to rust. The craftsman warned us that if we did not maintain the vessels they would not be fit for use in skilled labor. We did not heed his warnings, however, nor did we maintain the vessels. He began warning us that if we did not pay attention to the vessels they would be damaged beyond repair. But the laziness within us sapped our strength. We could see that the vessels were becoming more and more rusty and damaged but we did not scour them or wash them. We did nothing. Why should I go on at great lengths, may God greatly lengthen your days, Rabbi Israel. All the vessels were ruined and became useless. Even the workshop suffered a change for the worse. At first all its dimensions corresponded, then some were great and some average, and then they were all clenched tight and small. In the end nothing was left us but a little tavern. But by then we had nothing but one vessel to store the liquor. Now, the vessel has been damaged and has sprung a leak. The brandy trickles out, goes to waste. The craftsman tells us, 'I made you a large workshop and arranged within it beautiful and costly vessels that would fulfill all your needs. You lacked nothing from me. You did not inspect the vessels, however, and let them become damaged until nothing remained to you but one, to be used for brandy. Behold, you should have maintained it. But you paid it no mind. Now that it is damaged and does not hold what I put in it, what will I do with this defective vessel and with men like you?' In short, it is not good, Rabbi Israel, not good."

"If the vessel has a puncture it can still be repaired," said the Baal Shem Tov.

The villager replied, "Be repaired? Are we then able to repair it? Please, Rabbi Israel, tell us how."

He answered, "One could try to plug up the leak."

"With what?" asked the villager. "Please, Rabbi Israel, tell us with what to plug up the leak."

He replied, "Tell me what you have in your home."

"We have nothing at home but bread and some lead coins," he said.

The Baal Shem told him, "Take a slice of bread, stop up the leak, and press a coin onto the bread. You will find that the vessel will hold whatever the craftsman pours into it. Perhaps the craftsman will be satisfied and will not leave you."

Said the villager, "Rabbi Israel, may you live forever, you have counseled me well. I will go home and proclaim your advice."

After obtaining the Baal Shem Tov's permission the villager started to go. While the two of them were taking leave of each other, they stood and spoke among themselves. What did they speak of and what was spoken? If only we would know in the world to come just a tiny particle of what we are unable even to imagine in this world.

The villager went on his way and the Baal Shem Tov returned to his seat.

After the official ceremony marking the Sabbath's end they brought the Baal Shem his pipe. He sat and smoked. His students asked him, "With whom was our teacher speaking?"

He said to them, "He was none other than Elijah, may he be remembered for a blessing."

When they heard this their souls flew away. Had the Baal Shem not come to their aid, their souls surely would have departed forever.

After their souls had returned, his students pressed him, "About what did our teacher and Elijah discourse?"

He answered, "What does one speak of with Elijah? One speaks about the goodness of Israel."

"And what is that damaged vessel and that liquor that trickles out?" they asked him. "Who is the craftsman whose parting they so fear? And what is the meaning of that which our teacher said, 'One plugs the leak with a slice of bread and a coin'?"

The Baal Shem gazed at them and smoked with great energy. Finally he took the pipe from his mouth and put it down next to him. Then he said to them, "Elijah was greatly troubled, for he heard that an accusation had gone out against Israel. It was charged that even the few commandments they fulfill and good deeds they perform were insincere, from the lips outward. It was said that Israel is falling into the hands of the irreligious. Elijah fears that the Holy One, blessed be He, will say that He no longer wants this people. The Holy One gave my heart counsel to repair their deeds with a slice of bread to guests and charity to the poor. That is the meaning of my words to Elijah, that if the vessel is punctured and has a leak, one plugs it with a slice of bread and a coin, so the liquid will not trickle out and bring profit to the irreligious, God forbid."

The faces of the group rejoiced over the three sources of happiness. One, that they, the people Israel, were able to amend their deeds. Second, that they had seen Elijah. And lastly, that Israel had been honored in that every Jew had been found worthy to be worn like a garment by Elijah, may he be remembered for a blessing. He might appear at times in the guise of an old man and at times in the likeness of a villager.

A great joy came to them and they danced.

Something we did not mention earlier we will relate now. Rabbi David, and Rabbi David, Rabbi David, and Rabbi David, the four Rabbis David from the "palace" of the Baal Shem Tov, danced that dance. Even Rabbi David the Elder, the Maggid of Kolomyya, who chanced to be there that Sabbath, even he danced with the disciples. And the same old man whom they called Elijah the Prophet came and danced with them.

Translated from the Hebrew
by Jeremy Garber

The Poor Man and Eliyahu the Prophet

by Kamelia Shahar

A husband and wife used to be wretched. Not only were they poor and childless, the husband was blind (God help us). One day the man, sad and worn out, began to walk very slowly, till he came to the edge of the sea. There, helping himself with his cane, he found a spot, sat down, and started thinking about his miserable luck. Thinking, thinking, suddenly he felt a person touching his shoulder (the person was Eliyahu the Prophet, who appears always for our good, amen), and Eliyahu the Prophet said to him:

"The Lord of the world has taken pity on you and wants to help you. Speak: say what you want and God will satisfy you, but on the condition that you make only one request."

The man thought long and hard, and he didn't know how to put in one request all that he wanted, so he replied to Eliyahu the Prophet:

"Look, I beg you, give me till tomorrow. I'll give you the answer then."

"Fine," Eliyahu the Prophet said to him, and they parted, each going his own way.

The good man returned home, told his wife what was going through his mind, and asked her:

"Tell me, woman, what are we going to do? How in one request can I ask for all we need?"

His wife answered him:

"My husband, don't torture yourself, come and eat now, rest yourself, God is great even till tomorrow, I'll tell you what you're going to say."

The man ate and went to sleep. In the morning he rose, washed and dressed, took his little cane, and his wife told him what he should say. Again, very slowly, he made his way to the edge of the sea. There already waiting for him was Eliyahu the Prophet.

"Eh, good man," he said, "did you bring the answer? Do you know what you want?"

"Yes," the man replied, "I would like the Lord of the world to let me see my child eat off a plate of gold."

Surprised by the good answer, Eliyahu the Prophet said to him, "Since you knew how to put in one request the three things that you lack, the Holy One, blessed be He, will fulfill your wish."

And each one went his own way, joyful and satisfied.

May good fortune be heaped on them and on us too.

Translated from the Judezmo
by Stephen Levy

The Apprentice
by Dan Tsalka

At the close of the 19th century there lived in Jerusalem, near Yokhanan Ben-Zakkay synagogue—its ram-horn waiting for Elijah the Prophet, its oil can to anoint Messiah—a poor cobbler called Shaul Berachyah Azuz. His grandfather belonged to the Shabtaite Denme sect in Salonica and had come to Jerusalem in vague circumstances. The cobbler remembered queer prayers and odd songs. After the death of his parents he lived where they'd lived, in a half-ruined house supported by black beams.

Azuz was a fat bald man who liked eating hot bread and drinking arak. Few came to his house. One of them before daybreak and at midnight blew the ram-horn, short and strong like a bugle, through the empty synagogue and lingered by the chair of Elijah the Prophet and the cabinet with its can of oil.

For a long time Azuz had dreamed of an apprentice who would clean his tiny workroom, take out the shoes to dry, do odd jobs. Someone he could order about, look after, and tell stories to. But he was too poor. Usually he mended shoes and did not make new ones, for he was not very skillful or hardworking. Time passed and Azuz forgot his hopes for an apprentice.

One winter's day Azuz was wakened at daybreak by thunder and by rain and hail drumming on the roof and against the panes of the narrow windows. Apparently someone was knocking at the door. He got up, wrapped himself in blankets, and opened the door. Outside sharp raindrops lashed his face and bare hands, black clouds descended on the lonely roofs of Shiloah village. Azuz wanted to go back to his room, when suddenly he saw in the tiny square near the town wall something that stopped him. In the square, shivering and dripping wet, stood a naked angel in a puddle, changing from one bare foot to the other. Once Azuz had got the blood back in his face, he began walking toward the square. He didn't dare look at the angel and raised his eyes only when he saw him reflected in the puddle. Seen close the angel resembled a man of medium height. Azuz wrapped him in a blanket and took him to his house, walking by his side in respect and silence.

Once inside his room Azuz wiped the tears off the angel's face, heated some water, washed his feet, dried his hair, and put an old white shirt on his back. He gave him a small cup of tea with two lumps of sugar and himself drank several glasses of arak from embarrassment and wonder.

When the angel had drunk the tea his face glowed strangely, his eyes shone, and filled with joy Azuz said to him, recalling his grandfather's words and the murmuring of the man with the ram-horn about Paradise—same heaven, same earth, as in a mirror. The angel shook his head and again wept copious tears. Azuz continued to ask about heaven, but the angel answered in unintelligible signs, till Azuz grasped that he was dumb. That night he dreamed that he stood outside his house at daybreak, angels raining down around him. He started up afraid it was merely a dream. But he saw in the corner of the room the angel's white shirt and heard his tranquil breathing.

From that day the angel stayed with Azuz. At first, he wouldn't do anything in the workshop but he'd willingly run errands, bring customers their shoes, fetch water or herbs. On one occasion he collected wooden nails scattered over the floor of the tiny room, another time he covered thread with wax. In the summer he'd take the shoes out to dry on the sloping roof, and when Azuz fell ill, the angel sewed new soles on a neighbor's shoes. The years passed and everyone got used to the new apprentice. Azuz hummed his grandfather's tunes and told him stories. The angel, smiling in silence, drank arak with him.

Translated from the Hebrew
by Hannah Amit-Kochavi

The Magician

by I. L. Peretz

1

Once upon a time a magician came to a village.

And even though it was before Passover, when a Jew has more troubles than hairs on his head, the magician's arrival created a great stir.

What a mystery this man was! Bedraggled and shabby, he wore a crushed top hat on his head. His was a clean-shaven Jewish face. No one ever saw him eat any food, neither kosher nor unkosher. Who was he, one wondered?

If asked, "Where are you from?" he would reply, "From Paris." "Where are you going?" "To London!" "What brings you here?" "I'm lost!" Apparently he had walked there! If approached or encircled by people, he would suddenly vanish as if the earth had swallowed him whole and spat him out on the other side of the marketplace.

Meanwhile he rented a hall and started to perform tricks.

And what tricks! He swallowed live coals and drew colored ribbons from his mouth—red ones, green ones, whatever color you pleased. From his boots sixteen pairs of turkeys flew out, and what turkeys—big as bears and alive, running all over the place. Then he lifted his leg and scraped off gold coins from the sole of his boot, a whole plate of gold coins! The audience applauded, "Bravo!" He whistled and up flew Sabbath breads and loaves like birds dancing a jig under the ceiling. He whistled again and it all disappeared—the breads, the ribbons, the turkeys—all gone as if they had never been!

How could it be explained? Why was this man so poor? He could scrape coins from his soles but couldn't pay for his lodgings. With a whistle, he could produce more breads and loaves than the greatest baker. Turkeys appeared from his boots and yet his face was drawn and haggard as a corpse and starvation burned in his eyes like a flame! People started to say, "It's the fifth question of Passover."

But before we attempt to answer this question, let us leave the magician and turn our attention to Chaim-Yoneh and his wife, Rivke-Beile.

2

Chaim-Yoneh had once been a lumber merchant. He had bought a timber forest but it had been confiscated, so the poor man lost everything but the shirt on his back. He also lost a job as a lumber accountant and remained without a livelihood for many months. They survived the winter, but Passover was coming! Every item in the house from the chandeliers to the last pillow had been pawned.

Said Rivke-Beile, "Go! Ask for charity." But Chaim-Yoneh said he had faith that God would provide and would spare him the humiliation.

Again Rivke-Beile searched in every nook and cranny till she found an old, worn-out silver spoon which had been missing for years! Chaim-Yoneh sold the spoon but donated the few groschen to the poor for Passover. "Poor people," he said, "come first."

Time passed. Only a few weeks were left till Passover, but Chaim-Yoneh had faith. "God," said he, "never fails anyone!" Rivke-Beile remained silent; a wife must obey her husband. But another day went by and another. Rivke-Beile couldn't sleep and wept quietly so that Chaim-Yoneh would not hear. There was not a thing for Passover. Days were even worse than nights—at least at night she could relieve her soul's burden with tears, but during the day she had to pinch her cheeks so they would appear rosy. The neighbors stared at her, their mouths agape, their eyes pricking her with glances of pity. Others asked, "Aren't you going to bake matzos?" Her friends wondered, "What is it, what is happening to you, Rivke-Beile? If you are in need, we can lend you whatever you want."

But Chaim-Yoneh refused to accept gifts from people, and Rivke-Beile would not oppose her husband, so she made up any excuse she could think of, but her face was aflame with embarrassment and shame.

The neighbors, realizing something was amiss, ran to the rabbi and reported the problem. The rabbi, poor soul, heard them out, groaned as he thought it over carefully, and came to the conclusion that Chaim-Yoneh was a God-fearing man and was justified in his faith.

Rivke-Beile was left without so much as a candle for the Sabbath blessing. And—it was already Passover!

3

Walking home from the synagogue, Chaim-Yoneh saw all the windows brightly lit with holiday joy. Only his house was standing like a blind person amid the sighted. But he persisted in his faith. "If God wills it, there will be a Passover for us!" he thought. He entered and cheerfully said, *"Goot yomtov!"* and again, *"Goot yomtov* to you, Rivke-Beile!" Rivke-Beile's tear-choked voice answered him from a dark corner, *"Goot yomtov, goot yor,"* and her eyes glowed from the dark corner like two live coals.

He approached her and said, "Rivke-Beile, today is *yomtov,* do you understand? It is forbidden to be sorrowful. And what is there to sorrow for? If God didn't wish for us to have a seder of our own, we must accept His wish and sit at someone else's seder. We will celebrate the seder somewhere else. We are welcome anywhere. All doors are open to us. The Jews say, 'Let anyone who is hungry enter and be fed.' Come, put on your shawl and we will go to the first Jewish house on the way."

And Rivke-Beile, who always obeyed her husband, held back her tears with all her might so that they remained choked in her throat. She wrapped a ragged shawl about her shoulders and was ready to go, when the door suddenly opened and a person entered.

"Goot yomtov!" he said.

They completed the traditional greeting, *"Goot yor,"* without being able to make out who their guest was.

The unseen visitor said, "I have come to sit at your seder table with you."

Chaim-Yoneh replied, "We ourselves have no seder."

The voice answered that he had brought the seder with him.

"But we have no candles—it is dark!" Rivke-Beile sobbed, unable to hold back any longer.

"God forbid!" the visitor answered. "We will have light!"

He gesticulated with his hands—Hocus-pocus!—and two pairs of silver candlesticks with lighted candles appeared in the middle of the room, floating in the air! The room became bright with light, and Chaim-Yoneh and Rivke-Beile realized that it was the magician. Their mouths fell open with astonishment and fear; they could not utter a sound. Clasping one another's hands, they stood staring, their mouths agape.

Meanwhile, the magician approached the bare little table which almost seemed to be hiding itself in a corner for shame. "Come, little one, cover yourself and come over here to us!" As he said these words, a snow-white tablecloth dropped from the ceiling and covered the table, which then slid across the floor to the center of the room, where it came to a stop directly under the candles and silver candlesticks, whereupon they lowered themselves onto the table.

"Now," said the magician, "we need large sofas on which to recline. Let there be sofas!" Three benches from three corners of the room floated to three sides of the table. The magician commanded them to become wider and they stretched themselves till they were transformed into easy chairs. He called out, "Softer!" and they became draped with red velvet at the same time that snow-white pillows dropped from the ceiling on the easy chairs and were ready to be reclined upon! There also appeared magically red wineglasses, beakers of wine, matzos, and all that was required for a kosher and joyous seder, even gilt-edged Haggadahs.

"Is there no water for washing?" the magician asked. "I can provide water too!"

Only then were they jolted out of their shocked state. Rivke-Beile whispered to Chaim-Yoneh, "Is it allowed? What do you think?" Chaim-Yoneh did not know what to tell her. "Go, husband," she urged, "and ask the rabbi's advice." He replied that he couldn't leave her alone with the magician and suggested she go to the rabbi. But she felt that the rabbi would never believe a silly woman and would think she had gone mad. So the two of them went together to the rabbi, leaving the magician at the seder.

The rabbi proclaimed that whatever was produced by magic was worthless because magic is an illusion. He instructed them to go home and if the matzo could be broken and if the wine could be poured into the glasses and if the pillows could be felt, these would be sure signs that the seder was acceptable, a gift from God to be enjoyed.

That was what the rabbi decided. Their hearts pounding, the two returned home. They entered the house but the magician was gone. The seder stood as before. The pillows were soft to the touch, the wine could be poured, the matzos broke apart. It was only then that they realized they had been visited by Eliyahu Hanavi, Elijah the Prophet, and they celebrated their most joyous *yomtov!*

Translated from the Yiddish
by Aliza Shevrin

The Golem

by I. L. Peretz

Great men would sometimes perform great miracles . . . When the Prague ghetto was attacked with the intention of defiling the women, roasting the children, and slaughtering everyone else; when all hope appeared to be lost, the Maharal put aside the Gemara and went out into the streets. He went over to the first best clay mound, which happened to be in front of a *melamed*'s doorway, and fashioned a clay dummy. He blew into the Golem's nose—the Golem started to move; he whispered a name into his ear—and the Golem strode out of the ghetto. The Maharal returned to his learning and the Golem turned to our enemies who had besieged the ghetto, thrashing his stumps about. . . . Men started falling like flies!

Prague started filling up with dead. It went on, so it is said, all of Wednesday and Thursday; Friday came, the clock struck twelve, and still the Golem continued to go about his business.

Rabbi, the community pleaded, the Golem will kill off all of Prague! Who will remain to heat the stoves on the Sabbath or remove the candlesticks!

The Maharal again interrupted his learning, approached the altar, and began to say "A psalm, a song for the Sabbath day."

The Golem stopped his work. He returned to the ghetto, to the synagogue, and went over to the Maharal. The Maharal again whispered in his ear, and the Golem's eyes closed, the breath went out of him, and he became a clay dummy once more.

To this day the Golem lies in an upper alcove of the Prague synagogue, hidden by spider webs which reach out from all four walls and extend across the entire arcade, so that no eyes may gaze on him, especially not the pregnant women from the ladies' gallery. That in fact is the reason that the spider web must not be disturbed, and whoever does disturb it dies. The elders no longer remember the Golem; only the Chacham Zvi, the Maharal's grandson, still wonders whether the Golem may be included in the quorum of ten or the company of three.

The Golem, you see, has not been forgotten . . . he exists! But the Name, without which the Golem cannot be animated in times of need, it is as if the Name had sunk to the bottom of the seas! And the spider web grows and grows and must not be disturbed. Do something!

Translated from the Yiddish
by Evelyn Abel

How the Golem Was Created
by Rabbi Yudl Rosenberg

Yitzchak ben Simeon Cohen, the son-in-law of the Great Rabbi Loew, relates as follows:

The Maharal prayed that he might be told in a dream how to fight against the ritual accusation. He received from the heavens a reply in ten words, the initial letters of which corresponded to the sequence of the Hebrew alphabet: create an image (Golem) out of clay and you shall destroy the evil design of those who want to tear Israel to pieces. The Maharal was convinced that from those ten letters words could be formed which would enable a living Golem to be created out of clay.

The Maharal secretly called me and his oldest pupil, Jacob ben Chayim Sasson Levy, told us of the heavenly answer which he had prayed for, and disclosed to us the secret, how to create the Golem from clay and dust. We had to be his assistants, because such a creation required the power of the four elements, fire, air, water, and earth. He himself, he said, had been created by the power of the element air (spirit), I by the power of fire, and his pupil by the power of water. We three, therefore, could complete the creation of the Golem out of earth. We were enjoined not to divulge the secret to anyone and he gave us strict instructions how to behave during the week preceding the creation.

In the year 5340 (1580), on the 20 Adar the three of us went out of Prague at four o'clock in the morning to the river Moldavka. On its bank we found a spot containing sticky clay. We made out of it a human form, three ells long, with face, hands, and feet, and it lay there like a man on his back. We then stood at the Golem's feet, our faces turned to its face. The Maharal ordered me first of all to walk seven times round the clay form, from right to left, starting from the head towards the feet. I had to recite a formula which he had taught me. When I finished the body was glowing red like fire. After that the pupil had to walk round seven times, pronouncing a different formula. When he had finished the fire became extinguished, because water entered the body and issued as steam. Then the body became covered with hair, like a man of thirty, and the tips of the fingers and toes with nails. Now the Maharal himself performed the seven circuits and the three of us pronounced simultaneously the verse: "And the Lord God . . . breathed into his nostrils the breath of life; and man became a living creature."

The Golem opened his eyes and looked at us with wonder. The Maharal called in a loud voice: "Stand on your feet." The Golem rose and stood at once on his feet. We dressed him in the clothes which we had brought with us and which were suitable for a servant of the synagogue. We also put shoes on his feet, so that he looked exactly like a man. He saw, heard, and understood everything, but he did not have the power of speech.

Towards six o'clock, before the dawn, we returned home, the four of us. On the way the Maharal told the Golem: "Know that we have created you out of the dust of the earth in order that you may liberate the Jews from all the misery and sufferings which they have to endure from their enemies and oppressors. You will be called Joseph. You shall stay with me and live in my courtroom, where your duties will be those of an usher. You must fulfill all my commands, even to walk through fire, to descend into deep waters, or jump from a tower, until you have carried out my orders, no matter where I send you." The Golem inclined his head to show that he agreed.

The Maharal told us that he had named him Joseph because he was a kind of continuation of the being mentioned in the Talmud, Joseph Seda, half man, half spirit, who served the Talmudic sages and often delivered them from great danger. To the members of his household the Maharal explained that he had met this poor dumb man in the street, had noticed his great simplicity, and had taken him into the house out of pity, to be of service to him in his courtroom.

The Golem always sat in a corner of the courtroom, at the edge of the table, his head resting on his hands, just like a vessel of clay, without any mind, without any thought about anything. People called him "Dumb Yossel," or "Yossel the Clay," which means the same as "Yossel the Golem."

Translated from the Yiddish
by Frederic Thieberger

The End of the Golem

by Rabbi Yudl Rosenberg

Yitzchak ben Simeon Cohen, the son-in-law of the Great Rabbi Loew, relates as follows:

After the Emperor Rudolf had issued an Edict that in his domain there must be no more cases of blood accusation, the Great Rabbi Loew felt that now the Passover Festival would proceed peacefully. So he called me, his son-in-law, Yitzchak Cohen, and his pupil Yacob Sasson Levy, the two of us who had taken part in the creation of the Golem, and declared that from now onwards the Golem would not be required any longer. He ordered the Golem not to sleep that night on his usual bed in the courtroom, but to make it up in the loft of the Great Synagogue.

Towards two in the morning we went up to the loft where the Golem was sleeping. The old synagogue beadle, Abraham Chayim, also had the Maharal's permission to follow upstairs, carrying two lighted candlesticks, but he had to stand a little on one side.

The three of us placed ourselves, contrary to what we had done at his creation, at the head of the Golem, with our faces turned towards his feet, and we began to circle round him from left to right. There were seven circuits, the same as before. After each circuit we stopped and pronounced the formula which the Maharal had taught us. They were the same formulae as at the creation of the Golem, only they were recited in the opposite order.

Anyone versed in the practical Kabbalah and conversant with the *Book of the Creation (Sefer Yetsirah)* knows the secret of the manner of creation and also of dissolution. After the seventh circuit the Golem remained lying like a mass of clay with the shape of a human being. The Maharal called the synagogue servant and took the two candlesticks from him, and we removed the clothes from the Golem, leaving only the shirt. Having wrapped him in two old prayer shawls, a number of which were lying about in the loft, we took the heavy mass and hid it amongst the many fragments of books in the loft, so that nothing of it could be seen. The synagogue servant was ordered to burn the Golem's bed and clothes secretly.

Next day the news spread in the town that the Golem had run away and no one knew where. Only very few people were aware of what actually had taken place. A fortnight later the Great Rabbi Loew issued an order that no one was to enter the loft of the synagogue to deposit praying shawls or books which had become useless. People thought this was a precaution against the risk of fire, but the confidants of the Rabbi knew the real reason: it should not become known that Yossel the Golem was lying there.

Translated from the Yiddish
by Frederic Thieberger

The Moon, the Mercenary, and the Ring
by Lajos Szabolcsi

The clock struck midnight in the Jews' Street of Prague. It sounded like the thin, quiet ring of a bell. Above the steeples and chimneys the moon appeared, covering the sleeping houses with a blanket of green rays.

A mercenary of the emperor's army, walking with resounding steps, turned into the street. He wore a hussar's cap, and had a sword that hung from his waist, and a musket which he carried on his back. Two bludgeons were stuck into his big boots. His face was pockmarked, his eyes bloodshot.

The mercenary stopped briefly in front of a house. Then in front of another. He stared at the moon and let out a whistle before breaking into a battle song. Then he walked on.

In front of the synagogue he lapsed into a pensive mood. The old synagogue was asleep; its tall columns and white stones were dreaming restlessly in the quivering moonlight. Next to the synagogue a single-story house stood. In one of its windows a light was burning.

The rabbi lived there. Rabbi Loew. Whatever was he doing in his room at midnight?

The mercenary pulled out a bludgeon and knocked on the window. It gave a small clinking sound. Then he pulled out the other bludgeon and knocked on the window again.

The light went out in the window.

The mercenary shook. A shudder passed over him. The houses stood dark and silent. On the roofs cats were meowing, their backs curved in the direction of the moon. Suddenly the rabbi's window stopped clinking. Terror-stricken, the mercenary turned around. There he stood, next to him, the rabbi.

Rabbi Loew. He was a tall, gray-haired man. He wore a black garment, with a palm-sized yellow patch on his chest, and a hat.

"What do you want, soldier?" he asked the emperor's mercenary.

"Are you the rabbi of Prague, that famous Loew?" the mercenary responded in a brusque tone.

"I'm the rabbi of Prague. What made you come to the Jews' Street at midnight?"

"I'm just passing through. I was on my way from one inn to another when I decided to drop in on you. We arrived from Spain this morning. We'd seized Barcelona and carried off all three of the prince's daughters. Tomorrow we'll march against Düsseldorf. There are three more young countesses there and two thousand barrels of wine in the cellar. But tonight we'll only take a rest here after our labors in the inn."

A quiet, deep, sad sigh fluttered through the Jews' Street. The rabbi stood motionless. The mercenary looked around.

"Go on, soldier."

"Listen, rabbi, I've got a ring for sale. A dying blue-uniformed hussar gave it to me during a battle in Westphalia. He told me to take it home and sell it. I would get a lot of money for it. It's made of some strange metal. So soft that even your breath will leave a mark on it; yet it's harder than iron. That blue hussar was a spy, and he used to carve messages and orders in this soft stuff when he snuck from one camp to another. If only I could read, rabbi! What do I need this thing for? I want money! Emperor Rudolph's talers! That's what women and wine are measured out for in Prague. Understand, rabbi?"

"Go on," the rabbi said.

"I will. Don't rush me! Last night I showed the ring to the bartender. I asked how much he'd give for it. He looked at the ring, turning it around and examining it closely. Then he gave it back. That fool! How much he'd give? Nothing. I should take it to the rabbi. The rabbi? Why the rabbi? Because this ring is a Jewish ring. From Palestine. From the mines of Damascus. The rabbi would buy it. Would he buy it tonight? Sure, tonight, I should just go to him. I took a good look at the bartender. He had a red beard. A wretched Jew! You Jews are in cahoots with one another! It doesn't matter. I'm a decent fellow, and you, rabbi . . . all I'm going to tell you . . ."

The mercenary leaned against the wall of the synagogue and gazed at the moon.

"All I'm going to tell you . . ." he said in a hoarse voice. "Buy my ring now that I'm here. Give me two hundred gold pieces for it. Otherwise, I'll beat you to a pulp."

The rabbi reached for the ring. He took a good look at it. It was a thick circlet. Its color was golden green. The rabbi examined it more thoroughly, holding it against the moon. Was he reading something that had been inscribed in it?

The mercenary was still leaning against the wall. Suddenly, he burst out laughing. The moon was shining brighter and brighter, its rays falling into silvery streams. The clock struck at the half hour. The rabbi turned around.

"Soldier!" he shouted angrily. "Soldier! Where is your shadow?"

The mercenary jumped away from the wall. Where was his shadow?

He started whirling and jumping, dancing and bending. He shook his hat and twirled his musket; he brandished his sword and flailed his arms. All was to no avail. His shadow had disappeared.

He threw himself to the ground as if his money had rolled away. He sniffed the wall as if he wanted to lick the stone for water. He stamped his feet as if he wanted to jolt his shadow out of the ground. Nothing helped. His shadow had disappeared. He was alone. Alone! The sun would shine on him in vain; the moon would turn its face toward him in vain. His shadow had disappeared. It was gone! It had preceded him to Hell. And he would follow it within a month.

"Soldier!" the rabbi shouted again. "Where did you leave your shadow?"

Where did he leave it? Where, indeed? In Westphalia? On the battleground? No, he still had it even after he had been there. In Regensburg he had even marveled at the fine shadow his lance had cast. Could he have left it in the castle? Or the town?

"Where were you this evening?" the rabbi shouted.

"In the barracks. I didn't leave it there. I still had it there."

"Where else?"

"In the inn. But I didn't leave it there, either."

"Where else?"

"Nowhere."

The rabbi was holding the ring against the moon.

"You're lying, soldier! You're lying, hussar! I can read the message on the ring. You're lying! You left the barracks and went with a gunner to the cemetery. A Christian cemetery."

"That's true. We did."

"You stole a dead body from the mortuary."

"That's true. We did."

"You took the body of a Christian child from the catafalque and brought it to this street. You threw it into a cellar. So that it would be found with the Jews."

"Only so that they would find it, but . . ."

"Why did you do it, soldier?"

"We were paid . . . we were paid. But we spent all of it on drinks "

"You'd like to get your shadow back, soldier, wouldn't you?"

"What would I do without a shadow? I'm not worth a thing without it. I'll die within a month if I don't get it back."

"Do you know who took your shadow? Do you know who has it? That catafalque in the cemetery, that's who."

"Oh my! The catafalque!"

"You took the dead body from it, and out of revenge he pulled your shadow, like a cape, off you. What are you going to do about it?"

"I will take the dead body back to it."

"Do you know where you threw it?"

"Into a cellar, at the corner to the right, next to the bridge. I'll pull it out of the cellar. Oh my! I'm going to run now and take it back."

"Here's your ring, soldier."

"I don't need a Jewish ring. I don't need anything Jewish. I don't need anything from any Jew. All I want is to get my shadow back. My shadow! My shadow!"

Moaning, the drunken mercenary stumbled along the street. From time to time he bumped into a house. Roused by his moans, the cats stuck their heads out from behind the chimneys. Then he disappeared in an alley by the bridge.

The rabbi looked at the synagogue. Then he raised his eyes to the moon. His hand clutching the ring, he bent over slightly and he stepped through the low gate.

His window lit up again.

Above the sleeping ghetto, the clock struck once.

Translated from the Hungarian
by Andrew Handler

The House of Demons

by Martin Buber

On the main square of a city in Poland, there was a large and stately house that was quite old but, in its graystone manner, strong and handsomely fashioned. As long as could be remembered it had been unoccupied and stood like a sleeping colossus with its locked shutters and doors. The family to whom it belonged had lived for many decades in a distant city and scarcely concerned itself with this property. Nobody in the city knew why the members of the family disdained to live in so handsome a building. If there ever had been a reason, none of the townspeople remembered it, and the family themselves never discussed it. Nevertheless it was very odd that a line so widely branched and so rich in children in all of its generations should prefer to seek its dwelling among strangers, and even more curious that they never attempted to find a tenant and extract some profit from their property.

This might not have been so easy, since for some time many dark rumors concerning the house had circulated among the townspeople. These rumors were increased by a remarkable and tragic event that had taken place there several years before. A bold child had managed to penetrate the thick hedge at the rear of the building, had climbed onto the terrace, and, after breaking open a rotten shutter, entered the house through one of the lower windows. His companions, who had remained behind, heard the sound of many voices crying out as if in pain; there was much noise and a confused running back and forth. Suddenly they saw the boy, flung by an invisible hand, fly through the window in a wide arc and fall heavily to the ground. When they climbed over the low wall to help their playmate to his feet, they found that he was dead. The people who were attracted by their cries gave little credence to the children's account of the affair but considered it remarkable that the boy, whose neck they found to be broken, had been fatally injured by a fall from such an insignificant height onto the soft grass.

In any event, from that time on both house and garden were more assiduously avoided, although now and then one heard of various observations that some passerby had made rather hastily at a late hour. The enlightened members of the community had little more than a smile for these tales. Nevertheless everyone was surprised when word came that one of the younger sons of the family was on his way to take possession of the house for himself and his newlywed bride. It was rumored that the young man had made this decision independently and against the wishes of his family. They had discouraged him with all manner of dark words, alluding to a misfortune that an ancestor had experienced in the house, making it unlucky for all of them.

Presently the young man arrived. The house filled with industrious workmen of all sorts, and after a few weeks, when both inside and outside had been thoroughly cleaned, emerged polished and livable. The peculiar stories that had grown up around it were given new life by the artisans, who had some strange tales to tell. For example, the men were afraid to go into the cellar ever since some of their fellows, who were working down there, had been showered with earth and stones, had their hair pulled and been thrown to the ground, without once having encountered or observed any traces of a human being. As a result, the new owner had no other choice than to dispense with the use of the cellar, since in its present dirty and disordered state it was unsuitable for household purposes. Although this was not very convenient, he hoped that in the course of time, when the townspeople's foolish fantasies, as he termed them, had subsided, he would be able to hire other workmen to put the place in order.

With his affairs in this state, he and his young wife moved in, taking with them all the servants they had brought from their previous household. For a while everything was peaceful and pleasant for the newly married couple, except that several times the young wife was disturbed in her sleep by a plaintive, bitter crying. When she told this to her husband, who loved her tenderly, he made every effort to discover the source of the disturbance, but was unsuccessful, since he himself never heard a sound. On one occasion it seemed to her that someone was pulling on her hair, which lay draped over the pillow. Another time she thought that someone she couldn't see was blowing heavily in her face. When she awoke, her eyes were swollen shut, and although they didn't pain her, they remained swollen for the rest of the day. These things made the pretty young bride pale and nervous, and her husband grew seriously worried. But, since it was soon evident that the young woman was pregnant, people were inclined to explain these oddities as the result of her condition. Many women assured her that they had had similar, and even worse, hallucinations, and that all this would come to a natural conclusion.

It wasn't long before a happy, healthy child was born. The mother rejoiced, but the birth put no end to the inexplicable manifestations, which the others now also perceived. Sometimes they found the child turned over in the cradle with his face buried in the pillow, or asleep on the floor under the bed. Though nothing serious ever happened, they hardly dared leave him alone for a second. Similarly, in the kitchen and parlor, securely fastened dishes and cups would suddenly fall clattering to the floor for no particular reason, and there were days when the servant had nothing else to do but pick up broken pieces of porcelain. Just as the family sat down to eat, the kitchen maid would come running in tears, wailing that she no sooner left the stove for a minute to get something from the cupboard, than an evil spirit spilled garbage and ashes into the pot. On occasion, all the doors flew open, and hurried steps sounded in the rooms without anyone being seen. If a house guest chanced to walk down the corridor at night, he had the candle violently torn from his fingers and thrown to the floor, so that he stood in the dark where invisible hands pulled and tore at his hair and clothes until he called pitifully for help or ran back to the others. Neither master nor servants found relief or rest.

An ominous anxiety hung over the house, since no one was certain that he would be able to attend to his work in peace, take his meals, or get his rest without being disturbed by the tormenting spirits. But, inasmuch as nothing really serious occurred, things were permitted to continue in this way for some time, particularly because the young owner was reluctant to humiliate himself in public by acknowledging that the people who had warned him were right. Finally, however, the complaints of his wife and servants proved too much for him, and he appealed to the congregation for help. They advised him to consult the much celebrated miracle worker Rabbi Joel of Zamosc, who was reported to have power over the creatures of the unearthly realms.

The troubled young man immediately sent a messenger to Zamosc, and it was not long before Rabbi Joel arrived, prepared for his task. He ordered the occupants to vacate the house, leaving only the owner with him. The two of them prepared themselves by praying and fasting for a day and a night. On the midnight of the second day, the holy man lit the candles and threw herbs in the chafing dish. With strong and commanding words he invoked the spirits in the name of the Ruler of All Worlds; he promised them justice and, if possible, the dissolution of their earthly bonds.

The air trembled perceptibly, and a voice answered, "I am here, the chief of my people, the demons who have inhabited this house for two hundred years. Know that the possession and right of this house belong to us and not to the earthly race who have come to take what is rightfully ours. We are prepared to prove our claim. Therefore, draw up a tribunal and grant us a hearing as you have promised."

Rabbi Joel then assured the demon that if he returned at the same hour the next night, he would receive a formal hearing. To this the demon agreed.

At the appointed hour, the great master arrived, accompanied by two judges from the community and the owner of the house. Rabbi Joel invoked the demon, and the voice in the air answered, "I am here."

"Then," said the master, "lay your case before the court as is usual." And the voice told the following story:

"Long ago this house belonged to a Jew who had traveled through many lands in his youth and who, in the practice of his trade as a goldsmith and jewelry merchant, had acquired a considerable reputation for his skill in setting and polishing precious stones. He was already a man of years when he returned to the homeland of his childhood, where, after building this house and marrying a pious daughter of the Jewish community, he settled down for the rest of his days. He soon won favor with the rich and powerful, and many noble works of art issued from his hand. Also, as his behavior indicated, he had remained a religious Jew, although the people of the community found much that was strange in his habits and bearing, and continued to regard him with suspicion in spite of his property and wealth.

"For his part the goldsmith, having seen and experienced much richness and elegance in other lands, felt alien in the narrowness of the town and its people. When not completely occupied with his work, he could often be seen walking in his garden or strolling somewhere outside the city, deeply absorbed in his unhappiness. His imagination dwelt ceaselessly on distant lands to which he could not travel because of his wife and children. Once, while standing in this manner and gazing absently into a deep well that was located in a remote corner of his garden, he heard a rippling in the water and, when he looked up, saw a fair, naked woman emerging from its depths. She seated herself on the embankment and smiled at him so pleasantly that he lost his heart to her at once and never afterward desired to part from her.

"That same night he brought this daughter of the race of demons into his house and concealed her in a secret room in the cellar, that was frequented by no one but himself and where he kept the jewels of his trade secured behind iron doors. Between the mortal and the demon woman there grew a deep love. His being was bound to hers, and he no longer yearned for far-off lands. They lived together many years, and his happiness never abated. His strange wife bore him children of his and her blood, who were at once both men and demons. The goldsmith kept all of them concealed in the depths of the house with their mother, and no one else knew of their existence.

"His legal wife, however, who was neither lovely in body nor soul, who was grave, cross and sharp, who scolded fiercely and gave orders harshly, shared the impression of the townspeople that there was something odd about her husband, but as she scarcely concerned herself with him, she had no particular explanation for it. She was content that he provided properly for her and her children, and was grateful that his labor steadily increased their wealth. He also seemed to follow all the rules of the faith, though occasionally, in the midst of prayer in the synagogue, an irresistible desire for his demon woman seized him, and he rushed home to her.

"This happened once on the first night of Passover, while he was celebrating the seder. In the middle of the meal, he imagined that he heard the voice of the demon woman luring him with her silvery laughter. The meal became disgusting to him, and he could no longer endure the faces of his family. Without a word he rose from the table and hurried from the room. His wife watched in amazement; this time she considered his behavior a bit too strange, and she followed him secretly when he went down to the cellar. She watched him disappear behind the iron doors, and consumed with curiosity and wonder, she tiptoed after. When she bent down to the keyhole, she saw a very splendid chamber, the appointments of which were so lavish they seemed the products of fantasy. Lying on a divan in the center of the room was a fair creature that her husband kissed and caressed. The wife was momentarily overcome with rage and pain, but she quickly drew herself together and returned to her family.

"When her husband rejoined her some time later, she had managed to calm herself completely and was as quiet and withdrawn as usual. But the next day, without saying a word to her husband, she rushed to the rabbi and told him the whole story. She begged him to make her husband leave the strange woman—but in such a manner that no scandal would touch her house. The rabbi promised to do this and sent for the goldsmith as soon as she left. He accused the man of living with an unearthly creature and commanded him to drive the demon woman from the house. To protect him from the demon's entreaties, the rabbi placed on the goldsmith's neck an amulet inscribed with powerful spells. The man, who had surrendered his will to the rabbi, drove the demon woman and her children from the house that very night, and forced them to descend into the well from which she had originally come. That night his happiness disappeared.

"Although he lived for some time afterward, the goldsmith was always troubled and depressed, and he became feeble before his time. One night as he lay on his deathbed, unable to sleep, the door opened, and the demon entered. She sat down on the bed and placed her hand on his brow. For a moment he became animated and happy. She was still young and radiant, just as she had been on the day she emerged from the dark well. But, although she was smiling at him, her eyes were full of tears. When he saw this, he asked her why she was unhappy. She explained that it was because of her children. Being of his blood, they could not follow her into the realm of demons, but, because she was their mother, they were also unable to find a home among men. In this plight they were forced to wander peacelessly and precariously for the rest of their lives. She looked at him and entreated him with gentle words. For her sake she begged him to find some place for them before he died, where they could live out their years without suffering pain and oppressions—for their lives, though not so short as men's, were not of infinite duration like the lives of demons.

"The man swore that after his death, her children could return to his house and remain there forever. She thanked him sweetly and disappeared. The next day the man called his eldest son to his bedside and made him swear that after his father's death, he would depart from the house with his family and possessions, and insure that it would remain empty throughout his lifetime and in all future generations. The son took an oath to this effect, and, when his father died, he and his family departed. That very same night, the demons returned from the well and took possession of their property.

"And now hear me, Rabbi Joel; I am here to speak for my unhappy race.

"Equally son of man and demon, at home in no realm of earth and in no other realm, I and mine live in twilight and shadow and are driven by mortals from the one place granted us. Therefore, give us our right."

Then Rabbi Joel delivered this verdict:

"Let the man of the goldsmith's family depart, let the house be emptied and locked, and let no hand touch it any more."

Translated from the German
by David Antin

The Dybbuk

by Romain Gary

There is the merest trifle that I have not told my friend Schatz about our history and our beliefs, and he ignores nothing about this well-known phenomenon, which all who have studied our traditions have encountered: the dybbuk. Commissioner First Class Schatz knows he is being inhabited by a dybbuk. This is an evil spirit, a demon who seizes you, who installs himself within you and sets himself to reigning there like a master. To expel him you need prayers, you need ten pious Jews, venerable ones, known for their sanctity, who throw their weight into the scales and put the demon to flight. He himself went so far as to prowl around for several hours in the vicinity of a synagogue, but he never dared enter. What holds true for the first time in the history of thought and of religion is that a pure Aryan, an old SS man, is inhabited by a Jewish dybbuk. It may be necessary for me to speak up, to go find myself a rabbi, and to entreat him to free me of my abominable destiny: of being obliged to haunt the German conscience. That is why, out of sheer habit, Schatz is full of solicitude toward me. He wants to win me over. He wants me to liberate him, under pretext of liberating myself. But this time, aided by alcohol and exasperation, he is truly losing all caution. He is no longer in control of himself. He is no longer even afraid of being seen by witnesses in the act of talking to someone who is not there.

"You, Cohn, you're taking advantage of our situation. First of all, I have been denazified. I have papers to prove it. And furthermore, I keep telling you: I drink to forget, and not to remember! People, Cohn, drink in order to *forget.* Come on, grant me the point, and be quick about it. All this is beginning to resemble blackmail. All you're doing is provoking me. One of these fine days I'll get hopping mad, and I'm going to show you that despite your interesting state, you're not a touch-me-not! I'm going to let you have one of those sound cudgelings . . . just like that; you'll see that I have no remorse whatever. Hard as a rock!"

The Count, at these words, threw his unfortunate friend a compassionate glance.

"There is no need to talk of a rope in the house of a hanged man," he murmured.

"I beg your humble pardon," the Baron protested. "Those are perfectly uncalled-for insinuations! It happens I'm on excellent terms with my wife!"

"He, he, he!"

I couldn't restrain myself: these "excellent terms," I don't wish them on my best friends.

"I protest!" the Baron jawed. "I will not let myself be insulted!"

"Get lost, Cohn," said the Commissioner, making a very pretty gesture with his arm toward the door. "You think that just because they scrawled a few swastikas here and there, because they desecrated a few graves, they need you again in Germany, you can make yourself useful? Get going; on with you; out!"

"He is having visions," said the Count.

"Naughty, naughty!" went Johann, wagging a menacing finger at that little scamp of the absolute, which he could see so clearly.

Schatz put his head between his hands.

"There is no way to drink in peace and quiet anymore," he murmured.

"You should quit," said the Count. "You have the delirium tremens."

"When happy folk have the delirium tremens they see some spiders, snakes, rats, but as for me . . ."

He threw me a black glance, full of swastikas.

"As for me, I see some real filth."

He drives me back; sighs deeply, then rings. Enter a policeman, stiffly at attention.

"Governor?"

"Nothing. I just wanted to see something wholesome, simple, clean. . . ."

"Thanks, Governor."

The cop salutes, makes a half-about-face, then goes on his way. The two doctors—Schatz is sure, for now, that these are the psychiatrists whom Frau Müller had underhandedly sent him—are perplexed. They have never seen a parallel case. In all their careers they have never yet come upon an old SS man inhabited by a Jewish dybbuk. They don't even know it's a question of a dybbuk. For them, without a doubt, the Commissioner is undergoing a crisis of hallucinatory paranoia, supported by solid historical experiments. But the patient presents a ticklish ethical case. Schatz knows that the two psychiatrists, aware of the precedent created by Dr. Mendele and by the genocidal doctors, are in the midst of asking themselves whether they have a right to cure a German citizen of his remorse, or whether a possible suppression of the culpability complex does not risk being interpreted as a resurgence of Nazism. Do German physicians have a right to suppress a Jewish dybbuk? It is certain that from a strictly national point of view, the final solution of the problem posed by the presence of these six million psychic parasites on the German mind is desirable; it is a task of public health. There exist some new drugs, notably pramazine, administered in massive doses—extremely efficacious in this field. But the decision should be made at the top; it can be nothing short of a governmental decision. The great coalition should assume its responsibilities. Already the national parties demand, with a great hue and cry, the radical elimination of these psychic parasites, who hold the country in a state of impotence and will not let up with their foreign propaganda. Besides, the whole world knows that the Jews were not murdered. They died *voluntarily*. I'm keeping up on current events; you'd think I had nothing to do but that; and to top that I have just found some altogether reassuring things in that book by a certain Jean-François Steiner, *Treblinka*—we are joining the queue in front of the gas chambers. There were hardly any who revolted; here, there, *in extremis*, notably in the Warsaw ghetto, but on the whole there was eagerness, obedience, the will to vanish. There was the will to die. This was a collective suicide, it was. Before long someone is going to speak the full truth about our case. A new best-seller will show that the Nazis were nothing but an instrument in the hands of the Jews who wanted to die, *while at the same time completing a business transaction*. They could not, in effect, commit suicide by their own hands because the insurance monies would not have been paid, and the survivors would not have been able to touch the damage payments. It is time that someone finally wrote a definitive work on the problem, showing how we may well have manipulated the Germans in order to fulfill our dream of self-annihilation, and to have ourselves at the same time reimbursed for our losses. There will probably be found the author to disclose the diabolical maneuver which we have carried out, in transforming the Nazis into a blind and obedient instrument in our hands.

"Feet," the Commissioner murmured.

"I beg your pardon?"

"I'm feeling over my face some enormous feet, shaggy and circumcised. . . ."

"He is having hallucinations. It's the last stage."

"I feel them over my chest, my heart. . . . Feet, I tell you, feet without heart and without pity. . . . What do they want of me? I was a zealous functionary, obedient. I yelled *Fire!* because I had orders. I had orders! *Orders*, Cohn! I did nothing but my duty. I would like to be washed clean of all these accusations, once and for all. All I want is to feel clean."

Clean? Fine, very well—your humble servant. Right away I appear before Schatz, a bar of soap in my hand. I like to be of service; I'm a good dybbuk. The Commissioner looks at the soap, lets out a scream, stands up with a leap, and overturns his chair.

"Soap? Why soap? No! For twenty-two years now I haven't touched any soap; *you never know who is inside it!*"

I offer him the soap, with an inviting gesture. The Commissioner points a trembling finger at the thing.

"*Who is this, eh?*" he howls. "*Who is it, this soap?*"

I shrug my shoulders. How do I know? This was from mass production; they manufactured the soap in quantity, they didn't mark it on top *Jasza Gesundheit* or *Tsatsa Sardinenfisch*. They made it in bulk. Times were difficult. Germany lacked products of the first necessity.

"I refuse!" the Commissioner shouts. "For me, it has a very filthy mouth, your soap! It doesn't have a Catholic air about it at all!"

Oh, shucks. If it's now Catholic soap he needs, we'll never finish with that one. That requires enormous resources. They are six hundred million strong in the world, those Catholics. There is nothing for it but to turn to the Chinese. But he is wrong. This is deluxe soap. I heard an SS man at Auschwitz say it himself, with a good big laugh: *"This is deluxe soap; it is made from the Chosen People."* In German this is a *khokhmé*, that is to say, a *Witz*. I put my bar of soap back into my pocket and vanish.

Translated from the French
by Emery George

The Wandering Spirit of Léon Mitrani

by Isaac Goldemberg

Toward the middle of 1934, Jacobo Lerner began to feel that he had been possessed by the spirit of Léon Mitrani, that Mitrani had taken refuge within him and was nourishing himself with his blood. From that moment on, his life, until then discrete, defined by a walk in the evening through the Parque de la Reserva or by an afternoon of love with Doña Juana, began to be disturbed by strange events, until the compact order of his days tumbled like a castle made of sand.

Since 1929, when after his second return to Lima he decided to open the *prostíbulo* of La Victoria, Jacobo had shown up at the Synagogue of Breña on several occasions. The last time had been when he handed the *Sefer Torah* to Rabbi Schneider. After that, he never returned, and was completely cut off from his religion. By his own will he had been expelled from the ancestral matrix, had cut the umbilical cord that tied him to the universe. Not even in the nervous solitude of his own home did he fulfill his obligations as a Jew, which he had once considered the only source of order in his chaotic life.

During those five years he seldom visited his brother Moisés. Each time he did his visit had an almost religious nature; his return home was too suffocating. He preferred to spend his leisure time at the house of Marcos Geller, who was married to Juana Paredes' sister. In Marcos' company, Jacobo felt freer, distant from the life that he had planned for himself and that now belonged to Moisés. To visit Marcos Geller meant returning unharmed, with his feet firmly planted on the cobblestones of the street, while leaving his brother's house made him feel a musty figure, hesitating at every step, his soul full of old shipwrecks.

With Doña Juana, it was as if he were in a familiar landscape, on a wide plain that reminded him of Bertila's diffused shyness. With Juana he didn't feel the anxiety that he felt with Sara, nor the deep loneliness of dirty pillows and rented rooms.

After Marcos Geller died, Jacobo cultivated the friendship of other Jews who, like him, had no family. Men deformed by solitude, whose dreams were shaped by illusions. They met, usually, at Jacobo's whorehouse, where they would give themselves heart and soul to the dissonant atmosphere. On these nights their lust went unbounded, and they left the marks of their emptiness on the bodies of the courtesans.

It was during this period that Jacobo Lerner began to feel that he was possessed by a dybbuk, specifically the wandering soul of Léon Mitrani.

The first consequence of this belief was that he left Abraham Singer in charge of the brothel and locked himself in his house, where he spent all his time studying the Bible and the Talmud. Or he floated through the rooms of his house listening at the walls, peering into the darkness of each corner.

As time went on, the emptiness of his past life began to fill with something he scarcely understood, but to which he gave himself without hesitation. It was like diving into a well of warm, comforting waters. Moved by his fervor, Jacobo began to go to the synagogue every day for both morning and afternoon prayers. With his shawl on his shoulders, he would walk from his house to the temple, arousing first astonishment and then mockery from the people in the neighborhood. He seemed not to notice those who stopped in the street to look at him, nor those who made jokes at his expense. He walked slowly, holding a corner of the *tallis* in each hand, his head high, his mind full of images of Chepén as he relived, step by step, the route from Mitrani's house to his store. When the ash-colored synagogue came into his view he breathed deeply and hurried his step. The synagogue became the new vessel for all of Jacobo Lerner's emotions. There, protected from the disquieting murmurs that issued from the walls of his house, he found he could give himself wholly to God.

During one of the religious holidays, incited by a mysterious force that he could not resist, Jacobo went to the synagogue to reprimand the congregation for their sinful lives. For weeks he had been terrified by images of total destruction; his head was full of horrendous scenes in which the Jewish community of Lima perished in enormous columns of fire.

It was the second day of Shevuoth when Jacobo Lerner rushed into the temple and began shouting verses from the Prophets in his strong, powerful voice. The rabbi, who was praying in front of the tabernacle, stopped and tried to talk to him above the din of his imprecations and above the laughter and voices of the others telling Jacobo to shut up and go home.

Finally, the rabbi was able to convince him to leave, but Jacobo did not go home. Instead he sat outside the door of the temple, exhausted and thoughtful. When, some time later, people began to leave, Jacobo resumed his diatribe. His voice breaking with anger, he asked them to notice the luxury of their dress; he reproached them for their devotion to everything material; he dared them to think of the way they had abandoned everything spiritual. When the rabbi saw Jacobo in the middle of the street wielding his index finger as if it were a threatening whip of fire, prophesying the Last Judgment, he thought he understood, with a fleeting shudder, just what was wrong with him. Calmly he walked toward Jacobo, and with a loving tone in his voice, offered him his help.

But Jacobo insisted he could not be helped by a false representative of God.

One week after this incident, his brother Moisés took him to see Doctor Bernardo Rabinowitz. When, after long and careful observation, the doctor concluded that Jacobo should be hospitalized so that he might get the rest he needed, and avoid the possibility of harming himself, Moisés Lerner congratulated himself on his good luck. Thus, on the afternoon of June 2, 1934, Jacobo Lerner was admitted to the hospital at Orrantia del Mar.

The only person who visited Jacobo Lerner while he was at Orrantia del Mar Hospital was his sister-in-law. Moved by his misfortune, she had promised herself not to abandon him to his luck. She did not know she had assumed a responsibility she didn't really want, one that filled her with anxiety each time she went to the hospital, against her husband's wishes. She would arrive with a bunch of flowers, assuming an air of optimism to crush the disgust that Jacobo's wasted appearance produced within her. From the beginning, her visits were absurd little dramas played to the same conclusion. Shaken by the depths to which Jacobo had descended, she decided to resist all possibilities of getting close to him.

Once she found him resting in the shade of a fig tree. He was leaning against the trunk, his legs bent against his chest, his hands weakly clasping his knees, his head sunk, and his eyes fixed on nothing. He had been in that position for hours, imagining he was in Léon Mitrani's orchard, surrounded by dry, spiny bushes, ignoring the blind woman. Sara sat down next to him. Vaguely perceiving his sister-in-law's presence, Jacobo remained motionless and said nothing. He continued thinking of Chepén, trying to look through the thick fog. Nevertheless, all the muscles in his body tightened in response to the woman sitting next to him.

She began to talk mechanically about the day before when there had been a dinner in honor of Moisés. She described in detail the atmosphere of the Hebrew Union and gave the name of every guest. Carried on by the flow of her own words, she commented on the dresses worn by the women, admiring the taste of some, and sarcastically reproving that of others. Tenderly, she spoke of how proud and content Moisés had been, seeing the affection that was felt for him by the community.

With each passing second Jacobo went deeper into regions peopled by barely recognizable silhouettes. Indefinite streets and houses waved in his mind as he relived events from his past. Sometimes he saw himself with a cane in his hand, walking down the streets of Chepén. Other times he was praying in a room with shuttered windows, or preaching in the square in front of the church. He was publicly reproved by the priest. Guards took him from his house and dragged him through the streets. He was almost murdered by the people of Chepén. They dragged him to the square in the middle of the village. He had a cloak over his shoulders, and thin drops of blood were flowing down his forehead, clouding his eyes. Above the sea of ashen faces he saw the shape of a cross raised in the middle of the square. He broke away and began to run toward the outskirts of the village, followed by guards with whips and clubs.

On his first night in the hospital, Jacobo had had this same vision. Roused by his screams, two nuns had come into his room and found him crouching on the ground, his eyes tightly shut, shaking with fear. One of them had stayed by his side the rest of the night. The next morning, Jacobo asked her to remove the plaster crucifix from his room.

Jacobo's condition continued to deteriorate. He began to argue with the nuns about certain passages in the Bible. With vehement tone, he maintained that nowhere in the New Testament are the Jews blamed for the crucifixion of Christ. Each time he started on one of his speeches, the nuns listened to him with feigned attention, shaking their heads in compassionate agreement, not needing to contradict his words. But when Jacobo began to talk to them in Yiddish, the nuns stared at him, confused and frightened, because they believed they were in the presence of someone for whom there was no help.

After three months Jacobo had not improved, so Doctor Rabinowitz decided to release him. Convinced there was nothing more that medical science could do, he asked Rabbi Schneider to help his patient. Thus, on the 3rd of August, 1934, Jacobo left the hospital still believing the spirit of Léon Mitrani inhabited his body. Accompanied by Doctor Rabinowitz, he went to the house of Rabbi Schneider, who had promised to exorcise Mitrani's spirit and force him to find another dwelling place.

The rabbi, who lived about four blocks away from the synagogue, received Jacobo with great warmth and offered Jacobo lodging in his house until the exorcism began to take effect. It would be a difficult task. While the maid prepared a room, he told Jacobo with excitement that it had been a long time since he had had a chance to deal with a dybbuk. The last time had been in Poland, in 1915, when he practiced an exorcism on a young girl who thought herself possessed by the spirit of a whore.

The room they prepared for Jacobo was on the second floor. The furniture was scant and modest: under the window there was an old wooden bed, and next to it, on the wall, a shelf with a copper candelabra whose candles gave out a weak but turbulent light and leaden smoke. Jacobo saw only the maid, who came up three times a day to bring him his meals, and the rabbi, who came up every night in his black cloak and bonnet. He would ask Jacobo to undress and stand in the middle of the room, then walk around him, reciting obscure kabbalistic formulas.

On the third night, Jacobo began to feel a change. Mitrani's spirit suddenly became imperious. Jacobo's condition worsened: for seven days and seven nights his body was racked by tremors; he saw strange images in front of his eyes; he thought the maid was a blind woman who came to give him evil potions; he mistook the rabbi for the priest of Chepén. Jacobo began to pray to God to come to his rescue.

One night Jacobo Lerner saw himself surrounded by insects that came in under the door, and he became convinced that God would never again listen to him. To escape from his prison he opened the window, went out on the ledge, opened his arms wide, and flexed his knees in order to jump. But Rabbi Schneider, who had chanced to come in, grabbed him by his shirttails and stopped him from jumping. It was then that Jacobo realized God had in fact listened to his prayers, and had sent an angel to stop him from fleeing so that he might become completely exorcised.

Jacobo slowly began to regain his sense of reality. Recognizable faces and places once again filled his memory, and his imagination brought up images that were familiar and well defined. He saw his parents' house. He remembered a crossing on a ship. Bertila, the son he did not know, Juana Paredes and Sara Lerner, his brother Moisés, Daniel Abramowitz who had committed suicide, Marcos Geller, buried in the Cemetery of the Angels, his whorehouse, all came to mind.

But although he was regaining his sanity, he was sunk into a deeper depression than ever, because all these images were of a reality that he did not want to confront.

On the night of the 17th of August, Rabbi Schneider finally succeeded, and the spirit of Léon Mitrani abandoned Jacobo's body through the big toe of his right foot. With a restless flame in his eyes, the rabbi invoked Mitrani by his Hebrew name, and asked him to depart from Jacobo's body. There was a strangely familiar tone in the rabbi's invocation, as if he himself had known Léon Mitrani in the old days. Then Jacobo remembered what Mitrani had told him one afternoon in Chepén: a rabbi had come to the village on a donkey and stayed at his house for a few days. He had taught him some kabbalistic formulas that enabled him to fly. What Jacobo had then thought to be the product of a diseased mind now had a meaning of its own, and reentered his mind as a real fact. When the exorcism was over, Jacobo noticed that blood was flowing from a small opening in his toe.

The next morning as Jacobo was getting ready to leave the rabbi's house, the rabbi told him, in an admonishing voice, that dybbuks pursued those who kept a secret sin, and that if he had been possessed by a wandering soul, it was to atone for his guilt.

Translated from the Spanish
by Robert S. Picciotto

Watch Night

by Israel Zangwill

One night the Baal Shem and his disciples came to an inn, where he found the host sitting sadly in a room ablaze festally with countless candles and crowded with little boys, rocking themselves to and fro with prayer.

"Can we lodge here for the night?" asked the Baal Shem.

"Nay," answered the host dejectedly.

"Why art thou sad? Perchance I can help thee," said the Baal Shem.

"Tonight, as thou seest, is watch night," said the man; "for tomorrow my latest-born is to be circumcised. This is my fifth child, and all the others have died suddenly at midnight, although up to then there has been no sign of sickness. I know not why Lilith should have such a grudge against my progeny. But so it is, the devil's mother, she kills them every one, despite the many charms and talismans hung round my wife's bed. Every day since the birth, these children have come to say the *Shema* and the Ninety-first Psalm. And tonight the elders are coming to watch and study all night. But I fear they will not cheat Lilith of her prey. Therefore am I not in the humor to lodge strangers."

"Let the little ones go home; they are falling asleep," said the Master. "And let them tell their fathers to stay at home in their beds. My pupils and I will watch and pray."

So said, so done. The Baal Shem told two of his men to hold a sack open at the cradle of the child, and he instructed the rest of his pupils to study holy law ceaselessly, and on no account to let their eyelids close, though he himself designed to sleep. Should anything fall into the sack the two men were to close it forthwith and then awaken him. With a final caution to his disciples not to fall asleep, the master withdrew to his chamber. The hours drew on. Naught was heard save the droning of the students and the sough of the wind in the forest. At midnight the flames of the candles wavered violently, though no breath of wind was felt within the hot room. But the watchers shielding the flames with their hands strove to prevent them being extinguished. Nevertheless they all went out, and a weird gloom fell upon the room, the firelight throwing the students' shadows horribly on the walls and ceiling. Their blood ran cold. But one, bolder than the rest, snatching a brand from the hearth, relit the candles. As the last wick flamed again, a great black cat fell into the sack. The two men immediately tied up the mouth of it and went to rouse the Baal Shem.

"Take two cudgels," said he, "and thrash the sack as hard as you can."

After they had given it a sound drubbing, he bade them unbind the sack and throw it into the street. And so the day dawned, and all was well with the child. That day they performed the ceremony of Initiation with great rejoicing, and the Baal Shem was made godfather or *sandek*. But before the feasting began, the father of the child begged the Baal Shem to tarry, "for," said he, "I must needs go first to the lord of the soil and take him a gift of wine. For he is a cruel tyrant, and will visit it upon me if I fail to pay him honor on this joyous occasion."

"Go in peace," said the Baal Shem.

When the man arrived at the seigneur's house, the lackeys informed him that their master was ill, but had left instructions that he was to be told when the gift was brought. The man waited, and the seigneur ordered him to be admitted, and received him very affably, asking him how business was, and if he had guests at his inn.

"Ay, indeed," answered the innkeeper; "there is staying with me a very holy man who is from Poland, and he delivered my child from death."

"Indeed!" said the seigneur, with interest, and the man thereupon told him the whole story.

"Bring me this stranger," commanded the seigneur; "I would speak with him."

The innkeeper went home very much perturbed.

"Why so frightened an air?" the Baal Shem asked him.

"The seigneur desires thee to go to him. I fear he will do thee a mischief. I beseech thee, depart at once, and I will tell him thou hadst already gone."

"I will go to him," said the Baal Shem.

He was ushered into the sickroom. As soon as the seigneur had dismissed his lackeys he sat up in bed, thus revealing black-and-blue marks in his flesh, and sneered vengefully—

"Doubtless thou thinkest thyself very cunning to have caught me unawares."

"Would I had come before thou hadst killed the other four," replied the Baal Shem.

"Ho! ho!" hissed the magician; "so thou feelest sure thou art a greater wizard than I. Well, I challenge thee to the test."

"I have no desire to contend with thee," replied the Baal Shem calmly; "I am no wizard. I have only the power of the Holy Name."

"Bah! My witchcraft against thy Holy Name," sneered the wizard

"The Name must be vindicated," said the Baal Shem. "I accept thy challenge. This day a month I will assemble my pupils. Do thou and thy brethren gather together your attendant spirits. And thou shalt learn that there is a God."

In a month's time the Baal Shem with all his pupils met the wizard with his fellows in an open field; and there, under the blue circle of Heaven, the Baal Shem made two circles around himself and one in another place around his pupils, enjoining them to keep their eyes fixed on his face, and, if they noticed any change in it, immediately to begin crying the Penitential Prayer. The arch-wizard also made a circle for himself and his fellow-wizards at the other end of the field, and commenced his attack forthwith. He sent against the Baal Shem swarms of animals, which swept towards the circle with clamorous fury. But when they came to the first circle, they vanished. Then another swarm took their place—and another—and then another—lions, tigers, leopards, wolves, griffins, unicorns, and unnamable creatures, all dashing themselves into nothingness against the holy circle. Thus it went on all the long day, every instant seeing some new bristling horde vomited and swallowed up again.

Towards twilight the arch-magician launched upon the Baal Shem a herd of wild boars, spitting flames; and these at last passed beyond the first circle. Then the pupils saw a change come over the Baal Shem's face, and they began to wail the Penitential Prayer.

Still the boars sped on till they reached the second circle. Then they vanished. Three times the wizard launched his boars, the flames of their jaws lighting up the gathering dusk, but going out like blown candles at the second circle. Then said the wizard, "I have done my all." He bowed his head. "Well, I know one glance of thine eyes will kill me. I bid life farewell."

"Nay, look up," said the Baal Shem; "had I wished to kill thee, thou wouldst long ago have been but a handful of ashes spread over this field. But I wish to show thee that there is a God above us. Come, lift up thine eyes to Heaven."

The wizard raised his eyes towards the celestial circle, in which the first stars were beginning to twinkle. Then two thorns came and took out his eyes. Till his death was he blind; but he saw that there was a God in Heaven.

Lilith

by Moyshe Kulbak

And in the night, Benye was lying on his bed at home, as in a deep grave. He was barely breathing, and he was drenched with sweat, he lay among the foul rags, disheveled and stretched out like a carcass.

He held out his hands in the darkness, trying to grab on to something, to keep from falling; a stench arose from him and the drool was running from his mouth.

Benye, the saint of his generation, was drooling.

He untangled his hands from the darkness, and he stretched his hands into the darkness, but then he quickly pulled them back.

Benye seemed to have touched someone next to his bed.

He peered deep into the room. Someone was really standing not far from him, a stiff shape, a tall, warm shape.

Benye sat up in terror.

It was obviously a female; her hips and breasts were curving out of the stiff, black cloth.

He asked her softly:

"What are you doing here?"

She didn't answer. Slowly, unhurriedly, she walked over to the door, where she turned around to face him and remained standing in that position.

A yellow radiance poured through the room like a fine dust.

"Benye," she said, "once you summoned me."

Her voice was burning hot, it was lulling and it drew his body to her.

"I?"

"Yes, once, when you were still a little boy."

Benye stuck out his tangled beard.

"I? I was a little boy?"

"Yes, yes, Benye, you were wandering around the cows in pasture, you had a big swollen belly and calflike eyes. Do you remember? Whenever a bull would lust for a cow, you would wring your hands, and weep in pain, and start counting on your fingers to see how many years it was till you could marry."

Benye began recollecting, but he didn't want to answer.

"Benye, you summoned me then . . . but I don't come to little children," and she added with a smile: "Now you're a solid adult, a man . . . a strong, handsome man . . . handsome and dear! I want to put my head on your young chest . . . I want your hot hands embracing me, darling! I want to feel the fresh breath of your body. . . ."

Benye's calflike eyes bulged in the dark. He stammered:

"Woman, you must be mistaken."

"Look," she cried ecstatically, "you're the only man for me! Look at my fresh young body. . . ."

And wordlessly she began tearing off her clothes.

"Benye, my hips are still chaste, virginal, solid, and my thighs are supple and straight. . . . The nipples of my breasts are stiff, and my breasts have never suckled a child . . . never suckled . . . never suckled . . ."

And she wept with passion, wept, glowed, and her naked body sparkled in the yellow darkness, like the scales of a serpent.

Benye heard the benumbing voice, and in the yellow twilight he saw her, Lilith, standing at the door, bending slightly, her hands over her head, framed in the doorposts.

Benye grabbed the sides of the bed and clenched his teeth. He felt drawn to her. He was choking, and suddenly he screamed, and an alien voice yelled out of him:

"Get out! Get out of my house!"

He started throwing the rags and the pillows at her.

"Go away, you monster!"

He spat, tore his shirt; all at once he sprang from the bed and, in confusion, began beating his head and his chest.

Lilith stood at the door in silence, staring gravely with a grave smile on her lips. She was waiting until Benye calmed down.

"You whore! Get away!"

Benye realized he was practically naked in front of this woman, so he jumped back into bed, pulling the covers over him, closing his eyes, and turning his face to the wall.

He groaned softly.

Lilith stood there quietly for a while, then she slowly tiptoed over to him, and gently tickled his armpit.

Benye bit his lips; the pleasure ran through his entire body, every nook and cranny. He wouldn't turn around, but he gradually stopped groaning.

Lilith sat down on his bed, smiled, and began tickling the soles of his feet. It was so delicious that it dazed him.

Benye knew that Lilith was sitting next to him, so he held back his deep laughter, and lay there as mute as a wooden beam.

She began stroking his hair, and her slender fingers curled up the disheveled strands. He couldn't bear it anymore, he turned around to her, and his thick yellow teeth were grinding with his sweet sufferings.

He tittered like an old goat: "Darling, sweetest . . . !"

Lilith said: "Your beautiful face drives me crazy, Benye, darling! Don't smile at me like that!"

Suddenly Benye realized it was Lilith, and he started laughing and grinding his teeth all the harder, to drive her away.

She moved away from the bed.

"You slut!"

He leaped after her, dropping his rags in his excitement, but she managed to elude him.

"I'm going to get you, Lilith," he shouted, "I'm going to get you."

Benye dashed after her through the yellow light, storming like a wind, panting, screaming, until he caught her with his right hand, in a corner.

He dug his brown, dirty fingers into her white body and thrust his tangled beard into her face. Lilith curved away from him, but he pressed her closer and yelled with foaming lips:

"Deborah, you Deborah, you!"

For his dead wife's name was Deborah.

Lilith tried to fight back. She was delighted, but she fought back. Suddenly she grabbed his dirty beard and kissed him so hard on the thick parched lips that Benye nearly fell over, then she lifted him up on her hot shoulders and carried him off to his bed. . . .

"Oh God! Oh God! And the rooster hasn't crowed!"

It grew dark in the room, their breath merged, sparks were flashing in the darkness, and slippery limbs were wrapped around the body with green eyes, and with a faint flickering. . . . There is no salvation, oh God!

And Benye was struggling, he didn't know with whom, he fell down and reached out in the darkness to take hold of something, he dashed off the bed, but it was quiet in the room, and no one was there.

And his blood stopped in his veins, it curdled, froze.

Lilith, fresh, young Lilith, the wife of Satan, had killed him.

Adam's first wife.

Benye dragged himself across the room, climbed up on the oven, and then climbed down again. He sat naked, as he was, on the floor, sat and sat, and then stood up again with his head drooping, crept over to the pail of water, thrust in his hands, and then kept dragging around the room. . . .

He stumbled over to the door and opened it. The cold air refreshed him. He opened the door to the porch and stepped out. A cold, silvery blueness enveloped his face and naked body.

At first he didn't notice that a Jew was standing there with a sack and a staff in his hand—it was one of the three guests that had once visited him, and now the man touched his hand.

"Benye, you didn't resist!"

Benye remained cold, he didn't care, but then all at once he turned to the guest, and his eyes filled with blood:

"Thieves! Damn you all!"

And he burst into moans:

"Why don't you leave me alone?! You monsters!"

And he dashed back into the house, grabbed a stick of wood, and ran out again to the porch. But the guest was gone.

Benye hurried down the road after him.

Translated from the Yiddish
by Joachim Neugroschel

Lilith in the Lager

by Primo Levi

In the space of a few minutes the sky had turned black and it began to rain. Very soon the rain increased until it became a stubborn downpour and the thick grass of the workyard changed to a layer of mud, a handsbreadth deep. It became impossible not only to work with a shovel but downright impossible to keep your footing. Our *Kapo* spoke to the civilian foreman, then turned to us; people were to take shelter wherever they could. Scattered all around there were lengths of iron pipe, about seventeen to eighteen feet long and over a yard in diameter. I crawled into one of these and halfway along it I met Tischler, who had had the same idea and entered from the opposite end.

"Tischler" means carpenter, and this was the only name by which he was known to us. There were also The Blacksmith, The Russian, The Fool, two Tailors (respectively The Tailor and The Other Tailor), The Galician, and The Tall Man. For a long time I was The Italian, then, indiscriminately, Primo or Alberto, because they confused me with another Italian.

So the Tischler was Tischler and nothing more, but he didn't look like a carpenter and we all suspected that he was no such thing. At that time it was common practice for an engineer to have himself listed as a mechanic, or a journalist to put himself down as a printer. That way you could hope for better work than that of a common laborer without unleashing the Nazi wrath reserved for intellectuals. However it had come about, Tischler had been placed at the carpenters' bench and had managed to acquit himself fairly well. Most unusually for a Polish Jew, he spoke a little Italian. It had been taught to him by his father, who was taken prisoner by the Italians in 1917 and taken to a camp—a concentration camp, in fact—somewhere near Turin. Most of his father's fellow prisoners had died of Spanish influenza. You can still, as a matter of fact, read their exotic names today, Hungarian, Polish, Croat and German names, on a columbarium in the Big Cemetery. It is a visit that fills the visitor with pain at the thought of those lost men, dead so far from home. Tischler's father caught the flu too, but he recovered.

Tischler's Italian was amusing and full of errors, consisting chiefly as it did of snatches of librettos of operas which his father greatly admired. Often, at work I had heard him singing arias: *"sconto col sangue mio"* and *"libiamo nei lieti calici."* His mother tongue was Yiddish but he also spoke German and we had no trouble understanding one another. I liked the Tischler because he never succumbed to laziness. His step was brisk in spite of his wooden clogs, his speech was careful and precise, and he had an animated face, merry and sad at the same time. Sometimes in the evening he staged entertainments in Yiddish and I was sorry I didn't understand. Occasionally he went so far as to sing, and though no one applauded at the time and everyone kept his eyes on the ground, when he was through they begged him to continue.

That encounter of ours, on all fours, almost like dogs, cheered him. If only it could rain like that every day! But this happened to be a special day: it had rained for his benefit because it was his birthday. He was twenty-five years old. Now by sheer chance I was twenty-five that day too; we were twins. The Tischler said it was a date that called for a celebration since it was most unlikely that we would be together to celebrate our next birthday. He took half an apple out of his pocket, cut off a slice, and gave it to me, and that was the only time in a year of imprisonment that I tasted fruit.

We chewed in silence, as attentive to the precious acidulous flavor as we would have been to a symphony. In the meantime, a young woman all bundled up in dark clothes, who was perhaps Ukrainian, had taken refuge in the pipe in front of ours. She was very probably a member of the Todt Organization which consisted of "volunteer" (they had little or no choice) foreign laborers recruited for war work. The woman had a broad rosy face, shiny with rain, and she kept looking at us and laughing. She was scratching herself lazily, in a provocative way, under her jacket, then she let down her hair, combed it quite calmly, and began to rebraid it. In those days it was a rare experience to see a woman at close hand, an experience both sweet and fierce, and the effect was devastating.

The Tischler noticed that I was staring at her and asked if I was married. No, I wasn't. He looked at me with mock severity: to be celibate at our age was a sin. However, he turned around and stayed that way for some time, looking at the girl. She had finished braiding her hair, had crouched down in her pipe, and was humming, and swaying her head in time with the music.

"It's Lilith," the Tischler suddenly said to me.

"You know her? Is that her name?"

"I don't know her but I recognize her. She's Lilith, Adam's first wife. Don't you know the story of Lilith?"

I didn't know it and he laughed indulgently: everyone knows that western Jews are all Epicureans—*Apikorsim*, unbelievers. Then he continued: "If you had read the Bible carefully, you would remember that the business of the creation of woman is told twice, in two different ways. But you people—they teach you a little Hebrew when you reach thirteen and that's the end of it."

A typical situation, and a kind of game that I enjoyed, was developing: the dispute between the pious man and the unbeliever, who is by definition ignorant, and is made to gnash his teeth by the adversary in the course of being shown his error. I accepted my role and answered with the required insolence.

"Yes, it's told twice but the second time is only the commentary on the first."

"Wrong. That's the way the man who doesn't probe below the surface understands it. Look: if you read attentively and reason about what you're reading, you'll realize that in the first account it says only: "God created them male and female." That is to say, He created them equal, with the same dust. However, it says on the next page that God forms Adam, then decides it isn't good for man to be alone, takes one of Adam's ribs, and with the rib He fashions a woman, actually a *Männin*, a she-man. You'll notice that now we have no more equality. There are even people who believe that not only are the two stories different but there were two different women, and the first one wasn't Eve, man's rib, but Lilith. Now the story of Eve is written down and everybody knows it, but the story of Lilith is only told orally; that's why few people know it—know *them* rather, because there are many different stories. I'll tell you some of them, first because it's our birthday and it's raining, and then because today my role is to tell and to believe; today you are the unbeliever.

"The first story is that the Lord not only made man and woman equal, but He made a single figure with the clay—really a Golem, a formless form, a figure with two spines: the man and woman were already joined together. Then he cut them apart but they longed to reunite, and right off the bat Adam wanted Lilith to lie down on the ground. Lilith wouldn't hear of it: 'Why should I be underneath? Aren't we supposed to be equal? Two halves of the same material?' Adam tried to force her to do it but they were also equal in strength and he did not succeed. Then he asked God for help. God was male too and surely He would take Adam's part. Which in fact he did, but Lilith rebelled: equal rights or nothing, and since the two males wouldn't yield, she cursed and blasphemed the Lord's name, became a she-devil, flew off like an arrow, and went to live at the bottom of the sea. There are people who claim to know exactly where she lives, to wit, the Red Sea. Every night she rises up and flies all around the world, rustles against the windows of houses where there are newborn babies, and tries to smother them. You have to be on the lookout: if she gets in, you must catch her under an overturned bowl. Then she can no longer do any harm.

"At other times she enters the body of a man, and the man becomes listless. In that case the best remedy is to take him before a notary or a rabbinical tribunal, and have them draw up the necessary form in which the man declares that he wants to repudiate the she-devil. Why are you laughing? I don't believe this, naturally, but I love to tell these stories. I loved having them told to me, and I would hate to see them lost. Moreover, I can't guarantee that I too haven't embellished them; that's the way stories are born."

We heard a distant racket and shortly afterwards a caterpillar-tread tractor passed close to us. It was dragging a snowplow. But the mud it cleaved, immediately joined together again behind the machine. Like Adam and Lilith, I thought to myself. So much the better for us; we could go on resting for some time to come.

"Then there's the story of the seed. Lilith is greedy for man's seed, and she is always lying in wait wherever it may get spilled, especially in bed. All the semen that doesn't end in the only approved place—which is to say, inside a man's wife—belongs to her: all the semen that every man has wasted in his lifetime, through dreams or bad habits or adultery. Since she is the recipient of so much of it, you can understand why she is always pregnant and forever giving birth. Being a she-devil, she produces devils but they don't do much harm even if, heaven knows, they would dearly like to. They're malign imps, with no bodies. They turn milk and wine sour, and at night they run around in garrets and snarl girls' hair.

"However, they are the children of man and of every man, illegitimate, it's true, but when their fathers die they come to the funeral along with the legitimate children who are their stepbrothers and stepsisters. They swoop around the funeral candles like nocturnal moths, wail, and claim their portion of the inheritance. You're laughing, precisely because you're an unbeliever and it's your role to laugh. Or maybe you've never spilled your seed. But it could happen that you will get out of here alive. Then you'll see that at certain funerals the rabbi and his followers circle the dead man seven times. That's so as to erect a barrier to keep his bodiless children from coming to cause trouble for him.

"But I still have to tell you the strangest story of all, and it's not strange that it's strange because it's written down in the books of the Kabbalists, and they were men who didn't know the meaning of the word fear. You know that God created Adam, and immediately afterwards He realized it wasn't good for man to be alone and He placed a companion at his side. Well, the Kabbalists said that it wasn't good even for God Himself to be all alone, and at that time, right from the very beginning, He took as His companion the Shekhinah, which is to say, His own presence in the Universe. Consequently the Shekhinah became the wife of God and therefore the mother of all peoples. When the Temple in Jerusalem was destroyed by the Romans and we were scattered and became slaves, the Shekhinah became angry, left God, and came with us into exile. I can tell you that at times I myself have believed this: that the Shekhinah also became a slave and is here with us, in this exile within exile, in this home of mud and pain.

"This left God alone and, as happens to so many, He couldn't hold out against loneliness and temptation and He took a mistress. You know who? Her, Lilith, the she-devil, an unheard-of scandal. It seems, in short, that it happened the way things happen in altercations when one of the parties responds to an offense with a still more serious one, so that the altercation never ends but keeps on growing, like a landslide. Because you must know that this indecent relationship has not ended, and will not end in a hurry. In a way it's the cause of all the evil that occurs on this earth; in another way, it is its effect. As long as God continues to sin with Lilith, there will be blood and trouble on Earth. But one day a powerful being will come—the one we are all waiting for. He will put an end to Lilith and to God's lust, and to our exile. Yes, even to yours and mine, Italian. *Mazel tov.* Good fortune."

Fortune has indeed been sufficiently good to me but not to the Tischler. And it just so happens that, many years later, I found myself at a funeral that took place exactly in the way he had described to me, with the protective dance around the coffin. It is inexplicable that fate chose an unbeliever to repeat this pious and impious fable, woven of poetry, ignorance, foolhardy sharpness of mind, and the irremediable sadness that grows on the ruins of lost civilizations.

Translated from the Italian
by Ruth Feldman

From the Rabbi's Dreambook
by David Meltzer

In his dream the rabbi is wrapped in layers of Torah whose parchment is filled with light and the calligraphed letters move against his body with a million new senses and soon he is part of the mystic union his devotions hoped for.

But then the baby cries and his wife sleeps as if dead and the rabbi rolls out of bed, awkward and unsure of where the sound comes from. He stumbles through the rooms filled with books whose smells are perfume and gardens and for a moment he can not hear the baby and turns on a light to reach for a volume of the Zohar, for night is the real time to open those books like opening the bed, drawing the sheets down, to tangle and collide with her mysteries, her paradoxical measures. But the baby cries louder, almost like a cat, when he opens the book whose sighing ancient binding is like his wife uncoupling all that holds her inward and regal to one world to reveal her true concealed majesty.

And he runs through more rooms and up a small flight of stairs to the nursery, opens the door and surrounding the baby's bed are three *lilin* who, like their source, have red hair not braided or bunned but loose and flowing and alive in the light upon it, and their blouses are open as if to feed the baby and their mouths are lacquered red and shine like secret starlight in his groin, which he finds himself placing his palm against, and they all, as he touches himself, turn to him and flap their thighs together and massage their breasts and the baby is not crying. The baby watches the *lilin* writhe and the rabbi begins to intone the invoking words against them but his ears are wet with the steam of their breath which burrows back through his nerve-ends to the root his palm pulls away from.

The Woman in the Forest

by Jiri Langer

The holy Rebbe Reb Melech had also been a young man once. In his youth he often used to walk from the town to a nearby village. His way took him through a forest. One spring day he stayed in the village rather later than usual, and it was already night when he returned through the forest. Melech was unafraid. He knew no fear save before Almighty God. The forest murmured sadly and mysteriously. Melech continued on his way stumbling from time to time over tree stumps. The forest seemed never to end, but Melech had no fear. None the less a strange feeling overcomes a person who walks alone at night through a deep forest. At last Melech saw a light in the distance. As he drew closer, the light grew. A human dwelling!—Had he lost his way? He had never noticed anybody living in the forest before. A few more steps and Melech pushed aside a branch and found himself in a glade. And lo! in the middle of the glade was a cottage, beautifully painted like a toadstool. By now Melech was able to see without difficulty. The moon was shining as sweetly as the cottage window. Melech walked in—and stood on the threshold as though bewitched. At first he thought he must be dreaming. Never in his life had he seen such beauty. In the middle of the room stood a young girl. She was almost naked and yet seemed quite unashamed. Her golden hair reached down to the ground. Dear God, how long it was! She was evidently still a maiden, since her hair was not cut like that of married Jewish women.

"Yes," she said, "I am single and live entirely alone here. I have often watched you going through the forest—always so alone, like me. I have often wondered when you would come and see me. But you have always continued on your way without heeding me at all. Be not shy, I am clean, I have bathed at a spring in the forest, and I have long since had a soft bed ready. No, I am not learned, but this much at least I know: the sin will be only a slight one, but the enjoyment will be abundant, oh so abundant. Come!"

Her voice sounded as sweet as the silver bells on the parchment scroll of the Law of God, on festival days in the synagogue, but at the same time it was as powerful as the throb of blood in Melech's temples. Only gradually did Melech grasp the meaning of the words that flowed from her red lips, like little wavelets on a brook.

He stood still, not knowing what was happening to him. Can God take pleasure in such a union, when there is no rabbi's blessing, no wedding ring, and no wedding canopy?

"Come! I have bathed at the spring, I have made ready the softest of beds, the enjoyment will be abundant."

The girl's hair quivered like the forest grass fanned by a spring breeze. On the tips of her breasts something seemed to grow red, like two strawberries under their leafy green.

"No!" shouted Melech. It was the shout of a drowning man.

"No-o!" came the deep echo from the forest.

Then Melech found himself alone, so alone, on the green forest sward. The girl had disappeared and the cottage seemed to have fallen together. Only a cluster of glowworms was to be seen, dancing their mysterious dance in the thick grass.

Mere temptation it had been, a delicious prelude devised by Satan, like everything else that leads us astray in this world, to make us sin, and forget God.

The holy Rebbe Reb Melech did not forget Him. May the Light of his merits protect us!

Translated from the Czech
by Stephen Jolly

The Tale of the Duck

by Jeremy Garber

Once there was a man and wife, Haim and Rachel, who lived in peaceful isolation on the estate of a great Polish landowner north of the town Sando-mierz on the river Wisla. They were pious Jews, faithful to God's command-ments and mindful of ancient traditions. Among the hundreds of laws and customs that they did not forsake was the ceremony of *tashlich*—"thou shalt cast"—wherein a Jew approaches a body of water on the first day of the New Year and empties out the contents of his pockets into the current. He thereby demonstrates the belief that although he may be empty of good deeds, if he truly repents, his sins will be carried away by God, as the water carries off the bits of paper and crumbs that tumble from his garments. How distant is this custom from that of the uncircumcised ones who, every spring, make a straw body in the form of a woman and toss it into a river! And you will now hear of how a daughter of Israel was enchanted by a servant of the spirit of the Wisla, a witch, may all such troublers of Israel meet her terrible end, speedily in our days, Amen.

This Rosh Hashanah was different from all others for Haim and Rachel. For on all other New Years' the couple would lodge in town among their fellow Jews, whereas on this occasion Rachel was about to bring forth her first child and therefore remained in the wilderness with her husband. All the good Jewish midwives were busy preparing for the holiday, so they were obliged to hire an old Polish woman who was, it must be said, not without useful skills. She was rumored to be a witch whose potions and spells had helped many a woman survive the travails of labor.

"A witch shall surely die" was a biblical verse that Haim knew well, but he reflected instead on the story of King Saul, who sought out the sorceress of En Dor in his distress. And was not his own distress as great as King Saul's? For his wife was frail and might not survive childbirth. Burdened with these thoughts, Haim walked to the river alone, performed the *tashlich* ritual, and returning to his cottage saw that the old woman had observed everything.

"Jew," she cried, "I saw you throwing poison into the river. You wish to kill us as we bathe or launder our clothes downstream. I will tell the lord of the estate and he will surely kill you, your wife, and the Jews of Sandomierz."

Astonished by her outburst, Haim attempted to explain the meaning of this Jewish custom. She only laughed and repeated her words. Haim offered her money to keep silent, but she refused with disdain. Finally Haim became angry and forgetting the holiness of the day, rushed over to the old woman and tried to grab her around the waist. He had a strong grip, but it was like holding on to a stream. She slipped from his hands, leaving them covered with a gray slime. Haim then realized that she truly was a witch, a powerful one, who could certainly carry out her threat.

Trembling he said, "Take anything I have, even my life, only spare my family and my people."

"Do as I say and all will be well," spoke the witch. "Your wife will give birth to a daughter in three days' time. I am leaving today, but when the hour of birth arrives I will return, and you must give me the baby to raise as my own. And when she has passed through eighteen winters I will marry her off to the spirit of the river."

Haim had no intention of giving up his daughter, but nevertheless told the witch that he accepted her conditions. The old woman went off and he trudged home. When he told his wife what had happened, she insisted that as soon as two stars appeared in the sky on the morrow, signaling the end of Rosh Hashanah, they must harness their horse to a wagon and flee. They would travel to her brother in Volpe, Lithuania—far from the witch, the landowner, and the river. He argued with her that she was in no condition to make a journey, that he would find a way to outsmart the witch, but his words had no effect. They set off the next evening just as Rachel was struck by her first agonizing birth pangs. Two days later as they stopped briefly at an inn, she gave birth to a baby girl, Rivka, and died. Haim soon fell ill from grief and strain. He passed away seven days later on Yom Kippur, a light atonement for his transgressions. For he had promised to sell a Jewish soul, his own daughter, to a gentile, and for this same crime we, the children of Israel, sat in slavery in Egypt for four hundred years to gain forgiveness. Before his death Haim had told the innkeeper to deliver his baby to his brother-in-law Label, to whom they were journeying. Label owned a tavern in Volpe, and there Rivka grew to be a beautiful young woman.

Eighteen winters passed. Yossel, a young man, an orphan who studied in the yeshivah of Sandomierz, was disturbed by a recurring dream and went to his rebbe, Reb Zalman the Sandomierzer.

Said Yossel, "Rebbe, I dream the same dream night after night, that I am thirsty and go to the well by the yeshivah to drink but when I raise the bucket and bring it to my lips, it is empty."

Reb Zalman was silent a moment, then replied, "It is time for you to marry. Go north to the shtetl Volpe and wait for a young woman to offer you water. She will be your bride."

That afternoon Yossel set out on foot for Volpe. He walked and was given rides by wagoners, and all four days of the journey he pictured himself standing by the town well waiting for his destined one to offer him water. When he finally reached the outskirts of Volpe, however, it was dusk and he was tired and thirsty, so he entered a tavern to rest before heading for the well in the central square. He sat on a hard bench by the door and a young serving girl approached him with a clay pitcher of water and set it down before him. Without looking up, he took the pitcher and drank. But his hands shook with weariness and it fell and shattered on the floor. A man nearby shouted "Mazel tov" as if Yossel had just smashed the wedding glass. Suddenly the youth remembered his rebbe's instructions, glanced up at the lovely maiden, and asked her name. She replied that she was Rivka bas Haim of Sandomierz. He rushed out to find a matchmaker, for his heart was already burning with love. The arrangements proceeded swiftly, since both she and Yossel were penniless orphans. No dowry was requested and none was given. Yossel left for Sandomierz with a joyful spirit and was followed a week later by Rivka.

The Jewish women of Sandomierz gave themselves over willingly to the preparations for the orphans' wedding, especially after they discovered that Rivka was the daughter of Rachel and Haim. Yossel's fellow students, not to be outdone, cleaned up the yeshivah, their school and home, to make it fitting for a celebration.

The day before the wedding, a group of pious women led Rivka to the ritual bath house, the *mikvah*, which stood on the banks of the Wisla. Her head was shaved and her nails pared, and she was brought to the murky pool where the water of the Wisla mingled with pure rainwater in accordance with the Holy Law. They watched as Rivka went under and came up, under and up, but the third time she dipped herself beneath the water she did not come up. The women waited a few moments, then began screaming and swishing their hands through the water to find her body, but it was all to no avail. She had vanished. Outside the *mikvah*, a white duck appeared swimming on the surface of the water.

The women were ashamed to return to town with the news that the bride had disappeared, perhaps drowned. So they continued to wade along the riverbank calling out, "Rivka, Rivka!"

The apprentice slaughterer of the town, Pesach, was a dear friend of Yossel's, and like him was very poor. Shortly after Rivka disappeared he was wandering alongside the Wisla wondering what wedding present he would be able to give Yossel. Suddenly he spotted a white duck caught in the branches of a thorny bush which reached out over the water. He pulled the duck out of the thicket, and brought it back to the shop where he worked. There he slaughtered it, dressed it, cooked it, and took the roast duck and a jar containing its rendered fat to the yeshivah. He arrived to find much wailing and despair. Not even on Yom Kippur had he seen so many men weeping and beseeching God before the open Ark of the Torah. He felt ashamed to be carrying food into such an awesome assembly, so he left his gifts on a bench and hurried away.

Yossel stood by the ark in silence. He remained awake far into the night until all his comforters had fallen asleep on the benches around him. He too wished to sleep but was seized by restlessness. This was to have been his wedding night. He paced up and down the room and felt himself drawn by the aroma of the duck. He approached the fowl, his lips touched the golden skin, and his teeth sank into the breast meat. A flavor both succulent and nauseating filled his mouth, and he quickly withdrew without pulling off a bite.

He resumed his pacing through half the night until at last he fell into a weary slumber. He dreamed he was in a dungeon and before him was his beloved Rivka, standing naked with a scar over her breast. Beside her crouched an old woman who screamed at him, "Eat her! Eat her!" He awoke with a shudder, filled with fear and horror, but he knew not why. For he had forgotten his dream.

He waited until sunrise, then went to rouse Reb Zalman and ask him what he had dreamed and what it meant. The rebbe replied, "I am not Daniel whom God granted the power to know both a forgotten dream and its interpretation. You must remember and understand by yourself, Yossel."

But Yossel pleaded with his rebbe to help him remember until Reb Zalman agreed, saying, "Take the fat of the duck, put a wick within the jar, and by its light study the *Maftir*, the last lines, of Parshas Kedoshim (Lev.20:25-27), which you chanted on your bar mitzvah. Study these verses until they become one, then come to me. But if they do not become one before the candle goes out, all is lost."

Yossel read these verses:

"Ye shall therefore separate between the clean beast and the unclean, and between the unclean fowl and the clean; and ye shall not make your souls detestable by beast, or by fowl, or by any thing wherewith the ground teemeth, which I have set apart for you to hold unclean. And ye shall be holy unto Me; for I the Lord am holy, and have set you apart from the peoples, that ye should be Mine. A man also or a woman that divineth by a ghost or a familiar spirit, shall surely be put to death; they shall stone them with stones; their blood shall be upon them."

He recited and pondered the lines again and again but could not grasp how they were connected. What did dividing between clean and unclean fowls have to do with witches or sorcerers? Hours passed and the last droplets of fat were ascending the wick when Yossel's eyes were opened. He suddenly recalled his dream and understood its meaning. The duck which he had bitten was unclean because it contained the soul of a young woman, his bride. She had been enchanted by a witch and turned into a fowl. The evil woman desired that he should eat the duck so that he too would fall under her spell and serve the spirit of the Wisla.

Yossel ran to the rebbe's house and told him both the dream and its interpretation. Reb Zalman nodded and ordered him to gather together all the Jews of Sandomierz by the river. As the crowd was assembling, the rebbe went to the chamber of the burial society in the synagogue, took a large linen shroud, went to the yeshivah, wrapped the duck in the cloth, and set out for the river. Although it was a normal, profane weekday, he said the *tashlich* prayer and cast the duck out onto the water. A moment later, Rivka, dressed in the linen sheet, floated to the surface alive and well, except for the scar, which no one could see. The crowd was silent at first, then broke into cheers and shouts.

The witch, who had been watching the massive gathering from a narrow bridge overlooking the river, stamped her feet in anger, fell through a rotten board, and was smashed on the rocky bank. A wave reached up and pulled her body into the rushing water.

Rivka and Yossel were married that day. They prospered and had many fine children great in Torah and good deeds.

The Golden Bird

by *Howard Schwartz*

Now it was the custom of Reb Nachman of Bratslav to take long walks in the forest alone, as did his great-grandfather, the Baal Shem Tov. One day Reb Nachman was walking among the majestic trees, deep in thought, when he heard the trill of a bird in the distance. And that melody was so sweet and resonant that Reb Nachman did not hesitate, but hurried further into the forest, in the hope that he might catch a glimpse of the bird that had such a beautiful song. He traveled an untold distance, ignoring the way as he went, so great was his curiosity. But although his ears sought out the slightest sound, the forest was strangely silent, and Reb Nachman did not hear as much as a rustling leaf, for even the wind seemed to be holding its breath.

At last Reb Nachman concluded that he had set off in the wrong direction, and in despair he sat down at the base of one of those towering trees, whose upper branches seemed to reach into heaven. Perhaps because he was leaning there, a verse from Proverbs suddenly came into his mind: *The Torah is a Tree of Life to those who cling to it,* and at that moment a feather fluttered down through the branches of that tree, and fell beside Reb Nachman, where he sat, and at the same instant he heard clearly the haunting trill of the bird that had lured him to that place. Then Reb Nachman jumped up and searched in the branches, in the certainty that the bird must be in that tree, but nothing was to be seen. He continued to look long after it was apparent that the bird had eluded him once more, then he sat down and picked up the feather, and was amazed to discover that it was golden, and that it shone in the sun like a mirror. And when he saw that golden feather he knew it must have come from the bird with the enchanting song, and once again he was overwhelmed with longing to seek out that golden bird. But then Reb Nachman noticed that the rays of the sun were slanted through the trees, and he realized that the afternoon was coming to an end, and that it would soon be night. He knew very well how dangerous it would be to be caught in the forest after dark, and with great reluctance he left that place and made his way back. Then, to his amazement, he seemed led as if by an unseen guide, for he flew through that forest as if he had made his home there all of his days, and before the sun reached the horizon he emerged from it, with the golden feather in his hand. And with one look backward, he returned to his home in Bratslav, nor did he reveal the events of that day to anyone. And that night, before he went to sleep, he placed the golden feather beneath his pillow.

So it was that no sooner did Reb Nachman fall asleep than he found himself in that forest once more, the golden feather still in his possession. And in the distance he saw a circular pool, and realized that he was very thirsty. Then he went to the pool, bent down, and drank from the clear water, which satisfied him to his soul, and when he stood up he saw in the water the reflection of the golden bird, flying overhead, more wonderful than anything he had ever imagined. But when he raised his eyes, it had already disappeared. And once again Reb Nachman knew that he could not rest until he had seen that bird with his own eyes. And it was then that he woke up.

All the next day Reb Nachman wondered if he would be permitted to continue that night the quest for the golden bird that had so far evaded him. For he sensed that nothing would be served by searching for it in the forest outside Bratslav, but that it was his destiny to seek out that bird in the kingdom of dreams. And that night it did happen that he found himself walking in that forest once more. This time he reached a place where he glimpsed a garden in the distance. But no matter from whence he tried to approach it, it would vanish before he was able to find an entrance. And each time the garden reappeared, Reb Nachman heard the haunting song of the golden bird, which pierced him to his soul. And he knew that if he could only find a way to that garden, he might well find the golden bird, for no other could have such an unearthly song. Yet although he continued to glimpse the garden from time to time, he was never able to find any entrance, no matter how many times he circled the area in which it appeared.

It was then that Reb Nachman remembered the golden feather, and how it had shone like a mirror in the sun. And he took it out, and held it so that it faced the direction in which he had glimpsed the garden, and saw at once that in the mirror of the golden feather the garden did not disappear from his sight, but remained clearly in his vision. He then circled the garden once more, this time viewing it from the mirror of the feather, and in this way he was able to discern the gate, which had previously been invisible. And he saw how that gate opened and closed in the blink of an eyelash. So he made his way there, and stood before the gate and closed his eyes, and when he opened them he found, to his dismay, that he had awakened. Once more the dream had ended before he had achieved his goal. But this time he was confident that the quest had not come to its end, and that he might still find his way into the garden of the golden bird.

So it was that when Reb Nachman closed his eyes to sleep on the third night, he opened them to find himself standing inside that glorious garden, where he heard the haunting song of the golden bird clearly once more. And in the distance he saw a tree that was so wide he estimated it would take five hundred years' journey to travel around it. Beneath the tree flowed four streams, that spread throughout the garden, one in each direction. And high in that tree Reb Nachman saw the golden bird, glowing in the branches like a golden star. And when the bird started to sing, its song carried his soul to the heights.

It was then that Reb Nachman saw a man walking in the garden, whose face was glowing, and whose eyes cast such a great light that they seemed to illumine the path on which he walked. This man approached Reb Nachman, who cast down his eyes, knowing he was in the presence of a holy man. And the man said: "Welcome to this garden, Reb Nachman. I have been waiting for you to arrive ever since you found the golden feather, for I knew that you would not rest until you found the bird from which it came. As for me, I am the gardener here; it is my blessing to tend the sacred fruits and flowers and to see that they grow ripe."

And Reb Nachman said: "Peace be with you. I had longed to find one who could guide me in this enchanted garden, and who knows the ways of the garden better than the gardener? But tell me, what is your name, and how is it that you have come to tend this garden?"

And the man said: "I am the Ari. Just as I was a gardener of the Torah, and found the hidden meanings buried beneath the surface, and understood how scattered sparks can take root and bring forth a harvest of abundance, so it is that I have been rewarded by being made gardener of this garden, in which the golden bird makes its home."

And Reb Nachman was overwhelmed to find himself in the presence of the Ari, as Rabbi Issac Luria, of blessed memory, was known. At first Reb Nachman was silent, but then he found the courage to speak, for at last he had the opportunity to discover the secret of the golden bird, whose golden feathers reflected in the sunlight like the facets of a jewel, and whose melody had lured him the way a flame attracts a moth. And he asked if the Ari could share this secret, and the Ari said in reply: "That golden bird, Reb Nachman, is the beloved bird of the Messiah. For the song of that bird translates the prayers of Israel into a haunting music that fills the heavens."

It was then that Reb Nachman suddenly remembered something that had completely slipped his mind until that moment. It was a tale about his great-grandfather, the Baal Shem, who once was praying with his Hasidim when he prolonged the Eighteen Benedictions for a long time, and his Hasidim grew impatient, and one by one they departed from the House of Prayer. Later the Baal Shem told them that their leaving had caused a great separation to take place. For while he had prayed he had climbed the ladder of their prayers to reach a place where he had seen a vision of a golden bird, with a song that could not but bring peace of mind to all who heard it. And he was certain that if such a song were brought to the world of men, it would surely bring peace everywhere it was heard. And the Baal Shem told them that by stretching forth his hand he had come within reach of taking the bird from that tree. But just then the ladder of their prayers had broken, and he fell back to this world and the bird flew away.

Then the Ari, who could read his thoughts, spoke and said: "Yes, Reb Nachman, this is the same golden bird that the Baal Shem saw. Nor was it any accident that his Hasidim grew impatient, for heaven made certain of this, so that the Baal Shem did not succeed in taking the bird before the time had arrived for the Messiah to be born among men. For it is in this garden that the Messiah makes his home, and that is why his palace is known as the Bird's Nest, for it is the song of that bird that sustains the worlds above and below. And had the Baal Shem succeeded in bringing back even one golden feather, peace would have followed for many generations. And had he brought back the golden bird, the Messiah would surely have followed, so little can he bear being separated from its song."

Now Reb Nachman was startled when he heard this, and he became very solemn, for like the Baal Shem he longed for nothing more than that the Messiah should usher in the End of Days. At last he said to the Ari: "What if I should attempt to bring the golden bird out of this garden?" But no sooner had he spoken these words than a sudden wind arose, and plucked the golden feather from his hand, and carried it off, so that Reb Nachman knew that it was gone. Nor was that warning lost to him, for he recognized he might be expelled from there as swiftly as that feather in the wind. Then the Ari replied: "You, Reb Nachman, have entered this kingdom as a dreamer, while the Baal Shem came here as one awake. Therefore that path is closed to you, for even if you succeeded in capturing the golden bird, you could not carry it beyond the gate of the kingdom of dreams, for nothing that has its source here could survive to reach the waking world. At the very instant you touch its feathers, you would find yourself alone and empty-handed in the world of men, and that all that has transpired so far would be lost to you, like a dream lost between sleeping and waking."

Now Reb Nachman was not surprised to hear these words, for he had not forgotten that he had entered the kingdom of dreams. And the last thing he wanted was to be expelled from that kingdom. Then he said to the Ari: "But tell me, if I am permitted to know—how may I make my way back to this garden in order to hear the sacred song of the golden bird as it translates the prayers that ascend from the world below? Nor does it matter if I come here as a dreamer or as one awake, as long as I am permitted to be in its presence and to hear that haunting melody."

And the Ari smiled and said: "For you that will be very simple, Reb Nachman. You need only turn to the verse in which it is written that *The Torah is a Tree of Life*, and this will serve as your key to this kingdom. For on that night you will travel to this world in a dream, and share in the presence of the golden bird and the song that tranforms the prayers of men, which as you see, are themselves the keys of heaven."

And no sooner did the Ari finish speaking than Reb Nachman awoke and found himself in the world of men once more. But this time he did not feel that the quest was incomplete; on the contrary, he understood that his roots among the living were just as deep as those that drew him to the world above, where the song of the golden bird filled the heavens. And from that time forward his Hasidim noticed that Reb Nachman left the Holy Scriptures by his bed every night, opened to the Psalms. And from that time on they also noticed a divine smile that could be seen on his lips and in his eyes when he awoke. And all who knew him marveled at how peaceful he was every morning, as if he had returned from a journey to a faraway kingdom of peace.

The Seamstress of Safed

by Yehuda Yaari

There was a young girl in Safed by the name of Deborah. The girl was from a fine and wealthy family, but her parents perished in an epidemic, and all the wealth they had left her was plundered and looted. Deborah was left poor and alone, so she decided to learn the art of sewing, in order to keep herself alive. She was both sensible and intelligent, and she learned the skill easily.

Once she had completed her training, she secured a room for herself from an elderly couple who lived in the poor section on the edge of town; and there in that narrow and dark room she would sit every day and sew garments for the women of Safed. She sewed clothing for others, but for herself she never sewed a single thing. Old and tattered clothes, left after the looting, these were what Deborah wore. And because she was a good seamstress from a good family, the women of Safed used to prefer her to the other seamstresses in the town, and they would order their important clothing from her—bridal gowns, and holiday dresses. Even so, Deborah lived a life of poverty and suffering, and she wasn't able to make any new clothes for herself. A person has only two hands, and on each hand there are five fingers, but you can only hold one needle with these fingers, and in order to sew one garment it is necessary to traverse a distance greater than one mile with this one tiny little needle—even though Deborah sat and sewed and sewed without ceasing, from dawn's early rising until the rooster crowed, she was not able to provide for herself more than a meager living.

Deborah sat day after day, stooped and weary over the garments of others, until her beauty faded, her back became bent, and the light in her eyes dimmed. And when she reached the marriageable age, she received no proposals; not even one family from among the families of Safed considered her for marriage. Deborah remained in her poverty and loneliness, and she sewed for others while for herself she sewed nothing—until the earthquake struck.

When the earthquake struck Safed, the people of the town were gathered together in the synagogues and houses of study for the afternoon prayer. Even the old couple with whom Deborah lived were in the synagogue. At that very hour, Deborah sat alone in her narrow little room, sewing a wedding gown for a bride-to-be who was a member of an important family and whose wedding was soon to take place. As she bent over the cool and rustling silk material, the earth suddenly trembled, the houses shook, and their foundations collapsed. Deborah heard the loud and terrible noise, she dropped her needle and the dress she was working on, and she tried to flee outside to escape for her life, but she couldn't get out the front door. It was closed off by the top floor of the house, which had collapsed. Deborah lived on the bottom floor. Deborah cried out in a loud voice, but no one heard her and no one came to save her. Many souls, from among her neighbors, lay at that moment under the debris of the collapsed floor; they screamed and screamed but their screams could not penetrate the mounds of dirt and stones that buried them alive.

Deborah sat for a few days, which were to her as one long night in her sealed-off room, and she waited for them to come and get her out of her living grave. When the air in the house became heavy, so that Deborah felt a choking in her throat, she got up and took from her sewing bag a white sheet of her mother's, which she had been able to salvage from the looting, and she sewed herself a shroud. When she had finished sewing, she put it on; she lay down on her bed, and she lit candles at either side of her head. When the air in the house quit, and the candles were snuffed out, so too was the candle of Deborah's breath.

When they came twenty-four days after the earthquake, and they cleared away the ruins, they found Deborah lying on her bed dressed in her shroud, which shone brilliantly from its whiteness; the blown-out candles stood by her head. The silk dress she had not finished sewing was thrown on the ground, and embroidered on it in black letters were these words: "All my days I sewed for others, and for myself I did not sew a thing. Now I have sewed myself a dress, not a gown to wear under the *chupah* did I sew, but a gown for my death. In happiness did I sew it, and in happiness have I put it on."

They said: If you did not see the face of Deborah in her death, then you have not seen a truly beautiful face in all your life.

Translated from the Hebrew
by Pamela Altfeld Malone

The Legend of the Dead Poppy
by Zvi Kolitz

> . . . and know that trees and plants and flowers have
> language, feeling and prayer of their own.
>   Israel Ba'al Shem Tov

God created the plants and the flowers in order to provide a tangible expression of the new life led by those of His children who have returned to the dust from which they were taken. The flowers that entwine themselves and grow on the roots of graveyard cypress trees, the anemones, the violets, the chrysanthemums, and, most of all, the poppies that flourish in the abundant and sweet-smelling grass among the graves—these are flowers of the soul, whose purpose it is to reveal a very small part of the beauty of the eternal fields.

In the beginning, the poppies grew only on the graves of the dead. But as the dead multiplied and the earth became the sacrificial altar of its children, flowers grew and poppies flourished at every step, for the Creator knew that the world was only a great cemetery for the best of His creatures.

But since the days of creation there have never blossomed such beautiful and vibrant poppies as those that grew in the regions of the death camps set up by the Nazis in the land of Poland.

Around the dwellings near Treblinka of Hitler's officers who had been ordered to destroy the sons and daughters of God's people, the poppies flourished exceedingly. The earth was fat and good, enriched with the bones of thousands. On festive nights when Hitler's officers were carousing in their rooms, these poppies decorated their well-laid tables and their dance rooms. So it was in the beginning. Then something came to pass.

There was a woman whose daughter had been burned alive in the camp oven. The daughter, a child of fourteen, caught trying to escape from the camp, had been thrown alive into the fire before the eyes of her mother, who, with thousands of other prisoners, had been compelled to witness the punishment.

The child had been beautiful. Treblinka had taken her beauty from her, leaving only her large, lustrous eyes. When her little mouth contracted from hunger and her lips withered like those of an old woman, when her rosy skin became yellow and her teeth decayed, she was left with only those wondrous eyes.

The mother loved her daughter madly, and when they were sent together to the death camp, the mother, who had just given birth to a stillborn child of a husband who had been killed shortly before, fed her hungry daughter on the milk of her breasts. It was when the child could no longer bear the anguish of her mother's love that she decided to escape from the camp.

The burning of the child lasted only a few minutes, and the skeleton was placed immediately thereafter in the machine used for crushing bones into chemical fertilizer. The mother knew of this final process, and for several months the idea grew in her that, with the coming of spring, she would seek the flower that would grow from her daughter's bones.

The spring came and perfumed the air of the whole world. Do not be surprised, my friends. It is the same sun, precisely the same sun that we know, that shone over the living dead at Treblinka. Only the flowers that blossomed there were different from those that grow here. They were more beautiful.

That spring the flowers at Treblinka were more glorious than ever. They grew about the electrified fence like a bouquet, and beyond the fence, outside the camp area, flowers could be seen as far as the eye could reach. Their odor mingled with the odor of the dead, creating a gruesome mixture of flowering and putrefaction, filling the mind at once with visions of hell and dreams of paradise.

On one of those spring nights the mother went out to search for the flower of her daughter. The moon gleamed, and numberless stars, like glowworms, flickered across the horizon. The woman left the hut very quietly and, like a sleepwalker, crossed the area which was "out of bounds." She went swiftly and purposefully, led to her heart's desire. She doubled herself up and, like a mole, crept through the electrified fence.

Suddenly she found herself in a wide field, filled from end to end with poppies. A light breeze played over the flowers and in the pale light of the moon the mighty host bowed their childlike heads together. The mother stopped among the poppies and in a whisper called the name of her daughter. "Hannah," she said, "Hannah, where are you?" The flowers rustled slightly in the breeze, as though in whispered consultation.

For a long while the mother called her daughter, but, hearing no answer, went down on her knees and began to cry and plead, "Hannah, child, apple of my eye, where are you? Tell me . . . Don't hide from me . . . I shall not be afraid to see you as you are . . . I know it is as a poppy that you will appear before me . . . But you are not the only one . . . There are so many here . . . It is so good for you here . . . so much better than for me . . . Answer me, my child . . . Show me where you are . . . Let me hear your voice."

She knelt thus for a long time, embracing the earth of the poppy field. Then she rose and saw before her a divine spectacle: in the middle of the field, among thousands of poppies, there appeared two beautiful, bright eyes, which she recognized at once as those of her daughter.

She approached them cautiously, and as she knelt before them she was able to distinguish the long double stem which gave forth two poppies. From the depths of the flowers the eyes stared out—the eyes of her daughter. They were more beautiful, clearer and fresher than ever before. The mother looked at them and the eyes looked back at her. She began to caress them and to kiss them.

"Embrace me, Hannah, my child," she said. "Embrace me." The stems looked like two arms opened to receive her, and the mother put her head between them. They twined round her head with tender eagerness. She felt on her neck their revivifying coolness as she laid her head almost on the ground, her hands smoothing and caressing the earth that covered the roots of the flower. "Hannah, my little Hannah'le!" she cried.

Then the breeze dropped and the light rustle of the flowers was stilled. The poppies stood silent, unmoving, their heads turned towards the daughter embracing her mother. All living things that night had to see, and they turned in reverence on the scene of reunion. It was as though it were not only in the field that the wind had dropped, but that all creation was holding its breath.

For a long time the embrace of mother and daughter continued, but, as dawn drew near, the mother felt that her daughter wished her to leave. Before sunrise, the alarm sirens shook the death camp. The mother knew what that meant, but she would not run away. "I shall die by your side now that I have seen your face," she said. But the poppies writhed and twisted to show their desire that the mother should not remain with them in danger. Time after time the mother tried to place her head again within the poppies' arms, but the flowers drew away in a movement of pleading and despair. In the brightness of the rising sun, the light of the daughter's eyes was dimmed. The redness of the poppies' petals gave way to a blue-blackness, and the two stems bent over until their heads reached the ground, as though they were kneeling in supplication before the mother.

Meanwhile the fields were surrounded by Nazis, and the mother, seeing them in the distance, began fiercely to draw round her neck the "arms" of her daughter. Maddened by love and fear, she grasped the stems as though they were really arms. She shook them and pulled them and all at once she fell back, then jumped quickly to her feet: in her hand lay fading and dying the bloom of her daughter, torn out by the roots, and drops of blood were coming out at the place of the tearing as from an opened vein.

The mother burst into a loud cry—the cry of one who has killed by accident and sees his victim lying dead before him—an earth-rending cry. The poppies stirred and bowed their hands earthwards in a silent prayer for the soul of their sister-flower. The mother, deciding suddenly to accept her punishment, clasped the dead poppies firmly in her arms and turned towards the camp.

She went slowly but steadfastly, knowing well what awaited her, and with utter calm she gave herself up to her murderers. The same day she was consigned to the oven, her arms still grasping the remains of her daughter.

In honor of Hitler's birthday, which occurred a few days later, the Nazis in the neighborhood of Treblinka picked bunches of poppies and put them in crystal vases. These vases they set out on the enormous, swastika-shaped table loaded with all manner of wines and fruits for the enjoyment of all the high officers in the neighborhood; but suddenly the water in the vases began to go red and in a few minutes it looked like blood. The order was given for the water to be changed, but it congealed and the poppies withered instantly.

After that night no more poppies adorned the festive tables; the poppies multiplied exceedingly in the neighborhood and their redness covered the landscape.

The Last Living Jew

by Elie Wiesel

This is the story of a ghetto that stopped living, and of a beadle who lost his mind.

It was the beadle's custom to rush to the synagogue each morning, to ascend the *bimah* and shout first with pride, and then with anger: "I have come to inform you, Master of the Universe, that we are here."

Then came the first massacre, followed by many others. The beadle somehow always emerged unscathed. As soon as he could, he would run to the synagogue, and pounding his fist on the lectern, would shout at the top of his voice: "You see, Lord, we are still here."

After the last massacre, he found himself all alone in the deserted synagogue. The last living Jew, he climbed the *bimah* one last time, stared at the Ark, and whispered with infinite gentleness: "You see? I am still here."

He stopped briefly before continuing in his sad, almost toneless voice: "But You, where are You?"

Translated from the French
by Lily Edelman and the author

The Wandering Jew
by David Slabotsky

Rabbi Mikhal related the following tale:

There was once a Jew who had been wandering for hundreds of years in search of his death. From time to time he would stay in one place then in another, but no matter where he settled, those he loved and cared for passed away, and soon he chose to wander again, rather than endure the grief of separation.

One particular night, he found himself in the woods outside of Berditchev by an old, abandoned synagogue. The walls were almost entirely collapsed and little of the building remained except for the principal structure. The iron fence which surrounded the courtyard had fallen down and rusted. Rotted beams and pieces of stone lay hidden in the grass.

The Jew made his way inside through the wreckage and came at last to what remained of the sanctuary. He found a prayer book and stood in the light of the moon and began to pray.

Whenever he came to a word with the letter Aleph, the Aleph rose from the page and hovered about his heart, emitting a droning sound and giving off a light which he had never seen before. Before too long, the Jew stood in the moonlight with a cluster of Alephs about his heart like so many shining bees. It caused him pain, an almost exquisite grief which captivated him entirely.

His meditation was interrupted by the sound of hoofbeats. A horse was carrying him into battle. By the scarlet uniform he wore he understood that he was a cavalry officer, and by the ribbons on his breast he understood that he had been in battle before and that he had been brave.

The battle began at dawn, concluded at sunset, and when the moon hung full in the sky he found himself riding alone through a Jewish village. He spent the night at an inn where he was served by a young Jewess, the kind he had been taught to openly despise and secretly covet. That same night she came to his room and they were lovers.

They stayed together for many years and he lived to be an old man. The woman died, their children died, their grandchildren died, their great-grandchildren died, their great-great-grandchildren died, and he chose to wander again, rather than endure the grief of separation.

One particular night, he found himself in the woods outside of Berditchev by an old abandoned synagogue. The walls were almost entirely collapsed and little of the building remained except for the principal structure. The iron fence which surrounded the courtyard had fallen down and rusted. Rotted beams and pieces of stone lay hidden in the grass.

The Jew made his way inside through the wreckage and came at last to what remained of the sanctuary. He saw before him an old, decrepit Jew who stood in the moonlight. About the old man's heart he saw and heard a cluster of Alephs like so many shining bees. The sight of a man so old filled him with disgust.

He moved closer and saw that the Alephs were so arranged as to create an archway above a path which led directly into the old man's heart. Uttering the traveler's prayer, he set his feet upon the path.

He traveled until he came to the center of the old man's heart and sat himself down and prepared a glass of tea. There a weariness came upon him which nothing could dispel.

He tried to think of people he had known and loved, but he could not. He tried to conjure up recollections of times and places when he had been happy, but he could not. He tried to laugh or cry, but he could not. He tried to pray, but he could not. Nothing could dispel the weariness which had settled upon him.

In a corner of the old man's heart he discovered a tattered bag. He lifted it up and a cloud of dust and straw rose up, from which he understood that it had been lying in that particular place for many years. Inside the tattered bag he discovered a bird's nest.

He looked inside the nest and discovered a bird. He saw that the bird had only one eye. In the center of the eye he discovered an Aleph.

As he drew the bird closer to him, it flew away suddenly, passing through the chambers of the old man's heart, and past the Alephs, and disappeared at last into the sky. But it left two sounds behind. The first sound was like the clapping of hands. The second sound was like the stamping of feet.

He followed the sounds. The first sound, the sound like the clapping of hands, led him to his own hands which indeed were clapping. The second sound, the sound like the stamping of feet, led him to his own feet which indeed were stamping on the old, wooden floor of the synagogue.

He understood that he was dancing and that his dance was a joyful one. At the tip of his smallest finger he saw a handkerchief extending seven feet. At the end of the handkerchief he saw the finger of the decrepit Jew who was dancing, like himself, a joyful dance.

Large tears rolled out of their eyes and splashed onto the synagogue floor—tears of the lover and the beloved.

He drew the old man close to him as they danced and he recognized at last that he was that same old man. Laughing and weeping he danced past the Alephs, clapped and stamped, and danced into the center of the old man's heart, where he toppled over dead.

And that was how the Jew who had been wandering for hundreds of years in search of his death found his death.

The Shawl

by Cynthia Ozick

Stella, cold, cold, the coldness of hell. How they walked on the roads together, Rosa with Magda curled up between sore breasts, Magda wound up in the shawl. Sometimes Stella carried Magda. But she was jealous of Magda. A thin girl of fourteen, too small, with thin breasts of her own, Stella wanted to be wrapped in a shawl, hidden away, asleep, rocked by the march, a baby, a round infant in arms. Magda took Rosa's nipple, and Rosa never stopped walking, a walking cradle. There was not enough milk; sometimes Magda sucked air; then she screamed. Stella was ravenous. Her knees were tumors on sticks, her elbows chicken bones.

Rosa did not feel hunger; she felt light, not like someone walking but like someone in a faint, in trance, arrested in a fit, someone who is already a floating angel, alert and seeing everything, but in the air, not there, not touching the road. As if teetering on the tips of her fingernails. She looked into Magda's face through a gap in the shawl: a squirrel in a nest, safe, no one could reach her inside the little house of the shawl's windings. The face, very round, a pocket mirror of a face: but it was not Rosa's bleak complexion, dark like cholera, it was another kind of face altogether, eyes blue as air, smooth feathers of hair nearly as yellow as the Star sewn into Rosa's coat. You could think she was one of *their* babies.

Rosa, floating, dreamed of giving Magda away in one of the villages. She could leave the line for a minute and push Magda into the hands of any woman on the side of the road. But if she moved out of line they might shoot. And even if she fled the line for half a second and pushed the shawl-bundle at a stranger, would the woman take it? She might be surprised, or afraid; she might drop the shawl, and Magda would fall out and strike her head and die. The little round head. Such a good child, she gave up screaming, and sucked now only for the taste of the drying nipple itself. The neat grip of the tiny gums. One mite of a tooth tip sticking up in the bottom gum, how shining, an elfin tombstone of white marble gleaming there. Without complaining, Magda relinquished Rosa's teats, first the left, then the right; both were cracked, not a sniff of milk. The duct crevice extinct, a dead volcano, blind eye, chill hole, so Magda took the corner of the shawl and milked it instead. She sucked and sucked, flooding the threads with wetness. The shawl's good flavor, milk of linen.

It was a magic shawl, it could nourish an infant for three days and three nights. Magda did not die, she stayed alive, although very quiet. A peculiar smell, of cinnamon and almonds, lifted out of her mouth. She held her eyes open every moment, forgetting how to blink or nap, and Rosa and sometimes Stella studied their blueness. On the road they raised one burden of a leg after another and studied Magda's face. "Aryan," Stella said, in a voice grown as thin as a string; and Rosa thought how Stella gazed at Magda like a young cannibal. And the time that Stella said "Aryan," it sounded to Rosa as if Stella had really said, "Let us devour her."

But Magda lived to walk. She lived that long, but she did not walk very well, partly because she was only fifteen months old, and partly because the spindles of her legs could not hold up her fat belly. It was fat with air, full and round. Rosa gave almost all her food to Magda, Stella gave nothing; Stella was ravenous, a growing child herself, but not growing much. Stella did not menstruate. Rosa did not menstruate. Rosa was ravenous, but also not; she learned from Magda how to drink the taste of a finger in one's mouth. They were in a place without pity, all pity was annihilated in Rosa, she looked at Stella's bones without pity. She was sure that Stella was waiting for Magda to die so she could put her teeth into the little thighs.

Rosa knew Magda was going to die very soon; she should have been dead already, but she had been buried away deep inside the magic shawl, mistaken there for the shivering mound of Rosa's breasts; Rosa clung to the shawl as if it covered only herself. No one took it away from her. Magda was mute. She never cried. Rosa hid her in the barracks, under the shawl, but she knew that one day someone would inform; or one day someone, not even Stella, would steal Magda to eat her. When Magda began to walk Rosa knew that Magda was going to die very soon, something would happen. She was afraid to fall asleep; she slept with the weight of her thigh on Magda's body; she was afraid she would smother Magda under her thigh. The weight of Rosa was becoming less and less; Rosa and Stella were slowly turning into air.

Magda was quiet, but her eyes were horribly alive, like blue tigers. She watched. Sometimes she laughed—it seemed a laugh, but how could it be? Magda had never seen anyone laugh. Still, Magda laughed at her shawl when the wind blew its corners, the bad wind with pieces of black in it, that made Stella's and Rosa's eyes tear. Magda's eyes were always clear and tear-less. She watched like a tiger. She guarded her shawl. No one could touch it; only Rosa could touch it. Stella was not allowed. The shawl was Magda's own baby, her pet, her little sister. She tangled herself up in it and sucked on one of the corners when she wanted to be very still.

Then Stella took the shawl away and made Magda die.

Afterward Stella said: "I was cold."

And afterward she was always cold, always. The cold went into her heart: Rosa saw that Stella's heart was cold. Magda flopped onward with her little pencil legs scribbling this way and that, in search of the shawl; the pencils faltered at the barracks opening, where the light began. Rosa saw and pursued. But already Magda was in the square outside the barracks, in the jolly light. It was the roll-call arena. Every morning Rosa had to conceal Magda under the shawl against a wall of the barracks and go out and stand in the arena with Stella and hundreds of others, sometimes for hours, and Magda, deserted, was quiet under the shawl, sucking on her corner. Every day Magda was silent, and so she did not die. Rosa saw that today Magda was going to die, and at the same time a fearful joy ran in Rosa's two palms, her fingers were on fire, she was astonished, febrile: Magda, in the sunlight, swaying on her pencil legs, was howling. Ever since the drying up of Rosa's nipples, ever since Magda's last scream on the road, Magda had been devoid of any syllable; Magda was a mute. Rosa believed that something had gone wrong with her vocal cords, with her windpipe, with the cave of her larynx; Magda was defective, without a voice; perhaps she was deaf; there might be something amiss with her intelligence; Magda was dumb. Even the laugh that came when the ash-stippled wind made a clown out of Magda's shawl was only the air-blown showing of her teeth. Even when the lice, head lice and body lice, crazed her so that she became as wild as one of the big rats that plundered the barracks at daybreak looking for carrion, she rubbed and scratched and kicked and bit and rolled without a whimper. But now Magda's mouth was spilling a long viscous rope of clamor.

"Maaaa—"

It was the first noise Magda had ever sent out from her throat since the drying up of Rosa's nipples.

"Maaaa . . . aaa!"

Again! Magda was wavering in the perilous sunlight of the arena, scribbling on such pitiful little bent shins. Rosa saw. She saw that Magda was grieving for the loss of her shawl, she saw that Magda was going to die. A tide of commands hammered in Rosa's nipples: Fetch, get, bring! But she did not know which to go after first, Magda or the shawl. If she jumped out into the arena to snatch Magda up, the howling would not stop, because Magda would still not have the shawl; but if she ran back into the barracks to find the shawl, and if she found it, and if she came after Magda holding it and shaking it, then she would get Magda back, Magda would put the shawl in her mouth and turn dumb again.

Rosa entered the dark. It was easy to discover the shawl. Stella was heaped under it, asleep in her thin bones. Rosa tore the shawl free and flew—she could fly, she was only air—into the arena. The sunheat murmured of another life, of butterflies in summer. The light was placid, mellow. On the other side of the steel fence, far away, there were green meadows speckled with dandelions and deep-colored violets; beyond them, even farther, innocent tiger lilies, tall, lifting their orange bonnets. In the barracks they spoke of "flowers," of "rain": excrement, thick turd-braids, and the slow stinking maroon waterfall that slunk down from the upper bunks, the stink mixed with a bitter fatty floating smoke that greased Rosa's skin. She stood for an instant at the margin of the arena. Sometimes the electricity inside the fence would seem to hum; even Stella said it was only an imagining, but Rosa heard real sounds in the wire: grainy sad voices. The farther she was from the fence, the more clearly the voices crowded at her. The lamenting voices strummed so convincingly, so passionately, it was impossible to suspect them of being phantoms. The voices told her to hold up the shawl, high; the voices told her to shake it, to whip with it, to unfurl it like a flag. Rosa lifted, shook, whipped, unfurled. Far off, very far, Magda leaned across her air-fed belly, reaching out with the rods of her arms. She was high up, elevated, riding someone's shoulder. But the shoulder that carried Magda was not coming toward Rosa and the shawl, it was drifting away, the speck of Magda was moving more and more into the smoky distance. Above the shoulder a helmet glinted. The light tapped the helmet and sparkled it into a goblet. Below the helmet a black body like a domino and a pair of black boots hurled themselves in the direction of the electrified fence. The electric voices began to chatter wildly. "Maamaa, maaamaaa," they all hummed together. How far Magda was from Rosa now, across the whole square, past a dozen barracks, all the way on the other side! She was no bigger than a moth.

All at once Magda was swimming through the air. The whole of Magda traveled through loftiness. She looked like a butterfly touching a silver vine. And the moment Magda's feathered round head and her pencil legs and balloonish belly and zigzag arms splashed against the fence, the steel voices went mad in their growling, urging Rosa to run and run to the spot where Magda had fallen from her flight against the electrified fence; but of course Rosa did not obey them. She only stood, because if she ran they would shoot, and if she tried to pick up the sticks of Magda's body they would shoot, and if she let the wolf's screech ascending now through the ladder of her skeleton break out, they would shoot; so she took Magda's shawl and filled her own mouth with it, stuffed it in and stuffed it in, until she was swallowing up the wolf's screech and tasting the cinnamon and almond depth of Magda's saliva; and Rosa drank Magda's shawl until it dried.

The Tale of the Lucky Daaz
by Pinhas Sadeh

One day the heavenly messengers, the angels, came to present themselves before God, and Satan also came among them. And when God asked him: "Whence have you come?" Satan answered and said that he was returning from his daily walk, going to and fro on the earth. And the Lord asked him: "And what did you see?" "I saw men," said Satan, "and they live like pigs, and they are dispersed like the foolish sheep on the earth, eating and playing, accumulating wealth and honor, paying no attention. And when the day comes and all these are gone, their hearts break. They are mere clowns, my Lord." Hearing that, saith the Lord: "Not so is my servant Daaz, a man innocent of vice who will not get ensnared by the forgeries of the would-be-wise." So Satan went forth to see wherein lay Daaz's strength. Daaz, at that hour, finished his seven years of labor, as he was a day laborer, and got from his master a chest full of silver. He was on his way to his house, when Satan, who took on the shape of an Ishmaelite, met him. And Satan said to Daaz: "Why are you on foot, carrying on your back your burden? It is better to ride a horse, without carrying a burden." So did Satan seduce Daaz to give away his money in exchange for a horse. Daaz was happy in the luck that met him, mounted the horse and rode away. Next day Satan again met him, now clothed as a peasant, seducing Daaz to sell his horse for a sheep, saying that a sheep gives milk while a horse does not. Daaz was duped once again, then, and going on his way at the side of his grazing sheep he felt happy in his heart since every new day brought on his deeds a new blessing. On the third day Satan came clothed as a miller and said: "I do advise you to give your sheep away in exchange for my millstone, as the sheep's end is to die, while my millstone will not." Daaz agreed to the deal once again, and went on his way joyfully. So the hours of the day passed and Daaz, who went bent under his burden, reached the shores of a river. Daaz sat down to drink, and the stone rolled off his shoulders into the river and sank. Daaz stood up and said: "Blessed are You, my Lord, and I am the most lucky fellow on earth! Now I am free of the heavy stone, and ready to go fleetly and sweetly to my home."

Translated from the Hebrew
by Moshe Genen

The Wager and the Tiny Shining Star
by Alfredo Sarano

On a winter day, in the days when King David reigned, some young men were talking, saying that nobody wearing only a shirt was capable of staying outside the whole night in the garden in the cold. One of the young men said that he could do it, and he made a bet of ten ducats with his friends.

And he did spend the entire night naked to the cold in the garden. The morning after, when his friends, amazed, asked him how he could have spent the night in such a way, he answered that by looking far off at the light of a tiny shining star glistening against a window, he had diverted himself and succeeded in passing the time. Hearing this, the friends refused to pay him the ten ducats on the pretext that he had warmed himself from the light of the tiny shining star and so had been able to stay outside throughout the night. The poor young man, who had done this bold act and was now seeing it denied, appealed to King David to judge his case.

But King David, after studying the case, supported the friends' view, and the young man left the proceedings in misery.

Returning home, he met Shelomo, the king's son, who asked him why he was in such distress. After hearing why, Shelomo promised to help him.

Shelomo went back to the palace and ordered the king's cook to light a fire in a corner of the garden, in another corner to put pieces of lamb through a roasting spit, and to keep turning the spit around. And so it was done.

Walking in the garden, King David saw the fire on one side and the shish kabob on the other. He was dumbfounded and asked the cook:

"Who ordered you to do this?"

When he found out, he called Shelomo and asked him:

"How can this shish kabob get cooked if the fire is so far away?"

And Shelomo asked him in turn:

"My father, how can someone warm himself from a tiny star shining from so far off?"

King David understood the allusion, summoned the young men, and judged in favor of the young man after all.

Recorded by Matilda Koen;
translated from the Judezmo
by Stephen Levy

Challahs in the Ark

by Rabbi Zalman Schachter

At the beginning of the sixteenth century Jews who had been expelled from Spain tried to settle all over. Some traveled to Salonika in Greece, some to France, some to Germany. One man, whose name was Jacobo, and his wife Esperanza, settled in Sfat, the city where Kabbalah flourished. When he came to Sfat, the only language he spoke was Spanish, so when he went to *shul* and listened to the rabbi's sermons he didn't really understand everything he heard. One Shabbos the rabbi, who was sixty years old, gave a sermon in which he mentioned that in the Holy Temple God was offered twelve loaves of bread each week before Shabbos. Jacobo didn't understand everything about that sermon, but when he came home he said to 'Speranza,

"Next week, Friday morning, I want you to bake twelve loaves of *pan de Dios*, and I am going to bring it to the synagogue. The old rabbi said that God likes to have special bread for Shabbos, and I know that you bake the best *challah* in the whole country, so next Shabbos I am going to bring Him some of your *challah*." That week 'Speranza baked especially good *challahs*. She kneaded the dough until it was extra smooth, and put all her good intentions into the dough along with the special ingredients. Then, Friday morning, Jacobo wrapped them all up in a nice white tablecloth and took them to *shul*.

When he got to the synagogue, Jacobo looked around to make sure nobody was there, went up to the Holy Ark, kissed the curtain in front of the ark, and said, "Señor Dios, I bring you twelve *challahs* that my 'Speranza baked. She is really a good baker, and I hope you will like her *challah*. Tomorrow morning when they take out the *Sefer Torah*, I am going to look inside the ark, and I expect to see every crumb gone, because my 'Speranza, she really bakes good *challah*." Then he opened the ark, put the twelve *challahs* inside, arranged them neatly, said *"Bueno apetito,"* closed the ark, kissed the curtain, stepped back seven steps, and walked out of the synagogue very happy that God would have such good *challahs* to eat.

A few minutes later the *shammes* came in with his broom, talking to God. "Seven weeks already with no pay I'm cleaning up the synagogue, and Dear Lord, you know I only want one thing in my life, I just want to be here in your house. I don't want another job, I just want to be the *shammes* here, but Dear Lord, my children are getting so hungry. I know you can do miracles. Please make a miracle for me, I need a miracle so badly. I am going to open up the Holy Ark and I know you will make a miracle. I will find something inside that will help me and my family."

He walks over, opens up the *Aron Kodesh*, the Holy Ark, and sure enough, there is the miracle. "I knew it! I knew it! The *Ribbono shel Olam* never forsakes anyone." He took the twelve *challahs* and made his way home. When he got home he said, "Easy, easy, not yet. Tonight we will have two *challahs* for the Shabbos table. In the morning, after davening we will have two more *challahs*. For third meal we will have two more *challahs*, and there will be one *challah* for each day of the week. Next week we will see what happens."

Next morning Jacobo came to synagogue, Esperanza went upstairs to the women's section, and they both waited anxiously to see what would happen. When they open up the ark, will the *challahs* still be there? Or will God have really liked the *challah*, and have cleaned up every crumb? When the rabbi opened the ark, and reached in to take out the Torah, Jacobo, who had crept up behind the rabbi, peeked in and saw the *challahs* were gone. "Oh, Baruch ha-Shem! Thank God!" He winked up at his wife 'Speranza and went back to his seat.

During the next week Esperanza got the best ingredients she could find. Thursday evening she started making the dough. Friday morning she baked them, fresh and delicious, Jacobo wrapped them up and took them to the synagogue and left them in the *Aron Kodesh* just like the week before. A few minutes later the *shammes* came and picked up his miracle *challahs*. This scene repeated itself every week. The *shammes* found out that if he came too early, or if he hung around the *shul*, no miracle. He learned that he had to rely on God, and not show up until about ten o'clock on Friday, and then he'd find his *challahs* there.

Thirty years passed. One Friday as Jacobo was bringing the *challahs* to the Holy Ark he prayed to God, "Señor Dios, my poor 'Speranza, she is getting arthritis. Her fingers are not so good anymore for kneading the *challahs*. But if you don't like the lumps in the *challahs*, you better fix up my 'Speranza. I hope you enjoy them anyway." He leaves the twelve *challahs*, kisses the hem of the curtain over the ark, walks back his customary seven backward steps, and—aargh!!—the long bony hand of the old rabbi, now ninety years old, grabs poor frightened Jacobo by the neck.

"What is this that you just did?" yelled the rabbi angrily.

"I brought God His *pan de Dios*, His weekly bread."

"Whatever made you do that?"

"You did, sir. Thirty years ago you gave a sermon about *pan de Dios* in the Holy Temple, and ever since then I've brought God bread."

"Are you crazy? God doesn't eat!"

"Señor Rabino," Jacobo says, "you may be a rabbi, and you may know lots of things better, but He does too eat!"

"What do you mean, 'He does too eat'?"

"For thirty years not a crumb was left in the *Aron Kodesh*."

"Let's hide in the back of the synagogue and see what happens," said the rabbi.

Sure enough, a few minutes later in came the *shammes*, saying, "Dear Lord, I don't know what it is, but something is going wrong with the angels up there. Lately the *challah* has been very lumpy. For thirty years I've been sustained by your angels, so I can't complain, but I just thought you might like to know. Maybe you can ask the angels to bake a little better. Thank you anyways." He goes up to the *Aron Kodesh*, takes out the *challahs*, closes the ark, walks back a few steps, and—aargh!!—"You terrible man!" the rabbi yells, shaking the poor *shammes*. "On account of you this man has sinned the great sin of anthropomorphism! What do you think you are doing?"

"Listen," the *shammes* explained, "you haven't paid me. This is my *pa'nassa*, my living. Every week God makes a miracle for me."

Soon the *shammes* was crying, because he knew he wouldn't find any more *challahs*. Jacobo was crying because he just wanted to do good. The rabbi began to cry, "How could such a terrible thing come from my good sermon? I never said God eats; it goes against what the Rambam says. God has no body, God doesn't eat. Oy, what terrible people I have in my congregation."

Suddenly Reb Chaim Vital, disciple of the great Kabbalist Isaac Luria, came into the synagogue. "My master, the Ari ha-Kadosh, wants all of you to come to his house." They all went to the Ari's house, and the Ari said to the rabbi, "Go home, make sure your will is in order, because you will die before Shabbos. Thirty years ago your time had come to die. Do you know why you got thirty more years to live? Because since the destruction of the Holy Temple God didn't have as much fun as He has had every Friday morning watching what goes on in your *shul*. He would call all the angels together and they would watch that scene of the man bringing the *challahs*, the *shammes* coming to get them, and God getting all the credit. Since God so enjoyed it, He called the Angel of Death off, and let you live thirty more years. Now that you have spoiled God's fun, go home and get ready, so they can bury your body before Shabbos."

Then the Ari turned to Jacobo and said to him, "Now that you know who has been eating your *challah*, it is going to be a little bit harder, but I want you to believe with perfect faith that if you bring the *challahs* directly to the *shammes*, God will be pleased no less."

BOOK VII
HASIDIC
THEMES

The Seven Beggars

by Rabbi Nachman of Bratslav

Once upon a time there was a king, and he had an only son. The king decided to have his son reign in his stead, while the king himself was still in the prime of his life. He prepared a great banquet, and he invited all the noblemen in the kingdom to the banquet, every duke and earl, and there was great rejoicing there. It was a well-known fact that every time the king had a banquet, a great jubilation reverberated throughout the courtyards of his kingdom. All the greater was the joy this time, because the king was transferring rulership to his son, while he, the father, still lived. Even though they were not invited to the banquet, the multitudes of people that dwelt in that country experienced a profound happiness and pride, because it was a great honor for their king to be transferring his kingdom to his son while he, the father, still lived.

Now there were at that banquet every kind of musical instrument, bands of minstrels and jesters, and everything imaginable to enliven the occasion.

When the mirth and merrymaking had reached its highest point, the king rose and said to his son, "I want you to know, my son, that I am an astrologer, I interpret the stars. And behold, I saw in the stars that the day will come in the future when you will have to step down from your throne. Therefore take care, my son, that when that day comes, you do not grieve or feel sorry, but fortify yourself with gladness. Because when you are happy, so too am I. However, it is true that if you are besieged by trouble, I will be glad that you are no longer king, because such trouble will indicate that you shouldn't be king. And when you are again filled with happiness, I will be all the happier."

Then the king's son sat upon the throne, and he ruled his kingdom proudly. He appointed noblemen, established dukedoms and elected generals and built up a great army.

Now this young king was noted for his wisdom, he loved learning and held all wise men in great esteem, and he attracted them to him. Anyone who came before the king and brought him some kind of new knowledge was received very favorably and was given much honor and wealth. To one, the king would give material things, and to another, prestige—each man according to what he asked for and what he really wanted. Because wisdom was so highly regarded by the king, everyone began to busy himself with wisdom: one because he longed for material things, and another because he wanted honor to be bestowed upon himself. They became so immersed in philosophy that they forgot the tactics of war. So great was their knowledge that even the slightest among their wise men would be thought a great wise man in another state; it isn't necessary therefore to say that a superior wise man of theirs would be thought in another state to be a man without equal. And because they spent all their days studying diverse philosophies, they became heretical, and reached a point of religious denial.

The young king, who was so attracted to the wise men that were in his country, also suffered from heresy and his religious faith was shattered. However, the king had a good background, his roots were solid; he had been educated with good and moral ethics, so from time to time he would stir himself up, take an accounting of his soul, and say, "Where am I in this world? What's this that has become of me?" He would sigh with a broken heart until he would fall down, entangling himself in his own confusion. And so he would sigh this way and go on and on, until he would again turn to his mind for an answer, and as soon as he did this, immediately the various philosophies became important to him, and again he would sink into the void of the perplexed.

1

Now one day a great misfortune came to the residents of a certain state, they were seized by fear and dread, and all of them fled for their lives. On their flight, they passed through a thick and terrible forest, and there in that forest two little children became lost—one was a boy and the other a girl. The two of them were very young, four or five years old, and they were very hungry and had nothing to eat. They began to cry and shout, "Food, food!"

While they were still standing there crying and shouting, a beggar came along carrying sacks full of bread on his shoulders. The children came up to him crying out, "Food, food!" He immediately gave them some bread, and after they had eaten it he asked them, "How did you get here?"

They answered, "We don't know." They were very young and they didn't know where they had come from. When he started to leave them, the children attached themselves to him and begged him to take them with him. He said to them: "This I will not do. I don't want you to come with me." It was at that moment that they realized the man was blind. And they were amazed that a blind man knew how to find his way all by himself. True they were little, but they understood that it was a wondrous thing that a blind man knew how to find his own way. Then the man blessed them, saying that they should be like him, that they should grow to be old like him. Afterward he gave them more bread to eat and then he went off.

Then the children understood that the Lord, praised be He, had taken pity on them, and had sent them this blind beggar to give them bread so they could stay alive in the forest.

The day passed and the night came and they slept there that night.

The next morning, when they woke from their sleep, the children again began to cry and shout for food, because the bread that the blind beggar had given them the day before was already all gone. Immediately another beggar appeared and this one was deaf. How did they know that he was deaf? Because when they were talking to him, he made signs with his hands as if to say, "I can't hear you." The deaf beggar also gave them bread to eat. And when he was about to leave them, the children also wanted him to take them with him and he refused. He also blessed them, saying that they should be like him.

On the next day the bread that the deaf beggar had given them ran out, and again the children began to cry and shout. Immediately another beggar appeared, and this one stuttered. He stuttered and stammered so badly they couldn't figure out what he was saying. And this beggar also gave them bread to eat and blessed them, saying that they should be like him.

On the fourth day, another beggar came, this one with a twisted neck, and on the fifth day a humpbacked beggar, and on the sixth, a beggar with no hands, and on the seventh, one with no feet. And every one of them gave the children bread to eat and blessed them by saying they should be like the beggars.

Now on the eighth day, the children again saw that they had nothing to eat and this time no beggar came to give them bread, so they said one to the other, "Let's leave this place. Maybe we can find a place to stay." Though they were small, they had the intelligence to understand that if they remained there in the forest, they would eventually perish from hunger. They walked and walked, wandering among the trees of the forest, until they came to a road. They followed that road, until they came to a village. They walked this way and that, on the outskirts of the village, and finally they went up to one of the houses. The people in the house took pity on them, and gave them something to eat. Afterward they entered another house, and there they were given something to eat also, and so they went, all day long, from one house to another, begging for whatever the people would give them. They saw that this was a good thing to do, and they agreed to stay together always. They even made themselves typical beggars' sacks, and they traveled from place to place. From city to city and town to town, they would return to the same gates, being invited to celebrations—*brises* and weddings. And in every place, people were kind to them and happily gave them whatever they needed. They used to go to fairs, in the larger towns, that lasted for days. There they would sit by the side of the road, their alms plates in front of them—just like all the other beggars—until they became well known among the beggars. By this time everyone knew them as the two little children who had become lost in the forest at the time of the Great Flight.

One day the rumor reached the ears of all the beggars that there was going to be a great fair in one of the big cities. Immediately they hurried there, all of them as one, and the two children went with them.

When they reached the large city, the beggars got the idea that they should betroth the two young people, and that the two should be married. They all thought it was a very good idea, and they didn't leave that place until they had completed the betrothal. But they didn't know how the wedding feast could be arranged. They consulted among themselves until they figured out what to do: on a certain day of a certain month there would be a great celebration in the king's court, to honor the king's birthday; they would all go to the celebration and use whatever they could beg for the wedding feast. And that is what they did.

All of the beggars went to the king's birthday, and they got a great quantity of bread and meat; they even picked up most of the leftovers from the feast. Afterward, they went and dug a deep pit that could hold a hundred men or more; it was covered with sticks, tree branches, and dirt, and it was there that they gathered together for the wedding of the two children. The beggars saw that the children were properly married, and there was a great rejoicing. The beggars were happy, and so too were the bride and groom.

But in the middle of their happiness, the young couple remembered the favor the Lord, praised be He, had shown them, when they were lost in the woods, and they started to cry with longing, saying, "If only the Blind Beggar could be here, the one who kept us alive in the forest by giving us bread to eat!"

While they were still crying with longing for him, he came, saying, "Behold, here I am! You see I came to you on the day of your wedding, and I bring you the gift that you should be like me. There in the forest, I blessed you with this blessing, and now I am giving it to you as a gift for your wedding, that you should have as long a life as I.

"You believe that I am blind? I am not blind at all. It is just that all the time that is in this world is to me nothing more than the blink of an eye. Therefore I seem blind, because I have no sight or vision in this world. And although I am extremely old, I am still a mere infant, and I have yet hardly begun to live. It is not just I who says this, I have the affirmation of the Great Eagle. Let me tell you a story:

"Once upon a time, some people sailed out on the sea in boats. A storm came up and broke their boats. But the people in the boats were saved, and they managed to get to one of the many islands in the sea. There on the island was a tall tower. They climbed up the tower, and they found all kinds of food and drink, clothing, and everything else they needed. In the tower they all agreed that each of them would tell an old story, the most ancient story that each of them could remember; that is to say, what each of them could remember from the moment that memory begins. There were both old and young there, and the oldest man in the group was honored with telling the first tale.

"He answered and said, 'What can I tell you? I remember the moment when they plucked the apple from the branch.' They did not understand what he was saying. But the wise men among them explained, 'This is indeed an old story.' Next they asked a second man to tell his story. And the second, who was younger than the first, answered by saying, 'You think that is an old story? I remember that story and also the moment that the candle burned.' The wise men said, 'This story is older than the first.' Everyone was amazed. How could this man, who was younger than the first, remember a story that was older than the first man's? They invited the third man to tell his story. The third man, who was younger than the second, answered by saying, 'I remember the precise moment when the fruit was formed.' The wise men said, 'This is the oldest story.' When it came the turn of the fourth man, who was younger than the third, he said, 'I remember the moment that they extracted the seed to plant the fruit.' And the fifth, who was even younger, said, 'I remember the wise men who discovered the seed.' And the sixth said he remembered the taste of the fruit before it entered the fruit; while the seventh said he remembered the fragrance of the fruit before it entered the fruit; and the eighth claimed that he remembered the appearance of the fruit before it attached itself to the fruit. And I," so continued the Blind Beggar, "I was then a small child, and I was there too. And when they invited me to stand up and tell the story of my first memory, I said, 'I remember all of your stories, and I also remember the time before there was anything—that is the Void.' And the wise men said, 'This is indeed a truly ancient story—more ancient than any of the others.' And it was a wondrous thing to everyone there, that a mere child could remember more than those older and more mature than he.

"Meanwhile the Great Eagle came and he beat with his wings on the gate of the tower, and said, 'Cease your poverty! Return to your treasure chests! Use your wealth! Leave this tower!'

"And he instructed them to leave the tower according to age; that is, that the oldest should leave first and the youngest last. And he took me, a little child, and put me in front, and the oldest man in the group, he put last.

"After everyone had left the tower, the Great Eagle continued speaking. 'Come and I will explain to you the tales that were told here. The one who said he remembered when they cut the apple from the branch, the meaning is that he remembers the hour of his birth, when they cut his umbilical cord. The one who says he remembers the time the candle glowed, that means he remembers what it was like to be inside his mother, at that time when the candle burned over his head. The one who remembers when the fruit began to form, he remembers when the body of the child was formed at the time of conception. The one who remembered the time the seed was extracted from the fruit, he remembers when the drop was drawn at the time of the coupling. And the wise men that discovered the seed, the meaning of this is, when the drop was still in the mind. Now the taste, that is the soul, and the fragrance, that is the spirit, and the appearance, that is the breath. And this child, who said he remembered when there was no thing, he is the superior, because he remembers what was before the mind, soul, spirit, and breath. What he remembers is the exact point of nothingness.

" 'And now,' continued the Great Eagle, 'return to your boats, because they are your bodies, which were broken, and it is now time for them to be rebuilt.'

"And after he said these words, he blessed everyone, and to me he said, 'You come with me, because you are like me. You are ancient, while still a mere babe, and in fact, you have hardly begun your life at all.'

"So you see, I have the guarantee of the Great Eagle that I will live a very long life. And behold, I am giving you as a wedding gift that you should live a life as long as mine."

And there was a great rejoicing there that night.

2

On the second day of the seven-day wedding feast, the young couple remembered the other beggar, the one who was deaf, who had also kept them alive in the forest by giving them bread to eat. And they began to cry with longing, saying, "If only the Deaf Beggar could be here!" And at that moment he appeared, saying, "Behold, here I am!" And he fell on their necks, hugged and kissed them, and said, "I want you to know, I came to your wedding to bring you the gift that you should be like me; that is, that you should live a good life as I do. There in the woods, I gave you this blessing, and now I give you my good life as a wedding present.

"You are sure that I am deaf? I am not the least bit deaf. It is just that it isn't worth it for me to hear of the world's loss. Because all of the sounds in this world come from loss, because everyone cries about what he lacks. And even the sounds of gladness come from loss, because everyone is happy when what he lacks is supplied. But no sense of loss enters my ears at all, because I live the good life, in which there is no sense of anything lacking. And I have the affirmation of this from the Land of the Wealthy.

"There is a state that is blessed with unusual riches, and great and dazzling treasures are found there. Once the richest men in the state gathered together, and they began to boast of their riches and their good lives. And I, having been there, stood up and said, 'My good life is better than your good lives. If your lives are as good as you say, come with me and we shall see if you can help the people of a certain country who are in trouble. Because far from here is a country in which there was a magnificent garden. It was possible to taste all the heavenly tastes in the world from the fruit which grew in that garden, and to smell all of the beautiful fragrances that existed in the world. In that garden there was everything beautiful to look at, every hue and color; the most beautiful array of flowers in the world. A trusty gardener was appointed to work and care for the garden. Because of the splendor of their garden, the citizens of that state led truly good lives.

" 'And then one day, the gardener disappeared, and no one knew where he had gone. With the gardener gone, the splendor of the garden was soon gone also. The fruits spoiled, and fell off, and the flowers began to wilt one after the other. And yet in spite of this, the people in that state could still live off of the garden, their lives were still good, because of the vines in the garden.

" 'Now there was a cruel king who decided to conquer this state. And as soon as he discovered that he couldn't overcome it, he decided to corrupt the good life they had there. What did he do? He dispatched three groups of men there and instructed them to do what he told them. The men in the first group were ordered to do something that would damage the sense of taste, the second group was ordered to corrupt the sense of smell, and the third group's mission was to corrupt vision. Things got to the point that all the food that was eaten tasted putrid and smelled like bitter resin. And this king's servants corrupted vision, so that everyone's eyes were dimmed, and it seemed as if heavy clouds were covering the sky.

" 'So if you all live such a good life, let us see if you can save the people of that country from their trouble. Because this you should know, if you are not able to save them, then in the future this corruption of taste, smell and sight will spread to other places until you also will be harmed.'

"As soon as they had heard this, the rich men got up early and went to the country and I went with them.

"On the way, everyone behaved as his good life had accustomed him. But when they arrived near that state, their own senses of taste and smell and sight became corrupted, until they could no longer taste the expensive food and drink that they had brought for the trip, and their eyes clouded up and they couldn't see straight. I stood up and said, 'See for yourselves! Now, when you still have not even entered the borders of that state, your senses of taste, smell, and sight have already been damaged. Will it not be even worse once you have entered the borders? How are you going to be of any help to them?' So I gave them my bread and water, because harm had not come to my food and drink. When they ate my bread and water, they tasted all the good tastes that are in this world and smelled the most beautiful smells

"In a while we lifted our eyes and saw a band of men coming toward us.

We waited until they came near, then we asked them, 'Where are you coming from and where are you going?'

"The men answered, 'We come from that country whose name is known far and wide because of her wonderful garden.' Then the men told us that the leaders of their state had bestirred themselves, and decided that from now on they were going to endeavor to set things right, to purify everything that had become corrupted. But when they saw to what extent the damage had been done, and that the citizens of the state could no longer help themselves, they appointed messengers to go to the Land of the Wealthy. Since the people in the Land of the Wealthy also know how to live the good life, the two states coming from the same kind of stock, perhaps the rich men would be able to save them. 'And we,' so continued those men, 'we are the messengers, and we are on our way to the Land of the Wealthy.'

"The rich men heard this, and they said in unison, 'We ourselves are citizens of the Land of the Wealthy, and we are on our way to you.'

"And I," continued the Deaf Beggar, "I spoke up and said, 'They don't need you; after all, I already proved to you that you haven't the power to save them. I am whom they need. You remain here, while I go with these messengers, and I will save this state from her troubles.'

"And so I went with the messengers to their country. I arrived at a city, and I saw crowds of people gathering on the outskirts of the city. They seemed to be amusing themselves, laughing hysterically. I asked, 'Why are they laughing like this?' They answered, 'They tell each other funny things and that makes them laugh.' I cocked my ears to hear what was so funny, and I found out that they were saying obscene things. All of their utterances were base, one would say something one way and another the same thing in another way, and this would bring them to their knees laughing.

"After this, I went to another city, and there I saw two men arguing with each other, because of some business transaction. Since they could not agree between themselves, they went and brought the matter before the court. The judges heard their arguments and then decreed, 'This one is innocent and this one is guilty.' But as soon as they had left the courthouse they again began to argue with each other, and so they went to be judged before another court. Then I realized how many people were quarreling and disagreeing with each other, and bringing their disagreements before the court, until the whole city was full of courts. I checked into the matter, and I discovered that there was no truth in this place, because the judges tilted the scales of justice, by showing partiality and taking bribes.

"From there I went to another city, and I saw that it was so full of public lewdness that there was no shame.

"After I had seen all of these things, I gathered together the leaders of the state who wanted to improve their grave situation, and I told them, 'You should know that the cruel king who wanted to demean your country sent three groups of men to your borders and commanded them to corrupt your state. It is they who have accustomed your citizens to foul language and because of obscenities uttered by the mouth, your sense of taste was destroyed. It was they who taught your judges to take bribes, and because of this, your vision was damaged and your eyes clouded over, because bribes can blind the eyes of the wise. And it was they who introduced public lewdness to your country, and it is because of the lewdness that your sense of smell was harmed. So now go out and cleanse your state from these three evils! Seize these servants of the cruel king, and banish them from your borders. Once you have purified your state from these three evils, your sense of taste will be restored, and your senses of smell and vision also, and the gardener who is lost will be found.'

"They went and did as I had told them. They purged the state of those three evils, they seized the servants of that king, and banished them from the land. As soon as they had finished their task, they became anxious that the lost gardener be found, and they became very sorry and wondered aloud, 'What has become of our faithful gardener? Is he still alive? What will become of our garden without its rightful gardener?'

"Then one of them stood up and said, 'Perhaps that crazy man who walks back and forth outside claiming again and again that he is the gardener, the one that people mock and throw stones at, maybe he is indeed the gardener!' Then others stood up after him, and they too said as he had, 'Perhaps in truth that is the gardener.' When they all agreed, they had him brought before them so they could question him.

"As soon as I saw him, I immediately rose to my feet saying, 'This is the one! He is your gardener in truth!'

"So I have the agreement from the people of the Land of the Wealthy that I live a good life, and by my hand were the people of a country saved. And now for your wedding gift, I give you my good life."

And the joy and gaiety increased at the gathering. The young couple now had two precious gifts: a long life and a good life.

3

On the third day, the young couple remembered the third beggar who came to them in the forest and gave them bread to eat. And they began to cry and long for him, saying, "If only the beggar who stutters could be here!" At that moment he appeared and said, "Behold me!" And he fell upon their necks, and kissed and hugged them and said, "You see that I have come to your wedding, and my gift for you is that you should be like me. There in the woods I blessed you with this blessing, and now I am giving you this blessing for your wedding gift.

"Are you certain that I stutter? I really have no speech impediment of any kind. It is just that those things said in this world, which do not have the praise of the Lord, praised be He, in them, are not complete. That is why I make my tongue stutter and stammer; because when it comes to utterances that don't have the praise of the Lord, praised be He, in them, I want to stutter. The truth is, I am not the least bit of a stutterer or stammerer. On the contrary, I am a renowned speaker, an orator and poet. When I begin to recite poems and tell riddles, there isn't a creature in this world that is not drawn to hear me. Because in my poems and riddles all the wisdom of the world is contained. And I have the affirmation of this from the great man who is called the Man of True Righteousness. There is an entire tale regarding this.

"Once upon a time, there was a gathering of wise men, and each of them boasted of his wisdom. One bragged that with his wisdom he had discovered how to make iron, another claimed that he was so smart he could make silver. Still another boasted that he knew how to make gold, and another, all kinds of weaponry. And there was a man there who said that he knew how to make all of those metals in a way different from theirs. And so they were boasting back and forth, until one man got up and said, 'I am wiser than all of you, because I am as wise as the day.' And since they didn't understand what he was talking about, he explained, 'All wisdom is taken from one certain day, just as there was specific creating on each of the six days of Creation. Even if you were able to gather up all of the knowledge that you are boasting of they wouldn't last longer than one hour, whereas I am as wise as one entire day.'

"And I, who happened to be there," continued the Stammering Beggar, "asked him, 'You are as wise as what day?' And he answered, 'The man who asks this question is wiser than I. I am as wise as any day you choose.' And again it was too difficult for the others to understand, and they looked to me to explain it to them. So I said, 'You should know that everything in the world has a heart, and the world itself, as a whole, has its own heart. Now the Heart of the World is a physical entity, just like the body of a man, with a face and hands and feet. Only, even the nail on the baby toe of the Heart of the World beats more than any other heart.

" 'There is at the edge of the world a tall mountain, and on that mountain is a huge rock, and a spring gushes forth from that rock. And on the other side of the world there is another tall mountain, and the Heart of the World is there. And the Heart of the World continually stands and waits for the Spring, and the Heart longs and pines to come to the Spring; and the Spring for her part longs to come to the Heart. But the Heart has two weaknesses: one weakness is from the sun which beats down on the Heart and burns him, and the second weakness is from these longings and pinings. When the Heart of the World needs some respite to restore its spirit, a great bird comes and spreads its wings and shelters the Heart from the sun. But even in his hour of rest, the Heart waits for the Spring and cries and moans from so much aching and longing. And since the Heart pines and longs so much to come to the Spring, why doesn't the Heart just go there? Because every time the Heart stands on the mountain peak, he can see the top of the other mountain, where the Spring is; but if the Heart wanted to come closer, he would have to descend the mountain, and then he would not be able to see the top of the other mountain, and he wouldn't be able to see the Spring; and if the Heart of the World doesn't see the Spring, for even one second, his soul will expire and, God forbid, he will start to die. And if the Heart dies, the whole world will cease, because the Heart is the source of all life in the world.

" 'The Spring has no time of her own, because she is not found in time at all, and she exists from the time that the Heart gives her as a gift. And the matter of time is put together by the righteous men of truth. And I,' " so the Stammering Beggar continued his story, " 'I am the one who travels this world, bringing together all the righteous men of truth, and bringing them to that great man, the Man of True Righteousness, and he makes time from them. As soon as he has finished making one day, he immediately brings it as a gift to the Heart of the World, and the Heart of the World gives it as a gift to the Spring. And every single day, when the day begins to turn to night, the righteous men go their separate ways, parting with love, trembling, and anguish, because if there are not enough righteous men for the great man, the Man of True Righteousness, to use for a new day, then this will be their last day, and they too will disappear when the day disappears. And they tell each other riddles and sing songs and recite wondrous poems of the longing and pining of the soul. And the disappearing day also leaves on the wings of poetry and song, and there are wrapped up, in those songs and poems, all the wisdom that is in the world. Every day is different from the other; there are days that are holidays and festivals, and there are days of fasting and mourning. Each day has its own song; each day a poem for it alone.

" 'And so you see,' " concluded the Stammering Beggar as he spoke to the wise men, " 'I am wiser than any of you, including the one who said he was as wise as any day you choose. Because he is only as wise as one single day, whereas I am as wise as all of the days. Because I am the one who brings the righteous men of this earth together, and takes them to the great man, the Man of True Righteousness, so that he can make time from them, forming the days from their riddles, poetry, and song.'

"Verily, I have the affirmation from the same great man, the Man of True Righteousness, that I know how to tell riddles, sing songs, and recite poems. And I am giving this to you for your wedding day, that you should be like me."

Immediately a great gaiety and rejoicing rose up among those assembled.

They all burst forth into songs of praise, and began to dance. And so they sang and danced the night away.

4

On the fourth day of the wedding feast, the young couple remembered the fourth beggar, who had given them bread to eat when they were lost in the woods, and again they began to cry with longing, "If only the Beggar with the Twisted Neck could be here!" And while they were still crying, he appeared and said, "Here I am! I have come to your wedding and I have brought you a gift: that you should be like me. I blessed you with this blessing there in the forest, and now I am giving it to you on your wedding day.

"Do you really think I have a twisted neck? My neck isn't twisted at all. On the contrary, I have a very straight and beautiful neck. It is just that the world is full of vanity and I do not wish to breathe so much as one whiff of this vain world. That is why my neck appears as if it were twisted. Not only that, but I have a truly beautiful voice, and I can make all the sounds of the world with my throat, wonderful sounds without words. And I have the acknowledgment of this from a certain state.

"Once upon a time there was a country in which all the inhabitants were experts in the art of music. All of the people, young and old, studied music, and they had attained such expertise that even the most novice among them was thought a veritable lion among musicians in another country. And suffice it to say that the king, the wise men, and the musicians in the orchestras were so great in the art of music that it defies description.

"One day, the greatest men in the state got together to boast of their musicianship. One said he could play wondrously on a certain instrument, another that he could do the same on another instrument, another that he knew how to play many instruments, and still another that he could play any instrument. Then a man bragged that he could imitate many instruments with his voice, another said that he could imitate the sound of the drum, and another the sound of the cannon going off. And I," so said the Beggar with the Twisted Neck, "I was there, and I stood up and said, 'My voice is greater than yours. And I will instantly prove it to you.

" 'If you are truly as talented musically as you say, come and let us see if you can save two states.

" 'Because there are two countries, and they are at least four thousand miles or more apart. And the people in both of these states cannot sleep at night, because every night, at sundown, all of them begin to wail in one horrible voice; men, women, and children—everyone wailing, until even the stones in the walls crumble from the sound. And it is the same in both these states, even though they are more than four thousand miles apart. Why do they wail so? Because of the sound of wailing that they hear.

" 'So if you are really as talented in the art of music as you say, come and let us see if you can help the people in these two states. Because only someone who can precisely imitate the sound of wailing that is heard there can save them.'

"They asked me, 'Can you take us there?' And I answered, 'I will take you there most assuredly.'

"And so we set off on the road to one of the two states. When we arrived, night fell, and the people in that state began their wailing. And the men that were with me also began to wail just like them. Immediately they realized that they didn't have the ability to help the people of those states. As soon as I saw this, I said to them, 'Perhaps, in any event, you would like to ask me where this sound of night wailing comes from?' So they asked me, 'Do you know?' And I answered, 'Yes, indeed I do.

" 'There are in this world two special birds, one male and one female. They are a unique couple, there is none other like them in this world. And behold, one fateful day, the female became lost. Her lover looked for her and could not find her. And she, upon finding herself lost, sought to find her loved one and could not find him. And so these two birds began wandering all over the world, seeking each other until they had gone astray and could no longer find their way. So each stayed where he was, and made himself a nest. The male built himself a nest near one of the two states, and the female built hers near the other. Although they are not anywhere near each other, they are close enough for their voices to carry from one state to the other. And so every evening, when night falls, the two birds begin to wail a mighty wail. He wails and weeps for the loved one he has lost, and she weeps that her lover is no more. And when the inhabitants of the two countries hear this terrible sound, they cannot restrain themselves, and so they too begin to wail, and sleep evades them.'

"The musicians heard my words," continued the Beggar with the Twisted Neck, "but they didn't want to believe me. They said, 'Can you take us to this place where the birds are nesting?' I answered, 'I could take you there, but you wouldn't be able to go there. If you cannot even take their wailing in this place, which is far from them, imagine how much worse it will be when you come closer! And don't bother suggesting that we go there during daylight hours. Because you should be advised that you wouldn't be able to get close even in the daytime, because you wouldn't be able to take the force of the great joy that takes place there. Because in the daytime hours, multitudes of birds gather around each of the two love birds, and they soothe them and make them happy with all kinds of merrymaking, and they tell them things to comfort them such as "The day will yet come when you will find each other." It is impossible to stand all that joy there. It is just that the sound of the merrymaking isn't heard at a distance, only the wailing that the two lovers do at night.'

"So the musicians asked me, 'Can you do something about this problem?' And I answered, 'Naturally. I can set the matter straight, because I can imitate all the sounds in the world. I can also throw my voice a great distance, so that it isn't heard in the place where I am standing, but instead it is heard far away. And it is true that I can imitate the sound of the female bird's voice, and I can send it to the place where the male bird is, and I can imitate his voice and send it to her. This way, they can be brought closer and closer together until the people in these two states will be relieved from their distress.'

"And again they didn't believe me, until I took them to the forest, and there they heard the sound of a door being opened and closed, and the rattling of the lock when it was locked. Afterward they heard the sound of a hunting rifle firing, and the voice of the hunter ordering his dog to run and fetch the game, and the sound of the dog as he pawed through the snow with difficulty. They looked here and there, and they could see nothing, nor did they hear the sounds as they came from my mouth, but only from a distance. So they were finally convinced that I could imitate all of these sounds, and carry my voice a great distance."

(Our rebbe did not continue this story, and it appears that he intentionally skipped over it.)

"So you see I have agreement from that state that I have a wondrous voice, and I can imitate every kind of sound in the world. And so I give you as a wedding gift that you should be like me."

And there was again a great gaiety and rejoicing at the wedding feast.

5

On the fifth day, the young couple remembered the fifth beggar who had appeared to them in the forest and had given them bread to eat. So again they cried with longing, saying, "If only the Humpbacked Beggar were here! If he were with us, how much greater would be our happiness." And just then he came and said, "Here I am at your wedding, and my gift for you is that you should be like me. That was the blessing I gave you there in the forest, and now I am giving it to you as a marriage gift.

"Do you think that I am a humpback? I am not at all humpbacked! It is just that my shoulders prove that the small conquers the large. And I have proof of this.

"Once upon a time, a group of men gathered together to talk, and they were telling tale after tale. Their conversation turned to boasting, and they said that they were blessed with the trait of the small being mightier than the large. The first one who said this was regaled with laughter and they all mocked him, but then others said the same thing, and they were listened to.

"The first boasted that his mind proved that the small conquers the large, because in his mind he carried thousands of men with their needs, their worries and experiences, all of them carried in his one small brain. Thus, his mind proved that the small is mightier than the large. They all laughed at him and said, 'Thousands of men my foot! You are nothing, and your so-called men are nothing!' Then one of them said, while still laughing, 'I too know an example of the small being greater than the large. Because once I saw a tall mountain on which was piled up all kinds of dirt and garbage. I was quite amazed and wondered from where all the filth and garbage could have come. Just then a man came up to me, and he said to me that all of this came from him, because he dwelt near the mountain and he threw all his refuse there; it consisted of all the garbage that collected in his house day after day. If so, he too proves that the small is greater than the large. He is like you!' And again they all laughed.

"Afterward another said that he too believed that the small conquers the large. He inherited a field that yields much fruit, and if you reckoned and piled up all the fruit that is grown there, you would find that there was no room on his land to hold so much fruit. Surely that proved that the small outweighed the large. And his listeners praised him.

"After him, another man got up and he said that he had an orchard that was very lovely, and in the summertime multitudes of people came to his orchard from all corners of the state; from earls and other aristocrats down to the simple folk, all of them came to refresh themselves in the shade of the trees and to stroll the paths between the rows. But in fact there wasn't enough room for his orchard to hold all of these people at once. So surely this showed that the small was greater than the large. And what he said was well received.

"Still another boasted that he could prove that the small was greater than the large, because he served as the minister to a great king, and every day people came to him from every end of the state—some came to praise the king, some to lay before him their difficulties, others to submit their claims— and he, the king's minister, listened to all of them and repeated what they said to the king, and the king's minister did this in very few words. In a few short sentences he covered all of the praise, requests, and claims that had been brought before the king. So it seemed his economy of words showed that the small is greater than the large.

"Then another stood up, after him, saying that his silence proved that the small conquers the large. Many accusers denounced him, slandering him and speaking evil about him, while he remained silent. And with his silence, he closed the mouths of his accusers; with his silence he was victorious. And that proves that his silence was the small conquering the large.

"Still another boasted that he could prove the small was greater than the large, because he led a poor blind man, who could not find his way alone. And whereas the poor blind man was very big in size, this one, who led him along the road, was very small in size. And that proved that the small was greater than the large.

"Then I," continued the Humpbacked Beggar, "I was among them, and I got up and spoke: 'Behold, I have heard your words, and I know what each of you is expressing. Truly all of you have some of the measure of the small being greater than the large. And this last man, who said he led a blind man, means that he guided the wheel of the moon. Because the moon, which has no light of its own, is like a poor blind man. Therefore the strength of this last man is greater, in the trait of the small being mightier than the large, than the rest of you. Because this little man guides the wheel of the great moon, and because of him the world can exist, because the world needs the moon. But I am greater than all of you, in this virtue, even greater than the last man. And I will show you my proof of this.

" 'Once upon a time there was a group of men who belonged to a certain sect that inquired until they found out that every living thing in the world has a particular place of shade, in which it alone longs to go for shelter and rest; and every bird in the world has a particular branch on which it wants to dwell. Therefore, they asked, is there in the world one special tree whose shade would be chosen by all living things for refuge, and whose branches would be chosen as a nesting place by all the birds in the sky? They questioned and studied until they found that there was indeed a tree such as this. And once they had contemplated in their minds the great delight it would be to find shelter in the shade of such a tree, they all wanted to go there. But they argued in their opinions as to which was the best route to travel. Some of them said one had to get to the tree from the east, others said from the west; some said this way and others that, and they couldn't reach a decision among themselves, until a wise man said to them, "Since you cannot agree about the way to get there, it is better that you think about who will be going, because not every man can go to that tree. Only those men whose virtues are like the virtues of the tree itself can go to it. This tree has three roots. The first root is faith, the second reverence, and the third humility. Now the body of the tree is truth and from it all of the branches ramify. And a man cannot reach this tree unless he has attained all of these virtues."

" 'So did the wise man speak to the members of that sect, and his words went right to their hearts, since they knew, themselves, that all of them were not worthy enough to go to the tree: some of them had some of these virtues but some of them did not. To separate into two groups—one to go and one to stay—was unacceptable to them, because they felt love, friendship, and unity for each other, and therefore they did not leave. Instead, they struggled and worked very hard, until all of them attained those virtues. And when they had come to have these virtues, they no longer disagreed in their opinions, but instead they all agreed as to the way to travel to reach the tree.

" 'And so they set off, all of them as one, and they walked for some time until they saw the tree from the distance. They stood there looking, and behold, they saw that the tree was not standing in place, because the tree did not take up space at all. And they were amazed and confused and they didn't know what to think; for if the tree was not standing in a place, how would they be able to get to it?'

"And I, who was with them there," continued the Humpbacked Beggar, "I told them, 'I can bring you to the tree. Even though all of you can prove that the small is greater than the large, you still need to take up space, that is, you are dependent upon a small place to hold many. And since this tree is in the dimension beyond place, you cannot get there by yourselves. But I am on a superior level of the small being greater than the large; I can be found at the end of place, on the border between place and nonplace. So I can take you from place to beyond place.' And I took them, and carried them to the tree.

"So it is known that I have the agreement from the men of that sect that I am superior when it comes to the small being mightier than the large. And that is why I look humpbacked, because I carry so much on my shoulders. And now I am giving you, as a wedding gift, that you should be like me."

And there was a great gaiety and rejoicing there.

6

On the sixth day, amidst all their happiness, the young couple remembered the beggar who had no hands, who had appeared to them in the forest and who had given them bread to eat, and again they began to cry and say with longing, "If only the Beggar with No Hands could be brought here!" And while they so cried, he came and said, "Look, here I am!" And he hugged and kissed them and said, "I have come to your wedding, and your gift from me is that you should be like me.

"Do you believe me to be a handicapped man with no hands? I am not at all handicapped and I have great strength in my hands. It is just that I choose not to use the strength in my hands in this world, because I need them for something else. And I have the proof of this from the palace which is known as the Water Palace.

"Once upon a time, a certain number of men gathered together, and each was boasting of the strength in his hands. One said that when he shot an arrow he could retrieve it with the strength that was in his hands. I asked him, 'Which kind of arrow can you retrieve, as there are ten kinds of arrows? That is, every arrow is dipped in a special poison and there are ten kinds of poisons; some harm more and some less.' And I also asked him if he could cause the arrow to come back, before it reached the target, or if he could also retrieve it after it had hit the target. He answered, 'Even after it reaches the target, I can remove it with my bare hands.' I asked again, 'But which kind of arrow is it that you can return?' He answered me, 'The kind of arrow that is dipped in such and such a poison is the kind I can retrieve with my bare hands.' I said to him, 'If so, you cannot heal the princess, because you can retrieve only one kind of arrow.'

"Another boasted that he had such strength in his hands that what he takes he is in fact giving: that is, his receiving is giving. I said to him, 'It is said that you are a philanthropist; but what kind of charity do you give, as there are ten kinds of charity?' He said that he gave money. I said, 'If so, you cannot heal the princess, because you cannot go to the place where she is. You could only pass one of the many walls that surround the place where she is.'

"Still another boasted that he imparted wisdom to all of the rulers in the world, by laying his hands on them. Such was the strength in his hands. So I asked him, 'What kind of wisdom can you give, as there are ten measures of wisdom?' He answered, 'This kind of wisdom.' I said to him, 'If so, you cannot heal the princess either, because you cannot feel her pulse. There are ten kinds of pulses and you know only one.'

"Now another bragged that he could stop a severe storm with his bare hands; and he could temper it until it was nothing more than an ordinary breeze. I asked this one, 'Which kind of wind can you stop with your hands, as there are ten different kinds of wind?' He answered, 'Such and such kind of wind.' So I said to him, 'If so, you can't heal the princess either, because you cannot play more than one tune for her, and there are ten different tunes. Music is the cure for the princess, and you, who can only play one of the ten kinds of melody, cannot cure her.'

"So finally they said to me, 'So what can *you* do?' And I answered them, 'I can do everything that you can't do. I have all nine of the talents that you are lacking. Let me tell you a story:

" 'Once there was a king who was obsessed with a particular princess. And he kept coming to see her and he tried all kinds of tricks to win her, until finally he won her. He brought her to his castle and he lived there happily with her.

" 'One night the king had a dream in which the princess rose up against him and killed him. The king awoke from his sleep, and his mind was very unsettled. He immediately called his wise men, the dream interpreters, so that they could interpret his dream for him. The wise men interpreted it, in the most obvious way: that is, that the dream would come true in the future, and that the princess would turn against him and kill him. And the king didn't know what to do. What should be done with her? Should she be killed? He was very distressed about her. Should she be banished? Then another man might come and take her. How hard he had tried to win her, and now would someone else be able to take her away from him? Was it possible? And how did he know that just because he had her sent away, the dream wouldn't come true anyway? Couldn't she come back in secret and kill him?

" 'The king was completely confused; he didn't know what to do. Meanwhile his love for her died, because of the dream, and her love for him changed until it became a strong hate. Because the princess could no longer stand this hatred she felt, she fled from the castle, and nobody knew where she had gone.

" 'The king sent messengers to find her, and they returned, and told the king that they had seen her walking about near the Water Palace.

" 'There exists a palace that is made entirely of water. Ten walls surround it, one in front of the other, and all of them are made of water. And the bridge that leads to the palace is also made of water. Within the palace is a large courtyard and there are oak trees and fruit trees, and they too are water. And no living creature can enter this palace, because anyone who does, instantly drowns in the water. How can I describe it? So rare is the beauty of the palace it cannot be described or imagined at all.

" 'As soon as the king heard that the princess was to be found near the Water Palace, he took his home guard and went out to recapture her.

" 'The princess saw the king and his men as they came near, and she said to herself, "I will run into the palace, because it is better that I drown in this water than fall into his hands. And there is always the chance that I will be lucky, and I will succeed in entering the palace."

" 'As soon as the king saw that the princess was fleeing into the water, he said to his men, "If that's the way it is, shoot her! If she dies, she dies!" And they shot at her with all ten kinds of arrows that had been dipped in ten different kinds of poison. Then the king and his soldiers pursued her, and they all drowned in the water. But the princess succeeded in entering the palace. She passed through all of the gates, and their ten walls, until she had entered the palace. And when she had come into the palace, she collapsed.'

"And I," continued the Beggar with No Hands, "I am the doctor who is chosen to heal the princess. Because I have in my hands all ten kinds of charity, and that is how I can get past the ten walls of the palace. Because the walls are the waves of the sea, and they stand like walls because the winds hold them up and make them stand. And I can take out all ten kinds of arrows from her body. And I know all ten pulses, because in each of my ten fingers, I can feel one of each of the ten pulses. And I can heal her with the ten kinds of melody. Therefore, I am the one who will cure the princess.

"So you see, I have great strength in my hands. And now, I am offering us for your wedding gift that you should be like me."

And there was a great rejoicing and gaiety there.

7

Our Rebbe said, "This tale is very difficult for me to tell, but since I have begun, I am obliged to finish. In this story, there is not even one word that does not have in it a special meaning. And those who are knowledgeable about stories can understand some of the allusions that are in it."

In spite of this, our Rebbe did not tell the end of the story. We were not worthy to hear from his lips the story of the seventh day, with the Beggar that had No Feet, nor the end of the story about the son of the king and his father, the king who had transferred his kingdom to his son while the father was still alive. Nor will we be worthy to hear it until the Messiah comes in his mercy, may he come speedily in our days, Amen.

Retold from the Yiddish and Hebrew sources
by Yehuda Yaari
translated from the Hebrew by
Pamela Altfeld Malone

The Seventh Beggar's Tale
by Richard Siegel

On the seventh and final day of the wedding feast—the Shabbat—a new level of joy pervaded the cave, for the world was at rest and peace permeated the earth. The great words of unification had been pronounced, the king was with the queen, and shortly the bride and bridegroom were to be joined for now and for eternity. Yet the pair sat together silently and shared a common thought: "If only we could once again see our old friend from the forest, the lame beggar who cared for us on the seventh day of our first journey together. Then would our joy be complete." As they thought these words, a soft shadow covered the entrance to the cave and the lame beggar stood straight and tall between shadow and sun, between the inside and the outside. "Here I am—to join in your wedding celebration. Was there any doubt that I would come? At that time when we first met, I offered you my blessing that you might be like me. Today I offer this to you as my gift. You think that my legs are crippled and that I cannot walk. Rather, my legs are straight and strong. But the places of this world are of no importance and its roads hold no attraction for me. Rather than follow the false paths and vain strivings of others, I am my own path. And as I go, my legs carry me—but in my going I bring together the distant and unite the separated. For this my legs are strong. And of this ability, I have testimony from the great men who live in the kingdom of Knowledge.

"There was a time when all the great men gathered together to tell of their experiences in order to determine who had the greatest knowledge. For it was reasoned that from experience derives knowledge and from knowledge the world can be saved. One, who was white-haired with age and had a weather-beaten face, rose and said, 'For seventy years I have traveled the seven seas and I have knowledge of the seas—their tides and their depths and of all matter concerning them!' And I asked, 'Tell me, wise and withered man, can you swim up on the land?' He was serene as he answered, 'Of the sea I know much; with the waters I can do much; and as for swimmers, none can surpass the surety of my stroke—but of the land I know nothing, neither how to walk nor swim upon it.' 'Then,' I replied, 'you cannot keep the world from drowning. Your knowledge will not save her.'

"Now, a husky, muscular man stood and claimed, 'I have traveled the seven lands and have all the keys to their nature. So I may walk where I wish and know the truth of the way.' But I questioned even this knowledge: 'Can you, honored sir, walk on the air? For if you cannot, the world is in danger of fracturing.' He answered gravely, 'I have knowledge of the lands, as I have told, but this I cannot do, for I know nothing of the air and its vapors.' There followed a third mighty man, thin with long fingers, and with his neck stiffened back, who spoke that he had traversed the seven mountains and had knowledge of the highest heights which can be seen. But when I asked if he had ever descended to the valley, he answered that in his experience he had only ascended to the peaks, and the valleys were not his concern. I knew then that he could not keep the world from putrefying in its own dung. As the fourth man rose to speak, everyone froze rigid and silent, for he had an aura of awful mystery about him, and shadows covered his face, even in the sun. Slowly and in a whisper, he spoke: 'Others indeed are well experienced and possess great knowledge, but only I have secured the knowledge of true consequence to the world. Into the seven levels below I have descended, and I know the traps and illusions which plague mankind.' 'And can you look up from the depths?' I challenged. 'There is no "up" in the depths,' he spit back. 'All is down, for each disillusionment, each horror, leads down to another, and the darkness is so complete there is no light—no "up."' His words weighed so heavily upon me that I could hardly breathe, but I screamed out, 'Your knowledge cannot save the world even from its own night. But know: day follows night as night follows day—and as the night gets darker and darker, the day approaches closer and closer.' For a long time all were silent—until, in a surprisingly soft but resounding voice, the fifth man rose and began to speak: 'You have all traveled far and experienced wondrous things. I, however, have been where you have been and also where you have not been—for I have ascended through the seven rooms above and have reached the highest heights.' I recognized him and asked with great reverence, 'Will you not stay with us and teach us of your knowledge?' 'I cannot,' he replied, 'for the force which lifts is so great that I can no longer bear to resist. To remain with you is now beyond my will.' It was not easy for me to respond. Already the others were marveling at his wisdom, thinking that no one could be more knowledgeable and believing that his experience covered all ground. 'Yet,' I protested, 'not even you can save the world—for it may soon die of deceit and hatred.'

"In one body, the five rose up against me, and with a threatening voice they demanded of me, 'You who question our lives and the worth of our existence, what do you know? You who are lame, where have you been, and how is your experience greater than ours? In what manner can you save the world?'

" 'Of who I am and of what my knowledge consists, you will learn quite soon—but for now, come with me, each with his own knowledge and experiences, and let us set foot in the king's garden. However, know first that in the king's garden is a vast maze covering acres and acres of land, and sea and air. Few who enter ever find their way out but spend the rest of their lives in constant torment. For the mystery of this maze is that he who enters always finds himself in an unfamiliar place and his past experience is of no value in such a situation. But those who break the maze and free themselves are rewarded with an eternal life of peace and harmony.'

"Each man still believed that his knowledge was of superior worth in the world and that if he could not save the world (which he still thought he could), at least he was certain that his experience would always bring him comfort and aid in any situation. So, undaunted by my warning, each entered the king's garden and maze. But once inside, it seemed to each that the world had begun to spin inside out. Nowhere could rest be found but at every turn were unfamiliar surroundings, hostile and terrifying. To add to the misery they realized that there was no turning back, and every moment increased the fear that there would be no way out. For the sailor, there was only land; for the land traveler, there was only air; for the mountaineer, there were only valleys; for the depth seeker, there were only elevations; and for the heights attainer, there were only depths. And each despaired and cried out at his fate. All reason departed from them and they soon began thrashing about, beating whatever was near in the fading hope that something would yield. Even to observe them was unbearable, for their agony was so great. They were totally consumed in misery and fear, and the horror of being forever strangers in a strange land—never wanting to be where they were, never knowing how to get where they wanted to go.

"I also entered and lay down among the grass and bushes. I knew the grass, and it shifted to make a soft bed for my body when I needed rest. And I knew and loved the trees, and they gave me shade when the sun was too hot. I also knew and loved and respected the sun, and it gave me warmth when I was cold and light when I had enough of darkness. In this way, I knew and loved and respected them all—grass, trees, sun, moon, rain, clouds, flowers, wind. And I was exceedingly happy—so that my entire body shed news of my joy. I thought only of the glory of Creation, and the love of the Creator, and the mystery of the Infinity of Infinities. In turn, each man in his agony caught a glimpse of me and saw in the radiance of my Being an aspect of his own life, but saw the joy and beauty of it rather than the pain and suffering which he experienced. As they froze there, mystified and awed at my Presence, I tried to reveal the mystery to them.

" 'Wherever you have been and wherever you go, you gather the insights and knowledge of that place, but when you must depart in a different direction, you are lost and stumble, and curse out of your ignorance. All of your knowledge will never bring peace to any part of the world. It is not enough to know the "center," for to truly know the sea, land, mountains, depths, or heights, you must also know the shoreline, the horizon, the downslope, the brink of the abyss, and the limits of the void. And can the sea-line be distinguished from the shoreline, or the edge of land from the edge of sky, or the ascent from the descent, or the brink of the abyss from the ledge of existence, or the limits of the void from the limits of the fullness? To know this, then, is to bring peace to the world.

" 'You once asked me who I am, where I have been, and what is my knowledge. The answers stand before you. I am suspended in air, and I am supported by earth; I am carried by the water, and I carry the water; my thoughts reach up and are met by thoughts reaching down; I am falling in the vastness of love, and I support through the offering of love; from where I am there is no mountain and no valley except for the mountain and valley. I have brought down the heavens and I have lifted the earth and I bind them with Love. And wherever I am there is Peace, but can you say where I am not? Am I not like you?'

"The men were silent for a long time after this—an eternity passed as each slowly realized that I was in him and he was in me. We were of one nature and it is a vast and marvelous one. After the stillness, each rose to embrace me and one another—and each returned to his place of former agony. But now, they lay down in peace—for each could see what was not seen before. From the land, water could be seen, and thank God for the land for if there were only water, there would be nothing; but the land gives shape to water and the water gives shape to the land. They love each other and take pleasure in the sharing. So, also, with the others. From this time, there were no traps and no maze. Each man was where he wanted to be. Each was joyous in himself—beyond the need or testimony of words. Peace and Harmony arose from their joy and filled each day to overflowing.

"But now, my children, my lovers, the Shabbat has almost passed and all your guests must leave. I depart, leaving my gift—may you have the power of my legs and may you be like me. May you soon know the joy and peace which the Shabbat brings to the week and the week to the Shabbat and each of you to the other."

Amen and Amen

Two Worlds

by M. J. Berditchevsky

It happened a long time ago, in the beginning of the fifth century of the fifth millennium. There was a religious Jew who lived in the land of Walachia. His name was Eliezer. Now this man was of a good family and very learned. A God-fearing man from his youth, he observed all of the commandments to the letter of the law. He lived far from the men of the city, in a small inn built on the outskirts of the town within the circle of a mountain where a narrow path led to the riverbank. The river divided two ranges of hilly mountains, and between these mountains passed the ships that were loaded with the sheep and the wolves of mankind. They came from near and far. Most of the travelers did not detain themselves for long at that riverbank; only those whose provisions had run out on the road turned to the inn-keeper, who gave them food and drink. He dealt with everyone in an up-right and honest manner, and made each and every man feel welcome. So too was his wife observant and pure of heart in all her deeds. She did her husband's bidding, and she had no quarrel with the Lord even though he had closed up her womb. She rose early to do her work, serving the guests and doing what her husband wanted of her, for she thought of her husband as the most important guest of all. Yet another man lived in their house; he was part slave and part free, and his job was to accompany all passersby in time of danger, until they were safely on their way.

Day followed day, and night, night, and in the inn peace and tranquillity reigned. Early in the morning, before either the sun or man rose to do their daily work, the innkeeper immersed his flesh in water, on hot days as well as rainy ones, and then prayed in a fixed place at the moment of sunrise; so that he could take upon himself the yoke of the Kingdom of Heaven, and with all his heart reach at once all that is both above and below, the Four Winds of Heaven. Then at midnight, that hour when all the world rests from the toil of the day, he would ascend the roof and there he would prostrate himself in the dust and weep over the disappearance of the Divine Presence.

And behold, on one of those warm nights, when the sky was dressed in blue, and so too the face of the water reflected that sparkling blue, at that time of night when the Holy One, praised be He, sits on His throne and roars like a lion, "Woe to them, to the children who were exiled," pirates of the night came and captured the innkeeper while he was yet sitting in his sackcloth and ashes, and they took him across the seas and sold him into slav-ery, there among those nations where an Israelite is forbidden to go, yea, it is a capital offense.

There among those people he spent many days.

As his years lengthened, he began to think about fleeing and returning to his homeland, but he was stopped by means of a dream in the night: "Do not press the hour!"

After some time, he came to serve one of the king's ministers. And his master saw that God was with the slave, so he released him from his work in the house and the field once a day; so that when the master came from the king's gate, he was to greet him and bring him a vessel of water in which he would wash his hands and feet.

Every day when his master came from the king's palace, he was happy and of good heart. Only once did he come home depressed and his face did not reflect its usual gladness.

Eliezer asked him, "Why has your face fallen?"

"Danger hovers over my land, and I am afraid the enemy is mightier than we. I must lead my people on the day of battle, and I do not know how we can be victorious over the enemy, because the war surrounds us on all sides."

"Do not fear, salvation is the Lord's!"

That night, after Eliezer recited the *Shema* at his bedside, an Angel of the Lord appeared to him and revealed to him the military strategy with which to overcome the enemy. The next morning, before his master rose to go to the king, Eliezer hurried to tell him of what had been revealed to him from Heaven. His military advice was straightforward and wise, and it was well received by his master.

Then the minister made haste to run to the king to tell him of his slave's vision.

"This is good counsel," cried out the king in good spirits. "Let the crown of victory rest upon his head!"

And so it was.

Because of this Eliezer was freed from slavery and became one of the king's ministers, and the king advanced him above all his other advisers. Eliezer was made a wealthy nobleman. He had much property, much silver and gold, and he lived as one of the privileged noblemen in the king's court. But he did not profane the Sabbath, nor did he defile himself with forbidden foods, and under his purple cloak he wore sackcloth.

The king gave him a wife from among the most beautiful maidens in the land. She was pure in all her deeds. She felt in her heart that this man, who had tied the wedding knot with her, was a foreigner, and this foreigner pleased her and won her heart. They lived in her house for many years, but he did not touch her.

God was with him, and he was successful in everything he did. Because of him, the land was blessed, all enemies who rose up against them were defeated. There was peace without fear and the land flourished. But Eliezer remembered and longed for his land, when he saw this city built on its high hill, while the city of God was humbled, dashed to the bottom of Sheol.

And when the sun would sink in the evening, he would look out the window of his castle at the clouds coming from a faraway land to cover the tops of all the hills that dotted this capital city, and a silent sadness would press against his heart. He remembered his people, his wife and the land of his birth, there in the farthest corner of the world, and his spirit mourned.

"Why do you look so unhappy?" his wife would press him daily.

"Because I am a Hebrew! I was kidnapped from the land of the Hebrews," he suddenly revealed to her.

She was seized with terror and fright. A catastrophic fear threatened to envelop her. When she regained her strength and steadied herself on her feet, her face expressed amazement and her heart was torn with anger. Her soul was bound to his, and yet there now was a deep chasm that lay between them. For a moment her anger raged and stormed, and she threatened to send both of them before the king: Let her die with him! And then she said she would risk her life and go wherever he went. Should she give up her people and her native land for a strange people, because he did not recognize the god of her fathers?

Love and hate, fear and rage tore at her heart. Finally, she sent him away secretly, providing him with many provisions for his journey. But when he left, desolation pierced her heart.

He wandered a very long time, going from city to city and kingdom to kingdom. Forests and wild places prolonged his journey. But God was with him at all times so that nothing stood as a stumbling block to him. Many days passed before he reached his home, and when at last he did, he was one hundred and one years old. His wife still lived in the inn and rose early to do her work. The Lord remembered her in her old age, and she bore Eliezer a son, and the night he was born a great star appeared in the sky, and around the star a crown glowed in the distance. The child Israel grew to be a beautiful lad, with golden curls. He played in the forests and skipped on the hills, for there were many lovely mountains where the birds of the heavens dwelled and so too the sweet bird of freedom.

In the glory of his advanced age, the old man came to see Elijah, the Tishbite, who spoke to Eliezer in the name of God:

"This son, who was born to you, will be a Lamp unto Israel!" Before the young lad went out into the world to be with his brethren, and before he became great, a "Lamp unto Israel," a "Master of the Divine Name," he lived a simple life, a most pure and innocent existence. It was as if life itself spoke to him, as if he could make all things speak. In the heavens above and the earth below, in the quiet of the hills, and the waves of the sea, and in the recesses of his heart—he could hear the sound of all living things.

When the day's shadows fell, the boy would go off to be alone among the rocks that cut into the mountain, leading to a small woods below, and he would wander far from his father's house. And his likeness would rise above the rocky place and penetrate the red sky of sunset, which covered most of the canopy of Heaven above his head. At that time he did leave his world, as if he were not of this world at all.

So too when he was in the house, sitting at the table with his mother and father, then too it was as if he were not in this world, but his likeness hovered far away from them, there among the rocks above and the waves of the sea below.

One day, early in the morning, his mother died suddenly. At the time of her death, and when she lay with the candles burning, and later when they carried her to her grave there in the clefts of the rocks, and later still, when they had set the last stone in place, the boy was perplexed as if he did not know what had happened to him on that day.

Some time later the father was told by Heaven: "Set your house in order, for you will be gathered to your forefathers!"

On that day, between sunset and sunrise, the father sat with his son, the old man and the young man, under a red sky, and Heaven and all its hosts were gathered, the clouds were rent, and here and there they came together as if to darken the edge of the sky.

The father was dressed in white, he wrapped himself in a white shroud and prepared himself for a long rest, the setting of his sun. His large black eyes darted to and fro, looking in splendor at the boy who sat quietly on the tooth of a rock. The boy had blue eyes, and his face reflected that beauty which comes from a sense of wonder. Neither were his eyes calm and still, for there was reflected in them a great question. But the two of them, the father and the son, neither asked any questions nor gave any answers.

A peaceful sadness filled the heart of the old man. He was ready to enter the world to come while still feeling the two worlds touch. He knew that his young son was destined for greatness—that he would be a Lamp unto Israel—but now, while he was still with his father, he would be left abandoned to himself, totally alone. Suddenly Eliezer's lips moved and he whispered: "My son, I see that you will light my candle—remember that God is with you."

The boy was silent. All around a mute sadness, the stillness that is in splendor. And now the end . . . the clouds gathered, turning black, and then from above the Angel of Death swooped down. He had many eyes like lightning bolts, they were like waves of fire on a black sea.

A great wind came from the north at that time, seconds before his death.

Night, light and death

The wind subsided. The breath of that righteous man went out in purity, and he was gathered to his forefathers in a ripe old age. Even the flowing river was quiet in that stillness. There at the edge of the bed, which was covered in white sheets, between pillars of fire, the boy and the night stood at the foot of the bed.

And at its head, the Divine Presence.

Translated from the Hebrew
by Pamela Altfeld Malone

The Besht and P'ney Yehoshua
by Rabbi Zalman Schachter

There was a little town, not too far from Lemberg, where the Besht officiated as a *shochet* and as a *chazan* during the High Holy Days. The Rabbi of Lvov was at that time the P'ney Yehoshua, a great *tzaddik*, whose fame in Torah spread throughout the lands of the Council of the Four Countries. He made a decree, and a wise one it was, that all the folk who lived in the little villages in Galicia which belonged to Lvov's area were to assemble for the High Holy Days, in that city, in order to have services, to be instructed in the ways of the Lord in piety and *mussar*, and to pay their rightful share of the communal taxes and assessments. Then, to his dismay, he heard that in the town of Yozlovitz, a young man was conducting services for the High Holy Days. After Rosh Hashanah had passed, he sent the beadle of the court to Yozlovitz to tell that congregation and their leader to assemble in their holiday garb, in the city of Lvov, and to repeat the service in full view of the entire congregation of Lvov, and, of course, of all the schoolchildren. When the poor people of Yozlovitz raised the point of obedience with their rabbi (this was the Besht, yet in those silent years before he became renowned), he said, "Of course, we must show our obedience to the Rabbi, and furthermore we have nothing to fear." The good folk feared the ridicule more than anything else, but upon their leader's agreement to be obedient to the *beit din* of Lvov, they all traveled into town.

What hooting and noises greeted them when they entered the town! All the *cheder* children vied with one another in heaping those abuses that children can permit themselves in the anonymity of childhood, and the vulgar righteousness that they experience in doing so. The Besht continued on, and began in the synagogue his recital of the poetic portions of the prayers with the proper melodies. When he was to do the recitation of the *Amidah*, the Rabbi feared that soon the mocking would turn from the mocking of a person and a disobedient community to the mocking of the sacred service, and surveyed the congregation with a glance. Whereupon the Besht said, "Now that I am about to continue with the poetry of the *Amidah*, only those who have fully amended the sins of their youth by *teshuvah* can remain." Then he began. First the children felt the tremor of awe, and left the synagogue, then their elders, until only the Rabbi remained. He walked over to the prayer desk and said to the Besht, "Young man, I commend you for your obedience. People who know how to conduct prayer like you have my permission to do so, even outside of Lemberg."

Reb Zusheh and the Dowry
by Rabbi Zalman Schachter

The holy Rebbe, Reb Zusheh, surely deserves a double title, as does his brother who always is called the holy Rebbe, Reb Melech, and their master who is known as the Rebbe, Reb Baer. You want to know why he deserves a double title? Sha, there was a man who once asked Reb Shneur Zalman of Liadi, the author of the *Tanya*, why he addressed Reb Zusheh in a letter, as *HaRav HaGa'on*, the mighty master and prince of the Torah, since Reb Zusheh was said not to have been able to master all the great finesses of Torah scholarship. Reb Shneur Zalman replied, "There are *mitzvot*, commandments that can be fulfilled with the limbs of the body. He who knows all the commandments, their interpretations, their laws, details, knows them from the ground up, surely deserves to be called Ga'on. There are some other commandments known as the commandments of the heart, and Reb Zusheh is fairly accomplished in all of these and he is the master of this entire generation in the duties of the heart. It is for this reason that he deserves the title Ga'on." But then, among those who knew, it was said that the Rebbe Reb Zusheh also had within him the soul of Rebbe Yishmael, the high priest, and it was because of that soul that he did not lack anything, even in the manifest part of the Torah dealing with the duties of the limbs.

A great humble soul was the Rebbe, Reb Zusheh. His wife once asked him, before he became known, to see to it that he could marry off his daughters; that he should raise the necessary dowry. So how was he to make the money? His wife suggested that he visit his master, Rebbe Reb Baer, get from him a letter, addressed generally to all men of good heart, to solicit their support for Reb Zusheh, so that the man might accomplish his mission, marry off his daughters and return to the service of the Lord, to his study of the Torah, and meditation. Since the *mitzvah* of marrying off daughters is a very great one, Reb Zusheh listened to his wife, and traveled to his master, Rebbe Reb Baer. Rebbe Reb Baer said, "Zusheh, no need for you to travel." His master very well knew of Zusheh's custom never to eat before he begged God that He provide him with food out of His mercy. Mind you, Rebbe

Reb Zusheh did this even when the food was already served in front of him, so thoroughly did he depend on God's blessing, and so deep was his reliance. So the Rebbe Reb Baer said, "Reb Zusheh, you stay here. What you need will come to you." Whereupon Rebbe Reb Zusheh made off to the Beit Hamidrash and soon enough got started on his Torah and prayers.

In a few weeks, a rich man, from whom the blessing of children had been withheld, came to the Rebbe and solicited his blessings. Said the Rebbe Reb Baer, "There is one person whose blessing can help you. He sits in my Beit Hamidrash; he, too, has a concern about children, but these are his own. You give him three hundred rubles with which to marry off his daughters, and you can rest assured that his blessing will be powerful for you to become a father within a year." The rich man went to Reb Zusheh. Reb Zusheh thanked him for the *mitzvah,* and said that his master, Rebbe Reb Baer, had already integrated a blessing into his life and he need not fear. He would also give him his own blessing, although it wasn't even necessary.

Reb Zusheh went to take leave of his master and started for home on foot. The master was then in Rovneh. When he came to the edge of town, Reb Zusheh noticed a group of people standing around a woman who had fainted. He soon found out that she had brought some 300 rubles to town to do shopping for her little store, and then as she came to town she had noticed that she had either lost her money, or it had been stolen. Reb Zusheh, being the owner of 300 rubles, couldn't stand to see the despair and the pain of the woman. When they revived her he said, "I have found your money, my dear woman, and I will give it to you." He counted off 290 rubles and he gave them to her. She began to scream, asking for the other ten, and Reb Zusheh said that was all that he had, having spent the other ten. The woman began to scream again, and soon enough the police were at her side, she filed a complaint against Reb Zusheh, and placed handcuffs around Reb Zusheh as he was led through town to the jeers of children and abuse from adults.

The noise of this procession brought the Rebbe Reb Baer to the stoop, and upon seeing Reb Zusheh being led in handcuffs by the gendarme, he inquired. As soon as he was told what had happened he surmised, of course, that Reb Zusheh had given his daughters' dowry away. Reb Baer paid the ten rubles, got the woman to withdraw the complaint, and, finally asked Reb Zusheh, "Zusheh, Zusheh, my child. You didn't spend the ten rubles yet. If you had decided to be so generous as to give her your daughters' dowry, why did you not give her all 300 rubles?" Reb Zusheh, in a warm smile, replied, "Had I given her the 300 rubles she would have thanked me profusely. Everybody would have thought that this is very nice and decent of me to return the money to the woman, and while I still would have had a *mitzvah,* it would have been tainted by the praise of flesh and blood, and by my reaction to the praise. So I decided to have the *mitzvah* and the abuse in order to do what I did purely for His sake, be He blessed."

Ah, that was a *tzaddik*, Rebbe Zusheh. You want to know what happened to his daughters? Simply this. The Maggid of Mezeritch, Rebbe Reb Baer, collected the sum himself and sent it on to Reb Zusheh's wife, thus making sure that Zusheh would not encounter another set of *mitzvot* on his way home.

A Good Laugh

by S. Ansky

Frankly, I just don't feel like telling you any more stories. And do you know why? Because when you hear my stories, you get too excited.

At the close of the Sabbath, I told you how the holy rabbi, the Baal Shem Tov, speaking the words, "Liberator of prisoners," in the Eighteen Benedictions, broke down the iron gates of a prison and liberated Jews who had been arrested for a blood libel. Your eyes shone, you smacked your lips, you cried: "What a miracle!"

But for me, it was as if you had said that when Jews are imprisoned and tortured because of a libel, that's natural, but when they're set free, that's a miracle! You concluded from my story that the Good Lord introduced injustice as a natural thing, but luckily there are wonder-rabbis who prevent His injustice with miracles.

Just look at the slough one can get stuck down in from too much fervor and excitement!

Well, you will ask me, where does the power of wonder-rabbis lie if not in miracles? And I'll say to that: Their power isn't as great as you may think. No greater than the strength of an angel. Now angels are no more than messengers, and wonder-rabbis merely carry the messages of the Good Lord, blessed be His Name. A greater one does something important, a lesser one something less important. And that's all. None of them work miracles! There are no wonders! Everything is quite natural.

However, if I tell you that you have to listen to a hasidic tale without ardor or excitement, that doesn't mean that you can take it lightly—like a fairy tale about how once upon a time there was a rabbi and a rebbetsin, and all that. No! On the contrary. If you restrain your ardor and excitement, then you have to listen very attentively, you have to get into it fully. A hasidic tale has to be studied almost religiously, the way you pore over the Talmud, and perhaps even more profoundly. . . .

But now, listen to a story about the Baal Shem Tov.

1

One wintery day, the Baal Shem Tov and his followers were relaxing from their religious studies. They were sitting together, having drinks, smoking pipes, singing, and talking a bit. They talked about this and that, but their words were filled with a strange force. No matter what they talked about, even the deepest mysteries of the Kabbalah, everyone understood. Each word of theirs had windows to all levels of understanding.

And that was the secret of why their voices could be heard from one end of the world to the other.

When Hasids drink and croon, they are sure to be merry. And when they are merry—they laugh.

Whereupon Dovid Leykes said:

"Laughter is a fine thing. One can serve the Creator better with laughter and joy than with bitter tears."

The Baal Shem Tov heard him and said, almost to himself:

"There is an even greater level of humor, when, instead of laughing, you are laughed *at*. . . ."

Having spoken, he said no more.

His followers crooned to his words and meditated on them as though unrolling a scroll of the Torah.

Wolf Kitses responded:

"When I laugh for joy, I feel a widening of my soul. But when someone else laughs at me, I become like a stool under his feet, a footstool on which the man who's laughing can stand and put himself higher. And that puts me on a higher level."

But Dovid Firkes protested:

"No! There's something else behind it! If someone laughs at me, it means that what I've said or done is a surprise to the man who's laughing. And the instant I've done something surprising in the world, I've raised myself to a higher level."

But then, Ber Mezeritsher explained in his faint voice:

"If you add up the numerical values of the Hebrew letters in the word *tskhok* [laughter] and in *nitsokhn* [victory], they work out to equal sums. Now since victory can only come at the end of a war and is based on things that have happened, it belongs to the category of the past. And since the laughter of victory is a cruel thing, it is material in nature. And thus, the opponent, the one that's laughed at, is of the future and spiritual in nature."

The Baal Shem Tov smiled and said:

"You know what? Why don't we go for a drive? Perhaps on the way, someone, somewhere, will laugh at us, and you'll understand what it's all about."

The Hasids were delighted. Going for a drive with the Baal Shem Tov was always a holiday, and there was sure to be a surprise in store for them.

So they told Alexei, the Baal Shem Tov's manservant, to harness the horse.

2

Some people think there was something sublime about Alexei. But they're mistaken. He was a simple peasant, like any peasant, and a drunkard to boot. Still, he had the good quality of obeying without talking or questioning. If the Baal Shem Tov told him to sit with his back to the horse, he did so. If he had told Alexei to harness the horse with its tail in front and its head to the wagon, he would have gone and done it naively, and never even dreamt of asking why. And not because you don't ask the Baal Shem Tov any questions, but simply because he was incapable of asking questions. And he was incapable because he hadn't reached the level of will. Some people even speculated that Alexei was in the image of the Golem of Rabbi Levi of Prague. Be that as it may, the Baal Shem Tov was very fond of Alexei for obeying without questions, and at times the master would even tell his disciples to learn that fine quality from the servant. Once, when he was pondering the phenomenon of two existences that meet and do not meet, he said:

"The highest level of spirituality must bring you to the same denial of your own will and of all existence, which Alexei has attained on the lowest level of materiality."

Alexei harnessed the horse to a sleigh and—where were they driving to? That was up to the horse. Alexei was nestled up in fur, with his back to the horse, and sleeping. The frost burned and singed, the snow crackled, screamed, and ground under the sleigh. The wind blasted, and the trees in the forest popped like gunfire. But the Hasids couldn't care less. Even Ber Mezeritsher, an invalid, forgot to wrap his scarf around his neck. They were absorbed in their debate. About what? Reward and punishment.

The Baal Shem Tov listened, smiled, as was his wont, and said, almost in passing:

"If punishment atones for a sin, then a reward atones for a good deed. . . ."

The Hasids promptly fell silent.

Dovid Firkes cried out:

"If a reward nullifies a good deed, then the pleasure of doing a good deed requires no reward!"

Wolf Kitses countered:

"Isn't pleasure a reward?"

To which Ber Mezeritsher softly replied:

"Then let's forget about pleasure! Let's put an end to good deeds and rewards! Let there be fulfillment of the Will of the Lord God, blessed be He, as the only place of the life-spirit, that is to say: 'We must live with these laws.' "

Dovid Leykes asked:

"Well, then how are we to understand the question of sin?"

There was a silence. No one knew what to answer. The Baal Shem Tov put in a helping hand.

"If you can have a person without good deeds," he said, "then you can have a sin without a person."

And he quoted Exodus:

" 'He looked and he looked, and he saw that no one was there.' For the looking and looking are the shape of the sin. And as soon as a sin is committed, we can see that the man is no one. For he loses his life-spirit and becomes as dead."

Jacob-Joseph grumbled:

"What about repentance?"

The master replied:

"Repentance is the resurrection of the dead."

3

Their talk was done, and they drove on. All at once, the horse stopped. And when a horse stops, it stops. It may have been necessary, even though they were in the middle of the woods.

So they climbed out of the sleigh. And since it was time for evening prayers, they prayed. Suddenly, they saw someone in the distance driving their way. They peered closer. There were two people. From far away, they looked like children. When the sleigh came nearer, they turned out to be a boy and a girl, snuggling together, nearly frozen. And their horse was on its last legs, it could barely drag itself along.

The Hasids stopped the horse, took the young people out of the sleigh, shook them awake, revived them a bit. They gave them a few drops of brandy, and the youngsters came to their senses. When the Hasids asked them where they were driving, they burst into tears. Upon calming down, the boy told them the story.

He and the girl had been working for a tavernkeeper as his servant and maid. Since both were orphans and all alone in the world, they decided to marry, and so they got engaged. But then one day, the tavernkeeper's wife lost her temper at the girl and began hitting and beating her. And even though the boy was just a servant, he stood up for his bride. Their boss got so angry that he beat them and threw them out. Now since they had saved up enough rubles, they bought a horse and a little sleigh, and drove into the world. They kept driving, week after week, from place to place, without finding a haven. Meanwhile, they spent their last kopek and for two days now they hadn't had a bite to eat—and it got colder and colder outside, and they were at the end of their rope. . . .

The Hasids gave them food. And when they were full, Jacob-Joseph asked them gruffly:

"How come a boy and a girl are traveling alone—without a chaperon?"

The girl was embarrassed, and the boy started explaining.

But the Baal Shem Tov smiled and said:

"Then we'll drive to an inn and have a wedding."

So they piled into the sleighs, with Wolf Kitses joining the youngsters to chaperon them, and off they went. After a short drive, they halted at an inn. Upon seeing it, the boy and girl realized that this was the tavern where they had worked. They shivered and were amazed at returning here so fast.

Meanwhile, out came the tavernkeeper and his wife. Laying eyes upon their former servants, they screamed:

"So you've come back, you scoundrels! Get your sleigh out of here!"

The Baal Shem Tov began calming them:

"There's no reason to get angry. We've taken them along with us."

The woman laughed:

"You've got yourself a real bargain."

But the Baal Shem Tov went on:

"Since the boy and girl are engaged to marry, we would like to hold their wedding here."

The tavernkeeper guffawed. The very idea of having a wedding for the two scoundrels he had thrown out! He told the Baal Shem Tov to keep driving.

To which the Baal Shem Tov quietly said:

"No, we really want to have the wedding in your inn. And you will be so kind as to prepare a fine supper."

The tavernkeeper and his wife roared with laughter. A fine supper indeed!

"Yes," repeated the Baal Shem Tov. "You will prepare a fine supper, with the loveliest dishes, the choicest wines, and I will pay whatever it costs."

The tavernkeeper, his curiosity aroused, asked:

"And about how much will you pay?"

"Whatever you charge."

And the Baal Shem Tov showed him a pile of ducats.

When they saw the money, they stopped laughing. The tavernkeeper looked at his wife, and she at him. Both of them were wondering whether the money was stolen. And both of them answered the question themselves: "It's none of our business!" And the tavernkeeper said:

"If you really pay us well, we'll prepare a supper as you want us to."

So they entered the tavern and prepared for the wedding. And when everything was ready, they began the ceremony, which the Baal Shem Tov himself performed. When it was over, they all sat down at the table with the bride and groom at the head. And the company ate and drank and made merry.

4

When the seven nuptial blessings were spoken and the feast was over, the Baal Shem Tov stood up and said to his Hasids:

"We have to give our newlyweds presents." And he called out: "I'll give them this tavern and all its furnishings, and the surrounding buildings, the horses, cattle, sheep, and other livestock."

The innkeeper and his wife, upon hearing him, broke into loud guffaws, and they sent for the peasants living nearby to come and watch the fine comedy.

And the Baal Shem Tov and his Hasids did what they had to do.

After the Baal Shem Tov, Jacob-Joseph stood up:

"And I," he said, "I'll give the newlyweds the forest around the inn."

"And I'll give them the stone mill down by the river," cried Ber Mezeritsher.

"And I'll give them the brewery," cried Wolf Kitses.

And Dovid Leykes gave them the barn with all its grain, which stood in the duke's courtyard. And Dovid Firkes gave them a hundred barrels of wine from the duke's wine cellar.

And thus each Hasid gave them his gift. And each time, the tavernkeeper, his wife, and the peasants laughed louder and louder. At last, the tavernkeeper himself went over to the table, and choking with mirth, he shouted:

"And I'll give the fine couple the ten thousand rubles that the duke just got from his tavernkeepers today!"

His wife didn't want to be any less generous than her husband, and she shouted mirthfully:

"And I'll give the lovely young bride the precious brooch and the earrings that the duchess has on!"

The Baal Shem Tov said to them:

"Why don't you give them something of your own? After all, they did work for you for so many years."

The tavernkeeper screamed with laughter.

But his wife cried out sarcastically:

"Give them the old ruin behind the village!"

Everyone laughed. The ruin had no doors or windows, and the roof had caved in.

"Is that all you're giving them?" asked the Baal Shem Tov.

"That's all."

The Baal Shem Tov sighed, stood up, and paid hard cash for the supper. He added a ruble for the tablecloth.

Then he told the young man:

"Take all the food and drink left over from the supper and wrap them up in the cloth. Put it all in your sleigh, and then get in with your wife, and go in peace."

The young man asked:

"Where should we go?"

And the Baal Shem Tov replied:

"To the right. The Good Lord will take care of everything else."

And he wouldn't speak another word. He and his Hasids piled into the sleigh—and off they drove. And before they could even think, they were back in Medjibuzh.

5

The young man did what the Baal Shem Tov had told him to do. He put all the leftovers in the tablecloth, got into the sleigh with his wife, and drove off. And the tavernkeeper and his wife and the peasants accompanied them with mockery and abuse. And they drove without knowing what was happening. Everything seemed like a dream. But they did remember the people laughing at them, and they felt miserable, and wept.

Meanwhile, dawn was coming. And when it was daylight, the horse stopped all at once and refused to go any farther. The young man climbed out of the sleigh and looked for a twig to whip the horse. Suddenly, in the distance, he saw someone lying in the snow. He hurried over and realized it was a young nobleman, almost frozen, but still alive. The young groom called to his bride, and they started reviving the stranger, rubbing him with snow. The young nobleman opened his eyes. The bride remembered that they had some wine from the supper in the tablecloth. She ran back to the sleigh, got the wine, and poured a few drops into his mouth to refresh him. He came to his senses, and faintly asked for food. The bride remembered that they had a lot of food from the supper in the tablecloth and she gave him some. And he ate ravenously and drank up a whole bottle of wine. And, when he was full, he told them what had happened to him.

It turned out that he was the only son of the duke. The day before, he had gone out hunting, and the horse had run wild and thrown him, and then galloped off. He remained alone in the woods—and the farther he walked, the more he went astray in the depths of the forest. He had called out, but no one heard him. He wandered about for a day and a night, until his strength was gone, and he was so worn out, cold, and hungry that he collapsed and almost froze to death.

As he spoke, there was a sudden blare of trumpets, shouting, and the galloping of hooves. And then a troop of horsemen rode up with a carriage. When the horsemen sighted the young duke, they broke into a wild joy. They dashed over and kissed his hands, and then they picked him up and took him to the carriage and put him inside. And with a great commotion and a blaring of trumpets, they quickly drove away.

The young bride and groom remained alone in the middle of the forest. They still didn't know what had happened. Again, it all seemed like a dream.

6

When they brought the young duke back to the court, the old duke and duchess ran up and kissed and hugged him, and they ordered a huge meal. And the rejoicing had no end.

When everyone had calmed down a bit, the young duke remembered the young couple who had rescued him from death, and he asked for them. But no one knew where they were. So the duke sent out a great number of horsemen to look for them. When they found the young couple, they brought them back to the court in triumph and led them into the largest hall. And the duke and duchess thanked them over and over again for saving their only son from death. The old duke asked them who they were. The young man told him that he and his wife had worked for the tavernkeeper, but that he had gotten angry at them and thrown them out into the cold. Upon hearing this, the duke became furious and shouted:

"Since the tavernkeeper threw you out, I'll turn over his tavern to you for all time, with all the furnishings, the surrounding buildings, the horses, cattle, sheep, and other livestock."

And the duchess cried out:

"And I'll give them the forest around the tavern."

And the young duke said:

"And I'll give them the stone mill down by the river, and the brewery, and the barn with all the grain and a hundred barrels of wine from our wine cellar."

And then the old duke went on:

"They have to have some cash for the start of their marriage. I'll give them the ten thousand rubles that I got yesterday from my tavernkeepers."

And the duchess added:

"Since the young wife has only just married, she has to have jewelry."

And she unpinned her diamond brooch and diamond earrings and gave them to the young bride.

And the young couple stood there, dazed by their great fortune; it all seemed like a dream. And when they came to their senses, they started thanking their patrons for the wonderful presents, and the old duke asked the young man what he wanted. The young man remembered the tavern-keeper and his wife, and feeling sorry for them, he said:

"What's going to happen to the tavernkeeper and his wife?"

The duke laughed:

"Why should you worry about them?"

And the duchess, laughing, cried out to the duke:

"Give them the ruin behind the village!"

And everyone burst out laughing.

Upon hearing the laughter, the young couple thought it was still the tavernkeeper and his wife and the peasants, and they felt miserable and they wept. . . .

A short time later, when the Hasids were talking about the whole thing at the Baal Shem Tov's table, the master said:

" 'Even when they were laughing at me, my heart took pity on those who were laughing. The poor things were doubly pitiful.' "

And he heaved a heavy sigh. . . .

Translated from the Yiddish
by Joachim Neugroschel

The Wanderings of the Childless

by Martin Buber

A pious Hasid, an admirer of the Maggid of Kosnitz, used to visit his master every month. At each visit for many years he made the same request of the rabbi. Both he and his wife were approaching old age and were still without children. The Hasid begged the rabbi to release him from this fate, so that when he died some earthly part of him would still remain. Rabbi Israel always listened patiently and dismissed him in a friendly way, but without saying a word about the man's request.

One evening, while the man and his wife were discussing their misfortune, the woman was unable to control her grief and began crying bitterly. The man was deeply touched by his wife's emotion, and he seemed to see her for the first time. He finally understood how terribly the shame of this barrenness weighed upon her and was overcome with pity. This time he resolved to press the rabbi even more urgently and not to cease until the rabbi had given his promise. When he told this to his wife, she stopped crying and seized at the idea joyfully and impatiently. She pointed out many reasons why he should not delay his journey till the next month and begged him to leave at once. Unable to resist her frantic pleas, he hastened to Kosnitz the next day and opened his heart to the Maggid.

This time Rabbi Israel seemed well disposed. As the man spoke he felt encouraged and hopeful. But after he had finished, there was a very long silence, and his hopes began to fade. At last the rabbi said, "My friend, there is a way for you, but I am afraid to direct you toward it. You and your wife are approaching your declining years. To achieve your wish, you will have to sacrifice all that you have gained in your years of labor, all the possessions and security of your old age. If you would hold a son in your arms, you will have to watch over his youth in poverty, with much hardship and worry. Go and discuss this with your wife. If she is agreeable, I will direct you to your way."

The Hasid returned and told his wife all that the Maggid had said. His wife smiled through tear-wet eyes. For a moment she seemed as young and beautiful as she had been when he had married her many years before. She told him she was willing to undertake any necessary task and would never complain if she were allowed to hold in her arms a child of her own flesh. "People without children," she said, "freeze in the shadow of death even while they're still alive. What's the use of having money if you die and leave nothing behind you on earth?" When he heard what his wife said, the Hasid turned patiently around and hurried back to Kosnitz, expecting that the Maggid would point out his way.

But the Master said, "Take all your wealth and valuables, and whatever goods or property you possess, and convert them into money. Then prepare yourself to go to Rabbi Jacob Isaac in Lublin. Tell him that I sent you, and you will hear from his mouth the words that will direct your fate."

The man went home and sold all his possessions. His wife helped willingly and surrendered all her jewels and luxuries without regret. She assured him she would be able to support herself by her own labor while he was gone. Without hesitation then, the man took all the money they had collected, and putting it into a wallet that he wore under his shirt, he set out on his journey.

When he arrived at Lublin, he presented himself at the house of Rabbi Jacob Isaac, as the Maggid had instructed him to do. The rabbi seemed very detached and not overly sympathetic. He advised the man, somewhat coolly, to take lodgings in the city and wait until the time was ripe. He told him he would send for him in due time and dismissed him without much ceremony. The man found lodgings in an inn and waited patiently for several weeks.

After a while he began to fear that the rabbi had forgotten him and his affairs. Hoping to catch the rabbi's eye, the Hasid went to his house several times, together with a crowd of scholars. But the master seemed determined to ignore him, and all the man's hopes were turned to despair. The days passed drearily for the Hasid. He was very worried about his wife who was struggling to make ends meet, while he remained idle in obedience to the

Maggid's instructions. As he waited for the message from the rabbi, his money was dwindling. Although he tried to live as cheaply as possible, he was afraid he would end up a beggar before the rabbi sent for him.

At last, when he had almost stopped expecting it, the long-awaited message came. The rabbi said: "Because of the respect I bear your master, the Maggid of Kosnitz, I will help you untie the knot in which your fate is caught. Recollect how in your childhood your parents betrothed you to a girl whom you later left for another who pleased you better. On your account an innocent creature suffered the bitterness and pain of rejection. You, however, went your way unheedingly and dismissed from your mind all memory of the pain you caused another. That act sealed your fate. The rejected woman's tears have made your wife barren. The only way to escape this fate is to go and seek out this girl that you hurt so deeply and to beg her forgiveness. But you will not succeed unless she forgives you so completely that all the bitterness in her soul is forgotten. Understand also that the place of her residence is very distant, and the road beset with difficulty.

"Go now to Balta to the fair called 'The Green Sunday.' Search for her diligently and spare no effort. You must not hesitate, and you must continue your search without wearying or stopping for rest. If you find her, remember, you must do whatever she asks by way of expiation."

The man expressed his gratitude and returned to the inn. He prepared himself hurriedly and journeyed to Balta, where he awaited the first day of the fair with great anxiety. Before the sun came up he was out on the street. The workmen were putting up the last few booths. Soon the people began arriving. At first there was only a handful or so, but gradually they filled the square until the crowded streets throbbed and echoed with the dizzying clamor of the market. The man wasn't used to all this noise, and it made him nervous. But he remained at his post all day long and did not leave until everyone else had gone home and the square was deserted. In this manner the first day passed, and the second, and the others. He listened to every voice and looked at every face and asked whoever would listen whether they had seen any trace of the woman to whom he had once been engaged.

Day after day passed in the same manner, without a word or a look that brought him any closer to his goal. Tired and hungry, heartsore with disappointment, he wandered hour after hour among the stalls, surrounded by barkers and hagglers. Finally the last day arrived. The merchants were packing up their wares, loading their wagons with sacks and chests. Large numbers of foreign merchants were already leaving. As evening drew near, the Hasid could see the workmen taking down the last booths. He had spent this day feverishly combing all the back alleys and inns, looking anxiously into every female face and listening to every distant voice. All in vain. The fair was coming to its end. Time was running out, and his last hopes faded.

Suddenly, the sky darkened, and the day passed all at once—without any twilight—into the blackness of night. It began to rain heavily, and everyone left what he was doing and scrambled for cover from the furious downpour. It was not until he was soaked to the skin that the Hasid realized what was happening and began to look for shelter. Nearby he noticed a large, dark archway and made a dash for it. As he came out of the rain, he would have leaned against the wall to rest, but he heard a faint, rustling sound, as if he had brushed lightly against a silken dress. He retreated timidly to place a proper distance between himself and the wearer. Looking up cautiously, now that his eyes had become accustomed to the dark, he was able to make out two women whom he had not seen previously because of his hurry.

He had more or less ceased to concern himself with them—he was so entangled in his troubled thoughts—when a strange sound startled him. One of the women had laughed, the one standing next to him. Her laughter seemed to combine a painful hollowness with the piercing quality of gently breaking glass. Although she spoke in a very low voice, he heard every word.

"Look," she said, "there is the man to whom I was betrothed when I was a child. When he grew up he left me. Even now he finds me so repulsive he can only think to escape."

The man's heart stood still. With feverish eyes, he looked at the speaker through the darkness. She was a tall, thin woman, pale and festively dressed in stiff, black clothes. Her face and hair were partially obscured by veils, but her hands and garments glittered with costly jewels. The longer the man looked, the more frightened he became.

At length he summoned up his courage and was able to approach her. Although he did not dare to look her in the face, he asked haltingly, "What were you saying, madam?"

Her voice trembled and seemed to float away into space: "Have you forgotten me, then, like the dead? I am the girl to whom you were betrothed as a child, and who seemed so worthless to you afterward. But why are you here?"

"Very simply, I have come because of you. I will hide nothing from you. My marriage was unblessed. My wife and I have had no children. We were unhappy for many years, but my eyes have been opened by the Rabbi of Lublin. The wrong that I did you darkened our marriage. We cannot hope to have children and be happy in our old age, unless you are willing to forgive me completely for the wrong I have done you. I have suffered greatly to bring this day to pass. Please be merciful. Ask anything of me. I will do anything to atone."

The woman turned toward him and spoke softly, but so distinctly that he caught every word. "Our God," she said, "has been more merciful to me than you can imagine. I no longer need the goods of this world, and my peace does not depend on any atonement. But I have a brother living far from here, in a town near Suvalki. He is honest and pious, but he has become very poor. Right now he has a daughter ready to be married, but he doesn't have the money to make the necessary arrangements. What happened to me will happen to her. She will be scorned, and her family will suffer great anguish. If you wish me to forgive you, go there and prevent that misfortune. Two hundred gulden are all that is needed. If you give them the money, all will be well."

"Gladly," said the Hasid. "Here, take the money yourself. What would be the use of my going to your brother? You give him the money, or send it with a messenger. Do whatever you think best, but let me go my way, for I am homesick."

The woman shook her head gently and answered, "No, that isn't possible. I can only instruct you, but you are the one who has to do it. Give my brother my greetings, and put the gold in his hands. My time is up. Farewell."

She motioned to her companion, and the two women walked into the street and were swallowed up in the darkness. The Hasid, bewildered by the woman's words and hasty departure, ran out, hoping to detain her. In the distance, he could just make out her face as she turned it toward him. She spoke sadly, "My friend, it is useless for you to follow me. My journey is long, and I must hurry." Raising her hand, she waved a hasty farewell and was gone.

The next morning the Hasid set out and, after weeks of tedious traveling, arrived at Suvalki, where he immediately checked on the present location of the woman's brother. He was told the name of the village and, without stopping to rest, went on to the man's house. The Hasid found him very dejected and withdrawn, and hardly disposed to bare his heart to his unknown caller. It was not until his guest had directed many kind words to him and exhibited a sympathetic interest, that the host spoke about his troubles. He explained how heavily they had fallen upon him now that he had to marry off his daughter. Through a series of accidents—because of the poor harvest and his landlord's greediness—he had used up his daughter's dowry to support his family. The engagement had been contracted in her childhood, while he and his family were still wealthy. But their many misfortunes had now reduced their wealth far below that of the bridegroom's family. If he was unable to meet the terms of the marriage contract, the young man's parents would jump at this excuse to prevent the marriage. They had been viewing it with disfavor for some time now because of the bride's poverty, and only their honor and a strong sense of propriety had held them to their bond. His daughter took this rejection to heart and sat in her room for weeks, weeping inconsolably.

"My friend," said the Hasid, "do not be so downcast. Perhaps I can help you."

The man smiled bitterly in disbelief. "How can a stranger like yourself help me?"

"It so happens," said the Hasid, "that I have two hundred gulden with me. I have no better use for them than to give them to you for as long as you need them." The Hasid's honest appearance appealed to the man; gradually he came to trust his guest's intentions though he was still not able to understand why a perfect stranger should be so generous to him.

The Hasid now felt obliged to tell his host the history and purpose of his mission. He began by explaining, "Your sister, Esther Shiffra, sent me here to help you."

When his host heard this, he turned away and asked in a sinking voice, "Where did you see my sister last, and when did she tell you to do this?"

"Several weeks ago at the great fair in Balta. It was the first time I had seen her in many years. She told me how troubled she was by your misfortune and commanded me to help you. Then I came here."

"Idiot," the man screamed, "how dare you come into my house and laugh at me! My sister has been dead for fifteen years. I buried her with my own hands."

The Hasid sighed heavily and looked away. Finally, with a great effort, he found the words to explain what had happened. When he described the woman's appearance and the clothes she was wearing as she stood in the doorway, the man's eyes filled with tears.

"Yes," he said, "that was the way she looked when I buried her fifteen years ago. In that case I need not be ashamed to accept your help."

The Hasid stayed on for the wedding, and after exchanging blessings with his host, he departed in peace. From that time on, the Hasid and his wife lived in great poverty, though their marriage was blessed. For before old age was upon them, they had a son.

Translated from the German
by David Antin

The Burning of the Torah

by Meyer Levin

Then the Enemy, tormented as he saw Rabbi Israel doing good on earth, schemed to overcome the Master. He called all the angels of darkness into conclave about him and said, "This is my plan:

"I will station dark angels on all the roads that lead to heaven. And whenever and wherever a prayer rises seeking to go upward and enter the Gates of Heaven, the dark angels will seize it and throttle it and prevent it from reaching the Gates. Those prayers that have already wandered many years in limbo, they as well as the new prayers shall be prevented from arriving. And thus, no prayers will come before the Throne.

"When many days shall have passed with not a single prayer attaining the Throne, I will go up to God and say to Him, 'Look, how Your people have deserted you. They no longer send prayers up to You. Even your favorite among the puppets, Your devoted Rabbi Israel, has ceased to worship You. Take back Your wisdom from Rabbi Israel, and deprive his people of your Torah!'"

This was the plan of Satan.

At once his ministers of evil crept out upon all the roads that led to heaven. No turning point, no bypath was left unguarded. Silent and invisible, they lay in wait. Before the Gates of Heaven, a great army of them was in ambush. No prayer could pass.

As the prayers came upward, the angels seized them from behind, and leaped upon them, and throttled them. They could not kill the prayers, but flung them sidewards into chaos. All space was filled with the whimpering and moaning of wounded prayers that stumbled in search of their way.

But every Friday, the prayers came forward in such swarms that all the angels of evil were not numerous enough to stop them. Then many prayers escaped along the roads, and made their way to the Gates of Heaven. But here, the army that lay in wait before the Gates of Heaven stopped them, and did not allow them to enter.

Thus, weeks went by, and no prayers came up to the Throne.

Then Satan went to God and said, "Take away the Torah from the Jews."

God said, "Give them until the Day of Atonement."

But Satan was impatient. "Send out the command at once!" he said. "Though it be not done until the Day of Atonement."

God gave the terrible command.

Then, on earth, the Archbishop issued a proclamation to all his bishops. "In ten days' time," he said, "seize all of the Hebrew books of learning. Go among the Jews and take their Torah out of their synagogues and out of their houses. Heap the books into pyres, and burn them."

The Bishop of Kamenitz-Podolsky was the most zealous to follow the commands of the Archbishop. He sent his servants into all the houses of the Jews. The Bishop of Lemberg was also zealous. And all of the bishops did as they had been commanded to do.

The tenth day would be the Day of Atonement. And on that day, in a thousand pyres lighted in every corner of the land, the Torah would burn.

When the Torah began to be taken from the Jews, the Baal Shem knew that Satan had done a terrible work. Yet he could not find out what strange evil the Enemy had done, and he did not know how to battle against him,

Each day, the suffering and the horror among the Jews became greater. As the Torah was wrenched from their arms, they wept and beat themselves as mothers whose babes are torn from their breasts. And they said, "On the Day of Atonement we will go into the flames with our Torah!"

Fasting, and sleepless, night and day the Baal Shem strove for his people. Day and night he sent mighty prayers heavenward; they rose colossal on powerful wings and shot upward with incredible speed. But the Enemy was on guard every instant in every crevice of the heavens, the Enemy himself caught the prayers of the Baal Shem, and threw them from their way.

The heart of the Baal Shem was become a gusty cave of grief.

At last came the Day of Atonement.

Rabbi Israel went into the synagogue to hold the prayer service. At his side stood Rabbi Yacob.

And all those who were in the synagogue saw the terrible fever of struggle that lay over the face of the Baal Shem Tov. Hope came into their bleak hearts. "He will save us today," they said.

When the moment came for the utterance of *Kol Nidre*, Rabbi Israel lifted his voice, his voice sang through the shreds of his torn heart; all who listened were frozen with sorrow.

In the service of the lamentations it was the custom for Rabbi Yacob to read each verse aloud, then Rabbi Israel would repeat the verse after him. And so they began the lamentations.

But when Rabbi Yacob read out the verse, "Open the Portals of Heaven!" there was no sound from Rabbi Israel. Rabbi Yacob waited. The synagogue quaked in a terrific silence. And Rabbi Israel remained silent. Rabbi Yacob repeated, "Open the Portals of Heaven!" But still the Master did not utter a word.

Then, in that fever of silence, Rabbi Israel threw himself upon the ground, and beat his head against the ground, and out of him there came a cry that was like the roar of a dying lion.

Rabbi Israel remained doubled upon the ground. His body quivered with the might of the struggle. For two hours he remained with his head bent upon the ground.

And those who were in the house of prayer could not take their eyes from him; they did not dare to approach him, but watched him, and were silent.

At last Rabbi Israel raised himself. His face was a face of wonders.

He said, "The Portals of Heaven are open!"

And thus he ended the service.

Long afterward, what he had done during the two hours when he lay with his head to the ground became known.

He had gone up to the Palace of the Eternal. He had gone up to the greatest of Gates, that stands over the road that leads directly to the Throne. There, huddled before the Gate, he had found hundreds and thousands of prayers. Some of them were maimed, some lay gasping as though they had just ended a terrible struggle, some were emaciated and old, some were blind through wandering in darkness.

"What are you waiting for!" asked the Baal Shem. "Why don't you go in, and approach the Throne of the Almighty?"

They said, "Until this moment, the angels of darkness were on guard, and would not let us approach the Gate. But as they saw you coming, they fled. Now we are waiting for your prayer, to take us within the Portals."

"I will take you in," said the Baal Shem Tov.

But just at the moment when he sought to pass through the Gate, the army of Evil ones who had rushed behind the Gate when they saw his approach pushed the Gate forward, and closed it. Then the Enemy himself came out. In his two hands he carried a lock. He hung the lock upon the great Portal.

The Gate is as big as the world. And the lock was as big as a city.

The Baal Shem went up to the lock and walked around it, seeking some crack through which he might enter, and through which he might lead the prayers. But the lock was of solid iron, and there was no crack anywhere.

The road to the Throne was closed.

But the Baal Shem did not despair.

It is known that for each of us on earth there lives a being in heaven. And that being is exactly as we are.

Into that nether region of heaven the way was open. Then Rabbi Israel went in there, and sought out his counterpart, who was the Rabbi Israel of heaven.

And Rabbi Israel of the earth said to him, "What shall I do, to bring the prayers before the Name?"

Rabbi Israel of heaven said, "There is only one thing to do. Let us go to the palace of Messiah."

They came to the palace where Messiah sits awaiting the day when he may go down to earth.

And as soon as the Baal Shem entered, Messiah cried out to him, "Be joyous! I will help you!" And he gave the Baal Shem a token.

The Baal Shem took the token, and went back to the Gate that was locked. Before the token, the lock fell away, and the Portals opened wide as the earth is large, and all the prayers entered and went straight to the Throne of the Name.

Then there was joy all through the heavens, and the good angels sang paeans of joy, while the dark angels crept and slunk away to the farthest corners of chaos.

In that moment, the Bishop of Kamenitz-Podolsky kindled a fire on earth. He stood by the fire that he had kindled. At his side was a great pile of volumes of Hebrew writings, hundreds of tractates of the Talmud were there in that pyramid.

The Bishop of Kamenitz-Podolsky took a tractate of the Talmud, and hurled it into the fire. It began to burn. The Bishop took another book, and hurled it into the flames. They rose higher, they leaped mightily upward. Again and again the Bishop hurled the Talmud into the flames. But when he had thrown seven tractates into the flames, and was about to throw the eighth, his hand was seized with a trembling, and then his whole body was seized with shaking, and he fell in an epileptic fit.

All the multitude shivered with terror, and ran from the burning-place. The fire died down, and went out.

And the news of this spread swiftly, as a pestilence on the wind. Then all those bishops who had builded pyres of holy books, and prepared to burn them, were frightened, fearing that the curse of the Baal Shem would come upon them, and they would be seized with horrible spasms. They left the books in their marketplaces, and ran into their towers for safety.

Thus the Talmud was saved for the Jews on the Day of Atonement.

The Story of the He-Goat
Who Couldn't Say No
by I. L. Peretz

Reb Nachumke was standing outside, looking in on us, his Hasidim, inside. He had suddenly left us, and gone away to ponder some deep matter in solitude. Now he had returned, and stood by the window, leaning on the ledge, his eyes shining, and the moon stood like a crown on his head. That was how he told us the story of the he-goat.

"Once upon a time," he began, "there was a he-goat. At first sight a he-goat like all he-goats. Who was to know? He kept himself to himself, lived alone, loved solitude, showed himself rarely—how could people know? He kept away even from his own kind. He had no goat friends. He was an old bachelor. How was one to know?

"There was an old ruin outside the town. It had been there for generations. People said—and it was true—that it was the ruin of a synagogue. Once Jews had worshiped there, studied the Holy Word. And when it was laid waste Jews had probably perished there for His Name's sake.

"Tales of long ago. Today grass grows there. Strange grass, that no one sows and no one cuts.

"The he-goat lived in this ruin. He ate the grass.

"They say the strange grass that grows in ruins has a peculiar quality that makes a goat's horns grow, grow very long, very high. They can be wound back, and concealed, so that nobody sees, nobody knows. But when they are unwound they reach to the skies!

"Our he-goat was a Nazarite. He never touched any other grass. Not even a nibble. Only that grass in the ruin. Nor just anywhere in the ruin— only in one particular spot, where the Holy place had been, where the word of the Torah had been said; or in a second spot, where Jewish blood had been shed for His Name's sake. Especially in the second.

"The horns grew and grew. He kept them wound back and concealed—a Nazarite, and a hermit.

"But at midnight, when the town was asleep, and pious Jews sat in the *beth hamedrash* saying the midnight prayer, and the heartbreaking chant 'By the Waters of Babylon' came through the windows and spread over earth and heaven, then the he-goat was filled with irresistible longing—he stood on his hind legs, unwound his horns, and let them rise, especially when there was a young new moon whose appearance Jews had just blessed, hooked the points of his horns round the moon, to hold her, and asked:

" 'Isn't it time yet for Messiah to come?'

"Then the moon repeated his question to the stars, and the stars trembled and stopped still in their courses. Everything became still. The night was still. Its song stopped.

"They couldn't understand round God's Mercy Seat what had happened, why they didn't hear the song of the night. They sent someone down to find out. The messenger came back and reported that the moon and the stars had stopped to ask if it wasn't yet time for the Redemption.

"A great sigh went up round God's Mercy Seat.

"Things like that can do a great deal."

Reb Nachumke's voice broke. He covered his eyes with his hands, and his hands were trembling. The moon that stood like a crown on his head also trembled.

After a while he lifted his head. His face was white. His voice trembled as he continued his tale.

"His staying here was itself a great favor, an act of grace," he went on. "Any other goat with such horns would have hooked them on the moon and somersaulted up into heaven, a living goat into Paradise! Why worry about us down below?

"But he was pitiful and compassionate. He was sorry for our community, and wouldn't forsake us.

"There were times—years of hunger and want, when our community was in trouble. Women sold their trinkets, men the silver ornaments on their *tallitim*—they sold Hanukah lamps, Sabbath candlesticks, their Sabbath and festival clothes. Many left the town. When things got worse they took their children from the *chedar*, because they couldn't pay the teachers' fees. There was actual starvation! People were on the point of death. At such a time he *had* to help!

"There is in heaven a Milky Way—that's what the stargazers call the white patches scattered across the skies. It isn't really a Way. No one walks along it, no one rides there.

"They are fields, planted with precious stones, diamonds and rubies and emeralds from the crowns that the saints wear in Paradise. No one counts them, no one keeps any record of them. They just grow there, keep increasing, more and more—and the number of saints grows less. So they spread all over the fields.

"Our he-goat with the long horns went out one quiet midnight, when the town was asleep, except for the sound of wailing over the exile of the Shekhinah coming from the windows of the *beth hamedrash*, and he stood up on his hind legs, unwound his horns, sent them up into the Milky Way, and tore out a precious jewel and dropped it into the middle of the market. It broke into a thousand fragments. Jews going home from midnight prayer saw the market glittering with jewels, and picked them up; they had enough to live on for a time.

"That is why he can't go up there!

"It was his compassion that was his undoing," Reb Nachumke went on, with a trembling voice. "It was the cause of his losing his horns. Do you know how, over what? Over a pinch of snuff."

There was a sudden change in his voice, and you couldn't be sure if it was weeping or laughing.

"Everybody started taking snuff," he said. "It was said to be good for your eyes, and for your mind. It cleared the brain. Now if people take snuff they must have snuffboxes. A Jew walked along the road and found a bit of horn, and made a snuffbox out of it. Another came across a goat or a cow, and asked it for a bit of horn. What he got was a butt with the horn in his side.

"Then one Jew walking through the ruin met our he-goat, and when he spoke to him, and asked him for a bit of his horn to make a snuffbox out of it, the he-goat couldn't say no.

"So the Jew cut off a bit of horn. He came to the *beth hamedrash*, and handed his snuffbox round. People asked him where he had got that lovely horn from. And he told them.

"The result was that everybody went to ask the he-goat for a bit of horn, and he couldn't say no. He bent his head, and everybody cut off a bit of horn, to make snuffboxes.

"The horn got a great reputation everywhere. People came from all parts for it. From every corner of the Diaspora. There were snuffboxes galore.

"But there is no horn left to reach up to heaven to ask when Messiah will be coming. Not even to bring down a precious jewel from the Milky Way. All because of a pinch of snuff."

He stopped. A cloud floated over the moon and hid it from sight. And a sense of sadness fell over us all.

Translated from the Yiddish
by Joseph Leftwich

A Messiah in Every Generation
by Jiri Langer

There is a Messiah in every generation. He leads a solitary life and no one knows of his existence. He may not reveal himself to the world because of our guilt. But at that time the whole world knew that a Messiah was there, living at Belz, and that his name was Aaron.

The whole world knew about it and was glad, both those on earth and those in heaven.

Only the Devil did not rejoice. He could not reconcile himself to the idea of having to bid farewell to his rule over the world and hand over his scepter to a Messiah.

So the Devil changed himself into a woman, a woman of outstanding beauty and—this is what was unusual—wisdom. Thus disguised he set out on his road.

He went from town to town and wherever he came to he started learned discussions with distinguished rabbis. No one surmised who this erudite woman could be. But all the savants whom she induced to talk with her were confounded by her arguments, whatever the subject discussed. Her fame flew round the world.

Reb Aaron Messiah also desired to cross swords with this wondrous woman.

Dear me, what an occasion that was, this battle of words between a Messiah and the Devil! It is a wonder they did not burn each other up with the fire of their breath. In their wit and wisdom they overturned rocks by their roots and ground each other to pulp.

Finally the woman produced a question which even the Messiah was unable to answer.

"I will tell you when we are alone," she said. "It's a great secret. No one must know it except us."

Not knowing whom he had before him, the Messiah ordered everyone present to leave the room. Not even a child was allowed to remain, so sublime was the secret!

It was not until he had shut the door after the last person that the Messiah saw his error. In the heat of the learned dispute he had forgotten the words of the holy scholars in the Talmud which forbid us to be alone with a strange woman for a single moment.

It was too late. The Messiah's holy mission had been profaned and his journey on this earth came to an end. It was the sixth day of the month of Tishri. The Devil celebrated his victory.

As a result we have longer to wait for our salvation. It will be a long time yet, a very long time, perhaps.

Only an old tombstone in the Belz cemetery shows us that a Messiah really lived there: Reb Aaron Messiah.

It was the holy Reb Sholem who succeeded the Messiah.

Translated from the Czech
by Stephen Jolly

Daughter of Heaven
by Pascal Thémanlys

The Baal Shem Tov disseminated light among the righteous and made them into suns. When he left this world, his followers were growing in numbers in the towns and villages of Poland, the Ukraine and Austria. The Divine Presence moved from Medzhibozh, where the Baal Shem Tov had lived, to Mezhirech, the home of the Great Maggid, Rabbi Dov Baer. This was stated by none other than the man who himself claimed to be the Baal Shem Tov's senior disciple, Rabbi Jacob Joseph Katz of Polonnaye, the author of the first book of hasidic doctrine.

Mezhirech was like a humming beehive, where the honey of wisdom was gathered by the masters.

Almost all the future hasidic leaders came to hear the teachings of the Great Maggid. The warriors of King Solomon were stationed about his litter and assembled around his table. He himself occupied the royal chair and he lit the lamps. Messianic fervor, the joy of the commandments, study, and prayer were as brilliant as they had been in the time of the Baal Shem Tov. The clear spring had become a river. The waters of the Torah poured forth and flooded even the most isolated and impoverished communities. The Hasidim had made a revolution: they overthrew the pride of the wealthy and the learned. Now the love of Heaven, the love of Torah, and the love of Israel were the rule for both individual and communal behavior. Mystical intention, which had been raised high by the great masters of Kabbalah, became the goal and also the means. Who could measure the quality of a man's intentions? Who could imbue his prayer with fervor, the mark of this inner value? The great contest was open to all, and sages were prepared to give advice and show the way.

Nevertheless, Rabbi Dov Baer was apprehensive. The Frankist heresy had seduced mystical and naive souls from the straight way. Renowned masters opposed the hasidic movement. The Gaon of Vilna reproached the Hasidim for divulging mysteries and seeking to propagate the holy spirit among people who were inadequately prepared. Was it not written in the Talmud that an ignoramus cannot be a Hasid? On the other hand, the prophet Joel had proclaimed that one day the spirit would rest on all flesh: "Your sons and your daughters shall prophesy; your old men shall dream dreams, your young men shall see visions."

Had that day really come?

In Mezhirech, the Great Maggid was gravely concerned about his only son, Abraham, who was known as the Angel. The boy was absorbed totally in study and prayer. He preferred to devote himself to the study of hidden wisdom; when he spent long hours studying with his friend Rabbi Shneur Zalman, the future master of Habad, it was the esoteric, and the deeper side of the Talmud he loved to uncover.

The Great Maggid was disturbed by his son's total detachment from worldly matters. Had not the Baal Shem Tov himself warned against excessive asceticism? And now his son, impatient in his desire to hasten the Liberation and to rise from rung to rung on the ladder of holiness, had returned to the old way. He declined to marry, and stubbornly refused to acknowledge the existence of women.

At that time an important event took place at Mezhirech. Rabbi Feibush, who was famous for his work on the Talmud, paid a visit to the Great Maggid, seeking his guidance about the meaning of a particular legal passage. Rabbi Feibush used to fast whenever the solution to a problem eluded him, and he would receive an answer from heaven in a dream. This time no answer had been forthcoming, and, although he had always reserved his judgment concerning the hasidic movement, he decided to go to Rabbi Dov Baer. The Great Maggid, without waiting for the rabbi to complete the presentation of his question, cast light into the innermost chambers of his heart. And then Rabbi Feibush spoke to him about the spiritual fervor of his daughter.

Some months later Rabbi Dov Baer conceived a great plan. In the eyes of some, it could have been construed as a political act: would not a match between the families of the Great Maggid and of Rabbi Feibush strengthen the status of hasidic teaching, which had long been under threat of anathema? However, his motive was deeper than this, and lay elsewhere. Rabbi Dov

Baer sought such a young woman for his son; he hoped that a soul of such quality would join his family and his household.

He spoke to his son. "No one is absolved from observing the first of all the commandments. 'Be fruitful and multiply.' In the Talmud it is written that a bachelor is not a complete man, and that the Divine Presence cannot rest on him."

On a less solemn note he added. "Abramele, we had a family tree that traced our ancestry back to Rashi, and from him back to King David. The chart was destroyed in a fire. My saintly mother of blessed memory wept bitterly, but I consoled her by making a solemn promise: an even more illustrious family tree will descend from me . . . Abramele, you must help me keep that promise . . . Will not the Messiah himself, like us, be a descendant of King David? Do you have the right to sever such a noble lineage? Who knows? Who can know?"

His son answered sadly. "Is it not true that the elements must be true to their nature? Must not fire rise, just as water must flow downwards? I, father, am nothing but fire striving upwards to Heaven."

The Great Maggid replied, "You are not being asked to descend into carnal pleasure, to lower yourself among daughters of the earth. There are daughters of Heaven, too. You must fulfill the commandment that brings a man closer to God, that makes him into a creator of men. Remember, my son, that even though marital relations are forbidden on the eve of Yom Kippur, the high priest, the most holy of men who alone could enter the Holy of Holies on the holiest of days, he, of all men, had to be married. And remember, the one hundred and twenty years that Adam spent in solitude were the source of many evils; and that one of the reasons that Aaron's two sons were punished was their refusal to marry."

"Father, Adam gave himself over to impure thoughts. And as for Aaron's sons, is it not also said that they were, in a certain sense, superior even to Moses and Aaron? And is it not written in the Zohar that Moses parted from his wife in order to dedicate himself to the Divine Presence?"

"Everything you say is true, Abramele, but the Zohar also states that Moses would not have been permitted to do so had he not already had two sons. Furthermore, there is a time for every task. David and Solomon acted in a different way. Our movement needs new generations of leaders, and the Baal Shem Tov himself wished for your own birth.

"True, fire must rise, and may not descend," he went on. "But you bear the name of my father Abraham, and Abraham is the master of water, which is the glorious symbol of divine mercy."

With the consent of Abraham, the Angel, Rabbi Dov Baer sent a group of his Hasidim to Kremnitz, to discuss the matter with Rabbi Feibush. A painful intuition impelled him to act quickly.

The delegation bore a royal message. They were to ask for the hand of the rabbi's daughter for the son of their master. If the suit was accepted, they were to return with the betrothed.

The visionary child, so young, so frail, so lovely, accepted the proposal that her father conveyed to her. He had asked for a year's betrothal, according to old custom. But the messengers could not agree.

The child's name is not given in most of the accounts where she is mentioned, but according to an oral tradition it was Gittel.

She left with her mother for Mezhirech. The quick decision, the journey towards the unknown, engendered a dull feeling of melancholia in the mother's heart. The maiden remained silent as she looked at the sad countryside, the like of which she had never seen. As they approached the home of the Great Maggid, crowds of Hasidim came to meet them. The young daughter of princes of the Torah understood the royal character of the nuptials, and her mother was comforted by the magnificence of their reception. The Great Maggid himself and his most glowing disciples greeted them kindly. Shortly afterwards the marriage was celebrated with great joy.

At first the Angels of Light were frightening, but later, it is said, they were consoling. Gittel was troubled by the appearance of her husband, but she soon became attached to him with all her being. She became, in a way, the pupil of her father-in-law, and she sought comfort and advice from him.

Sometimes, from an adjacent room, Gittel would overhear the Master teaching his disciples. She was surprised that she understood. He did not speak, he chanted; and his voice penetrated the depths of her being.

" 'The righteous shall flourish like the palm tree.' Now there are two kinds of righteous men. One is constantly attached to God, but his righteousness is for himself alone, for it does not influence other people. He is like a cedar tree, which bears no fruit. But the righteous man who is compared to a palm tree bears much fruit. He is a master of repentance. The reward of the second is much greater than that of the first."

The great sage Nachum of Chernobyl, the illustrious rabbi Levi-Yitzhak of Berditchev, the holy brothers, Zussia of Annopol and Elimelekh of Lyzhansk, the masters of Polish Hasidism, came frequently to Mezhirech, as did Rabbi Menachem Mendel of Vitebsk, who was preparing to depart for Eretz Israel. Other visitors were young visionaries like Rabbi Solomon of Karlin, Rabbi Israel of Kozienice, and the future Seer of Lublin, all of whom showed great promise for the coming generation.

Shortly after his marriage, Rabbi Abraham fell ill. His sickness gave rise to much concern. Then one morning he was suddenly very much better. That very morning, Rabbi Dov Baer said to his daughter-in-law:

"Thank you for what you have done. You saved Abramele."

"I hope so," she replied. "I shall tell you what I dreamed. I ascended to the celestial throne to entreat for his recovery; the answer that I received was that as a result of my prayers, he would be granted twelve more years of life."

"Perhaps in twelve years' time, you will be able to do the same again," murmured Dov Baer.

"Amen," said Gittel.

The young couple had two sons. In their hasidic fervor, they named one of them Israel, after the Baal Shem Tov, and the other Shalom, which is one of the names of the Redeemer, the Bearer of Peace, like King Solomon, son of King David.

Young Gittel entered the study of the Great Maggid with greater ease than his most eminent disciples. He would ask her gaily, "Has our dreamer of dreams received any precious visions?"

Rabbi Dov Baer himself had been initiated by the Baal Shem Tov into the seeing of lightning flashes from Sinai. One evening, he had been listening, while reclining on a divan, to the Baal Shem Tov, who was reading and explaining to him a text that he thought he already understood well—and he saw the Divine Voices. Then the Baal Shem Tov had murmured, "This evening you have received the Torah close to your soul, like Israel at Sinai."

But the household of the Great Maggid was to remain the center of Hasidism for no more than a few years. The storm that burst forth from Vilna, with the fearful anathema of the venerable Gaon, was soon to darken the Field of Apple Trees, and cloud the thoughts of those who were awaiting the dawn.

In the face of the apparent indifference of the Master, the disciples formed a secret conclave and decided to return blow for blow. They cast an anathema of their own against the great commentator on the Zohar, who had accused them of laying waste the plantations of the Garden of Eden. The next day, the Great Maggid murmured, "You have, perhaps, won a victory, but you have lost your general."

Shortly afterwards the Great Maggid died, at Annopol.

Only Gittel continued to see him and to hear him. It was with her, and not with his greatest disciples, that he was able to communicate.

Knesset Israel, the young visionary girl, was able to hear the righteous ones of the past who do not always speak in the language of the righteous ones of the present.

Abraham had no ambition to succeed his father, who had been the uncontested leader of the Hasidim. He remained constantly drawn towards Heaven, but when he was asked to accept a rabbinical post at Hovatow, he agreed. Gittel strongly opposed this move, and said that her father-in-law did not approve of it. On a number of occasions she had warned the Great Maggid's disciples in such a fashion, but they rarely heeded her. As she opposed her husband's move, but was unable to prevent it, she decided not to accompany him. All the efforts of the disciples to persuade her to take her children to Hovatow were of no avail. Rabbi Abraham was accorded great honor by his new community, who also took care of all his needs, but he fell ill as soon as he arrived, and shortly afterwards he left this world.

When the Great Maggid's disciples learned of this sad event, they finally recognized that Gittel was a true visionary. They dared not tell her about her husband's death, but they told the young Shalom to say Kaddish. Gittel followed her son to the synagogue, and she understood what was being kept from her. She immediately left for Hovatow, where she was welcomed with great respect. She fell into silence and dejection, but she continued to see beautiful visions; in one of them, Rabbi Abraham came to beg her forgiveness for having left her behind and for not having heeded her. She rented a small shop, and managed to support her family with the income.

Rabbi Nachum of Chernobyl helped her by assuming responsibility for the education of young Shalom. From his youth Shalom had loved to mix with men, and he dreamt of a sumptuous hasidic life, worldly and well organized. His son, Rabbi Israel of Ruzhin, was later to put that ideal into practice.

Shalom's brother Israel married a daughter of Rabbi Solomon of Karlin, who was known as the Messiah son of Joseph . . .

When Rabbi Nachum of Chernobyl's wife died, he wanted to marry the daughter of kings, Gittel, who had been so dear to his master, the Great Maggid. He asked Shalom to go and discuss the matter with his mother, but Rabbi Abraham appeared before his son on the way and forbade him to convey the suit to his mother: "She promised to remain faithful to me."

Shalom obeyed his father. Nevertheless, some time later he himself wed a granddaughter of Rabbi Nachum, and so the house of Chernobyl was raised by being bound in marriage with Mezhirech.

When Gittel saw that her sons were set on the right path, she heard a new call, that of the Holy Land.

Cut off from the great leaders of her generation, the Daughter of Princes, Knesset Israel, dreamed of returning to Zion.

Some of the disciples of the Great Maggid had by that time settled in Tiberias, but she did not wish to join them. She knew that their life was hard, and were they to take her in, they would try to honor her. She did not wish to impose upon them. "I shall work," she thought.

Gittel collected her savings for the journey. She blessed her children, bid her friends farewell, and left the snowy life of Eastern Europe. She disembarked at Acre, among crowds of Arabs under an iron sun. Is the Divine Presence not blinding at times?

She recalled the center in Galilee, where Cordovero, the Ari, and Haim Vital had revealed the secrets of Heaven and earth, and had prepared the way for the Messiah. She reached Tiberias and humbly sought work among the oriental Jews. She did not understand their language, for they spoke Arabic, and she was surprised by their customs. Some people took her for a laundress, but others discerned the hidden saint in her. For in addition to the thirty-six unknown righteous men who maintain the world, are there not also prophetesses and visionary women? Is it not possible that the approach of messianic days will entail the renewal of the mystical role of women?

She is fair, this daughter of Jerusalem. She shuns the Hasidim. Is it out of love, or disappointment? She who daily hears the voice of the Great Maggid, and who humbly follows his counsel . . .

She takes in washing to support herself, and sometimes, in the pitiless heat of the Tiberias summer, she fasts in piety.

Knesset Israel, far from her masters and inspired by Heaven, works in the land of her ancestors. She feels that she has come near to Heaven. But it is not her own salvation that she is seeking. She hopes to make ready the day when Rabbi Shalom, or, perhaps, one of his descendants, will enter Jerusalem on a white or a many-colored ass.

But the asses are gray, Jerusalem is far away, and the Daughter of Kings takes in washing for ungenerous merchants. She remembers the festivals at Mezhirech, how the crowds, the singing and the dancing seemed to enhance the hopes of each individual. How different were the silent, modest prayers of the oriental sages. Nevertheless, they too are building a bridge between Heaven and earth.

Knesset Israel, alone, unrecognized, courageous, bows under her daily tasks and under the Asian sun. The low houses are clustered together in heat and silence.

Tiberias is calm, secretive, celestial. Nearby and distant hills are reflected in the lake.

Near Safed lie Bar Yohai, the Holy Lamp, and the Masters of the Zohar, the Ari, the Holy Lion, and his cubs.

In Tiberias Gittel climbs up to the tomb of Rabbi Meir Baal HaNes, the Master of the Miracle. The tiny synagogue looks down upon the lake, where hours are translated into shifting colors. There Rabbi Dov Baer appears to her once again . . . And the water promises a future blossoming, when the Righteous Ones and Knesset Israel will live in renewed harmony, and the Righteous Ones will heed the voice of the young inspired woman. Meanwhile, doves and gulls fly over the lake. . . .

Translated from the French
by Jeffrey Green and Jonathan Omer-man

A Bratslaver Hasid

by Joseph Opatshau

At midnight the Warsaw-Kiev train began to approach the Polish border. The third-class cars, which had left Warsaw packed, were almost empty now. There were only three passengers in the last car. Two of them lay on the lower benches, heads thrown to the side, arms outspread, as though dead. The third passenger, a deep-chested individual with a sparse, blond beard, looked like a Russian peasant. Lightly, he jumped down from an upper bench, dragging a bag after him, out of which rolled a loaf of black bread and a tin of honey. The two sleeping passengers awoke, looked at one another, and asked the third man:

"What, are we at the border already?"

The third man did not answer; he did not seem to have heard or understood the question. Absorbed in what he was doing, he repacked the bread and honey and retied the bag. His fellow passengers agreed out loud that their companion was deaf and dumb. Turning their heads to the wall, they fell asleep again. Not until then did the deaf-mute open the car window; he put out his head for a moment, then pulled it back in. It was raining. The rain drummed on the roof, splattering against the panes.

The deaf-mute picked up the bag by its straps and threw it over his shoulder. Quietly, he left the car. He stood on the steps of the running board. The rain and wind blowing through the fields assailed him, but he stood motionless for a while. When his eyes had penetrated the darkness and his body had caught the vibrations of the chugging locomotive, the wheels biting into the rails, and the pounding rain, the deaf-mute climbed up the iron ladder to the wagon roof. For a moment he considered whether to remain on this car or to move on to another. A door scraped; the deaf-mute stretched out on his stomach and lay flat against the roof. The rain beat harder, the darkness thickened. The wind blew away every sound, the rain drenched every view. The deaf-mute had not expected the night to be so bad. He saw it as an act of God.

Going uphill, the train slowed. In the darkness, tongues of flame appeared, indicating the Polish border. The locomotive whistle shrilled, and the train screeched to a halt.

The deaf-mute's ears were so wide open and alert that he could distinguish in the rain and wind the merest scraping of a door, the lightest footstep. Nor was this to be wondered at. This was Wolf's twentieth illegal crossing of the border in the guise of a deaf-mute. Every Rosh Hashanah the Hasid made the trip to Uman to the grave of his former master, Rabbi Nachman of Bratslav. He traveled with neither passport nor visa. Together with bread and honey, the bag over his shoulder contained a volume of Rabbi Nachman's famous folk tales. He was certain in his heart that his rabbi had not really died—he was riding in the train with him. It was as though the rabbi had merely changed cars; one had only to call out—and he would hear. The journey from Warsaw to Uman was a difficult one—as difficult as "the throes of the grave." Moving from car to car in mid-journey, always fighting, always taking chances, Wolf's life was constantly in danger—both on the Polish and the Soviet sides of the border. Nevertheless, not once in the nineteen years since Rabbi Nachman's death had Wolf failed to visit his master's grave in Uman. This was the twentieth trip. Up to this point the journey had been fairly easy. God Himself was on his side. What a rain, what a wind, what darkness! Is the passport check over?

The locomotive shrieked. The cars lurched sideways. The rain lashed at Wolf's wet feet and drenched shoulders; the roof was too slippery for him to sit down. Wolf crept over to the iron ladder and stood under the roof, holding tight to the wet railing. Shutting his eyes, he pressed his lips, and wordlessly, soundlessly, recited some of Rabbi Nachman's sayings. The urgency to reach Uman and be received by the rabbi at his grave—this was sufficient motive to keep Wolf warm. He no longer felt his feet soaking up water like a blotter, no longer feared to be pulled off the moving train at any moment. Joy rose in his breast, as though he were making a pilgrimage to Jerusalem. It was not as if he were undergoing a complete spiritual reformation—that was not the cause of this joy. Rather, he was happy because it was a sufficient achievement for a human being to lift up one shoulder toward heaven—and the rain, the darkness, the danger disappeared. Because man, after all, was created to raise up heaven. Otherwise, it would have been impossible for Rabbi Nachman to be sitting inside the car while his disciple, Wolf, stood on the roof. The Soviet border already?

Wolf fell prone. But this time he did not stay on the roof of the last car. Pushing his bag ahead of him to wipe a path through the wetness, he crept forward over the car roofs.

At the fourth car from the locomotive, Wolf stopped. There was no iron ladder on this car; no one would take the trouble to crawl up to the roof to check. The wind, blowing from the field and forest, angrily flung sheets of rain at him.

Wolf heard the passengers leave the cars and move toward customs. There, after their baggage and passports had been checked, they would transfer to a Russian train for Kharkov.

Not he. Wolf would remain lying on the roof of the Polish train, until the station lamps were extinguished and the railroad attendants left. Then he would descend, and set forth through the wood to Shepetovka.

The locomotive began chugging again; smoke issuing from the chimneys sprayed the wet air with sparks. The train switched rails, moved on into the fields, and there stopped. It grew silent after a while. The only sound was the beating of the rain, the groaning and whistling wind. Then the Russian train departed.

Wolf had reached the roof of the last car. Light on his feet as a cat, the forty-year-old Hasid dropped down from the roof and lay under the car. He considered a moment the alternative of taking the highway toward Shepetovka, then thought better of it and decided on the fields. He crawled some two hundred feet on hands and knees, then straightened up. His arms and legs creaked as he began to walk. Yet, soaked through and through though he was, a warm glow entered his heart: he was to spend Rosh Hashanah with Rabbi Nachman's followers in Uman for the twentieth time.

Wolf passed through a field where the potatoes were dug up. There were small holes in the ground, mounds of dirt and puddles of water everywhere he put his feet. The night was full of rain and din; it was hard to tell where the noise was coming from. Suddenly, a dog started to bark. Wolf stood stock still. When the barking stopped, he moved on, to trudge, out of breath, toward the smithy that stood at the entry to Shepetovka.

Wolf knocked at the smithy window, then at the door. He heard steps, a voice:

"Who is it?"

"It is me, Wolf."

"From Warsaw?"

"Yes, Mendel."

A lock creaked open. The door opened; Wolf was struck by the warmth of the hearth. The two men greeted one another in the darkness, embracing. Thus standing, words were exchanged.

"Was it a hard journey?"

"This was an easy one. When do we go to Uman to visit the rabbi?"

"Tomorrow, if you wish."

The two men had a short drink in the darkness. Hastily, news was exchanged, tidings of the rabbi's Hasidim in Warsaw, Berdishev, and Uman. When the smith's wife went into the kitchen to sleep, both men got into the warm bed and immediately fell asleep.

Translated from the Yiddish
by Jacob Sloan

The Dancing of Reb Hershl
with the Withered Hand

by Leslie A. Fiedler

It was in the time of my grandfather that the small but prosperous Jewish community of M. was threatened with extinction. My grandfather had known as a young man many of the leading scholars of that town; and he would speak of them to me with tears in his eyes. "Such learned men," he would say ruefully, "no longer exist!" But grandfathers have always talked in this way, and I suppose such remarks must be taken only as the tribute paid by the guilty living to the dead, who in dying have made amends for everything. At any rate, one black year just as the final preparations were being made for the Passover Seder, which was held annually at the house of the eminent Reb Yankele, a gentile child was discovered lying under the table, quite dead. His throat had been cut, but he was otherwise untouched and he lay there in all the apparent innocence of childish beauty. What was to be done?

The dead boy was obviously part of a well-planned provocation. If his body had remained undiscovered, soldiers would have broken into the house at the height of the Seder, led by the father of the boy, a peasant who might, indeed, have killed his own son in the drunken fury of his poverty, and then—woe! The nightmare of the gentiles would have been proved a fact, and the burning, murder and pillage for which they longed as for a feast would have seemed to them only the execution of justice. It had been a difficult winter with much inexplicable disease and with food scarce because of the poor crops of the previous summer.

"But we have heard of this before," Reb Yankele protested. "It is a story which our fathers have told us. It is not something which happens but which is *told!*"

"Only what is told happens. Nothing which occurs for a first time really is." This was the way Reb Hershl talked when he was a young man, in riddles and for the learned; later, he was different, his words like a drink of water—refreshing to any throat. But at this time Reb Hershl was still the student of Reb Yankele, and he had been married for just three days. It was for this reason that he protested bitterly against the decision of the Community, crying out that he wanted to stay with his bride, and to face with her whatever might come.

But it had been decided that the five men in whom was vested the wisdom of the Community must at all costs be saved from the destruction which no one could see any way to forestall. A hiding-place had been secretly prepared long before, against precisely such an event; for rightly or wrongly, the people of M. felt that they had been entrusted by God with the most learned men of their time in the Court of Reb Yankele. It was to this secret place, a cave in the side of the hill only a mile distant from the town, that Reb Hershl was driven, along with Reb Yankele himself, Reb Eliezar, Reb Shloimo and Reb Nahum.

They made an oddly contrasting group, those five: Reb Yankele with his fine, blue eyes and his serene face from which a white beard flowed like the waters of peace; Reb Hershl burly and golden-blond, but with those terrible black eyes from which the guilty (and even sometimes the innocent, for who can ever be sure) flinched; Reb Eliezar who was so old that he seemed always half asleep, or perhaps, as some said, already half transported into the World-to-come. He was without flesh as the result of severe fasting and seemed scarcely to exist beside the fleshiness of Reb Shloimo, a man with two chins and a belly that bounced rhythmically as he walked. Reproached once for loving a glutton, Reb Yankele is said to have answered that only in his seventieth year had he learned that the fat man, too, has a share in the World-to-come. Reb Nahum was the bitterest of the five, a prey to extraordinary rages. One cursed by God, he was accustomed to call himself, with his four daughters; but it was really his eternally renewed surprise at the evil of the world which kept him enraged.

A sixth man was also saved, though inadvertently; almost, you might say, by mistake. For it had been necessary to find a driver for the five rabbis, the Torah, and the dead body of the gentile boy, which they had decided, unwisely perhaps in their panic, to carry along with them. The driver had been selected by lot, and the choice had fallen on the *Roite* Moishe, a dull fellow with the flaming hair his name indicated, an ignorant drunken lout, always the butt of his fellow drivers, scarcely a Jew! Such was the will of God.

It was Moishe who rolled away the mossy stone which concealed the mouth of the cave, Moishe who winked back over his shoulder, showing his mountebank's face to the trembling rabbis, Moishe who went in with a lantern to make sure there were no poisonous reptiles in the damp darkness of the cavern. The rabbis, grouped around the dead body of the boy which they had dropped on the grass, waited impatiently for the driver to emerge, but there was no sign of him, though they could hear him singing loudly inside.

"An irreverent idiot!" Reb Nahum cried finally, "with his tavern songs in this hour of destruction," and he burst into the cave followed closely by the others. Moishe appeared to be dancing when they entered, his bloodflushed face and bright hair shining strangely in the light of the lantern, so that it seemed as if he were on fire. They could make out only uncertainly the words of his song:

Dark rabbis, let the dance begin,
The dance you do not know you do.
The dance of David was his sin;
The dance you dance is you, is you!

The dance he danced before the Ark,
Bathsheba taught him in the dark;
The dance you dance is you!

When Absalom hung by his hair
And danced his dying in the air,
God's mercy fell like dew!

Reb Nahum struck him a blow across the back of the head that knocked him to the floor. "Blasphemer," Reb Nahum cried in his metallic voice, "be silent if you cannot speak the words of God!"

"It's black magic, necromancy," Reb Shloimo screamed shrilly, wiping his bald head and his thick black jowls with the back of one fat hand, for he was a timid man. "This fellow may be Ashmodai himself, sent in this blackest hour to complete our torments."

But Reb Yankele made a sign for quiet, while the driver grovelled and begged for pardon from the floor. "What shall we do with *this?*" He held out in his arms the limp body of the gentile boy, from which they all shrank back. No one could remember any longer why they had decided to bring it.

"A miracle," Reb Eliezar answered, in his ghost of a voice, in words that seemed spent when they reached the ear, as if they had traveled for a long time, "only a miracle."

"It is told," Reb Shloimo put in eagerly, "that once, I think it was in Worms, a child killed just so, and concealed just so beneath the table, rose at the Seder and sang with all the faithful like one of the living, so that the searchers were baffled. . . ."

"There are no miracles for us," Reb Nahum cut him off indignantly. "An age of miracles is followed by an age of plagues. This is the time of the left hand and not of the right!"

"Why are we talking like children of miracles?" Reb Yankele said then. "The story of the dead child who sang we are not required to believe like infants. It is a parable, a way of presenting for the simple the mercy of God which no one is complicated enough to understand."

"It is the pagans who ask for miracles. Wonders can be done by the magicians of Pharaoh as well as by the Masters of the Holy Name. We must believe without evidence, believe in the Silence of God. All else is worshipping idols."

It was seldom that Reb Eliezar made so extended an effort, and they all listened without a word, remaining hushed afterwards until Reb Hershl, unable to bear it any longer, cried out, "Why are we not worthy of a sign? For

God's sake and not our own!" But he was embarrassed to find the red-headed driver chuckling from where he crouched beside him like a toad.

"Put the child in the center of the floor," Reb Hershl said to change the subject, "and let us see in this effigy of death the image of our own sons, how in a little while they will all be."

"Reb Hershl, forgive me, but you have no children yourself. Otherwise you would not talk so." Reb Nahum strode over as he spoke, and taking the body of the boy laid him almost tenderly on the floor in their midst.

"But I do have a wife and she, also, is already dead. It is only because I am a coward that I do not rend my clothes even now. She is my life and my wisdom and she is already dead. We should have brought the women with us."

"Ah yes, the women, the women!" The driver licked his lips comically and began to sing with vulgar gestures another verse:

> The dance he danced before the Ark,
> Bathsheba taught him in the dark!

He held one hand up before his face, to protect himself from the expected blow, but no one paid any attention to him.

"We have brought the only true Bride of Israel," Reb Eliezar whispered, and turning to him, they saw he held in his shrivelled arms the Torah in its dress of blue and silver.

"Your wife will be waiting for you in the World-to-come," Reb Nahum said. "This is the virtue of women, to wait. And you will not be without a footstool. Meanwhile, there will be other women to bear you sons."

"She is more worthy than I to be saved," Reb Hershl cried humbly.

"Why, then," Reb Nahum answered him, "do you thank God each morning that He has not made you a woman?"

"And is it not written," Reb Shloimo added, "that each man must think of his own wife as he utters those words of thanks." It was well known that the wife of Reb Shloimo was a shrew, a woman as passionately thin as he was placidly fat; and it was even reported that she beat him.

"This commentary is a mystery and not a joke!" Reb Yankele admonished him.

But Reb Hershl at least was not content to leave this, or indeed anything, a mystery. "When we thank God that He has not made us women, we think of our own wives certainly, for it is the difference which permits us to go to them as the Eternal goes to His Shekhina, so that what is above forever may be sustained by what is below for only a moment. . . ."

In the midst of Reb Hershl's remarks, Moishe had begun to sing very softly:

In the wood there is a rose,
That lives when all the roses die;
Who plucks her petals no one knows,
No one knows but I!

but Reb Nahum roared him down with the cry of "Silence!"

"It is the Passover," Reb Yankele reminded them, for, indeed, they had forgotten; and they sat down together to tell how they had come up out of Egypt, saying the bare words without the unleavened bread or the wine, or the bitter herb to memorialize suffering or the green to be the sign of hope. Only the child lay in their midst, his white throat gashed, as if the terrible old lie of the gentiles were true, and that dead flesh were the paschal sacrifice.

They repeated the text, of course from memory, running through the service without any pause for exegesis, as if they were in a hurry to be through, imagining perhaps the children squirming in their places at the odor of the feast wafted from the kitchen. There were tears in their eyes, it is true, at the words:

For not only one has risen up against us, but in every generation they have raised themselves up to destroy us; yet the Most Holy, Blessed be He, has always delivered us out of their hands!

But only when they sang the *Dayenu,* and paused with the verse: *If he had slain their first-born and not bestowed their wealth upon us, it would have been enough!* did the discussion begin.

"I do not understand," Reb Hershl said softly, almost to himself, "why it is written here 'bestowed their wealth upon us,' when in the Torah we find simply 'plundered the Egyptians,' which is to say, stole from them like common thieves their gold and jewels."

Reb Shloimo answered first, "The looting of the Egyptians must not be interpreted as vindictive or senseless plunder, only as the assertion of a just claim. For surely the total treasure of the Egyptians could not have come to one-tenth of what was owing the children of Israel for their long years of labor in the brick-kilns. It is a lesson forever that the laborer must be given his due hire!"

"Not so," Reb Eliezar whispered, "the plundering of the Egyptians can be understood only as the Ten Plagues are rightly understood, as a blessing disguised as a curse. Since each plague in depriving the Egyptians of what held them down in their mud, what bound them to the darkness, made it possible for them to know the Truth; for they also, they *especially,* were slaves in their own land to be freed by the Holy One, blessed be He. . . ."

"And yet the despoiling of the Egyptians," Reb Yankele went on, picking up the train of thought of the old man, whose voice had thinned to an invisible thread, "is the greatest blessing of all, greater even than the death of the First Born; for even the final curse of the Ten destroyed only a last human vanity. But that which was stolen from the Egyptians is not to be understood as mere treasure but as the golden stuff of their idols, as their lying gods themselves!"

"It is absurd," Reb Nahum roared in his habitual tone of wrath, "to complicate the Torah needlessly. God *commanded* the Children of Israel to spoil their spoilers, and it is not necessary to understand a command, only to obey it, to obey even when, and especially when, what is ordered seems repugnant to everyday morality. If to steal from the rich seems to you wrong, what of sacrificing your own son as was required of Abraham?"

He stabbed a nervous arm out toward Reb Hershl, who insisted stubbornly, "No! No! We will never understand the meaning of the act unless we begin by admitting it was *wrong!* In every enterprise no matter how noble, there are woven the threads of evil. This action was the ignoble revenge of a people who were still slaves in their hearts, and to call it the command of God is foolish pride. Twice the Children of Israel fell into pride in the moment of their Going Out of Egypt, first in the looting and second in their rejoicing over the drowning of the hosts of Pharaoh, who were also the children of God!"

"To hear the wisdom of Reb Hershl the angels of the heavenly host have descended to the sill of this world!" The extraordinary words appeared to come from the driver, but the voice was no longer his mocking snarl, and though each scholar attempted separately to step forward and hush him, they were incapable of moving a step toward him. "These words are true, but they are not the whole truth. Hear me, masters! If there had been no looting of the Egyptians, the Children of Israel would have had no gold to make the image set up in the desert while Moses was with God on Sinai; and this is the beginning.

"For if there had been no Golden Calf, the first tables of the Law would not have been destroyed, and the second, or bitter, Law would never have been given.

"And if the bitter Law had not been given, the Jews would no longer have been chosen among the people; for the first Law was so gentle a yoke that the Seventy Nations who were also present at Sinai would have gladly accepted it.

"And if Israel had been no longer alone in the Promise, the gentiles would not have persisted in their hatred of us.

"And if they had not persisted in their hatred, there would have been no pogrom today. . . ."

At this, all of the others, except for Reb Hershl, cried out "Abomination!" and Reb Yankele even held his hands over his ears.

But Reb Hershl pushed the absurd argument on to its conclusion, in a voice only half mocking, for such riddling explanations were then his special vice. "And if there had been no pogrom, we should not have been in this black hole together, and the question we are asking might never have been asked, the answer never known. The reason that we seek is our being here to discover the reason."

Reb Eliezar, lifting his tired head, pleaded with him, "Please! Some jokes must never be made."

And Reb Shloimo cried out, "This is the Adversary as I have said, and he has bewitched our brother Hershl!"

But the driver, who had seemed truly to grow taller in the gloom as a shadow grows with the decline of the sun, went on in a terrible voice that hushed them all. "Reb Hershl is exactly right. If the end of reason is to know the limits of reason, all right reasoning must close in on itself, making a circle which is Zero, or God!"

At these words, Reb Nahum struck the driver across the face, a blow whose sound rang out in the dark cave, but Moishe did not flinch.

"If you do not like this interpretation, masters," he said, glowing now like a ruddy jewel, until the surrounding darkness seemed heated to an intolerable scarlet, "let us say, then, that the Israelites stole the Egyptians' gold so that you might today be blessed with the death of your children and your wives." At this, Reb Hershl raised his hand as if he, too, would strike the driver, but he let it fall again embarrassedly. "Let God be so good to all of us!" the *Roite* Moishe finished, and this time Reb Shloimo slapped him, the flesh of his hand quivering as it met hard bone.

"Or rather, masters, let us say that only what is robbed is given by God, even as Jacob came into his portion only by robbing Esau. As it is written: to him who takes shall be given."

"This is the argument of the Serpent to Eve," Reb Shloimo screamed. "I knew him from the first."

"The words which you say are not written at all," Reb Yankele said firmly, and this time he himself struck the driver a blow whose force left his own body trembling and weak; but the driver did not move. Under the growing light and the rain of blows, his face had lost its malice and dullness, had become almost beautiful.

"Let us say, then, masters," he continued, "that it is for the salvation of Edom that the gold was taken. For if Israel had been perfect, the gentiles would have been lost forever. Venting their evil upon each other, they would have plunged forever into the darkness of Gehinnom; but turning their spite upon us, they are saved. For even as Isaiah tells us, the Kings of the Gentiles cry out concerning Israel. 'By his stripes we are healed, and his chastisement is our peace!' "

"This is blasphemy," Reb Eliezar whispered hoarsely, the tears streaming down his cheeks; and lifting the staff on which he was accustomed to lean, with what strength remained to him he managed to strike the final blow. But the driver only seized his nerveless hand as it fell again, kissing it, while Reb Hershl, moved by an impulse he did not quite understand, cried out, "Thou shalt be as the sandalwood, perfuming the ax which cuts it down."

He began to dance slowly, tentatively, more as if he dreamed he danced than as if he actually moved. But the driver, who seemed now to tower above and beyond the cave into a dimension where rocks have no reality, cried out like thunder, "Let the hand that has given no offense be withered!"

Looking down, Reb Hershl could see that his right hand had turned a scaly yellow-white, his scabbed fingers hanging limply, and the arm within his sleeve withered to a flaking stick. And now the man who they had thought was Moishe shone with an intolerable beauty that was like a blow and a consolation at once; and each lifting his mantle, covered his head, except for Reb Hershl, who stood gazing down upon his ruined hand with the wonder of a child who thinks he does not know why he is being punished.

"It is Elijah!" Reb Yankele more sighed than said, while the voice of the revealed Elijah flowed once more over and around and within them: "Lay the blasted hand upon the throat of the child!"

Reb Hershl, moving still as in a dream, but now as if in one from which he feared at any moment to awake, knelt beside the dead boy, touched the open wound, lifting his withered arm with his still strong left hand, and the wound was closed up. The color returned in a warm flush to the cheek of the child who was dead, and his eyes opened slowly, though for the moment he did not move.

At the cry of exultation that burst from Reb Hershl, each of the others unmuffled his head, looked, and shouted out in praise. First Reb Nahum: "The Lord may chastise me, but He has not given me over to death!" Then Reb Shloimo, "Thy mighty power didst Thou wonderfully display on the Passover," followed by Reb Eliezar, who murmured, "Let those who fear the Lord now say that His mercy endureth forever," while Reb Yankele shouted with mingled laughter and tears, "Therefore the limbs of which Thou hast formed us, the spirit and soul which Thou hast breathed into us, the tongue Thou has placed in our mouth shall worship, bless, praise, glorify, extol, reverence, sanctify and acknowledge Thy overwhelming power, our King!"

Only Reb Hershl seemed unable to find a text after his first cry of joy and relief, but looked still in anguish at his unchanged and ruined hand. "Why?" he began, turning toward Elijah, who paid him no heed, but sang with all the simple blitheness of a child the last verse of *Hagadyah:*

> Then came the Most Holy, Blessed be He,
> And did to death the Angel of Death,
> Who slew the slaughterer

Who had slain the ox,
Which had drunk the water,
Which had put out the fire,
Which had burnt the stick,
Which had beaten the dog,
Which had bit the cat,
Which had eaten the kid
My father bought for two pennies!
A kid, a kid, an only kid!

Reb Nahum had already run to the entrance of the cave, and had rolled away the rock that barred it, so that from within they could see across the plain to their village. It was already morning, for the night had passed without their noticing it. At just this moment, there arose the first shaft of smoke from over the Jewish quarter, while through the still air cries of lust and terror could be clearly heard, and soon within the calmly billowing smoke the nervous little tongues of flame showed palely.

A low moan moved from rabbi to rabbi as the wind moves, but the voice of Elijah was unmoved in its terrible joy, standing as a stone stands under the wind: "Wherefore I praised the dead which are already dead more than the living which are alive!"

Reb Hershl tried to begin the *Kaddish*, but he had said only three words when, attempting to raise his lifeless hand, he stuttered to a full stop, looking from his dead, flaking fingers to the greasy column of smoke on the horizon. There were no more cries. "Why?" he asked again hoarsely. "Why?"

But Elijah cast back at him his own earlier words. " 'Why are we not worthy of a sign? For God's sake and not our own!' Here is your sign: that you are not healed! Because in the hour of death you are able to reproach God for your right arm, as in the moment of resurrection you are able to cry out against Him for the lives of your wife and friends, be assured that your wife is dead, that they are all, *all* dead! That which is to be hath already been and God requireth that which is past!"

As the prophet spoke, the ruddy light about him faded and his form shrunk in upon itself until it had become the absurd insignificant frame of the *Roite* Moishe, while the unbearable music of his voice had blurred to the mocking raucous tones of the carter (and who could have sworn that he was ever anything else!), "Besides, rabbi, the physicians have to live, too. Is it God's place to compete with a poor Jew?"

At the word "Jew," the forgotten child rose to its feet like a sleepwalker, and began to sing in the shrill sweet voice of one trained for singing in the churches of the gentiles:

Where is Hugh, my pretty Hugh
That played with me at ball?

The Jew's black daughter lured him in
Behind her garden wall.

She soothed him with a lully-loo,
She stroked his golden head;
She cut his throat from ear to ear,
And laughed when he was dead!

He never said a single word,
He never made a moan,
The only sound was of her knife
That grated on the bone.

She caught his blood in a silver cup,
She caught his only tear.
Her father kissed his darling girl,
He called her dove and dear.

They threw Hugh's body in the well,
They weighted it with stones;
Green and oozy grows the moss
On Hugh's forgotten bones.

And when the springtime comes again,
The daughter of the Jew
Combs out her hair on the garden wall
To lure another Hugh.

Still tangled in a legend and a dream, the boy did not seem to see the dark, bearded men who stood about him until Reb Yankele shouted, "Why is this child alive and my sons dead!" He raised a fist into the air as if prepared to strike down the boy, who began to yell in a passion of fear, "I want my mama! I want my mama! I want my mama!"

The rabbis had closed in around him, cutting off all the morning light with their greater height, until it seemed as if he were sealed again in the darkness from which he had just been delivered. "I want my mama!" he sobbed now almost incomprehensibly; and it was then that Reb Hershl opened a path for him through his colleagues, holding up his withered hand in his good one like a talisman or a banner. "Why not?" Reb Hershl said, as if to himself, "After all, why not?"

At this, the voice of the carter swelled again to a climax of joy: LAST YEAR YOU WERE SLAVES, THIS YEAR YOU ARE FREE!

But when they looked around, neither driver nor prophet was to be seen, only the boy framed in the entryway as he ran off across the fields toward the burning village. At first the child ran headlong in terror, but in a little while he was pausing to pick a flower or to throw a rock at a bird—for it was spring and he was alive.

Then Reb Hershl began truly to dance, moving as the boy moved and as the wind moved past him, moving as the earth moved under them all and as the sun moved through the immaculate heavens toward the ending of another day. Only his withered arm did not move, hanging motionless in the midst of the motion, as if it were somehow the center and the meaning of the dance. But whether that meaning was joy or sorrow, knowledge or bafflement, or some strange marriage of them all, it would have been difficult to say. Certainly, *I* shall not try to say, though I have seen Reb Hershl dance that dance, as he danced it again every year after the Seder, when the old men commented on the Song of Songs. I went once to the village of M. with my grandfather, a little boy walking, it seemed to me then, forever along the road, while beside us in wagons and handcarts, on foot and on the shoulders of friends, the lame, the blind, the afflicted came in the hope of springtime to see the dancing of Reb Hershl with the withered hand.

The Shortest Friday of the Year

by Hayim Nachman Bialik

1

If we praise the man who on a plain Friday hastens to prepare for the Sabbath, he who does so on the shortest Friday of the year deserves twofold praise. On that day carelessness is forbidden. One slip and the Sabbath might be desecrated, God forbid. After all, Satan purposely does his worst during times of danger.

It was no surprise, then, that Rabbi Lipa, may he live and be well, a man weak by nature and easily alarmed, set out to outwit that short Friday even before sunrise. Very strict with himself was he and very fearful lest he be late by a split second and thereby ruin the entire order of his day.

Do not take the order of his day lightly. There were midnight prayers, Psalms, meditations, the morning service itself, chapters from the Mishnah, a page of the Talmud, some sections of the Code of Law, and, finally, the weekly portion of the Torah and its Aramaic Targum. All that was for Him in heaven. Then he had to tend to himself and prepare a meal. What could one do? A man of flesh and blood had to eat. After twelve noon a new order of activities began: the ritual bath, nail-paring, preparing snuff in honor of the Sabbath, and so on. In addition, people came with questions of law, and occasionally a dispute had to be settled. Conflict, as is well known, comes just on the eve of the Sabbath. In the meantime, the day slips by; before one turns around it's sunset.

No wonder, then, that Rabbi Lipa girded his strength like a lion and rose early on that shortest Friday of the year, washed his hands, and began his day's activities. Would that it would come and go without hindrance! He was afraid to waste a moment and occasionally glanced at the large old clock on the wall, terrified that he might skip something in the order of his day, God forbid, and come to the Sabbath with anxiety in his heart.

But as our sages have said: everything depends on *mazel*. And nothing, not speed, not counsel, not wisdom, can countervail *mazel*.

Listen to this awesome tale!

2

After Rabbi Lipa had finished all his meditations and was preparing to begin the morning prayers, the door suddenly groaned open and a peasant, bringing a column of vapor with him, entered the house.

What's he doing here so early? the rabbi wondered, somewhat alarmed, backing away from the wave of cold.

The peasant placed his whip next to the *mezzuzah* on the doorpost, removed his gloves, and slid his hand into his coat, from which he removed a folded letter, wrinkled and smudged, and handed it to the rabbi. The rabbi read it and shrugged.

The devil's own doings! His heart had warned him. Reb Getzi, the rich tax collector in the next village, was inviting him to a circumcision feast. Reb Getzi wrote that he was bringing his first grandson, the firstborn of his eldest daughter, into the Covenant of Abraham; hence, he was requesting the worthy rabbi to be the godfather. The honorable rabbi would have to inconvenience himself and come to the village right away. The sleigh was waiting.

But unfortunately, tax collector Reb Getzi wasn't a writer of short notes. A reader couldn't race through his letters. Attached to this epistle were three copious footnotes.

Footnote number one: a three-ruble banknote in an envelope, a brand-new bill transferred from the hand of the peasant (forgive the proximity) to the hand of the rabbi.

Footnote number two: a bagful of potatoes and, tied to it, a fattened, cackling goose. The maid removed this comely pair from the sleigh and in no time they were both in the kitchen.

Footnote number three: a warm and heavy coat of fur and a pair of felt boots which Reb Getzi had sent with the peasant. These came from his own stock of winter clothing so that the rabbi, long life to him, would be well wrapped and warm on the journey.

These three explicit footnotes opened the rabbi's eyes and in a flash everything fell into place. "Well, what can you do?" the rabbi sighed. "It must be

God's will. A circumcision. What a *mitzvah*! But, in any case, I must consult my wife.''

Rabbi Lipa went to see his wife in the other room, stayed awhile, did what he had to do, and emerged dressed in a white smock and a Sabbath cloak, ready for the trip. In the front room, he covered the cloak with the fur coat, pulled the yellow boots over his black shoes, donned his Sabbath fur hat over his skullcap, girded himself with the red belt that Ivan had also brought, and, dressed in this mixture of weekday and Sabbath clothing, Rabbi Lipa kissed the *mezzuzah* and left the house.

The large sleigh in front of the house was lined with lots of straw. Rabbi Lipa climbed in and sat down comfortably, feeling quite at home. The peasant covered the rabbi's legs with straw and climbed in too. He whistled once—and the sleigh was sliding over the snow.

3

The road was smooth and the mare quick. Just a short jump, really.

An hour later the sun still hadn't risen, and the rabbi arrived in the village and came to Reb Getzi's house.

The guests had already assembled. They had hot drinks and began to pray in a *minyan*. A butcher, who had come by chance into town to buy calves, was found to have a pleasant voice and served as cantor. But his Hebrew pronunciation was somewhat faulty. He also mixed up parts of the prayer: he asked for dew in the season of rain. Still, it wasn't so terrible. Finally, they rushed through the concluding *Alenu*, and amid general good cheer the rites of circumcision began.

The baby was swaddled and passed from hand to hand. The uncle handed him to the father's uncle. He to the nephew. The nephew to the father's father, and he to the mother's father. So it went until the baby came to the godfather, Rabbi Lipa. There they did what they had to do. Then the return trip. Again they picked up the little red body, wrapped hand and foot, which twitched and cried softly. They sent him back the same way. From the hands of the godfather to the father, from the father to the maternal grandfather, and so on—until he was returned to his cradle, where he quieted down.

Tax collector Reb Getzi was a hospitable man, kind and openhanded by nature. These traits were enhanced now that the Lord had granted him his first grandson. Obviously, then, the feast was a grand one. Fish aplenty. A veritable Leviathan. Meat—a whole calf, a dozen ducks, and three fattened geese. No need to mention the side dishes—stuffed derma, tongues and kidneys, dishes fried and roasted, as well as a host of mouth-watering delicacies, including the renowned candied turnips.

Now we move from edibles to potables. Reb Getzi, you must understand, was a straightforward, simple man. When he said whiskey he meant whiskey. No less than 95 proof and aged too. Whiskey that had been stored in his cellar, buried underground for years, set aside for the day he would celebrate the arrival of his first grandson. "Have another glass, rabbi, just this little tumbler." Reb Getzi pushed a pint bottle into the rabbi's hand. "Please. Go ahead. Drink, rabbi! Don't be afraid. Do you think this is whiskey? It isn't whiskey at all! It's olive oil! It flows into the glass without a sound. Pure olive oil! So help me—as my name is Getzi. *L'chayim!* Here's to your health, rabbi, your health!"

Getzi became a bit high. His fat and hairy face glittered and shone like a polished samovar. His eyes were sunk in fat. From time to time he jabbed a finger into his chest, clucking and muttering to himself with a thickened tongue. "Getzi . . . you know? Now you're an old man . . . a grandpa. Do you hear? Ha, ha, ha! You've become a grandpa. And what's your wife? A g . . . g . . . grandma! Where are you, g . . . g . . . grandma? Come here. Grandpa will drink to your health. Come, come, don't be shy. The rabbi will say amen. Right, rabbi?"

Here Reb Getzi grabbed Rabbi Lipa's arm, held his shoulders with all his might, and shook him like a bag of potatoes. Then he suddenly fell on the rabbi and kissed him ardently, at once crying and laughing for joy at the honor—ha, ha, ha—the honor that Rabbi Lipa had done him. "As I live and breathe, it's an honor! If it weren't for you, rabbi," and Getzi began sniffling.

"All right, enough! To your health!" Rabbi Lipa soothed the crying Getzi and took a careful sip from the bottle. "*L'chayim!* What's the crying for? No need for tears. No need."

Reb Getzi calmed down and wiped his tears with his sleeve. "As my name is Getzi that was well said, rabbi. There's no need for tears. No need. *L'chayim!* To health and life! And to health and life once more! A life of health and prosperity. Oh . . . r . . . r . . . rabbi!" Here Getzi burst into a renewed flood of tears. "Oh . . . pros-per-i-ty!"

Rabbi Lipa, by nature a kind and tenderhearted man, couldn't bear Getzi's sadness and favored him by taking another drop and yet another drop. . . .

In the meantime, the day rolled on—the shortest Friday of the year. Rabbi Lipa, who was now a little high himself, stirred once, twice, and tried to stand on his weak legs in front of the table. "Oh, oh," he murmured, spreading his hands. "It's the eve of Sabbath—the short Friday." But Reb Getzi neither listened nor cared. He held Rabbi Lipa with both hands and wouldn't let him go.

All this time the driver, Ivan, was sitting peacefully in the kitchen, enjoying his share of the festive meal. He was delighted that this little baby had become a Jew. He sent one drink after another down his gullet. One and one was two and one was three . . .

The clock tolled three. In a rush Rabbi Lipa stood up. But his legs were in no rush. When he had bundled himself into his wraps—the bearcoat, the sheepskin coat, the red belt—and stepped once more into those two barrels—the heavy boots—his legs wouldn't obey him at all.

Instead of uprooting himself, the bundled-up Rabbi Lipa found himself sitting in the middle of the room. He tried to move. But he couldn't budge.

The "olive oil" spreading through Rabbi Lipa's bones had had its effect. But Rabbi Lipa had no regrets. On the contrary, his thoughts were merry and his heart was glad. While he tried, with outstretched hands and moving fingers, to pluck himself from his place by his own strength, he chuckled in a soft, birdlike voice, tittering to himself. "Hee, hee, hee, Reb Getzi . . . my legs . . ."

"Hee . . . hee . . . hee," laughed the others. "The rabbi."

Finally, with the help of Him Who aids the weary and with that of the guests, the bundled form was lifted from its place. Then the two happy creatures, Rabbi Lipa and (forgive the proximity) his attendant, Ivan, left the house, assisting each other and leaning on each other's shoulders, and clambered up on the sleigh. Once again our rabbi sat comfortably in the sleigh, his body and legs covered. Again Ivan sat in the driver's seat. He emitted a loud, merry whistle—and the mare lifted her legs. . . .

And now we're getting to the heart of the tale.

4

From the moment the sleigh began to move and Rabbi Lipa was comfortably settled in his overcoats, he felt a pleasant warmth, sweet as honey, spreading through his body. His eyelids began to droop and his head began to nod. "Hee, hee, hee, the oil," the rabbi laughed into his chest and felt as if sand were falling on his eyelids. "Pure olive oil." And the moment the sleigh crossed the little bridge at the edge of the village he sank into a deep slumber.

Ivan, on the driver's seat, was talking to his mare, chattering amiably, promising her all sorts of good things if she would only go straight and not stray from the path. But while talking to the mare, the whip and reins slipped from his hands, and his head, with its sheepskin hat, sank to his chest. A minute later he was snoring like a sow.

The mare, sensing she was free, immediately forgot all her master's preaching and all his pleasant promises. At a fork in the road she hesitated a moment, as if thinking which way to go. Suddenly she pulled the sleigh with all her might and went straight ahead into the field.

Meanwhile clouds came by and darkened the way. A thick, wet snow fell heavily, confusing creation and wiping away all signs of a road. The mare, doubting she had done the right thing, was beginning to repent. But because the animal saw no solution, she resigned herself to Heaven and continued walking in the darkness, sad and ashamed, stepping gingerly as if with closed eyes, through snowdrifts and thickets of thorns, dragging the sleigh and its riders. Who knows where she would have gone had she not stumbled suddenly, causing the sleigh to overturn. Our two travelers woke up in a fright in a pile of snow, surrounded by all-pervasive darkness.

"What's this?" the rabbi wondered and tried to scramble out of the snow. Suddenly he remembered everything and, as if an ax had struck his head, he cried out: "The Sabbath!"

Rabbi Lipa wanted to let out a loud and bitter wail—but could not. His one and only terror-stricken thought was—Sabbath! When his power of speech returned, a cry burst from his throat: "Ivan, *ay vey!*" This cry, from the depths of his heart, expressed the only words the rabbi knew in the peasant's language. It combined an outburst of woe, a request for pity, his awe of God, his resignation to God's will, sorrow and complaint, and much more which could not be put into words.

Meanwhile, swearing lustily, Ivan was working on the overturned sleigh and the tangled reins. From time to time he kicked the poor mare's belly and cursed her ancestors. When the repairs were done, he invited the rabbi to take his seat. The rabbi looked into the night. From whence would come his salvation? None was forthcoming. For a moment he thought of not moving, come what may. Here in the open field he would lodge and spend his Sabbath. He would die rather than break the Torah commandment. Weren't there stories of Hasidim and men of good deeds who spent the Sabbath in woods and deserts? He remembered the story of Ariel. Didn't the Holy One, blessed be He, call forth a lion to guard him in the desert until the end of Sabbath and to serve as a beast of burden thereafter?

But when Rabbi Lipa considered the howling storm and the total darkness of the night his heart sank. To his left lay a dense forest full of deafening sounds. He knew that a forest was dangerous—marauders and wild beasts made their homes there. To his right stretched a broad, desolate field, wrapped in white shrouds. Strange black and white shapes that looked like tombstones emerged from the snow. God knows what they were: demons, beasts, corpses—or perhaps only thorn bushes. From out of the blackness, from every corner and every side, hosts of panthers and serpents were advancing toward him.

"No," Rabbi Lipa said, "according to the Law, when there is a danger to life the laws of Sabbath are suspended. You shall live by the law, the Torah states, not die by it. And one must not count on miracles. Who knows if I am worthy of having a miracle performed for me?" At that moment Rabbi Lipa saw a huge, awesome panther before him, shooting sparks from his eyes and grinding his crooked teeth. Rabbi Lipa's skin bristled with fear and his eyes protruded in horror. "No, no," the rabbi decided and, teeth chattering, climbed into the sleigh. "According to the Law, I'm not obliged to give up my life for the Sabbath. On the contrary, I must ride. The Torah does not forbid riding on the Sabbath; it is a prohibition added by the rabbis.''

The sleigh went slowly on its way through the slippery darkness. Rabbi Lipa, depressed and attempting to make himself uncomfortable, honored the arrival of the Sabbath with silent prayer. For him the night stretched on endlessly. The weary mare plodded along. The sleigh joggled over the bumpy path and shook the crushed Rabbi Lipa. His bones were just about scattered along the way. The old thick-branched, snow-covered trees of the forest seemed to reprimand him, and the young fir trees stood astonished. Who *is* this Rabbi Lipa, who *is* this rabbi who dares to travel on the Sabbath? Briars pressed their heads to the snow in shame and the wind among the ancient, snow-laden trees wept and wailed: "Woe, woe to the desecration of God's name! Woe that the Torah has been shamed!''

5

About midnight the sleigh finally reached a roadside inn on a hilltop. The snow was so high it covered the windowsills. The vapor of the exhausted mare turned into flecks of frost. The two passengers were battered and spent. The rabbi's beard, earlocks, mustache, and hat were frozen into one glassy piece. It was impossible to go any further. From the inn an old gentile attendant came out to them. The rabbi then entered the inn and the sleigh was taken into the yard.

The room which Rabbi Lipa entered was cold and drab; it was lit by the light of a small, sooty lantern. From the adjoining room he could hear the snores of the innkeepers. On the table stood two brass candlesticks whose candles had burned out. On the thick, hand-woven tablecloth crumbs and bones were scattered—leftovers of the Friday-night meal. Rabbi Lipa turned away. Frozen through and through, weighted down by his heavy clothing, he fell with his last ounce of strength on a plain hard bench near the wall and bent his head toward his chest.

He had profaned the Sabbath. How would he show his face tomorrow? And what would he say on Judgment Day? Oh the shame of it!

Tears poured from his eyes. His earlocks and mustache thawed somewhat and dripped water too. The rabbi's head and limbs were as heavy as bars of lead. He wanted to move but could not. Perhaps the hour of death had come, thought the terror-stricken rabbi, his teeth chattering. Yes, it was death. Time to confess.

The rabbi's lips whispered the prayer of confession. "Oh God, merciful and gracious, slow to anger and abounding in kindness and truth. Please, God, have pity. Sovereign of the Universe, pardon and forgive, for we're only flesh and blood; we are mere worms, human beings. I have sinned and transgressed and have gone astray. But the innocent lambs, my wife and children, how have they done wrong?"

For a long time the poor man tossed and turned. He perspired and his bones burned like fire. In the delirium of fever he whispered various verses: he mixed passages from the Mishnah with those in the Bible, sayings of the sages with snatches of prayer. Lofty thoughts of reward and punishment, heaven and hell, the torments of the grave and the angel of Gehenna ran about in his confused mind with thoughts of his family: his widow, orphans, a grown daughter, his position as rabbi, the yeast tax . . .

With these troubled thoughts the rabbi wearied himself. He groaned and sighed till morning. But with the coming of the dawn he sank into a deep, confused sleep, a tortured and heavy slumber.

6

While Rabbi Lipa was lying on the bench of the desolate inn, curled into his coat, soaked with perspiration, water dripping from his beard and earlocks, the Lord was sitting in Heaven doing what had to be done—making the roosters herald the morning and rolling the darkness away from the light.

When the rooster crowed and the cold light of a winter morning came into the house through the small frost-covered windows, Fivke, the proprietor, sneezed, belched, and woke up. With one jump he was out of bed; he put on his heavy boots, threw on his jacket, and went out into the public room to see who had arrived during the night. When he entered and saw what he saw, he became petrified: before him on the bench was the rabbi.

At first he thought he was dreaming. Then he bent closer and inspected him from all sides. "As I live and breathe, it *is* the rabbi. What's this? On the Sabbath? The rabbi? Am I drunk or crazy?" Suddenly he struck his head with his fist. "Oh Fivke, you ass! You've made a mistake. An awful mistake in reckoning the days of the week! Oh yes, Fivke, woe unto you and your life. You've been living among the heathen. For your great sins you've lost track of time. Here's a pretty fix, as you're alive. Tomorrow everyone will know it—fool!"

Fivke knew what he had to do: quickly remove all signs of the Sabbath before the rabbi awoke and saw the depths of Fivke's degradation. First, he took away the brass candlesticks, the remains of the meal, and the white tablecloth. Then he ran into the bedroom and rushed his wife and daughter out of their beds.

"Hurry up, you geese, the devil take you!"

"What is it? Who's here?" His wife woke up in a fright.

"To the blazes with you, you cow! Don't holler! Get up now and take the food out of the oven!"

For a moment she didn't know what her husband was talking about. But when he explained with a poke of his fist, she jumped up, dressed, and dashed to the oven.

"All of it! Take it all out, the plague take you!" her husband said. "Throw it away—every bit of it! The pudding, the stew. Everything."

In a flash the house changed character: gone was the Sabbath, replaced by the weekday. In the open-mouthed stove a fire was burning. The big-bellied samovar was filled with hot coals and started humming. The sounds of an ax and hammer were heard in the house. Yochim, the servant, was splitting logs and driving pegs and hammering nails, whether there was a need for it or not. Fivke himself was bent over the kneading trough working the dough with all his might. His daughter, a tall girl in her teens with a puffy, soot-covered face, stood in a daze in the middle of the room, not knowing what was happening. In the meantime, she managed to get slapped twice and pinched once by her father's dirty, dough-covered hands. Then she began peeling potatoes into a big, water-filled pot.

"Peel, peel, the devil take you," Fivke cried and hurried them on, working away himself. He expected the rabbi to wake at any moment. When he had finished kneading the dough and the rabbi was still asleep, Fivke hurriedly put on his shabby, crushed hat; he bared his arm and began to put on *tefillin*, chanting the weekday morning prayers in a loud voice.

Meanwhile, the door kept swinging on its hinges, and farmers, wearing their overcoats and carrying whips, were coming and going. The chill of snow, the smoke of pipes, the smell of overcoats, the noise of stamping feet and conversation filled the room.

Fivke purposely walked by the rabbi's bench while praying, chanting "Hallelujah" in a loud voice. While so doing, he threw a glance at the rabbi as if to say: "Sleep, sleep, rabbi. Sleep in good health. Now I'm not afraid anymore. Now you can even get up."

And, indeed, at that very moment the rabbi stirred. "Be strong now," Fivke urged himself. "Don't spoil it now."

7

With the rabbi's awakening, all his pains woke with him and he groaned. His head hurt and all his bones seemed crushed. With difficulty he sat up and opened his eyes. Where was he? In the bathhouse? No, in an inn! Where was the Sabbath? There was no hint of the Sabbath. Farmers. A weekday crowd. And there, in front of him, a samovar was boiling.

"If so"—an awful thought frightened the rabbi and his gloomy face darkened even more—"if so, I've slept through the whole Sabbath. Here on the bench, in front of Fivke and the peasants, I was stretched out and asleep for twenty-four hours. Without *Kiddush*, without prayers, without *havdalah*. O God, what are you doing to Lipa?" A black pall of fear came over him. God had caused him much agony, too much suffering. "Why? Tell me why?" he asked in despair.

In the midst of the thick cloud of pipe smoke Ivan came, whip in hand, and said, "It's time to go, rabbi. The sleigh is ready."

Sighing, the rabbi stood up and faced the doorway. He tottered like a drunkard, and barely made his way through the farmers. At the doorway Fivke's broad hand suddenly shook his. "Goodbye . . . r . . . r . . . rabbi."

"Goodbye, goodbye." The rabbi slipped out quickly. "No time . . ."

This separation pleased both and neither delayed it. Fivke slammed the door as though to say "Good riddance!"

The rabbi climbed up into his sleigh. "Hey, Ivan, Ivan!" the rabbi urged on the driver.

But what was the rush? Where could he flee to? Rabbi Lipa did not know the answer. At that moment he asked nothing and thought of nothing. Everything he did was seemingly done of its own accord, without knowledge, without foresight. He only had one wish and prayed for it with all his might: "Sovereign of the Universe, perform a miracle for me and stretch the way home into thousands of miles. Let years and centuries pass and let me travel on and on. If I'm not worthy of this, take my soul from me and I'll forgive you, God, take my soul!"

But Rabbi Lipa's prayer was not answered. The sleigh carried him swiftly as if on eagle's wings and the smooth and polished path ran by. After the cloudy night, a winter sun shone gaily on the snow-covered ground. Crows at the roadside flew away from the flying sleigh and welcomed it with hoarse screams—kraa, kraa, kraa.

Rabbi Lipa, ashamed before the crows, the bright sun, the white snow, bent his head, lost again in his despairing thoughts. From that moment on, he neither heard nor saw nor felt a thing. He gave his spirit to the God of Spirits and his broken body to the flying sleigh. "Whatever will be, will be."

8

At noon, the congregation was leaving the synagogue and walking in Sabbath peace on both sides of the street and in the middle too, greeting one another with Sabbath blessings. At that very moment there suddenly appeared from a lane a quick and graceful sleigh. The congregation blinked in disbelief: in it sat their rabbi—Rabbi Lipa.

Translated from the Hebrew
by Curt Leviant

Reb Yeshaiah Argues with God

by Yehuda Yaari

> The sacrifices of God are a broken spirit:
> A broken and a contrite heart, O God,
> Thou wilt not despise.
>
> Psalms 51:19

There is a story about a Rabbi Yeshaiah of Dennewitz, may he be remembered as a righteous man, who came before God, blessed be He, with an argument: Why was it that the Lord did not provide him with his Sabbath needs, either on Wednesday or Thursday, but instead always on Friday when the day was already half over? This same Rabbi Yeshaiah, although renowned as a righteous and God-fearing man, a man of God in every way, lived all of his days in wretched poverty. He did not serve as a rabbi, nor did he lead a congregation. He ran a tavern at the edge of the town, and he would serve vodka and other alcoholic drinks to the peasants from the surrounding area. And because he was preoccupied all day long serving the Lord with religious fervor, awe, and spiritual ecstasy, at the same time that he was serving his customers, the peasants used to dread coming to his place. For they said, "This Jew deadens our joy with his sorrowful mutterings and his heavy sighs. Not just vodka but tears he pours for us."

Needless to say, a tavern which gets a reputation for dampening the spirits of all who cross its threshold does not make a good impression on its patrons. Rabbi Yeshaiah, who felt the glow of Sabbath all the days of the week, used to worry anxiously from the beginning of the week to its end: from where would they get their Sabbath needs, from where? It is true that on the nonholy days one can get by on the most meager fare, a little water and stale bread. But on the Sabbath! And so he would worry and worry day after day until Friday came. As soon as Friday arrived, around the middle of the day, the Holy One, praised be He, would always send to Rabbi Yeshaiah some peasants who were just passing through, and who did not know of the rebbe's peculiar ways. They drank whatever they drank and they paid whatever they paid, until a coin or two crossed the rebbe's palm. As soon as he had enough money to cover the cost of the Sabbath, he immediately sent the peasants on their way, closed his tavern, and gave the money to his humble wife so that she could go to the market and buy whatever she could.

When his wife came to the market at this time, of course, she could not find the choicest meats and vegetables, and she had to make due with what she could get: fish that wasn't fresh, a scrawny chicken with more bones than meat on it, and the like. And not only this, but because she came at such a late hour, so close to the Sabbath's arrival, the merchants got the best of her and they demanded exorbitant prices from her, twice what she would have had to pay if she'd bought better goods a day before.

The saintly rebbe used to feel a great sorrow about this and so he took his case before the Lord, blessed be He. And thus he argued: "Master of the Universe! Being as You in Your great mercy always send me my Sabbath needs with Your holy and outstretched hand, I have come to You with a request. I beseech Thee, O Lord! Please do not send them to me again on Friday, Sabbath Eve, when the day is almost over, but send me whatever You will send me on Wednesday or Thursday. Because if You do this, it won't cost You any more, because believe me with a sum smaller than what you usually send me, I could get better provisions for the Sabbath, and I wouldn't feel such sorrow and anguish in my soul." The Holy One, blessed be He, answered him: "As for what you have said, that this would not cost Me more, do not worry, My son. I have the silver and I have the gold. But what about your anguishing soul? This, precisely, is what I want."

Translated from the Hebrew
by Pamela Altfeld Malone

The Laws of Partnership

by Fishel Schneersohn

When Rabbi Hayim of Volozhin, the founder of the famous yeshivah of Volozhin, died, there was great excitement in heaven. The host of angels who came out to greet him told him that there would be no need of a trial and that he would be admitted into heaven immediately, so rich was he in good deeds. But Rabbi Hayim brushed aside the invitation and insisted that there had to be a trial for him, just as there is for everyone else, and he cited the passage in the Talmud which says that all must be treated equally by the Law.

At the trial they said that, of course, he should be admitted and given a seat of honor in heaven for having established this mighty academy. But Rabbi Hayim argued, on the basis of a passage in the Talmud that deals with the Laws of Partnership, that if he was entitled to a reward then surely the students of the yeshivah were as well, for he could not have accomplished what he did without them. The court conferred and came to the conclusion that he was right, that the students were also entitled to a share of his glory. But Reb Hayim then argued that he would not enter heaven unless and until all of the people of Volozhin were admitted too, for it was they who had taken the students in and given them "days" to eat so that they could study. Without them, he said, the yeshivah could not have succeeded and so they, too, deserved a share of the reward.

The heavenly court conferred and they checked all the references that the rabbi had cited in the Laws of Partnership and came to the conclusion that he was right, that the people of Volozhin were entitled to a share in his glory. But Rabbi Hayim was not finished yet. He said: "The people of Volozhin at least had the satisfaction of seeing the results of their charity. They saw the students who studied. But what about all those Jews in all the many communities that I visited who gave me donations for the yeshivah without ever having the satisfaction of seeing the school and its results? Surely they too deserve a share in the reward as great as mine, for without them I could not have done it." He cited the passages in the Laws of Partnership that deal with this issue and he said: "I refuse. I will not enter heaven until and unless they are admitted too." The court conferred and checked the passages that he had cited and again concluded that he was right.

Then Reb Hayim argued that all Jews should be admitted with him, since all Jewish householders everywhere contribute in some way to the maintenance of the Torah. But even this did not satisfy him. He argued further that the gentiles too have provided a home for the Jews and therefore they, too, have a share in the Torah. This time he was told that he had asked too much, that there simply was not room enough in heaven for all, and that what he was asking was not possible until the Messiah comes.

"In that case," said Rabbi Hayim, "I will stay outside with them and wait." And until this day his great soul waits patiently at the portals, studying the Law with intensity and praying for the ultimate redemption of all mankind.

Retold from the Hebrew
by Rabbi Jack Riemer

Gedali

by Isaac Babel

On Sabbath eves the thick sadness of memories torments me. On such evenings, long ago, my grandfather used to stroke the volumes of Ibn Ezra with his yellow beard. My grandmother, in a lace kerchief, would make magic over the Sabbath candles with her knotty fingers and sob sweetly. On those evenings my childish heart would rock like a little ship on enchanted waves. Oh, the moldered Talmuds of my childhood! Oh, the thick sadness of memories!

I roam through Zhitomir looking for a shy star. Beside the ancient synagogue, beside its yellow and indifferent walls, old Jews sell chalk, wicks,
washing blue—Jews with prophets' beards and passionate rags on their
sunken chests.

Here, before me, is the market place and the death of the market place.
Killed is the fat soul of abundance. Dumb padlocks hang on the stalls and the
granite of the pavement is as clean as the bald spot of a dead man. The shy
star twinkles and goes out.

Success came to me later, success came just before sunset. Gedali's shop
was tucked away in a row of closed stores. Dickens, where was your friendly
shade that day? You should have seen in this old curiosity shop a pair of gilt
slippers and ships' cables, an ancient compass and a stuffed eagle, a Win-
chester with the date 1810 engraved on it and a battered saucepan.

Old Gedali, the proprietor, walks around his treasures in the pink vacuum
of evening, a little man in cloudy glasses and a green frock coat that reaches
to the ground. He rubs his small white hands, plucks at his little gray beard
and, cocking his head, listens to invisible voices that float down to him.

This shop resembles the treasure box of a solemn boy with a craving for
knowledge who will grow up to be a professor of botany. There are buttons
in it and a dead butterfly, and the name of its tiny proprietor is Gedali.
Everyone has left the market place, Gedali has stayed on. He slips in and out
of a labyrinth of globes, skulls and dead flowers, waving a bright duster of
cock's feathers and flicking the dust off flowers that have died.

And now we sit on two empty beer barrels. Gedali twists and untwists his
scanty beard. His high hat sways above us like a little black tower. Warm air
floats past us. The sky changes color. Up above gentle blood flows from an
overturned bottle, and a light odor of decay enfolds me.

"The Revolution—let us say aye to it, but are we to say nay to the Sabbath?" thus Gedali begins, winding about me the silken thongs of his cloudy
eyes. "I cry yes to the Revolution; I cry yes to her, but she hides from Gedali
and her only messengers are bullets. . . ."

"Sunlight does not enter closed eyes," I answer the old man. "But we will
rip open the eyes that are closed."

"The Pole has closed my eyes," the old man says in a barely audible whisper. "The Pole, vicious dog that he is. He takes the Jew and tears out his
beard, the cur! And now the vicious dog is getting a beating himself. That's
fine, that's—Revolution. And then those who have given the Pole a beating
say to me: 'Turn your gramophone over to us, Gedali, we're going to register it.' 'But I love music, madam,' I say to the Revolution. 'You don't know
what you love, Gedali; I'm going to shoot you, and then you'll know. And I
can't help shooting because I am the Revolution.' "

"She can't help shooting, Gedali," I say to the old man, "because she is
the Revolution."

"But the Pole did his shooting, kind sir, because he was the Counterrevolution; you shoot because you are the Revolution. But surely the Revolution is joy. And joy doesn't like orphans in the house. Good deeds are done by good men. Revolution is the good deeds of good men. But good men do not kill. So it is bad men that are making the Revolution. But Poles, too, are bad men. Who, then, will tell Gedali which is Revolution and which is Counterrevolution. I used to study the Talmud, I love Rashi's commentaries and the books of Maimonides. And there are yet other men of understanding in Zhitomir. And here all of us, learned men, fall upon our faces and cry out at the top of our voices: 'Woe unto us, where is our sweet Revolution?' "

The old man fell silent. And we beheld the first star that sprang up along the Milky Way.

"The Sabbath has begun," Gedali brought out solemnly; "time for Jews to go to synagogue. . . . Mr. Comrade," he said, rising, and his high hat, like a black tower, swayed on his head, "bring a few good men to Zhitomir. Oh, they are scarce in our town, oh, how scarce! Bring good men and we'll turn all our gramophones over to them. We are no dunces. The International—we know what the International is. I want an International of good men, I want to have every soul registered and given the biggest ration. There, soul, take your fill, please, and enjoy life. The International, Mr. Comrade, you're the one who doesn't know what sauce goes with it."

"Gunpowder's the sauce that goes with it and it's spiced with the best blood. . . ."

And lo! the young Sabbath ascended its throne, coming out of the blue darkness.

"Gedali," I said, "today is Friday and it's already evening. Where can you get a Jewish cookie, a Jewish glass of tea and in the glass of tea a little taste of that God who has been asked to step down?"

"Nowhere," Gedali answered me, hanging the padlock on his little treasure box, "nowhere. There is a tavern next door, and good people used to run it, but nobody eats there nowadays, they just weep."

He buttoned three bone buttons of his green frock coat, flicked himself with the cock's feathers, sprinkled a little water on his soft palms, and was gone—a tiny, lonely dreamer in a black top hat and with a large prayer book under his arm.

The Sabbath has arrived. Gedali, founder of a Utopian International, has gone to synagogue to pray.

Translated from the Russian
by Abraham Yarmolinsky

The Rabbi

by Isaac Babel

". . . All are mortal. The mother alone is destined to eternal life. And when she passes on, she leaves a memory behind which no one as yet has dared to sully. The memory of the mother feeds our compassion even as the ocean, the boundless ocean, feeds the rivers that carve the world. . . ."

Those were Gedali's words. He uttered them solemnly. The evening that was being snuffed out ensphered him in the pink haze of its sadness. The old man went on:

"The doors and windows of Hasidism, that passionate edifice, are smashed, but it is as deathless as the mother's soul. With empty eye sockets Hasidism still stands firmly at the crossroads swept by history's fierce winds."

Thus spoke Gedali and, having said his prayers in the synagogue, took me to see Rabbi Motele, the last of the Chernobyl dynasty.

Gedali and I walked up the main street. White churches gleamed in the distance like buckwheat fields. The wheel of a gun carriage groaned round the corner. Two pregnant Ukrainian women came out of a gateway, their coin necklaces jingling, and sat down on a bench. A shy star began to gleam on the sunset's orange battlefield, and peace, Sabbath peace, rested upon the crooked roofs of the Zhitomir ghetto.

"Here," whispered Gedali, pointing to a sprawling house with a shattered façade.

We entered a room, as stony and naked as a morgue. Rabbi Motele sat at a table, surrounded by liars and madmen. He wore a sable *strammel* and a white robe belted with rope. He sat with closed eyes, digging his thin fingers into the yellow down of his beard.

"Where do you come from, Jew?" he asked, and raised his eyelids.

"From Odessa," I answered.

"A pious city," said the Rabbi with unusual vehemence, "the star of our exile and, against its will, the well of our misfortunes. What is the Jew's occupation?"

"I put the adventures of Hersh of Ostropol into verse."

"A mighty and worthy task," murmured the Rabbi and dropped his eyelids. "The jackal howls when he is hungry, every fool has folly enough to be despondent, and alone the wise man rends the veil of being with laughter. . . . What did the Jew study?"

"The Torah."

"What is the Jew seeking?"

"Joy."

"Reb Mordkhe," said the *tzaddik*, and shook his beard, "let the young man be seated at the table, let him eat with other Jews, this Sabbath eve, let him rejoice that he is alive and not dead, let him clap his hands when his neighbors dance, let him drink wine if he is given wine."

And Reb Mordkhe, an old buffoon, a hunchbacked old man, no taller than a boy of ten, with everted eyelids, darted up to me.

"Oh, my dear and so very young man," said the ragged Reb Mordkhe and winked at me, "how many rich fools have I known in Odessa, and how many penniless sages have I known in Odessa! Sit down at the table, young man, and drink the wine that won't be offered you. . . ."

We all seated ourselves one next to the other, the liars, the madmen and the loafers. In the corner brawny Jews who looked like fishermen and apostles moaned over their prayer books. Gedali in his green frock coat was dozing against the wall like a bright-feathered bird. And suddenly behind his back I caught sight of a youth, a youth with the look of Spinoza, with Spinoza's powerful brow and with the sickly face of a nun. He was smoking and shivering, like an escaped prisoner whom his captors had brought back to his cell. Ragged Mordkhe stole up to him from behind, snatched the cigarette from his mouth and ran to my side.

"That's Ilya, the rabbi's son," Mordkhe muttered hoarsely, and brought closer to me the bleeding flesh of his everted eyelids. "The accursed son, the last son, the disobedient son."

And Mordkhe shook his little fist threateningly at the youth and spat in his face.

"Blessed be the Lord," rang out the voice of Rabbi Motele Bratzlavsky, and he broke the bread with his monkish fingers. "Blessed be the God of Israel who has chosen us from among all the nations of the earth. . . ."

The Rabbi blessed the food, and we sat down to eat. Beyond the window horses were neighing and Cossacks were shouting. The wilderness of war yawned beyond the window. The rabbi's son smoked one cigarette after another through prayers and silence. When supper was over, I was the first to get up.

"My dear and so very young man," mumbled Mordkhe behind my back and tugged my belt, "if there were nobody in the world except the wicked rich and the penniless tramps, how would the saintly live?"

I gave the old man some money and went out into the street. I parted from Gedali and made my way back to the depot. In the propaganda train of the First Cavalry Corps there awaited me the glare of hundreds of lights, the magical brilliance of the radio station, the persistent pounding of printing presses, and my unfinished story for the paper, "The Red Cavalry Man."

Translated from the Russian
by Abraham Yarmolinsky

The Rabbi's Son

by Isaac Babel

. . . Do you remember Zhitomir, Vasily? Do you remember the Teterev, Vasily, and that evening when the Sabbath, the young Sabbath, tripped stealthily along the sunset, her little red heel treading on the stars? The slender horn of the moon bathed its arrows in the black waters of the Teterev. Funny little Gedali, founder of the Fourth International, was taking us to Rabbi Motele Bratzlavsky's for evening service. Funny little Gedali swayed the cock's feathers of his high hat in the red haze of the evening. The candles in the Rabbi's room blinked their predatory eyes. Bent over prayer books, brawny Jews were moaning in muffled voices, and the old buffoon of the *tzaddikim* of Chernobyl jingled coppers in his torn pocket. . . .

. . . Do you remember that night, Vasily? Beyond the windows horses were neighing and Cossacks were shouting. The wilderness of war was yawning beyond the windows, and Rabbi Motele Bratzlavsky was praying at the eastern wall, his decayed fingers clinging to his *tallit*. Then the curtain of the Ark was drawn aside, and in the funereal light of the candles we saw the scrolls of the Torah gowned in purple velvet and light blue silk, and suspended above the Torahs the lifeless face, meek and beautiful, of Ilya, the Rabbi's son, the last prince of the dynasty. . . .

Well, the day before yesterday, Vasily, the regiments of the Twelfth Army left the front at Kovel exposed. The victors' scornful cannonade thunderously broke out in the city. Our troops quaked and were thrown into confusion. The propaganda train started crawling away across the field's dead back. And a monstrous Russia in bast shoes shuffled past on either side of the cars, as incredible as a herd of lice. A typhus-ridden peasant mob trudged along, carrying on its shoulders the usual hump of soldiers' death. They jumped on the steps of our train and dropped off, knocked down by butt ends of rifles. They grunted, scratched themselves and moved on in silence.

At the twelfth verst, having run out of potatoes, I tossed a batch of Trotzky's leaflets down to them. But only one of them stretched out a dirty, dead hand for a leaflet. And I recognized Ilya, the son of the rabbi of Zhitomir. I recognized him at once, Vasily. And it was so painful to see the prince, trouserless and doubled up under his soldier's pack, that, in defiance of the rules, we pulled him into our car. His bare knees, as helpless as a woman's, knocked against the rusty iron of the steps; two full-breasted typists in sailor suits dragged the long, bashful body of the dying man along the floor. We laid him on the floor of the editorial office. Cossacks, in red loose trousers, straightened what was left of his clothes. The girls, bearing down on their bandy legs, the legs of simple-minded females, stared drily at his private parts, the tender curly maleness of a spent Semite. And I who had seen him one night during my wanderings began to collect in a little box the scattered belongings of Bratzlavsky, Red Army man. There were all sorts of things here, helter-skelter—the instructions of a propagandist and the notebooks of a Jewish poet. Portraits of Lenin and Maimonides lay side by side: the gnarled iron of Lenin's skull and the dull silk of Maimonides' likeness. A lock of woman's hair lay in a volume of the resolutions of the Sixth Congress of the Party, and crooked lines of Hebrew verse crowded the margins of Communist leaflets. Like a sad and niggardly rain they fell upon me—pages from the Song of Songs and revolver cartridges. The sad rain of sunset washed my dusty hair, and I said to the youth who lay there dying on a torn mattress:

"One Friday evening four months ago, Gedali who owns the curiosity shop took me to your father, Rabbi Motele, but you were not a member of the Party then, Bratzlavsky. . . ."

"I was in the Party," the boy answered, scratching his chest and writhing with fever, "but I couldn't leave my mother."

"And now, Ilya?"

"In a revolution a mother is a mere episode," he whispered, growing quieter. "My turn came, and the organization sent me to the front."

"And you found yourself in Kovel, Ilya?"

"I found myself in Kovel," he cried out in despair. "The rats exposed the front. I took command of a scratch regiment, but it was too late. I didn't have enough artillery."

He died before we reached Rovno. He died, the last prince, in the midst of verses, phylacteries and foot-clouts. We buried him near a forgotten railway station. And I, who am hardly able to hold the tempests of my imagination within this immemorial body, I was with my brother as he breathed his last.

Translated from the Russian
by Abraham Yarmolinsky

A Tale of Piety

by Albert Goldbarth

The Hasidim say in the Days of His Splendor that always Was and Will Be, in the town of Drovsk, was a Jewish ghetto no larger than a *minyan*, the women saw to the long black radish and tended the Sabbath flames, the men saw to the small squeaks in their tin Balance-pans and studied the Clear Mystic Word, they were small but happy. Now one day the Regent of Drovsk dreamed a dream, a hard thrust of light from a fierce magenta cloud knocked his crown from his head, and he was a kindly man but his adviser told him: "This means the foreign accoutrement of the Jews will topple your rule one day if you do not seize the means of their praying." And so the Regent commanded, on pain of death, that the holy ones burn publicly the wool *talissim* that draped their shoulders in prayer, and the dark leather spools of *tefillin* they laced up their arms so their pulse would throb devoutly against the sign of the Lord. Long into the night they bickered, the tea grew chilled, and many vowed on the next morn they would refuse, though it meant death, they would not part with these symbols. Now this was the time of year when the trees, even trees so deep green the green seemed as hard and impervious as a sword, flushed the colors of meat, then dropped their leaves before the Cold Sleep and Reawakening, which is their way of kneeling; for there is no end to the many forms of piety. And the Rabbi of Drovsk studied this and said, "The tree is more secret in winter but keeps itself ready to bloom in His Splendor again; and we shall not murder ourselves who can simply whisper our Adoration in plainer and safer garb; for His ear is such that the joy of the root is no less a roar than the joy of the blossom; His eye is such that the good prayer is good clear water, it will wake and cleanse, though the shape of the vessel change daily; and His heart is such that the clandestine heart of the icewhipped tree, in His service through adversity, is more of a bounty to Him than the garish sacrificial heart offered from one's own breast, on a platter; and this conversion I have seen." So the elders burned their wool and leather in the square, and smiled, and said, "We will observe you, oh Regent, in this for your land is good to us, let us even toil for you as a sign in a grueling and menial task; once a week we will even labor diligently at the stables and the slaughterers' for although we are given over to the Balance-pan and the Book we would demonstrate calculated obeisance." And it was so. Once a week they would help deliver the suckling-calf from the birthing-cow; they would stretch taut the neck for the butchery blade; and the two bloods, of arrival and departure, oiled their bodies as if in a ritual. For there is no end to the many external devices of veneration. For *talissim* they gripped the primal, wooltuft, living backs in the sheep pens; for *tefillin* their arms would accept, long before it was leather, the hot pulsing sleeve of cow body. And the prayer in their hearts did not alter, though the signs did. Though the winter was long, with many a death, that spring the humus was thick, and rich, and every blossom a trumpet.

The Three Souls of Reb Aharon

by Howard Schwartz

In Memory of Rabbi Arnold Asher

Among the Hasidim of Buczacz there was none more beloved than Reb Aharon ben Pinhas. After his death at an age as early as that of Reb Nachman of Bratslav, it was said by many that he, like the Bratslaver, had been one of the *Lamed-vov*, the Thirty-six Just Men who serve as the pillars on which the world stands. But he was not a simple man. He was a man who wrestled with his own soul, as Jacob had wrestled with the Angel.

After Reb Aharon's death it became apparent that his mantle had passed to Reb Zvi. Reb Hayim Elya had been a Hasid of Reb Aharon. He had been in the Holy Land at the time Reb Aharon had died, and thus he had not been present at his funeral, which had been the largest in the history of the Jews of Buczacz, and there had been an outpouring of grief such as had never been seen before. So it was said by all those who had been present. When the news of Reb Aharon's death had reached him, Reb Hayim Elya had been stricken like a man drowning. But then he had felt the soul of Reb Aharon lift him up from below and carry him to the heights. And after the time of mourning had passed, Reb Hayim Elya was among those Hasidim who came to Reb Zvi. For it is the custom among Hasidim to seek out a new rebbe, once the first one has passed away.

Then it happened one night in a dream that Reb Hayim Elya was told that Reb Aharon was one of those who had three souls. Although there may have been more to his dream message, that is all Hayim Elya remembered when he woke up. Puzzled, he went to Reb Zvi and asked him to interpret the dream. When he heard this question Reb Zvi seemed to grow angry, and he told Hayim Elya: "Why have you come to me with this question? Let Reb Aharon answer this question himself!"

"But Rebbe," pleaded Hayim Elya, "Reb Aharon is dead. How is it possible to speak to the dead?"

"This is something you must find out for yourself," said Reb Zvi, and turned away.

Reb Hayim Elya was confused as he left Reb Zvi's study, but by the time he had passed through the doorway of Reb Zvi's house he was already on his way to seek out Reb Aharon, as if it were still possible to go to his house and find him there. That night Hayim Elya had a dream which came to haunt him for many days afterwards. In that dream he found himself walking in an ancient city. And the road he took in that city was round, and it was known that all those who started out on this road would one day meet all of the others who followed this path. And Hayim Elya could not tell if the city was Safed or Jerusalem, for it had qualities of both places, and yet at the same time was unlike either of them. But there was one thing in that dream that Hayim Elya was absolutely certain of—that if he continued on that path he would meet Reb Aharon. Yet even in the dream he had not forgotten that Reb Aharon was no longer among the living. And then the thought came to him that he might be walking in the City of the Dead. And this thought frightened him, for he was not certain how he might make his way back to the Land of the Living. And so it happened that in his fright he crossed from one world back to the other, and woke up.

When he woke up and remembered this dream, Reb Hayim Elya was distressed, for he had traveled that far to reach Reb Aharon and had lost his chance for a meeting because he had become frightened. And he was angry and disappointed, and anxious for another meeting to take place.

Then it happened the next day that there was a strange occurrence. A messenger arrived early in the morning, and delivered to Hayim Elya a letter from Reb Aharon, almost eleven months after his death. How was this possible? It happened that Reb Aharon had written the letter while he was among the living, shortly before his death, but it had never been sent. And now it had been found among his papers, and delivered belatedly. And in the letter Reb Aharon answered the question that Hayim Elya had not asked until eleven months after his death. But this did not surprise Hayim Elya, for he believed that the Bratslaver had told the truth when he had said that a question may be asked in one time, in one place, and answered in another time, in another place. And in that letter Reb Aharon told the tale of how he had come to have three souls. And this is the tale that was written there:

"When the world was created, one Jewish *neshamah* was given to every Jew. But due to the tragedies that have plagued the Jews in every generation, from the destruction of the Temple to the pogroms of the tyrant Chmelnicki, the population of the Jews had become depleted, and now the number of living Jews was far less than the number of available *neshamahs*. And for a *neshamah* to remain apart from a human being is to make it one of the Captive Souls, and to deny its destiny to be born, like a flame that is forced to burn invisibly, when it longs to reveal the myriad shapes and forms of its burning.

"So the angel Raziel was sent for by the King of the Kingdom of the Captive Souls, and given a message to deliver to the Holy One, Blessed be He, a plea from the Captive Souls to have their destinies fulfilled. And so it was that the Holy One heard their plea, and after that saw to it that it became possible for a Jew to have more than one soul. And among them there were many who were given a double portion, and became bearers of two souls. But among very few of them, only among the *Lamed-vov*, did it happen that three souls were bequeathed to the same person. And it is both a blessing and a curse to be born with three souls. For so much abundance and so much responsibility is fraught with danger.

"Now it happened that I was one of these, who are both cursed and blessed at the same time. For each of my souls was fully developed, and sought to dominate the other, and each was so strong that they nearly tore me apart. It is in this way that my heart has become weakened. Of the three souls, one is the soul of the High Priest Aharon, brother of Moses; and one is the soul of Jacob, our Father; and the third one is the Angel with whom Jacob wrestled. And when this soul of Jacob would dominate over the Angel, my life was a great blessing and it was possible for the soul of Aharon to perform the duties of the High Priest. Yes, then it was as if the High Priest had been restored to the Temple, and the Temple rebuilt. But when the Angel held sway, the walls of the Temple were once more reduced to rubble.

"Now it happened in my life that the soul of Jacob struggled endlessly with the Angel. Yet sometimes I hoped to come to terms with the Angel. And I wanted to know what Angel it was, if it had been sent by the Messiah, the Prince of Light, or by the Prince of Darkness. Then I would meet the Angel face to face and look into its eyes, and at that moment I would fall under the Angel's spell. That is how I learned that the Angel lost its power over me if I did not meet its eyes. As long as I looked away I was safe. But sometimes my curiosity grew strong, and I wished to know what Angel this was, and I would meet the eyes of the Angel, and then it would hold sway until I could turn away once more.

"This is the lot that befalls every *Lamed-vov*, nor is it an accident. For the souls of the *Lamed-vov* must contend to keep the world in existence. For if pure peace should settle in the heart of even one of the *Lamed-vov Tzaddikim*, the world would sink beneath the weight of darkness. So it is that the heart of every one of the *Lamed-vov* holds back the waters of the Abyss. And sometimes, when the pressure of the waters grows too great to bear, the heart of a *Lamed-vov* breaks."

Reb Hayim Elya read all the words of this letter with complete amazement. But even more amazing to him was the fact that as soon as he had finished reading it the words and letters began to dissolve, and soon disappeared. And then there was nothing left but dark powder on the white paper. And then Reb Hayim Elya woke up, and discovered that it was still the middle of the night, for he had fallen back to sleep and dreamed that a messenger had delivered a letter from Reb Aharon to him. And he knew that the meeting he had sought after had taken place. And he lay back on his bed and a light played around his face.

The Death of Rabbi Yoseph
by David Slabotsky

Rabbi Yoseph was astounded to discover that he was dead. Far below him, the crumbling ghetto of Zlochtov slumbered under a blanket of thick, wet snow, and a chorus of pious snores floated dreamily past him, wending their sleepy way to the Kingdom of Heaven. The snores were collected in a basket by a bird he had never seen before but had dreamed of once on the night of a Holy Day he no longer recalled. As in the dream, the bird wore curly sidelocks like an orthodox Jew and a skullcap embroidered with beads and small, round mirrors. Because of this odd familiarity, Rabbi Yoseph imposed upon the bird and begged permission to look through the basket for one particular snore, hinting that it was utterly important for reasons which he was obliged to keep secret for the moment but, at length, would reveal. The bird toyed with his sidelocks as he pondered the request and consulted a manual written in Yiddish and Hebrew and a language Rabbi Yoseph had never seen before. He furrowed his brow as birds will do when poring over questions of a legal nature, moved the skullcap back and forth on his head, and grudgingly consented. At that, a nest fluttered down beneath him and, tucking his bill into his wings, he was instantly asleep.

Rabbi Yoseph searched through the snores with particular care. Some felt warm to the touch like tiny kittens, others tickled him so that he nearly cried out, others were so drenched with tears that they nearly slipped through his fingers like water and escaped completely, and then at last he came to the snore he was looking for, that of his wife, his Merriam, who lay sleeping beside his mortal remains in the nest of rags and shredded linen which had been their wedding bed for so many years. In the morning she would discover him there and at night her snores would be dripping, heartbroken snores like so many the bird had collected before.

He held the snore cupped tightly in his hands for a very long time, afraid that it might float away the moment he opened them again, but at last contrived a way of opening just one finger enough so that he could see it clearly but not enough so that it could slip out. The snore was warm, and gray, and wrinkled, with a mole on its chin. As it lay in his hands like a tiny bird snuggled safely in a shell, its gentle buzzing was sometimes interrupted by snatches from the tune of a Sabbath prayer, once by incoherent words concerning a poppyseed cookie so wondrous that it could only be baked in the kitchen of dreams, and once it spoke Rabbi Yoseph's name with such a rich and boundless love that the snore nearly consumed itself in a sigh.

Rabbi Yoseph addressed the snore tenderly, tearfully, recalling vows of love and years of devotion, finishing first with a kiss and lastly with a blessing. He was intending to send the snore back to the sleeping ghetto of Zlochtov, along the tumbling streets and laneways, up the creaking stairs, and down the dark, damp corridor to the room where Merriam lay with the dust of her husband. How she would rejoice to know that he held in his hands at that moment her gentle snore! Tears clouded his eyes and a terrible sorrow tugged at his heart. Overcome with grief, he squeezed the snore so tightly that it suddenly popped right out of his hands and before he could catch it again it was floating over the head of the sleeping bird who, awakening suddenly, gathered it into his basket like a hen with a wayward chick, took the handle of the basket in his bill, and flew off into eternity. Rabbi Yoseph watched him disappear and then looked down at his hands which only a moment ago had held his Merriam's warm and beloved snore. He pressed his palms to his cheeks and wept without shame.

In the moments which followed, Rabbi Yoseph struggled with a curious event: The entire ghetto of Zlochtov was tangled in his beard like a fly on a hot summer day. He looked down his nose which was hooked and twisted at the end as if the tip had rebelled against the rest and taken a random course of its own, and screwing his eyes up and straining until he was faint, he was obliged to accept this strange occurrence as fact, though with misgivings on certain points. For instance, the ghetto of Zlochtov which lay before him at the foot of the wayward hill of his nose had not been diminished in size, and yet his beard, which admittedly was long, was no longer than usual, and he was certain, to the best of his knowledge, that not even once in his lifetime had the ghetto of Zlochtov ever grown tangled in his beard. The only time it might have happened was on a certain Day of Atonement when it had been an especially difficult fast and many strange things had happened—or had seemed to have happened; but since everything under Heaven was the working of the Holy Name there had seemed little point in trying to distinguish between the real and imagined events of the day. Furthermore, it had always been he, Rabbi Yoseph, who had been entangled in the ghetto of Zlochtov, and much like a fly at that, a humble almost unnoticed buzz in the life of that small community of Jews who made a home for their God in the vast Diaspora. And finally, since he had enemies (what man hasn't?), if this strange event had happened in the course of his lifetime, surely his enemies would have reproached him. Would Mendel the baker have spent one minute in his beard, one second in his beard, without giving him a slap? Or Hayim the tailor? And so it had never happened before and was happening now for the very first time. How this had all transpired was beyond the range of his intellect but within the bounds of belief, and uttering special prayers for the occasion he gazed at the ghetto of Zlochtov with new curiosity.

How very wonderful it seemed. How much like a miracle. Merriam was still the most beautiful woman and now he could see little prints of her feet showing every step she had taken in the ghetto throughout her life, the faintest being the smallest steps she had taken in childhood, the brightest being the ones she had taken that day to the market and back to their room. All her steps, even the first, smelled vaguely of onions and fish and this brought a deep, warm smile to his face as he closed his eyes and remembered her.

Rabbi Yoseph was distracted by the sound of a wagon rumbling towards him with a loadful of snores on their way to the Kingdom of Heaven. The wagonmaster was a pious frog with dark green sidelocks, a skullcap and the four-fringed vest of an orthodox Jew. Inquiring after the bird, Rabbi Yoseph learned that it had finally passed away and, since it had not appointed a successor, after much debate the task was given to the frog who rode on the wagon which stood before him. Rabbi Yoseph realized at once that a great deal of time had passed and instinctively put a hand to his beard and fumbled through it frantically for the ghetto of Zlochtov. To his dismay it had vanished without a trace. And where had it gone? And how had it gone? Loneliness came down upon him like a mountain collapsing on a fly and a giant, deadening ache overwhelmed him entirely. He looked around and saw as if for the very first time the vast expanse of the heavens. He gazed at the planets, and stars and constellations, and wondered whether in all that endless night there were Jews, or if there was a Sabbath.

In the years that followed, Rabbi Yoseph wandered from star to star and from world to world and returned to earth as a minor figure in a parable uttered by the Miracle Rabbi of Lublin. From tiny cracks in the story, Rabbi Yoseph looked out briefly into a world which reminded him of Zlochtov and fell in love with the rabbi's daughter whose name was not Merriam but might easily have been. Unfortunately, the Lublin Rabbi only recounted the parable twice in his life, once as a very young man and once on his deathbed, and since the Lubliner lived to a very ripe age, Rabbi Yoseph only managed to see his daughter twice, once as a girl and once as a very old woman. However, since his role in the parable was of a man who extolled the virtue of constancy, Rabbi Yoseph loved her faithfully all the time they were separated and praised her beauty the moment the parable rose to the lips of the dying Lublin sage.

Because of this, Rabbi Yoseph was given lives in other parables uttered by such great men as Lev of Grenoble and Raphael of Bershad and others greater still, and since the Jews were being driven from place to place, from cracks in their stories he managed to see a good deal of the world and in this way acquired a measure of wisdom of his own.

It was Rabbi Yoseph's honor to live in a parable uttered daily by Rabbi Judah, the Lion of Minsk, who was told of Rabbi Yoseph's presence in a dream. For his special benefit, Rabbi Judah created such wide cracks in his story (often to the point where his own disciples considered him a fool) that

Rabbi Yoseph was able to leave the parable completely at times and sit in the study hall disguised as a shadow or a draft of air.

Late one night, Rabbi Judah was astounded to discover that he was dead. Overcome with grief, he recited the parable in which Rabbi Yoseph had lived for so many years and found him suddenly there at his side. Rabbi Yoseph explained to him the pious task of the hare who collected snores in a barrow and how he had replaced the frog who had once collected snores in a wagon and how he had replaced the bird who had once collected snores in a basket. He showed Rabbi Judah the proper manner of searching through the barrow of snores to find the snore of his wife whose name, oddly enough, was Merriam, and how to cup it gently in his hands and peer at it by opening just one finger so that it would not float away. He showed him how to screw up his eyes to behold the ghetto of Minsk entangled in his beard and, when it vanished, clasped him to his bosom with heartfelt compassion.

Thus they became fast friends and wandered together from star to star and from world to world. Whenever they came to a difficulty, Rabbi Yoseph recited a parable which he had lived in and Rabbi Judah commented on it, whereupon Rabbi Yoseph related another parable, and so on, often for years at a time, until at last they reached the Kingdom of Heaven. The details of their journey are much like a dream and have no place in this story recounting the actual events of Rabbi Yoseph's adventures following his death. It can be told, however, that as they approached the Kingdom of Heaven they were greeted by a smell which reminded them greatly of onions and fish. And this can be told because it was no dream at all.

NOTES
ON THE STORIES

BOOK I
BIBLICAL THEMES

Page 111
"The Tale of the Menorah"
by Rabbi Nachman of Bratslav

The menorah is a seven-branched candelabrum whose use is specified in Numbers (8:2): *When thou lightest the lamps, the seven lamps shall give light in front of the candle-stick.* The menorah traditionally symbolizes the creation of the universe in seven days (Gen. 1:1-2:4), the center light representing the Sabbath. If this interpretation is brought to Rabbi Nachman's tale, the craftsman can be seen as representing God, and the menorah of defects the world, with all its imperfections. The craftsman also represents the rebbe, who must reveal the defects of his Hasidim to them, so that they may begin the process of *Tikkun*, or restoration. For further discussion of this tale, see pp. 45-46.

Page 111
"The Seven Lights of the Lamp"
by Moshe ben Yitzhak HaPardesan

This is a chain midrash, which links together previously unrelated midrashim. The story establishes a precedent for the menorah prior to its creation by Bezalel. The requirement to light the menorah is found in Numb. 8:1-2. The reference to the light at creation is to Gen. 1:3 and 1:14-19. The image of God wrapping Himself in a *tallit* (prayer shawl) of light is found in a midrash on Ps. 104:2 found in *Genesis Rabbah* 3:4. See also *Pesikta de Reb Kahana* 21:5. The legend that Adam saw all future generations is found in *Genesis Rabbah* 24:2 and *Midrash Tanhuma*, ed. Buber, Ber. 28. The legend that the primordial light shone for thirty-six hours appears in the Jerusalem Talmud (Ber. 8:8). The complete legend of the primordial light is found in the Zohar (1:31b). For more information about the legend of the *Lamed-vov*, the

Thirty-six Just Men, see stories pp. 204–231 and the appropriate notes. The legend that Adam and Eve were created in one body appears in *Genesis Rabbah* 8:1. The light burning in the womb appears in *Tanhuma Pekude* 3 and *The Chronicles of Jerahmeel* 9:1-8 (for a further discussion of this midrash, see p. 64). The legend that Noah fetched a precious stone from the River Pishon appears in the Jerusalem Targum to Gen. 6:16. The light of the Ark known as the *Tzohar* is found in *Genesis Rabbah* 31:11. The legend of Moses raising Joseph's coffin from the Nile is found in *Mekilta de Rabbi Ishmael, Beshallah,* based on Ex. 14:19: *And Moses took the bones of Joseph with him.* The story of Joseph's cup being carried by his brothers is found in Gen. 14. The image of the many-colored flames of the burning bush is found in a *genizah* fragment of *Midrash Tanhuma.* The image of the lights of the menorah bowing toward the center of the lamp is found in *Midrash Hagadol* to Numb. 8:2 and the idea that the lamp still burns in *Numbers Rabbah* 15:6. Other examples of chain midrashim are those concerning the Foundation Stone, which was believed to hold back the waters of the Abyss (Y. Yom. 5:23, B. Yom. 54b), which also figures in the legend about King David and the Shafts of the Temple (Y. Sanh. 29b); or the chain of legends concerning the garments worn by Adam and Eve, the Staff of Moses, and the Book of Raziel. It seems likely that J. R. R. Tolkien made use of some of these same legends in *The Silmarillion,* in which the central motif concerns jewels containing the last of a primordial light.

Page 114
"In the Beginning"
by Zalman Shneur

The biblical description of the creation of the world in Genesis (Gen. 1:1-31) was regarded as one of the ultimate mysteries of the Bible, along with the vision of Ezekiel. It was known as *Maaseh Bereshith,* or the Work of Creation, while the vision of Ezekiel was known as *Maaseh Merkavah,* or the Work of the Chariot. Aggadic exegesis of the creation tended to become anthropomorphic, as in the image of the garment of God from *Genesis Rabbah* (3:4) quoted in the previous note. In the kabbalistic period this kind of personification reached major proportions, especially in a long section of the Zohar (3:127b-145a) known as the Greater Holy Assembly which has separate sections on aspects of God's anatomy. (One translation of this text into English, by Roy A. Rosenberg, is titled *The Anatomy of God.)* These sections include "The Skull of the Ancient One," "The Nose of the Ancient One," "The Mouth of the Ancient One," and "The Forehead of the Ancient One." One section, "The Body of the Small Countenance, and His Union with the Bride," describes "the Matrona cleaving to the King to form one body." It is difficult to be more anthropomorphic than this. This excerpt from a longer story of the same title by Zalman Shneur was clearly intended to belong to this tradition, in which God is envisioned both in human terms (after all, man was made in God's image—Gen. 1:27) and in cosmic terms at the same time.

Page 115
"In the Beginning"
by Lilly Rivlin

Like the previous tale by Zalman Shneur, this is a creation story with echoes of both the biblical version (Gen. 1:1-31) and the kabbalistic. The force that Lilly Rivlin identifies as "Throbbing Spirit" seems parallel in all respects with the kabbalistic concept of the Shekhinah, the Divine Presence, which is identified as the feminine aspect of the divinity, and the subject of extensive legends in the kabbalistic era. For a discussion of the evolution of the concept of the Shekhinah, see pp. 20–23. The allegorical method here, so close to pure myth, is also like that found in the Zohar (2:96a) referred to in the previous note. The earliest personification of the forces of creation is found in rabbinic commentaries on *tohu* and *bohu*. These are Hebrew for "unformed" and "void" from Gen. 1:2: *Now the earth was unformed and void, and darkness was upon the face of the deep.* These are the forces that become the focus for the personification here of masculine and feminine entities, which evolve, as a result of the act of creation, creating the world in the process. In the Talmud (B. A. Z. 8a), Adam, on seeing the first nightfall, expresses the fear that "the world will return to *tohu* and *bohu*." For Ms. Rivlin as well as for the kabbalists, the primary consequences of such a myth were the restoration of the feminine to an equal position with the masculine, and a demonstration of how they must interact in order to bring existence into being.

Page 116
"The Creation of Man"
by Morris Rosenfeld

The resistance of the angels to the creation of man is a prominent theme, found, for example, in *Genesis Rabbah* (8:3-9). The passage from the Psalms (8:5) *What is man, that Thou art mindful of him, and the son of man, that Thou thinkest of him* is attributed to the ministering angels (*Genesis Rabbah* 8:6). Rosenfeld follows the traditional sources closely until he adds to the legend the notion that only poets will be given wings—wings of song. That God consulted the angels about creation is not stated, but the use of *Elohim*, which translates as "us" (actually it is a plural name of God), was interpreted by the rabbis as referring to the angels. See Gen. 1:26.

Page 117
"Before"
by Penina Villenchik

The "before" of the title refers to a prelapsarian state, closely resembling the vision of *Gan Eden* (the Garden of Eden) found in rabbinic sources, such as *Midrash Hagadol Bereshith*. The lack of consciousness "that we were man or woman, human or animal, male or female" echoes the biblical assertion about Adam and Eve that *they were both naked, the man and his wife, and were not ashamed* (Gen. 3:25). That such a state was markedly different from that after the Fall is emphasized in legends that assert, for example, that the cloud of glory that had surrounded the man and woman then departed: "When he ate of the fruits of the tree . . . the cloud of glory departed from him and he saw himself naked" (*Pirke de Rabbi Eliezer* 14).

Page 117
"In the End"
by Rabbi Jack Riemer

Using the description of the creation of the world found in Genesis (1:1-23) as its source, this apocalyptic piece describes the world "in the end." Here the world that God created is systematically destroyed by man, until "on the last day, a great cloud went up over all the face of the earth . . . and then man, and all of his doings, was no more."

Page 118
"The Arrival of Eve"
by Francine Prose

The biblical description of the creation of woman (Gen. 3:21-25) is here called into question, and an alternate offered, as is so often the case in aggadic disputations. Although the notion that Eve "was created in another place, a distant country" does not appear in the rabbinic legends, there were alternate accounts of the creation of man and woman, such as that in *Genesis Rabbah* (8:1) which asserts: "When the Holy One, blessed be He, created Adam, He created him double-faced, then He split him and made him of two backs, one back on this side and one back on the other side." See the discussion of the legend of Lilith, pp. 3-4.

Page 119
"Before the Law"
by Franz Kafka

This famous parable by Kafka from *The Trial* can be read as a religious allegory or as an allegory of justice. The doorkeeper guarding the gate to the Law is reminiscent of the angel God placed at the east of the Garden of Eden, with *the flaming sword which turned every way, to keep the way to the Tree of Life* (Gen. 3:24). Like that angel, the doorkeeper refuses to admit the man from the country. Also echoed is the popular Christian conception of St. Peter serving as the doorkeeper at the Gates of Heaven. Gershom Scholem has also pointed out parallels between this parable and passages in the Hekhaloth texts about guards at the gates of the palaces of heaven, such as this passage from *Hekhaloth Rabbati* (15:8): "At the gate of the seventh palace stand angry all the gatekeepers, warlike, strong, harsh, fearful, terrific, taller than mountains and sharper than peaks. Their bows are strung and stand before them; their swords are sharpened and in their hands. And lightnings flow and issue forth from the balls of their eyes, and spiderwebs of fire from their nostrils and torches of fiery coals from their mouths. And they are equipped with helmets and with coats of mail, and javelins and spears are hung upon their muscles." Compare this passage with Kafka's description of the doorkeeper: " 'I am powerful. And I am only the least of the doorkeepers. From hall to hall there is one doorkeeper after another, each more powerful than the last. The third doorkeeper is already so terrible that even I cannot bear to look at him.'. . . as he now takes a closer look at the doorkeeper in his fur coat, with his sharp nose and long, thin, black Tartar beard, he decides that it is better to wait until he gets permission to enter." Since this Hekhaloth text was very little known, however, it is not possible to assume that Kafka had any direct knowledge of it, and it is only the remarkable parallel that may be commented on. Another perspective, one rarely considered, is suggested by a passage from the Zohar (1:7b): *"Open to me the gates of righteousness. . . . This is the gate of the Lord* (Ps. 68: 19-20). Assuredly, without entering through that gate one will never gain access to the most high King. Imagine a king greatly exalted who screens himself from the common view behind gate upon gate, and at the end, one special gate, locked and barred. Saith the king: 'He who wishes to enter into my presence must first of all pass through that gate.' " Still another parallel, of a source probably also unknown to Kafka, is found in Ibn Gabirol's treatise written in the 11th century, *The Book of the Selection of Pearls* (ch. 8): "The following laconic observations are said to have been addressed to a king, by one who stood by the gate of the royal palace, but who failed to obtain access. First: Necessity and hope prompted me to approach thy throne. Second: My dire distress admits of no delay. Third: My disappointment would gratify the malice of my enemies. Fourth: Thine acquiescence would confer advantages, and even thy refusal would relieve me from anxiety and suspense."

Page 120
"Paradise"
by Franz Kafka

Kafka's notion that "Paradise was not destroyed" is very much parallel to the rabbinic notion that the Garden of Eden, which is regarded as the Earthly Paradise, still exists, although the gate to it is guarded by an angel with a *flaming sword which turned every way, to keep the way to the Tree of Life* (Gen. 3:24). This is emphasized by the recurrent legends about sages, such as Rabbi Joshua ben Levi, who managed to reenter the Garden of Eden. Joshua ben Levi was said to have tricked the Angel of Death into bringing him to the wall of the Garden of Eden, from which place he leaped down into the Garden, and refused to return (B. Ket. 77b). The famous passage about the four who entered *Pardes* (B. Hag. 14b) is also interpreted to mean that they entered an orchard (the literal meaning of *pardes*), which is readily identified with the Garden of Eden. This notion of the Garden of Eden having an eternal existence is stated quite explicitly in the Zohar (4:150a): "The Garden was planted by the Holy One . . . and made an exact likeness of its prototype, the Paradise above, and all supernal forms were fashioned and shaped in it. . . . All the images and forms of all the things in this world were fashioned there, and this is the abode of those who have come into this world, and those who have not yet come into this world." For a discussion of archetypal elements in rabbinic literature, see pp. 40-41.

Page 122
"The Eden Angel"
by Nachmann Rapp

The notion that an angel of God observed the transgression of Adam and Eve, and sympathized to the extent of also tasting the fruit, is original, although there is a tradition that Adam and Eve were watched in the Garden by angels, and that Adam heard what the angels were saying to one another about the Fall, and what they were saying to God (*Genesis Rabbah* 19:8). Rapp's apparent transformation of the angel into a human being after tasting the forbidden fruit is an especially fine touch.

Page 126
"Generation"
by Nessa Rapoport

Here the Fall is identified with sexual desire, and it is Adam, rather than Eve, who "plucks the fruit"—i.e., knows Eve's ripeness. Such an identification between sex and the Fall is also found in rabbinic sources, such as in this passage from *Genesis Rabbah*: "And the man knew Eve his wife (Gen. 4:1): Adam knew that he had been robbed of his tranquillity; he knew what his serpent (i.e., Eve, his tempter) had done to him."

Page 127
"The Tree of Id"
by Rabbi Harold S. Kushner

Rabbi Kushner offers a version of how the Genesis story would read had Adam and Eve obeyed God and not eaten of the Tree of Knowledge, but eaten, instead, "from the Tree of Id, which some call the Tree of Life." In this way they would have retained their primal innocence and perceptions, and evil would have receded as a danger after "the grass grew high around the Tree of Knowledge of Good and Evil till it covered it completely and hid it from view." The fact that Adam and Eve ate instead from the Tree of Knowledge, in this view, prevented them from reaching an understanding of the Id, here identified with the Tree of Life—i.e. from coming to an understanding of the nature of the forces of the unconscious Freud identified as the Id. From a Jungian perspective this negative and threatening aspect of the unconscious is only one pole of the bipolar unconscious. The other is the pole of balance and harmony. The kabbalistic parallel is the notion that God's Left Hand symbolizes His aspect of justice, and His Right Hand His aspect of mercy. A more conventional interpretation would likely identify the Tree of Knowledge, rather than the Tree of Life, with the unconscious forces the Id represents.

Page 128
"The Tree of Life and the Tree of Death"
by Howard Schwartz

This parable was inspired by James G. Frazer's theory about the Tree of Knowledge in *Folklore in the Old Testament* (pp. 16–17), which proposes that it was the Tree of Death in the original myth on which the text in Genesis (2:9 ff.) is based, and that the reason God blocks the way to the Tree of Life is that once having eaten from the Tree of Death, Adam and Eve had lost the opportunity to eat from the Tree of Life. A legend suggesting a similar view of the story of the two trees is found in *Vita Adae and Evae* (*The Books of Adam and Eve* 28:1–4): "But the Lord turned to Adam and said: 'I will not suffer thee henceforward to be in Paradise.' And Adam answered and said: 'Grant me, O Lord, of the Tree of Life that I may eat of it, before I be cast out.' Then the Lord spake to Adam: 'Thou shalt not take of it now, for I have commanded the cherubim with the flaming sword that turneth every way to guard it from thee that thou taste not of it.' " The earliest rabbinic reference to the Tree of Knowledge as a Tree of Death appears in *Midrash Konen*. The identification of the Tree of Knowledge and the Tree of Death is explicitly made in the Zohar (1:35b):

"This Tree . . . was a Tree of Death insofar that he who ate of it was bound to die, since he took poison." For a further discussion of Frazer's theory of the two trees, see pp. 12–14.

Page 129
"Lilith Recollects Genesis"
by Wendy Laura Frisch

While Lilith came to represent everything the rabbis found sexually threatening about women, this parable presents the story of Lilith as a victim of male sexual greed, implying that the subsequent stories, perpetuated by men, twisted the truth. For further discussion of the legend of Lilith, see pp. 3–4.

Page 130
"Adam and Eve Return to the Garden"
by Itzik Manger

This tale is excerpted from *The Book of Paradise*, pp. 95–98. In the afterlife Adam and Eve have returned to Paradise, and in this episode they return to the Garden of Eden from which they were expelled in Gen. 3:23–24. Manger implies that Adam and Eve are still quarreling over the causes of their expulsion from Eden, like an old married couple, as well as reminiscing about the pleasures of Paradise. But when a wind shakes the Tree of Knowledge—a symbol of the presence of God—they become frightened and run off "as fast as they could go." There is no tradition of Adam and Eve returning to the Garden together, although in *Vita Adae et Evae (The Books of Adam and Eve* 40:1–2) there is a description of Eve returning to the gates of the Garden with Seth to implore mercy for Adam, who was dying: "But Seth and his mother walked to the regions of Paradise for the oil of mercy to anoint the sick Adam; and they arrived at the gates of Paradise, and they took dust from the earth and placed it on their heads, and bowed themselves with their faces to the earth and began to lament and make loud moaning, imploring the Lord God to pity Adam in his pains and to send His angel to give them the oil from the 'tree of His mercy.' " There is some question about whether *Vita Adae et Evae* is a Jewish text, but Louis Ginzberg concludes that it is of Jewish origin, with Christian interpolations. For further discussion of *The Book of Paradise*, see pp. 64–65.

Page 131
"True Joy"
by Kamelia Shahar

This tale is an example of a folktale in which Eliyahu (Elijah) the Prophet assists those in need. Here the poor couple assert that they would not have succumbed to temptation as did Adam and Eve. Eliyahu quickly tests them, letting them find three buried boxes, the first two of which bestow great treasures on them (much as Adam and Eve were given the Garden of Eden to live within), while the third box has written on it: "Whoever opens me loses all that he has." The parallel to the Tree of Knowledge and the forbidden fruit is apparent, and of course the couple succumbs to temptation and a storm comes which washes away their riches. This tale demonstrates the princi ple in folklore of presenting a narrative which is intended to have an obvious parallel to another, well-known narrative. This is the same literary principle used by a good many of the authors represented in this book, whose works are intended both to echo and diverge from other well-known (and sometimes lesser-known) sources.

Page 133
"The Story of Lilith and Eve"
by Jakov Lind

In this tale Lind manages to combine the previously separate legends of Lilith and Eve. He has recognized each of the legends as projections of polar aspects of one woman, and has traced the projections back to their original source. For further discussion of the legend of Lilith, see pp. 3–4. For further discussion of this tale, see p. 60.

Page 135
"The Poet of Irsahab"
by Else Lasker-Schüler

Very little is said about Methuselah, apart from the brief mention of him in Genesis (5:22–27), where he is identified as having lived longer than anyone else—969 years. But this was enough for the rabbis to identify him as a very righteous man, and to make him the focus of a highly developed rabbinic tradition, much like that centered around Enoch. (For further discussion of the legend of Enoch, see p. 4.) In this parable of Lasker-Schüler's, Enoch is reincarnated as a raven, in contrast to the rabbinic tradition that he was transformed into the angel Metatron (*2 Enoch* 15). It is in this form that Enoch speaks to his grandson Grammaton, a figure not mentioned in the biblical genealogy, although the name is probably intended to echo the word "Tetragrammaton," the primary Name of God. Also, the notion that Grammaton was a poet is echoed in the tradition that holds that Methuselah composed 230 parables in praise of God for every word he uttered (*Chronicles of Jerahmeel* 23:5). See "The Jewbird" by Bernard Malamud for an interesting parallel.

Page 136
"The City Coat of Arms"
by Franz Kafka

Here Kafka puts the blame for the failure to complete the building of the Tower of Babel firmly on the builders rather than on God, as does the biblical account (Gen. 11:1–9). The rabbinic sources, on the other hand, almost unanimously view the people as motivated by a desire to overthrow heaven, as in this passage from *Mekilta de Rabbi Ishmael, Mispatim* 20: "We will take axes and cleave the heavens, that all the water that is stored there shall run out below; then He will not be able to treat us as He did the generation of the Flood. We will break heaven up into pieces. We will also wage war against Him in heaven and not permit Him to dwell there. We will dwell there in His place, and there we will introduce idolatry." The closed fist on the city's coat of arms is a sign that they recognized the evil in their pursuit, and the inevitable apocalypse that would surely follow, which does conform to the rabbinic image of the builders, who are referred to as "The Generation of the Division." For a further discussion of the Tower of Babel, see p. 16. Compare Kafka's story "The Great Wall and the Tower of Babel" in *Parables and Paradoxes*, pp. 25–27.

Page 137
"Legend of the Third Dove"
by Stefan Zweig

This tale is based on the biblical passage in Genesis (8:8–12) about Noah's sending out a dove to see if the waters had receded. In the biblical version it appears that the same dove was sent out three times, but Zweig assumes that three different doves were sent. In the midrashic tradition that a story must be completed, he then tells the rest of the story of the third dove, up to the point of its becoming a symbol of peace. In *Genesis Rabbah* 33 it is said that the olive branch the dove brought back came from the Garden of Eden, because "the gates of Paradise were opened for her, and from there she brought it." The dove is also interpreted in rabbinic literature as a symbol of Israel: "After Israel is delivered from the war of God it will never again return to exile (*Torah Shlemah* 8:50)." For a further discussion of this tale, see pp. 68–69.

Page 140
"The Fleeting Rainbow"
by Ladislav Grosman

The kinds of questions Yidele Froechlich raises with the three boys he is attempting to educate are all midrashic in nature. He asks "why God appeared to Moses in the bushes rather than in a garden, a meadow or an orchard." The rabbis considered the purpose of the bush very carefully, and gave several reasons for its choice. In *Exodus Rabbah* (2:10) the fire is said to symbolize Israel, while the bush represents the heathens. Thus, while the fire of Israel cannot consume the heathens, neither can the heathens extinguish the fire of Israel, i.e., the Torah. Another interpretation was given by Rabbi Bahya ben Asher, who suggested that the bush was identified with Mt. Sinai, since fire burned on both. The central episode of the quest for the rainbow in this story brings in focus the contrary perspectives of Yidele Froehlich and the boys. The boys have their own pagan folklore about the rainbow's origin and believed that could they reach a river while a newborn rainbow was still drinking from it, they could capture the rainbow. The rich tradition of the rainbow as the covenant between God and man and as a gift from God is lost on them. Even so, their own folklore has its own legitimate attractions, and cannot but serve to remind those who doubt the divine origin of the Torah that Jewish beliefs and symbols had their origin in such an imaginative manner as well.

Page 144
"The Ark"
by Cecil Helman

Rather than forty days and nights, as in Genesis (8:6), Helman suggests that the Flood lasted for forty years. For forty years "tired generations of doves have returned, every evening—their beaks empty." Finally the doves return with "an olive branch, a crumb, or a piece of cloth," and deliverance comes after forty years. The effect is to blend into one the legend of Noah and that of the Israelites wandering in the wilderness for forty years. Their relief at entering the Promised Land after all that time is parallel, in this view, to the moment Noah realized that the waters were receding at last. This kind of parallel drawn between two periods is commonly done in the rabbinic literature. For example, in order to explain the childhood of Abraham, which does not appear in the Bible, a parallel was drawn between the childhood of Moses and that of Abraham.

Page 144
"The Rainbow"
by Aaron Sussaman

The rainbow is a sign of the Covenant between God and man, as stated in Gen. 8:6. The rainbow was intended to serve as a reminder of this covenant, as stated in Gen. 9:14-16. The fragile rainbow seen in the propped-up legs of the dead donkey in this tale is a sign used in the same way—not merely to signify that the donkey has died, but as a confirmation of the dream in which the milkman states his intention to continue working in the world above, but in a new business: "Down below I was in the milk business. Up above I'm in the rainbow business." Such a role in the celestial Paradise follows a long tradition of giving especially righteous figures, such as Enoch, roles to perform in heaven. See "Heaven's Wagon Driver" by Péter Ujvári.

Page 146
"Abraham"
by Franz Kafka

Kafka imagines an Abraham who, while willing to go through with the sacrifice of his son, "was unable to bring it off because he could not get away, being indispensable." In the abundant literature concerned with the *Akedah*, the binding of Isaac, there are given ways in which Abraham tried to evade the terrible order. In *Genesis Rabbah* (55:7), for example, Abraham pretends he does not know which son God means: " '*Take thy son* (Gen. 22:2).' 'Which son?' he asked. '*Thine only son* (ibid.).' 'But each is the only one of his mother.' '*Whom thou lovest* (ibid.)' 'Is there a limit to affection?' '*Even Isaac* (ibid.).' " For an inspired study of the *Akedah* legends, see *The Last Trial* by Sholem Spiegel. See also the variations on this theme in the parables at the beginning of Søren Kierkegaard's *Fear and Trembling*.

Page 147
"The Near Murder"
by Jakov Lind

The pagan and barbaric dimension of the *Akedah* is muted by the fact that in the end Isaac was not sacrificed, and because it is a kind of mythology, from which we do not usually make literal comparisons. The power of Lind's parable is that he presents an Abraham stripped of the mythic aura, who is compelled by "a voice behind him: 'Take your son and kill him.' " Here the underlying madness is underscored, and the horror of the deed Abraham was prepared to undertake laid bare. Retold in this perspective, the story becomes simply horrifying. Perhaps to mute this fact, tradition has identified the test on Mt. Moriah as a new Covenant between God and the Jews, in which human sacrifice is brought to an end, and replaced with animal sacrifice (which itself is still practiced by some Jews in the *kaparot* ceremony).

Page 149
"The Dream of Isaac"
by Howard Schwartz

This tale, formerly titled "The Sacrifice," replaces the ram caught in the bush in Gen. 22:13 with a goose. This happens in a dream attributed to Isaac, dreamed thirty years after the *Akedah*. (According to one tradition, Isaac was 10 years old at the time of the journey to Mt. Moriah.) The purpose of this extreme example of midrashic license is to link the sacrifice of the goose with the cutting of the umbilical cords of Esau and Jacob by Isaac. The effect is to link the two episodes, a common midrashic device, and to imply a link between the sacrifice that saves the son and the cutting of the cord that is necessary for the child to live. The fact that the cord of Esau is blood-red is deduced from the description of Esau at his birth, when he emerged red all over (Gen. 25:25). The pure white of Jacob's cord symbolizes the purity that Jacob is considered to represent in the Aggadah, despite his frequent use of trickery (Gen. 27:5–23; 30:35–43).

Page 150
"Isaac"
by Michael Strassfeld

Here, too, Isaac is haunted by the *Akedah* in a dream, this one recurring. The blurring of Abraham and the ram in the dream completes the circle of figures present in the biblical episode (Gen. 22), except for God and the angels. This tale links the episode of the binding of Isaac with that of the blessing of Jacob, disguised as Esau. In both cases something that was about to happen was changed in the course of the event, and Strassfeld implies that the changing of his father's face to that of the ram in the dream prefigures the substitution of Jacob for Esau in the blessing of the firstborn.

Page 151
"Isaac"
by Barry Holtz

This tale expands on the description of the blessing of the firstborn by Isaac in Gen. 27, and also links the binding of Isaac with the episode in which Jacob steals the blessing of Esau by disguising himself as his older brother. Holtz suggests that in facing death ("the terrible future before his eyes") Isaac's "mind returns to an unescaped past." The memory is so vivid for the blind Isaac that he "grasps for Esau," who is "safe from all but natural terrors, his life defined by taste and smell." According to *Genesis Rabbah* (65:10), Isaac was blinded either by the tears of the angels or by the glimpse he had into the heavens while he lay bound on his back. In *Pirke de Rabbi Eliezer* 32 this notion is made even more explicit: "Rabbi Simeon said: 'In the hour when Isaac was bound, he lifted up his eyes heavenwards and saw the glory of the Shekhinah, as it is written *For man shall not see me and live* (Ex. 33:20). Instead of death his eyes grew dim in his old age (Gen. 27:1).' " By linking the episodes of the *Akedah* and that of the blessing and its attendant deception, Holtz implies that they are connected in meaning, perhaps because Abraham deceived Isaac by not admitting his intention to sacrifice him (Gen. 22:7–8), while Jacob deceived him by pretending to be Esau (Gen. 27:32).

Page 152
"The Tale of the Ram"
by Rabbi Tsvi Blanchard

According to *Sefer Yashar* (23:70), "Abraham lifted up his eyes and saw a ram was caught in a thicket by his horns; that was the ram which the Lord God had created on the day that He made earth and heaven." After having created the ram, it was necessary to keep it in Paradise until the time came to bring it down to earth. This is "the small back section of heaven" referred to in this tale by Tsvi Blanchard, where other pre-created figures are also to be found, including the Messiah. One list of ten such premundane creations can be found in *Pirke de Rabbi Eliezer* 2, another in *Pirke Avot* 5, where the ram is mentioned. The 12th-century commentator Machson Vitry offered as a proof-text of the ram's preexistence Gen. 22:13: *And behold, before him a ram caught in the thicket by his horns.* Here "before" is taken to mean "in the past." The punishment of the ram for goring the Messiah is derived from the laws about a goring ox in Exodus (21:28–36). The wounding of the Messiah also serves as a reason—one of a multitude that have been given—to explain why the coming of the Messiah has been delayed.

Page 152
"Rivka on Mount Moriah"
by Laya Firestone

The births of Jacob and Esau are described in Gen. 25. According to *Midrash Rabbah* (63:6) the struggle of Jacob and Esau began in the womb: "Rabbi Yohanan said: 'Each ran to slay the other.' Resh Lakish said: 'Each annulled the laws of the other.' Rabbi Berekiah observed in Rabbi Levi's name: 'Do not think that only after issuing into the light of the world was Esau antagonistic to Jacob, but even while still in his mother's womb his fist was stretched out against him, as it is written: *The wicked stretch out their fists from the womb* (Ps. 58:4). When she stood near synagogues or schools, Jacob struggled to come out. While when she passed idolatrous temples, Esau eagerly struggled to come out.' " The assertion of Rivka (Rebecca) that "with such suffering, would that I had not conceived" derives from the same section of *Midrash Rabbah*. Rivka's journey to Moriah parallels that of the *Akedah* (Gen. 22). Such a journey, for the purpose of having Rivka conceive, is suggested in *Genesis Rabbah* (63:5) and made overt in *Pirke de Rabbi Eliezer* 32: "Rabbah Yehuda said: 'Rebecca was barren for twenty years. After twenty years Isaac took Rebecca and went with her to Mt. Moriah, to the place where he had been bound, and he prayed on her behalf concerning the conception of the womb.' "

Page 155
"Jacob at the River"
by Joel Rosenberg

This retelling of Gen. 32:23–33 proposes that rather than wrestling with an angel, Jacob wrestled the spirit of the river Yabbok and in this way exorcised his own double. (The notion of wresting with the spirit of a river is also found in "The Hermit and the Bear" by I. L. Peretz.) Eventually the waters take the form of a man, much as the waves turn into a bear in Peretz's parable. This interpretation of the enigmatic wrestling of Jacob with the angel has distinct kabbalistic elements, such as Jacob's "trying to shape its crests and swells into the letters of the alphabet and into words, to carve out names with fingernails, and shape the flowing stream into a text and into commentaries." The meaning, in this context, is perhaps that Jacob was attempting to make sense of the revelation he had at the river, which Rosenberg interprets as a mystical experience. There are a wide range of interpretations of this incident, which include an assertion that the angel with whom Jacob wrestled was God. The most common identification, however, is that the angel was the archangel Michael, although the angel Metatron is sometimes substituted. In *Genesis Rabbah* (77:3) the angel is identified as the guardian angel of Esau.

Page 157
"The Plague of Darkness"
by Dan Jacobson

The ninth plague of Ex. 10:21–23, which was sent on Egypt because they refused to let the Israelites depart from Egypt, here recurs in South Africa, in the form of widespread blindness, blurring the distinction between the colors of the races, which the whites of the country put so much store in. In this way the story serves as an allegory of that country's reluctance to let the black people go, and makes explicit the parallel between their plight and that of the Israelites in Egypt. In *Exodus Rabbah* (14:1–2) this darkness is interpreted as follows: "It came from the darkness of Gehinnom . . . our sages conjectured that it was as thick as a *dinar*." And in *Midrash Hagadol*: "The darkness which befell the Egyptians was of a material character . . . and even all the lamps and all the torches in the world gave them no light. When one lit a lamp it was extinguished, just as travelers relate of the Mountains of Darkness: lamps cannot burn there, they are extinguished by the darkness." In both these descriptions, the darkness resembles that of the blind. The seriousness of this plague is emphasized by the fact that it is next to last, the last being the killing of the firstborn sons of the Egyptians. Jacobson's story implies that as in Exodus, if this plague is not heeded, the next will take place.

Page 160
"In the Wilderness"
by Aharon Appelfeld

This story of the travels of refugees during the Second World War has been constructed to provide careful parallels to the biblical narrative about the wandering of the Israelites in the wilderness, as the title suggests. For an analysis of this parallel, see pp. 67–68.

Page 164
"The Third Tablet of the Covenant"
by Moshe ben Yitzhak HaPardesan

This legend draws its inspiration from both the Written Torah and the Oral Torah. Moses' forty-day sojourn on Mt. Sinai is well known from the Bible, while the remarkable detail that the tablets of the covenant, given to Moses, were written by the finger of God is related in Ex. 31:18. On the other hand, in the Oral Torah we find the tradition that Moses learned the Written Torah during the day and the Oral Torah at night; see, for example, *Pirke de Rabbi Eliezer* 46. The description of the Written Torah as black fire on white fire, and its comparison to curly locks of (God's?!) hair (S. of S. 5:11) is found in the beginning of *Midrash Tanhuma* (Ber. 1). Moreover, *The Midrash on the Ten Commandments* (*Beit ha-Midrash*, ed. Jellinek, I:62) notes that before the creation of the world the Torah, written in black fire on white fire, was set on the arm of God Himself. The idea that there are seventy ways or facets (*panim*) of interpreting the Torah is found in *Numbers Rabbah* 13:15–16 (see also *Zohar Pinhas* 216a and Ex. 83b); however, according to other sources, such as Soferim 16, the Torah was given to Moses in forty-nine different interpretations. For the notion that the Oral Torah contains even the questions that each disciple may ask of his master, see, for example, *Exodus Rabbah* 47:1. *Exodus Rabbah* (41:6 and 57:7) also grapples with the problem of the impossibility of Moses' learning all the Torah in just forty days. Moses' request to commit not just the Written Torah but also the Oral Torah to writing is related in *Midrash Tanhuma* (Ki Tissa 34), while the ascent of the letters from the broken tablets is found, for example, in B. Pes. 87b. No previous literary source for the tradition of a third tablet of the covenant has yet come to light. However, the existence of such a tradition may have been suggested by the curious depiction of Moses handing down from Sinai no less than five tablets, found in the Birds' Head Haggadah (Bezalel National Museum of Israel), folio 23r. Some scholars have suggested that these five tablets represent the five books of the Pentateuch; but they could equally represent the Torah, Prophets, and Writings which make up the Written Torah plus the Halakhah and the Aggadah which together make up the Oral Torah. Another possibility is that the five tablets represent the Torah and its four modes of interpretation known by the acronym *PaRDeS* (see pp. 83–87). (Note supplied by Marc Bregman.)

Page 166
"The Flying Letters"
by David Einhorn

The flight of the letters first appears in connection with the tablets received by Moses on Mt. Sinai. When Moses descended with the tablets in his hands and saw the people worshiping the golden calf, he did not immediately break the tablets, according to Y. Taan. 4:68c and *The Fathers According to Rabbi Nathan* 2:11, but "he looked at the tablets and saw that the writing had disappeared from them." A similar tradition holds that when the fire in the Temple reached the Ark, the letters also took flight.

Page 167
"The Chest of Herbs and the Golden Calf"
by Martin Buber

This tale is found in *Maaysiot Varsha*, ed. by Rabbi Abraham Biyalkamin, Warsaw, 1904, pp. 22–31. The impure spirit of the Golden Calf that remains within the chest, substituted for the one of the healing herbs, represents the decision of the Israelites to abandon the ways of God at Mt. Sinai and mold the Golden Calf, substituting the poisonous (the Golden Calf) for the nourishing (the Torah). The description of the formation of the Golden Calf is found in Exodus (32:4): *And Aaron said unto them: "Break off the golden rings, which are in the ears of your wives, of your sons, and of your daughters, and bring them unto me." All the people broke off the golden rings which were in their ears, and brought them unto Aaron. And he received them at their hand, and fashioned it with a graving tool, and made it a molten calf; and they said: "This is thy god, O Israel, which brought thee out of the land of Egypt."* The notion of the Golden Calf as an evil spirit that the people evoked appears in the Zohar (4:192b): "When [Aaron] took the gold from their hands they began their magical manipulations and incantations and so drew down the spirit of impurity from the 'other side,' and caused two spirits to come together, one male and the other female. The male was disguised in the form of an ox and the female in that of an ass, and these two became one." Another legend in the Zohar (3:113b) tells of a tidal wave that would have inundated the world had Moses not burned the Golden Calf. That legend is parallel in many respects to the legend of King David and the Foundation Stone that held back the waters of the Abyss (B. Yom 54b). This passage has distinct parallels to the description of the Golden Calf at the end of Buber's tale: "Before the eyes of the assembled rabbis, there arose a creature of horrible aspect, somewhat like the image of a calf but with the wings and fangs of a monstrous bird of prey. The creature hovered trembling in the air. . . . Its eyes were formless liquid fire and its breath a mist of ice and cloud." The same legend that is told in "The Chest of Herbs and the Golden Calf" is retold in S. Ansky's story "The Tower of Rome," which can be found in *Yenne Velt: The Great Works of Jewish Fantasy and the Occult.*

Page 173
"A Tent of Dolphin Skins"
by Rabbi Marc A. Gellman

Among the very explicit directions in Ex. 26–27 for the construction of the Tabernacle, there is the passage that serves as the epigram of this story (Ex. 26:14): *And make for the tent a covering of tanned ram skins, and a covering of dolphin skins above.* It is not certain if *takash*, the term for dolphin, means exactly that—it is alternately translated as porpoise or seal. Working from the translation "dolphin skins," as it appears in *The Torah: The Five Books of Moses,* Rabbi Gellman links the assistance of the dolphins at the Red Sea and their subsequent death on the spears of the Egyptians—which he invents—to the requirement that dolphin skins be used in the tent that covered the Tabernacle. There is a tradition that dolphins are half man and half fish, and represent humans in the water. In Tosefta B. Bek. 1:11 it is stated that dolphins give birth to their children in the same manner as human beings do.

Page 174
"The Death of Moses"
by Franz Werfel

There is a rich literature concerning the death of Moses, who is said to have greatly resisted the attempts to end his life. This story by Werfel is based directly on a legend that appears in *Deuteronomy Rabbah* (21:10) in which Moses resists the attempt by Samael (Satan) to rob him of his soul. Werfel remains very true to the sources. The circle that Moses draws to protect himself is like that drawn by Honi the Circlemaker (B. Taan. 23a). The tradition that "God kissed him and took the soul from his mouth with that kiss" is referred to in rabbinic literature as "the Kiss of the Shekhinah" (B. Bab. Bat. 17a) and differs from every other kind of death, since it does not involve the Angel of Death, as explained in this passage from *Pirke de Rabbi Eliezer* (4b): "Six there were over whom the Angel of Death had no dominion, namely Abraham, Isaac, and Jacob, Moses, Aaron, and Miriam . . . Moses, Aaron, and Miriam because it is written in connection with them that they died *by the mouth of the Lord* (Numb. 33:38)." A talmudic passage (B. Sot. 13b) describes Moses as being carried, after his death, "on the wings of the Shekhinah," echoing Ex. 19:14, in which God says to Moses: *Ye have seen. . . . now I have you on eagles' wings, and brought you unto Myself.* Other versions of the death of Moses can be found in *The Fathers According to Rabbi Nathan*, ch. 12, and in *Falasha Anthology: The Black Jews of Ethiopia*, pp. 107–11, which has been translated from Geez, the same language in which the oldest extant manuscript of *The Book of Enoch* is found.

BOOK II
APOCRYPHAL THEMES

Page 181
"The Royal Messenger"
by Rabbi Nachman of Bratslav

Tales about kings who represent God are found throughout Jewish literature. This can be said to be the parable of the agnostic, who sees the letter—i.e., the evidence of God's creation—but who remains unsatisfied unless he is able to see the sender of the letter. In Jewish legend, the first example of the messenger given a message to deliver to the world is Jonah. But the role given to Enoch in the Enoch literatures is almost identical to that of the royal messenger in Nachman's parable. In *The Slavonic Book of Enoch* (*2 Enoch*, also known as *The Book of the Secrets of Enoch*) 33:8 this role is specified: "Give them the books of the handwriting, and they will read them and will know Me for the Creator of all things, and will understand how there is no other God but Me."

Page 182
"The Menorah"
by Theodor Herzl

This story, written in 1897, is about Herzl's return to Judaism. The menorah of the title is the eight-branched candelabrum (plus the ninth branch, known as the *shammes*) used on Hanukah, known as the *Hanukiah*, in contrast with the seven-branched menorah used for Sabbath services. (See "The Tale of the Menorah" by Rabbi Nachman of Bratslav and "The Seven Lights of the Lamp" by Moshe ben Yitzhak HaPardesan and the appropriate notes.) Hanukah celebrates the remarkable victory of the Jews over the Greeks on the 25th of Kislev, which is reported in the apocryphal *First and Second Books of the Maccabees*. However, the miracle that is the focus of the central Hanukah ritual, that of lighting an additional candle for each night of the eight-day celebration, does not appear in the books of the Maccabees, but is referred to in the Talmud (B. Shab. 21b): "What is the origin of the feast of Hanukah? Our rabbis taught: 'On the twenty-fifth day of Kislev the eight days of Hanukah begin. When the heathens entered the Temple they defiled all the holy oil they found in it; but when the Maccabees prevailed and conquered the heathens, they sought and found one remaining jar of oil, stamped with the seal of the high priest. Though the oil contained in the jar would have sufficed for one day only, a miracle occurred, and it lasted for eight days. On the anniversary of this occasion a feast was instituted with the reciting of Hallel and other praises.'" The Talmud (B. Yom. 58b) also reports a debate between the schools of Hillel and Shammai over the proper way to light the Hanukah candles: "The school of Shammai hold that on the first day eight lights are lit and thereafter they are gradually reduced. But the school of Hillel maintain that on the first day one is lit and thereafter they are progressively increased up to eight." As always, the ruling of the school of Hillel was accepted. This story first appeared in *Die Welt* on December 31, 1897. It was later collected in Herzl's *Zionistische Schriften*.

Page 185
"The Seventh Millennium"
by Der Nister

This tale has been excerpted from the novel *Di Mishpoche Mashber* (2:313). The notion that the messianic era will begin in the seventh millennium appears in *Vita Adae et Evae* 51:1 (*The Books of Adam and Eve*), after the death of Adam: "When they had been mourning for four days, Michael the archangel appeared and said to Seth: 'Man of God, mourn not for thy dead more than six days, for on the seventh day is the sign of the resurrection and the rest of the age to come: on the seventh day the Lord rested from all His works.'" A parallel to this also appears in *The Apocalypse of Moses* 43:3–4. See R. H. Charles, *The Apocrypha and Pseudepigrapha of the Old Testament*, vol. 2, pp. 153–54. These millennia are further defined in the Talmud (Sanh. 97a): "The world is to exist for six thousand years, the first two thousand of which were chaos, the second two thousand of Torah, and the third two thousand are the days of the Messiah." The seventh millenium, in this view, will take place after the End of Days.

Page 185
"Sabbath in Gehenna"
by Isaac Bashevis Singer

The earliest Jewish concept of the underworld was Sheol, the abode of the dead (Numb. 16:32–33). This was replaced by Gehenna, which more closely resembles the notion of Hell, in that it is a place where souls are cleansed and purified before they enter the lower Paradise" (Zohar 4:211b). The origin of the term is the Valley of Hinnom, outside of Jerusalem (2 Chron. 28:3). But it is first in *The Book of Enoch* and other apocryphal texts that the evolution from the Valley of Hinnom (Gai Hinnom) to Gehenna takes place. *1 Enoch* 27:1-2 describes "The accursed valley which is for those who are accursed for ever." And *1 Enoch* 90:26-27 describes Enoch's vision of the judgment of the accursed: "And I saw at that time how an abyss was opened in the midst of the earth, full of fire, and they brought those blinded sheep, and they were all judged and found guilty and cast into this fiery abyss, and they burned." Gehenna is referred to by name in *The Assumption of Moses* (10:10): "And thou shalt look from on high and shalt see thy enemies in Gehenna, and thou shalt recognize them and rejoice." It is in the Talmud, however, that the concept of Gehenna is fully developed as the counterpart of the Celestial Paradise, as, for example, in B. Ber. 28b, where Rabban Yohanan ben Zakkai tells his disciples that "there are two paths before me, one leading to the Garden of Eden and the other leading me to Gehenna, and I do not know along which I shall be led." This concept is expanded in the midrashic literatures; see especially *The Chronicles of Jerahmeel* 14-17. The primary legend about Sabbath in Gehenna is found in the Zohar 2:251a. See p. 56-57 for a translation of this legend and further discussion of this story. For a thorough discussion of Gehenna, see *Hell in Jewish Literature* by Samuel J. Fox.

Page 189
"The Book of Mysteries"
by Meyer Levin

The immediate source for Levin's retelling is *Shivhei ha-Besht*, the earliest collection of legends about the founder of Hasidim (available in English as *In Praise of the Baal Shem Tov*), where it is said in the fifth tale that "Rabbi Adam had found these manuscripts containing the hidden secrets of the Torah in a cave." The tale of the transmission of this book to the Baal Shem is number 7, "The Secret Manuscripts and Rabbi Adam's Son." However, the history of the Book of Mysteries (also known as the Book of Reb Adam) is itself based on the famous legend of the Book of Raziel, which the angel Raziel is said to have given to Adam so that he could read in it the history of the future generations. The origin of the legend of the Book of Raziel seems to derive from *2 Enoch* (33:5-12), also known as *The Book of the Secrets of Enoch*, which was preserved only in Slavonic. However, here the book originates with Enoch, who was said to have written it based on the teachings he was said to have received in heaven, although Enoch, like Adam, receives the book from the angel Raziel. The fullest expression of the legend of the Book of Raziel appears in the Zohar 1:37b, 1:55b, and 1:58b, where it is linked to the biblical passage *This is the book of the generations of Adam* (Gen. 5:1). In the Zohar (1:37b) it is suggested that the book given to Adam and that written by Enoch were two different books, but the subsequent tradition blended them into the same book, which was believed to have been used by Noah in building the ark, which he also took with him, and in this way preserved it to reach the Patriarchs, and, eventually, King Solomon, who derived his wisdom from it and referred to it in the building of the Temple. According to the legend, the book was destroyed along with the Temple. Therefore the Hasidim could not assert that it had come into the possession of the Baal Shem, and so created the legend of the Book of Mysteries, which is otherwise identical in motif. This is underscored by the fact that the Baal Shem receives the book from the son of Reb Adam, which cannot but echo the legend that the Book of Raziel was first received and then handed down by Adam. Clearly the intent of the hasidic legend is to link up the Baal Shem with the sages of the past, as well as to offer a source for his great knowledge of the mysteries.

Page 195
"Angel Rolling the Heavens Together"
by Jerred Metz

This apocalyptic piece is reminiscent of the cosmic upheavals portrayed in several apocryphal texts, such as this vision of the final judgment found in *The Book of Enoch*: "And He will summon all the host of the heavens, and all the holy ones above, and the host of God, the Cherubim, Seraphim and Ophanim, and all the angels of power . . . shall on that day raise one voice, and bless and glorify and exalt in the spirit of faith . . . and all shall say with one voice: 'Blessed is He, and may the Name of the Lord of Spirits be blessed for ever and ever' " (*1 Enoch* 61:10–11). The mythic type of behavior of the angel who rolls the heavens together has many parallels, such as this from the Hekhaloth text *3 Enoch* (36:2): "And all the ministering angels first go down into the river of fire, and they dip themselves in the fire and dip their tongue and their mouth seven times."

BOOK III
AGGADIC THEMES

Page 199
"The Spider and the Fly"
by Rabbi Nachman of Bratslav

God's guardianship of Israel, in the form of a Covenant between them, which is the Torah, is a recurrent aggadic theme. The Torah, as represented by the page in Rabbi Nachman's tale, rises up as a protector when set in force by the Holy One, whose presence is represented by the wind. This is the same wind of which it is written: *And the spirit of God hovered over the face of the waters* (Gen. 1:2). Thus the king's dream is an allegory in which the fly represents Israel, and the spider the enemies of Israel. The mountain that must be climbed to reach the tablet is clearly intended to represent Mt. Sinai, and the tablet, the tables received by Moses, which were inscribed with the finger of God. Such allegories are common in the aggadic literatures. One example, in which God also intercedes to protect Israel in a time of danger, is found in the Talmud (B. Ber. 54a): "The stone which Og, King of Bashan, tried to throw upon Israel is delivered by tradition as follows: 'The camp of Israel,' said he, 'extends three miles. I shall therefore go and uproot a mountain three miles in extent, throw it upon them and kill them.' He went and uprooted a mountain three miles wide, and raised it above his head. But the Holy One, praised be He, sent a host of ants to the mountain and they bored a hole in it, causing it to fall over his head and rest on his shoulders. He tried to throw it off, but his teeth protruding one into the other had riveted it upon him and he was not able to throw it off. What was Moses' height? Ten cubits: he seized an axe ten cubits long, sprang up ten cubits, and struck Og's ankle a mighty blow which killed him." Here an unprepossessing force, the ants, succeeds in overcoming the giant Og; clearly they represent Israel, which succeeded, as in the victory of the Maccabees over the Greeks, in defeating a more powerful enemy. (See note to "The Menorah" by Theodor Herzl, p. 660.) For another parallel legend, see B. Bab. Bat. 74b. There is also a variety of legends and folktales concerning kings who are dissuaded from harming Jews. Often their revelation comes in a dream, as in this tale by Rabbi Nachman or "Three Vows" by S. Y. Agnon. One of the tales in *Shivhei ha-Ari*, for example, concerns a king who is transported by the power of the Ari to a pit, from which the Ari has him pulled out, still lying in his bed, by ropes. Then he is made to affix his royal seal to a proclamation protecting the Jews. Later, when he awakes, this decree is presented to him, and he acknowledges that it is authentic. A parallel to this tale is the king's dream which can be found in *Mimekor Yisrael* (1:477–8).

Page 204
"The Prince Who Was Made Entirely of Precious Stones"
by Rabbi Nachman of Bratslav

This tale is based on the tradition of the *Lamed-vov Tzaddikim*, the Thirty-six Just Men in every generation. The earliest reference to this tradition appears in the Talmud, and is attributed to Abbaye: "There are not less than thirty-six righteous men in the world who receive the Divine Presence" (B. Sanh. 97b and B. Suk. 45b). Because of the centrality of the concept of the *tzaddik*, this tradition became particularly important to the Hasidim, whose tales include many reports of encounters with these hidden *tzaddikim*.

Page 208
"The Hidden Tzaddik"
by S. Y. Agnon

According to the tradition, the hidden *tzaddikim* were usually modest figures such as the stove maker in this tale. This inherent modesty and desire to remain hidden is reflected in the stove maker's wish to be buried "in the plot where the stillborn are buried" and "not to place a tombstone on my grave." It is understood that when the hidden *tzaddik* dies another will take his place, so that there always remain thirty-six *tzaddikim* alive in the world. Tales of hidden *tzaddikim* are commonly found in hasidic literature. See, for example, "The Hidden Tzaddikim" in Martin Buber's *Tales of the Hasidim: The Early Masters*, p. 263, and "Of a Hidden Tzaddik" in *Tales of the Hasidim: The Later Masters*, p. 65. Sholem Asch's novella *Kiddush Ha-Shem* also concerns one of these hidden saints.

Page 217
"The Stars of Heaven"
by S. Y. Agnon

This tale is a clever parable about the nature of the Oral Law, and its relationship to the Written Law. Reb Moses, who has a book published after his death called *The*

Words of Moses, seeks out the Rabbi of Polonnoye, whose teacher was the Baal Shem, and they discuss for many hours a saying of the Baal Shem that Reb Moses was unable to understand. Reb Moses is readily identified with Moses the Redeemer, whose words are always cited to demonstrate their authenticity as part of the Oral Law: "Go and tell them I have a tradition . . . reaching from Moses at Mt. Sinai" (B. Hag. 3). This tale is precisely parallel to the famous talmudic legend of Moses sitting in the school of Rabbi Akiba, where he is unable to understand a point that he is credited with (B. Men. 29b). For a translation and discussion of this legend see p. 7. The Rabbi of Polonnoye expounds on the saying of the Baal Shem in the same way that the Oral Law expounds on the Written. The metaphor of the stars of the rabbi applies equally well to the words of the Torah, and justifies the extensive commentary of the Oral Law. The story also reinforces the belief among Hasidim that the teachings of their rebbes, especially the Baal Shem, were of the sacred caliber of the previous generations, including those of the time of the Torah. For more on the Oral Law, see pp. 6–8.

Page 218
"The Legend of the Just Men"
by André Schwarz-Bart

Schwarz-Bart revises the basic nature of the tradition of the *Lamed-vov* in this story by making the Just Men descendants in a single lineage which he traces back to 1185 C.E. The notion of the hidden identity of the *tzaddikim* is also abandoned. Schwarz-Bart also focuses on the martyrlike quality of these descendants, whereas martyrdom is not an essential aspect of the original tradition. The role of the hidden *tzaddik* was rather to serve and assist others in a self-effacing manner, and thus to serve as an example of those who, though having great power at their command, do not use it for personal gain.

Page 231
"One of the Just Men"
by Elie Wiesel

This tale deviates from the *Lamed-vov* tradition in that it describes a Just Man who "walked the streets and markets preaching against greed and theft, falsehood and indifference," which is contrary to the custom of the hidden *tzaddik,* who remains unknown. As in most of Elie Wiesel's writings, the tale may be seen as a projection of the present into the past, in which the Just Man may well represent Wiesel. From this perspective, Wiesel is presenting his rationale for continuing his work as a writer and speaker, even in the face of indifference: "In the beginning I thought I could change man. Today, I know I cannot. If I still shout today, if I still scream, it is to prevent man from ultimately changing me." The true model for this figure is, rather than the *Lamed-vov,* the prophets of the Bible.

Page 231
"The Unrecognized Just Men"
by Albert Memmi

Memmi refers to an authentic tradition about the *Lamed-vov Tzaddikim*—that they remain unknown to all, even perhaps to themselves, "for, were they to know this anonymity, they would not be anything anymore." For more on the issue of the "hid-denness" of the *Lamed-vov*, see Gershom Scholem's article "The 36 Hidden Tzad-dikim" in *The Messianic Idea in Judaism*. Memmi interprets this belief to mean that any and every man, including himself, might be one of the Just Men, and therefore we all have the responsibility to act as if we were in fact one of the *Lamed-vov*: "But, for precisely this reason, should I not be on the watch over all things: Over my royal cousin, over the public weal, and over my own person?" This meaning could well be seen to be implicit in the tradition of the hidden *tzaddik*, and in making it explicit, Memmi is performing the same kind of exegesis as is found in the midrash-im.

Page 232
"The Holy of Holies"
by Albert Memmi

The absence of God from the Holy of Holies of the Tabernacle when invaded by conquerors is used here to provide a meditation on the Jewish conception of God, "so mysterious, of Whom we hardly speak." This, in turn, leads Memmi to ask "if they have been so loquacious about this nothing, what could they have said, had there been something there?" This question is replied to in a well-known but highly enigmatic talmudic passage (B. Ber. 7a) about a vision of God in the Holy of Holies, by Rabbi Ishmael ben Elisha, the high priest: "Once, when I entered the Holy of Holies to burn the incense, I saw Akatriel Yah, Lord of all Hosts sitting on a high and exalted throne, and He said to me, 'Ishmael, My son, bless Me!' I replied, 'Sovereign of the Universe! may it be Thy will that Thy mercy overcome Thy anger, and Thy compassion overrule Thy other attributes; let Thy conduct toward Thy children be with the attribute of loving kindness and stop short of the line of justice; and, out of regard to them mayest Thou overlook Judgment!' The Lord then inclined His head toward me as a sign confirming my prayer." The identity of Akatriel Yah has been widely debated. Some commentators assume that it is a name for God, while others feel it refers to an elevated angel. This vision in the Holy of Holies is unique in Jewish literature. See *Jewish Gnosticism, Merkabah Mysticism, and Talmudic Tradition* by Gershem Scholem, ch. 7.

Page 233
"The Building of the Temple"
by Franz Kafka

That Kafka, who had very little exposure to the Midrash, often thought in an aggadic manner is demonstrated by the remarkable parallel of his parable "The Building of the Temple" and a legend from the Zohar (174a). Kafka says, for example, "No building ever came into being as easily as did this Temple," while the legend from the Zohar states, "In reality it was made of itself, by a miracle. . . . It was built of its own accord . . . it showed the workers a design which guided their hands and from which they did not turn their eyes until the whole building of the Temple was completed." The model for the Temple was, according to the kabbalistic belief, the Celestial Tem-ple in the heavenly Jerusalem. The existence of such a heavenly Jerusalem is stated in the Talmud (B. Bat. 75b): "Rabbah said in the name of Rabbi Yohanan: 'Jerusalem of the World to Come will not be like Jerusalem of this world. Anyone who wishes to can ascend to Jerusalem of this world, but only those invited will go to that of the world to come.' " Other legends about the Celestial Jerusalem, including one proposing that the earthly Jerusalem will one day ascend three parasangs, are found in the same folio of the Talmud.

Page 233
"Temple-Builders"
by Dennis Silk

The tradition that the Temple was built by "unruly djinns," as Silk puts it, derives from the legend of the capture of Asmodeus, King of Demons, by Beniah, servant of King Solomon, in the Talmud (B. Git. 68b). Solomon was reputed to have power over the demons that derived from his magic ring, on which the Name of God (the Tetragrammaton) was inscribed, and he used this power over them to compel the demons to assist in constructing the Temple. See the previous note.

Page 233
"Scroll of Fire"
by Hayim Nachman Bialik

The destruction of the Temple in Jerusalem is dealt with extensively in rabbinic literature, especially in *Lamentations Rabbah*. Other passages about the destruction of the Temple include Seder 'Olam 27 and B. Taan. 29a, as well as Y. 4:69c. In this excerpt from Bialik's epic poem "Scroll of Fire," reference is made to the legend that God descended to mourn over the ruins of the Temple. (See Ginzberg, *Legends of the Jews*, vol. 4, p. 305.) The Exile of the Shekhinah takes place when she "arose from over the ruins and went into the hidden places." In B. Rosh Hashana (31a) the great reluctance with which the Shekhinah removed herself from the Temple is described. The Exile of the Shekhinah is also described in *Lamentations Rabbah* 25. For discussion of the evolution of the concept of the Shekhinah, see pp. 20–23.

Page 235
"The Angel and the World's Dominion"
by Martin Buber

The independence of the angels is a common theme in the Aggadah. The angels resisted the creation of man, stole the Book of Raziel from Adam and threw it into the sea, and tried to prevent Moses from receiving the Torah. In one infamous passage (B. Hag. 15a), Elisha ben Abuyah sees the angel Metatron sitting on a throne in Paradise, and comes to the false conclusion that "there are two powers in heaven." The inadequacy of the angels to undertake the work of God on their own is pointedly made in Buber's tale. A possible source for it is a passage in the Talmud (B. Taan. 24) in which an angel turns sand into flour, much as the flour of the angel in Buber's story is later turned to clay: "Once I stood on the bank of the River Papa and observed angels clad like sailors, who took sand, and filled the ships therewith. The sand was turned to fine flour, and the whole world came to buy. I said to the persons of my household: 'Do not buy of it, for it is only because of a miracle, and I wish to derive no benefit from miracles.' On the morrow, ships laden with actual wheat arrived from Parzina, of which all bought."

Page 236
"Yaish Meets the Angels"
by Hayim Hazaz

This excerpt from the novel *Yaish* is based on the talmudic legend about Moses and the angels (B. Shab. 88b–89a). This legend and a discussion of "Yaish Meets the Angels" can be found on pp. 63–64. In a passage about the four who entered *Pardes* (B. Hag. 14b—see pp. 83–87) the resistance of the angels to Rabbi Akiba is described: "Rabbi Akiba ascended in peace and descended in peace. And Rabbi Akiba too the ministering angels sought to thrust away, but the Holy One, blessed be He, said to them: 'Let this Elder be, for he is worthy to avail himself of My glory' " (B. Hag. 15b).

Page 243
"The Angel"
by Jiri Langer

This hasidic legend, excerpted from *Nine Gates to the Chassidic Mysteries*, p. 218, probably derives from Mishnah Avot (3:2): "If two sit together and words of the Law are spoken between them, the Divine Presence rests between them." The notion of angels being born and perishing is found in the Talmud (B. Hag. 14): "Every single day ministering angels are created from the stream Dinar, who after uttering one song before God, perish. A different opinion holds that with every word which comes forth from the mouth of the Holy One, blessed be He, an angel is created."

Page 243
"The Sacrifice"
by I. L. Peretz

The figure of the Angel of Death, the subject of this tale, derives from the passage in Exodus about the slaying of the Egyptian firstborn (Ex. 12:29). Here the Angel of Death is identified as "the destroyer" (Ex. 12:23). Numerous legends about the Angel of Death are found in the Talmud, and in the subsequent literatures, especially that of folk and hasidic lore. The most famous legend about the Angel of Death in the Talmud concerns King David's means of eluding him (B. Shab. 30b). The transfer of life from Sarah to the dying young man in "The Sacrifice" is a common motif of folklore. For an interesting literary parallel, see Edgar Allan Poe's story "The Portrait." The role of the Angel of Death is described in the Zohar (4:150a): "When the time comes for a spirit to take leave of this world, it cannot do so until the Angel of Death has taken off the garment of the body." In the pseudepigraphical work *The Testament of Abraham* (A17), Abraham convinces the Angel of Death, who has disguised himself, to reveal his true appearance: "And he showed Abraham seven fiery heads of dragons, and fourteen faces of most flaming fire and of every fierceness, and a dark face and a most gloomy viper's face, and the face of a most terrible precipice, and the fiercer face of an asp, and the face of a fearsome lion, and the face of a cerastes and of a basilisk. . . . in short, he showed him great fierceness and unendurable bitterness and every deadly sickness as of the odor of death. And from the great bitterness and fierceness about seven thousand male and female servants died, and the righteous Abraham entered the faint of death, as if his spirit had departed." In the *Maaseh Book*

(195) there is the story of a bride who saved her husband from the Angel of Death and obtained a reprieve for seven years—without having to give up her life, as in the Peretz story. In *Shivhei ha-Besht* there is also the story of how the wife of Abraham the Angel argued for his soul in Paradise, and obtained twelve more years of life for him. See "Daughter of Heaven" by Pascal Thémanlys and the appropriate note.

Page 246
"From the Beyond"
by Sholem Asch

Baruch Mordecai's vision in Paradise before he returned to this world and came back to life contains many traditional elements of the rabbinic conception of the World to Come. The presence of the Dark Angel (the Angel of Death) and the intercession of the archangel Gabriel who "flicked me with his finger on my nose, and said: 'Baruch Mordecai, you're not wanted here yet' " fully resembles the rabbinic conception of the heavenly hierarchy. The angel flicking him on the nose is an echo of the midrash on the formation of a child in *Tanhuma Pekude* 3 in which the angel "fillips the baby on the nose" when he is born, causing him to forget all the knowledge he carried with him from the *Yenne Velt* (the Other World). This same theme is also found in Itzik Manger's novel *The Book of Paradise*. Baruch Mordecai's description of being conducted by the Angel of Death is very much like that in *Midrash on Psalms* (Ps. 6:7; 51b–52a): "As soon as a person dies his spirit issues forth and cries and weeps before the Holy One, blessed be He, saying: 'Lord of the Universe! Whither am I being led?' Immediately Dumah, the Angel of Death, takes and conducts him to the court of death among the spirits." Asch also works in a subtle satire on the aggadic method of embellishing tales when Baruch Mordecai begins to embellish his encounter in Paradise. For example, he satirizes the use of the Oral Law for justification of any additions or changes in an established tale: "And Moses himself taught me the Torah and the word of God at the foot of Sinai." Additional visions of the Celestial Paradise and the Angel of Death are found in hasidic literature. See *Shivhei ha-Besht* 41 ("The Besht in the Messiah's Heavenly Palace") and 91 ("The Besht and the Angel of Death"). Stories of those who return from death are also common hasidic lore. See "The Bride in Her Grave," a tale of the Baal Shem in *Classic Hasidic Tales*, pp. 45–57.

Page 250
"The Star and the Angel of Death"
by Itzik Manger

This poignant tale, excerpted from Manger's novel *The Book of Paradise*, pp. 65–68, underscores, as does the previous tale by Peretz, the essentially heartless character of the Angel of Death. The star who argues with the angel to spare a bride starts to succeed only when he reminds the angel of the song *Dayyenu* from the end of the Passover seder, in which it is written, "And the Holy One, blessed be He, came and slaughtered the Angel of Death." This provides the remarkable moment in which the Angel of Death shudders at the thought of his own death. The legend in the song *Dayyenu* derives from the Talmud (B. Suk. 52): "In the future the Holy One, blessed be He, will bring the evil angel and slaughter him in the presence of the upright and unfolted."

Page 252
"The Six Days and the Seven Gates"
by Yitzhak Navon

There is a lengthy aggadic tradition of God's holding dialogue with the angels concerning important decisions, such as the creation of man, or the Giving of the Torah, as in this example from *Midrash Tehillim* (*Midrash on Psalms* 68:9), attributed to Rabbi Nathan: "When the Holy One, blessed be He, sought to give the Torah to the children of Israel, Mt. Carmel came from Aspamea and Mt. Tabor came from Bethelim. The one said: 'I am called Mt. Tabor. It is fitting that the Shekhinah should dwell upon me, for I am the highest of all the mountains, and not even the water of the deluge overwhelmed me.' And the other said: 'I am called Mt. Carmel. It is fitting that the Divine Presence should rest upon me, for I put myself in the middle of the Red Sea, and it was by my help that the children of Israel got across.' The Holy One, blessed be He, replied: 'By the blemish of arrogance in you, you have already made yourselves unworthy of My Presence.' The mountains asked: 'Are You partial to another? Is it possible that You will deprive us of our due?' The Holy One, blessed be He, replied: 'Because you put yourselves to trouble for My honor, I shall give you a reward. Behold, in the time of Deborah I shall give deliverance to the children of Israel upon Mt. Tabor, as it is said, *Go and draw toward Mt. Tabor* (Judg. 4:6); and I shall also give deliverance to Elijah upon Mt. Carmel, as it is said, *Ahab . . . gathered the prophets together unto Mt. Carmel* (1 Kings 18:20).' Then all the other mountains began to thunder protests and to make a commotion, as it is said, *the mountains quaked in the presence of the Lord* (Judg. 5:5). Thereupon the Holy One, blessed be He, said: . . . 'My wish is to dwell only on Sinai, because Sinai is the lowliest among you for, as Scripture says, *I dwell in the high and holy place, with him also that is of a contrite and lowly spirit* (Isa. 57:15).' " The letters of the Hebrew alphabet are also involved in such dialogues, such as in *Lamentations Rabbah* 24, where "The Holy One, blessed be He, said to Abraham, 'Let the twenty-two letters come and testify against Israel.' Forthwith the twenty-two letters appeared. The Aleph came to testify that Israel had transgressed against the Torah. . . ." The immediate source for this tale is probably the legend of the alphabet that appears in the Zohar (1:2b–3b): "When the Holy One, blessed be He, was about to make the world, all the letters of the Alphabet were still embryonic, and for two thousand years the Holy One, blessed be He, had contemplated them and toyed with them. When He came to create the world, all the letters presented themselves before Him in reversed order. . . ." A partial translation of this legend can be found on pp. 72–73. Rabbi Levi Yitzhak of Berditchev tells a tale about Moses' having witnessed "the tall mountains come before God, and each beg for the privilege of being the one on which the revelation should come to pass" (Buber, *Tales of the Hasidim* 1:221). See the following note.

Page 256
"The Golden Gates of Jerusalem"
by Matti Megged

In structure this tale is parallel to "The Six Days and the Seven Gates." Here, however, the issue is the coming of the Messiah rather than the retaking of Jerusalem in 1967, and here the seven gates of Jerusalem "correspond to the seven days of the week as well as to the seven ages between the war of God and Magog and the coming of the Messiah." (See "The Seventh Millennium" by Der Nister, and the appropriate note.) Since the Messiah will pass through one of the gates of Jerusalem, the notion of the gates vying for the right to have him pass through them is probably the basis of this tale and that of Yitzhak Navon. The belief that the Messiah will pass through one of the gates of Jerusalem derives, perhaps, from the passage in Daniel (9:24–26) which asserts that the Messiah will arrive sixty-two weeks after Jerusalem is rebuilt. There is also a talmudic legend (B. Bab. Bat. 75a) about precious stones of enormous size that "in the future the Holy One will . . . set up in the gates of Jerusalem." This appears to refer to the time of the messianic era.

Page 257
"The Messiah at the Gates of Rome"
by Der Nister

This is a portrayal of the famous talmudic legend (B. Sanh. 98a) which establishes a tradition of the Messiah as a leper or a beggar, such as those found in *Sefer Sippurim Noraim* 9a–10b and *Sippure Yakov*, pp. 35–36. The original talmudic legend of the Messiah at the gates of Rome is as follows: "Rabbi Yehoshua ben Levi once met Elijah standing at the entrance of the cave of Rabbi Shimon bar Yohai. He asked him: 'When will the Messiah come?' Elijah said to him: 'Go, ask him yourself. He sits at the entrance of the city of Rome.' Yehoshua ben Levi said: 'How will I recognize him?' And Elijah replied: 'He sits among the poor who suffer from diseases, and while all of them unwind and rewind their bandages all at once, he unwinds and rewinds them one at a time, for he says, "Should I be summoned, there must be no delay." ' Rabbi Yehoshua ben Levi went to him and said: 'Peace be with you.' The Messiah replied: 'Peace be with you, ben Levi.' Then Rabbi Yehoshua asked: 'When will the Master come?' And he replied: 'Today.' Rabbi Yehoshua then returned to Elijah, who asked him: 'What did he tell you?' Rabbi Yehoshua replied: 'He said to me, "Peace be with you, ben Levi." ' Elijah said: 'By saying this he assured the World to Come for you and your father.' Rabbi Yehoshua then said to Elijah: 'The Messiah lied to me, for he said that he shall come today, and he has not come.' Elijah said: 'He told you *Today, if you but hearken to His voice* (Ps. 95:7).' "

Page 258
"Forcing the End"
by Hugh Nissenson

This story is a reworking of the escape of Rabbi Yohanan ben Zakkai from Jerusalem during the Roman siege found in B. Git. 56a-b. For a translation of the original text and a discussion of this story, see p. 65–66.

Page 263
"On the Life and Death of Abbaye"
by David Shahar

The following are just a few of the many talmudic passages where Abbaye begins with "the matriarch said to me": B. Shab. 133b, B. Ket. 50a, B. M. K. 12a, B. M. K. 18b, and B. Yeb. 25a. On Abbaye's rejoicing, see B. Ber. 30b. The statement about Abbaye's juggling appears in B. Suk. 53a. The episode of the boys pointing to the roof appears in B. Ber. 48a. The lamb that accompanied Abbaye to the outhouse is mentioned in B. Ber. 62a: "The mother of Abbaye trained a lamb for him to go with him into the privy." The prayer in the privy is based on B. Ber. 60b: "On entering a privy one should say: 'Be honored, ye honored and holy ones that minister to the Most High. Give honor to the God of Israel. Wait for me till I enter and do my needs, and return to you.' " This is based on the belief that in the privy a man is abandoned by the angels and thus open to the approach of demons. Abbaye's prayer in the privy appears in B. Ber. 60b. That certain privies are the homes of demons derives from B. Ber. 62a: "There was a certain privy in Tiberias which if two persons entered together, even by day, they came to harm." The exorcism against demons appears in B. Shab. 67a. The window through which Rava's wife placed her hand on his head is mentioned in B. Ber. 62a. The two previous husbands of Abbaye's wife are mentioned in B. Yeb. 64b. The old man who consoled Abbaye about his passion for women is mentioned in B. Suk. 52a: "A certain old man came up to him and taught him: 'The greater the man, the greater his *Yetzer Hara* (Evil Inclination).' " Tradition identifies the anonymous old man with Elijah. The legend of the rocks of the Tigris kissing each other after the death of Abbaye appears in B. M. K. 25b. The attack on Abbaye's wife Homa is reported in B. Ket. 65a. This is based on the belief that when a wife outlives three husbands there is the presumption that she was some-how responsible for their deaths (B. Yeb. 64b). (Note prepared by Jeremy Garber.)

Page 269
"The Temptations of Rabbi Akiba"
by David Pinski

There are a considerable number of tales about demonic female spirits who attempt, and often succeed, in seducing men. This tale by Pinski expands on a brief talmudic legend, as follows: "Rabbi Akiba used to scoff at transgressors. One day Satan appeared to him as a woman at the top of a palm tree. Grasping the tree, he went climbing up, but when he had reached halfway up the tree Satan resumed his normal shape, saying: 'Had they not proclaimed in heaven, "Take heed of Rabbi Akiba and his learning," I would have valued your life as worthless' (B. Kid. 81a)." A parallel legend to this one about Rabbi Akiba, concerning Rabbi Meir, is found in B. Kid. 80a. (For a translation of it, see the note to "A Messiah in Every Generation," p. 715.) Still another parallel is found in B. Kid. 81a, concerning Rabbi Amram, who moved a ladder in order to reach a woman, and stopped when he had climbed up halfway. This legend is retold in the *Masseh Book* (106). Another such legend is found in *Midrash Tanhuma*, ed. Buber, 1:20, as follows: "A tale is told of a Hasid who en-countered a demon in the shape of a woman and she seduced him and copulated with him on the Day of Atonement. Later the Hasid was very much grieved, until he en-countered Elijah, who asked him, 'Why are you grieving?' He told him all that had happened to him. Elijah replied: 'You are free from sin. It was a succubus.' " In gen-eral, these tales are an expression of the Lilith legend. (See pp. 506–517 and the ap-propriate notes.) That Akiba starts to give in to the final temptation in Pinski's story, which retells the talmudic source, is surely intended to signify that the power of these succubi and of sexual lust is so great that not even Akiba, who was regarded as incor-ruptible and an expert at overcoming illusions (as in B. Hag. 14b), could resist it.

Page 274
"The Garden of *Shir Hashirim*"
by Arthur Waskow

This is the first of several tales concerned with explicating the enigmatic passage in B. Hag. 14b about the four sages who entered *Pardes*, a translation of which appears on p. 84. In form it is very much of a *drash*, with Waskow first linking *Pardes*, which means "orchard," with the garden of the Song of Songs, and, by implication, with the Garden of Eden. In this way he links and provides explanation for two enigmatic texts: the Song of Songs, because of its pronounced erotic aspect, and the *Pardes* passage, which because of its terseness and mystery has always been considered highly enigmatic. The passage, then, in Waskow's view, is about the experience of sexuality without the sense of the presence of God—as symbolized by the fact that God's Name does not appear in the Song of Songs. Traditionally, *Pardes* has been understood to mean mystical contemplation; here Waskow reinterprets it in a modern sense as sexuality, making the pointed observation that this remains a difficult matter for human beings to come to terms with.

Page 275
"The Four Who Entered *Pardes*"
by Howard Schwartz

This tale about the four who entered *Pardes* (B. Hag. 14b) starts with the assumption that *Pardes* refers to Paradise, of which it is the root word in Greek, and interprets the whole passage to refer to an attempt to enter *Gan Eden*. Such an interpretation links the orchard which *Pardes* denotes to the Garden of Eden, which is also the Earthly Paradise. While this interpretation is not unusual, *Pardes* is more commonly taken to denote the Celestial Paradise, and the Hagigah passage to refer to a heavenly journey, although there may remain an awareness that the journey is itself a metaphor for mystical contemplation and spiritual ascent. This is the interpretation of *Pardes* that is found in the Hekhaloth texts. (See Book IV, "Themes of Merkavah Mysticism.") The notion that the Tree of Life covered a five-hundred-year journey derives from *Genesis Rabbah* (15:6). The references to the left and right echo the kabbalistic doctrine of Justice (symbolized by the left side) and Mercy (symbolized by the right). In cleaving to the right, then, at all times, Rabbi Akiba places his faith in God's Mercy, and since he alone succeeded in the quest, it is implied that he was correct.

Page 276
"The Cave of Machpelah"
by Howard Schwartz

Because the patriarchs Abraham, Isaac, and Jacob and their wives are said to be buried in the Cave of Machpelah in Hebron, this cave was regarded as one of the holiest sites on earth. The tradition that Adam and Eve are also buried there, in an inner chamber, is found in the Talmud (B. Bab. Bat. 57b–58a): "Rabbi Bana'a used to mark caves of the deceased Rabbis. When he came to the cave of Abraham the Patriarch he found Eliezer, his servant, standing outside the door. 'What is Abraham doing now?' he asked. 'He sleeps in Sarah's lap, and she looks on his head,' was the reply. Rabbi Bana'a said to him: 'Go and inform Abraham that Bana'a is waiting at the door.' He communicated that to Abraham, whereupon the latter said: 'Let him come in, for he knows perfectly well that the evil inclination does not exist in this place.' Bana'a then entered, took the measure of the cave, and went out; when he arrived at the cave of Adam, he heard a *bat kol*, a heavenly voice, saying: 'Thou hast been permitted to see the likeness of My image (Abraham), but My real image itself (Adam) thou canst not see.' 'But I need to mark the measure of the cave,' protested Rabbi Bana'a. 'The measure of the outside equals the inside,' came the reply. After Rabbi Bana'a left the cave, he said: 'I have seen the heels of Adam and they appear to me as two sun globes.' " This tradition is also reported in *Pirke de Rabbi Eliezer* 36: "When the angels appeared to Abraham he thought them ordinary travelers. He ran to greet them, and desired to entertain them with a great feast. . . . He ran to procure a calf, but it fled into the cave of Machpelah. He followed it and found Adam and Eve lying on couches, asleep; lamps burned near them, and a fragrant, incenselike odor enveloped them. Therefore he longed for the cave of Machpelah as a family sepulcher." The notion that the cave of Machpelah was near the entrance to the Garden of Eden is found in *Zohar Hadash Ruth* 79. The history of the cave of Machpelah is reported in the Zohar (1:57b): "When God decreed Adam's death, He took pity on him and allowed him to be buried near the Garden of Eden, where Adam had previously made a cave and hidden with his wife." The belief that the souls of those who have died must pass through the cave of Machpelah on the way to *Gan Eden* is found in the Zohar (2:250b): "The souls that are worthy pass before the patriarchs in the cave so that they (the patriarchs) may awake and behold the seed which they have left in the world, and rejoice before the Almighty." The notion of the upside-down world derives from the Talmud (B. Pes. 50). Rabbi Joseph, the son of Rabbi Joshua ben Levi, once became sick and fell into a trance, and upon awakening, was asked by his father what he had seen; and he answered: "I saw a world reversed. The uppermost, below, and those below, uppermost." "My son," said his father, "thou has seen a rightly conducted world! But how do we scholars appear there?" "Just as we are esteemed here, so are we esteemed there," was Rabbi Joseph's answer. This episode is excerpted from a novel-in-progress, *The Four Who Entered Paradise*, which, taking *Pardes* to mean Paradise, describes the quest of the four sages of B. Hag. 14b to reach Paradise in order to recover the lost Book of Raziel.

Page 279
"The Four Who Sought to Re-enter the Garden"
by Moshe ben Yitzhak HaPardesan

It is characteristic of the Aggadah that all generations exist simultaneously. In this tale the four sages of B. Hag. 14b seek to reenter the Garden, only to discover that a later Torah master already inside has distracted the angel who serves as the gatekeeper as well as the gardener. That the four sages are unable to reenter the garden implies that the pattern established by the four sages in B. Hag. 14b of entering Paradise has become ritualized in succeeding generations, who may not always recall that their knowledge is built on that of the previous generations.

Page 280
"Ben Azzai"
by M. J. Berditchevsky

There are two opinions about the nature of the death of Ben Azzai, who "looked and died" in the legend of the four who entered *Pardes*. One view holds that Ben Azzai was somehow flawed, and therefore unable to survive the pure light of Paradise. This parable by Berditchevsky presents this interpretation, while the other view, that Ben Azzai was a great saint who chose to give up his spirit in a mystical union, is presented in the subsequent tale, "The Death of Ben Azzai" by Milton Steinberg. According to Berditchevsky, Ben Azzai used the biblical verse *Who has measured the waters in the hollow of his hand* (Isa. 40:12) to meditate on in order to delve "into the matter of the Divine Chariot until the morning broke." This verse calls up Akiba's warning in B. Hag. 14b not to call out "Water, water." Ben Azzai's sin, in Berditchevsky's view, is that he does not acknowledge the presence of his wife, the daughter of Rabbi Akiba, during the vision, although she has somehow witnessed his vision of Paradise; i.e., he is denying the feminine dimension, identified with the Shekhinah. For a discussion of the links between the Shekhinah and the Jungian concept of the *anima*, see pp. 40.

Page 280
"The Death of Ben Azzai"
by Rabbi Milton Steinberg

This episode, excerpted from *As a Driven Leaf,* takes the view that Ben Azzai's death, as mentioned in B. Hag. 14b, was the result of a mystical union so complete that his soul could not return to the world of the living. Rabbi Steinberg has Ben Azzai explain that he had concluded that he could not achieve complete spiritual union while alive: "Long ago I concluded that my body was a wall between us." And his description of the moment of death is clearly intended to be understood as a mystical union: "The veil is lifting. The wall is breaking through. Light flows over me and an intoxication as of wine. . . ."

Page 283
"The Fate of Ben Zoma"
by Rabbi Milton Steinberg

This passage, also excerpted from *As a Driven Leaf,* explains that the madness of Ben Zoma, who "looked and lost his reason" in the legend of the four who entered *Pardes* (B. Hag. 14b), derived from his journey into Paradise—i.e., mystical contemplation—in that he was subsequently unable to take his mind off the mystical ascent. Although Steinberg's description of Ben Zoma's obsession is original, it is virtually parallel to the talmudic legend that describes Ben Zoma's madness and death, as follows: "Once Rabbi Yehoshua was walking down a road when he saw Ben Zoma approaching. Rabbi Yehoshua greeted him, but Ben Zoma did not respond. Rabbi Yehoshua then asked: 'Whither the feet Ben Zoma?' (i.e., where are you coming from?). Ben Zoma replied: 'Between the upper waters and the lower waters there are but three finger-breadths.' Rabbi Yehoshua said to his disciples, 'Alas, Ben Zoma is gone.' And within a few days Ben Zoma had died (B. Hag. 15a)." A parallel version is found in Y. Hag. 77a–b. See the note to "Mysteries of the Chariot" by Rabbi Milton Steinberg, p. 680.

Page 284
"The Fire at Elisha's Grave"
by Rabbi Milton Steinberg

This excerpt from *As a Driven Leaf* is a retelling of the following talmudic legend (B. Hag. 15b): "When Aher (Elisha ben Abuyah) died, they said: 'Let him not be judged, nor let him enter the World to Come. Let him not be judged, because he engaged in the study of the Torah; nor let him enter the World to Come, because he sinned.' Rabbi Meir said: 'It were better that he should be judged and that he should enter the world to come. When I die I shall cause smoke to rise from his grave.' When Rabbi Meir died, smoke rose up from Aher's grave. Rabbi Yohanan said: 'What a mighty deed to burn his master! One among us went astray, yet all of us together have not the power to save him! If I were to take him by the hand, who would snatch him from me? But when I die, I shall extinguish the smoke from Aher's grave, as a sign that he has been forgiven.' When Rabbi Yohanan died, the smoke ceased from Aher's grave." For more on the sin of Aher, see the following note.

Page 286
"The Pagan Rabbi"
by Cynthia Ozick

Elisha ben Abuyah, one of the greatest talmudic sages, who became an apostate, might well be seen as the model for Isaac Kornfeld. Isaac, like Elisha, was famous for his brilliance and imagination: "His imagination was so remarkable he could concoct holiness out of the fine line of a serif." And like Elisha, Isaac read not only sacred Jewish texts, but other works as well: "No sooner did I catch his joy in Saadia Gaon than he had already sprung ahead to Yehudah Halevi. One day he was weeping with Dostoyevski and the next leaping in the air over Thomas Mann. He introduced me to Hegel and Nietzsche while our fathers wailed." In a famous episode, Greek books fell from beneath Elisha's robe: "It is told of Aher that when he used to rise from the schoolhouse, many heretical books used to fall from his lap" (B. Hag. 15b). Elisha's attraction to Greek thought in contrast to the rabbis' intense rejection of it was legendary: "Greek song did not cease from his mouth" (B. Hag. 15b). In Isaac Kornfeld's notebook, there is found "Greek writing which had the shape of verse." The paradox about Elisha is that his commentaries were so apt that they were retained in the Talmud even after the decision had been made to refer to Elisha as Aher—the Other. Likewise, Isaac Kornfeld published two books of *responsa* that were widely recognized for their brilliance, and made him famous in the world of Jewish scholars. Elisha's apostasy was, it is widely believed, in becoming a Gnostic, while Isaac Kornfeld's was in becoming a pagan, writing in his notebook: "Great Pan lives." Elisha saw the angel Metatron seated in Paradise and proclaimed: "There are two powers in heaven!" (B. Hag. 15a), and like Elisha's, Isaac's world view is distinctly dualistic: there are two kinds of souls, the free and the indwelling. Objects in nature are possessed of free souls, while humans are cursed with the indwelling kind. In contrast, the Zohar (2:141b) speaks of three aspects of the soul, *Nefesh* (life), *Ruach* (spirit), and *Neshamah* (soul), with two additional higher levels, *Hayyah* and *Yehidah*, which only the elect can obtain. In addition, the human soul has sparks of other souls in it. Like Elisha, Isaac comes to his view reluctantly, over a period of time, accepting it finally in the spirit of a searcher who will not allow himself to be deceived, no matter how unsatisfactory the conclusion he has reached is to him: "His intention was not to accumulate mystery but to dispel it." Isaac's paganism is very much that associated with Greek religion, and parallel to Elisha's attraction to Greek thought. And like Elisha, Isaac's conclusions brought him isolation and alienation, from which there was no turning back. Elisha told Rabbi Meir, "I have already heard from behind the *Pargod*: *'Return ye backsliding children'*—except Aher." After coupling with the dryad, Isaac loses his soul: "your body is now an empty packet, that is why it is so light." The tragedy of both figures is brought home in Elisha's implicit regret, and in Isaac's discovery from the nymph that "you, poor man, do not know your own soul." Both are at heart reverent, observant Jews who have somehow been led astray from their true nature. Isaac's soul takes the form of "an ugly old man . . . with a matted beard and great fierce eyebrows," who "reads as he goes." Isaac's inner conflict is thus represented in the epigram to the story from *Pirke Avot* (3:7). (Although it might appear that the whole story grew out of this epigram, the author has said that she discovered it after the story had already been written.) Isaac's soul, the old man, "reads the Law and breathes the dust and doesn't see the flowers," while Isaac's body cannot put the beauty of the flowers out of his sight. In this way the age-old conflict between body and soul is represented, as unresolved as ever, leading Isaac Kornfeld, inevitably, to his destruction. As a suicide, Isaac had to be buried outside the fence, and Aher, it was believed, was denied the World to Come until after the death of Rabbi Meir, who said: "It is better that he should be judged and that he should enter the World to Come" (B. Hag. 15b). See the previous note for a translation of this legend.

Page 310
"Outfoxing the Fox"
by Cynthia Ozick

The storyteller's retelling of the legend of the fox in the ruins of the Temple, excerpted from *The Cannibal Galaxy*, is an accurate recounting of the legend that appears in *Lamentations Rabbah* (5:18). The conclusion drawn from the legend, "to predict not from the first text, but from the second," enlarges the meaning of the original legend in much the same way that aggadic legends expand on the proof-texts to which they tie themselves. Prophecy of better times to come in a time of despair stands behind the entire tradition of messianic longing. For a further discussion of this tradition, see pp. 25–26.

Page 311
"The Homily of the Roses"
by Arthur A. Cohen

The use of homilies is pervasive in rabbinic literature. Frequently the moral of the homily is presented as a parable, such as this one by Arthur A. Cohen, excerpted from *In the Days of Simon Stern*, pp. 363–65. The dual interpretations appended to it are typical of the multiple interpretations found in the Talmud and the Midrash. The garden, because of its identification with *Gan Eden* and *Pardes*, is the subject itself of innumerable rabbinic similes. A chapter is devoted to some of these in *The Parables and Similes of the Rabbis* by Rabbi Asher Feldman, pp. 84–99. The identification of Israel with the roses is found in commentaries on several passages from the Song of Songs, such as *A rose among thorns* (S. of S. 2:2). In *Genesis Rabbah* (S. of S. 2:3) a parable very similiar to that of Cohen's is found: "A king once had an orchard in which they planted a row of fig trees and rows of vines and apples and pomegranates, and then he turned it over to a keeper and went away. After a time the king came and inspected the orchard to see how it was getting on, and he found it full of thorns and briars. So he brought wood-cutters to cut it down. Seeing in it a beautiful rose, he took and smelt it and was appeased, and said: 'For the sake of this rose the orchard shall be spared.' So the world was created only for the sake of Israel. After twenty-six generations the Holy One, blessed be He, inspected His garden to see how it was getting on, and He found it one mass of water. The generation of Enosh was wiped out with water; the generation of the dispersion was punished with water. So He brought wood-cutters to cut it down, but He saw a beautiful rose, namely Israel, and He took and smelt it, at the time when Israel received the Ten Commandments, and He was appeased. Said the Holy One, blessed be He: 'For the sake of this rose, let the garden be spared; for the sake of the Torah and those who study it, let the world be saved.' "

Page 313
"A Song of Children"
by David Meltzer

This tale is based on the legend of the formation of the child, from *Tanhuma Pekude* 3. It also appears in *The Chronicles of Jerahmeel* 9. For a translation of the appropriate text, see p. 64. The legend also serves as the framework for Itzik Manger's novel *The Book of Paradise*. For a discussion of its use in that novel, see. pp. 64–65.

BOOK IV
THEMES OF
MERKAVAH MYSTICISM

Page 317
"The Portrait"
by Rabbi Nachman of Bratslav

The king in this allegory is clearly intended to be God, and the portrait in the tale almost certainly was intended to represent the *Pargod*, the curtain that was believed to hang before the Throne of Glory, separating God from the angels. This concept derives from the Hekhaloth texts. One passage in *Masekhet Hekhaloth* (ch. 7) holds that "the seven angels that were created first" continue to exist behind the *Par-*

god. According to Gershom Scholem, there is also present in the Hekhaloth literature the belief that the *Pargod* serves as a "curtain of souls," and that all souls "are initially woven into (this) curtain *(Pargod)* that hangs before the Throne of Glory." Furthermore, "the entire past history and future destiny of each single soul is recorded in this curtain." See Scholem, *Kabbalah,* p. 18 and p. 159. In *Sefer Hekhaloth* (*3 Enoch* 5:187–188) the *Pargod* is described as follows: "Rabbi Ishmael said: 'Metatron said to me: "Come and I shall show you the *Pargod* which is spread out before the Holy One, on which are engraved all the generations of the world and their deeds, whether they did them or will do them until the end of all generations. . . . And I saw them all with my own eyes." ' "

Page 319
"The Wandering of a Soul"
by Mendele Mokher-Seforim

Although the primary objective of Mendele in writing this story was to satirize hasidic visionary literature, the example of the vision he presents is actually quite representative of such visions, which originate in the Hekhaloth texts as descriptions of heavenly journeys. Take, for example, the vision of the heavenly palace as Mendele describes it: "And I looked up and saw a palace before me five hundred leagues high, all of marble and fine gold. And the palace had five hundred enormous gates, and each enormous gate five hundred tiny gates. Between them stood the Angels of Wisdom, the Angels of Intelligence, the Angels of the Talmud, the Guardian Angels of Hasidism, the Guardian Angels of Enthusiasm, the Guardian Angels of Religious Ecstasy. And I saw something like two fearfully long flashes of lightning crackle out of the palace, and a shape of a hand clutched a heap of black fire and made crowns for the letters in the Torah." Compare Mendele's satire with an actual Hekhaloth text, such as the following chapter from *The Hebrew Book of Enoch* (*3 Enoch* 7): "When the Holy One, blessed be He, took me away from the generation of the Flood, He lifted me on the winds of the Shekhinah into the highest heaven and brought me into the great palaces of the highest heaven, Araboth, where is the glorious Throne of the Shekhinah, the Merkavah, the troops of anger, the armies of vehemence, the fiery Accusers, the flaming servants, the servants of burning coal and firebrands, the servants of sparks and lightning." Mendele apparently believed that these visionary texts were satirical enough as it was not to need changing in any substantial way, although he did permit an ironic tone unlike the original to enter the dialogue. As in the hasidic visions of ascent, there is a purpose accomplished by the ascent—it is not described for its own sake, as in the Hekhaloth texts. Here a cure is effected for the barren wife of him who makes the ascent. As in the writing of Joseph Perl, Mendele more preserves the spirit of the original than he satirizes it, at least from our present perspective. Proof that Mendele based his passage on the ascent into Paradise on authentic texts can be determined by the inclusion of an ice angel: "I could feel a frost run over my whole body, my teeth were chattering with cold, and, getting to my feet, I saw a cold angel before me, a hunk of ice!" This is a clear reference to the ice angel in *The Slavonic Book of Enoch* (*2 Enoch* 37:1): "And the Lord called up one of the older angels, terrible and menacing, and placed him by me, in appearance of a great frost, and he froze my face, because I could not endure the terror of the Lord." This treatment of traditional texts may well have served as the model for Itzik Manger's *The Book of Paradise*, which satirizes a variety of midrashim. See "Adam and Eve Return to the Garden" and "The Star and the Angel of Death" by Itzik Manger, and also the discussion of *The Book of Paradise*, pp. 64–65. See also "My Grandfather" by Arnold Kiss, p. 327 and "From the Beyond" by Sholem Asch, p. 246.

Page 326
"Mysteries of the Chariot"
by Rabbi Milton Steinberg

This episode is excerpted from *As a Driven Leaf.* In it Ben Zoma, one of the four sages who entered Paradise (B. Hag. 14b), performs a kind of mystical meditation known as *Maaseh Bereshith*, or Work of the Creation, which probes the meaning of the passages about the creation in Genesis (1:1–2:3). He then shifts to a second kind of mystical meditation, *Maaseh Merkavah* or Work of the Chariot, referring to Ezekiel's vision of the Divine Chariot. Meditation and teachings concerning the Work of the Chariot are found in the Talmud, such as in Y. Hag. 77a, where Rabbi Yohanan ben Zakkai discusses *Maaseh Merkavah* with Rabbi Elazar ben Akakn and suddenly "fire descended from heaven and enveloped them, and ministering angels danced before them like people attending a wedding who rejoice before the bridegroom." Further discussion of *Maaseh Merkavah* is also found in Y. Hag. 77a and 77c. Steinberg has Ben Zoma meditate on the meaning of the description of the wheels of the Merkavah (Ezek. 1:15–17). Ben Zoma tries to visualize this image, but fails because "it is too complex to be conceived"—a comment that has general relevance to much Hekhaloth and kabbalistic literature. He succeeds, however, in visualizing the description of *a firmament like the color of a terrible ice* (Ezek. 2:22) and has a vision of the Holy One sitting on His Throne of Glory (Ezek. 2:26). Here Ben Zoma has a mystical experience, "leaving him only the dizzy intertwining of myriad threads that lost themselves in convolutions about one another." This echoes a famous talmudic legend (Y. Hag. 77a–b) in which Ben Zoma states: "I was contemplating the Work of Creation, and found that there was between the upper waters and the lower waters not more than a hand's breadth." A parallel version of this legend is found in B. Hag. 15a. See the note to "The Fate of Ben Zoma" by Milton Steinberg, p. 675. These two mysteries on which Ben Zoma meditates are the foundation stones of all of Jewish mysticism, beginning with the Hekhaloth texts of Merkavah Mysticism, and the further evolution of the kabbalistic period. The kind of meditation performed by Ben Zoma is typical of Merkavah mystics, who sought to ascend to Paradise in the Divine Chariot. Gershom Scholem describes other aspects of this meditation for purposes of ascent, such as the singing of hymns and use of special positions, in *Jewish Gnosticism, Merkabah Mysticism, and Talmudic Tradition*, ch. 4 and elsewhere.

Page 327
"My Grandfather"
by Arnold Kiss

The grandfather's vision of Paradise, filled with his ancestors and all the great sages, is representative in every respect of the thorough vision of Paradise that can be reconstructed from the Hekhaloth and kabbalistic texts. See, for example, *The Chronicles of Jerahmeel (Sefer ha-Zikhronot)* 18–24. It also resembles a number of talmudic descriptions of *Gan Eden*, the earthly Paradise. It is important to observe that in the Bible the concept of Paradise is expressed by the Garden of Eden, and that this remains true for the Talmud as well. But beginning with the Hekhaloth texts, which interpret Ezekiel's vision to refer to a Celestial Paradise, there is a progressive mapping out of the nature of the world above, which was said to consist of seven heavens.

Page 333
"Heaven's Wagon Driver"
by Péter Ujvári

This tale begins by presenting a vision of Rabbi Meir of Promishlan which is clearly intended to echo, in a satirical way, Ezekiel's vision of the Divine Chariot. In Ezekiel's vision the Merkavah travels in *a great cloud, with a fire flashing up, so that a brightness was round about it* (Ezek. 1:4), while the wagon driver in Ujvári's story is "allowed to trot his horses in Heaven as if he were on the road." There follows the story of the good deed of the otherwise evil wagon driver which results in his becoming heaven's wagon driver. This follows a tradition of stories in which a single good deed is enough to reverse the judgment in heaven. Ujvári uses the term "Merkavah" in the story itself to describe the ascent of the soul of the *tzaddik* of Belz after his death. In this context the use of "Merkavah" is not only intended to echo the chariot of Ezekiel's vision, but also the vision of the Throne of Glory which is somehow a part of the Merkavah later in the same vision: *And above the firmament that was over their heads was the likeness of a throne, as the appearance of a sapphire stone; and upon the likeness of the throne was a likeness as the appearance of a man upon it above* (Ezek. 2:26). This story is based on a hasidic tale told among the Lubavitch Hasidim. One version told by Rabbi Shlomo Weinberg goes as follows: "We only reach in the World to Come to the place we strive for in this world. There was once a wagon driver who was good at what he did. When he died he went to heaven. But what was heaven for him? A smooth, straight, endless road over which he rode with his carriage and horses at great speed." This is seen as being sad and ironic, just like Bontshe Schweig, in the story by I. L. Peretz, who, when given the opportunity to have any wish granted by heaven, asked for a hot roll every day.

Page 335
"The Celestial Orchestra"
by Howard Schwartz

The chariot which sweeps down from heaven in Rabbi Nachman's vision in this story is the Merkavah, the Divine Chariot of Ezekiel's vision. In the terms of the Merkavah mystics, the ascent into heaven is known as the "Descent of the Merkavah." Perhaps the enigmatic meaning of this term is simply meant to describe the descent of the chariot which must precede the ascent, as in this story. The talmudic legend of the existence of the heavenly Jerusalem (B. Bab. Bat. 75b) is echoed in the kabbalistic doctrine "as above, so below.": This means that just as there is an Earthly Paradise, *Gan Eden*, so too is there a Celestial Paradise, in which everything that exists below is mirrored above. See also *2 Baruch* 4:2-7. The danger facing Rabbi Nachman in the celestial heights is the same as in the talmudic legend of the four who entered Paradise (B. Hag. 14b). The notion of a celestial music is common to the rabbinic vision of Paradise. Isaiah has a vision of a choir of seraphim (Is. 6:3). In the Talmud (B. Hag. 14a) it is stated: "Every day ministering angels are created from the fiery stream, and utter song, and cease to be." A celestial choir is described in *The Book of Enoch* (61:11): "And He will summon all the host of the heavens, and all the holy ones above, and the host of God, the Cherubim, Seraphim and Ophanim, and all the angels of power . . . on that day shall raise one voice, and bless and glorify and exalt in the spirit of faith." In the Hekhaloth texts, the angels are frequently described as singing hymns, whose lyrics are given. (Some of these can be found in *The Penguin Book of Hebrew Verse*, edited by T. Carmi, pp. 195–200.) The singing of hymns by angels and other Holy Living Creatures is described in *Hekhaloth Rabbati* 8a: "Accordingly do they strengthen themselves and make themselves splendid and purify themselves in fire seventy times and do all of them stand in cleanliness and holiness and sing songs and hymns, praise and rejoicing and applause, with one voice, with one utterance, with one mind, and with one melody." See also Zohar 2:123a: "Everything that the Holy One has created sings songs and praises before Him, both on high and here below." A similar song sung in unison is described in the legends about the song at the Sea. See *The Song at the Sea* by Judah Goldim, a partial translation of *Mekilta de Rabbi Ishmael*. In *Sichos ha-Ran* 96 Rabbi Nachman of Bratslav attributes the music of the celestial choir to a single angel: "There is an angel with a thousand heads. Each head has a thousand tongues. Each tongue has a thousand melodies. Imagine the indescribable beauty of this angel's song."

Page 339
"The Tale of the Amulet"
by Howard Schwartz

Hekhaloth texts describe four methods of ascent into the Celestial Paradise. These are via the Merkavah; pronouncing the Tetragrammaton, God's secret Name; ascending Jacob's Ladder; and with the assistance of magical amulets and invocations. The Zohar (3:79b) also identifies a sign that makes passage through the celestial realms possible: "He who is united with Him in worship has on him a sign inscribed from above to make it known. . . . that he can pass through all the supernal gates without hindrance." This story describes ascent with the aid of an amulet. The eating of the text of the amulet is, as observed in the tale, from Ezekiel (3:1–3). The *Sefer Raziel* that is spoken of is a book that has been commonly found in Jewish libraries since the Middle Ages, but though it took the title of the legendary Book of Raziel that the angel Raziel gave to Adam, it was, of course, a separate text. As in all of the Hekhaloth and kabbalistic texts concerned with heavenly journeys, the ascent is a metaphor for the spiritual ascent, although it is presented in an essentially literal manner. In a letter written to his brother-in-law, Rabbi Gershom, the Baal Shem Tov described such a heavenly ascent: "On Rosh Hashanah 5507 (1747) I made an adjuration of heavenly ascent. . . . This time I saw such visions that I had never previously seen. . . . I rose from rung to rung until I entered into the palace of the Messiah, where the Messiah teaches Torah with all of the authors of the Mishnah, the saints and the seven shepherds." This letter is reprinted in *Sefer ha-Hasidut*, edited by A. Kahana, pp. 73–74.

Page 344
"The Apocalyptic Chariot Race"
by Aaron Sussaman

The fierce chariot race that is at the crux of this tale is clearly intended to echo the Merkavah of Ezekiel's vision. It personifies the conflict between God and Satan, with Hitler as the personification of the Evil One. God's chariot has only one wheel in this tale, perhaps to symbolize His Unity, while in Ezekiel the chariot has four wheels. Underlying the whole is the question of the existence of evil, a question much more difficult to address since the Holocaust.

BOOK V
KABBALISTIC THEMES

Page 349
"The Lost Princess"
by Rabbi Nachman of Bratslav

This tale of Rabbi Nachman's is an allegory about the Exile of the Shekhinah and the effort that is required in order to end her exile, which, according to the kabbalistic tradition, will take place only when the Messianic era begins. It is possible to identify the minister who seeks the lost princess with the Messiah, in which case the role of the Messiah in ending the Exile of the Shekhinah would be active. In fact, in this reading the struggle to bring the Shekhinah out of exile becomes the central quest of the Messiah. For the evolution of the myth of the Shekhinah from the talmudic to the kabbalistic periods, see pp. 20–23. For further discussion of the sources and meaning of "The Lost Princess," see pp. 37–38 and 87–88.

Page 353
"A Letter"
by Rabbi Nachman of Bratslav

This rich parable may be understood in several ways. It can be read as an allegory of the relationship between God and a *tzaddik*, symbolized by the king and his son, in which the *tzaddik* recognizes the presence of God through His creations. It can also be read as an allegory of the Giving of the Torah, in which the Torah is symbolized by the letter that the king writes to his son. The letter from the king may also be seen as a symbol for creation itself—i.e., the handwriting of God that can be read in His creations. Because the prince is able to recognize his father's handwriting, a bond is created between them. This is the situation of the believer. For a parable by Nachman depicting the agnostic, see his "The Royal Messenger." For further discussion of this tale see p. 91.

Page 354
"The King Who Loved Music"
by Rabbi Levi Yitzhak of Berditchev

This is an allegory in which the king represents God and the musicians represent observant Jews who pray before God every morning. The inability of the sons to take the place of their fathers points up the failure of the Jews of the present to take the place of their fathers in God's eyes. Using the playing of music to symbolize prayer points up Levi Yitzhak's positive view of the interaction between man and God. The mechanical playing of the sons of the musicians is the kind of rote ritual that the Hasidim accused the Mitnagdim of—approaching the *mitzvot* without *kavanah*. The musicians who decide to correct the situation, who often arrive late, symbolize the Hasidim, with their less fixed approach. The fact that their efforts were good in the king's eyes, "even though they did not play with the same talent as their fathers," presents Levi Yitzhak's view that the ways of the Hasidim were accepted in the eyes of the Lord. Parables about music are not uncommon in Hasidic literature. The Baal Shem retold the famous parable of the deaf man watching people dance to music, who cannot understand the reasons for their movement. See S. Y. Agnon's story "The Orchestra" in *Twenty-one Stories*, in which God is represented as being the conductor of an orchestra, and the players all of the people Agnon has known in his life. This story develops along the lines of Levi Yitzhak's allegory, and may well have been inspired by it.

Page 355
"An Imperial Message"
by Franz Kafka

This famous parable has been subjected to a wide variety of interpretations. In terms of religious allegory, the Emperor may be seen as God, and the humble subject, man. In this case the messenger can be identified as the Jewish Messiah, whom Jews firmly believe is going to come, but who has not yet arrived. This puts this parable in the category of allegories about God, such as the following story, "Illusion," and other tales in this section, such as "The Castle in the Kingdom" and "The Tale of the Palace." "An Imperial Message" may also be read as an allegory of the process any dreamer goes through in receiving messages from his unconscious mind. The Emperor gives the message to the faithful messenger before his death, but because of the delay between the sending and the receiving, the messenger is delivering "a message from a dead man." The dead king, then, may be viewed as a symbol of the past, which preserves itself in memory and the unconscious mind, and sends messages into the future through dreams, works of art, etc. The fact that the messenger never appears with the message, although the man who dreams it to himself is certain he is on the way, signifies the fact that we can never fully comprehend the meaning of such unconscious messages; i.e., we can never pin down their symbolism to a precise interpretation. For further discussion of this parable, see pp. 43–44.

Page 356
"Illusion"
by M. J. Berditchevsky
Like the previous parable by Kafka, "Illusion" is an allegory about God and man.
Here the king, i.e. God, creates a great palace around himself, i.e. all of his creation,
which is in essence only an illusion, although very few are able to recognize this. This
is an allegorical expression of the kabbalistic concept of *Alma d'Shikra*—World of Illusion, or World of Lies. This concept differs from the Hindu concept of *maya*,
which is commonly translated as illusion, only in that it emphasizes this world as a
delusion, which must be recognized in order to be freed from it, while *maya* emphasizes a more neutral concept of illusion, in which this world is simply not what it appears to be. The Hebrew title of this story is *"Ahizat Enayim"* (literally, "seizing the
eyes"), an archaic term that can be translated as either illusion or delusion. This tale is
a reworking of a well-known allegorical teaching of the Baal Shem found in *Kether
Shem Tov (The Crown of the Good Name)*, a collection of the Baal Shem's sayings, compiled by Aaron ben Tzur HaCohen from the works of Rabbi Jacob Joseph Cohen.
For a translation of the original text and a further discussion of this story, see pp.
69–70. The Hindu teaching story that defines the meaning of *maya* can be found in
Zimmer's *Myths and Symbols of Indian Art and Civilization*, pp. 31–33. See the following note for "Three Vows" by S. Y. Agnon. "The Tale of the Palace" by Tsvi
Blanchard is also based on this same parable of the Baal Shem; see it and the appropriate note. This tale of an illusory palace has an interesting parallel among the tales of
the Maharal, Rabbi Judah Loew, in the 16th century in Prague. This is one of the
tales included in Yudl Rosenberg's *Niflaot Maharal* (see note p. 704). A translation of
another version of this tale can be found in *The Great Rabbi Loew*, pp. 140–46. This
same tale is also found in *Shivhei ha-Besht*, where the illusion of the palace is credited
to Rabbi Adam, who was said to have transmitted the Book of Mysteries (also
known as the Book of Rabbi Adam) to the Baal Shem Tov. (See "The Book of Mysteries" by Meyer Levin and the appropriate note.) Because of the questions concerning the authenticity of Yudl Rosenberg's collection of Maharal legends, it is difficult
to assess which version of this legend is the earliest, that concerning the Maharal or
that about Rabbi Adam. It is likely, however, given the hasidic practice of retelling
legends and substituting their own rabbis, that it was part of the earlier legend cycle
of the Maharal.

Page 358
"Three Vows"
by S. Y. Agnon
The scribe's interpretation in the second paragraph of this story is based on B. Ket.
111a. The same verse beginning "I have made you swear" appears in the Song of
Songs three times, hence the three vows. This story, like Berditchevsky's "Illusion,"
illustrates the kabbalistic concept of *Alma d'Shikra*, World of Illusion. This is the
world that the old man, who is the reluctant leader of his generation (in the model of
one of the *Lamed-vov*—see pp. 664–666), pulls the king into, in which time is com-
pressed and a few minutes appears to be many years. At the same time, the fact that
the king returns circumcised emphasizes that all that occurred did in fact occur, although in a different time dimension. Agnon attributes this tale to the Baal Shem
Tov, as does Berditchevsky with "Illusion." In fact, it is a retelling of a famous

folktale whose best-known version is the Hindu, and can be found in *Myths and Symbols in Indian Art and Civilization*, ed. Joseph Campbell, pp. 31–33. This folktale defines the meaning of *maya* or illusion, a concept very close to that of *Alma d'Shikra* as well as *ahizat enayim*. (See pp. 69–70.) For further discussion of *Alma d'Shikra*, see the note to the preceding story, "Illusion" by J. Berditchevsky. Another variant of this tale can be found in *Tales of the Dervishes*, ed. by Idries Shah, pp. 35–38.

Page 363
"The Tale of Rabbi Gadiel the Infant"
by S. Y. Agnon

There is a legend in *Shulhan Aruch* of Rabbi Isaac Luria (in contrast to the *Shulhan Aruch* of Joseph Caro), a translation of which can be found in *Mimekor Yisrael* 2:828, about a Rabbi Gadiel who dwells in the Garden of Eden, in the palace of the Secret and Concealed Illumination, which is near the palace of the Messiah, known as the Bird's Nest. He is the head of a Torah Academy. It is he who reveals the hidden meanings of the Torah, for he serves as the vessel through which they are transmitted. His pure soul had been set free when he was seven years old, and when God saw the illumination of his soul, He swore to reveal through him secrets and mysteries of the Torah. It is this pure soul that is incarnated in Agnon's story, which perpetuates the notion that this soul was too pure for this world, and was confronted with insurmountable obstacles when he wore the human raiment. Unique births, such as Rabbi Gadiel's, are a standard feature of both mythology and folklore, including that of the Jews. When only twenty days old, Abraham was already fully developed, both in mind and spirit, and had already intuited the existence of God (*Beit ha-Midrash*, Jellinek, 2:18). Similar miracles are attributed to Noah and Moses, and also appear in Christian legends. There are numerous examples of births in which the child has been born circumcised. In the *Maaseh Book* (2:168) there is a brief tale of Rabbi Amitai, who was born with the word *emeth* ("truth") imprinted on his forehead. This word was also said to be inscribed on the forehead of the Golem, as part of the process of bringing it to life. Itzik Manger uses the theme of the child born with its knowledge intact as the premise of his satire *The Book of Paradise* (see pp. 64–65). There are also obvious parallels to the biblical story of Jonah and the whale (Jon. 2:1–11).

Page 366
"The Castle in the Kingdom"
by Francis Landy

This is another allegory in which the king may be seen to represent God, and his kingdom, in which "the chamber was a hemisphere . . . engraved with stars and constellations," the universe. In such a reading the true Covenant between God and the Jewish people is even more profound than that acknowledged among the people as a whole, existing between God and every individual, each of whom believes he has been singled out to be favored. If the king is taken to represent a human ruler, then the story concerns the issue of the rebellion of the Jews against the rulers of nations, which is one of the primary themes of S. Y. Agnon's "Three Vows" (see this tale and the appropriate note). The commentary incorporated in the parable follows the form of Jewish textural exegesis, such as that found in the *Midrash Rabbah* and *Pirke de*

Rabbi Eliezer. The four kinds of interpretations may be viewed as an analysis of the tale from each of the four levels of *Pardes.* For a discussion of these levels, see pp. 83–87.

Page 368
"The Tale of the Palace"
by Rabbi Tsvi Blanchard

The use of allegories about a king who builds a palace, representing God and His creation, the world, is often found in kabbalistic texts, as in the following example from the Zohar (1:3b): "The Holy and Mysterious One graved in a hidden recess one point. In that He enclosed the whole of Creation as one who locks up all his treasures in a palace, under one key, which is therefore as valuable as all that is stored up in that palace; for it is the key which opens and shuts. In that palace there are hidden treasures, one greater than the other. The palace is provided with fifty mystic gates. . . . All these gates have one lock, and there is one tiny spot for the insertion of the key, which is only marked by the impress of the key." See the note to "Illusion" by M. J. Berditchevsky, p. 685.

Page 369
"Kabbalists"
by I. L. Peretz

With the example given in B. Hag. 14b about the four sages who entered *Pardes* (see pp. 83–87), the mystical contemplations that are the essence of the kabbalistic approach were regarded as dangerously obsessive. Examples of the potential dangers are also demonstrated in the tale of the son of Reb Adam, retold here as "The Book of Mysteries" by Meyer Levin. A famous example also appears in S. Ansky's play *The Dybbuk,* about a yeshivah student whose longing for a young girl, combined with his kabbalistic studies, produces madness and death. This story by Peretz is in that tradition. Peretz seems to imply that their difficulties of poverty and hunger play an important role in driving them to the other world that Kabbalah offers, and also drives the rebbe's student to a mystical vision of a celestial music and to the discovery that "they require a new singer in the celestial choir," at which time the student expires. For more on the tradition of celestial music, see p. 681. The parallels to the legend of the four who entered *Pardes* are quite clear in this conclusion, which presents the reward (the mystical vision) and the danger (death) of this kind of mystical contemplation. The specific parallel seems to be to the death of Ben Azzai in B. Hag. 14b, who "looked and died." See the stories pp. 274–310 and the appropriate notes. Compare as well the stories and texts in Book IV, "Themes of Merkavah Mysticism."

Page 373
"The Hermit and the Bear"
by I. L. Peretz

Kabbalistic teachings take as their basic assumption the power of the word. (See Rabbi Nachman's "A Letter.") This is emphasized, for example, in the midrash of the alphabet from the Zohar (2b–3b; see pp. 72–73 for a partial translation of this text). The most powerful word is the ineffable Name of God, known as the Tetra-

grammaton. To a considerable extent kabbalistic knowledge was equated with para-
normal powers, which were sometimes practiced as a kind of magic. "The Hermit
and the Bear" demonstrates the extent and danger of these powers as practiced by the
hermit, who is a master of kabbalistic mysteries. For a further discussion of this tale
see pp. 88–89.

Page 376
"The Amulet"
by M. Z. Feierberg

Kabbalistic invocations, prayers, and spells were often inscribed inside of amulets
made up for magical purposes—especially to protect from demonic dangers or to accomplish some enchanted purpose, such as ascending into Paradise or bringing a man
of clay to life, as in the case of the Golem. (See the tales concerning Lilith and the
Golem in Book VI, "Themes of Folklore.") In "The Amulet" the boy Hofni has a
recurrent dream of his great-grandfather as a holy man and martyr. When the dreams
become an obsession, and other remedies fail, Hofni is brought to Shemaiah the Kabbalist. The Kabbalist first checks for the possible causes of the boy's melancholy—
whether he studies properly, says the *Shema*, and has *tsitsis* of his *tallis* in order, and
the condition of the *mezzuzah* in the house. As a remedy the Kabbalist offers the boy
an amulet, which he ties around his neck. This, then, is his protection against the
forces of Evil that are everywhere, in the vision of the Kabbalist, and Hofni finds the
solution eminently satisfactory. Such was the power attributed to amulets, especially
in the late Middle Ages. For the translation of the text of an amulet to ward off the
demon Lilith, see p. 96. The most extensive book in English on the subject of such
amulets is *Hebrew Amulets: Their Decipherment and Interpretation*, by T. Schrire. See
also Joshua Tractenberg's *Jewish Magic and Superstition*.

Page 382
"The Rebbe's Whip"
by S. Ansky

This tale is excerpted from the first act of S. Ansky's drama *The Dybbuk*. It portrays
the kabbalistic concept of the *Nahash Hakadmoni*, the primal or primeval serpent.
Perhaps the earliest link between Satan and the serpent in the Garden of Eden is
found in *The Greek Apocalypse of Baruch* (*3 Baruch* 9:7): "At the transgression of the
first Adam . . . Samael took the serpent as a garment." In *Pirke de Rabbi Eliezer* 21
the assertion is made that "Samael riding on the serpent came to Eve, and she conceived Cain; afterwards Adam came to her, and she conceived Abel." This explanation for the power of the *Yetzer Hara*, or Evil Impulse, of Cain, is expanded into a
cosmic principle in the Zohar, where the *Nahash Hakadmoni* comes to represent the
active principle of evil in existence. In this passage from the Zohar (1:49b) the serpent
is equated with the Evil Inclination: "*And the serpent was more subtle* (Gen. 3:1). After
the man had addressed all these words to the woman, the Evil Inclination awoke,
prompting him to seek to unite with her in carnal desire, and to entice her to things
in which the Evil Inclination takes delight." In other passages from the Zohar, such as
this from 1:63b, the serpent has already been abstracted into a principle of evil: "(In
the generation of the deluge) the scum of the serpent had not yet been removed from
the world, and Noah's generation did not believe in the Holy One, blessed be He,

and all of them clung to the 'lower leaves of the tree and were clothed with an unclean spirit.' " In the Ansky tale, Reb Shmelke of Nikolsburg is so righteous he is able
to utilize the primal snake as a whip, without the risk of its powers being loosened on
him. This fits in appropriately with the kabbalistic tradition, which did not seek to
destroy evil, but to overcome its power, and, if possible, master it, as Reb Shmelke
does in this case.

Page 383
"The Death of the Little God"
by David Shahar

This story utilizes the kabbalistic concept of *zimzum* in a very original manner, linking it to the sense of the haunted character who believes that "The world is growing
bigger" and "God is growing smaller." *Zimzum* is an esoteric concept that refers to
the contraction of God at the time of the creation of the world in order to make a
space in which creation could exist. This doctrine is found in *Sefer ha-Iyyun*: "How
did God produce and create this world? Like a man who gathers in and contracts his
breath, so that the smaller might contain the larger, so He contracted His light into a
hand's breadth, according to His own measure, and the world was left in darkness,
and in that darkness He cut boulders and hewed rocks." (See Gershom Scholem,
Kabbalah, pp. 129–35.) For further discussion of this story, see pp. 70–71.

Page 390
"The Disappearance"
by Edmond Jabès

This excerpt from *Elya* refers to the kabbalistic concept of *zimzum* as a cosmological
explanation for the origin of existence. Jabès symbolizes the contraction of God with
a circle that turns into a point: " 'This circle,' he said, 'which the blotter has made
into a point invaded by night, is God.' " His reference to a time when all existence
was "one insignificant point in space" (which is parallel to Hubbel's theory that at
one time all of the universe was contracted in a single point) is to the kabbalistic concept of *Ein Sof*, the highest, unknowable aspect of the concept of Divinity. In this
way Jabès demonstrates the link between these two highly abstract concepts: after
having contracted to a single point, the *Ein Sof*, God then began the process of emanation spoken of in conjunction with the *Sefirot*.

Page 391
"Mirror and Scarf"
by Edmond Jabès

This parable from *The Book of Questions* is a meditation on the subject of *Maaseh
Bereshith*, or the Work of Creation, one of the two primary subjects of Kabbalah,
along with *Maaseh Merkavah*, or the Work of the Chariot. It is cast in the form of a
rabbinic dialogue, such as that found in the Talmud, *Midrash Rabbah*, or the Zohar.
However, the rabbis are apocryphal, invented by Jabès. The mirror that divides God
from man and man from God is reminiscent of the firmament between the upper
waters and lower waters of Gen. 1:7, as well as of the curtain hanging before the
Throne of Glory, known as the *Pargod* (see p. 40). Among the interpretations that

are offered is that of Reb Alsem: "We live out the dream of creation, which is God's dream." This echoes the kabbalistic concept of *Alma d'Shikra*, the World of Illusion. See "Illusion" by M. J. Berditchevsky, and the appropriate note.

Page 392
"The Angel of the Alphabet"
by David Meltzer

In the kabbalistic cosmology, the letters of the alphabet are like the stars and planets of the heavens, according to the primary kabbalistic principle of "as above, so below." In this parable the letters of the alphabet emerge onto the page almost independently of the author, who regards them almost as an observer. This reflects the attitude of creation as divinely inspired, and the role of the artist as that of a vessel through which the divine spirit may pass. The writing of the Finger of God on the tablets of Moses, described as "black fire on white fire" in the Zohar (3:84a), is refracted in the image of the two angels, one black, one white, who accompany the words. This, in turn, echoes the talmudic legend (B. Sot. 11:9b) about the two angels who accompany a man home on the Sabbath: "Two ministering angels accompany a man on the eve of the Sabbath from the synagogue to his home; one a good angel and one an evil one. And when he arrives home and finds the candle burning, the table laid, and his bed made up, the good angel exclaims, 'May it be the will of God that it be even thus on another Sabbath,' and the evil angel unwillingly responds, 'Amen.' But if not, the evil angel exclaims, 'May it be the will of God that it be thus on another Sabbath,' and the good angel unwillingly responds, 'Amen.' " While the angel of the alphabet is not identified, the angel most closely associated with the alphabet is Raziel, who delivered the divine book to Adam in which he foresaw the future (Zohar 1:37b and 1:55b).

Page 394
"Midrash of the Alphabet"
by Rabbi Yehiel Poupko

This parable retells the legend of the alphabet from the Zohar (1:2b–3b) from a post-Holocaust perspective in which the forces of evil are dominant. An earlier version of this legend is found in the Jerusalem Talmud (Y. Ber.). For further discussion and a partial translation of its text, see pp. 72–73. The role of the letters of the alphabet in the creation is remarked on in the Talmud (B. Ber. 55a): "Bezalel knew how to arrange the letters with which heaven and earth were created." Another interesting parallel legend is also found in the Zohar (1:55b): "All the letters of the alphabet but the last two were reversed as a result of the Fall. And these letters remained reversed until Israel stood before Mount Sinai, when they regained their proper order."

Page 396
"The Mind of Genesis"
by David Slabotsky

In this tale Rabbi Yehuda meditates on a single letter of the Hebrew alphabet, Aleph, and through it comes to an understanding of cosmic mysteries, although he perceives them through "the mind of Genesis," meaning prior to the Creation which begins with the second letter, Bet. Such meditation, a form of *Maaseh Bereshith*, which often produces dramatic results such as those described here, is commonly reported in the Hekhaloth and kabbalistic literatures.

Page 397
"Aleph/Bet"
by Jorge Plescoff

One of the primary tenets of the Kabbalah is that the letters of the Hebrew alphabet were the vessels through which God created the world. Great truths, then, are contained by these letters, and especially by the first two, Aleph and Bet—Aleph because it is the first letter, and Bet because it is the first letter of the first word of the Bible, *Bereshith*, "In the beginning." One kabbalistic technique was to meditate on individual letters, especially Bet. How, for example, the letter Bet served as a vessel for the creation is described in this passage from the Zohar (1:7b): "The letter Bet indicates two things joined together, namely two points, one shrouded in mystery and one capable of being revealed; and as they are inseparable they therefore are both joined in the single term *reshith* (beginning), i.e. they are one and not two, and he who takes away the one takes away the other as well." Here the explicit dualism of the Gnostics is transformed into a kind of polar monotheism, such as that found in the Zohar concerning God's merciful Right Hand and Left Hand of Justice.

Page 399
"The Alphabet Came to Me"
by Jerome Rothenberg

This brief tale, which the author describes as a dream, clearly echoes the famous parable of the letters of the alphabet found in the Zohar (1:2b–3b). For a translation of a portion of this text, see p. 72. The reference to the Work of Creation is to mystical meditation on the mysteries of creation, known as *Maaseh Bereshith*, which along with *Maaseh Merkavah* or the Work of the Chariot (referring to the Divine Chariot in the vision of Ezekiel) constitute the two primary biblical sources on which the texts of the Kabbalah are based.

Page 400
"Staraya Ushitza's Rabbi"
by Isaac Goldemberg

The model for a sage retreating to a cave for meditation is found in the Talmud (B. Shab. 33b), and the sage is Simeon bar Yohai, who was said to have sat for thirteen years in a cave with his son, Rabbi Eleazar, buried up to their necks in sand, immersed in mystical contemplation. The Zohar purports to be the book Simeon bar Yohai wrote during the thirteen years he was in that cave. Instead, it was almost certainly composed in the 13th century by Moshe de Leon. Kabbalistic exercises normally required some physical dimension. There were various means of purification, including the use of fasting, ritual immersion, prescribed positions, the chanting of hymns, etc. The madness that overtakes Staraya Ushitza's rabbi is the most prominent danger facing the kabbalists, among whom it was common to look upon the celestial mysteries and lose their mind as did Ben Zoma. The passage in B. Hag. 14b about the four sages who entered *Pardes* best represents this danger. (For further discussion of this legend see pp. 83–87.)

Page 400
"The Number of the Name"
by Mario Satz

The premise of this story is that the number tattooed on the arm of a former inmate of a concentration camp is, when calculated by *gematria*, the Tetragrammaton, the four-letter Name of God, YHVH or Yahweh. (For a discussion of *gematria*,, see p. 79. Reference to the Tetragrammaton can be found in *The Book of Enoch* 61:3, *The Prayer of Manessah*, and *Ecclesiastes Rabbah* 3.) It was believed that the true pronunciation of this ultimate Name has been lost, and that those who knew it possessed the power of God, including the power to create and destroy. This is the Name invoked by kabbalists chiefly for purposes of the mystical ascent, but for other magical purposes as well. Rabbi Judah Loew is said to have created the Golem, a man made out of clay, by uttering, at the culmination of the invocation to bring the man of clay to life, the Tetragrammaton. Variations of this legend claim that he did not know how to pronounce the Name—so long had its true pronunciation been lost—but merely that Rabbi Loew wrote the Name on a slip of paper and inserted it into the mouth of the Golem. The power of the Name is demonstrated in a tale in which Rabbi Semel the pious uses it to summon a lion (*Maaseh Book* 2:161).

Page 403
"The Generation of the Flood"
by Mark Mirsky

This tale has been excerpted from *The Secret Table*. It expands on the passage from the Zohar (1:19b) which serves as its epigraph. The evil of the generation of the Deluge is an explicit theme of the biblical narrative: *And the Lord saw that the wickedness of man was great in the earth, and that every imagination of the thoughts of his heart was only evil* (Gen. 6:5). This theme is repeated in the subsequent literature, with the evil acts vividly portrayed. In the Talmud (B. Sanh. 107b–108a) there is a discussion of the fate of this evil generation. In *Genesis Rabbah* (27:3) this generation is said to have marked the spots most favorable for breaking in during the daylight, then returning at night to complete the theft. So wicked were they, according to *Pesikta Rabbati* 5, that "the Shekhinah departed to the fourth heaven." In the Zohar the evil generation becomes an expression of the very principle of evil, what is referred to as the "evil side." Here (Zohar 61a) the Removal of the Shekhinah, as it is referred to, made the world vulnerable to an evil spirit: "They thrust the Shekhinah out of the world, and the earth is left in a corrupt state. With the Shekhinah thrust out, another spirit comes and hovers over the world, bringing with it corruption." The passage from the Zohar quoted at the end of the story is from 1:66a.

Page 407
"The Coming of the Messiah"
by Franz Kafka

There are two conditions, according to a variety of legends, under which the Messiah might usher in the End of Days. One proposes that the Messiah will come only after great upheaval and destruction in a war known as the War of Gog and Magog, and the other that the Messiah will come only when all Jews are righteous. The notion of the war of Gog and Magog is found as early as the Jerusalem Targum to Numb. 11:26: "In the End of Days, Gog and Magog and their armies will fall into the hands of King Messiah, and for seven years the Children of Israel will light fires from their weapons." Kafka reflects the tradition of the second condition for the coming of the Messiah, that of general perfection: "The Messiah will come only when he is no longer necessary; he will come only on the day after his arrival; he will come, not on the last day, but on the very last." In a sense Kafka is commenting on this tradition, and observing that having achieved perfection, they would have achieved a messianic state without the Messiah, therefore he "will come only when he is no longer necessary." In his novel *Gog and Magog* (p. 232), Martin Buber boils down these two types of conditions for the coming of the Messiah by asking "whether the way for the inner fulfillment should be paved by magical procedures or by an inner transformation." Kafka here firmly takes the side of inner transformation. Kafka's statement that "hence the graves will open themselves" is a traditional image for the Resurrection of the Dead, a common feature of messianic myths. A uniquely Jewish image is the legend that since the Resurrection of the Dead is to take place in Jerusalem, the dead will roll to Jerusalem in underground caves, where they will be judged by King Messiah (*Pesikta de Reb Kahana*, ed. Mandelbaum, pp. 299–300). For more on the great resurrection of the messianic era, see *The Hafety Hayyim: Stories and Parables*, pp. 46–47.

Page 408
"Rabbi Joseph Della Reina"
by Asher Barash

According to kabbalistic doctrine, methods exist to hasten the coming of the Messiah, which are referred to as "Forcing the End." The notion that the messianic age could be hastened was a tradition established in the Talmud (B. Bab. Met. 85): "Elijah used to appear frequently in the college of Rabbi (Judah ha-Nasi). On one of the days during new moon, a bright day, Elijah did not appear; and when he was questioned thereafter for the reason of his absence he said: 'It takes time until I awake Abraham, wash his hands, wait until he prays, and bring him to sleep again. The same I do with Isaac, and the same with Jacob.' Rabbi then questioned him: 'Why do you not awaken all of them at the same time?' 'This I am not allowed, as it is to be feared that if they should all pray together, they would bring the Messiah before his time.' And Rabbi asked him: 'Is their equal to be found in this world?' And he said: 'Yea! there are R. Chiya and his sons.' Rabbi then ordered a fast day, and placed R. Chiya and his sons on the altar. When they came to the section of the Eighteen Benedictions, *He who causes the wind to blow*, a wind came; and when they came to the words *He who causes rain*, rain came. When, thereafter, they were about to say the third section of resurrection, the world began to tremble, and in heaven it was questioned: 'Who has revealed this secret to the world?' 'Elijah did it!' " Elijah was brought and was punished with sixty fiery lashes. (This is the same punishment that was received by Metatron in B. Hag. 15a.) Elijah then appeared at the place where R. Chiya was praying in the form of an angry bear, and scattered them. The archetypal legend for this attempt is that of Rabbi Joseph Della Reina. There is no agreement on where the real Joseph Della Reina lived and in what century. But the legend reached its peak of popularity in the 16th century in Safed. One source for this legend, which exists with several variants, is *Sefer Hasidim*, ed. Wistynezki, par. 545. For variants and sources see Bin Gorion (Berditchevsky), *Mimekor Yisrael* 2:837–854, English-language edition. Compare the version of Barash, which sticks closely to the sources, combining variants to flesh out the narrative, and Dan Tsalka's novella *The Terrible Tale of Joseph de la Reina*, in *New Writings in Israel.* The Hasidim tended to be sympathetic toward the excessive piety of those intent on hastening the End of Days, and the attempt to do this was attributed to a number of rebbes, including the Baal Shem Tov. See the following note.

Page 415
"The Fettered Messiah"
by Yehoshua Bar-Yoseph

This story is also based on the legend of Joseph Della Reina, and retells it in more fragmentary fashion, within a frame about the inability of the Messiah to free himself in order to bring about the End of Days. The notion of "Forcing the End," i.e. hastening the coming of the Messiah, is indicated in a literal fashion by presenting the Messiah as shackled, and Joseph Della Reina as attempting "to swoop down to the dark dungeon of the Messiah and undo his shackles." Bar-Yoseph's version minimizes the challenge to the heavens made explicit in the full legend of Joseph Della Reina, and presents him, instead, as a pure figure who was trapped into making one mistake: "Unwittingly Rabbi Joseph de la Reina had offered incense to the Prince of Pollution." For further discussion of this legend and its sources, see the previous note.

Page 418
"The Pangs of the Messiah"
by Moshe Smilanski

There are clusters of legends associated with every sacred site in Israel. The best English-language source for these is Zev Vilnay's three-volume *The Sacred Land.* This story is built on the legends associated with the cave in which Simeon bar Yohai was said to have stayed for thirteen years, as described in the Talmud (B. Shab. 33b). Some of these legends are included in vol. 3 of the Vilnay set, *Legends of Galilee, Jordan and Sinai*, pp. 221–24. The close attention Reb Yose pays to every sign is characteristic of the kabbalistic approach to existence. The tradition of the pangs that will precede the coming of the Messiah is stated in the Zohar (3:7b): "Then shall pangs overtake Israel, and all nations and their kings shall furiously rage together and take counsel against her." The reference to the belief that the Eternal Lamp over the grave of Simeon bar Yohai must not be extinguished, lest the world return to void and emptiness, echoes a long tradition of the central importance of the Eternal Light of the Tabernacle in the desert and in the Temple in Jerusalem, which is often associated with the light of the Shekhinah. Those who came into the presence of the Lamp of the Ark were said to have become quite fertile (*Mekilta de Rabbi Ishmael*, Vayassa 6:52a–52b). The notion that Reb Yose's granddaughter is a reincarnation of the mysterious woman he had met is an illustration of the primary kabbalistic concept of *gilgul*, or the transmigration of souls. This concept, of which there is no reference in the Talmud, first appears in *Sefer ba-Babir* in the 12th century. One such passage (1:195) is as follows: " 'Why is there a righteous person who has good, and another righteous person who has evil? Because the second was wicked in a previous life, and is now being punished. . . . I am not speaking of his present lifetime. I am speaking about what he has already been, previously.' His colleagues said to him: 'How long will you conceal your words?' He replied: 'Go and see. What is this like? A person planted a vineyard and hoped to grow grapes, but instead sour grapes grew. He saw that his planting and harvest were not successful, so he tore it up and planted it again.' 'How many times?' they asked. He said to them: 'For a thousand generations. It is written *The word that He commanded for a thousand generations* (Ps. 105:8).' " *Gilgul*, then, is the harsh punishment the soul must undergo in order to purify itself. A Sufi teaching story about the nature of transmigration, "The Tale of the Sands," can be found in *Tale of the Dervishes*, ed. Idries Shah, pp. 23–24. A related concept is that of the dybbuk, the spirit of one who has died, that enters the body of one of the living. (See stories pp. 492–501 and the appropriate notes.) It was also possible for a male soul to enter a female body, resulting in barrenness. More positively, the souls of *tzaddikim* were believed to break into sparks that were received by great men in later generations. Thus, for example, Rabbi Nachman of Bratslav believed that sparks of the souls of the Ari and the Baal Shem, among others, were in his soul.

Page 434
"A Message from the Messiah"
by Howard Schwartz

For further discussion of the Shattering of the Vessels and the Gathering of the Sparks, see pp. 23–26. This story is based on a dream of Hayim Vital (*Sefer ha-Hezyonot*, pp. 71–72): "In the dream I saw a man who brought me a letter written in Hebrew characters, similar to the letters of the Torah. He put it in my hand and said: 'You have always wanted to see the handwriting of the Messiah. Behold, I have brought it to you from a land more distant than two years' journey, from where the ten lost tribes live. It is written by the hand of the Messiah himself, and he sent it to you.' " Vital was the primary disciple of the Ari, and the author of *Etz Hayim (The Tree of Life)*, in which he presents his understanding of the central teachings of the Ari. The teachings of the Ari were of particular importance to Rabbi Nachman of Bratslav, who constructed his own philosophy around them to a considerable extent. The Ari, Hayim Vital, and Rabbi Nachman all shared an intense longing for the coming of the Messiah, which in many ways was the central passion of their lives, and it is possible they each may have had messianic aspirations of their own. See pp. 35–36 for further discussion. Other models for this tale are Rabbi Nachman's "The Royal Messenger" and Franz Kafka's "An Imperial Message." The flying of the letters at the end of the story echoes the letters flying from the broken tablets. See the note to "The Flying Letters" by David Einhorn, p. 658.

Page 436
"The Two Souls of Professor Scholem"
by Howard Schwartz

The central text of the Kabbalah is the Zohar, which was written by Moshe de Leon in the 13th century, and not by Simeon bar Yohai in the 2nd century, as claimed by de Leon. From then until this century, the attribution of the Zohar to Simeon bar Yohai was fully accepted, and many Orthodox Jews still maintain that Simeon bar Yohai was the author. Although Professor Scholem was not the first to question the authenticity of the Zohar—the historian Graetz had earlier raised the issue—he was the first to demonstrate convincingly that it was an artful work of pseudepigrapha. The fictional premise of "The Two Souls of Professor Scholem" is that there was a disciple of Moshe de Leon who knew that he was the true author of the Zohar, and kept this secret faithfully in his lifetime, but carried it with him throughout the subsequent transmigrations of his soul. This belief in reincarnation, or *gilgul*, is a primary kabbalistic doctrine. For a further discussion of *gilgul*, see the note for "The Pangs of the Messiah" by Moshe Smilanski, p. 694. The soul of the disciple of Moshe de Leon is ultimately incarnated along with the soul of a German scholar as Professor Scholem, and their discovery of how to exist in harmony is offered as a metaphorical explanation for Professor Scholem's mastery of kabbalistic studies.

Page 437
"The Messiah's Overcoat"
by Aaron Sussaman

Many of the kabbalistic legends concerning the Messiah have a pronounced aspect of cosmic mythology. The Messiah lives, for example, in a celestial palace known as the Bird's Nest. The Messiah is also identified as Son of the Clouds in the Talmud (B. Sanh. 96b–97a). In the Zohar (2:8a–9a) the Messiah is identified as a star: "A fearsome star will rise in the middle of the firmament—by day it will radiate and glow purple before the eyes of the whole world." From this conception to the notion that the overcoat of the Messiah consists of the stars is a natural mythic evolution that Sussaman makes with great skill, inventing in the process a new but seemingly authentic myth about why the coming of the Messiah has been delayed.

Page 438
"The True Waiting"
by Elie Wiesel

The tradition of attempting to hasten the coming of the Messiah is taken a step further in this parable, in which a rebbe "knocked at the Messiah's gate" to ask, "Why are you taking so long?" The Messiah reveals that he feels the people do not really care about him, but about the benefits of his coming. The rebbe is deeply shocked to learn this, and accuses the Messiah of arrogance, since he symbolizes all those benefits to the people. He concludes: "If you have not understood all this and more: that every wait is a wait for you, then you are telling the truth: indeed, it is not you that mankind is waiting for." The true waiting that the rebbe refers to at the end of the tale is a waiting without hope that the Messiah will ever come. This tale, then, postulates an end to the ancient belief that the Messiah will come. Even though the Messiah exists—the rebbe speaks to him—he seems incapable of understanding and fulfilling the needs of the people, and therefore they in turn must give up hope for him. It is not difficult to recognize that the desperation in this parable is a reflection of the psychological state induced by the tragedies of the Nazi Holocaust, in which God's—and thus the Messiah's—silence became unbearable, forcing some people to abandon belief rather than sustain it under the circumstances. Such despair is rarely found in rabbinic literature, since it verges on disbelief.

Page 439
"The Palace of Pearls"
by Penina Villenchik

The palace of pearls in this story refers to "the palace of pearls on a golden mountain" in Rabbi Nachman's tale "The Lost Princess." This tale takes up the quest of Nachman's tale to find that palace of pearls on a golden mountain, which is "the abode of the Shekhinah." Like Nachman's tale, this one is also an internal allegory, and the process of finding the palace is one of internal discovery. Above all, the tale is an attempt to make explicit the role of the Shekhinah as an *anima* figure, which is the implicit meaning of Rabbi Nachman's "The Lost Princess." For further discussion of the evolution of the concept of the Shekhinah, see pp. 20–23. Further discussion of this tale can be found on pp. 23.

Page 444
"The Tale of the Garden"
by Rabbi Tsvi Blanchard

Because of the Garden of Eden and the legend about the four who entered *Pardes* (which refers, literally, to an orchard), gardens and orchards became somewhat interchangeable symbols for the mystic realm that Kabbalists find so alluring. This attraction is vividly portrayed in this story, where the true role of the woman in the garden remains indeterminate—on the one hand promising spiritual fulfillment, on the other only the kind of mirage for which Lilith and her cohorts are famous. Unlike clearcut stories such as Pinski's "The Temptation of Rabbi Akiba," Reb Zvi's ultimate resistance to the woman and the garden has a tragic dimension—cutting him off from the sister of his soul, but protecting him, at the same time, from the dangers associated with mystical contemplation. For a discussion of these dangers, see p. 86.

Page 446
"The Tale of the Spark"
by Rabbi Tsvi Blanchard

The core of this tale retells in allegorical fashion the essential myth of the Shattering of the Vessels and the Gathering of the Sparks of the Ari. This myth is expanded on from a notion appearing in a text of the Zohar known as *Maaseh Merkavah* (not to be confused with the earlier texts of Merkavah Mysticism). This description also refers to the shape of the diagram of the kabbalistic Tree of Life as it is commonly drawn: "The source of the sea's water and the water stream proceeding thereupon to spread itself are Two. A great reservoir is thus formed, just as if a huge hollow had been dug; this reservoir is called the sea, and is the Third. The unfathomable deep divides itself into Seven streams, resembling seven vessels. The source, the water stream, the sea and the seven streams together make Ten. And when the master breaks the vessels which He has made, the waters return to the source, and then only the shattered vessels remain dried up and without water." From *The Secret Garden*, ed. David Meltzer, p. 150. Translated by Rabbi Zalman Schachter. For further discussion of this myth, see pp. 23–26. The writer Hayim's ability to turn a drop into an ocean derives from the primary nature of the oral tradition, which enables the implicit (the drop) to be made explicit (the ocean). Or, using the same metaphor as the Ari, the dryness of the present makes the wood even more susceptible to a single spark, which thus is able to ignite a blazing fire. This means that the sparks—i.e. the rituals, the myths, and the legends—are still a potent force, capable of igniting interest even among those who are not observant, since they are an even drier wood, and thus easier to ignite.

Page 447
"The Magic Spark"
by Miriam Goldman

This is an excerpt from a novel in progress, *The Magic Spark*. Here the myth of the Ari (see pp. 23–26), which itself was an attempt to simplify the kabbalistic concept of creation, is further simplified without any loss of profundity, much as it was in its transmission to those outside the esoteric circles of the Kabbalists: "The sparks flew everywhere. Some were lost eternally. But others fell in a shower of sparks to earth. . . . Then magic sparks are all around us? Yes, they are all around us. Why can't we see them? They are buried, hidden." This explanation of the Ari's myth in terms that a child could comprehend demonstrates the short distance between an esoteric language such as is used in Kabbalah and the universal and accessible language of fairy tales. The link between the two is the role of myth in both of these languages, which is their most essential aspect. Above all, this was the primary role of Kabbalah in the Jewish tradition—restoring the mythic dimension that had been considerably curtailed by the need to affirm monotheism and to remove any possible threats to this central principle. In the kabbalistic period, on the other hand, a way was found to maintain the essential monotheism within a mythic context, where figures such as the Shekhinah could be recognized as aspects of the Divinity rather than as independent figures, despite the appearance of the myths and legends concerning her. For further discussion of the evolution of the Shekhinah, see pp. 20–23.

Page 451
"How the Rabbi of Kalev Freed a Song"
by Manasseh Unger

In the myth formulated by the Ari, vessels filled with primordial light were contained within fragile vessels which shattered at a crucial point in the creation of the world that is equivalent to the Fall. The sparks of light within those vessels were scattered throughout the world, and as a result "Every soul comes to the earth to accomplish a purpose," as Manasseh Unger puts it. This purpose is to locate and set free these scattered and imprisoned sparks. In the case of this tale, the Rabbi of Kalev takes a melody used by a shepherd who is unaware of its sacred nature, and puts it to sacred lyrics concerning the Shekhinah, thus freeing it. Thus this is an example of the Gathering of the Sparks. The process described in this story is virtually identical to that concerning St. John of the Cross, who heard a peasant's songs while imprisoned, and wrote sacred lyrics to accompany the melody. The important role of the *nigun*, the sacred melody, is also emphasized in Unger's version of this story. Hasidim in general, and Rabbi Isaac of Kalev and Rabbi Nachman of Bratslav in particular, held melody in great reverence because of its inherent beauty and purity. See the note to

"The Celestial Orchestra," by Howard Schwartz, p. 681. Additional tales about the Rabbi of Kalev can be found in Martin Buber's *Tales of the Hasidim: The Later Masters*, including the original legend that is retold in this tale, which Buber titles "The Song of the Gooseboy," p. 100. A volume of tales about the Rabbi of Kalev by various Hungarian authors has been translated into English by Andrew Handler. It is *Rabbi Eizik: Hasidic Stories about the Zaddik of Kallo* (Kakev). Another version of this legend, "The Rebbe's Song," by Albert Neumann will be found in this book on p. 23.

BOOK VI
THEMES OF FOLKLORE

Page 457
"Harvest of Madness"
by Rabbi Nachman of Bratslav

The parallel between this tale of Rabbi Nachman's and the Sufi tale known as "When the Waters Were Changed" is so pronounced as to assure the folk origin of the tale on which Rabbi Nachman based his own. For a further discussion of this parallel, see p. 44. The nature of madness is the subject of a number of talmudic legends, concerning, in particular, Ben Zoma, who "looked and lost his mind" (B. Hag. 14b), and Elisha ben Abuyah, known as Aher, who "cut the shoots" (ibid.)—i.e. became an apostate. For further discussion of these legends, see pp. 83–87. The rabbis were attracted and mystified by the phenomenon of madness, and open-minded enough to consider that there might be some validity in a madman's perspective; at least it deserved to be explored. Rabbi Nachman seems to be saying that the ideas of sanity and madness are relative, since the perspective of the people before and after eating of the wheat is radically different. Yet this does not mean that truth does not exist, only that it is difficult to identify, and once identified, hard to keep in focus. The Torah, of course, symbolizes for Judaism the pole of absolute truth, the perfect North of the soul.

Page 458
"The Prince Who Thought He Was a Rooster"
by Rabbi Nachman of Bratslav

This is also a tale about the nature and cure of madness (see previous note). The wise man who imitates the prince's behavior represents the *tzaddik* for Rabbi Nachman, who, in his view, must descend to the level of his Hasidim in order to influence them deeply. For the modern reader, the wise man is an archetype for the psychiatrist, who, according to the theories of R. D. Laing, among others, must share his patients' madness so as to fully comprehend what it is that they are experiencing, in order to lead them away from that place. There are many parallels between the role of the *tzaddik* and the modern therapist. See Rabbi Zalman Schachter's *The Yehidut: A Study of Counselling in Hasidism.* For further discussion of this tale, see p. 45. There is an entire category of Jewish folktales about people who are transformed into animals. See Dov Noy, *Motif-Index of Talmudic-Midrashic Literature,* pp. 202-50. The Aggadah contains extensive examples of animal folklore. In the Kabbalah there are examples of evil people who are reincarnated as animals as a punishment, in the process known as *gilgul,* or the transmigration of souls. See also the fox fables of Berechiah ha-Nakdan in *Fables of a Jewish Aesop,* translated by Moses Hudas. A parallel Hasidic motif is found in a tale of the Baal Shem's in which "a wise man caused his dress and speech to resemble those of the prince, and so step by step won his favor, until he brought him back to his father." See Birnbaum, *The Life and Sayings of the Baal Shem,* p. 82.

Page 459
"Fable of the Goat"
by S. Y. Agnon

There are five variants of this tale in the collection of the Israel Folktales Archive (IFA) in Haifa. One of these is translated in full on pp. 51-52, where a further discussion of this tale can also found. See also the note to "The Cave of Machpelah" by Howard Schwartz, p. 673.

Page 461
"The Animal in the Synagogue"
by Franz Kafka

There is a large category of mythical animals in the aggadic literature and medieval folklore, which can be found on pp. 202-14 of Dov Noy's *Motif-Index of Talmudic-Midrashic Literature.* These include the man-plant Adne Sadeh, who could travel no farther than the circle of its navel cord; Leviathan, the great fish that will be eaten at the End of Time; and mythical birds such as the Ziz. There does not appear to be a precise parallel to the animal Kafka describes. The animal symbolizes the sexual tension in the synagogue, despite the fact that the women have been separated from the men behind a partition. The ambivalence of the women toward the animal—alternate fear and attraction—also signifies the sexual dimension of the tale. The separation of men and women was intended to permit all the focus on the spiritual relationship between God and man, but in this satire Kafka suggests that the resulting tension causes the opposite to happen, only intensifying the attraction between the sexes.

Page 464
"The Jewbird"
by Bernard Malamud

The black bird in this tale is easily identified as a raven, around which there is a rich folklore, especially involving legends of pointed debates between Noah and the raven he sent out at the end of forty days, which *went forth to and fro, until the waters were dried up from off the earth* (Gen. 8:7). In the Talmud (B. Sanh. 108b) there is recorded a bitter argument between Noah and the raven, not unlike those of the protagonists—man and bird—in Malamud's tale: *"And he sent forth a raven* (Gen. 8:7). Resh Lakish said: 'The raven gave Noah a triumphant retort. It said to him: "Thy Master hateth me, and thou hatest me. Thy Master hateth me since He commanded seven pairs to be taken of the clean creatures, but only two of the unclean. Thou hatest me seeing that thou leavest the species of which there are seven, and sendeth one of which there are only two. Should the angel of heat or of cold smite me, would not the world be short of one kind? Or perhaps thou desirest my mate!" ' " A similar argument is found in *Genesis Rabbah* (33:5): "The raven began arguing with Noah: 'Of all the birds that you have here, why do you send me?' Noah replied: 'What need, then, has the world of you? For food? For a sacrifice?' " See also *Pirke de Rabbi Eliezer* 32, where the raven is viewed as an evil creature; "Noah sent forth the raven to ascertain what was the state of the world. It went forth and found a carcase of a man cast upon the summit of a mountain, and it settled thereon for its food, and did not return with its message to its sender." The unacknowledged need that man and bird have for each other in Malamud's tale is not apparent in the sources concerning Noah and the raven, but in both cases man and bird are thrown together. Noah's sending forth of the raven also prefigures the expulsion of the Jewbird in Malamud's tale. A speaking dove is found in B. Sanh. 95a. See also B. Sanh. 108. The notion that the bird is a Jew who has been reincarnated is representative of the kabbalistic notion of *gilgul,* or the transmigration of souls. See also "Legend of the Third Dove" by Stefan Zweig.

Page 471
"Eliyahu the Prophet"
by Sholom Aleichem

This story derives from the Passover custom of leaving a full wineglass on the seder table for Eliyahu (Elijah), and opening the door at one point for him to enter. This custom reflects the high esteem in which Elijah is held, and the countless legends in Jewish folklore in which Elijah appears, often in disguise, to provide a magical salvation. In this story, however, Elijah is given a less illustrious role, being used by the boy's parents as a means of frightening him into staying awake during the long seder by telling him that on "Pesach night Eliyahu the Prophet goes around looking for anyone who falls asleep at the seder table and takes him away in his sack." This warning, which probably reflects a common local custom, leads the boy to dream after falling asleep at the seder table that Elijah has arrived to carry him off: "Bent over, leaning on a huge staff, with a sack on his back, he silently, oh so silently, without a word, comes straight toward me." Elijah gives the boy an impossible choice—to come with him (leaving his family) or sleep forever. The boy's only salvation in this case will come when he awakes. Although the biblical Elijah is a stern figure, the Elijah of Jewish folklore is full of compassion. The harsh role given him by the boy's parents here, therefore, that of a seder enforcer who makes certain that the child remains awake, is an exception to the rule. See "The Prophet Elijah in Modern Jewish Folktales" by Beatrice Silverman Weinreich (M.A. thesis, Columbia University, 1957).

Page 474
"The Revelation of Elijah"
by S. Y. Agnon

The presence of Elijah at every circumcision and at every seder was assumed, although the prophet would most often appear disguised as a stranger, usually a poor
man. According to the legends of the Baal Shem, his birth was announced by Elijah,
and he maintained a close relationship with the prophet all his life, often seeing him
in visions, such as in *Shivhei ha-Besht* 114, where "on one side stood Elijah the
Prophet, God bless his memory, and on the other side stood my rabbi, Ahijah, the
prophet of Shiloh. They spoke to me and I passed it on to you." Although the untu-
tored Elijah in this story by Agnon is called Elijah the Prophet by everyone, the Baal
Shem's disciples, who do not come across as very perceptive in this tale, do not consider associating him with the actual prophet, present in another one of his disguises.
They continue to resist making this connection until the Baal Shem reveals that it
was the case. After this Elijah reappears in another disguise, that of a poor bartender
whose vessels have become rusty and broken. Actually he is there to transmit to the
Baal Shem an allegorical message about the present spiritual condition of the Jews—
that they have been accused of lacking *kavanah,* and that Elijah is afraid God will
withdraw his blessings from the people. The Baal Shem acknowledges this allegory,
referring to the bread and coin Elijah has directed him to use to repair the vessels:
"The Holy One gave my heart counsel to repair their deeds with a slice of bread to
guests and charity to the poor." The restoration of *kavanah* for prayer and all other
rituals was the primary goal of the Baal Shem, and this tale presents the Baal Shem's
motivation—the knowledge that the vessels, i.e. the people, had become broken, i.e.
were no longer able to maintain an authentic spiritual harmony with the Creator.
Another valid interpretation is that the rusty and broken vessels refer to the Ari's
myth of the Shattering of the Vessels and the Gathering of the Sparks. (For a discussion of this myth see pp. 23-26.) In this case the meaning is the same: the work of
Tikkun—which the restoration of the broken vessels represents—needs to be undertaken at once. Compare this story with "The King Who Loved Music" by Rabbi
Levi Yitzhak of Berditchev, in which the inability of subsequent generations of musicians to play as well as their ancestors serves as an allegory making the same point as
that of the vessels in this tale.

Page 480
"The Poor Man and Eliyahu the Prophet"
by Kamelia Shahar

This folktale about Eliyahu (Elijah) was collected orally in Israel by Kamelia Shahar
for the Israel Folktales Archives. Three of these orally collected tales have been included in the anthology to demonstrate the continuing oral transmission of Jewish
folklore, even in the present. (The other two tales are "True Joy" by Kamelia Shahar
and "The Wager and the Tiny Shining Star" by Alfredo Sarano.) One of the common categories of folktales about Elijah concerns his assisting the poor (see the following note). The three things that the poor couple lacked were a child, sight (the
husband was blind), and gold. His request "to let me see my child eat off a plate of
gold" fulfilled all three wishes, even though he was permitted only one request. Note
also that the poor man directed his wish to "the Lord of the World," and not to

Eliyahu, understanding well that the source of the bounty was God. It is details such as this that characterize Jewish folklore, and distinguish it from that of others. This tale first appeared in the Judezmo-language magazine *Aki Yerushalayim*, No. 2, July 1979. Kamelia Shahar recorded the tale from a Judezmo-speaking woman in Or-Yehuda, who had heard it from her grandmother in Izmir.

Page 481
"The Apprentice"
by Dan Tsalka

Elijah provides salvation, often miraculous, for those in need in a multitude of medieval folktales. Here a cobbler wishes, when lingering by the chair of Elijah in the empty synagogue, for an apprentice. His prayer is answered when a naked angel appears at his door, who turns out to be unable to speak. This reply to his prayers is somewhat unconventional, in that in most cases it is Elijah himself who appears, often in disguise, to fulfill the prayer of someone in need and deserving of assistance. The biblical model for angels descending to earth is the episode of Abraham and the three angels in Genesis (18:1-16). Usually the appearance of an angel is for a short time, to deliver a message, as when the angel Raziel delivered the Book of Raziel to Adam. This story is parallel in many respects to the story "An Old Man with Enormous Wings" by Gabriel García Marquez.

Page 482
"The Magician"
by I. L. Peretz

The visit of Elijah, disguised as a magician, to a village before Passover is typical of the role Elijah plays in medieval and Jewish folklore. Here, in the Peretz tale, Elijah, disguised as a beggar with immense powers at his command, brings his assistance to a devout but impoverished family at the time of Passover, the observance with which Elijah is most closely associated. In his four-volume collection of the legends of Elijah, *Stories of Elijah the Prophet* (4:7-132), Yisroel Yaakov Klapholtz includes more than two dozen tales concerned with Elijah feeding the hungry and enriching the poor. These include stories such as one from *Even Shtiya* in which Elijah appears to a needy *tzaddik* in the form of a visitor and provides him with his needs for the festival.

Page 485
"The Golem"
by I. L. Peretz

The most famous legend-cycle of medieval Jewish folklore concerns the creation of a man out of clay, known as the Golem. Created, according to tradition, by Rabbi Judah Loew of Prague, the purpose of the Golem was to protect the Jewish population of the ghetto from the accusation of the blood libel—i.e. of using the blood of a Christian, usually a child, for the Passover service. These accusations often led to pogroms against the Jews. The creation of a man out of clay obviously parallels the creation of man by God in Genesis (2:7). A report of such a creation is found in the Talmud (B. Sanh. 65b): "Rabba created a man, and sent him to Rabbi Zora. Rabbi Zora spoke to him but received no answer. Therefore he said to him, 'You are a creature of the magicians. Return to your dust.' " The creation of a calf is also reported in the same folio, and in B. Sanh. 67b: "Rabbi Haina and Rabbi Oshaia spent every Sabbath eve studying the *Sefer Yetsirah (The Book of Creation)*, by means of which they created a third-grown calf and ate it." The key element in the creation of the Golem is the use of the Divine Name (the Tetragrammaton). That the Golem is inferior to God's creation, man, is emphasized by the fact that he was unable to speak or reproduce. Because the powers involved in such a creation are difficult to control, there are many legends about the Golem's running amok, as in this tale by Peretz, where the Golem continued killing after the danger had subsided, and was in danger of killing off all Prague. In these cases the only way to stop him was to kill him and return him to clay, as the Maharal (Rabbi Loew) does in this case. The notion of the Golem's running amok is a common motif in the Golem legends. In *Journal for Hermits*, published in 1808, Jakob Grimm reports the following Golem legend: "One man's Golem once grew very tall, and he let him grow so long that he was unable to reach his forehead to erase the first letter of *emeth*, so that he would collapse and turn to clay again. Once he ordered the Golem to take off his boots, thinking to reach his forehead when he bent down. But when he erased the letter, the whole heap of clay fell on the Jew and crushed him." There also exist fragmentary legends concerning Golems that were said to have been made by Ibn Gabirol and Ibn Ezra in the 11th century. Amazingly, Ibn Gabirol was said to have created a woman who served him, possibly in sexual respects as well as domestic. When he was denounced to the authorities, he convinced them that she was not a complete creature, and broke her down to the component parts (*Mimekor Yisrael*, 2:752). See Cynthia Ozick's novella *Puttermesser and Xanthippe* in *Levitation: Five Fictions*. Ibn Ezra is said to have created a creature and have said: " 'See what the Holy One has given me by means of the holy letters!' Then he turned to the creature and said, 'Turn back!' and it became what it had been before it was created" (*Mimekor Yisrael*, 2:752).

Page 486
"How the Golem Was Created"
by Rabbi Yudl Rosenberg

The most famous cycle of the legends of the Golem is *Niflaot Maharal*, by Yudl Rosenberg, first published in 1909. The entire cycle can be found in English translation in *Yenne Velt: The Great Works of Jewish Fantasy and the Occult*, pp. 163-225. This text serves as the primary source for Chaim Block's *The Golem*. Rosenberg claimed that he had found a manuscript, but modern critics, including Dov Sadan and Yossi Dan, claim that the work is fiction, created by Rosenberg; Gershom Scholem suggests that it was not written until after the blood libels of the 1890s (see *Kabbalah*, p. 354). In any case, Rosenberg's text incorporates many elements traditionally associated with the legend of the Golem. Assuming that Rosenberg's text is largely a work of pseudepigrapha, as Professors Sadan and Dan insist, it then joins an illustrious tradition of pseudepigraphical works, including the most famous example, the Zohar, which Moshe de Leon claimed was written in the 3rd century by Simeon bar Yohai, but which Gershom Scholem and others insist was his own creation. In most accounts of the creation of the Golem the key element in its creation is the use of the Divine Name. See Frederic Thieberger's important collection of Golem legends in

The Great Rabbi Loew of Prague. Niflaot Maharal also serves as the basis for *The Golem of Prague* by Gershom Winkler.

Page 488
"The End of the Golem"
by Rabbi Yudl Rosenberg

In order to destroy the Golem it was necessary to reverse the process by which it had been created (see the previous two notes). At this point the Golem collapsed back into clay. In other descriptions of the creation and destruction of the Golem other than Yudl Rosenberg's, the word *emeth* ("truth") is inscribed on the forehead of the Golem, and a slip of paper on which the Divine Name has been written is inserted in its mouth. When the time comes to destroy the Golem, the first letter (Aleph) of *emeth* is erased, leaving *meth* ("death"), and the Golem collapses. Clearly the creation and destruction of the Golem are intended to be parallel to that of man, about whom it is written *dust thou art, and unto dust thou shalt return* (Gen. 3:19).

Page 489
"The Moon, the Mercenary, and the Ring"
by Lajos Szabolcsi

This story retells a legend about Rabbi Judah Loew, in which he is able to distinguish from the ring a mercenary tries to sell him that another attempt has been made to accuse the Jews of a blood libel. As in other stories about the Maharal (Rabbi Loew), his powers and perceptions are far beyond the ordinary. In fact he is the subject of many legends deriving from the 16th century. Many of these legends are found in *Niflaot Maharal*, edited by Yudl Rosenberg (see note to "How the Golem Was Created"), which confuses the issue of their authenticity. The soldier's loss of his shadow is a common consequence of evil behavior in folklore, and a sign that one is doomed.

Page 492
"The House of Demons"
by Martin Buber

One of the richest strains of Jewish folklore concerns tales about demons. Belief in demons can be traced back to the Talmud (B. Kid. 29b), where the following legend about exorcising a demon is found: "Rabbi Acha entered to sleep in a school, and the demon appeared to him in the shape of a seven-headed dragon. Every time Rabbi Acha knelt down to pray he caused the throwing off of one of those heads, thus having killed the serpent after he knelt down seven times." In the Zohar (1:14a and 48a) the following legend about the origin of demons is found: "After the Sabbath was sanctified there was left a residue of spirits for which no bodies had been created. . . . These creatures are rejected both above and below, and therefore they have no pure resting place. They all have their origin in the side of the left (the side of evil); they are invisible to men and hover around them to do them mischief." As in the talmudic legend of Rabbi Acha, demons have taken possession of a house, and will not leave unless exorcised. The formal hearing the demon receives from a *beit din*, a court of rabbis, parallels that in S. Ansky's drama *The Dybbuk*. Such hearings are reported to have taken place. The demon lover in the story told by the Jewish demon has strong echoes of the legends associated with Lilith. In particular, the notion that the demoness confronts the Jew on his deathbed with the children he has fathered with her echoes the belief that on his deathbed the demons a man has fathered flock around him, calling out his name. For protection from the evil offspring Psalm 91 is recited. The decision of Rabbi Joel to permit the demons possession of the house comes from the vow made by the dying Jew, giving it to them. Such vows are inviolate, even if they are delivered to demons. The story ends with a description of the nature of the being the Jew had fathered among the demons: "Equally son of man and demon, at home in no realm of earth and in no other realm, I and mine live in twilight and shadow and are driven by mortals from the one place granted us." This reflects the belief in various categories of demons and spirits, including those demons fathered through the spilling of a man's seed, which, since a human is one parent, will have qualities of both the father and the mother. This story is a reworking of a medieval folktale which can be found in Nathan Ausubel's *A Treasury of Jewish Folklore*, pp. 617-20, where the judgment of the *Beit Din* is opposite that of Buber's retelling. A tale about demonic possession of a ruin is found in *Otsar Midrashim* (2:339-40) and in *Mimekor Yisrael* (3:1094-6). See also *Mishle Sendebar*, lines 461–544.

Page 498
"The Dybbuk"
by Romain Gary

This story has been excerpted from *The Dance of Genghis Cohn*. One of the most prominent themes in Yiddish folklore, in particular, is that of the dybbuk, a spirit of one dead who enters and takes possession of the body of another. S. Ansky's drama *The Dybbuk* describes a case of such possession between a young woman and the dybbuk of a *yeshivah* student who loved her. Gary gives a new twist to the motif of the dybbuk by having the spirit of a murdered Jew enter and possess one of the Nazi murderers. In this way does Gary bring out the psychological aspects of the dybbuk legends, where a man's guilt comes to take possession of him. Also, in a peculiar way, the murdered Jew remains alive by virtue of possessing the body of the Nazi. A variety of dybbuk stories can be found in *Mimekor Yisrael* 2:861-70.

Page 501
"The Wandering Spirit of Léon Mitrani"
by Isaac Goldemberg

This story is an excerpt from the novel *The Fragmented Life of Don Jacobo Lerner*. Lerner becomes possessed by the spirit of Léon Mitrani, which causes his entire outlook to become transformed and embittered. The subtle infestation of the alien spirit and the consequent change in perspective is especially well portrayed. This again highlights the psychological aspect of this kind of demonic possession. A typical Yiddish folktale about possession by a dybbuk is found in the *Maaseh Book* (1:152): "An evil spirit had entered the body of a young man. Thereupon he was adjured to reveal his name or that of his wife. When they mentioned his wife, he began to scream and said that his was an *agunah* and had lost her right to remarry because he had lost his life at sea." The tradition is that the dybbuk remains in this world, possessing another, until he is able to resolve an unfinished matter of great importance. Another good example of this motif is found in *Shivhei ha-Ari* in a story about an adulterer whose soul sought refuge in a widow living in Safed. The dybbuk carries on a conversation with the rabbi sent to exorcise him, recounting a tale within a tale about his own history and infamy. There is also the description of his suffering as a wandering spirit, before he took possession of the widow: "Three evil angels drag me by a heavy chain and torment me pitilessly and cry out: 'Thus is a Jew punished who leads a woman to violate her marriage vows!' " See *Mimekor Yisrael* 2:861-65. The classic literary expression of the dybbuk motif is S. Ansky's drama *The Dybbuk*.

Page 506
"Watch Night"
by Israel Zangwill

This tale of the Baal Shem Tov is excerpted from Zangwill's novella *Master of the Good Name*, which retells the best-known legends of the Baal Shem, especially those in the earliest collection, *Shivhei ha-Besht*. To protect infants from Lilith and her cohorts, women wore amulets during pregnancy and hung them on the cradles of the infants once they were born. When an infant was regarded as being in danger, due to ill health or a frail nature, and required protection even greater than an amulet, a guard was posted beside it all night, to protect the child from the evil spirits. The transformation of the evil magician into the black cat is a common motif of medieval folk magic. The battle of the power of the Name against the powers of black magic is parallel to the rain-making contest won by Elijah over the prophets of Baal (1 Kings 18). The magic circles that the Baal Shem drew are common in folk magic, and were believed to have been used by King Solomon, who was said to know how to control the forces of enchantment. Such circles within circles are also kabbalistic symbols for phases of emanation, known as *Sefirot*, and illustrations of these circles are commonly found. Rabbi Nachman of Bratslav reports a dream vision in which such circles play a prominent part: "There was a man lying on the ground, and about him people sat around in a circle. Outside that circle was another circle, then another, and yet several more. . . . The one seated in the center was moving his lips, and all those in the circles moved their lips after him. Then I saw that he was gone, and everyone's lips had stopped moving" (*Likkutim* 20). For the text of an amulet used to ward off Lilith, see p. 96. Another tale of a watch night, by Ayzik-Meyer Dik, is found in *The Shtetl* by Diane K. and David G. Roskies, pp. 143-46. A parallel to the enchantment of the wizard into a cat is found in "The Black Cat," an orally collected folktale in *Seven Bags of Gold*, ed. Otto Schnitzler, no. 6.

Page 508
"Lilith"
by Moyshe Kulbak

For a discussion of the evolution of the legend of Lilith, see pp. 3–4. Various legends about Lilith can be found in *The Alphabet of Ben Sira*, and, in particular, in the Zohar, such as this example about Lilith the Seducer from 1:148a-b: "The female of Samael is the Serpent, called Woman of Harlotry, End of All Flesh, End of the Days. . . . She adorns herself with many jewels like a despicable harlot, and she stands at the crossroads and on the paths to seduce the sons of man. . . . That fool goes astray after her, and drinks from her cup of wine, and commits fornications with her, and goes astray after her. Then she leaves him asleep on the couch and when the fool awakens and thinks to make sport with her as before, she removes her ornaments, and turns into a menacing giant. She is full of glittering eyes, a drawn sword in her hand, and bitter drops hang from that sword. And she kills that fool and casts him into Gehenna." Here Lilith is revealed to be the Angel of Death in disguise, and this accurately reflects the rabbinic attitude toward her. This very aspect of Lilith is alluded to in Kulbak's tale, when Benye wakes up and realizes that "Lilith, fresh, young Lilith, the wife of Satan, had killed him."

Page 512
"Lilith in the Lager"
by Primo Levi

For a discussion of this tale see p. 29.

Page 516
"From the Rabbi's Dreambook"
by David Meltzer

There are two separate but related traditions about Lilith: one of Lilith the seducer, and the other of Lilith the child-destroying witch. In both traditions Lilith plays a destructive role, but in different ways. Meltzer, in this tale, brings those separate strands of the legend together for the first time, and weaves them into one legend, much as Jakov Lind weaves together the legends of Lilith and Eve in "The Story of Lilith and Eve." Lilith enters as a witch, intent on strangling the rabbi's child, but when he confronts her she protects herself by switching to her second persona, and attempts to seduce him, and in this way weakens his resolve to expel her—leaving his child in danger. These two aspects are so thoroughly interrelated in this tale that it is apparent that Meltzer has made explicit a tie that always existed implicitly in both of these roles of Lilith. For a further discussion of the legend of Lilith, see pp. 3–4.

Page 517
"The Woman in the Forest"
by Jiri Langer

This tale, excerpted from *Nine Gates to the Chassidic Mysteries*, pp. 133-34, follows the pattern of Lilith or a Lilith-like demon who attempts to seduce and destroy the piety of righteous men. See "The Temptations of Rabbi Akiba" by David Pinski. The fact that the woman is blond is a revealing fact about the sexual fantasy that lies at the bottom of such legends about encounters with Lilith, implying a longing for the "forbidden fruit" of non-Jewish women. See the previous tales about Lilith and their appropriate notes.

Page 518
"The Tale of the Duck"
by Jeremy Garber

This story was modeled on the 18th- and 19th-century folktales told by the Hasidim. The libel of the witch, that the Jews were poisoning the water, affected the Jews throughout the Middle Ages, especially during the 14th-century black-plague outbreaks. The harsh punishment of the father for agreeing to sell his daughter stems from the midrashic tradition concerning the gravity of the crime of selling Joseph (Gen. 37:27): "Because ye have sold Joseph to be a slave, therefore shall ye say year after year 'Slaves were we unto Pharaoh in Egypt' " (*Midrash on Psalms*, ed. Buber, 10:93). The situation that befalls the heroine partakes of the motif of *gilgul* or transmigration of the soul, a primary kabbalistic doctrine. It also resembles a standard fairy tale type of enchantment.

Page 523
"The Golden Bird"
by Howard Schwartz

One of the essential types of Jewish folklore is the fairy tale. One of the earliest of such tales is the Book of Esther, in which the Queen (Esther) discovers the plot of the evil vizier (Haman) against her native people (the Jews), and saves them by using her influence over the King (Ahasuerus). Other early fairy tales are those found in the Talmud concerning King David and Ishbi-benob (B. Sanh. 95a), King Solomon and Asmodeus (B. Git. 68b), and Honi, who drew a magic circle and invoked the rain, and then fell asleep for seventy years (B. Taan. 23a). The prime period for fairy tales came in the Middle Ages, and there are several dozen extant tales from this period. Examples of four such tales, including "The Princess with Golden Hair," can be found in Moses Gaster's *Studies and Texts*, vol. 2, pp. 922–41. Another, more recent source of fairy tales are those collected in two important Yiddish volumes edited by Y. L. Cahan: *Yiddische Folkmayses* and *Yiddische Folklore*. Finally, the major collection of fairy tales and other folklore from the modern period is that of the Israel Folktale Archives in Haifa. A unique case, discussed elsewhere (pp. 35–48), is that of Rabbi Nachman of Bratslav, who told fairy tales to his Hasidim, including "The Lost Princess" and "The Seven Beggars," both of which are presented in this collection. In "The Golden Bird" Rabbi Nachman is given a role similar to that of the prince in the standard fairy tale. This tale is a variation on the widely found motif of the quest for the golden bird. See, for example, "The Golden Bird" in *Grimm's Fairy Tales*. The source for this particular tale is a legend about the Baal Shem Tov, one version of which can be found in Martin Buber's *Tales of the Hasidim: The Early Masters*, pp. 54–55, and another in *The Hasidic Anthology* by Louis I. Newman, p. 247. See also *Menorah Journal*, vol. 10, p. 521. Here the Baal Shem tells his Hasidim a parable about a king who climbs a living ladder and almost captures a glorious bird, when those near the bottom of the ladder tire and depart, causing the ladder to collapse. The identification of the golden bird with the bird of the Messiah who transforms the prayers of Israel into song is linked to the kabbalistic term for the hidden palace of the Messiah, known as the Bird's Nest, and the talmudic legend about the angel Sandalphon: "His name is Sandalphon; he is higher than his fellow angels by a distance of five hundred years' journey, and he stands behind the Chariot (Merkavah) and wreathes crowns for his Maker" (B. Hag. 13b). Reference to the bird that inhabits the Bird's Nest is found in the Zohar (2:8a): "The Holy One, blessed be He, beckons that bird, and it enters its nest, and comes to the Messiah, and it calls what it calls, and stirs up what it stirs up, until that Bird's Nest and the Messiah are called three times from inside the Holy Throne, and all ascend."

Page 527
"The Seamstress of Safed"
by Yehuda Yaari

This tale is based on a legend deriving from the earthquake of 1837 in Safed. Such realistic folktales inevitably emerge from major upheavals, such as earthquakes, wars, or messianic stirrings. The suffering of the poor seamstress, who was condemned to sew bridal dresses for others but not for herself, and whose only consolation was sewing her own shroud, is made poignantly. Safed is the second-holiest city in Israel, after Jerusalem, and it is regarded as a symbol of purity, and of the presence of the Shekhinah. These symbolic echoes are implicit in this tale, part of the background of the city of Safed and the extensive legends associated with it, which are found, for example, in *Shivhei ha-Ari*, translated into English as *In Praise of the Ari*.

Page 529
"The Legend of the Dead Poppy"
by Zvi Kolitz

The notion of *gilgul*, or the transmigration of souls, is commonly found in folklore as well as in kabbalistic texts. The transformation of the eyes of the girl, who "had been burned alive in the camp oven," into two poppies can be seen as a miracle or as an expression of her mother's madness. So closely entwined are the magical and the mad in this tale that they cannot be sorted out, much as in "The Shawl" by Cynthia Ozick. The poppies are also an appropriate symbol for the blood shed.

Page 532
"The Last Living Jew"
by Elie Wiesel

The issue of the persistence of evil in the world and God's passivity in the face of it is a theme found as early as the Talmud, in the story of Elisha ben Abuyah, who is said to have lost his faith after witnessing a man killed attempting to perform a good deed. As a result of the Holocaust some Jews lost their faith, unable to comprehend how God could permit the horrors of the Holocaust to take place. This sense of the absence of God is summarized in the final words of this tale: "But You, where are You?"

Page 533
"The Wandering Jew"
by David Slabotsky

In origin the Wandering Jew is a Christian legend, although it is largely prefigured by the legend of the wandering of Cain (see note 35 to the Introduction, p. 100, for a discussion of it). Hundreds of accounts of sightings of the Wandering Jew exist, and a rich folklore. Slabotsky suggests that the quest that motivates his life is the search for his death. His realization of that quest gives the legend a conclusion.

Page 535
"The Shawl"
by Cynthia Ozick

For a discussion of "The Shawl," see pp. 73–74.

Page 538
"The Tale of the Lucky Daaz"
by Pinhas Sadeh

This tale is a retelling of the story of Job, with the important distinction that the figure being tested is not the devout and worthy Job, but rather Daaz, an innocent who can easily be fooled. The opening passage is identical to that in Job (1:7): *And the Lord said unto Satan: "Whence comest thou?" Then Satan answered the Lord, and said: "From going to and fro in the earth, and from walking up and down on it."* Satan dupes Daaz again and again, but each subsequent loss takes on a positive aspect from the perspective of Daaz. The contrast with Job is striking—since Daaz does not value his possessions, he cannot be damaged by losing them, and "free of the heavy stone" he can "go fleetly and sweetly to my home." Most folklores contain stories of such innocents. The best-known tradition in Jewish folklore is the cycle of legends associated with the residents of the city of Chelm, who attempt things like capturing the moon in a barrel of water. Daaz is also somewhat parallel to the Sufi character Mulla Nastrudin, although it is never certain if Nastrudin is really a fool or simply playing the fool.

Page 539
"The Wager and the Tiny Shining Star"
by Alfredo Sarano

This is the third orally collected folktale included in this volume. It is a variant of a well-known tale about the childhood of King Solomon, and presents one of the first instances in which King Solomon demonstrates his wisdom. Medieval Jewish folklore has an abundance of tales about King David, and, especially, King Solomon. Perhaps the most famous story about Solomon is that concerning the capture of the demon Asmodeus found in the Talmud (Git. 68b). Bialik collected and retold many of the legends about David and Solomon in *And It Came to Pass*, including another version of this tale, which Bialik entitled "The Egg."

Page 540
"Challahs in the Ark"
by Rabbi Zalman Schachter

This is a retelling of one of the tales of the Ari (Isaac Luria) from *Shivhei ha-Ari*. The offering of the dozen *challahs* is represented as perfect, since it brings satisfaction both to the giver and the receiver for thirty years. The rabbi who condemns this exchange because he thinks it has encouraged anthropomorphism is blind to its positive dimension, and, as Hayim Vital, the disciple of the Ari, tells him, in condemning it he has signed his own death warrant. The story implies a willingness of the Ari to permit anthropomorphic thinking on the part of the common people, as long as it assisted in sustaining their faith in God. It also echoes the biblical injunctions to bring offerings to the Temple, although this requirement was suspended with the destruction of the Temple. This legend suggests that the satisfaction received by those who made such offerings came from their belief that they were offering nourishment to God, much as God had nourished them. It also points out the distinction between the literal (*peshat*) and the symbolic (*remez* and *drash*), as well as the tolerance among Jewish sages for those who prefer to understand at the metaphorical level. See the discussion of *Pardes*, pp. 83–87. The moral seems to be that denial of the literal level, even in a case where it may not seem to have legitimacy, is unacceptable. A translation of the tale retold here can be found in Chaim Bloch's *Legends of the Ari* under the title "The Holy Sin." See *Menorah Journal*, vol. 14, p. 472–74, 1928. This is a good example of the religious, in contrast to the secular, folktale. See p. 27 for a further discussion of this point.

BOOK VII
HASIDIC THEMES

Page 547
"The Seven Beggars"
by Rabbi Nachman of Bratslav

This most famous of Rabbi Nachman's tales was also the last one that he told. It is incomplete in that the seventh beggar does not appear. Some have attributed this to Rabbi Nachman's severe illness, others to his intention, since the seventh beggar represents the Messiah, and since Rabbi Nachman's tales are believed by his Hasidim to contain hidden mysteries. It is possible that Nachman may have felt that the tale of the seventh beggar might have contained secrets which could possibly hasten the coming of the Messiah, a dangerous sin. (See "Rabbi Joseph Della Reina" by Asher Barash and "The Fettered Messiah" by Yehoshua Bar-Yoseph and the appropriate notes.) There is a long tradition of secrets so potent that grave danger can result from revealing them. There are also mysteries so hidden that heaven does not want them revealed, according to a famous story about the Ari: "One day the Ari was explaining a passage in the Zohar. Suddenly he stopped short and said: 'The sentence I have just read conceals a deeper, more secret meaning.' Thereupon he said: 'I told you it was perilous for me to reveal the secret meaning of this passage. But you would give me no peace. Already I hear the punishment proclaimed in Heaven: "Thy son, Moses, shall die in seven days (*Shivhei ha-Avi*)." ' " This terrible punishment takes place, indicating the severity of the sin. Each of the seven beggars represents a different aspect of the *tzaddik*, whose role it is to impart understanding of the true nature of existence. For further discussion of "The Seven Beggars," see pp. 39–40.

Page 566
"The Seventh Beggar's Tale"
by Richard Siegel

This tale should be read in conjunction with the previous tale, "The Seven Beggars" by Rabbi Nachman of Bratslav. It completes the unfinished tale by presenting the tale of the seventh beggar (see the previous note). The author credits Rabbi Zalman Schachter with the suggestion of writing this tale, and adds that it is based on two related dreams. Certainly it has the style and texture of the Nachman tale, and is a convincing and likely interpretation, identifying the seventh beggar with the Messiah.

Page 570
"Two Worlds"
by M. J. Berditchevsky

This story combines and retells the first three tales in *Shivhei ha-Besht*, which concern Rabbi Eliezer, the father of the Baal Shem Tov. The considerable obstacles Rabbi Eliezer overcomes in order to obtain his freedom have parallels in many fairy tales, and thus attribute an enchanted quality to the birth of the Baal Shem, whose pure soul is identified as a reward for the righteousness of his father during his long trial. Rabbi Eliezer's wanderings are also clearly intended to parallel those of Joseph, who also was sold as a slave and became the trusted adviser of a ruler. See Gen. 37–50.

Page 574
"The Besht and P'ney Yehoshua"
by Rabbi Zalman Schachter

The Besht (Baal Shem Tov) did not reveal himself as a *tzaddik* until the age of thirty. Before that he served as the coachman for his brother-in-law, Rabbi Gershon. *Shivhei ha-Besht* contains two tales about the Besht revealing himself (tales 14 and 15, *In Praise of the Baal Shem Tov*, pp. 27–31). In "The Besht and P'ney Yehoshua" Rabbi Schachter presents an additional legend, not included in *Shivhei ha-Besht*, concerning a prior incident of the Besht's revealing himself to the P'ney Yehoshua, who alone among his congregation was able to remain when the Baal Shem prayed the *Amidah*, since he alone had amended the sins of his youth by *teshuvah*, or repentance. Rabbi Schachter's source for this story is *Hutim ha-M'shulasuim* by Rabbi Abraham Stern, p. 10.

Page 575
"Reb Zusheh and the Dowry"
by Rabbi Zalman Schachter

Reb Zusheh is a unique figure among hasidic masters—he displays qualities of a simpleton, but in a canny manner. For example, he sets free an innkeeper's caged birds when no one is looking, and then acknowledges his deed and takes a beating without complaint (Buber, *Tales of the Hasidim: The Early Masters*, p. 245). Here his sympathy for the woman's despair translates directly into his own punishment, but he still manages to retain the purity of his *mitzvah*. Rabbi Schachter heard this tale from Reb Elya Simpson of Brooklyn, Gabbai of the late Lubavicher Rebbe.

Page 577
"A Good Laugh"
by S. Ansky

The ability of the Baal Shem either to perceive future events or to somehow influence them is a common theme in the tales about him. Here the many deprivations of the boy and girl are in the end rewarded precisely in the form of the mock blessings given them at their wedding by the innkeeper and his wife, who were responsible for much of their suffering, while the latter are punished for their evil by losing their inn. Although this tale does not appear in *Shivhei ha-Besht*, it is a well-known story associated with the Baal Shem, and another version of it by I. L. Peretz, entitled "The Wedding Gift," can be found in *The Book of Fire*, translated by Joseph Leftwich, pp. 91–98. A parallel motif is found in one of the tales of Reb Shmelke of Nikolsburg, titled "David's Harp," which can be found in Buber's *Tales of the Hasidim* (1:182).

Page 585
"The Wandering of the Childless"
by Martin Buber

The breaking of a betrothal was regarded as one of the most serious sins, since matches were believed to be arranged by God: "Forty days before the formation of a child a voice goes forth out of Heaven to announce that this one will marry that one. And each match is as difficult for the Holy One to arrange as was the dividing of the Red Sea (B. Sot. 2a)." In addition, vows of all kinds were regarded as unbreakable, without the permission of the other to whom it was made. For the sin of rejecting his betrothed, the Hasid in this story was cursed with a barren wife. Finally Rabbi Jacob Isaac reveals to him the reason for her barrenness, and directs him to seek permission from the woman he has wronged. He meets with her and resolves the matter by agreeing to assist her poor brother in paying for the wedding of his daughter—a kind of poetic justice. Then he discovers that she was a spirit who appeared to him so that the matter could be resolved. The appearance of such spirits is a common motif both in medieval folklore and in hasidic tales. Almost always they return to earth to resolve an unfinished matter. It is the ability of the rebbe to perceive the reason for the obstruction that makes the Hasid's salvation possible. Such powers and abilities were commonly attributed to the hasidic masters, beginning with the Baal Shem Tov, who reported visions of ascents into Paradise, and of seeing the presence of figures such as Elijah and the Angel of Death. (See *Shivhei ha-Besht* 24, 41, and 114.)

Page 590
"The Burning of the Torah"
by Meyer Levin

This is a version of a tale that appears in *Shivhei ha-Besht*, known as "The Besht in the Messiah's Heavenly Palace" (*In Praise of the Baal Shem Tov* 41, pp. 54–58). On several occasions the Baal Shem is described as making a spiritual ascent into Paradise to argue the case of those on earth. See, for example, "The Bride in Her Grave" in *Classic Hasidic Tales*, pp. 45–57. Note the parallels in Levin's version to the story of Job. In the original the role of Satan is not as pronounced, although an angel does place a lock on a gate to prevent the entrance of the Baal Shem into Paradise. But in the original, the prayers failed to ascend because the people did not pray with the proper *kavanah*—spiritual intensity—rather than because of a plot of Satan.

Page 594
"The Story of the He-Goat Who Couldn't Say No"
by I. L. Peretz

This story is based on a tale attributed to Reb Menahem Mendel of Kotzk, a version of which appears in Martin Buber's *Tales of the Hasidim: The Later Masters*, pp. 288–89, as "The Sacred Goat." This tale and a discussion of its relationship to that of Peretz will be found on pp. 88–89. The horn of the ram that reaches the heavens recalls the *shofar*, the ram's horn that is blown on the New Year. It is believed that this blast is also heard in heaven. The legend giving the reasons for the custom of blowing the ram's horn is found in *Pirke de Rabbi Eliezer* 46.

Page 597
"A Messiah in Every Generation"
by Jiri Langer

The belief that there is a potential Messiah in every generation derives from the tradition of the two Messiahs, Messiah ben Joseph and Messiah ben David. Since according to one tradition the Messiah will become a martyr and according to another he will bring in the End of Days, two separate traditions rose up. The Messiah who will be martyred is known as Messiah ben Joseph. It is he who is the potential Messiah in his generation. If the conditions are right, and this *tzaddik* is righteous enough, he will have the opportunity to pave the way for the heavenly Messiah. If the conditions are not right, then the role is taken up by another potential Messiah in the next generation. This tale by Jiri Langer, from *Nine Gates to the Chassidic Mysteries*, pp. 34–35, describes the fate of one of these potential Messiah ben Josephs, who is tricked by Satan, disguised as a beautiful woman. He is trapped into choosing to be alone with this woman, thus contradicting the talmudic dictum that a man may not be alone in a room with a woman who is not his wife for as long as a minute (Mishnah Kid. 80b). Satan often comes in disguise to trick righteous Jews, and Hasids in particular, since the righteousness of the Hasidim endangers Satan's position, and could hasten the coming of the Messiah. In B. Kid. 81a "Satan appeared to Rabbi Meir in the appearance of a woman standing on the opposite side of the river. As there was no ferry, he seized the rope and proceeded across. When he had reached halfway along the rope, Satan let him go, by resuming his normal shape, saying: 'Had they not proclaimed in heaven "Take heed of Rabbi Meir and his learning," I would have destroyed you as a worthless thing.' " In one hasidic collection, *Noster Teenah* (15), the fast on the Ninth of Ab of the saintly Rabbi Jacob Joseph of Polonnoye is broken when Satan disguises himself as a student, who convinces him that his mourning is so extreme that he ought interrupt the fast in order not to commit suicide. When he had done this, the rabbi realized that he had been tricked, and that the student must certainly be a demon. He then said: "Depart, impure one!" and the student, who was in fact a demon, vanished. See *Mimekor Yisrael* 2·978–79

Page 598
"Daughter of Heaven"
by Pascal Thémanlys

In addition to legends about the Baal Shem, there are also to be found in *Shivhei ha-Besht* legends of other rebbes, including Rabbi Adam, the precursor of the Baal Shem; Rabbi Gershon, the Besht's brother-in-law; the Great Maggid (Rabbi Dov Baer); and the Besht's disciple, Rabbi Jacob Joseph, and his son, who was known as Abraham the Angel. This story by Thémanlys links together a variety of legends concerning Abraham the Angel and his wife, who was herself recognized as a visionary of great spiritual accomplishment. Some of these legends include *Shivhei ha-Besht*, 72-75 (pp. 91-98 in the English translation, *In Praise of the Baal Shem Tov*). Because of his intense piety and short life, Rabbi Jacob Joseph's son Abraham became known as the Angel, as if he had been an angel incarnated in this world for a short time. Abraham's *drash* on *The righteous shall flourish like the palm tree* (Ps. 92:12), in which he describes two kinds of righteous men, one "like a cedar tree, which bears no fruit," and the other like "a palm tree" who "bears much fruit," echoes a dream attributed to his namesake, the Patriarch Abraham, in a fragmentary legend about Abraham's journey in Egypt, based on Gen. 20, which was found at Qumran: "The first night after we had arrived in Egypt, I, Abram, had a dream of a cedar and a palm tree. Some men came and tried to cut down and uproot the cedar, leaving the palm tree on its own. But the palm tree cried out, 'Do not cut down the cedar. Whoever fells it will be cursed.' So the cedar was spared because of the palm tree." (See *Apocrypha: Jewish Literature of the Hellenistic Age* by Nicholas de Lange, p. 62.) Here the cedar symbolizes Abraham, and the palm Sarah, who at that point seemed infertile. But from the *drash* of Abraham the Angel it becomes apparent that like the palm tree Sarah would prove fertile.

Page 605
"A Bratslaver Hasid"
by Joseph Opatshau

It is the custom among the Hasidim of Rabbi Nachman of Bratslav to attempt, at least once in their lives, the journey to Uman, where Rabbi Nachman's grave is to be found. This journey usually involves great distances and obstacles, but has been persisted in by present-day Bratslavers, including those stationed in Jerusalem. The success or failure of a Bratslav Hasid in this quest is usually regarded as a sign from the spirit of Rabbi Nachman about the worthiness of the Hasid, although even those Hasidim who were unable to complete the journey are admired by the others for undertaking it. The description of the journey in Opatshau's story is very likely an accurate one, based on an account he heard. In 1980 two articles appeared in the Israeli newspaper *Ma'ariv* describing such journeys by present-day Bratslaver Hasidim. In one case Meyer Deutch was arrested as a spy and jailed for several months before being released; in the other a *baal teshuvah* (a Jew who has returned to the traditional fold), Moshe Shilge, a violinist, succeeded in reaching Rabbi Nachman's tomb with a large group of Bratslav Hasidim from around the world, and played hasidic melodies at the grave.

Page 608
"The Dancing of Reb Hershl with the Withered Hand"
by Leslie A. Fiedler

Throughout the Middle Ages the blood libel, accusing the Jews of using the blood of a Christian for the Passover seder, has been repeated, usually accompanied by pogroms in the Jewish communities. In this story the blood libel occurs in a hasidic community, who decide to send "the five men in whom was vested the wisdom of the Community" to a cave, so that at least they would survive the impending pogrom. The five take with them the body of the murdered child left in their community with them. This is the theme out of which grew the legend-cycle of the Golem. See the stories pp. 485-489 and their appropriate notes. In the cave the rabbis proceed with the Passover service, beginning with a discussion about the meaning of the biblical passage *And they despoiled the Egyptians* (Ex. 12:36). In fact, this passage posed rabbinic difficulties. In *The Fathers According to Rabbi Nathan* 41 it is explained by saying that "The wealth of Egypt returned to its place." Another interpretation is that in this way the Egyptians paid the Israelities for their centuries of labor in Egypt (B. Sanh. 91a): " 'Six hundred thousand men served them two hundred and ten years. Let them pay us for their labor at the rate of a *dinar* per day.' Thereupon mathematicians sat and calculated what was owing for their labor, and they had not calculated that due for a hundred years before Egypt was found to be forfeit for the sum due." The exegetical form of the discussion follows very closely that of the standard talmudic disputation. The assertion of the driver that "To hear the wisdom of Reb Hershl, the angels of the heavenly host have descended to the sill of this world" repeats the description of what occurs when Rabbi Joshua discussed the Mysteries of the Chariot with Rabbi Jose: "the ministering angels assembled and came to listen like people who assemble and come to watch the entertainment of a bridegroom and bride" (B. Hag. 14b). When the driver, who is Elijah in disguise, causes Reb Hershl's hand to be withered, and thus gives it the power to bring to life, it echoes motifs found in the Talmud, such as this one about a magical diamond that could bring the dead to life: "We had salted birds, and we wanted to see whether the diamond would bring them to life, so we placed the gem on them, and they became animated, and flew away with the gem" (B. Bab. Bat. 74). A similiar motif is found in the talmudic legend about Simeon bar Yohai and his son, Rabbi Eliezer; on leaving the cave in which they had been hidden for many years, they had no patience for human imperfection, and "wherever they directed their eyes, everything was consumed by fire" (B. Shab. 33b).

Page 618
"The Shortest Friday of the Year"
by Hayim Nachman Bialik

In order not to desecrate the Sabbath, observant Jews are careful to complete their Sabbath preparations before the sun sets and the Sabbath begins. At the time of the winter solstice, when the day grows short, it becomes especially difficult to complete the Sabbath preparations on time. In this tale Rabbi Lipa is a devout Jew who takes special pride in observing the Sabbath, and when he is unwittingly forced to desecrate it, he is devastated and prays that God should "perform a miracle for me and stretch the way home into thousands of miles. Let years and centuries pass and let me travel on and on." Instead "the sleigh carried him swiftly as if on eagle's wings," bringing the rabbi face to face with his congregation at the very moment they left the synagogue after saying the Sabbath blessings, and could observe him violating the Sabbath. Bialik recounts this tale in a satirical manner, in which fate seems to conspire against the rabbi to make him sin twice—once by riding on the Sabbath to the inn, and again when he wakes up and believes, mistakenly, that he has slept through the whole Sabbath, and thus leads him to arrive right in the middle of the Sabbath, a terrible humiliation. The rabbi has not really sinned, although he permitted himself to be influenced by the gifts he received for attending the circumcision, and into drinking too much. This illustrates the belief about the Evil Impulse that "In the beginning, the *Yetzer Hara* appears insignificant and thin as a cobweb, and finally it becomes as thick as a wagon rope (B. Suk. 52)."

Page 628
"Reb Yeshaiah Argues with God"
by Yehuda Yaari

This tale, which has an ironic edge, suggests that God treasures the anguish that some of his children experience in their efforts to meet the commandments. Reb Yeshaiah, like Rabbi Lipa in Bialik's "The Shortest Friday of the Year," treasures the Sabbath, but has great anxiety over whether he and his wife will have enough money to properly prepare for the Sabbath. God does provide a weekly miracle—every Friday, shortly before closing, the rebbe receives enough money to afford the cost of the Sabbath food. Reb Yeshaiah asks God to move the miracle up one or two days to relieve his anxiety, but God replies by denying his request and explaining that He treasures the rabbi's anguish. Such a relationship between God and man—intimate and enigmatic—is frequently recorded, especially in hasidic literature, as is the idea that miracles can be counted on. When the horse of the Besht was stolen, for example, he insisted, "The horse will be returned to me," which happened after a year (*Shivhei ha-Besht* 30).

Page 629
"The Laws of Partnership"
by Fishel Schneersohn

The principle by which benefits—including admission into Paradise—may extend to those whose participation was passive rather than active is established by the example of the tribes of Zebulun and Issachar, of which it is written in Genesis (49:13-15): *Zebulun shall dwell at the shore of the sea and he shall be a shore for ships, and his flank shall be upon Zidon. Issachar is a large-boned ass, couching down between the sheep-folds. For he saw a resting-place that it was good, and the land that it was pleasant; and he bowed his shoulder to bear, and became a servant under task-work.* It is Rashi's commentary on this passage that links the destinies of the two tribes: "Zebulun engaged in trade, and provided sustenance for the tribe of Issachar, while the latter engaged in the study of the Torah. That is what Moses said: *Rejoice, Zebulun, in thy going out, and Issachar, in thy tents* (Deut. 33:18). For Zebulun goes out for trade, while Issachar engages in the study of Torah in his tents." The extensive laws on the subject of partnership are found in the Mishnah, especially in Baba Batra and also in Baba Metzia. This parable concerns a Mitnagdid rather than a hasidic community.

Page 630
"Gedali"
by Isaac Babel

The conflict between the traditional ways, as symbolized by the observance of the Sabbath, and the need for change, as symbolized by the revolution, is here presented in the person of the old man Gedali, who is both an observant Jew and the founder of a Utopian International. The description of the Sabbath in the story, the memory of which Babel cherishes, reflects the traditional view of the Sabbath as God's great gift to the Jewish people. The transformation that takes place as the Sabbath begins echoes the belief of the arrival of the Sabbath Queen, who is said to descend every Sabbath. This seems to be the specific reference of "the young Sabbath ascended its throne." In the Talmud (B. Shab. 119a) the welcome of the Sabbath Queen is described: "Rabbi Hanina used to wrap himself in festive clothes towards evening on Friday and say: 'Come, let us go to receive the Sabbath Queen.' Rabbi Yannai used to put on festive clothes on the eve of the Sabbath and say: 'Come, O bride, come, O bride.' " In the Zohar (3:272b) the greeting of the Sabbath Queen is further described: "The Sabbath is a queen and a bride. . . . One must sing and rejoice at the table in her honor. One must receive the Lady with many lighted candles, many enjoyments, beautiful clothes, and a house embellished with many fine arrangements, for through this rejoicing one causes the Evil Handmaid (i.e. Lilith) to remain in the dark, hungry, crying and wailing, wrapped in mourning clothes like a widow. For when the one is fulfilled, the other is destroyed."

Page 633
"The Rabbi"
by Isaac Babel

The Jewish determination to maintain the traditional ways even in the midst of war and destruction are described in this story, a sequel to the previous one. Here the old man Gedali takes Babel to see Reb Motele of Chernobyl, who affirms the need to fulfill the commandments of the Sabbath even in the face of overwhelming opposition, where "the wilderness of war yawned beyond the window" and "the doors and windows of Hasidism . . . are smashed." The sense that the vision and accomplishments of Hasidism would remain despite this destruction, which has proved to be true, is stated by Gedali: "With empty eye sockets Hasidism still stands firmly at the crossroads swept by history's fierce winds."

Page 635
"The Rabbi's Son"
by Isaac Babel

In this, the third of three related stories (see "Gedali" and "The Rabbi"), Ilya, the son of Reb Motele of Chernobyl, is killed while serving as a soldier, a fate that radically contrasts with his background and apparent destiny as "the last prince of the dynasty." The contrast between Ilya's intended and actual fate brings home for Babel and the reader the depravity of war.

Page 636
"A Tale of Piety"
by Albert Goldbarth

Compelled by the Regent of Drovsk to burn their *talissim (tallitim)* and *tefillin*, on threat of death, the Jews obey the order after the Rabbi of Drovsk concludes that "we shall not murder ourselves who can simply whisper our Adoration in plainer and safer garb." In so doing the rabbi is supported by the principle of *Pikku'ah Nefesh* (Hebrew for "regard for human life"), the rabbinic term applied to the duty to save human life in any situation in which it is imperiled. It is a biblical injunction deriving from the verse *Neither shalt thou stand idly by the blood of thy neighbor* (Lev. 19:16). According to the Talmud it supersedes even the Sabbath laws (B. Yom. 85a). Thus for the Jews of Drovsk "the prayer in their hearts did not alter."

Page 638
"The Three Souls of Reb Aharon"
by Howard Schwartz

Reb Aharon is identified as one of the *Lamed-vov*, the Thirty-six Just Men. For a discussion on this legend, see the note to "The Prince Who Was Made Entirely of Precious Stones" by Rabbi Nachman of Bratslav, p. 664, and the following six notes. The principle of a struggle within the soul is suggested by the talmudic legend that two angels accompany a man home on the eve of the Sabbath, a good angel and an evil one (B. Shab. 11:9b). A similar notion is found in one of the tales of the Baal Shem in *Shivhei ha-Besht* (196), where it is stated that "angels were at the right hand of Jacob, our Patriarch, and demons were at his left hand. Angels were also on the right side of the Besht, and demons were on his left side." The talmudic legend of the two angels is abstracted in the Zohar (1:12b) into the notion of two guardians: "Along with the souls as they arise there appear many winged beings who fly about all over the world, and whenever a soul descends into this world the winged beings that issued together with it from that tree accompany it. Two accompany each soul, one on its right hand, and one on its left." The notion that it is possible to ignore such beings, as does Reb Aharon when he chooses to, is also found in the hasidic tale: "But the Besht refused to use the angels because they were holy, and he refused to use the demons because they were liars." According to the Midrash the 600,000 souls created at the creation of the world were also present at the Revelation at Mt. Sinai. The souls are also equated with the 600,000 letters of the Torah. See *Zohar Hadash, Shir ha-Shirim* 74d. Assuming that many Jewish souls were deprived of being born because of "the tragedies that have plagued the Jews in every generation," and specifically because of the Holocaust, there evolves the possibility of one person's bearing multiple souls. The identity of the angel with whom Jacob wrestled (Gen. 32:23-33) has been the subject of many interpretations. See the note to "Jacob at the River" by Joel Rosenberg, p. 656.

Page 641
"The Death of Rabbi Yoseph"
by David Slabotsky

The retention of the soul with its earthly identity and memory is one of the assumptions of rabbinic literature about the nature of the afterlife. According to the traditional belief, the soul of one who has departed hovers in this world for a period of eleven months, then departs for the World to Come. This is why the prayer of the *Kaddish* is repeated for eleven months after the death of a parent. The wagonmaster who bears "a loadful of snores on their way to the Kingdom of Heaven" echoes in a satirical way the role of the angel Sandelphon, who collects the prayers of the Jewish people and weaves them into a crown of prayers, which the angel then charms so that it rises of its own accord until it reposes on the head of the Lord (B. Hag. 13b and *Maayam ba-Hokmah* 58-60). See also "Heaven's Wagon Driver" by Péter Ujvári. The notion that Rabbi Yoseph attains immortality in a parable uttered by the Miracle Rabbi of Lublin seems one of the premises of Jewish literature, in which it is implicitly understood that the act of remembering brings a kind of immortality.

INDEX OF
TRANSLATORS

722

G

Ganen, Moshe—from Hebrew: Sadeh
Garber, Jeremy—from Hebrew: Agnon, Berditchevsky, D. Shahar
        from Yiddish: Ansky
George, Emery—from French: Gary, Memmi
        from German: Zweig
Ginsburg, Elliot—from Yiddish and Hebrew: Nachman
Goldberg, Isaac—from Yiddish: Pinski
Green, Jeffrey—from French: Thémanlys
Greenberg, Clement—from German: Kafka

H

Halkin, Hillel—from Hebrew: Feierberg
Handler, Andrew—from Hungarian: Kiss, Szabolcsi, Ujvári

J

Jolly, Stephen—from Czech: Langer

K

Kaiser, Ernst—from German: Kafka

L

Leftwich, Joseph—from Yiddish: Peretz
Leviant, Curt—from Hebrew: Bialik
Levin, Meyer—from Yiddish and Hebrew: Nachman
Levy, Stephen—from Judezmo: Sarano, K. Shahar
Louvish, Misha—from Hebrew: Navon

M

Malone, Pamela Altfeld—from Hebrew: Berditchevsky, Nachman, Smilanski, Yaari
Megged, Matti—from Hebrew: Megged
Muir, Willa and Edwin—from German: Kafka

N

Neugroschel, Joachim—from German: Lasker-Schüler, Werfel
          from Yiddish: Ansky, Kulbak, Mokher-Seforim

O

Omer-man, Jonathan—from French: Thémanlys

P

Pashin, Gertrude—from Yiddish: Einhorn
Picciotto, Robert S.—from Spanish: Goldemberg

R

Rappoport, A. S.—from Yiddish: Peretz
Riemer, Jack—from Yiddish: Nachman, Schneersohn
Robbin, Edward—from Hebrew: Unger
Roston, Murry—from Hebrew: Barash
Rothenberg, Jerome—from German: Buber
Rubin, Barney—from Hebrew: Agnon

S

Samuel, Maurice—from Yiddish: Asch
Sandbank, Tirza—from Hebrew: Appelfeld
Schwartz, Howard—from Hebrew: Megged, Nachman
Schwartz, Tsila—from Hebrew: Nachman
Shevrin, Aliza—from Yiddish: Aleichem, Peretz
Silver, Miriam—from Yiddish: Rapp
Singer, Isaac Bashevis—from Yiddish: Singer
Sloan, Jacob—from Yiddish: Opatshau
Spicehandler, Ezra—from Hebrew: Hazaz
Spiegel, Moshe—from Hebrew: Schneur

T

Thieberger, Frederic—from Yiddish: Rosenberg
Tobin, Yishai—from Spanish: Plescoff, Satz

U

Unger, David—from Spanish: Goldemberg

W

Waldrop, Rosemarie—from French: Jabès
Wiener, Leo—from Yiddish: Rosenfeld
Wiesel, Elie—from French: Wiesel
                from Yiddish and Hebrew: Nachman
Wilkins, Eithne—from German: Kafka
Wolf, Leonard—from Yiddish: Manger, Schwartz

Y

Yarmolinsky, Abraham: from Russian—Babel

Z

Zohn, Harry—from German: Herzl

NOTES
ON THE AUTHORS
AND INDEX OF STORIES

S. Y. Agnon was born in 1888 in Galicia, the southernmost district of Poland. He received a traditional religious education, and at the age of twenty left home for Palestine. Agnon's novels and stories became classics of Hebrew literature in his lifetime. Six of his books have been translated into English: *The Bridal Canopy, A Guest for the Night, Two Tales, In the Heart of the Seas, Twenty-one Stories,* and *Days of Awe.* The last is a collection of oral and written legends pertaining to the High Holy Days. Four of the six stories of Agnon collected here appear in their first English publication. They are "The Stars of Heaven," "Three Vows," "The Tale of Rabbi Gadiel the Infant," and "The Revelation of Elijah." "The Hidden Tzaddik" was first published in *Modern Hebrew Literature.* Agnon shared the Nobel Prize for Literature in 1966 with Nelly Sachs. He died in Jerusalem in 1970.

"The Hidden Tzaddik," p. 208; "The Stars of Heaven," p. 217; "Three Vows," p. 358; "The Tale of Rabbi Gadiel the Infant," p. 363; "Fable of the Goat," p. 459; "The Revelation of Elijah," p. 474

Sholom Aleichem was the pseudonym of Sholom Rabinovitz, who was born in the Russian village of Voronko in 1859. He began writing in Hebrew and Russian in his youth, but, influenced by the writing of Mendele Mokher-Seforim, he turned to writing in Yiddish. He became a great folk figure to the Jews of Eastern Europe, who read his work in the Yiddish newspapers. Many volumes of his stories and novels have been translated into English, including *The Best of Sholom Aleichem, Old Country Tales, Some Laughter, Some Tears, The Adventures of Menahem-Mendel,* and the novel *Wandering Star.*

"Eliyahu the Prophet," p. 471

S. Ansky was the pseudonym of Shloyme Zanvl Rappoport, who was born in Vitebsk, Russia, in 1863. He led a life of wandering, roaming the cities and villages of Russia, collecting folktales. *The Dybbuk,* which is one product of these travels, was the only drama he wrote. Ansky died in 1920, shortly before its first performance. His collected works appeared in Yiddish in fifteen volumes, and include stories based on themes of folklore and hasidic lore. The bulk of the folktales collected by Ansky have remained unpublished in a Russian archive, and when released are certain to constitute a major work in themselves.

"The Rebbe's Whip,". p. 382; "A Good Laugh," p. 577

Aharon Appelfeld was born in Czernowitz, Bukovina, in 1932. He was deported to a concentration camp in Transnistria during World War II. He immigrated to Palestine in 1947. He graduated from Hebrew University in Jerusalem, and from 1959 on his stories appeared in various journals. His central theme is the Holocaust, presented allegorically with highly symbolic characterization. Two novels, *Badenheim 1945* and *The Age of Wonders*, have been translated into English, as has a book of stories, *In the Wilderness*. Several other books are in the process of being translated.

"In the Wilderness," p. 160

Sholem Asch was born in Kutno, Poland, in 1880, where he received a traditional education and was introduced into general culture by his wife. His early stories depict life in the *shtetl*. He subsequently lived in Paris and New York, and published more than fifty books, including novels, plays, travelogues, and apologias. His books include *The Little Town, Salvation, Three Cities, Mottke the Thief*, and *Children of Abraham*, as well as a novel on the life of the false Messiah, Shabbatai Zevi, *Kiddush Ha-Shem*. Asch became embroiled in a bitter controversy over novels he wrote on Christian subjects, including *The Nazarene* and *The Apostle*. However, he is generally ranked as one of a handful of major Yiddish authors, along with I. L. Peretz, Sholom Aleichem, and I. B. Singer.

"From the Beyond," p. 246

Isaac Babel was born in Odessa in 1894, and grew up in the atmosphere of a lower-middle-class Jewish family. At the age of twenty-one he went to St. Petersburg, where he was encouraged by Maxim Gorky, who printed two of his stories in the magazine *Letopis*. During the Revolution Babel fought with the cavalry, then later operated a printing press in Odessa. In 1923 he published a number of short stories in periodicals, and their success encouraged him to publish two volumes of stories: *Tales of Odessa* and *Red Cavalry*. Although recognized in the Soviet Union as a major writer, he was regarded by the authorities with suspicion, and was permitted to publish little after 1930. Shortly before his arrest during the purges of the late 1930s he spoke of how he had become "a master of silence." The exact nature of his fate is unknown. He died in a concentration camp in 1939 or 1940. His *Collected Stories* is available in English, as are two other collections of his stories, *Benya Krik, the Gangster* and *You Must Know Everything*.

"Gedali," p. 630; "The Rabbi," p. 633; "The Rabbi's Son," p. 635

Asher Barash was born in Lopatin, Eastern Galicia, in 1889. Most of his juvenilia was written in Yiddish, the rest in German and Polish. At the age of sixteen, Barash left home and wandered all over Galicia. At that time he began to publish his literary works, first in Yiddish and then in Hebrew. His first poems and a long story appeared in Hebrew in 1910. In 1914 he moved to Palestine, where he taught in Tel Aviv and Haifa. He established himself as an important critic, but left his primary mark as a writer of fiction. He also retold medieval folklore and was a collector and reteller of Arabic tales. Examples of these tales have been translated as *A Golden Treasury of Jewish Tales* and *Arabic Folk Tales*. Some of his stories have been translated into English in *Though He Slay Me* and *Pictures from a Brewery*. He died in 1952.

   "Rabbi Joseph Della Reina," p. 408

Yehoshua Bar-Yoseph was born in Safed in 1912. He is one of the leading native writers in Israel. Most of his stories deal with the life of the "Yishuv," that is, the religious community which antedated the Zionist movement. His trilogy *Enchanted City* tells the saga of the Hasidim of Safed from the early part of the 19th century until the First World War.

   "The Fettered Messiah," p. 415.

Micha Joseph Berditchevsky was born in Mezibuz, Poland, in 1865. He lived in a hasidic environment, attended the famous yeshivah in Volozshin, and began at an early age to contribute essays and stories to Hebrew periodicals. He later also wrote in German and Yiddish. During the later part of his life he lived in Berlin and Breslau. Among his unique contributions are interpretative renderings of aggadic literature. Berditchevsky was also an important early collector of aggadic texts and folklore. The three-volume *Mimekor Yisrael*, available in English, collects much of this material. Berditchevsky's collected Hebrew works appeared between 1922 and 1926 in twenty volumes. He died in Berlin in 1921.

   "Ben Azzai," p. 280; "Illusion," p. 356; "Two Worlds," p. 570

Hayim Nachman Bialik was born in 1873 to a poor family in the Ukraine. He received the traditional Jewish training in Talmud. After establishing himself in literary and publishing circles in Odessa, Bialik translated classics of European literature into Hebrew, edited the Aggadah and the Hebrew poets of Spain, established the Dvir publishing house, and became the leading poet of the Hebrew renaissance. Before settling in Palestine in 1924, he wrote in both Hebrew and Yiddish. He died in 1924. *Aftergrowth and Other Stories* has been translated into English, as has a translation of his *Selected Poems*. Also of interest is *Bialik Speaks: Words from the Poet's Lips, Clues to the Man*, edited by Mordecai Ovadyahu.

   "Scroll of Fire," p. 233; "The Shortest Friday of the Year," p. 618

Rabbi Tsvi Blanchard was born in Rochester, New York, in 1945. He attended Washington University, where he received a doctoral degree in philosophy. He later taught philosophy and courses in Jewish studies at Washington University. He founded the Mossad Or Yeshivah, and presently is principal of the Ida Crown Jewish Academy in Chicago. His parables and hasidic tales have appeared in journals such as *Holy Beggar's Gazette* and *Webster Review*, and in the anthology *Imperial Messages*, as well as in the Conservative Movement's new Passover Haggadah. He is presently preparing a volume of his stories.

   "The Tale of the Ram," p. 152; "The Tale of the Palace," p. 368; "The Tale of the Garden," p. 444; "The Tale of the Spark," p. 446

Martin Buber was born in Vienna in 1878 and raised in Galicia in the home of his grandfather, Solomon Buber, a noted Hebrew scholar. It was here that he was first exposed to Hasidism. He studied philosophy and the history of art at the Universities of Vienna, Berlin, and Zurich. In 1900 he joined the Zionist movement and made the decision to dedicate his life to the cause of Judaism. At the age of twenty-six he took up the study of Hasidism, and in 1906 he published his first book, *The Tales of Rabbi Nachman*. Two years later he published *The Legend of the Baal Shem*. He later edited the classic collection of hasidic stories and tales entitled *Tales of the Hasidim* (Early Masters and Later Masters). In 1923 Buber published *I & Thou*, a major philosophical-theological statement about the relationships between man and man as well as between man and God. His later books on the religious message of Hasidism include *The Origin and Meaning of Hasidism* and *Hasidism and Modern Man*. Buber was also the author of one novel, *For the Sake of Heaven*, and of a book of short stories, *Tales of Angels, Spirits, and Demons*, both based on hasidic themes and legends.

"The Chest of Herbs and the Golden Calf," p. 167; "The Angel and the World's Dominion," p. 235; "The House of Demons," p. 492; "The Wanderings of the Childless," p. 585

Arthur A. Cohen was born in New York City in 1928. He is the author of the novels *The Carpenter Years, In the Days of Simon Stern, A Hero in His Time* and *Acts of Theft*. He has also published several works on the history of modern Jewish thought, including *The Natural and the Supernatural Jew, Martin Buber*, and *The Myth of the Judeo-Christian Tradition*. His recent book, *The Tremendum: A Theological Interpretation of the Holocaust*, was published in 1981. *In the Days of Simon Stern* received the Edward Lewis Wallant Award in 1973. Mr. Cohen presently lives in New York City.

"The Homily of the Roses," p. 311

David Einhorn was born in a small town in Russia in 1886. His first volume of poems, *Quiet Songs*, was published in Vilna in 1909. Einhorn has also published a number of books of essays on Jewish and international problems, and starting in 1920 became a regular columnist for the *Jewish Daily Forward*. His *Selected Poems 1904–1951* appeared in 1952. "The Flying Letters" appears in *The Seventh Candle and Other Folk Tales of Eastern Europe*. David Einhorn died in 1973.

"The Flying Letters," p. 166

Mordecai Ze'ev Feierberg was born in Novograd-Volynsk, Russia, in 1874. His was a devoutly hasidic family. He was tutored by his father, a *shochet*. His stories concentrated mainly on talmudic, philosophical, and hasidic themes. His father eventually drove him out of the house when his secular studies caused a serious conflict between them. He worked for a while as a grocer, until contracting tuberculosis. His literary career began in 1896 when he went to Warsaw. His first story appeared in 1897. His major work is *Whither?* which appears in English translation in *Whither and Other Stories*. He was planning an extensive narrative on the Baal Shem Tov when he died of his disease in 1899, and the work was never written.

"The Amulet," p. 376

Leslie A. Fiedler was born in Newark, New Jersey, in 1917. He taught at the University of Montana, and since 1965 has been a Professor of English at the State University of New York at Buffalo. He has published books of short stories, such as *Pull Down Vanity* and *Nude Croquet*, and novels, including *The Second Stone, Back to China,* and *The Last Jew in America*. He is best known, however, for his literary studies and critical essays, which include *The Art of the Essay, Love and Death in the American Novel,* and various articles in journals such as *Encounter* and *Partisan Review.* Jewish themes play an important part in Fiedler's writing, notably in *The Image of the Jew in American Fiction* and *The Jew in the American Novel.*

"The Dancing of Reb Hershl with the Withered Hand," p. 608

Laya Firestone (Seghi) was born in Kansas City, Missouri, in 1947. She lived in Israel, Wisconsin, Illinois, and Canada before returning to live in Missouri. She has worked as a Hebrew teacher and translator, and is the author of the Hebrew-language Introduction in the anthology *Voices Within the Ark: The Modern Jewish Poets.* Her translations from the Hebrew have included poets such as Yehuda Amichai, Gabriel Preil, Shlomo Vinner, and Nathan Zach.

"Rivka on Mount Moriah," p. 152

Wendy Laura Frisch was born in New York in 1956 and raised in Detroit. She attended the University of Michigan, and is presently employed as an editor and publication designer at the university. She has published a small prose collection, *Hard Times on the Outskirts of Eden,* and independently edits Red Shoes Press.

"Lilith Recollects Genesis," p. 129

Jeremy Garber was born in Montreal in 1953. He attended Washington University and Columbia University, receiving a degree in Hebrew literature. He presently teaches at Indiana University. His articles and translations have appeared in magazines such as *Present Tense, Midstream,* and *Shdemot,* and in the anthology *Voices Within the Ark: The Modern Jewish Poets.* "The Tale of the Duck" is his first story to be published.

"The Tale of the Duck," p. 518

Romain Gary was born Roman Kacew in Vilna, then part of Russia, in 1914. His father abandoned the family when he was seven years old. He was greatly influenced by his mother. In 1928 the family moved to Nice, France. He attended the University of Paris, where he obtained a degree in law, and returned to Poland for a diploma in Slavic languages. He served as a fighter pilot in World War II. His novel *Education européene* was published in France in 1945, and acclaimed as one of the best novels to grow out of the war. His subsequent books include *Roots of Heaven* and *The Dance of Genghis Cohn,* both available in English translation. He committed suicide in 1980.

"The Dybbuk," p. 498

Rabbi Marc A. Gellman is the rabbi of Congregation Beth Am, Teaneck, New Jersey. He is a contributing editor of *Moment Magazine,* and the author of articles on Jewish thought, midrashim for adults and children, and philosophy. He has written two books of modern midrashim, *Into a Night Garden* and *A Tent of Dolphins*, both as yet unpublished. He is receiving his Ph.D. and teaches theology at the Hebrew Union College.

"A Tent of Dolphin Skins," p. 173

Albert Goldbarth was born in Chicago in 1948 and has since lived in Iowa, Utah, upstate New York, and currently Austin, Texas. He is the author of ten volumes of poetry, of which *Jan. 31* was nominated for a National Book Award and *Different Fleshes* is the most recent.

"A Tale of Piety," p. 636

Isaac Goldemberg was born in 1945 in Peru. At the age of sixteen he went to Israel, where he lived for a year and a half on a kibbutz. He then settled in New York City. He presently teaches courses in Spanish and Latin American literature at New York University. His first novel has been published in English translation as *The Fragmented Life of Don Jacobo Lerner*, and he has also published a book of poems, *De Chepen a Habana*, translated into English as *Just Passing Through*.

"Staraya Ushitza's Rabbi," p. 400; "The Wandering Spirit of Léon Mitrani," p. 501

Miriam Goldman was born in Malden, Massachusetts. She attended Radcliffe, majoring in music. Her short stories have been published in the O. Henry Prize collections and other anthologies, and she has received the Quill Award for Fiction. She teaches writing in prisons, and has recently completed her first novel, *The Magic Amethyst*.

"The Magic Spark," p. 447

Ladislav Grosman was born in 1921 in Humenne, Slovakia. He lived in Prague from the end of World War II until 1968. He studied philosophy and worked in bookshops and publishing houses. He has written several dozen stories and novels, the most famous of which is *The Shop on Main Street*, the film version of which won an Academy Award in 1966. Other books include *The Bride, Uncle David's Date, Head Against the Wall*, and *To Fly with Broken Wings*.

"The Fleeting Rainbow," p. 140

Moshe ben Yitzhak HaPardesan is the pseudonym for an American scholar who teaches in Jerusalem. He is presently completing a critical text of *Midrash Tanhuma*. These are the first of his modern midrashim to be published.

"The Seven Lights of the Lamp," p. 111; "The Third Tablet of the Covenant," p. 164; "The Four Who Sought to Reenter the Garden," p. 279

Hayim Hazaz was born in the Ukraine in 1898, where he was educated and witnessed the Bolshevik Revolution. He left Russia for Paris and Constantinople and settled in Palestine in 1931. He was soon recognized as one of the major writers of the new generation of Hebrew writers. Two of his novels, *Mori Sa'id* and *Gates of Bronze*, have been translated into English. He also wrote many stories on biblical episodes. Hazaz died in Jerusalem in 1972.

"Yaish Meets the Angels," p. 236

Cecil Helman was born in 1944 in Cape Town, South Africa, the grandson of rabbis. He graduated as a medical doctor at the University of Cape Town in 1967. Since then he has been self-exiled from South Africa and has lived in London. He has studied anthropology at the University of London, and at various times he has been a ship's doctor, illustrator of children's books, picture salesman, astronomer, and museum guide. He is the author of *The Emperor's Aversion and Other Fables* and *The Exploding Newspaper*.

"The Ark," p. 144

Theodor Herzl was born in Budapest in 1860. He is the founder of the Zionist Organization and the modern Zionist movement. He was first a lawyer, but soon devoted himself exclusively to journalism and literature. He was the Paris correspondent of the *Neue Freie Presse* and later its literary editor. He wrote many comedies and dramas that were produced on the Viennese stage and elsewhere. Herzl's Zionism was crystallized by the Dreyfus case, with its anti-Semitic overtones. The creation of the state of Israel was, of course, the culmination of Herzl's dream.

"The Menorah," p. 182

Barry Holtz was born in Boston and was educated at Tufts and Brandeis. He is currently co-director at the Melton Research Center of the Jewish Theological Seminary. His poetry and essays have been published in many journals, including *Response, Midstream*, and *The Jerusalem Post*. He has coedited (with Arthur Green) *Your Word Is Fire: The Hasidic Masters on Contemplative Prayer*.

"Isaac," p. 151

Edmond Jabès was born in Cairo in 1912. Being Jewish, he had to leave Egypt at the time of the Suez crisis. He now lives in Paris, where he received the Prix des Critiques in 1970. Two of his books, *The Book of Questions* and *Elya*, have appeared in English translation.

"The Disappearance," p. 390; "Mirror and Scarf," p. 391

Dan Jacobson was born in Johannesburg, South Africa, in 1929. He went to Kimberly Boys' High School and to the University of the Witwatersand, where he received a Bachelor of Arts degree. Jacobson worked as a laborer on a kibbutz in Israel and was a teacher in London and a journalist in Johannesburg. He presently lives in London. His novels include *The Trap, A Dance in the Sun, The Price of Diamonds, The Beginners, The Rape of Tamar, The Wonder-Worker*, and *The Confessions of Josef Baisz*. He has also published collections of short stories, including *Inklings*.

"The Plague of Darkness," p. 157

Franz Kafka was born in Prague in 1883. Kafka took his law degree in 1906 at the German University of Prague and later secured a minor position with the Austrian government. During his lifetime only a small portion of Kafka's writings were published. Before his death, of tuberculosis, in 1924, Kafka requested of his friend and literary mentor Max Brod that he burn his remaining manuscripts. However, Brod published all of them, and later edited Kafka's diaries. Many of his letters and notebooks have also been published. There are several editions of his stories available, including an edition of his *Complete Stories*. His three novels, all unfinished, are *Amerika, The Trial,* and *The Castle*. His *Parables and Paradoxes*, from which all of his stories included here have been selected, is certainly the classic volume of parables to be published so far in this century.

"Before the Law," p. 119; "Paradise," p. 120; "The City Coat of Arms," p. 136; "Abraham," p. 146; "The Building of the Temple," p. 233; "An Imperial Message," p. 355; "The Coming of the Messiah," p. 407; "The Animal in the Synagogue," p. 461

Arnold Kiss was an orator, poet, and rabbi who lived in Budapest, where he died in 1946. Except for the story "My Grandfather," which originally appeared in *Ararat: A Collection of Hungarian-Jewish Short Stories*, edited by Andrew Handler, his work has not been translated into English.

"My Grandfather," p. 327

Zvi Kolitz was born to a famous rabbinical family in Lithuania. Prior to World War II he went to Palestine, where he was twice arrested by the British for suspected membership in the underground. During the war he was chief recruiting officer for the New Zionist Organization in Jerusalem. His book *The Tiger Beneath the Skin*, in which "The Legend of the Dead Poppy" appears, was published in 1948. He is also the author of *Survival for What?* and the author and producer of the Israeli motion picture *Hill 24 Doesn't Answer*.

"The Legend of the Dead Poppy," p. 529

Moyshe Kulbak was born in Smorgon, Lithuania, in 1896. He initially wrote poetry in Hebrew, but soon switched to Yiddish, publishing his first book of poetry, *Songs*, in 1920. He emigrated to Byelorussia and became associated with the Minsk group of Soviet Yiddish poets. He exchanged his expressionism for the only style acceptable to the Soviet regime, socialist realism, in his novel *Zelmenianer* and his comic epic *Childe Harold of Dissen*. Nevertheless, he was arrested in 1937 and sent to a slave labor camp, where he died in 1940. In 1956 he was rehabilitated by the Soviet regime and his books once more appeared.

"Lilith," p. 508

Rabbi Harold S. Kushner is rabbi of Temple Israel of Natick, Massachusetts. He is editor of *Conservative Judaism* and author of the books *When Children Ask About God* and *When Bad Things Happen to Good People*.

"The Tree of Id," p. 127

Francis Landy was born in London in 1947. He lives in Brighton, where he is completing the book *Beauty and the Enigma: A Study of Some Related Passages in the Song of Songs*. His forthcoming books also include *The Tale of Aqhat*, translated from the Ugaritic, and *Poems by Avraham Shlonsky*, translated from the Hebrew. He edited the Ancient Egyptian, Ugaritic, and Mesopotamian sections in the book *Poetry of Asia*. He has also written a book of parables, *The Castle in the Kingdom*, as yet unpublished.

"The Castle in the Kingdom," p. 366

Jiri Mordecai Langer was born in Czechoslovakia in 1894. He was a friend of Kafka's and taught him Hebrew. At the age of eighteen he joined the Belz Hasidim, with whom he lived for five years. After returning he published a volume of hasidic lore, *Nine Gates to the Hasidic Mysteries*. After the Nazi occupation he entered Palestine as an illegal immigrant; there he published several volumes of poetry in Hebrew before his death in 1943.

"The Angel," p. 243; "The Woman in the Forest," p. 517; "A Messiah in Every Generation," p. 597.

Else Lasker-Schüler was born in 1876 in Elberfeld, Germany. She was prominent in the Berlin bohemia of the period 1910–1930, where she was regarded as a precursor of the Expressionists, and was notorious for her eccentric dress and behavior. She wrote plays and prose fantasies, as well as poems, mainly religious and confessional. She emigrated first to Switzerland, then to Palestine, and died in Jerusalem in 1945. *Hebrew Ballads and Other Poems* was recently published in English translation.

"The Poet of Irsahab," p. 135

Primo Levi was born in 1919 in Turin, and was trained as a chemist. His first book, *If This Is a Man*, described the Auschwitz extermination camp to which he had been sent by the Nazis in 1944. In *The Reawakening* he described his wanderings on the return journey to Italy at the end of World War II, when he also traveled through Soviet Russia. His collection of parables and fantastic tales, *Storie naturali*, was published in 1966 under the pseudonym Damianos Malabaila. His *Selected Poems* has recently appeared in English translation, and a translation of his stories into English is in preparation.

"Lilith in the Lager," p. 512

Rabbi Levi Yitzhak of Berditchev was born in 1740 into a distinguished rabbinic family. His father was rabbi in Hoshakov, Galicia. He became acquainted with the Hasidism of Israel ben Eliezer, the Baal Shem Tov, through Rabbi Shmelke of Nikolsburg. He studied under Dov Baer, the Maggid of Mezhirech. He won great renown as a rabbi, hasidic leader, and scholar. He was one of the few hasidic masters of his generation who did not oppose Rabbi Nachman of Bratslav. Rabbi Levi Yitzhak died in 1810. He is the focus of the book *Levi Yitzhak of Berditchev: Portrait of a Hasidic Master* by Samuel H. Dresner.

"The King Who Loved Music," p. 354

Meyer Levin was born in Chicago in 1905. He was educated at the University of Chicago and studied art in Paris. He worked in a Palestinian commune, where he wrote his first novel, *Yehuda*, and he served as a war correspondent in World War II. His books include *The Old Bunch, Compulsion, Eva, In Search*, and *The Settlers*. His tales of the Baal Shem and of Rabbi Nachman of Bratslav in *Classic Hasidic Tales* (originally *The Golden Mountain*) is one of the finest of such works available in English. Levin died in Jerusalem in 1981.

"The Book of Mysteries," p. 189; "The Burning of the Torah," p. 590

Jakov Lind was born in 1927 in Vienna. He was evacuated to Holland for safety in 1938. At the time of the German invasion he obtained false papers under the name of Jan Overbeek, returning to Germany as a deckhand on a Rhine barge. At the end of World War II he emigrated to Palestine, but returned to Europe a few years later. His first book, *Soul of Wood*, was an international literary sensation and was translated into fourteen languages. His subsequent books include three novels, *Landscape in Concrete, Ergo*, and *Travels to the Eno*, and three volumes of autobiography, *Counting My Steps, Numbers*, and *The Trip to Jerusalem*. The stories included here are from an as yet unpublished collection of parables entitled *The Stove*.

"The Story of Lilith and Eve," p. 133; "The Near Murder," p. 147

Bernard Malamud was born in Brooklyn in 1914 and educated at City College of New York and Columbia University. His novels include *The Natural, The Assistant, The Fixer*, and *Dubin's Lives*, and his collections of stories include *The Magic Barrel, Idiots First*, and *Rembrandt's Hat*. He has won the National Book Award for fiction. Selections from his novels and stories have been published in *A Malamud Reader*.

"The Jewbird," p. 464

Itzik Manger was born in 1901 in Bukovina, where he acquired a great interest in Yiddish folklore and German literature. His first collection of poetry was published in 1929. In addition to writing several volumes of poetry, Manger wrote several plays, including *The Megillah*, and one novel, *The Book of Paradise*, which is a satire on aggadic literature. After fleeing the Nazis, he lived in London until 1951, then in New York. He moved to Israel in 1967 and died there in 1969.

"Adam and Eve Return to the Garden," p. 130; "The Star and the Angel of Death," p. 250

Matti Megged was born in Poland in 1923 and was brought to Palestine in 1926. He was active in the Haganah and fought in the later Israeli wars. He is Professor of Jewish Mysticism and Literature and former Dean of Humanities at Haifa University. His works include poems, short stories, critical essays, anthologies, and translations of Genet and Beckett. He was awarded the Jerusalem Prize of Belles-Lettres.

"The Golden Gates of Jerusalem," p. 256

David Meltzer was born in Rochester, New York, in 1937. He had fully established himself as a West Coast Beat poet when he turned his attention to kabbalistic studies in the mid-1960s. He published the magazine *Tree*, concerned with kabbalistic revival, and *Tree Books*. His books of poetry include *The Dark Continent, Knots, Hero/Lil, Tens: Selected Poems*, and *The Eyes, the Blood*. The three fictions included here are from a book in progress to be titled *The Rabbi's Dreambook*. Meltzer has also edited an important selection of kabbalistic texts translated into English, *The Secret Garden*.

"A Song of Children," p. 313; "The Angel of the Alphabet," p. 392; "From the Rabbi's Dreambook," p. 516

Albert Memmi was born in 1920 in Tunis, where he spent his entire youth. During World War II he was arrested and interned in a forced-labor camp, from which he managed to escape. After the war he studied at the Sorbonne, where he received a degree in philosophy. Since that time he has taught both in Tunis and in Paris, where he now resides. His books of fiction include *The Pillar of Salt, The Scorpion*, and *Strangers*.

"The Unrecognized Just Men," p. 231; "The Holy of Holies," p. 232

Jerred Metz was born in Freehold, New Jersey, in 1943. He is the author of three books of poetry, *Speak Like Rain, The Temperate Voluptuary*, and *Angels in the House*. He has also written two plays, *Broker's Tip* and *Sousa*, and edited the book *Drinking the Dipper Dry*. He presently lives in St. Louis, where he is writing a biography of Earl Durand and is collecting material for an anthology of folk riddles.

"Angel Rolling the Heavens Together," p. 195

Mark Mirsky, born in Boston in 1939, is the great-grandson of Moses Mirsky, a Lithuanian Kabbalist. He was educated at the Boston Public Latin School, Harvard College, and Stanford University. He is a professor at the City College of New York and has published five books, *Thou Worm Jacob, Proceedings of the Rabble, Blue Hill Avenue, The Secret Table*, and *My Search for the Messiah*. He recently completed the study *Dante, Kabbalah and The New World* and is presently at work on the codex of the Rambaz, *Rayach Shel HaMaschiach*.

"The Generation of the Flood," p. 403

Mendele Mokher-Seforim was the pseudonym of Sholem Jakov Abramovitch, who was born in Kopyl, Lithuania, in 1836. He spent his boyhood studying in *yeshivot* in Slutsk and Vilna. He wrote both in Hebrew and Yiddish, but it was his Yiddish fiction that became both popular and controversial. The creator of a new style, he became known as the "grandfather" of modern Yiddish literature. His books include *The Travels and Adventures of Benjamin the Third; Fishke the Lame; The Parasite; The Mare*, a novella available in *Yenne Velt*, edited by Joachim Neugroschel; and the novella *Of Bygone Days*, available in *A Shtetl and Other Yiddish Novellas*, edited by Ruth Wisse. Mendele died in 1917.

"The Wandering of a Soul," p. 319

Rabbi Nachman of Bratslav was born in Medzibuz, Ukraine, in 1772, the great-grandson of the Baal Shem Tov, founder of Hasidism. He became a prominent, although controversial, hasidic rabbi; he began in the last years of his life to tell his Hasidim teaching stories that took the form of fairy tales and folklore. Five translations of Nachman's tales into English have been made, including Martin Buber's *The Tales of Rabbi Nachman* and Meyer Levin's *Classic Hasidic Tales*. For additional background information, see section III of the Introduction, "Rabbi Nachman of Bratslav: Forerunner of Modern Jewish Literature."

"The Tale of the Menorah," p. 111; "The Royal Messenger," p. 181; "The Spider and the Fly," p. 199; "The Prince Who Was Made Entirely of Precious Stones," p. 204; "The Portrait," p. 317; "The Lost Princess," p. 349; "A Letter," p. 353; "Harvest of Madness," p. 457; "The Prince Who Thought He Was a Rooster," p. 458; "The Seven Beggars," p. 547

Yitzhak Navon was born in Jerusalem in 1921, of a family that had lived in Jerusalem for more than three hundred years. He was educated in religious schools and at Hebrew University. He first taught, but in 1946 was asked to direct the Arabic department of the Haganah. In 1952 he was appointed the head of Prime Minister Ben-Gurion's office, and later headed the Department of Culture in the Ministry of Education. He was elected to the Knesset in 1965. In 1978 he was elected President of Israel. His books include *Romancero Sephardi*, a concert presentation of the sacred and secular songs of Sephardic Jewry, *Bustan Sephardi*, and *Six Days and Seven Gates*.

"The Six Days and the Seven Gates," p. 252

Hugh Nissenson was born in 1933 in Brooklyn, New York. He attended Swarthmore College. His books include *A Pile of Stones*, a collection of stories which received the Edward Lewis Wallant Award; *Notes from the Frontier*, a nonfiction account of life in a kibbutz; *In the Reign of Peace*, also a collection of stories; and *My Own Ground*, a novel. He is presently completing a second novel, *The Tree of Life*.

"Forcing the End," p. 258

Der Nister, the pseudonym of Pinhas Kahanovich, was born in 1884 in Berditchev, Ukraine. He received a traditional Jewish education but was also acquainted with secular Russian literature from an early age. His older brother, Aaron, was a Bratslaver Hasid. Aaron served as the model for the character Luzi in Der Nister's major work, *The Family Mashber*. I. L. Peretz assisted in the publication of his early work. In the period from 1906 to 1929, Der Nister (a term meaning "the concealed one" in Yiddish) wrote highly original mystical visions and fantastic tales. After 1929 he worked under the shadow of repression. He died in 1950. Several of his stories, as well as the novella "A Tale of Kings," are available in *Yenne Velt: The Great Works of Jewish Fantasy and Occult*, edited by Joachim Neugroschel.

"The Seventh Millennium," p. 185; "The Messiah at the Gates of Rome," p. 257

Joseph Opatshau was born in Mlave, Poland, in 1887. His father belonged to an old Hasidic family. Although he did not attend his religious classes, his father taught him religious lore. At fourteen he attended the commercial school in Warsaw and subsequently attended the polytechnic at Nancy in France. He went to America in 1907, where he completed his training as a civil engineer in 1914. His first story was pub lished in 1910, and altogether he published over three hundred stories. His novel *In the Polish Woods* placed him in the ranks of Yiddish literature. This novel and other works, including *The Last Revolt* and *A Day in Regensburg*, have appeared in English translation. Opatshau died in 1954.

"A Bratslaver Hasid," p. 605

Cynthia Ozick is the author of *Trust*, a novel; *The Pagan Rabbi and Other Stories* (nominated for a 1972 National Book Award); *Bloodshed and Three Novellas*; and *Levitation: Five Fictions*. A new novel, *The Cannibal Galaxy*, will be published in 1983. She has also published essays, poetry, criticism, reviews, and translations in numerous periodicals and anthologies, and has been the recipient of several prizes, including the Award for Literature of the American Academy of Arts and Letters. She lives in New Rochelle, New York.

"The Pagan Rabbi," p. 286; "Outfoxing the Fox," p. 310; "The Shawl," p. 535

I. L. Peretz was born in 1852 in Zamosc, Poland. Though raised in the Orthodox tradition, he also absorbed worldly knowledge. He was a prodigy, being advanced enough at the age of six to begin the study of the Talmud. He passed the bar in 1877, and for a decade he had a thriving practice in his home town. In 1890 he secured a position as a secretary to the Jewish community of Warsaw, a position he retained for the rest of his life. Although he experimented with Polish, Hebrew, and Yiddish, it was the last that was to become his chief literary medium. His poem "Monish," published in 1877, first demonstrated that Peretz was a literary craftsman. Before long, stories by Peretz began to appear regularly in the Yiddish dailies, and his popularity became immense. At his funeral in 1915 more than 100,000 mourners followed his coffin. Several collections of his stories, which were often based on folklore and hasidic legends, have appeared in English, including *In This World and the Next*, *The Book of Fire*, and, most recently, *Selected Stories of I. L. Peretz*.

"The Sacrifice," p. 243; "Kabbalists," p. 369; "The Hermit and the Bear," p. 373; "The Magician," p. 482; "The Golem," p. 485; "The Story of the He-Goat That Couldn't Say No," p. 594

David Pinski was born in 1872 in Mohilev, in White Russia. At the age of thirteen his parents moved to Moscow, where he studied both Jewish and general subjects. He played an active part in the early days of the Jewish Labor Movement, and brought Peretz into it. He also cooperated with Peretz in publishing educational books in Yiddish. He settled in New York in 1899, and became editor of the New York daily *Zeit*. Some of his plays, notably *The Treasure* and *King David and His Wives*, are well known, and he also published stories and novellas. A volume of Pinski's stories, *Temptations*, has been translated into English.

"The Temptations of Rabbi Akiba," p. 269

Jorge Plescoff was born in Santiago, Chile, in 1940. He has lived in Jerusalem since 1969. Plescoff is a poet, writer of fiction, and literary critic. He has published five volumes of poetry and edits the Spanish-language magazine *Cuadernos de Jerusalem*.

"Aleph/Bet," p. 397

Rabbi Yehiel Poupko is Area Director of the B'nai B'rith Hillel Foundation for the State of Illinois and has written on the Midrash and on the Holocaust. His writings have appeared in *The Third Jewish Catalogue* and *The National Jewish Monthly*.

"Midrash of the Alphabet," p. 394

Francine Prose was born in 1947 in Brooklyn. She attended Radcliffe College, went to graduate school for one year, and lived and traveled in India. She has taught creative writing at Harvard. Her first novel, *Judah the Pious*, was widely praised. Since then she has published three novels, *The Glorious Ones*, *Marie Laveau*, and *Household Saints*. She has also edited a book of Jewish tales, *Stories from Our Living Past*. She presently lives in upstate New York.

"The Arrival of Eve," p. 118

Nessa Rapoport was born in Toronto, Canada, in 1953, and currently lives in New York, where she works as a senior editor in a publishing house. Her stories have appeared in magazines such as *Shefa Quarterly* and *Lilith*, and in the anthology *The Woman Who Lost Her Names*. Her first novel, *Preparing for Sabbath*, was recently published. She is working on a second novel.

"Generation," p. 126

Nachmann Rapp works with the Yiddish-language department of the Israeli Radio Network. A collection of his stories, *Men in His Ways: Biblical Stories*, was published in English translation in 1973. "The Eden Angel" has been excerpted from the story "Man."

"The Eden Angel," p. 122

Rabbi Jack Riemer was ordained at the Jewish Theological Seminary. He was formerly rabbi of the Beth Abraham Synagogue of Dayton, and he is presently rabbi of Congregation Beth El in La Jolla. He edited the book *Jewish Reflections on Death*. He also coedited *New Prayers for the High Holidays* and is the author of numerous essays and reviews in Jewish and general journals here and abroad.

"In the End," p. 117

Lilly Rivlin is a seventh-generation Jerusalemite who now lives in New York. A feminist writer and filmmaker, she is presently working on a film about her family entitled *The Tribe*. She has also done extensive research on the legends associated with Lilith, and published a famous article on Lilith in *Ms.* magazine.

"In the Beginning," p. 115

Joel Rosenberg teaches Hebrew language and literature at Tufts University. His poetry and essays have appeared in *Response*, *Moment*, *National Jewish Monthly*, and other publications, and in anthologies such as *Voices Within the Ark: The Modern Jewish Poets* and *The Big Book of Jewish Humor*. He is currently writing a book on political allegory in the Bible. A first book of his poems, *The Violin Tree*, will appear in the near future.

"Jacob at the River," p. 155

Rabbi Yudl (Yehuda) Rosenberg was born in 1865 in Skarishev, Poland, into an important family of hasidic rabbis. He was a child prodigy and was known as the Skarishever Ilui. At seventeen he moved to Tarle, and at the age of twenty he was ordained as a rabbi. He was a rabbinical judge and teacher in Lublin, Warsaw, and Lodz. In 1912 he was invited by the Polish Jews of Toronto, Canada, to become their rabbi, and from there he moved to Montreal, where he became the Chief Rabbinic Judge of the Association of Orthodox Congregations of Montreal. He was the author of many rabbinic works and translated the Zohar from Aramaic into Hebrew. He is best known for his folk material, some written in Hebrew, but most in Yiddish, which includes *The Book of Elijah the Prophet, The Book of Raphael the Angel, The Wonders of the Maharal of Prague, The Splendor of the Maharal of Shpole,* and *The Chronicles of Solomon the King.* Rosenberg said that the original manuscript of the Golem stories came from a group of writings which a relative of his, a bookseller, found in the city library of Metz, written by the son-in-law of Rabbi Judah Loew of Prague, Rabbi Yitzhak Katz. Modern critics such as Gershom Scholem, Dov Sadan, Yossi Ðan, and others have cast doubts on this claim.

"How the Golem Was Created," p. 486; "The End of the Golem," p. 488

Morris Rosenfeld was a Yiddish poet born in Bolkshein in Russian Poland, 1852. He grew up in Warsaw and went to NYC in 1886, where he worked in a garment sweatshop. His first collection of poems was published in 1888. His sweatshop songs became famous and he became known as the "Poet Laureate of Labor." He published twenty volumes of poems and also wrote biographies of Judah Halevi and Henrich Heine. Rosenfeld died in 1923.

Jerome Rothenberg was born in New York City in 1929. He is the author of more than a dozen books of poetry, several books of translations, and four major anthologies. His books of poetry include *Poems for the Game of Silence, Poland/1931,* and *Vienna Blood.* His anthologies include *Technicians of the Sacred, Shaking the Pumpkin, America, A Prophecy,* and *A Big Jewish Book.*

"The Alphabet Came to Me," p. 399

Pinhas Sadeh was born in Lvov in 1929 and taken to Palestine in 1934. He has published poems, stories, and literary articles, and is presently one of the most respected literary figures in Israel. His fiction includes the novella *The Death of Abimelech* and the novel *Life As a Parable,* both of which have been translated into English.

"The Tale of the Lucky Daaz," p. 538

Alfredo Sarano was born in Aydin, Turkey, in 1906. In 1912 he moved with his family to Rhodes. In 1926 he went to study at the University of Bocconi in Milan, Italy, from which he received his doctorate in economics. For twenty-five years he served as Secretary-General of the Jewish Community of Milan. Dr. Sarano emigrated to Israel in 1969 and presently lives in Bene Brak, where he is writing his memoirs and a history of the Jews of Milan.

"The Wager and the Tiny Shining Star," p. 539

Mario Satz was born in 1944 in Buenos Aires, where he lived until 1966. He then traveled throughout various European countries, and settled in Jerusalem in 1970. There he completed the first volumes of a series called *Planetarium*. These are *Sol* and *Luna*, the first of which has appeared in English translation.

"The Number of the Name," p. 400

Rabbi Zalman Schachter was born in Zolkiew, Poland. He was raised in Vienna, Austria, and was interned as a youngster by the Vichy French government, and came via Belgium, Algeria, Morocco, and the West Indies to the Lubavitcher Yeshiva in the United States, where he was ordained in 1947. He is widely recognized as a rebbe in the classic mold. He has taught at the University of Manitoba, Canada, and worked as a Hillel Foundation director. He presently is a professor in the Department of Religion at Temple University. His books include *Fragments of a Future Scroll* and *The First Step*.

"Challahs in the Ark," p. 540; "The Besht and P'ney Yehoshua," p. 574; "Reb Zusheh and the Dowry," p. 575

Fishel Schneersohn was born in 1887 in Kamenety-Podolsk. He was the great-great-grandson of Rabbi Mendel Lubavitcher. He was raised in his grandfather's house and received a Habad hasidic education. He was ordained a rabbi at sixteen. At twenty-one he left for Berlin to study medicine. After a brief period in Kiev and Warsaw after the First World War, he settled in Berlin in 1922. That year his book *Catastrophic Periods and the Young Generation: The Effect of Social Catastrophes on the Psyches of Normal and Abnormal Children* appeared in Yiddish and German. In 1927 his book *Human Society* appeared in Yiddish, Hebrew, German, and English. His fictional works include the novel *Hayim Gravitser*, from which "The Laws of Partnership" has been excerpted and adapted, and which was published in 1922. In 1928 Schneersohn published the novella *Karabod: The Wanderings of Abraham Itsye the Kirzhner*. His novella *Lady Cotterfield's Biblical Soirée* has been translated into English.

"The Laws of Partnership," p. 629

Howard Schwartz was born in St. Louis in 1945. He attended Washington University and teaches at the University of Missouri–St. Louis. He is the author of two books of poetry, *Vessels* and *Gathering the Sparks*, and of several books of fiction, *A Blessing Over Ashes*, *Lilith's Cave*, and *Midrashim: Collected Jewish Parables*. *The Captive Soul of the Messiah: New Tales about Reb Nachman* will be published in 1983. A new book of stories, *Rooms of the Soul*, has recently been completed. He is presently working on a novel, *The Four Who Entered Paradise*, and collaborating with Rabbi Zalman Schachter on a book to be called *Tales of Reb Zalman*.

"The Tree of Life and the Tree of Death," p. 128; "The Dream of Isaac," p. 149; "The Four Who Entered *Pardes*," p. 275; "The Cave of Machpelah," p. 276; "The Celestial Orchestra," p. 335; "The Tale of the Amulet," p. 339; "A Message from the Messiah," p. 434; "The Two Souls of Professor Scholem," p. 436; "The Golden Bird," p. 523; "The Three Souls of Reb Aharon," p. 638

André Schwarz-Bart was born in Metz, France, in 1928 to a family of Polish Jews who had arrived in France in 1924. By 1941 his parents had been taken in a Nazi roundup and deported to an extermination camp. Schwarz-Bart joined the Resistance, was arrested in Limoges, escaped, and rejoined the Maquis. After the war he worked in a variety of jobs, and later entered the Sorbonne. His first novel, *The Last of the Just*, was a worldwide success. He has since published a second novel, *A Woman Named Solitude*.

"The Legend of the Just Men," p. 218

David Shahar is a native of Jerusalem. He won the Prime Minister's Award for Literature in 1969 and was elected Chairman of the Society of Hebrew Writers in Israel in 1972. In 1973 he was awarded the Agnon Prize. His novel *The Palace of Shattered Vessels* has been published in English translation, as has his volume of stories, *News from Jerusalem*.

"On the Life and Death of Abbaye," p. 263; "The Death of the Little God," p. 383

Kamelia Shahar was born in Izmir, Turkey, in 1926. Leading a group of Zionist activists, she emigrated to Israel in November 1948. Since 1955 she has worked as a broadcaster and editor in the Judezmo section of Israeli radio. She presently produces a weekly radio program featuring Judezmo stories and songs, and collects Judezmo folktales for the Israel Folktales Archives.

"True Joy," p. 131; "The Poor Man and Eliyahu the Prophet," p. 480

Zalman Shneur was born in Shklov, Russia, in 1887, a lineal descendant of Rabbi Shneur Zalman, the founder of Habad Hasidism. At the age of thirteen he left for Odessa, where he received encouragement from Hayim Nachman Bialik. He moved to Warsaw in 1902 and was employed in a large publishing house on Bialik's recommendation. In 1904 Shneur moved to Vilna and joined the editorial staff of the Hebrew daily *Ha-Zeman*. There he published his first collection of poetry, his first novel, and a collection of stories. From the first Shneur wrote in both Hebrew and Yiddish, and continued to write in both languages all of his life. Eventually Shneur became the last member of the distinguished trio of writers who created modern Hebrew literature and brought it to full maturity. The other two figures are Bialik and Shaul Tchernichovsky. *Restless Spirit*, a selection of Shneur's writings in both Hebrew and Yiddish, has been published in English translation. Shneur died in New York in 1959.

"In the Beginning," p. 114.

Richard Siegel is the Director of Arts Services for the National Foundation for Jewish Culture. He is coeditor of *The Jewish Catalog*, *The Jewish Calendar*, and the recently published *The Jewish Almanac*.

"The Seventh Beggar's Tale," p. 566

Dennis Silk was born in London in 1928, and has lived in Jerusalem since 1955. He has published two books of poetry, *Face of Stone* and *The Punished Land*, and has also published stories and plays in various periodicals. In addition, he has edited *Retrievements: A Jerusalem Anthology*, and coedited *Fourteen Israeli Poets*.

"Temple-Builders," p. 233

Isaac Bashevis Singer was born in Radzymin, Poland, in 1904. Singer is widely recognized as the last great Yiddish writer, and received the Nobel Prize for Literature in 1976. In Poland he worked for the Yiddish press, and since 1935 he has been a regular contributor to the *Jewish Daily Forward*, the principal Yiddish newspaper in the United States. His novels include *Satan in Goray, The Family Moskat, The Magician of Lublin, The Slave, The Manor* and its sequel, *The Estate, Enemies: A Love Story,* and *Shosha.* His collections of stories include *Gimpel the Fool, The Spinoza of Market Street, Short Friday, The Seance, A Crown of Feathers,* and *Passions.* His *Collected Stories* was recently published to much acclaim. Singer has also published four volumes of memoirs, *In My Father's Court, A Little Boy in Search of God, A Young Man in Search of Love,* and *Lost in America.* He is also the author of many children's books, including *Zlateh the Goat and Other Stories, Naftali the Storyteller and His Horse, Sus, The Power of Light,* and *The Golem.*

"Sabbath in Gehenna," p. 185

David Slabotsky was born in 1943 in Montreal, Canada. He is the author of four books of parables, *Parables, The Girl Without a Name, The Wandering Jew,* and *The Mind of Genesis,* the last his collected parables. His work has been published in periodicals in Canada and the United States, and has been produced by the CBC television and radio networks.

"The Mind of Genesis," p. 396; "The Wandering Jew," p. 533; "The Death of Rabbi Yoseph," p. 641

Moshe Smilanski was born in Russia in 1874 and died in Israel in 1953. At the age of sixteen he migrated to Palestine and settled in Rehovot. He worked as a farm laborer and in time became an authority on agriculture. He wrote numerous novels, short stories, and essays on the life of the early settlers. He also wrote widely on Arab life.

"The Pangs of the Messiah," p. 418

Rabbi Milton Steinberg was born in Rochester, New York, in 1903. He was ordained by the Jewish Theological Seminary in 1928. He served congregations in Indianapolis and New York. His book *Basic Judaism* is a fine introduction to the subject. Steinberg's novel *As a Driven Leaf* is considered one of the best novels written using the talmudic period as a background. The four selections in this anthology are excerpted from this novel. Steinberg died in 1950.

"The Death of Ben Azzai," p. 280; "The Fate of Ben Zoma," p. 283; "The Fire at Elisha's Grave," p. 284; "Mysteries of the Chariot," p. 326

Michael Strassfeld is chairperson of the National Havurah Coordinating Committee, coeditor of *The First Jewish Catalog, The Second Jewish Catalog* and *The Third Jew-*

ish Catalog and *The Jewish Calendar*, and editor of a Passover Haggadah for the Conservative Movement.

"Isaac," p. 150

Aaron Sussaman was born in Brooklyn in 1948. He attended schools in New York and Oregon, and graduated from Reed College in Portland. After college he joined the army, and since then has taught English and had other occupations. He is the author of *The Flying Ark: Little Jewish Tales* and of two forthcoming children's books.

"The Rainbow," p. 144; "The Apocalyptic Chariot Race," p. 344; "The Messiah's Overcoat," p. 437

Lajos Szabolcsi was born in Budapest in 1890. From the age of eighteen he wrote for his father's newspaper. In 1915 he succeeded his father as editor in chief, and retained the position until the paper ceased publication in 1938. He sought to root out anti-Semitism, and took positions that demonstrated considerable personal courage. He published *A History of Modern Hebrew Poetry* and translations of medieval and modern Hebrew verse. He also wrote fiction on Jewish subjects, including a historical novel on the life of Bar Kochba, *The Wedding in Levelek*, and a historical drama on Josephus. He died in 1943.

"The Moon, the Mercenary, and the Ring," p. 489

Pascal Thémanlys was born in Paris in 1907, descended from an old Bordeaux family. A Zionist and a mystic, he believed in the reestablishment of Israel as Jewry's spiritual center. He settled in Israel in 1949, and cofounded with Joseph Milbauer the Association des Amitiés Israel-France. His works include *Figures passionées, Les merveilles du Becht, Grands d'Israel, des Pharisiens a nos jours, Influences*, and *Un itinéraire de Paris à Jerusalem*.

"Daughter of Heaven," p. 598

Dan Tsalka was born in Warsaw in 1936 and came to Israel in 1957. Tsalka has published poetry, a novel, and short stories. He has also edited a poetry series, a newspaper literary supplement, and an arts quarterly. A novella, *The Terrible Tale of Joseph della Reina*, can be found in *New Writings in Israel*, edited by Ezra Spicehandler and Curtis Arnson. In 1976 he received the Brenner Prize.

"The Apprentice," p. 481

Péter Ujvári was born in Tolcsva, Hungary, in 1869. His father was rabbi of Erekujvar, Slovakia. He was educated in various yeshivot until the age of twenty, when he became a journalist in Szeged. By the time he moved to Budapest in 1907 he was already well known. His books give a realistic picture of Jewish life in the late 19th century. After World War I he wandered from one central European country to another before he returned to Budapest. His most successful enterprise was the creation of a Hungarian-Jewish encyclopedia. His books include *Legends and Stories, Across the River* and *By Candlelight*, the last of which has been translated into English.

"Heaven's Wagon Driver," p. 333

Manasseh Unger was born in Sabno, Galicia, in 1900, the descendant of a hasidic dynasty. He lived in Vienna for five years, left to work in a Palestinian commune, and then returned to Poland where he was active as a Yiddish publicist and an official of the Yiddish Scientific Society (YIVO) in Vilna, Lithuania. He wrote hasidic stories and essays for the New York Yiddish newspaper, *The Day*, and published several books on Hasidism, among them studies of the Baal Shem Tov and Rabbi Nachman of Bratslav. The story included here first appeared in the March 1929 issue of *The Menorah Journal*.

"How the Rabbi of Kalev Freed a Song," p. 451

Penina Villenchik (Adelman) was born in New York and studied at Hebrew University, the University of Pennsylvania, and Pardes Yeshiva in Jerusalem. She teaches Bible and Jewish folklore in college and high school. She has coauthored *Riding the Nightmare: Women and Witchcraft* under the name of Pamela J. Williams, and has written stories and poems for *Shefa*, *Response*, and *Agada*. Ms. Villenchik is married and lives in Boston, where she writes, tells stories, and studies Torah.

"Before," p. 117; "The Palace of Pearls," p. 439

Arthur Waskow is the author of *Godwrestling*, *The Freedom Seder*, *The Bush Is Burning*, and *Seasons of Our Joy*. He is also the editor of *Menorah, A Journal of Jewish Renewal*. "The Garden of *Shir Hashirim*" has been excerpted from *Godwrestling*.

"The Garden of *Shir Hashirim*," p. 274

Franz Werfel was born and educated in Prague in 1890. He was a member of Martin Buber's Neo-hasidic coterie. He later successively became an adherent of anarchism, communism, and Catholicism, and finally, as a result of Fascist persecution of the Jews, he fled to England and became a devout Jew. He was regarded as one of the finest poets and novelists of his time. His novels include *The Song of Bernadette*, *Star of the Unborn*, *The Forty Days of Musa Dagh*, and *The Pure in Heart*, all of which have been translated into English. Werfel died in California in 1945.

"The Death of Moses," p. 174

Elie Wiesel was born in 1928 in the town of Sighet in Transylvania. He was still a child when he was taken from his home and sent to Auschwitz and Buchenwald. After the liberation he made his way to Paris, where he studied at the Sorbonne. His work as a journalist took him to Israel and finally to the United States; he now makes his home in New York City. His books include *Night*, *Dawn*, *The Jews of Silence*, *The Accident*, *The Town Beyond the Wall*, *One Generation After*, *The Gates of the Forest*, *A Beggar in Jerusalem*, *The Oath*, *Zalman: Or the Madness of God*, and *Testament*. *A Beggar in Jerusalem* won the French Prix Médici in 1969. He has also published two volumes concerned with hasidic masters, *Souls on Fire* and *Somewhere a Master*, and one volume on the Midrash, *Messengers of God*.

"One of the Just Men," p. 231; "The True Waiting," p. 438; "The Last Living Jew," p. 532

Yehuda Yaari was born in Poland in 1900. He settled in Palestine immediately after World War I. He worked in a kibbutz as a farm laborer, road builder, and cattleman, before joining the staff of the National University Library in Jerusalem. He traveled widely, first visiting the United States in 1928 as a student at Pratt Institute. Upon his return to Palestine in 1933 he joined the staff of the Keren Hayesod, serving first as head of its Information and Publicity Department and later as Secretary-General until 1955, when he entered the Israel Foreign Ministry. He has been Cultural Attaché in Stockholm, head of the Foreign Ministry's Cultural Relations Department, and finally Consul-General in Amsterdam. He has published many novels and collections of stories, including *When the Candle Was Burning*, a novel, and *The Covenant: Ten Stories* and *Prisoners of Hope: Ten Stories*, all of which have been translated into English. Yaari also published a Hebrew translation of the tales of Rabbi Nachman of Bratslav which was widely acclaimed. English versions of several of these tales have appeared in *Ariel* magazine. Yaari was a close friend and associate of S. Y. Agnon, Martin Buber, and Gershom Scholem, and played a major role in the literature of his generation. Yaari died in Jerusalem in 1982.

"The Seamstress of Safed," p. 527; "Reb Yeshaiah Argues with God," p. 628

Israel Zangwill was born in London in 1864. He attended London University. He became best known as an interpreter of Jewish life, and his books about the London Jewish ghetto, including *Dreamers of the Ghetto, Children of the Ghetto*, and *The King of Schnorrers*, have become classics. Zangwill was also a playwright and critic, and allied himself with Theodor Herzl in the Zionist movement. He died in 1926.

"Watch Night," p. 506

Stefan Zweig was born in Vienna in 1881 and was later educated at the University of Vienna. His literary career was interrupted by the outbreak of World War I, when his pacifism took him to Switzerland. There he wrote his antiwar play, *Jeremiah*. He became a voluntary exile from Fascist Austria, lived for a while in London, and then sought refuge in Brazil, where, depressed by exile and war, he committed suicide. The author of thirty-nine books, Zweig excelled as a novelist, biographer, poet, short-story writer, dramatist, critic, and psychologist. His books translated into English include his volume of stories *Kaleidoscope*.

"Legend of the Third Dove," p. 137

INDEX OF
LANGUAGES

747

Asher Barash
Yehoshua Bar-Yoseph
M. J. Berditchevsky
Hayim Nachman Bialik
M. Z. Feierberg
Hayim Hazaz
Rabbi Levi Yitzhak of Berditchev
Matti Megged
Yitzhak Navon
Pinhas Sadeh
Fishel Schneersohn
David Shahar
Zalman Shneur
Moshe Smilanski
Dan Tsalka
Manasseh Unger
Yehuda Yaari

Hungarian

Arnold Kiss
Lajos Szabolcsi
Péter Ujvári

Judezmo

Alfredo Sarano
Kamelia Shahar

Russian

Isaac Babel

Spanish

Isaac Goldemberg
Jorge Plescoff
Mario Satz

Yiddish

Sholom Aleichem
S. Ansky
Sholem Asch
David Einhorn
Moyshe Kulbak
Itzik Manger
Mendele Mokher-Seforim
Rabbi Nachman of Bratslav
Der Nister
Joseph Opatshau
I. L. Peretz
David Pinski
Nachmann Rapp
Yudl Rosenberg
Isaac Bashevis Singer

GLOSSARY

This Glossary includes Hebrew words and a few Yiddish and Aramaic words; titles of works referred to in the Introduction and the Notes on the Stories; and abbreviations used for tractates of the Talmud. It will assist those who are unfamiliar with the terms and titles they encounter in the book, but it is not intended to bring order to the variations of transliteration and pronunciation that inevitably occur when a hundred different authors, or their translators, have been brought together. The transliterations used in the Introduction and the Notes on the Stories are those judged to be the most common and readable, and the Glossary lists these forms. In addition, a few variations in transliteration of the same word, such as *beder* and *cheder*, are listed, and some words pronounced differently by Sephardic and Ashkenazi Jews, such as *tallit* and *tallis*, have been listed in more than one form; but for reasons of space, variations that will pose no problem to the reader have not been included. Conventions for capitalization and italics also vary somewhat from author to author, since Hebrew has neither. The Glossary lists terms and titles as they appear in the Introduction, in the Notes on the Stories, and in stories newly translated for this volume, but the reader can expect variations in previously published material.

Adam Kadmon the term used for the kabbalistic concept of the Primordial Man, which serves as an intermediary link between the *Ein Sof* and the subsequent emanations of the Divinity.

Adar the twelfth month in the Jewish calendar.

Adne Sadeh a legendary figure identified as one of the prior creations of God, before the creation of man. He was said to be attached to the earth by a long navel cord, and able to move only within the circle of this cord. When the cord snapped, the creature died. All such creatures, sometimes identified as plant-men, were said to have been drowned in the Flood.

Adonai the name of God that is used most often in prayer to substitute for the unpronounceable four-letter Name known as the Tetragrammaton.

Aggadah a term referring to the non-halakhic material in the Talmud, primarily of a legendary character. In a broader sense, usually lowercased (pl. aggadot), it refers to the post-biblical legends found in both the Talmud and the Midrash. In the broadest sense, it is the kind of legendary material found throughout Jewish literature.

agunah a woman who is forbidden to remarry because her husband either has abandoned her without a divorce or is believed to have died without any proof that this has occurred.

abizat enayim literally, "seizing the eyes." A term meaning illusion, delusion, or mirage.

Akedah the binding of Isaac by Abraham on Mt. Moriah.

Alenu prayer that proclaims God's sovereignty over the Jewish people. It is included in all three daily and holiday services.

Aleph the first letter of the Hebrew alphabet.

Alma d' Shikra kabbalistic term for World of Illusion or World of Lies. It is often contrasted with the World to Come, *Olam o' Emeth*, World of Truth.

Alphabet of Ben Sira a treatise written in the 11th century but attributed to a 2nd-century author.

Amidah the prayers also known as *Shmoneh Esreh* or the Eighteen Benedictions, which are found in all daily, Sabbath, and holiday services. This prayer is recited while standing.

amora (pl. *amoraim*) the name given to the rabbinic teachers in Palestine and Babylonia during the period after the completion of the Mishnah and the compilation of the Talmud (c. 3rd to 6th centuries). The discussions of the *amoraim* are recorded in the Gemara.

Apikorsim a term based on the rabbinic version of the Greek name Epicurus, the philosopher who concluded that it was preferable to concentrate on wordly pleasures, since body and soul both come to an end upon death. The term was used to refer both to heretics and to nonbelievers, and is still in use.

The Apocalypse of Abraham a text of the 2nd century C.E., extant only in the Slavonic version of a Greek translation of a presumably Hebrew original.

Araboth the highest realm of heaven.

Aron HaKodesh lit. "the holy Ark." The Ark of the Covenant, in which the *Sefer Torah* is kept.

Asmodeus the king of demons, a familiar figure in Jewish folklore.

Av. Avoth, a tractate of the Talmud.

Ayin a letter of the Hebrew alphabet.

B. Babylonian. When used before the abbreviated name of a Talmud tractate, as in B. Bab. Bat., it identifies it as referring to the Babylonian rather than the Jerusalem Talmud.

baal teshuvah one who repents of his sins. The term is also used to refer to Jews who come to embrace Orthodox teachings for the first time in their lives.

Bab. Bat. Baba Batra, a tractate of the Talmud.

Bab. Met. Baba Metzia, a tractate of the Talmud.

2 Baruch an apocryphal text also known as the *Syriac Apocalypse of Baruch*, written in the 1st century C.E.

bat kol a heavenly voice.

beit din a rabbinic court convened to decide issues relating to the Halakhah.

beit knesset a house of prayer.

beit midrash (alt. *beit ha-midrash*) a house of study. Traditionally next to the *beit knesset*.

Ber. Berakoth, a tractate of the Talmud.

Bereshith lit. "in the beginning." The first word of the Torah.

Besht, BeSHT acronym for Baal Shem Tov (lit. "Master of the Good Name"), the founder of Hasidism.

Bet the second letter of the Hebrew alphabet, and the first letter of the first word of the Torah, *Bereshith*.

beth hamedrash see *beit midrash*.

bimah the podium where prayers are offered.

Book of Jubilees a Hebrew text following the chronology of the Torah that was written between 135 and 105 B.C.E.

Book of Mysteries a legendary book said to have been given by Rabbi Adam to the Baal Shem Tov, which the latter sealed in a mountain before his death. Also known as the Book of Rabbi Adam.

Book of Raziel a legendary book given by the angel Raziel to Adam at God's command, in which he learned of the future generations. A book of the same title, *Sefer Raziel*, appeared in the Middle Ages; it consists of charms and spells and merely took the title of the legendary book.

brit (alt. *bris*) lit. "Covenant." The circumcision given to every male Jewish child on the eighth day after birth. The complete term is *brit milah*, or "Covenant of the Circumcision."

Cabbala see **Kabbalah**.

challah bread baked for the Sabbath and holidays, which is often braided.

chazan (alt. *hazan*) a cantor.

chedar (alt. *cheder*, *heder*) lit. "a room." It has come to refer to the schoolroom where Jewish studies are taught to children.

The Chronicles of Jerahmeel see *Sefer ha-Zikhronot*.

chupah a wedding canopy used in Jewish wedding services.

daven, *davening* Yiddish for "to pray." Refers especially to the intense prayers of the Hasidim, who, following the dictum of the Baal Shem Tov, attempt to *daven* with *kavanah*, or spiritual intensity.

dayan a judge in a rabbinic court.

Dayyenu a popular song in the Passover seder.

Di Mishpoche Mashber a two-volume Yiddish novel by Der Nister.

drash an interpretation of a passage of the Bible. Also the third level of *Pardes*, the system of interpretation of sacred texts, representing allegory.

d'var Torah lit. "word of Torah." A concise lesson in Torah, interpreting a passage in the Bible or Talmud or another sacred text.

dybbuk the soul of one who has died that enters the body of one who is living and remains until exorcised.

Ein Sof lit. "endless" or "infinite." The highest, unknowable aspect of the Divinity.

Ein Yakov a collection of the Aggadah of the Talmud, compiled in the 16th century by Rabbi Jacob Ibn Chabib.

Elohim one of the primary names of God, representing God's aspect of Justice, as Adonai represents the aspect of God's Mercy.

emeth truth.

Eretz Yisrael the Land of Israel.

Erev Shavuot the eve on which the celebration of Shavuot begins.

Eruv. Eruvim, one of the tractates of the Mishnah, with commentary in both the Babylonian and Jerusalem Talmuds. It deals with the laws concerning Sabbath restrictions and methods to remove difficulties relating to these laws by the creation of *eruvim*, or boundaries.

esha woman.

etrog the citron, one of the four species of plants carried and symbolically shaken as part of the Sukkoth celebration.

Etz Hayim lit. "The Tree of Life," a text written in the 16th century in Safed by Hayim Vital.

Even Shtiya the Foundation Stone, which, according to Jewish legend, holds back the waters of the Abyss.

Exodus Rabbah see *Midrash Rabbah.*

gabbai a tax collector or collector for a charity. Also refers to an usher in a synagogue, who is appointed to distribute honors in the service.

Galut the forced exile of the Jewish people from the Land of Israel; the Diaspora.

Gan Eden the Garden of Eden; also a term for the Earthly Paradise, in conjunction with the Celestial Paradise.

gaon the title given to the heads of the two outstanding academies in Babylonia, after the closing of the Talmud. In more recent times it has referred to outstanding scholars and religious leaders, such as the Vilna Gaon.

Gehenna the place where the souls of the wicked are punished and purified; the equivalent of Hell in Jewish legend.

Gemara lit. "to study" in Aramaic. The commentary surrounding the Mishnah. The Gemara and Mishnah together make up the Talmud.

gematria a technique used by Jewish mystics to discern secret meanings in the Torah. In this system each Hebrew letter has a numerical value, and the commentator seeks out words or word combinations that have the same totals, which are then regarded as linked.

Genesis Rabbah see *Midrash Rabbah.*

genizah lit. "to hide." A storeroom in a synagogue for the storage of worn-out sacred texts.

gilgul the transmigration of souls. The kabbalistic equivalent of the belief in reincarnation.

Git. Gittin, a tractate of the Talmud.

Golem lit. "shapeless mass"; see Ps. 139:16. A creature, usually in human form, created by magical means, especially by use of the Tetragrammaton. The best-known legends are connected with the Golem created by Rabbi Judah Loew of Prague to protect the Jewish community against blood-libel accusations.

Hag. Haggigah, a tractate of the Talmud.

Haggadah the text used for the Passover seder.

Halakhah the code of Jewish religious law, which also includes ethical, civil, and criminal matters. A halakhah (lowercased, with the plural halakhot) is an individual law.

hamsa Arabic for five, referring to the hand.

Hanukiah the special menorah for Hanukah, which has eight candlesticks and a ninth for the *shammash* (server).

Hasid (pl. *Hasidim* or *Hasids*) lit. a "pious one." A follower of Hasidism, a Jewish sect founded by the Baal Shem Tov. Hasidim are usually associated with a religious leader, known as a rebbe, as disciples.

Haskalah lit. "enlightenment." A movement that originated in central Europe in the 18th century; it encouraged Jews to broaden their knowledge of the world through secular studies.

havdalah lit. "to distinguish" or "to separate." The ceremony performed at the end of the Sabbath, denoting the separation of the Sabbath from the rest of the week that follows.

Hayyah a high level of the soul which only the elect can attain.

hazan see *chazan*.

heder see *chedar*.

Hekhaloth lit. "palaces." Refers to the visions of the Jewish mystics of the palaces of heaven. The texts describing these visions and the ascent into Paradise are known as Hekhaloth texts.

Hekhaloth Rabbati one of the primary Hekhaloth texts.

Hoshanah Rabbah the seventh day of Sukkoth, on which seven circuits of the synagogue are made, carrying the four species of plants. See *lulav*.

Humash lit. "a fifth." Any one or all of the Five Books of Moses.

Iyar the second month of the Jewish religious calendar.

Kabbalah lit. "to receive." The term designating the texts of Jewish mysticism. A Kabbalist is one who devotes himself to the study of those texts.

Kaddish an ancient prayer, written in Aramaic, sanctifying the name of God, which is recited by mourners as a prayer for the dead.

kaparot lit. "expiation." A ceremony performed on the day before Yom Kippur in which a person's sins are symbolically transferred to a fowl.

kavanah lit. "intention." Spiritual intensity, especially in prayer. A common saying is "Prayer without *kavanah* is like a body without *neshamah* [soul]."

kehillah the term used to designate an organized Jewish community.

kelippot a kabbalistic concept referring to the empty shells which represent the concentrated forces of evil and obstruction. An individual shell is known as a *kelippa* (alt. *klipa*).

Keren Kayemet the Jewish National Fund.

Ket. Ketubah, a tractate of the Talmud.

Kether Shem Tov a collection of hasidic teachings compiled by Rabbi Aaron ben Zevi Hirsh Kohen in 1784.

ketubah a traditional marriage contract, written in Aramaic, which lists the groom's obligations to the bride.

Kid. Kiddushin, a tractate of the Talmud.

Kiddush the blessing over a cup of wine, preceding the Sabbath-eve or holiday-eve meal.

Kiddush ha-Shem a novel by the Yiddish author Scholem Asch.

kippah a skullcap worn by observant Jews.

klayzl a small group that meet in the synagogue.

klipa see *kelippot*.

Knesset Haggedolah The Great Assembly of the Sanhedrin, the supreme religious and judicial body of the Jews during the Temple period.

Knesset Israel lit. "the House of Israel." The quintessential, mystical community of Israel.

Kol Nidre the eve of Yom Kippur.

Kotel lit. "wall." The retaining wall which is the only remaining section of the Holy Temple still standing in Jerusalem. It is also known as the Western Wall and the Wailing Wall.

Lamed-vov; Lamed-vov Tzaddikim according to the tradition, there are thirty-six (*lamed-vov* in Hebrew) Just Men in every generation, and the world continues to exist because of the righteousness of these *Lamed-vov Tzaddikim,* as they are known.

lilin demons who are the offspring of Lilith.

Lilith Adam's first wife in Jewish legend. Later she became identified as a night demoness who attempts to seduce men and strangle newborn infants.

Litvak a Jew from Lithuania.

luluv a palm branch. It is used along with the *etrog* (citron), *hadasim* (myrtle), and *aravot* (willow) in the Sukkoth festival.

Maariv the evening prayer service, recited after nightfall.

maaseh a tale or story, often a folktale.

Maaseh Beresbith the Work of Creation. The mystical doctrine of the secrets of creation.

Maaseh Book a Yiddish collection of tales from talmudic and medieval sources.

Maaseh Merkavah the Work of the Chariot. The mystical doctrine associated with the vision of Ezekiel.

Maasekhet Hekhaloth one of the Hekhaloth texts, from the 4th century, describing the heavens, God's throne, the angels, etc.

Maayam ba-Hokmah one of the Hekhaloth texts, describing the encounter between Moses and the angels in heaven.

Machzor a festival prayer book.

Maftir the final section of the Sabbath and holiday reading of the Torah.

maggid a preacher who confined his talks to easily understood homiletics, such as the Maggid of Dubno.

Maharal acronym for Rabbi Judah Loew of Prague.

manna the divine food which fell from the heavens to sustain the Israelites in their wanderings. It was said to assume the flavor of whatever the one who ate it wished for.

mari a schoolteacher; rabbi.

mashumid an apostate.

mazel luck.

Mekilta de Rabbi Isbmael a midrashic commentary on Exodus; it is believed to be the earliest midrash in existence.

melamed a teacher, usually of young children.

melammu Akkadiam word representing a way that gods appeared in Babylonian mythology.

Men. Menahot, a tractate of the Talmud.

menorah the seven-branched candelabrum described in the Bible and used in Temple days.

merkavah lit. "chariot." The merkavah is the divine chariot in the vision of Ezekiel.

Merkavah Mysticism Hekhaloth and kabbalistic texts concerned with the mystical ascent, especially by means of the divine chariot.

metivta Aramaic term for yeshivah, the primary institution for Jewish learning, dating back to ancient times. It is devoted primarily to the study of the Talmud and rabbinic literature.

mezzuzah lit. "doorpost." A small case containing a piece of parchment upon which is written the prayer that begins "*Shema Yisrael.*" This case is affixed to the right doorpost of a Jew's home, in accordance with the biblical injunction.

middoth lit. "rules." The middoth is one of the tractates of the Mishnah, the division Kodashim, which deals primarily with the laws pertaining to the Temple.

Midrash a method of exegesis of the biblical text. Also refers to post-talmudic Jewish legends as a whole. A midrash (lowercased, with the plural midrashim) is an individual midrashic legend.

Midrash Hagadol a 13th-century rabbinic work on the Pentateuch, emanating from Yemen and consisting mainly of excerpts from older rabbinic texts of the talmudic period.

Midrash Konen a post-talmudic midrashic collection with elaborate descriptions of *Gan Eden* and Gehenna.

Midrash Rabbah a major midrashic collection, consisting of a series of individual volumes on the books of the Torah and the Five Megillot (Song of Songs, Ruth, Lamentations, Ecclesiastes, and Esther). These individual texts are divergent in character and originate from various circles and periods, ranging from the early to the very late.

Midrash Ribesh Tov a collection of hasidic legends edited by L. Abraham, published in Kecstemet in 1927.

Midrash Tanhuma a major midrashic collection on the books of the Torah, dating from the 9th or 10th century. It exists in two different compilations, and is also known as *Midrash Yelammedenu.* (alt. *Yelamdenu*). It includes a great deal of messianic contemplation.

Midrash Tebillim (Midrash on Psalms) a volume of midrashim on the Psalms, dating from the 4th to the 12th century.

Midrash Vayyosha a medieval midrash in Hebrew about the legendary wars of Jacob and his sons.

Mikra in talmudic literature, Mikra is the equivalent term for Torah or Hummash, the first five books of the Bible.

mikvah (alt. *mikweh*) the ritual bath in which women immerse themselves after menstruation has ended. It is also used occasionally by men for purposes of ritual purification.

Mimekor Yisroel lit. "Fountain of Israel." An extensive collection of rabbinic legends and medieval folklore assembled in this century by M. J. Berditchevsky, published under the pseudonym M. J. Bin Gorion.

Minbab the daily prayer service, which is recited after noon and before sunset.

minyan the quorum of ten males over the age of thirteen that is required for any congregational service.

Mishnah the earliest portion of the Talmud, consisting of six orders, each divided into tractates. The Mishnah is believed to contain the Oral Law transmitted from the time of the giving of the Torah at Mount Sinai.

Mitnagdid opponents of the hasidic movement.

mitzvah (pl. *mitzvot*) a divine commandment. There are 613 *mitzvot* listed in the Torah. The term has also come to mean a good deed.

M.K. Moed Katan, a tractate of the Talmud.

Modeh Ani the prayer recited on waking, which thanks God for giving life for another day.

Moloch Hamoves the Angel of Death.

mosbol (alt. *masbal*) a parable, often used by a preacher known as a *maggid* to explain some portion of the Torah or subsequent rabbinic literature.

Motze Shabbat the period at the end of the Sabbath.

mussar ethical literature.

Nakhash Hakadmoni the primal serpent, one manifestation of the Evil One, or Satan. Primarily a kabbalistic concept derived from the encounter of Eve and the serpent in Genesis.

Ned. Nedarim, a tractate of the Talmud.

Nefesh one of the three aspects of the soul, representing the animal soul, or life itself.

neshamah a soul.

Nid. Niddah, a tractate of the Talmud.

Niflaot Maharal a collection of legends about the Maharal (Rabbi Judah Loew of Prague) and the creation and use of the Golem against the blood-libel accusation, published in 1909 by Rabbi Yudl Rosenberg.

nigun traditional chant to a prayer.

Noster Teenah a hasidic collection published in Tarnow in 1900.

notarikon a system of interpretation in which every letter of a word is taken as an initial or abbreviation of a word, used primarily as a kabbalistic technique.

Numbers Rabbah see *Midrash Rabbah*.

Olam ha-Nigun the world of song.

or light.

or lagoyim "a light unto the nations." A phrase used by the biblical prophets to describe Israel.

Otsar Midrashim a library of 200 minor midrashim, edited and annotated by J. D. Eisenstein and published in 1915.

Parashah the weekly portion of the Torah that is read aloud during Sabbath (and festival) services, so divided that the reading begins and ends on Simhat Torah, then begins anew. It is also known as a *Sidrah*.

Pardes, PaRDeS lit. "orchard," and also a root term for "Paradise." Also an acronym of a system of textual exegesis, based on four levels of interpretation: *peshat* (literal), *remez* (symbolical), *drash* (allegorical), and *sod* (mystical).

Pargod lit. "curtain." In Jewish mysticism it refers to the curtain that is said to hang before the Throne of Glory.

Parochet the curtain that hangs before the Ark of the Covenant.

Pes. Pesahim, a tractate of the Talmud.

Pesach the festival of Passover, commemorating the Exodus from Egypt.

peshat a literal kind of textual exegesis. Also the first level of interpretation in the system known as *Pardes*.

Pesikta de Reb Kahana homiletical midrashim on the festivals of the year, written in Palestine in approximately the 5th century.

Pikku'ah Nefesh the duty to save an endangered life, which temporarily overrides the other commandments.

pilpul a discussion of a fine point of the law.

Pirke Avot (The Ethics of the Fathers) the most popular tractate of the Mishnah, dealing with the ethical principles established by the fathers of Jewish tradition, from the time of the last prophet to the end of the 2nd century.

Pirke de Rabbi Eliezer a midrashic collection on Genesis and parts of Exodus and Numbers. Some parts of it are said to be as late as the 8th century, although they contain older elements.

rabbi originally a title for addressing a scholar or sage. It now refers to an individual who has been ordained.

Rambam acronym for the name of Maimonides.

Razi Li a manuscript of the 17th century Kabbalist Rabbi Abraham Yakhini.

Raziel, Book of a legendary book, said to have been given to Adam by the angel Raziel, in which Adam saw the history of the future generations. To be distinguished from *Sefer Raziel*, a book with the same title from the Middle Ages that is a collection of various spells and incantations.

reb an honorific term used among Jews to address a man who is a scholar. It is also used among Hasidim to address each other.

rebbe the term used for hasidic leaders and masters. It is a Yiddish form of "rabbi."

rebbitzen the wife of a rabbi.

remez lit. "a hint." The second level of interpretation in the system known by the acronym *Pardes*. It implies the perception that the meaning has moved from the literal to the symbolic level.

reshith lit. "beginning." This word is part of the word *bereshith*, meaning "in the beginning."

responsa letters sent between rabbis discussing halakhic decisions.

roite Yiddish for red.

Rosh Hashanah the Jewish New Year, which takes place on the first day of Tishri. Tradition says that the world was created on Rosh Hashanah.

Ruach lit. "spirit" or "wind." One of the three primary aspects of the soul, representing spirit.

sandek he who receives the honor of holding the child during the circumcision ceremony.

Sanh. Sanhedrin, one of the tractates of the Talmud.

seder the traditional Passover ceremonial meal, during which the Haggadah describing the deliverance from Egypt is recited.

Seder Olam a midrashic work mentioned in the Talmud, ascribed to a Palestinian *tanna*, Yose ben Halaftag of the 2nd century.

sefer book.

Sefer ha-Aggadah a collection of talmudic and midrashic legends compiled by Bialik and Ravnitsky in this century.

Sefer ha-Bahir an ancient kabbalistic text attributed to Rabbi Nehuniah ben HaKana, 1st century.

Sefer ha-Hasidut a collection of hasidic texts compiled by A. Kahana and published in Warsaw in 1922.

Sefer ha-Hezyonot lit. "Book of Visions." A collection of autobiographical notes assembled by Hayim Vital between 1609 and 1612, containing stories and dreams concerning Rabbi Isaac Luria and himself.

Sefer Hatmunah a kabbalistic work written in the 13th century.

Sefer ha-Iyyun a book ascribed to Rav Hamai Gaon, composed in Provence in the 13th century, containing a kabbalistic theory of supernal essences.

Sefer ha-Razim an early theurgical and magical work, composed in Palestine, perhaps at the end of the talmudic period, containing descriptions of the firmaments greatly influenced by the Hekhaloth literature.

Sefer Hasidim a book of ethical, mystical, and ascetic teachings by Judah ben Samuel ha-Hasid of Regensburg, written in the 13th century.

Sefer ha-Zikhronot a collection of various minor midrashim compiled by Eleazar ben Asher, dating from the 14th century.

Sefer Hekhaloth (3 Enoch or *The Hebrew Book of Enoch)* the best-known Hekhaloth text, which is also the longest and most complex, of eclectic composition.

Sefer Pardes a lost book reputed to have been written by Moshe de Leon, author of the Zohar, concerning the system of interpretation represented by the acronym *Pardes.*

Sefer Raziel a collection of incantations and magic spells dating from the Middle Ages. Not to be confused with the legendary Book of Raziel that Adam is said to have received from the angel Raziel.

Sefer Yashar a midrashic chronicle of biblical history from Adam to the Judges deriving from the 12th century.

Sefer Yetsirah (The Book of Creation) widely regarded as the earliest kabbalistic text, deriving from the 8th century and containing mystical numerical formulas.

Sefirot emanations, ten in all, through which the world came into existence, according to kabbalistic theory.

Selichot penitential prayers recited around midnight on the Saturday night preceding the High Holy Days, and continued until Erev Yom Kippur.

selihah lit. "forgiveness." The term used to apologize.

Sephardi Machzor a festival prayer book of Sephardic origin. The prayers included differ slightly from those in the standard Ashkenazi Machzor.

Shab. Shabbat, one of the tractates of the Talmud.

Shabbat (alt. *Shabbas*) the Sabbath.

Shaddai one of the names of God.

Shaharets the morning prayers.

shammes (alt. *shamash* or *shammash*) lit. "servant." The beadle of a synagogue.

Shavuoth the Feast of Weeks festival, which falls exactly seven weeks after Passover.

Shehakol a prayer said before eating certain foods.

Shekhinah lit. "to dwell." The Divine Presence, usually identified as a feminine aspect of the Divinity, which evolved into an independent mythic figure in the kabbalistic period. Also identified as the Bride of God and the Sabbath Queen.

Shema; Shema Yisroel Shema Yisroel are the first two words of the central prayer in Judaism: "Hear, O Israel, the Lord our God, the Lord is One." Based on Deut. 6:4–9.

Sheol the underworld limbo of the dead.

Shin a letter of the Hebrew alphabet.

Shir Hashirim Song of Songs.

Shivah a week-long period of mourning following the funeral of a loved one.

Shivhei ha-Ari (In Praise of the Ari) a collection of legends concerning the Ari, Rabbi Isaac Luria, compiled in the 16th century in Safed.

Shivhei ha-Besht (In Praise of the Baal Shem Tov) the earliest collection of legends about the Baal Shem Tov, founder of Hasidism, compiled by Rabbi Dov Baer, the scribe of the Baal Shem Tov, first published in 1814 in Kopys, Poland.

Shivhei ha-Ran (In Praise of Rabbi Nachman) a volume of the teachings and travels to the Holy Land of Rabbi Nachman of Bratslav, written by Rabbi Nathan of Nemerov.

Shivhei Rabbi Hayim Vital (In Praise of Rabbi Hayim Vital) a collection of tales and legends about Hayim Vital, the primary disciple of the Ari, written in Safed in the 16th century.

sblimazel a Yiddish term for one without luck, or one who is easily fooled.

sbochet a ritual slaughterer.

sbofar a ram's horn trumpet used by the ancient Hebrews in battle; it is sounded as part of some high religious observances.

Sbolem Aleichem a greeting among Jews meaning "Peace to you." The reply is *Aleichem Sholem.*

sbtetl a small rural village inhabited almost exclusively by Jews.

sbul a synagogue.

Sbulhan Aruch (of the Ari) a collection of the teachings of the Ari, Rabbi Isaac Luria, written down in Safed in the 16th century.

Sbulhan Aruch (of Joseph Caro) an extensive and definitive commentary on the laws of the Halakhah, written by Joseph Caro in Safed in the 16th century.

Sichos ha-Ran (The Wisdom of Rabbi Nachman) a collection of the teachings of Rabbi Nachman of Bratslav written by his scribe, Rabbi Nathan of Nemerov, and published in the 19th century in Poland.

siddur prayer book.

Sifra the tannaitic commentary on Leviticus.

Sifré the tannaitic commentary on Numbers and Deuteronomy.

Simhat Torah the concluding day of the festival of Sukkot on which the cycle of reading from the Torah is concluded and begun again.

Sippur Maasiot the Hebrew and Yiddish edition of the thirteen primary tales of Rabbi Nachman of Bratslav, edited by Rabbi Nathan of Nemerov, his scribe, and first published in Poland in 1815.

Sivan the third month of the Jewish religious calendar, during which Shavouth falls.

sod the fourth, mystical level of the four-level system of interpretation represented by the acronym *Pardes.*

Soferim one of the minor tractates printed in some Talmud editions at the end of the order of Nezikin.

Song of Songs Rabbah see *Midrash Rabbah.*

sopher a scribe, whose duties included copying and repairing the *Sefer Torah,* and, among the Hasidim, recording the teachings of their rebbes. A famous scribe is Rabbi Nathan of Nemerov, scribe of Rabbi Nachman of Bratslav.

Sot. Sotah, a tractate of the Talmud.

strammel a fur hat worn by Hasidim.

Suk. Sukkah, a tractate of the Talmud.

sukkab a booth in which Jews were commanded to live for seven days so as to remember the Israelites who resided in booths during their exodus from Egypt. Its roof must be covered with boughs, through which the stars are visible and which are not attached.

Sukkoth the festival celebrating the completion of the harvest.

Taan. Taanith, a tractate of the Talmud.

tallit (alt. *tallis;* pl. *tallitim*) a four-cornered prayer shawl with fringes at the corners, worn by men during the morning prayer services. It is worn throughout the day on Yom Kippur. A *tallit katan* is a small *tallit.*

talmid hakham a wise student or scholar.

Talmud the second most sacred Jewish text, after the Bible. The term "Talmud" is the comprehensive designation for the Mishnah and the Gemara as a single unit. There are Babylonian and Jerusalem Talmuds, which have different Gemaras commenting on the same Mishnah. The material in the Talmud consists of both Halakhah and Aggadah, and there are in addition discussions on philosophy, medicine, agriculture, astronomy, and hygiene.

Tammuz the fourth month of the Jewish religious calendar.

Tanach an acronym for the Bible.

Tanhuma Bereshith see ***Midrash Tanhuma.***

Tanhuma Ki Tissa see ***Midrash Tanhuma.***

Tanhuma Pekude see ***Midrash Tanhuma.***

Tanhuma Yelamdenu see ***Midrash Tanhuma.***

tannaim early talmudic sages mentioned in the Mishnah.

Targum (pl. **Targumim**) lit. "translation" in Aramaic. The translation of the Bible into Aramaic. The best-known translation is that of Onkelos. The Targumim often inserted aggadic material into the biblical translation.

tashlich a custom whereby Jews proceed to the nearest body of water on the first day of Rosh Hashanah, and cast off their sins by emptying their pockets and throwing the contents into the water.

Tav the last letter of the Hebrew alphabet.

tefillin phylacteries worn at the morning services (except on the Sabbath) by men and boys over the age of thirteen.

temurah a kabbalistic technique in which one letter is substituted for another. Also, Temurah is a tractate of the Talmud, of the order of Kodashim, concerned with the substitution of one species for another.

teshuvah repentance.

The Testament of Abraham the apocryphal story of the death of Abraham. It is preserved in two Greek versions, and there are also Arabic, Coptic, Ethiopic, and Rumanian versions. It was composed by a Jew, and possibly based on a Hebrew or Aramaic original. The exact date of composition is unknown.

Tetragrammaton the four-letter Ineffable Name of God: YHVH. The true pronunciation is believed to have been lost, and the knowledge of it is believed to confer great power.

Tikkun restoration and redemption.

Tisha b'Av the ninth of Av, traditionally the day on which the first and second Temples were destroyed. It is a day on which disasters have recurred among the Jewish people.

Tohu va' Bohu lit. "unformed and void." A phrase used in Gen. 1:2 to refer to the unformed state of the world prior to creation.

Torah the Five Books of Moses. In a broader sense the term refers to the whole Bible and the Oral Law. And in the broadest sense it refers to all of Jewish culture and teaching.

Torah Shlemah an extensive, 30-volume collection of aggadot edited by Menahem Kasher, published in Jerusalem in this century. It follows the biblical chronology.

Tosefta (pl. **Tosafot**) lit. "addition." The outer column of commentaries found in all editions of the Talmud, which are additions to the traditional commentary of Rashi. These commentaries date from the 12th to the 14th century and originated in northern France.

tsadik see *tzaddik.*

tsitsit (alt. *tsitsis*) the fringes of the prayer shawl.

tzaddik (pl. *tzaddikim*) an unusually righteous and spiritually pure person. Hasidim believed their rebbes to be *tzaddikim*. A *tzaddik ba-dor* is the leading *tzaddik* of his generation, sometimes identified with Messiah ben Joseph, who, if the time is right, will pave the way for the coming of Messiah ben David.

tzedakab charity.

tziruf a kabbalistic technique in which a word is rearranged into another—i.e., an anagram.

Tzobar the legendary gem which was hung by Noah in the ark to light it in the darkness during the forty days of the Flood.

Urim and Thumin the breastplate worn by the High Priest, which was believed capable of divination.

Vita Adae et Evae an apocryphal account of the lives of Adam and Eve after the expulsion from Eden. It is regarded as an essentially Jewish text with Christian interpolations.

Y. Jerusalem. When used before the abbreviated name of a Talmud tractate, it identifies it as referring to the Jerusalem (rather than the Babylonian) Talmud.

yad hand.

Yalqut Reubeni an anthology of aggadic commentary by the Kabbalists compiled by Reuben Hoeshke.

yartzeit Yiddish term meaning the anniversary of the death of a close relative.

Yeb. Yebamoth, a tractate of the Talmud.

Yebidab the highest level of the soul, possessed only by the elect.

The Yebidut a volume on hasidic counseling written by Rabbi Zalman Schachter.

Yeme Mabarnat a collection of the teachings of Rabbi Nachman of Bratslav compiled by his scribe, Rabbi Nathan of Nemerov.

yetzer lit. "impulse." *Yetzer Hara* is the Evil Impulse, and *Yetzer Tov* is the Good Impulse.

Yod a letter of the Hebrew alphabet, which appears in the Tetragrammaton.

Yom. Yoma, a tractate of the Talmud.

Yom Kippur the most solemn day of the Jewish religious year, spent in fasting and prayer. It is regarded as the Day of Judgment, on which God decides whether or not a person will be inscribed in the Book of Life for the coming year.

yomtov lit. "good day." An expression used by Jews to greet each other on various festivals.

zimzum lit. "contraction." The contraction of God at the time of the creation of the universe. A kabbalistic concept.

Zohar lit. "illumination" or "splendor." The central text of Kabbalah, written in the 13th century by Moshe de Leon, but attributed to the talmudic sage Simeon bar Yohai.

Zohar Hadash in printed editions the Zohar is composed of five volumes. The first three are the text of the Zohar as attributed to Shimon bar Yohai, the fourth bears the title *Tikkunei ba-Zohar*, and the fifth is entitled *Zohar Hadash*. This is a collection of sayings and texts found in the manuscripts of the Safed Kabbalists. *Zohar Hadash Ruth* is part of this fifth volume.

Zohar Sitre Torah verses from the Book of Genesis which were printed in separate columns, parallel to the main text of the Zohar.

SELECTED BIBLIOGRAPHY
OF BOOKS IN ENGLISH

I. BIBLICAL

A. Primary Sources (including Targumim)

Aberbach, Moses, and Grossfeld, Bernard, ed. *Targum Onkelos for Genesis.* New York: Ktav, 1981.

Bates, Sutherland, ed. *The Bible.* New York: Simon and Schuster, 1949.

Ben Isaiah, Rabbi Abraham, and Sharfman, Benjamin, trans. *The Pentateuch and Rashi's Commentary.* New York: S.S. & R. Publishing, 1949.

Cohen, A., ed. *The Soncino Books of the Bible.* Surrey, England: Soncino, 1947.

Cohen, A., ed. *The Soncino Chumash: The Five Books of Moses with Haftaroth.* London: Soncino, 1947.

De La Mare, Walter, ed. *Stories from the Bible.* New York: Knopf, 1961.

Drazin, Israel. *Targum Onkelos on Deuteronomy.* New York: Ktav, 1981.

Greenberg, Moshe, ed. *The Book of Job.* Philadelphia: Jewish Publication Society, 1980.

Hadas, Gershon, tr. *The Book of Psalms.* New York: Jonathan David, 1964.

Hertz, J. H., ed. *The Pentateuch and Haftorahs.* London: Soncino, 1947.

The Holy Scriptures. Philadelphia: Jewish Publication Society, 1955.

Kaplan, Aryeh. *The Living Torah.* New York: Maznaim, 1981.

Mitchell, Stephen, tr. *Into the Whirlwind: The Book of Job.* New York: Doubleday, 1979.

Orlinsky, Harry M., ed. *Genesis.* New York, Harper & Row, 1962.

The Torah: The Five Books of Moses. Philadelphia: Jewish Publication Society, 1962.

Zlotowitz, Meir. *Genesis.* New York: Mesorah Publications, 1977.

B. Secondary Sources (including Targum commentaries)

Albright, William Foxwell. *Archaeology and the Religion of Israel.* Baltimore: Johns Hopkins University Press, 1942.

———. *From the Stone Age to Christianity.* New York: Doubleday, 1957.

762

———. *Yahweh and the Gods of Canaan.* New York: Doubleday, 1968.

Alter, Robert. *The Art of Biblical Narrative.* New York: Basic Books, 1981.

Bever, Julius A. *The Literature of the Old Testament in Its Historical Development.* New York: Columbia University Press, 1922.

Bowker, John. *The Targums and Rabbinic Literature.* Cambridge, England: Cambridge University Press, 1969.

Buber, Martin. *The Prophetic Faith.* New York: Harper and Row, 1949.

———. *On the Bible.* New York: Schocken, 1982.

Driver, S. R. *Introduction to the Literature of the Old Testament.* New York: Scribners, 1895.

Eissfeldt, O. *The Old Testament: An Introduction.* New York: Harper & Row, 1965.

Frazer, James George. *Folk-lore in the Old Testament.* London: Macmillan & Co., 1919. Three volumes. Reprinted, New York: Hart Publishing, 1975.

Freud, Sigmund. *Moses and Monotheism.* New York: Vintage, 1955.

Gaster, Theodor, ed. *Myth, Legend and Custom in the Old Testament.* New York: Harper & Row, 1969.

Grossfeld, Bernard. *A Critical Commentary on Targum Neofiti I to Genesis.* New York: Ktav, 1981.

Gunkel, Hermann. *The Legends of Genesis.* New York: Schocken, 1970.

Hastings, James, ed. *Dictionary of the Bible.* New York: Scribner's, 1946.

Heidel, Alexander. *The Gilgamesh Epic and Old Testament Parallels.* Chicago: University of Chicago Press, 1949.

Heschel, Abraham J. *The Prophets.* New York: Harper & Row, 1955. Two volumes.

Kluger, Rivkah Scharf. *Satan in the Old Testament.* Evanston, Ill.: Northwestern University Press, 1967.

Leibowitz, Nehama. *Studies in Bereshit.* Jerusalem: World Zionist Organization, 1974.

Mendenhall, George E. *The Tenth Generation.* Baltimore: Johns Hopkins University Press, 1973.

Morganstern, Julian. *The Book of Genesis.* New York: Schocken, 1965.

Petuchowski, Jacob J. *Ever Since Sinai: A Modern View of Torah.* New York: Scribe Publications, 1961.

Sarna, Nahum M. *Understanding Genesis.* New York: Schocken, 1976.

Thieberger, Frederic. *King Solomon.* New York: East and West Library, 1947.

II. APOCRYPHAL

A. Primary Sources

Box, G.H., and Charles, R. H. *The Apocalypse of Abraham and Ascension of Isaiah.* New York: Macmillan, 1918.

Charles, R.H., ed. *The Apocrypha and Pseudepigrapha of the Old Testament.* Oxford: Clarendon Press, 1913. Two volumes.

———, trans. *The Book of Enoch.* London: SPCK, 1917.

Charlesworth, J.H. *The Odes of Solomon.* New York: Oxford University Press, 1973.
Enslin, M.S., and Zeitlin, S. *The Book of Judith.* New York: Ktav, 1973.
Fischel, H.A. *The First Book of Maccabees.* New York: Schocken, 1948.
Goodenough, E.R. *An Introduction to Philo Judaeus.* Naperville, Ill.: Alec R. Allenson, 1962.
Goodspeed, Edgar J. *The Apocrypha: An American Translation.* New York: Vintage, 1959.
Hadas, Moses. *The Third and Fourth Books of Maccabees.* New York: Ktav, 1953.
———, ed. *Aristeas to Philocrates.* New York: Ktav, 1951.
Lawrence, Richard, trans. *The Book of Enoch the Prophet.* Minneapolis: Wizards Bookshelf, 1976.
Leslau, Wolf. *Falasha Anthology: The Black Jews of Ethiopia.* New York: Schocken, 1951.
Metzger, Bruce M., ed. *The Apocrypha of the Old Testament.* New York: Oxford University Press, 1965.
Reider, J. *The Book of Wisdom.* New York: Ktav, 1957.
Robinson, M. James, ed. *The Nag Hammadi Library.* New York: Harper and Row, 1977.
Sanders, J.A. *The Dead Sea Psalms Scroll.* Oxford: Clarendon, 1965.
Stone, Michael E., trans. *The Testament of Abraham: The Greek Recensions.* Missoula, Montana: Society of Biblical Literature, 1972.
———, *Scriptures, Sex and Visions.* Philadelphia: Fortress Press, 1980.
Tedesche, S., and Zeitlin, S. *The First Book of Maccabees.* New York: Ktav, 1950.
Vermes, G., trans. *The Dead Sea Scrolls in English.* New York: Penguin, 1968.
Zeitlin, S., and Tedesche, S. *The Second Book of Maccabees.* New York: Ktav, 1954.
Zimmerman, F. *The Book of Tobit.* New York: Ktav, 1958.

B. Secondary Sources

Bamberger, Bernard J. *Fallen Angels.* Philadelphia: Jewish Publication Society, 1952.
Davidson, Gustav. *A Dictionary of Angels.* New York: Free Press, 1971.
Delange, Nicholas. *Apocrypha: Jewish Literature of the Hellenistic Age.* New York: Viking, 1978.
Goodenough, E.R. *By Light, Light: The Mystic Gospel of Hellenistic Judaism.* New Haven: Yale University Press, 1935.
Goodspeed, E.J. *The Story of the Apocrypha.* Chicago: University of Chicago Press, 1939.
Herford, R.T. *Talmud and Apocrypha: A Comparative Study of the Ethical Teachings in the Rabbincal and Non-Rabbinical Sources.* New York: Ktav, 1971.
Metzger, B.M. *An Introduction to the Apocrypha.* New York: Oxford University Press, 1957.
Rankin, O.S. *Israel's Wisdom Literature.* New York: Schocken, 1936.
Schmithals, Walter. *The Apocalyptic Movement.* Nashville: Abingdon, 1975.
Schurer, Emil. *The Literature of the Jewish People in the Time of Jesus.* New York: Schocken, 1972.
Smolar, Leivy, Aberbach, Moses, and Churgin, Pinkhos. *Studies in Targum Jonathan to the Prophet.* New York: Ktav, 1981.

Torrey, C.C. *The Apocryphal Literature.* New Haven: Yale University Press, 1945.
Wolfson, H.A. *Philo: Foundations of Religious Philosophy in Judaism, Christianity and Islam.* Cambridge, Mass.: Harvard University Press, 1962.

III. AGGADIC

A. *Primary Sources*

Braude, William G. *The Midrash on Psalms (Midrash Tehillim).* New Haven: Yale University Press, 1959. Two volumes.
———. *Pesikta Rabbati: Discourses for Feasts, Fasts, and Special Sabbaths.* New Haven: Yale University Press, 1968. Two volumes.
———, and Kapstein, Israel J *Pesikta de-Rab Kahana.* Philadelphia: Jewish Publication Society, 1975.
———, and Kapstein, Israel J. *Tanna Debe Eliyyahu.* New York: Jewish Publication Society, 1981.
Danby, Herbert. *The Mishnah.* London: Oxford University Press, 1938.
———. *Tractate Sanhedrin: Mishnah and Tosefta.* New York: Macmillan, 1919.
Epstein, I., ed. *The Babylonian Talmud.* London: Soncino, 1935–52. Thirty-six volumes.
Freedman, H., and Simon, Maurice, eds. *Midrash Rabbah.* London: Soncino, 1939. Ten volumes.
Friedlander, Gerald. *Pirke de Rabbi Eliezer.* New York: Hermon Press, 1970.
Gaster, Moses. *The Chronicles of Jerahmeel or The Hebrew Bible Historiale (Sefer ha-Zikhronot).* New York: Ktav, 1971.
———, *The Exempla of the Rabbis.* New York: Ktav, 1968.
Glatzer, Nahum N. *Hammer on the Rock: A Midrash Reader.* New York: Schocken, 1962.
Glick, S. H., tr. *En Jacob: Aggadah of the Babylonian Talmud.* New York: Hebrew Publishing Co., 1921. Five volumes.
Goldin, Hyman E. *Mishnah: Baba Kamma (First Gate).* New York: Hebrew Publishing Co., 1913.
———. *Mishnah: Baba Mezia (Middle Gate).* New York: Hebrew Publishing Co., 1913.
———. *Mishnah: Baba Batra (Last Gate).* New York: Hebrew Publishing Co., 1913.
Goldin, Judah. *The Living Talmud.* Chicago: Chicago University Press, 1957.
———. *The Song at the Sea (Mekilta de-Rabbi Ishmael).* New Haven: Yale University Press, 1971.
———, tr. *The Fathers According to Rabbi Nathan (Avot de Rabbi Nathan).* New York: Schocken, 1924.
Gore, Norman C. *Tzeenah U-Reenah: A Jewish Commentary on the Book of Exodus.* New York: Vantage, 1965.
Herford, R. Travers. *The Ethics of the Talmud: Sayings of the Fathers (Pirke Avot).* New York: Schocken, 1945.

Hertz, Joseph H., tr. *Sayings of the Fathers (Pirke Avot)*. New York: Behrman House, 1945.

Kasher, Menahem M. *Encyclopedia of Biblical Interpretation*. New York: American Biblical Encyclopedia Society, 1980. Nine volumes.

Klapholz, Yisroel Yaakov. *From Our Torah Treasury*. Tel Aviv: Orly, 1972. Two volumes.

Kravitz, Nathaniel, ed. *Pirke Avot: Sayings of the Fathers*. Chicago: Ophir, 1951.

Lauderbach, Jacob Z., tr. *Mekilta de-Rabbi Ishmael*. Philadelphia: Jewish Publication Society, 1935. Three volumes.

Lysman, Eugene J., tr. *The Mishnah: Oral Teachings of Judaism*. New York: Schocken, 1974.

Matter, Henry, tr. *Ta'anit: The Treatise of the Babylonian Talmud*. Philadelphia: Jewish Publication Society, 1928.

Neusner, Jacob, tr. *The Tosefta*. New York: Ktav, 1981. Six volumes.

Noah, Mordechai Manuel, tr. *The Book of Yashar (Sefer Yashar)*. New York: Hermon, 1972.

Rapaport, Samuel. *A Treasury of the Midrash*. New York: Ktav, 1968.

Runes, Dagobert D. *The Talmud of Jerusalem*. New York, Philosophical Library, 1956.

B. Secondary Sources

Abelson, J. *The Immanence of God in Rabbinical Literature*. New York: Hermon, 1969.

Adler, Morris. *The World of the Talmud*. New York: Schocken, 1963.

Agnon, S. Y. *Days of Awe*. New York: Schocken, 1965.

Ben-Amos, Dan. *Narrative Forms in the Haggadah: Structural Analysis*. Ann Arbor: University Microfilm, 1973.

Chajes, Z. H. *The Student's Guide Through the Talmud*. Trans. Jacob Schacter. New York: Feldheim, 1960.

Cohen, A. *Everyman's Talmud*. New York: Schocken, 1975.

Corre, Alan. *Understanding the Talmud*. New York: Ktav, 1975.

Culi, Yaakov. *The Torah Anthology*. New York: Maznaim, 1977. Two volumes.

Darmester, Arsene. *The Talmud*. Philadelphia: Jewish Publication Society, 1897.

Deutsch, Emanuel. *The Talmud*. Philadelphia: Jewish Publication Society, 1869.

Feldman, Asher. *The Parables and Similes of the Rabbis*. Cambridge, England: Cambridge University Press, 1927.

Finkelstein, Louis. *Akiba: Scholar, Saint, and Martyr*. Philadelphia: Jewish Publication Society, 1962.

Fischel, Henry A. *Essays in Greco-Roman and Related Talmudic Literature*. New York: Ktav, 1980.

———. *Rabbinic Literature and Greco-Roman Philosophy*. Leiden: E. J. Brill, 1973.

Fox, Samuel J. *Hell in Jewish Literature*. Wheeling, Ill.: Whitehall, 1972.

Gaer, Joseph. *The Lore of the Old Testament*. Boston: Little, Brown, 1952.

Gerhardson, Birger. *Memory and Manuscript*. Uppsala: Gleenup, 1961.

Gersh, Harry. *The Sacred Books of the Jews*. New York: Stein and Day, 1968.

Ginzberg, Louis. *The Legends of the Jews.* Philadelphia: Jewish Publication Society, 1909–35. Seven volumes.

——. *On Jewish Law and Lore.* New York: Atheneum, 1955.

Glenn, G. Mendel, ed. *Jewish Tales and Legends.* New York: Hebrew Publishing Co., 1929.

Goldin, Hyman E. *The Book of Legends.* New York: Hebrew Publishing Co., 1938.

Goodblatt, David M. *Rabbinic Instruction in Sasanian Babylonia.* Leiden: E. J. Brill, 1975.

Goodenough, E. R. *Jewish Symbols in the Greco-Roman Period.* New York: Pantheon, 1953–68. Thirteen volumes.

Halper, B., tr. *Post-Biblical Hebrew Literature.* Philadelphia: Jewish Publication Society, 1921.

Heineman, Joseph, and Noy, Dov, eds. *Studies in Aggada and Folk-literature.* Jerusalem: Magnes, 1971.

Jacobs, Louis. *Teyku: The Unsolved Problem in the Babylonian Talmud.* London: Cornwall, 1981.

Jastrow, Marcus. *A Dictionary of the Targumim, the Talmud Babli and Yerushalmi, and the Midrashic Literature.* Brooklyn: Traditional Press, 1903.

Kadushin, Max. *The Rabbinic Mind.* New York: Bloch, 1972.

Klausner, J. *The Messianic Idea in Israel from its Beginning to the Completion of the Mishnah.* New York: Macmillan, 1955.

Kushner, Lawrence. *Honey From the Rock.* New York: Harper and Row, 1977.

——. *The River of Light.* New York: Harper & Row, 1981.

Landman, Leo. *Messianism in the Talmudic Era.* New York: Ktav, 1979.

Lauterback, Jacob Zallel. *Rabbinic Essays.* Cincinnati: Hebrew Union College, 1957.

——. *Studies in Jewish Law, Custom and Folklore.* New York: Ktav, 1970.

Lehrman, S. M. *The World of the Midrash.* New York: Yoseloff, 1961.

Maccoby, Hyam. *The Day God Laughed.* London: Robson, 1978.

Marmorstein, Alfred. *The Doctrine of Merits in Old Rabbinic Literature.* New York: Ktav, 1968. Three volumes.

Mielziner, Moses. *Introduction to the Talmud.* New York: Bloch, 1968.

Mikliszanski, J. K. *The Saga of Traditional Judaism: A Survey of Post-Biblical Literature.* Los Angeles: Zahavia, 1977.

Miller, Amos W. *Understanding the Midrash.* New York: Jonathan David, 1965.

Montefiore, C. G., and Loewe, H., eds. *A Rabbinic Anthology.* New York: Schocken, 1974.

Neusner, Jacob. *Development of a Legend: Studies on the Traditions Concerning Yohanan ben Zakkai.* Leiden: E. J. Brill, 1970.

——. *Eliezer ben Hyrcanus.* Leiden: E. J. Brill, 1973. Two volumes.

——. *First Century Judaism in Crisis.* Nashville: Abingdon, 1975.

——. *The Formation of the Babylonian Talmud.* Leiden: E. J. Brill, 1970.

——. *Invitation to the Talmud.* New York: Harper & Row, 1973.

——. *A Life of Yohanan ben Zakkai.* Leiden: E. J. Brill, 1962.

——. *Understanding Rabbinic Judaism.* New York: Ktav, 1974.

Newman, Louis J. *The Talmudic Anthology.* New York: Behrman House, 1945.

Noy, Dov. "Motif Index of Talmudic-Midrashic Literature." Unpublished dissertation, Indiana University, 1954.

Oesterley, W. O. E. and Box, G. H. *A Short Survey of Literature of Rabbinic and Medieval Judaism.* New York: Macmillan, 1920.

Polano, H., tr. *The Talmud.* New York: Warne, 1978.

Rappoport, A. S. *Myth and Legend of Ancient Israel.* London: Gresham, 1928. Three volumes.

―――. *The Psalms in Life, Legend and Literature.* London: Centenary, 1935.

Sandmel, Samuel. *Philo of Alexandria.* New York: Oxford University Press, 1979.

Saperstein, Marc. *Decoding the Rabbis: A Thirteenth Century Commentary on the Aggadah.* Cambridge: Harvard University Press, 1980.

Schechter, Solomon. *Aspects of Rabbinic Theology: Major Concepts of the Talmud.* New York: Schocken, 1961.

―――. *Studies in Judaism.* Philadelphia: Jewish Publication Society, 1908. Three volumes.

Segal, Yocheved. *Our Sages Showed the Way.* Jerusalem: Feldheim, 1976. Two volumes.

Shrock, A. *Rabbi Jonah ben Abraham of Gerona.* London: Goldstom, 1948.

Silverman, B. William. *Rabbinic Stories for Christian Ministers and Teachers.* New York: Abingdon, 1968.

Spiegel, Shalom. *The Last Trial.* Philadelphia: Jewish Publication Society, 1967.

Steinsaltz, Adin. *The Essential Talmud.* New York: Basic Books, 1976.

Strack, Herman L. *Introduction to the Talmud and Midrash.* Philadelphia: Jewish Publication Society, 1931.

Towner, Wayne Sibley. *The Rabbinic Enumeration of Scriptural Examples.* Leiden: E. J. Brill, 1973.

Unterman, Isaac. *The Talmud: An Analytical Guide to Its History and Teachings.* New York: Bloch, 1952.

Urbach, Ephraim E. *The Sages: Their Concepts and Beliefs.* Jerusalem: Magnus, 1975. Two volumes.

Waskow, Arthur. *Godwrestling.* New York: Schocken, 1978.

Weiss, L. *Talmudic and Other Legends.* New York: Streltiner, 1888.

Wiesel, Elie. *Messengers of God: Biblical Portraits and Legends.* New York: Random House, 1976.

Wright, Addison G. *The Literary Genre Midrash.* Staten Island, N.Y.: Alba, 1967.

IV. MERKAVAH MYSTICISM

A. Primary Sources

Odeberg, Hugo. *3 Enoch or The Hebrew Book of Enoch.* New York: Ktav, 1973.

Scholem, Gershom, ed. *Hekhaloth Rabbati,* trans. by Morton Smith. Unpublished manuscript.

B. Secondary Sources

Blumenthal, David R. *Understanding Jewish Mysticism—The Merkabah Tradition and the Zoharic Tradition.* New York: Ktav, 1978.
Bokser, Ben Zion. *The Jewish Mystical Tradition.* New York: Pilgrim, 1981.
Gruenwald, Ithamar. *Apocalyptic and Merkavah Mysticism.* Leiden: E. J. Brill, 1980.
Halpern, David Joel. *The Merkabah in Rabbinic Literature.* New York: American Oriental Society, 1980.
Kaufman, William. *Journeys.* New York: Bloch, 1981.
Jacobs, Louis. *Jewish Mystical Testimonies.* New York: Schocken, 1976.
Scholem, Gershom G. *Jewish Gnosticism, Merkabah Mysticism, and Talmudic Tradition.* New York: Jewish Theological Seminary, 1960.
Segal, Alan. *Two Powers in Heaven.* Leiden: E. J. Brill, 1979.

V. KABBALISTIC

A. Primary Sources

Abulafia, Abraham ben Samuel. *The Path of the Names.* Berkeley: Trigram, 1976.
Bension, Ariel. *The Zohar in Moslem and Christian Spain.* New York: Hermon, 1974.
Ben Zion, Raphael, ed. *An Anthology of Jewish Mysticism.* New York: Judaica Press, 1981.
Franck, Adolphe. *The Kabbalah.* New Hyde Park, N.Y.: University Books, 1967.
Friedman, Irving. *The Book of Creation.* New York: Samuel Weiser, 1977.
Gaster, M. *The Sword of Moses.* New York: Weiser, 1970.
Jacobs, Louis. *The Palm Tree of Deborah.* London: Vallentine-Mitchell, 1960.
Kaplan, Aryeh. *The Bahir.* New York: Weiser, 1979.
Luzzatto, Moses Chaim. *The Path of the Just.* Jerusalem: Feldheim, 1966.
———. *The Way of God.* Jerusalem: Feldheim, 1978.
Manhar, Nurho De, trans. *Zohar Genesis.* San Diego: Wizards Bookshelf, 1978.
Meltzer, David. *The Secret Garden: An Anthology in the Kabbalah.* New York: Seabury, 1976.
Montefiore, C. G., and Loewe, H. *A Rabbinic Anthology.* Philadelphia: Jewish Publication Society, 1963.
Mordell, Pineas. *Sefer Yetzirah.* New York: Weiser, 1975.
Rosenberg, Roy A. *The Anatomy of God.* New York: Ktav, 1973.
Runes, D. Dagobert. *The Wisdom of the Kabbalah.* New York: Citadel, 1967.
Scholem, Gershom, ed. *Zohar: The Book of Splendor.* New York: Schocken, 1949.
Sperling, Harry, and Simon, Maurice, eds. *Zohar.* London: Soncino, 1931–34.
Steinsaltz, Adin. *The Thirteen Petalled Rose.* New York: Basic Books, 1980.
Stenring, Knut. *The Book of Formation (Sefer Yetzirah).* New York: Ktav, 1978.
Zahavy, Zev, ed. *Ibn Zuzu Kadlibu.* New York: Sage, 1977.

B. Secondary Sources

Abelson, J. *Jewish Mysticism.* London: Bell, 1913.

Ashlag, Rabbi Yehuda. *An Entrance to the Tree of Life.* Jerusalem: Research Centre of Kabbalah, 1977.

————. *An Entrance to the Zohar.* Jerusalem: Research Centre of Kabbalah, 1974.

————. *The Kabbalah.* Jerusalem: Research Centre of Kabbalah, 1972.

Bakan, David. *Sigmund Freud and the Jewish Mystical Tradition.* New York: Schocken, 1958.

Ben Bezalel, Rabbi Yehudah Leove. *The Book of Divine Power.* Jerusalem: Feldheim, 1975.

Biale, David. *Gershom Scholem: Kabbalah and Counter-History.* Cambridge, Mass.: Harvard University Press, 1979.

Bokser, Ben Zion. *From the World of the Cabbalah.* New York: Philosophical Library, 1954.

Epstein, Perle. *Kabbalah, the Way of the Jewish Mystic.* New York: Doubleday, 1978.

Franck, Adolphe. *The Kabbalah: The Religious Philosophy of the Hebrews.* New York: Bell, 1940.

Ginzberg, Simon. *The Life and Works of Moses Hayyim Luzzatto.* Philadelphia: Dropsie College Press, 1931.

Godwin, David. *Cabbalistic Encyclopedia.* St. Paul, Minn.: Llewellyn, 1979.

Gonzalez, Wippler Migene. *A Kabbalah for the Modern World.* New York: Bantam, 1974.

Greenstone, Julius H. *The Messiah Idea in Jewish History.* Philadelphia: Jewish Publication Society, 1906.

Jacobs, Louis. *Jewish Ethics: Philosophy and Mysticism.* New York: Behrman House, 1969.

————. *Jewish Mystical Testimonies.* New York: Schocken, 1978.

Klausner, Joseph. *The Messianic Idea in Israel.* New York: Macmillan, 1955.

Kook, Abraham Isaac. *The Lights of Penitence, the Moral Principles, Lights of Holiness, Essays, Letters, and Poems.* New York: Paulist Press, 1978.

Levi, Elyshas. *The Mysteries of the Kabalah.* New York: Weiser, 1974.

Luzzatto, Rabbi Moses. *General Principles of the Kabbalah.* New York: Press of the Research Centre of Kabbalah, 1970.

Meltzer, David. *The Secret Garden: An Anthology in the Kabbalah.* New York: Seabury, 1976.

Muller, Ernst. *History of Jewish Mysticism.* New York: Yessod Publishing.

Pick, Bernhard. *The Cabala.* La Salle, Ill.: Open Court, 1974.

Safran, Alexandre. *The Kabbalah.* Jerusalem: Feldheim, 1975.

Sarachek, Joseph. *The Doctrine of the Messiah in Medieval Jewish Literature.* New York: Jewish Theological Seminary, 1932.

Schaya, Leo. *The Universal Meaning of the Kabbalah.* Baltimore: Penguin, 1974.

Scholem, Gershom. *Kabbalah.* Jerusalem: Keter, 1974.

————. *Major Trends in Jewish Mysticism.* New York: Schocken, 1964.

————. *The Messianic Idea in Judaism and Other Essays on Jewish Spirituality.* New York: Schocken, 1971.

————. *On Jews and Judaism in Crisis.* New York: Schocken, 1976.

————. *On the Kabbalah and Its Symbolism.* New York: Schocken, 1965.

———. *Shabbatai Sevi: The Mystical Messiah.* Princeton: Schocken, 1973.

Suares, Carlo. *The Cipher of Genesis.* Boulder, Colo.: Shambhala, 1978.

———. *The Resurrection of the Word.* Boulder, Colo.: Shambhala, 1975.

———. *The Sepher Yetsira.* Boulder, Colo.: Shambhala, 1976.

Unterman, Alan. *The Wisdom of the Jewish Mystics.* New York: New Directions, 1976.

Waite, A. E. *The Holy Kabbalah.* Secaucus, N.J.: University Books, Inc., 1960.

Weinner, Herbert. *Nine and a Half Mystics: The Kabbalah Today.* New York: Collier, 1969.

Werblowsky, R. J. Zwi. *Joseph Karo, Lawyer and Mystic.* Philadelphia: Jewish Publication Society of America, 1977.

VI. FOLKLORE

A. Primary Sources

Ausubel, Nathan, ed. *A Treasury of Jewish Folklore.* New York: Crown, 1948.

Barash, Asher, ed. *A Golden Treasury of Jewish Tales.* Tel Aviv: Masada, 1965.

Bialik, Hayim Nachman. *And It Came to Pass: Legends and Stories About King David and King Solomon.* New York: Hebrew Publishing Co., 1938.

Bin-Gorion, Micha Joseph [Berditchevsky]. *Mimekor Yisrael: Classical Jewish Folktales.* Bloomington: Indiana University Press, 1976. Three volumes.

Bloch, Chayim. *The Golem: Legends of the Ghetto of Prague.* Vienna, 1945.

Einhorn, David. *The Seventh Candle and Other Folk Tales of Eastern Europe.* New York: Ktav, 1968.

Epstein, Morris. *Tales of Sendebar.* Philadelphia: Jewish Publication Society of America, 1967.

Gaster, M. *Studies and Texts in Folklore, Magic, Medieval Romance, Hebrew Apocrypha and Samaritan Archeology.* New York: Ktav, 1971.

———. *The Sword of Moses.* London: D. Nutt, 1896.

———. *Ma'aseh Book of Jewish Tales and Legends.* Philadelphia: Jewish Publication Society, 1934. Two volumes.

Goitein, S. F. *From the Land of Sheba: Tales of the Jews of Yemen.* New York: Schocken, 1947.

Hadas, Moses. *Fables of a Jewish Aesop.* New York: Columbia University Press, 1967.

Hanauer, J. E. *Folk-lore of the Holy Land.* London: Folcroft, 1977.

Kahana, S. Z. *Legends of Zion.* Ramat Hasharon, Israel: Royal Press, 1974.

Klapholtz, Yisroel Yaakov. *Stories of Elijah the Prophet.* Bnei Brak, Israel: Pe'er Hasefer, 1971–73. Four volumes.

Nahmad, Hayim Musa, ed. *A Portion in Paradise and Other Jewish Folktales.* New York: Norton, 1970.

Noy, Dov. *Folktales of Israel.* Chicago: University of Chicago Press, 1969.

———. *Moroccan Jewish Folktales.* New York: Herzl, 1966.

Pascheles, Wolff *Jewish Legends of the Middle Ages.* London: Shapiro Vallentine.

Posy, Arnold. *Israeli Tales and Legends.* New York: Jonathan David, 1966.

Rappoport, Angelo S. *Myth and Legend of Ancient Israel.* New York: Ktav, 1956. Three volumes.

Rush, Barbara, and Marcus, Eliezer, eds. *Seventy and One Tales.* New York: A.Z.Y.F., 1980.

Saben, Yona. *The Folk Literature of the Kurdistani Jews: An Anthology.* New Haven: Yale University Press, 1982.

St. John, Seymour D. *Tales of King Solomon.* London: Oxford University Press, 1924.

Vilnay, Zev. *Legends of Galilee, Jordon and Sinai.* Philadelphia: Jewish Publication Society of America, 1978.

———. *Legends of Jerusalem.* Philadelphia: Jewish Publication Society of America, 1973.

———. *Legends of Judea and Samaria.* Philadelphia: Jewish Publication Society of America, 1975.

Zabara, Joseph ben Meir. *The Book of Delight.* Philadelphia: Jewish Publication Society, 1912.

B. Secondary Sources

Ansky, S. *Between Two Worlds: The Dybbuk.* New York, 1926; South Bend, Ind.: Regnevy/Gateway, 1979.

Cohen, Isabel E. *Legends and Tales.* Philadelphia: Jewish Publication Society of America, 1905.

Cohn, Bernhard Emil. *Stories and Fantasies from the Jewish Past.* Philadelphia: Jewish Publication Society of America, 1951.

Davies, Thomas Witton. *Magic, Divination and Demonology Among the Hebrews and Their Neighbors.* New York: Ktav, 1909.

Fleg, Edmond. *The Life of Solomon.* New York: Dutton, 1930.

Gaer, Joseph. *The Legend of the Wandering Jew.* New York: Mentor, 1961.

Goitein, S. D. *From the Land of Sheba.* New York: Schocken, 1947.

Goldin, E. Hyman. *The Magic Ring.* New York: Hebrew Publishing Co., 1946.

Goldsmith, Arnold L. *The Golem Remembered, 1909–1980.* Detroit: Wayne State University Press, 1981.

Harlow, Jules. *Lessons from Our Living Past.* New York: Behrman House, 1972.

Heddy, Jason. *Conflict and Resolution in Jewish Sacred Tales.* Bloomington: Indiana University Press, 1968.

Ish Kishor, Judith. *Tales from the Wise Men of Israel.* Philadelphia: Lippincott, 1962.

Ish-Kishor, Shulamit. *The Master of Miracle: A Novel of the Golem.* New York: Harper and Row, 1971.

Jacobs, Joseph. *Jewish Ideals and Other Essays.* New York: Macmillan, 1896.

Lauterbach, Jacob Z. *Studies in Jewish Law, Custom and Folklore.* New York: Ktav, 1968.

Lehrman, S. M. *Jewish Customs and Folklore.* London: Routledge, 1964.

Maitlis, Jacob. *The Ma'aseh in the Yiddish Ethical Literature.* London, Shapiro-Vallentine, 1958.

Meyrink, Gustav. *The Golem.* New York: Dover, 1976.

Mouskopf, Aaron. *The Religious Philosophy of the Maharal of Prague.* New York: Morgenstern, 1966.

Neuman, [Noy] D. "Motif-Index of Talmudic- Midrashic Literature." Dissertation, Indiana University, 1954.

Noy, Dov, ed. *Studies in Biblical and Jewish Folklore.* Bloomington: American Folklore Society, 1959.

Prose, Francine. *Stories from Our Living Past.* New York: Behrman House, 1981.

Rappoport, Angelo S. *The Folklore of the Jews.* London: Soncino, 1937.

Scharzbaum, Haim. *Studies in Jewish and World Folklore.* Berlin: Walter de Gruyter, 1968.

Schrire, Theodore. *Hebrew Amulets: Their Decipherment and Interpretation.* London: Routledge, 1966.

Schwartz, Howard. *Lilith's Cave: Jewish Tales of the Supernatural.* San Francisco: Harper & Row, 1988.

Schwartz, Howard. *Miriam's Tambourine: Jewish Folk Tales from Around the Si World.* New York: Macmillan, 1987; New York: Oxford University Press, 1988.

Singer, I. B. *The Golem.* New York: Farrar, Straus & Giroux, 1983.

Simon, Solomon. *The Wise Men of Helm.* New York: Behrman House, 1945.

———. *More Wise Men of Helm.* New York: Behrman House, 1965.

———. *The Wandering Beggar.* New York: Behrman House, 1942.

Skulsky, S. *Legends of King Solomon.* New York: Shulsinger, 1957.

Talmage, Frank, ed. *Studies in Jewish Folklore.* Cambridge: Association for Jewish Studies, 1980.

Tenenbaum, Samuel. *The Wise Men of Chelm.* New York: Collier, 1965.

Thieberger, Frederic. *The Great Rabbi Loew of Prague.* London: East and West Library, 1955.

Trachtenberg, Joshua. *Jewish Magic and Superstition.* Philadelphia: Jewish Publication Society, 1961.

———. *The Devil and the Jews.* New Haven: Yale University Press, 1943.

Weinreich, B. S. "The Prophet Elijah in Modern Yiddish Folktales." Unpublished M.A. thesis, Columbia University, 1957.

Weinreich, Uriel and Beatrice. *Yiddish Language and Folklore: A Selective Bibliography for Research.* The Hague: Mouton, 1959.

Weinreich, Uriel, ed. *The Field of Yiddish: Studies in Yiddish Language, Folklore, and Literature.* New York: Columbia University Press, 1954.

Winkler, Gershom. *Dybbuk.* New York: Judaica Press, 1980.

Winkler, Gershom. *The Golem of Prague.* New York: Judaica Press, 1982.

VII. HASIDIC

A. Primary Sources

Aryeh, Isaiah, and Dvorkes, Joshua, eds. *The Baal Shem on Pirkey Avot.* Jerusalem: Feldheim, 1974.

Band, J. Arnold. *Nachman of Bratslav: The Tales.* New York: Paulist Press, 1978.

Ben-Amos, Dan, and Mintz, Jerome R., trans. and eds. *In Praise of the Baal Shem Tov (Shivhei ha-Besht).* Bloomington: Indiana University Press, 1970.

Buber, Martin. *The Tales of Rabbi Nachman.* New York: Avon, 1970.

――――. *Tales of the Hasidim.* New York: Schocken, 1947–48.

Cordovero, Moses. *The Palm Tree of Deborah.* New York: Sepher-Hermon, 1981.

Dov Baer of Lubavitch. *Tract on Ecstasy.* London: Vallentine-Mitchell, 1963.

Eliach, Yaffa. *Hasidic Tales of the Holocaust.* New York: Oxford University Press, 1982.

Heinemann, Benno. *The Maggid of Dubno and His Parables.* New York: Feldheim, 1967.

Kaplan, Aryeh. *The Light Beyond: Adventures in Hasidic Thought.* New York: Maznaim, 1981.

Klapholtz, Yisroel Yaakov. *Tales of the Baal Shem Tov.* Tel Aviv: Pe'er Hasefer, 1970. Five volumes.

Klein, Aaron, and Klein, Jenny Machlowitz. *Tales in Praise of the Ari (Shivhei ha-Ari).* Philadelphia: Jewish Publication Society, 1970.

Kramer, Mordechai, ed. *The Thirteen Stories of Rebbe Nachman of Breslev.* Jerusalem: Hillel Press, 1978.

Mintz, Jerome R. *Legends of the Hasidim: An Introduction to Hasidic Culture and Oral Tradition in the New World.* Chicago: University of Chicago Press, 1968.

Rabbi Nachman of Bratslav. *Outpouring of the Soul.* Jerusalem: Yeshiva Chasidei Breslov, 1980.

――――. *Rabbi Nachman's Wisdom (Shevachay Haran and Sichos Haran).* Brooklyn: Hermon, 1976.

――――. *Restore My Soul.* Jerusalem: Yeshiva Chasidei Breslov, 1980.

Weinbach, Mendel, ed. *Who Wants to Live: 101 Mesholim of the Chofetz Chaim.* Jerusalem: Nachat, 1968.

Zaretsky, David. *The Stories and Parables of the Hafetz Hayyim.* New York: Feldheim, 1976.

B. Secondary Sources

Birnbaum, Salomo. *The Life and Sayings of the Baal Shem.* New York: Maximilian Hurwitz, 1933.

Buber, Martin. *For the Sake of Heaven.* New York: Meridian and Jewish Publication Society, 1958.

――――. *Hasidim.* New York: Philosophical Library, 1948.

――――. *Hasidim and Modern Man.* New York: Horizon, 1958.

――――. *The Legend of the Baal-Shem.* New York: Schocken, 1977.

――――. *The Origin and Meaning of Hasidism.* New York: Horizon, 1960.

――――. *Tales of Angels, Spirits and Demons.* New York: Hawkswell, 1958.

――――. *The Tales of Rabbi Nachman.* New York: Horizon, 1956.

――――. *Ten Rungs.* New York: Schocken, 1947.

Dan, Joseph, ed. *Readings in Hasidism.* New York: Behrman House, 1979.

Dresner, Samuel H. *Levi Yitzhak of Berditchev: Portrait of a Hasidic Master.* Bridgeport, Conn.: Hartmore House, 1974.

――――. *The Zaddik: The Doctrine of the Zaddik According to the Writings of Rabbi Yaakov Yosef of Polnoy.* New York: Abelard-Schuman, 1960.

Elstein, Yoav. *Structuralism in Literary Criticism: A Method and Application in Two*

Representative Hasidic Tales. Unpublished doctoral dissertation, University of California, 1974.

Fleer, Gedaliah. *Rabbi Nachman's Fire.* New York: Hermon, 1972.

———. *Rabbi Nachman's Foundation.* New York: Sepher-Hermon, 1976.

Green, Arthur. *Tormented Master: A Life of Rabbi Nachman of Bratslav.* University, Ala.: University of Alabama Press, 1979.

———, and Holtz, Barry. *Your Word is Fire: The Hasidic Masters on Contemplation.* New York: Paulist Press, 1977.

Handler, Andrew. *Rabbi Eizik: Hasidic Stories About the Zaddik of Kallo.* Rutherford: New Jersey: Associated University Press, 1978.

Heifetz, Harold. *Zen and Hasidism.* Wheaton, Ill.: Theosophical Publishing House, 1978.

Heinemann, Benno. *The Maggid of Dubno and His Parables.* New York: Feldheim, 1967.

Horodezky, S. A. *Leaders of Hassidism.* London: Hasefer, 1928.

Jacobs, Louis. *Hasidic Prayer.* New York: Schocken, 1978.

———. *Hasidic Thought.* New York: Schocken, 1976.

Kaplan, Rabbi Aryeh. *Gems of Rabbi Nachman.* Jerusalem: Yeshiva Chasidei Breslov, 1980.

Langer, Jiri. *Nine Gates to the Chassidic Mysteries.* New York: Behrman House, 1976.

Levin, Meyer. *The Golden Mountain.* New York: Behrman House, 1932.

Lowenkopf, Anne N. *The Hasidim: Mystical Adventures and Ecstatics.* Los Angeles: Sherbourne, 1973.

Mindel, Nissan. *The Philosophy of Chabad.* New York: Chabad Research Center, Kehot Publication Society, 1974.

Minkin, Jacob S. *The Romance of Hasidism.* New York: Macmillan, 1935.

Mintz, Jerome R. *Legends of the Hasidim.* Chicago: University of Chicago Press, 1968.

Newman, Louis I., and Spitz, Samuel, eds. *The Hasidic Anthology.* New York: Bloch, 1944.

———. *Maggidim and Hasidim: Their Wisdom.* New York: Bloch, 1962.

Panko, Stephen M. *Martin Buber.* Waco: Word Books, 1976.

Rabinowicz, Harry M. *The World of Hasidism.* New York and Bridgeport: Hartmore House, 1970.

Rubin, Israel. *Satmar: An Island in the City.* Chicago: Quadrangle, 1972.

Schachter, Zalman M. *Fragments of a Future Scroll.* Germantown, Pa.: Leaves of Grass, 1975.

———. *The First Step.* New York: Bantam, 1982.

Schochet, Jacob Immanuel. *The Great Maggid: The Life and Teachings of Rabbi Dov Ber of Mezhirech.* New York: Kehot Publication Society, 1974.

———. *Rabbi Israel Baal Shem Tov.* Toronto: Lieberman, 1961.

Singer, Isaac B. *Reaches of Heaven.* New York: Farrar, Straus, & Giroux, 1980.

Steinman, Eliezer. *The Garden of Hasidism.* Jerusalem: World Zionist Organization, 1961.

Wiesel, Elie. *Four Hasidic Masters and Their Struggle Against Melancholy.* Notre Dame, Ind.: University of Notre Dame Press, 1978.

————. *Somewhere a Master: Further Hasidic Portraits and Legends.* New York: Summit, 1982.

————. *Souls on Fire: Portraits and Legends of Hasidic Masters.* New York: Random House, 1972.

VIII. THE MODERN PERIOD

A. Primary Sources

Agnon, Shmuel Yosef. *The Bridal Canopy.* New York: Doubleday, 1937.

————. *A Guest for the Night.* New York: Schocken, 1968.

————. *In the Heart of the Seas.* New York: Schocken, 1947.

————. *Twenty-one Stories.* New York: Schocken, 1970.

————. *Two Tales: Betrothed and Edo and Enam.* New York: Schocken, 1966.

Aleichem, Sholem. *Adventures of Mottel the Cantor's Son.* New York: Collier, 1961.

————. *The Best of Sholem Aleichem.* Washington: New Republic Books, 1979.

————. *Collected Stories of Sholem Aleichem.* New York: Crown, 1965. Two volumes.

————. *The Great Fair: Scenes from My Childhood.* New York: Collier, 1955.

————. *Hanukah Money.* New York: Greenwillow, 1978.

————. *Inside Kasrilevke.* New York: Schocken, 1948.

————. *Marienbad.* New York: Putnam, 1982.

————. *The Old Country.* New York: Crown, 1953.

————. *Old Country Tales.* New York: Crown, 1966.

————. *Selected Stories.* New York: Modern Library, 1956.

————. *Some Laughter, Some Tears.* New York: Putnam, 1969.

————. *Stories and Satires.* London: Collier, 1959.

————. *Tovye's Daughter.* New York: Crown, 1965.

————. *Wandering Star.* New York: Crown, 1952.

Ansky, S. *The Dybbuk.* Los Angeles: Nash Publishing, 1974.

Appelfeld, Aharon. *The Age of Wonders.* Boston: Godine, 1981.

————. *Badenheim 1939.* Boston: Godine, 1980.

————. *In the Wilderness.* Jerusalem: Ah'shav, 1965.

Asch, Sholem. *Children of Abraham.* New York: Putnam, 1942.

————. *In the Beginning.* New York: Schocken, 1966.

————. *Kiddush Ha'shem: An Epic of 1648 and Sabbatai Zevi.* Philadelphia: Jewish Publication Society of America, 1926.

————. *Mottke the Thief.* Westport, Conn.: Greenwood, 1970.

————. *A Passage in the Night.* New York: Putnam, 1953.

————. *The Prophet.* New York: Putnam, 1955.

————. *Sabbatai Zevi: A Tragedy in Three Acts and Six Scenes.* Philadelphia: Jewish Publication Society, 1930.

————. *Salvation.* New York: Putnam, 1933.

————. *Tales of My People.* New York: Putnam, 1948.

————. *Three Cities: A Trilogy.* New York: Putnam, 1933.

Babel, Isaac. *Benya Krik, the Gangster*. New York: Schocken, 1948.

———. *The Collected Stories*. New York: Criterion, 1955.

———. *You Must Know Everything*. New York: Farrar, Straus & Giroux, 1969.

Barash, Asher. *Pictures from a Brewery*. Tel Aviv: Institute for the Translation of Hebrew Literature and Massada Publishing Co., 1971.

———. *Though He Slay Me*. Tel Aviv: Massada–P.E.C. Press, 1963.

Baron, Dvora. *The Thorny Path*. Jerusalem: Institute for the Translation of Hebrew Literature and Israel Universities Press, 1969.

Bialik, Hayim Nachman. *Aftergrowth and Other Stories*. Philadelphia: Jewish Publication Society of America, 1939.

———. *Complete Poetic Works*. New York: Bloch, 1948.

Bloch, Chayim. *The Golem: Mystical Tales from the Ghetto of Prague*. New York: Steiner, 1972.

Buber, Martin. *For the Sake of Heaven*. Philadelphia: Jewish Publication Society, 1945.

Cohen, Arthur A. *A Hero in His Time*. New York: Random House, 1976.

———. *In the Days of Simon Stein*. New York: Random House, 1972.

———. *The Myth of the Judeo-Christian Tradition*. New York: Harper and Row, 1969.

———. *The Natural and the Supernatural Jew*. New York: Pantheon, 1962.

Feierberg, Mordecai Ze'ev. *Whither and Other Stories*. Philadelphia: Jewish Publication Society, 1978.

Fiedler, Leslie A. *Back to China*. New York: Stein & Day, 1965.

———. *The Collected Essays of Leslie Fiedler*. New York: Stein & Day, 1971.

———. *A Fiedler Reader*. New York: Stein & Day, 1977.

———. *The Jew in the American Novel*. New York: Herzl, 1959.

———. *The Last Jew in America*. New York: Stein & Day, 1966.

———. *No! in Thunder: Essays on Myth and Literature*. Boston: Beacon, 1960.

———. *Nude Croquet: The Stories of Leslie A. Fiedler*. New York: Stein & Day, 1969.

———. *Pull Down Vanity and Other Stories*. Philadelphia: Lippincott, 1962.

Gary, Romain. *The Colors of the Day*. London: White Lion, 1976.

———. *The Company of Men*. New York: Simon and Schuster, 1950.

———. *The Dance of Genghis Cohn*. New York: World, 1968.

———. *The Enchanters*. New York: Putnam, 1975.

———. *Europa*. Garden City: Doubleday, 1978.

———. *The Guilty Head*. New York: World, 1969.

———. *The Roots of Heaven*. New York: Simon and Schuster, 1958.

Goldemberg, Isaac. *The Fragmented Life of Don Jacobo Lerner*. New York: Persea, 1978.

Grossman, Ladislav. *The Shop on Main Street*. Garden City, N.Y.: Doubleday, 1970.

Hazaz, Hayim. *Gates of Bronze*. Philadelphia: Jewish Publication Society, 1975.

———. *Mori Sa'id*. New York: Abelard-Schuman, 1956.

Helman, Cecil. *The Emperor's Aversion and Other Fables*. London: Caligula, 1977.

———. *The Exploding Newspaper*. London: Menard, 1977.

Herzl, Theodor. *Complete Diaries*. New York: Herzl, 1960.

———. *The Jewish State*. New York: American Zionist Emergency Council, 1946.

———. *Old-new Land*. New York: Bloch, 1960.

Jabès, Edmond. *The Book of Questions*. Middletown, Conn.: Wesleyan University Press, 1972.

Jacobson, Dan. *The Beginners*. New York: Macmillan, 1966.
———. *The Confessions of Josef Baisz*. London: Secker and Warburg, 1977.
———. *A Dance in the Sun*. London: Weidenfeld & Nicholson, 1956.
———. *Evidence of Love*. Boston: Little, Brown, 1960.
———. *Inklings: Selected Stories*. London: Weidenfeld & Nicolson, 1973.
———. *A Long Way from London*. London: Weidenfeld and Nicolson, 1958.
———. *The Price of Diamonds*. New York: Knopf, 1958
———. *The Rope of Tamar*. New York: Macmillan, 1970.
———. *The Trap*. London: Weidenfeld & Nicolson, 1955.
———. *The Wonder-Worker*. London: Weidenfeld & Nicolson, 1973.
———. *The Zulu and the Zeide*. Boston: Little, Brown, 1959.
Kafka, Franz. *The Castle*. New York: Knopf, 1930.
———. *The Complete Stories*. New York: Schocken, 1971.
———. *Diaries 1910–1913*. New York: Schocken, 1965.
———. *Diaries 1914–1923*. New York: Schocken, 1974.
———. *Letters to Felice*. New York: Schocken, 1973.
———. *Letters to Friends, Family and Editors*. New York: Schocken, 1977.
———. *Letters to Milena*. New York: Schocken, 1953.
———. *Letters to Ottla and the Family*. New York: Schocken, 1982.
———. *Letter to His Father*. New York: Schocken, 1953.
———. *Parables and Paradoxes*. New York: Schocken, 1961.
———. *The Penal Colony*. New York: Schocken, 1961.
———. *Stories and Reflections*. New York: Schocken, 1970.
———. *The Trial*. New York: Schocken, 1953.
———. *Wedding Preparations in the Country and Other Stories*. London: Penguin, 1978.
Kushner, Harold J. *When Bad Things Happen to Good People*. New York: Schocken, 1981.
Lasker-Schüler, Else. *Hebrew Ballads and Other Poems*. Philadelphia: Jewish Publication Society, 1980.
Levi, Primo. *Survival in Auschwitz*. New York: Collier, 1959.
———. *The Truce*. London: New English Library, 1965.
Levin, Meyer. *Compulsion*. New York: Simon and Schuster, 1956.
———. *The Fanatic*. New York: Simon and Schuster, 1964.
———. *My Father's House*. New York: Viking, 1947.
———. *The Obsession*. New York: Simon and Schuster, 1973.
———. *The Old Bunch*. New York: Citadel, 1944.
———. *The Settlers*. New York: Simon and Schuster, 1972.
———. *The Spell of Time*. New York: Praeger, 1974.
Lind, Jakov. *Counting My Steps*. New York: Macmillan, 1969.
———. *Landscape in Concrete*. New York: Grove Press, 1966.
———. *The Silver Foxes and Other Plays*. New York: Hill and Wang, 1969.
———. *Soul of Wood and Other Stories*. New York: Grove, 1964.
Malamud, Bernard. *The Assistant*. New York: Farrar, Straus & Cudahy, 1957.
———. *Dubin's Lives*. New York: Farrar, Straus & Giroux, 1979.
———. *The Fixer*. New York: Farrar, Straus & Giroux, 1966.
———. *Idiots First*. New York: Farrar, Straus, 1963.
———. *The Magic Barrel*. New York: Farrar, Straus & Cudahy, 1958.

————. *A Malamud Reader*. New York: Farrar, Straus & Giroux, 1967.

————. *The Natural*. New York: Farrar, Straus & Cudahy, 1952.

————. *A New Life*. New York: Farrar, Straus & Cudahy, 1961.

————. *Pictures of Fidelman*. New York: Farrar, Straus & Giroux, 1969.

————. *Rembrandt's Hat*. New York: Farrar, Straus & Giroux, 1973.

————. *The Tenants*. New York: Farrar, Straus & Giroux, 1971.

Manger, Itzik. *The Book of Paradise*. New York: Hill and Wang, 1965.

Meltzer, David. *Tens: Selected Poems 1961–1971*. New York: McGraw-Hill, 1973.

Memmi, Albert. *The Pillar of Salt*. New York: Criterion, 1955.

————. *The Scorpion*. New York: Grossman, 1971.

————. *Strangers*. New York: Orion, 1960.

Mendele Mokher-Seforim. *Fishke the Lame*. London: Stanley Paul, 1928.

————. *The Parasite*. New York: Yoseloff, 1956.

————. *The Travels and Adventures of Benjamin the Third*. New York: Schocken, 1949.

Minsky, Mark. *Thou Worm Jacob*. New York, Macmillan, 1967.

————. *Proceedings of the Rabble*. New York: Bobbs, Merrill, 1971.

————. *Blue Hill Avenue*. New York: Bobbs, Merrill, 1972.

————. *The Secret Table*. New York: Fiction Collective, 1975.

————. *My Search for the Messiah*. New York: Macmillan, 1977.

Nissenson, Hugh. *A Pile of Stones*. New York: Scribners, 1965.

————. *Notes from the Frontier*. New York: Dial, 1968.

————. *In the Reign of Peace*. New York: Farrar, Straus and Giroux, 1972.

————. *My Own Ground*. New York: Farrar, Straus and Giroux, 1976.

————. *The Tree of Life*. New York: Harper & Row, forthcoming, 1983.

Opatshau, Joseph. *A Day in Regensburg*. Philadelphia: Jewish Publication Society, 1968.

Ozick, Cynthia. *Bloodshed and Three Novellas*. New York: Knopf, 1976.

————. *The Pagan Rabbi and Other Stories*. New York: Knopf, 1971.

————. *Trust*. New York: New American Library, 1966.

Peretz, I.L. *The Book of Fire*. New York. Yoseloff, 1959.

————. *In This World and the Next: Selected Writings*. New York: Yoseloff, 1958.

————. *Keys to a Magic Door*. New York: Farrar, 1959.

————. *My Memories*. New York: Citadel, 1964.

Pinsky, David. *King David and His Wives*. New York, B. W. Huebsch, 1923.

————. *Temptations*. New York: Brentano's, 1919.

Prose, Francine. *Judah the Pious*. New York: Atheneum, 1973.

Rapoport, Nessa. *Preparing for Sabbath*. New York: Morrow, 1981.

Rapp, Nachman. *Men in His Ways: Biblical Stories*. Tel Aviv: Hamenorah, 1973.

Rothenberg, Jerome. *Poems for the Game of Silence, 1960–1970*. New York: Dial, 1971.

————. *Vienna Blood and Other Poems*. New York: New Directions, 1980.

Sadeh, Pinhas. *Life As a Parable*. London: A. Blond, 1966.

Schneersohn, Fishel. *Lady Cotterfield's Biblical Soirée*. Tel Aviv: Massadah, 1947.

Schwartz, Howard. *The Captive Soul of the Messiah: New Tales about Reb Nachman*. New York: Schocken, 1983.

————. *Midrashim: Collected Jewish Parables*. London: Menard, 1976.

Schwarz-Bart, André. *The Last of the Just*. New York: Atheneum, 1961.

Shahar, David. *News from Jerusalem*. Boston: Houghton Mifflin, 1974.

———. *The Palace of Shattered Vessels*. Boston: Houghton Mifflin, 1976.

Silk, Dennis. *The Punished Land*. New York: Viking, 1977.

Singer, Isaac Bashevis. *Alone in the Wild Forest*. New York: Farrar, Straus & Giroux, 1971.

———. *A Crown of Feathers*. New York: Farrar, Straus & Giroux, 1970.

———. *A Day of Pleasure*. New York: Farrar, Straus & Giroux, 1963.

———. *Enemies: A Love Story*. New York: Farrar, Straus & Giroux, 1972.

———. *The Estate*. New York: Dell, 1969.

———. *The Family Moskat*. New York: Noonday, 1950.

———. *A Friend of Kafka*. New York: Farrar, Straus & Giroux, 1962.

———. *Gimpel the Fool*. New York: Farrar, Straus & Giroux, 1953.

———. *An Isaac Bashevis Singer Reader*. New York: Farrar, Straus & Giroux, 1953.

———. *Joseph and Koza or the Sacrifice to the Vistula*. New York: Farrar, Straus & Giroux, 1969.

———. *The Magician of Lublin*. New York: Bantam, 1960.

———. *The Manor*. New York: Dell, 1967.

———. *Naftali the Storyteller and His Horse, Sus*. New York: Dell, 1979.

———. *Old Love*. New York: Farrar, Straus & Giroux, 1966.

———. *Passions*. New York: Farrar, Straus & Giroux, 1974.

———. *The Power of Light*. New York: Farrar, Straus & Giroux, 1980.

———. *Reaches of Heaven*. New York: Farrar, Straus & Giroux, 1980.

———. *Satan in Goray*. New York: Farrar, Straus & Giroux, 1979.

———. *The Seance*. London: Penguin, 1970.

———. *Short Friday*. Philadelphia: Jewish Publication Society, 1964.

———. *Shosha*. New York: Farrar, Straus & Giroux, 1978.

———. *The Slave*. New York: Farrar, Straus & Giroux, 1962.

———. *The Spinoza of Market Street*. New York: Avon, 1963.

Slabotsky, David. *The Mind of Genesis*. Ottawa: Valley Editions, 1975.

Steinberg, Milton. *As a Driven Leaf*. New York: Behrman House, 1939.

Sussaman, Aaron. *The Flying Ark*. St. Louis: Cauldron, 1980.

Ujvári, Péter. *By Candlelight*. London: Associated University Presses, 1978.

Waskow, Arthur. *The Bush Is Burning!* New York: Macmillan, 1971.

Werfel, Franz. *Between Heaven and Earth*. New York: Philosophical Library, 1944.

———. *The Death of a Poor Man*. London: Benn, 1927.

———. *Embezzled Heaven*. New York: Viking, 1940.

———. *The Forty Days of Musa Dagh*. New York: Viking, 1934.

———. *Hearken unto the Voice*. New York: Viking, 1938.

———. *The Pascarella Family*. New York: Viking, 1935.

———. *The Pure in Heart*. New York: Book League of America, 1931.

———. *The Song of Bernadette*. New York: Viking, 1946.

———. *Star of the Unborn*. New York: Viking, 1946.

Wiesel, Elie. *A Beggar in Jerusalem*. New York: Random House, 1970.

———. *Dawn*. New York: Hill & Wang, 1961.

———. *The Gates of the Forest*. New York: Holt, Rinehart & Winston, 1966.

———. *Night*. New York: Hill & Wang, 1960.

———. *The Oath*. New York: Random House, 1973.

———. *The Testament*. New York: Summit, 1981.

——. *The Town Beyond the Wall.* New York: Holt, Rinehart & Winston, 1964.

Yaari, Yehuda. *The Covenant: Ten Stories.* Jerusalem: Zionist Organization, 1965.

Zangwill, Israel. *The Bachelors' Club.* London: Henry, 1891.

——. *Children of the Ghetto.* New York: Macmillan, 1899.

——. *Dreamers of the Ghetto.* London: Heinemann, 1898.

——. *Ghetto Tragedies.* Philadelphia: Jewish Publication Society, 1899.

——. *The Gray Wig.* London: Heinemann, 1903.

——. *The King of Schnorrers.* New York: Macmillan, 1899.

——. *The Mantle of Elijah.* London: Heinemann, 1900.

——. *The Master.* New York: Harper, 1897.

——. *Selected Works of Israel Zangwill.* Philadelphia: Jewish Publication Society, 1938.

——. *The Voice of Jerusalem.* London: Heinemann, 1920.

Zweig, Stefan. *Amok.* New York: Viking, 1931.

——. *Beware of Pity.* New York: Viking, 1939.

——. *The Buried Candelabrum.* New York: Viking, 1937.

——. *Conflicts.* New York: Viking, 1927.

——. *Kaleidoscope.* New York: Viking, 1934.

——. *The Royal Game.* New York: Viking, 1944.

B. Secondary Sources

Abramowicz, Dina, ed. *Yiddish Literature in English Translation 1945–1967.* New York: YIVO Institute for Jewish Research, 1967.

Allentuck, M., ed. *The Achievements of Isaac Bashevis Singer.* Carbondale, Ill.: Southern Illinois University Press, 1969.

Alter, Robert. *After the Tradition: Essays on Modern Jewish Writing.* New York: Dutton, 1971.

——. *Defenses of the Imagination: Jewish Writers and Modern Historical Crises.* Philadelphia: Jewish Publication Society, 1977.

——. *Modern Hebrew Literature.* New York: Behrman House, 1966.

Band, Arnold J. *Nostalgia and Nightmare: A Study in the Fiction of S.Y. Agnon.* Berkeley: University of California Press, 1968.

Bein, Alex. *Theodore Herzl.* Philadelphia: Jewish Publication Society, 1940.

Bellow, Saul. *Great Jewish Short Stories.* New York: Dell, 1963.

Ben Shalom, Benzion. *Hebrew Literature Between the Two World Wars.* New York: Jewish Agency, 1953.

Blocker, Joel, ed. *Israeli Stories.* New York: Schocken, 1962.

Brod, Max. *Franz Kafka: A Biography.* New York: Schocken, 1964.

Buchen, Irving. *Isaac Bashevis Singer and the Eternal Past.* New York: New York University Press, 1968.

Canetti, Elias. *Kafka's Other Trial.* New York: Schocken, 1969.

Chapman, Abraham. *Jewish American Literature.* New York: New American Library, 1974.

Falstein, Louis. *The Man Who Loved Laughter: The Story of Sholem Aleichem.* Philadelphia: Jewish Publication Society, 1968.

Fiedler, Leslie. *The Jew in the American Novel.* New York: Herzl, 1959.

Frank, Helena. *Yiddish Tales.* Philadelphia: Jewish Publication Society, 1912.

Goell, Yohai. *Bibliography of Modern Hebrew Literature in Translation.* Tel Aviv: The Institute for the Translation of Hebrew Literature, 1975.

Grafstein, Melech, ed. *Sholom Aleichem Panorama.* London, Ontario, Canada: Jewish Observer, 1948.

Guttman, Allen. *The Jewish Writer in America: Assimilation and the Crisis of Identity.* New York: Oxford University Press, 1971.

Halkin, Simon. *Modern Hebrew Literature.* New York: Schocken, 1970.

Handler, Andrew. *Ararát: A Collection of Hungarian-Jewish Short Stories.* Rutherford, N.J.: Fairleigh Dickinson University Press, 1980.

Heschel, A.J. *The Earth Is the Lord's: The Inner World of the Jew in East Europe.* New York: Harper, 1966.

———. *Theology of Ancient Judaism.* London: Soncino, 1971. Two volumes.

Hochman, Baruch. *The Fiction of S.Y. Agnon.* Ithaca, N.Y.: Cornell University Press, 1970.

Howe, Irving, ed. *Jewish American Stories.* New York: New American Library, 1977.

———. *Isaac B. Singer: Selected Short Stories.* New York: Modern Library, 1966.

———, and Greenberg, E., eds. *A Treasury of Yiddish Stories.* New York: Viking, 1954.

———, eds. *Voices from the Yiddish.* Ann Arbor: University of Michigan Press, 1972.

Janouch, Gustav. *Conversations with Kafka.* New York: New Directions, 1972.

Kahn, Sholom J., ed. *A Whole Loaf: Stories from Israel.* Tel Aviv: Karni, 1957.

Kazin, Alfred, ed. *Selected Stories of Sholom Aleichem.* New York: Modern Library, 1956.

Kresh, Paul. *I.B. Singer: The Magician of West 86th Street.* New York: Dial, 1979.

Landis, J.C., ed. and trans. *The Dybbuk and Other Great Yiddish Plays.* New York: Bantam, 1966.

Lask, Israel Meir, ed. and trans. *Palestine Stories.* Jerusalem: Tarshish, 1942.

Leftwich, Joseph, ed. *The Way We Think: Jewish Essays at Mid-Century.* London: Yoseloff, 1969.

———, ed. *Yisröel: The First Jewish Omnibus.* New York: Yoseloff, 1952.

Lind, Jakov. *Ergo.* New York: Hill and Wang, 1968.

———. *The Trip to Jerusalem.* New York: Harper & Row, 1927.

Liptzin, Sol. *The Flowering of Yiddish Literature.* New York: Yoseloff, 1965.

———. *The History of Yiddish Literature.* New York: Yoseloff, 1972.

———. *The Jew in American Literature.* New York: Bloch, 1966.

———. *The Maturing of Yiddish Literature.* New York: Yoseloff, 1970.

Madison, Charles. *Yiddish Literature: Its Scope and Major Writers.* New York: Schocken, 1971.

Malin, Irving, ed. *Contemporary American-Jewish Literature: Critical Essays.* Bloomington: Indiana University Press, 1973.

———. *Critical Views of Isaac Bashevis Singer.* New York: New York University Press, 1969.

Mersand, Joseph. *Traditions in American Literature: A Study of Jewish Characters and Authors.* New York: Ktav, 1968.

Michener, James A., ed. *Firstfruits: A Harvest of 25 Years of Israeli Writing.* Philadelphia: Jewish Publication Society, 1973.

Miron, Dan. *A Traveler Disguised: A Study in the Rise of Modern Yiddish Fiction in the Nineteenth Century*. New York: Schocken, 1973.

Neugroschel, Joachim. *Great Works of Jewish Fantasy*. London: Pan, 1978.

———, ed. *The Shtetl*. New York: Marek, 1979.

Novak, William. *The Big Book of Jewish Humor*. New York: Harper & Row, 1981.

Ovadyahu, Mordecai. *Bialik Speaks*. New York: Herzl, 1969.

Patterson, David. *The Hebrew Novel in Czarist Russia*. Edinburgh: University of Edinburgh Press, 1964.

———, ed. *Studies in Modern Hebrew Literature Series*. New York: Cornell University Press, 1974.

Penueli, Shmuel Yeshayahu, and Azriel, Ukhmani, eds. *Hebrew Short Stories*. Tel Aviv: Institute for the Translation of Hebrew Literature and Megiddo Publishing Company, 1965. Two volumes.

Peretz, Isaac Leib. *My Memoirs*. New York: Citadel, 1964.

Pinsker, S. *The Schlemiel as Metaphor: Studies in the Yiddish and American Jewish Novel*. Carbondale: Southern Illinois University Press, 1971.

Ribalow, Harold W., ed. *A Treasury of American Jewish Stories*. New York: Yoseloff, 1952.

Ribalow, Menachem. *The Flowering of Modern Hebrew Literature*. New York: Twayne, 1959.

Roback, A.A. *I.L. Peretz: Psychologist of Literature*. Cambridge: Sci-Art, 1935.

———. *The Story of Yiddish Literature*. New York: YIVO, 1940.

Samuel, Maurice. *Prince of the Ghetto: The Stories of Y.L. Peretz Retold*. New York: Schocken, 1973.

———. *The World of Sholom Aleichem*. New York: Knopf, 1947.

Schwartz, Howard, ed. *Imperial Messages: One Hundred Modern Parables*. New York: Avon, 1976.

———, ed. *Voices Within the Ark*. New York: Avon, 1980.

Schwarz, Leo W. *Feast of Leviathon*. New York: Rinehart, 1956.

———, ed. *A Golden Treasury of Jewish Literature*. New York: Rinehart and Company, Inc., 1937.

———, ed. *The Jewish Caravan: Great Stories of Twenty-five Centuries*. New York: Schocken, 1976.

Siegel, B. *Isaac Bashevis Singer*. Minneapolis: University of Minnesota Press, 1969.

Silberschlag, Eisig. *From Renaissance to Renaissance*. New York: Ktav, 1981. Three volumes.

———. *Hebrew Literature: An Evaluation*. New York: Herzl, 1959.

Singer, Isaac Bashevis. *In My Father's Court*. New York: Signet/New American Library, 1967.

———. *A Little Boy in Search of God*. New York: Doubleday, 1976.

———. *Lost in America*. New York: Doubleday, 1981.

———. *A Young Man in Search of Love*. New York: Doubleday, 1978.

Slouschz, Nahum, trans. *The Renaissance of Hebrew Literature 1743–1885*. Philadelphia: Jewish Publication Society, 1909.

Spicehandler, Ezra, ed. *Modern Hebrew Stories*. New York: Bantam, 1971.

Tammuz, Binyamin, and Yudkin, Leon I., eds. *Meetings with the Angel: Seven Stories from Israel*. London: Deutsch, 1973.

Waife-Goldberg, Marie. *My Father Sholom Aleichem*. New York: Schocken, 1971.

Wallenrod, Rueben. *The Literature of Modern Israel.* New York: Abelard-Schuman, 1956.

Wiener, Leo. *The History of Yiddish Literature in the Nineteenth Century.* New York: Hermon, 1972.

IX. GENERAL AND REFERENCE

Adidin, Ben M. *Jewish Customs and Ceremonies.* New York: Hebrew Publishing Co., 1941.

Ausubel, Nathan. *The Book of Jewish Knowledge.* New York: Crown, 1964.

Ben, Sasson H.H., ed. *A History of the Jewish People.* Cambridge, Mass.: Harvard University Press, 1976.

Birnbaum, Philip. *A Book of Jewish Concepts.* New York: Hebrew Publishing Co., 1964.

———. *A Treasury of Judaism.* New York: Hebrew Publishing Co., 1957.

Buber, Martin. *Between Man and Men.* New York: Macmillan, 1947.

———. *On Judaism.* New York: Schocken, 1972.

———. *The Way of Men.* New York: Citadel, 1963.

Caplan, Samuel, ed. *The Great Jewish Books.* New York: Washington Square Press, 1963.

Carmi, T., ed. *The Penguin Book of Hebrew Verse.* New York: Penguin Books, 1981.

Cheyne, T.K. *Traditions and Beliefs of Ancient Israel.* London: Adam and Charles Black, 1907.

Chill, Abraham. *The Minhagim: The Customs and Ceremonies of Judaism, Their Origins and Rationale.* New York: Hermon, 1980.

———. *The Mitzvot: The Commandments and Their Rationale.* New York: Bloch, 1974.

Comay, Joan. *The Diaspora Story.* New York: Random House, 1980.

Davidson, I. *Parody in Jewish Literature.* New York: Columbia University Press, 1907.

Davidowicz, Lucy. *The Golden Tradition.* New York: Holt, Rinehart & Winston, 1968.

Davis, Enid. *Comprehensive Guide to Children's Literature with a Jewish Theme.* New York; Schocken, 1981.

Dresner, Samuel H. *The Sabbath.* New York: Burning Bush, 1963.

Epstein, Isidore. *Judaism.* New York: Penguin, 1959.

Finkelstein, Louis. *The Beliefs and Practices of Judaism.* New York: Devin-Adair, 1952.

———, ed. *The Jewish People, Past and Present.* New York: Cyco, 1952.

———, ed. *The Jews: Their Religion and Culture.* New York: Schocken, 1971.

Fohrer, Georg. *History of Israelite Religion.* Nashville: Abingdon, 1972.

Friedlander, M. *The Jewish Religion.* London: Shapiro-Vallentine, 1922.

Gaster, Theodor H. *Festivals of the Jewish Year.* New York: Morrow, 1974.

———. *The Holy and the Profane: Evolution of Jewish Folkways.* New York: Sloane, 1955.

———. *Passover: Its History and Traditions.* Boston: Beacon, 1962.

Gersh, Harry. *The Sacred Books of the Jews.* New York: Stein & Day, 1972.

Glatzer, Nahum N., ed. *A Jewish Reader in Time and Eternity.* New York: Schocken, 1969.

Glatzer, Nahum N., ed. *The Judaic Tradition.* Boston: Beacon, 1968.

Goldin, Judah, ed., *The Jewish Expression.* New Haven: Yale University Press, 1976.

Goodenough, Erwin R. *Jewish Symbols in the Greco-Roman Period.* New York: Pantheon, 1953. Thirteen volumes.

Goodman, Philip, ed. *The Passover Anthology.* Philadelphia: Jewish Publication Society, 1961.

———, ed. *The Purim Anthology.* Philadelphia: Jewish Publication Society, 1949.

———, ed. *The Rosh Hashana Anthology.* Philadelphia: Jewish Publication Society, 1970.

———, ed. *Sukkot and Simhat Torah Anthology.* Philadelphia: Jewish Publication Society, 1973.

———, ed. *The Yom Kippur Anthology.* Philadelphia: Jewish Publication Society, 1971.

Gordis, Robert. *Judaism for the Modern Age.* New York: Farrar, Straus, 1955.

Grayzel, Solomon. *A History of the Jews.* Philadelphia: Jewish Publication Society, 1963.

Hayman, Ronald. *Kafka: A Biography.* New York: Oxford, 1982.

Heilman, Samuel C. *Synagogue Life.* Chicago: University of Chicago Press, 1976.

Heinmann, Joseph, and Petuchowski, Jacob J., eds. *Literature of the Synagogue.* New York: Behrman House, 1976.

Heschel, Abraham J. *The Earth Is the Lord's.* New York: Schuman, 1950.

———. *God in Search of Man.* New York: Farrar, Straus & Giroux, 1955.

———. *Man Is Not Alone.* New York: Farrar, Straus & Giroux, 1976.

———. *Man's Quest for God.* New York: Scribners, 1981.

———. *The Sabbath: Its Meaning for Modern Man.* New York: Farrar, Straus & Young, 1951.

Jacobs, Louis. *Principles of the Jewish Faith.* New York: Basic Books, 1964.

Jung, Leo. *Fallen Angels in Jewish, Christian and Mohammedan Literature.* Philadelphia: Dropsie College, 1926.

———, ed. *The Jewish Library.* New York: Bloch, 1930.

Katz, Eliezer, ed. *A Classified Concordance.* Jerusalem: Central Press, 1964.

Katz, Steven T. *Jewish Ideas and Concepts.* New York: Schocken, 1977.

Kaufman, Yehezkel. *The Religion of Israel.* New York: Schocken, 1972.

Kitov, Eliyahu. *The Book of Our Heritage.* Jerusalem: 'A' Publishers, 1968. Three volumes.

Levy, Isaac. *The Synagogue: Its History and Function.* London: Vallentine-Mitchell, 1964.

Maccoby, Hyam. *Revolution in Judea: Jesus and the Jewish Resistance.* London: Ocean Books, 1973.

Maimonides, Moses. *The Guide for the Perplexed.* New York: Dover, 1956.

Margolis, Max L. *A History of the Jewish People.* New York: Meridian, 1958.

Millgram, Abraham Ezra. *Great Jewish Ideas.* New York: B'nai B'rith Department of Adult Jewish Education, 1964.

———. *Jewish Worship.* Philadelphia: Jewish Publication Society, 1971.

————, ed. *An Anthology of Medieval Hebrew Literature.* Philadelphia: Burning Bush Press, 1935.

————, ed. *Sabbath: The Day of Delight.* Philadelphia: Jewish Publication Society, 1944.

Morgenstern, Julian. *Rites of Birth, Marriage, Death and Kindred Occasions among the Semites.* New York: Ktav, 1973.

Pearl, Chaim, and Brookes, Reuben S. *A Guide to Jewish Knowledge.* London: Jewish Chronicle Publications, 1956.

Posner, Raphael. *Jewish Liturgy.* Jerusalem: Keter, 1975.

Riemer, Jack, ed. *Jewish Reflections on Death.* New York: Schocken, 1976.

Roth, Cecil. *The Concise Jewish Encyclopedia.* New York: New American Library, 1980.

————. *The Jewish Contribution to Civilization.* London: East and West Library, 1956.

————, and Wigoder, G., eds. *Encyclopedia Judaica.* Jerusalem: Keter, 1972. Sixteen volumes.

————, eds. *The New Standard Jewish Encyclopedia.* New York: Doubleday, 1977.

Rothenberg, Jerome. *A Big Jewish Book: Poems and Other Visions of the Jews from Tribal Times to Present.* New York: Anchor/Doubleday, 1978.

Rubenstein, Richard. *The Religious Imagination: A Study in Psychoanalysis and Jewish Theology.* Indianapolis: Bobbs-Merrill, 1968.

Runes, Dagobert D. *Concise Dictionary of Judaism.* New York: Philosophical Library, 1959.

Schauss, Hayyim. *The Jewish Festivals.* New York: Schocken, 1962.

Schechter, Solomon. *Studies in Judaism.* Philadelphia: Jewish Publication Society, 1908.

Schonfield, Hugh. *A Popular Dictionary of Judaism.* New York: Citadel, 1966.

Schwartz, Howard, and Rudolf, Anthony, eds. *Voices Within the Ark: The Modern Jewish Poets.* New York: Avon, 1980.

Schwartz, Leo, ed. *Great Ages and Ideas of the Jewish People.* New York: Modern Library, 1956.

————, ed. *Memoirs of My People.* Philadelphia: Jewish Publication Society, 1943.

————, ed. *The Menorah Treasury.* Philadelphia: Jewish Publication Society, 1964.

Siegel, Richard, and Strassfeld, Michael and Sharon, eds. *The Jewish Catalog.* Philadelphia: Jewish Publication Society, 1973.

Silk, Dennis, ed. *Retrievements: A Jewish Anthology.* Jerusalem: Keter, 1968.

Singer, Isador, ed. *Jewish Encyclopedia.* New York: Ktav, 1964. Twelve volumes.

Steinberg, Milton. *Basic Judaism.* New York: Harcourt, Brace, 1947.

Steinschneider, M. *Jewish Literature.* New York: Harmon, 1965.

Strassfeld, Sharon and Michael. *The Second Jewish Catalog.* Philadelphia: Jewish Publication Society, 1976.

————. *The Third Jewish Catalog.* Philadelphia: Jewish Publication Society, 1980.

Unterman, Alan. *Jews: Their Religious Beliefs and Practices.* Boston: Routledge, 1981.

Waskow, Arthur. *Seasons of Our Joy.* New York: Bantam, 1982.

Waxman, Meyer. *A History of Jewish Literature from the Close of the Bible to Our Own Days.* New York: Yoseloff, 1960. Six volumes.

Wigoder, Geoffrey, ed. *Encyclopedic Dictionary of Judaica.* New York: Amiel, 1974.

Yerushalmi, Yosef Hayim. *From Spanish Court to Italian Ghetto.* Seattle: University of Washington Press, 1971.

Zaehner, R.C., ed. *Living Faiths: Judaism or the Religion of Israel.* New York: Hawthorn, 1959.

Zinberg, Israel. *A History of Jewish Literature.* New York: Ktav, 1972. Twelve volumes.

ACKNOWLEDGMENTS

The editor has made every effort to trace copyright owners. Any additional information will be incorporated in future editions of this book. All rights for the original Hebrew versions are reserved by the authors, Copyright © 1982.

S. Y. AGNON: "The Hidden Tzaddik," "Three Vows," "The Revelation of Elijah," and "The Stars of Heaven" used by permission of Schocken Publishing House, Ltd., and Jeremy Garber. Translations Copyright © 1982 Schocken Books, Inc. "Fable of the Goat" reprinted by permission of Schocken Books, Inc. from *Twenty-one Stories* by S. Y. Agnon. Copyright © 1970 by Schocken Books, Inc. "The Tale of Rabbi Gadiel the Infant" is used by permission of Schocken Books, Inc. and Evelyn Abel. Copyright © 1982 by Schocken Books, Inc.

SHOLOM ALEICHEM: "Eliyahu the Prophet" used by permission of the Family of Sholom Aleichem and Aliza Shevrin. Translation Copyright © 1982 Aliza Shevrin.

S. ANSKY: "The Rebbe's Whip" used by permission of Jeremy Garber. Translation Copyright © 1982 Jeremy Garber. "A Good Laugh" is reprinted from *Yenne Velt: The Great Works of Jewish Fantasy and the Occult*, edited by Joachim Neugroschel. Reprinted by permission of Stonehill Publishing Co. Copyright © 1976 by Joachim Neugroschel.

AHARON APPELFELD: "In the Wilderness" from *In the Wilderness* by Aharon Appelfeld. Used by permission of Aharon Appelfeld and ACUM Ltd. Copyright © 1971 by Aharon Appelfeld.

SHOLEM ASCH: "From the Beyond" from *Children of Abraham* by Sholem Asch. Used by permission of the Estate of Sholem Asch. Copyright © 1982 the Estate of Sholem Asch.

ISAAC BABEL: "Gedali," "The Rabbi," and "The Rabbi's Son" reprinted from *Benya Krik, The Gangster and Other Stories* by Isaac Babel, edited by Avraham Yarmolinsky. Copyright © 1948 by Schocken Books, Inc. Reprinted by permission of Schocken Books, published by Pantheon Books, a Division of Random House, Inc.

ASHER BARASH: "Rabbi Joseph Della Reina" reprinted from *A Golden Treasury of Jewish Tales* by Asher Barash. Copyright © 1970 by Massada Ltd. Used by permission of Massada Ltd. and ACUM Ltd.

M. J. BERDITCHEVSKY: "Ben Azzai" used by permission of Jeremy Garber and ACUM Ltd. Translation Copyright © 1982 Jeremy Garber. "Illusion" and "Two Worlds" used by permission of Pamela Altfeld Malone and ACUM Ltd. Translations Copyright © 1982 Pamela Altfeld Malone.

HAYIM NACHMAN BIALIK: "The Shortest Friday of the Year" used by permission of Curt Leviant and ACUM Ltd. Translation Copyright © 1982 Curt Leviant. "Scroll of Fire" reprinted from *Selected Poems of H. N. Bialik*, edited by Israel Ephros. Copyright © 1948, 1965 by Bloch Publishing Co. Used by permission of Bloch Publishing Co. and ACUM Ltd.

RABBI TSVI BLANCHARD: "The Tale of the Ram," "The Tale of the Palace," "The Tale of the Garden," and "The Tale of the Spark" used by permission of Rabbi Tsvi Blanchard. Copyright © 1982 Tsvi Blanchard.

MARTIN BUBER: "The Chest of Herbs and the Golden Calf," "The Angel and the World's Dominion," "The House of Demons," and "The Wanderings of the Childless," from *Tales of Angels, Spirits and Demons* by Martin Buber. Used by permission of Raphael Buber and Jerome Rothenberg. Translations copyright © 1976, 1982 by Jerome Rothenberg. "The Sacred Goat" from *Tales of the Hasidim: The Later Masters* by Martin Buber, translated by Olga Marx. Copyright © 1947, 1948 and renewed 1975 by Schocken Books, Inc. Reprinted by permission of Schocken Books, published by Pantheon Books, A Division of Random House, Inc.

ARTHUR A. COHEN: "The Homily of the Rose" reprinted from *In the Days of Simon Stern* by Arthur A. Cohen. Used by permission of Arthur A. Cohen. Copyright © 1972, 1973, 1982 by Arthur A. Cohen.

DAVID EINHORN: "The Flying Letters" from *The Seventh Candle* by David Einhorn. Used by permission of Ktav Publishing House. Copyright © 1968 Ktav Publishing House.

M. Z. FEIERBERG: "The Amulet" from *Whither* by M. J. Feierberg. Used by permission of The Jewish Publication Society. Copyright © 1982 The Jewish Publication Society.

LESLIE A. FIEDLER: "The Dancing of Reb Hershl with the Withered Hand" used by permission of Leslie A. Fiedler. Copyright © 1982 Leslie A. Fiedler.

LAYA FIRESTONE: "Rivka on Mount Moriah" used by permission of Laya Firestone. Copyright © 1982 by Laya Firestone.

WENDY LAURA FRISCH: "Lilith Recollects Genesis" used by permission of Wendy Laura Frisch. Copyright © 1982 Wendy Laura Frisch.

JEREMY GARBER: "The Tale of the Duck" used by permission of Jeremy Garber. Copyright © 1982 by Emery George.

ROMAIN GARY: "The Dybbuk" from *La Danse de Genghis Cohen* by Romain Gary. Used by permission of Robert Lantz and Emery George. Translation Copyright © 1982 Emery George.

RABBI MARC A. GELLMAN: "A Tent of Dolphin Skins" used by permission of Rabbi Marc A. Gellman. Copyright © 1982 Marc A. Gellman.

ALBERT GOLDBARTH: "A Tale of Piety" used by permission of Albert Goldbarth. Copyright © 1982 Albert Goldbarth.

ZVI KOLITZ: "The Legend of the Dead Poppy" from *Tiger Beneath the Skin* by Zvi Kolitz. Used by permission of Zvi Kolitz. Copyright © 1982 Zvi Kolitz.

MOYSHE KULBAK: "Lilith" from "The Messiah of the House of Ephraim" by Moyshe Kulbak, from *Yenne Velt: The Great Works of Jewish Fantasy and the Occult*, edited by Joachim Neugroschel. Reprinted by permission of Stonehill Publishing Co. Copyright © 1976 by Joachim Neugroschel.

RABBI HAROLD S. KUSHNER: "The Tree of Id" used by permission of Rabbi Harold S. Kushner. Copyright © 1982 Harold S. Kushner.

FRANCIS LANDY: "The Castle in the Kingdom" used by permission of Francis Landy. Copyright © 1982 Francis Landy.

JIRI LANGER: "The Angel," "A Messiah in Every Generation," and "The Woman in the Forest" from *Nine Gates to the Chassidic Mysteries* by Jiri Langer. Reprinted by permission of James Clarke and Co. Ltd. Copyright © 1961, 1982 by James Clarke and Co. Ltd.

ELSE LASKER-SCHÜLER: "The Poet of Irsahab" used by permission of Joachim Neugroschel. Translation © 1982 Joachim Neugroschel.

PRIMO LEVI: "Lilith in the Lager" used by permission of Primo Levi and Ruth Feldman. Translation Copyright © 1982 Ruth Feldman.

RABBI LEVI YITZHAK OF BERDITCHEV: "The King Who Loved Music" from *Rabbi Levi Yitzhak of Berditchev* by Samuel S. Dresner. Copyright © 1979 by Samuel S. Dresner. Used by permission of Hartmore House Inc.

MEYER LEVIN: "The Book of Mysteries" and "The Burning of the Torah" reprinted from *Classic Hasidic Tales* (formerly *The Golden Mountain*) by Meyer Levin. Used by permission of Meyer Levin. Copyright © 1932 by Meyer Levin. Copyright © 1982 the Estate of Meyer Levin.

JAKOV LIND: "The Story of Lilith and Eve" and "The Near Murder" from *The Stove* by Jakov Lind. Used by permission of Jakov Lind. Copyright © 1982 Jakov Lind.

BERNARD MALAMUD: "The Jewbird" from *Idiots First*. Copyright © 1963 by Bernard Malamud. Reprinted by permission of Farrar, Straus & Giroux Inc.

ITZIK MANGER: excerpts from *The Book of Paradise*, trans. from the Yiddish by Leonard Wolf. Copyright © 1965 by Itzik Manger. Reprinted by permission of Hill and Wang, a division of Farrar, Straus & Giroux Inc.

MATTI MEGGED: "The Golden Gates of Jerusalem" used by permission of Matti Megged, Howard Schwartz, and ACUM Ltd. Translation Copyright © 1982 Howard Schwartz.

DAVID MELTZER: "A Song of Children," "The Angel of the Alphabet," and "From the Rabbi's Dreambook" used by permission of David Meltzer. Copyright © 1982 David Meltzer.

I. L. PERETZ: "The Sacrifice," "The Hermit and the Bear," and "The Story of the He-Goat Who Couldn't Say No" from *The Book of Fire* by I. L. Peretz, translated by Joseph Leftwich. Used by permission of A. S. Barnes & Co., Inc. Copyright © 1960 A. S. Barnes & Co., Inc. "The Magician" used by permission of Aliza Shevrin. Translation © 1982 Aliza Shevrin. "The Golem" used by permission of Evelyn Abel. Translation © 1982 Evelyn Abel.

JORGE PLESCOFF: "Aleph/Bet" used by permission of Jorge Plescoff and Yishai Tobin. Translation Copyright © 1982 Yishai Tobin.

RABBI YEHIEL POUPKO: "The Midrash of the Alphabet" used by permission of Yehiel Poupko. Copyright © 1981, 1982 Yehiel Poupko.

FRANCINE PROSE: "The Arrival of Eve" from *Judah the Pious* by Francine Prose. Used by permission of Francine Prose. Copyright © 1973 by Francine Prose.

NESSA RAPOPORT: "Generation" used by permission of Nessa Rapoport. Copyright © 1982 Nessa Rapoport.

NACHMANN RAPP: "The Eden Angel" has been excerpted from *Man in His Ways* by Nachmann Rapp, translated from the Yiddish by Miriam Silver. Used by permission of Nachmann Rapp. Copyright © 1982 by Nachmann Rapp.

JACK RIEMER: "In the End" used by permission of Jack Riemer. Copyright © 1982 Jack Riemer.

LILLY RIVLIN: "In the Beginning" used by permission of Lilly Rivlin. Copyright © 1982 Lilly Rivlin.

JOEL ROSENBERG: "Jacob at the River" used by permission of Joel Rosenberg. Copyright © 1982 Joel Rosenberg.

YUDL ROSENBERG: "How the Golem Was Created" and "The End of the Golem" from *The Great Rabbi Loew* by Frederic Thieberger. Copyright © 1963 by Horovitz Publishing Co. Used by permission of East-West Publishing Co.

JEROME ROTHENBERG: "The Alphabet Came to Me" from *The Notebooks* by Jerome Rothenberg. Used by permission of Jerome Rothenberg. Copyright © 1982 by Jerome Rothenberg.

PINHAS SADEH: "The Tale of the Lucky Daaz" used by permission of Pinhas Sadeh, Moshe Ganan and ACUM Ltd. Translation Copyright © 1982 Moshe Ganan.

ALFREDO SARANO: "The Wager and the Tiny Shining Star" used by permission of Stephen Levy. Translation Copyright © 1982 Stephen Levy.

MARIO SATZ: "The Number of the Name" used by permission of Mario Satz and Yishai Tobin. Translation Copyright © 1982 Yishai Tobin.

RABBI ZALMAN SCHACHTER: "Challahs in the Ark," "The Besht and P'ney Yehoshua," and "Reb Zusheh and the Dowry" used by permission of Rabbi Zalman Schachter. Copyright © 1982 Zalman Schachter.

INDEX